(Continued inside back cover)

Mathematical Applications
for Management, Life, and Social Sciences

Third Edition

Mathematical Applications

for Management, Life, and Social Sciences

Ronald J. Harshbarger

The Pennsylvania State University

James J. Reynolds

The Pennsylvania State University

D. C. HEATH AND COMPANY

Lexington, Massachusetts   Toronto

Acquisitions Editor: Mary Lu Walsh
Developmental Editor: Kathleen Sessa
Production Editor: Karen Potischman
Designer: Victor Curran
Production Coordinator: Lisa Arcese

Cover: © Berenholtz/The Stock Market

Published simultaneously in Canada.

Printed in the United States of America.

International Standard Book Number: 0-669-16263-9

Library of Congress Catalog Card Number: 88-80464

10 9 8 7 6 5

Preface

To paraphrase Alfred North Whitehead, the purpose of education is not to fill a vessel but to kindle a fire. This desirable goal is not always an easy one to realize with students whose primary interest is in an area other than mathematics. The purpose of this text, then, is to present mathematical skills and concepts and to apply them to areas that are important to students in the management, life, and social sciences. The applications included allow students to view mathematics in a practical setting relevant to their intended careers. Almost every chapter of this book includes a section or two devoted to the applications of mathematical topics. An index of these applications on the inside covers demonstrates the wide variety used in examples and exercises. Although intended for students who have completed two years, or the equivalent, of high school algebra, this text begins with a brief review of algebra, which, if covered, will aid in preparing students for the work ahead.

Pedagogical Features

Important pedagogical features that have been retained in this new edition are the following.

Intuitive Viewpoint. The book is written from an intuitive viewpoint, with emphasis on concepts and problem solving rather than on mathematical theory. Each topic is carefully explained and examples illustrate the techniques involved. Exercises stress computation and drill, but there are enough challenging problems to stimulate students.

Flexibility. At different colleges or universities the coverage and sequencing of topics may vary according to the purpose of this course. To accommodate this, the text has a great deal of flexibility in the order of topics.

Chapter Warmups. A Warmup appears at the beginning of each chapter and invites students to test themselves on the skills needed for that chapter. The Warmups present several prerequisite problem types that are taken from parts of upcoming problems. Each prerequisite problem type is keyed to the upcoming section where that skill is needed, and students who have difficulty with any particular skill are directed to specific sections of the text for review. Instructors may find the Warmups useful in creating a syllabus.

Applications. We have found that offering applied topics such as cost, revenue, and profit functions in a separate section brings the preceding mathematical discussions into clear and concise focus. There are 16 such sections in this book. Beyond this, there are over 1450 applied exercises and hundreds of applied examples throughout the text.

Objective Lists. Every section begins with a brief list of objectives that outlines the goals of that section for the student.

Procedure/Example Tables. Sprinkled throughout the text, Procedure/Example tables aid student understanding by giving step-by-step descriptions of important procedures with illustrative examples worked out beside the procedures.

Boxed Information. All important information is boxed for easy reference, and key terms are highlighted in boldface.

Review Exercises. At the end of each chapter, a set of Review Exercises offers the student extra practice on the topics in that chapter. These exercises are annotated with section numbers so that the student having difficulty can turn to the appropriate section for review.

Changes in the Third Edition

A major focus of this revision was to improve the exercise sets. This was achieved by providing the following: (1) a better balance between the odd- and the even-numbered exercises, (2) a smoother progression from easy exercises to difficult exercises, (3) better coverage of the topics within each section, and (4) the inclusion of numerous new applications. In fact, the number of exercises has been increased by more than 20% to over 4250 problems. The number of applications has also been increased by more than 20% to over 1450 applications.

Other significant improvements in the third edition are the following.

The discussion of radicals was expanded and placed in a separate section of Chapter 0.

In Chapter 1, the discussion of functions was expanded to include piecewise-defined functions. In addition, the simultaneous solution of three equations in three variables was added to this chapter.

In Chapter 3, the notation for the simplex method has been standardized so that it is more consistent with other linear programming discussions. The simplex method was extended to cases where infinitely many and no solutions occured.

Chapter 6 was rewritten with a stronger emphasis on the mathematics of finance. The discussion of sequences is now used to support the develoment of the mathematics of finance rather than as the central theme of the chapter. Sigma notation was moved from Chapter 6 to Chapter 13, where it is needed to develop the definite integral. Deferred annuities were added to the section on ordinary annuities. The discussion of depreciation has been updated to reflect changes brought about by the Tax Reform Law of 1986. The notation used in this chapter has been made consistent with the notation used in business textbooks and all important formulas have been boxed.

In Chapter 13, a new section on areas between curves follows the definite integral. This gives a firmer foundation to the notions of producer's and consumer's surplus. Also, a discussion of continuous income streams (both total income and present value) replaced and extended the subsection on present value of an annuity.

Throughout the text, exercises that are best worked with a calculator are now highlighted with the symbol 🖩 .

Supplements

Instructor's Guide. This booklet contains two forms of a test for each chapter of the text, with answers provided. In addition, the answers to all even-numbered exercises of the text are included.

Selected Solutions Guide. In addition to an answer section at the end of the text, the solutions to all odd-numbered exercises are included in this supplementary booklet.

Computerized Testing Program by Engineering Software Associates, Inc. Hardware requirements: IBM PC or compatible, two disk drives, IBM graphics-compatible dot-matrix printer or laser printer.

Items included: One program disk, test item disks, User Manual/Printed Test Item File.

This new, versatile test-generating program allows instructors to customize tests for their own classes. It contains over 1000 test items and offers full graphics capability (including mathematical symbols).

With this program, instructors can preview questions on-screen and then add each item to a test with one keystroke. Random generation of test items by chapter is possible. Additionally, instructors may edit existing items or add new items either to the database or to individual tests. Tests may be saved and then printed in multiple scrambled versions. Answer keys are automatically generated.

Interactive Finite Mathematics and Interactive Applied Calculus by The Math Lab. For use with the IBM PC or Apple II, this software program provides labwork for business, life, and social science majors. A total of 80 labs are provided, allowing instructors to select those labs appropriate for their use. Twenty-two of the labs are related to business and economic applications, while many others model real-life business problems and situations.

Related Texts

This book is one of three covering finite mathematics and applied calculus. All three texts heavily emphasize real-world applications of the mathematics featured as the students in these courses are typically majoring in management or the life or social sciences. The material in *Mathematical Applications* is also available in the following two separate texts.

Finite Mathematics for Management, Life, and Social Sciences, Third Edition.

This text is intended for a one-term course covering sets, matrices, inequalities and linear programming, mathematics of finance, probability, and statistics. A chapter on game theory has been added to this text.

Applied Calculus for Management, Life, and Social Sciences, Third Edition.

This text is designed for a one-term course covering a review of algebra, functions of one variable, derivatives, exponential and logarithmic functions, indefinite and definite integrals, and finally, functions of two or more variables. Sections on numerical methods of integration and double integrals have been added to this text.

Acknowledgements

We would like to thank the many people who have helped us at various stages of this project. The encouragement, criticism, and suggestions that have been offered have been invaluable to us. We are especially indebted to Samuel Laposata, Virginia Electric Power Company, who provided ideas and encouragement, and to Frank Kocher, The Pennsylvania State University, who provided support and reviews throughout the first edition's evolution. Our special thanks are due Gordon Shilling, University of Texas at Arlington, who carefully examined every exercise set; and to Stanley Chadick, Northwestern State University; James Runyon, Rochester Institute of Technology; and Ellen Wood, Stephen F. Austin State University; each of whom reviewed the entire manuscript and made many helpful comments. Survey respondents offered many valuable suggestions; our thanks to Patricia Blitch, Lander College; Louis Bush, San Diego City College; Nancy Fisher, University of Alabama; Mary Guffey, Auburn University; Ronald Rule, Georgia College; and Gary Taka, Santa Monica College. Our thanks also to Bill Bolem, Glenn Ostrowski, Patti Stacey, and Sheryl Rutkowski for their help with manuscript preparation. We would also like to express our appreciation to the editorial staff at D. C. Heath for their continued enthusiasm and support.

Ronald J. Harshbarger
James J. Reynolds

Contents

Part Four □ Probabilistic Models

7 Introduction to Probability 347

8 Introduction to Statistics 403

Part Five □ Calculus

9 Derivatives 465

Mathematical Applications
for Management, Life, and Social Sciences

Part One

Algebra Review

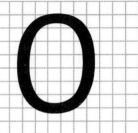

Algebra Concepts

This chapter provides a brief review of the algebraic concepts that will be used throughout the text. You should already be familiar with its topics, but it will be to your advantage to spend some time reviewing them. You will also find this chapter useful as a reference as you study related topics in later chapters.

0.1 Sets

A **set** is a well-defined collection of objects. We may talk about a set of books, a set of dishes, or a set of students. We shall be concerned with sets of numbers. There are two ways to tell what a given set contains. One way is by listing the **elements** (or **members**) of the set (usually between braces). We may say that a set A contains 1, 2, 3, and 4 by writing $A = \{1, 2, 3, 4\}$. To say that 4 is a member of set A, we write $4 \in A$.

If all the members of the set can be listed, the set is said to be a **finite set.** $A = \{1, 2, 3, 4\}$ and $B = \{x, y, z\}$ are examples of finite sets. Although we cannot list all the elements of an **infinite set,** we can use three dots to indicate the unlisted members of such a set. For example, $N = \{1, 2, 3, 4, \ldots\}$ is an infinite set. This set N is called the set of **natural numbers.** Although they are not all listed, we know $10 \in N$, $1121 \in N$, and $15,331 \in N$, but $\frac{1}{2}$ is not a member of N (that is, $\frac{1}{2} \notin N$) because $\frac{1}{2}$ is not a natural number.

Another way to specify the elements of a given set is by description. For example, we may write $D = \{x: x \text{ is a Ford automobile}\}$ to describe the set of all Ford automobiles. $F = \{y: y \text{ is an odd natural number}\}$ is read "F is the set of all y such that y is an odd natural number." Thus $3 \in F$, $5 \in F$, and $7 \in F$ because they are odd natural numbers, and $6 \notin F$ because 6 is not an odd natural number.

EXAMPLE 1 Write the following sets in two ways.
(a) The set A of natural numbers less than 6.
(b) The set B of natural numbers greater than 10.
(c) The set C containing only 3.

Solution   (a) $A = \{1, 2, 3, 4, 5\}$ or $A = \{x: x$ is a natural number less than 6$\}$
(b) $B = \{11, 12, 13, 14, \ldots\}$ or $B = \{x: x$ is a natural number greater than 10$\}$
(c) $C = \{3\}$ or $C = \{x: x = 3\}$

Note that set C of Example 1 contains one member, 3; set A contains five members; and set B contains an infinite number of members. It is possible for a set to contain no members. Such a set is called the **empty set** or the **null set,** and it is denoted by $\varnothing$ or by $\{\ \}$. The set of living veterans of the War of 1812 is empty because there are no living veterans of that war. Thus

$$\{x: x \text{ is a living veteran of the War of 1812}\} = \varnothing.$$

Special relations that may exist between two sets are defined as follows.

Relations with sets

Definition	Example
1. Sets X and Y are **equal** if they contain the same elements.	1. If $X = \{1, 2, 3, 4\}$ and $Y = \{4, 3, 2, 1\}$, then $X = Y$.
2. $A \subseteq B$ if every element of A is an element of B. A is called a **subset** of B. The empty set is a subset of every set.	2. If $A = \{1, 2, c, f\}$ and $B = \{1, 2, 3, a, b, c, f\}$, then $A \subseteq B$.
3. If C and D have no elements in common, they are called **disjoint.**	3. If $C = \{1, 2, a, b\}$ and $D = \{3, e, 5, c\}$, C and D are disjoint.

In the discussion of particular sets, the assumption is always made that the sets under discussion are all subsets of some larger set, called the **universal set** U. The choice of the universal set depends upon the problem under consideration. For example, in discussing the set of all students and the set of all female students, we may use the set of all humans as the universal set.

We may use **Venn diagrams** to illustrate the relationships among sets. We use a rectangle to represent the universal set and closed figures inside the rectangle to represent the sets under consideration. Figure 0.1 shows such a Venn diagram.

Figure 0.1 shows that B is a subset of A; that is, $B \subseteq A$. In Figure 0.2, M and N are disjoint sets. In Figure 0.3, sets X and Y overlap; that is, they are not disjoint.

The shaded portion of Figure 0.3 indicates where the two sets overlap. The set containing the members that are common to two sets is said to be the **intersection** of the two sets.

Set Intersection   The intersection of A and B, written $A \cap B$, is defined by

$$A \cap B = \{x: x \in A \text{ and } x \in B\}.$$

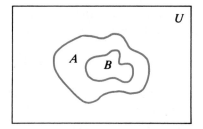

Figure 0.1

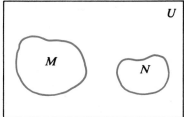

Figure 0.2

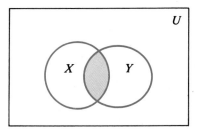

Figure 0.3

EXAMPLE 2   If $A = \{2, 3, 4, 5\}$ and $B = \{3, 5, 7, 9, 11\}$, find $A \cap B$.

Solution $A \cap B = \{3, 5\}$ because 3 and 5 are the common elements of A and B. Figure 0.4 shows the sets and their intersection.

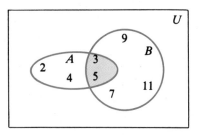

Figure 0.4

The **union** of two sets is the set that contains all members of the two sets.

Set Union   The union of A and B, written $A \cup B$, is defined by

$$A \cup B = \{x: x \in A \text{ or } x \in B \text{ (or both)}\}.*$$

EXAMPLE 3   If $X = \{a, b, c, f\}$ and $Y = \{e, f, a, b\}$, find $X \cup Y$.

Solution $X \cup Y = \{a, b, c, e, f\}$

EXAMPLE 4   Let $A = \{x: x \text{ is a natural number less than 6}\}$ and $B = \{1, 3, 5, 7, 9, 11\}$.
(a) Find $A \cap B$.
(b) Find $A \cup B$.

Solution   (a) $A \cap B = \{1, 3, 5\}$
(b) $A \cup B = \{1, 2, 3, 4, 5, 7, 9, 11\}$

*In mathematics, the word *or* means one or the other or both.

We can illustrate the intersection and union of two sets by the use of Venn diagrams. The shaded region in Figure 0.5 represents $A \cap B$, the intersection of A and B, while the shaded region in Figure 0.6 represents $A \cup B$.

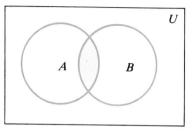

Figure 0.5

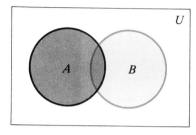

Figure 0.6

All elements of the universal set that are not contained in a set A form a set called the **complement** of A.

Set Complement   The complement of A, written A', is defined by

$$A' = \{x : x \in U \text{ and } x \notin A\}.$$

EXAMPLE 5   If $U = \{x \in N : x < 10\}$, $A = \{1, 3, 6\}$, and $B = \{1, 6, 8, 9\}$, find the following.
(a) A' (b) B' (c) $(A \cap B)'$ (d) $A' \cup B'$

Solution   (a) $U = \{1, 2, 3, 4, 5, 6, 7, 8, 9\}$ so $A' = \{2, 4, 5, 7, 8, 9\}$
(b) $B' = \{2, 3, 4, 5, 7\}$
(c) $A \cap B = \{1, 6\}$ so $(A \cap B)' = \{2, 3, 4, 5, 7, 8, 9\}$
(d) $A' \cup B' = \{2, 4, 5, 7, 8, 9\} \cup \{2, 3, 4, 5, 7\}$
   $= \{2, 3, 4, 5, 7, 8, 9\}$

We can use a Venn diagram to illustrate the complement of a set. The shaded region of Figure 0.7 represents A' and the *un*shaded region of Figure 0.5 represents $(A \cap B)'$.

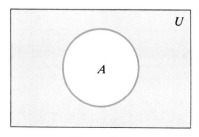

Figure 0.7

Exercise 0.1

Use $\in$ or $\notin$ to indicate whether the given object is an element of the given set in the following problems.

1. x $\{x, y, z, a\}$
2. 3 $\{1, 2, 4, 5, 6\}$
3. 12 $\{1, 2, 3, 4, \ldots\}$
4. 5 $\{x: x$ is a natural number greater than 5$\}$
5. 6 $\{x: x$ is a natural number less than 6$\}$
6. 3 $\varnothing$

In problems 7–12, write the following sets a second way.

7. $\{x: x$ is a natural number less than 8$\}$
8. $\{x: x$ is a natural number greater than 6 and less than 10$\}$
9. $\{n: n$ is a natural number greater than 4 and less than 3$\}$
10. $\{1, 2, 3, 4, 5, 6, 7, 8, 9\}$
11. $\{3, 4, 5, 6, 7\}$
12. $\{7, 8, 9, 10, \ldots\}$
13. If $A = \{1, 2, 3, 4\}$ and $B = \{1, 2, 3, 4, 5, 6\}$, is A a subset of B?
14. If $A = \{a, b, c, d\}$ and $B = \{c, d, a, b\}$, is A a subset of B?
15. Is $A \subseteq B$ if $A = \{a, b, c, d\}$ and $B = \{a, b, d\}$?
16. Is $A \subseteq B$ if $A = \{6, 8, 10, 12\}$ and $B = \{6, 8, 10, 14, 18\}$?

Use $\subseteq$ notation to indicate which set is a subset of the other in the following problems.

17. $C = \{a, b, 1, 2, 3\}, D = \{a, b, 1\}$
18. $E = \{x, y, a, b\}, F = \{x, 1, a, y, b, 2\}$
19. $A = \{1, \pi, e, 3\}, D = \{1, \pi, 3\}$
20. $A = \{2, 3, 4, e\}, \varnothing$
21. $A = \{6, 8, 7, 4\}, B = \{8, 7, 6, 4\}$
22. $D = \{a, e, 1, 3, c\}, F = \{e, a, c, 1, 3\}$

In problems 23–26, indicate whether the following pairs of sets are equal.

23. $A = \{a, b, \pi, \sqrt{3}\}, B = \{a, \pi, \sqrt{3}, b\}$
24. $A = \{x, g, a, b\}, D = \{x, a, b, y\}$
25. $D = \{x: x$ is a natural number less than 4$\}, E = \{1, 2, 3, 4\}$
26. $F = \{x: x$ is a natural number greater than 6$\}, G = \{7, 8, 9, \ldots\}$

27. From the following list of sets, indicate which pairs of sets are disjoint.

$$A = \{1, 2, 3, 4\}$$

$$B = \{x: x \text{ is a natural number greater than 4}\}$$

$$C = \{4, 5, 6, \ldots\}$$

$$D = \{1, 2, 3\}$$

28. If A and B are disjoint sets, what does $A \cap B$ equal?

In problems 29–32, find the intersection of sets A and B, $A \cap B$.

29. $A = \{2, 3, 4, 5, 6\}$ and $B = \{4, 6, 8, 10, 12\}$
30. $A = \{a, b, c, d, e\}$ and $B = \{a, d, e, f, g, h\}$
31. $A = \varnothing$ and $B = \{x, y, a, b\}$
32. $A = \{x: x$ is a natural number less than 4$\}$ and $B = \{3, 4, 5, 6\}$

In problems 33–36, find the union of sets A and B, $A \cup B$.

33. $A = \{1, 2, 4, 5\}$ and $B = \{2, 3, 4, 5\}$
34. $A = \{a, e, i, o, u\}$ and $B = \{a, b, c, d\}$
35. $A = \varnothing$ and $B = \{1, 2, 3, 4\}$
36. $A = \{x: x$ is a natural number greater than 5$\}$ and
    $B = \{x: x$ is a natural number less than 5$\}$

In problems 37–44, assume

$$A = \{1, 3, 5, 8, 7, 2\}, \qquad B = \{4, 3, 8, 10\},$$

and U is the universal set of natural numbers less than 11. Find the following.

37. A'	38. B'	39. $(A \cup B)'$	40. $A' \cap B'$
41. $A \cap B'$	42. $(A \cap B)'$	43. $A' \cup B'$	44. $A' \cup B$

The difference of two sets, $A - B$, is defined as the set containing all elements of A except those in B. That is, $A - B = A \cap B'$. Find $A - B$ for each pair of sets in problems 45–48.

45. $A = \{1, 3, 7, 9\}$ and $B = \{3, 5, 8, 9\}$
46. $A = \{1, 2, 3, 6, 9\}$ and $B = \{1, 4, 5, 6, 7\}$
47. $A = \{2, 1, 5\}$ and $B = \{1, 2, 3, 4, 5, 6\}$
48. $A = \{1, 2, 3, 4, 5\}$ and $B = \{7, 8, 9\}$

APPLICATIONS

49. The following persons were on the ballot for judge of River County.

    Republicans: $A = \{$Robbins, Swartz, Gonzales$\}$
    Democrats: $B = \{$Barth, McRoberts, Robbins$\}$

    If only one person named Robbins is running for judge,
    (a) list the elements of $A \cup B$ and describe this set.
    (b) list the elements of $A \cap B$ and describe this set.
50. In problem 49, suppose two judges are to be elected. Write the set that contains all possible pairs of winners.
51. A survey of 100 aides at the United Nations revealed that 65 could speak English, 60 could speak French, and 40 could speak both English and French.
    (a) Draw a Venn diagram representing the 100 aides. Use E to represent English-speaking and F to represent French-speaking aides.
    (b) How many aides are in $E \cap F$?
    (c) How many aides are in $E \cup F$?
    (d) How many aides are in $E \cap F'$?
52. Suppose that a survey of 100 advertisers in *U.S. News*, *These Times*, and *World* found the following.

    14 advertised in all three
    30 advertised in *Times* and *U.S. News*

26 advertised in *World* and *U.S. News*
27 advertised in *World* and *Times*
60 advertised in *Times*
52 advertised in *U.S. News*
50 advertised in *World*

(a) How many advertised in none of these?
(b) How many advertised only in *Times*?
(c) How many advertised in *U.S. News* or *Times*?

53. Records at a small college show the following about the enrollments of 100 freshmen in mathematics, fine arts, and economics.

38 take math
42 take fine arts
20 take economics
4 take economics and fine arts
15 take math and economics
9 take math and fine arts
3 take all three

Draw a Venn diagram representing this information and label all the areas. Use this diagram to answer the following.
(a) How many take none of these three courses?
(b) How many take math or economics?
(c) How many take exactly one of these three courses?

54. In a survey of the dining preferences of 110 dormitory students at the end of the spring semester, the following facts were discovered about Adam's Lunch (AL), Pizza Tower (PT), and the Student Union.

30 liked AL but not PT
21 liked AL only
63 liked AL
58 liked PT
25 liked PT and AL but not the Union
18 liked PT and the Union
22 liked home cooking (i.e., disliked all three)

Draw a Venn diagram representing this survey and label all the areas. Use this diagram to answer the following.
(a) How many liked PT or the Union?
(b) How many liked all three?
(c) How many liked only the Union?

0.2 The Real Numbers

The universal set for our discussion in this text is the set of **real numbers.** Since there is exactly one point on a straight line for each real number, we can represent the real numbers along a line called the **real number line.** This number line is a picture, or graph, of the real numbers. Two numbers are said to be equal whenever they are represented by the same point on the number line. The equation $a = b$ (a equals b) means that the symbols a and b represent the same real number. Thus $3 + 4 = 7$ means that $3 + 4$ and 7 represent the same number. Table 0.1 lists the subsets of the real numbers.

Table 0.1   Subsets of the set of real numbers

	Description	Example
Natural numbers	$\{1, 2, 3, \ldots\}$ The counting numbers	
Integers	$\{\ldots, -2, -1, 0, 1, 2, \ldots\}$ The natural numbers, 0, and the negatives of the natural numbers.	
Rational numbers	All numbers that can be written as the ratio of two integers, a/b, with $b \neq 0$. These numbers have decimal representations that either terminate or repeat.	
Irrational numbers	Those real numbers that *cannot* be written as the ratio of two integers. Irrational numbers have decimal representations that neither terminate nor repeat.	
Real numbers	The set of all rational and irrational numbers (the entire number line).	

The properties of the real numbers are fundamental to the study of algebra. These properties follow.

Properties of the Real Numbers

1. Addition and multiplication are commutative.
$$a + b = b + a \qquad ab = ba$$

2. Addition and multiplication are associative.
$$(a + b) + c = a + (b + c) \qquad (ab)c = a(bc)$$

3. The additive identity is zero.
$$a + 0 = 0 + a = a$$

4. The multiplicative identity is one.
$$a \cdot 1 = 1 \cdot a = a$$

5. Each element a has an additive inverse, denoted by $(-a)$.

$$a + (-a) = -a + a = 0$$

Note that there is a difference between a negative number and the negative of a number.

6. Each nonzero element a has a multiplicative inverse, denoted by a^{-1}.

$$a \cdot a^{-1} = a^{-1} \cdot a = 1$$

Note that $a^{-1} = 1/a$.

7. Multiplication is distributive over addition.

$$a(b + c) = ab + ac$$

Notice that property 5 provides the means to subtract by adding the additive inverse and property 6 provides a means to divide by multiplying by the multiplicative inverse. The number 0 has no multiplicative inverse, so division by 0 is undefined.

We say that a is less than b (written $a < b$) if the point representing a is to the left of the point representing b on the real number line. For example, $4 < 7$ because 4 is to the left of 7 on the number line. We may also say that 7 is greater than 4 (written $7 > 4$). We may indicate that the number x is less than or equal to another number y by writing $x \le y$. We may also indicate that p is greater than or equal to 4 by writing $p \ge 4$.

EXAMPLE 1   Use $<$ or $>$ notation to write
(a) 6 is greater than 5.
(b) 10 is less than 15.
(c) 3 is to the left of 8 on the number line.
(d) x is less than or equal to 12.

Solution   (a) $6 > 5$ (b) $10 < 15$ (c) $3 < 8$ (d) $x \le 12$

Sometimes we are interested in the *distance* a number is from the origin (0) of the number line, without regard to direction. The distance a number a is from 0 on the number line is the **absolute value** of a, denoted $|a|$. The absolute value of any nonzero number is positive, and the absolute value of 0 is 0.

EXAMPLE 2   Evaluate the following.
(a) $|-4|$ (b) $|+2|$ (c) $|0|$ (d) $|-5 - |-3||$

Solution   (a) $|-4| = +4 = 4$
(b) $|+2| = +2 = 2$
(c) $|0| = 0$
(d) $|-5 - |-3|| = |-5 - 3| = |-8| = 8$

Note that if a is a nonnegative number, then $|a| = a$, *but if a is negative, then* $|a|$ *is the positive number* $(-a)$. Thus,

$$|a| = \begin{cases} a & \text{if } a \geq 0 \\ -a & \text{if } a < 0 \end{cases}$$

In performing computations with real numbers, it is important to remember the rules for computations with signed numbers.

Operations with real (signed) numbers

Procedure	Example
1. (a) To add two signed numbers with the same sign, add their absolute values and affix their common sign.	1. (a) $(+5) + (+6) = +11$ $(-3) + (-4) = -7$ $\left(-\dfrac{1}{6}\right) + \left(-\dfrac{2}{6}\right) = -\dfrac{3}{6} = -\dfrac{1}{2}$
(b) To add two signed numbers with unlike signs, find the difference of their absolute values and affix the sign of the number with the larger absolute value.	(b) $(-4) + (+3) = -1$ $(+5) + (-3) = +2$ $\left(-\dfrac{11}{7}\right) + (+1) = -\dfrac{4}{7}$
2. To subtract one signed number from another, change the sign of the number being subtracted and proceed as in addition.	2. $(-9) - (-8) = (-9) + (+8) = -1$ $16 - (+8) = 16 + (-8) = +8$ $\left(-\dfrac{7}{12}\right) - \left(-\dfrac{5}{6}\right) = -\dfrac{7}{12} + \left(+\dfrac{10}{12}\right)$ $\quad\quad\quad = \dfrac{1}{4}$
3. (a) The product of two numbers with like signs is positive.	3. (a) $(-3)(-4) = +12$ $\left(+\dfrac{3}{4}\right)(+4) = +3$
(b) The product of two numbers with unlike signs is negative.	(b) $5(-3) = -15$ $(-3)(+4) = -12$
4. (a) The quotient of two numbers with like signs is positive.	4. (a) $(-14) \div (-2) = +7$ $+36/4 = +9$
(b) The quotient of two numbers with unlike signs is negative.	(b) $(-28)/4 = -7$ $45 \div (-5) = -9$

When two or more operations with real numbers are indicated in an evaluation, it is important that everyone agree upon the order in which the operations are performed so that a unique result is guaranteed.

The following **order of operations** is universally accepted.

1. Perform operations within parentheses.
2. Find indicated powers $(2^3 = 2 \cdot 2 \cdot 2 = 8)$
3. Perform multiplications and divisions from left to right.
4. Perform additions and subtractions from left to right.

EXAMPLE 3   Evaluate the following.
   (a) $-4 + 3$
   (b) $-4^2 + 3$
   (c) $(-4 + 3)^2 + 3$
   (d) $6 \div 2(2 + 1)$

Solution   (a) -1
   (b) $-16 + 3 = -13$
   (c) $(-1)^2 + 3 = 1 + 3 = 4$
   (d) $6 \div 2(3) = 3 \cdot 3 = 9$

Operations with real numbers can be performed with ease on a calculator. Calculator types vary widely, from those that perform only the four arithmetic operations to those that perform many operations automatically and those that can be programmed.

Two types of internal logic (methods of computation) are used in calculators: *algebraic* and *reverse Polish*. Reverse Polish logic is highly efficient and does not require parentheses; many people feel it is better for complex problems. Algebraic logic operates in a manner consistent with the order of operations and is easy to use for most elementary problems.

The text assumes that you have a scientific calculator that can perform the four arithmetic operations and can evaluate exponential and logarithmic expressions. Many differences exist among the various models of calculators, even those that use algebraic logic, so it is important that you refer to your manual to understand how to use function keys and devise your own plan for solving each problem type. For example, scientific calculators have a power button denoted $\boxed{y^x}$ or $\boxed{x^y}$ that can be used to calculate powers. Algebraic logic uses the following keystrokes to calculate 4^3:

$$4 \;\boxed{y^x}\; 3 \;\boxed{=}\; \text{gives the display} \quad \boxed{\qquad\qquad 64 \qquad}$$

Reverse Polish notation uses these keystrokes:

$$4 \;\boxed{\text{ENTER}}\; 3 \;\boxed{y^x}\; \text{gives the display} \quad \boxed{\qquad\qquad 64 \qquad}$$

EXAMPLE 4   Perform the following operations with an algebraic calculator.

(a) $(-3.72)(1.55)$ (b) $\dfrac{1}{\sqrt{1.5625}}$ (c) $\dfrac{(25)(36)(18) - (81)(14)}{(27)(20)}$

Solution   (a) The $\boxed{+/-}$ key is used to change the sign of a number:

3.72 $\boxed{+/-}$ $\boxed{\times}$ 1.55 $\boxed{=}$ gives the display $\boxed{-5.766}$.

(b) The $\boxed{\sqrt{x}}$ is used to find the square root and $\boxed{1/x}$ is used to find the reciprocal:

1.5625 $\boxed{\sqrt{x}}$ $\boxed{1/x}$ gives the display $\boxed{0.8}$.

(c) Note how the division is handled in this problem:

25 $\boxed{\times}$ 36 $\boxed{\times}$ 18 $\boxed{-}$ 81 $\boxed{\times}$ 14 $\boxed{=}$ $\boxed{\div}$ 27 $\boxed{\div}$ 20

gives the display $\boxed{27.9}$.

Exercise 0.2

In problems 1–8, indicate whether the given expression is one or more of the following types of numbers: rational, irrational, integer, natural. If the expression is meaningless, indicate this.

1. $\dfrac{-\pi}{10}$ *rat*   2. -9 *int*   3. $\dfrac{9}{3}$ *rat*   4. $\dfrac{0}{6}$ *rat*

5. $\dfrac{4}{0}$ *irr*   6. -1.2916 *irr*   7. 1.414 *irr*   8. $\dfrac{9}{6}$ *rat*

Which property of real numbers is being illustrated in problems 9–16?

9. $8 + 6 = 6 + 8$
10. $3 \cdot \frac{1}{3} = 1$
11. $(5 + 3) + 6 = 5 + (3 + 6)$
12. $-e \cdot 1 = -e$
13. $6(4 \cdot 5) = (6 \cdot 4) 5$
14. $5 + (-5) = 0$
15. $5(3 + 7) = 5 \cdot 3 + 5 \cdot 7$
16. $18 \div 18 = 1$

17. Graph the integers from -6 to 10 on a number line.
18. Graph the rational numbers $-\frac{1}{4}$ and $\frac{7}{4}$ on a number line.

In problems 19–24, insert the proper inequality sign to replace $\square$.

19. $\sqrt{16}$ $\boxed{\le}$ 5
20. $-\sqrt{15}$ $\square$ -3
21. $\dfrac{3}{4}$ $\boxed{\ge}$ $\dfrac{5}{6}$
22. $-3 + \sqrt{4}$ $\boxed{\ge}$ -5
23. -4 $\boxed{\le}$ -3
24. π $\boxed{\ge}$ 3

Evaluate each of the following.

25. $|-6|$ *6*

26. $|+5|$ *5*

27. $|-6 + 1|$ *5*

28. $|5 - 32|$ *27*

Compute the following.

29. $(-5) + (-2) + (-6)$

30. $(-3) + (+4) + 2$

31. $-6 + (-3) + (-7)$

32. $-3 + (2 + 1)$

33. $(+6) - (-7)$

34. $(-3) - (-8)$

35. $(-8) + (-6) - (+3)$

36. $-6 - (-3) - (-4)$

37. $(-2)(+6)(-5)$

38. $(+3)(-2)(-6)(-1)$

39. $\dfrac{(-33)(16)}{24}$

40. $\dfrac{6(-3)(-2)}{-9}$

Insert the proper sign from $<$, $=$, or $>$ to replace $\square$ in each of problems 41–46.

41. $0.333 \ \square \ \dfrac{1}{3}$

42. $\dfrac{1}{3} + \dfrac{1}{2} \ \square \ \dfrac{5}{6}$

43. $|-3| + |5| \ \square \ |-3 + 5|$

44. $|-9 - 3| \ \square \ |-9| + |3|$

45. $-\dfrac{1}{13} \ \boxed{\le} \ -0.08$

46. $\dfrac{1}{13} \ \square \ |-0.08|$

In problems 47–56 evaluate each expression.

47. $-3^2 + 1 \cdot 3$

48. $(-3)^2 + 10 \div 2$

49. $-6 \div 2 \cdot 3$

50. $\left(\dfrac{4 + 2}{2}\right)^2$

51. $\dfrac{4 + 2^2}{2}$

52. $\dfrac{(4 + 2)^2}{2}$

53. $\dfrac{16 - (-4)}{8 + (-2)}$

54. $\dfrac{(-5)(-3) - (-2)(3)}{2 - 9}$

55. $\dfrac{|5 - 2| - |-7|}{|5 - 2|}$

56. $\dfrac{8 \div 2 - 6}{6}$

In problems 57–66 use your calculator to evaluate each of the following. List all the digits on your display in the answer.

57. $(3.618)(2.998)$ *10.846764*

58. $(.06949)(-3.8649)$ *−3.79541*

59. $\dfrac{-1}{25916.8}$ *−0.0000385*

60. $\dfrac{51.412}{127.01}$

61. $(3.679)^7$

62. $(1.28)^{10}$

63. $\sqrt{423.98}$ *20.590774*

64. $\sqrt{0.049102}$ *0.2215897*

65. $(-0.3019)^5$

66. $(-3.8)^{12}$

0.3   Integral Exponents

If \$1000 is placed in a 5-year savings certificate that pays an interest rate of 10% per year, compounded annually, then the amount returned after 5 years is given by

$$1000(1.1)^5$$

The 5 in this expression is an **exponent.** Exponents provide an easier way to denote certain multiplications. For example

$$(1.1)^5 = (1.1)(1.1)(1.1)(1.1)(1.1)$$

An understanding of the properties of exponents is fundamental to the algebra needed to study functions and solve equations. Furthermore, the definition of exponential and logarithmic functions and many of the techniques in calculus also require an understanding of the properties of exponents.

For any real number a,

$$a^2 = a \cdot a, \ a^3 = a \cdot a \cdot a \quad \text{and} \quad a^n = a \cdot a \cdot a \cdot \ldots \cdot a \qquad (n \text{ factors})$$

for any positive integer n. The positive integer n is called the **exponent,** the number a is called the **base,** and a^n is read "a to the nth power."

Note that $4a^n$ means $4(a^n)$, which is different from $(4a)^n$. The 4 is the coefficient of a^n in $4a^n$.

Some of the rules of exponents follow.

Positive Integer Exponents

For any real numbers a and b and positive integers m and n,

1. $a^m \cdot a^n = a^{m+n}$

2. For $a \neq 0$, $\dfrac{a^m}{a^n} = \begin{cases} a^{m-n} & \text{if } m > n \\ 1 & \text{if } m = n \\ 1/a^{n-m} & \text{if } m < n \end{cases}$

3. $(ab)^m = a^m b^m$

4. $\left(\dfrac{a}{b}\right)^m = \dfrac{a^m}{b^m} \qquad (b \neq 0)$

5. $(a^m)^n = a^{mn}$

EXAMPLE 1   Use properties of positive integer exponents to rewrite each of the following. Assume all denominators are nonzero.

(a) $\dfrac{5^6}{5^4}$ (b) $\dfrac{x^2}{x^5}$ (c) $\left(\dfrac{x}{y}\right)^4$ (d) $(3x^2 y^3)^4$ (e) $3^3 \cdot 3^2$

Solution   (a) $\dfrac{5^6}{5^4} = 5^{6-4} = 5^2$ (b) $\dfrac{x^2}{x^5} = \dfrac{1}{x^{5-2}} = \dfrac{1}{x^3}$ (c) $\left(\dfrac{x}{y}\right)^4 = \dfrac{x^4}{y^4}$

(d) $(3x^2y^3)^4 = 3^4 (x^2)^4(y^3)^4 = 81 x^8 y^{12}$ (e) $3^3 \cdot 3^2 = 3^{3+2} = 3^5$

For certain calculus operations, use of negative exponents is necessary in order to write problems in the proper form. We can extend the rules for positive integer exponents to all integers by defining a^0 and a^{-n}. Clearly $a^m \cdot a^0$ should equal $a^{m+0} = a^m$, and it will if $a^0 = 1$.

Zero Exponent   For any nonzero real number a, we define $a^0 = 1$. We leave 0^0 undefined.

In Section 0.2, we defined a^{-1} as $1/a$ for $a \neq 0$, so we define a^{-n} as $(a^{-1})^n$, and for $a \neq 0$ and $b \neq 0$ we have

Negative Exponents

$$a^{-n} = (a^{-1})^n = \left(\frac{1}{a}\right)^n = \frac{1}{a^n}$$

$$\left(\frac{a}{b}\right)^{-n} = \left[\left(\frac{a}{b}\right)^{-1}\right]^n = \left(\frac{b}{a}\right)^n$$

EXAMPLE 2   Write each of the following without exponents:

(a) $6 \cdot 3^0$ (b) 6^{-2} (c) $\left(\frac{1}{3}\right)^{-1}$ (d) $-\left(\frac{2}{3}\right)^{-4}$ (e) $(-4)^{-2}$

Solution   (a) $6 \cdot 3^0 = 6 \cdot 1 = 6$ (b) $6^{-2} = \frac{1}{6^2} = \frac{1}{36}$ (c) $\left(\frac{1}{3}\right)^{-1} = \frac{3}{1} = 3$

(d) $-\left(\frac{2}{3}\right)^{-4} = -\left(\frac{3}{2}\right)^4 = \frac{-81}{16}$ (e) $(-4)^{-2} = \frac{1}{(-4)^2} = \frac{1}{16}$

Using the definitions of zero and negative exponents enables us to extend the rules of exponents to all integers and to express them more simply.

Rules of Exponents   For real numbers a and b and *integers m and n*,

1. $a^m \cdot a^n = a^{m+n}$ 2. $a^m/a^n = a^{m-n}$ $(a \neq 0)$

3. $(ab)^m = a^m b^m$ 4. $(a^m)^n = a^{mn}$

5. $(a/b)^m = a^m/b^m$ $(b \neq 0)$ 6. $a^0 = 1$ $(a \neq 0)$

7. $a^{-n} = 1/a^n$ $(a \neq 0)$ 8. $(a/b)^{-n} = (b/a)^n$ $(a, b \neq 0)$

Throughout the remainder of the text, we will assume all expressions are defined.

EXAMPLE 3   Use the rules of exponents and the definitions of a^0 and a^{-n} to simplify each of the following with positive exponents.

(a) $2(x^2)^{-2}$ (b) $x^{-2} \cdot x^{-5}$ (c) $\frac{x^{-8}}{x^{-4}}$ (d) $\left(\frac{2x^3}{3x^{-5}}\right)^{-2}$

Solution   (a) $2(x^2)^{-2} = 2x^{-4} = 2\left(\dfrac{1}{x^4}\right) = \dfrac{2}{x^4}$ (b) $x^{-2} \cdot x^{-5} = x^{-2-5} = x^{-7} = \dfrac{1}{x^7}$

(c) $\dfrac{x^{-8}}{x^{-4}} = x^{-8-(-4)} = x^{-4} = \dfrac{1}{x^4}$

(d) $\left(\dfrac{2x^3}{3x^{-5}}\right)^{-2} = \left(\dfrac{2x^8}{3}\right)^{-2} = \left(\dfrac{3}{2x^8}\right)^2 = \dfrac{9}{4x^{16}}$

EXAMPLE 4   Write $(x^2y)/(9wz^3)$ with all factors in the numerator.

Solution $\dfrac{x^2y}{9wz^3} = x^2y\left(\dfrac{1}{9wz^3}\right) = x^2y\left(\dfrac{1}{9}\right)\left(\dfrac{1}{w}\right)\left(\dfrac{1}{z^3}\right) = x^2y \cdot 9^{-1}w^{-1}z^{-3} = 9^{-1}x^2yw^{-1}z^{-3}$

EXAMPLE 5   Simplify the following so all exponents are positive.

(a) $(2^3x^{-4}y^5)^{-2}$ (b) $\dfrac{2x^4(x^2y)^0}{(4x^{-2}y)^2}$

Solution   (a) $(2^3x^{-4}y^5)^{-2} = 2^{-6}x^8y^{-10} = \dfrac{1}{2^6} \cdot x^8 \cdot \dfrac{1}{y^{10}} = \dfrac{x^8}{64y^{10}}$

(b) $\dfrac{2x^4(x^2y)^0}{(4x^{-2}y)^2} = \dfrac{2x^4 \cdot 1}{4^2x^{-4}y^2} = \dfrac{2}{4^2} \cdot \dfrac{x^4}{x^{-4}} \cdot \dfrac{1}{y^2} = \dfrac{2}{16} \cdot \dfrac{x^8}{1} \cdot \dfrac{1}{y^2} = \dfrac{x^8}{8y^2}$

Exercise 0.3

Compute problems 1–8. Write all answers without exponents.

1. $(-4)^3$ 2. -5^3 3. -2^4 4. $(-2)^5$

5. 3^{-2} 6. 6^{-1} 7. $-\left(\dfrac{3}{2}\right)^2$ 8. $\left(\dfrac{2}{3}\right)^3$

In problems 9–16 use rules of exponents to simplify the expressions. Express answers with positive exponents.

9. $6^5 \cdot 6^3$ 10. $\dfrac{7^8}{7^3}$ 11. $\dfrac{10^8}{10^9}$ 12. $\dfrac{5^4}{(5^{-2} \cdot 5^3)}$

13. $(3^3)^3$ 14. $(2^{-3})^{-2}$ 15. $\left(\dfrac{2}{3}\right)^{-2}$ 16. $\left(\dfrac{-2}{5}\right)^{-4}$

In problems 17–20, simplify by expressing answers with positive exponents.

17. $(x^2)^{-3}$ 18. x^{-4} 19. $xy^{-2}z^0$ 20. $(xy^{-2})^0$

In problems 21–36, use the rules of exponents to simplify.

21. $x^3 \cdot x^4$ 22. $a^5 \cdot a$ 23. $x^{-5} \cdot x^3$ 24. $y^{-5} \cdot y^{-2}$

25. $2^{-3} \cdot 2^{-4}$ 26. $a^3 \cdot a^2$ 27. $\dfrac{x^8}{x^4}$ 28. $\dfrac{a^5}{a^{-1}}$

29. $\dfrac{y^5}{y^{-7}}$ 30. $\dfrac{y^{-3}}{y^{-4}}$ 31. $(x^4)^3$ 32. $(y^3)^{-2}$

33. $(xy)^2$ 34. $(2m)^3$ 35. $\left(\dfrac{2}{x}\right)^4$ 36. $\left(\dfrac{8}{a^3}\right)^3$

In problems 37–46, compute and simplify so only positive exponents remain.

37. $(2x^{-2}y)^{-4}$ 38. $(-32x^5)^{-3}$

39. $(-8a^{-3}b^2)(2a^5b^{-4})$ 40. $(-3m^2y^{-1})(2m^{-3}y^{-1})$

41. $(2x^{-2}) \div (x^{-1}y^2)$ 42. $(-8a^{-3}b^2c) \div (2a^5b^4)$

43. $\left(\dfrac{x^3}{y^{-2}}\right)^{-3}$ 44. $\left(\dfrac{x^{-2}}{y}\right)^{-3}$

45. $\left(\dfrac{a^{-2}b^{-1}c^{-4}}{a^4b^{-3}c^0}\right)^{-3}$ 46. $\left(\dfrac{4x^{-1}y^{-40}}{2^{-2}x^4y^{-10}}\right)^{-2}$

In calculus it is often necessary to write expressions in the form cx^n, where c is a constant. In problems 47–54, write the expressions in this form.

47. $\dfrac{1}{x}$ 48. $\dfrac{1}{x^2}$ 49. $(2x)^3$ 50. $(3x)^2$

51. $\dfrac{1}{(4x^2)}$ 52. $\dfrac{3}{(2x^4)}$ 53. $\left(\dfrac{-x}{2}\right)^3$ 54. $\left(\dfrac{-x}{3}\right)^2$

In problems 55–58, use a scientific calculator to evaluate the indicated powers.

55. 1.2^4 56. $(-3.7)^3$ 57. $(-6)^5$ 58. $(-.8)^{-9}$

APPLICATIONS

If P is invested for n years at rate i, compounded annually, the compound amount that accrues is given by $A = P(1 + i)^n$, and the interest earned is $I = A - P$. In problems 59–62, find A and I for the given P, i, and n.

59. \$1200 for 5 years at 12%   60. \$1800 for 7 years at 10%

61. \$5000 for 6 years at 11.5%   62. \$800 for 20 years at 10.5%

0.4 Radicals and Rational Exponents

A process closely linked to that of raising numbers to powers is that of extracting roots. From geometry we know that if an edge of a cube is x units, its volume is x^3 cubic units. Reversing this process, we determine that if the volume of a cube is V cubic units, the length of an edge is the cube root of V, denoted

$$\sqrt[3]{V} \text{ units.}$$

When we seek the **cube root** of a number such as 8 (written $\sqrt[3]{8}$), we are looking for a number whose cube equals 8. Since $2^3 = 8$, we know that $\sqrt[3]{8} = 2$. Similarly, $\sqrt[3]{-27} = -3$ since $(-3)^3 = -27$. The expression $\sqrt[n]{a}$ is called a **radical,** where

$\sqrt{}$ is the **radical sign,** n the **index,** and a the **radicand.** When no index is indicated, the index is assumed to be 2 and the expression is called a **square root**; thus, $\sqrt{4}$ is the square root of 4 and represents the positive number whose square is 4.

Only one real number satisfies $\sqrt[n]{a}$ for a real number a and an odd number n; we call that number the **principal nth root,** or, more simply, the **nth root.**

For an even index n, there are two possible cases:

1. If a is negative, there is no real number equal to $\sqrt[n]{a}$. For example, there are no real numbers that equal $\sqrt{-4}$ or $\sqrt[4]{-16}$ because there is no real number b such that $b^2 = -4$ or $b^4 = -16$. In this case, we say $\sqrt[n]{a}$ is not a real number.

2. If a is positive, there are 2 real numbers whose nth power equals a. For example, $3^2 = 9$ and $(-3)^2 = 9$. In order to have a unique nth root, we define the (principal) nth root, $\sqrt[n]{a}$, as the *positive* number b satisfying $b^n = a$.

We summarize this discussion as follows.

nth Root of a	The **(principal) nth root** of a real number is defined as

$$\sqrt[n]{a} = b \qquad \text{only if} \qquad a = b^n$$

subject to the following conditions:

	$a = 0$	$a > 0$	$a < 0$
n even	$\sqrt[n]{a} = 0$	$\sqrt[n]{a} > 0$	$\sqrt[n]{a}$ not real
n odd	$\sqrt[n]{a} = 0$	$\sqrt[n]{a} > 0$	$\sqrt[n]{a} < 0$

When we are asked for the root of a number, we give the principal root.

EXAMPLE 1   Find the roots, if they are real numbers.

    (a) $\sqrt[6]{64}$ (b) $-\sqrt{16}$ (c) $\sqrt[3]{-8}$ (d) $\sqrt{-16}$

Solution   (a) $\sqrt[6]{64} = 2$ because $2^6 = 64$

    (b) $-\sqrt{16} = -\left(\sqrt{16}\right) = -4$

    (c) $\sqrt[3]{-8} = -2$

    (d) $\sqrt{-16}$ is not a real number because the even root of a negative number is not real.

To perform calculus operations on expressions involving radicals, it is sometimes necessary to rewrite the radicals in exponential form with fractional exponents.

We have stated that for $a \geq 0$ and $b \geq 0$,

$$\sqrt{a} = b \quad \text{only if} \quad a = b^2.$$

This means that $\left(\sqrt{a}\right)^2 = b^2 = a$, or $\left(\sqrt{a}\right)^2 = a$. In order to extend the properties of exponents to rational exponents, it is necessary to define

$$a^{1/2} = \sqrt{a}, \quad \text{so that } (a^{1/2})^2 = a.$$

For a positive integer n, we define
$$a^{1/n} = \sqrt[n]{a} \quad \text{if } \sqrt[n]{a} \text{ exists.}$$
Thus $(a^{1/n})^n = a^{(1/n)\cdot n} = a$.

Since we wish the properties established for integer exponents to extend to rational exponents, we make the following definitions.

For positive integer n and any integer m:

1. $a^{m/n} = (a^{1/n})^m = \left(\sqrt[n]{a}\right)^m$.

2. $a^{m/n} = (a^m)^{1/n} = \sqrt[n]{a^m}$ if a is nonnegative when n is even, and if $a \neq 0$ when $m \leq 0$.

Throughout the remaining discussion we assume all expressions are real.

EXAMPLE 2   Write the following in radical form and simplify.
(a) $16^{3/4}$ (b) $y^{-3/2}$ (c) $(6m)^{2/3}$

Solution   (a) $16^{3/4} = \sqrt[4]{16^3} = \left(\sqrt[4]{16}\right)^3 = (2)^3 = 8$

(b) $y^{-3/2} = 1/y^{3/2} = \dfrac{1}{\sqrt{y^3}}$

(c) $(6m)^{2/3} = \sqrt[3]{(6m)^2} = \sqrt[3]{36m^2}$

EXAMPLE 3   Write the following without radical signs.

(a) $\sqrt{x^3}$ (b) $\dfrac{1}{\sqrt[3]{b^2}}$ (c) $\sqrt{(ab)^3}$

Solution   (a) $\sqrt{x^3} = x^{3/2}$ (b) $\dfrac{1}{\sqrt[3]{b^2}} = \dfrac{1}{b^{2/3}} = b^{-2/3}$ (c) $\sqrt{(ab)^3} = (ab)^{3/2}$

As noted, our definition of $a^{m/n}$ guarantees that the rules for exponents will apply to fractional exponents. Thus, we can perform operations with fractional exponents as we did with integer exponents.

EXAMPLE 4   Simplify the following expressions.

(a) $a^{1/2} \cdot a^{1/6}$ (b) $a^{3/4}/a^{1/3}$ (c) $(a^3b)^{2/3}$ (d) $(a^{3/2})^{1/2}$

(e) $a^{-1/2} \cdot a^{-3/2}$

Solution   (a) $a^{1/2} \cdot a^{1/6} = a^{1/2+1/6} = a^{3/6+1/6} = a^{4/6} = a^{2/3}$

(b) $a^{3/4}/a^{1/3} = a^{3/4-1/3} = a^{9/12-4/12} = a^{5/12}$

(c) $(a^3b)^{2/3} = (a^3)^{2/3}b^{2/3} = a^2b^{2/3}$

(d) $(a^{3/2})^{1/2} = a^{3/4}$

(e) $a^{-1/2} \cdot a^{-3/2} = a^{-1/2-3/2} = a^{-2} = 1/a^2$

We can perform operations with radicals by first rewriting in exponential form, performing the operations with exponents, and then converting the answer back to radical form. Another option is to apply the following rules for operations with radicals directly.

Rules for Radicals	Examples
Given that $\sqrt[n]{a}$ and $\sqrt[n]{b}$ are real,*	
1. $\sqrt[n]{a^n} = (\sqrt[n]{a})^n = a$	1. $\sqrt[5]{6^5} = (\sqrt[5]{6})^5 = 6$
2. $\sqrt[n]{a} \cdot \sqrt[n]{b} = \sqrt[n]{ab}$	2. $\sqrt[3]{2}\,\sqrt[3]{4} = \sqrt[3]{8} = \sqrt[3]{2^3} = 2$
3. $\dfrac{\sqrt[n]{a}}{\sqrt[n]{b}} = \sqrt[n]{\dfrac{a}{b}}$ $(b \neq 0)$	3. $\dfrac{\sqrt{18}}{\sqrt{2}} = \sqrt{\dfrac{18}{2}} = \sqrt{9} = 3$

*Note that this means $a \geq 0$ and $b \geq 0$ if n is even.

Let us consider Rule 1 for radicals more carefully. Notice that if n is even and $a < 0$, then $\sqrt[n]{a}$ is not real, and Rule 1 does not apply. For example,

$$\sqrt{(-2)^2} \neq -2 \quad \text{since} \quad \sqrt{(-2)^2} = \sqrt{4} = 2 = -(-2).$$

We can generalize this observation as follows: If $a < 0$, then $\sqrt{a^2} = -a > 0$, so

$$\sqrt{a^2} = \begin{cases} a & \text{if } a \geq 0 \\ -a & \text{if } a < 0 \end{cases}$$

This means

$$\sqrt{a^2} = |a|$$

EXAMPLE 5   Simplify.

(a) $\sqrt[3]{8^3}$ (b) $\sqrt[5]{x^5}$ (c) $\sqrt{x^2}$

Solution   (a) $\sqrt[3]{8^3} = 8$ by Rule 1 for radicals   (b) $\sqrt[5]{x^5} = x$ (c) $\sqrt{x^2} = |x|$

Rule 2 for radicals $\left(\sqrt[n]{a} \cdot \sqrt[n]{b} = \sqrt[n]{ab}\right)$ provides a procedure for simplifying radicals.

EXAMPLE 6   Simplify the following radicals, assuming the expressions are real.

(a) $\sqrt[3]{72a^3b^4}$ (b) $\sqrt{48x^5y^6}$ $(y \geq 0)$

Solution   (a) $\sqrt[3]{72a^3b^4} = \sqrt[3]{8 \cdot 9a^3b^3b} = \sqrt[3]{8} \cdot \sqrt[3]{a^3} \cdot \sqrt[3]{b^3} \cdot \sqrt[3]{9b} = 2ab\sqrt[3]{9b}$

(b) $\sqrt{48x^5y^6} = \sqrt{16 \cdot 3 \cdot x^4xy^6} = \sqrt{16} \sqrt{x^4} \sqrt{y^6} \sqrt{3x} = 4x^2y^3 \sqrt{3x}$

Rule 2 for radicals $\left(\sqrt[n]{a} \cdot \sqrt[n]{b} = \sqrt[n]{ab}\right)$ also provides a procedure for multiplying two roots with the same index.

EXAMPLE 7   Multiply the following and simplify the answers, assuming nonnegative variables.

(a) $\sqrt[3]{2xy} \cdot \sqrt[3]{4x^2y}$ (b) $\sqrt{8xy^3z} \sqrt{4x^2y^3z^2}$

Solution   (a) $\sqrt[3]{2xy} \cdot \sqrt[3]{4x^2y} = \sqrt[3]{2xy \cdot 4x^2y} = \sqrt[3]{8x^3y^2} = \sqrt[3]{8} \cdot \sqrt[3]{x^3} \cdot \sqrt[3]{y^2} = 2x\sqrt[3]{y^2}$

(b) $\sqrt{8xy^3z} \sqrt{4x^2y^3z^2} = \sqrt{32x^3y^6z^3} = \sqrt{16x^2y^6z^2} \sqrt{2xz} = 4xy^3z\sqrt{2xz}$

Rule 3 for radicals $\left(\sqrt[n]{a}/\sqrt[n]{b} = \sqrt[n]{a/b}\right)$ indicates how to find the quotient of two roots with the same index.

EXAMPLE 8   Find the quotients and simplify the answers, assuming nonnegative variables.

(a) $\dfrac{\sqrt[3]{32}}{\sqrt[3]{4}}$ (b) $\dfrac{\sqrt{16a^3x}}{\sqrt{2ax}}$

Solution   (a) $\dfrac{\sqrt[3]{32}}{\sqrt[3]{4}} = \sqrt[3]{\dfrac{32}{4}} = \sqrt[3]{8} = 2$ (b) $\dfrac{\sqrt{16a^3x}}{\sqrt{2ax}} = \sqrt{\dfrac{16a^3x}{2ax}} = \sqrt{8a^2} = 2a\sqrt{2}$

Occasionally, we wish to express a fraction containing radicals in an equivalent form that contains no radicals in the denominator. This is accomplished by multiplying the numerator *and* denominator by the expression that will remove the radical. This process is called **rationalizing the denominator.**

EXAMPLE 9   Express each of the following with no radicals in the denominator. (Rationalize each denominator.)

(a) $\dfrac{15}{\sqrt{x}}$ (b) $\dfrac{2x}{\sqrt{18xy}}$ $(x, y > 0)$ (c) $\dfrac{3x}{\sqrt[3]{2x^2}}$

Solution   (a) We wish to create a perfect square under the radical in the denominator.

$$\frac{15}{\sqrt{x}} \cdot \frac{\sqrt{x}}{\sqrt{x}} = \frac{15\sqrt{x}}{x}$$

(b)

$$\frac{2x}{\sqrt{18xy}} \cdot \frac{\sqrt{2xy}}{\sqrt{2xy}} = \frac{2x\sqrt{2xy}}{\sqrt{36x^2y^2}} = \frac{2x\sqrt{2xy}}{6xy} = \frac{\sqrt{2xy}}{3y}$$

(c) We wish to create a perfect cube under the radical in the denominator.

$$\frac{3x}{\sqrt[3]{2x^2}} \cdot \frac{\sqrt[3]{4x}}{\sqrt[3]{4x}} = \frac{3x\sqrt[3]{4x}}{\sqrt[3]{8x^3}} = \frac{3x\sqrt[3]{4x}}{2x} = \frac{3\sqrt[3]{4x}}{2}$$

It is also sometimes useful, especially in calculus, to *rationalize the numerator* of a fraction. For example, we can rationalize the numerator of

$$\frac{\sqrt[3]{4x^2}}{3x}$$

by multiplying the numerator and denominator by $\sqrt[3]{2x}$, which creates a perfect cube under the radical:

$$\frac{\sqrt[3]{4x^2}}{3x} \cdot \frac{\sqrt[3]{2x}}{\sqrt[3]{2x}} = \frac{\sqrt[3]{8x^3}}{3x\sqrt[3]{2x}} = \frac{2x}{3x\sqrt[3]{2x}} = \frac{2}{3\sqrt[3]{2x}}.$$

Exercise 0.4

Unless stated otherwise, assume all variables are nonnegative and all denominators are nonzero.

In problems 1–8, find the powers and roots, if they are real numbers.

1. $\sqrt{256/9}$ 2. $\sqrt{1.44}$ 3. $\sqrt[5]{-32^3}$ 4. $\sqrt[4]{-16^5}$
5. $-8^{1/3}$ 6. $(-8)^{1/3}$ 7. $16^{3/4}$ 8. $32^{3/5}$

In problems 9–12, replace each radical with a fractional exponent. Do not simplify.

9. $\sqrt{m^3}$ 10. $\sqrt[3]{x^5}$ 11. $\sqrt[4]{m^2n^5}$ 12. $\sqrt[5]{x^3}$

In problems 13–16, write in radical form. Do not simplify.

13. $x^{7/4}$ 14. $y^{11/5}$ 15. $-(1/4)x^{-5/4}$ 16. $-x^{-5/3}$

In problems 17–30, use the properties of exponents to simplify each expression so only positive exponents remain.

17. $y^{1/4} \cdot y^{1/2}$ 18. $x^{2/3} \cdot x^{1/5}$ 19. $z^{3/4} \cdot z^4$ 20. $x^{-2/3} \cdot x^2$
21. $y^{-3/2} \cdot y^{-1}$ 22. $z^{-2} \cdot z^{5/3}$ 23. $x^{1/3}/x^{-2/3}$ 24. $x^{-1/2}/x^{-3/2}$
25. $y^{-5/2}/y^{-2/5}$ 26. $x^{4/9}/x^{1/12}$ 27. $(x^{2/3})^{3/4}$ 28. $(x^{4/5})^3$
29. $(x^{-1/2})^2$ 30. $(x^{-2/3})^{-2/5}$

In problems 31–36, simplify each expression by using the properties of radicals. Assume nonnegative variables.

31. $\sqrt{64x^4}$ 　　　　　　　32. $\sqrt[3]{-64x^6y^3}$ 　　　　　　　33. $\sqrt{128x^4y^5}$

34. $\sqrt[3]{54x^5z^8}$ 　　　　　　35. $\sqrt[3]{40x^8y^5}$ 　　　　　　　36. $\sqrt{32x^5y}$

In problems 37–44, perform the indicated operations and simplify.

37. $\sqrt{12x^3y} \cdot \sqrt{3x^2y}$ 　　　　　　　　　　38. $\sqrt[3]{16x^2y} \cdot \sqrt[3]{3x^2y}$

39. $\sqrt{63x^5y^3} \cdot \sqrt{28x^2y}$ 　　　　　　　　40. $\sqrt{10xz^{10}} \cdot \sqrt{30x^{17}z}$

41. $\dfrac{\sqrt{12x^3y^{12}}}{\sqrt{27xy^2}}$ 　　42. $\dfrac{\sqrt{250xy^7z^4}}{\sqrt{18x^{17}y^2}}$ 　　43. $\dfrac{\sqrt[4]{32a^9b^5}}{\sqrt[4]{162a^{17}}}$ 　　44. $\dfrac{\sqrt[3]{-16x^3y^4}}{\sqrt[3]{128y^2}}$

In problems 45–50, rationalize each denominator and simplify.

45. $\sqrt{2/3}$ 　　　　　　　46. $\sqrt{5/8}$ 　　　　　　　47. $\sqrt{m^2x}/\sqrt{mx^2}$

48. $5x^3w/\sqrt{4xw^2}$ 　　　　49. $\sqrt[3]{m^2x}/\sqrt[3]{mx^5}$ 　　　　50. $\sqrt[4]{mx^3}/\sqrt[4]{y^2z^5}$

In calculus it is frequently important to write an expression in the form cx^n, where c is a constant. In problems 51–54, write each expression in this form.

51. $\dfrac{-2}{3\sqrt[3]{x^2}}$ 　　　52. $\dfrac{-2}{3\sqrt[4]{x^3}}$ 　　　53. $3x\sqrt{x}$ 　　　54. $\sqrt{x} \cdot \sqrt[3]{x}$

In calculus problems, the answers are frequently expected to be in a simple form with a radical instead of an exponent. In problems 55–58, write each expression with radicals.

55. $\dfrac{3}{2}x^{1/2}$ 　　　56. $\dfrac{4}{3}x^{1/3}$ 　　　57. $\dfrac{1}{2}x^{-1/2}$ 　　　58. $\dfrac{-1}{2}x^{-3/2}$

APPLICATIONS

In problems 59 and 60, use the fact that the quantity of a radioactive substance after t years is given by $q = q_0(2^{-t/k})$, where q_0 is the original amount of radioactive material and k is its half-life (the number of years for half the radioactive substance to decay).

59. The half-life of strontium-90 is 25 years. Find the amount of strontium-90 remaining after 10 years if $q_0 = 98$ kg.

60. The half-life of carbon-14 is 5600 years. Find the amount of carbon-14 remaining after 10,000 years if $q_0 = 40.0$ g.

0.5 Operations with Algebraic Expressions

In algebra we are usually dealing with a combination of real numbers (such as 3, 6/7, $-\sqrt{2}$) and letters (such as x, a, m). Unless otherwise specified, the letters are symbols used to represent real numbers and are sometimes called **variables.** An expression obtained by performing additions, subtractions, multiplications, divisions, or extraction of roots with one or more real numbers or variables is called an

algebraic expression. Unless otherwise specified, the variables represent all real numbers for which the algebraic expression is a real number. Examples of algebraic expressions are

$$3x + 2y, \qquad \frac{x^3y + y}{x - 1}, \qquad \text{and} \qquad \sqrt{x} - 3.$$

Note that the variable x cannot be negative in the expression $\sqrt{x} - 3$, and that $(x^3y + y)/(x - 1)$ is not a real number when $x = 1$ because division by 0 is undefined.

Any product of a real number (called the **coefficient**) and one or more variables to powers is called a **term.** The sum of a finite number of terms with nonnegative integer powers on the variables is called a **polynomial.** If a polynomial contains only one variable x, then it is called a polynomial in x.

> The general form of a **polynomial in x** is
>
> $$a_nx^n + a_{n-1}x^{n-1} + \cdots + a_1x + a_0,$$
>
> where each coefficient a_i is a real number and where $i = 1, 2, \ldots, n$.

If $a_n \neq 0$, the **degree** of the polynomial is n, and a_n is called the **leading coefficient.** Thus $4x^3 - 2x + 3$ is a third-degree polynomial in x with leading coefficient 4. If two or more variables are in a term, the degree of the term is the sum of the exponents of the variables. The degree of a nonzero constant term is zero. Thus, the degree of $4x^2y$ is $2 + 1 = 3$, the degree of $6xy$ is $1 + 1 = 2$, and the degree of 3 is 0. The **degree of a polynomial** containing two or more variables is the degree of the term in the polynomial having the highest degree. Therefore $2xy - 4x + 6$ is a second-degree polynomial.

A polynomial containing two terms is called a **binomial** and one containing three terms is called a **trinomial.** A single term polynomial is a **monomial.**

Since monomials and polynomials represent real numbers, the properties of real numbers can be used to add, subtract, multiply, divide, and simplify polynomials. For example, we can use the distributive law to add $3x$ and $2x$.

$$3x + 2x = (3 + 2)x = 5x$$

Similarly, $9xy - 3xy = (9 - 3)xy = 6xy$.

Terms with exactly the same variable factors are called **like terms.** We can add or subtract like terms by adding or subtracting the coefficients of the variables.

EXAMPLE 1   Compute $(4xy + 3x) + (5xy - 2x)$.

Solution

$$
\begin{aligned}
(4xy + 3x) + (5xy - 2x) &= 4xy + 3x + 5xy - 2x \\
&= 9xy + x
\end{aligned}
$$

Subtraction of polynomials uses the Distributive Law to remove the parentheses.

EXAMPLE 2   Compute $(3x^2 + 4xy + 5y^2 + 1) - (6x^2 - 2xy + 4)$.

Solution   Removing the parentheses gives

$$3x^2 + 4xy + 5y^2 + 1 - 6x^2 + 2xy - 4,$$

which simplifies to

$$-3x^2 + 6xy + 5y^2 - 3.$$

Using the rules of exponents and the commutative and associative laws for multiplication, we can multiply and divide monomials, as the following example shows.

EXAMPLE 3   Perform the indicated operations.
(a) $(8xy^3)(2x^3y)(-3xy^2)$
(b) $-15x^2y^3 \div (3xy^5)$

Solution   (a) $8 \cdot 2 \cdot (-3)x \cdot x^3 \cdot x \cdot y^3 \cdot y \cdot y^2 = -48x^5y^6$

(b) $\dfrac{-15x^2y^3}{3xy^5} = -\dfrac{15}{3} \cdot \dfrac{x^2}{x} \cdot \dfrac{y^3}{y^5} = -5 \cdot x \cdot \dfrac{1}{y^2} = -\dfrac{5x}{y^2}$

Symbols of grouping are used in algebra in the same way that they are in the arithmetic of real numbers. We have removed parentheses in the process of adding and subtracting polynomials. Other symbols of grouping, such as brackets, [ ], are treated the same as parentheses.

When there are two or more symbols of grouping involved, we may begin with the innermost and work outward.

EXAMPLE 4   Simplify $3x^2 - [2x - (3x^2 - 2x)]$.

Solution

$$\begin{aligned}
3x^2 - [2x - (3x^2 - 2x)] &= 3x^2 - [2x - 3x^2 + 2x] \\
&= 3x^2 - [4x - 3x^2] \\
&= 3x^2 - 4x + 3x^2 \\
&= 6x^2 - 4x
\end{aligned}$$

By the use of the Distributive Law, we can multiply a binomial by a monomial. For example,

$$x(2x + 3) = x \cdot 2x + x \cdot 3 = 2x^2 + 3x.$$

We can extend the Distributive Law to multiply polynomials with more than two terms. For example,

$$5(x + y + 2) = 5x + 5y + 10.$$

EXAMPLE 5   Find the following products.
(a) $-4ab(3a^2b + 4ab^2 - 1)$ (b) $(4a + 5b + c)ac$

Solution   (a) $-4ab(3a^2b + 4ab^2 - 1) = -12a^3b^2 - 16a^2b^3 + 4ab$
(b) $(4a + 5b + c)ac = 4a \cdot ac + 5b \cdot ac + c \cdot ac = 4a^2c + 5abc + ac^2$

The Distributive Law can be used to show us how to multiply two polynomials. Consider the indicated multiplication $(a + b)(c + d)$. If we first treat the sum $(a + b)$ as a single quantity, then two successive applications of the Distributive Law gives

$$(a + b)(c + d) = (a + b) \cdot c + (a + b) \cdot d = ac + bc + ad + bd.$$

Thus we see that the product can be found by multiplying $(a + b)$ by c, $(a + b)$ by d, and then adding the products. This is frequently set up as follows.

Procedure	Example
To multiply two polynomials:	Multiply $(3x + 4xy + 3y)$ by $(x - 2y)$.
1. Write one of the polynomials above the other.	1. $3x + 4xy + 3y$ $\quad\quad x - 2y$
2. Multiply each term of the top polynomial by each term of the bottom one, and write the similar terms of the product under one another.	2. $3x^2 + 4x^2y + 3xy$ $\quad\quad\quad\quad\quad - 6xy - 8xy^2 - 6y^2$
3. Add like terms to simplify the product.	3. $3x^2 + 4x^2y - 3xy - 8xy^2 - 6y^2$

EXAMPLE 6   Multiply $(4x^2 + 3xy + 4x)(2x - 3y)$.

Solution

$$
\begin{array}{l}
4x^2 + 3xy + 4x \\
2x - 3y \\
\hline
8x^3 + 6x^2y + 8x^2 \\
 - 12x^2y - 9xy^2 - 12xy \\
\hline
8x^3 - 6x^2y + 8x^2 - 9xy^2 - 12xy
\end{array}
$$

Since the multiplications we must perform often involve binomials, the following special products are worth remembering.

A. $(x + a)(x + b) = x^2 + (a + b)x + ab$
B. $(ax + b)(cx + d) = acx^2 + (ad + bc)x + bd$

It is easier to remember these two special products if we note the structure of the result and realize that we can obtain this result by finding the products of the First terms, Outside terms, Inside terms, and Last terms, and adding the results. This is called the FOIL method of multiplying two binomials.

EXAMPLE 7   Multiply the following.

(a) $(x - 4)(x + 3)$ (b) $(3x + 2)(2x + 5)$

Solution   (a) $(x - 4)(x + 3) = (x^2) + (3x) + (-4x) + (-12) = x^2 - x - 12$
 First   Outside   Inside   Last

(b) $(3x + 2)(2x + 5) = (6x^2) + (15x) + (4x) + (10) = 6x^2 + 19x + 10$

Additional special products are as follows:

> C. $(x + a)^2 = x^2 + 2ax + a^2$ (binomial squared)
> D. $(x - a)^2 = x^2 - 2ax + a^2$ (binomial squared)
> E. $(x + a)(x - a) = x^2 - a^2$ (difference of two squares)
> F. $(x + a)^3 = x^3 + 3ax^2 + 3a^2x + a^3$ (binomial cubed)
> G. $(x - a)^3 = x^3 - 3ax^2 + 3a^2x - a^3$ (binomial cubed)

EXAMPLE 8   Multiply the following.

(a) $(x + 5)^2$ (b) $(3x - 4y)^2$ (c) $(x - 2)(x + 2)$
(d) $(x^2 - y^3)^2$ (e) $(x + 4)^3$

Solution   (a) $(x + 5)^2 = x^2 + 2(5)x + 25 = x^2 + 10x + 25$
(b) $(3x - 4y)^2 = (3x)^2 - 2(3x)(4y) + (4y)^2 = 9x^2 - 24xy + 16y^2$
(c) $(x - 2)(x + 2) = x^2 - 4$
(d) $(x^2 - y^3)^2 = (x^2)^2 - 2(x^2)(y^3) + (y^3)^2 = x^4 - 2x^2y^3 + y^6$
(e) $(x + 4)^3 = x^3 + 3(4)(x^2) + 3(4^2)(x) + 4^3 = x^3 + 12x^2 + 48x + 64$

All algebraic expressions can represent real numbers, so the techniques used to perform operations on polynomials and to simplify polynomials also apply to other algebraic expressions.

EXAMPLE 9   Perform the indicated operations.

(a) $3\sqrt{3} + 4x\sqrt{y} - 5\sqrt{3} - 11x\sqrt{y} - (\sqrt{3} - x\sqrt{y})$ (b) $x^{3/2}(x^{1/2} - x^{-1/2})$
(c) $(x^{1/2} - x^{1/3})^2$ (d) $(\sqrt{x} + 2)(\sqrt{x} - 2)$

Solution   (a) First we combine the terms containing $\sqrt{3}$ and then the terms containing $x\sqrt{y}$.

$(3 - 5 - 1)\sqrt{3} + (4 - 11 + 1)x\sqrt{y} = -3\sqrt{3} - 6x\sqrt{y}$

(b) $x^{3/2}(x^{1/2} - x^{-1/2}) = x^{3/2} \cdot x^{1/2} - x^{3/2} \cdot x^{-1/2} = x^2 - x$
(c) $(x^{1/2} - x^{1/3})^2 = (x^{1/2})^2 - 2x^{1/2}x^{1/3} + (x^{1/3})^2 = x - 2x^{5/6} + x^{2/3}$
(d) $(\sqrt{x} + 2)(\sqrt{x} - 2) = (\sqrt{x})^2 - (2)^2 = x - 4$

In later chapters we will need to write problems in a simplified form so that we can perform certain operations on them. We can often use division of one polynomial by another to obtain the simplification. The procedure for dividing one polynomial by another follows.

Procedure	Example

To divide one polynomial by another:

1. Write with both polynomials in descending powers of a variable. Include missing terms with coefficient 0 in the dividend.

2. (a) Divide the highest power of the divisor into the highest power of the dividend, and write this partial quotient above the dividend. Multiply the partial quotient times the divisor, write the product under the dividend, and subtract, getting a new dividend.

   (b) Repeat until the degree of the new dividend is less than the degree of the divisor. Any remainder is written over the divisor and added to the quotient.

Divide $4x^3 + 4x^2 + 5$ by $2x^2 + 1$.

1. $2x^2 + 1\overline{)4x^3 + 4x^2 + 0x + 5}$

2. (a)
$$
\begin{array}{r}
2x \\
2x^2 + 1\overline{)4x^3 + 4x^2 + 0x + 5} \\
\underline{4x^3 + 2x } \\
4x^2 - 2x + 5
\end{array}
$$

(b)
$$
\begin{array}{r}
2x + 2 \\
2x^2 + 1\overline{)4x^3 + 4x^2 + 0x + 5} \\
\underline{4x^3 + 2x } \\
4x^2 - 2x + 5 \\
\underline{4x^2 + 2} \\
- 2x + 3
\end{array}
$$

Degree $(-2x + 3) <$ degree $(2x^2 + 1)$

Quotient: $2x + 2 + \dfrac{-2x + 3}{2x^2 + 1}$

EXAMPLE 10   Divide $(4x^3 - 13x - 22)$ by $(x - 3)$, $x \neq 3$.

Solution
$$
\begin{array}{r}
4x^2 + 12x + 23 \\
x - 3\overline{)4x^3 + 0x^2 - 13x - 22} \\
\underline{4x^3 - 12x^2 } \\
12x^2 - 13x \\
\underline{12x^2 - 36x } \\
23x - 22 \\
\underline{23x - 69} \\
47
\end{array}
$$

($0x^2$ is inserted so that each power of x is present.)

The quotient is $4x^2 + 12x + 23$, with remainder 47, or

$$4x^2 + 12x + 23 + \frac{47}{x - 3}.$$

Exercise 0.5

For each polynomial in problems 1–4, (a) give the degree of the polynomial, (b) give the coefficient (numerical) of the highest degree term, (c) give the constant term, and (d) decide whether it is a polynomial of one or several variables.

1. $10 - 3x - x^2$ 2. $5x^4 - 2x^9 + 7$ 3. $7x^2y - 14xy^3z$ 4. $2x^5 + 7x^2y^3 - 5y^6$

In problems 5–14, simplify by combining like terms.

5. $7x^2 + 8x + 4x^2 + 11x - 6$
6. $(16pq - 7p^2) + (5pq + 5p^2)$
7. $(3x^3 + 4x^2y^2) + (3x^2y^2 - 7x^3)$
8. $(4m^2 - 3n^2 + 5) - (3m^2 + 4n^2 + 8)$
9. $(4a + 2b) - (3a + 3c) + (6b + 2c)$
10. $(4rs - 2r^2s - 11rs^2) - (11rs^2 - 2rs + 4r^2s)$
11. $[8 - 4 - (q + 5)]$
12. $x^3 + [3x - (x^3 - 3x)]$
13. $x^2 - [x - (x^2 - 1) + 1 - (1 - x^2)] + x$
14. $y^3 - [y^2 - (y^3 + y^2)] - [y^3 + (1 - y^2)]$

In problems 15–60, perform the indicated operations and simplify.

15. $(5x^3)(7x^2)$

16. $(-3x^2y)(2xy^3)(4x^2y^2)$

17. $(39r^3s^2) \div (13r^2s)$

18. $(-15m^3n) \div (5mn^4)$

19. $(3mx)(2mx^2) - (4m^2x)x^2$

20. $\dfrac{15y^3z^2}{yz^2} - \dfrac{8y^4z}{y^2z}$

21. $ax^2(2x^2 + ax + ab)$

22. $-3(3 - x^2)$

23. $(3y + 4)(2y - 3)$

24. $(4x - 1)(x - 3)$

25. $(1 - 2x^2)(2 - x^2)$

26. $(x^3 + 3)(2x^3 - 5)$

27. $(4x + 3)^2$

28. $(2y + 5)^2$

29. $\left(x^2 - \dfrac{1}{2}\right)^2$

30. $(x^3y^3 - 0.3)^2$

31. $(2x + 1)(2x - 1)$

32. $(5y + 2)(5y - 2)$

33. $(0.1 - 4x)(0.1 + 4x)$

34. $\left(\dfrac{2}{3} + x\right)\left(\dfrac{2}{3} - x\right)$

35. $(x - 2)(x^2 + 2x + 4)$

36. $(a + b)(a^2 - ab + b^2)$

37. $(x^3 + 5x)(x^5 - 2x^3 + 5)$

38. $(x^3 - 1)(x^7 - 2x^4 - 5x^2 + 5)$

39. $(18m^2n + 6m^3n + 12m^4n^2) \div (6m^2n)$

40. $(16x^2 + 4xy^2 + 8x) \div (4xy)$

41. $(24x^8y^4 + 15x^5y - 6x^7y) \div (9x^5y^2)$

42. $(27x^2y^2 - 18xy + 9xy^2) \div (6xy)$

43. $(x + 1)^3$

44. $(x - 3)^3$

45. $(2x - 3)^3$

46. $(3x + 4)^3$

47. $(0.1x - 2)(x + 0.05)$

48. $(6.2x + 4.1)(6.2x - 4.1)$

49. $(x^3 + x - 1) \div (x + 2)$

50. $(x^5 + 5x - 7) \div (x + 1)$

51. $(x^4 + 3x^3 - x + 1) \div (x^2 + 1)$

52. $(x^3 + 5x^2 - 6) \div (x^2 - 2)$

53. $x^{1/2}(x^{1/2} + 2x^{3/2})$

54. $x^{-2/3}(x^{5/3} - x^{-1/3})$

55. $(x^{1/2} + 1)(x^{1/2} - 2)$

56. $(x^{1/3} - x^{1/2})(4x^{2/3} - 3x^{3/2})$

57. $(\sqrt{x} + 3)(\sqrt{x} - 3)$

58. $(x^{1/5} + x^{1/2})(x^{1/5} - x^{1/2})$

59. $(2x + 1)^{1/2}[(2x + 1)^{3/2} - (2x + 1)^{-1/2}]$

60. $(4x - 3)^{-5/3}[(4x - 3)^{8/3} + 3(4x - 3)^{5/3}]$

0.6 Factoring

We can factor monomial factors out of a polynomial by using the Distributive Law in reverse; $ab + ac = a(b + c)$ is an example showing that a is a monomial factor of the polynomial $ab + ac$. But it is also a statement of the Distributive Law (with the sides of the equation interchanged). The monomial factor of a polynomial must be a factor of each term of the polynomial, so it is frequently called a common monomial factor.

EXAMPLE 1   Factor $-3x^2t - 3x + 9xt^2$.

Solution   1. We can either factor out $3x$ and obtain

$$-3x^2t - 3x + 9xt^2 = 3x(-xt - 1 + 3t^2)$$

2. or we can factor out $-3x$ (factoring out the negative will make the first term of the polynomial positive) and obtain

$$-3x^2t - 3x + 9xt^2 = -3x(xt + 1 - 3t^2).$$

If a factor is common to each term of a polynomial, we can use the above procedure to factor it out, even if it is not a monomial. For example, we can factor $(a + b)$ out of the polynomial $2x(a + b) - 3y(a + b)$. If we factor $(a + b)$ from both terms, we get $(a + b)(2x - 3y)$. The following example demonstrates the **factoring by grouping** technique.

EXAMPLE 2   Factor $5x - 5y + bx - by$.

Solution   We can factor this polynomial by the use of grouping. The grouping is done so that common factors (frequently binomial factors) can be removed. We see that we can factor 5 from the first two terms and b from the last two, giving

$$5(x - y) + b(x - y).$$

This gives two terms with the common factor $x - y$, so we get

$$(x - y)(5 + b).$$

We can use the formula for multiplying two binomials to factor certain trinomials. The formula

$$(x + a)(x + b) = x^2 + (a + b)x + ab$$

can be used to factor trinomials like

$$x^2 - 7x + 6.$$

EXAMPLE 3   Factor $x^2 - 7x + 6$.

Solution   If this trinomial can be factored into an expression of the form

$$(x + a)(x + b)$$

then we need to find a and b such that

$$x^2 - 7x + 6 = x^2 + (a + b)x + ab$$

That is, we need to find a and b such that $a + b = -7$ and $ab = 6$. The two numbers whose sum is -7 and whose product is 6 are -1 and -6. Thus

$$x^2 - 7x + 6 = (x - 1)(x - 6).$$

A similar method can be used to factor trinomials like $9x^2 - 31x + 12$. Finding the proper factors for this type of trinomial may involve a fair amount of trial and error because we must find factors a, b, c, and d such that

$$(ax + b)(cx + d) = acx^2 + (ad + bc)x + bd.$$

Another technique of factoring can be used to factor trinomials like those we have been discussing. It is especially useful in factoring more complicated trinomials, like $9x^2 - 31x + 12$. This procedure for factoring second-degree trinomials follows.

Procedure	Example
To factor a trinomial into the product of its binomial factors:	Factor $9x^2 - 31x + 12$.
1. Form the product of the second-degree term and the constant term.	1. $9x^2 \cdot 12 = 108x^2$
2. Determine if there are any factors of the product of step 1 that will sum to the middle term of the trinomial. (If the answer is no, the trinomial will not factor into two binomials.)	2. The factors $-27x$ and $-4x$ give a sum of $-31x$.
3. Use the sum of these two factors to replace the middle term of the trinomial.	3. $9x^2 - 31x + 12 = 9x^2 - 27x - 4x + 12$
4. Factor this four-term expression by grouping.	4. $\begin{aligned}&= (9x^2 - 27x) + (-4x + 12) \\ &= 9x(x - 3) - 4(x - 3) \\ &= (x - 3)(9x - 4)\end{aligned}$

In the example just completed, note that writing the middle term $(-31x)$ as $-4x - 27x$ rather than as $-27x - 4x$ (as we did) will still result in the correct factorization. (Try it.)

EXAMPLE 4 Factor $9x^2 - 9x - 10$.

Solution The product of the second-degree term and the constant is $-90x^2$. Factors of $-90x^2$ that sum to $-9x$ are $-15x$ and $6x$. Thus

$$\begin{aligned}
9x^2 - 9x - 10 &= 9x^2 - 15x + 6x - 10 \\
&= (9x^2 - 15x) + (6x - 10) \\
&= 3x(3x - 5) + 2(3x - 5) \\
&= (3x - 5)(3x + 2).
\end{aligned}$$

Checking gives

$$(3x - 5)(3x + 2) = 9x^2 + 6x - 15x - 10$$
$$= 9x^2 - 9x - 10.$$

Some special products that make factoring easier are

Special Factorizations

The perfect-square trinomials:

$$x^2 + 2ax + a^2 = (x + a)^2$$
$$x^2 - 2ax + a^2 = (x - a)^2$$

The difference of two squares:
$$x^2 - a^2 = (x + a)(x - a)$$

EXAMPLE 5

Factor $25x^2 - 36y^2$.

Solution

Since the binomial $25x^2 - 36y^2$ is the difference of two squares, the factorization is $(5x - 6y)(5x + 6y)$. These two factors are called binomial **conjugates** because they differ only in one sign.

EXAMPLE 6

Factor $4x^2 + 12x + 9$.

Solution

Although we can use the technique we have learned to factor trinomials, the factors come quickly if we recognize that this trinomial is a perfect square. It has two square terms, and the remaining term ($12x$) is twice the product of the square roots of the squares ($12x = 2 \cdot 2x \cdot 3$). Thus $4x^2 + 12x + 9 = (2x + 3)^2$.

Most of the polynomials we have factored have been second-degree polynomials, or **quadratic polynomials.** Some polynomials that are not quadratic are in a form that can be factored in the same manner as quadratics. For example, the polynomial $x^4 + 4x^2 + 4$ can be written as $a^2 + 4a + 4$, where $a = x^2$.

EXAMPLE 7

Factor $x^4 + 4x^2 + 4$ completely.

Solution

Since the trinomial is in the form of a perfect square, letting $a = x^2$ will give us $x^4 + 4x^2 + 4 = a^2 + 4a + 4 = (a + 2)^2$. Thus $x^4 + 4x^2 + 4 = (x^2 + 2)^2$.

EXAMPLE 8

Factor $x^4 - 16$ completely.

Solution

The binomial $x^4 - 16$ can be treated as the difference of two squares, $(x^2)^2 - 4^2$, so $x^4 - 16 = (x^2 - 4)(x^2 + 4)$. But $x^2 - 4$ can be factored into $(x - 2)(x + 2)$, so $x^4 - 16 = (x - 2)(x + 2)(x^2 + 4)$.

A polynomial is said to be factored completely if all possible factorizations have been completed. For example, $(2x - 4)(x + 3)$ is not factored completely because a 2 can still be factored out of $2x - 4$. Confining our attention to factors with integer coefficients, we can factor a number of polynomials completely by using the following procedure.

> Look for: Monomials first.
> Then for: Difference of two squares.
> Then for: Trinomial squares.
> Then for: Other methods of factoring trinomials.

EXAMPLE 9   Factor completely: $12x^2 - 36x + 27$.

Solution
$$12x^2 - 36x + 27 = 3(4x^2 - 12x + 9) \quad \text{(Monomial)}$$
$$= 3(2x - 3)^2 \quad \text{(Perfect square)}$$

EXAMPLE 10   Factor completely: $16x^2 - 64y^2$.

Solution
$$16x^2 - 64y^2 = 16(x^2 - 4y^2)$$
$$= 16(x + 2y)(x - 2y)$$

Note that factoring the difference of two squares immediately would give $(4x + 8y)(4x - 8y)$, which is not factored completely (since we could still factor 4 from $4x + 8y$ and 4 from $4x - 8y$).

Exercise 0.6

Factor the following completely.

1. $9ab - 12a^2b + 18b^2$
2. $8a^2b - 160x + 4bx^2$
3. $4x^2 + 8xy^2 + 2xy^3$
4. $12y^3z + 4yz^2 - 8y^2z^3$
5. $5(y - 4) - x^2(y - 4)$
6. $2(x + 1) - 5x(x + 1)$
7. $6x - 6m + xy - my$
8. $x^3 - x^2 - 5x + 5$
9. $x^2 + 8x + 12$
10. $x^2 + 6x + 8$
11. $x^2 - x - 6$
12. $x^2 - 2x - 8$
13. $2x^2 - 8x - 42$
14. $3x^2 - 21x + 36$
15. $7x^2 - 10x - 8$
16. $12x^2 + 11x + 2$
17. $x^2 - 10x + 25$
18. $4y^2 + 12y + 9$
19. $49a^2 - 144b^2$
20. $16x^2 - 25y^2$
21. $2x^3 - 8x^2 + 8x$
22. $x^3 + 16x^2 + 64x$
23. $2x^2 + x - 6$
24. $2x^2 + 13x + 6$
25. $3x^2 + 3x - 36$
26. $4x^2 - 8x - 60$
27. $2x^3 - 8x$
28. $16z^2 - 81w^2$

29. $10x^2 + 19x + 6$

30. $6x^2 + 67x - 35$

31. $9 - 47x + 10x^2$

32. $10x^2 + 21x - 10$

33. $9x^2 + 21x - 8$

34. $9x^2 + 22x + 8$

35. $y^4 - 16x^4$

36. $x^4 - 16$

37. $x^4 - 8x^2 + 16$

38. $81 - 18x^2 + x^4$

39. $4x^4 - 5x^2 + 1$

40. $x^4 - 3x^2 - 4$

The following factorization formulas involving cubes can be verified by multiplication.

$$a^3 + 3a^2b + 3ab^2 + b^3 = (a + b)^3 \qquad \text{Perfect cube}$$
$$a^3 - 3a^2b + 3ab^2 - b^3 = (a - b)^3 \qquad \text{Perfect cube}$$
$$a^3 - b^3 = (a - b)(a^2 + ab + b^2) \qquad \text{Difference of two cubes}$$
$$a^3 + b^3 = (a + b)(a^2 - ab + b^2) \qquad \text{Sum of two cubes}$$

In problems 41 – 48, use these cube formulas to factor each expression.

41. $x^3 + 3x^2 + 3x + 1$

42. $x^3 + 6x^2 + 12x + 8$

43. $x^3 - 12x^2 + 48x - 64$

44. $y^3 - 9y^2 + 27y - 27$

45. $x^3 - 64$

46. $8x^3 - 1$

47. $27 + 8x^3$

48. $a^3 + 216$

In problems 49 – 54, determine the missing factor.

49. $x^{3/2} + x^{1/2} = x^{1/2}(?)$

50. $2x^{1/4} + 4x^{3/4} = 2x^{1/4}(?)$

51. $x^{-3} + x^{-2} = x^{-3}(?)$

52. $x^{-1} - x = x^{-1}(?)$

53. $(-x^3 + x)(3 - x^2)^{-1/2} + 2x(3 - x^2)^{1/2} = (3 - x^2)^{-1/2}(?)$

54. $4x(4x + 1)^{-1/3} - (4x + 1)^{2/3} = (4x + 1)^{-1/3}(?)$

APPLICATIONS

55. Suppose squares of side x are cut from four corners of an 8- × -8-inch piece of cardboard, and an open-top box is formed (see Figure 0.8). The volume of the box is given by $64x - 32x^2 + 4x^3$. Factor this expression.

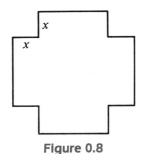

Figure 0.8

56. Factor the following expression for the maximum power in a certain electrical circuit: $(R + r)^2 - 2r(R + r)$.

0.7 Algebraic Fractions

Evaluating certain limits and graphing rational functions require an understanding of algebraic fractions. The fraction 6/8 can be reduced to 3/4 by dividing both the numerator and denominator by 2. In the same manner, the algebraic fraction

$$\frac{(x + 2)(x + 1)}{(x + 1)(x + 3)}$$

can be reduced to

$$\frac{x + 2}{x + 3}$$

by dividing both the numerator and denominator by $x + 1$, if $x \neq -1$.

> We *simplify* algebraic fractions by factoring the numerator and denominator and then dividing both the numerator and denominator by any common factors.*

EXAMPLE 1   Simplify $\dfrac{3x^2 - 14x + 8}{x^2 - 16}$, $x^2 \neq 16$.

Solution

$$\frac{3x^2 - 14x + 8}{x^2 - 16} = \frac{(3x - 2)(x - 4)}{(x - 4)(x + 4)}$$

$$= \frac{(3x - 2)\overset{1}{\cancel{(x - 4)}}}{\underset{1}{\cancel{(x - 4)}}(x + 4)}$$

$$= \frac{3x - 2}{x + 4}$$

We can multiply fractions by writing the product as the product of the numerators divided by the product of the denominators. For example,

$$\frac{4}{5} \cdot \frac{10}{12} \cdot \frac{2}{5} = \frac{80}{300},$$

which reduces to $\frac{4}{15}$.

---

*We assume all fractions are defined.

We can also find the product by reducing the fractions before we indicate the multiplication in the numerator and denominator. For example, in

$$\frac{4}{5} \cdot \frac{10}{12} \cdot \frac{2}{5},$$

we can divide the numerator and denominator by 5 and then by 4, giving

$$\frac{\overset{1}{\cancel{4}}}{\underset{1}{\cancel{5}}} \cdot \frac{\overset{2}{\cancel{10}}}{\underset{3}{\cancel{12}}} \cdot \frac{2}{5} = \frac{1}{1} \cdot \frac{2}{3} \cdot \frac{2}{5} = \frac{4}{15}.$$

> We *multiply* algebraic fractions by writing the product of the numerators divided by the product of the denominators, and then reduce to lowest terms. We may also reduce prior to finding the product.

EXAMPLE 2   Multiply: (a) $\dfrac{4x^2}{5y} \cdot \dfrac{10x}{y^2} \cdot \dfrac{y}{8x^2}$ (b) $\dfrac{-4x + 8}{3x + 6} \cdot \dfrac{2x + 4}{4x + 12}$

Solution   (a)

$$\frac{4x^2}{5y} \cdot \frac{10x}{y^2} \cdot \frac{y}{8x^2} = \frac{\overset{1}{\cancel{4x^2}}}{\underset{1 \cdot 1}{\cancel{5y}}} \cdot \frac{\overset{2}{\cancel{10x}}}{y^2} \cdot \frac{\overset{1}{\cancel{y}}}{\underset{2}{\cancel{8x^2}}}$$

$$= \frac{1}{1} \cdot \frac{\overset{1}{\cancel{2x}}}{y^2} \cdot \frac{1}{\underset{1}{\cancel{2}}} = \frac{x}{y^2}$$

(b)

$$\frac{-4x + 8}{3x + 6} \cdot \frac{2x + 4}{4x + 12} = \frac{-4(x - 2)}{3(x + 2)} \cdot \frac{2(x + 2)}{4(x + 3)}$$

$$= \frac{\overset{-1}{\cancel{-4}(x - 2)}}{3\cancel{(x + 2)}} \cdot \frac{2\overset{1}{\cancel{(x + 2)}}}{\underset{1}{\cancel{4}(x + 3)}}$$

$$= \frac{-2(x - 2)}{3(x + 3)}$$

In arithmetic we learned to divide one fraction by another by inverting the divisor and multiplying. The same rule applies to division of algebraic fractions.

(a) Divide $\dfrac{a^2b}{c}$ by $\dfrac{ab}{c^2}$.   (b) $\dfrac{6x^2 - 6}{x^2 + 3x + 2} \div \dfrac{x - 1}{x^2 + 4x + 4}$

(a)
$$\frac{a^2b}{c} \div \frac{ab}{c^2} = \frac{a^2b}{c} \cdot \frac{c^2}{ab} = \frac{\overset{a \cdot 1}{\cancel{a^2b}}}{\cancel{c}} \cdot \frac{\overset{c}{\cancel{c^2}}}{\underset{1 \cdot 1}{\cancel{ab}}} = \frac{ac}{1} = ac$$

(b)
$$\frac{6x^2 - 6}{x^2 + 3x + 2} \div \frac{x - 1}{x^2 + 4x + 4} = \frac{6x^2 - 6}{x^2 + 3x + 2} \cdot \frac{x^2 + 4x + 4}{x - 1}$$
$$= \frac{6(x - 1)(x + 1)}{(x + 2)(x + 1)} \cdot \frac{(x + 2)(x + 2)}{x - 1}$$
$$= 6(x + 2)$$

If two fractions are to be added, it is convenient that each be expressed with the same denominator. If the denominators are not the same, we can write the equivalents of each of the fractions with a common denominator. We usually use the lowest common denominator (LCD) when we write the equivalent fractions. The **lowest common denominator** is the lowest degree variable expression into which all denominators will divide. If the denominators are polynomials, then the LCD is the lowest degree polynomial into which all denominators will divide. We can find the lowest common denominator as follows.

Procedure	Example
To find the lowest common denominator of a set of fractions:	Find the LCD of $\dfrac{1}{x^2 - x}, \dfrac{1}{x^2 - 1}, \dfrac{1}{x^2}$.
1. Completely factor each denominator.	1. The factored denominators are $x(x - 1)$, $(x + 1)(x - 1)$, $x \cdot x$.
2. Write the LCD as the product of each of these factors used the maximum number of times it occurs in any one denominator.	2. x occurs a maximum of 2 times in one denominator, $x - 1$ occurs once, and $x + 1$ occurs once. Thus the LCD is $x \cdot x(x - 1)(x + 1) = x^2(x - 1)(x + 1)$.

The procedure for combining (adding or subtracting) two or more fractions is as follows.

Procedure	Example

To combine fractions:

Combine: $\dfrac{y-3}{y-5} + \dfrac{y-23}{y^2-y-20}$.

1. Find the LCD of the fractions.

1. $y^2 - y - 20 = (y-5)(y+4)$, so the LCD is $(y-5)(y+4)$.

2. Write the equivalent of each fraction with the LCD as its denominator.

2. The sum is $\dfrac{(y-3)(y+4)}{(y-5)(y+4)} + \dfrac{y-23}{(y-5)(y+4)}$.

3. Add or subtract as indicated.

3. $= \dfrac{y^2 + y - 12 + y - 23}{(y-5)(y+4)}$

$= \dfrac{y^2 + 2y - 35}{(y-5)(y+4)}$

4. Reduce the fraction, if possible.

4. $y - 5$ is a factor of the numerator, so the sum is

$\dfrac{y+7}{y+4}$,   if $y \neq 5$.

EXAMPLE 4   Add: $\dfrac{3x}{a^2} + \dfrac{4}{ax}$

Solution   1. The LCD is a^2x.

2. $\dfrac{3x}{a^2} + \dfrac{4}{ax} = \dfrac{3x}{a^2} \cdot \dfrac{x}{x} + \dfrac{4}{ax} \cdot \dfrac{a}{a}$

3. $\dfrac{3x^2}{a^2x} + \dfrac{4a}{a^2x} = \dfrac{3x^2 + 4a}{a^2x}$

4. The sum is in lowest terms.

EXAMPLE 5   Combine: $\dfrac{y-3}{(y-5)^2} + \dfrac{y-2}{y^2-y-20}$

Solution $y^2 - y - 20 = (y-5)(y+4)$, so the LCD is $(y-5)^2(y+4)$. Writing the equivalent fractions gives

$\dfrac{y-3}{(y-5)^2} + \dfrac{y-2}{(y-5)(y+4)} = \dfrac{(y-3)(y+4)}{(y-5)^2(y+4)} + \dfrac{(y-2)(y-5)}{(y-5)(y+4)(y-5)}$

$= \dfrac{(y^2 + y - 12) + (y^2 - 7y + 10)}{(y-5)^2(y+4)}$

$= \dfrac{2y^2 - 6y - 2}{(y-5)^2(y+4)}.$

We can simplify algebraic fractions whose denominators contain sums and differences involving square roots by rationalizing the denominator. Using the fact that $(x + y)(x - y) = x^2 - y^2$, we multiply the numerator and denominator of an algebraic fraction of this type by the conjugate of the denominator to simplify the fraction.

EXAMPLE 6   Rationalize the denominators.

(a) $\dfrac{1}{\sqrt{x} - 2}$ (b) $\dfrac{3 + \sqrt{x}}{\sqrt{x} + \sqrt{5}}$

Solution   Multiplying $\sqrt{x} - 2$ by $\sqrt{x} + 2$, its conjugate, gives the difference of two squares and removes the radical from the denominator in (a). We also use the conjugate in (b).

(a) $\dfrac{1}{\sqrt{x} - 2} \cdot \dfrac{\sqrt{x} + 2}{\sqrt{x} + 2} = \dfrac{\sqrt{x} + 2}{(\sqrt{x})^2 - (2)^2} = \dfrac{\sqrt{x} + 2}{x - 4}$

(b) $\dfrac{3 + \sqrt{x}}{\sqrt{x} + \sqrt{5}} \cdot \dfrac{\sqrt{x} - \sqrt{5}}{\sqrt{x} - \sqrt{5}} = \dfrac{3\sqrt{x} - 3\sqrt{5} + x - \sqrt{5x}}{x - 5}$

Exercise 0.7

Simplify the following fractions.

1. $\dfrac{18x^3y^3}{9x^3z}$

2. $\dfrac{15a^4b^5}{30a^3b}$

3. $\dfrac{x - 3y}{3x - 9y}$

4. $\dfrac{x^2 - 6x + 8}{x^2 - 16}$

5. $\dfrac{x^2 - 2x + 1}{x^2 - 4x + 3}$

6. $\dfrac{x^2 - 5x + 6}{9 - x^2}$

7. $\dfrac{6x^3y^3 - 15x^2y}{3x^2y^2 + 9x^2y}$

8. $\dfrac{x^2y^2 - 4x^3y}{x^3y - 2x^2y^2}$

In problems 9–38, perform the indicated operations and simplify.

9. $\dfrac{6x^3}{8y^3} \cdot \dfrac{16x}{9y^2} \cdot \dfrac{15y^4}{x^3}$

10. $\dfrac{25ac^2}{15a^2c} \cdot \dfrac{4ad^4}{15abc^3}$

11. $\dfrac{8x - 16}{x - 3} \cdot \dfrac{4x - 12}{3x - 6}$

12. $\dfrac{x^2 + 7x + 12}{3x^2 + 13x + 4} \cdot \dfrac{3x + 1}{x + 3}$

13. $(x^2 - 4) \cdot \dfrac{2x - 3}{x + 2}$

14. $\dfrac{4x + 4}{x - 4} \cdot \dfrac{x^2 - 6x + 8}{8x^2 + 8x}$

15. $\dfrac{x^2 - x - 2}{2x^2 - 8} \cdot \dfrac{18 - 2x^2}{x^2 - 5x + 4} \cdot \dfrac{x^2 - 2x - 8}{x^2 - 6x + 9}$

16. $\dfrac{x^2 - 5x - 6}{x^2 - 5x + 4} \cdot \dfrac{x^2 - x - 12}{x^3 - 6x^2} \cdot \dfrac{x - x^3}{x^2 - 2x + 1}$

17. $\dfrac{15ac^2}{7bd} \div \dfrac{4a}{14b^2d}$

18. $\dfrac{16}{x - 2} \div \dfrac{4}{3x - 6}$

19. $\dfrac{y^2 - 2y + 1}{7y^2 - 7y} \div \dfrac{y^2 - 4y + 3}{35y^2}$

20. $\dfrac{6x^2}{4x^2y - 12xy} \div \dfrac{3x^2 + 12x}{x^2 + x - 12}$

21. $(x^2 - x - 6) \div \dfrac{9 - x^2}{x^2 - 3x}$

22. $\dfrac{2x^2 + 7x + 3}{4x^2 - 1} \div (x + 3)$

23. $\dfrac{a}{a - 2} - \dfrac{a - 2}{a}$

24. $x - \dfrac{2}{x - 1}$

25. $\dfrac{x}{x + 1} + x + 1$

26. $\dfrac{x - 1}{x + 1} - \dfrac{2}{x^2 + x}$

27. $\dfrac{4a}{3x + 6} + \dfrac{5a^2}{4x + 8}$

28. $\dfrac{b - 1}{b^2 + 2b} + \dfrac{b}{3b + 6}$

29. $\dfrac{x - 7}{x^2 - 9x + 20} - \dfrac{x + 2}{x^2 - 5x + 4}$

30. $\dfrac{x + 1}{x^2 + x - 6} - \dfrac{2x - 1}{2 - x}$

31. $\dfrac{3x - 1}{2x - 4} + \dfrac{4x}{3x - 6} - \dfrac{4}{5x - 10}$

32. $\dfrac{2x + 1}{4x - 2} + \dfrac{5}{2x} - \dfrac{x + 1}{2x^2 - x}$

33. $\dfrac{1}{x^2 - 4y^2} - \dfrac{1}{x^2 - 4xy + 4y^2}$

34. $\dfrac{3x^2}{x^2 - 4} + \dfrac{2}{x^2 - 4x + 4} - 3$

35. $\dfrac{x}{x^2 - 4} + \dfrac{4}{x^2 - x - 2} - \dfrac{x}{x^2 + 3x + 2}$

36. $\dfrac{1}{y^2 + 5y - 14} - \dfrac{y}{y^2 - y - 2} + \dfrac{2}{y^2 + 8y + 7}$

37. $\dfrac{-x^3 + x}{\sqrt{3 - x^2}} + 2x\sqrt{3 - x^2}$

38. $\dfrac{3x^2(x + 1)}{\sqrt{x^3 + 1}} + \sqrt{x^3 + 1}$

In problems 39–42, rationalize the denominator of each fraction and simplify.

39. $\dfrac{1}{\sqrt{5} - 3}$

40. $\dfrac{3}{\sqrt{7} + 4}$

41. $\dfrac{1 - \sqrt{x}}{1 + \sqrt{x}}$

42. $\dfrac{x - 3}{x - \sqrt{3}}$

In problems 43 and 44, rationalize the numerator of each fraction and simplify.

43. $\dfrac{\sqrt{x + h} - \sqrt{x}}{h}$

44. $\dfrac{\sqrt{9 + 2h} - 3}{h}$

APPLICATIONS

45. Workers A, B, and C can complete a job in a, b, and c hours respectively. Working together they can complete

$$\frac{1}{a} + \frac{1}{b} + \frac{1}{c}$$

of the job in one hour. Add these fractions to obtain an expression for what they can do in one hour working together.

46. Two thin lenses with focal lengths p and q and that are a distance d apart have their focal length given by the reciprocal of

$$\frac{1}{p} + \frac{1}{q} - \frac{d}{pq}.$$

(a) Combine these fractions.

(b) Use the reciprocal of your answer in (a) to find the focal length.

Review Exercises

0.1

1. Is $A \subseteq B$, if $A = \{1, 2, 5, 7\}$ and $B = \{x: x$ is a positive integer, $x \leq 8\}$
2. Is it true that $3 \in \{x: x > 3\}$?
3. Are $A = \{1, 2, 3, 4\}$ and $B = \{x: x \leq 1\}$ disjoint?

In problems 4–7, use the sets $A = \{1, 2, 3, 9\}$, $B = \{1, 3, 5, 6, 7, 8, 10\}$, and $U = \{1, 2, 3, 4, 5, 6, 7, 8, 9, 10\}$ to find the elements of the sets described.

4. $A \cup B$ 5. $A \cap B$
6. A' 7. $A - B$

8. In an attempt to determine some off-the-job factors that might be indicators of on-the-job effectiveness, a company made a study of 200 of its employees. They were interested in whether the employees had been recognized for superior work by their supervisors within the past year, whether they were involved in community activities, and whether they followed a regular exercise plan. The company found the following.

   > 30 answered "yes" to all three
   > 50 were recognized and they exercised
   > 52 were recognized and were involved in the community
   > 77 were recognized
   > 37 were involved in the community but did not exercise
   > 95 were recognized or were involved in the community
   > 95 answered "no" to all three

   (a) Draw a Venn diagram that represents this information.
   (b) How many exercised only?
   (c) How many exercised or were involved in the community?

0.2

9. State the property of the real numbers illustrated in each case.

   (a) $6 + \dfrac{1}{3} = \dfrac{1}{3} + 6$ (b) $2(3 \cdot 4) = (2 \cdot 3)4$ (c) $\dfrac{1}{3}(6 + 9) = 2 + 3$

In problems 10–12, indicate whether the given expression is one or more of the following: rational, irrational, integer, natural, or meaningless.

10. π 11. 0/6   12. 6/0

For problems 13–20, evaluate each expression. Use a calculator when necessary.

13. $|5 - 11|$ 14. $44 \div 2 \cdot 11 - 10^2$

15. $(-3)^2 - (-1)^3$ 16. $\dfrac{(3)(2)(15) - (5)(8)}{(4)(10)}$

17. $2 - [3 - (2 - |-3|)] + 11$ 18. $-4^2 - (-4)^2 + 3$

19. $\dfrac{4 + 3^2}{4}$ 20. $\dfrac{(-2.91)^5}{\sqrt{3.29^5}}$

0.3

21. Evaluate each of the following without a calculator.

   (a) $\left(\dfrac{3}{8}\right)^0$ (b) $2^3 \cdot 2^4$ (c) $\dfrac{4^9}{4^3}$ (d) $\left(\dfrac{1}{7}\right)^3 \left(\dfrac{1}{7}\right)^{-4}$

22. Use the rules of exponents to simplify each of the following with positive exponents. Assume all variables are nonzero.

   (a) $x^5 \cdot x^{-7}$ (b) x^8/x^{-2} (c) $(x^3)^3$ (d) $(y^4)^{-2}$ (e) $(-y^{-3})^{-2}$

For problems 23–28 rewrite each expression so only positive exponents remain. Assume all variables are nonzero.

23. $\dfrac{-(2xy^2)^{-2}}{(3x^{-2}y^{-3})^2}$

24. $\left(\dfrac{2}{3}x^2y^{-4}\right)^{-2}$

25. $\left(\dfrac{x^{-2}}{2y^{-1}}\right)^2$

26. $\dfrac{(-x^4y^{-2}z^2)^0}{-(x^4y^{-2}z^2)^{-2}}$

27. $\left(\dfrac{x^{-3}y^4z^{-2}}{3x^{-2}y^{-3}z^{-3}}\right)^{-1}$

28. $\left(\dfrac{x}{2y}\right)\left(\dfrac{y}{x^2}\right)^{-2}$

0.4

29. Find the following roots.

    (a) $-\sqrt[3]{-64}$ (b) $\sqrt{4/49}$

30. Write each of the following with an exponent and with the variable in the numerator.

    (a) $\sqrt{x}$ (b) $\sqrt[3]{x^2}$ (c) $1/\sqrt[4]{x}$

31. Write each of the following in radical form and simplify.

    (a) $x^{2/3}$ (b) $x^{-1/2}$ (c) $-x^{3/2}$

32. Rationalize each of the following denominators and simplify.

    (a) $\dfrac{5xy}{\sqrt{2x}}$ (b) $\dfrac{y}{x\sqrt[3]{xy^2}}$

In problems 33–39, use the properties of exponents to simplify, so only positive exponents remain. Assume all variables are positive.

33. $x^{1/2} \cdot x^{1/3}$ 34. $y^{-3/4}/y^{-7/4}$ 35. $x^4 \cdot x^{1/4}$ 36. $1/(x^{-4/3} \cdot x^{-7/3})$

37. $(x^{4/5})^{1/2}$ 38. $(x^{1/2}y^2)^4$ 39. $\left(\dfrac{36x^{4/3}}{25y^{7/6}}\right)^{3/2}$

In problems 40–45, simplify each expression. Assume all variables are positive.

40. $\sqrt{12x^3y^5}$ 41. $\sqrt{1250x^6y^9}$ 42. $\sqrt[3]{24x^4y^4} \cdot \sqrt[3]{45x^4y^{10}}$

43. $\sqrt{16a^2b^3} \cdot \sqrt{8a^3b^5}$ 44. $\dfrac{\sqrt{52x^3y^6}}{\sqrt{13xy^4}}$ 45. $\dfrac{\sqrt{32x^4y^3}}{\sqrt{6xy^{10}}}$

0.5

In problems 46–64, perform the indicated operations and simplify.

46. $(3x + 5) - (4x + 7)$ 47. $x(1 - x) + x[x - (2 + x)]$

48. $(3x^3 - 4xy - 3) + (5xy + x^3 + 4y - 1)$

49. $(4xy^3)(6x^4y^2)$ 50. $(3x^{-3}y^2) \div (x^3y^{-3})$

51. $(3x - 4)(x - 1)$ 52. $(3x - 1)(x + 2)$

53. $(4x + 1)(x - 2)$ 54. $(3x - 7)(2x + 1)$

55. $(2x - 3)^2$ 56. $(4x + 3)(4x - 3)$

57. $(2x^2 + 1)(x^2 + x - 3)$ 58. $(2x - 1)^3$

59. $(x - y)(x^2 + xy + y^2)$ 60. $\dfrac{4x^2y - 3x^3y^3 - 6x^4y^2}{2x^2y^2}$

61. $(3x^4 + 2x^3 - x + 4) \div (x^2 + 1)$ 62. $(x^4 - 4x^3 + 5x^2 + x) \div (x - 3)$

63. $x^{4/3}(x^{2/3} - x^{-1/3})$ 64. $\left(\sqrt{x} + \sqrt{a - x}\right)\left(\sqrt{x} - \sqrt{a - x}\right)$

0.6

In problems 65–75, factor each expression completely.

65. $2x^4 - x^3$ 66. $4(x^2 + 1)^2 - 2(x^2 + 1)^3$ 67. $x^3 + x^2 - x - 1$

68. $4x^2 - 4x + 1$ 69. $16 - 9x^2$ 70. $2x^4 - 8x^2$

71. $x^2 - 4x - 21$ 72. $3x^2 - x - 2$ 73. $12x^2 - 23x - 24$

74. $16x^4 - 72x^2 + 81$ 75. $16 + 6x^3 - x^6$

0.7

76. Factor as indicated: $x^{-2/3} + x^{-4/3} = x^{-4/3}(?)$

77. Reduce each of the following to lowest terms:

(a) $\dfrac{2x}{2x + 4}$ (b) $\dfrac{4x^2y^3 - 6x^3y^4}{2x^2y^2 - 3xy^3}$

In problems 78–86, perform the indicated operations and simplify.

78. $\dfrac{x^2 - 4x}{x^2 + 4} \cdot \dfrac{x^4 - 16}{x^4 - 16x^2}$

79. $\dfrac{x^2 + 6x + 9}{x^2 - 7x + 12} \cdot \dfrac{x^2 - 3x - 4}{x^2 + 4x + 3}$

80. $\dfrac{x^2 - 9}{x^2 - x - 2} \div \dfrac{2x^2 + 7x + 3}{x^2 - 2x}$

81. $\dfrac{x^4 - 2x^3}{3x^2 - x - 2} \div \dfrac{x^3 - 4x}{9x^2 - 4}$

82. $1 + \dfrac{3}{2x} - \dfrac{1}{6x^2}$

83. $\dfrac{1}{x - 2} - \dfrac{x - 2}{4}$

84. $\dfrac{x}{3x + 6} + \dfrac{4}{x^2 + x - 2}$

85. $\dfrac{x + 2}{x^2 - x} - \dfrac{x^2 + 4}{x^2 - 2x + 1} + 1$

86. $\dfrac{x - 1}{x^2 - x - 2} - \dfrac{x}{x^2 - 2x - 3} + \dfrac{1}{x - 2}$

87. Rationalize the denominator of $\dfrac{3x - 3}{\sqrt{x} - 1}$ and simplify.

88. Rationalize the numerator of $\dfrac{\sqrt{x} - \sqrt{x - 4}}{2}$ and simplify.

Part Two

Linear Models

WARMUP

	Prerequisite problem type	Answer	Section for review
1.1, 1.2, 1.3, 1.5, 1.6	Evaluate: (a) $2(-1)^3 - 3(-1)^2 + 1$ (b) $3(-3) - 1$ (c) $14(10) - 0.02(10^2)$ (d) $\dfrac{3-1}{4-(-2)}$ (e) $\dfrac{-1-3}{2-(-2)}$ (f) $\dfrac{3(-8)}{4}$ (g) $2\left(\dfrac{23}{9}\right) - 5\left(\dfrac{2}{9}\right)$	(a) -4 (b) -10 (c) 138 (d) $\dfrac{1}{3}$ (e) -1 (f) -6 (g) 4	0.2 Signed numbers
1.2, 1.4, 1.6	Locate on a number line: (a) The integers from -1 to 3 inclusive (b) The integers from -3 to 2	(a) (b)	0.2 Real number line
1.3, 1.4	(a) $\dfrac{1}{x}$ is *un*defined for which real numbers? (b) $\sqrt{x-4}$ is a real number for which values of x?	(a) Undefined for $x = 0$ (b) $x \geq 4$	0.2 Real numbers 0.4 Radicals
1.1, 1.4, 1.5, 1.6, 1.7	Identify the coefficient of x and the constant term for (a) $y = -\frac{3}{2}x + 2$ (b) $R(x) = 9x$ (c) $P(x) = 7x - 300$	*Coeff. of x* *Const. term* (a) $-\frac{3}{2}$ 2 (b) 9 0 (c) 7 -300	0.5 Algebraic expressions
1.1, 1.3, 1.4, 1.5, 1.6, 1.7	Simplify: (a) $4(-c)^2 - 3(-c) + 1$ (b) $[3(x+h) - 1] - [3x - 1]$ (c) $12\left(\dfrac{3x}{4} + 3\right)$ (d) $9x - (300 + 2x)$ (e) $-\frac{1}{5}[x - (-1)]$ (f) $2(2y + 3) + 3y$	(a) $4c^2 + 3c + 1$ (b) $3h$ (c) $9x + 36$ (d) $7x - 300$ (e) $-\frac{1}{5}x - \frac{1}{5}$ (f) $7y + 6$	0.5 Algebraic expressions

1

Linear Equations
and Functions

A wide variety of problems from business, the social sciences, and the life sciences may be solved by using equations. Managers and economists use equations and their graphs to study costs, sales, national consumption, or supply and demand. Social scientists may plot demographic data or try to develop equations that predict population growth, voting behavior, or learning and retention rates. Life scientists use equations to model the flow of blood or the conduction of nerve impulses and to test theories or develop new ones by plotting experimental evidence.

In this chapter we begin by investigating linear equations and their graphs. We will also define the concepts of relation and function, introduce functional notation, and then relate all of these back to equations and graphs.

Numerous applications of mathematics are given throughout the text, but all chapters contain special sections emphasizing business and economics applications. In particular, this chapter introduces three important applications that will be expanded and used throughout the text as increased mathematical skills permit: national consumption; supply and demand as functions of price (market analysis); and total cost, total revenue, and total profit as functions of the quantity produced or sold (theory of the firm).

Linear equations are used by most businesses to predict such things as future revenues and costs. Linear functions are used in economics, biology, and sociology to relate data, and are also used to a large extent in accounting courses. Keynes used the linear function as the model for national consumption. In this chapter we discuss several important features of Keynesian analysis. We also formulate linear supply and demand functions and then determine the price and quantity at which market equilibrium occurs. We use linear revenue and cost functions to obtain profit functions and to find break-even points, and we solve problems involving linear equations from the social and life sciences.

1.1 Solution of Linear Equations in One Variable

Objectives   ☐   To solve linear equations in one variable
☐   To solve applied problems by using linear equations

A firm is said to break even if its total revenue *equals* its total cost. If we have an expression representing total revenue and an expression representing total cost for a product, these expressions are *equal* when the firm breaks even. An **equation** is a statement that two quantities or algebraic expressions are equal. The two quantities on either side of the equal sign are called **members** of an equation. For example, $2 + 2 = 4$ is an equation with members $2 + 2$ and 4; $3x - 2 = 7$ is an equation with $3x - 2$ as its left member and 7 as its right member. Note that the equation $7 = 3x - 2$ is the same statement as $3x - 2 = 7$. An equation with one literal number, such as $3x - 2 = 7$, is known as an equation in one variable. The literal number (x in this case) is called a **variable** because the value of the literal number determines whether the equation is true or not. For example, $3x - 2 = 7$ is true only for $x = 3$. Finding the value(s) of the variable that make the equation true is called **solving the equation.** The set of solutions to an equation is called a **solution set** of the equation. The variable in an equation is sometimes called the **unknown.**

Some equations involving variables are true only for certain values of the variables, while others are true for all values of the variables. Equations that are true for all values of the variable(s) are called **identities.** The equation $2(x - 1) = 2x - 2$ is an example of an identity. Equations that are true only for certain values of the variable(s) are called **conditional equations** or simply **equations.** The values of the variable(s) for which the equation is true are called **the solutions** of the equation.

Two equations are said to be **equivalent** if they have exactly the same solution set. For example,

$$4x - 12 = 16$$
$$4x = 28$$
$$x = 7$$

and

are equivalent equations because they all have the same solution, namely 7. We can often solve a complicated linear equation by finding an equivalent equation whose solution is easily found. We use the following properties of equality to reduce an equation to a simple equivalent equation.

Properties	Examples
Substitution Property The equation formed by substituting one expression for an equal expression is equivalent to the original equation.	$3(x - 3) - \frac{1}{2}(4x - 18) = 4$ is equivalent to $3x - 9 - 2x + 9 = 4$ and to $x = 4$. We say the solution set is {4}, or the solution is 4.

Addition Property

The equation formed by adding the same quantity to both sides of an equation is equivalent to the original equation.

$x - 4 = 6$ is equivalent to $x = 10$.
$x + 5 = 12$ is equivalent to $x = 7$.
(Subtracting 5 from both sides is equivalent to adding -5 to both sides.)

Multiplication Property

The equation formed by multiplying both sides of an equation by the same nonzero quantity is equivalent to the original equation.

$\frac{1}{3}x = 6$ is equivalent to $x = 18$. $5x = 20$ is equivalent to $x = 4$. (Dividing both sides by 5 is equivalent to multiplying both sides by $\frac{1}{5}$.)

If an equation contains one variable and if the variable occurs to the first degree, the equation is called a **linear equation in one variable.** The three properties above permit us to reduce any linear equation in one unknown to an equivalent equation whose solution is obvious. We may solve linear equations in one unknown by using the following procedure:

Procedure	Example
To solve a linear equation in one unknown:	Solve $\dfrac{3x}{4} + 3 = \dfrac{2(x-1)}{6}$.
1. If the equation contains fractions, multiply both sides by the least common denominator (LCD) of the fractions.	1. LCD is 12. $$12\left(\frac{3x}{4} + 3\right) = 12\left(\frac{2(x-1)}{6}\right)$$
2. Remove any parentheses in the equation.	2. $9x + 36 = 4x - 4$
3. Perform any additions or subtractions to get all terms containing the variable on one side and all other terms on the other side.	3. $9x + 36 - 4x = 4x - 4 - 4x$ $5x + 36 = -4$ $5x + 36 - 36 = -4 - 36$ $5x = -40$
4. Divide both sides of the equation by the coefficient of the variable.	4. $\dfrac{5x}{5} = \dfrac{-40}{5}$ $x = -8$
5. Check the solution by substitution in the original equation.	5. $\dfrac{3(-8)}{4} + 3 = -\dfrac{18}{6}$ ✓

EXAMPLE 1   Solve $2(3y - 1) = 4(y - 5)$ for y.

Solution   1. No fractions are involved.
2. $6y - 2 = 4y - 20$ Removing parentheses
3. $2y - 2 = -20$ Subtracting 4y from both sides
    $2y = -18$ Adding 2 to both sides
4. $y = -9$ Dividing both sides by 2

EXAMPLE 2   The relation between degrees Celsius and degrees Fahrenheit is given by

$176 = \frac{9}{5}C + 32$

$$F = \frac{9}{5}C + 32.$$

What Celsius temperature is equivalent to 176°F?

Solution   If $F = 176$, the equation is $176 = \frac{9}{5}C + 32$. Solving for C gives

$$880 = 9C + 160$$
$$720 = 9C$$
$$80 = C.$$

Thus 80°C is equivalent to 176°F.

EXAMPLE 3   Suppose a firm's profit function for a product is given by

$$P = \frac{5x}{4} - 300.$$

$150 = \frac{5x}{4} - 300$

$600 = 5x - 1200$ $+1200$

(a) How many units must be produced to make a profit of $150?
(b) Producing how many units will result in a profit of 0?

$x = 360$

Solution   (a) Setting $P = 150$ and solving for x gives

$$150 = \frac{5x}{4} - 300$$
$$600 = 5x - 1200$$
$$1800 = 5x$$
$$x = 360.$$

$0 = \frac{5x}{4} - 300$

$0 = 5x - 1200$

(b) Setting $P = 0$ and solving for x gives

$5x = 1200$

$$0 = \frac{5x}{4} - 300$$
$$0 = 5x - 1200$$
$$1200 = 5x$$
$$x = 240.$$

We say the firm breaks even at 240 units.

EXAMPLE 4   A bicycle costs the wholesaler $28.00. What will the retailer sell it for if the whole-saler's markup is 20% of the wholesale selling price and the retailer's markup is 30% of the retail selling price?

Solution   The wholesaler's markup of 20% means his or her cost ($28.00) is 80% of the wholesale selling price.

$$\$28.00 = 0.80\ S_w$$
$$\$35.00 = S_w \qquad \text{see Figure 1.1}$$

The wholesaler's selling price is $35.00, so the retailer's cost is $35.00. The retailer's markup is 30%, so the retail cost ($35.00) is 70% of the retail selling price.

$$\$35.00 = 0.70\, S_r$$
$$\$50.00 = S_r$$

The retailer will sell the bicycle for $50.00.

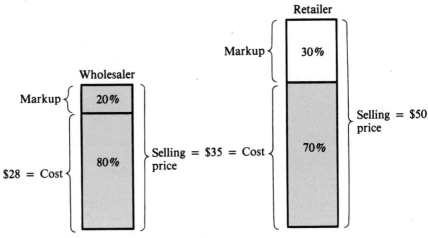

Figure 1.1

Exercise 1.1

In problems 1–30, solve each equation.

1. $x + 3 = 12$
2. $x + 8 = 7$
3. $2x - 3 = 5$
4. $4x + 2 = 5$
5. $4x - 7 = 8x - 2$
6. $3x + 2 = 7x + 2$
7. $15 - x = 3(x - 1)$
8. $4x - 1 = 3(x - 1)$
9. $8(x - 3) = 6(3x - 4)$
10. $3(x - 2) = 4(3 - x)$
11. $3x + \dfrac{1}{2} = 8$
12. $\dfrac{x}{2} + 4 = \dfrac{1}{3}$
13. $\dfrac{5x}{2} - 4 = \dfrac{2x - 7}{6}$
14. $\dfrac{2x}{3} - 1 = \dfrac{x - 2}{2}$
15. $\dfrac{5x - 1}{9} = \dfrac{5(x - 1)}{6}$
16. $\dfrac{6x + 5}{2} = \dfrac{5(2 - x)}{3}$
17. $0.4x = 16$
18. $0.4x + 5 = 9$
19. $2x + 0.6 = 4$
20. $0.3x + 0.4 = 1$
21. $2(x - 7) = 5(x + 3) - x$
22. $3(x - 4) = 4 - 2(x + 2)$
23. $2[x - (4 + 2x) + 3] = 2x + 2$
24. $3[2x - (2 + 4x) - 1] = 3(x - 4)$

25. $x + \dfrac{1}{3} = 2\left(x - \dfrac{2}{3}\right) - 6x$

26. $\dfrac{3x}{4} - \dfrac{1}{3} = 1 - \dfrac{2}{3}\left(x - \dfrac{1}{6}\right)$

27. $\dfrac{x + 3}{2x - 1} = 4$

28. $\dfrac{x - 2}{3x + 2} = 2$

29. $\dfrac{1}{x + 2} - \dfrac{1}{2} = \dfrac{x}{x + 2}$

30. $\dfrac{1}{4x} + \dfrac{2}{x} = \dfrac{5}{12}$

In problems 31–34, use a calculator to solve each equation. Round your answer to three decimal places.

31. $3.259x - 8.638 = -3.8(8.625x + 4.917)$

32. $3.319(14.1x - 5) = 9.95 - 4.6x$

33. $0.000316x + 9.18 = 2.1(3.1 - 0.0029x) - 4.68$

34. $3.814x = 2.916(4.2 - 0.06x) + 5.3$

APPLICATIONS

35. In wildlife management, the capture-mark-recapture technique is used to estimate the populations of fish or birds in an area or to measure the infestation of insects such as Japanese beetles. Suppose 100 individuals of the species being studied are caught, marked, and released, and one week later 100 more are caught. To estimate the total number of individuals, the following relationship is used:

$$\frac{\text{Total marked found in 2nd capture}}{\text{Total in 2nd capture}} = \frac{\text{Total number marked}}{\text{Total population}}.$$

   (a) If in the second capture of 100, it is found that 3 are marked, what is the total population?
   (b) Suppose that 1000 beetles are captured, marked, and released. Suppose further that in the second capture of 1000 it is found that 63 are marked. What is the population estimate?

36. Joe bought a radio for $99.95. He paid $19.95 down and agreed to pay the balance plus a finance charge of $2.00 in three months. What rate of simple interest did he pay? (Use the formula: interest = principal × rate × time.)

37. The equation $F = \frac{9}{5}C + 32$ describes the relation between temperature readings in Fahrenheit and Celsius. At what temperature will the two readings be the same?

38. The equation relating temperature readings in Fahrenheit and Celsius is given by

$$C = \frac{5}{9}(F - 32).$$

   (a) What Fahrenheit reading is equivalent to 0° Celsius?
   (b) What Fahrenheit reading is equivalent to 100° Celsius?

39. It has been noted that for adults over 5 feet tall in the northeast United States, their weight is related to their height according to

$$3w + 110 = 11(h - 20)$$

where w is measured in pounds and h is measured in inches. Use the formula above to answer the following.

(a) Find the weight of an adult whose height is 5 feet, 6 inches.

(b) Find the height of adults weighing 160 pounds.

40. A 90-minute recording tape is 10,125 inches long. How long is a 60-minute tape?

41. The manager of a hardware store marks all items so that the markup is 25% of the cost. How much would a saw sell for that costs the manager $25.50?

42. A firm produces two types of widgets, A and B. Each unit of A requires 3 work-hours and each unit of B requires 4 work-hours. If there are 430 work-hours available each week, how many units of A can be produced if 40 units of B are produced?

43. The Hillcrest Youth Organization determines the number of youths it has served by adding its active registrations and the number of dropouts. If the drop-out rate is one-third of the total served, find the total number of youths served when there are 6000 youths actively registered.

44. A city has a population P at the beginning of a year. The birth rate during the year was 10 per thousand and the death rate was 12 per thousand (of the year's original population). During the year, 360 people moved into the city and 190 moved away. If the population at the end of the year is 30,110, what was the population at the beginning of the year?

45. A realtor sells a house and receives a 5% commission on its selling price. If the realtor's commission is $4250, what is the selling price of the house?

46. The total price of a new car (including 6% sales tax) is $10,033. How much of this is tax?

47. A retailer wants a 30% markup on the selling price of an item that costs him $214.90. What selling price should he charge?

48. A toaster costs the Ace Department Store $22.74. If the store marks the toaster up by 40% of the selling price, what is the selling price?

49. A room air conditioner costs the wholesaler $154.98. If the wholesaler's markup is 10% of the wholesale selling price and if the retailer's markup is 30% of the retail selling price, for what does the retailer sell the air conditioner?

50. An electric mixer retails for $48.54, which includes a markup of 40% for the retailer and a markup of 20% for the wholesaler. If these markups are based on selling price,

(a) what did the mixer cost the retailer?

(b) what did the mixer cost the wholesaler?

51. A dinette set costs a wholesaler $189 and her markup is 10% of her selling price. If the retailer's markup is 30% of his selling price for the item, what is the retailer's selling price?

52. A wholesaler wants to establish a list price for an item so that his selling price gives a trade discount of 10% of the list price. If he makes a markup of 20% of this selling price, and if his cost is $160, what list price should he establish?

53. To earn an A in a course, a student must get at least a 90 average on four tests and a final exam, with the final exam weighted twice that of any one test. If the four test scores are 93, 69, 89, and 97, what is the lowest score the student can earn on the final exam and still get an A in the course?

54. Suppose a professor counts the final exam as being equal to each of the other tests in her course, and she will also change the lowest test score to match the final exam score if the final exam score is higher. If a student's four test scores are 83, 67, 52, and 90, what is the lowest score the student can earn on the final exam and still obtain at least an 80 average for the course?

55. An antique collector sold two pieces of furniture for $480 each. For one of them, this represented a 20% loss; for the other, it was a 20% profit (based on the cost of each item). How much did he make or lose on the transaction?

56. A woman making $2000 per month has her salary reduced by 10% due to sluggish sales. One year later, after a dramatic improvement in sales, she is given a 20% raise over her reduced salary. Find her salary after the raise. What percent change is this from the $2000 per month?

57. A car dealer purchases 20 new automobiles for $8000 each. If he sells 16 of them at a profit of 20%, for how much must he sell the remaining 4 to obtain an average profit of 18%?

1.2 Graphing Linear Equations

Objectives
- ☐ To graph linear equations by plotting points
- ☐ To graph linear equations by using intercepts

Equations may have more than one variable. The equation $y = 3x - 2$, for example, has two variables. There are an infinite number of solutions to this equation because any pair of values that satisfies the equation is a solution. For example, $x = 1$, $y = 1$ is a solution, as is $x = 4$, $y = 10$. We can find other solutions by substituting values for x and finding the value of y that satisfies the equation. For example, if we let $x = 5$, then letting $y = 3(5) - 2 = 13$ will satisfy the equation.

We denote an **ordered pair** of real numbers as (a, b), where a and b are real numbers. The number a is called the **first component** or **first coordinate** of the ordered pair, and b is called the **second component** or **second coordinate.** The ordered pairs (a, b) and (c, d) are said to be equal if and only if $a = c$ and $b = d$. We may write a **solution** to an equation in two variables x and y as an *ordered pair* of numbers (a, b), where the first number a is the x-value of the solution and the second number b is the y-value.

Just as we can use a number line to graph the real numbers (see Section 0.2), we can use a rectangular (or Cartesian) coordinate plane to graph ordered pairs of real numbers. The coordinate plane is especially useful, since it permits us to geometrically represent solutions to equations in two variables.

We construct the coordinate system by drawing two real number lines perpendicular to each other so that they intersect at their origins. (See Figure 1.2.) The point of intersection is called the **origin** of the system, and the two lines are called the **coordinate axes.** We call the horizontal axis the x-axis (or the first coordinate axis), and the vertical axis the y-axis (or the second coordinate axis). The scales on the two axes are frequently (but not always) the same. The axes divide the plane into four parts, called **quadrants.**

Any point in the plane can be represented by an ordered pair of real numbers. The point on the x-axis representing the real number a is denoted by the ordered pair $(a, 0)$, and the point on the y-axis representing the real number b is denoted by the ordered pair $(0, b)$. Any point P that is a units from the y-axis (right or left, depending on whether a is positive or negative) and b units from the x-axis (up or down, depending on whether b is positive or negative) is denoted by the ordered pair (a, b). (See Figure 1.2.)

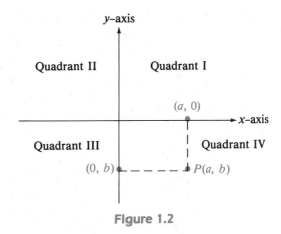

Figure 1.2

Note that the line drawn through the point denoted by (*a*, *b*) and perpendicular to the *x*-axis intersects the *x*-axis at (*a*, 0) and that the line drawn through (*a*, *b*) and perpendicular to the *y*-axis intersects the *y*-axis at (0, *b*). The values *a* and *b* in the ordered pair associated with the point *P* are called the **rectangular coordinates** of the point. The first coordinate of a point is called the **x-coordinate** (or **abscissa**), and the second coordinate is called the **y-coordinate** (or **ordinate**). To plot a point *P*(*a*, *b*) means to locate the point with *x*-coordinate *a* and *y*-coordinate *b*.

EXAMPLE 1   Plot the points *A*(5, 2), *B*(−4, 1), *C*(−4, −4), and *D*(1, −5).

Solution   See Figure 1.3.

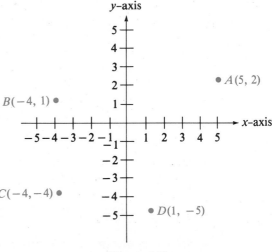

Figure 1.3

The **graph** of an equation is the picture that is drawn by plotting the points whose coordinates (x, y) satisfy the equation. Since there are an infinite number of such points, we cannot hope to plot them all. But we can plot enough points to determine the general outline of the graph. Then we usually connect the points with a smooth curve.

One very special equation is the **linear equation.** A linear equation can be written in the form $ax + by = c$ where a, b, and c are constants, and a and b are not both zero.

The graph of a linear equation may be drawn by plotting the points whose coordinates (x, y) satisfy the equation $ax + by = c$. Because the graph of a linear equation is always a straight line, only two points are required to determine its graph (two points determine a straight line). A third point may be plotted as a check on the graph.

EXAMPLE 2   Graph the equation $3x + y = 9$.

Solution   1. Plot any points that satisfy the equation.
   (a) If $x = 0$, $y = 9$, so $(0, 9)$ is one point.
   (b) If $x = 5$, $y = -6$, so $(5, -6)$ is another point.
2. Draw a straight line through the points. (See Figure 1.4.)
3. Plot a third point as a check: if $x = 2$, $y = 3$, so $(2, 3)$ should be on the line.

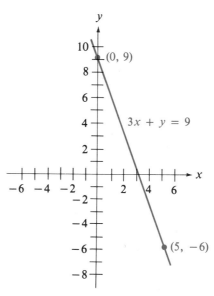

Figure 1.4

EXAMPLE 3   Graph (a) $x = 2$ and   (b) $y = 3$.

Solution   (a) We may think of this equation as $x + 0y = 2$, which indicates that $x = 2$ for all values of y. That is, y can have any value and x will still be 2. (See Figure 1.5.)

(b) Similarly $y = 3$ is the same as $0x + y = 3$. Hence, x may have any value and y will still be 3. (See Figure 1.5.)

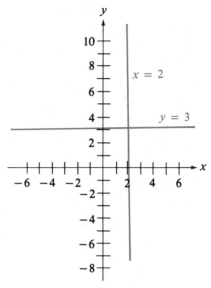

Figure 1.5

The points where $y = 0$ are points at which a graph intersects the x-axis, and are called the **x-intercepts** of the graph; **y-intercepts** are points where the graph intersects the y-axis.

| **Intercepts** | a. To find the **y-intercept(s)** of the graph of an equation, set $x = 0$ in the equation and solve for y. |
| | b. To find the **x-intercept(s)**, set $y = 0$ and solve for x. |

EXAMPLE 4   Find the x-intercept and y-intercept of the graph of $5x - 3y = 15$, and use them to sketch the graph of the equation.

Solution x-intercept: $y = 0$ gives $5x = 15$
$$x = 3.$$
Thus $(3, 0)$ is the x-intercept.
y-intercept: $x = 0$ gives $-3y = 15$
$$y = -5.$$
Thus $(0, -5)$ is the y-intercept.

A third point such as $(6, 5)$ can be used as a check. The graph is shown in Figure 1.6 on the following page.

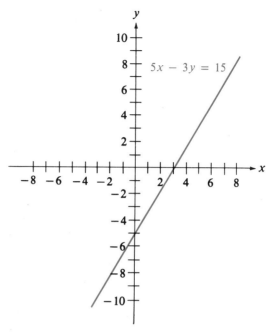

Figure 1.6

Despite the ease of using intercepts, this method is not always the best. For example, vertical lines, horizontal lines, or lines that pass through the origin may have a single intercept, and if a line has both intercepts very close to the origin, using the intercepts may lead to an inaccurate graph.

Exercise 1.2

Graph the following linear equations.

1. $y = 6x - 2$

2. $y = 2x + 8$

3. $y = \dfrac{x}{3} + \dfrac{2}{3}$

4. $y = \dfrac{4x}{5} - \dfrac{1}{2}$

5. $y = \dfrac{5 - x}{2}$

6. $y = \dfrac{7 - x}{3}$

7. $2x - 3y = 12$

8. $3x + 2y = 0$

9. $6x + 5y = 9$

10. $4x + 5y = 8$

11. $y = 3$

12. $x = -5$

13. $x = 0$

14. $y = 0$

15. $5y + 2x = 3(y - 1)$

16. $3x - 4(x - 3) = 2(y + x)$

17. $0.3x + 0.4y = 1.2$

18. $0.5x + 0.2y = 1$

19. $0.6x - 0.3y = 1.2$

20. $0.1x - 0.3y = 0.9$

21. $\dfrac{x}{4} - \dfrac{y}{6} = 1$

22. $\dfrac{y}{5} - \dfrac{x}{4} = 1$

23. $x + \dfrac{y}{2} = 2$

24. $\dfrac{x}{3} - \dfrac{y}{5} = 1$

25. $\dfrac{x}{2} - \dfrac{y}{4} = 1$

26. $\dfrac{x}{2} + \dfrac{y}{5} = 1$

APPLICATIONS

27. The fish population y in a certain river is related to the tons of pollutants x according to the following:

$$y = 100{,}000 - 1500x.$$

   (a) Sketch the graph of this equation.
   (b) Suppose that 17.5 tons of pollutants is deemed critical. How many fish would be in the stream at the critical level of pollution?

28. The activity of particles in a chemical reaction (such as digestion) or in the diffusion of a given solution is related to the concentration of the particles according to the formula $A = KC$, where A is the activity, C is the concentration, and K is the fraction of the concentration that is effective in determining the diffusion or the chemical reaction.
   (a) Sketch the graph of the equation if $K = 1$.
   (b) Sketch the graph of the equation if $K = 0.7$.

29. Body heat loss due to convection depends on a number of factors. If H_c is body-heat loss due to convection, A_c is the exposed surface area of the body, $T_s - T_a$ is skin temperature minus air temperature, and K_c is the convection coefficient (determined by air velocity and so on), then we have

$$H_c = K_c A_c (T_s - T_a).$$

When $K_c = 1$, $A_c = 1$, and $T_s = 90$, the equation is

$$H_c = 90 - T_a.$$

Sketch the graph.

30. The rate of oxygen consumption of the blood, x, measures the cardiac output (blood flow through the lungs), y, by

$$y = \frac{x}{A - V} = \left(\frac{1}{A - V}\right)x,$$

where A is the arterial concentration of oxygen and V is the venous concentration of oxygen. Sketch the graph for the above if $1/(A - V) = \frac{3}{4}$.

31. In psychology, the study of threshold levels of stimulus is of interest. If s is the amount of stimulus, then Δs is the required change in s so that the subject notices a change. Research has shown that

$$\Delta s = ks \quad (k = \text{constant}).$$

Sketch graphs of this equation ($s > 0$) for the values $k = \frac{1}{2}$, $k = 1$, and $k = 2$. Label the horizontal axis s and the vertical axis Δs.

32. The equation $C = \frac{5}{9}(F - 32)$ describes the relationship between temperature readings in degrees Centigrade and degrees Fahrenheit. Graph this equation with C on the vertical axis.

33. The distance d (in miles) to a thunderstorm is given by

$$d = \frac{t}{4.8}$$

where t is the number of seconds that elapse between seeing the lightning and hearing the thunder. Graph this equation for $0 \leq t \leq 20$.

34. The volume V (in cubic centimeters) of a certain gas depends on its temperature T (in °C) according to

$$V - 120 = \frac{3}{8}(T - 50).$$

Graph this equation.

35. A \$360,000 building is depreciated 5% per year by its owner. The value y of the building after x months of use is $y = 360,000 - 1500x$.
    (a) Graph this equation for $x \geq 0$.
    (b) How long before the building is completely depreciated (its value is zero)?

36. A study by a construction company showed that the strength s of concrete, measured by the percent of design strength attained, depends on the length of time t (in days) since it was poured. This value can be approximated using $s = 1.8t + 27$.
    (a) Graph this equation for $t \geq 0$.
    (b) How long before $s = 100$?
    (c) What is the significance of your answer to part (b)?

1.3 Functions

Objectives ☐ To determine if a relation is a function
              ☐ To state the domain and range of certain functions
              ☐ To use functional notation

It is reasonable to assume that a relation exists between the number of items a firm sells and its total revenue (the money brought into the firm by the sale of its product). It is frequently possible to express this relation by means of an equation. For example, if a firm sells its product for \$35 per unit, then the total revenue for a period of time could be expressed by the equation

$$R = 35x$$

where x represents the quantity sold by the firm during that period.

An equation containing two variables expresses a **relation** between those two variables. The equation $R = 35x$ expresses a relation between the variables x and R, and the equation $y = 4x - 3$ expresses a relation between the variables x and y.

In addition to defining a relation by an equation or rule of correspondence, we may also define it as any set of ordered pairs. The solutions to $y = 4x - 3$ are ordered pairs that also define the relation between x and y.

Relation	A **relation** is defined by a set of ordered pairs or by a rule that determines how the ordered pairs are found.

For example,

$$\{(1, 3), (2, 6), (3, 9), (4, 12)\}$$

expresses a relation between the set of first components, $\{1, 2, 3, 4\}$, and the set of second components, $\{3, 6, 9, 12\}$. The set of first components is called the **domain** of the relation, and the set of second components is called the **range** of the relation. Figure 1.7 uses arrows to indicate how the inputs from the domain (the first components) are associated with the outputs in the range (the second components).

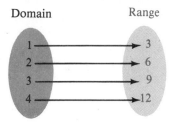

Figure 1.7

An equation frequently expresses how the second component (the output) is obtained from the first component (the input). For example, the equation

$$y = 4x - 3$$

expresses how the output y results from the input x. This equation expresses a special relation between x and y because each value of x that is substituted into the equation results in only one value for y. If each value of x put into an equation results in one value of y, we say that the equation expresses y as a **function** of x.

Definition of a Function	In general, a **function** is a relation between two sets such that to each element of the domain (input) there corresponds exactly one element of the range (output).

When a function is defined by an equation, the variable that represents the numbers in the domain (input) is called the **independent variable** of the function, and the variable that represents the numbers in the range (output) is called the **dependent variable** (because its values depend on the values of the independent variable). When we say "the equation $y = 4x - 3$ defines y as a function of x," we are saying that the equation defines a function with independent variable x and dependent variable y.

The equation $y = 4x^2$ defines y as a function of x, because only one value of y will result from each value of x that is substituted into the equation. Thus x is the independent variable and y is the dependent variable.

EXAMPLE 1   Does $y^2 = 2x$ express y as a function of x?

Solution   No, because for some values of x there is more than one value for y. In fact, there are two y-values for each $x > 0$. For example, if $x = 8$, $y = \pm 4$. The equation $y^2 = 2x$ expresses a relation between x and y, but y is not a function of x.

We can determine if a relation is a function by inspecting its graph. If the relation is a function, no two points on the graph will have the same first coordinate (component). Thus, no two points of the graph will lie on the same vertical line.

Vertical-Line Test   A curve in the coordinate plane is the graph of a function unless there exists a vertical line that intersects the curve in more than one point.

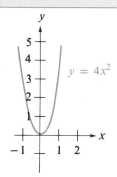

Figure 1.8

Performing this test on the graph of $y = 4x^2$ (Figure 1.8), we easily see that this equation describes a function. The vertical-line test indicates, however, that the equation $y^2 = 2x$ (which is graphed in Figure 1.9) is not a function. For example, a vertical line at $x = 2$ intersects the curve at $(2, 2)$ and $(2, -2)$.

We can use functional notation to indicate that y is a function of x. The function is denoted by f, and we write $y = f(x)$. This is read "y is a function of x" or "y equals f of x." For specific values of x, $f(x)$ represents the value of the function (that is, output or y-value) at those x-values. Thus, if

$$f(x) = 3x^2 + 2x + 1$$
$$f(2) = 3(2)^2 + 2(2) + 1 = 17$$

and

$$f(-3) = 3(-3)^2 + 2(-3) + 1 = 22.$$

Figure 1.10 represents this functional notation.

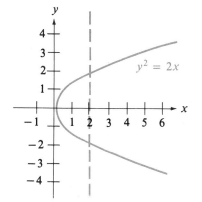

Figure 1.9

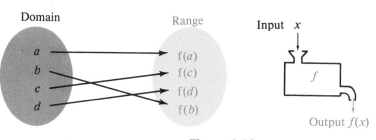

Figure 1.10

Letters other than f may also be used to denote functions. For example, $y = g(x)$ or $y = h(x)$ may be used.

EXAMPLE 2 If $y = f(x) = 2x^3 - 3x^2 + 1$, find the following.
(a) $f(0)$ (b) $f(3)$ (c) $f(-1)$

Solution (a) $f(0) = 2(0)^3 - 3(0)^2 + 1 = 1$. Thus $y = 1$ when $x = 0$.
(b) $f(3) = 2(3)^3 - 3(3)^2 + 1 = 2(27) - 3(9) + 1 = 28$. Thus $y = 28$ when $x = 3$.
(c) $f(-1) = 2(-1)^3 - 3(-1)^2 + 1 = 2(-1) - 3(1) + 1 = -4$. Thus $y = -4$ when $x = -1$.

EXAMPLE 3 If $g(x) = 4x^2 - 3x + 1$, find the following.
(a) $g(a)$ (b) $g(-a)$ (c) $g(b)$ (d) $g(a + b)$

Solution (a) $g(a) = 4(a)^2 - 3(a) + 1 = 4a^2 - 3a + 1$
(b) $g(-a) = 4(-a)^2 - 3(-a) + 1 = 4a^2 + 3a + 1$
(c) $g(b) = 4(b)^2 - 3(b) + 1 = 4b^2 - 3b + 1$
(d) $g(a + b) = 4(a + b)^2 - 3(a + b) + 1$

(a) $f(x) = 11$ when $x = 4$
(b) $f(x) = 3\lambda - 1$
(c)

EXAMPLE 4 Given $f(x) = 3x - 1$, find the following.
(a) $f(4)$ (b) $f(\lambda)$ (c) $\dfrac{f(x + h) - f(x)}{h}$, if $h \neq 0$

Solution (a) $f(4) = 3(4) - 1 = 11$ (b) $f(\lambda) = 3(\lambda) - 1 = 3\lambda - 1$

(c) $\dfrac{f(x + h) - f(x)}{h} = \dfrac{[3(x + h) - 1] - (3x - 1)}{h}$

$= \dfrac{3x + 3h - 1 - 3x + 1}{h} = \dfrac{3h}{h} = 3$

We will limit our discussion in this text to **real** functions, which are functions whose domains and ranges contain only real numbers. If the domain and range of a function are not specified, it is assumed that the domain consists of all real numbers that result in real numbers in the range, and the range is a subset of the real numbers.

In general, if the domain of a function is unspecified, it will include all real numbers except:

1. values that result in a denominator of 0, and
2. values that result in an even root of a negative number.

EXAMPLE 5 Find the domain of each of the following functions; find the range for the functions in (a) and (b).

(a) $y = 4x^2$ (b) $y = \sqrt{4 - x}$ (c) $y = 1 + \dfrac{1}{x}$

Solution
(a) There are no restrictions on the numbers substituted for x, so the domain consists of all real numbers. Since the square of any real number is nonnegative, $4x^2$ must be nonnegative. Thus the range is $y \geq 0$.

(b) We note the restriction that $4 - x$ cannot be negative. Thus the domain consists of only numbers less than or equal to 4. That is, the domain is the set of real numbers satisfying $x \leq 4$. Since $\sqrt{4 - x}$ is always nonnegative, the range is all $y \geq 0$.

(c) $1 + \dfrac{1}{x}$ is undefined at $x = 0$ since $\dfrac{1}{0}$ is undefined. Hence, the domain consists of all real numbers except 0.

Linear equations that can be written in the form $y = ax + b$ express y as a function of x. Thus, they are called **linear functions.** When $a = 0$, we have $y = f(x) = b$, which is a special linear function called a **constant** function. Figure 1.4 (Section 1.2) shows the graph of the linear function $y = -3x + 9$, and Figure 1.5 shows the graph of the constant function $y = 3$.

Another special function comes from the definition of $|x|$. The **absolute value function** can be written as

$$f(x) = |x| \text{ or } f(x) = \begin{cases} x & \text{if } x \geq 0 \\ -x & \text{if } x < 0 \end{cases}.$$

The graph of this function is shown in Figure 1.11. Since the absolute value function is defined by two equations, we say it is a **piecewise defined function.**

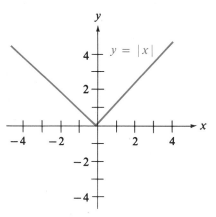

Figure 1.11

Equations may involve variables other than x and y. For example, we could use S to represent selling price and C to represent cost to write the selling price as a function of the cost, as follows.

$$S = f(C) = \begin{cases} 3C & \text{if } 0 \leq C \leq 20 \\ 1.5C + 30 & \text{if } C > 20 \end{cases}$$

piecewise function

Written in this way, the value of S depends on the value of C, so C is the independent variable and S is the dependent variable. The set of possible values of C (the domain) is the set of nonnegative real numbers (because cost cannot be negative), and the range is the set of nonnegative real numbers (since all values of C will result in nonnegative values for S).

Note that the selling price is defined piecewise by two different equations on two different intervals. For example, the selling price of a product that costs $15 would be $f(15) = 3(15) = 45$ (dollars) and the selling price of a product that costs $25 would be $f(25) = 1.5(25) + 30 = 67.50$ (dollars).

EXAMPLE 6   Graph the above selling price function.

Solution   Each of the two pieces of the graph of this function is a line and is easily graphed. It remains only to graph each in the proper interval. The graph is shown in Figure 1.12.

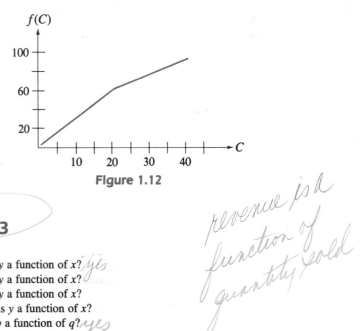

Figure 1.12

Exercise 1.3

1. If $y = 3x^3$, is y a function of x? *yes*
2. If $y = 6x^2$, is y a function of x?
3. If $y^2 = 3x$, is y a function of x?
4. If $y^2 = 10x^2$, is y a function of x?
5. If $p = 2q$, is p a function of q? *yes*
6. If $y = \sqrt{4x}$, is y a function of x?
7. If $p = \pm\sqrt{2q}$, is p a function of q? *yes*
8. If $R = \sqrt[3]{x}$, is R a function of x?
9. If $R(x) = 8x - 10$, find the following.
   (a) $R(0)$ (b) $R(2)$ (c) $R(-3)$ (d) $R(1.6)$
10. If $g(x) = 1 - 4x$, find the following.
    (a) $g(1)$ (b) $g(3)$ (c) $g(-4)$ (d) $g(-2.8)$
11. If $C(x) = 4x^2 - 3$, find the following.
    (a) $C(0)$ (b) $C(-1)$ (c) $C(-2)$ (d) $C\left(-\frac{3}{2}\right)$
12. If $h(x) = 3x^2 - 2x$, find the following.
    (a) $h(3)$ (b) $h(-3)$ (c) $h(2)$ (d) $h\left(\frac{1}{6}\right)$

revenue is a function of quantity sold

13. If $f(x) = x^3 - 4/x$, find the following.
    (a) $f\left(-\frac{1}{2}\right)$ (b) $f\left(\frac{3}{2}\right)$ (c) $f(0.16)$

14. If $f(x) = 2.89x^2 - \sqrt{1.06x}$, find the following.
    (a) $f(3.82)$ (b) $f(0.029)$ (c) $f\left(\frac{3}{7}\right)$

15. If $F(x) = \dfrac{|x|}{x}$, find the following.

    (a) $F\left(-\frac{1}{3}\right)$ (b) $F(10)$ (c) $F(0.001)$ (d) Is $F(0)$ defined?

16. If $H(x) = ||x| - 1|$, find the following.
    (a) $H(-1)$ (b) $H(1)$ (c) $H(0)$ (d) Does $H(-x) = H(x)$?

17. If $f(x) = \begin{cases} x^2 + 1 & \text{if } x < 1 \\ 3 - 1/x & \text{if } x > 1 \end{cases}$, find the following.
    (a) $f(-6)$ (b) $f(1)$ (c) $f(100)$ (d) $f(0.9)$

18. If $k(x) = \begin{cases} 2 & \text{if } x < 0 \\ x + 4 & \text{if } 0 < x < 1 \\ 1 - x & \text{if } x \geq 1 \end{cases}$, find the following, if they exist.

    (a) $k(-5)$ (b) $k(0)$ (c) $k(1)$ (d) $k(-0.001)$

19. If $f(x) = 1 + x + x^2$, find the following.
    (a) $f(2 + 1)$ (b) $f(x + 1)$ (c) $f(x + h)$

20. If $f(x) = 3x^2 - 6x$, find the following.
    (a) $f(3 + 2)$ (b) $f(x + 2)$ (c) $f(x + h)$

21. If $f(x) = x - 2x^2$, find the following.

    (a) $f(x + h)$ (b) $f(x + h) - f(x)$ (c) $\dfrac{f(x + h) - f(x)}{h}$

22. If $f(x) = 2x^2 - x + 3$, find the following.

    (a) $f(x + h)$ (b) $f(x + h) - f(x)$ (c) $\dfrac{f(x + h) - f(x)}{h}$

23. Does the graph in Figure 1.13 represent y as a function of x?
24. Does the graph in Figure 1.14 represent s as a function of t?

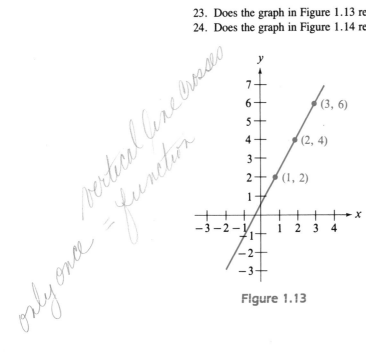

Figure 1.13

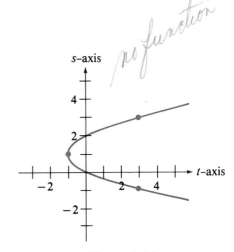

Figure 1.14

25. Does the graph in Figure 1.15 represent y as a function of x?
26. Does the graph in Figure 1.16 represent y as a function of x?

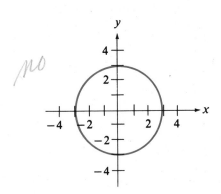

Figure 1.15

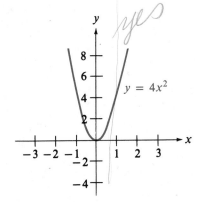

Figure 1.16

27. If $y = f(x)$ in Figure 1.13, what is $f(1)$?
28. If $y = f(x)$ in Figure 1.13, what is $f(2)$?
29. If $y = g(x)$ in Figure 1.16, what is $g(0)$?
30. Is there a value of x in the domain of the function represented by Figure 1.16 such that $g(x) = 0$?
31. The graph of $y = x^2 - 4x$ is shown in Figure 1.17.
    (a) If the coordinates of the point P on the graph are (a, b), how are a and b related?
    (b) What are the coordinates of the point Q? Do they satisfy the equation?
    (c) What are the coordinates of R? Do they satisfy the equation?
    (d) What are the x-values of the points on the graph whose y-coordinates are 0? Are these x-values solutions to the equation $x^2 - 4x = 0$?

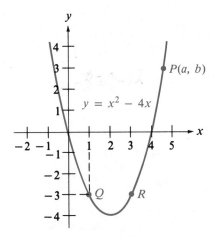

Figure 1.17

32. The graph of $y = 2x^2$ is shown in Figure 1.18.
    (a) If the point P, with coordinates (a, b), is on the graph, how are a and b related?
    (b) Does the point $(1,1)$ lie on the graph? Do the coordinates satisfy the equation?
    (c) What are the coordinates of point R? Do they satisfy the equation?
    (d) What is the x-value of the point whose y-coordinate is 0? Does this value of x satisfy the equation $0 = 2x^2$?

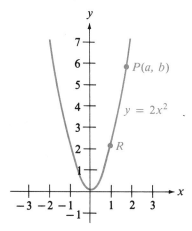

Figure 1.18

State the domain and range of each of the following functions.

33. $y = x^2 + 4$ 34. $y = x^2 - 1$
35. $y = \sqrt{x - 1}$ 36. $y = \sqrt{x^2 + 1}$

State the domain of each of the following functions.

37. $y = \dfrac{1}{x}$ 38. $R = \dfrac{3}{x + 3}$

39. $y = \dfrac{\sqrt{x - 1}}{x - 2}$ 40. $y = \dfrac{\sqrt{x^2 + 1}}{x}$

APPLICATIONS

41. The description of body-heat loss due to convection involves a coefficient of convection K_c, which depends on wind speed v according to the equation

$$K_c = 4\sqrt{4v + 1}.$$

    (a) Is K_c a function of v?
    (b) What is the domain?
    (c) What restrictions do nature and common sense put on v?

42. The efficiency E of a muscle performing a maximal contraction is related to the time t that the muscle is contracted according to

$$E = \frac{1 - 0.24t}{2 + t}.$$

(a) Is E a function of t?
(b) What is the domain?
(c) What restrictions do nature and common sense put on the domain?

43. The equation $C = \frac{5}{9}F - \frac{160}{9}$ gives the relation between temperature readings in Celsius and Fahrenheit.

(a) Is C a function of F?
(b) What is the domain?
(c) If we consider this equation as relating temperatures of water in its liquid state, what are the domain and range?
(d) What is C when $F = 40°$?

44. The pressure P of a certain gas is related to volume V according to

$$P = \frac{100}{V}.$$

(a) Is 0 in the domain of this function?
(b) What is $P(100)$?
(c) What is $P(50)$?
(d) As volume decreases, what happens to pressure?

45. The population size y of a certain organism at time t is given by

$$y = f(t) = 4t^2 + 2t.$$

(a) What is $f(1)$?
(b) What is $f(2)$?
(c) What is $f(3)$?

46. The reaction R to an injection of a drug is related to the dosage x according to

$$R(x) = x^2\left(500 - \frac{x}{3}\right),$$

where 1000 mg is the maximum dosage. What is $R(100)$?

47. The number of action potentials produced by a nerve t seconds after a stimulus may be described by

$$N(t) = 25t + \frac{4}{t^2 + 2} - 2.$$

(a) What is $N(2)$?
(b) What is $N(10)$?

48. The total cost of producing a product is given by

$$C = 300x + 0.1x^2 + 1200,$$

where x represents the number of units produced.

(a) What is the total cost of producing 10 units?
(b) What is the average cost per unit when 10 units are produced?

49. Suppose the cost C (in dollars) of removing p percent of the particulate pollution from the smokestacks of an industrial plant is given by

$$C(p) = \frac{7300p}{100 - p}.$$

(a) Find the domain of this function. Recall that p represents the percent of pollution that is removed.
(b) Find $C(45)$.
(c) Find $C(90)$.
(d) Find $C(99)$.
(e) Find $C(99.6)$.

50. If a test having reliability r is lengthened by a factor n ($n \geq 1$), the reliability R of the new test is given by

$$R(n) = \frac{nr}{1 + (n - 1)r} \qquad 0 < r \leq 1.$$

If the reliability is $r = 0.6$, the equation becomes

$$R(n) = \frac{0.6n}{0.4 + 0.6n}.$$

(a) Find $R(1)$.
(b) Find $R(2)$; that is, find R when the test length is doubled.
(c) What percentage improvement is there in the reliability when the test length is doubled?

51. If 100 feet of fence is to be used to fence in a rectangular yard, then the resulting area of the fenced yard is given by $A = x(50 - x)$, where x is the width of the rectangle.
(a) Is A a function of x?
(b) If $A = A(x)$, find $A(2)$ and $A(30)$.
(c) What restrictions must be placed on x (the domain) so the problem makes physical sense?

52. If a box with square cross-section is to be sent by the postal service, there are restrictions on its size such that its volume is given by $V = x^2(108 - 4x)$, where x is the length of each side of the cross-section (in inches).
(a) Is V a function of x?
(b) If $V = V(x)$, find $V(10)$ and $V(20)$.
(c) What restrictions must be placed on x (the domain) so the problem makes physical sense?

53. The monthly charge for water in a small town is given by

$$f(x) = \begin{cases} 18 & \text{if } 0 \leq x \leq 20 \\ 18 + 0.1\,(x - 20) & \text{if } x > 20 \end{cases}$$

where x is in hundreds of gallons and $f(x)$ is in dollars. Find the monthly charge for each of the following usages.
(a) 30 gallons   (b) 3000 gallons   (c) 4000 gallons

54. The monthly charge (in dollars) for x kilowatt hours (KWH) of electricity used by a commercial customer is given by the following function.

$$C(x) = \begin{cases} 7.52 + 0.1079x & \text{if } 0 \leq x \leq 5 \\ 19.22 + 0.1079x & \text{if } 5 < x \leq 750 \\ 20.795 + 0.1058x & \text{if } 750 < x \leq 1500 \\ 131.345 + 0.0321x & \text{if } x > 1500 \end{cases}$$

Find the monthly charge for the following usages.
(a) 5 KWH   (b) 6 KWH   (c) 3000 KWH

1.4 Applications of Functions in Business and Economics

Objectives
- ☐ To formulate and evaluate consumption functions
- ☐ To evaluate and graph supply and demand functions
- ☐ To formulate and evaluate total cost, total revenue, and profit functions

We will discuss numerous applications of mathematics in this text, but in this section we will introduce three important business applications, which will be expanded and used in different circumstances throughout the text as increased mathematical skills permit. These applications are national consumption (Keynesian analysis); supply and demand as functions of price (market analysis); and total cost, total revenue, and profit as functions of quantity sold (theory of the firm).

The Consumption Function

The consumption function is one of the basic ingredients in a larger discussion of how an economy can have persistent high unemployment or persistent high inflation. This study is often called Keynesian analysis after its founder, John Maynard Keynes. During the Great Depression of the 1930s, the United States suffered through many years of high unemployment that threatened the collapse of capitalism in this country. During this period, elements of Keynes's theories were used when the Roosevelt administration abandoned laissez-faire economics and instituted government-sponsored employment programs and governmental fiscal and monetary policies.

If we use the language of functions, we can write a consumption function as

$$C = f(y) = 0.8y + 6,$$

where y is disposable income (in billions of dollars) and C is consumption (in billions of dollars). This statement says that consumption is a function, and expresses exactly what the functional relationship is. **Consumption functions** are frequently assumed to be linear over short periods of time. Over longer periods of time, consumption functions will be nonlinear.

EXAMPLE 1   If the consumption function is given by $C = f(y) = 20 + 0.6y$, where C is the consumption and y is the disposable income (in billions of dollars),
(a) what is the consumption when disposable income is 0?
(b) what is the consumption when disposable income is $5 billion?
(c) sketch the graph of the consumption function.

Solution   (a) $f(0) = 20 + 0.6(0) = 20$ (billion dollars)
(b) $f(5) = 20 + 0.6(5) = 23$ (billion dollars)

(c) The graph in Figure 1.19 is the line passing through the points satisfying the equation $C = 20 + 0.6y$. Note that y cannot be negative.

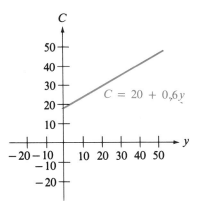

Figure 1.19

Supply and Demand Functions

It is a fact that consumers want more goods than they actually purchase. The goods that they actually buy are determined by (a) the price of the good desired, (b) the amount of money they have to spend on the item, (c) the strength of their tastes and preferences, (d) the prices of competing goods, and (e) their expectations of the future and its effect on this good.

If we concentrate on the relationship between the price of the good and the amount of the good a consumer is willing to purchase in a fixed period of time, the resulting function is called a **demand function.** Economists define demand for a commodity by using a schedule, or table, that shows the various amounts of the commodity that consumers are willing and able to purchase at specific prices in a set of possible prices during a specified period of time. The **law of demand** states that as price increases, the corresponding quantity demanded will fall or, as price decreases, the quantity demanded will increase.

Table 1.1 is a demand schedule that shows the relationship between the price of a particular brand of shirt and the number of shirts one person is willing and able to buy in a given period of time (the quantity demanded). This function (or schedule) is for only one person and for a fixed period (one month). Different people will have different demand schedules based on the other four factors mentioned. Usually we will be talking about the demand of a group of consumers. Note also that the demand schedule is for a specified period of time. The relationship from Table 1.1 is for a period of one month. Figure 1.20 shows its graph.

Table 1.1   One person's demand schedule for shirts for one month

q, Quantity demanded	p, Price of one shirt
0	24
1	21
2	18
3	15
4	12
5	9

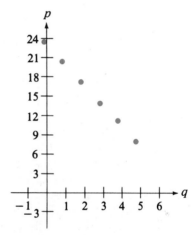

Figure 1.20

The relationship between the price of a commodity and the quantity demanded is functional; namely, quantity demanded is a function of price, which is denoted $q = f(p)$. However, economists traditionally have graphed the demand function on a two-dimensional graph with the quantity demanded on the horizontal axis and the price on the vertical axis, as we have done in Figure 1.20. Throughout the text, we will follow this tradition when graphing demand functions. Equations relating price and quantity demanded can be solved for either p or q, and we will have occasion to use the equations in both forms.

Although we only have a series of points as the graph of the demand function in Figure 1.20, it is common practice to draw a smooth curve joining the points and to call the curve the **demand curve.** In this case the smooth curve would be a straight line (see Figure 1.21) with the equation $p = 24 - 3q$. The graph implies that, for example, the consumer will buy 0.5 shirts per month if the cost is $22.50 per shirt. This can be interpreted as meaning he or she will buy 1 shirt every two months. Though some points on the graph, such as $\left(\sqrt{2}, 24 - 3\sqrt{2}\right)$, will not have much meaning in a business sense, the advantage of dealing with continuous demand curves far outweighs any possible disadvantages. Thus we assume that demand functions will have continuous curves.

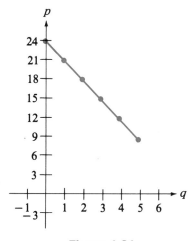

Figure 1.21

Except in very sophisticated economic models, negative price* and quantity have no meaning, so the graphs of demand curves will be in the first quadrant. The demand curve will normally slope downward toward the right because the quantity demanded will be larger as the price decreases. The demand curve may be a vertical line, however, if price is not a factor in demand. For example, a diabetic person must continue to buy insulin regardless of its cost. The demand curve could also be a horizontal line if the price remains constant regardless of the demand.

Just as a consumer's willingness to buy is related to price, so is a manufacturer's willingness to supply goods. Economists define **supply** as a schedule that shows the various amounts of a commodity that a producer is willing and able to produce and make available for sale at specific prices during a specified time.

Economists usually interpret supply as showing the quantity producers will offer at various prices, so quantity supplied is a function of price. As with demand, price is placed on the vertical axis on the graph of the **supply curve.** The horizontal axis now represents quantity supplied rather than quantity demanded.

The **law of supply** states that as price rises, the corresponding quantity supplied for sale will also rise. Because the producer will supply more goods if the price increases, the supply curve will normally rise as it moves to the right (see Figure 1.22). Of course, certain special circumstances may result in horizontal lines rep-

---

*Negative price values would result if buyers were paid to remove goods from the market.

resenting supply curves. For example, a consumer may be supplied with the right to make an unlimited number of local phone calls per month for a fixed fee, resulting in a horizontal supply curve (see Figure 1.23). As with the demand curve, the supply curves will have meaning for us only in the first quadrant.

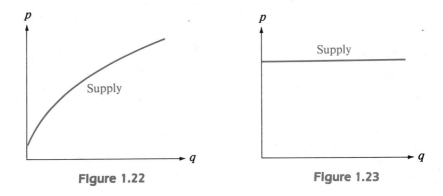

Figure 1.22   **Figure 1.23**

Total Cost, Total Revenue, and Profit Functions

Suppose you are the manager of a shoelace company that operates according to the following conditions:

1. It makes only shoelaces, and sells them for $.50 per pair.
2. Ten people are employed, and are paid $.10 for each pair of shoelaces they make. Note that they are paid *only* for what they produce.
3. Raw materials cost $.24 for each pair of shoelaces made.
4. Costs for equipment, plant, insurance, the manager's salary, and fringe benefits (these are called **fixed costs**) amount to $2000 per month.

If you were the manager of this shoelace factory, you would be interested in how many pairs of shoelaces you would have to make to break even. This means you would have to determine what your **total revenue** and your **total cost** would be at different levels of production. The information given is sufficient to formulate equations for the total revenue and the total cost, and from these equations we can formulate an equation that will determine the **profit** at different levels of production. From this equation you can determine when profit is 0; that is, when you break even. Let's discuss this problem in more detail.

The **total revenue function** states how much money is brought into the firm each month by the sale of its product. The total revenue for a month is the amount taken in before any expenses are paid. If x pairs of shoelaces are sold in a month, the total revenue for the shoelace factory is $0.50x$. Thus the total revenue function is

$$R = R(x) = 0.50x \quad \text{(in dollars)}.$$

Here x is the independent variable and R is the dependent variable. The graph of $R(x)$ for one month is shown in Figure 1.24. Note that the domain of the function is $\{x: x \geq 0\}$ because a negative quantity is meaningless.

We can also write the equation for the total cost function, which measures how many dollars the firm must pay to produce and sell its product. The total cost is comprised of two parts, fixed costs and variable costs. **Fixed costs** are those that remain constant regardless of the number of units produced. They include depreciation or rent on buildings, interest on investments, and so on. The fixed costs for the shoelace factory are given to be $2000 per month. Thus the cost for one month will always be at least $2000, even if no shoelaces are produced. The fixed costs are denoted by FC on the graph of Figure 1.25.

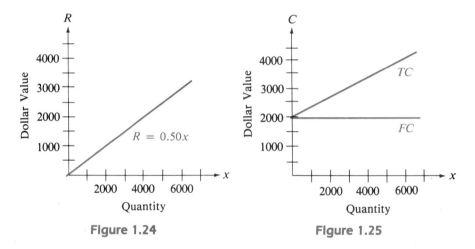

Figure 1.24   Figure 1.25

Variable costs are those directly related to the production of a commodity. The variable costs for producing x pairs of shoelaces are $0.10x$ for labor and $0.24x$ for raw materials, for a total of $0.34x$. The **total cost function** is the sum of the fixed and variable costs, or

$$C = C(x) = 2000 + 0.34x \qquad \text{(in dollars)}.$$

The total cost is denoted by TC on the graph of Figure 1.25. Note that the total cost equals the fixed cost when production is zero.

EXAMPLE 2   Find the total revenue and total cost if the shoelace factory produces and sells
(a) 10,000 pairs of shoelaces in a month.
(b) 15,000 pairs of shoelaces in a month.

Solution   (a) The total revenue is $R(10{,}000) = 0.50(10{,}000) = 5000$ (dollars)
The total cost is $C(10{,}000) = 2000 + 0.34(10{,}000) = 5400$ (dollars)
(b) The total revenue is $R(15{,}000) = 0.50(15{,}000) = 7500$ (dollars)
The total cost is $C(15{,}000) = 2000 + 0.34(15{,}000) = 7100$ (dollars)

We see that the profit or loss for a month can be found by subtracting the total cost from the total revenue. In the previous example, producing and selling 10,000 pairs of shoelaces results in a loss of $400 (that is, $5000 − 5400) while producing and selling 15,000 pairs results in a profit of $7500 − 7100 = $400. So the firm will break even at some point between 10,000 and 15,000 pairs of shoelaces.

If x units of a commodity are produced and sold, the profit is found by subtracting the total cost from the total revenue.*

$$\text{Profit (or loss)} = \text{total revenue} - \text{total cost}$$

We can define the **profit function** as follows:

$$P(x) = R(x) - C(x).$$

Thus for the total revenue function $R(x) = 0.50x$ and the total cost function $C(x) = 2000 + 0.34x$ in the shoelace example, the profit function is given by the equation $P(x) = 0.50x - (2000 + 0.34x)$, or $P(x) = 0.16x - 2000$.

Figure 1.26 is the graph of $P(x)$ for positive values of x. Note that the profit function is negative for some values of x (a loss is incurred) and positive for other values (a profit is made). For example, $P(10,000) = 1600 - 2000 = -400$, so a loss of $400 will result from producing and selling 10,000 pairs of shoelaces. Also, $P(15,000) = 400$, so a profit of $400 will result from selling 15,000 pairs of shoelaces.

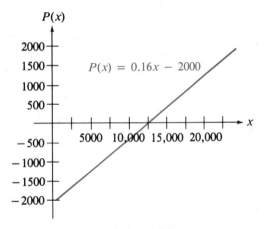

Figure 1.26

The point at which the profit function is zero is called the **break-even point.** Setting $P = 0$ and solving for x gives the break-even point.

$$0 = 0.16x - 2000$$
$$x = 12,500 \text{ units}$$

Note that this x-value corresponds to the x-intercept in Figure 1.20.

---

*The symbols generally used in economics for total cost, total revenue, and profit are TC, TR, and π, respectively. We do not use these symbols to avoid confusion, especially with the use of π as a variable.

EXAMPLE 3   Suppose the selling price of a commodity is $.40 per item. If fixed costs are $200 and the variable costs amount to $.20 per item, find
(a) the total revenue function.
(b) the total cost function.
(c) the profit function.

Solution   (a) The total revenue function is $R(x) = 0.40x$.
(b) The total cost function is $C(x) = 200 + 0.20x$.
(c) The profit function is

$$P(x) = 0.40x - (200 + 0.20x)$$

or

$$P(x) = 0.20x - 200.$$

Exercise 1.4

NATIONAL CONSUMPTION

1. If $C = f(y) = 3 + 0.7y$ (in billions of dollars),
   (a) what is the consumption when disposable income is 0?
   (b) what is the consumption when disposable income is $6 billion?
   (c) sketch the graph of the consumption function.
2. If $C = 4 + 0.65y$ (in billions of dollars),
   (a) what is the consumption when disposable income is 0?
   (b) what is the consumption when disposable income is $18 billion?
   (c) sketch the graph of the consumption function.
3. If $C = 5.6 + 0.6y$ (in billions of dollars),
   (a) what is the consumption when disposable income is 0?
   (b) what is the consumption when disposable income is $15 billion?
   (c) sketch the graph of the consumption function.
4. If $C = 9 + 0.5y$ (in billions of dollars),
   (a) what is the consumption when disposable income is 0?
   (b) what is the consumption when disposable income is $15 billion?
   (c) sketch the graph of the consumption function.
5. If the consumption function is given by

$$C(y) = 0.47y + 16 \quad \text{(in billions of dollars)},$$

   (a) what is the consumption when there is no disposable income?
   (b) what is the consumption when disposable income is $1 billion?
   (c) use the difference in the answers to parts (a) and (b) to find what percent of the $1 billion of disposable income was spent.
6. If the consumption function is given by

$$C(y) = 0.82y + 36 \quad \text{(in billions of dollars)},$$

   (a) what is the consumption when there is no disposable income?
   (b) what is the consumption when disposable income is $1 billion?
   (c) use the difference in the answers to parts (a) and (b) to find what percent of the $1 billion of disposable income was spent.

SUPPLY AND DEMAND FUNCTIONS

7. Plot the points in the demand schedule below.

Price	Quantity
$52	0
48	1
44	3
40	6
36	12

8. Do the points in the demand schedule in problem 7 lie on a straight line?
9. Plot the points in the supply schedule below.

Price	Quantity
$ 8	0
16	2
24	4
40	8
48	10

10. Do the points in the supply schedule in problem 9 lie on a straight line?
11. As the price of a commodity increases, what happens to demand?
12. As the price of a commodity increases, what happens to supply?

Figure 1.27 is the graph of the demand function for a product, and Figure 1.28 is the graph of the supply function for the same product. Use these graphs to answer questions 13 and 14.

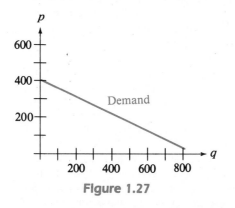

Figure 1.27

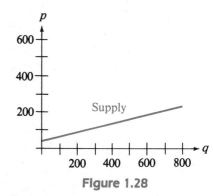

Figure 1.28

13. (a) How many units q are *demanded* when the price p is $100?
    (b) How many units q are *supplied* when the price p is $100?
    (c) Will there be a market surplus (more supplied) or shortage (more demanded) when $p = \$100$?
14. (a) How many units q are demanded when the price p is $200?
    (b) How many units q are supplied when the price p is $200?
    (c) Will there be a market surplus or shortage when the price p is $200?

15. If the demand for a pair of shoes is given by $2p + 5q = 200$ and the supply function for it is $p - 2q = 10$, compare the quantity demanded and supplied when the price is $60. Will there be a surplus or shortfall at this price?

16. If the demand function and supply function for Z-brand phones are $p + 2q = 100$ and $35p - 20q = 350$, respectively, compare the quantity demanded and the quantity supplied when $p = 14$. Are there surplus phones or not enough to meet demand?

TOTAL COST, TOTAL REVENUE, AND PROFIT FUNCTIONS

17. For a certain period, a calculator has fixed costs of $3400 and variable costs of $17 for each item produced.
    (a) Write the equation that represents total cost.
    (b) What will it cost to produce 200 units during the given period?

18. A stereo receiver has a fixed cost of $1650 and a variable cost of $105 for each item produced during a given month.
    (a) Write the equation that represents the total cost.
    (b) What will it cost to produce 215 items during the month?

19. Production of radios has a fixed cost of $1850 and a variable cost of $43 for each radio produced.
    (a) Write the equation that represents the total cost.
    (b) What is the cost if no units are produced?
    (c) What is the cost if 37 units are produced?

20. A computer has a fixed cost of $3300 and a variable cost of $85 for each item produced.
    (a) Write the equation that represents total cost.
    (b) What is the cost if no units are produced?
    (c) What is the cost if 300 units are produced?

21. A calculator is sold for $34 per unit.
    (a) Write the total revenue function as an equation.
    (b) What will the revenue be if 300 units are sold?

22. A stereo receiver is sold for $215 per item.
    (a) Write the equation that represents the revenue function.
    (b) What will the revenue be from the sale of 50 items?

23. A radio is sold for $80 per unit.
    (a) Write the equation that represents the revenue function.
    (b) What will the revenue be from the sale of 75 radios?

24. A computer is sold for $385 per item.
    (a) Write the equation that represents the revenue function.
    (b) What will the revenue be from the sale of 130 items?

25. Suppose a calculator has the total cost function $C(x) = 17x + 3400$ and the total revenue function $R(x) = 34x$.
    (a) What is the equation of the profit function for the calculator?
    (b) What is the profit on 300 units?
    (c) How many units must be sold to ensure no money will be lost during the period?

26. Suppose a stereo receiver has the total cost function $C(x) = 105x + 1650$ and the total revenue function $R(x) = 215x$.
    (a) What is the equation of the profit function for this commodity?
    (b) What is the profit on 50 items?
    (c) How many items must be sold in a month to avoid losing money?

27. Suppose radios have the total cost function $C(x) = 43x + 1850$ and the total revenue function $R(x) = 80x$.
    (a) What is the equation of the profit function for this commodity?
    (b) What is the profit on 30 units? Interpret your result.
    (c) How many radios must be sold to avoid losing money?   *fixed*

28. Suppose a computer has the total cost function $C(x) = 85x + 3300$ and the total revenue function $R(x) = 385x$.   *variable*
    (a) What is the equation of the profit function for this commodity?
    (b) What is the profit on 351 items?
    (c) How many items must be sold to avoid losing money?

a) $Pn = 385x - (85X + 3300)$

$Pn = 300X - 3300$

29. Figure 1.29 is the graph of a profit function for a product. Use the graph to answer the following.
    (a) How many units must be produced to break even? (Two values give the break-even points.)
    (b) How many units will give maximum profit?
    (c) What is the maximum possible profit?

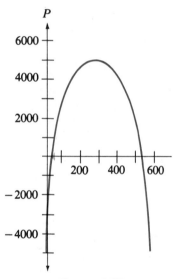

Figure 1.29

30. Refer to Figure 1.29.
    (a) How much money is lost if no units are produced?
    (b) Is it possible to lose more money than $4000? How?

1.5 Slope of a Line; Writing Equations of Lines

Objectives
☐ To find the slope of a line from its graph and from its equation
☐ To graph a line, given its slope and y-intercept or its slope and one point on the line
☐ To write the equation of a line, given information about its graph
☐ To find marginal cost, revenue, and profit, given linear total cost, total revenue, and profit functions
☐ To write the equations of linear total cost, total revenue, and profit functions, by using information given about the functions

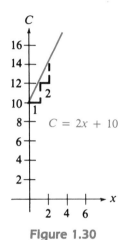

$C = 2x + 10$

Figure 1.30

The cost of producing one additional unit at any level of production is called **marginal cost.** If the cost function is linear, the marginal cost will be the same at all levels of production. For example,

$$C = 2x + 10$$

is the cost function for a good whose fixed cost is $10 and whose variable cost is $2 per unit. Because producing one more unit adds $2 to the cost, the marginal cost is $2. Looking at the graph of this function (Figure 1.30), we see that the C-value changes $+2$ units (from 10 to 12) while the x-value changes $+1$ unit (from 0 to 1). The ratio of this change in C to the corresponding change in x is called the **slope** of the line. The slope represents the rate of change in the total cost function.

We could also use points on the graph to find the slope of this line. To do this, we divide the change in C by the change in x for any two points on the line. For example, the points $(1, 12)$ and $(3, 16)$ lie on the line that represents the graph of $C = 2x + 10$. The C-value changes $+4$ units (from 12 to 16) while the x-value changes $+2$ units (from 1 to 3). Thus the slope, symbolized by m, is

$$m = \frac{\text{change in } C}{\text{change in } x} = \frac{4}{2} = 2.$$

Slope of a Line

In general, if a nonvertical line passes through the points $P_1(x_1, y_1)$ and $P_2(x_2, y_2)$ (see Figure 1.31), its **slope** is found by using the formula

$$m = \frac{y_2 - y_1}{x_2 - x_1}.$$

We may use this formula to find the slope of any line (that is not vertical) if we know the coordinates of two points on the line.

Note that it doesn't matter which point we choose as $P_2(x_2, y_2)$ when we use the formula, since

$$\frac{y_2 - y_1}{x_2 - x_1} = \frac{y_1 - y_2}{x_1 - x_2}.$$

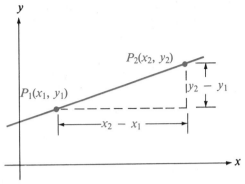

Figure 1.31

We may also write the slope by using the notation

$$m = \frac{\Delta y}{\Delta x},$$

where Δy means "change in y" and Δx means "change in x."

EXAMPLE 1   Find the slope of
(a) Line ℓ_1, passing through $(-2, 1)$ and $(4, 3)$.
(b) Line ℓ_2, passing through $(3, 0)$ and $(4, -3)$.

Solution   (a) $m = \dfrac{3 - 1}{4 - (-2)} = \dfrac{2}{6} = \dfrac{1}{3}.$

This means that a point 3 units to the right and 1 unit up from any point on the line is also on the line. Line ℓ_1 is shown in Figure 1.32.

(b) $m = \dfrac{0 - (-3)}{3 - 4} = \dfrac{3}{-1} = -3$

This means that a point 1 unit to the right and 3 units down from any point on the line is also on the line. Line ℓ_2 is also shown in Figure 1.32.

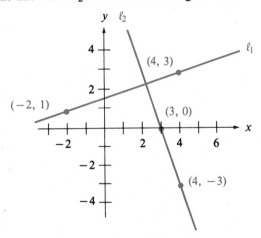

Figure 1.32

From the previous discussion we see that the slope describes the direction of a line as follows:

1. The slope is *positive* if the line slopes upward toward the right.

$$m = \frac{\Delta y}{\Delta x} > 0$$

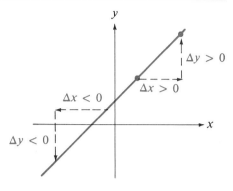

2. The slope is *negative* if the line slopes downward toward the right.

$$m = \frac{\Delta y}{\Delta x} < 0$$

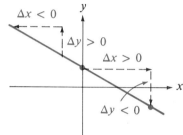

Two additional facts should be stated:

3. The slope of a *horizontal line* is 0 because the y-values are the same for any two points on the line ($y_2 - y_1 = 0$).

$$m = \frac{\Delta y}{\Delta x} = 0$$

since $\Delta y = 0$

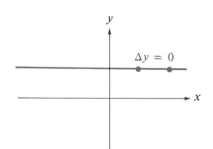

4. The slope of a *vertical line* is *undefined* because $x_2 - x_1$ would equal 0, and division by 0 is undefined. (Note: y is not a function of x here.)

$$m = \frac{\Delta y}{\Delta x}$$ is undefined

since $\Delta x = 0$

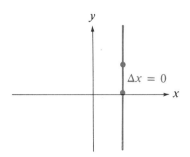

Clearly two distinct nonvertical lines that have the same slope are parallel and, conversely, two parallel lines have the same slope.

Slopes of Parallel Lines	Two distinct nonvertical lines are *parallel* if and only if their slopes are *equal*.

Because the slope of a vertical line is undefined, we cannot use slope in discussing parallel and perpendicular relations involving vertical lines. Two vertical lines are parallel, and any horizontal line is perpendicular to any vertical line.

Note that the lines ℓ_1 and ℓ_2 of Figure 1.32 (page 85) appear to be perpendicular and that the slope of ℓ_1, $\frac{1}{3}$, is the negative reciprocal of the slope of ℓ_2, -3. In fact, any two nonvertical lines that are perpendicular have slopes that are negative reciprocals of each other.

Slopes of Perpendicular Lines	A line with slope m ($m \neq 0$) is *perpendicular* to any line with slope $-1/m$, and conversely. (The slopes are *negative reciprocals*.)

If we are given the slope and y-intercept of a line, the following example illustrates the procedure used to sketch the graph of the line.

EXAMPLE 2   Graph the line that has slope $-\frac{1}{2}$ and y-intercept 4.

Solution   We plot the y-intercept, $(0, 4)$, first. The point $(2, 3)$ is on the line because it is 2 units to the right and 1 unit below $(0, 4)$. A third point (for a check) is plotted at $(4, 2)$. The graph is shown in Figure 1.33.

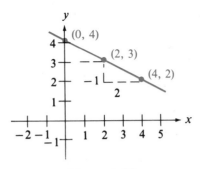

Figure 1.33

It is also possible to graph a straight line if we know its slope and a point through which it passes. We simply plot the point given and then use the slope to plot other points.

teacher likes this (handwritten margin note)

We can find the slope and y-intercept of a line from its equation if it is written in the proper form, and we can use this information to graph the line.

Slope-Intercept Form of Equation of a Line	The equation $y = mx + b$ is the **slope-intercept form** of the equation of a line. The coefficient of x, namely m, is the slope of the line, and the constant b is the value of y where the graph crosses the y-axis (b is called the y-intercept).

If we consider the total cost function

$$C = 2x + 10,$$

we see that the equation is in slope-intercept form. We noted earlier that the slope of the graph of this function is 2. As Figure 1.30 (page 84) shows, the graph crosses the C-axis at 10.

When a linear equation does not appear in slope-intercept form, it can be put into slope-intercept form by solving the equation for y.

EXAMPLE 3   Find the slope of the line whose equation is $3x + 2y = 4$.

Solution   We must solve the equation for y to put the equation in the slope-intercept form:

$$2y = -3x + 4$$
$$y = -\tfrac{3}{2}x + 2.$$

Thus the slope is $-\tfrac{3}{2}$. The y-intercept is 2.

EXAMPLE 4   Write the equation of the line with slope $\tfrac{1}{2}$ and y-intercept 3.

Solution   Substituting $m = \tfrac{1}{2}$ and $b = 3$ in the equation $y = mx + b$ gives $y = \tfrac{1}{2}x + 3$. The **general form** of the equation of a line is $ax + by + c = 0$, so the general form of this equation is $x - 2y + 6 = 0$.

If we know the slope of a line and a point (x_1, y_1) on it, we can use the fact that the slope between the fixed point (x_1, y_1) and any point (x, y) on the line is

$$m = \frac{y - y_1}{x - x_1}.$$

Multiplying both sides by $(x - x_1)$ gives the point-slope form.

Point-Slope Form of Equation of a Line	The equation of a line passing through the point (x_1, y_1) with slope m can be written in the **point-slope form** $$y - y_1 = m(x - x_1).$$

EXAMPLE 5   Write the equation of the line passing through $(1, -2)$ with slope $\frac{2}{3}$.

Solution   Here $m = \frac{2}{3}$, $x_1 = 1$, and $y_1 = -2$. So the equation is $y - (-2) = \frac{2}{3}(x - 1)$. Writing this equation in general form gives $2x - 3y - 8 = 0$.

$$y + 2 = \frac{2}{3}x - \frac{2}{3})$$

$$3y + 6 = 2x - 2$$

$$0 \cdot 2x - 3y - 8$$

EXAMPLE 6   Write the equation of the line passing through $(-1, 3)$ and $(4, 2)$.

Solution   Using the two points, we can find the slope of the line.

$$m = \frac{2 - 3}{4 - (-1)} = -\frac{1}{5}.$$

Using the slope of this line and *either* of the two points in the point-slope form of the equation, we can write the equation. Using the point $(-1, 3)$, we get $y - 3 = -\frac{1}{5}[x - (-1)]$, or $x + 5y - 14 = 0$. Note that using the point $(4, 2)$ would result in the same general equation of the line.

Table 1.2 summarizes the forms of equations of lines.

Table 1.2   Forms of linear equations

General form	$ax + by + c = 0$
Point-slope form	$y - y_1 = m(x - x_1)$
Slope-intercept form	$y = mx + b$
Vertical line	$x = a$
Horizontal line	$y = b$

For a linear total cost function the **slope** represents the *rate of change in total cost* with respect to the number of units produced, or the **marginal cost.** If we are given a linear total revenue function, then the slope of the line represents the *rate of change in the total revenue*. This rate of change is called the **marginal revenue.** The slope of a linear profit function is the **marginal profit.**

$$P(x) = R(x) - C(x)$$

$$P(x) = 9x - (300 + 2x)$$

$$9x - 300 - 2x$$

$$(7)x - 300$$

marginal profit

EXAMPLE 7   If the total cost function is given by $C(x) = 300 + 2x$ (dollars), and if the total revenue function is given by $R(x) = 9x$ (dollars), find (a) the marginal cost, (b) the marginal revenue, (c) the marginal profit.

Solution   (a) $C(x) = 300 + 2x$ is in slope-intercept form with $m = 2$ and $b = 300$. Thus the marginal cost is $2, so the production of each additional unit costs $2 at all levels of production. Note that $b = 300$ indicates that the fixed costs (when $x = 0$) are $300.

(b) $R(x) = 9x$ is also in slope-intercept form with $m = 9$ and $b = 0$. The slope represents the marginal revenue, which is $9. That is, the sale of each additional unit produces an additional $9 in revenue at all levels of production. Note that $b = 0$ indicates that if nothing is sold ($x = 0$), no revenue results.

(c) The profit function is

$$P(x) = R(x) - C(x)$$
$$P(x) = 9x - (300 + 2x)$$
$$P(x) = 7x - 300.$$

The profit function slope is equal to 7, so marginal profit is $7. That is, the sale of each extra unit results in $7 additional profit at all levels of production. Also note that $b = -300$ indicates that when no items have been sold ($x = 0$), the profit is $-$300; that is, there is a loss of $300.

We have seen that the slope of a linear total cost function is the marginal cost, and the C-intercept (where C lies along the vertical axis of the graph) represents the fixed cost. Thus, if we know that a linear cost function has a marginal cost of $30 and a fixed cost of $1000, we can write the equation that defines the function:

$$C = 30x + 1000.$$

Note that when total cost functions are linear, the marginal cost is the same as the variable cost. This is not the case, however, if the functions are not linear, as we shall see later.

EXAMPLE 8   Suppose the profit function for a good is linear, and the marginal profit is $5. If the profit is $200 when 125 units are sold, write the equation of the profit function.

Solution   The marginal profit gives us the slope of the line representing the profit function. Using this slope and the point (125, 200), we have the equation

$$P - 200 = 5(x - 125),$$

or

$$P = 5x - 425.$$

Exercise 1.5

Find the slopes of the lines passing through the following points.

1. (1, 2) and (0, 0)
3. (2, 1) and (3, −4)
5. (3, 2) and (−1, 2)

2. (−1, 2) and (2, −3)
4. (−1, −2) and (−2, −3)
6. (−4, 2) and (−4, −2)

Find the slopes and y-intercepts of the lines whose equations are given in problems 7−20.

7. $y = \frac{7}{3}x - \frac{1}{4}$
9. $y = 3$
11. $y = -\frac{1}{2}x - \frac{2}{3}$
13. $x = -8$

8. $y = \frac{4}{3}x + \frac{1}{2}$
10. $y = -2$
12. $y = \frac{2}{3}x + \frac{1}{2}$
14. $x = -\frac{1}{2}$

15. $x = 4y$

16. $x = 3y + 6$

17. $2x + 3y = 6$

18. $3x - 2y = 18$

19. $2.61x + 3.14y = 91.7$

20. $1.31x - 3.82y = 0.0213$

Write the equation and sketch the graph of each line with the given slope and y-intercept.

21. slope $\frac{1}{2}$ and y-intercept 3

22. slope 2 and y-intercept 3

23. slope -2 and y-intercept $\frac{1}{2}$

24. slope $\frac{2}{3}$ and y-intercept -1

25. slope 0 and y-intercept -4

26. slope -1 and y-intercept $\frac{3}{2}$

In problems 27–32, write the equation and graph the line that passes through the given point and has the slope indicated.

27. $(2, 0)$ with slope $\frac{1}{2}$

28. $(1, 1)$ with slope $-\frac{1}{3}$

29. $(-1, 3)$ with slope -2

30. $(3, -1)$ with slope 1

31. $(-1, 1)$ with undefined slope

32. $(1, 1)$ with 0 slope

Write the equations of the lines passing through the following pairs of points.

33. $(3, 2)$ and $(-1, -6)$

34. $(-4, 2)$ and $(2, 4)$

35. $(7, 3)$ and $(-6, 2)$

36. $(10, 2)$ and $(5, 7)$

37. $(10, 2)$ and $(5, 2)$

38. $(3, 6)$ and $(3, 8)$

39. Write the equation of the line through $(-2, -7)$ that is parallel to $3x + 5y = 11$.

40. Write the equation of the line through $(6, -4)$ that is parallel to $4x - 5y = 6$.

41. Write the equation of the line through $(3, 1)$ that is perpendicular to $5x - 6y = 4$.

42. Write the equation of the line through $(-2, -8)$ that is perpendicular to $x = 4y + 3$.

43. Write the equation of the line that is perpendicular to and has the same x-intercept as $5x - 8y = 80$.

44. Do the equations $4x - y = 2$ and $8x - 2y = 4$ represent parallel lines or the same line?

APPLICATIONS

45. Residential customers who heat their homes with natural gas have their monthly bill calculated by adding a base service charge of $5.19 per month and an energy charge of 51.91 cents per hundred cubic feet (CCF). Write an equation for the monthly charge y in terms of x, the number of CCF used.

46. An electric utility company determines the monthly bill for a residential customer by adding an energy charge of 8.38 cents per kilowatt hour (KWH) to its base charge of $4.95 per month. Write an equation for the monthly charge y in terms of x, the number of KWH used.

47. It has been estimated that a certain stream can support 85,000 fish if it is pollution-free. It has further been estimated that for each ton of pollutants in the stream, 1700 fewer fish can be supported. Write the equation that gives the population of fish p in terms of the tons of pollutants x.

48. Each day, a young person should sleep 8 hours plus $\frac{1}{4}$ hour for each year that the person is under 18 years of age. Assuming the relation is linear, write the equation relating hours of sleep y and age x.

49. A linear cost function is $C(x) = 5x + 250$.
    (a) What are the slope and C-intercept?
    (b) What is the marginal cost, and what does it mean?
    (c) What are the fixed costs?

(d) How are your answers to (a) and to (b) and (c) related?

(e) What is the cost of producing *one more* item if 50 are currently being produced? What is it if 100 are currently being produced?

50. A linear cost function is $C(x) = 21.75x + 4890$.

(a) What are the slope and C-intercept?

(b) What is the marginal cost, and what does it mean?

(c) What are the fixed costs?

(d) How are your answers to (a) and to (b) and (c) related?

(e) What is the cost of producing *one more* item if 50 are currently being produced? What is it if 100 are currently being produced?

51. A linear revenue function is $R = 27x$.

(a) What is the slope?

(b) What is the marginal revenue, and what does it mean?

(c) What is the revenue received from selling *one more* item if 50 are currently being sold? If 100 are being sold?

52. A linear revenue function is $R = 38.95x$.

(a) What is the slope?

(b) What is the marginal revenue, and what does it mean?

(c) What is the revenue received from selling *one more* item if 50 are currently being sold? If 100 are being sold?

53. What is the R-intercept for the revenue functions in problems 51 and 52? Explain why these are the same. Is this always the case? Explain.

54. A linear profit function is $P = 51x - 710$.

(a) What are the slope and P-intercept of the profit function?

(b) What is the marginal profit and what does it mean?

(c) What is the significance of the P-intercept?

(d) How much profit is expected if 20 items are produced and sold?

(e) How much *additional* profit would be expected if production and sales increased from 20 to 21?

55. Let $C(x) = 5x + 250$ and $R(x) = 27x$.

(a) Write the profit function $P(x)$.

(b) What is the slope of the profit function?

(c) What is the marginal profit?

(d) Interpret the marginal profit. What does this tell the manager of the firm with this profit function, if the objective is to make the most profit?

56. Given $C(x) = 21.95x + 1400$ and $R(x) = 10x$, find the profit function.

(a) What is marginal profit, and what does it mean?

(b) What should a firm with these cost, revenue, and profit functions do? (Hint: Graph the profit function and see where it goes.)

57. Suppose the total cost function for a radio is linear, that the marginal cost is $27, and that the fixed costs amount to $3000. Write the equation of this cost function and then graph it.

58. Suppose the total revenue function for a radio is linear, with marginal revenue $30. Write the total revenue function; recall that the revenue from 0 units is $0.

59. The R-value of insulation is a measure of its ability to resist heat transfer. For fiberglass insulation, $3\frac{1}{2}$ inches is rated at R-11 and 6 inches is rated at R-19. Assuming this relationship is linear, write the equation that gives the R-value of fiberglass insulation as a function of its thickness t (in inches).

60. Write the equation of the linear relationship between temperature in Celsius (C) and Fahrenheit (F) if water freezes at 0°C and 32°F and boils at 100°C and 212°F.

61. Suppose that the production and sale of each additional unit of a stereo system results in an increase of $50 in profit, regardless of the level of production. If the sale of 1000 units gives a profit of $40,000, write the equation of the profit function.

62. A company charting its profits notices the relationship between the number of units sold, x, and the profit, P, is linear. If 200 units sold results in $3100 profit and 250 units sold results in $6000 profit, write the profit function for this company. Find their marginal profit.

63. The particulate readings for a city have been found to follow a certain pattern for a given month.

> 7:00 A.M.–10:00 A.M.: an initial level of 100, with an increase of 15 units each hour
> 10:00 A.M.– 3:00 P.M.: stable reading
> 3:00 P.M.– 6:00 A.M.: increase of 15 units each hour
> 6:00 P.M.– 4:00 A.M.: decrease of 9 units per hour
> 4:00 A.M.– 7:00 A.M.: stable reading

Make a graph that represents this situation for a 24-hour period beginning at 7:00 A.M. Use time as the horizontal axis.

64. In psychology, the study of threshold levels of stimulus are of interest. If s is the amount of stimulus, then Δs is the required change in s so that the subject notices a change. Research has shown that

$$\Delta s = ks \qquad (k = \text{constant}).$$

What is the slope of the graph of this equation?

1.6 Solutions of Systems of Linear Equations

Objectives
- ☐ To solve systems of linear equations in two variables by graphing *yes*
- ☐ To solve systems of linear equations by substitution — *no*
- ☐ To solve systems of linear equations by elimination *yes*
- ☐ To solve systems of three linear equations in three variables *no*

In the previous sections we graphed linear equations in two variables, and observed that the graphs are straight lines. Each point on the graph represents an ordered pair of values (x, y) that satisfies the equation, so a point of intersection of two (or more) lines represents a solution to both (or all) the equations of those lines.

The equations are referred to as a **system of equations,** and the ordered pairs (x, y) that satisfy all the equations are the **solutions** (or **simultaneous solutions**) to the system. We can use graphing to find the solution to a system of equations.

EXAMPLE 1   Use graphing to find the solution of the system

$$\begin{cases} 4x + 3y = 11 \\ 2x - 5y = -1 \end{cases}$$

Solution   The graphs of the two equations intersect (meet) at the point (2, 1). (See Figure 1.34.) The solution of the system is $x = 2$, $y = 1$. Note that these values satisfy both equations.

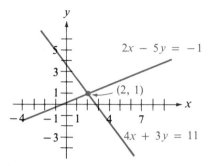

Two distinct nonparallel lines:
one solution

Figure 1.34

If the graphs of two equations are parallel lines, they have no point in common and thus the system has no solution. Such a system of equations is called **inconsistent.** For example,

$$\begin{cases} 4x + 3y = 4 \\ 8x + 6y = 18 \end{cases}$$

is an **inconsistent system** (see Figure 1.35).

It is also possible that two equations describe the same line. When this happens the equations are equivalent, and values that satisfy either equation are solutions to the system. For example,

$$\begin{cases} 4x + 3y = 4 \\ 8x + 6y = 8 \end{cases}$$

is called a **dependent system** because all points satisfying one equation also satisfy the other (see Figure 1.36).

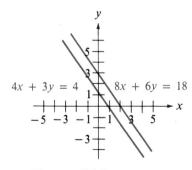

Two parallel lines:
no solution

Figure 1.35

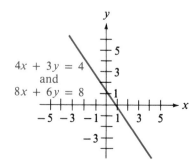

Two coincident lines:
infinitely many solutions

Figure 1.36

Figures 1.34, 1.35, and 1.36 represent the three possibilities that can occur when solving a system of two equations in two variables.

Algebraic methods are usually used for solving a system of equations because it is not practical to solve systems with graphs. These methods are based on the fact that equivalent systems result when any of the following operations are performed.

Equivalent Systems

Equivalent systems result when:

1. One expression is replaced by an equivalent expression
2. Two equations are interchanged
3. A multiple of one equation is added to another equation
4. An equation is multiplied by a nonzero constant

The **substitution method** is based on operation (1).

Procedure	Example
To solve a system of two equations in two variables by substitution:	Solve the system containing $2x + 3y = 4$ and $x - 2y = 3$.
1. Solve one of the equations for one of the variables in terms of the other.	1. Solving $x - 2y = 3$ for x gives $x = 2y + 3$
2. Substitute this expression into the other equation to give one equation in one unknown.	2. Replacing x by $2y + 3$ in $2x + 3y = 4$ gives $2(2y + 3) + 3y = 4$
3. Solve this linear equation for the unknown.	3. $4y + 6 + 3y = 4$ $\qquad 7y = -2$ $\qquad y = -\dfrac{2}{7}$
4. Substitute this solution into the equation in step 1 or into one of the original equations to solve for the other variable.	4. $x = 2\left(-\dfrac{2}{7}\right) + 3$ $\qquad x = \dfrac{17}{7}$
5. Check the solution by substituting for x and y in both original equations.	5. $2\left(\dfrac{17}{7}\right) + 3\left(-\dfrac{2}{7}\right) = 4 \checkmark$ $\dfrac{17}{7} - 2\left(-\dfrac{2}{7}\right) = 3 \qquad \checkmark$

EXAMPLE 2   Solve the system

$$\begin{cases} 4x + 5y = 18 & (1) \\ 3x - 9y = -12 & (2) \end{cases}$$

Solution   1. $x = \dfrac{9y - 12}{3} = 3y - 4$ Solving for x in equation (2)

2. $4(3y - 4) + 5y = 18$ Substituting for x in equation (1)

3. $12y - 16 + 5y = 18$ Solving for y

$$17y = 34$$
$$y = 2$$

4. $x = 3(2) - 4$ Using $y = 2$ to find x

$$x = 2$$

5. $4(2) + 5(2) = 18$ and $(2) - 3(2) = -4$ Checking

Note that if we graphed the two equations, they would intersect at the point $(2, 2)$.

We can also eliminate one of the variables in a system by the **elimination method,** which is based on the operations that lead to equivalent systems.

Procedure	Example

To solve a system of two equations in two variables by addition or subtraction:

Solve the system
$$\begin{cases} 2x - 5y = 4 & (1) \\ x + 2y = 3 & (2) \end{cases}$$

1. If necessary, multiply one or both equations by a nonzero number that will make the coefficients of one of the variables identical, except perhaps for signs.

1. Multiply (2) by -2.
$$2x - 5y = 4$$
$$-2x - 4y = -6$$

2. Add or subtract the equations to eliminate one of the variables.

2. Adding gives
$$0x - 9y = -2$$

3. Solve for the variable in the resulting equation.

3. $y = \dfrac{2}{9}$

4. Substitute the solution into one of the original equations and solve for the remaining variable.

4. $2x - 5\left(\dfrac{2}{9}\right) = 4$

$$2x = 4 + \dfrac{10}{9} = \dfrac{36}{9} + \dfrac{10}{9}$$

$$x = \dfrac{23}{9}$$

5. Check the solutions in both original equations.

$$5. \ 2\left(\frac{23}{9}\right) - 5\left(\frac{2}{9}\right) = 4 \ \checkmark$$

$$\frac{23}{9} + 2\left(\frac{2}{9}\right) = 3 \quad \checkmark$$

EXAMPLE 3   A person has \$200,000 invested, part at 9% and part at 8%. If the total yearly income from the two investments is \$17,200, how much is invested at 9%, and how much at 8%?

Solution   If x represents the amount invested at 9% and y represents the amount invested at 8%, then

$$x + y = 200,000$$

and

$$0.09x + 0.08y = 17,200.$$

We solve these equations as follows:

$$
\begin{array}{rl}
-8x - 8y = -1,600,000 & \text{Multiplying by } -8 \\
\underline{9x + 8y = 1,720,000} & \text{Multiplying by } 100 \\
x = 120,000 & \text{Adding}
\end{array}
$$

Thus \$120,000 is invested at 9%, and \$80,000 is invested at 8%.

EXAMPLE 4   Solve the systems:

(a) $\begin{cases} 4x + 3y = 4 \\ 8x + 6y = 18 \end{cases}$ (b) $\begin{cases} 4x + 3y = 4 \\ 8x + 6y = 8 \end{cases}$

Solution   (a) $\begin{array}{rl} -8x - 6y = -8 \\ \underline{8x + 6y = 18} \\ 0x - 0y = 10 \\ 0 = 10 \end{array}$

The system is solved when $0 = 10$. This is impossible, so there are no solutions to the system. The equations are inconsistent. (Their graphs are parallel lines; see Figure 1.35 on page 94.)

(b) $\begin{array}{rl} -8x - 6y = -8 \\ \underline{8x + 6y = 8} \\ 0x - 0y = 0 \\ 0 = 0 \end{array}$

This is an identity, so the two equations share infinitely many solutions. The equations are dependent. Their graphs coincide, and each point on this line represents a solution to the system; see Figure 1.36 on page 94.

EXAMPLE 5   A nurse has two solutions that contain different concentrations of a certain medication. One is a 12.5% concentration and the other is a 5% concentration. How many cubic centimeters of each should she mix to obtain 20 cc of an 8% concentration?

Solution   Let x equal the number of cc's of the 12.5% solution, and let y equal the number of cc's of the 8% solution. The total amount of substance is

$$x + y = 20$$

and the total amount of medication is

$$0.125x + 0.05y = (0.08)(20) = 1.6$$

Solving this pair of equations simultaneously gives

$$
\begin{array}{rcl}
50x + 50y & = & 1000 \\
-125x - 50y & = & -1600 \\
\hline
-75x \quad\quad & = & -600 \\
x & = & 8
\end{array}
$$

$8 + y = 20$, so $y = 12$.

Thus 8 cc of a 12.5% concentration and 12 cc of a 5% concentration yield 20 cc of an 8% concentration.

Three Equations in Three Variables

If a, b, c, and d represent constants, then

$$ax + by + cz = d$$

is an equation in three variables. When equations of this form are graphed in a three-dimensional coordinate system their graphs are planes. Two different planes may intersect in a line (like two walls) or may not intersect at all (like a floor and ceiling). Three different planes may intersect in a single point (as when two walls meet the ceiling), in a line (as in a paddle wheel), or may not have a common intersection. (See Figures 1.37, 1.38, and 1.39.) Thus, three equations in three variables may have a unique solution, infinitely many solutions, or no solution. For example, the solution to the system

$$
\begin{cases}
3x + 2y + z = 6 \\
x - y - z = 0 \\
x + y - z = 4
\end{cases}
$$

is $x = 1$, $y = 2$, $z = -1$, since these three values satisfy all three equations, and these are the only values that satisfy them. In this section, we will only discuss

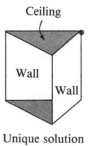
Ceiling

Wall

Wall

Unique solution

Figure 1.37

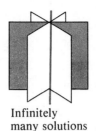
Infinitely
many solutions

Figure 1.38

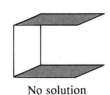
No solution

Figure 1.39

systems of three equations in three variables that have unique solutions. Additional systems will be discussed in Section 2.3.

We can solve three equations in three variables using a systematic procedure, called the **left-to-right elimination method.**

Procedure	Example

To solve a system of three equations in three variables by the left-to-right elimination method.

Solve: $\begin{cases} 2x + 4y + 5z = 4 \\ x - 2y - 3z = 5 \\ x + 3y + 4z = 1 \end{cases}$

1. If necessary, interchange two equations or use multiplication to make the coefficient of the first variable in equation (1) a factor of the other first variable coefficients.

1. Interchange the first two equations:

$$\begin{array}{ll} x - 2y - 3z = 5 & (1) \\ 2x + 4y + 5z = 4 & (2) \\ x + 3y + 4z = 1 & (3) \end{array}$$

2. Add multiples of the first equation to each of the following equations so that the coefficients of the first variable in the second and third equations become zero.

2. Add $(-2) \times$ equation (1) to equation (2) and add $(-1) \times$ equation (1) to equation (3):

$$\begin{array}{ll} x - 2y - 3z = 5 & (1) \\ 0x + 8y + 11z = -6 & (2) \\ 0x + 5y + 7z = -4 & (3) \end{array}$$

3. Add a multiple of the second equation to the third equation so that the coefficient of the second variable in the third equation becomes zero.

3. Add $\left(-\frac{5}{8}\right) \times$ equation (2) to equation (3):

$$\begin{array}{ll} x - 2y - 3z = 5 & (1) \\ 8y + 11z = -6 & (2) \\ 0y + \frac{1}{8}z = -\frac{2}{8} & (3) \end{array}$$

4. Solve the third equation and *back substitute* from the bottom to find the remaining variables.

4. $z = -2$ from equation (3)
$y = \frac{1}{8}(-6 - 11z) = 2$ from equation (2)
$x = 5 + 2y + 3z = 3$ from equation (1)
so $x = 3, y = 2, z = -2$.

EXAMPLE 6   Solve: $\begin{cases} x + 2y + 3z = 6 & (1) \\ 2x + 3y + 2z = 6 & (2) \\ -x + y + z = 4 & (3) \end{cases}$

Solution   Using equation (1) to eliminate x from the other equations gives the equivalent system:

$$\begin{cases} x + 2y + 3z = 6 & (1) \\ -y - 4z = -6 & (2) \\ 3y + 4z = 10 & (3) \end{cases}$$ $(-2) \times$ equation (1) added to equation (2)
Equation (1) added to equation (3)

Using equation (2) to eliminate y from equation (3) gives

$$\begin{cases} x + 2y + 3z = 6 & (1) \\ -y - 4z = -6 & (2) \\ -8z = -8 & (3) \end{cases}$$ (3) $\times$ equation (2) added to equation (3)

Solving for each **lead variable** gives

$$x = 6 - 2y - 3z$$
$$y = 6 - 4z$$
$$z = 1$$

and *back substituting* from the bottom gives

$$z = 1, \quad y = 6 - 4 = 2, \quad x = 6 - 4 - 3 = -1.$$

Hence, the solution is $x = -1, y = 2, z = 1$.

Exercise 1.6

In problems 1–4, solve the systems of equations by using graphical methods.

1. $\begin{cases} 4x - 2y = 4 \\ x - 2y = -2 \end{cases}$ 2. $\begin{cases} x - y = -2 \\ 2x + y = -1 \end{cases}$

3. $\begin{cases} 3x - y = 10 \\ 6x - 2y = 5 \end{cases}$ 4. $\begin{cases} 2x - y = 3 \\ 4x - 2y = 6 \end{cases}$

In problems 5–22, solve the systems of equations.

5. $\begin{cases} 4x - y = 3 \\ 2x + 3y = 19 \end{cases}$ 6. $\begin{cases} 5x - 3y = 9 \\ x + 2y = 7 \end{cases}$ 7. $\begin{cases} 2x - y = 2 \\ 3x + 4y = 6 \end{cases}$

8. $\begin{cases} x - y = 4 \\ 3x - 2y = 5 \end{cases}$ 9. $\begin{cases} 3x - 2y = 6 \\ 4y = 8 \end{cases}$ 10. $\begin{cases} 5x - 2y = 4 \\ 2x - 3y = 5 \end{cases}$

11. $\begin{cases} -4x + 3y = -5 \\ 3x - 2y = 4 \end{cases}$ 12. $\begin{cases} x + 2y = 3 \\ 3x + 6y = 6 \end{cases}$ 13. $\begin{cases} \frac{5}{2}x - \frac{7}{2}y = -1 \\ 8x + 3y = 11 \end{cases}$

14. $\begin{cases} 3m + 2n = 2 \\ m - 3n = 1 \end{cases}$

15. $\begin{cases} 0.3u - 0.2v = 0.5 \\ 0.9u - 0.6v = 0.1 \end{cases}$

16. $\begin{cases} x - \frac{1}{2}y = 1 \\ \frac{2}{3}x - \frac{1}{3}y = 1 \end{cases}$

17. $\begin{cases} 0.2x - 0.3y = 4 \\ 2.3x - y = 1.2 \end{cases}$

18. $\begin{cases} 0.5x + y = 3 \\ 0.3x + 0.2y = 6 \end{cases}$

19. $\begin{cases} 4x + 6y = 4 \\ 2x + 3y = 2 \end{cases}$

20. $\begin{cases} \dfrac{x}{4} + \dfrac{3y}{4} = 12 \\ \dfrac{y}{2} - \dfrac{x}{3} = -4 \end{cases}$

21. $\begin{cases} \dfrac{(x + y)}{4} = 2 \\ \dfrac{(y - 1)}{x} = 6 \end{cases}$

22. $\begin{cases} 3x + 4y = 8 \\ \dfrac{(16 - 6x)}{y} = 8 \end{cases}$

Use the left-to-right elimination method to solve the systems in problems 23–28.

23. $\begin{cases} x + 2y + z = 2 \\ 3x \quad\ \ - z = 4 \\ 4x + 3y \quad\ = 7 \end{cases}$

24. $\begin{cases} 4x - y + 2z = 9 \\ x \quad\ \ + 3z = 5 \\ 2y - 2z = -4 \end{cases}$

25. $\begin{cases} x - 2y + z = 0 \\ x + 4y - 2z = 9 \\ 2x - 3y + z = 1 \end{cases}$

26. $\begin{cases} 3x + 3y - z = 15 \\ 2x + 4y - 3z = 20 \\ x - y + 2z = -5 \end{cases}$

27. $\begin{cases} 4r + 2s + t = 7 \\ 3r - 3s - t = -1 \\ 2r - 3s + 4t = 3 \end{cases}$

28. $\begin{cases} 3r + s - 4t = -8 \\ 2r - s + 3t = 1 \\ 5r + s + 5t = 8 \end{cases}$

APPLICATIONS

29. One safe investment pays 10% per year and a more risky investment pays 18% per year. A woman who has $145,600 to invest would like to have an income of $20,000 per year from her investments. How much should she invest at each rate?

30. A bank loaned $118,500 to a company for the development of two products. If the loan for product A was for $34,500 more than that for product B, how much was loaned for each product?

31. A woman has $23,500 invested in two rental properties. One earns 10% on the investment and the other yields 12%. Her total income from the two properties is $2550. How much is her income from each property?

32. Mr. Jackson borrowed money from his bank and on his life insurance to start a business. His interest rate on the bank loan is 10% and his rate on the insurance loan is 12%. If the total amount borrowed is $10,000 and his total yearly interest payment is $1090, how much did he borrow from the bank?

33. Each ounce of substance A supplies 5% of the required nutrition a patient needs. Substance B supplies 12% of the required nutrition per ounce. If digestive restrictions require that the ratio of substance A to substance B be 3/5, how many ounces of each substance should be in the diet to provide 100% of the required nutrition?

34. A glass of skim milk supplies 0.1 mg of iron and 8.5 g of protein. A quarter pound of lean red meat provides 3.4 mg of iron and 22 g of protein. If a person on a special diet is to have 7.15 mg of iron and 73.75 g of protein, how many glasses of skim milk and how many quarter-pound servings of meat would provide this?

35. Bacteria of species A and species B are kept in a single test tube, where they are fed two nutrients. Each day the test tube is supplied with 10,600 units of the first nutrient and 19,650 units of the second nutrient. Each bacteria of species A requires 2 units of the

first nutrient and 3 units of the second, and each bacteria of species B requires 1 unit of the first nutrient and 4 units of the second. What populations of each species can coexist in the test tube so that all the nutrients are consumed each day?

36. A biologist has a 40% solution and a 10% solution of the same plant nutrient. How many cubic centimeters of each solution should be mixed to obtain 25 cc of a 28% solution?

37. A nurse has two solutions that contain different concentrations of a certain medication. One is a 20% concentration and the other is a 5% concentration. How many cubic centimeters of each should he mix to obtain 10 cc of a 15.5% solution?

38. Medication A is given every 4 hours and medication B is given twice each day. The total intake of the two medications is restricted to 50.6 mg per day, for a certain patient. If the ratio of the dosage of A to the dosage of B is 5 to 8, find the dosage for each administration of each medication.

Application problems 39–42 require systems of equations in three variables.

39. Each ounce of substance A supplies 5% of the required nutrition a patient needs. Substance B supplies 15% of the required nutrition per ounce, and substance C supplies 12% of required nutrition per ounce. If digestive restrictions require that substance A and C be given in equal amounts, and the amount of substance B is one-fifth of either of these other amounts, find the number of ounces of each substance that should be in the meal to provide 100% of the nutrition.

40. A glass of skim milk supplies 0.1 mg of iron, 8.5 g of protein, and 1 g of carbohydrates. A quarter pound of lean red meat provides 3.4 mg of iron, 22 g of protein, and 20 g of carbohydrates. Two slices of whole grain bread supply 2.2 mg of iron, 10 g of protein, and 12 g of carbohydrates. If a person on a special diet must have 10.5 mg of iron, 94.5 g of protein and 61 g of carbohydrates, how many glasses of skim milk, how many quarter-pound servings of meat, and how many two-slice servings of whole grain bread will supply this?

41. A social agency is charged with providing services to three types of clients, A, B, and C. A total of 500 clients are to be served, with $150,000 available for counseling and $100,000 available for emergency food and shelter. Type A clients require an average of $200 for counseling and $300 for emergencies, Type B clients require an average of $500 for counseling and $200 for emergencies, and Type C clients require an average of $300 for counseling and $100 for emergencies. How many of each type client can be served?

42. If funding for counseling is cut to $135,000 and funding for emergency food and shelter is cut to $90,000, only 450 clients can be served. How many of each type can be served in this case? (See problem 41.)

1.7 Business Applications of Linear Equations in Two Variables

Objectives
- ☐ To solve problems involving consumption functions
- ☐ To solve problems involving market equilibrium
- ☐ To solve problems involving break-even analysis

National Consumption

As we stated in Section 1.4, the national consumption function is frequently considered to be linear over short periods of time. Thus we may write the general form of the consumption function as $C = my + b$.

The value of b will always be greater than zero, for there is always some amount of consumption necessary to maintain life, even though disposable income (money) is zero. Mathematically, we say $b > 0$. Consumption will increase whenever income increases, but at a slower rate. Thus the slope m of the line representing the consumption function is greater than 0 but less than 1; that is, $0 < m < 1$.

We call m the **marginal propensity to consume** because it indicates the proportion of our income increases that we are willing to spend. The value of C for a given value of y is called the **aggregate consumption.**

EXAMPLE 1   Suppose that national consumption is $7 billion when national disposable income is zero, and that at each level of income above zero, consumption is 0.75 of disposable income.

(a) Write this consumption function as an equation.
(b) What is the marginal propensity to consume?
(c) Graph the consumption function.

Solution   (a) The line representing the consumption function has $m = 0.75$ and $b = 7$, so the equation is $C = 0.75y + 7$ (in billions of dollars).
(b) The marginal propensity to consume is $m = 0.75$.
(c) See Figure 1.40.

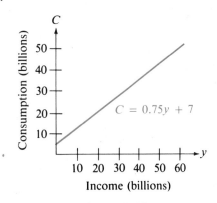

Figure 1.40

Market Equilibrium

We discussed demand functions and supply functions in Section 1.4. In many circumstances it is reasonable to assume that demand and supply functions are linear functions. Because demand will normally increase as price decreases, the slope of a demand curve (line) will be negative. On the other hand, a manufacturer will be willing to supply more goods as the price increases, so the supply curve will have a positive slope.

EXAMPLE 2   Suppose that the demand per month for a commodity is 24 if the price is $15 for each unit, 27 if the price is $13, 30 if the price is $11, and 33 if the price is $9. Assuming the demand curve is linear, write its equation. Graph the demand curve.

Solution   Using two of the points on the demand curve, say (24, 15) and (33, 9), we can find the slope of the line.

$$m = \frac{15 - 9}{24 - 33} = \frac{6}{-9} = -\frac{2}{3}$$

We can then use one of the points, say (24, 15), to write the equation of the demand curve as $p - 15 = -\frac{2}{3}(q - 24)$ or $p = -\frac{2}{3}q + 31$. The graph of the demand function is shown in Figure 1.41.

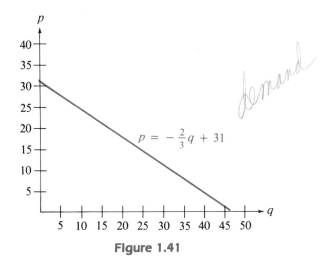

Figure 1.41

EXAMPLE 3   A manufacturer will supply 200 electric motors per month when the price is $30 and 300 per month when the price is $40. Assuming the supply curve is linear, write its equation and sketch its graph.

Solution   The slope of the line connecting the points (200, 30) and (300, 40) is

$$m = \frac{40 - 30}{300 - 200} = \frac{10}{100} = \frac{1}{10}.$$

The equation is

$$p - 30 = \tfrac{1}{10}(q - 200) \qquad \text{or} \qquad p = \tfrac{1}{10}q + 10.$$

The graph is shown in Figure 1.42.

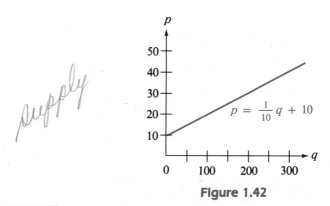

Figure 1.42

Producers of a commodity like high prices and consumers like low prices, but an agreement is made between these two opposing forces in something called a "market" (thus this area is called *market analysis*). The effects on prices of gasoline and natural gas shortages are painfully apparent to all consumers, and the effects of farm surpluses have led many small farmers to stop producing.

Table 1.3

Demand schedule		Supply schedule	
Price per unit	*Quantity demanded*	*Price per unit*	*Quantity supplied*
$15	24	$15	60
13	27	13	45
11	30	11	30
9	33	9	15

Consider the demand and supply schedules (Table 1.3) for a commodity over a period of one month. We can see from these schedules that when the price is $15, the producers are willing to supply many more units than consumers are willing to purchase. The $15 could not be the prevailing market price, for the producers would be producing many more than consumers are willing to buy at that price. This price would create a *surplus* of 36 units of this commodity each month. Eventually this surplus would force the price down below $15. If the price drops to $13, the demand is still less than the supply, so there will still be a surplus on the market, and this will force the price even lower. So the market prices of $15 and $13 will be unstable because they are too high. The price that will put the market in balance will have to be lower than $13.

On the other hand, if the price is $9, consumers will be willing to buy 33 units per month but producers will only supply 15 units. Thus the market will experience a *shortage*. Competition among consumers for the small number of items will force the price higher than the $9 price.

If the price is $11, consumers will be willing to purchase the same number of units (30) that the producers are willing to supply. So the market will be in balance if the price is $11.

When the quantity of a commodity demanded is equal to the amount supplied, **market equilibrium** is said to occur. If the demand and supply curves are graphed on the same coordinate system, with the same units, the point at which they intersect represents the **equilibrium point.** The price at that point is the **equilibrium price,** and the quantity at that point is the **equilibrium quantity.**

Graphing the curves associated with the schedules of Table 1.3 on the same graph, we see that the two lines intersect at (30, 11). This corresponds to the solution we have already found. (See Figure 1.43.)

In general, the equilibrium price and the equilibrium quantity must both be positive for the market equilibrium to have meaning.

We can find the market equilibrium by graphing the demand and supply functions on the same coordinate system, but solving the two equations simultaneously by algebraic methods will generally provide more accurate results.

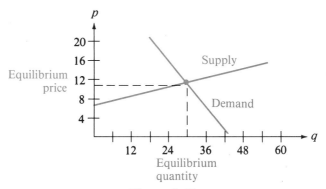

Figure 1.43

EXAMPLE 4   Find the equilibrium point for the following supply and demand functions:

$$\text{Demand:} \quad p = -3q + 26$$
$$\text{Supply:} \quad p = 4q - 9$$

Solution   Solving simultaneously by substitution gives

$$-3q + 26 = 4q - 9$$
$$35 = 7q$$

so $q = 5, \quad p = 11.$

The equilibrium point is (5, 11).

EXAMPLE 5   A group of wholesalers will buy 50 dryers per month if the price is $200 and 30 per month if the price is $300. The manufacturer is willing to supply 20 if the price is $210 and 30 if the price is $230. Assuming the resulting supply and demand functions are linear, find the equilibrium point for the market.

Solution   Demand function:

$$m = \frac{300 - 200}{30 - 50} = -5$$

$$p - 200 = -5(q - 50)$$
$$p = -5q + 450$$

Supply function:

$$m = \frac{230 - 210}{30 - 20} = 2$$

$$p - 230 = 2(q - 30)$$
$$p = 2q + 170$$

Solving simultaneously gives (by substitution)

$$-5q + 450 = 2q + 170$$
$$280 = 7q$$
$$q = 40$$
$$p = 250.$$

The equilibrium point is (40, 250). See Figure 1.44 for the graph of the functions.

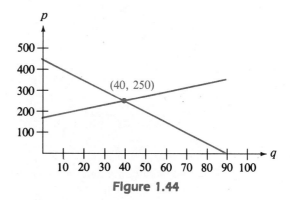

Figure 1.44

Break-Even Analysis

As we stated in Section 1.4, the profit that a firm makes on its product is the difference between its total revenue (the total amount it receives from sales) and its total cost (both fixed and variable).

$$\text{Profit (or loss)} = \text{total revenue} - \text{total cost}$$

We can solve the equations for total revenue and total cost simultaneously to find the point where cost and revenue are equal. This point is called the **break-even point.** Figure 1.45 is called a break-even chart. The quantity produced is measured along the horizontal axis; the vertical axis represents the dollar value of the costs or revenue. We will use x to represent the quantity produced and y to represent the dollar value of revenue *and* cost. The line C represents the sum of the fixed and variable costs. The line R represents the total revenue. Note that the total revenue is zero when no units are produced, and it increases more rapidly than the total cost line. (If it didn't, the firm would never make a profit.) The point where the total revenue line crosses the total cost line is called the break-even point. To the left of this point the total revenue is less than the total cost (resulting in a loss), and to the right of this point the total revenue is greater than the total cost (resulting in a profit).

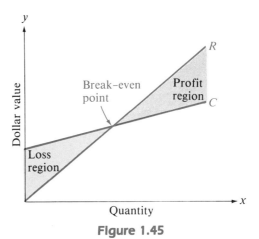

Figure 1.45

EXAMPLE 6   A manufacturer sells a product for $10 per unit. The manufacturer's fixed costs are $1200 per month, and the variable costs are $2.50 per unit. How many units must be produced each month to break even?

Solution   The total revenue for x units of the product is $10x$, so the equation for total revenue is $R = 10x$. The fixed costs are $1200, so the total cost for x units is $2.50x + 1200$. Thus the equation for total cost is $C = 2.50x + 1200$. We find the break-even point by solving the two equations simultaneously ($R = C$ at the break-even point).
    By substitution,

$$10x = 2.50x + 1200$$
$$7.5x = 1200$$
$$x = 160.$$

Thus the manufacturer will break even if 160 units are produced per month. The manufacturer will make a profit if more than 160 units are produced. (See Figure 1.46.)

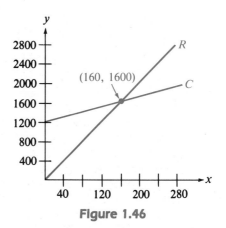

Figure 1.46

Using the fact that the profit function is found by subtracting the total cost function from the total revenue function, we can form the profit function for the previous example. The profit function is given by

$$P(x) = 10x - (2.50x + 1200) \qquad \text{or} \qquad P(x) = 7.50x - 1200.$$

We can find the point where the profit is zero (the break-even point) by setting $P(x) = 0$ and solving for x.

$$0 = 7.50x - 1200$$
$$1200 = 7.50x$$
$$x = 160$$

Note that this is the same break-even point that was found by solving the total revenue and total cost equations simultaneously.

EXAMPLE 7   Suppose a firm requires a 15% return on its investment (fixed costs) to break even. (a) If the good sells for $1, the variable cost is $.50 per unit, and the fixed cost is $20,000, find the quantity the firm must produce to break even. (b) If the capacity of the firm's plant is 40,000 units, should it start production?

Solution   The firm's minimum desired profit is 15% of its fixed costs, so the desired profit is $0.15(20,000) = 3000$. If this desired profit is added to fixed costs, the break-even quantity is the quantity that will provide the firm with its 15% return. Thus we seek the quantity that makes $P = 3000$, where

$$P = R - C$$
$$3000 = 1x - (0.50x + 20,000)$$
$$3000 = 0.50x - 20,000$$
$$0.50x = 23,000$$
$$x = 46,000.$$

(a) The break-even quantity is 46,000.
(b) No, the plant does not have the capacity to produce enough units to reach the desired profit.

Exercise 1.7

NATIONAL CONSUMPTION

1. Suppose that national consumption is $8 billion when national disposable income is zero, and that at each level of income above zero, consumption is 0.6 of disposable income.
   (a) Write this consumption function as an equation.
   (b) What is the marginal propensity to consume?
2. Suppose that national consumption is $10 billion when national disposable income is zero, and that at each level of income above zero, consumption is 0.7 of disposable income.
   (a) Write this consumption function as an equation.
   (b) What is the marginal propensity to consume?
3. Graph the equation from problem 1.
4. Graph the equation from problem 2.
5. If the national consumption function is given by the equation

$$C = 0.65y + 5 \qquad \text{(billions of dollars)},$$

   (a) what is the marginal propensity to consume?
   (b) what is the national consumption when disposable income is zero?
6. If the national consumption function is given by the equation

$$C = 0.55y + 9 \qquad \text{(billions of dollars)},$$

   (a) what is the marginal propensity to consume?
   (b) what is the national consumption when disposable income is zero?
7. Graph the consumption function in problem 5.
8. Graph the consumption function in problem 6.
9. What is the relation between the marginal propensity in problem 5 and the slope of the graph in problem 7?
10. If the national consumption is $7 billion when national disposable income is zero, and if the marginal propensity to consume is 0.8, write the linear consumption function as an equation.

MARKET EQUILIBRIUM

11. Figure 1.47 shows a supply function and a demand function.
    (a) Label each function.
    (b) Label the equilibrium point and determine the price and quantity at which market equilibrium occurs.

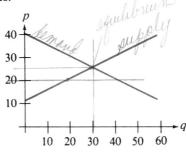

Figure 1.47

12. Use Figure 1.47 to answer the following questions.
    (a) If the price is $30, what quantity is demanded?
    (b) If the price is $30, what quantity is supplied?
    (c) Is there a surplus or shortage when the price is $30? How many units is this surplus or shortage?

13. Use Figure 1.47 to answer the following questions.
    (a) If the price is $20, what quantity is supplied? 20
    (b) If the price is $20, what quantity is demanded? 40
    (c) Is there a surplus or shortage when the price is $20? How many units is this surplus or shortage? 20

14. Will a price above the equilibrium price result in a market surplus or shortage?

15. Will a price below the equilibrium price result in a market surplus or shortage?

16. Suppose the demand per month for a product is 5 if the price is $310, 10 if the price is $300, and 15 if the price is $290. Assuming the demand curve is linear, graph the curve.

17. Suppose the demand per month for a commodity is 24 if the price is $16, 20 if the price is $18, 16 if the price is $20, and 12 if the price is $22. Assuming the demand curve is linear, graph the curve.

18. Write the equation of the demand curve in problem 16.

19. Write the equation of the demand curve in problem 17.

20. A manufacturer will supply the product in problem 16 as follows:

    5 if the price is $42
    10 if the price is $82
    15 if the price is $122

    Assuming the supply curve is linear, graph it.

21. A manufacturer will supply the commodity of problem 17 as follows:

    8 if the price is $14
    14 if the price is $16
    20 if the price is $18
    26 if the price is $20

    Assuming the supply curve is linear, graph the curve.

22. Write the equation of the supply curve in problem 20.

23. Write the equation of the supply curve in problem 21.

24. Find the equilibrium point for the demand and supply functions in problems 18 and 22.

25. Find the equilibrium point for the demand and supply functions in problems 19 and 23.

26. Find the equilibrium point for the following supply and demand functions:

$$\text{Demand:} \quad p = 480 - 3q$$
$$\text{Supply:} \quad p = 17q + 80$$

27. Find the equilibrium point for the following supply and demand functions:

$$\text{Demand:} \quad p = -4q + 220$$
$$\text{Supply:} \quad p = 15q + 30$$

28. Retailers will buy 45 Z-brand phones from a wholesaler if the price is $10 each, and will buy 20 if the price is $60 each. The wholesaler is willing to supply 35 phones at $30 each and 70 at $50 each. Assuming the resulting supply and demand functions are linear, find the market equilibrium point.

29. A group of retailers will buy 80 televisions from a wholesaler if the price is $350 and 120 if the price is $300. The wholesaler is willing to supply 60 if the price is $280 and

140 if the price is $370. Assuming the resulting supply and demand functions are linear, find the equilibrium point for the market.

30. A shoestore owner will buy 10 pairs of a certain shoe if the price is $75 per pair, and 30 pairs if the price is $25 per pair. The supplier of the shoes is willing to provide 35 pairs if the price is $80 per pair, and 5 pairs if the price is $20 per pair. Assuming the supply and demand functions for the shoes are linear, find the market equilibrium point.

If a supplier is taxed K per unit sold, then the tax is passed on to the consumer by adding K to the selling price of the product. If the original supply function is $p = f(q)$, then passing the tax on gives a new supply function, $p = f(q) + K$. Because the value of the product is not changed by the tax, the demand function is unchanged. Figure 1.48 shows the demand function and the supply functions for this case. Use this information to answer problems 31–34 and Figure 1.48 to answer problems 31 and 32.

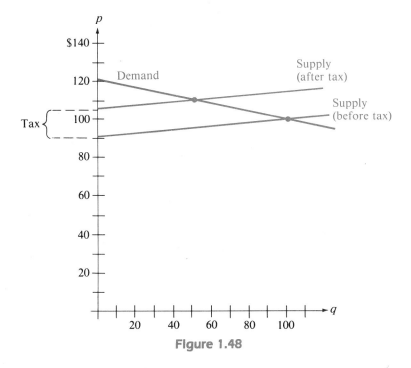

Figure 1.48

31. (a) What is the amount of the tax?
    (b) What is the original equilibrium price and quantity?
    (c) What is the new equilibrium price and quantity?
    (d) Does the supplier suffer from the tax even though it is passed on?
32. (a) If the tax is doubled, how many units will be sold?
    (b) Can a government lose money by increasing taxes?
33. If a $38 tax is placed on each unit of the product of problem 27, what is the new equilibrium price and quantity?

34. If a $56 tax is placed on each unit of the product of problem 26, what is the new equilibrium point?

BREAK-EVEN ANALYSIS

35. Figure 1.49 shows graphs of the total cost function and the total revenue function for a commodity.
    (a) Label each function correctly.
    (b) Determine the fixed costs.
    (c) Locate the break-even point and determine the number of units sold to break even.
    (d) Estimate the marginal cost and marginal revenue.

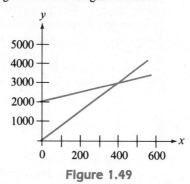

Figure 1.49

36. A manufacturer of shower-surrounds has a revenue function of

$$R(x) = 81.50x$$

and a cost function of

$$C(x) = 63x + 1850.$$

Find the number of units that must be sold to break even.

37. A jewelry maker incurs costs for a necklace according to

$$C(x) = 35x + 1650.$$

If the revenue function for the necklaces is

$$R(x) = 85x,$$

how many necklaces must be sold to break even?

38. A small business recaps and sells tires. If a set of four tires has the revenue function

$$R(x) = 89x$$

and the cost function

$$C(x) = 1400 + 75x,$$

find the number of sets of recaps that must be sold to break even.

39. A manufacturer sells belts for $12 per unit. The fixed costs are $1600 per month, and the variable costs are $8 per unit.
    (a) Write the equations of the revenue and cost functions.
    (b) Find the break-even point.

40. A manufacturer sells watches for $50 per unit. The fixed costs related to this product are $10,000 per month, and the variable costs are $30 per unit.
    (a) Write the equations of the revenue and cost functions.
    (b) How many watches must be sold to break even?
41. (a) Write the profit function for problem 39.
    (b) Set profit equal to zero and solve for x. Compare this x-value with the break-even point from 39(b).
42. (a) Write the profit function for problem 40.
    (b) Set profit equal to zero and solve for x. Compare this x-value with the break-even point from 40(b).
43. Suppose a firm will not begin production of a product unless it returns a 20% return on its investment for fixed costs. If the fixed costs are $50,000, the variable costs are $2 per unit, and the product sells for $5 per unit, how many units must be produced to break even (that is, make the required return)?
44. Suppose a firm requires a 10% return on its investment for fixed costs to break even. If the product sells for $2 per unit, the variable costs are $.50 per unit, and the fixed costs are $30,000, how many units must be produced to break even?

Review Exercises

1.1

Solve the equations in problems 1–8.

1. $x + 7 = 14$
2. $3x - 8 = 23$
3. $2x - 8 = 3x + 5$
4. $\dfrac{6x + 3}{6} = \dfrac{5(x - 2)}{9}$
5. $2x + \dfrac{1}{2} = \dfrac{x}{2} + \dfrac{1}{3}$
6. $0.6x + 4 = x - 0.02$
7. $\dfrac{3}{x} - 2 = 3 + \dfrac{1}{x}$
8. $2.81\,(3.62x - 4.02) = \dfrac{0.061x - 3.82}{412}$

1.2

In problems 9–14, sketch the graph of each equation.

9. $y = 3x$
10. $y = 5$
11. $x = -2$
12. $2x - 3y = 6$
13. $5x + 3y = 6$
14. $2(y + 1) = \frac{1}{2}x + \frac{1}{2}$

1.3

15. If $p = 3q^3$, is p a function of q?
16. If $y^2 = 9x$, is y a function of x?
17. If $R = \sqrt[3]{x + 4}$, is R a function of x?
18. What are the domain and range of the function $y = \sqrt{9 - x}$?
19. What is the domain of $y = \dfrac{\sqrt{x + 3}}{x}$?

20. If $f(x) = x^2 + 4x + 5$, find the following.
    (a) $f(-3)$ (b) $f(4)$ (c) $f\left(\frac{1}{2}\right)$
21. If $g(x) = x^2 + 1/x$, find the following.
    (a) $g(-1)$ (b) $g\left(\frac{1}{2}\right)$ (c) $g(0.1)$
22. If $f(x) = \begin{cases} -x^2 & \text{if } x \le 0 \\ 1/x & \text{if } x > 0 \end{cases}$, find the following.

    (a) $f(0)$ (b) $f(0.0001)$ (c) $f(-5)$ (d) $f(10)$
23. If $f(x) = 9x - x^2$, find the following.
    (a) $f(-4 + 1)$ (b) $f(x + 1)$ (c) $f(x + h)$
24. If $f(x) = 9x - x^2$, find $\dfrac{f(x + h) - f(x)}{h}$.

25. Does the graph in Figure 1.50 represent y as a function of x?
26. Does the graph in Figure 1.51 represent y as a function of x?

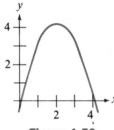

Figure 1.50   **Figure 1.51**

27. For the function f graphed in Figure 1.50, what is $f(2)$?
28. For the function f graphed in Figure 1.50, for what values of x does $f(x) = 0$?
29. For the relation whose graph is in Figure 1.51, when $x = 1$, what values does y assume?

1.5

In problems 30–32, find the slope of the line passing through each pair of points.

30. $(-1, 2)$ and $(3, -1)$
31. $(2, -1)$ and $(-1, -4)$
32. $(-3.8, -7.16)$ and $(-3.8, 1.16)$

In problems 33 and 34, find the slope and y-intercept of each line.

33. $2x + 5y = 10$ 34. $x = -\frac{3}{4}y + \frac{3}{2}$

In problems 35–42, write the equation of each line described.

35. Slope 4 and y-intercept 2   36. Slope $-\frac{1}{2}$ and y-intercept 3
37. Through $(-2, 1)$ with slope $\frac{2}{3}$ 38. Through $(6, -11)$ with slope -1
39. Through $(-2, 7)$ and $(6, -4)$ 40. Through $(-1, 8)$ and $(-1, -1)$
41. Through $(1, 6)$ and parallel to $y = 4x - 6$
42. Through $(-1, 2)$ and perpendicular to $3x + 4y = 12$

In problems 43–50, solve each system of equations.

43. $\begin{cases} 4x - 2y = 6 \\ 3x + 3y = 9 \end{cases}$ 44. $\begin{cases} 2x + y = 19 \\ x - 2y = 12 \end{cases}$

45. $\begin{cases} 3x + 2y = 5 \\ 2x - 3y = 12 \end{cases}$ 46. $\begin{cases} 6x + 3y = 1 \\ y = -2x + 1 \end{cases}$

47. $\begin{cases} 4x - 3y = 253 \\ 13x + 2y = -12 \end{cases}$ 48. $\begin{cases} 0.6x + y = 2.2 \\ 0.3x - 0.1y = 0.5 \end{cases}$

49. $\begin{cases} -2x - 3y + 5z = 11 \\ 3x + y = 2 \\ x + 2y + 3z = 5 \end{cases}$ 50. $\begin{cases} x + 2y - z = 12 \\ 3x - y + z = 2 \\ 4x + 3y - 4z = -2 \end{cases}$

APPLICATIONS

51. In a certain course, grades are based on three tests worth 100 points each, three quizzes worth 50 points each, and a final exam worth 200 points. A student has test grades of 91, 82, and 88, and quiz grades of 50, 42, and 42. What is the lowest percent the student can get on the final and still earn an A (90% or more of the total points) in the course?

52. The owner of a small construction business needs a new truck. He can buy a diesel truck for $18,000 and figures it will cost him $0.16 per mile to operate it. He can buy a gas engine truck for $16,000 and figures it will cost him $0.21 per mile to operate. Find the number of miles he must drive before the costs are equal. If he normally keeps a truck for 5 years, which is the better buy?

53. Suppose the national consumption is described by $C = 0.8y + 2$, in billions of dollars.
    (a) What is consumption when disposable income is 0?
    (b) What is consumption when disposable income is $5 billion?

54. Graph the consumption function in problem 53.

55. A certain product has supply and demand functions $p = 4q + 5$ and $p = -2q + 81$, respectively.
    (a) If the price is $53, how many units are supplied and how many are demanded?
    (b) Does this give a shortfall or a surplus?
    (c) Is the price likely to increase from $53 or decrease from it?

56. Suppose that a commodity has fixed costs of $500 and variable costs of $2 per unit.
    (a) Find the total cost function for this commodity.
    (b) What is the cost of producing 100 units?

57. Suppose that the commodity of problem 56 sells for $4 per unit.
    (a) Find the total revenue function for the commodity.
    (b) Find the revenue if 100 units are sold.

58. (a) Form the total profit function for the commodity in problems 56 and 57.
    (b) Find the profit if 100 units are produced and sold.
    (c) Find the number of units required before no money is lost.

59. A retired couple has $150,000 to invest and wants to earn $15,000 per year in interest. The safest investment yields 9.5%, but they can supplement by investing some of their money at 11%. How much should they invest at each rate to earn $15,000 per year.

60. A botanist has a 20% solution and a 70% solution of an insecticide. How much of each must be used to make 4.0 liters of a 35% solution?

61. Of the equations $p + 6q = 420$ and $p = 6q + 60$, one is supply function for a product and one is the demand function for that product.

(a) Graph these equations on the same set of axes.

(b) Label the supply function and the demand function.

(c) Find the market equilibrium point.

62. A national consumption function is given by $C = 4 + 0.6y$ (billions of dollars).

    (a) What is the consumption when disposable income is zero?

    (b) What is the marginal propensity to consume?

    (c) Graph the consumption function.

63. The total costs and total revenues of a certain product are given by the following.

    $C(x) = 38.80x + 4500$

    $R(x) = 61.30x$

    (a) Find the marginal cost.

    (b) Find the marginal revenue.

    (c) Find the marginal profit.

    (d) Find the number of units required to break even.

64. A certain commodity has the following costs for a period:

$$\begin{aligned} &\text{Fixed costs:} \quad \$1500 \\ &\text{Variable costs:} \quad \$22 \text{ per unit} \end{aligned}$$

If the commodity is sold for $52 per unit,

    (a) what is the total cost function?

    (b) what is the total revenue function?

    (c) what is the profit function?

    (d) what is the marginal cost?

    (e) what is the marginal revenue?

    (f) what is the marginal profit?

    (g) what is the break-even point?

65. The supply function and the demand function for a product are linear and determined by the tables below. Find the price that will give market equilibrium.

Supply Function		Demand Function	
Price	Quantity	Price	Quantity
100	200	200	200
200	400	100	400
300	600	0	600

WARMUP

Prerequisite problem type	Answer	Section for review
2.1, 2.2, 2.3, 2.4, 2.5	Evaluate: (a) $4 - (-2)$ (b) $-4\left(\frac{2}{3}\right) + 3$ (c) $(-5)(4) + (8)(1) + (2)(5)$ (d) Multiply each of the numbers 0, -3, -3, -2, 2 by $-\frac{1}{3}$.	(a) 6 (b) $\frac{1}{3}$ (c) -2 (d) $0, 1, 1, \frac{2}{3}, -\frac{2}{3}$	0.2 Signed numbers

| 2.3, 2.4, 2.5 | Write the coefficients of x, y, and z and the constant term in each equation:
 (a) $2x + 5y + 4z = 4$
 (b) $x - 3y - 2z = 5$
 (c) $3x + y = 4$ | | 0.5 Algebraic expressions |

		Coefficients of			Constant term	
		x	y	z		
	(a)	2	5	4	4	
	(b)	1	-3	-2	5	
	(c)	3	1	0	4	

| 2.3, 2.4, 2.5 | Solve
 (a) $x_1 - 2x_3 = 2$ for x_1
 (b) $x_2 + x_3 = -3$ for x_2 | (a) $x_1 = 2 + 2x_3$
 (b) $x_2 = -3 - x_3$ | 1.1 Linear equations |

| 2.3, 2.4, 2.5 | Solve the system:
 $\begin{cases} x - 0.25y = 11{,}750 \\ -0.20x + y = 10{,}000 \end{cases}$ | $x = 15{,}000$
 $y = 13{,}000$ | 1.6 Systems of linear equations |

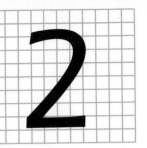

Matrices

A business may collect and store or analyze various types of data as a regular part of its record-keeping procedures. The data may be presented in tabular form. For example, a building contractor who builds four different styles of houses may catalog the number of units of certain materials needed to build each style in a table like Table 2.1.

Table 2.1

| Required units | House style | | | |
	Ranch	Colonial	Split level	Cape Cod
Wood	20	25	22	18
Siding	27	40	31	25
Roofing	16	16	19	16

If we write the numbers from Table 2.1 in the rectangular array

$$A = \begin{bmatrix} 20 & 25 & 22 & 18 \\ 27 & 40 & 31 & 25 \\ 16 & 16 & 19 & 16 \end{bmatrix},$$

we say A is a **matrix** (plural: matrices) representing Table 2.1. In addition to storing data in a matrix, we can analyze data and make business decisions by defining the operations of addition, subtraction, and multiplication for matrices.

Matrices are very useful in solving systems of linear equations in two or more variables. We will see how matrices can be used to solve two linear equations in two unknowns, and will extend the method to solve systems involving three and more variables.

2.1 Matrices

□   To organize and interpret data stored in matrices
         □   To add and subtract matrices

As we noted in the introduction to this chapter, matrices can be used to store data and to perform operations with the data. We have noted that the matrix

$$A = \begin{bmatrix} 20 & 25 & 22 & 18 \\ 27 & 40 & 31 & 25 \\ 16 & 16 & 19 & 16 \end{bmatrix}$$

represents the data from Table 2.1. Matrix A contains the heart of the information from Table 2.1, without the labels. This rectangular array refers to very specific information, but the organizational format is useful in an assortment of problems. In general, any rectangular array of numbers is called a **matrix.**

The *rows* of the matrix A correspond to the types of building materials and the *columns* correspond to the types of houses. The rows of a matrix are numbered from the top to the bottom and the columns are numbered from left to right.

$$\begin{array}{c} \\ \text{Row 1} \\ \text{Row 2} \\ \text{Row 3} \end{array} \begin{array}{cccc} \text{Column 1} & \text{Column 2} & \text{Column 3} & \text{Column 4} \\ \begin{bmatrix} 20 & 25 & 22 & 18 \\ 27 & 40 & 31 & 25 \\ 16 & 16 & 19 & 16 \end{bmatrix} \end{array}$$

Matrices are classified by the number of rows and columns they have. The matrix A has three rows and four columns, so we say this is a 3×4 (read "three by four") matrix.

The matrix

$$A = \begin{bmatrix} a_{11} & a_{12} & a_{13} & \cdots & a_{1n} \\ a_{21} & a_{22} & a_{23} & \cdots & a_{2n} \\ & \vdots & & & \vdots \\ a_{m1} & a_{m2} & a_{m3} & \cdots & a_{mn} \end{bmatrix}$$

has m rows and n columns, so it is an $m \times n$ matrix. When we designate A as an $m \times n$ matrix, we are indicating the size of the matrix. Two matrices are said to have the same **order** (be the same size) if they have the same number of rows and the same number of columns.

The numbers in a matrix are called its **entries** or **elements.** Note that the subscripts on an entry in matrix A correspond respectively to the row and column in which the entry is located. Thus a_{23} represents the entry in the second row and the third column, and we refer to it as the "two-three entry." In matrix B on page 121 the entry denoted by b_{23} is 1.

Some matrices take special names because of their size. If the number of rows equals the number of columns, we say the matrix is a **square matrix.** Matrix B is an example of a 3×3 square matrix.

$$B = \begin{bmatrix} 4 & 3 & 0 \\ 0 & 0 & 1 \\ -4 & 0 & 0 \end{bmatrix}.$$

A matrix with one row, such as $[9 \quad 5]$ or $[3 \quad 2 \quad 1 \quad 6]$, is called a **row matrix,** and a matrix with one column, such as

$$\begin{bmatrix} 1 \\ 3 \\ 5 \end{bmatrix},$$

is called a **column matrix.** Row and column matrices are also called **vectors.**

Any matrix in which *every* entry is zero is called a **zero matrix;** examples are

$$\begin{bmatrix} 0 & 0 \\ 0 & 0 \end{bmatrix}, \begin{bmatrix} 0 & 0 \\ 0 & 0 \\ 0 & 0 \end{bmatrix}, \begin{bmatrix} 0 & 0 & 0 & 0 \\ 0 & 0 & 0 & 0 \end{bmatrix}.$$

We define two matrices to be **equal** if they are the same order and if each entry in one equals the corresponding entry in the other.

EXAMPLE 1 Are $A = \begin{bmatrix} 1 & 3 & 2 \\ 4 & 1 & 2 \end{bmatrix}$ and $B = \begin{bmatrix} 1 & 4 \\ 2 & 1 \\ 3 & 0 \end{bmatrix}$ the same order matrices?

Solution No. A is a 2×3 matrix and B is a 3×2 matrix.

EXAMPLE 2 (a) Which element of

$$A = \begin{bmatrix} 1 & 2 & 3 \\ 4 & 5 & 6 \\ 7 & 8 & 9 \end{bmatrix}$$

is represented by a_{32}?
(b) Is A a square matrix?

Solution (a) a_{32} represents the element in row 3 and column 2; that is, 8.
(b) Yes, it is a 3×3 (square) matrix.

If two matrices have the same number of rows and columns, we can add the matrices by adding their corresponding entries. More formally,

Sum of Two Matrices

If matrix A and matrix B are the same order and have elements a_{ij} and b_{ij}, respectively, then their **sum** $A + B$ is a matrix C whose elements are $c_{ij} = a_{ij} + b_{ij}$ for all i and j.

That is,

$$
\begin{bmatrix}
a_{11} & a_{12} & \cdots & a_{1n} \\
a_{21} & a_{22} & \cdots & a_{2n} \\
\vdots & & & \vdots \\
a_{m1} & a_{m2} & \cdots & a_{mn}
\end{bmatrix}
+
\begin{bmatrix}
b_{11} & b_{12} & \cdots & b_{1n} \\
b_{21} & b_{22} & \cdots & b_{2n} \\
\vdots & & & \vdots \\
b_{m1} & b_{m2} & \cdots & b_{mn}
\end{bmatrix}
$$

$$
=
\begin{bmatrix}
a_{11} + b_{11} & a_{12} + b_{12} & \cdots & a_{1n} + b_{1n} \\
a_{21} + b_{21} & a_{22} + b_{22} & \cdots & a_{2n} + b_{2n} \\
\vdots & & & \vdots \\
a_{m1} + b_{m1} & a_{m2} + b_{m2} & \cdots & a_{mn} + b_{mn}
\end{bmatrix}.
$$

EXAMPLE 3   Find the sum of A and B if

$$
A = \begin{bmatrix} 1 & 2 & 3 \\ 4 & -1 & -2 \end{bmatrix} \quad \text{and} \quad B = \begin{bmatrix} -1 & 2 & -3 \\ -2 & 0 & 1 \end{bmatrix}.
$$

Solution $A + {}'B = \begin{bmatrix} 1 + (-1) & 2 + 2 & 3 + (-3) \\ 4 + (-2) & -1 + 0 & -2 + 1 \end{bmatrix} = \begin{bmatrix} 0 & 4 & 0 \\ 2 & -1 & -1 \end{bmatrix}.$

The matrix $-B$ is called the **negative** of the matrix B, and each element of $-B$ is the negative of the corresponding element of B. For example, if

$$
B = \begin{bmatrix} -1 & 2 & -3 \\ -2 & 0 & 1 \end{bmatrix}, \quad \text{then} \quad -B = \begin{bmatrix} 1 & -2 & 3 \\ 2 & 0 & -1 \end{bmatrix}.
$$

Using the negative, we can define the difference $A - B$ (when A and B have the same order) by $A - B = A + (-B)$, or by subtracting corresponding elements.

EXAMPLE 4   For matrices A and B of Example 3, find $A - B$.

Solution $A - B$ can be found by subtracting corresponding elements.

$$
A - B = \begin{bmatrix} 1 - (-1) & 2 - 2 & 3 - (-3) \\ 4 - (-2) & -1 - 0 & -2 - 1 \end{bmatrix} = \begin{bmatrix} 2 & 0 & 6 \\ 6 & -1 & -3 \end{bmatrix}.
$$

EXAMPLE 5   Suppose the purchase prices and delivery costs (per unit) for wood, siding, and roofing used in construction are given by Table 2.2. If the supplier decides to raise the purchase prices by $.60 per unit, and the delivery costs by $.05 per unit, write the matrix that describes the new unit costs.

Table 2.2

	Wood	Siding	Roofing
Purchase	6	4	2
Delivery	1	1	0.5

Solution The matrix representing the original unit costs is

$$C = \begin{bmatrix} 6 & 4 & 2 \\ 1 & 1 & 0.5 \end{bmatrix},$$

and the matrix representing the increases is given by

$$H = \begin{bmatrix} 0.60 & 0.60 & 0.60 \\ 0.05 & 0.05 & 0.05 \end{bmatrix}.$$

The new unit cost for each item is its former cost plus the increase, so the new unit cost matrix is given by

$$C + H = \begin{bmatrix} 6 + 0.60 & 4 + 0.60 & 2 + 0.60 \\ 1 + 0.05 & 1 + 0.05 & 0.5 + 0.05 \end{bmatrix} = \begin{bmatrix} 6.60 & 4.60 & 2.60 \\ 1.05 & 1.05 & 0.55 \end{bmatrix}.$$

Note that the sum of C and H in Example 5 could be found by adding the matrices in either order. That is, $C + H = H + C$. This is known as the **commutative law of addition** for matrices. We will see in the next section that multiplication of matrices is *not* commutative.

Exercise 2.1

In problems 1–4, find x, y, z, and w.

1. $\begin{bmatrix} x & 1 & 0 \\ 0 & y & z \\ w & 2 & 1 \end{bmatrix} = \begin{bmatrix} 3 & 1 & 0 \\ 0 & 2 & 3 \\ 4 & 2 & 1 \end{bmatrix}$

2. $\begin{bmatrix} 0 & x & 1 \\ 3 & y & y \\ z & 0 & 2 \end{bmatrix} = \begin{bmatrix} 0 & 4 & 1 \\ 3 & 1 & y \\ 1 & 0 & w \end{bmatrix}$

3. $\begin{bmatrix} x & 3 & (2x - 1) \\ y & 4 & 4y \end{bmatrix} = \begin{bmatrix} 2x - 4 & z & 7 \\ 1 & (w + 1) & (3y + 1) \end{bmatrix}$

4. $\begin{bmatrix} x & y & (x + 3) \\ z & 4 & 4y \end{bmatrix} = \begin{bmatrix} (2x - 1) & -1 & w \\ x & (5 + y) & -4 \end{bmatrix}$

Use the following matrices in problems 5–26.

$$A = \begin{bmatrix} 1 & 0 & 2 \\ 3 & 2 & 1 \\ 4 & 0 & 3 \end{bmatrix} \quad B = \begin{bmatrix} 1 & 1 & 3 & 0 \\ 4 & 2 & 1 & 1 \\ 3 & 2 & 0 & 1 \end{bmatrix} \quad C = \begin{bmatrix} 5 & 3 \\ 1 & 2 \end{bmatrix}$$

$$D = \begin{bmatrix} 4 & 2 \\ 3 & 5 \end{bmatrix} \quad E = \begin{bmatrix} 1 & 0 & 4 \\ 5 & 1 & 0 \end{bmatrix} \quad F = \begin{bmatrix} 1 & 2 & 3 \\ -1 & 0 & 1 \\ 2 & -3 & -4 \end{bmatrix}$$

$$Z = \begin{bmatrix} 0 & 0 & 0 \\ 0 & 0 & 0 \\ 0 & 0 & 0 \end{bmatrix}$$

5. Which of the matrices A, B, C, D, E, F, and Z are square?
6. Which pairs of matrices, if any, are equal?
7. Which pairs of matrices, if any, are the same order?
8. Write the matrix that is the negative of matrix F.
9. Using matrix A, find all possible answers to each of the following:
   (a) $a_{23} = ?$ (b) $a_{3j} = ?$, if $1 \le j \le 3$ (c) if $a_{i2} = 2$, then $i = ?$
   (d) if $a_{i2} = 0$, then $i = ?$ (e) if $a_{ij} = 1$, then $i = ?$ and $j = ?$
10. Using matrix B, find all possible answers to each of the following:
    (a) if B is $m \times n$, then $m = ?$ and $n = ?$ (b) $b_{32} = ?$
    (c) if $b_{2j} = 1$, then $j = ?$ (d) if $b_{ij} = 4$, what are i and j?
    (e) if $b_{ij} = 0$, then $i = ?$ and $j = ?$
11. Find the negative of A.
12. Find the sum of A and its negative.
13. Write a 2×5 zero matrix.
14. If a matrix is added to its negative, what kind of matrix results?

In problems 15–26, compute the sums and differences if possible.

15. $C + D$ 16. $A + F$ 17. $A - F$ 18. $C - D$
19. $A + B$ 20. $D - C$ 21. $D - E$ 22. $B + F$
23. $A + Z$ 24. $A - Z$ 25. $Z + C$ 26. $Z + F$
27. Solve for x, y, and z if

$$\begin{bmatrix} x & y \\ y & z \end{bmatrix} + \begin{bmatrix} 2x & -y \\ 3y & -4z \end{bmatrix} = \begin{bmatrix} 6 & 0 \\ 8 & 9 \end{bmatrix}.$$

28. Find x, y, z, and w if

$$\begin{bmatrix} x & 4 \\ 4y & w \end{bmatrix} - \begin{bmatrix} 4x & 2z \\ -3 & -2w \end{bmatrix} = \begin{bmatrix} 12 & 8 \\ y & 6 \end{bmatrix}.$$

APPLICATIONS

Operating from two plants, the Book Equipment Company (BEC) produces bookcases and filing cabinets. Matrix A summarizes its production for a week, with row 1 representing the number of bookcases and row 2 representing the number of filing cabinets. Matrix B gives the production for the second week, and matrix C that of the third and fourth weeks combined.

$$A = \begin{bmatrix} 50 & 30 \\ 36 & 44 \end{bmatrix} \quad B = \begin{bmatrix} 30 & 45 \\ 22 & 62 \end{bmatrix} \quad C = \begin{bmatrix} 96 & 52 \\ 81 & 37 \end{bmatrix}$$

If column 1 in each matrix represents production from plant 1 and column 2 represents production from plant 2, answer the following questions.

29. How many bookcases were produced in the first week?
30. How many filing cabinets were produced in the first week?
31. How many units were produced by plant 1 in the first week?
32. How many units were produced by plant 2 in the first week?
33. If production during the second week is given by matrix B, write a matrix that describes production for the first two weeks.
34. If production over the next two-week period is given by matrix C, describe production for the four-week period.
35. If BEC sells the bookcases and filing cabinets for the same price, was the week described by matrix A or the one described by matrix B better for the company?
36. Was total production better during the first two weeks or the last two described?
37. If matrix D

$$D = \begin{bmatrix} 40 & 26 \\ 29 & 42 \end{bmatrix}$$

describes the shipments made during the first week, write the matrix that describes the units added to the plants' inventories.
38. If D also describes the shipments during the second week, describe the change in inventory. What happened at plant 1?

In a computer simulation, three groups of baby laboratory animals were used. Group I had an enriched diet, group II (control) had the regular diet, and group III had a deficient diet. At the beginning of the simulation the animals were weighed and measured according to their group, with group I averaging 140 g with a length of 5.5 cm. Group II and group III weighed 151 g and 141 g, with lengths of 5.7 cm and 5.5 cm, respectively.

39. Make a matrix that displays this information.
40. At the end of two weeks, the same measurements were made, with the following results: 12.5 cm, 250 g; 11.8 cm, 215 g; 9.8 cm, 190 g. Make a matrix that displays this information. Make sure the matrix is the same size as your answer in problem 39.
41. Calculate the changes in weight and length from problem 40 by using matrix subtraction.
42. The table below gives the years of life expected at birth for blacks and whites born in the U.S. in the years 1920, 1940, 1960, and 1980.

	Whites		Blacks	
	Males	Females	Males	Females
1920	54.4	55.6	45.5	45.2
1940	62.1	66.6	51.5	54.9
1960	67.4	74.1	61.1	67.4
1980	70.7	78.1	65.3	73.6

(*Source*: National Center for Health Statistics)

Make a matrix A containing the information for whites and a matrix B for blacks. Use these to find how many more years whites in each category are expected to live than blacks.

43. (a) From the data in the table below make a matrix A that gives the value (in millions of dollars) of imports for the various country groupings in the years 1983–1985.
    (b) Make a matrix B that gives the value of exports (in millions of dollars) for the same groupings in the same years.
    (c) Find the trade balance for each country grouping in each year by finding $A - B$.

Countries	Imports			Exports		
	83	84	85	83	84	85
Developed	122,822	135,884	134,018	152,117	200,714	223,314
Developing	72,342	74,421	72,673	102,266	119,790	116,161
Communist	5,085	7,214	7,091	3,604	5,221	5,801
Other	289	369	365	1	1	0

(*Source*: U.S. Bureau of Census)

2.2   Multiplication of Matrices

Objectives   □   To multiply a matrix by a scalar (real number)
    □   To multiply two matrices

We have seen (in Section 2.1) how we can use matrices to store data, and how addition and subtraction of matrices can be used to gain new information from the data. In this section we will see how multiplication involving matrices can provide information about data. We will begin our discussion with scalar multiplication of a matrix.

Consider the matrix

$$A = \begin{bmatrix} 3 & 2 \\ 1 & 1 \\ 2 & 0 \end{bmatrix}.$$

Since $2A$ is $A + A$, we see that

$$2A = \begin{bmatrix} 3 & 2 \\ 1 & 1 \\ 2 & 0 \end{bmatrix} + \begin{bmatrix} 3 & 2 \\ 1 & 1 \\ 2 & 0 \end{bmatrix} = \begin{bmatrix} 6 & 4 \\ 2 & 2 \\ 4 & 0 \end{bmatrix}.$$

Note that $2A$ could have been found by multiplying each entry of A by 2. In the same manner,

$$3A = A + A + A = \begin{bmatrix} 3 & 2 \\ 1 & 1 \\ 2 & 0 \end{bmatrix} + \begin{bmatrix} 3 & 2 \\ 1 & 1 \\ 2 & 0 \end{bmatrix} + \begin{bmatrix} 3 & 2 \\ 1 & 1 \\ 2 & 0 \end{bmatrix}$$

$$= \begin{bmatrix} 9 & 6 \\ 3 & 3 \\ 6 & 0 \end{bmatrix} = \begin{bmatrix} 3(3) & 3(2) \\ 3(1) & 3(1) \\ 3(2) & 3(0) \end{bmatrix}.$$

We can define **scalar multiplication** as follows:

> Multiplying a matrix by a real number (called a *scalar*) results in a matrix in which each entry of the original matrix is multiplied by the real number.

Thus, if

$$A = \begin{bmatrix} a_{11} & a_{12} \\ a_{21} & a_{22} \end{bmatrix}, \quad \text{then} \quad cA = \begin{bmatrix} ca_{11} & ca_{12} \\ ca_{21} & ca_{22} \end{bmatrix}.$$

EXAMPLE 1 If

$$A = \begin{bmatrix} 4 & 1 & 4 & 0 \\ 2 & -7 & 3 & 6 \\ 0 & 0 & 2 & 5 \end{bmatrix},$$

find $5A$ and $-2A$.

Solution

$$5A = \begin{bmatrix} 5 \cdot 4 & 5 \cdot 1 & 5 \cdot 4 & 5 \cdot 0 \\ 5 \cdot 2 & 5(-7) & 5 \cdot 3 & 5 \cdot 6 \\ 5 \cdot 0 & 5 \cdot 0 & 5 \cdot 2 & 5 \cdot 5 \end{bmatrix} = \begin{bmatrix} 20 & 5 & 20 & 0 \\ 10 & -35 & 15 & 30 \\ 0 & 0 & 10 & 25 \end{bmatrix}$$

$$-2A = \begin{bmatrix} -2 \cdot 4 & -2 \cdot 1 & -2 \cdot 4 & -2 \cdot 0 \\ -2 \cdot 2 & -2(-7) & -2 \cdot 3 & -2 \cdot 6 \\ -2 \cdot 0 & -2 \cdot 0 & -2 \cdot 2 & -2 \cdot 5 \end{bmatrix}$$

$$= \begin{bmatrix} -8 & -2 & -8 & 0 \\ -4 & 14 & -6 & -12 \\ 0 & 0 & -4 & -10 \end{bmatrix}$$

EXAMPLE 2 Suppose the purchase prices and delivery costs (per unit) for wood, siding, and roofing used in construction are given by Table 2.3.

Table 2.3

	Wood	Siding	Roofing
Purchase	6	4	2
Delivery	1	1	0.5

Then the table of unit costs may be represented by the matrix

$$C = \begin{bmatrix} 6 & 4 & 2 \\ 1 & 1 & 0.5 \end{bmatrix}.$$

If the supplier announces a 10% increase on both purchase and delivery of these items, find the new unit cost matrix.

Solution   A 10% increase means that the new unit costs are the former costs plus 0.10 times the former cost. That is, the new costs are 1.10 times the former, so the new unit cost matrix is given by

$$1.10C = 1.10 \begin{bmatrix} 6 & 4 & 2 \\ 1 & 1 & 0.5 \end{bmatrix}$$

$$= \begin{bmatrix} 6.60 & 4.40 & 2.20 \\ 1.10 & 1.10 & 0.55 \end{bmatrix}.$$

Suppose one store of a firm has 30 washers, 20 dryers, and 10 dishwashers in its inventory. If the value of each washer is \$300, each dryer is \$250, and each dishwasher is \$350, then the value of this inventory is

$$30 \cdot 300 + 20 \cdot 250 + 10 \cdot 350 = \$17,500.$$

If we write the value of each of the appliances in the *row matrix*

$$A = [300 \quad 250 \quad 350]$$

and the number of each of the appliances in the *column matrix*

$$B = \begin{bmatrix} 30 \\ 20 \\ 10 \end{bmatrix},$$

then the value of the inventory may be represented by

$$AB = [300 \quad 250 \quad 350] \begin{bmatrix} 30 \\ 20 \\ 10 \end{bmatrix}$$

$$= [300 \cdot 30 + 250 \cdot 20 + 350 \cdot 10]$$

$$= [\$17,500].$$

This useful way of operating with a row matrix and a column matrix is called the **product** of A times B.

In general, we can multiply the row matrix

$$A = [a_1 \quad a_2 \quad a_3 \quad \cdots \quad a_n]$$

times the column matrix

$$B = \begin{bmatrix} b_1 \\ b_2 \\ b_3 \\ \vdots \\ b_n \end{bmatrix}$$

if A and B have the same number of elements. The product A times B is

$$AB = [a_1 \quad a_2 \quad a_3 \quad \cdots \quad a_n] \begin{bmatrix} b_1 \\ b_2 \\ b_3 \\ \vdots \\ b_n \end{bmatrix} = [a_1b_1 + a_2b_2 + a_3b_3 + \cdots + a_nb_n].$$

Suppose the firm has a second store, with 40 washers, 25 dryers, and 5 dish-washers. We can use matrix C to represent the inventories of the two stores.

$$C = \begin{matrix} & \text{Store I} & \text{Store II} & \\ & \begin{bmatrix} 30 & 40 \\ 20 & 25 \\ 10 & 5 \end{bmatrix} & \begin{matrix} \text{Washers} \\ \text{Dryers} \\ \text{Dishwashers} \end{matrix} \end{matrix}$$

Suppose the values of the appliances are \$300, \$250, and \$350, respectively. We have already seen that the value of the inventory of store I is \$17,500. The value of the inventory of store II is

$$300 \cdot 40 + 250 \cdot 25 + 350 \cdot 5 = \$20,000.$$

Because the value of the inventory of store I can be found by multiplying the row matrix A times the first column of the matrix C, and the value of the inventory of store II can be found by multiplying matrix A times the second column of matrix C, we can write this result as

$$AC = [300 \quad 250 \quad 350] \begin{bmatrix} 30 & 40 \\ 20 & 25 \\ 10 & 5 \end{bmatrix} = [17,500 \quad 20,000].$$

The matrix we have represented as AC is called the **product** of the row matrix A and the 3×2 matrix C. We should note that matrix A is a 1×3 matrix, matrix C is a 3×2 matrix, and their product is a 1×2 matrix. In general, we can multiply an $m \times n$ matrix times an $n \times p$ matrix and the product will be an $m \times p$ matrix, as follows:

Product of Two Matrices

Given an $m \times n$ matrix A and an $n \times p$ matrix B, the **matrix product** AB is an $m \times p$ matrix C, with the ij entry of C given by the formula

$$c_{ij} = a_{i1}b_{1j} + a_{i2}b_{2j} + \cdots + a_{in}b_{nj},$$

which is illustrated in Figure 2.1 on the following page.

$$
\begin{bmatrix} a_{11} & a_{12} & \cdots & a_{1n} \\ a_{21} & a_{22} & \cdots & a_{2n} \\ & \vdots & & \\ a_{i1} & a_{i2} & \cdots & a_{in} \\ & \vdots & & \\ a_{m1} & a_{m2} & \cdots & a_{mn} \end{bmatrix}
\begin{bmatrix} b_{11} & b_{12} & \cdots & b_{1j} & \cdots & b_{1p} \\ b_{21} & b_{22} & \cdots & b_{2j} & \cdots & b_{2p} \\ & \vdots & & & & \vdots \\ b_{n1} & b_{n2} & \cdots & b_{nj} & \cdots & b_{np} \end{bmatrix}
$$

$$
= \begin{bmatrix} c_{11} & c_{12} & \cdots & c_{1j} & \cdots & c_{1p} \\ c_{21} & c_{22} & \cdots & c_{2j} & \cdots & c_{2p} \\ & \vdots & & & & \vdots \\ c_{i1} & c_{i2} & \cdots & c_{ij} & \cdots & c_{ip} \\ & \vdots & & & & \vdots \\ c_{m1} & c_{m2} & \cdots & c_{mj} & \cdots & c_{mp} \end{bmatrix}
$$

Figure 2.1

EXAMPLE 3   Find AB if

$$
A = \begin{bmatrix} 3 & 4 \\ 2 & 5 \\ 6 & 10 \end{bmatrix} \quad \text{and} \quad B = \begin{bmatrix} a & b & c & d \\ e & f & g & h \end{bmatrix}.
$$

Solution A is a 3×2 matrix and B is a 2×4 matrix, so the number of columns of A equals the number of rows of B. Thus we can find the product AB, which is a 3×4 matrix. That is, $A_{32} \times B_{24} = C_{34}$.

$$
AB = \begin{bmatrix} 3 & 4 \\ 2 & 5 \\ 6 & 10 \end{bmatrix} \begin{bmatrix} a & b & c & d \\ e & f & g & h \end{bmatrix}
$$

$$
= \begin{bmatrix} 3a + 4e & 3b + 4f & 3c + 4g & 3d + 4h \\ 2a + 5e & 2b + 5f & 2c + 5g & 2d + 5h \\ 6a + 10e & 6b + 10f & 6c + 10g & 6d + 10h \end{bmatrix}
$$

This example shows that if $AB = C$, element c_{32} is found by multiplying each entry of A's *third* row by the corresponding entry of B's *second* column, and then adding these products.

EXAMPLE 4   Find AB and BA if

$$
A = \begin{bmatrix} 3 & 2 \\ 1 & 0 \end{bmatrix} \quad \text{and} \quad B = \begin{bmatrix} 1 & 2 \\ 3 & 1 \end{bmatrix}.
$$

Solution Both A and B are 2×2 matrices, so both AB and BA are defined.

$$AB = \begin{bmatrix} 3 & 2 \\ 1 & 0 \end{bmatrix} \begin{bmatrix} 1 & 2 \\ 3 & 1 \end{bmatrix} = \begin{bmatrix} 3 \cdot 1 + 2 \cdot 3 & 3 \cdot 2 + 2 \cdot 1 \\ 1 \cdot 1 + 0 \cdot 3 & 1 \cdot 2 + 0 \cdot 1 \end{bmatrix} = \begin{bmatrix} 9 & 8 \\ 1 & 2 \end{bmatrix}$$

$$BA = \begin{bmatrix} 1 & 2 \\ 3 & 1 \end{bmatrix} \begin{bmatrix} 3 & 2 \\ 1 & 0 \end{bmatrix} = \begin{bmatrix} 1 \cdot 3 + 2 \cdot 1 & 1 \cdot 2 + 2 \cdot 0 \\ 3 \cdot 3 + 1 \cdot 1 & 3 \cdot 2 + 1 \cdot 0 \end{bmatrix} = \begin{bmatrix} 5 & 2 \\ 10 & 6 \end{bmatrix}$$

Note that for these matrices the two products AB and BA are the same size matrices, but they are not equal. That is, $BA \neq AB$. Thus we say that *matrix multiplication is not commutative*.

EXAMPLE 5 Suppose products A and B are made from plastic, steel, and glass, with the number units of each raw material required for each product given by Table 2.4.

Table 2.4 *Units Required*

	Plastic	*Steel*	*Glass*
Product A	3	1	0.50
Product B	4	0.50	2

Because of transportation costs to the firm's two plants, X and Y, the unit costs for some of the raw materials are different. Table 2.5 gives the unit costs for each of the raw materials at the two plants.

Table 2.5 Unit Costs

	Plant X	*Plant Y*
Plastic	10	9
Steel	22	26
Glass	14	14

Using the information just given, find the total cost of producing each of the products at each of the factories.

Solution Table 2.4, which gives the units of raw material required for each of the products, may be represented by the *production matrix*

$$P = \begin{bmatrix} 3 & 1 & 0.50 \\ 4 & 0.50 & 2 \end{bmatrix},$$

and Table 2.5, which gives the unit costs of the raw materials at each of the sites, may be represented by the *unit cost matrix*

$$C = \begin{bmatrix} 10 & 9 \\ 22 & 26 \\ 14 & 14 \end{bmatrix}.$$

To find the total cost of product A at plant X, we must multiply the number of units of raw materials required for product A by the unit cost for the respective raw materials at plant X, and add these costs together. Note that the entry in the first row and the first column of the matrix product PC gives this cost.

$$PC = \begin{bmatrix} 3 & 1 & 0.50 \\ 4 & 0.50 & 2 \end{bmatrix} \begin{bmatrix} 10 & 9 \\ 22 & 26 \\ 14 & 14 \end{bmatrix}$$

$$= \begin{bmatrix} 30 + 22 + 7 & 27 + 26 + 7 \\ 40 + 11 + 28 & 36 + 13 + 28 \end{bmatrix} = \begin{bmatrix} 59 & 60 \\ 79 & 77 \end{bmatrix}.$$

We can see that the second entry of the first row gives the cost of product A at plant Y. The first entry of the second row is the cost of product B at plant X and the second entry in the second row is the cost of product B at plant Y. Thus matrix PC summarizes the costs for the products at each plant.

$$PC = \begin{matrix} & \text{X} & \text{Y} & \\ & \begin{bmatrix} 59 & 60 \\ 79 & 77 \end{bmatrix} & \begin{matrix} A \\ B \end{matrix} \end{matrix}$$

An $n \times n$ (square) matrix (where n is any natural number) that has 1s down its diagonal and 0s everywhere else is called an **identity matrix.** The matrix

$$I = \begin{bmatrix} 1 & 0 & 0 \\ 0 & 1 & 0 \\ 0 & 0 & 1 \end{bmatrix}$$

is a 3×3 identity matrix. The matrix I is called an identity matrix because for any 3×3 matrix A, $AI = IA = A$. That is, if I is multiplied times a 3×3 matrix A, the product matrix is A. Note that when one of the matrices being multiplied is an identity matrix, the product *is commutative*.

EXAMPLE 6   (a) Write the 2×2 identity matrix.

(b) Given $A = \begin{bmatrix} 4 & -7 \\ 13 & 2 \end{bmatrix}$, show $AI = IA = A$

Solution   (a) We use I to denote the 2×2 identity matrix.

$$I = \begin{bmatrix} 1 & 0 \\ 0 & 1 \end{bmatrix}$$

(b) $AI = \begin{bmatrix} 4 & -7 \\ 13 & 2 \end{bmatrix} \begin{bmatrix} 1 & 0 \\ 0 & 1 \end{bmatrix} = \begin{bmatrix} 4 + 0 & 0 - 7 \\ 13 + 0 & 0 + 2 \end{bmatrix} = \begin{bmatrix} 4 & -7 \\ 13 & 2 \end{bmatrix}$

$IA = \begin{bmatrix} 1 & 0 \\ 0 & 1 \end{bmatrix} \begin{bmatrix} 4 & -7 \\ 13 & 2 \end{bmatrix} = \begin{bmatrix} 4 & -7 \\ 13 & 2 \end{bmatrix}$

Therefore, $AI = IA = A$.

Exercise 2.2

1. Is matrix multiplication commutative?
2. Is multiplication by the identity matrix commutative?

In problems 3–28, use matrices A through F to perform the indicated operations when possible.

$$A = \begin{bmatrix} 1 & 0 & 2 \\ 3 & 2 & 1 \\ 4 & 0 & 3 \end{bmatrix} \quad B = \begin{bmatrix} 1 & 1 & 3 & 0 \\ 4 & 2 & 1 & 1 \\ 3 & 2 & 0 & 1 \end{bmatrix} \quad C = \begin{bmatrix} 5 & 3 \\ 1 & 2 \end{bmatrix}$$

$$D = \begin{bmatrix} 4 & 2 \\ 3 & 5 \end{bmatrix} \quad E = \begin{bmatrix} 1 & 0 & 4 \\ 5 & 1 & 0 \end{bmatrix} \quad F = \begin{bmatrix} 1 & 0 & -1 & 3 \\ 2 & -1 & 3 & -4 \end{bmatrix}$$

3. $3A$
4. $4D$ *scaler*
5. $4C + 2D$
6. $5C - 3D$
7. $2A - 3B$
8. If the product CF is an $m \times p$ matrix, what are m and p?
9. CD
10. DE
11. DC
12. CF
13. Does $CD = DC$? (see problems 9 and 11)
14. DF
15. AB
16. EC
17. BA
18. CE
19. EB
20. BE
21. EA
22. AE
23. A^2
24. A^3
25. C^3
26. F^2 *can't be done*
27. Are $\left(\frac{1}{4}A\right)B$ and $\frac{1}{4}(AB)$ equal?
28. Are $(CD)E$ and $C(DE)$ equal?

In problems 29–34, use the matrices below. Perform the indicated operations.

$$A = \begin{bmatrix} 2 & 5 & 4 \\ 1 & 4 & 3 \\ 1 & -3 & -2 \end{bmatrix} \quad B = \begin{bmatrix} -1 & 2 & 1 \\ -5 & 8 & 2 \\ -7 & 11 & -3 \end{bmatrix} \quad I = \begin{bmatrix} 1 & 0 & 0 \\ 0 & 1 & 0 \\ 0 & 0 & 1 \end{bmatrix}$$

$$C = \begin{bmatrix} 3 & 0 & 4 \\ 1 & 7 & -1 \\ 3 & 0 & 4 \end{bmatrix} \quad D = \begin{bmatrix} 4 & 4 & -8 \\ -1 & -1 & 2 \\ -3 & -3 & 6 \end{bmatrix}$$

$$F = \begin{bmatrix} 0 & 1 & 2 \\ 0 & 0 & -4 \\ 0 & 0 & 0 \end{bmatrix} \quad Z = \begin{bmatrix} 0 & 0 & 0 \\ 0 & 0 & 0 \\ 0 & 0 & 0 \end{bmatrix}$$

29. AB
30. BA
31. CD
32. DC
33. F^3
34. AZ
35. AI
36. IA
37. ZCI
38. IFZ

39. Is it true for matrices (as it is for real numbers) that AB equals a zero matrix if and only if either A or B equals a zero matrix? Refer to problems $29-34$.

40. Is it true for matrices (as it is for real numbers) that multiplication by a zero matrix gives a result of a zero matrix?

41. Find AB and BA if

$$A = \begin{bmatrix} a & b \\ c & d \end{bmatrix} \quad \text{and} \quad B = \frac{1}{ad - bc} \begin{bmatrix} d & -b \\ -c & a \end{bmatrix}.$$

42. For B (in problem 41) to exist, what restriction must $ad - bc$ satisfy?

APPLICATIONS

A salesman's expense account for the first week of a certain month has the daily expenses (in dollars) shown in matrix A. Use this matrix for problems 43 and 44.

	Meals	Lodging	Travel	Other	
	22	40	100	5	Monday
	20	40	20	0	Tuesday
$A =$	28	70	45	0	Wednesday
	15	70	20	10	Thursday
	20	0	100	5	Friday

43. The salesman finds that his expenses for the second week are 5% more (in each category) than for the first week. Find his expenses matrix for the second week (note that this is $1.05A$).

44. Find the salesman's expenses matrix for the third week if his expenses for that week are 10% more (in each category) than they were in the first week.

45. Two departments of a firm, A and B, need differing amounts of the same products. The following table gives the amounts of the products needed by the departments.

	Steel	Plastic	Wood
Department A	30	20	10
Department B	20	10	20

These three products are supplied by two suppliers, Ace and Kink, with the unit prices given in the table.

	Ace	Kink
Steel	300	280
Plastic	150	100
Wood	150	200

(a) Use matrix multiplication to find how much these two orders will cost at the two suppliers. The result should be a 2 × 2 matrix.

(b) From which supplier should each department make its purchase?

46. A furniture manufacturer produces four styles of chairs, and has orders for 1000 of style A, 4000 of style B, 2000 of style C, and 1000 of style D. The table lists the number of units of raw material the manufacturer needs for each style.

	Wood	Nylon	Velvet	Spring
Style A	10	5	0	0
Style B	5	0	20	10
Style C	5	20	0	10
Style D	5	10	10	10

(a) Form a 1 × 4 matrix containing the number of units of each style ordered.

(b) Use matrix multiplication to determine the total number of units of each raw material needed.

47. Suppose, in problem 46, wood costs the manufacturer $5 per unit, nylon costs $3 per unit, velvet costs $4 per unit, and springs cost $4 per unit.

(a) Write a 4 × 1 matrix representing the costs for the raw materials.

(b) Use matrix multiplication to find the 1 × 1 matrix that represents the total investment to fill the orders.

48. Use matrix multiplication and the information given in problems 46 and 47 to determine the cost for materials for each style of chair.

49. In problem 40 of Exercise 2.1, we found the weights and measures of the laboratory animals to be given by matrix A, where column 1 gives the measures.

$$A = \begin{bmatrix} 12.5 & 250 \\ 11.8 & 215 \\ 9.8 & 190 \end{bmatrix}$$

If the increase in both weight and length over the next two weeks is 20% for group I, 7% for group II, and 0% for group III, then the increases in the measures of the groups during the two weeks can be found by computing GA, where

$$G = \begin{bmatrix} 0.20 & 0 & 0 \\ 0 & 0.07 & 0 \\ 0 & 0 & 0 \end{bmatrix}.$$

(a) What are the increases in respective weights and measures at the end of these two weeks?

(b) Find the matrix that gives the new weights and measures at the end of this period by computing

$$(I + G)A,$$

where I is the 3 × 3 identity matrix.

50. Matrix A below gives the fraction of the world's area and the fraction of its population for five continents. Matrix B gives the earth's area (in square miles) and its 1985 population. Find the area and population of each given continent by finding AB.

$$A = \begin{array}{c} \text{Fraction} \\ \text{of Area} \end{array}\begin{array}{c} \text{Fraction of} \\ \text{Population} \end{array}$$

$$A = \begin{bmatrix} .162 & .082 \\ .119 & .054 \\ .066 & .139 \\ .298 & .608 \\ .202 & .111 \end{bmatrix} \begin{array}{l} \text{North America} \\ \text{South America} \\ \text{Europe} \\ \text{Asia} \\ \text{Africa} \end{array} \qquad B = \begin{array}{c} \begin{array}{cc} \text{Area} & \text{Population} \end{array} \\ \begin{bmatrix} 57{,}850{,}000 & 0 \\ 0 & 4{,}843{,}000{,}000 \end{bmatrix} \end{array} \begin{array}{l} \text{Area} \\ \text{Population} \end{array}$$

(*Source*: Rand McNally and Co.; World Almanac, p. 544)

In an ecological model, matrix A gives the fraction of several types of plants consumed by the herbivores in the ecosystem. Similarly, matrix B gives the fraction of each type of herbivore that is consumed by the carnivores in the system. Each row of matrix A refers to a type of plant and each column refers to a kind of herbivore. Similarly, each row of matrix B is a kind of herbivore and each column is a kind of carnivore.

$$A = \overset{\text{Herbivores}}{\begin{bmatrix} 0.2 & 0.1 & 0.4 \\ 0.3 & 0.3 & 0.1 \\ 0.2 & 0.1 & 0.1 \\ 0.1 & 0.2 & 0.5 \\ 0.4 & 0.4 & 0 \end{bmatrix}} \text{Plants} \qquad B = \overset{\text{Carnivores}}{\begin{bmatrix} 0.1 & 0.1 & 0.2 \\ 0.2 & 0 & 0.4 \\ 0.1 & 0.5 & 0.1 \end{bmatrix}} \text{Herbivores}$$

The matrix AB gives the fraction of each plant that is consumed by each carnivore. Use these matrices in problems 51–53.

51. Find AB.
52. What fraction of plant type 1 (row 1) is consumed by each carnivore?
53. Identify the plant type that each carnivore consumes the most.

2.3 Gauss-Jordan Elimination: Solving Systems of Equations

Objective □ To use matrices to solve systems of linear equations

Systems with Unique Solutions

There are many occasions in business when the simultaneous solution of linear equations is important. We have already seen examples of this in Chapter 1 when we found market equilibrium and break-even points by the simultaneous solution of two linear equations in two variables.

Other application problems were solved by using the left-to-right elimination method with larger systems of linear equations. In solving systems with this method, we operated on the coefficients of the variables (x, y, and z in Example 5 of Section 1.6) and the constants. If we keep the coefficients of the variables x, y, and z in distinctive columns, we do not need to write the equations. This leads us to consider a solution method using **matrices.**

We write the coefficients and constants from the system (on the left) in the **augmented matrix** (on the right).

$$\begin{cases} a_1x + b_1y + c_1z = d_1 \\ a_2x + b_2y + c_2z = d_2 \end{cases} \qquad \left[\begin{array}{ccc|c} a_1 & b_1 & c_1 & d_1 \\ a_2 & b_2 & c_2 & d_2 \end{array}\right]$$

In the augmented matrix, the numbers on the left side of the solid line form the **coefficient matrix,** with each column containing the coefficients of a variable (0 represents any missing variable). The column on the right side of the line (called the *augment*) contains the constants. Each row of the matrix gives the corresponding coefficients of an equation.

The augmented matrix associated with the system

$$\begin{cases} x + 2y + 3z = 6 \\ x \quad\quad - z = 0 \\ x - y - z = -4 \end{cases} \quad \text{is} \quad A = \left[\begin{array}{ccc|c} 1 & 2 & 3 & 6 \\ 1 & 0 & -1 & 0 \\ 1 & -1 & -1 & -4 \end{array}\right].$$

We can use matrices to solve systems of linear equations by performing the same operations on the rows of a matrix to reduce it as we do on equations in a linear system. The three different operations we can use to reduce the matrix are called **elementary row operations** and are similar to the operations with equations that result in equivalent systems. These operations are:

1. Interchange two rows.

2. Add a multiple of one row to another row.

3. Multiply a row by any nonzero constant.

When a new matrix results from one or more of these elementary row operations being performed on a matrix, the new matrix is said to be **equivalent** to the original because both these matrices represent equivalent systems of equations.

The process that we use to solve a system of equations using matrices (called the **elimination method**) is not always the fastest way, but it is a systematic procedure similar to the left-to-right elimination method discussed in Section 1.6. This method uses these row operations to attempt to reduce the coefficient matrix to an identity matrix. Example 1 illustrates this process, called the **Gauss-Jordan Elimination Method.**

EXAMPLE 1   Use matrices to solve the system

$$\begin{cases} 2x + 5y + 4z = 4 \\ x + 4y + 3z = 1 \\ x - 3y - 2z = 5. \end{cases}$$

Solution   The augmented matrix for this system is

$$\begin{bmatrix} 2 & 5 & 4 & 4 \\ 1 & 4 & 3 & 1 \\ 1 & -3 & -2 & 5 \end{bmatrix}.$$

Note that this system has 3 equations in 3 variables, but the reduction procedure and row operations apply regardless of the size of the system.

The following display shows a series of step-by-step goals for reducing a 3×3 matrix and shows a series of row operations that reduces this matrix.

Goal (for each step)	Row operation	Equivalent matrix
1. Get a 1 in row 1, col. 1.	Interchange row 1 and row 2.	$\begin{bmatrix} 1 & 4 & 3 & 1 \\ 2 & 5 & 4 & 4 \\ 1 & -3 & -2 & 5 \end{bmatrix}$
2. Use row 1 *only* to get zeros in other entries of col. 1.	Add -2 times row 1 to row 2, and add -1 times row 1 to row 3.	$\begin{bmatrix} 1 & 4 & 3 & 1 \\ 0 & -3 & -2 & 2 \\ 0 & -7 & -5 & 4 \end{bmatrix}$
3. Use rows below row 1 to get a 1 in row 2, col. 2.	Multiply row 2 by $-\frac{1}{3}$.	$\begin{bmatrix} 1 & 4 & 3 & 1 \\ 0 & 1 & \frac{2}{3} & -\frac{2}{3} \\ 0 & -7 & -5 & 4 \end{bmatrix}$
4. Use row 2 *only* to get other entries in col. 2 zeros.	Add -4 times row 2 to row 1, and add 7 times row 2 to row 3.	$\begin{bmatrix} 1 & 0 & \frac{1}{3} & \frac{11}{3} \\ 0 & 1 & \frac{2}{3} & -\frac{2}{3} \\ 0 & 0 & -\frac{1}{3} & -\frac{2}{3} \end{bmatrix}$
5. Use row below row 2 to get a 1 in row 3, col. 3.	Multiply row 3 by -3.	$\begin{bmatrix} 1 & 0 & \frac{1}{3} & \frac{11}{3} \\ 0 & 1 & \frac{2}{3} & -\frac{2}{3} \\ 0 & 0 & 1 & 2 \end{bmatrix}$
6. Use row 3 *only* to get other entries in col. 3 zeros.	Add $-\frac{1}{3}$ times row 3 to row 1, and add $-\frac{2}{3}$ times row 3 to row 2.	$\begin{bmatrix} 1 & 0 & 0 & 3 \\ 0 & 1 & 0 & -2 \\ 0 & 0 & 1 & 2 \end{bmatrix}$

The system of equations corresponding to this final augmented matrix follows.

$$\begin{aligned} x + 0y + 0z &= 3 \\ 0x + y + 0z &= -2 \\ 0x + 0y + z &= 2 \end{aligned}$$

Thus the solution is $x = 3$, $y = -2$, and $z = 2$.

This Gauss-Jordan Elimination Method (outlined in Example 1) may be used with systems of any size.

EXAMPLE 2   Solve the system

$$\begin{cases} x_1 + x_2 + x_3 + 2x_4 = 6 \\ x_1 + 2x_2 + x_4 = -2 \\ x_1 + x_2 + 3x_3 - 2x_4 = 12 \\ x_1 + x_2 - 4x_3 + 5x_4 = -16. \end{cases}$$

Solution   First note that there is a variable missing in the second equation. When we form the augmented matrix, we must insert a zero in this place so that each column represents the coefficients of one variable.

To solve this system, we must reduce the augmented matrix.

$$\left[\begin{array}{cccc|c} 1 & 1 & 1 & 2 & 6 \\ 1 & 2 & 0 & 1 & -2 \\ 1 & 1 & 3 & -2 & 12 \\ 1 & 1 & -4 & 5 & -16 \end{array}\right]$$

The reduction process follows. The entry in row 1, column 1 is 1. To get zeros in the first column, add -1 times row 1 to each of the other rows.

$$\left[\begin{array}{cccc|c} 1 & 1 & 1 & 2 & 6 \\ 1 & 2 & 0 & 1 & -2 \\ 1 & 1 & 3 & -2 & 12 \\ 1 & 1 & -4 & 5 & -16 \end{array}\right] \begin{array}{l} \text{Add } (-1)R_1 \text{ to } R_2 \\ \text{Add } (-1)R_1 \text{ to } R_3 \\ \hline \\ \text{Add } (-1)R_1 \text{ to } R_4 \end{array} \left[\begin{array}{cccc|c} 1 & 1 & 1 & 2 & 6 \\ 0 & 1 & -1 & -1 & -8 \\ 0 & 0 & 2 & -4 & 6 \\ 0 & 0 & -5 & 3 & -22 \end{array}\right]$$

The entry in row 2, column 2 is 1. To get zeros in the second column, add -1 times row 2 to row 1.

$$\begin{array}{c} \\ \text{Add } (-1)R_2 \text{ to } R_1 \\ \hline \\ \end{array} \left[\begin{array}{cccc|c} 1 & 0 & 2 & 3 & 14 \\ 0 & 1 & -1 & -1 & -8 \\ 0 & 0 & 2 & -4 & 6 \\ 0 & 0 & -5 & 3 & -22 \end{array}\right]$$

The entry in row 3, column 3 is 2. To get a 1 in this position, multiply row 3 by $\frac{1}{2}$.

$$\begin{array}{c} \\ \frac{1}{2}R_3 \\ \hline \\ \end{array} \left[\begin{array}{cccc|c} 1 & 0 & 2 & 3 & 14 \\ 0 & 1 & -1 & -1 & -8 \\ 0 & 0 & 1 & -2 & 3 \\ 0 & 0 & -5 & 3 & -22 \end{array}\right]$$

Using row 3, add -2 times row 3 to row 1; add row 3 to row 2; and add 5 times row 3 to row 4.

$$\begin{array}{c} \text{Add } (-2)R_3 \text{ to } R_1 \\ \text{Add } R_3 \text{ to } R_2 \\ \hline \\ \text{Add } 5R_3 \text{ to } R_4 \end{array} \left[\begin{array}{cccc|c} 1 & 0 & 0 & 7 & 8 \\ 0 & 1 & 0 & -3 & -5 \\ 0 & 0 & 1 & -2 & 3 \\ 0 & 0 & 0 & -7 & -7 \end{array}\right]$$

Multiplying $-\frac{1}{7}$ times row 4 gives a 1 in row 4, column 4.

$$\xrightarrow{-\frac{1}{7}R_4} \left[\begin{array}{cccc|c} 1 & 0 & 0 & 7 & 8 \\ 0 & 1 & 0 & -3 & -5 \\ 0 & 0 & 1 & -2 & 3 \\ 0 & 0 & 0 & 1 & 1 \end{array}\right]$$

Adding appropriate multiples of row 4 to the other rows gives the following:

$$\begin{array}{c} \text{Add } (-7)R_4 \text{ to } R_1 \\ \text{Add } 3R_4 \text{ to } R_2 \\ \xrightarrow{\hspace{2cm}} \\ \text{Add } 2R_4 \text{ to } R_3 \end{array} \left[\begin{array}{cccc|c} 1 & 0 & 0 & 0 & 1 \\ 0 & 1 & 0 & 0 & -2 \\ 0 & 0 & 1 & 0 & 5 \\ 0 & 0 & 0 & 1 & 1 \end{array}\right].$$

This corresponds to the system

$$\begin{array}{rcr} x_1 & = & 1 \\ x_2 & = & -2 \\ x_3 & = & 5 \\ x_4 & = & 1. \end{array}$$

So the solutions are $x_1 = 1$, $x_2 = -2$, $x_3 = 5$, and $x_4 = 1$.

EXAMPLE 3   The Walters Manufacturing Company makes three types of metal storage sheds. The company has three departments: stamping, painting, and packaging. The following table gives the number of hours each division requires for each shed.

		Shed	
Departments	Type I	Type II	Type III
Stamping	2	3	4
Painting	1	2	1
Packaging	1	1	2

Using the information in the table, determine how many of each type of shed can be produced if the stamping department has 3200 hours available, the painting department has 1700 hours, and the packaging department has 1300 hours.

Solution   If we let x_1 be the number of type I sheds, x_2 be the number of type II sheds, and x_3 be the number of type III sheds, the equation

$$2x_1 + 3x_2 + 4x_3 = 3200$$

represents the hours used by the stamping department. Similarly,

$$1x_1 + 2x_2 + 1x_3 = 1700$$

and

$$1x_1 + 1x_2 + 2x_3 = 1300$$

represent the hours used by the painting and packaging departments, respectively. The augmented matrix for this system of equations is

$$\begin{bmatrix} 2 & 3 & 4 & | & 3200 \\ 1 & 2 & 1 & | & 1700 \\ 1 & 1 & 2 & | & 1300 \end{bmatrix}.$$

Reducing this augmented matrix proceeds as follows.

$$\begin{bmatrix} 2 & 3 & 4 & | & 3200 \\ 1 & 2 & 1 & | & 1700 \\ 1 & 1 & 2 & | & 1300 \end{bmatrix} \xrightarrow{\text{Switch } R_1 \text{ and } R_3} \begin{bmatrix} 1 & 1 & 2 & | & 1300 \\ 1 & 2 & 1 & | & 1700 \\ 2 & 3 & 4 & | & 3200 \end{bmatrix}$$

$$\xrightarrow[\text{Add } (-2)R_1 \text{ to } R_3]{\text{Add } (-1)R_1 \text{ to } R_2} \begin{bmatrix} 1 & 1 & 2 & | & 1300 \\ 0 & 1 & -1 & | & 400 \\ 0 & 1 & 0 & | & 600 \end{bmatrix}$$

$$\xrightarrow[\text{Add } (-1)R_2 \text{ to } R_3]{\text{Add } (-1)R_2 \text{ to } R_1} \begin{bmatrix} 1 & 0 & 3 & | & 900 \\ 0 & 1 & -1 & | & 400 \\ 0 & 0 & 1 & | & 200 \end{bmatrix}$$

$$\xrightarrow[\text{Add } R_3 \text{ to } R_2]{\text{Add } (-3)R_3 \text{ to } R_1} \begin{bmatrix} 1 & 0 & 0 & | & 300 \\ 0 & 1 & 0 & | & 600 \\ 0 & 0 & 1 & | & 200 \end{bmatrix}$$

Thus the solution to the system is

$$x_1 = 300$$
$$x_2 = 600$$
$$x_3 = 200.$$

Thus the company should make 300 type I, 600 type II, and 200 type III sheds.

Systems with Nonunique Solutions

While all the systems considered so far had unique solutions, it is also possible for a system of linear equations to have an infinite number of solutions or no solution at all. Although coefficient matrices for systems with an infinite number of solutions or no solution will not reduce to identity matrices, row operations can be used to obtain a reduced form from which the solutions, if they exist, can be determined.

A matrix is said to be in **reduced form** when it is in the following form:

1. The first nonzero element in each row is 1.

2. Every column containing a first nonzero element for some row has zeros everywhere else.

3. The first nonzero element of each row is to the right of the first nonzero element of every row above it.

4. All rows containing zeros are grouped together below the rows containing non-zero entries.

The following matrices are in reduced form because they satisfy these conditions:

$$\left[\begin{array}{cc|c} 1 & 0 & 4 \\ 0 & 1 & 2 \\ 0 & 0 & 0 \end{array}\right] \qquad \left[\begin{array}{ccc|c} 1 & 0 & 0 & 0 \\ 0 & 1 & 0 & 3 \\ 0 & 0 & 1 & 0 \\ 0 & 0 & 0 & 1 \end{array}\right] \qquad \left[\begin{array}{ccc|c} 1 & 4 & 0 & 1 \\ 0 & 0 & 1 & 2 \\ 0 & 0 & 0 & 0 \end{array}\right].$$

The following matrices are *not* in reduced form:

$$\left[\begin{array}{cc|c} 1 & ① & 0 \\ 0 & 1 & 3 \\ 0 & 0 & 0 \end{array}\right] \qquad \left[\begin{array}{cc|c} 1 & 0 & 1 \\ 0 & ② & 1 \\ 0 & 0 & 0 \end{array}\right] \qquad \left[\begin{array}{cc|c} 0 & 1 & 0 \\ 1 & 0 & 0 \\ 0 & 0 & 1 \end{array}\right].$$

In the first two matrices the circled element must be changed to obtain a reduced form. Can you see what row operations would transform each of these matrices into reduced form? The third matrix does not satisfy point 3 above.

We can solve a system of linear equations by using row operations on the augmented matrix until the coefficient matrix is transformed to an equivalent matrix in reduced form.

EXAMPLE 4   Solve the system

$$\begin{cases} x_1 + x_2 - x_3 + x_4 = 3 \\ x_2 + x_3 + x_4 = 1 \\ x_1 \quad\quad - 2x_3 + x_4 = 6 \\ 2x_1 - x_2 - 5x_3 - 3x_4 = -5. \end{cases}$$

Solution   To solve this system we must reduce the augmented matrix

$$\left[\begin{array}{cccc|c} 1 & 1 & -1 & 1 & 3 \\ 0 & 1 & 1 & 1 & 1 \\ 1 & 0 & -2 & 1 & 6 \\ 2 & -1 & -5 & -3 & -5 \end{array}\right].$$

Attempting to reduce the coefficient matrix to an identity matrix requires the following.

$$\left[\begin{array}{cccc|c} 1 & 1 & -1 & 1 & 3 \\ 0 & 1 & 1 & 1 & 1 \\ 1 & 0 & -2 & 1 & 6 \\ 2 & -1 & -5 & -3 & -5 \end{array}\right] \xrightarrow[\text{Add } (-2)R_1 \text{ to } R_4]{\text{Add } (-1)R_1 \text{ to } R_3} \left[\begin{array}{cccc|c} 1 & 1 & -1 & 1 & 3 \\ 0 & 1 & 1 & 1 & 1 \\ 0 & -1 & -1 & 0 & 3 \\ 0 & -3 & -3 & -5 & -11 \end{array}\right]$$

$$\xrightarrow[\substack{\text{Add } (-1)R_2 \text{ to } R_1 \\ \text{Add } R_2 \text{ to } R_3 \\ \text{Add } 3R_2 \text{ to } R_4}]{} \left[\begin{array}{cccc|c} 1 & 0 & -2 & 0 & 2 \\ 0 & 1 & 1 & 1 & 1 \\ 0 & 0 & 0 & 1 & 4 \\ 0 & 0 & 0 & -2 & -8 \end{array}\right]$$

The entry in row 3, column 3 cannot be made 1 using rows *below* row 2. Moving to column 4; the entry in row 3, column 4 is a 1. Using row 3 gives the following.

$$\begin{array}{c} \text{Add } (-1)R_3 \text{ to } R_2 \\ \xrightarrow{\hspace{2cm}} \\ \text{Add } 2R_3 \text{ to } R_4 \end{array} \quad \left[\begin{array}{cccc|c} 1 & 0 & -2 & 0 & 2 \\ 0 & 1 & 1 & 0 & -3 \\ 0 & 0 & 0 & 1 & 4 \\ 0 & 0 & 0 & 0 & 0 \end{array}\right]$$

The augmented matrix is now reduced; this matrix corresponds to the system

$$\begin{cases} x_1 - 2x_3 = 2 \\ x_2 + x_3 = -3 \\ x_4 = 4 \\ 0 = 0. \end{cases}$$

If we solve each of these equations for the leading variable (the variable corresponding to the first 1 in each row of the reduced form of the matrix), we obtain

$$\begin{aligned} x_1 &= 2 + 2x_3 \\ x_2 &= -3 - x_3 \\ x_4 &= 4. \end{aligned}$$

In this form we have the values of x_1 and x_2 dependent on the value of x_3, so we can get many different solutions to the system by specifying different values for x_3. For example, if $x_3 = 1$, then $x_1 = 4$, $x_2 = -4$, $x_3 = 1$, and $x_4 = 4$ is a solution to the system; if we let $x_3 = -2$, then $x_1 = -2$, $x_2 = -1$, $x_3 = -2$, and $x_4 = 4$ is a solution. The **general solution** to the system is given by

$$\begin{aligned} x_1 &= 2 + 2x_3 \\ x_2 &= -3 - x_3 \\ x_3 &= x_3 \\ x_4 &= 4, \end{aligned}$$

where x_3 is arbitrary (any real number).

We have seen two different possibilities for solutions to systems of linear equations. In Examples 1–3, there was only one solution, whereas in Example 4 we saw that there were many solutions. A third possibility exists, namely that the system will have no solution. Recall that these three possibilities also existed for two equations in two unknowns, as discussed in Chapter 1.

EXAMPLE 5   Solve the system

$$\begin{cases} x + 2y - z = 3 \\ 3x + y = 4 \\ 2x - y + z = 2. \end{cases}$$

Solution   The augmented matrix is

$$\left[\begin{array}{ccc|c} 1 & 2 & -1 & 3 \\ 3 & 1 & 0 & 4 \\ 2 & -1 & 1 & 2 \end{array}\right].$$

This can be reduced as follows.

$$\begin{bmatrix} 1 & 2 & -1 & 3 \\ 3 & 1 & 0 & 4 \\ 2 & -1 & 1 & 2 \end{bmatrix} \xrightarrow[\text{Add } (-2)R_1 \text{ to } R_3]{\text{Add } (-3)R_1 \text{ to } R_2} \begin{bmatrix} 1 & 2 & -1 & 3 \\ 0 & -5 & 3 & -5 \\ 0 & -5 & 3 & -4 \end{bmatrix}$$

$$\xrightarrow{\left(-\frac{1}{5}\right)R_2} \begin{bmatrix} 1 & 2 & -1 & 3 \\ 0 & 1 & -\frac{3}{5} & 1 \\ 0 & -5 & 3 & -4 \end{bmatrix}$$

$$\xrightarrow[\text{Add } (5)R_2 \text{ to } R_3]{\text{Add } (-2)R_2 \text{ to } R_1} \begin{bmatrix} 1 & 0 & \frac{1}{5} & 1 \\ 0 & 1 & -\frac{3}{5} & 1 \\ 0 & 0 & 0 & 1 \end{bmatrix}.$$

The system of equations corresponding to the reduced matrix is

$$\begin{cases} x + \frac{1}{5}z = 1 \\ y - \frac{3}{5}z = 1 \\ 0 = 1. \end{cases}$$

Thus we see that this system has $0 = 1$ as an equation. This is clearly an impossibility, so there is no solution.

Now that we have seen examples of each of the different solution possibilities, let us consider what we have learned. In all cases the solution procedure began by setting up and then reducing the augmented matrix. Once the matrix is reduced, we can write the corresponding reduced system of equations. The solutions, if they exist, are easily found from this reduced system.

Exercise 2.3

In problems 1–4, write the augmented matrix associated with each system of linear equations.

1. $\begin{cases} 3x + 2y + 4z = 0 \\ 2x - y + 2z = 0 \\ x - 2y - 4z = 0 \end{cases}$

2. $\begin{cases} x - 3y + 4z = 0 \\ 2x + 2y + z = 1 \\ 3x - 4y + 2z = 9 \end{cases}$

3. $\begin{cases} x - 3y + 4z = 2 \\ 2x + 2z = 1 \\ x + 2y + z = 1 \end{cases}$

4. $\begin{cases} x + 2y + 2z = 3 \\ x - 2y = 4 \\ y - z = 1 \end{cases}$

The system of equations in problems 5–18 have unique solutions. Use matrices to solve each system.

5. $\begin{cases} 3x - 2y = 0 \\ x + y = 5 \end{cases}$

6. $\begin{cases} 2x + 5y = 1 \\ 3x - 4y = 10 \end{cases}$

7. $\begin{cases} 7x - 2y = -1 \\ 3x + 6y = 11 \end{cases}$

8. $\begin{cases} 6x + 7y = 55 \\ 5x - 37y = 3 \end{cases}$

9. $\begin{cases} x + y - z = 0 \\ x + 2y + 3z = -5 \\ 2x - y - 13z = 17 \end{cases}$

10. $\begin{cases} x + 2y - z = 3 \\ 2x + 5y - 2z = 7 \\ -x + y + 5z = -12 \end{cases}$

11. $\begin{cases} 2x - 6y - 12z = 6 \\ 3x - 10y - 20z = 5 \\ 2x \qquad - 17z = -4 \end{cases}$

12. $\begin{cases} -3x + 6y - 9z = 3 \\ x - y - 2z = 0 \\ 5x + 5y - 7z = 63 \end{cases}$

13. $\begin{cases} x - 3y + 3z = 7 \\ x + 2y - z = -2 \\ 3x + 2y + 4z = 5 \end{cases}$

14. $\begin{cases} 3x + 2y + z = 0 \\ x + y + 2z = 1 \\ 2x + y - z = -1 \end{cases}$

15. $\begin{cases} x_1 + 3x_2 + 2x_3 + 2x_4 = 3 \\ x_1 + x_2 + 3x_3 \qquad = 4 \\ 2x_1 \qquad + 2x_3 - 3x_4 = 4 \\ x_1 - 3x_2 \qquad = 1 \end{cases}$

16. $\begin{cases} x_1 + x_2 + x_3 + 2x_4 = 1 \\ x_1 \qquad - 3x_3 \qquad = 2 \\ x_1 - 3x_2 \qquad + x_4 = -2 \\ x_2 - 4x_3 + x_4 = 0 \end{cases}$

17. $\begin{cases} x - 2y + 3z + w = -2 \\ x - 3y + z - w = -7 \\ x - y \qquad = -2 \\ x \qquad + z + w = 2 \end{cases}$

18. $\begin{cases} x + 4y - 6z - 3w = 3 \\ x - y \qquad + 2w = -5 \\ x \qquad + z + w = 1 \\ y + z + w = 0 \end{cases}$

19. Solve $\begin{cases} a_1x + b_1y = c_1 \\ a_2x + b_2y = c_2 \end{cases}$ for x.

20. Solve the system in problem 19 for y.

The systems of equations in problems 21–40 may have unique solutions, an infinite number of solutions, or no solution. Use matrices to find the general solution to each system, if a solution exists.

21. $\begin{cases} x + y + z = 0 \\ 2x - y - z = 0 \\ -x + 2y + 2z = 0 \end{cases}$

22. $\begin{cases} 2x - y + 3z = 0 \\ x + 2y + 2z = 0 \\ x - 3y + z = 0 \end{cases}$

23. $\begin{cases} 2x - 4y + 2z = 2 \\ x - 2y + z = 1 \\ x - 5y + 3z = 0 \end{cases}$

24. $\begin{cases} x + 3y + 2z = 2 \\ 2x - y - 2z = 1 \\ 3x + 2y = 3 \end{cases}$

25. $\begin{cases} 2x + 2y + z = 2 \\ x - 2y + 2z = 1 \\ -x + 2y - 2z = -1 \end{cases}$

26. $\begin{cases} x + 2y + 3z = 1 \\ 2x - y = 3 \\ x + 2y + 3z = 2 \end{cases}$

27. $\begin{cases} 2x + 3y + 4z = 2 \\ x + 2y + 2z = 1 \\ x + y + 2z = 2 \end{cases}$

28. $\begin{cases} 2x + y - z = 0 \\ x - y - z = 0 \\ 3x + 2y - 2z = 0 \end{cases}$

29. $\begin{cases} x - y + z = 0 \\ x + 2y + z = 0 \\ x - 4y + 2z = 0 \end{cases}$

30. $\begin{cases} 2x + y - z = 2 \\ x - y + 2z = 3 \\ x + y - z = 1 \end{cases}$

31. $\begin{cases} 2x - 5y + z = -9 \\ x + 4y - 6z = 2 \\ 3x - 4y - 2z = -10 \end{cases}$

32. $\begin{cases} 2x - y + z = 2 \\ 3x + y - 6z = -7 \\ x - y + 2z = 3 \end{cases}$

33. $\begin{cases} x + y + z = 3 \\ x - y + z = 4 \\ x + y - z = 5 \end{cases}$

34. $\begin{cases} 3x + 2y + z = 3 \\ x - y - z = 2 \\ 2x + y - 2z = 1 \end{cases}$

35. $\begin{cases} -0.6x_1 + 0.1x_2 + 0.3x_3 = 0 \\ 0.4x_1 - 0.7x_2 + 0.2x_3 = 0 \\ 0.2x_1 + 0.6x_2 - 0.5x_3 = 0 \end{cases}$

36. $\begin{cases} 0.1x_1 - 0.1x_2 - 0.3x_3 = 0 \\ 0.2x_1 + 0.3x_2 + 0.1x_3 = -0.3 \\ 0.3x_1 + 0.7x_2 + 0.5x_3 = -0.6 \end{cases}$

37. $\begin{cases} x_1 + 2x_2 - x_3 + x_4 = 3 \\ x_1 + 3x_2 + 4x_3 + x_4 = -2 \\ 2x_1 + 5x_2 + 2x_3 + 2x_4 = 1 \\ 2x_1 + 3x_2 - 6x_3 + 2x_4 = 3 \end{cases}$

38. $\begin{cases} x_1 + 2x_2 + 3x_3 + 4x_4 = 2 \\ x_1 + 2x_2 + 4x_3 + 3x_4 = 2 \\ 2x_1 + 4x_2 + 6x_3 + 8x_4 = 4 \\ x_1 + 4x_2 + 3x_3 = 4 \end{cases}$

39. $\begin{cases} x_1 + 3x_2 + 4x_3 - x_4 = 1 \\ x_1 - x_2 - 2x_3 + x_4 = 2 \\ x_1 - 2x_2 + 3x_3 + x_4 = 0 \\ 2x_1 + 2x_2 + 2x_3 = 3 \end{cases}$

40. $\begin{cases} 2x_1 - x_2 + x_3 = 6 \\ x_1 + x_2 + x_3 + 2x_4 = 0 \\ 2x_1 + x_2 - x_3 + x_4 = -3 \\ x_1 + 2x_2 - 2x_3 + x_4 = -9 \end{cases}$

APPLICATIONS

Application problems 41–51 involve systems with unique solutions.

41. A bank loaned $118,500 to a company for the development of two products. If the loan for product A was for $34,500 more than that for product B, how much was loaned for each product?

42. A man has $23,500 invested in two rental properties. One earns 15% on the investment and the other yields 16%. His total income from the two properties is $3,625. How much is his income from each property?

43. The King Trucking Company has an order for three products to be delivered to a destination. The table below gives the particulars for the products.

	Type I	Type II	Type III
Unit volume (cu ft)	10	8	20 -6000
Unit weight (lb)	10	20	40 =11000
Unit value ($)	100	20	200 36900

If the carrier can carry 6,000 cu ft, 11,000 lbs, and is insured for $36,900, how many units of each type can be carried?

44. Mr. Jackson borrowed money from his bank and on his life insurance to start a business. His interest rate on the bank loan is 15% and his rate on the insurance loan is 16%. If the total amount borrowed is $10,000 and his total yearly interest payment is $1,545, how much did he borrow from the bank?

45. A psychologist studying the effects of nutrition on the behavior of laboratory rats is feeding one group a combination of three foods, I, II, and III. Each of these foods contains three additives, A, B, and C, that are being used in the study. Each additive is a certain percentage of each of the foods as follows.

	Foods		
	I	II	III
Additive A	10%	30%	60%
Additive B	0	4	5
Additive C	2	2	12

If the diet requires 53 g per day of A, 4.5 g per day of B, and 8.6 g per day of C, find the number of grams per day of each food that must be used.

46. A young couple with a $120,000 inheritance wants to invest all this money. They plan to diversify their investments, choosing some of each of the following.

Type	Cost/share	Expected total yield/share
Growth stocks	$ 30	$ 4.60
Blue-chip stocks	100	11.00
Utility stocks	50	5.00

Their strategy is to have the total investment in growth stocks equal to the sum of the other investments, and their goal is a 13% return on their investment. How many shares of each type of stock should they purchase?

47. An airline company has three types of aircraft that carry three types of cargo. The payload of each type is summarized in the table below.

	Plane type		
Units carried	Passenger	Transport	Jumbo
First class mail	100	100	100
Passengers	150	20	350
Air freight	20	65	35

Suppose that on a given day the airline must move 1100 units of first class mail, 460 units of air freight, and 1930 passengers. How many aircraft of each type should be scheduled?

48. A brokerage house offers 3 stock portfolios. Portfolio I consists of 2 blocks of common stock and 1 municipal bond. Portfolio II consists of 4 blocks of common stock, 2 municipal bonds, and 3 blocks of preferred stock. Portfolio III consists of 7 blocks of common stock, 3 municipal bonds, and 3 blocks of preferred stock. A customer wants 21 blocks of common stock, 10 municipal bonds, and 9 blocks of preferred stock. How many of each portfolio should be offered?

49. Suppose that portfolios I and II in problem 48, are unchanged and portfolio III consists of 2 blocks of common stock, 2 municipal bonds, and 3 blocks of preferred stock. A customer wants 12 blocks of common stock, 6 municipal bonds, and 6 preferred stock. How many of each portfolio should be offered?

50. Each ounce of substance A supplies 5% of the required nutrition a patient needs. Substance B supplies 15% of the required nutrition per ounce and substance C supplies 12% of required nutrition per ounce. If digestive restrictions require that substances A and C be given in equal amounts and that the amount of substance B be one-fifth of these other amounts, find the number of ounces of each substance that should be in the meal to provide 100% nutrition.

51. A glass of skim milk supplies 0.1 mg of iron, 8.5 g of protein, and 1 g of carbohydrates. A quarter pound of lean red meat provides 3.4 mg of iron, 22 g of protein, and 20 g of carbohydrates. Two slices of whole-grain bread supply 2.2 mg of iron, 10 g of protein, and 12 g of carbohydrates. If a person on a special diet must have 12.1 mg of iron, 97 g of protein, and 70 g of carbohydrates, how many glasses of skim milk, how many quarter-pound servings of meat, and how many two-slice servings of whole-grain bread will supply this?

Application problems 52–57 involve systems with nonunique solutions.

52. A botanist can purchase plant food of 4 different types, I, II, III, and IV. Each food comes in the same size bag and the following table summarizes the number of grams of each of three nutrients that each bag contains.

	Foods			
	I	*II*	*III*	*IV*
Nutrient A	5	5	10	5
Nutrient B	10	5	10	10
Nutrient C	5	15	10	25

The botanist wants to use a food that has these nutrients in a different proportion and determines that he will need a total of 400 g of A, 1200 g of B, and 1000 g of C. Find the number of bags of each type of food that should be ordered.

53. In the analysis of traffic flow, a certain city estimates the following situation for an area of its downtown district. Figure 2.2 indicates the traffic flow, with the arrows indicating the flow of traffic. If x_1 represents the number of cars traveling between intersections A and B, x_2 represents the number of cars traveling between B and C, x_3 the number between C and D, and x_4 the number between D and A, we can formulate equations based on the principle that the number of vehicles entering an intersection equals the number leaving it. That is, for intersection A we obtain

$$200 + x_4 = 100 + x_1.$$

(a) Formulate equations for the traffic at B, C, and D.
(b) Solve the system of these four equations.

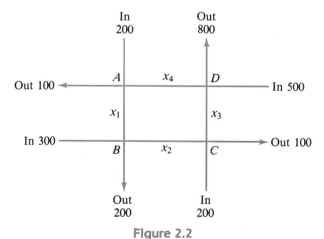

Figure 2.2

54. An investment club has set a goal of earning 15% of the money they invest in stocks. They are considering purchasing four possible stocks, with their cost per share (in dollars) and their earnings per share (in dollars) summarized in the following table.

	Oil	Bank	Computer	Retail
Cost/share	100	40	30	20
Total yield/share	10.00	3.60	6.00	2.40

If they have $102,300 to invest, how many shares of each stock should they buy to meet their goal?

55. Three different bacteria are cultured in one dish and feed on three nutrients. Each individual of species I consumes one unit of each of the first and second nutrients and two units of the third nutrient. Each individual of species II consumes two units of the first nutrient and two units of the third nutrient. Species III consumes two units of the first nutrient, three units of the second nutrient, and five units of the third nutrient. If the culture is given 5100 units of the first nutrient, 6900 units of the second nutrient, and 12,000 units of the third nutrient, how many of each species can be supported so all of the nutrients are consumed?

56. An irrigation system allows water to flow in the pattern shown in Figure 2.3. Water flows into the system at A and exits at B, C, D, and E with the amounts shown. Using the fact that at each point the water entering equals the water leaving, formulate an equation for water flow at each of the five points and solve the system.

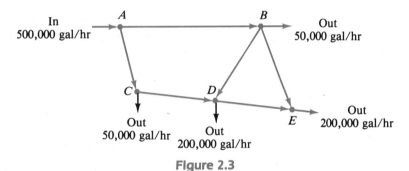

Figure 2.3

57. A brokerage house offers 3 stock portfolios. Portfolio I consists of 2 blocks of common stock and 1 municipal bond. Portfolio II consists of 4 blocks of common stock, 2 municipal bonds, and 3 blocks of preferred stock. Portfolio III consists of 2 blocks of common stock, 1 municipal bond, and 3 blocks of preferred stock. A customer wants 16 blocks of common stock, 8 municipal bonds, and 6 blocks of preferred stock. If the numbers of each portfolio offered must be integers, find all possible offerings.

2.4   Inverse of a Square Matrix

Objectives   ☐   To find the inverse of a square matrix
              ☐   To use inverse matrices to solve systems of linear equations

An algebraic equation of the form $ax = b$ $(a \neq 0)$ is solved for x by dividing both sides of the equation by a. But dividing by a is really the same as multiplying by the multiplicative inverse of the number a.

In a similar fashion, some matrix equations of the form $AX = C$ can be solved by multiplying both sides by the matrix B satisfying $BA = I$, where I is an identity matrix. This gives

$$(BA)X = BC \qquad \text{or} \qquad IX = BC,$$

so the solution is $X = BC$.

The matrix B is called the **inverse matrix** of A, denoted A^{-1}.

Inverse Matrices   Two square matrices, A and B, are called **inverses** of each other if

$$AB = I \qquad \text{and} \qquad BA = I.$$

EXAMPLE 1   Is B the inverse of A if $A = \begin{bmatrix} 1 & 2 \\ 1 & 1 \end{bmatrix}$ and $B = \begin{bmatrix} -1 & 2 \\ 1 & -1 \end{bmatrix}$?

Solution

$$AB = \begin{bmatrix} 1 & 2 \\ 1 & 1 \end{bmatrix} \cdot \begin{bmatrix} -1 & 2 \\ 1 & -1 \end{bmatrix} = \begin{bmatrix} 1 & 0 \\ 0 & 1 \end{bmatrix} = I$$

$$BA = \begin{bmatrix} -1 & 2 \\ 1 & -1 \end{bmatrix} \cdot \begin{bmatrix} 1 & 2 \\ 1 & 1 \end{bmatrix} = \begin{bmatrix} 1 & 0 \\ 0 & 1 \end{bmatrix} = I$$

Thus, B is the inverse of A, or $B = A^{-1}$. We also say A is the inverse of B, or $(A^{-1})^{-1} = A$.

We have seen how to use elementary row operations on augmented matrices to solve systems of linear equations. We can also find the inverse of a matrix using elementary row operations.

If the inverse exists for a square matrix A, we find A^{-1} as follows.

Procedure	Example
To find the inverse of the square matrix A:	Find the inverse of matrix $A = \begin{bmatrix} 1 & 2 \\ 1 & 1 \end{bmatrix}$.
1. Form the augmented matrix $[A\|I]$ where A is the $n \times n$ matrix and I is the $n \times n$ identity matrix.	1. $\begin{bmatrix} 1 & 2 & \vert & 1 & 0 \\ 1 & 1 & \vert & 0 & 1 \end{bmatrix}$
2. Perform elementary operations on $[A\|I]$ until we have an augmented matrix of the form $[I\|B]$; that is, until the matrix A on the left is transformed into the identity matrix.	2. $\begin{bmatrix} 1 & 2 & \vert & 1 & 0 \\ 1 & 1 & \vert & 0 & 1 \end{bmatrix} \rightarrow \begin{bmatrix} 1 & 2 & \vert & 1 & 0 \\ 0 & -1 & \vert & -1 & 1 \end{bmatrix}$ $\rightarrow \begin{bmatrix} 1 & 0 & \vert & -1 & 2 \\ 0 & 1 & \vert & 1 & -1 \end{bmatrix}$

3. The matrix B (on the right) is the inverse of matrix A.

3. The inverse of A is $B = \begin{bmatrix} -1 & 2 \\ 1 & -1 \end{bmatrix}$.

We have verified this in Example 1.

Note that if A has no inverse, the reduction process on $[A|I]$ will yield a row of zeros in the left half.

In Example 1 of Section 2.3, we solved the system

$$\begin{cases} 2x + 5y + 4z = 4 \\ x + 4y + 3z = 1 \\ x - 3y - 2z = 5. \end{cases}$$

This system can be written as the following matrix equation.

$$\begin{bmatrix} 2x + 5y + 4z \\ x + 4y + 3z \\ x - 3y - 2z \end{bmatrix} = \begin{bmatrix} 4 \\ 1 \\ 5 \end{bmatrix}$$

This matrix equation is often written as follows.

$$\begin{bmatrix} 2 & 5 & 4 \\ 1 & 4 & 3 \\ 1 & -3 & -2 \end{bmatrix} \begin{bmatrix} x \\ y \\ z \end{bmatrix} = \begin{bmatrix} 4 \\ 1 \\ 5 \end{bmatrix}$$

We can see that this second form of a matrix equation is equivalent to the first if we carry out the multiplication. With the system written in this second form, we could also solve the system by multiplying both sides of the equation by the inverse of

$$\begin{bmatrix} 2 & 5 & 4 \\ 1 & 4 & 3 \\ 1 & -3 & -2 \end{bmatrix}.$$

EXAMPLE 2   (a) Find the inverse of

$$\begin{bmatrix} 2 & 5 & 4 \\ 1 & 4 & 3 \\ 1 & -3 & -2 \end{bmatrix}.$$

(b) Solve the system

$$\begin{cases} 2x + 5y + 4z = 4 \\ x + 4y + 3z = 1 \\ x - 3y - 2z = 5 \end{cases}$$

by using inverse matrices.

Solution   (a) To find the inverse of the given matrix we reduce

$$\left[\begin{array}{ccc|ccc} 2 & 5 & 4 & 1 & 0 & 0 \\ 1 & 4 & 3 & 0 & 1 & 0 \\ 1 & -3 & -2 & 0 & 0 & 1 \end{array}\right]$$

until the left side is an identity matrix.

$$\xrightarrow{\text{Switch } R_1 \text{ and } R_2} \left[\begin{array}{rrr|rrr} 1 & 4 & 3 & 0 & 1 & 0 \\ 2 & 5 & 4 & 1 & 0 & 0 \\ 1 & -3 & -2 & 0 & 0 & 1 \end{array}\right]$$

$$\begin{array}{c} \text{Add } -2R_1 \text{ to } R_2 \\ \xrightarrow{\hspace{2cm}} \\ \text{Add } -R_1 \text{ to } R_3 \end{array} \left[\begin{array}{rrr|rrr} 1 & 4 & 3 & 0 & 1 & 0 \\ 0 & -3 & -2 & 1 & -2 & 0 \\ 0 & -7 & -5 & 0 & -1 & 1 \end{array}\right]$$

$$\xrightarrow{-\frac{1}{3}R_2} \left[\begin{array}{rrr|rrr} 1 & 4 & 3 & 0 & 1 & 0 \\ 0 & 1 & \frac{2}{3} & -\frac{1}{3} & \frac{2}{3} & 0 \\ 0 & -7 & -5 & 0 & -1 & 1 \end{array}\right]$$

$$\begin{array}{c} \text{Add } -4R_2 \text{ to } R_1 \\ \xrightarrow{\hspace{2cm}} \\ \text{Add } 7R_2 \text{ to } R_3 \end{array} \left[\begin{array}{rrr|rrr} 1 & 0 & \frac{1}{3} & \frac{4}{3} & -\frac{5}{3} & 0 \\ 0 & 1 & \frac{2}{3} & -\frac{1}{3} & \frac{2}{3} & 0 \\ 0 & 0 & -\frac{1}{3} & -\frac{7}{3} & \frac{11}{3} & 1 \end{array}\right]$$

$$\begin{array}{c} \text{Add } R_3 \text{ to } R_1 \\ \text{Add } 2R_3 \text{ to } R_2 \\ \xrightarrow{\hspace{2cm}} \\ -3R_3 \end{array} \left[\begin{array}{rrr|rrr} 1 & 0 & 0 & -1 & 2 & 1 \\ 0 & 1 & 0 & -5 & 8 & 2 \\ 0 & 0 & 1 & 7 & -11 & -3 \end{array}\right]$$

The inverse we seek is

$$\left[\begin{array}{rrr} -1 & 2 & 1 \\ -5 & 8 & 2 \\ 7 & -11 & -3 \end{array}\right].$$

(b) To solve the system we multiply both sides of the associated matrix equation by the inverse.

$$\left[\begin{array}{rrr} -1 & 2 & 1 \\ -5 & 8 & 2 \\ 7 & -11 & -3 \end{array}\right]\left[\begin{array}{rrr} 2 & 5 & 4 \\ 1 & 4 & 3 \\ 1 & -3 & -2 \end{array}\right]\left[\begin{array}{c} x \\ y \\ z \end{array}\right] = \left[\begin{array}{rrr} -1 & 2 & 1 \\ -5 & 8 & 2 \\ 7 & -11 & -3 \end{array}\right]\left[\begin{array}{c} 4 \\ 1 \\ 5 \end{array}\right]$$

Notice that we must be careful to multiply both sides *from the left* since matrix multiplication is not commutative. If we carry out the multiplications, we obtain

$$\left[\begin{array}{rrr} 1 & 0 & 0 \\ 0 & 1 & 0 \\ 0 & 0 & 1 \end{array}\right]\left[\begin{array}{c} x \\ y \\ z \end{array}\right] = \left[\begin{array}{r} 3 \\ -2 \\ 2 \end{array}\right],$$

which yields $x = 3$, $y = -2$, $z = 2$, the same solution as that found in Example 1 of Section 2.3.

Thus inverse matrices can be used to solve systems of equations. Unfortunately, this method will work only if the solution to the system is unique. In fact, a system $AX = C$ has a unique solution if and only if A^{-1} exists.

The technique of reducing $[A|I]$ can be used to find A^{-1} or to find that A^{-1} doesn't exist for any square matrix A. However, problem 41 of Exercise 2.2 provides a special formula that can be used to find the inverse of a 2 × 2 matrix, if the inverse exists.

Inverse of a 2 × 2 matrix

If $A = \begin{bmatrix} a & b \\ c & d \end{bmatrix}$, then $A^{-1} = \dfrac{1}{ad - bc} \begin{bmatrix} d & -b \\ -c & a \end{bmatrix}$

provided $ad - bc \neq 0$. If $ad - bc = 0$, A^{-1} does not exist.

This result can be verified by direct calculation or by reducing $[A|I]$.

EXAMPLE 3   Find the inverse, if it exists, for each of the following:

(a) $A = \begin{bmatrix} 3 & 7 \\ 2 & 5 \end{bmatrix}$ (b) $B = \begin{bmatrix} 2 & -1 \\ -4 & 2 \end{bmatrix}$

Solution   (a) For A, $ad - bc = (3)(5) - (2)(7) = 1 \neq 0$, so A^{-1} exists.

$$A^{-1} = \frac{1}{1} \begin{bmatrix} 5 & -7 \\ -2 & 3 \end{bmatrix} = \begin{bmatrix} 5 & -7 \\ -2 & 3 \end{bmatrix}$$

(b) For B, $ad - bc = (2)(2) - (-4)(-1) = 4 - 4 = 0$, so B^{-1} does not exist.

EXAMPLE 4   Solve the system

$$\begin{cases} 7x - 5y = 12 \\ 2x - 3y = 6 \end{cases}$$

using inverse matrices.

Solution   This system can be written

$$\begin{bmatrix} 7 & -5 \\ 2 & -3 \end{bmatrix} \begin{bmatrix} x \\ y \end{bmatrix} = \begin{bmatrix} 12 \\ 6 \end{bmatrix}$$

and for the coefficient matrix A, $ad - bc = -21 - (-10) = -11$. Thus, A^{-1} exists.

$$A^{-1} = -\frac{1}{11} \begin{bmatrix} -3 & 5 \\ -2 & 7 \end{bmatrix} = \begin{bmatrix} \frac{3}{11} & -\frac{5}{11} \\ \frac{2}{11} & -\frac{7}{11} \end{bmatrix},$$

so multiplying *from the left* gives the solution.

$$\begin{bmatrix} \frac{3}{11} & -\frac{5}{11} \\ \frac{2}{11} & -\frac{7}{11} \end{bmatrix} \begin{bmatrix} 7 & -5 \\ 2 & -3 \end{bmatrix} \begin{bmatrix} x \\ y \end{bmatrix} = \begin{bmatrix} \frac{3}{11} & -\frac{5}{11} \\ \frac{2}{11} & -\frac{7}{11} \end{bmatrix} \begin{bmatrix} 12 \\ 6 \end{bmatrix}$$

$$\begin{bmatrix} 1 & 0 \\ 0 & 1 \end{bmatrix} \begin{bmatrix} x \\ y \end{bmatrix} = \begin{bmatrix} \frac{6}{11} \\ -\frac{18}{11} \end{bmatrix}$$

So $x = \frac{6}{11}$, $y = -\frac{18}{11}$.

Exercise 2.4

1. If $A = \begin{bmatrix} 1 & 2 & 1 \\ 0 & 0 & 3 \\ 1 & 0 & 1 \end{bmatrix}$ and $B = \begin{bmatrix} 0 & -\frac{1}{3} & 1 \\ \frac{1}{2} & 0 & -\frac{1}{2} \\ 0 & \frac{1}{3} & 0 \end{bmatrix}$, does $B = A^{-1}$?

2. If $D = \begin{bmatrix} 0 & 2 & -6 \\ -3 & 0 & 3 \\ 0 & -2 & 0 \end{bmatrix}$ and $C = -\frac{1}{3}\begin{bmatrix} 2 & 4 & 2 \\ 0 & 0 & 6 \\ 2 & 0 & 2 \end{bmatrix}$, does $C = D^{-1}$?

3. What is the inverse of $A = \begin{bmatrix} 3 & 0 & 0 \\ 0 & 3 & 0 \\ 0 & 0 & 3 \end{bmatrix}$?

4. What is the inverse of $B = \begin{bmatrix} 4 & 0 & 0 \\ 0 & 3 & 0 \\ 0 & 0 & -1 \end{bmatrix}$?

In problems 5–12, find the inverse matrix for each matrix that has an inverse. Use the formula for 2 × 2 matrices.

5. $\begin{bmatrix} 4 & 7 \\ 1 & 2 \end{bmatrix}$

6. $\begin{bmatrix} 4 & 5 \\ 7 & 9 \end{bmatrix}$

7. $\begin{bmatrix} 2 & -1 \\ -4 & 2 \end{bmatrix}$

8. $\begin{bmatrix} 3 & 12 \\ 1 & 4 \end{bmatrix}$

9. $\begin{bmatrix} 2 & 2 \\ 4 & 5 \end{bmatrix}$

10. $\begin{bmatrix} 6 & -4 \\ -1 & 1 \end{bmatrix}$

11. $\begin{bmatrix} 4 & 7 \\ 2 & 1 \end{bmatrix}$

12. $\begin{bmatrix} 1 & 2 \\ 3 & 0 \end{bmatrix}$

In problems 13–20, find the inverse matrix for each matrix that has an inverse.

13. $\begin{bmatrix} 0 & 1 & 0 \\ 1 & 1 & 0 \\ 0 & 1 & 1 \end{bmatrix}$

14. $\begin{bmatrix} 0 & 2 & 1 \\ 3 & 0 & 1 \\ 1 & 1 & 1 \end{bmatrix}$

15. $\begin{bmatrix} 3 & 1 & 2 \\ 1 & 2 & 3 \\ 1 & 1 & 1 \end{bmatrix}$

16. $\begin{bmatrix} 1 & 2 & 3 \\ -1 & 5 & 6 \\ -1 & 3 & 3 \end{bmatrix}$

17. $\begin{bmatrix} 1 & 3 & 5 \\ -1 & -1 & 2 \\ 1 & 5 & 12 \end{bmatrix}$

18. $\begin{bmatrix} 1 & -1 & 4 \\ -1 & 0 & -2 \\ -1 & -3 & 4 \end{bmatrix}$

19. $\begin{bmatrix} 1 & 2 & 4 \\ 1 & -1 & -3 \\ 2 & 1 & 1 \end{bmatrix}$

20. $\begin{bmatrix} 3 & 4 & -1 \\ 4 & 2 & 2 \\ 2 & 6 & -4 \end{bmatrix}$

21. Use the inverse found in problem 13 to solve

$$\begin{bmatrix} 0 & 1 & 0 \\ 1 & 1 & 0 \\ 0 & 1 & 1 \end{bmatrix}\begin{bmatrix} x \\ y \\ z \end{bmatrix} = \begin{bmatrix} 1 \\ 2 \\ 3 \end{bmatrix}.$$

22. Use the inverse found in problem 14 to solve

$$\begin{bmatrix} 0 & 2 & 1 \\ 3 & 0 & 1 \\ 1 & 1 & 1 \end{bmatrix} \begin{bmatrix} x \\ y \\ z \end{bmatrix} = \begin{bmatrix} 1 \\ 0 \\ 4 \end{bmatrix}$$

In problems 23–30, use inverse matrices to solve each system of linear equations.

23. $\begin{cases} x + 2y = 4 \\ 3x + 4y = 10 \end{cases}$

24. $\begin{cases} 3x - 4y = 11 \\ 2x + 3y = -4 \end{cases}$

25. $\begin{cases} 2x + y = 4 \\ 3x + y = 5 \end{cases}$

26. $\begin{cases} 5x - 2y = 6 \\ 3x + 3y = 12 \end{cases}$

27. $\begin{cases} x + y + z = 3 \\ 2x + y + z = 4 \\ 2x + 2y + z = 5 \end{cases}$

28. $\begin{cases} 2x - y - 2z = 2 \\ 3x - y + z = -3 \\ x + y - z = 7 \end{cases}$

29. $\begin{cases} x + y + 2z = 8 \\ 2x + y + z = 7 \\ 2x + 2y + z = 10 \end{cases}$

30. $\begin{cases} x - 2y + z = 0 \\ 2x + y - 2z = 2 \\ 3x + 2y - 3z = 2 \end{cases}$

APPLICATIONS

Multiplication by a matrix can be used to encode messages, and multiplication by its inverse can be used to decode messages. Given the code

a	b	c	d	e	f	g	h	i	j
1	2	3	4	5	6	7	8	9	10

k	l	m	n	o	p	q	r	s
11	12	13	14	15	16	17	18	19

t	u	v	w	x	y	z	blank
20	21	22	23	24	25	26	27

and the code matrix

$$A = \begin{bmatrix} 5 & 9 \\ 6 & 11 \end{bmatrix},$$

we can encode a message by separating it into number pairs (since A is 2×2) and multiplying by A. For example, the message "my eye" is written

m	y	blank	e	y	e
13	25	27	5	25	5

and encoded by writing each pair of numbers as a column matrix, and multiplying this matrix by the matrix A.

$$\begin{bmatrix} 5 & 9 \\ 6 & 11 \end{bmatrix} \begin{bmatrix} 13 \\ 25 \end{bmatrix} = \begin{bmatrix} 290 \\ 353 \end{bmatrix}$$

$$\begin{bmatrix} 5 & 9 \\ 6 & 11 \end{bmatrix} \begin{bmatrix} 27 \\ 5 \end{bmatrix} = \begin{bmatrix} 180 \\ 217 \end{bmatrix}$$

$$\begin{bmatrix} 5 & 9 \\ 6 & 11 \end{bmatrix} \begin{bmatrix} 25 \\ 5 \end{bmatrix} = \begin{bmatrix} 170 \\ 205 \end{bmatrix}$$

Thus 290, 353, 180, 217, 170, and 205 are sent.

    To decode any message encoded by A, we multiply by A^{-1} in a similar fashion.

31. Use matrix A to encode the message "The die is cast."
32. Use matrix A to encode the message "To be or not to be."
33. Find A^{-1} for the coding matrix A above and use it to decode the message

$$49, 59, 133, 161, 270, 327, 313, 381.$$

34. If the code matrix is

$$A = \begin{bmatrix} 3 & 5 \\ 1 & 2 \end{bmatrix},$$

    find A^{-1} and use it to decode

$$157, 59, 73, 29, 147, 58, 63, 24, 119, 44.$$

35. If the code matrix is

$$A = \begin{bmatrix} 0 & 2 & 1 \\ 3 & 0 & 1 \\ 1 & 1 & 1 \end{bmatrix},$$

    find A^{-1} and use it to decode

$$47, 22, 34, 28, 87, 46, 63, 66, 55, 56, 44, 43, 17, 14, 15.$$

Since A and A^{-1} are 3×3 matrices, use triples of numbers.

In problems 36–40, set up each system of equations then solve it by using inverse matrices.

36. One safe investment pays 10% per year and a more risky investment pays 18% per year. A woman has $145,600 to invest and would like to have an income of $20,000 per year from her investments. How much should she invest at each rate?
37. A biologist has a 40% solution and a 10% solution of the same plant nutrient. How many cubic centimeters of each solution should be mixed to obtain 25 cc of a 28% solution?
38. A nurse has two solutions that contain different concentrations of a certain medication. One is a 20% concentration and the other is a 5% concentration. How many cubic centimeters of each should he mix to obtain 10 cc of a 15.5% solution?
39. Medication A is given every 4 hours and medication B is given twice a day. For patient I, the total intake of the two medications is restricted to 50.6 mg per day, and for patient II the total intake is restricted to 92 mg per day. The ratio of dosage of A to the dosage of B is always 5 to 8. Find the dosage for each administration of each medication for both patient I and patient II.
40. The Ace Freight Company has an order for two products to be delivered to two stores of a company. The matrix below gives information regarding the two products.

Product	I	II
Unit volume (cu ft)	20	30
Unit weight (lb)	100	400

If truck A can carry 2350 cu ft and 23,000 lbs, and truck B can carry 2500 cu ft and 24,500 lbs, how many of each product can be carried by each truck?

2.5 Applications of Matrices: Leontief Input-Output Models

Objectives
- ☐ To interpret Leontief technology matrices
- ☐ To use Leontief models to solve input-output problems

One interesting application of matrices is the Leontief Input-Output model, named for Wassily Leontief. Just as an airplane model approximates the real thing, a *mathematical model* attempts to approximate a real-world situation. Models that are carefully constructed from past information may often provide remarkably accurate forecasts. The model Leontief developed was useful in predicting the effects to the economy of price changes or shifts in government spending.*

Leontief's work divided the economy into 500 sectors and in a subsequent article in *Scientific American* (October 1951), this was further reduced to a more manageable 42 departments of production. We can examine the workings of input-output analysis with a very simplified view of the economy.

Suppose we consider a simple economy as being based on three commodities: agricultural products, manufactured goods, and fuels. Suppose further that production of 10 units of agricultural products requires 5 units of agricultural products, 2 units of manufactured goods, and 1 unit of fuels; production of 10 units of manufactured goods requires 1 unit of agricultural products, 5 units of manufactured products, and 3 units of fuels; and production of 10 units of fuels requires 1 unit of agricultural products, 3 units of manufactured goods, and 4 units of fuels.

Table 2.6 summarizes this information in terms of production of one unit. The first column represents the units of agricultural products, manufactured goods, and fuels, respectively, that are needed to produce one unit of agricultural products. Column 2 represents the units required to produce one unit of manufactured goods, and column 3 represents the units required to produce one unit of fuels.

Table 2.6

| | Outputs | | |
Inputs	Agricultural products	Manufactured goods	Fuels
Agricultural products	0.5	0.1	0.1
Manufactured goods	0.2	0.5	0.3
Fuels	0.1	0.3	0.4

Note that the sum of the units of agricultural products, manufactured goods, and fuels required to produce 1 unit of fuels (column 3) does not add up to 1 unit. This is because not all commodities or industries are represented in the model. In particular, it is customary to omit labor from these models.

---

*Leontief's work dealt with a massive analysis of the American economy. He was awarded a Nobel Prize in Economics in 1973 for his study.

EXAMPLE 1   Use Table 2.6 on the previous page to answer the following questions.
(a) How many units of fuels were required to produce 100 units of manufactured goods?
(b) Production of which commodity is least dependent on the other two?
(c) If fuel costs rise, which two industries will be most affected?

Solution   (a) Referring to column 2, manufactured goods, we see that one unit requires 0.1 unit of agricultural products and 0.3 unit of fuels. Thus 100 units of manufactured goods require 10 units of agricultural products and 30 units of fuels.
(b) Looking down the columns, we see that one unit of agricultural products requires 0.3 unit of the other two commodities; one unit of manufactured goods requires 0.4 unit of the other two; and one unit of fuels requires 0.4 unit of the other two. Thus production of agricultural products is less dependent on the others.
(c) A rise in the cost of fuels would most affect those industries using the larger amount of fuels. One unit of agricultural products requires 0.1 unit of fuels, while a unit of manufactured goods requires 0.3 unit, and fuels requires 0.4 of its own units. Thus manufacturing and the fuel industry would be most affected by a cost increase in fuels.

From Table 2.6 we can form matrix A, called a **technology matrix** or a **Leontief matrix.**

$$A = \begin{bmatrix} 0.5 & 0.1 & 0.1 \\ 0.2 & 0.5 & 0.3 \\ 0.1 & 0.3 & 0.4 \end{bmatrix}$$

or input / output

For this simplified model of the economy, not all information is contained within the technology matrix. In particular, each industry has a gross production. The **gross production matrix** for the economy can be represented by the column matrix.

$$X = \begin{bmatrix} x_1 \\ x_2 \\ x_3 \end{bmatrix},$$

where x_1 is the gross production of agricultural products, x_2 is the gross production of manufactured goods, and x_3 is the gross production of fuels.

Those units of gross production not used by these industries are called **final demands** or **surpluses,** and may be considered as being available for consumers, the government, or export. If we place these surpluses in a column matrix D, then the surplus can be represented by the equation

$$X - AX = D, \quad \text{or} \quad (I - A)X = D,$$

where I is an identity matrix. This matrix equation is called the **technological equation** for an open Leontief model.

EXAMPLE 2   Use matrix A from Table 2.6 as the technology matrix. If we wish to have a surplus of 85 units of agricultural products, 65 units of manufactured goods, and 0 units of fuels, what should the gross outputs be?

Solution   Let X be the matrix as above. Then the technological equation is $(I - A)X = D$.

$$I - A = \begin{bmatrix} 1 & 0 & 0 \\ 0 & 1 & 0 \\ 0 & 0 & 1 \end{bmatrix} - \begin{bmatrix} 0.5 & 0.1 & 0.1 \\ 0.2 & 0.5 & 0.3 \\ 0.1 & 0.3 & 0.4 \end{bmatrix} = \begin{bmatrix} 0.5 & -0.1 & -0.1 \\ -0.2 & 0.5 & -0.3 \\ -0.1 & -0.3 & 0.6 \end{bmatrix}$$

Hence we must solve the matrix equation

$$\begin{bmatrix} 0.5 & -0.1 & -0.1 \\ -0.2 & 0.5 & -0.3 \\ -0.1 & -0.3 & 0.6 \end{bmatrix} \begin{bmatrix} x_1 \\ x_2 \\ x_3 \end{bmatrix} = \begin{bmatrix} 85 \\ 65 \\ 0 \end{bmatrix}.$$

The augmented matrix is

$$\begin{bmatrix} 0.5 & -0.1 & -0.1 & | & 85 \\ -0.2 & 0.5 & -0.3 & | & 65 \\ -0.1 & -0.3 & 0.6 & | & 0 \end{bmatrix}.$$

If we reduce this as in Section 2.3, we obtain

$$\begin{bmatrix} 1 & 0 & 0 & | & 300 \\ 0 & 1 & 0 & | & 400 \\ 0 & 0 & 1 & | & 250 \end{bmatrix},$$

so the gross outputs for the industries are

Agriculture: $x_1 = 300$
Manufacturing: $x_2 = 400$
Fuels: $x_3 = 250$.

A few comments are in order. First, the surplus matrix must contain positive or zero entries. If this is not the case, then the gross production of one or more industries is insufficient to supply the needs of the others. That is, the economy cannot use more of a certain commodity that it produces.

Second, the model we have considered is referred to as an **open Leontief model** because not all inputs and outputs were incorporated within the technology matrix. In particular, since labor was omitted, some (or all) of the surpluses must be used to support this labor.

If a model is developed in which all inputs and outputs are used within the system, then such a model is called a **closed Leontief model.** In such a model, labor (and perhaps other factors) must be included. Labor is included by considering a new industry, households, which produces labor. When such a closed model is developed, all outputs are used within the system and the sum of the entries in each column equals 1. In this case, there is no surplus, so $D = 0$, and $X - AX = 0$. Thus the technological equation is

$$AX = X. \qquad \text{(closed Leontief model)}$$

EXAMPLE 3   The following closed Leontief model with technology matrix A might describe the economy of the entire country, with x_1 equal to the government's budget, x_2 the value of industrial output (profit-making organizations), x_3 the budget of nonprofit organizations, and x_4 the household's budget.

$$A = \begin{array}{c} \\ \end{array} \begin{array}{cccc} \text{G} & \text{I} & \text{N} & \text{H} \\ \end{array}$$

$$A = \begin{bmatrix} 0.4 & 0.2 & 0 & 0.3 \\ 0.2 & 0.2 & 0.2 & 0.1 \\ 0.2 & 0 & 0.2 & 0.1 \\ 0.2 & 0.6 & 0.6 & 0.5 \end{bmatrix} \begin{array}{l} \text{Govt.} \\ \text{Ind.} \\ \text{Nonprof.} \\ \text{Hshld.} \end{array}$$

Find the total budgets (or outputs) x_1, x_2, x_3, and x_4.

Solution   Since this is a closed Leontief model, we must solve the system given by $AX = X$, that is,

$$0.4x_1 + 0.2x_2 + 0x_3 + 0.3x_4 = x_1 \qquad (1)$$
$$0.2x_1 + 0.2x_2 + 0.2x_3 + 0.1x_4 = x_2 \qquad (2)$$
$$0.2x_1 + 0x_2 + 0.2x_3 + 0.1x_4 = x_3 \qquad (3)$$
$$0.2x_1 + 0.6x_2 + 0.6x_3 + 0.5x_4 = x_4. \qquad (4)$$

If we put this system in the form where the constants occur as the right members [by subtracting x_1 from both sides of equation (1), and so on], and then form the augmented matrix, we have

$$\begin{bmatrix} -0.6 & 0.2 & 0 & 0.3 & | & 0 \\ 0.2 & -0.8 & 0.2 & 0.1 & | & 0 \\ 0.2 & 0 & -0.8 & 0.1 & | & 0 \\ 0.2 & 0.6 & 0.6 & -0.5 & | & 0 \end{bmatrix}.$$

If we multiply each entry by 5 and rearrange the rows we can obtain the matrix

$$\begin{bmatrix} 1 & 0 & -4 & 0.5 & | & 0 \\ -3 & 1 & 0 & 1.5 & | & 0 \\ 1 & -4 & 1 & 0.5 & | & 0 \\ 1 & 3 & 3 & -2.5 & | & 0 \end{bmatrix}.$$

Then, if we reduce this matrix by the methods of Section 2.3, we obtain

$$\begin{bmatrix} 1 & 0 & 0 & -\frac{53}{86} & | & 0 \\ 0 & 1 & 0 & -\frac{15}{43} & | & 0 \\ 0 & 0 & 1 & -\frac{12}{43} & | & 0 \\ 0 & 0 & 0 & 0 & | & 0 \end{bmatrix}.$$

The system of equations that corresponds to this augmented matrix is

$$\begin{array}{ll} x_1 -\frac{53}{86}x_4 = 0 & x_1 = \frac{53}{86}x_4 \\ x_2 -\frac{15}{43}x_4 = 0 \quad \text{or} & x_2 = \frac{15}{43}x_4. \\ x_3 -\frac{12}{43}x_4 = 0 & x_3 = \frac{12}{43}x_4 \end{array}$$

no unique
solution
if I throw
out

Note that the economy satisfies the given equation if the government's budget is $\frac{53}{86}$ times the household's budget, if the value of industrial output is $\frac{15}{43}$ times the household's budget, and if the budget of nonprofit organizations is $\frac{12}{43}$ times the household's budget. The dependency here is expected. The fact that the system is closed suggests the dependency, but even more obvious is the fact that industrial output is limited by labor supply.

We have examined two types of input-output models as they pertain to the economy as a whole. Since Leontief's original work with the economy, various other applications of input-output models have been developed. Consider the following parts-listing problem.

EXAMPLE 4   A storage shed consists of 4 walls and a roof. The walls and roof are made from stamped aluminum sheeting and are reinforced with 4 braces, each of which is held with 6 bolts. The final assembly joins the walls to each other and to the roof using a total of 20 more bolts. The parts listing for these sheds can be described by the following matrix.

$$Q = \begin{bmatrix} & S & W & R & Sht & Br & Bo & \\ & 0 & 0 & 0 & 0 & 0 & 0 & \text{Sheds} \\ & 4 & 0 & 0 & 0 & 0 & 0 & \text{Walls} \\ & 1 & 0 & 0 & 0 & 0 & 0 & \text{Roofs} \\ & 0 & 1 & 1 & 0 & 0 & 0 & \text{Sheets} \\ & 0 & 4 & 4 & 0 & 0 & 0 & \text{Braces} \\ & 20 & 24 & 24 & 0 & 0 & 0 & \text{Bolts} \end{bmatrix}$$

This matrix is a form of input-output matrix, with the rows representing inputs that are used directly to produce the items that head the columns. We note that the entries here are quantities used rather than proportions used.

Thus to produce a shed requires 4 walls, 1 roof, and 20 bolts, and to produce a roof requires 1 aluminum sheet, 4 braces, and 24 bolts.

Suppose that an order is received for 4 completed sheds and spare parts including 2 walls, 1 roof, 8 braces, and 24 bolts. How many of each of the assembly items are required to fill the order?

Solution   If matrix D represents the order and matrix X represents the gross production, we have

$$D = \begin{bmatrix} 4 \\ 2 \\ 1 \\ 0 \\ 8 \\ 24 \end{bmatrix} \begin{matrix} \text{Sheds} \\ \text{Walls} \\ \text{Roofs} \\ \text{Sheets} \\ \text{Braces} \\ \text{Bolts} \end{matrix} \qquad X = \begin{bmatrix} x_1 \\ x_2 \\ x_3 \\ x_4 \\ x_5 \\ x_6 \end{bmatrix} = \begin{bmatrix} \text{total sheds required} \\ \text{total walls required} \\ \text{total roofs required} \\ \text{total sheets required} \\ \text{total braces required} \\ \text{total bolts required} \end{bmatrix}.$$

Then X must satisfy $X - QX = D$, which is the technological equation for an open Leontief model.

We can find X by solving the system $(I - Q)X = D$, which is represented by the augmented matrix

$$
\left[
\begin{array}{cccccc|c}
1 & 0 & 0 & 0 & 0 & 0 & 4 \\
-4 & 1 & 0 & 0 & 0 & 0 & 2 \\
-1 & 0 & 1 & 0 & 0 & 0 & 1 \\
0 & -1 & -1 & 1 & 0 & 0 & 0 \\
0 & -4 & -4 & 0 & 1 & 0 & 8 \\
-20 & -24 & -24 & 0 & 0 & 1 & 24
\end{array}
\right].
$$

Although this matrix is quite large, it is easily reduced and yields the following:

$$
\left[
\begin{array}{cccccc|c}
1 & 0 & 0 & 0 & 0 & 0 & 4 \\
0 & 1 & 0 & 0 & 0 & 0 & 18 \\
0 & 0 & 1 & 0 & 0 & 0 & 5 \\
0 & 0 & 0 & 1 & 0 & 0 & 23 \\
0 & 0 & 0 & 0 & 1 & 0 & 100 \\
0 & 0 & 0 & 0 & 0 & 1 & 656
\end{array}
\right].
$$

This matrix tells us that the order will have 4 complete sheds. The 18 walls from the matrix include the 16 from the complete sheds and the 5 roofs include the 4 from the complete sheds. The 23 sheets, 100 braces, and 656 bolts are the total number of *primary assembly items* (bolts, braces, and sheets) required to fill the order.

Exercise 2.5

The following technology matrix describes the relationship of certain industries within the economy to each other.

A&F	RM	M	F	U	SI	
0.410	0.008	0	0.002	0	0.006	Agriculture and food
0.025	0.493	0.190	0.024	0.030	0.150	Raw materials
0.015	0.006	0.082	0.009	0.001	0.116	Manufacturing
0.097	0.096	0.040	0.053	0.008	0.093	Fuels industry
0.028	0.129	0.039	0.058	0.138	0.409	Utilities
0.043	0.008	0.010	0.012	0.002	0.095	Service industries

Use this matrix in problems 1–8.

1. For each 1000 units of raw materials produced, how many units of agricultural and food products were required?
2. For each 1000 units of raw materials produced, how many units of service were required?
3. How many units of fuels were required to produce 1000 units of manufactured goods?

4. How many units of fuels were required to produce 1000 units of power (utilities' goods)?
5. Which industry is most dependent on its own goods for its operations? Which industry is least dependent on its own goods?
6. Which industry is most dependent on the fuels industry?
7. Which three industries would be most affected by a rise in the cost of raw materials?
8. Which industry would be most affected by a rise in the cost of manufactured goods?
9. Suppose a primitive economy consists of two industries, farm products and farm machinery. Suppose also that their technology matrix is

$$A = \begin{matrix} & \text{P} & \text{M} \\ \begin{bmatrix} 0.5 & 0.1 \\ 0.1 & 0.3 \end{bmatrix} & \begin{matrix} \text{Products} \\ \text{Machinery} \end{matrix} \end{matrix}$$

If the surpluses of 96 units of farm produce and 8 units of farm machinery are desired, find the gross production of each industry.

10. Suppose an economy has two industries, agriculture and minerals. Suppose further that the technology matrix for this economy is A.

$$A = \begin{matrix} & \text{Ag} & \text{M} \\ \begin{bmatrix} 0.3 & 0.1 \\ 0.1 & 0.2 \end{bmatrix} & \begin{matrix} \text{Agriculture} \\ \text{Minerals} \end{matrix} \end{matrix}$$

If a surplus of 60 agricultural units and 70 mineral units is desired, find the gross production for each industry.

11. Suppose the economy of an underdeveloped country has an agricultural industry and an oil industry, with technology matrix

$$A = \begin{matrix} & \text{A} & \text{O} \\ \begin{bmatrix} 0.3 & 0.1 \\ 0.2 & 0.1 \end{bmatrix} & \begin{matrix} \text{Agr. prod.} \\ \text{Oil prod.} \end{matrix} \end{matrix}$$

If a surplus of 0 units of agricultural products and 610 units of oil products are desired, find the gross production of each industry.

12. Suppose a simple economy with only an agricultural industry and a steel industry has the following technology matrix.

$$A = \begin{matrix} & \text{Ag} & \text{St} \\ \begin{bmatrix} 0.5 & 0.2 \\ 0.1 & 0.6 \end{bmatrix} & \begin{matrix} \text{Agriculture} \\ \text{Steel} \end{matrix} \end{matrix}$$

If surpluses of 15 units of agricultural products and 33 units of steel are desired, find the gross production of each industry.

13. Suppose an economy has the same technological matrix as that used in Example 2. If surpluses of 110 units of agricultural goods and 50 units each of manufactured goods and fuels are desired, find the gross production of each industry required to satisfy this.

14. Suppose that an economy has the same technological matrix as that used in Example 2. If surpluses of 180 units of agricultural goods, 90 units of manufactured goods, and 40 units of fuels are desired, find the gross production of each industry required to satisfy this.

15. Suppose that the economy of a small nation has an electronics industry, a steel industry, and an auto industry, with the following technology matrix.

$$\begin{array}{ccc} \text{El} & \text{St} & \text{Au} \end{array}$$
$$A = \begin{bmatrix} 0.6 & 0.2 & 0.2 \\ 0.1 & 0.4 & 0.5 \\ 0.1 & 0.2 & 0.2 \end{bmatrix} \begin{array}{l} \text{Electronics} \\ \text{Steel} \\ \text{Autos} \end{array}$$

If the nation wishes to have surpluses of 100 units of electronics production, 200 units of steel production, and 200 automobiles, find the gross production of each industry.

16. Suppose an economy has the same technology matrix as that in problem 15. If surpluses of 540 units of electronics, 30 units of steel, and 140 autos are desired, find the gross production for each industry.

17. Suppose that for the primitive economy in problem 9 we form a closed model by including households. Suppose further that the resulting technology matrix is

Closed

$$\begin{array}{ccc} \text{P} & \text{M} & \text{H} \end{array}$$
$$A = \begin{bmatrix} 0.5 & 0.1 & 0.2 \\ 0.1 & 0.3 & 0 \\ 0.4 & 0.6 & 0.8 \end{bmatrix} \begin{array}{l} \text{Farm products} \\ \text{Farm machinery} \\ \text{Households} \end{array}$$

Find the gross productions for these industries.

18. In Example 3 we gave a closed Leontief model for the economy. In the following matrix we combined the nonprofit organizations with industry (viewing nonprofit organizations as a service industry). Find the gross productions for the industries in this revised closed model.

Closed

$$\begin{array}{ccc} \text{G} & \text{I} & \text{H} \end{array}$$
$$A = \begin{bmatrix} 0.4 & 0.1 & 0.3 \\ 0.4 & 0.3 & 0.2 \\ 0.2 & 0.6 & 0.5 \end{bmatrix} \begin{array}{l} \text{Govt.} \\ \text{Ind.} \\ \text{House.} \end{array}$$

19. Suppose the technology matrix for a closed model of a simple economy is given by matrix A. Find the gross productions for the industries.

$$\begin{array}{ccc} \text{G} & \text{I} & \text{H} \end{array}$$
$$A = \begin{bmatrix} 0.4 & 0.2 & 0.2 \\ 0.2 & 0.3 & 0.3 \\ 0.4 & 0.5 & 0.5 \end{bmatrix} \begin{array}{l} \text{Govt.} \\ \text{Ind.} \\ \text{House.} \end{array}$$

20. Suppose the technology matrix for a closed model of an economy is given by matrix A. Find the gross productions for the industries.

$$\begin{array}{cccc} \text{G} & \text{P} & \text{N} & \text{H} \end{array}$$
$$A = \begin{bmatrix} 0.3 & 0.2 & 0.1 & 0.05 \\ 0.2 & 0.3 & 0.1 & 0.1 \\ 0.2 & 0.1 & 0.2 & 0.1 \\ 0.3 & 0.4 & 0.6 & 0.75 \end{bmatrix} \begin{array}{l} \text{Govt.} \\ \text{Profit sector} \\ \text{Nonprof.} \\ \text{House.} \end{array}$$

21. For the storage shed in Example 4, find the number of each primary assembly item required to fill an order of 24 sheds, 12 braces, and 96 bolts.

22. Card tables are made by joining 4 legs and a top using 4 bolts. The legs are each made from a steel rod. The top has a frame made from 4 steel rods. A cover and four special clamps that brace the top and hold the legs are joined to the frame using a total of 8 bolts. The parts-listing matrix for the card table assembly is given by

$$A = \begin{bmatrix} & \text{CT} & \text{L} & \text{T} & \text{R} & \text{Co} & \text{Cl} & \text{B} \\ 0 & 0 & 0 & 0 & 0 & 0 & 0 \\ 4 & 0 & 0 & 0 & 0 & 0 & 0 \\ 1 & 0 & 0 & 0 & 0 & 0 & 0 \\ 0 & 1 & 4 & 0 & 0 & 0 & 0 \\ 0 & 0 & 1 & 0 & 0 & 0 & 0 \\ 0 & 0 & 4 & 0 & 0 & 0 & 0 \\ 4 & 0 & 8 & 0 & 0 & 0 & 0 \end{bmatrix} \begin{matrix} \text{Card table} \\ \text{Legs} \\ \text{Top} \\ \text{Rods} \\ \text{Cover} \\ \text{Clamps} \\ \text{Bolts} \end{matrix}$$

If an order is received for 10 card tables, 4 legs, 1 top, 1 cover, 6 clamps, and 12 bolts, how many of each primary assembly item are required to fill the order?

23. A sawhorse is made from 2 pairs of legs and a top joined with 4 nails. The top is a 2″ × 4″ board 3 ft long. Each pair of legs is made from two 2″ × 4″ boards 3 ft long, a brace, and a special clamp, with the brace and the clamp joined using 8 nails. The parts-listing matrix for the sawhorse is given by

$$A = \begin{bmatrix} & \text{SH} & \text{T} & \text{LP} & 2 \times 4 & \text{B} & \text{C} & \text{N} \\ 0 & 0 & 0 & 0 & 0 & 0 & 0 \\ 1 & 0 & 0 & 0 & 0 & 0 & 0 \\ 2 & 0 & 0 & 0 & 0 & 0 & 0 \\ 0 & 1 & 2 & 0 & 0 & 0 & 0 \\ 0 & 0 & 1 & 0 & 0 & 0 & 0 \\ 0 & 0 & 1 & 0 & 0 & 0 & 0 \\ 4 & 0 & 8 & 0 & 0 & 0 & 0 \end{bmatrix} \begin{matrix} \text{Sawhorse} \\ \text{Top} \\ \text{Leg pair} \\ 2 \times 4\text{s} \\ \text{Brace} \\ \text{Clamp} \\ \text{Nails} \end{matrix}$$

How many of each primary assembly item are required to fill an order for 10 sawhorses, 6 extra 2 × 4s, 6 extra clamps, and 100 nails.

24. A log carrier has a body made from a 4-ft length of reinforced material having a patch on each side and a dowel slid through each end to act as handles. The parts-listing matrix for the log carrier is given by

$$A = \begin{bmatrix} & \text{LC} & \text{B} & \text{H} & \text{C} & \text{P} \\ 0 & 0 & 0 & 0 & 0 \\ 1 & 0 & 0 & 0 & 0 \\ 2 & 0 & 0 & 0 & 0 \\ 0 & 1 & 0 & 0 & 0 \\ 0 & 2 & 0 & 0 & 0 \end{bmatrix} \begin{matrix} \text{Log carrier} \\ \text{Body} \\ \text{Handles} \\ \text{Cloth} \\ \text{Patch} \end{matrix}$$

How many of each primary assembly item are required to fill an order for 500 log carriers and 20 handles?

Within a company there is a (micro) economy that is monitored by the accounting procedures. In terms of the accounts, the various departments "produce" costs, some of which are internal and some of which are direct costs. Problems 25–27 show how an open Leontief model can be used to determine departmental costs.

25. Suppose the development department of a firm charges 10% of its total monthly costs to the promotional department, and the promotional department charges 5% of its total

monthly costs to the development department. The direct costs of the development department are $20,400, and the direct costs of the promotional department are $9,900. The solution to the matrix equation

$$\begin{bmatrix} 20{,}400 \\ 9{,}900 \end{bmatrix} + \begin{bmatrix} 0 & 0.05 \\ 0.1 & 0 \end{bmatrix} \begin{bmatrix} x \\ y \end{bmatrix} = \begin{bmatrix} x \\ y \end{bmatrix}$$

for the column matrix $\begin{bmatrix} x \\ y \end{bmatrix}$ gives the total costs for each department. Note that this equation can be written in the form

$$D + AX = X \quad \text{or} \quad X - AX = D,$$

which is the form for an open economy. Find the total costs for each department in this (micro) economy.

26. Suppose the shipping department of a firm charges 10% of its total monthly costs to the printing department, while the printing department charges 20% of its total monthly costs to the shipping department. If the direct costs of the shipping department are $16,500 and the direct costs of the printing department are $11,400, find the total costs for each department.

27. Suppose the engineering department of a firm charges 20% of its total monthly costs to the computer department, and the computer department charges 25% of its total monthly costs to the engineering department. If during a given month the direct costs were $11,750 for the engineering department and $10,000 for the computer department, what are the total costs of each department?

Review Exercises

Using the matrices

$$A = \begin{bmatrix} 4 & 4 & 2 & -5 \\ 6 & 3 & -1 & 0 \\ 0 & 0 & -3 & 5 \end{bmatrix}, \quad B = \begin{bmatrix} 2 & -5 & -11 & 8 \\ 4 & 0 & 0 & 4 \\ -2 & -2 & 1 & 9 \end{bmatrix},$$

$$C = \begin{bmatrix} 4 & -2 \\ 5 & 0 \\ 6 & 0 \\ 1 & 3 \end{bmatrix}, \quad D = \begin{bmatrix} 3 & 5 \\ 1 & 2 \end{bmatrix}, \quad E = \begin{bmatrix} 1 & 1 \\ 1 & 1 \\ 4 & 6 \\ 0 & 5 \end{bmatrix},$$

$$F = \begin{bmatrix} -1 & 6 \\ 4 & 11 \end{bmatrix}, \quad G = \begin{bmatrix} 2 & -5 \\ -1 & 3 \end{bmatrix}, \quad I = \begin{bmatrix} 1 & 0 \\ 0 & 1 \end{bmatrix},$$

in problems 1–22, determine the following.

2.1

1. Find a_{12} in matrix A.
2. Find b_{23} in matrix B.
3. Which of the matrices, if any, are 3 × 4?
4. Which of the matrices, if any, are 2 × 4?

2.2

5. $A + B$ 6. $C - E$ 7. $2A$
8. $3C$ 9. $4I$ 10. $-2F$
11. $D - I$ 12. $F + 2D$ 13. $3A - 5B$
14. AC 15. CD 16. DF
17. FD 18. FI 19. IF
20. DG 21. $(DG)F$ 22. Are D and G inverse matrices?

2.3

In problems 23–28, solve each system using matrices.

23. $\begin{cases} x - 2y = 4 \\ -3x + 10y = 24 \end{cases}$

24. $\begin{cases} x + y + z = 4 \\ 3x + 4y - z = -1 \\ 2x - y + 3z = 3 \end{cases}$

25. $\begin{cases} -x + y + z = 3 \\ 3x - z = 1 \\ 2x - 3y - 4z = -2 \end{cases}$

26. $\begin{cases} x + y - 2z = 5 \\ 3x + 2y + 5z = 10 \\ -2x - 3y + 15z = 2 \end{cases}$

27. $\begin{cases} x - y = 3 \\ x + y + 4z = 1 \\ 2x - 3y - 2z = 7 \end{cases}$

28. $\begin{cases} x_1 + x_2 + x_3 + x_4 = 3 \\ x_1 - 2x_2 + x_3 - 4x_4 = -5 \\ x_1 - x_3 + x_4 = 0 \\ x_2 + x_3 + x_4 = 2 \end{cases}$

2.4

Find the inverse of each of the following matrices.

29. $\begin{bmatrix} 7 & -1 \\ -10 & 2 \end{bmatrix}$

30. $\begin{bmatrix} 1 & 0 & 2 \\ 3 & 4 & -1 \\ 1 & 1 & 0 \end{bmatrix}$

31. $\begin{bmatrix} 3 & 3 & 2 \\ -1 & 4 & 2 \\ 2 & 5 & 3 \end{bmatrix}$

Solve the following systems of equations by using inverse matrices.

32. $\begin{cases} x + 2z = 5 \\ 3x + 4y - z = 2 \\ x + y = -3 \end{cases}$
(See problem 30)

33. $\begin{cases} 3x + 3y + 2z = 1 \\ -x + 4y + 2z = -10 \\ 2x + 5y + 3z = -6 \end{cases}$
(See problem 31)

34. $\begin{cases} x + 3y + z = 0 \\ x + 4y + 3z = 2 \\ 2x - y - 11z = -12 \end{cases}$

APPLICATIONS

The Burr Cabinet Company manufactures bookcases and filing cabinets at two plants, A and B. Matrix M gives the production for the two plants during June and matrix N gives the production for July.

$$M = \begin{bmatrix} A & B \\ 150 & 80 \\ 280 & 300 \end{bmatrix} \begin{matrix} \text{Bookcases} \\ \text{Files} \end{matrix} \qquad N = \begin{bmatrix} A & B \\ 100 & 60 \\ 200 & 400 \end{bmatrix}$$

$$S = \begin{bmatrix} 120 & 80 \\ 180 & 300 \end{bmatrix} \qquad P = \begin{bmatrix} 1000 & 800 \\ 600 & 1200 \end{bmatrix}$$

35. Write the matrix that represents total production at the two plants for the two months.

36. If matrix P represents the inventories at the plants at the beginning of June and matrix S represents shipments from the plants during June, write the matrix that represents the inventories at the plants at the end of June.

37. If the company sells its bookcases to wholesalers for $100 and its filing cabinets for $120, for which month was the value of production higher at (a) plant A? (b) plant B?

A small church choir is made up of men and women who wear choir robes in the sizes shown in matrix A.

$$A = \begin{array}{c} \\ \\ \\ \end{array} \overset{\text{Men \quad Women}}{\begin{bmatrix} 1 & 14 \\ 12 & 10 \\ 8 & 3 \end{bmatrix}} \begin{array}{c} \text{Small} \\ \text{Medium} \\ \text{Large} \end{array} \qquad B = \overset{\text{S \quad\; M \quad\; L}}{\begin{bmatrix} 25 & 40 & 45 \\ 10 & 10 & 10 \end{bmatrix}} \begin{array}{c} \text{Robes} \\ \text{Hoods} \end{array}$$

Matrix B contains the prices (in dollars) of new robes and hoods according to size. Use these matrices in problems 38–40.

38. Find the product BA and label the rows and columns to show what each entry represents.

39. To find a matrix that gives the cost of new robes and the cost of new hoods, find

$$BA \begin{bmatrix} 1 \\ 1 \end{bmatrix}.$$

40. A matrix that gives the total cost of purchasing new robes and new hoods is given by

$$[1 \quad\;\; 1] \, BA \begin{bmatrix} 1 \\ 1 \end{bmatrix}.$$

Find this total.

41. A woman has $50,000 to invest. She has decided to invest all of it by purchasing some shares of stock in each of three companies: a fast-food chain that sells for $50 per share and has an expected growth of 11.5% per year, a software company that sells for $20 per share and has an expected growth of 15% per year, and a pharmaceutical company that sells for $80 per share and has an expected growth of 10% per year. She plans to buy twice as many shares of stock in the fast-food chain as in the pharmaceutical company. If her goal is 12% growth per year, how many shares of each stock should she buy?

42. A biologist is growing three different types of slugs (types A, B, and C) in the same laboratory environment. Each day, the slugs are given a nutrient mixture that contains three different ingredients (I, II, and III). Each type A slug requires 1 unit of I, 3 units of II, and 1 unit of III per day. Each type B slug requires 1 unit of I, 4 units of II, and 2 units of III per day. Each type C slug requires 2 units of I, 10 units of II, and 6 units of III per day. If the daily mixture contains 2000 units of I, 8000 units of II, and 4000 units of III, find the number of slugs of each type that can be supported.

43. A look at the industrial sector of an economy can be simplified to include three industries: the mining industry, the manufacturing industry, and the fuels industry. The technology matrix for this sector of the economy is given by

$$A = \overset{\text{Mi \quad\;\; Mf \quad\;\; F}}{\begin{bmatrix} 0.4 & 0.4 & 0.2 \\ 0.2 & 0.4 & 0.2 \\ 0.1 & 0.2 & 0.4 \end{bmatrix}} \begin{array}{c} \text{Mining} \\ \text{Mfg.} \\ \text{Fuels.} \end{array}$$

Find the gross production of each industry if a surplus of 10 units of mined goods, 40 units of manufactured goods, and 140 units of fuels is desired.

44. Suppose a closed Leontief model for a nation's economy has the following technology matrix.

$$
A = \begin{matrix}
 & G & A & M & H & \\
 & \begin{bmatrix} 0.4 & 0.2 & 0.2 & 0.2 \\ 0.2 & 0.4 & 0.1 & 0.2 \\ 0.2 & 0.1 & 0.3 & 0.1 \\ 0.2 & 0.3 & 0.4 & 0.5 \end{bmatrix} & & & & \begin{matrix} \text{Govt.} \\ \text{Agr.} \\ \text{Mfg.} \\ \text{House.} \end{matrix}
\end{matrix}
$$

Find the gross productions for this closed model.

WARMUP

	Prerequisite problem type	Answer	Section for review
3.1	(a) Solve $3x - 2 = 7$. (b) Solve $2(x - 4) = \dfrac{x - 3}{3}$.	(a) $x = 3$ (b) $x = \frac{21}{5}$	1.1 Linear equations
3.1	Graph the equation $y = \frac{3}{2}x - 2$.	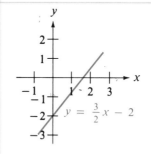	1.2 Graphing linear equations
3.2, 3.3	Solve the systems: (a) $\begin{cases} x + 2y = 10 \\ 2x + y = 14 \end{cases}$ (b) $\begin{cases} x + 0.5y = 16 \\ x + y = 24 \end{cases}$	(a) $x = 6, y = 2$ (b) $x = 8, y = 16$	1.6 Systems of linear equations
3.4	Write the system in an augmented matrix: $\begin{cases} x + 2y + s_1 = 10 \\ 2x + y + s_2 = 14 \\ -2x - 3y + f = 0 \end{cases}$	$\begin{bmatrix} 1 & 2 & 1 & 0 & 0 & 10 \\ 2 & 1 & 0 & 1 & 0 & 14 \\ -2 & -3 & 0 & 0 & 1 & 0 \end{bmatrix}$	2.3 Gauss-Jordan Elimination
3.4	Write a matrix equivalent to matrix A with the entry in row 1, column 2 equal to 1 and with all other entries in column 2 equal to 0. First multiply row 1 by $\frac{1}{2}$. $A = \begin{bmatrix} 1 & 2 & 1 & 0 & 0 & 10 \\ 2 & 1 & 0 & 1 & 0 & 14 \\ -2 & -3 & 0 & 0 & 1 & 0 \end{bmatrix}$	$\begin{bmatrix} \frac{1}{2} & 1 & \frac{1}{2} & 0 & 0 & 5 \\ \frac{3}{2} & 0 & -\frac{1}{2} & 1 & 0 & 9 \\ -\frac{1}{2} & 0 & \frac{3}{2} & 0 & 1 & 15 \end{bmatrix}$	2.3 Gauss-Jordan Elimination

3

Inequalities and Linear Programming

A firm frequently requires several components for the manufacture of the items it produces, and there are usually several stages for each item's assembly and final shipment. The company's costs and profits depend on the availability of the components (for example, labor and raw materials), the costs of these components, the unit profit for each product, and how many products are required. If the relationships among the various resources, the production requirements, the costs, and the profits are all linear, then these activities may be planned (or programmed) in the best possible (optimal) way by means of **linear programming.**

Because linear programming is useful in solving the problem of allocating limited resources among various activities in the best possible way, its impact has been tremendous. Although it is a relatively recent development, it is a standard tool for companies of all sizes, and its application has been responsible for saving many thousands of dollars. Numerous textbooks have been written on the subject; our intention here is to provide an introduction to the method.

Because the restrictions (constraints) on most business operations can often be expressed as linear inequalities, we begin this chapter by introducing methods for solving and graphing linear inequalities. We will show how graphs of the constraint inequalities can be used to solve linear programming problems. The simplex method provides a technique for converting a system of inequalities into a system of equations that can be used to solve linear programming problems.

3.1 Linear Inequalities in One Variable

Objective ☐ To graph and solve linear inequalities in one variable.

An **inequality** is a statement that one quantity is greater than (or less than) another quantity. We have already encountered some very simple inequalities. For example, the number of items a firm produces and sells, x, must be a nonnegative quantity. Thus x is greater than or equal to zero, which is written $x \geq 0$. The inequality $3x - 2 > 2x + 1$ is a first-degree (linear) inequality that states that the left member is greater than the right member. Certain values of the variable will satisfy the inequality. These values form the solution set of the inequality. For example, 4 is in the solution set of $3x - 2 > 2x + 1$ because $3 \cdot 4 - 2 > 2 \cdot 4 + 1$. On the other hand, 2 is not in the solution set because $3 \cdot 2 - 2 \not> 2 \cdot 2 + 1$. *Solving* an inequality means finding its solution set, and two inequalities are *equivalent* if they have the same solution set. As with equations, we find the solutions to inequalities by finding equivalent inequalities from which the solutions can be easily seen. We use the following properties to reduce an inequality to a simple equivalent inequality.

Properties	Examples

Substitution Property

The inequality formed by substituting one expression for an equal expression is equivalent to the original inequality.

$$5x - 4x < 6$$
$$x < 6$$

The solution set is $\{x: x < 6\}$.

Addition Property

The inequality formed by adding the same quantity to both sides of an inequality is equivalent to the original inequality.

$$2x - 4 > x + 6$$
$$2x - 4 + 4 > x + 6 + 4$$
$$2x > x + 10$$
$$2x + (-x) > x + 10 + (-x)$$
$$x > 10$$

Multiplication Property I

The inequality formed by multiplying both sides of an inequality by the same *positive* quantity is equivalent to the original inequality.

$$\tfrac{1}{2}x > 8 \qquad\qquad 3x < 6$$
$$\tfrac{1}{2}x(2) > 8(2) \qquad 3x\left(\tfrac{1}{3}\right) < 6\left(\tfrac{1}{3}\right)$$
$$x > 16 \qquad\qquad x < 2$$

Multiplication Property II

The inequality formed by multiplying both sides of an inequality by a *negative* number and reversing the sense of the inequality is equivalent to the original inequality.

$$-x < 6 \qquad\qquad -3x > -27$$
$$-x(-1) > 6(-1) \qquad -3x\left(-\tfrac{1}{3}\right) < -27\left(-\tfrac{1}{3}\right)$$
$$x > -6 \qquad\qquad x < 9$$

We may graph the solutions to inequalities in one unknown on the real number line. For example, the graph of $x < 2$ consists of all points to the left of 2 on the number line. The open circle on the graph in Figure 3.1 indicates that all points up to but *not* including 2 are in the solution set.

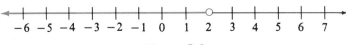

Figure 3.1

EXAMPLE 1   Solve the inequality

$$-2\left(\frac{s}{-2}\right) < -4 \quad x - 2$$

$$s > 8$$

and graph the solution set.

Solution

$$\frac{s}{-2} < -4$$

$$\frac{s}{-2}(-2) > -4(-2)$$

$$s > 8$$

The solution set is $\{s: s > 8\}$. The graph of the solution set is shown in Figure 3.2.

Figure 3.2

Some inequalities will require several operations to find their solution set. In this case, the order in which the operations are performed is the same as that used in solving linear equations.

EXAMPLE 2   Solve the inequality $2(x - 4) < \dfrac{x - 3}{3}$.

Solution

$$2(x - 4) < \frac{x - 3}{3}$$

$$3\left(2x - 8\right) < \left(\frac{x-3}{3}\right)3$$

$$6x - 24 < x - 3$$

$$\qquad\qquad +24 \qquad +24$$

$6(x - 4) < x - 3$	Cleared fractions $\quad 6x < x + 21$
$6x - 24 < x - 3$	Removed parentheses
$5x < 21$	Performed additions and subtractions $\quad 5x < 21$
$x < \dfrac{21}{5}$	Multiplied by $\dfrac{1}{5}$ $\qquad x < \dfrac{21}{5}$

Now, if we want to check that this solution is a reasonable one, we can substitute the integer values around 21/5 into the original inequality. Note that $x = 4$ satisfies the inequality because

$$2[(4) - 4] < \frac{(4) - 3}{3},$$

but $x = 5$ does not:

$$2[(5) - 4] \not< \frac{(5) - 3}{3}.$$

Thus, $x < 21/5$ is a reasonable solution.

We may also solve inequalities of the form $a \leq b$. This means "a is less than b or $a = b$." The solution of $2x \leq 4$ is $x \leq 2$, since $x < 2$ is the solution of $2x < 4$ and $x = 2$ is the solution of $2x = 4$.

EXAMPLE 3   Solve the inequality $3x - 2 \leq 7$.

Solution   This inequality states that $3x - 2 = 7$ or that $3x - 2 < 7$. By solving in the usual manner, we get $3x \leq 9$, or $x \leq 3$. Then $x = 3$ is the solution to $3x - 2 = 7$ and $x < 3$ is the solution to $3x - 2 < 7$, so the solution set for $3x - 2 \leq 7$ is $\{x: x \leq 3\}$.

The graph of the solution set includes the point $x = 3$ and all points $x < 3$ (see Figure 3.3).

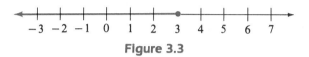

Figure 3.3

We may use the notation $-2 < x < 4$ to state that x satisfies the two conditions $-2 < x$ and $x < 4$. This **compound inequality** represents an **interval** on the number line. The graph of this compound inequality is called an **open interval** because neither *endpoint* (-2 or 4) is included in the graph (see Figure 3.4). We may denote the interval $-2 < x < 4$ by $(-2, 4)$.

Figure 3.4

The graph in Figure 3.5 of $-1 \leq x \leq 3$ is a **closed interval** because both endpoints are included. This closed interval may be denoted $[-1, 3]$.

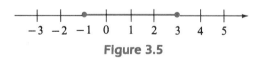

Figure 3.5

The interval determined by $-2 < x \leq 4$ is denoted $(-2, 4]$ and is called **half-open** because one endpoint is excluded (see Figure 3.6).

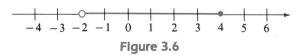

Figure 3.6

In general, we denote the closed interval $a \leq x \leq b$ as $[a, b]$, the open interval $a < x < b$ by (a, b), and the half-open interval $a \leq x < b$ by $[a, b)$.

Exercise 3.1

Solve the following inequalities.

1. $x + 2 < 4$

2. $x - 3 > 5$

3. $x - 3 \geq 2x + 1$

4. $2x - 1 \leq 3x + 4$

5. $3(x - 1) < 2x - 1$

6. $2(x + 1) > x - 1$

7. $2(x - 1) - 3 > 4x + 1$

8. $7x + 4 \leq 2(x - 1)$

9. $\dfrac{x}{3} > x - 1$

10. $\dfrac{x - 3}{4} \geq 2x$

11. $\dfrac{3(x - 1)}{2} \leq x - 2$

12. $\dfrac{x - 1}{2} + 1 > x + 1$

13. $\dfrac{5 (2 - x)}{3} \geq \dfrac{6x + 5}{2}$

14. $\dfrac{3(x - 1)}{4} \leq \dfrac{4 - x}{2}$

15. $2.9 (2x - 4) \geq \dfrac{3.6x - 8.5}{5}$

16. $2.2 (3.1x - 5) \leq \dfrac{3(4.6 - 6.1x)}{8}$

Graph the solutions to the following inequalities.

17. $2x + 1 < x - 3$

18. $3x - 1 \geq 2x + 2$

19. $3(x - 1) < 2x$

20. $3(x + 2) \geq 4x + 1$

21. $2x + \dfrac{1}{2} \geq x - 3$

22. $5x - 2 > 3(x + 3)$

23. $\dfrac{3x}{4} - \dfrac{1}{6} < x - \dfrac{2(x - 1)}{3}$

24. $\dfrac{4x}{3} - 3 > \dfrac{1}{2} + \dfrac{5x}{12}$

25. $\dfrac{3x}{4} - \dfrac{1}{3} < 1 - \dfrac{2}{3}\left(x - \dfrac{1}{2}\right)$

26. $\dfrac{x}{2} - \dfrac{4x}{5} > \dfrac{3(x - 1)}{10} - 2$

In problems 27–38, express each inequality or graph using interval notation and name the type of interval.

27. $1 < x \leq 3$

28. $-4 \leq x \leq 3$

29.

30.

31.

32.

33. $-4 < x < 3$

34. $-6 \leq x \leq -4$

35. $4 \leq x \leq 6$

36. $-2 \leq x \leq -1$

37. $4 \leq x < 9$

38. $5 < x \leq 8$

In problems 39–42, write an inequality that describes each interval or graph.

39. $(1, 4)$

40. $[3, 7]$

41.

42.

APPLICATIONS

43. **Normal body temperature is 98.6°F. What Celsius temperature C corresponds to $F \geq 98.6°$ if $F = \frac{9}{5}C + 32$?**

44. A saleswoman has monthly income I given by $I = 1000 + 0.062S$, where S is the monthly sales volume. How much must she sell to make at least $3500 in a month?

45. The traffic flow problem illustrated in Figure 3.7 appeared as problem 53 of Section 2.3, where x_1, x_2, x_3, and x_4 represent the number of cars on the indicated streets.

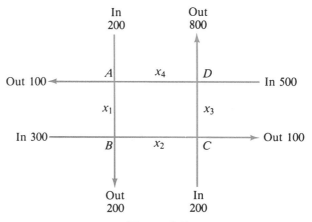

Figure 3.7

The solution to this problem is described as follows.

$$x_1 = x_4 + 100$$
$$x_2 = x_4 + 200$$
$$x_3 = x_4 + 300$$

Since the total number of cars in the system is 1200 and each variable must be nonnegative we can develop the following inequalities.

$$x_4 + 100 \leq 1200 \quad (1)$$
$$x_4 + 200 \leq 1200 \quad (2)$$
$$x_4 + 300 \leq 1200 \quad (3)$$
$$x_4 \geq 0 \quad (4)$$

(a) Solve each inequality for x_4.
(b) Determine an interval for x_4 that satisfies all these inequalities. (Hint: Find the intersection of the solution graphs.)
(c) Use the interval from (b) to develop an interval for each of the other variables.

46. Problem 52 of Section 2.3 described a botanist who could purchase 4 different plant foods with various nutrient values. If x_1 represents the number of bags of food I that were purchased, x_2 the number of bags of food II, and so on, then the number of bags of each food that the botanist can purchase and satisfy the requirements given in problem 52 of Section 2.3 can be described by the following.

$$x_1 = 160 - x_4$$
$$x_2 = 2x_4 - 220$$
$$x_3 = x_4 + 70$$

Since each variable must be nonnegative we can develop the following inequalities.

$$160 - x_4 \geq 0$$
$$2x_4 - 220 \geq 0$$
$$x_4 + 70 \geq 0$$
$$x_4 \geq 0$$

(a) Solve each inequality for x_4.
(b) Determine an interval for x_4 that solves all these inequalities.
(c) Develop an interval for each of the other variables.

3.2   Linear Inequalities in Two Variables

Objectives   ☐   To graph linear inequalities in two variables
                 ☐   To solve systems of linear inequalities in two variables

We solved and graphed the solutions of linear inequalities in one variable in Section 3.1. We now consider linear inequalities in *two* variables. The inequality $y < x$ is a linear inequality in two variables. The solutions to this inequality are the ordered pairs (x, y) that satisfy the inequality. Thus $(1, 0)$, $(3, 2)$, $(0, -1)$, and $(-2, -5)$ are solutions to $y < x$ but $(3, 7)$, $(-4, -3)$, and $(2, 2)$ are not. The graph of $y < x$ consists of all points whose y-value is less than the x-value. Thus the graph consists of all points below the line $y = x$ (the shaded area in Figure 3.8). Selecting any "test point" in the shaded region and using it to discover if it satisfies the inequality serves as a check.

Note that the points on the line $y = x$ do not satisfy the inequality, so they are not part of the graph. This is indicated by the dashed line in Figure 3.8.

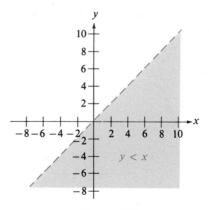

Figure 3.8

EXAMPLE 1   Graph the inequality $3x + y < 3$.

Solution   If we solve the inequality for y, we get $y < 3 - 3x$. Thus the graph of this inequality will consist of all points *below* the line $y = 3 - 3x$. The graph is shown in Figure 3.9 on the following page. Note that any point (such as $(0, 0)$) that is in the shaded region will satisfy the original inequality.

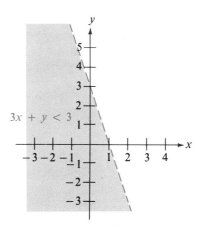

Figure 3.9

EXAMPLE 2   Graph the inequality $4x - 2y \le 6$.

Solution   Solving the inequality for y gives $y \ge 2x - 3$. Because y is greater than or equal to $2x - 3$, the graph consists of all points *on* or *above* the graph of $y = 2x - 3$. The line representing $y = 2x - 3$ is solid in Figure 3.10 to indicate that it is included in the solution.

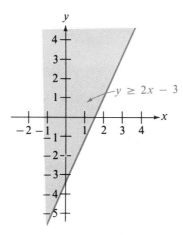

Figure 3.10

If we have two inequalities in two variables, we can find the solutions that satisfy both inequalities. We call the inequalities a **system of inequalities,** and the solution to the system can be found by finding the intersection of the solution sets of the two inequalities.

The solution set of the system of inequalities can be found by graphing the inequalities on the same set of axes and noting their points of intersection.

EXAMPLE 3   Graph the solution to the system

$$\begin{cases} 3x - 2y \geq 4 \\ x + y - 3 > 0. \end{cases}$$

Solution   The inequalities can be written in the form

$$y \leq \tfrac{3}{2}x - 2$$
$$y > -x + 3.$$

The graph of $y \leq \tfrac{3}{2}x - 2$ consists of all points on or below the line $y = \tfrac{3}{2}x - 2$. The graph of $y > -x + 3$ consists of all points above the line $y = -x + 3$. The points that satisfy both of these inequalities lie in the intersection of the two solution regions. This intersection is the heavily shaded region of Figure 3.11. This **solution region** is the graph of the solution to the system containing these two inequalities.

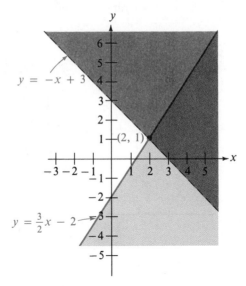

Figure 3.11

The point (2, 1) in Figure 3.11, where the two regions form a "corner," is found by solving the *equations* $y = \tfrac{3}{2}x - 2$ and $y = -x + 3$ simultaneously.

EXAMPLE 4   Graph the solution to the system

$$\begin{cases} x + 2y \leq 10 \\ 2x + y \leq 14 \\ x \geq 0 \\ y \geq 0 \end{cases}$$

Solution   We seek points in the first quadrant (on or above $y = 0$ and on or to the right of $x = 0$) that satisfy $x + 2y \le 10$ *and* $2x + y \le 14$. We can write these inequalities in their equivalent forms $y \le 5 - \frac{1}{2}x$ and $y \le 14 - 2x$. The points that satisfy these inequalities (in the first quadrant) are shown by the heavily shaded area in Figure 3.12. We can observe from the graph that the points $(0, 0)$, $(7, 0)$, and $(0, 5)$ are corners of the heavily shaded region. The corner $(6, 2)$ is found by solving the *equations* $y = 5 - \frac{1}{2}x$ and $y = 14 - 2x$ simultaneously as follows.

$$5 - \frac{1}{2}x = 14 - 2x$$
$$\frac{3}{2}x = 9$$
$$x = 6$$
$$y = 2$$

We will see that the corners of the solution region are important in solving linear programming problems.

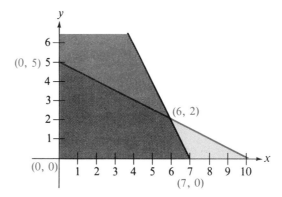

Figure 3.12

Exercise 3.2

In problems 1–10, graph each inequality.

1. $y > x$

2. $y < 3x$

3. $y \le 2x - 1$

4. $y \ge 4x - 5$

5. $\dfrac{x}{2} + \dfrac{y}{4} < 1$

6. $x - \dfrac{y}{3} < \dfrac{-2}{3}$

7. $2(x - y) \le y + 3$

8. $2(x - y) \ge x + 4$

9. $0.4x \ge 0.8$

10. $\dfrac{-y}{8} > \dfrac{1}{4}$

In problems 11–16, the graph of the solution to each system of inequalities is shown below that system. Find the corners of each solution region.

11. $\begin{cases} x + 4y \leq 60 \\ 4x + 2y \leq 100 \\ x \geq 0 \\ y \geq 0 \end{cases}$

$(0, 15)$ $4x + 2y \leq 100$

$(20, 10)$

$x + 4y \leq 60$

$\dfrac{x}{20} \Big| \dfrac{y}{0}$ 30

$5 \ 10 \ 15 \ 20 \ 25 \ (25, 0)$

12. $\begin{cases} 4x + 3y \leq 240 \\ 5x - y \leq 110 \\ x \geq 0 \\ y \geq 0 \end{cases}$

$4x + 3y = 240$

$5x - y = 110$

13. $\begin{cases} -x + y \leq 4 \\ x + 3y \leq 20 \\ 5x + 2y \leq 35 \\ x \geq 0 \\ y \geq 0 \end{cases}$

$-x + y = 4$

$x + 3y = 20$

$5x + 2y = 35$

$\dfrac{x}{0} \Big| \dfrac{y}{4}$

14. *constraints*

$\begin{cases} x + 2y \leq 20 \\ 3x + 4y \leq 48 \\ 3x + 2y \leq 42 \\ x \geq 0 \\ y \geq 0 \end{cases}$

Corner Points

$3x + 2y = 42$

$x + 2y = 20$

$3x + 4y = 48$

x	y
0	0
0	10
14	0
12	3
8	6

15. $\begin{cases} x + 3y \geq 6 \\ 2x + 4y \geq 10 \\ 3x + y \geq 5 \\ x \geq 0 \\ y \geq 0 \end{cases}$

$(0, 5)$

$3x + y = 5$

$x + 3y = 6$

$2x + 4y = 10$

$2x + 4 =$
$2x = 6$

16. $\begin{cases} x + 4y \geq 10 \\ 4x + 2y \geq 10 \\ x + y \geq 4 \\ x \geq 0 \\ y \geq 0 \end{cases}$

$4x + 2y = 10$ $x + 4y = 10$

$x + y = 4$

In problems 17–32, graph the solution to each system of inequalities.

17. $\begin{cases} y < 2x \\ y > x - 1 \end{cases}$

18. $\begin{cases} y > 3x - 4 \\ y < 2x + 3 \end{cases}$

19. $\begin{cases} 2x + y < 3 \\ x - 2y \geq -1 \end{cases}$

20. $\begin{cases} 3x + y > 4 \\ x - 2y < -1 \end{cases}$

21. $\begin{cases} y \geq 3 - 2x \\ y \geq \frac{1}{2}x + \frac{1}{2} \\ y \geq 3 \end{cases}$

22. $\begin{cases} y \leq x + 1 \\ y \geq 2x - 1 \\ x \geq 0 \\ y \geq 0 \end{cases}$

23. $\begin{cases} x + 5y \leq 200 \\ 2x + 3y \leq 134 \\ x \geq 0, y \geq 0 \end{cases}$

24. $\begin{cases} -x + y \leq 2 \\ x + 2y \leq 10 \\ 3x + y \leq 15 \\ x \geq 0, y \geq 0 \end{cases}$

25. $\begin{cases} x + 2y \leq 48 \\ x + y \leq 30 \\ 2x + y \leq 50 \\ x \geq 0, y \geq 0 \end{cases}$

26. $\begin{cases} 3x + y \leq 9 \\ 3x + 2y \leq 12 \\ x + 2y \leq 8 \\ x \geq 0, y \geq 0 \end{cases}$

27. $\begin{cases} x + 2y \geq 19 \\ 3x + 2y \geq 29 \\ x \geq 0, y \geq 0 \end{cases}$

28. $\begin{cases} 4x + y \geq 12 \\ x + y \geq 9 \\ x + 3y \geq 15 \\ x \geq 0, y \geq 0 \end{cases}$

29. $\begin{cases} x + 3y \geq 3 \\ 2x + 3y \geq 5 \\ 2x + y \geq 3 \\ x \geq 0, y \geq 0 \end{cases}$

30. $\begin{cases} x + 2y \geq 10 \\ 2x + y \geq 11 \\ x + y \geq 9 \\ x \geq, y \geq 0 \end{cases}$

31. $\begin{cases} x + 3y \geq 6 \\ 3x + 4y \geq 13 \\ x \geq 0 \\ y \geq 0 \end{cases}$

32. $\begin{cases} x + 2y \leq 8 \\ 5x + 4y \leq 28 \\ x \geq 0 \\ y \geq 0 \end{cases}$

APPLICATIONS

33. A company manufactures two types of electric hedge-trimmers, one of which is cordless. The cord-type trimmer requires 2 hours to make, and the cordless model requires 4 hours. The company has only 800 work hours to use in manufacturing each day, and the packing department can package only 300 trimmers per day.
    (a) Write the inequalities that describe these constraints on production.
    (b) Graph the region determined by these constraint inequalities.
34. A firm manufactures bumper bolts and fender bolts for cars. One machine can produce 130 fender bolts and another machine can produce 120 bumper bolts per day. The combined number of fender bolts and bumper bolts the packaging department can handle is 230 per day.

(a) Write the inequalities that describe these constraints on production.

(b) Graph the region determined by these constraint inequalities.

35. A candidate wishes to use a combination of radio and television advertisements in his campaign. Research has shown that each 1-minute spot on television reaches 0.09 million people and each 1-minute spot on radio reaches 0.006 million. The candidate feels he must reach at least 2.16 million people, and he must buy a total of at least 80 minutes of advertisements.

(a) Write the inequalities that describe his needs.

(b) Graph the region determined by these constraint inequalities.

36. In a hospital ward, the patients can be grouped into two general categories depending on their condition and the amount of solid foods they require in their diet. A combination of two diets is used for solid foods because they supply essential nutrients for recovery. The table below summarizes the patient group and minimum daily requirements.

	Diet A	Diet B	Daily requirements
Patient group #1	4 oz per serving	1 oz per serving	26 oz
Patient group #2	2 oz per serving	1 oz per serving	18 oz

(a) Write the inequalities that describe these needs.

(b) Graph the region determined by these constraint inequalities.

3.3 Linear Programming: Graphical Methods

Objective ☐ To use graphical methods to find the optimum value of a linear function subject to constraints

Many practical problems in business and economics involve complex relationships between capital, raw material, manpower, and so forth. For example, we may want to find the maximum possible sales or the minimum operating costs subject to certain conditions (constraints), such as available raw material, manpower, and production capacities. If the constraints can be expressed as linear inequalities and if the function that is to be maximized or minimized (called the **objective function**) is a linear function, the problem fits a special mathematical model and can be solved by a technique called **linear programming.** Linear programming can be (and often is) used with nonlinear systems that can be approximated by linear systems, but we will consider only linear functions and inequalities in our discussion.

Frequently linear programming problems involve many variables, but in this section we restrict our discussion to problems involving two variables. With two variables we can use graphical methods to help solve the problem. The constraints form a system of linear inequalities in two variables that we can solve by graphing. The solution to the system of inequalities determines a region, any point of which may yield the *optimum* (maximum or minimum) value for the objective function.* Hence any point in the region determined by the constraints is called a **feasible solution,** and the region itself is called the **feasible region.**

In a linear programming problem, we seek the feasible solution that maximizes (or minimizes) the objective function. For example, suppose we wish to maximize the function $C = 2x + y$ subject to the constraints $x \geq 0$, $y \geq 0$, $x + 3y \leq 6$, and $x + y \leq 4$. The solution set (feasible region) for the system of constraints is shown in Figure 3.13(a). *Any* point inside the shaded region or on its boundary is a feasible solution to the problem. To determine which point will maximize the objective function, we graph $C = 2x + y$, for different values of C, on the same graph containing the feasible region. The different values of C change the position of the line, *but the slope* of the line does not change. Letting $C = 0, 2, 3, 7$, and 8, we get the graphs shown in Figure 3.13(b). If any part of the line lies within the feasible region, we have feasible solutions.

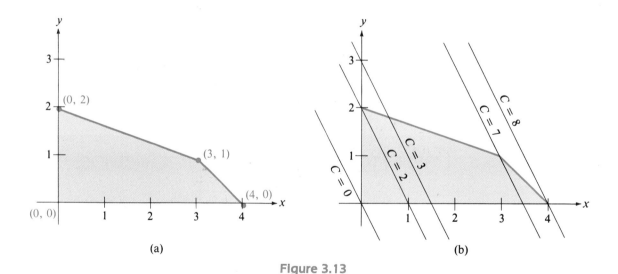

(a)

(b)

Figure 3.13

Since we seek the values of x and y that will maximize $2x + y$, subject to the constraints, we keep trying larger values of C while keeping some part of the line intersecting the feasible region. It is clear from Figure 3.13(b) that any value of C

---

*The region determined by the constraints must be *convex* for the optimum to exist. A convex region is one such that for any two points in the region, the segment joining those points lies entirely within the region. We restrict our discussion to convex regions.

larger than 8 will cause the line $C = 2x + y$ to "miss" the region, and so the maximum value for $2x + y$, subject to the constraints, is 8. The point where the line $8 = 2x + y$ intersects the feasible region is $(4, 0)$, so the function $2x + y$ is maximized when $x = 4$, $y = 0$. Note that the objective function was maximized at one of the "corners" (or vertices) of the feasible region.

The feasible region in Figure 3.13 is an example of a closed and bounded region because it is entirely enclosed by, and includes, the lines associated with the constraints. When the feasible region for a linear programming problem is closed and bounded, the objective function has a maximum value and a minimum value. When the feasible region is not closed and bounded, the objective function may have a maximum only, a minimum only, or no solution. However, if a solution exists, we have the following.

> If a linear programming problem has a solution, then the optimum (maximum or minimum) value of an objective function occurs at a corner of the feasible region determined by the constraints.

Thus, to find the maximum or minimum value of the objective function, we need only evaluate the function at each of the corners of the feasible region formed by the solution of the constraint inequalities. If the objective function has its optimum values at two corners, then it also has that optimum value at any point on the line (boundary) connecting those two corners.

EXAMPLE 1   Maximize $C = 2x + 3y$ subject to the constraints

$$\begin{cases} x + 2y \le 10 \\ 2x + y \le 14 \\ x \ge 0 \\ y \ge 0. \end{cases}$$

Solution   The feasible region determined by the constraint inequalities is shown in Figure 3.14 on the following page. (Note that the region is identical to that in Example 4 of Section 3.2—see Figure 3.12.) We can find the maximum value by evaluating $C = 2x + 3y$ at each of the corner points.

$$\begin{array}{lll} \text{At } (0, 0), & 2x + 3y = & 0 \\ \text{At } (0, 5), & 2x + 3y = & 15 \\ \text{At } (6, 2), & 2x + 3y = & 18 \\ \text{At } (7, 0), & 2x + 3y = & 14 \end{array}$$

Thus we see that C is maximized when $x = 6$ and $y = 2$ and has a maximum value of $C = 18$. See Figure 3.14 on the following page.

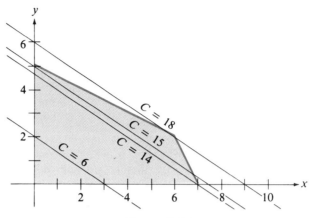

Figure 3.14

The steps involved in solving a linear programming problem are as follows.

Procedure	Example
To solve a linear programming problem:	Example 1 (again)
1. Write the objective function and constraint inequalities from the problem.	1. Objective function: $C = 2x + 3y$ Constraints: $x + 2y \leq 10$ $2x + y \leq 14$ $x \geq 0$ $y \geq 0$
2. Graph the solution to the constraint system.	2. See Figure 3.14.
3. Find the corners of the resulting feasible region. This may sometimes require simultaneous solution of two boundary equations.	3. Corners are $(0, 0)$, $(0, 5)$, $(6, 2)$, $(7, 0)$.
4. Evaluate the objective function at each corner of the feasible region determined by the constraints.	4. At $(0, 0)$, $2x + 3y = 0$. At $(0, 5)$, $2x + 3y = 15$. At $(6, 2)$, $2x + 3y = 18$. At $(7, 0)$, $2x + 3y = 14$.
5. If two corners give the optimum value for the objective function, all points on the boundary line joining these two corners also maximize the function.	5. The function is maximized at $x = 6$, $y = 2$. The maximum value is 18.

Although the examples so far have sought to maximize an objective function, the same procedures apply when a minimum is sought.

EXAMPLE 2   Minimize $C = x + y$ subject to the constraints

$$\begin{cases} 3x + 2y \geq 12 \\ x + 3y \geq 11 \\ x \geq 0, y \geq 0. \end{cases}$$

Solution   The graph of the constraint system is shown in Figure 3.15. Notice that even though the feasible region is not an enclosed polygon, the corners still hold the key to the solution.

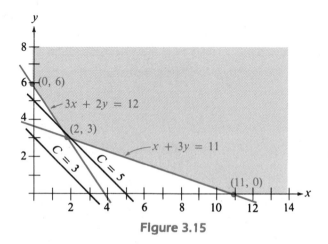

Figure 3.15

The corners $(0, 6)$ and $(11, 0)$ can be identified from the graph. The third corner, $(2, 3)$, can be found by solving the equations of the two lines

$$3x + 2y = 12 \quad \text{and} \quad x + 3y = 11$$

simultaneously, as follows.

$$\begin{array}{r} 3x + 2y = 12 \\ -3x - 9y = -33 \\ \hline -7y = -21 \\ y = 3 \\ x = 2 \end{array}$$

Examining the value of C at each corner point, we have

$$\text{At } (0, 6), \quad C = x + y = 6$$
$$\text{At } (11, 0), \quad C = x + y = 11$$
$$\text{At } (2, 3), \quad C = x + y = 5.$$

So C is minimized at $(2, 3)$ with minimum value $C = 5$. Notice that for any smaller value of C, the graph of $C = x + y$ misses the feasible region.

EXAMPLE 3   A small firm manufactures necklaces and bracelets. The combined number of necklaces and bracelets that it can handle per day is 24. Each bracelet takes 1 hour of labor to make and each necklace takes a half hour. The total number of hours of labor available per day is 16. If the profit on the bracelet is $2 and the profit on the necklace is $1, how many of each product should be produced daily to maximize profit?

Solution   Let x be the number of bracelets produced per day and y be the number of necklaces produced per day. Then the daily profit function is given by the equation $P = 2x + 1y$. Thus we seek to maximize $2x + y$, subject to the constraints.

The constraint on labor indicates that the total number of hours per day is 16, so if x bracelets and y necklaces are made, $1x + \frac{1}{2}y$ must be no more than 16. That is, $x + \frac{1}{2}y \leq 16$. Since only 24 items can be handled each day, the second constraint is expressed as $x + y \leq 24$. Since all quantities must be nonnegative, two additional constraints are $x \geq 0$ and $y \geq 0$.

Thus we seek to solve the following problem.

Maximize $P = 2x + y$ *objective function*

Subject to $\begin{cases} x + \frac{1}{2}y \leq 16 \\ x + y \leq 24 \\ x \geq 0, y \geq 0. \end{cases}$

The set that satisfies the constraints is the shaded area in Figure 3.16.

Convert to slope intercept

$P = x + 2y$

maximum value for objective function well be found at one of the corners

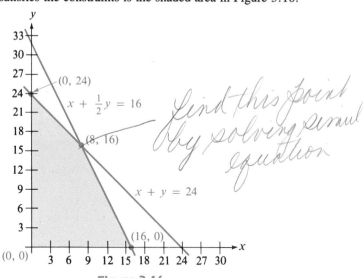

find this point by solving simul. equation

Figure 3.16

The corners of the polygon are $(0, 0)$, $(0, 24)$, $(16, 0)$, and $(8, 16)$. All of these are obvious except for $(8, 16)$, which can be found by solving $x + \frac{1}{2}y = 16$ and $x + y = 24$ simultaneously. Testing the objective function at the corners gives

At $(0, 0)$, $2x + y = 0$
At $(0, 24)$, $2x + y = 24$
At $(16, 0)$, $2x + y = 32$
At $(8, 16)$, $2x + y = 32$.

Thus the maximum value of the function occurs at *either* $x = 16$, $y = 0$ or $x = 8$, $y = 16$, which means that the profit will be maximized at any point on the line joining (8, 16) and (16, 0). For example, the point (12, 8) is on this line, and $2x + y = 32$ at $x = 12$, $y = 8$.

EXAMPLE 4   Two chemical plants produce three grades (A, B, and C) of a certain chemical in a single operation, so the various grades are in fixed proportions. Assume Plant 1 produces 1 unit of A, 2 units of B, and 3 units of C in a single operation, and it charges $300 for what is produced in one operation. Assume one operation at Plant 2 costs the consumer $500 and produces 1 unit of A, 5 units of B, and 1 unit of C. A consumer needs 100 units of A, 260 units of B, and 180 units of C. How should the consumer place orders so that costs are minimized?

Solution   If x represents the number of operations requested from Plant 1 and y represents the number of operations requested from Plant 2, then we seek to minimize cost

$$C = 300x + 500y.$$

The following table summarizes production capabilities and requirements.

	Plant 1	*Plant 2*	*Requirements*
Units of A	1	1	100
Units of B	2	5	260
Units of C	3	1	180

Using the number of operations requested and the fact that requirements must be met or exceeded, we can formulate the following constraints:

$$\begin{cases} x + y \geq 100 \\ 2x + 5y \geq 260 \\ 3x + y \geq 180 \\ x \geq 0, \ y \geq 0. \end{cases}$$

Graphing this system gives the feasible set shown in Figure 3.17 on the following page. The corners are (0, 180), (40, 60), (80, 20), and (130, 0), where (40, 60) is obtained by solving $x + y = 100$ and $3x + y = 180$ simultaneously, and where (80, 20) is obtained by solving $x + y = 100$ and $2x + 5y = 260$ simultaneously.

Evaluating $C = 300x + 500y$ at each corner we obtain

At (0, 180), $C = 90{,}000$
At (40, 60), $C = 42{,}000$
At (80, 20), $C = 34{,}000$
At (130, 0), $C = 39{,}000.$

So to minimize costs the consumer should place orders requiring 80 operations of Plant 1 and 20 operations of Plant 2.

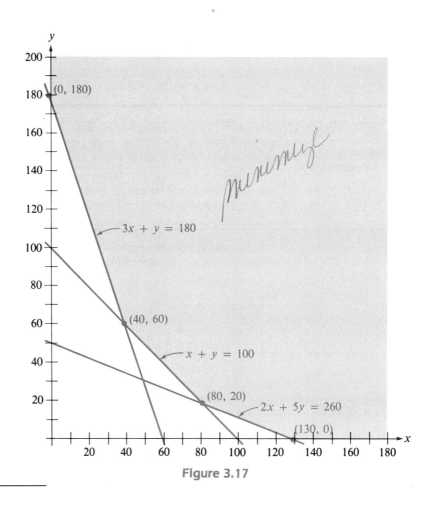

Figure 3.17

Exercise 3.3

In problems 1–6, use the given feasible regions determined by the constraint inequalities to find the maximum and minimum of the given objective function (if they exist).

1. $c = 2x + 3y$

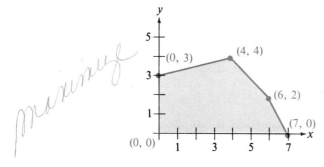

2. $f = 6x + 4y$

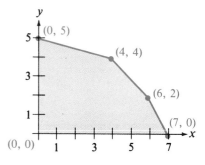

3. $c = 5x + 2y$

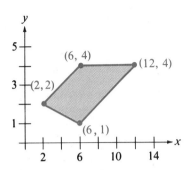

4. $c = 4x + 7y$

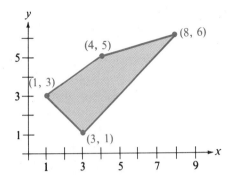

5. $f = 3x + 4y$

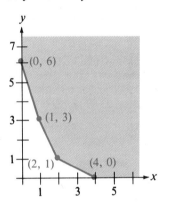

6. $f = 4x + 5y$

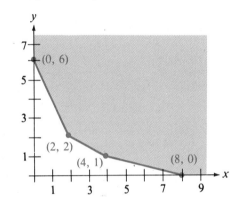

In each of problems 7–10, the graph of the feasible region is shown. Find the corners of each feasible region, and maximize or minimize the function as directed.

7. Maximize $f = 3x + 2y$

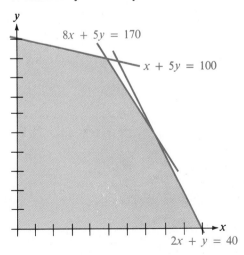

8. Maximize $f = 5x + 8y$

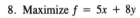
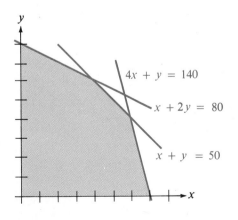

9. Minimize $g = 3x + 2y$

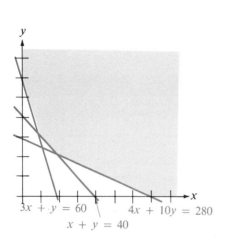

$3x + y = 60$ $4x + 10y = 280$
$x + y = 40$

10. Minimize $g = x + 3y$

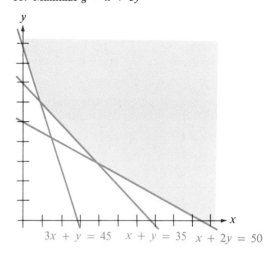

$3x + y = 45$ $x + y = 35$ $x + 2y = 50$

In problems 11–18, find the indicated maximum or minimum value of the objective function in the linear programming problem. Note that the feasible regions for these problems are the solution regions sketched in problems 23–30 of Exercise 3.2.

11. Maximize $f = 4x + 9y$ subject to

$$x + 5y \leq 200$$
$$2x + 3y \leq 134$$
$$x \geq 0, y \geq 0.$$

12. Maximize $f = 2x + y$ subject to

$$-x + y \leq 2$$
$$x + 2y \leq 10$$
$$3x + y \leq 15$$
$$x \geq 0, y \geq 0.$$

13. Maximize $f = 3x + 2y$ subject to

$$x + 2y \leq 48$$
$$x + y \leq 30$$
$$2x + y \leq 50$$
$$x \geq 0, y \geq 0.$$

14. Maximize $f = 7x + 10y$ subject to

$$3x + y \leq 9$$
$$3x + 2y \leq 12$$
$$x + 2y \leq 8$$
$$x \geq 0, y \geq 0.$$

15. Minimize $g = 9x + 10y$ subject to

$$x + 2y \geq 19$$
$$3x + 2y \geq 29$$
$$x \geq 0, y \geq 0.$$

16. Minimize $g = 5x + 2y$ subject to

$$4x + y \geq 12$$
$$x + y \geq 9$$
$$x + 3y \geq 15$$
$$x \geq 0, y \geq 0.$$

17. Minimize $g = 12x + 48y$ subject to

$$x + 3y \geq 3$$
$$2x + 3y \geq 5$$
$$2x + y \geq 3$$
$$x \geq 0, y \geq 0.$$

18. Minimize $g = 12x + 8y$ subject to

$$x + 2y \geq 10$$
$$2x + y \geq 11$$
$$x + y \geq 9$$
$$x \geq 0, y \geq 0.$$

In problems 19–34, solve the following linear programming problems.

19. Maximize $f = x + 3y$ subject to

$$x + 2y \leq 4$$
$$2x + y \leq 4$$
$$x \geq 0, y \geq 0.$$

20. Maximize $f = 3x + 2y$ subject to

$$2x + y \leq 8$$
$$2x + 3y \leq 12$$
$$x \geq 0, y \geq 0.$$

21. Maximize $f = x + 2y$ subject to

$$x + y \geq 4$$
$$2x + y \leq 8$$
$$y \leq 4.$$

22. Maximize $f = 3x + 5y$ subject to

$$2x + 4y \geq 8$$
$$3x + y \leq 7$$
$$y \leq 4.$$

23. Maximize $f = 3x + 4y$ subject to

$$x + y \leq 6$$
$$2x + y \leq 10$$
$$y \leq 4$$
$$x \geq 0, y \geq 0.$$

24. Maximize $f = x + 3y$ subject to

$$x + 4y \leq 12$$
$$y \leq 2$$
$$x + y \leq 9$$
$$x \geq 0, y \geq 0.$$

25. Maximize $f = 2x + 6y$ subject to

$$x + y \leq 7$$
$$2x + y \leq 12$$
$$x + 3y \leq 15$$
$$x \geq 0, y \geq 0.$$

26. Maximize $f = 4x + 2y$ subject to

$$x + 2y \leq 20$$
$$x + y \leq 12$$
$$4x + y \leq 36$$
$$x \geq 0, y \geq 0.$$

27. Minimize $g = 7x + 6y$ subject to

$$5x + 2y \geq 16$$
$$3x + 7y \geq 27$$
$$x \geq 0, y \geq 0.$$

28. Minimize $g = 22x + 17y$ subject to

$$8x + 5y \geq 100$$
$$12x + 25y \geq 360$$
$$x \geq 0, y \geq 0.$$

29. Minimize $g = 3x + y$ subject to

$$4x + y \geq 11$$
$$3x + 2y \geq 12$$
$$x \geq 0, y \geq 0.$$

30. Minimize $g = 50x + 70y$ subject to

$$11x + 15y \geq 225$$
$$x + 3y \geq 27$$
$$x \geq 0, y \geq 0.$$

31. Minimize $g = 3x + 4y$ subject to

$$3x + y \geq 8$$
$$x + y \geq 6$$
$$2x + 5y \geq 18$$
$$x \geq 0, y \geq 0.$$

32. Minimize $g = 3x + 4y$ subject to

$$2x + y \geq 16$$
$$x + y \geq 12$$
$$5x + 8y \geq 75$$
$$x \geq 0, y \geq 0.$$

33. Minimize $g = 51x + 34y$ subject to

$$4x + y \geq 80$$
$$3x + 2y \geq 110$$
$$x + 4y \geq 70$$
$$x \geq 0, y \geq 0.$$

34. Minimize $g = 27x + 63y$ subject to

$$x + y \geq 60$$
$$2x + y \geq 70$$
$$3x + 7y \geq 100$$
$$x \geq 0, y \geq 0.$$

APPLICATIONS

35. A company manufactures two types of electric hedge-trimmers, one of which is cordless. The cord-type trimmer requires 2 hours to make, and the cordless model requires 4 hours. The company has only 800 work hours to use in manufacturing each day, and the packing department can package only 300 trimmers per day. If the company sells the cord-type model for $30 and the cordless model for $40, how many of each type should it produce per day to maximize its sales? (See problem 33 of Exercise 3.2.)

36. A firm manufactures bumper bolts and fender bolts for cars. One machine can produce 130 fender bolts and another machine can produce 120 bumper bolts per day. The combined number of fender bolts and bumper bolts the packaging department can handle is 230 per day. How many of each type of bolt should the firm produce daily to maximize its sales if fender bolts sell for $1 and bumper bolts sell for $2? (See problem 34 of Exercise 3.2.)

37. A privately owned lake contains two types of game fish, I and II. The owner provides two types of food, A and B, for these fish. Species I requires 2 units of food A and 4 units of food B, and species II requires 5 units of food A and 2 units of food B. If the owner has 800 units of each food, find the maximum number of fish that the lake can support.

38. A company makes two different products, Wigbats and Widgets, each of which is begun at one factory and finished at a second factory. Factory A has 1000 labor hours available per day and Factory B has 1200 labor hours available per day. Factory A works 10 hours on each Wigbat and 5 hours on each Widget while Factory B works 6 hours on each Wigbat and 10 hours on each Widget. If only 100 Widgets can be sold, and if the profit on Wigbats is $50 and the profit on Widgets is $25, producing how many of each of these products will maximize profit?

39. A bank has two types of branches. A satellite branch employs 3 people, requires $100,000 to construct and open, and generates an average daily revenue of $10,000. A full-service branch employs 6 people, requires $140,000 to construct and open, and generates an average daily revenue of $18,000. The bank has up to $2.98 million available to open new branches, and has decided to limit the new branches to a maximum of 25. If the bank further decides to hire at most 120 new employees, how many branches of each type should the bank open in order to maximize the average daily revenues?

40. In a zoo, there is a natural habitat containing several feeding areas. One of these areas serves as a feeding area for two species, I and II, and it is supplied each day with 120 pounds of food A, 110 pounds of food B, and 57 pounds of food C. Each individual of species I requires 5 lb of A, 5 lb of B, and 2 lb of C, and each individual of species II requires 6 lb of A, 4 lb of B, and 3 lb of C. Find the maximum number of these species that can be supported.

41. A candidate wishes to use a combination of radio and television advertisements in his campaign. Research has shown that each 1-minute spot on television reaches 0.09 million people and each 1-minute spot on radio reaches 0.006 million. The candidate feels he must reach at least 2.16 million people, and he must buy a total of at least 80 minutes of advertisements. How many minutes of each medium should be used to minimize costs if television costs $500/minute and radio costs $100/minute? (See problem 35 of Exercise 3.2.)

42. In a hospital ward, the patients can be grouped into two general categories depending on their condition and the amount of solid foods they require in their diet. A combination of two diets is used for solid foods because they supply essential nutrients for recovery, but each diet has an amount of a substance deemed detrimental. The table summarizes

the patient group, minimum diet requirements, and the amount of the detrimental substance. How many servings from each diet should be given each day in order to minimize the intake of this detrimental substance? (See problem 36 of Exercise 3.2.)

	Diet A	Diet B	Daily requirements
Patient group #1	4 oz per serving	1 oz per serving	26 oz
Patient group #2	2 oz per serving	1 oz per serving	18 oz
Detrimental substance (oz per serving)	0.18 oz	0.07 oz	

43. Two factories produce three different types of kitchen appliances. The table below summarizes the production capacity, the number of each type of appliance ordered, and the daily operating costs for the factories. How many days should each factory operate to fill the orders at minimum cost?

	Factory 1	Factory 2	Number ordered
Appliance 1	80 per day	20 per day	1600
Appliance 2	10 per day	10 per day	500
Appliance 3	20 per day	70 per day	2000
Daily cost	$10,000	$20,000	

44. In a laboratory experiment, two separate foods are given to experimental animals. Each food contains essential ingredients, A and B, for which the animals have a minimum requirement, and each food also has an ingredient C, which can be harmful to the animals. The table below summarizes this information.

	Food 1	Food 2	Requirements
Ingredient A	10 units per g	3 units per g	49 units
Ingredient B	6 units per g	12 units per g	60 units
Ingredient C	3 units per g	1 unit per g	

How many grams of foods 1 and 2 should be given to the animals in order to satisfy the requirements for A and B while minimizing the amount of ingredient C ingested?

45. The Janie Gioffre Drapery Company makes three types of draperies at two different locations. At location I, they can make 10 pairs of deluxe drapes, 20 pairs of better drapes, and 13 pairs of standard drapes per day. At location II, they can make 20 pairs of deluxe, 50 pairs of better, and 6 pairs of standard per day. The company has orders for 2000 pairs of deluxe drapes, 4200 pairs of better drapes, and 1200 pairs of standard drapes. If the daily costs are $500 per day at location I and $800 per day at location II, how many days should Janie schedule at each location in order to fill the orders at minimum costs? Find the minimum costs.

46. Two foods contain only proteins, carbohydrates, and fats. Food A costs $1 per pound, and contains 30% protein and 50% carbohydrates. Food B costs $1.50 per pound, and contains 20% protein and 75% carbohydrates. What combination of these two foods provides at least 1 pound of protein, $2\frac{1}{2}$ pounds of carbohydrates, and $\frac{1}{4}$ pound of fat at the lowest cost?

3.4 The Simplex Method: Maximization

Objective   ☐   To use the simplex method to maximize functions subject to constraints

The graphical method for solving linear programming problems is suitable only when there are three or fewer variables. If there are more than three variables, we could still find the corners of the convex region by simultaneously solving the equations of the boundaries. The objective function could then be evaluated at these corners. However, as the number of variables and the number of constraints increases, it becomes increasingly difficult to discover the corners and extremely time consuming to evaluate the function. Furthermore, some problems have no solution, and this cannot be determined by using the method of solving the equations simultaneously.

The method discussed in this section is called the **simplex method** for solving linear programming problems. Basically, this method gives a systematic way of moving from one feasible corner of the convex region to another one in such a way that the value of the objective function increases until an optimum value is reached or it is discovered that no solution exists.

The simplex method was first developed by George Dantzig in the late 1940s. One of the earliest applications of the method was to the scheduling problem that arose in connection with the Berlin airlift, begun in 1948. There the objective was to maximize the amount of goods delivered, subject to such constraints as the number of personnel, the number and size of available aircraft, and the number of runways.

In discussing the simplex method, we initially restrict ourselves to linear programming problems satisfying the following conditions.

1. The objective function is to be maximized.

2. All variables are nonnegative.

3. The constraints are of the form

$$a_1x_1 + a_2x_2 + \cdots + a_nx_n \leq b,$$

where $b > 0$.

These may seem to restrict unduly the types of problems, but in applied situations where the objective function is to be maximized, the constraints generally satisfy conditions 2 and 3.

Before outlining a procedure for the simplex method, let us develop that procedure and investigate its rationale by seeing how the simplex method compares to the graphical method.

EXAMPLE 1   Maximize $2x + 3y = f$ subject to

$$\begin{aligned} x + 2y &\leq 10 \\ 2x + y &\leq 14. \end{aligned}$$

Since we assume $x \geq 0$ and $y \geq 0$ in these problems, we shall no longer state these conditions.

Solution   The simplex method uses matrix methods on systems of equations, so we convert the constraint inequalities to equations by using **slack variables.** When we write $x + 2y \leq 10$, this means that some nonnegative number, say s_1, added to $x + 2y$ equals 10. This variable s_1 is called a slack variable because it changes with x and y so that the sum is always 10. Thus

$$x + 2y + s_1 = 10.$$

We can use another slack variable s_2 to write

$$2x + y \leq 14 \quad \text{as} \quad 2x + y + s_2 = 14.$$

If we write the objective function as an equation in the form

$$-2x - 3y + f = 0,$$

then we have a system of equations that describes the problem.

$$\begin{cases} x + 2y + s_1 & = 10 \\ 2x + y & + s_2 & = 14 \\ -2x - 3y & + f = 0 \end{cases}$$

We seek to maximize f in the last equation subject to the constraints in the first two equations.

We can place this system of equations in a matrix called a **simplex matrix** or **simplex tableau.** Note that the objective function is in the last row of this matrix with all variables on the left side, and that the first two rows correspond to the constraints.

$$A = \begin{array}{c} \\ \end{array} \begin{array}{ccccc} x & y & s_1 & s_2 & f \\ \end{array}$$

$$A = \left[\begin{array}{ccccc|c} 1 & 2 & 1 & 0 & 0 & 10 \\ 2 & 1 & 0 & 1 & 0 & 14 \\ -2 & -3 & 0 & 0 & 1 & 0 \end{array} \right] \begin{array}{l} \text{constraint 1} \\ \text{constraint 2} \\ \text{objective} \end{array}$$

From the graph in Figure 3.18, we know that $(0, 0)$ is a feasible solution giving a value of 0 for f. Since the origin is always a feasible solution to the type of linear

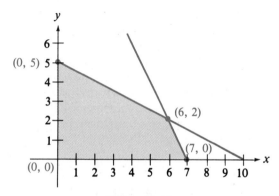

Figure 3.18

programming problems we are considering, the simplex method begins there and systematically moves to new corners while increasing the value of f.

Notice that if $x = 0$ and $y = 0$, then from rows 1, 2, and 3 we can read the values of s_1, s_2, and f, respectively.

$$s_1 = 10, \quad s_2 = 14, \quad f = 0$$

Recall that the last row still corresponds to the objective function $f = 2x + 3y$. If we seek to improve (that is, increase the value of) $f = 2x + 3y$ by changing the value of only one of the variables, then since the coefficient of y is larger, the greatest improvement can be made by increasing y.

> In general, we can find the variable that will improve f most by looking for the *most negative* value in the last row of the simplex matrix. The column containing this value is called the **pivot** column.

The simplex matrix A is shown again below with the y column indicated as the pivot column.

$$A = \begin{array}{c} \\ \end{array} \begin{array}{ccccc} x & y & s_1 & s_2 & f \\ \left[\begin{array}{cc|ccc} 1 & \boxed{2} & 1 & 0 & 0 \\ 2 & 1 & 0 & 1 & 0 \\ \hline -2 & -3 & 0 & 0 & 1 \end{array}\right. & \left.\begin{array}{c} 10 \\ 14 \\ 0 \end{array}\right] \end{array}$$

most negative entry, so pivot column

The amount by which y can be increased is limited by the constraining equations (rows 1 and 2 of the simplex matrix). As the graph in Figure 3.11 (on page 179) shows, the constraints limit y to no larger than $y = 5$. Note that when the positive coefficients in the y-column of the simplex matrix are divided into the constants in the augment, the *smallest* quotient is $10/2 = 5$. The 2 (circled) in row 1, column 2 of the matrix A is called the **pivot entry.** The quotient $y = 5$ is found by setting $x = 0$ and $s_1 = 0$ in the row 1 equation. The point $(0, 5)$ corresponds to a corner adjoining $(0, 0)$ on the constraint region.

We will see that if we continue this method, then the next values for x and y will correspond to another corner of the constraint region.

To continue the solution, note that we used row 1 to determine the largest value for y. We can "transform" the simplex matrix into an equivalent simplex matrix by eliminating y from the remaining rows. If we also multiply the first row by $\frac{1}{2}$, we obtain the equivalent matrix B.

$$B = \begin{array}{ccccc} x & y & s_1 & s_2 & f \\ \left[\begin{array}{cc|ccc} \frac{1}{2} & 1 & \frac{1}{2} & 0 & 0 \\ \boxed{\frac{3}{2}} & 0 & -\frac{1}{2} & 1 & 0 \\ \hline -\frac{1}{2} & 0 & \frac{3}{2} & 0 & 1 \end{array}\right. & \left.\begin{array}{c} 5 \\ 9 \\ 15 \end{array}\right] \end{array}$$

When we look at this transformed simplex matrix, we notice that the function $f = 15 + \frac{1}{2}x - \frac{3}{2}s_1$ depends on x and s_1 and $f = 15$ if $x = 0$ and $s_1 = 0$. Since x was held at 0 and s_1 must be nonnegative, the maximum value of f occurs at this point when $s_1 = 0$. Using $x = 0$ and $s_1 = 0$, rows 1, 2, and 3 allow us to read the values of y, s_2, and f, respectively.

$$y = 5, \qquad s_2 = 9, \qquad f = 15$$

This solution corresponds to the corner $(0, 5)$ in Figure 3.11 on page 179. We also see that the value of f can be increased by increasing the value of x while holding the value s_1 at 0. This is clear from the equation

$$f = 15 + \frac{1}{2}x - \frac{3}{2}s_1$$

or by observing that the most negative number in the last row occurs in the x column of the new matrix B.

The amount of the increase for x is limited by the constraints. We can discover the limitations on x by dividing the coefficient of x (if positive) into the constant term in the augment of each row and choosing the smaller quotient.

$$5 \div \frac{1}{2} = (5)(2) = 10 \qquad \text{from row 1}$$

$$9 \div \frac{3}{2} = (9)\left(\frac{2}{3}\right) = 6 \qquad \text{from row 2}$$

The smaller quotient is 6, so the pivot entry is in row 2, column 1 of B (circled). Note that if we move to a corner adjoining $(0, 5)$ on the region in Figure 3.11, the largest x-value is 6 [at $(6, 2)$].

Let us again transform the simplex matrix B by eliminating x from all but the pivot row (the second row) in B and then multiplying the second row by $\frac{2}{3}$. The new simplex matrix is C.

$$C = \begin{array}{c c} & \begin{array}{ccccc} x & y & s_1 & s_2 & f \end{array} \\ & \left[\begin{array}{ccccc|c} 0 & 1 & \frac{2}{3} & -\frac{1}{3} & 0 & 2 \\ 1 & 0 & -\frac{1}{3} & \frac{2}{3} & 0 & 6 \\ \hline 0 & 0 & \frac{4}{3} & \frac{1}{3} & 1 & 18 \end{array} \right] \end{array}$$

The last row of this new matrix C corresponds to

$$f = 18 - \frac{4}{3}s_1 - \frac{1}{3}s_2$$

so any increase in s_1 or s_2 will cause a *decrease* in f. Observing this, or the fact that all entries of the last row are nonnegative, tells us that we have the optimum solution when $s_1 = 0$ and $s_2 = 0$. Using this, rows 1, 2, and 3 give the values for y, x, and f, respectively.

$$y = 2, \qquad x = 6, \qquad f = 18$$

This corresponds to the corner $(6, 2)$ on the graph and to the graphical solution of $f = 18$ at this corner (which was found in Example 1 of Section 3.3).

As we review the simplex solution in Example 1, observe that each of the feasible solutions corresponded to a corner (x, y) of the feasible region, and that two of the four variables x, y, s_1, and s_2 where equal to 0 at each feasible solution.

At $(0, 0)$: x and y were equal to 0.
At $(0, 5)$: x and s_1 were equal to 0.
At $(6, 2)$: s_1 and s_2 were equal to 0.

The values that were set equal to zero at each feasible solution are called the **nonbasic variables** for that feasible solution, and the other variables are called the **basic variables** for that feasible solution. At each step in the simplex method, we can identify the basic variables directly from the simplex matrix by noting that their columns contain a single entry of 1 with all other entries zeros. (Check this.) The remaining columns identify the nonbasic variables. Thus the values of the basic variables and of the objective function can be read from the rows of the simplex matrix, because the nonbasic variables are set equal to 0 at each step.

The simplex method involves a series of decisions and operations using matrices. It involves three major tasks.

Simplex Method Tasks	Task A:	Setting up the matrix for the simplex method.
	Task B:	Determining necessary row operations and implementing those to reach a solution.
	Task C:	Reading the solution from the simplex matrix.

From Example 1, it should be clear that the pivot selection and row operations of Task B are designed to move the system to the new corner that achieves the greatest increase in the function and at the same time is sensitive to the nonnegative limitations on the variables. The procedure that combines these three tasks to maximize a function is given below.

Procedure	Example
To use the simplex method to solve linear programming problems:	Maximize $f = 2x + 3y$ subject to $$x + 2y \le 10$$ $$2x + y \le 14$$
1. Use slack variables to write the constraints as equations with positive constants on the right side.	1. $x + 2y \le 10$ becomes $x + 2y + s_1 = 10$ $2x + y \le 14$ becomes $2x + y + s_2 = 14$ Maximize f in $-2x - 3y + f = 0$.
2. Set up the simplex matrix. Put the objective function in the last row with all variables on the left and coefficient 1 for f.	2. $\quad x \quad\; y \quad\; s_1 \quad s_2 \quad\; f$ $$\begin{bmatrix} 1 & 2 & 1 & 0 & 0 & 10 \\ 2 & 1 & 0 & 1 & 0 & 14 \\ \hline -2 & -3 & 0 & 0 & 1 & 0 \end{bmatrix}$$

3. Find the pivot:
   (a) The pivot column has the most negative number in the last row. (If a tie occurs, use either column.)

   (b) The positive coefficient in the pivot column that gives the smallest quotient when divided into the constant in the constraint rows of the augment is the pivot entry. If there is a tie, either coefficient may be chosen. If there are no positive coefficients in the pivot column, no solution exists and we stop.

4. Use row operations with only the row containing the pivot entry to make the pivot entry a 1 and all other entries in the pivot column zeros. This makes the variable basic.

5. The numerical entries in the last row are the indicators of what to do next.
   (a) If there is a negative indicator, return to step 3.
   (b) If all indicators are positive or zero, an optimum value has been obtained for the objective function.

6. Read the values of the basic variables and the objective function from the rows of the matrix (after setting the nonbasic variables equal to 0).

---

3. (a)
$$\begin{bmatrix} 1 & 2 & 1 & 0 & 0 & | & 10 \\ 2 & 1 & 0 & 1 & 0 & | & 14 \\ -2 & -3 & 0 & 0 & 1 & | & 0 \end{bmatrix}$$

$\uparrow$ most negative entry, so pivot column

(b) Row 1 quotient: $\dfrac{10}{2} = 5$

Row 2 quotient: $\dfrac{14}{1} = 14$

Therefore, pivot row is row 1.

$$\begin{bmatrix} 1 & ⓶ & 1 & 0 & 0 & | & 10 \\ 2 & 1 & 0 & 1 & 0 & | & 14 \\ -2 & -3 & 0 & 0 & 1 & | & 0 \end{bmatrix}$$

Pivot entry is circled.

4. Row operations:
Multiply row 1 by $\frac{1}{2}$.
Add -1 times new row 1 to row 2.
Add 3 times new row 1 to row 3.

Result:
$$\begin{bmatrix} \frac{1}{2} & 1 & \frac{1}{2} & 0 & 0 & | & 5 \\ \frac{3}{2} & 0 & -\frac{1}{2} & 1 & 0 & | & 9 \\ -\frac{1}{2} & 0 & \frac{3}{2} & 0 & 1 & | & 15 \end{bmatrix}$$

Indicators

5. $-\frac{1}{2}$ is negative, so we identify a new pivot column and reduce again.

$$\begin{bmatrix} \frac{1}{2} & 1 & \frac{1}{2} & 0 & 0 & | & 5 \\ ⓷ & 0 & -\frac{1}{2} & 1 & 0 & | & 9 \\ -\frac{1}{2} & 0 & \frac{3}{2} & 0 & 1 & | & 15 \end{bmatrix}$$
$5 \div \frac{1}{2} = 10$
$9 \div \frac{3}{2} = 6*$

Pivot column   *6 is smaller quotient

The new pivot entry is $\frac{3}{2}$ (circled). Now reduce, using the new pivot row, to obtain:

$$\begin{bmatrix} 0 & 1 & \frac{2}{3} & -\frac{1}{3} & 0 & | & 2 \\ 1 & 0 & -\frac{1}{3} & \frac{2}{3} & 0 & | & 6 \\ 0 & 0 & \frac{4}{3} & \frac{1}{3} & 1 & | & 18 \end{bmatrix}$$
y
x
max value for f

Indicators all 0 or positive, so the solution is complete.

6. f is maximized at 18 when $y = 2$, $x = 6$, $s_1 = 0$, and $s_2 = 0$.

As we look back over our work, we can observe the following:

1. Steps 1 and 2 complete Task A.
2. Steps 3–5 complete Task B.
3. Step 6 completes Task C.

EXAMPLE 2   Complete Tasks A, B, and C to find the maximum value of $f = 4x + 3y$ subject to

$$x + 2y \le 8$$
$$2x + y \le 10.$$

Solution   *Task A:* Introducing the slack variables gives the system of equations

$$\begin{cases} x + 2y + s_1 \qquad\qquad\quad = 8 \\ 2x + y \qquad + s_2 \qquad = 10 \\ -4x - 3y \qquad\qquad + f = 0 \end{cases}$$

Writing this in a matrix with the objective function in the last row gives

$$A = \begin{bmatrix} x & y & s_1 & s_2 & f & \\ 1 & 2 & 1 & 0 & 0 & 8 \\ \boxed{2} & 1 & 0 & 1 & 0 & 10 \\ -4 & -3 & 0 & 0 & 1 & 0 \end{bmatrix} \begin{array}{l} 8/1 = 8 \\ 10/2 = 5* \\ \\ \end{array}$$

$$\uparrow$$
Most negative

Task B: The most negative entry in the last row is -4 (indicated by the arrow), so the pivot column is column 1. The smallest quotient formed by dividing the positive coefficients from column 1 into the constants in the augment is 5 (indicated by the asterisk), so row 2 is the pivot row. Thus, the pivot entry is in row 2, column 1 (circled in matrix A above).

Next use row operations with row 2 only to make the pivot entry equal 1 and all other entries in column 1 equal zero. The row operations are:

(a) Multiply row 2 by $\frac{1}{2}$.

(b) Add -1 times the new row 2 to row 1.

(c) Add 4 times the new row 2 to row 3.

This gives

$$B = \begin{bmatrix} x & y & s_1 & s_2 & f & \\ 0 & \boxed{\tfrac{3}{2}} & 1 & -\tfrac{1}{2} & 0 & 3 \\ 1 & \tfrac{1}{2} & 0 & \tfrac{1}{2} & 0 & 5 \\ 0 & -1 & 0 & 2 & 1 & 20 \end{bmatrix} \begin{array}{l} 3 \div \tfrac{3}{2} = 2* \\ 5 \div \tfrac{1}{2} = 10 \\ \\ \end{array}$$

$$\uparrow$$
Most negative

Since the last row contains a negative entry, we locate another pivot column and continue. The pivot column is indicated with an arrow, and the smallest quotient is indicated with an asterisk. The new pivot entry is circled.

The row operations using this pivot row are:

(a) Multiply row 1 by $\frac{2}{3}$.

(b) Add $-\frac{1}{2}$ times the new row 1 to row 2.

(c) Add the new row 1 to row 3.

This gives

$$
C = \begin{array}{c} \\ \\ \\ \\ \end{array}
\begin{array}{ccccc}
x & y & s_1 & s_2 & f \\
\end{array}
\left[
\begin{array}{ccccc|c}
0 & 1 & \frac{2}{3} & -\frac{1}{3} & 0 & 2 \\
1 & 0 & -\frac{1}{3} & \frac{2}{3} & 0 & 4 \\
0 & 0 & \frac{2}{3} & \frac{5}{3} & 1 & 22 \\
\end{array}
\right]
$$

Because there are no negative indicators in the last row, the solution is complete.

   Task C: s_1 and s_2 are nonbasic variables, so they equal zero. f is maximized at 22 when $y = 2$, $x = 4$, $s_1 = 0$, and $s_2 = 0$.

EXAMPLE 3   A firm manufactures three different types of hand calculators and classifies them as small, medium, and large according to their calculating capabilities. The three types have production requirements given by the following table.

	Small	Medium	Large
Electronic circuit components	5	7	10
Assembly time (h)	1	3	4
Cases	1	1	1

The firm has a monthly limit of 90,000 circuit components, 30,000 hours of labor, and 9000 cases. If the profit is $6 for the small, $13 for the medium, and $20 for the large calculators, how many of each should be produced to yield maximum profit? What is the maximum profit?

Solution   Let x_1 be the number of small calculators produced, x_2 the number of medium calculators produced, and x_3 the number of large calculators produced. Then the problem is to maximize the profit $f = 6x_1 + 13x_2 + 20x_3$ subject to

Inequalities	*Equations with slack variables*

$$
\begin{aligned}
5x_1 + 7x_2 + 10x_3 &\le 90{,}000 \\
x_1 + 3x_2 + 4x_3 &\le 30{,}000 \\
x_1 + x_2 + x_3 &\le 9{,}000
\end{aligned}
$$

and

$$
\begin{aligned}
5x_1 + 7x_2 + 10x_3 + s_1 &= 90{,}000 \\
x_1 + 3x_2 + 4x_3 + s_2 &= 30{,}000 \\
x_1 + x_2 + x_3 + s_3 &= 9{,}000
\end{aligned}
$$

The simplex matrix, with the pivot entry circled, is shown on the following page.

Slack variables

$$\begin{bmatrix} x_1 & x_2 & x_3 & s_1 & s_2 & s_3 & f & \\ 5 & 7 & 10 & 1 & 0 & 0 & 0 & 90,000 \\ 1 & 3 & \boxed{4} & 0 & 1 & 0 & 0 & 30,000 \\ 1 & 1 & 1 & 0 & 0 & 1 & 0 & 9,000 \\ -6 & -13 & -20 & 0 & 0 & 0 & 1 & 0 \end{bmatrix}$$

$90,000/10 = 9,000$
$30,000/4 = 7,500*$
$9,000/1 = 9,000$

↑
Most negative   *Smallest quotient

We now use row operations to change the pivot entry to 1 and create zeros elsewhere in the pivot column. The row operations are

1. Multiply row 2 by $\frac{1}{4}$ to convert the pivot entry to 1.
2. Using the new row 2,
   (a) add -10 times new row 2 to row 1.
   (b) add -1 times new row 2 to row 3.
   (c) add 20 times new row 2 to row 4.

The result is the second simplex matrix:

$$\begin{bmatrix} x_1 & x_2 & x_3 & s_1 & s_2 & s_3 & f & \\ \frac{5}{2} & -\frac{1}{2} & 0 & 1 & -\frac{5}{2} & 0 & 0 & 15,000 \\ \frac{1}{4} & \frac{3}{4} & 1 & 0 & \frac{1}{4} & 0 & 0 & 7500 \\ \boxed{\frac{3}{4}} & \frac{1}{4} & 0 & 0 & -\frac{1}{4} & 1 & 0 & 1500 \\ -1 & 2 & 0 & 0 & 5 & 0 & 1 & 150,000 \end{bmatrix}$$

$15,000 \div \frac{5}{2} = 6000$
$7500 \div \frac{1}{4} = 30,000$
$1500 \div \frac{3}{4} = 2000*$

↑
Most negative   *Smallest quotient

For this new simplex matrix, we check the last row indicators. Since there is an entry that is negative, we repeat the simplex process. Again the pivot entry is circled and we apply row operations similar to the above. What are the row operations this time? The resulting matrix is

$$\begin{bmatrix} x_1 & x_2 & x_3 & s_1 & s_2 & s_3 & f & \\ 0 & -\frac{4}{3} & 0 & 1 & -\frac{5}{3} & -\frac{10}{3} & 0 & 10,000 \\ 0 & \frac{2}{3} & 1 & 0 & \frac{1}{3} & -\frac{1}{3} & 0 & 7000 \\ 1 & \frac{1}{3} & 0 & 0 & -\frac{1}{3} & \frac{4}{3} & 0 & 2000 \\ 0 & \frac{7}{3} & 0 & 0 & \frac{14}{3} & \frac{4}{3} & 1 & 152,000 \end{bmatrix}$$

Checking the last row, we see all the entries are 0 or positive, so the solution is complete. Setting $x_2 = 0$, $s_2 = 0$, and $s_3 = 0$ (the nonbasic variables), we see from the matrix that $x_1 = 2000$, $x_3 = 7000$, $s_1 = 10,000$, and $f = 152,000$.

Thus the number of calculators that should be produced is ⟩ *correct answer*

$$x_1 = 2000 \text{ small calculators,}$$
$$x_2 = 0 \text{ medium calculators,}$$
$$x_3 = 7000 \text{ large calculators,}$$

in order to obtain a maximum profit of \$152,000 for the month. Note that s_1 being nonzero means that some circuit components are not used in this optimal situation.

Nonunique Solutions

Note all linear programming problems result in unique solutions. In fact, we have seen that the problem in Example 3 of Section 3.3 had an infinite number of solutions (on the line between (8, 16) and (16, 0)). Let us solve this same problem using the simplex method.

The objective function to be maximized is

$$f = 2x + y$$

subject to the constraints

$$x + \tfrac{1}{2}y \le 16$$
$$x + y \le 24 \cdot$$

The simplex matrix (with the slack variables introduced) is

$$
\begin{array}{ccccc}
x & y & s_1 & s_2 & f \\
\end{array}
$$
$$
\left[
\begin{array}{ccccc|c}
① & \tfrac{1}{2} & 1 & 0 & 0 & 16 \\
1 & 1 & 0 & 1 & 0 & 24 \\
\hline
-2 & -1 & 0 & 0 & 1 & 0 \\
\end{array}
\right].
$$

The most negative value in the last row is -2, so the x column is the pivot column. The smallest quotient occurs in row 1; the pivot entry (circled) is 1. Making x a basic variable gives the following transformed simplex matrix.

$$
\begin{array}{ccccc}
x & y & s_1 & s_2 & f \\
\end{array}
$$
$$
\left[
\begin{array}{ccccc|c}
1 & \tfrac{1}{2} & 1 & 0 & 0 & 16 \\
0 & \tfrac{1}{2} & -1 & 1 & 0 & 8 \\
\hline
0 & 0 & 2 & 0 & 1 & 32 \\
\end{array}
\right]
$$

This simplex matrix has no negative indicators, so the optimum value of f has been found ($f = 32$ when $x = 16$, $y = 0$). Note that one of the nonbasic variables

(y) has a zero indicator. When this occurs, there frequently are multiple solutions to the linear programming problem. (We have seen that $x = 16$, $y = 0$ and $x = 8$, $y = 16$ are solutions in Section 3.3.)

> When the simplex matrix for the optimum value of f has a nonbasic variable with a zero indicator in its column, there may be multiple solutions giving the *same* optimum value for f. We can discover if another solution exists by using the column of that nonbasic variable as the pivot column.

Thus in the example above, if we use the y-column as the pivot column, then we could find the second solution. You will be asked to do this in problem 39 of Exercise 3.4.

It is also possible for a linear programming problem to have an unbounded solution (and thus no maximum value for f). This is identified by the following conditions in the simplex method.

> If, after finding the pivot column, there are no positive coefficients in that column, no maximum solution exists.

EXAMPLE 4   Maximize $f = 2x_1 + x_2 + 2x_3$ subject to

$$x_1 - 3x_2 + x_3 \leq 3$$
$$x_1 - 6x_2 + 2x_3 \leq 6$$

if a maximum exists.

Solution   The simplex matrix for this problem (after introduction of slack variables) is

$$
\begin{array}{cccccc}
x_1 & x_2 & x_3 & s_1 & s_2 & f \\
\end{array}
$$

$$
\left[
\begin{array}{cccccc|c}
1 & -3 & \boxed{1} & 1 & 0 & 0 & 3 \\
1 & -6 & 2 & 0 & 1 & 0 & 6 \\
\hline
-2 & -1 & \boxed{-2} & 0 & 0 & 1 & 0 \\
\end{array}
\right]
$$

We see that the x_1 column and the x_3 column have the same most negative number, so we can use either column as the pivot column.

Using the x_3 column as the pivot column, we see that the smallest quotient is 3. Both coefficients give this quotient, so we can use either coefficient as the pivot entry. Using the element in row 1, we can make x_3 basic. The new simplex matrix is

$$
\begin{array}{cccccc}
x_1 & x_2 & x_3 & s_1 & s_2 & f \\
\end{array}
$$

$$
\left[
\begin{array}{cccccc|c}
1 & -3 & 1 & 1 & 0 & 0 & 3 \\
-1 & 0 & 0 & -2 & 1 & 0 & 0 \\
\hline
0 & -7 & 0 & 2 & 0 & 1 & 6 \\
\end{array}
\right]
$$

The most negative value in the last row of this matrix is -7, so the pivot column is the x_2 column. But there are no positive coefficients in the x_2 column, so no solution exists for this problem. That is, there is no maximum value for f.

Some difficulties can arise in using the simplex method to solve linear programming problems. In the solution process, it is possible for the same simplex matrix to recur before an optimum value for the objective function is obtained. These "degeneracies" are discussed in more advanced courses. They rarely occur in applied linear programming problems, and we shall not encounter them in this text.

Exercise 3.4

Task A: In problems 1–6 set up the simplex matrix used to solve each linear programming problem.

1. Maximize $f = 2x + 4y$ subject to
$$2x + 5y \le 30$$
$$x + 5y \le 25.$$

2. Maximize $f = x + 5y$ subject to
$$3x + 7y \le 20$$
$$7x + 4y \le 44.$$

3. Maximize $f = 4x + 9y$ subject to
$$x + 5y \le 200$$
$$2x + 3y \le 134.$$

4. Maximize $f = x + 3y$ subject to
$$5x + y \le 50$$
$$x + 2y \le 50.$$

5. Maximize $f = 2x + 5y + 2z$ subject to
$$2x + 7y + 9z \le 100$$
$$6x + 5y + z \le 145$$
$$x + 2y + 7z \le 90.$$

6. Maximize $f = 3x + 5y + 11z$ subject to
$$2x + 3y + 4z \le 60$$
$$x + 4y + z \le 48$$
$$5x + y + z \le 48.$$

Task B: In problems 7–10, a simplex matrix is given. In each case identify the pivot element.

7. $$\begin{bmatrix} 2 & 4 & 1 & 0 & 0 & | & 24 \\ 1 & 1 & 0 & 1 & 0 & | & 5 \\ -4 & -11 & 0 & 0 & 1 & | & 0 \end{bmatrix}$$

8. $$\begin{bmatrix} 3 & 1 & 1 & 1 & 0 & 0 & | & 100 \\ 4 & 3 & 6 & 0 & 1 & 0 & | & 250 \\ -5 & -3 & -4 & 0 & 0 & 1 & | & 0 \end{bmatrix}$$

9. $$\begin{bmatrix} 10 & 27 & 1 & 0 & 0 & 0 & | & 200 \\ 4 & 51 & 0 & 1 & 0 & 0 & | & 400 \\ 15 & 27 & 0 & 0 & 1 & 0 & | & 350 \\ -6 & -7 & 0 & 0 & 0 & 1 & | & 0 \end{bmatrix}$$

10. $$\begin{bmatrix} 5 & 5 & 7 & 1 & 0 & 0 & 0 & | & 12 \\ 4 & 0 & 6 & 0 & 1 & 0 & 0 & | & 48 \\ 0 & 1 & 1 & 0 & 0 & 1 & 0 & | & 8 \\ -1 & -3 & -1 & 0 & 0 & 0 & 1 & | & 0 \end{bmatrix}$$

Task B: In problems 11–18, a simplex matrix is given. Examine the indicators and determine if the solution is complete or not. If it is not complete, find the next pivot element; if it is complete, indicate this.

11.
$$\begin{bmatrix} 2 & 0 & 1 & -\frac{3}{4} & 0 & 12 \\ 3 & 1 & 0 & \frac{1}{3} & 0 & 15 \\ -4 & 0 & 0 & 3 & 1 & 15 \end{bmatrix}$$

12.
$$\begin{bmatrix} 0 & 4 & 1 & -\frac{1}{5} & 0 & 2 \\ 1 & 2 & 0 & 1 & 0 & 4 \\ 0 & 2 & 0 & 2 & 1 & 12 \end{bmatrix}$$

13.
$$\begin{bmatrix} 4 & 1 & 0 & 0 & \frac{3}{4} & 4 & 0 & 14 \\ -2 & 0 & 0 & 1 & -\frac{5}{8} & -2 & 0 & 6 \\ 3 & 0 & 1 & 0 & 2 & 6 & 0 & 11 \\ 4 & 0 & 0 & 0 & 2 & \frac{1}{2} & 1 & 525 \end{bmatrix}$$

14.
$$\begin{bmatrix} 2 & 1 & 1 & 0 & 0 & 0 & 12 \\ -2 & 0 & -1 & 0 & 1 & 0 & 5 \\ 4 & 0 & 2 & 1 & 0 & 0 & 6 \\ -2 & 0 & 5 & 0 & 0 & 1 & 30 \end{bmatrix}$$

15.
$$\begin{bmatrix} 4 & 4 & 1 & 0 & 0 & 2 & 0 & 12 \\ 2 & 4 & 0 & 1 & 0 & -1 & 0 & 4 \\ -3 & -11 & 0 & 0 & 1 & -1 & 0 & 6 \\ -3 & -3 & 0 & 0 & 0 & 4 & 1 & 150 \end{bmatrix}$$

16.
$$\begin{bmatrix} 0 & 0 & -3 & 4 & -4 & 0 & 12 \\ 0 & 1 & -4 & 2 & 5 & 0 & 100 \\ 1 & 0 & -1 & -6 & -3 & 0 & 40 \\ 0 & 0 & 6 & -1 & -3 & 1 & 380 \end{bmatrix}$$

17.
$$\begin{bmatrix} 4 & -1 & 0 & 1 & -5 & 0 & 0 & 5 \\ 1 & 0 & 1 & 0 & 1 & 0 & 0 & 12 \\ 3 & -3 & 0 & 0 & -2 & 1 & 0 & 6 \\ -2 & -5 & 0 & 0 & 10 & 0 & 1 & 120 \end{bmatrix}$$

18.
$$\begin{bmatrix} 0 & 20 & -6 & 1 & 0 & -3 & 0 & 4 \\ 0 & 5 & -6 & 0 & 1 & -2 & 0 & 2 \\ 1 & -1 & 0 & 0 & 0 & 4 & 0 & 6 \\ 0 & -9 & -12 & 0 & 0 & 10 & 1 & 20 \end{bmatrix}$$

Task C: In problems 19–24, a simplex matrix is given. In each case the solution is complete, so identify the maximum value of f and a set of values of the variables that gives this maximum value.

19.
$$\begin{bmatrix} 1 & 0 & \frac{3}{4} & -\frac{3}{4} & 0 & 11 \\ 0 & 1 & \frac{5}{12} & \frac{11}{12} & 0 & 9 \\ 0 & 0 & 2 & 4 & 1 & 20 \end{bmatrix}$$

20. $\begin{bmatrix} 0 & 4 & 1 & -\frac{1}{5} & 0 & 2 \\ 1 & 2 & 0 & 1 & 0 & 4 \\ 0 & 2 & 0 & 2 & 1 & 12 \end{bmatrix}$

21. $\begin{bmatrix} 4 & 1 & 0 & 0 & \frac{3}{4} & 43 & 0 & 14 \\ -2 & 0 & 0 & 1 & -\frac{8}{5} & -2 & 0 & 6 \\ 3 & 0 & 1 & 0 & 2 & 6 & 0 & 11 \\ 4 & 0 & 0 & 0 & 2 & \frac{1}{2} & 1 & 525 \end{bmatrix}$

max f=525 when x=0, y=14, z=11

22. $\begin{bmatrix} 0 & 1 & 0 & -3 & -1 & -4 & 0 & 12 \\ 1 & 0 & 0 & -2 & -1 & -5 & 0 & 16 \\ 0 & 0 & 1 & -1 & 2 & 1 & 0 & 22 \\ 0 & 0 & 0 & 4 & 1 & 2 & 1 & 150 \end{bmatrix}$

23. $\begin{bmatrix} 1 & 0 & 3 & 0 & 6 & 0 & 50 \\ 0 & 0 & 4 & 1 & -4 & 0 & 6 \\ 0 & 1 & -2 & 0 & 2 & 0 & 10 \\ 0 & 0 & 9 & 0 & 0 & 1 & 100 \end{bmatrix}$

max f=100 when x=50, y=10, z=0

24. $\begin{bmatrix} 0 & 1 & 2 & 1 & 0 & 0 & 20 \\ 1 & 0 & 6 & 1 & 0 & 0 & 50 \\ 0 & 0 & -1 & -2 & 1 & 0 & 10 \\ 0 & 0 & 4 & 0 & 0 & 1 & 88 \end{bmatrix}$

In problems 25–38, use the simplex method to maximize the given functions. Assume $x \geq 0$, $y \geq 0$ in all problems.

25. Maximize $f = 3x + 10y$ subject to
$$14x + 7y \leq 35$$
$$5x + 5y \leq 50.$$

26. Maximize $f = 7x + 10y$ subject to
$$14x + 14y \leq 98$$
$$8x + 10y \leq 100.$$

27. Maximize $f = 2x + 3y$ subject to
$$x + 2y \leq 10$$
$$x + y \leq 7.$$

28. Maximize $f = 5x + 30y$ subject to
$$2x + 10y \leq 96$$
$$x + 10y \leq 90.$$

29. Maximize $f = x + 3y$ subject to
$$x + 2y \leq 12$$
$$y \leq 5$$
$$x + y \leq 9.$$

30. Maximize $f = 2x + 6y$ subject to
$$2x + 5y \leq 30$$
$$x + 5y \leq 25$$
$$x + y \leq 11.$$

31. Maximize $f = 2x + y$ subject to
$$-x + y \leq 2$$
$$x + 2y \leq 10$$
$$3x + y \leq 15.$$

32. Maximize $f = 3x + 2y$ subject to
$$x + 2y \leq 48$$
$$x + y \leq 30$$
$$2x + y \leq 50$$
$$x + 10y \leq 200.$$

In problems 33–38, assume $x \geq 0$, $y \geq 0$, and $z \geq 0$.

33. Maximize $f = 7x + 10y + 4z$ subject to
$$3x + 5y + 4z \leq 30$$
$$3x + 2y \leq 4$$
$$x + 2y \leq 8.$$

34. Maximize $f = 64x + 36y + 38z$ subject to
$$4x + 2y + 2z \leq 40$$
$$8x + 10y + 5z \leq 90$$
$$4x + 4y + 3z \leq 30.$$

$\begin{bmatrix} 14 & 7 & 1 & 0 & 0 & 35 \\ 5 & 5 & 0 & 1 & 0 & 50 \\ -3 & -10 & 0 & 0 & 1 & 0 \end{bmatrix}$

$\begin{bmatrix} 1 & 2 & 1 & 0 & 0 & 10 \\ 1 & 1 & 0 & 1 & 0 & 7 \\ -2 & -3 & 0 & 0 & 1 & 0 \end{bmatrix}$

$\begin{bmatrix} 1 & 2 & 1 & 0 & 0 & 0 & 12 \\ 0 & 1 & 0 & 1 & 0 & 0 & 5 \\ 1 & 1 & 0 & 0 & 1 & 0 & 9 \\ -1 & -3 & 0 & 0 & 0 & 1 & 0 \end{bmatrix}$

$\begin{bmatrix} -1 & 1 & 1 & 0 & 0 & 0 & 2 \\ 1 & 2 & 0 & 1 & 0 & 0 & 10 \\ 3 & 1 & 0 & 0 & 1 & 0 & 15 \\ -2 & -1 & 0 & 0 & 0 & 1 & 0 \end{bmatrix}$

$\begin{bmatrix} 3 & 2 & 0 & 1 & 0 & 0 & 0 & 4 \\ 1 & 2 & 0 & 0 & 1 & 0 & 0 & 8 \\ 3 & 5 & 4 & 0 & 0 & 1 & 0 & 30 \\ 7 & -10 & -4 & 0 & 0 & 0 & 1 & 0 \end{bmatrix}$

35. Maximize $f = 20x + 12y + 12z$
subject to

$$x +   z \le 40$$
$$x + y \le 30$$
$$y + z \le 40.$$

36. Maximize $f = 10x + 5y + 4z$
subject to

$$2x + y + z \le 50$$
$$x + 3y \le 20$$
$$y + z \le 15.$$

37. Maximize $f = 10x + 8y + 5z$
subject to

$$2x + y + z \le 40$$
$$x + 2y \le 10$$
$$y + 3z \le 80.$$

38. Maximize $f = x + 3y + z$ subject to

$$x + 4y \le 12$$
$$3x + 6y + 4z \le 48$$
$$y + z \le 8.$$

Problems 39–44 involve linear programming problems that have nonunique solutions.

The simplex matrices shown in problems 39 and 40 indicate that an optimal solution has been found, but that a second solution is possible. Find the second solution.

39. $$\begin{bmatrix} 1 & \frac{1}{2} & 1 & 0 & 0 & 16 \\ 0 & \frac{1}{2} & -1 & 1 & 0 & 8 \\ 0 & 0 & 2 & 0 & 1 & 32 \end{bmatrix}$$

40. $$\begin{bmatrix} 1 & 2 & 0 & 1 & 0 & 40 \\ 0 & 1 & 1 & 2 & 0 & 15 \\ 0 & 0 & 0 & 4 & 1 & 90 \end{bmatrix}$$

In problems 41–44, use the simplex method to maximize each function (whenever possible) subject to the given constraints. If there is no solution, indicate this; if multiple solutions exist, find two of them.

41. Maximize $f = 3x + 2y$ subject to

$$x - 10y \le 10$$
$$-x + y \le 40.$$

42. Maximize $f = 10x + 15y$ subject to

$$-5x + y \le 24$$
$$2x - 3y \le 9.$$

43. Maximize $f = 3x + 12y$ subject to

$$2x + y \le 120$$
$$x + 4y \le 200.$$

44. Maximize $f = 8x + 6y$ subject to

$$4x + 3y \le 24$$
$$10x + 9y \le 198.$$

APPLICATIONS

45. An experiment involves placing the males and females of a laboratory animal species in two separate controlled environments. There is a limited time available in these environments, and the experimenter wishes to maximize the number of animals subject to the constraints described.

	Males	Females	Time available
Environment A	20 min	25 min	800 min
Environment B	20 min	15 min	600 min

How many males and how many females will maximize the total number of animals?

t = # of crates of tomatoes
p = # of crates of peaches

$.5t + 1.25p \le 2500$
$60t + 50p \le 120,000$
$f = t + 2p$ (47)

$$\begin{bmatrix} .5 & 1.25 & 1 & 0 & 0 & 2500 \\ 60 & 50 & 0 & 1 & 0 & 120000 \\ 1 & -2 & 0 & 0 & 1 & 0 \end{bmatrix}$$

x = newspaper ads
y = radio ads

$100x + 300y \le 6000$
$x \le 21$
$y \le 28$
$z = 6000x + 8000y$

46. A firm produces two products, both of which use two departments of its factory. Product X requires one hour in department A and 5 hours in department B, while product Y requires 2 hours in department A and 3 hours in department B. Two hundred hours are available in department A and 134 are available in department B. If the profit on product X is $4 and the profit on product Y is $9, how many of each product should be produced to maximize the profit for the firm?

47. A produce wholesaler has determined that it takes $\frac{1}{2}$ hour of labor to sort and pack a crate of tomatoes, and it takes $1\frac{1}{4}$ hours to sort and pack a crate of peaches. The crate of tomatoes weighs 60 pounds, and the crate of peaches weighs 50 pounds. The wholesaler has 2500 hours of labor available each week and can ship 120,000 pounds per week. If profits are $1 per crate of tomatoes and $2 per crate of peaches, how many crates of each should be sorted, packed, and shipped to maximize profits? What is the maximum profit?

48. A manufacturer has two resources available, R_1 and R_2. These resources can be used to produce two different products, A and B, in the following way.

2 units of R_1 and 5 units of R_2 give 1 unit of A
5 units of R_1 and 5 units of R_2 give 1 unit of B
30 units of R_1 and 25 units of R_2 are available

The profit for A is $2 per unit, and the profit for B is $4 per unit. How many units of product A and B should be produced to maximize profit?

49. Tire Corral has $6000 available per month for advertising. Newspaper ads cost $100 each and can occur a maximum of 21 times per month. Radio ads cost $300 each and can occur a maximum of 28 times per month at this price. Each newspaper ad reaches 6000 men over 20 years of age and each radio ad reaches 8000 of these men. The company wants to maximize the number of ad exposures to this group. How many of each ad should it purchase?

50. A bicycle manufacturer makes a ten-speed and a regular bicycle. The ten-speed requires 2 units of steel and 6 units of aluminum in its frame and 12 special components for the hub, sprocket, and gear assembly. The regular bicycle requires 5 units each of steel and aluminum for its frame and 5 of the special components. Shipments are such that steel is limited to 100 units per day, aluminum is limited to 120 units per day, and the special components are limited to 180 units per day. If the profit is $30 on each ten-speed and $20 on each regular bike, how many of each should be produced to yield maximum profit? What is the maximum profit?

51. The total advertising budget for a firm is $200,000. The following table gives the costs per ad package for each medium and the number of exposures per ad package (with all numbers in thousands).

$f = 3100x_1 + 2000x_2 + 2400x_3$
$x_1 \le 18$
$x_2 \le 10$
$x_3 \le 12$
$x_1 + x_2 + x_3 \le 200,000$

	x_1 Medium 1	x_2 Medium 2	x_3 Medium 3
Cost/package	10	4	5
Exposures/ package	3100	2000	2400

If the maximum number of medium 1, medium 2, and medium 3 packages that can be purchased is 18, 10, and 12, respectively, how many of each ad package should be purchased to maximize the number of ad exposures?

$$\begin{bmatrix} 10 & 4 & 5 & 1 & 0 & 0 & 0 & 0 & 200,000 \\ 1 & 0 & 0 & 0 & 1 & 0 & 0 & 0 & 18 \\ 0 & 1 & 0 & 0 & 0 & 1 & 0 & 0 & 10 \\ 0 & 0 & 1 & 0 & 0 & 0 & 1 & 0 & 12 \\ -3100 & -2000 & -2400 & 0 & 0 & 0 & 0 & 1 & 0 \end{bmatrix}$$

52. The Laposata Pasta Company has $12,000 available for advertising. The following table gives the cost per ad and number of people exposed to its ads in three different media (with numbers in thousands).

Ad packages	Newspaper	Radio	TV
Cost	2	2	4
Total audience	30	21	54
Working mothers	6	12	8

If the total available audience is 420,000, and if it wishes to maximize the number of exposures to working mothers, how many ads of each type should it purchase?

53. A firm has decided to discontinue production of an unprofitable product. This will create excess capacity, and the firm is considering one or more of three possible new products, A, B, and C. The available weekly hours in the plant will be 477 hours in tool and die, 350 hours on the drill presses, and 150 hours on lathes. The hours of production required in each of these areas are as follows for each of the products.

[handwritten notes in margin:]
$f = 30A + 9B + 15C$

$A \geq 0$
$B \leq 20$
$C \geq 0$

$\begin{bmatrix} 9 & 3 & .5 & 1 & 0 & 0 & 0 & 477 \\ 5 & 4 & 0 & 0 & 1 & 0 & 0 & 350 \\ 3 & 0 & 2 & 0 & 0 & 1 & 0 & 150 \end{bmatrix}$

	Tool and die	Drill press	Lathe
A	9	5	3
B	3	4	0
C	0.5	0	2

[handwritten under table:] 477   350   150

Furthermore, the sales department foresees no limitations on the sale of products A and C, but sees sales of only 20 or fewer per week for B. If the unit profits expected are $30 for A, $9 for B, and $15 for C, how many of each should be produced to maximize profits? What is the maximum profit?

54. A medical clinic performs three types of medical tests that use the same machines. Tests A, B, and C take 15 minutes, 30 minutes, and 1 hour, respectively, with respective profits of $30, $50, and $100. The clinic has 4 machines available. One person is qualified to do test A, two to do test B, and one to do test C. If the clinic has a rush of customers for these tests, how many of each type should it schedule in a 12-hour day to maximize its profit?

3.5 The Simplex Method: Minimization

Objectives
- ☐ To formulate the dual for minimization problems
- ☐ To solve minimization problems using the simplex method on the dual

We have solved both maximization and minimization problems using graphical methods, but the simplex method, as discussed in Section 3.4, applies only to maximization problems. Now let us turn our attention to extending the use of the simplex method to solve minimization problems. Such problems might arise when a company seeks to minimize its production costs yet fill customer's orders or purchase items necessary for production.

As with maximization problems, we shall limit our discussion of minimization problems to only those in which the constraints satisfy the following conditions.

1. All variables are nonnegative.

2. The constraints are of the form

$$a_1y_1 + a_2y_2 + \cdots + a_ny_n \geq b,$$

where b is positive.

In this section, we will show how minimization problems of this type can be solved using the simplex method.

EXAMPLE 1   Minimize $g = 11y_1 + 7y_2$ subject to

$$y_1 + 2y_2 \geq 10$$
$$3y_1 + y_2 \geq 15.$$

Solution   Since the simplex method specifically seeks to increase the objective function, it does not apply to this minimization problem. So, rather than solve this problem, let us solve a different but related problem called the **dual problem.**

In forming the **dual problem,** we write a matrix A that has a form similar to the simplex matrix, but without slack variables and with positive coefficients for the variables in the last row (and with the function to be minimized in the augment).

$$A = \begin{bmatrix} 1 & 2 & 10 \\ 3 & 1 & 15 \\ 11 & 7 & g \end{bmatrix}$$

The matrix for the dual problem is formed by interchanging the rows and columns of matrix A. Matrix B is the result of this procedure, and we say that B is the *transpose* of A.

$$B = \begin{bmatrix} 1 & 3 & 11 \\ 2 & 1 & 7 \\ 10 & 15 & g \end{bmatrix}$$

Notice that row 1 of A became column 1 of B, row 2 of A became column 2 of B, and row 3 of A became column 3 of B.

In the same way that we formed matrix A, we can now "convert back" from the matrix B to the maximization problem that is the dual of the original minimization problem. We state this dual problem, using different letters to emphasize that this is a different problem from the original.

Maximize $f = 10x_1 + 15x_2$ subject to

$$x_1 + 3x_2 \leq 11$$
$$2x_1 + x_2 \leq 7.$$

The simplex method does apply to this maximization problem, with the following simplex matrix.

$$\begin{array}{ccccc} x_1 & x_2 & s_1 & s_2 & f \\ \left[\begin{array}{ccccc|c} 1 & 3 & 1 & 0 & 0 & 11 \\ 2 & 1 & 0 & 1 & 0 & 7 \\ \hline -10 & -15 & 0 & 0 & 1 & 0 \end{array}\right] \end{array}$$

Successive matrices that occur using the simplex method are shown below with each pivot entry circled.

Beside the maximization problem is the solution to the original minimization problem, obtained using graphical methods.

Maximization Problem		Minimization Problem

1.
$$\begin{array}{ccccc} x_1 & x_2 & s_1 & s_2 & f \\ \left[\begin{array}{ccccc|c} 1 & ③ & 1 & 0 & 0 & 11 \\ 2 & 1 & 0 & 1 & 0 & 7 \\ \hline -10 & -15 & 0 & 0 & 1 & 0 \end{array}\right] \end{array}$$

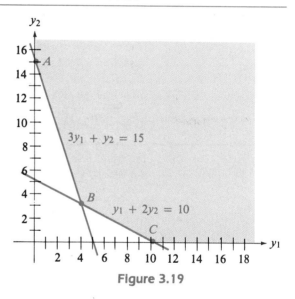

Figure 3.19

2.
$$\left[\begin{array}{ccccc|c} \frac{1}{3} & 1 & \frac{1}{3} & 0 & 0 & \frac{11}{3} \\ ⑤⁄₃ & 0 & -\frac{1}{3} & 1 & 0 & \frac{10}{3} \\ \hline -5 & 0 & 5 & 0 & 1 & 55 \end{array}\right]$$

Corners:

$A = (0, 15)$ ⎱ obtained by solving
$B = (4, 3)$ ⎰ simultaneously
$C = (10, 0)$

3.
$$\left[\begin{array}{ccccc|c} 0 & 1 & \frac{2}{5} & -\frac{1}{5} & 0 & 3 \\ 1 & 0 & -\frac{1}{5} & \frac{3}{5} & 0 & 2 \\ \hline 0 & 0 & 4 & 3 & 1 & 65 \end{array}\right]$$

$g = 11y_1 + 7y_2;$
at A, $g = 105$
at B, $g = 65$
at C, $g = 110$

Maximum $f = 65$ occurs at $x_1 = 2, x_2 = 3$.

Minimum $g = 65$ occurs at $y_1 = 4, y_2 = 3$.

In comparing the solutions to the previous two problems the first thing to notice is that the maximum value for f in the maximization problem and the minimum value for g in the minimization problem are the same. Furthermore, looking at the final simplex matrix, we can also find the values of y_1 and y_2 that give the minimum value for g by looking at the last row of the matrix.

$$
\begin{array}{ccccc}
x_1 & x_2 & s_1 & s_2 & f \\
\end{array}
$$

$$
\left[
\begin{array}{ccccc|c}
0 & 1 & \frac{2}{5} & -\frac{1}{5} & 0 & 3 \\
1 & 0 & -\frac{1}{5} & \frac{3}{5} & 0 & 2 \\
\hline
0 & 0 & 4 & 3 & 1 & 65
\end{array}
\right]
$$

These values give the values for y_1 and y_2
in the minimization problem.

From this example we see that the given minimization problem and its dual maximization problem are very closely related. Furthermore, it appears that when problems enjoy this relationship, the simplex method might be used to solve them both. The question is whether the simplex method will always solve them both. The answer is yes. This fact was proved by John von Neuman, and it is summarized by the Principle of Duality.

Principle of Duality	1. When a minimization problem and its dual have a solution, the maximum value of the function to be maximized is the same value as the minimum value of the function to be minimized.
	2. When the simplex method is used to solve the maximization problem, the values for the variables that solve the corresponding minimization problem are *the last entries in the columns corresponding to the slack variables.*

EXAMPLE 2   Given the problem

$$\text{Minimize } 18y_1 + 12y_2 = g \text{ subject to}$$

$$2y_1 + y_2 \geq 8$$
$$6y_1 + 6y_2 \geq 36$$

(a) State the dual of this minimization problem.
(b) Use the simplex method to solve the given problem.

Solution   (a) The dual of this minimization problem will be a maximization problem. To form the dual, write the matrix A (without slack variables and with positive coefficients for the variables in the last row) for the given problem.

$$
A = \left[
\begin{array}{cc|c}
2 & 1 & 8 \\
6 & 6 & 36 \\
\hline
18 & 12 & g
\end{array}
\right]
$$

Transpose matrix A to yield matrix B.

$$B = \begin{bmatrix} 2 & 6 & | & 18 \\ 1 & 6 & | & 12 \\ 8 & 36 & | & 8 \end{bmatrix}$$

Write the dual maximization problem, renaming the variables and the function.

Dual problem

Maximize $f = 8x_1 + 36x_2$ subject to

$$2x_1 + 6x_2 \leq 18$$
$$x_1 + 6x_2 \leq 12.$$

(b) To solve the given minimization problem, we use the simplex method on its dual maximization problem. The complete simplex matrix for each step is given and each pivot entry is circled:

1. $\begin{bmatrix} 2 & 6 & 1 & 0 & 0 & | & 18 \\ 1 & ⑥ & 0 & 1 & 0 & | & 12 \\ -8 & -36 & 0 & 0 & 1 & | & 0 \end{bmatrix}$

2. $\begin{bmatrix} ① & 0 & 1 & -1 & 0 & | & 6 \\ \frac{1}{6} & 1 & 0 & \frac{1}{6} & 0 & | & 2 \\ -2 & 0 & 0 & 6 & 1 & | & 72 \end{bmatrix}$

$\quad\quad x_1 \quad x_2 \quad s_1 \quad s_2 \quad f$

3. $\begin{bmatrix} 1 & 0 & 1 & -1 & 0 & | & 6 \\ 0 & 1 & -\frac{1}{6} & \frac{2}{6} & 0 & | & 1 \\ 0 & 0 & 2 & 4 & 1 & | & 84 \end{bmatrix}$

The last entries in the slack variable columns give the values of y_1 and y_2. Thus $y_1 = 2$, $y_2 = 4$, and $g = 84$.

EXAMPLE 3   A beef producer is considering two different types of feed. Each feed contains some or all of the necessary ingredients for fattening beef. Brand 1 feed costs 2 cents per pound and brand 2 costs 3 cents per pound. The producer would like to determine how much of each brand to buy in order to satisfy the nutritional requirements at minimum cost. Table 3.1 contains all the relevant data about nutrition and cost of each brand and the minimum requirements per unit of beef.

Table 3.1

	Brand 1	Brand 2	Minimum requirement
Ingredient A	3 lb	5 lb	40 lb
Ingredient B	4 lb	3 lb	46 lb
Cost per pound	2 ¢	3 ¢	

Solution   Let y_1 be the number of pounds of brand 1 and y_2 the number of pounds of brand 2. Then we can formulate the problem as follows:

$$\text{Minimize costs } C = 2y_1 + 3y_2 \text{ subject to}$$
$$3y_1 + 5y_2 \geq 40$$
$$4y_1 + 3y_2 \geq 46.$$

The original linear programming problem is usually called the **primal problem.** If we write this in an augmented matrix, without the slack variables, then we can transpose to find the dual problem.

<table>
<tr><td colspan="2"></td><td colspan="2" align="center">*Primal*</td><td colspan="2" align="center">*Dual*
(with function renamed)</td></tr>
</table>

$$
\begin{array}{c}
\text{Primal}\\
\left[\begin{array}{cc|c}
3 & 5 & 40\\
4 & 3 & 46\\
2 & 3 & C
\end{array}\right]
\end{array}
\qquad
\begin{array}{c}
\textit{Dual}\\
\textit{(with function renamed)}\\
\left[\begin{array}{cc|c}
3 & 4 & 2\\
5 & 3 & 3\\
40 & 46 & f
\end{array}\right]
\end{array}
$$

Thus the dual maximum problem here is

$$\text{maximize } f = 40x_1 + 46x_2 \text{ subject to}$$
$$3x_1 + 4x_2 \leq 2$$
$$5x_1 + 3x_2 \leq 3.$$

The simplex matrix for this maximum problem, with slack variables *included,* is

1.
$$
\left[\begin{array}{ccccc|c}
3 & 4 & 1 & 0 & 0 & 2\\
5 & 3 & 0 & 1 & 0 & 3\\
\hline
-40 & -46 & 0 & 0 & 1 & 0
\end{array}\right]
$$

Solving the problem gives

2.
$$
\left[\begin{array}{ccccc|c}
\frac{3}{4} & 1 & \frac{1}{4} & 0 & 0 & \frac{1}{2}\\
\frac{11}{4} & 0 & -\frac{3}{4} & 1 & 0 & \frac{3}{2}\\
\hline
-\frac{11}{2} & 0 & \frac{23}{2} & 0 & 1 & 23
\end{array}\right]
$$

3.
$$
\left[\begin{array}{ccccc|c}
0 & 1 & \frac{5}{11} & -\frac{3}{11} & 0 & \frac{1}{11}\\
1 & 0 & -\frac{3}{11} & \frac{4}{11} & 0 & \frac{6}{11}\\
\hline
0 & 0 & 10 & 2 & 1 & 26
\end{array}\right]
$$

The solution to this problem is

$$y_1 = 10 \text{ lb of brand 1}$$
$$y_2 = 2 \text{ lb of brand 2}$$
$$\text{Minimum cost} = 26 \text{ cents per unit of beef.}$$

In a more extensive study of linear programming, the duality relationship that we have used in this section as a means to solve minimization problems could be shown to have more properties than we have mentioned. For example, in applied problems where the objective is to minimize costs, it is possible to interpret the variables in the dual as "shadow prices" and interpret their values as marginal costs. Moreover, if the given problem is a profit maximization problem, then we can also form its dual, a minimization problem, by using matrix transposition, and we can think of the dual variables as representing "shadow prices" and interpret their values as marginal profits. Linear programming, the simplex method, and duality are topics of depth and beauty, and we have provided only a brief introduction to their terminology, areas of application, and power.

Exercise 3.5

In problems 1–6, form the matrix associated with each problem and find the transpose of the matrix.

1. Minimize $g = 5y_1 + 2y_2$ subject to

$$\begin{bmatrix} 1 & 1 & 9 \\ 1 & 3 & 15 \\ 5 & 2 & 0 \end{bmatrix}$$

$y_1 + y_2 \geq 9$
$y_1 + 3y_2 \geq 15.$

$\begin{bmatrix} 1 & 1 & 5 \\ 1 & 3 & 2 \\ 9 & 15 & 9 \end{bmatrix}$ $x_1 + x_2 \leq 5$ $x_1 + 3x_2 \leq 2$ $f = 9x_1 + 15x_2$

2. Minimize $g = 9y_1 + 10y_2$ subject to

$$y_1 + 2y_2 \geq 21$$
$$3y_1 + 2y_2 \geq 27.$$

$$\begin{bmatrix} 4 & 1 & 11 \\ 3 & 2 & 12 \\ 3 & 1 & 6 \\ 3 & 1 & 9 \end{bmatrix}$$

3. Minimize $g = 3y_1 + y_2$ subject to

$$4y_1 + y_2 \geq 11$$
$$3y_1 + 2y_2 \geq 12$$
$$3y_1 + y_2 \geq 6.$$

$\begin{bmatrix} 4 & 3 & 3 & 3 \\ 1 & 2 & 1 & 1 \\ 11 & 12 & 6 & 9 \end{bmatrix}$ $4x_1 + 3x_2 + 3x_3 \leq$ $x_1 + 2x_2 + x_3 \leq$ $f = 11x_1 + 12x_2 + 6x_3$

4. Minimize $g = 2y_1 + 5y_2$ subject to

$$4y_1 + y_2 \geq 12$$
$$y_1 + y_2 \geq 9$$
$$y_1 + 3y_2 \geq 15.$$

$$\begin{bmatrix} 1 & 3 & 0 & 1 \\ 4 & 6 & 1 & 3 \\ 0 & 4 & 1 & 1 \\ 12 & 48 & 8 & 9 \end{bmatrix}$$

5. Minimize $g = 12y_1 + 48y_2 + 8y_3$ subject to

$$y_1 + 3y_2 \qquad\ \geq 1$$
$$4y_1 + 6y_2 + y_3 \geq 3$$
$$4y_2 + y_3 \geq 1.$$

$\begin{bmatrix} 1 & 4 & 0 & 12 \\ 3 & 6 & 4 & 48 \\ 0 & 1 & 1 & 8 \\ 1 & 3 & 1 & 9 \end{bmatrix}$ $x_1 + 4x_2 \leq 12$ $3x_1 + 6x_2 + 4x_3 \leq$ $x_2 + x_3 \leq$ $f = x_1 + 3x_2 +$

6. Minimize $g = 12y_1 + 8y_2 + 10y_3$ subject to

$$y_1 + \qquad\ 2y_3 \geq 10$$
$$y_1 + y_2 \qquad\ \geq 12$$
$$2y_1 + 2y_2 + y_3 \geq 8.$$

7–12. Write the dual problem for problems 1–6. Be sure to rename the variables and the function.

13–18. Solve the linear programming problem given in problems 1–6. Use the simplex method.

19. Minimize $g = 2x + 10y$ subject to

$$2x + y \geq 11$$
$$x + 3y \geq 11$$
$$x + 4y \geq 16.$$

20. Minimize $g = 8x + 4y$ subject to

$$3x - 2y \geq 6$$
$$2x + y \geq 11.$$

21. Minimize $g = 8x + 7y + 12z$ subject to

$$x + y + z \geq 3$$
$$y + 2z \geq 2$$
$$x \qquad \geq 2.$$

22. Minimize $g = 20x + 30y + 36z$ subject to

$$x + 2y + 3z \geq 48$$
$$2x + 2y + 3z \geq 70$$
$$2x + 3y + 4z \geq 96.$$

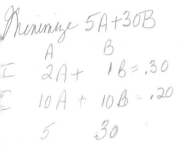

APPLICATIONS

23. A nutritionist wants to find the least expensive combination of two foods that meet daily vitamin requirements, which are 5 units of A and 30 units of B. Each ounce of food I provides 2 units of A and 1 unit of B, and each ounce of food II provides 10 units of A and 10 units of B. If food I costs 30 cents per ounce and food II costs 20 cents per ounce, find the number of ounces of each food that will provide the vitamins and minimize the cost.

24. A small company produces two products, I and II, at 3 facilities, A, B, and C. They have orders for 2000 of product I and 1200 of product II. The production capacity and cost per week to operate each facility are summarized in the following table.

	A	B	C
I	200	200	400
II	100	200	100
Cost/week	$1,000	$3,000	$4,000

How many weeks should each facility operate to fill the company's orders, and what is the minimum cost?

25. In a hospital ward, the patients can be grouped into two general categories depending on their condition and the amount of solid foods they require in their diet. A combination of two diets is used for solid foods because they supply essential nutrients for recovery, but each diet has an amount of a substance deemed detrimental. The table on page 220 summarizes the patient group, diet requirements, and the amount of the detrimental substance. How many servings from each diet should be given each day in order to minimize the intake of this detrimental substance?

	Diet A	Diet B	Daily requirements
Patient group 1	4 oz per serving	1 oz per serving	26 oz
Patient group 2	2 oz per serving	1 oz per serving	18 oz
Detrimental substances (ounces per serving)	0.18 oz	0.07 oz	.

26. Two factories produce three different types of kitchen appliances. The table summarizes the production capacity, the number of each type of appliance ordered, and the daily operating costs for the factories. How many days should each factory operate to fill the orders at minimum cost?

	Factory 1	Factory 2	Number ordered
Appliance 1	80 per day	20 per day	1600
Appliance 2	10 per day	10 per day	500
Appliance 3	20 per day	70 per day	2000
Daily cost	$10,000	$20,000	

27. In a laboratory experiment, two separate foods are given to experimental animals. Each food contains essential ingredients, A and B, which have minimum requirements for the animals, and each food also has an ingredient C, which can be harmful to the animals. The table summarizes this information.

	Food 1	Food 2	Requirements
Ingredient A	10 units per g	3 units per g	49 units
Ingredient B	6 units per g	12 units per g	60 units
Ingredient C	3 units per g	1 unit per g	

How many grams of foods 1 and 2 should be given to the animals in order to satisfy the requirements for A and B, and in order to minimize the amount of ingredient C that is ingested?

28. A political candidate wishes to use a combination of radio and TV advertisements in her campaign. Research has shown that each 1-minute spot on TV reaches 0.9 million people and each 1 minute on radio reaches 0.6 million. The candidate feels she must reach 63 million people, and she must buy at least 90 minutes of advertisements. How many minutes of each medium should be used if TV costs $500 per minute and radio costs $100 per minute, and the candidate wishes to minimize costs?

29. The James MacGregor Mining Company owns three mines, I, II, and III. Three ores, A, B, and C, are mined at these mines. For each ore, the number of tons per week available from each mine and the number of tons per week required to fill orders are given in the table.

		I	II	III	Required tons/week
Ore Types	A	10	10	10	90
	B	0	10	10	50
	C	10	0	10	60
Cost/day		$6000	$8000	$12000	

Find the number of days the company should operate each mine so that orders are filled at minimum cost. Find the minimum cost.

30. A hospital wishes to provide at least 24 units of nutrient A and 16 units of nutrient B in a meal, while minimizing the cost of the meal. If three types of food are available, with the nutritional value and costs (per ounce) given in the following table, how many ounces of each food should be served?

	Units of nutrient A	Units of nutrient B	Cost
Food I	2	1	1
Food II	2	5	5
Food III	2	1	2

31. Each nurse works 8 consecutive hours at the Beaver Medical Center. The center has the following staffing requirements for each 4-hour work period.

Work Period	Nurses Needed
1 (7–11)	40
2 (11–3)	20
3 (3–7)	30
4 (7–11)	40
5 (11–3)	20
6 (3–7)	10

(a) If y_1 represents the number of nurses starting in period 1, y_2 the number starting in period 2, and so on, write the linear programming problem that will minimize the total number of nurses needed. (Note that the nurses who begin work in period 6, work periods 6 and 1 for their 8-hour shift.)

(b) Solve the problem in (a).

Review Exercises

3.1

1. Solve $3x - 9 \le 4(3 - x)$ and graph the solution.
2. Solve $\frac{2}{5}x \le x + 4$ and graph the solution.
3. Solve $5x + 1 \ge \frac{2}{3}(x - 6)$ and graph the solution.
4. Solve $\dfrac{4(x - 2)}{3} \ge 3x - \dfrac{1}{6}$ and graph the solution.
5. Determine if the following represent open, closed, or half-open intervals. Write each in interval notation.
   (a) $0 \le x \le 5$ (b) $3 \le x < 7$ (c) $-3 < x < 2$
6. Write the inequality represented by each of the following.
   (a) $(-1, 16)$ (b) $(-12, -8]$

   (c)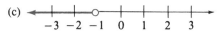

3.2

In problems 7–10, graph the solutions sets of each inequality or system of inequalities.

7. $2x + 3y \le 12$

8. $4x + 5y \ge 100$

9. $\begin{cases} x + 2y \le 20 \\ 3x + 10y \le 80 \\ x \ge 0,\ y \ge 0 \end{cases}$

10. $\begin{cases} 3x + y \ge 4 \\ x + y \ge 2 \\ -x + y \le 4 \\ x \qquad \le 5 \end{cases}$

3.3

Solve the following linear programming problems using graphical methods. Restrict $x \ge 0$ and $y \ge 0$.

11. Maximize $f = 5x + 6y$ subject to

$$x + 3y \le 24$$
$$4x + 3y \le 42$$
$$2x + y \le 20.$$

12. Maximize $f = 9x + 5y$ subject to the constraints in problem 11.

13. Maximize $f = x + 4y$ subject to

$$7x + 3y \le 105$$
$$2x + 5y \le 59$$
$$x + 7y \le 70.$$

14. Maximize $f = 2x + y$ subject to the constraints in problem 13.

15. Minimize $g = 5x + 3y$ subject to

$$3x + y \ge 12$$
$$x + y \ge 6$$
$$x + 6y \ge 11.$$

16. Minimize $g = 3x + 5y$ subject to the constraints in problem 15.

17. Minimize $g = x + 5y$ subject to

$$8x + y \ge 85$$
$$x + y \ge 50$$
$$x + 4y \ge 80$$
$$x + 10y \ge 94.$$

18. Minimize $g = 7x + y$ subject to the constraints in problem 17.

3.4

Use the simplex method to solve the following linear programming problems. Assume all variables are nonnegative.

19. Maximize $f = 7x + 12y$ subject to the conditions in problem 13.

20. Maximize $f = 3x + 4y$ subject to
$$x + 4y \leq 160$$
$$x + 2y \leq 100$$
$$4x + 3y \leq 300.$$

21. Maximize $f = 3x + 8y$ subject to the conditions in problem 20.

22. Maximize $f = 39x + 5y + 30z$ subject to
$$x + z \leq 7$$
$$3x + 5y \leq 30$$
$$3x + y \leq 18.$$

Problems 23 and 24 have nonunique solutions. If there is no solution, indicate this; if there are multiple solutions, find two different solutions. Use the simplex method.

23. Maximize $f = 4x + 4y$ subject to
$$x + 5y \leq 500$$
$$x + 2y \leq 230$$
$$x + y \leq 160.$$

24. Maximize $f = 2x + 5y$ subject to
$$-4x + y \leq 40$$
$$x - 7y \leq 70.$$

3.5

Form the dual and use the simplex method to solve the minimization problems 25–28.

25. Minimize $g = 7y_1 + 6y_2$ subject to
$$5y_1 + 2y_2 \geq 16$$
$$3y_1 + 7y_2 \geq 27.$$

26. Minimize $g = 3y_1 + 4y_2$ subject to
$$3y_1 + y_2 \geq 8$$
$$y_1 + y_2 \geq 6$$
$$2y_1 + 5y_2 \geq 18.$$

27. Minimize $g = 2y_1 + y_2$ subject to the conditions of problem 26.

28. Minimize $g = 12y_1 + 48y_2 + 8y_3$ subject to
$$y_1 + 3y_2 \geq 1$$
$$4y_1 + 6y_2 + y_3 \geq 3$$
$$4y_2 + y_3 \geq 1.$$

APPLICATIONS

3.3

29. A company manufactures two different size backyard swing sets. The larger requires 5 hours of labor to complete, the smaller requires 2 hours, and there are 700 hours of labor each day. The packing department can pack at most 185 swing sets per day. If the profit is $4 on each larger set and $2 on each smaller set, how many of each should be produced to yield maximum profit? What is the maximum profit? Use graphical methods.

30. A company produces two different grades of steel, A and B, at two different factories, 1 and 2. The table on the following page summarizes the production capabilities of the factories, the cost per day, and the number of units of each grade of steel that is required to fill orders.

	Factory 1	*Factory 2*	*Required*
Grade A steel	1 unit	2 units	80 units
Grade B steel	3 units	2 units	140 units
Cost per day	$5000	$6000	

How many days should each factory operate in order to fill the orders at minimum cost? What is the minimum cost? Use graphical methods.

Use the simplex method to solve problems 31–34.

3.4

31. A small industry produces two items, I and II. They operate at capacity and make a profit of $6 on each item I and $4 on each item II. The following table gives the hours required to produce each item and the hours available per day.

	I	*II*	*Hours available*
Assembly	2 hours	1 hour	100
Packaging & Inspection	1 hour	1 hour	60

Find the number of each item that should be produced each day to maximize profits, and find the maximum daily profit.

32. A manufacturer of blenders produces three different sizes: Regular, Special, and Kitchen Magic. The production of each type requires the materials and amounts given in the table.

	Regular	*Special*	*Kitchen Magic*
Electrical components	5	12	24
Units of aluminum	1	2	4
Blending containers	1	1	1

Suppose the manufacturer is opening a new plant, and anticipates weekly supplies of 90,000 electrical components, 12,000 units of aluminum, and 9000 containers. If the unit profit is $3 for the Regular, $4 for the Special, and $8 for the Kitchen Magic, how many of each should be produced to maximize profits? What is the maximum profit?

3.5

33. A laboratory wishes to purchase two different feeds, A and B, for their animals. The table summarizes the nutritional content of the feeds, the required amounts of each ingredient, and the cost of each type of feed.

	Feed A	*Feed B*	*Requirements*
Carbohydrates	1 unit/lb	4 units/lb	40 units
Protein	2 units/lb	1 unit/lb	80 units
Cost	14¢/lb	16¢/lb	

How many pounds of each type of feed should the laboratory buy in order to satisfy their needs at minimum cost?

34. A company makes three products I, II, and III at three different factories. At factory A, they can make 10 units of each product per day. At factory B, they can make 20 units of II and 20 units of III per day. At factory C, they can make 20 units of I, 20 units of II, and 10 units of III per day. The company has orders for 200 units of I, 500 units of II, and 300 units of III. If the daily costs are $200 at A, $300 at B, and $500 at C, find the number of days that each factory should operate in order to fill their orders at minimum cost. Find the minimum cost.

Part Three

Nonlinear Models

WARMUP

	Prerequisite problem type	Answer	Section for review
4.1, 4.2	Find $b^2 - 4ac$ if (a) $a = 1, b = 2, c = -2$ (b) $a = -2, b = 3, c = -1$ (c) $a = -3, b = -3, c = -2$	(a) 12 (b) 1 (c) -15	0.2 Signed numbers
4.1	(a) Factor $6x^2 - x - 2$. (b) Factor $6x^2 - 9x$.	(a) $(3x - 2)(2x + 1)$ (b) $3x(2x - 3)$	0.6 Factoring
4.1	Is $\dfrac{1 + \sqrt{-3}}{2}$ a real number?	No	0.4 Radicals
4.2	(a) Find the y-intercept of $\quad y = x^2 - 6x + 8$. (b) Find the x-intercepts of $\quad y = 3x(2x - 3)$.	(a) 8 (b) $0, \frac{3}{2}$	1.2 x- and y-intercepts

4

Quadratic Functions

In previous chapters we studied linear equations and inequalities and their applications in detail, including their analysis by using matrices and linear programming. Even though linear equations are relatively easy to formulate and to use, they are not sufficient to solve all problems that arise in business, the social sciences, or the life sciences. Thus we now direct our attention to equations of second degree, called quadratic equations.

In this chapter, we solve quadratic equations in one variable; that is, equations of the form $ax^2 + bx + c = 0$. We also graph quadratic functions of the form $y = ax^2 + bx + c$, whose graphs are parabolas. We will apply our knowledge about these equations and these functions to solve problems that arise in the management, life, and social sciences.

The use of these quadratic functions makes it possible to greatly expand our study of the special business functions we have been discussing in detail. In particular, we will see that the mathematical principles governing market equilibrium and break-even analysis still apply, but now the functions are quadratics. Furthermore, our analysis allows us to find maximum values for revenue and profit functions, which are quadratic functions of the form $f(x) = ax^2 + bx + c$.

4.1 Quadratic Equations

Objective

□ To solve quadratic equations

It is important for us to know how to solve the equations that arise as we study different types of functions and consider their graphs and applications. This was true for linear equations and is again true for quadratic equations.

In general, a **quadratic equation** in one variable is an equation that can be written in the *general form*

$$ax^2 + bx + c = 0 \qquad (a \neq 0),$$

where a, b, and c represent constants. For example, the equations

$$3x^2 + 4x + 1 = 0 \qquad \text{and} \qquad 2x^2 + 1 = x^2 - x$$

are quadratic equations; the first of these is in general form, and the second may easily be rewritten in general form.

When we solve quadratic equations we will only be interested in real number solutions and will consider two methods of solution: factoring and the quadratic formula. We will discuss solving quadratic equations by factoring first. (For a review of factoring, see Section 0.6.)

Solution by factoring is based on the fact that, in our number system, when the product of two factors equals zero, then one of the factors (or both) must equal zero. Hence, to solve by factoring, the equation must be written with zero on one side.

EXAMPLE 1   Solve $6x^2 + 3x = 4x + 2$.

Solution

$$6x^2 + 3x = 4x + 2$$
$$6x^2 - x - 2 = 0 \qquad \text{Proper form for factoring}$$
$$(3x - 2)(2x + 1) = 0 \qquad \text{Factored}$$

$$3x - 2 = 0 \quad \text{or} \quad 2x + 1 = 0 \qquad \text{Factors equal to zero}$$
$$3x = 2 \qquad\qquad 2x = -1$$
$$x = \frac{2}{3} \qquad\qquad x = -\frac{1}{2} \qquad \text{Solutions}$$

We now check that these values are, in fact, solutions to our original equation.

$$6\left(\frac{2}{3}\right)^2 + 3\left(\frac{2}{3}\right) \overset{?}{=} 4\left(\frac{2}{3}\right) + 2 \qquad\qquad 6\left(-\frac{1}{2}\right)^2 + 3\left(-\frac{1}{2}\right) \overset{?}{=} 4\left(-\frac{1}{2}\right) + 2$$

$$\frac{24}{9} + 2 \overset{?}{=} \frac{8}{3} + 2 \qquad\qquad\qquad 6\left(\frac{1}{4}\right) - \frac{3}{2} \overset{?}{=} -2 + 2$$

$$\frac{14}{3} = \frac{14}{3} \quad \checkmark \qquad\qquad\qquad\qquad 0 = 0 \quad \checkmark$$

EXAMPLE 2   Solve $6x^2 = 9x$.

Solution

$$6x^2 = 9x$$
$$6x^2 - 9x = 0$$
$$3x(2x - 3) = 0$$

$$3x = 0 \quad \text{or} \quad 2x - 3 = 0$$
$$x = 0 \qquad\qquad 2x = 3$$
$$x = \frac{3}{2}$$

CHECK: $6(0)^2 = 9(0) \quad \checkmark \qquad 6\left(\frac{3}{2}\right)^2 = 9\left(\frac{3}{2}\right) \quad \checkmark$

Thus, the solutions are $x = 0$ and $x = \frac{3}{2}$.

Note that in the previous example (and always) it is incorrect to divide both sides of the equation by x, since this results in the loss of the solution $x = 0$.

EXAMPLE 3 Solve $(y - 3)(y + 2) = -4$ for y.

Solution Note that the left side of the equation is factored, but the right member is not 0. Therefore we must multiply the factors before we can rewrite the equation in general form.

$$(y - 3)(y + 2) = -4$$
$$y^2 - y - 6 = -4$$
$$y^2 - y - 2 = 0$$
$$(y - 2)(y + 1) = 0$$

$$y - 2 = 0 \quad \text{or} \quad y + 1 = 0$$
$$y = 2 \quad | \quad y = -1$$

CHECK: $(2 - 3)(2 + 2) = -4$ ✓ $\quad (-1 - 3)(-1 + 2) = -4$ ✓

We may use the quadratic formula to solve quadratic equations in which factorization is difficult or impossible to see.

Quadratic Formula   If $ax^2 + bx + c = 0$, where $a \neq 0$, then

$$x = \frac{-b + \sqrt{b^2 - 4ac}}{2a} \quad \text{or} \quad x = \frac{-b - \sqrt{b^2 - 4ac}}{2a}.$$

Note that the equation *must* be in general form to begin the solution. Here the proper identification of values for a, b, and c to be substituted into the formula requires that the equation be in general form.

EXAMPLE 4 Use the quadratic formula to solve $2x^2 - 3x - 6 = 0$ for x.

Solution The equation is already in general form, with $a = 2$, $b = -3$, and $c = -6$. Hence,

$$x = \frac{-b \pm \sqrt{b^2 - 4ac}}{2a}$$

$$= \frac{-(-3) \pm \sqrt{(-3)^2 - 4(2)(-6)}}{2(2)}$$

$$= \frac{3 \pm \sqrt{9 + 48}}{4}$$

$$= \frac{3 \pm \sqrt{57}}{4}.$$

Thus, the solutions are

$$x = \frac{3 + \sqrt{57}}{4} \quad \text{and} \quad x = \frac{3 - \sqrt{57}}{4}.$$

EXAMPLE 5   Using the quadratic formula, find all real solutions to $x^2 = x - 1$.

Solution   We must rewrite the equation in general form before we can determine the values of a, b, and c.

$$x^2 = x - 1$$
$$x^2 - x + 1 = 0 \qquad \text{Note: } a = 1, b = -1, \text{ and } c = 1.$$
$$x = \frac{-(-1) \pm \sqrt{(-1)^2 - 4(1)(1)}}{2(1)}$$
$$x = \frac{1 \pm \sqrt{1 - 4}}{2}$$
$$x = \frac{1 \pm \sqrt{-3}}{2}$$

Since $\sqrt{-3}$ is not a real number, the values of x are not real. Hence, there are no real solutions to the given equation.

In the previous example, there were no real solutions to the given quadratic equation because the radicand of the quadratic formula was negative. In general, when solving a quadratic equation, we can use the sign of the radicand in the quadratic formula, i.e., the sign of $b^2 - 4ac$, to determine how many real solutions there are. Thus, we refer to $b^2 - 4ac$ as the **quadratic discriminant.**

> Given $ax^2 + bx + c = 0$ \qquad and \qquad $a \neq 0$,
>
> if $b^2 - 4ac > 0$, the equation has 2 distinct real solutions.
> if $b^2 - 4ac = 0$, the equation has 1 real solution.
> if $b^2 - 4ac < 0$, the equation has no real solutions.

if $b^2 - 4ac$ is positive perfect square, original problem could have been factored.

Exercise 4.1

Write the following equations in general form.

1. $x^2 + 5x = 3$
2. $y^2 + 4y = 2$
3. $2x^2 + 3 = x^2 - 2x + 4$
4. $x^2 - 2x + 5 = 2 - 2x^2$
5. $(y + 1)(y + 2) = 4$
6. $(z - 1)(z - 3) = 1$

In problems 7–20, solve each equation by factoring.

7. $9 - 4x^2 = 0$
8. $25x^2 - 16 = 0$
9. $x = x^2$
10. $t^2 - 4t = 3t^2$
11. $0.05x^2 = 7x$
12. $0.8y^2 + 6.4y = 0$
13. $z^2 - z = z + 3$
14. $x^2 + 10x = 18x - 15$
15. $x^2 + 5x = 21 + x$
16. $x^2 + 17x = 8x - 14$
17. $4t^2 - 4t + 1 = 0$
18. $49z^2 + 14z + 1 = 0$
19. $(x - 1)(x + 5) = 7$
20. $(x - 3)(1 - x) = 1$

In problems 21–30, solve each equation by using the quadratic formula. Give real answers (a) exactly and (b) rounded to two decimal places.

21. $6x^2 = x + 1$ 22. $3y^2 + 5y = 2$
23. $x^2 - 4x - 4 = 0$ 24. $x^2 - 6x + 7 = 0$
25. $2w^2 + w + 1 = 0$ 26. $z^2 + 2z + 4 = 0$
27. $16z^2 + 16z - 21 = 0$ 28. $10y^2 - y - 65 = 0$
29. $5x^2 = 2x + 6$ 30. $3x^2 = -6x - 2$

In problems 31–48, find the real solutions to each equation. Give any approximate answers from a calculator rounded to two decimal places.

31. $y^2 = 7$ 32. $z^2 = 12$
33. $y^2 + 9 = 0$ 34. $z^2 + 121 = 0$
35. $49x^2 + 28x + 4 = 0$ 36. $25x^2 + 120x + 144 = 0$
37. $21x + 70 - 7x^2 = 0$ 38. $4x^2 + 12x + 8 = 0$
39. $x(4 - 3x) = 7$ 40. $(2x + 1)(x + 2) = -2$
41. $3x^2 - 11x + 6 = 0$ 42. $6x^2 + 5x - 6 = 0$
43. $300 - 2x - 0.01x^2 = 0$ 44. $-9.6 + 2x - 0.1x^2 = 0$
45. $25.6x^2 - 16.1x - 1.1 = 0$ 46. $6.8z^2 - 4.9z - 2.6 = 0$
47. $x - 3/x = 5$ 48. $2 + 1/x = 4x$

APPLICATIONS

49. The speed at which water travels in a pipe can be measured by directing the flow through an elbow and measuring the height it spurts out the top. If the elbow height is 10 cm, the equation relating the height of the water above the elbow (in centimeters) and its velocity v (in centimeters per second) is given by

$$v^2 = 1960(h + 10).$$

(a) Find v if $h = 2$.
(b) Find v if $h = 18$.
(c) The height h is a function of the velocity v. Solve the equation for h to express this function.

50. Weather forecasters frequently report wind chill factors because a body exposed to wind loses heat due to convection. The amount of loss depends on many factors, but for a given situation there is a positive number called the coefficient of convection, K_c, which depends on the wind velocity v. The approximate relationship between K_c and v is given by

$$\frac{(K_c)^2}{64} - \frac{1}{4} = v.$$

(a) Find the coefficient of convection when the wind velocity is 10 mph.
(b) Find K_c when $v = 40$ mph.
(c) What is the change in K_c for the change in v from 10 mph to 40 mph?

51. The velocity of a blood corpuscle in a vessel depends on how far the corpuscle is from the center of the vessel. Let R be the constant radius of the vessel, v_m the constant maximum velocity of the corpuscle, r the distance from the center to a particular blood

corpuscle (variable), and v_r the velocity of that corpuscle. Then the velocity v_r is related to the distance r according to

$$v_r = v_m \left(1 - \frac{r^2}{R^2} \right).$$

(a) Find r when $v_r = \frac{1}{2}v_m$.
(b) Find r when $v_r = \frac{1}{4}v_m$.
(c) Find v_r when $r = R$.

52. A ladder 13 feet long is leaning against a wall with its foot 5 feet from the wall. If the foot of the ladder is pulled 4 feet farther from the wall, how much does the top of the ladder slide down the wall?

53. A flower bed 32 feet by 42 feet is bordered by a walk of uniform width (see Figure 4.1). The area of the walk is 656 feet. Find the width of the walk.

32′
42′

Figure 4.1

54. The flower border around a rectangular plot of grass is of uniform width, and its area is three-fifths the area of the grass. If the plot of grass is 18 by 30 feet, what is the width of the border?

55. A fissure in the earth appeared after an earthquake. To measure its vertical depth a stone was dropped into it, and the sound of the stone's impact was heard 3.9 seconds later. The distance (in feet) the stone fell is given by $s = 16t_1^2$, and the distance (in feet) the sound traveled is given by $s = 1090t_2$. In these equations, the distances traveled by the sound and the stone are the same, but their times are not. Using the fact that the total time is 3.9 seconds, find the depth of the fissure.

56. Two projectiles are shot into the air over a lake. The paths of the projectiles are given by

(a) $y = -0.0013x^2 + x + 10$, and
(b) $y = -\frac{x^2}{81} + \frac{4}{3}x + 10$.

Determine which projectile travels farther by substituting $y = 0$ in each equation and finding x.

57. The Ace Jewelry Store sold a necklace for $144. If the percentage of profit (based on cost) equals the cost of the necklace to the store, how much did the store pay for it? (Use

$$P = \left(\frac{C}{100} \right) C$$ where P is profit and C is cost.)

4.2 Quadratic Functions: Parabolas

Objectives
- ☐ To determine if a vertex is a maximum point or a minimum point
- ☐ To find the vertex of the graph of a quadratic function
- ☐ To find the zeros of a quadratic function
- ☐ To graph quadratic functions

The equation $y = f(x)$, where $f(x)$ is a polynomial in the variable x, is called a polynomial function. One special class of polynomial functions is the linear function (or first degree function) $y = mx + b$, studied in Chapter 1. Increasing the degree of a linear function by one gives a **second-degree polynomial function,** or **quadratic function.** The general equation of a quadratic function has the form

$$y = ax^2 + bx + c,$$

where a, b, and c are real numbers and $a \neq 0$. Quadratic functions can be used to model many applications such as suspension bridges; paths of projectiles; and cost, revenue, and profit.

In Chapter 1, we noted that the total cost of producing a product could be given by the equation

$$C = C(x) = 300x + 0.1x^2 + 1200,$$

where x represented the number of units produced. That is, the cost of this product is represented by a quadratic function. We can find the cost of producing 10 units by evaluating

$$C(10) = 300(10) + 0.1(10)^2 + 1200 = 4210.$$

EXAMPLE 1   Suppose the profit in dollars from the production and sale of x units of a product is modeled by $P(x) = -x^2 + 60x - 50$. Find the profit if
(a) 20 units are produced.
(b) 30 units are produced.
(c) 40 units are produced.

Solution   (a) $P(20) = -(20)^2 + 60(20) - 50 = \$750$
(b) $P(30) = -(30)^2 + 60(30) - 50 = \$850$
(c) $P(40) = -(40)^2 + 60(40) - 50 = \$750$

Note that the profit function of Example 1 indicates that as production and sale increases from 20 to 40 units, the profit first increases and then decreases. Thus the graph of this (and other) quadratic function is not a line. However, the graph of a quadratic function does have a distinctive shape, called a **parabola.**

The quadratic function

$$y = ax^2 + bx + c \qquad (a \neq 0)$$

has a graph that is a parabola that opens upward if $a > 0$ (see Figure 4.2). If $a < 0$, the parabola opens downward (see Figure 4.3).

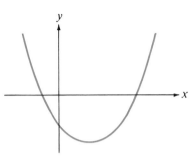

Graph of $y = ax^2 + bx + c$, $a > 0$

Figure 4.2

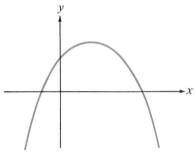

Graph of $y = ax^2 + bx + c$, $a < 0$

Figure 4.3

The following example will help us discover more properties of quadratic functions.

EXAMPLE 2   (a) Evaluate the function $y = x^2 - 4x + 3$ for integer values of x from -1 to 5 and display the results in a table.

(b) Use the points obtained in (a) to graph the function.

Solution   (a)

x	$y = x^2 - 4x + 3$	Points (x, y)
-1	$(-1)^2 - 4(-1) + 3 = 8$	$(-1, 8)$
0	$0^2 - 4(0) + 3 = 3$	$(0, 3)$
1	$1^2 - 4(1) + 3 = 0$	$(1, 0)$
2	$2^2 - 4(2) + 3 = -1$	$(2, -1)$
3	$3^2 - 4(3) + 3 = 0$	$(3, 0)$
4	$4^2 - 4(4) + 3 = 3$	$(4, 3)$
5	$5^2 - 4(5) + 3 = 8$	$(5, 8)$

(b) The graph is shown in Figure 4.4.

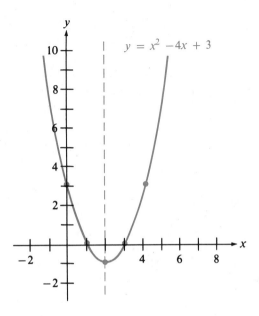

Figure 4.4

From the graph of the equation in Example 2, we can make the following observations:

1. The graph opens upward ($a = 1 > 0$), so it has a minimum (lowest) point. (A parabola that opens downward will have a maximum, or highest point.)

2. One half of the parabola is a reflection (mirror image) of the other about some line. We say the parabola is **symmetric** about the line, called its **axis of symmetry.** In Example 1, the axis of symmetry is the vertical line with equation $x = 2$ (shown as a dashed line).

3. The parabola has its minimum point where the axis of symmetry intersects the curve, at $(2, -1)$. Since the axis of symmetry lies midway between any two points on the curve with the same y-coordinate, we can easily determine the x-coordinate of the minimum point. A parabola that opens downward will have a maximum (highest) point. The point where a parabola has its maximum point or minimum point is called the **vertex** of the parabola.

4. The parabola crosses the x-axis at points whose y-coordinates are zero. Thus, the x-intercepts are solutions to the equation $0 = x^2 - 4x + 3$.

From the graph, the solutions to the equation $0 = x^2 - 4x + 3$ are $x = 1$ and $x = 3$. Solving the equation by factoring gives $0 = (x - 1)(x - 3)$, so $x = 1$ and $x = 3$ are the solutions. These values are called the **zeros** of the function.

Again, the axis of symmetry is a vertical line that passes through the minimum point $(2, -1)$. Note that we can find the x-coordinate of the minimum point, namely $x = 2$, by taking the value midway between the two x-coordinates where the curve crosses the x-axis. This value, $x = 2$, represents the average of the numbers 1 and 3; that is, $\frac{1}{2}(1 + 3) = 2$.

More generally, if we are given $y = ax^2 + bx + c$, then the zeros are solutions to $ax^2 + bx + c = 0$, and they are given by the quadratic formula as

$$x = \frac{-b + \sqrt{b^2 - 4ac}}{2a} \quad \text{and} \quad x = \frac{-b - \sqrt{b^2 - 4ac}}{2a}.$$

If we average these x-values (that is, take one-half their sum), then we obtain the equation of the axis of symmetry and the x-coordinate of the vertex of the parabola,

$$x = \frac{-b}{2a}.$$

We can summarize the information we have learned about quadratic functions as follows.

Graphs of Quadratic Functions

Form: $y = ax^2 + bx + c$ Graph: parabola

$a > 0$ $\begin{cases} \text{opening upward} \\ \text{vertex is a minimum point} \end{cases}$

$a < 0$ $\begin{cases} \text{opening downward} \\ \text{vertex is a maximum point} \end{cases}$

Vertex: $x = \dfrac{-b}{2a}, \quad y = f\left(\dfrac{-b}{2a}\right)$

Zeros (if real): $x = \dfrac{-b + \sqrt{b^2 - 4ac}}{2a}, \quad x = \dfrac{-b - \sqrt{b^2 - 4ac}}{2a}$

See Figure 4.5.

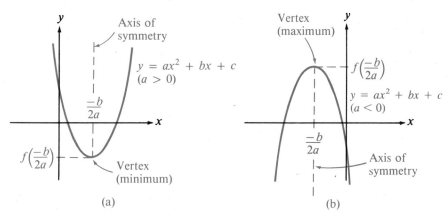

Figure 4.5

EXAMPLE 3   For the function $y = 4x - x^2$: determine if its vertex is a maximum point or minimum point and find the coordinates of this point; find the zeros, if any exist, and sketch the graph.

Solution   The proper form is $y = -x^2 + 4x + 0$, so $a = -1$. Thus, the parabola opens downward, and the vertex is the highest (maximum) point.

The vertex occurs at $x = \dfrac{-b}{2a} = \dfrac{-4}{2(-1)} = 2$.

The y-coordinate of the vertex is $f(2) = -(2)^2 + 4(2) = 4$.
The zeros for the parabola are solutions to

$$-x^2 + 4x = 0$$
$$x(-x + 4) = 0,$$

or $x = 0$ and $x = 4$.

Plotting these three points (and others to ensure accuracy) gives the graph (see Figure 4.6).

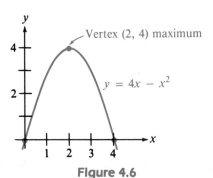

Figure 4.6

The vertex is the most important point on a parabola because it is the place where the graph changes direction. With the ability to locate the vertex, we need very few other points to make a good sketch.

EXAMPLE 4   For the function $f(x) = -2x^2 + 4x - 4$: determine if its vertex is a maximum point or minimum point and find the coordinates of this point; find the zeros, if any exist, and sketch the graph.

Solution   Since $a = -2$, the parabola opens downward and the vertex is a maximum point. The coordinates of the vertex are:

$$x = \frac{-b}{2a} = \frac{-4}{2(-2)} = 1$$
$$y = f(1) = -2(1)^2 + 4(1) - 4 = -2.$$

The zeros are the solutions to $f(x) = 0$:

$$-2x^2 + 4x - 4 = 0.$$

If we use the quadratic formula, we obtain

$$x = \frac{-4 \pm \sqrt{(4)^2 - 4(-2)(-4)}}{2(-2)}$$
$$= \frac{-4 \pm \sqrt{16 - 32}}{-4}$$
$$= \frac{-4 \pm \sqrt{-16}}{-4}.$$

These solutions are not real numbers, so the function has no zeros and hence its graph does not cross the x-axis.

The parabola opens downward, because the x^2 term has a negative coefficient. A table of values for x's on either side of $x = 1$ (the x-coordinate of the vertex) will allow us to accurately sketch the graph. (See Figure 4.7.)

x	y
-1	-10
0	-4
1	-2
2	-4
3	-10

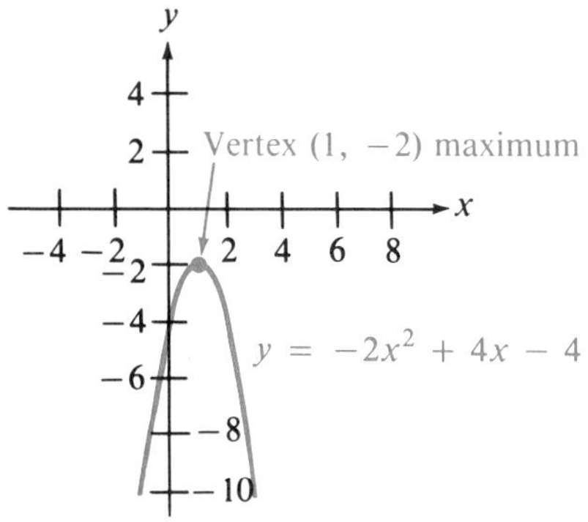

Figure 4.7

Note that the graph of $y = x^2 + k$ (see Figure 4.8(b) where $k = 2$) has the same shape as the graph of $y = x^2$ (see Figure 4.8(a)), but the graph is shifted up k units if $k > 0$. This is because for each value of x, the value of $y = x^2 + k$ will be k units more than the corresponding y-value of $y = x^2$.

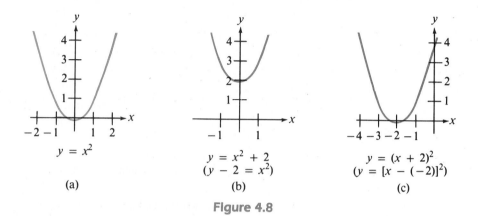

$$y = x^2$$

(a)

$$y = x^2 + 2$$
$$(y - 2 = x^2)$$

(b)

$$y = (x + 2)^2$$
$$(y = [x - (-2)]^2)$$

(c)

Figure 4.8

We can also say that any function of the form $y - k = x^2$ will be shifted k units in the y-direction. Similarly, a function of the form $y = (x - h)^2$ has the same shape as $y = x^2$, but with the graph shifted h units in the x-direction (see Figure 4.8(c) where $h = -2$).

Thus far we have discussed quadratic functions of the form $y = ax^2 + bx + c$. More generally, we define any equation that has at least one second-degree term and no term with degree higher than 2 as a **quadratic equation.**

The general form of a quadratic equation in two unknowns is

$$Ax^2 + Bxy + Cy^2 + Dx + Ey + F = 0,$$

with A, B, and C not all 0. The graphs of some of these equations will not be parabolas, but all equations that can be written in the form $y = ax^2 + bx + c$, where $a \neq 0$, will have parabolas as their graphs.

Techniques exist that make graphing the other forms of quadratic equations fairly easy, but we are primarily interested in parabolas, so we will not discuss those techniques. We can graph quadratic equations in two variables that are not of the form $y = ax^2 + bx + c$ by plotting a number of points or by using techniques we will learn in later chapters.

Perhaps a word should also be said about **polynomial functions,** such as $y = 3x^3 + 4x^2 + 5x + 2$ or $y = x^4 + 3x^2$. These functions can be graphed by plotting a (large) number of points and drawing a smooth curve through the points. Their graphs can be sketched more easily using the techniques of calculus, so we will defer further discussion of their graphs until Chapter 10.

Exercise 4.2

In problems 1–4, find the vertex of the graph and determine if it is a maximum point or minimum point.

1. $y = \frac{1}{2}x^2 + x$

2. $y = x^2 - 2x$

3. $y = 8 + 2x - x^2$

4. $y = 6 - 4x - 2x^2$

In problems 5–8, find the zeros of each function and sketch its graph. (See problems 1–4 for information.)

5. $y = \frac{1}{2}x^2 + x$

6. $y = x^2 - 2x$

7. $y = 8 + 2x - x^2$

8. $y = 6 - 4x - 2x^2$

In problems 9–18, determine whether each function's vertex is a maximum point or minimum point and find the coordinates of this point. Find the zeros, if any exist, and sketch the graph of the function.

9. $y = x^2 - 4$

10. $y = x^2 - 2$

11. $y = x - \frac{1}{4}x^2$

12. $y = -2x^2 + 18x$

13. $y = x^2 + 4x + 4$

14. $y = x^2 - 6x + 9$

15. $x^2 + 5x - y + 4 = 0$

16. $y - x^2 - 10x = 16$

17. $\frac{1}{4}x^2 + x - y + 4 = 0$

18. $x^2 + x + y + 2 = 0$

In problems 19–26, sketch the graph of each function.

19. $y = x^2 + 5$

20. $y = x^2 + 4$

21. $y = -4 + 7x - 4x^2$

22. $y = \frac{1}{2}x^2 + x - 1$

23. $y = -30 + 4x - 0.1x^2$

24. $y = -9 + x - 0.01x^2$

25. $y = 0.2x^2 + 0.4x + 1.8$

26. $y = 9 - 0.2x - 0.1x^2$

27. Graph (a) $y = x^2$ (b) $y = -x^2$ (c) $y = x^2 - 1$ (d) $y = (x - 1)^2$

28. Graph (a) $y = 2x^2$ (b) $y = -2x^2$ (c) $y = 2x^2 - 2$ (d) $y = 2(x - 2)^2$

APPLICATIONS

29. The amount of particulate pollution x depends on the wind velocity v, among other things. If the relationship between x and v can be approximated by

$$x = 20 - 0.01v^2,$$

    sketch the graph relating these quantities, with v on the horizontal axis.

30. In problem 51 of Exercise 4.1 we saw that the velocity of a blood corpuscle in a vessel, v_r, depends on the distance of the corpuscle from the center of the vessel, r, according to

$$v_r = v_m \left(1 - \frac{r^2}{R^2} \right),$$

    where v_m is the maximum velocity and R the radius of the vessel.

The blood pressure also affects the velocity of a corpuscle. If we make some simplifications in the formula, namely, let $v_m = 1$ and let $x^2 = r^2/R^2$, then we can observe the following.

Pressure	Equation
$p = 20$ mm	$v(x) = 8(1 - x^2)$
$p = 10$ mm	$v(x) = 3(1 - x^2)$
$p = 5$ mm	$v(x) = 1 - x^2$

Graph each of these equations on the same set of axes.

31. The yield from a grove of orange trees is given by $Y = x(800 - x)$, where x is the number of orange trees per acre. How many trees will maximize the yield?

32. One of the early results in psychology relating the magnitude of a stimulus x to the magnitude of a response y is expressed by the equation

$$y = kx^2,$$

where k is an experimental constant. Sketch this graph for $k = 1$, $k = 2$, and $k = 4$.

33. The sensitivity S to a drug is related to the dosage x by

$$S = 1000x - x^2.$$

Sketch the graph of this function and determine what dosage gives maximum sensitivity. Use the graph to determine the maximum sensitivity.

34. If 100 feet of fence is used to fence in a rectangular yard, then the resulting area is given by

$$A = x(50 - x),$$

where x is the width of the rectangle and $50 - x$ is the length. Graph this equation and determine the length and width that give maximum area.

35. The rate of photosynthesis R for a certain plant depends on the intensity of light x according to

$$R = 270x - 90x^2.$$

Sketch the graph of this function, and determine the intensity that gives the maximum rate.

36. A ball thrown vertically into the air has its height above ground given by

$$s = 112t - 16t^2.$$

Find the maximum height the ball reaches.

37. Two projectiles are shot into the air from the same location. The paths of the projectiles are parabolas and given by
   (a) $y = -0.0013x^2 + x + 10$, and
   (b) $y = \dfrac{-x^2}{81} + \dfrac{4}{3}x + 10$.

Determine which projectile goes higher by locating the vertex of each parabola.

38. A projectile shot vertically into the air has its height above ground given by

$$s = 100 + 960t - 16t^2.$$

Find its maximum height.

39. In problem 49 of Exercise 4.1 we saw that the speed of flowing water could be measured according to the equation

$$v^2 = 1960(h + 10).$$

Solve this equation for h and graph the result, using the velocity as the independent variable.

40. When a stone is thrown upward, it follows a parabolic path given by some form of the equation

$$y = ax^2 + bx + c.$$

If $y = 0$ represents ground level, find the equation of a stone thrown from ground level at $x = 0$ and landing on the ground 40 units away if the stone reaches a maximum height of 40 units. (*Hint:* Find the coordinates of the vertex of the parabola and two other points.)

41. A rectangular field is to be fenced off along a river and no fence is required along the river. The material for the fence costs $4 per running foot for the two ends and $6 per running foot for the side x. Express the area of the field as a function of x if $1800 worth of fence can be used. What is the maximum area?

42. The Quick Car Rental Company can rent 100 cars per day at a rate of $10 per day. For each $1.00 increase in rate, five fewer cars are rented. If x represents the increase in rate, express the total income in terms of x. What is the maximum income?

4.3 Business Applications of Quadratic Functions

Objectives   ☐ To graph quadratic supply and demand functions
☐ To find market equilibrium by using quadratic supply and demand functions
☐ To find break-even points by using quadratic cost and revenue functions
☐ To maximize quadratic revenue and profit functions

Supply, Demand, and Market Equilibrium

The first-quadrant parts of parabolas or other quadratic equations are frequently used to represent supply and demand functions. For example, the first-quadrant part of $p = q^2 + q + 2$ (Figure 4.9) may represent a supply curve, while the first-quadrant part of $q^2 + 2q + 6p - 23 = 0$ (Figure 4.10) may represent a demand curve.

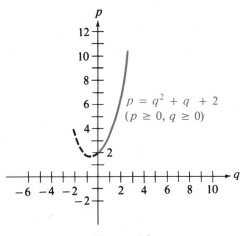

Figure 4.9

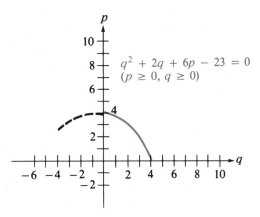

Figure 4.10

When quadratic equations are used to represent supply or demand curves, we can solve their equations simultaneously to find the market equilibrium as we did with linear supply and demand functions. As in Section 1.6, we can solve two equations in two variables by eliminating one variable and obtaining an equation in the other variable. When the functions are quadratic, the substitution method of solution is perhaps the best, and the resulting equation in one unknown will usually be quadratic.

EXAMPLE 1   If the supply function for a commodity is given by $p = q^2 + 100$ and the demand function is given by $p = -20q + 2500$, find the point of market equilibrium.

Solution   At market equilibrium, both equations will have the same p-value. So substituting $q^2 + 100$ for p in $p = -20q + 2500$, we get

$$q^2 + 100 = -20q + 2500$$
$$q^2 + 20q - 2400 = 0$$
$$(q - 40)(q + 60) = 0$$
$$q = 40 \quad \text{or} \quad q = -60.$$

Since a negative quantity has no meaning, the equilibrium point occurs when 40 units are sold, at (40, 1700). The graphs of the functions are shown (in the first quadrant only) in Figure 4.11.

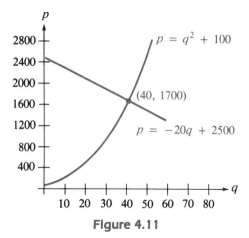

Figure 4.11

EXAMPLE 2   If the demand function for a commodity is given by $p(q + 4) = 400$ and the supply function is given by $2p - q - 38 = 0$, find the market equilibrium.

Solution   First note that the demand is defined by a quadratic equation, but its graph is not a parabola. This causes no problems for us in trying to solve the equations simultaneously; we proceed as before. Solving $2p - q - 38 = 0$ for p gives $p = \frac{1}{2}q + 19$. Substituting for p in $p(q + 4) = 400$ gives

$$\left(\tfrac{1}{2}q + 19\right)(q + 4) = 400$$
$$\tfrac{1}{2}q^2 + 21q - 324 = 0.$$

Multiplying both sides of the equation by 2 gives $q^2 + 42q - 648 = 0$. Factoring gives

$$(q - 12)(q + 54) = 0$$
$$q = 12 \quad \text{or} \quad q = -54.$$

Thus the market equilibrium occurs when 12 items are sold, at a price of $25 each. The graphs of the demand and supply functions are shown in Figure 4.12.

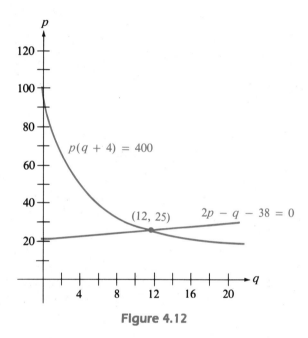

Figure 4.12

Break-Even Points and Profit Maximization

In Chapter 1, we discussed linear total cost and total revenue functions. Many total revenue functions may be linear, but costs tend to increase sharply after a certain level of production. Thus functions other than linear functions, including quadratic functions, are used to predict the total costs of products.

For example, the monthly total cost curve for a commodity may be the parabola with equation $C(x) = 360 + 40x + 0.1x^2$. If the total revenue function is

$R(x) = 60x$, we can find the break-even point by finding the quantity x that makes $C(x) = R(x)$. (See Figure 4.13.)

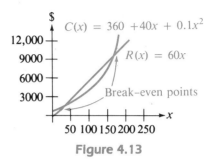

Figure 4.13

Setting $C(x) = R(x)$, we have

$$360 + 40x + 0.1x^2 = 60x$$
$$0.1x^2 - 20x + 360 = 0$$
$$x^2 - 200x + 3600 = 0$$
$$(x - 20)(x - 180) = 0$$
$$x = 20 \quad \text{or} \quad x = 180.$$

Thus $C(x) = R(x)$ at $x = 20$ and at $x = 180$. If 20 items are produced and sold, $C(x)$ and $R(x)$ are both \$1200; if 180 items are sold, $C(x)$ and $R(x)$ are both \$10,800. Thus, there are two break-even points.

EXAMPLE 3   Suppose that the total cost per week of producing Ace electric shavers is given by $C(x) = 360 + 10x + 0.2x^2$. If the price per unit sold is $50 - 0.2x$, at what level(s) of production will the break-even point(s) occur?

Solution   The total cost function is $C(x) = 360 + 10x + 0.2x^2$, and the total revenue function is $R(x) = (50 - 0.2x)x = 50x - 0.2x^2$.

Setting $C(x) = R(x)$ and solving for x gives

$$360 + 10x + 0.2x^2 = 50x - 0.2x^2$$
$$0.4x^2 - 40x + 360 = 0$$
$$4x^2 - 400x + 3600 = 0$$
$$x^2 - 100x + 900 = 0$$
$$(x - 90)(x - 10) = 0$$
$$x = 90 \quad \text{or} \quad x = 10.$$

Does this mean the firm will break even at 10 units and at 90 units? Yes. Figure 4.14 shows the graphs of $C(x)$ and $R(x)$. From the graph we can observe that the firm makes a profit after $x = 10$ *until* $x = 90$. At $x = 90$, the profit is 0, and the firm loses money if more than 90 units are produced per week.

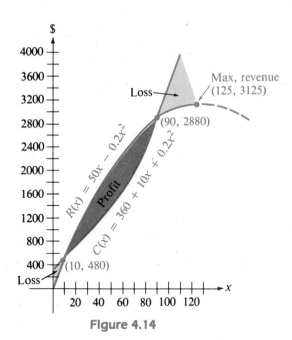

Figure 4.14

Notice that for Example 3, the revenue function

$$R(x) = 50x - 0.2x^2$$

is a parabola that opens downward. Thus the vertex is the point at which revenue is maximum. We can locate this vertex by using the methods discussed in the previous section.

$$\text{Vertex: } x = \frac{-b}{2a} = \frac{-50}{2(-0.2)} = \frac{50}{0.4} = 125 \text{ (units)}$$

It is interesting to note that when $x = 125$, the firm achieves its maximum revenues of

$$R(125) = 50(125) - 0.2(125)^2 = 3125 \text{ (dollars)},$$

but the costs when $x = 125$ are

$$C(125) = 360 + 10(125) + 0.2(125)^2 = 4735 \text{ (dollars)},$$

which results in a loss. This illustrates that maximizing revenue is not a good goal. We should seek to maximize profit.

EXAMPLE 4   If total costs are given by $C(x) = 360 + 10x + 0.2x^2$ and total revenues are given by $R(x) = 50x - 0.2x^2$, form the profit function and find the maximum profit.

Note that these are the same cost and revenue functions that appear in the previous example.

$$\text{Profit} = \text{revenue} - \text{cost},$$

so we have

$$P(x) = (50x - 0.2x^2) - (360 + 10x + 0.2x^2),$$

or

$$P(x) = -360 + 40x - 0.4x^2.$$

Now, this profit function is a parabola that opens downward, so the vertex will be the maximum point.

$$\text{Vertex: } x = \frac{-b}{2a} = \frac{-40}{2(-0.4)} = \frac{-40}{-0.8} = 50$$

Furthermore, when $x = 50$, we have

$$P(50) = -360 + 40(50) - 0.4(50)^2 = 640 \text{ (dollars)}.$$

Thus, when 50 items are produced and sold, a maximum profit of \$640 results (see Figure 4.15).

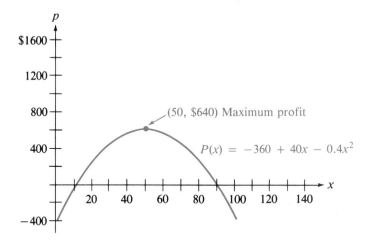

Figure 4.15

Comparing Figures 4.14 and 4.15, notice first that the maximum profit of \$640 at 50 units in Figure 4.15 corresponds to the vertical distance between revenue and cost at 50 units in Figure 4.14. In addition, the break-even points at $x = 10$ and $x = 90$ in Figure 4.14 correspond to x-intercepts (Profit = 0) in Figure 4.15.

It is important to note that the procedures for finding maximum revenue and profit in these examples depend on the fact that these functions are parabolas. For more general functions, procedures for finding maximum or minimum values are discussed in Chapter 10.

Exercise 4.3

SUPPLY, DEMAND, AND MARKET EQUILIBRIUM

1. Sketch the first quadrant portions of the following on the same set of axes.
   (a) The supply function whose equation is $p = \frac{1}{4}q^2 + 10$.
   (b) The demand function whose equation is $p = 86 - 6q - 3q^2$.
   (c) Label the market equilibrium point.
   (d) Algebraically determine the equilibrium point for the supply and demand functions.
2. Sketch the first-quadrant portions of the following on the same set of axes.
   (a) The supply function whose equation is $p = q^2 + 8q + 16$.
   (b) The demand function whose equation is $p = 216 - 2q$.
   (c) Label the market equilibrium point.
   (d) Algebraically determine the equilibrium point for the supply and demand functions.
3. Sketch the first quadrant portions of the following on the same set of axes.
   (a) The supply function whose equation is $p = 0.2q^2 + 0.4q + 1.8$.
   (b) The demand function whose equation is $p = 9 - 0.2q - 0.1q^2$.
   (c) Label the market equilibrium point.
   (d) Algebraically determine the market equilibrium point.
4. Sketch the first-quadrant portions of the following on the same set of axes.
   (a) The supply function whose equation is $p = q^2 + 8q + 22$.
   (b) The demand function whose equation is $p = 198 - 4q - \frac{1}{4}q^2$.
   (c) Label the market equilibrium point.
   (d) Algebraically determine the market equilibrium point for the supply and demand functions.
5. If the supply function for a commodity is $p = q^2 + 8q + 16$ and the demand function is $p = -3q^2 + 6q + 436$, find the equilibrium quantity and equilibrium price.
6. If the supply function for a commodity is $p = q^2 + 8q + 20$ and the demand function is $p = 100 - 4q - q^2$, find the equilibrium quantity and equilibrium price.
7. If the demand function for a commodity is given by the equation $p^2 + 4q = 1600$ and the supply function is given by the equation $300 - p^2 + 2q = 0$, find the equilibrium quantity and equilibrium price.
8. If the supply and demand functions for a commodity are given by $4p - q = 42$ and $(p + 2)q = 2100$, respectively, find the price that will result in market equilibrium.
9. If the supply and demand functions for a commodity are given by $q = p - 10$ and $q = 1200/p$, what is the equilibrium price and what is the corresponding number of units supplied and demanded?
10. If the supply and demand functions for a certain product are given by the equations $2p - q + 6 = 0$ and $(p + q)(q + 10) = 3696$, respectively, find the price and quantity that give market equilibrium.

11. The supply function for a product is $2p - q - 10 = 0$. The demand function for the product is $(p + 10)(q + 30) = 7200$. Find the market equilibrium point.

12. Supply and demand for a product are given by $2p - q = 50$ and $pq = 100 + 20q$, respectively. Find the market equilibrium point.

13. For the product in problem 11, if a $22 tax is placed on production of the item, then the supplier passes this tax on by adding $22 to his selling price. Find the new equilibrium point for this product when the tax is passed on. (The new supply function is given by $p = \frac{1}{2}q + 27$.)

14. For the product in problem 12, if a $12.50 tax is placed on production and passed through by the supplier, find the new equilibrium point.

BREAK-EVEN POINTS AND MAXIMIZATION

15. The total costs for a company are given by

$$C(x) = 2000 + 40x + x^2$$

and the total revenues are given by

$$R(x) = 130x.$$

Find the break-even points.

16. If a firm has the following cost and revenue functions,

$$C(x) = 3600 + 25x + \frac{1}{2}x^2; \qquad R(x) = \left(175 - \frac{1}{2}x\right)x,$$

find the break-even points.

17. If a company has total costs given by $C(x) = 15,000 + 35x + 0.1x^2$ and total revenues given by $R(x) = 385x - 0.9x^2$, find the break-even points.

18. If total costs are $C(x) = 1600 + 1500x$ and total revenues are $R(x) = 1600x - x^2$, find the break-even points.

19. Given $C(x) = 150 + x + 0.09x^2$ and $R(x) = 12.5x - 0.01x^2$, and given that production is restricted to fewer than 75 units, find the break-even points.

20. If the profit function for a firm is given by $P(x) = -1100 + 120x - x^2$ and limitations on space require that production is less than 100 units, find the break-even points.

21. Find the maximum revenue for the revenue function $R(x) = 385x - 0.9x^2$.

22. Find the maximum revenue for the revenue function $R(x) = 1600x - x^2$.

23. If the profit function for a product is given by $P(x) = 92x - x^2 - 1760$, find the maximum profit.

24. Find maximum revenue for $R(x) = (175 - \frac{1}{2}x)x$.

25. The profit function for a certain commodity is $P(x) = 110x - x^2 - 1000$. Find the level of production that yields maximum profit, and find the maximum profit.

26. The profit function for a firm making widgets is $P(x) = 88x - x^2 - 1200$. Find the number of units at which maximum profit is achieved and find the maximum profit.

27. (a) Form the profit function for the cost and revenue functions in problem 17, and find maximum profit.
    (b) Compare the level of production to maximize profit with the level to maximize revenue (see problem 21). Do they agree?
    (c) How do the break-even points compare with the zeros of $P(x)$?

28. (a) Form the profit function for the cost and revenue functions in problem 18, and find maximum profit.
   (b) Compare the level of production to maximize profit with the level to maximize revenue (see problem 22). Do they agree?
   (c) How do the break-even points compare with the zeros of $P(x)$?

29. Suppose a company has fixed costs of \$28,000 and variable costs of $\frac{2}{3}x + 222$ dollars per unit, where x is the total number of units produced. Suppose further that the selling price of its product is $1250 - \frac{3}{5}x$ dollars per unit.
   (a) Find the break-even points.
   (b) Find the maximum revenue.
   (c) Form the profit function from the cost and revenue functions and find maximum profit.
   (d) Compare the level of production to maximize profit with the level to maximize revenue. Do they agree?

30. Suppose a company has fixed costs of \$300 and variable costs of $\frac{3}{4}x + 1460$ dollars per unit, where x is the total number of units produced. Suppose further that the selling price of its product is $1500 - \frac{1}{4}x$ dollars per unit.
   (a) Find the break-even points.
   (b) Find the maximum revenue.
   (c) Form the profit function from the cost and revenue functions and find maximum profit.
   (d) Compare the level of production to maximize profit with the level to maximize revenue. Do they agree?

Review Exercises

4.1

In problems 1–14, find the real solutions to each quadratic equation. Give exact answers.

1. $3x^2 + 10x = 5x$
2. $4x - 3x^2 = 0$
3. $x^2 + 5x + 6 = 0$
4. $11 - 10x - 2x^2 = 0$
5. $(x - 1)(x + 3) = -8$
6. $4x^2 = 3$
7. $4z^2 + 25 = 0$
8. $z(z + 6) = 27$
9. $3x^2 - 18x - 48 = 0$
10. $3x^2 - 6x - 9 = 0$
11. $20x^2 + 3x = 20 - 15x^2$
12. $8x^2 + 8x = 1 - 8x^2$
13. $7 = 2.07x - 0.02x^2$
14. $46.3x - 117 - 0.5x^2 = 0$
15. Solve $x^2 + ax + b = 0$ for x.
16. Solve $xr^2 - 4ar - x^2c = 0$ for r.

In problems 17 and 18, approximate the real solutions to each quadratic equation to two decimal places.

17. $23.1 - 14.1x - 0.002x^2 = 0$
18. $1.03x^2 + 2.02x - 1.015 = 0$

4.2

For each function in problems 19–24, find the vertex and determine if it is a maximum or minimum point, find the zeros if they exist, and sketch the graph.

19. $y = \frac{1}{2}x^2 + 2x$
20. $y = 4 - \frac{1}{4}x^2$
21. $y = 6 + x - x^2$
22. $y = x^2 - 4x + 5$
23. $y = x^2 + 6x + 9$
24. $y = 12x - 9 - 4x^2$

In problems 25–30, graph each function. Be sure to label the maximum or minimum point.

25. $y = \frac{1}{3}x^2 - 3$ 26. $y = \frac{1}{2}x^2 + 2$
27. $y = x^2 + 2x + 5$ 28. $y = -10 + 7x - x^2$
29. $y = 20x - 0.1x^2$ 30. $y = 50 - 1.5x + 0.01x^2$

APPLICATIONS

31. A rectangular lot is to be fenced in, then divided down the middle to create two identical fenced lots (see Figure 4.16).

Figure 4.16

If 1200 ft of fence is to be used, the area of each lot is given by

$$A = x\left(\frac{1200 - 3x}{4}\right)$$

(a) Find the x value that maximizes this area.
(b) Find the maximum area.

4.3

32. Graph the first-quadrant portion of the supply function

$$p = 2q^2 + 4q + 6.$$

33. Graph the first-quadrant portion of the demand function

$$p = 18 - 3q - q^2.$$

34. (a) Suppose the supply function for a product is $p = 0.1q^2 + 1$ and the demand function is $p = 85 - 0.2q - 0.1q^2$. Sketch the first quadrant portion of the graph of each function. Use the same set of axes for both and label the market equilibrium point.
    (b) Use algebraic methods to find the equilibrium price and quantity.
35. The supply function for a product is given by $p = q^2 + 300$, and the demand is given by $p + q = 410$. Find the equilibrium quantity and price.
36. If the demand function for a commodity is given by the equation $p^2 + 5q = 200$ and the supply function is given by $40 - p^2 + 3q = 0$, find the equilibrium quantity and price.
37. If total costs for a product are given by $C(x) = 1760 + 8x + 0.6x^2$ and total revenues are given by $R(x) = 100x - 0.4x^2$, find the break-even points.
38. If total costs for a commodity are given by $C(x) = 900 + 25x$ and total revenues are given by $R(x) = 100x - x^2$, find the break-even points.
39. Find the maximum revenue and maximum profit for the functions described in problem 38.
40. Given total profit $P(x) = 1.3x - 0.01x^2 - 30$, find maximum profit and the break-even points and sketch the graph.

41. Given $C(x) = 360 + 10x + 0.2x^2$ and $R(x) = 50x - 0.2x^2$, find the level of production that gives maximum profit and find the maximum profit.

42. A certain company has fixed costs of $15,000 for its product and variable costs given by $140 + 0.04x$ dollars per unit, where x is the total number of units. The selling price of the product is given by $300 - 0.06x$ dollars per unit.
    (a) Formulate the functions for total cost and total revenue.
    (b) Find the break-even points.
    (c) Find the level of sales that maximizes revenue.
    (d) Form the profit function and find the level of production and sales that maximizes profit.
    (e) Find the profit (or loss) at the production levels found in parts (c) and (d).

WARMUP

	Prerequisite problem type	Answer	Section for review
5.1, 5.2, 5.3	Write the following with positive exponents: (a) x^{-3} (b) $\dfrac{1}{x^{-2}}$ (c) $\sqrt{x}$	(a) $\dfrac{1}{x^3}$ (b) x^2 (c) $x^{1/2}$	0.3, 0.4 Exponents and radicals
5.1, 5.2, 5.3	Simplify: (a) 2^0 (b) x^0 $(x \neq 0)$ (c) $49^{1/2}$ (d) 10^{-2}	(a) 1 (b) 1 (c) 7 (d) $\frac{1}{100}$	0.3, 0.4 Exponents
5.1, 5.2	Answer true or false. (a) $\left(\frac{1}{2}\right)^x = 2^{-x}$ (b) $\sqrt{50} = 50^{1/2}$ (c) If $8 = 2^y$, then $y = 4$. (d) If $x^3 = 8$, then $x = 2$.	(a) True (b) True (c) False; $y = 3$ (d) True	0.3, 0.4 Exponents and radicals
5.1, 5.2, 5.3	(a) If $f(x) = 2^{-2x}$, what is $f(-2)$? (b) If $f(x) = 2^{-2x}$, what is $f(1)$? (c) If $f(t) = (1 + 0.02)^t$, what is $f(0)$? (d) If $f(t) = 100(0.03)^{0.02^t}$, what is $f(0)$?	(a) 16 (b) $\frac{1}{4}$ (c) 1 (d) 3	1.3 Functional notation

5

Exponential and Logarithmic Functions

In this chapter we study exponential and logarithmic functions, which provide models for many applications that at first seem remote and unrelated. For example, a business manager uses these functions to study the growth of money or corporations or the decay of new sales volume. A social scientist uses exponential and logarithmic functions to study the growth of organizations or populations or the dating of fossilized remains. And a biologist uses these functions to study the growth of microorganisms in a laboratory culture, the spread of disease, the measurement of pH, or the decay of radioactive material.

In our study of exponential and logarithmic functions we will examine their description, their properties, their graphs, and the special inverse relationship between these two functions. We will see how these functions are applied to some of the concerns of social scientists, business managers, and life scientists. In these applications, the inverse relationship of the exponential and logarithmic functions is used to solve some of the equations that arise. The work with these functions will be much easier if you have a calculator that computes powers of e and logarithms to the base e (denoted e^x and $\ln x$, respectively), but tables have been provided in the appendix in case you do not have such a calculator.

5.1 Exponential Functions

Objective □ To graph exponential functions

Suppose we observe a culture of bacteria to have the characteristic that each minute, every microorganism present splits into two new organisms. Then we can describe the number of bacteria present in the culture as a function of time. That is, if we begin the culture with just one microorganism, then we know that after one minute we will have two organisms, after two minutes, four, and so on. Table 5.1 on the following page gives a few of the values that describe the growth.

257

Table 5.1

Minutes passed	0	1	2	3	4
Number	1	2	4	8	16

If x represents the number of minutes that have passed and y represents the number of organisms, the points (x, y) lie on the graph of the function with equation

$$y = 2^x.$$

This equation is an example of a special group of functions called **exponential functions.** In general, we define these functions as follows.

If a is a positive real number, then the function

$$f(x) = a^x$$

is an **exponential function.**

A table of some values satisfying $y = 2^x$ and the graph of this function are given in Figure 5.1. This function is said to model the growth of the number of organisms in the discussion above even though some points on the graph do not correspond to a time and a number of organisms. For example, time x could not be negative, and the number of organisms y could not be fractional.

We have defined rational powers of x in terms of radicals in Chapter 0, so 2^x makes sense for any rational power x. It can also be shown that the laws of exponents apply for irrational numbers. We will assume that if we graphed $y = 2^x$ for irrational values of x, those points would lie on the curve in Figure 5.1. Thus, in general, we can graph an exponential function by plotting easily calculated points, such as those in the table for Figure 5.1, and drawing a smooth curve through the points.

x	$y = 2^x$
-3	$2^{-3} = \frac{1}{8}$
-2	$2^{-2} = \frac{1}{4}$
-1	$2^{-1} = \frac{1}{2}$
0	$2^0 = 1$
1	$2^1 = 2$
2	$2^2 = 4$
3	$2^3 = 8$

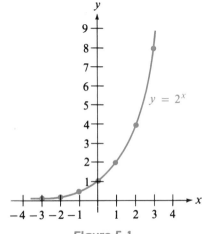

Figure 5.1

EXAMPLE 1   Graph $y = 10^x$.

Solution   A table of values and the graph are given in Figure 5.2.

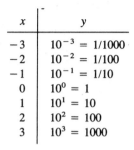

x	y
-3	$10^{-3} = 1/1000$
-2	$10^{-2} = 1/100$
-1	$10^{-1} = 1/10$
0	$10^0 = 1$
1	$10^1 = 10$
2	$10^2 = 100$
3	$10^3 = 1000$

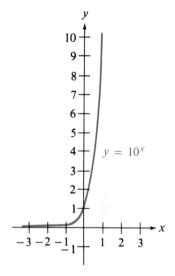

Figure 5.2

Note that the graphs of $y = 2^x$ and $y = 10^x$ are very similar. In each case there is no x-value that makes 2^x or 10^x less than or equal to zero. Each graph approaches, but never touches, the x-axis on the left. (We call the x-axis an **asymptote** for these curves.) The domain of each function contains all real numbers, and the range contains all positive real numbers. Both graphs pass through the point $(0, 1)$. In fact, the only difference between the graphs of $y = 2^x$ and $y = 10^x$ is that $y = 10^x$ rises more rapidly than $y = 2^x$.

The shapes of the graphs of equations of the form $y = a^x$, with $a > 1$, are similar to those for $y = 2^x$ and $y = 10^x$. Exponentials of this type model growth in diverse applications, and their graphs have the following basic shape:

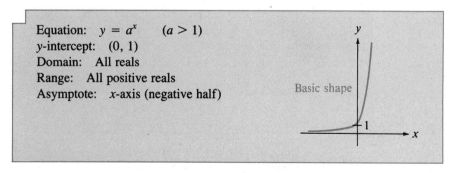

Equation: $y = a^x$ $(a > 1)$
y-intercept: $(0, 1)$
Domain: All reals
Range: All positive reals
Asymptote: x-axis (negative half)

Basic shape

A special function that occurs frequently in economics and biology is $y = e^x$, where e is a fixed irrational number (approximately $2.71828\ldots$). We will see how *e* arises in Section 6.2 when we discuss interest that is compounded continuously, and we will formally define *e* in Section 9.2.

Since $e > 1$, the graph of $y = e^x$ will have the same basic shape as other growth exponentials. We can calculate the *y*-coordinate for points on the graph of this function with a calculator or Table I in the Appendix. A table of some values (with *y*-values rounded to two places) and the graph are shown in Figure 5.3.

Exponential functions with base *e* often arise in natural ways. As we will see in Section 6.2, the growth of money that is compounded continuously is given by $A = P_0 e^{rt}$, where P_0 is the original principal, *r* the annual interest rate, and *t* the time in years. Certain populations (of insects, for example) grow exponentially, and the number of individuals can be closely approximated by the equation $y = P_0 e^{ht}$, where P_0 is the original population size, *h* is a constant that depends on the type of population, and *y* is the population size at any instant *t*. These are both examples of exponential growth with base *e*.

Exponentials whose base is between 0 and 1, such as $y = \left(\frac{1}{2}\right)^x$, have graphs different from the exponentials just discussed. Using the properties of exponents, we have

$$y = \left(\frac{1}{2}\right)^x = (2^{-1})^x = 2^{-x}.$$

This suggests that exponentials of the form $y = b^x$, where $0 < b < 1$, can be rewritten in the form $y = a^{-x}$, where $a > 1$.

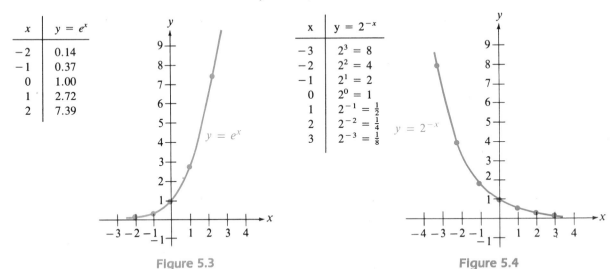

x	$y = e^x$
-2	0.14
-1	0.37
0	1.00
1	2.72
2	7.39

Figure 5.3

x	$y = 2^{-x}$
-3	$2^3 = 8$
-2	$2^2 = 4$
-1	$2^1 = 2$
0	$2^0 = 1$
1	$2^{-1} = \frac{1}{2}$
2	$2^{-2} = \frac{1}{4}$
3	$2^{-3} = \frac{1}{8}$

Figure 5.4

EXAMPLE 2   Graph $y = 2^{-x}$.

Solution   A table of values and the graph are given in Figure 5.4.

EXAMPLE 3   **Graph $y = e^{-2x}$.**

Solution   Using a calculator or Table I in the Appendix to find the values of powers of e (to two decimal places), we get the graph shown in Figure 5.5.

x	y
-3	$e^6 = 403.43$
-2	$e^4 = 54.60$
-1	$e^2 = 7.40$
0	$e^0 = 1.00$
1	$e^{-2} = 0.14$
2	$e^{-4} = 0.02$

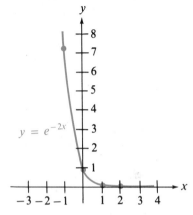

Figure 5.5

Exponential functions of the form $y = a^{-x}$, where $a > 1$, all have a similar basic shape. They fall rapidly to the right, approaching but not touching the positive x-axis. Functions of this type model decay for various phenomena. For example, the number of atoms y of a radioactive element at an instant in time t is given by

$$y = w_0 e^{-h(t - t_0)},$$

where w_0 is the number of atoms at time t_0 and h is a constant that depends on the element.

There are some important exponential functions that use base e, but whose graphs are different from those we have discussed. For example, the standard normal probability curve, which will be studied in Section 8.6, is the graph of an exponential function with base e (see Figure 5.6).

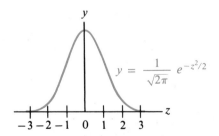

Standard normal probability curve

Figure 5.6

Later in this chapter we will study other exponential functions that model growth, but whose graphs are also different from those discussed above.

Exercise 5.1

In problems 1–10, use a calculator or table to evaluate each expression.

1. $10^{0.5}$ 2. $10^{3.6}$
3. $5^{-2.7}$ 4. $8^{-2.6}$
5. $3^{1/3}$ 6. $2^{11/6}$
7. e^2 8. e^5
9. e^{-3} 10. $e^{-1.5}$

In problems 11–22, graph each function.

11. $y = 4^x$ 12. $y = 8^x$
13. $y = 2(x^3)$ 14. $y = 3(2^x)$
15. $y = 5^x$ 16. $y = 3^{x-1}$
17. $y = e^x$ 18. $y = 2e^x$
19. $y = 3^{-x}$ 20. $y = 3^{-2x}$
21. $y = e^{-x}$ 22. $y = \frac{1}{3}e^x$

In problems 23–28, use the graph of $y = 2^x$ (see Figure 5.1) to sketch each graph.

23. $y = 2^{x+1}$ 24. $y = 2^{x-2}$
25. $y = 3(2^x)$ 26. $y = \frac{1}{4}(2^x)$
27. $y + 1 = 2^x$ 28. $y - 1 = 2^x$
29. Graph $y = 1 + e^x$ 30. Graph $y = 2 + e^{-x}$
31. How does the graph in problem 29 differ from the graph of $y = e^x$?
32. How does the graph in problem 30 differ from the graph of $y = e^{-x}$?

APPLICATIONS

33–36. World population can be considered as growing according to the equation

$$N = N_0(1 + r)^t$$

where N_0 is the number of individuals at time $t = 0$, r is the yearly rate of growth, and t is the number of years.

33. Sketch the graph for $t = 0$ to $t = 10$ when the growth rate is 2% and N_0 is 4.1 billion.
34. Sketch the graph for $t = 0$ to $t = 10$ when the growth rate is 3% and N_0 is 4.1 billion.
35. Repeat problem 33 when the growth rate is 5%.
36. Repeat problem 34 when the growth rate is 7%.
37. The number of molecules of a certain substance that have enough energy to activate a reaction is given by

$$y = 100,000 \, e^{-1/x},$$

where y is the number of molecules and x is the (absolute) temperature of the substance. Plot the graph of this equation for $x > 0$.
38. When a body is moved from one medium to another, its temperature T will change according to the equation

$$T = T_0 + ce^{kt},$$

where T_0 is the temperature of the new medium, c the temperature difference between the mediums (old − new), t the time in the new medium, and k a constant. Given that $T_0 = 70$, $c = 23$, and $k = -0.2$, sketch the graph for $t \geq 0$.

39. We will show in Chapter 6 that if $P is invested for n years at 10% compounded continuously, the total amount returned on the investment is given by

$$S = Pe^{0.1n}.$$

Use $P = 1000$ and graph this function for $0 \leq n \leq 20$.

40. A single bacterium splits into two bacteria every half hour, so that the number of bacteria in a culture quadruples every hour. Thus the equation by which a colony of 10 bacteria multiplies in t hours is given by

$$y = 10(4^t).$$

Graph this equation for $0 \leq t \leq 8$.

41. The concentration y of a certain drug in the bloodstream at any time t is given by the equation

$$y = 100(1 - e^{-0.462t}).$$

Graph this equation for $0 \leq t \leq 10$.

42. A statistical study shows that the fraction of television sets of a certain brand that are still in service after x years is given by $f = e^{-0.15x}$. Graph this equation for $0 \leq x \leq 10$.

43. The atmospheric pressure P (in lbs/sq in.) is given by

$$P = 14.7e^{-0.2x},$$

where x is the number of miles above sea level. Graph this equation for $0 \leq x \leq 20$.

5.2 Logarithmic Functions and Their Properties

Objectives
- [ ] To convert equations for logarithmic functions from logarithmic to exponential form and vice versa
- [ ] To evaluate some special logarithms
- [ ] To graph logarithmic functions
- [ ] To use properties of logarithmic functions to simplify expressions involving logarithms

Before the development and easy availability of calculators and computers, certain arithmetic computations, such as $(1.37)^{13}$ and $\sqrt[16]{3.09}$, were difficult to perform. The computations could be performed relatively easily using **logarithms,** which were developed in the sixteenth century by John Napier, or by using a slide rule, which is based on logarithms. The use of logarithms as a computing technique has all but disappeared today, but the study of **logarithmic functions** is still very important because of the many applications of these functions.

For example, let us again consider the culture of bacteria described at the beginning of Section 5.1. If we know that the culture is begun with one microorganism and that each minute every microorganism present splits into two new ones, then we can find the number of minutes it takes until there are 1024 organisms by solving

$$1024 = 2^y.$$

The solution of this equation may be written in the form

$$y = \log_2 1024,$$

which is read "y equals the logarithm of 1024 to the base 2."

In general, we may express the equation $x = a^y$ ($a > 0$, $a \neq 1$) in the form $y = f(x)$ by defining a **logarithmic function.**

Logarithmic Function	For $a > 0$ and $a \neq 1$, the **logarithmic function**

For $a > 0$ and $a \neq 1$, the **logarithmic function**

$$y = \log_a x \quad \text{(logarithmic form)}$$

has domain $x > 0$, and is defined by

$$a^y = x \quad \text{(exponential form).}$$

The a is called the **base** in both $\log_a x = y$ and $a^y = x$, and y is the *logarithm* in $\log_a x = y$ and the *exponent* in $a^y = x$. Thus, **a logarithm is an exponent.**

Table 5.2 shows some logarithmic equations and their equivalent exponential form.

Table 5.2

Logarithmic form	Exponential form
$\log_{10} 100 = 2$	$10^2 = 100$
$\log_{10} 0.1 = -1$	$10^{-1} = 0.1$
$\log_2 x = y$	$2^y = x$
$\log_a 1 = 0 \quad (a > 0)$	$a^0 = 1$
$\log_a a = 1 \quad (a > 0)$	$a^1 = a$

EXAMPLE 1   (a) Write $64 = 4^3$ in logarithmic form.
(b) Write $\log_4 \left(\frac{1}{64}\right) = -3$ in exponential form.
(c) If $4 = \log_2 x$, find x.

Solution   (a) $64 = 4^3$ is equivalent to $3 = \log_4 64$.
(b) $\log_4 \left(\frac{1}{64}\right) = -3$ is equivalent to $4^{-3} = \frac{1}{64}$.
(c) If $4 = \log_2 x$, then $2^4 = x$ and $x = 16$.

EXAMPLE 2   Evaluate: (a) $\log_2 8$ (b) $\log_3 9$ (c) $\log_5 \left(\frac{1}{25}\right)$.

Solution   (a) If $y = \log_2 8$, then $8 = 2^y$. Since $2^3 = 8$, $\log_2 8 = 3$.
(b) If $y = \log_3 9$, then $9 = 3^y$. Since $3^2 = 9$, $\log_3 9 = 2$.
(c) If $y = \log_5 \left(\frac{1}{25}\right)$, then $\frac{1}{25} = 5^y$. Since $5^{-2} = \frac{1}{25}$, $\log_5 \left(\frac{1}{25}\right) = -2$.

We can use the exponential form of a logarithmic equation to sketch its graph.

EXAMPLE 3   Graph $y = \log_2 x$.

Solution   We may graph $y = \log_2 x$ by graphing $x = 2^y$. The table of values (found by substituting values in for y and calculating x) and the graph are shown in Figure 5.7.

$x = 2^y$	y
$\frac{1}{8}$	-3
$\frac{1}{4}$	-2
$\frac{1}{2}$	-1
1	0
2	1
4	2
8	3

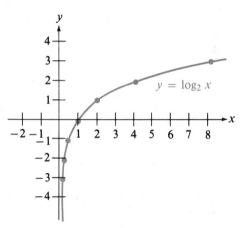

Figure 5.7

From the definition of logarithms, we see that all logarithms have a base. Yet most applications of logarithms involve logarithms to the base 10 (called **common logarithms**) or logarithms to the base e (called **natural logarithms**). In fact, logarithms to the base 10 and to the base e are the only ones that have function keys on scientific calculators. Thus it is important to be familiar with their names and their designation.

Common Logarithms: $\log x$ means $\log_{10} x$

Natural Logarithms: $\ln x$ means $\log_e x$

Values of the natural logarithm function are found in Table II in the Appendix.

EXAMPLE 4   Graph $y = \ln x$.

Solution   We can graph $y = \ln x$ by writing the equation in its exponential form, $x = e^y$, and
then finding x for integer values of y. We can also graph by evaluating $y = \ln x$
for $x > 0$ (including some values $0 < x < 1$) with a calculator or Table II of the
Appendix. The graph is shown in Figure 5.8.

y	$x = e^y$		x	$y = \ln x$
-3	0.050		0.05	-3.000
-2	0.135		0.10	-2.303
-1	0.368		0.50	-0.693
0	1.000		1	0.000
1	2.718		2	0.693
2	7.389		3	1.099
3	20.086		5	1.609
			10	2.303

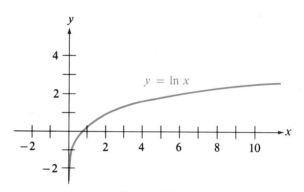

Figure 5.8

Note that the graphs of $y = \log_2 x$ and $y = \ln x$ are very similar. The shapes
of graphs of equations of the form $y = \log_a x$ with $a > 1$ are similar to these two
graphs.

Equation: $y = \log_a x$ $(a > 1)$
x-intercept: $(1, 0)$
Domain: All positive reals
Range: All reals
Asymptote: y-axis (negative half)

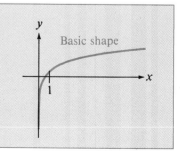

The definition of the logarithmic function and the previous examples suggest a special relationship between the logarithmic function $y = \log_a x$ and the exponential function $y = a^x$ $(a > 0, a \neq 1)$. Since we can write $y = \log_a x$ in exponential form as $x = a^y$, we see that the connection between

$$y = \log_a x \qquad \text{and} \qquad y = a^x$$

is that x and y have been interchanged from one function to the other. This is true for the functional description and hence for the pairs that satisfy these functions. This is illustrated in Table 5.3 for the functions $y = \log_{10} x$ and $y = 10^x$.

Table 5.3

| $y = \log_{10} x$ | | $y = 10^x$ | |
Coordinates	Justification	Coordinates	Justification
$(1000, 3)$	$3 = \log_{10} 1000$	$(3, 1000)$	$1000 = 10^3$
$(100, 2)$	$2 = \log_{10} 100$	$(2, 100)$	$100 = 10^2$
$\left(\frac{1}{10}, -1\right)$	$-1 = \log_{10} \frac{1}{10}$	$\left(-1, \frac{1}{10}\right)$	$\frac{1}{10} = 10^{-1}$

In general, we say $y = f(x)$ and $y = g(x)$ are **inverse functions** if, whenever the pair (a, b) satisfies $y = f(x)$, then the pair (b, a) satisfies $y = g(x)$. Furthermore, because the values of the x and y coordinates are interchanged for inverse functions, their graphs are reflections of each other in the line $y = x$.

Thus for $a > 0$ and $a \neq 1$, the logarithmic function $y = \log_a x$ (also written $x = a^y$) and the exponential function $y = a^x$ are inverse functions.

The logarithmic function $y = \log x$ is the inverse of the exponential function $y = 10^x$. Thus the graphs $y = \log_{10} x$ and $y = 10^x$ are reflections of each other about the line $y = x$. Some values of x and y for these functions are given in Table 5.3, and their graphs are shown in Figure 5.9.

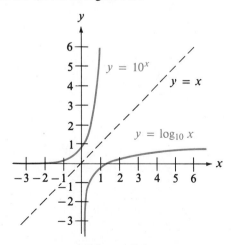

Figure 5.9

As we stated previously, if $y = \log_a x$, then $x = a^y$. This means that the logarithm y is an exponent. For example, $\log_3 81 = 4$ because $3^4 = 81$. In this case the logarithm 4 was the exponent to which we had to raise the base to obtain 81. In general, if $y = \log_a x$, then y is the exponent to which the base a must be raised to obtain x.

Since logarithms are exponents, the properties of logarithms can be derived from the properties of exponents. (The properties of exponents are discussed in Chapter 0.) The following properties of logarithms are useful in simplifying expressions containing logarithms.

Logarithm Property I   If $a > 0$, $a \neq 1$, then $\log_a a^x = x$, for any real number x.

EXAMPLE 5   Use Property I to simplify each of the following.
(a) $\log_4 4^3$ (b) $\log_e e^x$

Solution   (a) $\log_4 4^3 = 3$
CHECK: The exponential form is $4^3 = 4^3$.
(b) $\log_e e^x = x$
CHECK: The exponential form is $e^x = e^x$.

We note that two special cases of Property I are used frequently; these are when $x = 1$ and $x = 0$.

Since $a^1 = a$,   we have $\log_a a = 1$.
Since $a^0 = 1$,   we have $\log_a 1 = 0$.

Logarithm Property II   If $a > 0$, $a \neq 1$, then $a^{\log_a x} = x$, for any positive real number x.

EXAMPLE 6   Use Property II to simplify each of the following.
(a) $2^{\log_2 4}$ (b) $e^{\ln x}$

Solution   (a) $2^{\log_2 4} = 4$
CHECK: The logarithmic form is $\log_2 4 = \log_2 4$.
(b) $e^{\ln x} = x$
CHECK: The logarithmic form is $\log_e x = \ln x$.

Logarithm Property III	If $a > 0$, $a \neq 1$, and M and N are positive real numbers, then $\log_a (MN) = \log_a M + \log_a N$.

EXAMPLE 7   (a) Find $\log_2 (4 \cdot 16)$, if $\log_2 4 = 2$ and $\log_2 16 = 4$.
(b) Find $\log_{10} (4 \cdot 5)$ if $\log_{10} 4 = 0.6021$ and $\log_{10} 5 = 0.6990$.

Solution   (a) $\log_2 (4 \cdot 16) = \log_2 4 + \log_2 16 = 2 + 4 = 6$
CHECK: $\log_2 (4 \cdot 16) = \log_2 (64) = 6$, because $2^6 = 64$.
(b) $\log_{10} (4 \cdot 5) = \log_{10} 4 + \log_{10} 5 = 0.6021 + 0.6990 = 1.3011$
CHECK: Using a calculator, we can see that $10^{1.3011} = 20 = 4 \cdot 5$.

Logarithm Property IV	If $a > 0$, $a \neq 1$, and M and N are positive real numbers, then $\log_a (M/N) = \log_a M - \log_a N$.

EXAMPLE 8   (a) Evaluate $\log_3 \left(\frac{9}{27}\right)$.
(b) Find $\log_{10} \left(\frac{16}{5}\right)$, if $\log_{10} 16 = 1.2041$ and $\log_{10} 5 = 0.6990$ (to 4 decimal places).

Solution   (a) $\log_3 \left(\frac{9}{27}\right) = \log_3 9 - \log_3 27 = 2 - 3 = -1$
CHECK: $\log_3 \left(\frac{1}{3}\right) = -1$ because $3^{-1} = \frac{1}{3}$.
(b) $\log_{10} \left(\frac{16}{5}\right) = \log_{10} 16 - \log_{10} 5 = 1.2041 - 0.6990 = 0.5051$
CHECK: Using a calculator, we can see that $10^{0.5051} = 3.2 = \frac{16}{5}$.

Logarithm Property V	If $a > 0$, $a \neq 1$, M is a positive real number, and N is any real number, then $\log_a (M^N) = N \log_a M$.

EXAMPLE 9   (a) Simplify $\log_3 (9^2)$.
(b) Simplify $\ln 8^{-4}$, if $\ln 8 = 2.0794$ (to 4 decimal places).

Solution   (a) $\log_3 (9^2) = 2 \log_3 9 = 2 \cdot 2 = 4$
CHECK: $\log_3 81 = 4$ because $3^4 = 81$.
(b) $\ln 8^{-4} = -4 \ln 8 = -4(2.0794) = -8.3176$

Natural logarithms, $y = \ln x$ (and the inverse exponential with base e), have many practical applications, some of which are considered in the next section. Common logarithms, $y = \log x$, were widely used for computation before computers and calculators became popular. They also have several applications to scaling variables, where the purpose is to reduce the scale of variation when a natural physical variable covers a wide range.

EXAMPLE 10   The Richter scale is used to measure the intensity of an earthquake. The magnitude on the Richter scale of an earthquake of intensity I is given by

$$R = \log (I/I_0),$$

where I_0 is a certain minimum intensity used for comparison.
(a) Find R if I is 3,160,000 times as great as I_0.
(b) The 1964 Alaskan earthquake measured 8.5 on the Richter scale. Find the intensity of the 1964 Alaskan earthquake.

Solution   (a) With $I = 3{,}160{,}000 \, I_0$, then $I/I_0 = 3{,}160{,}000$. Hence

$$\begin{aligned} R &= \log (3{,}160{,}000) \\ &= 6.5 \qquad \text{(to one decimal place).} \end{aligned}$$

(b) For $R = 8.5$, it follows that

$$8.5 = \log (I/I_0).$$

Rewriting this in exponential form gives

$$10^{8.5} = I/I_0,$$

and from a calculator we obtain

$$I/I_0 = 316{,}000{,}000 \qquad \text{(approximately).}$$

Thus the intensity is 316,000,000 times I_0.

Notice that a Richter scale measurement that is 2 units larger means that the intensity is $10^2 = 100$ *times* greater.

Exercise 5.2

In problems 1–4, write each equation in exponential form.

1. $4 = \log_2 16$ 2. $3 = \log_3 27$
3. $\frac{1}{2} = \log_4 2$ 4. $-2 = \log_3 \left(\frac{1}{9}\right)$

In problems 5–8, solve for x.

5. $\log_2 x = 3$ 6. $\log_4 x = -2$
7. $\log_8 x = -\frac{1}{3}$ 8. $\log_{25} x = \frac{1}{2}$

In problems 9–12, write each equation in logarithmic form.

9. $2^5 = 32$ 10. $5^3 = 125$

11. $4^{-1} = \frac{1}{4}$ 12. $9^{1/2} = 3$

In problems 13–18, graph the functions.

13. $y = \log_3 x$ 14. $y = \log_4 x$
15. $y = \ln x$ 16. $y = \log_9 x$
17. $y = \log_2 (-x)$ 18. $y = \ln (-x)$

Evaluate the following:

19. $\log_3 27$ 20. $\log_4 16$
21. $\log_9 3$ 22. $\log_5 \left(\frac{1}{5}\right)$
23. $\log_3 3^4$ 24. $\log_5 5^{2/3}$
25. $\ln e^x$ 26. $\ln e^5$
27. $\log 10$ 28. $\ln e$
29. $\log 100$ 30. $\ln \sqrt{e}$
31. $3^{\log_3 x}$ 32. $4^{\log_4 5}$
33. $10^{\log 2}$ 34. $e^{\ln 3}$

35. Find $\log (3 \cdot 4)$, if $\log 3 = 0.4771$ and $\log 4 = 0.6021$ (to 4 decimal places).
36. Find $\log (12 \cdot 43)$, if $\log 12 = 1.0792$ and $\log 43 = 1.6335$ (to 4 decimal places).
37. Find $\log \left(\frac{13}{4}\right)$, if $\log 13 = 1.1139$ and $\log 4 = 0.6021$ (to 4 decimal places).
38. Find $\log_3 \left(\frac{27}{9}\right)$, if $\log_3 27 = 3$ and $\log_3 9 = 2$. Does the answer equal $\log_3 3$?
39. Find $\log (16^{-2})$, given that $\log 16 = 1.2041$ (to 4 decimal places).
40. Find $\log \sqrt{351}$, given $\log 351 = 2.5453$ (to 4 decimal places).
41. Find $\ln 16^3$, if $\ln 16 = 2.773$ (to 4 decimal places).
42. Find $\ln \sqrt{50}$, if $\ln 50 = 3.912$ (to 4 decimal places).

Write each expression in problems 43–46 as the sum or difference of two logarithmic functions containing no exponents.

43. $\log \left(\dfrac{x}{x + 1}\right)$ 44. $\ln[(x + 1)(4x + 5)]$

45. $\log_7 (x \sqrt[3]{x + 4})$ 46. $\log_5 \left[\dfrac{x^2}{\sqrt{x + 4}}\right]$

47. Prove Logarithm Property I. (*Hint:* Let $v = \log_a a^x$, and write the expression in exponential form.)
48. Prove Logarithm Property II. (*Hint:* Let $u = \log_a x$, and write the expression in exponential form.)
49. Prove Logarithm Property III. (*Hint:* Let $u = \log_a M$ and $v = \log_a N$, write them in exponential form, and find the product MN.)

APPLICATIONS

Use the formula $R = \log (I/I_0)$ in problems 50–55.

50. Find the Richter scale reading of an earthquake with intensity 20,000 times I_0.
51. Find the Richter scale reading of an earthquake with intensity 800,000 times I_0.

52. In May 1983, an earthquake measuring 7.7 on the Richter scale occurred in Japan. This was the first major earthquake in Japan since 1948, when one registered 7.3 on the Richter scale. How many times more severe was the 1983 shock?

53. The strongest earthquake ever to strike Japan occurred in 1933 and measured 8.9 on the Richter scale. How many times more severe was this 1933 quake than the one in May 1983? (See problem 52.)

54. Two earthquakes measure 5.8 and 6.4 on the Richter scale. Calculate the ratio of their intensities.

55. The largest earthquakes ever recorded measured 8.9 on the Richter scale; the San Francisco earthquake of 1906 measured 8.25. Calculate the ratio of their intensities. (These readings correspond to devastating quakes.)

56–59. The loudness of sound (in decibels) perceived by the human ear depends upon intensity levels according to

$$L = 10 \log (I/I_0),$$

where I_0 is the threshold of hearing for the average human ear.

56. Find the loudness when I is 10,000 times I_0. This is the intensity level of the average voice.

57. A sound that causes pain has intensity about 10^{14} times I_0. Find the decibel reading for this threshold.

58. Graph the equation for loudness. Use I/I_0 as the independent variable.

59. A relatively quiet room has a background noise level of about $L_1 = 32$ decibels, and a heated argument has a decibel level of about $L_2 = 66$. Find the ratio I_2/I_1 of the associated intensities.

60–64. Chemists use the pH (hydrogen potential) of a solution to measure its acidity or basicity. The pH is given by the formula

$$pH = -\log [H^+],$$

where $[H^+]$ is the concentration of hydrogen ions in moles per liter.

60. Most common solutions have a pH range between 1 and 14. What values for H^+ are associated with these extremes?

61. Find the approximate pH of each of the following.
    (a) blood: $[H^+] = 3.98 \times 10^{-8} = 0.0000000398$
    (b) beer: $[H^+] = 6.31 \times 10^{-5} = 0.0000631$
    (c) vinegar: $[H^+] = 6.3 \times 10^{-3} = 0.0063$

62. Sometimes pH is defined as the logarithm of the reciprocal of the concentration of hydrogen ions. Write an equation that represents this sentence, and explain how it and the equation given above can both represent pH.

63. Find the approximate hydrogen ion concentration $[H^+]$ for each of the following.
    (a) apples: $pH = 3.0$
    (b) eggs: $pH = 7.79$
    (c) neutral water: $pH = 7.0$

64. A solution is considered acidic if $[H^+] > 10^{-7}$ or basic if $[H^+] < 10^{-7}$. What pH values correspond to acids and what values correspond to bases?

5.3 Applications of Exponential and Logarithmic Functions

Objectives
□ To solve exponential growth or decay equations when sufficient data are known
□ To solve exponential and logarithmic equations representing demand, supply, total revenue, or total cost when sufficient data are known

Growth and Decay

In business, economics, biology, and the social sciences, the growth of money, bacteria, or population is frequently of interest. If growth can be described by a function of the form

$$f(x) = ma^x,$$

with $a > 0$ and $m > 0$, the growth is called **exponential growth.**

As we mentioned in Section 5.1, the curve that models the growth of some populations is given by $y = P_0e^{ht}$, where P_0 is the population size at a particular time t, h is a constant that depends on the population involved, and y is the total population at time t. This function may be used to model population growth for humans, insects, or bacteria.

EXAMPLE 1   The population of a certain city was 30,000 in 1970 and 40,500 in 1980. If the formula $y = P_0e^{ht}$ applies to the growth of the city's population, what should the population be in 2000?

Solution   We can first use the data from 1970 and 1980 to find the value of h in the formula. Letting $P_0 = 30,000$ and $t = 10$, we get

$$40{,}500 = 30{,}000e^{h(10)}$$
$$1.35 = e^{10h}.$$

Writing this in logarithmic form gives

$$\log_e 1.35 = 10h$$
$$0.3001 = 10h$$
$$h = 0.0300.$$

Thus the formula for this population is $y = P_0e^{0.03t}$. To predict the population for the year 2000, we use $P_0 = 40,500$ (for 1980) and $t = 20$. This gives

$$y = 40{,}500e^{0.03(20)}$$
$$= 40{,}500e^{0.6}$$
$$= 40{,}500(1.8221)$$
$$= 73{,}795.$$

One family of curves that has been used to describe human growth and development, the growth of organisms in a limited environment, and the growth of many types of organizations is the family of **Gompertz curves.** These curves are graphs of equations of the form

$$N = Ca^{R^t},$$

where t represents the time, R $(0 < R < 1)$ is a constant depending on the population, a represents the proportion of initial growth, C is the maximum possible number of individuals, and N is the number of individuals at a given time t.

For example, the equation $N = 100(0.03)^{0.2^t}$ could be used to predict the size of a deer herd introduced on a small island. Here the maximum number of deer C would be 100, the proportion of the initial growth a is 0.03, and R is 0.2. For this example, t represents time, measured in decades. The graph of this equation is given in Figure 5.10.

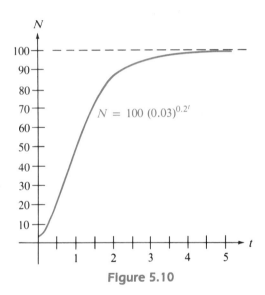

$$N = 100\,(0.03)^{0.2^t}$$

Figure 5.10

EXAMPLE 2   A hospital administrator predicts that the growth in the number of hospital employees will follow the Gompertz equation

$$N = 2000(0.6)^{0.5^t},$$

where t represents the number of years after the opening of a new facility.
(a) What is the number of employees when the facility opens $(t = 0)$?
(b) How many employees are predicted after one year of operation $(t = 1)$?
(c) Graph the curve.
(d) What is the maximum value for N that the curve will approach?

Solution   (a) If $t = 0$, $N = 2000(0.6)^1 = 1200$.

(b) If $t = 1$, $N = 2000(0.6)^{0.5} = 2000\sqrt{0.6} = 2000(0.7746) = 1549.20 \approx 1549$.

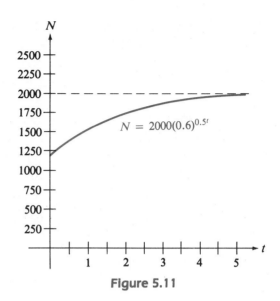

Figure 5.11

(c) The graph is shown in Figure 5.11.
(d) From the graph we can see that as larger values of t are substituted in the function, the values of N approach, but never reach, 2000. We say that the line $N = 2000$ (dashed) is an **asymptote** for this curve, and that 2000 is the maximum possible value.

If the function modeling some situation is given by an equation of the form $f(x) = ma^{-x}$, with $a > 1$ and $m > 0$, we say the function represents **exponential decay.** We have already mentioned that radioactive decay has this form, as do the demand curves discussed later. Another example of this phenomenon occurs in the life sciences when the valves to the aorta are closed, and blood flows into the heart. During this period of time, the blood pressure in the aorta falls exponentially. This is illustrated in the following example.

EXAMPLE 3   Medical research has shown that over short periods of time when the valves to the aorta of a normal adult close, the pressure in the aorta is a function of time and can be modeled by the equation

$$P = 95e^{-0.491t},$$

where t is in seconds.
(a) What is the aortic pressure when the valves are first closed ($t = 0$)?
(b) What is the aortic pressure after 0.1 seconds?
(c) How long will it be before the pressure reaches 80?

Solution   (a) If $t = 0$, the pressure is given by

$$P = 95e^0 = 95.$$

(b) If $t = 0.1$, the pressure is given by

$$P = 95e^{-0.491(.01)}$$
$$= 95e^{-0.0491}$$
$$= 95(0.952)$$
$$= 90.44.$$

(c) Setting $P = 80$ and solving for t gives us the length of time before the pressure reaches 80.

$$80 = 95e^{-0.491t}$$
$$\frac{80}{95} = e^{-0.491t}$$

Rewriting this equation in logarithmic form gives

$$\ln\left(\frac{80}{95}\right) = -0.491t.$$

Using tables or a calculator, we have $-0.172 = -0.491t$, so $t = 0.35$ seconds.

Another example of exponential decay is the decline in the volume of new sales after the end of a sales campaign. This *sales decay* is illustrated by the following example.

EXAMPLE 4   A company finds that the number of its sales begins to fall after the end of an advertising campaign, and the rate of the decline is such that the number of sales x days after the end of the campaign is $S = 2000(2^{-0.1x})$.
(a) How many sales will be made 10 days after the end of the campaign?
(b) How many sales will be made 100 days after the end of the campaign?
(c) If they do not want sales to drop below 500 per day, when should they start a new campaign?

Solution   (a) If $x = 10$, sales are given by $S = 2000(2^{-1}) = 1000$.
(b) If $x = 100$, sales will be $S = 2000(2^{-10}) = 2000(0.0010) = 2$.
(c) Setting $S = 500$ and solving for x will give us the number of days after the end of the campaign when sales will reach 500.

$$500 = 2000(2^{-0.1x})$$
$$0.25 = 2^{-0.1x}$$

Since the base of this exponential is 2 rather than e or 10, we choose to take the logarithm, base 10, of both sides of the equation instead of rewriting in logarithmic form.

$$\log(0.25) = \log(2^{-0.1x})$$

$$\log(0.25) = (-0.1x)(\log 2) \qquad \text{(Property V)}$$

$$\frac{\log(0.25)}{\log 2} = -0.1x$$

$$\frac{-0.6021}{0.3021} = -0.1x$$

$$-1.993 = -0.1x$$

$$x \approx 20$$

Thus sales will be 500 on the twentieth day after the end of the campaign. If a new campaign isn't begun on or before the twenty-first day, sales will drop below 500. (See Figure 5.12.)

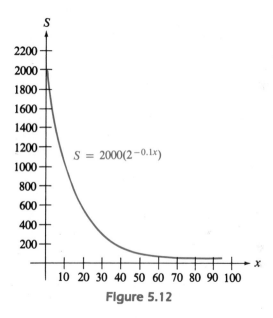

Figure 5.12

Example 4 is typical of many exponential decay models. In particular, once some action is completed, such as an advertising campaign, its effect on sales volume diminishes, or decays, with time.

Economic and Management Applications

In Section 4.3, we discussed quadratic cost, revenue, demand, and supply functions. But cost, revenue, demand, and supply may also be modeled by exponential or logarithmic equations. For example, suppose the demand for a product is given by $p = 30e^{-q/2}$, where q is the number of units demanded at a price of p dollars per unit. Then the graph of the demand curve is as given in Figure 5.13 on the following page.

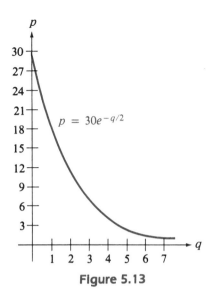

Figure 5.13

EXAMPLE 5   If the demand function for a certain commodity is given by $p = 30e^{-q/2}$,
(a) at what price per unit will the demand equal 4 units?
(b) how many units, to the nearest unit, will be demanded if the price is $18.20?

Solution   (a) If $q = 4$, then $p = 30e^{-4/2}$
$$= 30(0.1353)$$
$$= 4.06 \text{ (dollars).}$$
(b) If $p = 18.20$, then $18.20 = 30e^{-q/2}$
$$0.6067 = e^{-q/2} \qquad \text{Exponential Form}$$
$$\ln 0.6067 = -q/2 \qquad \text{Logarithmic Form}$$
$$-2 \ln 0.6067 = q$$
$$-2(-0.4997) = q$$
$$1 \approx q.$$
The number of units demanded would be 1, to the nearest unit.

EXAMPLE 6   If the total cost function for a product is $C(x) = 1000 + 300 \ln (x + 1)$, find the total cost of producing 8099 units.

Solution   The total cost is given by

$$C(8099) = 1000 + 300 \ln (8100)$$
$$= 1000 + 300(8.996) = 3698.80 \text{ (dollars).}$$

EXAMPLE 7   If the demand function for a commodity is given by $p = 100e^{-x/10}$, where p is the price per unit when x units are sold,
(a) what is the total revenue function for the commodity?
(b) what would be the total revenue if 30 units are demanded and supplied?

Solution   (a) The total revenue can be computed by multiplying the quantity sold times the price per unit. Since the demand function gives the price per unit when x units are sold, the total revenue for x units is $x \cdot p = x(100e^{-x/10})$. Thus the total revenue function is $R(x) = 100xe^{-x/10}$.

(b) If 30 units are sold, the total revenue is $R(30) = 100(30)e^{-30/10} = 100(30)(0.0498)$
$= 149.40$ (dollars).

Exercise 5.3

GROWTH AND DECAY

1. If the population of a certain county was 100,000 in 1970 and 110,517 in 1980, and if the formula $y = P_0e^{ht}$ applies to the growth of the county's population, estimate the population of the county in 1995.

2. The population of a certain city grows according to the formula $y = P_0e^{0.03t}$. If the population was 250,000 in 1980, estimate the population in the year 2100.

3. The president of a company predicts that sales will increase after she assumes office, and that the number of monthly sales will follow the curve given by $N = 3000(0.2)^{0.6^t}$, where t represents the months since she assumed office.
   (a) What were sales when she assumed office?
   (b) What will be the sales after three months?
   (c) What will be the maximum sales she hopes to achieve?
   (d) Graph the curve.

4. Because of a new market opening, the number of employees of a firm is expected to increase according to the equation $N = 1400(0.5)^{0.3^t}$, where t represents the number of years after the new market opens.
   (a) What is the level of employment when the new market opens?
   (b) How many employees should be working at the end of two years?
   (c) What is the expected upper limit on the number of employees?
   (d) Graph the curve.

5. If the equation $N = 500(0.02)^{0.7^t}$ represents the number of employees working t years after 1977, in what year will at least 100 employees be working?

6. A firm predicts that sales will increase during a promotional campaign, and that the number of daily sales will be given by $N = 200(0.01)^{0.8^t}$, where t represents the number of days after the campaign begins. How many days after the beginning of the campaign would the firm expect to sell at least 60 units per day?

Gompertz curves describe situations in which growth is limited. There are other equations that describe this phenomenon under different assumptions. Two examples are

(a) $y = c(1 - e^{-ax})$, $\quad a > 0$ (b) $y = \dfrac{A}{1 + ce^{-ax}}$, $\quad a > 0$ (logistic curve)

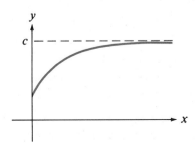

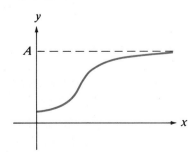

These equations have many applications. In general both (a) and (b) can be used to describe learning or sales of new products, and (b) can be used to describe the spread of epidemics. Problems 7–9 illustrate applications.

7. The concentration y of a certain drug in the bloodstream at any time t is given by the equation

$$y = 100(1 - e^{-0.462t}).$$

   (a) What is y after one hour ($t = 1$)?
   (b) How long does it take for y to reach 50?

8. The number of people $N(t)$ in a community who are reached by a particular rumor at time t is given by the equation

$$N(t) = \frac{50{,}500}{1 + 100e^{-0.7t}}.$$

   (a) Find $N(0)$.
   (b) What is the upper limit on the number of people affected?
   (c) How long before 75% of the upper limit is reached?

9. On a college campus of 10,000 students, a single student returned to campus infected by a disease. The spread of the disease through the student body is given by

$$y = \frac{10{,}000}{1 + 9999e^{-0.99t}},$$

   where y is the total number infected at time t (in days).
   (a) How many are infected after 4 days?
   (b) If the school will shut down if 50% of the students are ill, during what day will it close?

10. The sales of a product decline after the end of an advertising campaign, with the sales decay given by $S = 100{,}000e^{-0.5x}$, where S represents the weekly sales and x represents the number of weeks since the end of the campaign.
   (a) What will be the sales for the tenth week after the end of the campaign?
   (b) During what week after the end of the campaign will sales drop below 400?

11. The sales decay for a product is given by $S = 50{,}000e^{-0.8x}$, where S is the monthly sales and x is the number of months that have passed since the end of a promotional campaign.
   (a) What will be the sales 4 months after the end of the campaign?
   (b) How many months after the end of the campaign will sales drop below 1000, if no new campaign is initiated?

12. A statistical study shows that the fraction of television sets of a certain brand that are still in service after x years is given by $f = e^{-0.15x}$.
   (a) What fraction of the sets are still in service after 5 years?
   (b) What fraction can be expected to be replaced in the sixth year?

13. Radioactive carbon-14 can be used to determine the age of fossils. Carbon-14 decays according to the equation

$$y = y_0 e^{-0.00012378t},$$

   where y is the amount of carbon-14 at time t, in years, and y_0 is the original amount.
   (a) How much of the original amount would be left after 3000 years?
   (b) If a fossil is found to have $\frac{1}{100}$ the original amount of carbon-14, how old is the fossil?

14. A breeder reactor converts stable uranium-238 into the isotope plutonium-239. The decay of this isotope is given by

$$A(t) = A_0 e^{-0.00002876t},$$

where $A(t)$ is the amount of the isotope at time t, in years, and A_0 is the original amount.
    (a) If $A_0 = 500$ lb, how much will be left after a human lifetime (use $t = 70$ years)?
    (b) How long before half the original amount has disintegrated? This time is called the *half-life* of this isotope.

ECONOMIC AND MANAGEMENT APPLICATIONS

15. If the demand function for a certain commodity is given by $p = 100e^{-q/2}$,
    (a) at what price per unit will the quantity demanded equal 6 units?
    (b) if the price is \$1.83 per unit, how many units will be demanded, to the nearest unit?
16. If the demand function for a product is given by $p = 3000e^{-q/3}$,
    (a) at what price per unit will the quantity demanded equal 6 units?
    (b) if the price is \$149.40 per unit, how many units will be demanded, to the nearest unit?
17. If the supply function for a product is given by $p = 100e^q/(q + 1)$, where q represents the number of hundreds of units, what will be the price when the producers are willing to supply 300 units?
18. If the supply function for a product is given by $p = 200(2^q)$, where q represents the number of hundreds of units, what will be the price when the producers are willing to supply 500 units?
19. If the demand function for a product is $p = 1000/\ln (q + 1)$,
    (a) what will be the price if 19 units are demanded?
    (b) how many units, to the nearest unit, will be demanded if the price is \$200?
20. If the supply function for a product is given by $p = 100 \ln (q + 1)$, then
    (a) at what price will 9 items be supplied?
    (b) how many units, to the nearest unit, will be supplied if the price is \$346.57?
21. If the total cost function for a product is $C(x) = e^{0.1x} + 400$, where x is the number of items produced, what is the total cost of producing 30 units?
22. If the total cost for a product is given by $C(x) = 400 \ln (x + 10) + 100$, what is the total cost of producing 100 units?
23. If the demand function for a product is given by $p = 200e^{-0.02x}$, where p is the price per unit when x units are demanded, then what is the total revenue when 100 units are demanded and supplied?
24. If the demand function for a product is given by $p = 4000/\ln (x + 10)$, where p is the price per unit when x units are demanded, then what is total revenue when 40 units are demanded and supplied?

ADDITIONAL APPLICATIONS

25. When two chemicals, A and B, react to form another chemical C (such as in the digestive process), this is a special case of the **law of mass action,** which is fundamental to studying chemical reaction rates.
    Suppose chemical C is formed from A and B according to

$$x = \frac{120 \left[1 - (0.6)^{3t}\right]}{4 - (0.6)^{3t}},$$

where x is the number of pounds of C formed in t minutes.
(a) How much of C is present when the reaction begins?
(b) How much of C is formed in 4 minutes?
(c) How long does it take to form 10 lbs of C?

26. A certain object at 90° F that is allowed to cool in a room where the temperature is 20° F has its temperature T given as a function of time t (in minutes) according to

$$T = 20 + 70e^{-0.056t}.$$

(a) Find the temperature of the object 30 seconds after it is in the room.
(b) How long does it take before the temperature of the object is 20.5° F?

27. In a building the ventilation system operates when the concentration of carbon dioxide (CO_2) reaches a certain level. Suppose that when the ventilation system operates, the cubic feet of CO_2, x, in an 8000 cu ft room depends on time t (in minutes) according to

$$x = 4.8 + 11.2e^{-t/4}.$$

(a) Find the initial amount of CO_2 in the room, and find the concentration of CO_2 at this time.
(b) How long does it take to have a concentration of 0.07% CO_2?
(c) The steady-state or equilibrium concentration is what would result if the ventilation system were left on indefinitely. By using large values for t, determine the steady-state concentration.

28. If $1000 is invested at 10% compounded continuously, then the compound amount A at any time t (in years) is given by $A = 1000e^{0.1t}$.
(a) What is the amount after 1 year?   (b) How long before the investment doubles?

29. If $5000 is invested at 9% per year compounded monthly, then the compound amount A at any time t (in months) is given by $A = 5000(1.0075)^t$.
(a) What is the amount after 1 year?   (b) How long before the investment doubles?

30. If $10,000 is invested at 1% per month, then the compound amount A at any time t (in months) is given by $A = 10,000(1.01)^t$.
(a) What is the amount after 1 year?   (b) How long before the investment doubles?

Review Exercises

5.1, 5.2

1. Write each statement in logarithmic form.
   (a) $2^x = y$ (b) $3^y = 2x$
2. Write each statement in exponential form.
   (a) $\log_7\left(\frac{1}{49}\right) = -2$ (b) $\log_4 x = -1$

Graph the following functions.

3. $y = e^x$ 4. $y = e^{-x}$
5. $y = \log_2 x$ 6. $y = 2^x$
7. $y = 4^x$ 8. $y = \ln x$
9. $y = \log_4 x$ 10. $y = 3^{-2x}$
11. $y = \log x$ 12. $y = \log (x + 2)$
13. $y = \ln (x - 3)$ 14. $y = 10 (2^{-x})$

In problems 15–22 evaluate each logarithm without using a calculator.

15. $\log_5 1$ 16. $\log_8 64$ 17. $\log_{25} 5$ 18. $\log_3\left(\frac{1}{3}\right)$
19. $\log_3 3^8$ 20. $\ln e$ 21. $e^{\ln 5}$ 22. $10^{\log 3.15}$

If log 16 = 1.2041 and log 4 = 0.6021 (to 4 decimal places), find each of the following by using the properties of logarithms.

23. log (16 ÷ 4)   24. log $\sqrt{16}$ 25. log (16 · 4)   26. log 4^3

In problems 27–28, use the properties of logarithms to write each expression as the sum or difference of two logarithmic functions containing no exponents.

27. log(yz)

28. ln $\sqrt{\dfrac{x+1}{x}}$

29. Is it true that ln x + ln y = ln($x + y$) for all values of x?
30. If $f(x) = \ln x$, find $f(e^{-2})$.
31. If $f(x) = 2^x + \log(7x - 4)$, find $f(2)$.
32. If $f(x) = e^x + \ln(x + 1)$, find $f(0)$.
33. If $f(x) = \ln(3e^x - 5)$, find $f(\ln 2)$.

APPLICATIONS

5.2

34. The stellar magnitude M of a star is related to its brightness B as seen from earth according to

$$M = -\frac{5}{2} \log (B/B_0),$$

where B_0 is a standard level of brightness (the brightness of the star Vega).
(a) Find the magnitude of Venus if its brightness is 36.3 times B_0.
(b) Find the brightness of the North Star if its magnitude is 2.1 (as a multiple of B_0).
(c) If the faintest stars have magnitude 6, find their brightness (as a multiple of B_0).
(d) Is a star with magnitude -1.0 brighter than a star with magnitude $+1.0$?

5.3

35. Because of a new advertising campaign, a company predicts that sales will increase, and that the yearly sales will be given by the equation

$$N = 10{,}000(0.3)^{0.5^t},$$

where t represents the number of years after the start of the campaign.
(a) What are the sales when the campaign begins?
(b) What are the predicted sales for the third year?
(c) What are the maximum predicted sales?

36. The sales decay for a product is given by $S = 50{,}000e^{-0.1x}$, where S is the weekly sales and x is the number of weeks that have passed since the end of an advertising campaign.
(a) What will sales be 6 weeks after the end of the campaign?
(b) How many weeks will pass before sales drop below 15,000?

37. The sales decay for a product is given by $S = 50{,}000e^{-0.6x}$, where S is the monthly sales and x is the number of months that have passed since the end of an advertising campaign. What will sales be 6 months after the end of a campaign?

38. If $1000 is invested at 12%, compounded monthly, the compound amount A at any time t (in years) is given by

$$A = 1000(1.01)^{12t}.$$

How long will it take for the amount to double?

39. If $5000 is invested at 13.5%, compounded continuously, then the compound amount A at any time t (in years) is given by $A = 5000e^{0.135t}$.
(a) What is the amount after 9 months?   (b) How long before the investment doubles?

WARMUP

Prerequisite problem type	Answer	Section for review
6.2 What is $\dfrac{(-1)^n}{2n}$, if (a) $n = 1$ (b) $n = 2$ (c) $n = 3$	 (a) $-\frac{1}{2}$ (b) $\frac{1}{4}$ (c) $-\frac{1}{6}$	0.2 Signed numbers
6.2 (a) What is $(-2)^6$? (b) What is $\dfrac{\frac{1}{4}\left[1 - \left(\frac{1}{2}\right)^6\right]}{1 - \frac{1}{2}}$?	(a) 64 (b) $\frac{63}{128}$	0.2 Signed numbers
6.1 If $f(x) = \dfrac{1}{2x}$, what is (a) $f(2)$? (b) $f(4)$?	 (a) $\frac{1}{4}$ (b) $\frac{1}{8}$	1.3 Functional notation

6

Mathematics of Finance

Regardless of whether or not your career is in business, understanding how interest is computed on investments and loans is important to you as a consumer. We begin by studying simple interest, sometimes used on short-term investments or loans. Most investments (for example, savings accounts or bonds) pay compound interest, where the interest is calculated over short periods of time and added to the principal. Most loans are not simple interest loans because they are repaid by making partial payments of both principal and interest during the period of the loan; one such method of repaying a loan is called **amortization.**

The goal of this chapter is to provide some understanding of the methods used to determine the interest and amount (principal plus interest) resulting from savings plans and the methods used in repayment of debts. We will also study sequences, and pay special attention to arithmetic and geometric sequences because of their applications in mathematics of finance. From these we will develop formulas for computing compound interest, the amount of annuities, amortization of debts, and the amount paid into a sinking fund to discharge a debt. The depreciation of business assets is also discussed.

6.1 Simple Interest; Sequences

Objectives
- □ To compute simple interest
- □ To write a specified number of terms of a sequence
- □ To find specified terms of arithmetic sequences
- □ To find sums of specified numbers of terms of arithmetic sequences

Simple Interest

If a sum of money (called the **principal**) P is invested for a time period t (frequently years) at an interest rate r per period, the **simple interest** is given by the following formula.

Simple Interest $I = Prt$

I = interest (in dollars)
P = principal (in dollars)
r = annual interest rate (written as a decimal)
t = time (in years)*

Simple interest is paid on investments involving time certificates issued by banks and on certain types of bonds, such as U.S. government series H bonds and municipal bonds. The interest for a given period is paid to the investor and the principal remains the same.

EXAMPLE 1   If $4000 is invested for 2 years at an annual interest rate of 9%, how much interest will be received at the end of the 2-year period?

Solution   The interest is

$$I = \$4000(0.09)(2) = \$720.$$

The **amount of an investment** at the end of an interest period is the sum of the principal and the interest. Thus in Example 1, the amount is

$$S = \$4000 + \$720 = \$4720.$$

Interest on loans may also be calculated using simple interest.

EXAMPLE 2   If $4000 is borrowed for 6 months at an annual interest rate of 15%, how much interest is due at the end of the six months?

Solution   The principal is $P = 4000$ (dollars).
The annual interest rate is $r = 15\% = 0.15$.
The time in years is $t = \frac{1}{2}$.
The interest due is $I = 4000\,(0.15)\left(\frac{1}{2}\right)$
$\qquad\qquad = 30$ (dollars).

The amount of money that would have to be repaid at the end of six months in the loan of Example 2 is the principal plus the interest, or

$$A = \$4000 + \$30 = \$4030.$$

This is called the **amount of the loan.**

---

*Periods of time other than years can be used, as can other monetary systems.

If we use the letter S to denote the amount of an investment and the letter A to denote the amount of a loan, we have the following:

Amount of investment: $S = P + I$

Amount of loan: $A = P + I$

where P is the principal (in dollars) and I is the interest (in dollars).

The principal P of a loan is also called the **face value** of the **note** or the **present value** of the loan, and the amount A is also called the **future value** of the loan.

EXAMPLE 3 If $2000 is invested for 5 months at a simple interest rate of 1% per month, what is the amount of the investment at the end of the 5-month period?

Solution The interest for the 5-month period is $I = \$2000(0.01)(5) = \$100$. Thus, the amount of the investment for the period is $S = \$2000 + \$100 = \$2100$.

Sequences — *forget this*

Let us look at the amount of the investment in the previous example at the end of each of the 5 months it was invested.

Month	Interest ($I = Prt$)	Amount of the investment
1	($2000)(0.01)(1) = $20	$2000 + $20 = $2020
2	($2000)(0.01)(1) = $20	$2020 + $20 = $2040
3	($2000)(0.01)(1) = $20	$2040 + $20 = $2060
4	($2000)(0.01)(1) = $20	$2060 + $20 = $2080
5	($2000)(0.01)(1) = $20	$2080 + $20 = $2100

We can describe the value of the investment with the equation

$$f(n) = \$2000 + (\$2000)(0.01)n = \$2000 + (\$20)n,$$

where $f(n)$ is the amount of the investment at the end of the nth month. That is,

for $n = 1,$ we have $f(1) = \$2020$

$n = 2,$ $\quad f(2) = \$2040$

$n = 3,$ $\quad f(3) = \$2060$

$n = 4,$ $\quad f(4) = \$2080$

$n = 5,$ $\quad f(5) = \$2100.$

Note that in this example, we have not calculated $f(n)$ for $n > 5$ because the money is invested for only 5 months.

Suppose we ignore the investment situation and the resulting restriction on n. That is, let us consider the function $f(n) = 2000 + 20n$ for all positive integers n. Then, the values $f(n)$ form the **sequence**

$$2020, 2040, 2060, 2080, 2100, 2120, 2140, \ldots.$$

We define a **sequence function** as follows.

    A **sequence function** is a function whose domain is the set of positive integers.

Because these functions are very special, it is customary to use the notation a_n to represent the functional value $f(n)$. The n is used to remind us that the domain contains only positive integers. The set of functional values $a_1, a_2, a_3, \ldots$ of the sequence function is called a **sequence.** The values $a_1, a_2, a_3, \ldots$ are called **terms** of the sequence, with a_1 the first term, a_2 the second term, and so on.

EXAMPLE 4   Write the first four terms of the sequence whose nth term is $a_n = (-1)^n/2n$.

Solution   The first four terms of the sequence are as follows:

$$a_1 = \frac{(-1)^1}{2(1)} = -\frac{1}{2}$$

$$a_2 = \frac{(-1)^2}{2(2)} = \frac{1}{4}$$

$$a_3 = \frac{(-1)^3}{2(3)} = -\frac{1}{6}$$

$$a_4 = \frac{(-1)^4}{2(4)} = \frac{1}{8}$$

We usually write these terms in the form $-\frac{1}{2}, \frac{1}{4}, -\frac{1}{6}, \frac{1}{8}$.

EXAMPLE 5   If the nth term of a sequence is

$$a_n = \frac{n - 2}{n(n + 1)},$$

write the first four terms and the eighth term of the sequence.

Solution The first four terms and the eighth term of the sequence are as follows:

$$a_1 = \frac{1 - 2}{1(1 + 1)} = -\frac{1}{2}$$

$$a_2 = \frac{2 - 2}{2(2 + 1)} = 0$$

$$a_3 = \frac{3 - 2}{3(3 + 1)} = \frac{1}{12}$$

$$a_4 = \frac{4 - 2}{4(4 + 1)} = \frac{1}{10}$$

$$a_8 = \frac{8 - 2}{8(8 + 1)} = \frac{1}{12}$$

Arithmetic Sequences

Earlier in this section, we described the sequence

$$2020, 2040, 2060, 2080, 2100, 2120, 2140, \ldots$$

with the equation $a_n = 2000 + 20n$. This function can also be described in the following way:

$$a_1 = 2020, \; a_n = a_{n-1} + 20 \text{ for } n > 1.$$

This sequence is an example of a special kind of sequence called an **arithmetic sequence.** In such a sequence, each term after the first can be found by adding a constant to the preceding term. Thus, we have the following definition.

Arithmetic Sequence   A sequence is called an **arithmetic sequence (progression)** if there exists a number d, called the **common difference,** such that

$$a_n = a_{n-1} + d \qquad \text{for } n > 1.$$

EXAMPLE 6   Write the next three terms of the following arithmetic sequences:

(a) $1, 3, 5, \ldots$ (b) $9, 6, 3, \ldots$ (c) $\frac{1}{2}, \frac{5}{6}, \frac{7}{6}, \ldots$

Solution   (a) The common difference is 2, so the next three terms are 7, 9, 11.
(b) The common difference is -3, so the next three terms are 0, -3, -6.
(c) The common difference is $\frac{1}{3}$, so the next three terms are $\frac{3}{2}, \frac{11}{6}, \frac{13}{6}$.

Since each term after the first in an arithmetic sequence is obtained by adding d to the preceding term, the second term is $a_1 + d$, the third is $(a_1 + d) + d = a_1 + 2d, \ldots$ and the nth term is $a_1 + (n - 1)d$. Thus we have the following formula.

> **The nth term of an arithmetic sequence** (progression) is given by
>
> $$a_n = a_1 + (n - 1)d,$$
>
> where a_1 is the first term and d is the common difference between successive terms.

EXAMPLE 7   Find the eleventh term of the arithmetic sequence with first term 3 and common difference -2.

Solution   The eleventh term is $a_{11} = 3 + (11 - 1)(-2) = -17$.

EXAMPLE 8   If the first term of an arithmetic sequence is 4 and the ninth term is 20, find the fifth term.

Solution   Substituting the values $a_1 = 4$, $a_n = 20$, and $n = 9$ in $a_n = a_1 + (n - 1)d$ gives $20 = 4 + (9 - 1)d$. Solving this equation gives $d = 2$. Therefore, the fifth term is $a_5 = 4 + (5 - 1)2 = 12$.

Consider the arithmetic sequence with first term a_1, common difference d, and nth term a_n. The first n terms of an arithmetic sequence can be written from a_1 to a_n as

$$a_1, a_1 + d, a_1 + 2d, a_1 + 3d, \ldots, a_1 + (n - 1)d$$

or backwards from a_n to a_1 as

$$a_n, a_n - d, a_n - 2d, a_n - 3d, \ldots, a_n - (n - 1)d.$$

If we let s_n represent the sum of the first n terms of the sequence described above, then we have

$$s_n = a_1 + (a_1 + d) + (a_1 + 2d) + \cdots + [a_1 + (n - 1)d], \qquad (1)$$

or alternately,

$$s_n = a_n + (a_n - d) + (a_n - 2d) + \cdots + [a_n - (n - 1)d]. \qquad (2)$$

If we add equations (1) and (2) together, term by term, we obtain the equation

$$2s_n = (a_1 + a_n) + (a_1 + a_n) + (a_1 + a_n) + \cdots + (a_1 + a_n),$$

in which $(a_1 + a_n)$ appears as a term n times. Thus,

$$2s_n = n(a_1 + a_n)$$

$$s_n = \frac{n}{2}(a_1 + a_n).$$

We may state this result as follows.

> The **sum of the first n terms of an arithmetic sequence** is given by the formula
>
> $$s_n = \frac{n}{2}(a_1 + a_n),$$
>
> where a_1 is the first term of the sequence and a_n is the nth term.

EXAMPLE 9   Find the sum of the first 10 terms of the arithmetic sequence with first term 2 and common difference 4.

Solution   We are given the values $n = 10$, $a_1 = 2$, and $d = 4$. Thus, the tenth term is $a_{10} = 2 + (10 - 1)4 = 38$, and the sum is

$$s_{10} = \frac{10}{2}(2 + 38) = 200.$$

EXAMPLE 10   Find the sum of the first 7 terms of the arithmetic sequence $\frac{1}{4}, \frac{7}{12}, \frac{11}{12} \cdots$.

Solution   The first term is $\frac{1}{4}$ and the common difference is $\frac{1}{3}$. Therefore, the seventh term is $a_7 = \frac{1}{4} + (7 - 1)\left(\frac{1}{3}\right) = \frac{9}{4}$. The sum is $s_7 = \frac{7}{2}\left(\frac{1}{4} + \frac{9}{4}\right) = \frac{35}{4} = 8\frac{3}{4}$.

Exercise 6.1

SIMPLE INTEREST

1. If $10,000 is invested for 6 years at an annual simple interest rate of 16%,
   (a) how much interest will be earned?
   (b) what is the amount of the investment at the end of the 6 years?

2. If $800 is invested for 5 years at an annual simple interest rate of 14%,
   (a) how much interest will be earned?
   (b) what is the amount of the investment at the end of the 5 years?

3. If $1000 is invested for 3 months at an annual simple interest rate of 12%,
   (a) how much interest will be earned?
   (b) what is the amount of the investment after 3 months?

4. If $1800 is invested for 9 months at an annual simple interest rate of 15%,
   (a) how much interest will be earned?
   (b) what is the amount of the investment after 9 months?

5. If you borrow $800 for 6 months at 16%, simple interest, how much must you repay at the end of the 6 months?

6. If you borrow $1600 for 2 years at 14%, simple interest, how much must you repay at the end of the 2 years?

7. If you loan $3500 to a friend for 15 months at 8% simple interest, find the future value of the loan.

8. Mrs. Gonzalez loaned $2500 to her son Luis for 7 months at 9% simple interest. What is the future value of this loan?

9. A couple bought some stock for $30 per share that pays an annual dividend of $.90 per share. After one year the price of the stock was $33. Find the simple interest rate they earned on their investment.

10. Jenny Reed bought SSX stock for $16 per share. If the annual dividend was $1.50 per share and after one year SSX was selling for $35 per share, find the simple interest rate of growth of her money.

11. (a) To buy a treasury bill (T-bill) that matures to $10,000 in 6 months, you must pay $9685.23. What rate does this earn?
    (b) If the bank charges a fee of $40 to buy a T-bill, what is the actual interest rate you earn?

12. Janie Christopher loaned $6000 to a friend for 90 days at 12%. After 30 days, she sold the note to a third party for $6000. What interest rate did the third party receive? Use 360 days in a year.

13. A firm buys 12 file cabinets at $140 each, with the bill due in 90 days. How much must the firm deposit now to have enough to pay the bill if money is worth 12% per year? Use 360 days in a year.

14. A student has a savings account earning 9% simple interest. She must pay $1500 for first semester tuition by September 1 and $1500 for second semester on January 1. How much must she earn in the summer (by September 1) in order to pay the first semester bill on time and still have the remainder of her summer earnings grow to $1500 between September 1 and January 1?

15. A retailer owes a wholesaler $500,000 due in 45 days. If the bill is 15 days late, there is a 1% penalty charge. The retailer can get a 45-day certificate paying 6% or a 60-day certificate paying 7%. Is it better to take the 45-day certificate and pay on time or the 60-day certificate and pay late with the penalty?

16. An investor owns several apartment buildings. The taxes on these buildings total $30,000 per year and are due before April 1. The late fee is 1/2% per month up to 6 months, at which time the buildings are seized by the authorities and sold for back taxes. If the investor has $30,000 available on March 31, will he save money by paying the taxes at that time or by investing the money at 8% and paying the taxes and the penalty on September 30?

SEQUENCES

17. Write the first 10 terms of the sequence defined by $a_n = 3n$.
18. Find the first six terms of the sequence defined by $a_n = 4n$.
19. Write the first eight terms of the sequence defined by $a_n = n/3$.
20. Write the first seven terms of the sequence defined by $a_n = 2/n$.
21. Write the first six terms of the sequence whose nth term is $(-1)^n/4$.
22. Write the first five terms of the sequence whose nth term is $(-1)^n/3$.
23. Write the first six terms of the sequence whose nth term is $(-1)^n/(2n)$.
24. Write the first five terms of the sequence whose nth term is

$$a_n = \frac{(-1)^n}{n + 1}.$$

25. Write the first four terms and the tenth term of the sequence whose nth term is

$$a_n = \frac{n - 4}{n(n + 2)}.$$

26. Write the sixth term of the sequence whose nth term is

$$a_n = \frac{n(n - 1)}{n + 3}.$$

ARITHMETIC SEQUENCES

27. Write three additional terms of the arithmetic sequence 2, 5, 8, ...
28. Write three additional terms of the arithmetic sequence 3, 9, 15, ...
29. Write four additional terms of the arithmetic sequence, 3, $\frac{9}{2}$, 6, ...
30. Write four additional terms of the arithmetic sequence 2, 2.75, 3.5, ...
31. Find the 8th term of the arithmetic sequence with first term -3 and common difference 4.
32. Find the 11th term of the arithmetic sequence with first term 7 and common difference 4.
33. Find the 8th term of the arithmetic sequence with first term 6 and common difference $-\frac{1}{2}$.
34. Find the 6th term of the arithmetic sequence with first term $\frac{1}{2}$ and common difference $-\frac{1}{3}$.
35. Find the sixth term of the arithmetic sequence with first term 5 and eighth term 19.
36. Find the sixth term of the arithmetic sequence with first term 20 and tenth term 47.
37. Find the sum of the first eight terms of the arithmetic sequence with first term 2 and the common difference 3.
38. Find the sum of the first seven terms of the arithmetic sequence with first term 6 and the common difference 4.
39. Find the sum of the first six terms of the arithmetic sequence with first term 10 and common difference $\frac{1}{2}$.
40. Find the sum of the first eight terms of the arithmetic sequence with first term 12 and common difference -3.
41. Find the sum of the first five terms of the arithmetic sequence 2, 4, 6, ...
42. Find the sum of the first six terms of the arithmetic sequence 6, 9, 12, ...
43. Find the sum of the first eight terms of the arithmetic sequence 6, $\frac{9}{2}$, 3, ...
44. Find the sum of the first seven terms of the arithmetic sequence 12, 9, 6, ...

APPLICATIONS

45. A female bee hatches from a fertilized egg while a male bee hatches from an unfertilized egg. Thus a female bee has a male parent and a female parent while a male bee only has a female parent. Therefore the number of ancestors of a male bee follows the *Fibonacci sequence*

$$1, 2, 3, 5, 8, 13, \ldots .$$

Observe the pattern and write three more terms of the sequence.

46. Suppose you are offered a job with a relatively low starting salary but with a $1500 raise each year for each of the next 7 years. How much more than your starting salary would you be making in the eighth year?

47. A new firm loses $2000 in its first month, but its profit increases by $400 in each succeeding month for the next year. What is its profit in the twelfth month?

48. If you are making $27,000 and are given $1800 raises each year, in how many years will your salary double?

49. Suppose you are offered two identical jobs: one paying a starting salary of $20,000 with yearly raises of $1000 and one paying a starting salary of $18,000 with yearly raises of $1200. Which job will be paying you more for your tenth year on the job?

50. A new firm loses $2000 in its first month, but its profit increases by $400 in each succeeding month for the next year. What is its profit for the year?

51. If you are an employee, would you rather be given a raise of $1000 at the end of each year (Plan I) or $300 at the end of each 6-month period (Plan II)? To answer the question, consider the following table for an employee whose base salary is $20,000 per year (or $10,000 per 6-month period).

| Period | Salary received per 6-month period | |
(in months)	Plan I	Plan II
0–6	$10,000	$10,000
6–12	10,000	10,300
12–18	10,500	10,600
18–24	10,500	10,900
24–30	11,000	11,200
30–36	11,000	11,500

(a) Find the sum of the raises for Plan I for the first 3 years.
(b) Find the sum of the raises for Plan II for the first 3 years.
(c) Which plan is better, and by how much?
(d) Find the sum of the raises in Plan I for 5 years.
(e) Find the sum of the raises in Plan II for 5 years.
(f) Which plan is better, and by how much?
(g) Do you want Plan I or Plan II?

52. As an employee, would you prefer being given a $1200 raise each year for 5 years or a $200 raise each quarter for 5 years?

6.2   Compound Interest; Geometric Sequences

Objectives
☐   To find the compound amount and compound interest of money invested where interest is compounded at regular intervals
☐   To find compound amount and interest on money where interest is compounded continuously
☐   To find the effective annual interest rate of money invested at compound interest
☐   To find specified terms of geometric series
☐   To find the sums of specified numbers of terms of geometric sequences

Compound Interest

In Section 6.1 we discussed simple interest. A second method of paying interest is the **compound interest** method, where the interest for each period is added to the principal before interest is calculated for the next period. With this method the principal grows as the interest is added to it. This method is used in investments such as savings accounts and U.S. government series E bonds.

An understanding of compound interest is important not only for people planning careers with financial institutions, but also for anyone planning to invest money. To see how compound interest is computed, we will first calculate the *amount* that will result if $20,000 is invested for three years at 10%, *compounded annually* (each year).

The principal for the first year is $20,000.
The interest at the end of the first year is

$$I = \$20,000(0.10)(1) = \$2000.$$

The amount at the end of the first year is

$$S = P + I = \$20,000 + \$2000 = \$22,000.$$

Thus the principal for the second year is $22,000.
The interest at the end of the second year is

$$I = \$22,000(0.10)(1) = \$2200.$$

The amount at the end of the second year is

$$S = \$22,000 + \$2200 = \$24,200.$$

Thus, the principal for the third year is $24,200.
The interest at the end of the third year is

$$I = \$24,200(0.10)(1) = \$2420.$$

The amount at the end of the third year is

$$S = \$24,200 + \$2420 = \$26,620.$$

We see that calculation of compound amount (and compound interest) is very tedious if we proceed in this manner. But notice that the compound amount for each year can be found by multiplying the amount from the preceding year by 1.10, or $1 + 0.10$. That is, the compound amounts at the end of the first, second, and third years are, respectively,

$$\$20,000(1.10) = \$22,000,$$
$$[\$20,000(1.10)](1.10) = \$20,000(1.10)^2 = \$24,200,$$
and
$$[\$20,000(1.10)^2](1.10) = \$20,000(1.10)^3 = \$26,620.$$

This suggests that if we maintained this investment for n years, the compound amount at the end of this time would be $\$20,000(1.10)^n$. Thus, we have the following general formula.

> If $\$P$ is invested at an interest rate of i per year, compounded annually, the compound amount S at the end of the nth year is
>
> $$S = P(1 + i)^n.$$

EXAMPLE 1   If $3000 is invested for 4 years at 9%, compounded annually, how much interest is earned?

Solution   The compound amount is

$$S = \$3000(1 + 0.09)^4$$
$$= \$3000(1.4115816)$$
$$= \$4234.7448$$
$$= \$4234.74, \text{ to the nearest cent.}$$

Since $3000 of this amount was the original investment, the interest earned is $4234.74 - \$3000 = \$1234.74$.

Some accounts have the interest compounded semiannually, quarterly, monthly, or daily. Unless specifically stated otherwise, a stated interest rate is the rate per year, and is called the **nominal annual rate.** The interest rate *per period* is the nominal rate divided by the number of interest periods per year. The interest periods are also called *conversion periods.* Thus, if $100 is invested for five years at 6% compounded semiannually (twice a year), it has been invested for $n = 10$ periods (5 years × 2 periods per year) at $i = 3\%$ per period (6% per year ÷ 2 per year). The compound amount on investments of this type is found using the following formula.

> **Compound Amount**
>
> If $\$P$ is invested for t years at a nominal interest rate, j, compounded m times per year, then the total number of compounding periods is
>
> $$n = mt,$$
>
> the interest rate per compounding period is
>
> $$i = \frac{j}{m},$$
>
> and the compound amount is
>
> $$S = P(1 + i)^n = P\left(1 + \frac{j}{m}\right)^{mt}.$$

Because compound interest is used so frequently in business, tables are available that give the compound amount of $1 invested for different periods and at different rates. Table IV in the Appendix is a sample of such a table. Note that the left hand column of this table lists values for the total number of compounding periods, n, and the top row lists values for the interest rate per period, i. The compound amount can also be calculated from the formula using a calculator.

EXAMPLE 2   If $8000 is invested for 6 years at 8%, compounded quarterly, find (a) the compound amount, (b) the compound interest.

Solution   (a) Since $P = \$8000$, $t = 6$ years, $j = 0.08$, and $m = 4$ compounding periods per year, the compound amount is given by

$$S = P\left(1 + \frac{j}{m}\right)^{mt}$$

$$= \$8000\left(1 + \frac{0.08}{4}\right)^{4 \cdot 6} = \$8000(1 + 0.02)^{24}$$

$$= \$8000(1.608437) = \$12,867.50$$

To use Table IV in the Appendix, we must find the total number of compounding periods ($n = (4)(6) = 24$) and the interest rate per period ($i = 0.08/4 = 0.02$). From Table IV we see that the compound amount of $1 invested for 24 periods at 2% per period is $1.608437. Thus, the compound amount is

$$S = \$8000(1.608437) = \$12,867.50.$$

(b) The compound interest is given by $12,867.50 − $8000 = $4867.50.

EXAMPLE 3   If $500 is invested for 3 years at 8%, compounded quarterly (four times a year), what interest is earned?

Solution   Since $P = \$500$, $t = 3$ years, $j = 0.08$, and $m = 4$ compounding periods per year, the total number of compounding periods is

$$n = (4)(3) = 12,$$

the interest rate per period is

$$i = \frac{0.08}{4} = 0.02,$$

and the compound amount is

$$\begin{aligned} S &= P(1 + i)^n \\ &= \$500(1 + 0.02)^{12} \\ &= \$500(1.2682418) \\ &= \$634.1209 \\ &= \$634.12. \end{aligned}$$

Thus the interest is $\$634.12 - \$500 = \$134.12$.

Suppose $1 is invested for one year at a nominal rate of 8%, compounded semiannually. Then the compound amount will be $\$1(1.04)^2 = \$1.0816$, and the interest for the year will be $\$1.0816 - \$1 = \$.0816$. Note that this amount of interest represents a *simple* interest rate of 8.16%. Since over one year the nominal rate of 8%, compounded semiannually, is equivalent to a simple interest rate of 8.16%, we say that the effective annual rate in this case is 8.16%. We can find the effective annual rate with the following formula.

Effective Annual Rate   If j represents the nominal rate and m the number of compounding periods per year, then the effective annual rate, r, is given by

$$r = \left(1 + \frac{j}{m}\right)^m - 1.$$

Thus, although we cannot directly compare two nominal rates having different compounding periods, we can compare their equivalent simple interest rates, i.e., their corresponding effective annual rates.

To prove that this formula gives the true (effective) interest rate, consider the following: If I, S, and P represent interest, compound amount, and principal, respectively, for a 1-year period, then

$$I = S - P$$
$$I = P\left(1 + \frac{j}{m}\right)^{mt} - P$$
$$\frac{I}{P} = \left(1 + \frac{j}{m}\right)^{mt} - 1$$

But if the time is 1 year, then $mt = m(1)$ and $I = Prt = Pr(1)$. Thus, the true yearly rate is

$$r = \frac{I}{P} = \left(1 + \frac{j}{m}\right)^m - 1.$$

EXAMPLE 4   Find the effective annual rate equivalent to the nominal rate of 6% compounded quarterly.

Solution   Since the number of periods per year is $m = 4$ and the nominal rate is $j = 0.06$, the rate per period is $j/m = 0.06/4 = 0.015$. Thus,

$$r = (1 + 0.015)^4 - 1 = 1.061364 - 1$$
$$= 0.061364$$
$$= 6.14\%.$$

It is reasonable to assume that the more frequently the interest is compounded, the larger the compound amount will become. In order to determine the interest that results from *continuous* compounding (compounding every instant), consider an investment of $1 for one year at a 100% interest rate. If the interest is compounded m times per year, the compound amount is given by

$$S = \left(1 + \frac{1}{m}\right)^m.$$

Table 6.1 shows the compound amount that results as the number of compounding periods increases.

Table 6.1

Compounded	Number of periods per year	Compound amount
Annually	1	$\left(1 + \frac{1}{1}\right)^1 = 2$
Monthly	12	$\left(1 + \frac{1}{12}\right)^{12} = 2.6130\cdots$
Daily	360 (business year)	$\left(1 + \frac{1}{360}\right)^{360} = 2.7145\cdots$
Hourly	8640	$\left(1 + \frac{1}{8640}\right)^{8640} = 2.71812\cdots$
Each minute	518,400	$\left(1 + \frac{1}{518400}\right)^{518400} = 2.71827\cdots$

It is clear that as the number of periods per year increases, the compound amount increases, although not very rapidly. In fact, no matter how often the interest is compounded, the compound amount will never exceed $2.72. We say that as the number of periods increases, the compound amount in this case approaches a **limit,** which is the number e:

$$e = 2.7182818\cdots.$$

We have discussed the number e and the function $y = e^x$ in Chapter 5. The discussion here shows one way the number we call e may be derived. We will define e more formally later.

Compound Amount (continuous compounding)	In general, if P is invested for t years at a nominal rate, j, compounded continuously, then the compound amount is given by the exponential function $$S = Pe^{jt}.$$

need log buttons on calculator.

EXAMPLE 5   Find the compound amount if $1000 is invested for 20 years at 8%, compounded continuously.

Solution   The amount is

$$S = \$1000e^{(0.08)(20)} = \$1000e^{1.6}$$
$$= \$1000(4.95303) \quad \text{(since } e^{1.6} = 4.95303)$$
$$= \$4953.03.$$

EXAMPLE 6   How much more will you earn if you invest $1000 for 5 years at 8% compounded continuously instead of 8% compounded quarterly?

Solution   If the interest is compounded continuously, the compound amount at the end of the 5 years is

$$S = \$1000e^{(0.08)(5)} = \$1000e^{0.4} = \$1000(1.49182)$$
$$= \$1491.82.$$

If the interest is compounded quarterly, the amount at the end of the 5 years is

$$S = \$1000(1.02)^{20} = \$1000(1.485947)$$
$$= \$1485.95, \text{ to the nearest cent.}$$

Thus the extra interest earned by compounding continuously is

$$\$1491.82 - \$1485.95 = \$5.87.$$

Geometric Sequences — *don't bother*

If P is invested at an interest rate of i per year, compounded at the end of each year, the *compound amount* at the end of each succeeding year is

$$P(1 + i), P(1 + i)^2, P(1 + i)^3, \ldots, P(1 + i)^n, \ldots.$$

The compound amounts for each of the succeeding years form a sequence in which each term (after the first) is found by multiplying the previous term by the same number. Such a sequence is called a **geometric sequence.**

A sequence is called a **geometric sequence (progression)** if there exists a number r, called the **common ratio**, such that

$$a_n = ra_{n-1} \qquad \text{for } n > 1.$$

EXAMPLE 7   Write the next three terms of the following geometric sequences:

(a) $1, 3, 9, \ldots$ (b) $4, 2, 1, \ldots$ (c) $3, -6, 12, \ldots$

Solution   (a) The common ratio is 3, so the next three terms are $27, 81, 243$.

(b) The common ratio is $\frac{1}{2}$, so the next three terms are $\frac{1}{2}, \frac{1}{4}, \frac{1}{8}$.

(c) The common ratio is -2, so the next three terms are $-24, 48, -96$.

Because each term after the first in a geometric sequence is obtained by multiplying the previous term by r, the second term is $a_1 r$, the third is $a_1 r^2, \ldots$ and the nth term is $a_1 r^{n-1}$. Thus we have the following formula.

The **nth term of a geometric sequence** (progression) is given by

$$a_n = a_1 r^{n-1},$$

where a_1 is the first term of the sequence and r is the common ratio.

EXAMPLE 8   Find the seventh term of the geometric sequence with first term 5 and common ratio -2.

Solution   The seventh term is $a_7 = 5(-2)^{7-1} = 5(64) = 320$.

EXAMPLE 9   A ball is dropped from a height of 125 feet. If it rebounds $\frac{3}{5}$ of the height from which it falls every time it hits the ground, how high will it bounce after it strikes the ground for the fifth time?

Solution   The first rebound is $\frac{3}{5}(125) = 75$ feet; the second rebound is $\frac{3}{5}(75) = 45$. The heights of the rebounds form a geometric sequence with first term 75 and common ratio $\frac{3}{5}$. Thus the fifth term is

$$a_5 = 75\left(\frac{3}{5}\right)^4 = 75\left(\frac{81}{625}\right) = \frac{243}{25} = 9\frac{18}{25} \text{ feet.}$$

The sum of the first n terms of a geometric sequence is

$$s_n = a_1 + a_1 r + a_1 r^2 + \cdots + a_1 r^{n-1}. \qquad (1)$$

If we multiply equation (1) by r, we have

$$rs_n = a_1 r + a_1 r^2 + a_1 r^3 + \cdots + a_1 r^n. \qquad (2)$$

Subtracting equation (2) from equation (1), we obtain

$$s_n - rs_n =$$
$$a_1 + (a_1r - a_1r) + (a_1r^2 - a_1r^2) + \cdots + (a_1r^{n-1} - a_1r^{n-1}) - a_1r^n.$$

Thus

$$s_n(1 - r) = a_1 - a_1r^n$$

$$s_n = \frac{a_1 - a_1r^n}{1 - r}, \qquad \text{if } r \neq 1.$$

This gives the following.

> The **sum of the first n terms of the geometric sequence** with first term a_1 and common ratio r is
>
> $$s_n = \frac{a_1(1 - r^n)}{1 - r}, \qquad \text{provided } r \neq 1.$$

EXAMPLE 10   Find the sum of the first 5 terms of the geometric progression with first term 4 and common ratio -3.

Solution   We are given that $n = 5$, $a_1 = 4$, and $r = -3$. Thus,

$$s_5 = \frac{4[1 - (-3)^5]}{1 - (-3)} = \frac{4[1 - (-243)]}{4} = 244.$$

EXAMPLE 11   Find the sum of the first six terms of the geometric sequence $\frac{1}{4}, \frac{1}{8}, \frac{1}{16}, \ldots$.

Solution   We know that $n = 6$, $a_1 = \frac{1}{4}$, and $r = \frac{1}{2}$. Thus,

$$s_6 = \frac{\frac{1}{4}\left[1 - \left(\frac{1}{2}\right)^6\right]}{1 - \frac{1}{2}} = \frac{\frac{1}{4}\left(1 - \frac{1}{64}\right)}{\frac{1}{2}} = \frac{1 - \frac{1}{64}}{2} = \frac{64 - 1}{128} = \frac{63}{128}.$$

Exercise 6.2

COMPOUND INTEREST

1. Find the amount that will accrue if $8000 is invested for 10 years at 12%, compounded annually.   *24846.80*
2. Find the interest that will be earned if $5000 is invested for 3 years at 10%, compounded annually.

3. Find the interest that will be earned if $10,000 is invested for 3 years at 9%, compounded monthly.

4. What amount will result if $8600 is invested for 8 years at 10%, compounded semiannually?

5. What amount will result if $3200 is invested for 5 years at 8%, compounded quarterly?

6. What interest will be earned if $6300 is invested for 3 years at 12%, compounded monthly?

7. Find the interest that will be earned if $8600 is invested for 6 years at 10%, compounded semiannually.

8. Find the amount that will result if $3500 is invested for 6 years at 8%, compounded quarterly.

9. Find the amount that will result if $5100 is invested for 4 years at 9%, compounded continuously.

10. Find the interest that will result if $8000 is invested at 7%, compounded continuously, for 8 years.

11. What is the compound interest if $410 is invested for 10 years at 8%, compounded continuously?

12. If $8000 is invested at 8.5%, compounded continuously, find the amount that results after $4\frac{1}{2}$ years.

13. Which investment will earn more money, a $1000 investment for 5 years at 8%, compounded annually, or a $1000 investment for 5 years, compounded continuously at 7%?

14. How much more interest will be earned if $5000 is invested for 6 years at 7%, compounded continuously, instead of 7%, compounded quarterly?

15. What is the effective annual rate equivalent to a nominal rate of 8%, compounded quarterly?

16. If money is invested at 9%, compounded monthly, what is the equivalent effective annual rate?

17. If money is invested at 6% compounded continuously, what is the effective annual rate?

18. What is the effective annual rate equivalent to a nominal rate of 10%, compounded continuously?

19. How long (in years) would $700 have to be invested at 11.9%, compounded continuously, to earn $300 interest?

20. How long (in years) would $600 have to be invested at 8%, compounded continuously, to amount to $970?

21. At what nominal rate, compounded quarterly, would $20,000 have to be invested to amount to $26,425.82 in 7 years?

22. At what nominal rate, compounded annually, would $10,000 have to be invested to amount to $14,071 in 7 years?

23. For her first birthday, Polly's grandparents invested $1000 in an 18-year certificate for her that pays 8% compounded annually. How much will the certificate be worth on Polly's 19th birthday?

24. To help their son buy a car on his 16th birthday, his parents invest $1500 on his tenth birthday. If the investment pays 9%, compounded continuously, how much is available on his 16th birthday?

25. A forty-year-old man no longer qualifies for additional IRAs. If his present IRAs have a balance of $12,860 and if he expects them to earn interest at 7.5%, compounded annually, how much does he expect to have when he retires at age 62?

26. The purchase of Alaska cost the U.S. $7 million in 1869. If this money had been placed in a savings account paying 6%, compounded annually, how much money would be

available from this investment in 1989? Do you think this amount would purchase Alaska in 1989?

27. If a couple needs $15,000 as a down payment for a home and if they invest the $10,000 they have at 8%, compounded quarterly, how long will it take for the money to grow into $15,000?

28. If the couple in problem 27 invests the $10,000 at 10%, compounded continuously, how long will it take to grow into $15,000?

GEOMETRIC SEQUENCES

29. Write four additional terms of the geometric sequence 3, 6, 12, ...
30. Write four additional terms of the geometric sequence 4, 12, 36, ...
31. Write three additional terms of the geometric sequence 81, 54, 36, ...
32. Write three additional terms of the geometric sequence 32, 40, 50, ...
33. Find the sixth term of the geometric sequence with first term 10 and common ratio 2.
34. Find the fifth term of the geometric sequence with first term 6 and common ratio 3.
35. Find the fifth term of the geometric sequence with first term 4 and common ratio $\frac{3}{2}$.
36. Find the fifth term of the geometric sequence with first term 3 and common ratio -2.
37. Find the sum of the first six terms of the geometric sequence with first term 6 and common ratio 3.
38. Find the sum of the first four terms of the geometric sequence with first term 3 and common ratio 4.
39. Find the sum of the first six terms of the geometric sequence with first term 4 and common ratio $-\frac{1}{2}$.
40. Find the sum of the first five terms of the geometric sequence with first term 9 and common ratio $\frac{1}{3}$.
41. Find the sum of the first five terms of the geometric sequence 1, 3, 9, ...
42. Find the sum of the first four terms of the geometric sequence 16, 64, 256, ...
43. Find the sum of the first five terms of the geometric sequence 6, 4, $\frac{8}{3}$, ...
44. Find the sum of the first five terms of the geometric sequence 9, -6, 4, ...

APPLICATIONS

45. A house worth $160,000 twenty years ago has increased in value by 4% each year because of inflation. What is its worth today?

46. If inflation causes the cost of automobiles to increase by 10% each year, what should a car that costs $5000 six years ago cost today?

47. Suppose a country has a population of 20 million and it projects a growth rate of 2% per year for the next 20 years. What will the population of this country be in 10 years?

48. Suppose a country is so devastated by the AIDS epidemic that its population decreases by 0.5% each year for a four-year period. If the population was originally 10 million, what is the population at the end of the four-year period?

49. If the rate of growth of a population continues at 2%, in how many years will the population double?

50. If a population of 8 million begins to increase at a rate of 0.1% each month, in how many months will it be 10 million?

51. A ball is dropped from a height of 128 feet. If it rebounds $\frac{3}{4}$ of the height from which it falls every time it hits the ground, how high will it bounce after it strikes the ground for the fourth time?

52. A pump removes $\frac{1}{3}$ of the water in a container with every stroke. What amount of water is still in a container after 5 strokes if it originally contained 81 cm^3?

53. A machine is valued at $10,000. If the depreciation at the end of each year is 20% of its value at the beginning of the year, find its value at the end of 4 years.

54. Suppose a new business makes a $1000 profit in its first month and has its profit increase by 10% each month for the next 2 years. How much profit will the business earn in its twelfth month?

55. The size of a certain bacteria culture doubles each hour. If the number of bacteria present initially is 5000, how many would be present at the end of 6 hours?

56. If a bacteria culture increases by 20% every hour and 2000 are present initially, how many will be present at the end of 10 hours?

57. If changing market conditions cause a company earning $8,000,000 in 1985 to project a loss of 2% of its profit in each of the next 5 years, what profit does it project in 1990?

58. Suppose a new business makes a $1000 profit in its first month and has its profit increase by 10% each month for the next 2 years. How much profit will it earn in its first year?

59. An interest-free loan of $12,000 requires monthly payments of 10% of the outstanding balance. What is the outstanding balance after 18 payments?

60. If Sherri must repay a $9000 interest-free loan by making monthly payments of 15% of the unpaid balance, what is the unpaid balance after one year?

61. Suppose you receive a chain letter with six names on it, and to keep the chain unbroken you are to mail a dime to the person whose name is at the top, cross out the top name, add your name to the bottom, and mail it to five friends. If your friends mail out five letters each, and no one breaks the chain, you will eventually receive dimes. How many dimes would you receive? (This is a geometric sequence with first term 5.)

62. Mailing chain letters through the mail was declared illegal because most people would receive nothing while a comparative few would profit. If the chain letter in problem 61 were to go through 12 unbroken progressions,
    (a) how many people would receive money?
    (b) how much money would these people receive as a group?

63. How many letters would be mailed if the chain letter in problem 61 went through 12 unbroken progressions?

6.3 Annuities

Objectives
 □ To compute the amount of an ordinary annuity
 □ To compute the amount of an annuity due
 □ To compute the present value of an ordinary annuity
 □ To compute the present value of a deferred annuity

Ordinary Annuities

In Section 6.2 we learned how to compute the compound amount and interest if a fixed sum of money was deposited in an account that pays interest that is compounded periodically or continuously. But not many people are in a position to deposit a large sum of money at one time in an account. Most people save (or invest) money by depositing relatively small amounts at different times. If a depositor makes equal deposits at regular intervals, he or she is contributing to an **annuity.** The payments (deposits) may be made weekly, monthly, quarterly, yearly, or for any other period of time. The sum of all payments plus all interest earned is called the **amount of the annuity** or **future value** of the annuity.

Annuities may be classified into two categories—annuities certain and contingent annuities. An **annuity certain** is one in which the payments begin and end on fixed dates. In a **contingent annuity** the payments are related to events that cannot be paced regularly, so the payments are not regular. We will deal with annuities certain in this text, and we will deal first with annuities in which the payments are made at the end of each of the equal payment intervals. This type of annuity certain is called an **ordinary annuity.** The ordinary annuities we will consider have payment intervals that coincide with the compounding period of the interest.

Suppose you invested $100 at the end of each year for five years in an account that paid interest at 10%, compounded annually. How much money would you have in the account at the end of the five years?

Because you are making payments at the end of each period (year), this annuity is called an **ordinary annuity.**

To find the value of your annuity at the end of the five years, we compute the compound amount of each payment separately, and add the amounts. (See Figure 6.1.) The $100 invested *at the end* of the first year will draw interest for 4 years, so it will amount to $100(1.10)^4$. The $100 invested at the end of the second year will draw interest for 3 years, so it will amount to $100(1.10)^3$. Similarly, the $100 invested at the end of the third year will amount to $100(1.10)^2$, and the $100 invested at the end of the fourth year will amount to $100(1.10)$. The $100 invested at the end of the fifth year will draw no interest, so it will amount to $100.

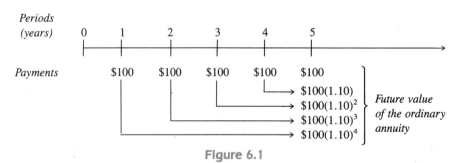

Figure 6.1

Thus the amount of the annuity is given by

$$S = 100 + 100(1.10) + 100(1.10)^2 + 100(1.10)^3 + 100(1.10)^4.$$

The terms of this sum are the first five values of the geometric progression having $a_1 = 100$ and $r = 1.10$. Thus,

$$S = \frac{100[1 - (1.10)^5]}{1 - 1.10} = \frac{100(-0.61051)}{-0.10}$$

$$= 610.51.$$

Thus the investment ($100 at the end of each year for 5 years, at 10%, compounded annually) would return $610.51.

Because every such annuity will take the same form, we can state that if a periodic payment R is made for n periods at an interest rate i *per period,* the **amount of the annuity,** or its **future value,** will be given by

$$S = R \cdot \frac{1 - (1 + i)^n}{1 - (1 + i)}.$$

This simplifies to the following.

Future Value of an Ordinary Annuity

If $\$R$ are deposited at the end of each period for n periods in an annuity that earns interest at a rate of i per period, the future value of the annuity will be

$$S = R \cdot s_{\overline{n}|i} = R \cdot \left[\frac{(1 + i)^n - 1}{i} \right],$$

where $s_{\overline{n}|i}$ represents the future value of an ordinary annuity of $\$1$ per period for n periods with an interest rate of i per period.

The value of $s_{\overline{n}|i}$ can be computed directly with a calculator or found in a table like Table V in the Appendix.

EXAMPLE 1 Ruth Gearhart deposits $500 at the end of each year in a savings account that pays 6%, compounded annually. How much money will she have in the account at the end of 10 years?

Solution Her savings form an ordinary annuity with $R = \$500$, $i = 6\%$, and $n = 10$. Thus, we have

$$S = \$500 \cdot s_{\overline{10}|6\%} = \$500 \cdot \frac{(1 + 0.06)^{10} - 1}{0.06}.$$

Using Table V in the Appendix, we see that $s_{\overline{10}|6\%}$, the future value of an ordinary annuity of $\$1$ per period for 10 periods with an interest rate of 6% per period, is 13.180795. Therefore,

$$S = \$500(13.180795) = \$6590.40.$$

EXAMPLE 2 Richard Lloyd deposits $100 at the end of each month in an account that pays 12%, compounded monthly. How much money will he have in his account in a year and a half?

Solution The number of periods is $n = 18$, and the rate *per period* is $i = 1\%$. At the end of 18 months the value of the annuity will be

$$S = \$100 \cdot s_{\overline{18}|1\%} = \$100(19.614748)$$

$$= \$1961.47.$$

Annuities Due

Deposits in saving accounts, rent payments, and insurance premiums are examples of **annuities due.** An annuity due differs from an ordinary annuity in that the periodic payments are made at the *beginning* of the period with an annuity due. The *term* of an annuity due is from the first payment to the end of one period after the last payment. Thus an annuity due draws interest for one period more than the ordinary annuity.

We can find the future value of an annuity due by treating each payment as if it were made at the *end* of the preceding period in an ordinary annuity. Thus we calculate $s_{\overline{n}|\,i}$ for one additional period. But increasing the number of periods also adds one more payment than should be paid. To compensate for this, we subtract the amount of one payment (see Figure 6.2).

Thus the future value of an annuity due with n payments can be found by using a calculator or Table V to find the future value of an ordinary annuity for $n + 1$ periods and by subtracting one annuity payment.

Of course, calculating $s_{\overline{n}|i}$ for one additional period gives $s_{\overline{n+1}|i}$ and gives one more payment than should be paid. Thus the formula for an annuity due is as follows.

Annuity Due	$S_{\text{due}} = R\, s_{\overline{n+1}|i} - R$
	$= R\, \dfrac{(1 + i)^{n+1} - 1}{i} - R$

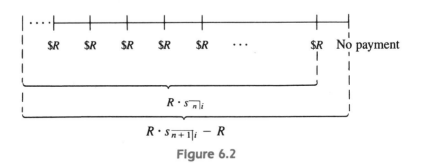

$R \cdot s_{\overline{n}|i}$

$R \cdot s_{\overline{n+1}|i} - R$

Figure 6.2

EXAMPLE 3   Find the amount of an annuity due of \$1 for 3 years at 8%, compounded quarterly.

Solution   The number of quarterly periods in 3 years is $n = 12$ and the interest rate per period is $i = 2\%$. The future value of the annuity due is

$$S_{\text{due}} = R\, s_{\overline{n+1}|i} - R = \$1\, s_{\overline{13}|2\%} - \$1.$$

$s_{\overline{13}|2\%}$ can be found using Table V or $\dfrac{(1.02)^{13} - 1}{i}$ to obtain

$$\$14.680332 - \$1 = \$13.680332.$$

What is the future value of a savings account if $50 is deposited at the beginning of every 6 months for 5 years and the account pays interest at the rate of 6%, compounded semiannually?

This is an annuity due with 10 periods at 3% per period. The future value is

$$
\begin{aligned}
S_{\text{due}} &= R\, s_{\overline{n+1}|i} - R \\
&= \$50\, s_{\overline{11}|3\%} - \$50 \\
&= \$50(12.807796) - \$50 \\
&= \$590.39
\end{aligned}
$$

Present Value of an Annuity

We have been discussing how contributing to an annuity program will result in a sum of money, and we have called that sum the future value of the annuity. Just as the term *annuity* is used to describe an account into which a person makes equal periodic payments (deposits), this term is also used to describe an account from which a person receives equal periodic payments (withdrawals); that is, if you invest a lump sum of money in an account today, so that at regular intervals you will receive a fixed sum of money, you have established an annuity. We call this lump sum the **present value** of the annuity.

Many people who are retiring purchase an annuity to supplement their income. This annuity pays them a fixed sum of money at regular intervals (usually each month). The single sum of money required to purchase an annuity that will provide these payments at regular intervals is the **present value** of the annuity. For example, you could receive $1000 at the end of each year for 16 years if you invested a lump sum of $10,837.77 in an annuity that paid interest at 5%, compounded annually. This lump sum is called the present value of the annuity. But how do we determine that the present value of this annuity (of $1000 per year) is $10,837.77?

Suppose we wish to invest a lump sum of money (which we will denote A_n) in an annuity for n periods at an interest rate of i per period, so that we will receive (withdraw) a payment of R at the end of each period.

To find a formula for A_n, we must first note that the value today of a series of payments is the same whether we call these payments withdrawals or deposits. This means that A_n also represents the present value of an annuity in which we deposit R at the end of each period for n periods with an interest rate of i per period.

Thus, we can express the future value of A_n in two ways. The future value is the compound amount that would result if the lump sum of A_n were invested and left in an account for n periods at an interest rate of i per period:

$$S = A_n(1 + i)^n;$$

and it is also the total amount that would result if $R are deposited at the end of each period for n periods in an annuity that earns interest at a rate of i per period:

$$S = R \cdot s_{\overline{n}|i}.$$

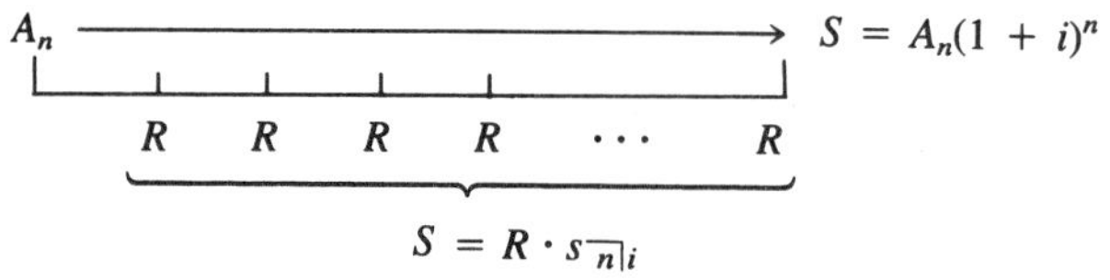

Figure 6.3

Equating these two expressions for S, we have

$$A_n (1 + i)^n = R \cdot s_{\overline{n}|i},$$

or

$$A_n (1 + i)^n = R \cdot \frac{(1 + i)^n - 1}{i}.$$

Multiplying both sides of this equation by $(1 + i)^{-n}$, we obtain a formula for the present value:

$$A_n = R \cdot \frac{1 - (1 + i)^{-n}}{i}.$$

Thus, we have the following.

Present Value of an Ordinary Annuity

If a payment of $R is made at the end of each period for n periods, into (or out of) an annuity that earns interest at a rate of i per period, the present value of the annuity is

$$\left([1 - (1+i)^{-n}]/i \right)$$

$$A_n = R \cdot a_{\overline{n}|i} = R \cdot \left[\frac{1 - (1 + i)^{-n}}{i} \right],$$

where $a_{\overline{n}|i}$ represents the present value of an ordinary annuity of $1 per period for n periods, with an interest rate of i per period.

The values of $a_{\overline{n}|i}$ can be computed directly with a calculator or found in a table like Table VI in the Appendix.

The present value of the annuity we discussed earlier (paying $1000 at the end of each year for 16 years) is

$$A_n = \$1000 \cdot a_{\overline{16}|5\%}$$

$$= \$1000 \cdot \frac{1 - (1.05)^{-16}}{0.05}$$

$$= \$1000 \cdot 10.83777$$

$$= \$10{,}837.77.$$

EXAMPLE 5   What lump sum would have to be invested at 6%, compounded annually, to provide an ordinary annuity of $1000 per year for 10 years?

Solution   We are given that $i = 6\%$, $R = \$1000$, and $n = 10$. Thus,

$$A_n = \$1000 \cdot a_{\overline{10}|6\%} = \$1000 \cdot \frac{1 - (1.06)^{-10}}{.06}$$

Using Table VI in the Appendix or a calculator, we see that $a_{\overline{10}|6\%}$ is $7.360087. Therefore,

$$A_n = \$1000(7.360087)$$
$$= \$7360.087$$
$$= \$7360.09, \text{ to the nearest cent.}$$

EXAMPLE 6   What is the present value of an annuity of $1500 payable at the end of each 6-month period for 2 years if money is worth 8%, compounded semiannually?

Solution   We are given that $R = \$1500$ and $i = 8\%/2 = 4\%$. Since a payment is made twice a year for 2 years, the number of periods is $n = (2)(2) = 4$. Thus,

$$A_n = \$1500 \cdot a_{\overline{4}|4\%}$$
$$= \$1500(3.69895)$$
$$= \$5444.84, \text{ to the nearest cent.}$$

Deferred Annuities

A **deferred annuity** is one in which the first payment is not made at the beginning or end of the first period, but at some later date. An annuity that is deferred for k periods and then has payments of $\$R$ per period at the end of each of the next n periods can be illustrated by Figure 6.4.

Deferred Annuity

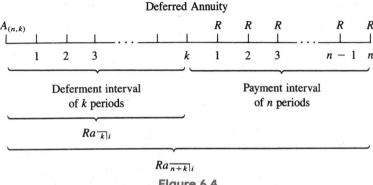

Figure 6.4

We now consider how to find the present value of such a deferred annuity when the interest rate is i per period. If we first assume that payments are made for the

$k + n$ periods, then the annuity is an ordinary annuity with present value $Ra_{\overline{n+k}|i}$. However, for an annuity that is deferred for k periods, $Ra_{\overline{n+k}|i}$ must be reduced by an amount equal to the present value of the first k payments, $Ra_{\overline{k}|i}$, since these payments are not made. Thus, the present value of the deferred annuity is found by subtracting the present value for the period of deferment.

Present Value of a Deferred Annuity

The present value of a deferred annuity of $\$R$ per period for n periods deferred for k periods with interest rate i per period is given by

$$A_{(n,k)} = Ra_{\overline{n+k}|i} - Ra_{\overline{k}|i} = R(a_{\overline{n+k}|i} - a_{\overline{k}|i})$$

$$= R\left[\frac{1 - (1+i)^{-(n+k)}}{i} - \frac{1 - (1+i)^{-k}}{i}\right]$$

The formula for $A_{(n,k)}$ can be written in the form

$$A_{(n,k)} = R\left[\frac{1 - (1+i)^{-n}}{i}\right](1+i)^{-k};$$

this may be easier to use with a calculator.

EXAMPLE 7   A deferred annuity is purchased that will pay $\$10,000$ per year for 15 years after being deferred for 5 years. If money is worth 6% per year, what is the present value of this annuity?

Solution   We have $R = \$10,000$, $n = 15$, $k = 5$, and $i = .06$. The present value is

$$A_{(15,5)} = \$10,000\,(a_{\overline{20}|6\%} - a_{\overline{5}|6\%})$$
$$= \$10,000(11.469921 - 4.212364)$$
$$= \$72,575.57.$$

As Figure 6.4 shows, the deferment interval ends **one** period before the first payment.

EXAMPLE 8   Find the present value of an annuity of $\$1000$ every month for 2 years if the first payment is to be made one year after the annuity is established, and money is worth 12%, compounded monthly.

Solution   The first payment is made at the end of 12 months, so the payment is deferred 11 months; that is, $k = 11$. Using $n = 24$, $i = .01$, and $R = \$1000$, we have

$$A_{(24,11)} = \$1000\,(a_{\overline{35}|.01} - a_{\overline{11}|.01})$$
$$= \$1000(28.408580 - 10.367628)$$
$$= \$14,040.95.$$

Homework
1-8 Ordinary
15-7 Due
23-26 Present
33-34 Deferred

$1 * \left[\dfrac{(1 + .07)^6 - 1}{.07} \right] - 1$

Exercise 6.3

ORDINARY ANNUITIES

1. Find the future value of an annuity of $1 paid at the end of each year for 10 years, if it earns interest at 8%, compounded annually.

2. Find the future value of an ordinary annuity of $1 paid every 6 months for 3 years, if the interest rate is 6%, compounded semiannually.

3. Find the future value of an annuity of $1300 paid at the end of each year for 5 years, if interest is earned at a rate of 6%, compounded annually.

4. Find the future value of an annuity of $50 paid at the end of each year for 10 years, if it earns 9%, compounded annually.

5. Find the future value of an ordinary annuity of $80 paid quarterly for 3 years, if the interest rate is 8%, compounded quarterly.

6. Find the future value of an ordinary annuity of $300 paid quarterly for 5 years, if the interest rate is 12%, compounded quarterly.

7. Find the future value of an ordinary annuity of $40 paid at the end of each 6-month period for 10 years, if the interest rate is 6%, compounded semiannually.

8. Find the future value of an ordinary annuity of $75 paid every 6 months for 7 years, if the interest rate is 8%, compounded semiannually.

9. Mr. Gordon plans to invest $300 at the end of each year for 12 years in a savings account. If the account pays 9%, compounded annually, how much will he have at the end of the 12 years?

10. Sam deposits $500 at the end of every 6 months into an account that pays 8%, compounded semiannually. How much will he have at the end of 8 years?

11. Parents agree to invest $500 for their son (at 10%, compounded semiannually) on the December 31 or June 30 following each semester that he makes the Dean's list during his four years in college. If he makes the Dean's list in each of the eight semesters, how much money will his parents have to give him when he graduates?

12. Jake Werkheiser qualifies to invest $2000 in an IRA each April 15 for the next ten years. If he makes these investments, and if the certificates pay 12%, compounded annually, how much will he have at the end of the ten years?

13. Patty Stacey deposited $2000 at the end of each of the 5 years she qualified for an IRA. If she leaves the money that has accumulated in the IRA account for 25 additional years, how much is in her account at the end of the 30-year period? Assume an interest rate of 9%, compounded annually.

14. Suppose that Patty's husband delayed starting an IRA for the first 10 years he worked, but he made $2000 deposits at the end of each of the next 15 years. If the interest rate is 9%, compounded annually, and if he leaves the money in his account for 5 additional years, how much will be in his account at the end of the 30-year period? Does Patty or her husband have more IRA money? (See problem 13.)

ANNUITIES DUE

15. Find the future value of an annuity due of $1 payable at the beginning of each year for 5 years if the interest rate is 7%, compounded annually.

16. Find the future value of an annuity due of $1 payable at the beginning of each 6-month period for 7 years if the interest rate is 8%, compounded semiannually.

17. Find the future value of an annuity due of $100 each year for 2½ years at 12%, compounded quarterly.
18. Find the future value of an annuity due of $1500 each month for 3 years if the interest rate is 12%, compounded monthly.
19. Find the future value of an annuity due of $200 paid at the beginning of each 6-month period for 8 years if the interest rate is 6%, compounded semiannually.
20. For 3 years $400 is placed in a savings account at the beginning of each 6-month period. If the account pays interest at 10%, compounded semiannually, how much will be in the account at the end of the 3 years?
21. Jane Adele deposits $500 in an account at the beginning of each 3-month period for 9 years. If the account pays interest at the rate of 8%, compounded quarterly, how much will she have in her account?
22. A house is rented for $900 per quarter, with each quarter's rent payable in advance. If money is worth 8%, compounded quarterly and the rent is deposited in an account, what is the future value of the rent for one year?

PRESENT VALUE OF AN ANNUITY

$$100 * \left[\frac{1-(1+.07)^{-17}}{.07} \right]$$

23. Find the present value of an annuity of $100 paid at the end of each year for 17 years if the interest rate is 7%, compounded annually.
24. Find the present value of an annuity of $800 paid at the end of each year for 15 years if the interest rate is 12%, compounded annually.
25. Find the present value of an annuity of $100 paid at the end of each 6-month period for 8 years if the interest rate is 8%, compounded semiannually.
26. Find the present value of an annuity that pays $300 at the end of each 6-month period for 6 years if the interest rate is 6%, compounded semiannually.
27. What lump sum would have to be invested at 8%, compounded quarterly, to provide an annuity that pays $200 at the end of each quarter for 3 years?
28. A woman buying a home paid $10,000 down and agreed to make 18 quarterly payments of $500 beginning in 3 months. If money is worth 12%, compounded quarterly, how much should the house cost if she paid for it in cash?
29. Joe Burkhart inherited a sum of money. He wants to purchase an annuity that will give him $1000 at the end of each 6-month period for 9 years. If money is worth 10%, compounded semiannually, how much will he have to pay for the annuity?
30. Is it more economical to buy an automobile for $3900 cash or to pay $800 down and $400 each quarter for 2 years, if money is worth 8%, compounded quarterly?
31. Suppose a state lottery prize of $5 million is to be paid in 20 payments of $250,000 each at the end of the next 20 years. If money is worth 10%, compounded annually, what is the present value of the prize?
32. Suppose Becky has her choice of $10,000 per month for life or a single prize of $1.5 million. She is 35 years old and her life expectancy is 40 more years. (a) Find the present value of the annuity if money is worth 7.2%, compounded monthly. (b) If she takes the $1.5 million, spends $700,000 of it, and invests the remainder at 7.2%, what monthly annuity will she receive?

DEFERRED ANNUITIES

33. Find the present value of an annuity of $2000 per year at the end of each of 8 years after being deferred for 6 years, if money is worth 7%, compounded annually.

$$2000 \times \left[\frac{1-(1+.07)^{-14}}{.07} - \frac{1-(1+.07)^{-6}}{.07} \right] \qquad 2000 \times \left[8.7454714 - 4.7665429 \right]$$

34. Find the present value of an annuity of $2000 per quarter at the end of each of 5 years after being deferred for 3 years, if money is worth 8%, compounded quarterly.

35. The terms of a single parent's will indicate that a child will receive an ordinary annuity of $16,000 per year from age 18 to age 24 (so the child can attend college) with the balance of the estate going to a niece. If the parent dies on the child's 15th birthday, how much money must be removed from the estate to purchase the annuity? (Assume an interest rate of 6%, compounded annually.)

36. On his 48th birthday, a man wants to set aside enough money to provide an income of $300 per month at the end of each month from his 60th birthday to his 65th birthday. If he earns 6%, compounded monthly, on his money, how much will this supplemental retirement plan cost him on this 48th birthday?

37. The semiannual tuition payment at a major university is expected to be $10,000 for the four years beginning in the year 2008. What lump sum payment should the university accept on January 1, 1990, in lieu of tuition payments beginning on July 1, 2008? Assume money is worth 7%, compounded semiannually, and tuition is paid on July 1 and January 1 of the four years.

38. A grateful alumnus wishes to provide a scholarship of $2000 per year for 5 years to his alma mater, with the first scholarship awarded on his 60th birthday. If money is worth 6%, compounded annually, how much money must he donate on his 50th birthday?

If the present value of a deferred annuity $A_{(n,k)}$ is known, we can use the formula

$$A_{(n,k)} = R\left[a_{\overline{n+k}|i} - a_{\overline{k}|i}\right]$$

to find the size of the deferred periodic payment, R.

39. Danny Metzger's parents invested $1600 when he was born. This money is to be used for Danny's college education and is to be withdrawn in four equal annual payments beginning when Danny is age 18. Find the amount that will be available each year, if money is worth 6%, compounded annually.

40. Carol Goldsmith received a trust fund inheritance of $10,000 on her 30th birthday. She plans to use the money to supplement her income with 20 quarterly payments beginning on her 60th birthday. If money is worth 7.6%, compounded quarterly, how much will each quarterly payment be?

6.4 Loans; Amortization; Sinking Funds

Objectives
- ☐ To find interest and payments on installment loans
- ☐ To find the regular payments required to amortize a debt
- ☐ To find the amount that must be invested periodically in a sinking fund to discharge a debt

Installment Loans

Just as we invest money to earn interest, banks and lending institutions loan money and collect interest for its use. While your aunt may loan you money with the understanding that you will repay the full amount of the money plus simple interest at the end of a year, financial institutions generally expect you to make partial payments on a regular basis (frequently monthly).

Most consumer loans (for automobiles, appliances, televisions, and the like) are classed as **installment loans.** On one type of installment loan, interest is charged on the full principal of the loan for the full period of the loan, even though the principal is repaid in installments. This interest is then added to the principal to determine the total amount that must be repaid. The size of each payment is determined by dividing the number of payments into the total amount. This method of computing interest is called the **add-on method.**

EXAMPLE 1   Mrs. Sentz obtained a loan from a finance company for $1200 plus add-on interest at 12% (per year) to be repaid in 12 monthly installments. What are her monthly payments?

Solution   The add-on interest for one year is

$$I_A = Prt = \$1200 \times 0.12 \times 1 = \$144,$$

so the amount of the loan is $1200 + $144 = $1344. Thus the monthly payments are $1344 ÷ 12 = $112.

At first glance, it may appear that Mrs. Sentz paid 12% interest on her loan, but she really paid a much higher rate because her unpaid balance was less than $1200 in each month of the year except for the first month (in the last month, she owed only $100).

Federal law requires that the full cost of the loan and the **true annual percentage rate (APR)** be disclosed with each loan.

The APR gives the interest rate as though the interest is always charged on the unpaid balance. For example, if a charge customer is charged 1% of the unpaid balance each month when he/she makes a payment, the true interest rate is 12% per year, but the stated add-on interest rate is not the true interest rate. The formula used by the Federal Reserve System to determine the APR is the following constant ratio formula.

The **true annual percentage rate** is

$$APR = \frac{2mI}{P(n + 1)}$$

where

m = number of payments *per year* (12 for monthly, 52 for weekly)
I = interest charged (in dollars) *per year*
P = amount financed
n = *total* number of payments required

If we represent the APR by j, then j/m is the interest rate per period and P/n is the payment size. The unpaid balance before the first payment is $n(P/n) = P$, the unpaid balance before the second payment is $(n - 1)(P/n) = P - P/n$, and so on, with the balance before the last payment equal to $1(P/n)$.

We can write the total interest I as the sum

$I = n(P/n)(j/m) + (n - 1)(P/n)(j/m) + \cdots + (2)(P/n)(j/m) + (1)(P/n)(j/m)$
$I = (P/n)(j/m)[n + (n - 1) + \cdots + 2 + 1]$
$I = (P/n)(j/m)[(n/2)(n + 1)]$ sum of arithmetic sequence

Solving for j gives the APR formula.

$$\text{APR} = j = \frac{2Imn}{nP(n + 1)} = \frac{2mI}{P(n + 1)}$$

The 12-month add-on loan at 12% in Example 1 has

$$\text{APR} = \frac{2(12)(144)}{1200(12 + 1)} = 0.2215 = 22.15\%.$$

Some installment loans are set up on a *discounted* basis. As with add-on loans, the interest is charged on the full amount for the full period of the loan, but the interest on the loan is deducted *before* the borrower receives the loan. The interest that is deducted in advance is called **bank discount, D**, and the amount the borrower receives for his or her use is called the **proceeds of the loan, P_B**.

The amount to be repaid by the borrower is called the **maturity value** of the loan, S, where

$$S = P_B + D.$$

When a loan is discounted, the bank discount is calculated as a percentage of the maturity value S rather than the amount the borrower receives.

The bank discount is

$$D = Sdt$$

where

> S is the maturity value of the loan,
> d is the discount rate (per year), and
> t is the time (in years).

The proceeds of the loan are

$$P_B = S - D.$$

EXAMPLE 2   If $2000 is the maturity value of a loan for 2 years at a 10% bank discount rate,
(a) what is the bank discount?
(b) how much does the consumer receive to spend?

Solution   (a) The bank discount is

$$D = \$2000(0.10)(2) = \$400.$$

(b) The consumer receives the proceeds of the loan,

$$P_B = S - D = \$2000 - \$400 = \$1600.$$

With a discount loan, for a person to have $\$P_B$ to spend, the maturity value of the loan must be larger than $\$P_B$. That is, the maturity value must be such that $\$P_B$ remains after the bank discount is taken. Thus for the proceeds to be $\$P_B$, the maturity value of the loan, S, must satisfy:

$$S - D = P_B$$
or
$$S - Sdt = P_B$$
so
$$S(1 - dt) = P_B$$

This gives the following.

> The maturity value (amount to be repaid) of a loan of $\$P_B$ for t years at bank discount rate d is
>
>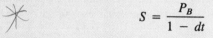
>
> $$S = \frac{P_B}{1 - dt}$$

EXAMPLE 3   What is the maturity value of the loan if Jake borrows $1000 for 1 year at a discount rate of 6%?

Solution   The maturity value of the loan is

$$S = \frac{P_B}{1 - dt} = \frac{\$1000}{1 - 0.06(1)} = \$1063.83.$$

The true annual percentage rate (APR) for a discounted loan is even higher than that for an add-on loan. If the loan of Example 1 were given on a discounted basis, Mrs. Sentz would have to repay $1363.64 rather than $1344, and the APR would be

$$\text{APR} = \frac{2(12)(163.64)}{1200(12 + 1)} = 25.18\%$$

Amortization

Home mortgages and long-term commercial loans are usually paid off by a series of partial payments with interest charged on the unpaid balance at the end of each payment period. In this case, the stated interest rate is the same as the APR.

A loan of this type can be made in one of two ways. One repayment plan applies an equal amount to the principal each payment period plus the interest for that period, which is the interest on the unpaid balance. For example, a loan of $120,000 for 10 years at 12% could be repaid in 120 payments of $1000 plus 1% of the remaining balance of the loan. When this payment method is used, the payments will decrease as the unpaid balance decreases.

This type of loan can also be repaid by making all payments (including principal and interest) of equal size. The process of repaying this type of loan is called **amortization.**

When a bank makes a loan of this type, it is purchasing an ordinary annuity that pays a fixed return each payment period. The lump sum the bank gives to the borrower (i.e., the principal of the loan) is the present value of the annuity, and each payment the bank receives from the borrower is a payment from the annuity. To find the size of these periodic payments, we solve the formula for the present value of an ordinary annuity, $A_n = R \cdot a_{\overline{n}|i}$, for R. Thus, we have the following.

Amortization Formula

If a debt of $\$A_n$, with interest at a rate of i per period, is amortized by n equal, periodic payments (each payment being made at the end of a period), the size of each payment is

$$R = A_n \cdot \frac{1}{a_{\overline{n}|i}} = A_n \cdot \left[\frac{i}{1 - (1 + i)^{-n}} \right],$$

where $1/a_{\overline{n}|i}$ represents the periodic payment necessary to amortize $1 over n periods, at an interest rate of i per period.

Note that in the formula above, we can divide by $a_{\overline{n}|i}$ or multiply by $1/a_{\overline{n}|i}$. Values for $a_{\overline{n}|i}$ can be found in Table VI in the Appendix, and values for $1/a_{\overline{n}|i}$ can be found in Table VII.

EXAMPLE 4   A debt of $1000 with interest at 16%, compounded quarterly, is to be amortized by 20 quarterly payments (all the same size) over the next 5 years. What will the size of these payments be?

Solution   The 20 equal payments form an annuity whose present value is $1000. Therefore, $A_n = \$1000$ and $n = 20$. Since we are given that the nominal interest rate is 16% and the number of compounding periods per year is $m = 4$, we know that the rate per period $i = j/m = 16\%/4 = 4\%$. Thus, using Table VI or a calculator, we have

$$R = \frac{\$1000}{a_{\overline{20}|4\%}} = \$1000 \left[\frac{.04}{1 - (1.04)^{-20}} \right]$$

$$= \frac{\$1000}{13.590326}$$

$$= \$73.58, \text{ to the nearest cent.}$$

EXAMPLE 5   A man buys a house for $200,000. He makes a $50,000 down payment and agrees to amortize the rest of the debt with quarterly payments over the next 10 years. If interest on the debt is 12%, compounded quarterly, what will be the size of the quarterly payments?

Solution   We know that $A_n = \$200{,}000 - \$50{,}000 = \$150{,}000$, $n = (4)(10) = 40$, and $i = 12\%/4 = 3\%$. Thus, using Table VII or a calculator, we have

$$R = \$150{,}000 \cdot \frac{1}{a\,\overline{_{40}|}\,3\%} = \$150{,}000 \cdot 0.043262 = \$6489.30.$$

The quarterly payment is $6489.30.

We can construct an amortization schedule that summarizes all the information regarding the amortization of a loan.

For example, a loan of $10,000 with interest at 10% could be repaid in 5 equal annual payments of size

$$R = \$10{,}000 \left(\frac{1}{a\,\overline{_{5}|}\,10\%} \right) = \$10{,}000(0.263797)$$
$$= \$2{,}637.97.$$

Each time this $2637.97 payment is made, some is used to pay the interest on the unpaid balance and some is used to reduce the principal. For the first payment, the unpaid balance is $10,000, so the interest payment is 10% of $10,000, or $1000. The remaining $1,637.97 is applied to the principal. Hence, after this first payment, the unpaid balance is $10,000 - \$1637.97 = \$8,362.03$.

For the second payment of $2,637.97, the amount used for interest is 10% of $8,362.03, or $836.20; the remainder, $1801.77, is used to reduce the principal.

This information for these two payments and for the remaining payments is summarized in the amortization schedule below, which gives the payment, the interest on the unpaid balance, the reduction of the balance, and the remaining unpaid balance for each payment period.

Period	Payment	Interest	Balance reduction	Unpaid balance
				10000.00
1	2637.97	1000.00	1637.97	8362.03
2	2637.97	836.20	1801.77	6560.26
3	2637.97	656.03	1981.94	4578.32
4	2637.97	457.83	2180.14	2398.18
5	2638.00	239.82	2398.18	0.00
Total	13189.88	3189.88	10000.00	

Note that the last payment was increased by 3¢ so that the balance was reduced to $0 at the end of the five years. Such an adjustment is normal in amortizing a loan.

Many people who borrow money, such as for a car or a home, do not pay on the loan for its entire term, but pay off the loan early by making a final lump sum payment. The unpaid balance found in the amortization schedule is the "payoff amount" of the loan and represents the lump sum payment that must be made to complete payment on the loan. When the number of payments is large, we may wish to find the unpaid balance of a loan without constructing an amortization schedule.

EXAMPLE 6   In Example 5, find the unpaid balance immediately after the fifteenth payment.

Solution   The unpaid balance after the fifteenth payment is the present value of the annuity with $40 - 15 = 25$ payments to be made. So the principal is the payment times $a_{\overline{25}|3\%}$ (from Table VI or a calculator):

$$A_n = \$6489.30 \cdot a_{\overline{25}|3\%} = \$6489.30 \cdot 17.413148$$
$$= \$112,999.14$$

The unpaid balance is $112,999.14. Thus, he could pay off the loan after the fifteenth payment by making a lump sum payment of $112,999.14.

Sinking Funds

Some borrowers, such as municipalities, may have a debt that must be paid in a single large sum on a specified date. If they make periodic deposits that will produce that sum on the specified date, we say they have established a **sinking fund.**

If the deposits are all the same size and are made regularly, they form an ordinary annuity whose future value (on a specified date) is the amount of the principal of the debt. To find the size of these periodic deposits, we solve the equation for the future value of an ordinary annuity, $S = R \cdot s_{\overline{n}|i}$, for R. Thus, we have the following.

Sinking Fund Formula

Suppose n equal, periodic payments are deposited into a sinking fund earning interest at a rate of i per period so that at the end of n periods, the fund contains enough money to pay off a debt of $\$S$. If each deposit is made at the end of a period, the size of each payment is

$$R = S \cdot \frac{1}{s_{\overline{n}|i}} = S \cdot \left[\frac{i}{(1 + i)^n - 1} \right],$$

where $1/s_{\overline{n}|i}$ represents the periodic payment into a sinking fund that would amount to $1 over n periods, at an interest rate of i per period.

Note that in the formula above, we can divide by $s_{\overline{n}|i}$ or multiply by $1/s_{\overline{n}|i}$. Values for $s_{\overline{n}|i}$ can be found in Table V in the Appendix and values for $1/s_{\overline{n}|i}$ can be found in Table VIII.

EXAMPLE 7   How much will have to be invested at the end of each year at 8%, compounded annually, to pay off a debt of $60,000 in 5 years?

Solution   We are given that $i = 8\%$, $S = \$60,000$, and $n = 5$. Using Table V, we have

$$R = \frac{\$60,000}{s_{\overline{5}|8\%}} = \frac{\$60,000}{5.866601}$$
$$= \$10,227.39, \text{ to the nearest cent.}$$

Note that an annuity of $10,227.39 for 5 years at 8% compounded annually will amount to $\$10,227.39 \cdot 5.866601 = \$60,000.01$.

EXAMPLE 8   A company establishes a sinking fund to discharge a debt of $100,000 due in 5 years by making equal semiannual deposits, the first due in six months. If the deposits are placed in an account that pays 6%, compounded semiannually, what is the size of the deposits?

Solution   We know that $S = \$100,000$, $n = (2)(5) = 10$, and $i = 6\%/2 = 3\%$. Using Table VIII, we have

$$R = \$100,000 \cdot \frac{1}{s_{\overline{10}|3\%}} = \$100,000 \cdot .087231 = \$8723.10.$$

The semiannual deposit is $8723.10.

Notice that a sinking fund is really a savings plan used to discharge a future debt, but it can also be used to provide a lump sum at a future date for any purpose, such as a college education.

Exercise 6.4

INSTALLMENT LOANS

1. A man borrowed $1800 from a bank and agreed to repay the loans plus add-on interest at 10% by making 12 monthly payments.
   (a) What is the interest charge?
   (b) How much must be repaid?
   (c) What are the monthly payments?
2. A woman obtained a car loan of $3600 and agreed to repay the loan plus add-on interest at 8% by making monthly payments over a 3-year period. How much are her payments?
3. A bank loans $2000 for 2 years at an add-on interest rate of 10%.
   (a) What is the interest charge?
   (b) If this charge is added to the principal of the loan and the amount then owed is divided into monthly payments, what are the monthly payments?
   (c) Is this the same as a simple interest loan?
4. A bank loans $1600 for 18 months at an add-on interest rate of 8%.
   (a) What is the interest charge?
   (b) If this charge is added to the principal of the loan and the amount then owed is divided into monthly payments, what are the monthly charges?

5. Suppose $2000 is the maturity value of a loan for 2 years at a 10% discount rate.
   (a) What is the discount?
   (b) How much does the consumer receive to spend?
   (c) Is discounting the loan a better or worse deal for the consumer than being charged add-on interest?

6. Suppose the maturity value of a loan is $1600 for 18 months at a discount rate of 8%.
   (a) What is the amount of the discount?
   (b) How much does the consumer receive to spend?
   (c) What are the monthly payments on the loan?

7. Ye Olde Yankee Bank will give a 9-month discounted loan of $1800 to Sam Laposata, at a discount rate of 10%.
   (a) What is the maturity value of the loan if Sam receives the $1800?
   (b) What are his monthly payments?

8. Suppose a man needs $4968 and can borrow it by making monthly payments for a year and paying a discount rate of 8%.
   (a) What is the maturity value of the loan?
   (b) What are the monthly payments?

9. Find the APR for a loan of $1800 with add-on interest at 10%, if 12 monthly payments are made.

10. Find the APR for a loan of $3600 with add-on interest at 8%, if 36 monthly payments are made.

11. What is the APR for a discounted loan of $1800 with a discount rate of 10%, if 9 monthly payments are made?

12. What is the APR for a discounted loan of $4968 with a discount rate of 8%, if 12 monthly payments are made?

AMORTIZATION

13. A debt of $10,000 is to be amortized by equal payments at the end of each year for 5 years. If the interest charged is 8%, compounded annually, find the periodic payment.

14. A debt of $15,000 is to be amortized by equal payments at the end of each year for 10 years. If the interest charged is 9%, compounded annually, find the periodic payment.

15. A debt of $8000 is to be amortized with 8 equal semiannual payments. If the interest rate is 12%, compounded semiannually, what is the size of each payment?

16. A loan of $10,000 is to be amortized with 10 equal quarterly payments. If the interest rate is 6%, compounded quarterly, what is the periodic payment?

17. Develop an amortization schedule for a loan of $100,000 to be repaid in 3 annual payments of equal size. The interest rate is 9%.

18. Develop an amortization schedule for a loan of $30,000 to be repaid in 5 annual payments of equal size. The interest rate is 7%.

19. Develop an amortization schedule for a loan of $20,000 with interest at 12%, compounded quarterly, if it is to be repaid by 4 quarterly payments of equal size.

20. Develop an amortization schedule for a loan of $50,000 with interest at 10%, if it is to be repaid in $2\frac{1}{2}$ years by making equal semiannual payments.

21. A debt of $10,000 is to be amortized by equal payments of $2504.56 at the end of each year for 5 years. Find the outstanding principal (unpaid balance) immediately after the third payment. Interest is 8%, compounded annually.

22. A debt of $15,000 is to be amortized by equal payments of $2337.30 at the end of each year for 10 years. Find the unpaid balance immediately after the eighth payment. Interest is 9%, compounded annually.

23. A debt of $8000 is to be amortized with 8 equal semiannual payments of $1288.29. If the interest rate is 12%, compounded semiannually, find the unpaid balance immediately after the fifth payment.
24. A loan of $10,000 is to be amortized with 10 equal quarterly payments of $334.27. If the interest rate is 6%, compounded quarterly, what is the unpaid balance immediately after the sixth payment?
25. A man buys a house for $75,000. He makes a $25,000 down payment and amortizes the rest of the debt with semiannual payments over the next 10 years. If the interest rate on the debt is 12%, compounded semiannually, what are the payments?
26. Sean Lee purchases $20,000 worth of supplies for his restaurant by making a $3000 down payment and amortizing the rest with quarterly payments over the next 5 years. If the interest rate is 16%, compounded quarterly, what is the size of the quarterly payments?
27. John Fare purchased $10,000 worth of equipment by making a $2000 down payment and promising to pay the remainder of the cost in semiannual payments over the next 4 years. If the interest rate on the debt is 10%, compounded semiannually, what are the payments?
28. A woman buys an apartment house for $250,000 by making a down payment of $100,000 and amortizing the rest of the debt with semiannual payments over the next 10 years. If the interest rate is 12%, compounded semiannually, what will be the size of the payments?
29. A man buys a car for $12,000. If the interest rate on the loan is 12%, compounded monthly, and he wants to make monthly payments of $300 for 36 months, how much must he put down?
30. A woman buys a car for $15,000. If the interest rate on the loan is 12%, compounded monthly, and she wants to make monthly payments of $500 for 3 years, how much must she have for a down payment?
31. A couple purchasing a home wants their payment to be $500 per month. If they have $15,000 available for a down payment and the mortgage rate on a 25-year loan is 12%, compounded monthly, how much can they spend on a house?
32. An investor interested in purchasing an apartment building determines that she can make payments of $3000 per month. If a loan is available at 15%, compounded monthly for 20 years, how much can she afford to pay for the building?
33. Suppose the man of problem 25 receives an inheritance and wishes to pay off his loan after he has made 10 payments. Find the payoff amount.
34. What is the payoff amount for Sean Lee's loan (see problem 26) immediately after the eleventh payment?

SINKING FUNDS

35. What amount will have to be invested at the end of each year for 10 years to form a sinking fund of $100,000 if the interest rate is 10%, compounded annually?
36. What amount will have to be invested at the end of each year for 5 years to form a sinking fund of $25,000 if the interest rate is 12%, compounded annually?
37. How much will have to be invested at the end of each year at 10%, compounded annually, to pay off a debt of $50,000 in 8 years?
38. How much will have to be invested at the end of each year at 12%, compounded annually, to pay off a debt of $30,000 in 6 years?
39. A company establishes a sinking fund to discharge a debt of $75,000 due in 8 years by making equal semiannual deposits, the first due in 6 months. If their investment pays 12%, compounded semiannually, what is the size of the deposits?

40. A sinking fund is established to discharge a debt of $80,000 in 10 years. If deposits are made at the end of each 6-month period and interest is paid at the rate of 8%, compounded semiannually, what is the size of the deposits?

41. A sinking fund is established by a working couple so that they will have $20,000 to pay for part of their daughter's education when she enters college. If they make deposits at the end of each three-month period for 10 years, and if interest is paid at 12%, compounded quarterly, what size deposits must they make?

42. The Weidmans want to save $20,000 in two years for a down payment on a house. If they make monthly deposits into an account paying 12%, compounded monthly, what size payments are required to meet their goal?

43. A company can borrow $100,000 for ten years to purchase new equipment. They can either amortize the loan at an annual rate of 12% or they can pay interest on the loan at 11% for each of the ten years and set up a sinking fund at 10% per year, compounded annually. Which method of repayment costs less per year?

44. A company borrows $200,000 to be repaid in equal payments at the end of each semi-annual period for 10 years. Find the total semiannual cost if:
    (a) the loan is amortized at an interest rate of 12%.
    (b) the interest on the loan is paid at 12% in each of the 20 semiannual periods, and a sinking fund paying 10%, compounded semiannually, is set up to discharge the debt.

6.5 Depreciation of Property Purchased Before 1981 (Optional)

Objectives
- ☐ To compute depreciation on business assets using the straight-line method
- ☐ To compute depreciation using the units-of-production method
- ☐ To compute depreciation using the double-declining-balance method
- ☐ To compute depreciation using the sum-of-the-years-digits method

Certain business properties wear out and must be replaced, so businesses are allowed tax deductions for the decrease in value of these assets. This decrease in value over time is called **depreciation.** To be depreciable, the property must be for business use and it must have a limited useful lifespan. Land is not depreciable, but buildings, trucks, and equipment are.

The Economic Recovery Act of 1981 provided new methods for depreciating property. Under the act, items purchased after 1980 must be depreciated using one of the methods in the new Accelerated Cost Recovery System, which will be discussed in Section 6.6, and items purchased before 1981 must continue to be depreciated using the methods in effect before 1981. These methods included the *straight-line method,* the *double-declining-balance method,* and the *sum-of-the-years-digits method.* In these methods, we must know the item's useful life (how long it is expected to be used) and its basis (original cost plus improvements). For these methods we must also know the *resale* or *salvage value* of the property.

The 1986 Tax Reform Act made some changes in how depreciation is computed, and the new method is called the Modified Accelerated Cost Recovery System (MACRS). It will also be discussed in Section 6.6.

Straight-Line Methods

One method of computing depreciation is the straight-line method. One of the most frequently used methods, it is calculated by assuming equal depreciation over each year of the asset's useful life. We calculate the annual depreciation by the **straight-line method** as follows.

Procedure	Example
To calculate depreciation by the straight-line method:	Find the annual depreciation of a truck costing $10,500, with salvage value $1000, over a 5-year period.
1. Subtract the salvage value from the basis (cost) to get the total depreciation.	1. $10,500 − $1000 = $9500
2. Divide the total depreciation by the useful life (in years) to get the annual depreciation.	2. $9500 ÷ 5 = $1900 per year

The estimated life of a business asset is frequently converted to an *annual rate of depreciation,* which is stated as a percent. The rate of depreciation is usually based on the cost of the asset. Thus, in the previous example, we would divide the annual depreciation by the cost to get the annual rate of depreciation. This rate would be

$$\$1900 \div \$10,500 = 18.1\%.$$

EXAMPLE 1   Find the annual depreciation and annual rate of depreciation of a stamping machine that has a cost of $10,000, a useful life of 16 years, and a salvage value of $1200.

Solution   Total depreciation is $10,000 − $1200 = $8800.
Annual depreciation is $8800 ÷ 16 = $550.
Annual rate of depreciation is $550 ÷ $10,000 = 5.5%.

A second straight-line method of computing depreciation is the **units-of-production method.** This method relates depreciation to the estimated productive capacity of the property. An automobile or truck may be depreciated on the basis of the number of miles the company plans to run it, and a machine may be depreciated on the number of units it is estimated to produce or the number of hours it is expected to function.

EXAMPLE 2   A machine is expected to stamp 5,000,000 units during its life. Its cost was $53,000 and its resale value is $3000.
(a) What is the depreciation per unit of production?
(b) If the machine produces 339,500 units in a given year, what is the depreciation for that year?

Solution   (a) The total depreciation is $53,000 − $3000 = $50,000. The depreciation per unit is $50,000 ÷ 5,000,000 = $.01.
(b) The depreciation for the specified year is 339,500 × $.01 = $3395.

Double-Declining-Balance Method

Both methods of depreciation mentioned so far are *straight-line* methods, which assume that the relationship between the value of the asset and the number of years it is owned (or the number of units it has produced) is linear. But, in many cases, equipment (such as company trucks, etc.) depreciates very fast in the first few years, then more slowly in succeeding years. One method that will permit a larger charge for depreciation in the first years and less in later years is the **double-declining-balance method.** In this method, the depreciation at the end of each year is computed as a fixed percentage of its value at the beginning of the year. Because the value at the beginning of each year (called the *book value*) is multiplied by a fixed percentage, the book values and the yearly depreciations form geometric sequences.

The Internal Revenue Service permits businesses to use a maximum rate equal to *twice* the straight-line rate when computing depreciation by the double-declining-balance method on property purchased before 1981. Thus the most common practice in using this method is to apply twice the straight-line depreciation rate to the book value for the year. The straight-line rate can be calculated (as a percentage) by dividing the number of years of useful life into 100%. Thus an asset with an estimated life of four years has a straight-line depreciation rate of 100%/4 = 25%, and the rate used in the double-declining-balance method for a four-year useful life would be twice 25%, or 50%. The procedure for this method is outlined as follows.

Procedure	Example
To calculate depreciation by the double-declining-balance method:	Use the double-declining-balance method to compute the depreciation on a $10,500 truck with an estimated useful life of 5 years and salvage value of $1000.
1. Divide the number of years of useful life into 100%.	1. 100% ÷ 5 = 20%
2. Double this rate (from step 1).	2. 20% · 2 = 40%
3. The first year's depreciation is the cost times this double rate.	3. $10,500 · 0.40 = $4200 is the first year's depreciation.
4. Find the book value by subtracting the depreciation from the cost.	4. Book value is $10,500 − $4200 = $6300.
5. Take the double rate times the present book value to get the next year's depreciation, then subtract to find the book value at the end of that year.	5. $6300 · 0.40 = $2520 is the depreciation for the second year. $6300 − $2520 = $3780 is the book value at the end of the second year.

6. Repeat step 5 until the useful life is finished *or* until the book value is equal to the salvage value. (Frequently the depreciation for the final year will be the difference between the book value and the salvage value.)

6. $3780 \cdot 0.40 = \$1512$ is the depreciation for the third year. $\$3780 - \$1512 = \$2268$ is the book value at the end of the third year. $\$2268 \cdot 0.40 = \$907.20$ is the depreciation for the fourth year. $\$2268 - \$907.20 = \$1360.80$ is the book value at the end of the fourth year. $\$1360.80 \cdot \$0.40 = \$544.32$ is the depreciation for the fifth year. $\$1360.80 - \$544.32 = \$816.48$ is the book value at the end of the fifth year. *But* the salvage value is $1000, so the company can only claim depreciation down to a book value of $1000.

Thus the depreciation for the fifth year is limited to $\$1360.80 - \$1000 = \$360.80$.

This example can be put in tabular form, called a depreciation schedule (see Table 6.2). Note that the salvage value is used only to put a lower limit on the book value. It is not used as it was in the straight-line depreciation.

Table 6.2 Double-declining-balance depreciation schedule

Year	Book value at beginning of year	Rate	Depreciation for year	Book value at end of year
1	$10,500 (cost)	40%	$4,200.00	$6,300.00
2	6,300.00	40	2,520.00	3,780.00
3	3,780.00	40	1,512.00	2,268.00
4	2,268.00	40	907.20	1,360.80
5	1,360.80	—	360.80	1,000.00 (salvage)
		Total depreciation $9500.00		

We see that the book values at the end of each of the years form a geometric sequence with a common ratio of $60\% = 0.60$ (resulting from 100% minus the 40% depreciation rate), except for the last term, which is the salvage value. Similarly, the yearly depreciations (except for the last year) form a geometric sequence with ratio 0.60. This knowledge can be helpful in computing the depreciation.

EXAMPLE 3   A machine costing $156,250 has an estimated life of 10 years and an estimated salvage value of $18,000. Develop a depreciation schedule using the double-declining-balance method to find the book value and depreciation for each year.

Solution   The straight-line rate is $100\% \div 10 = 10\%$, so the double-declining-balance rate is twice 10%, or 20%. Then the book values will form a geometric sequence with common ratio 0.80. The depreciation schedule is given in Table 6.3.

Table 6.3 Double-declining-balance depreciation schedule

Year	Book value at beginning of year	End of year	Depreciation
1	$156,250 (cost)	$125,000	$31,250
2	125,000	100,000	25,000
3	100,000	80,000	20,000
4	80,000	64,000	16,000
5	64,000	51,200	12,800
6	51,200	40,960	10,240
7	40,960	32,768	8,192
8	32,768	26,214.40	6,553.60
9	26,214.40	20,971.52	5,242.88
10	20,971.52	18,000 (salvage)	2,971.52

Note that neither the book value nor the depreciation for the tenth year fit their respective sequences because the book value cannot fall below the salvage value.

EXAMPLE 4 The Ace Tool Company purchased an automobile for $8300. If the car is depreciated over 4 years with a salvage value of $500, use the double-declining-balance method to develop the depreciation schedule.

Solution **Table 6.4** Double-declining-balance depreciation schedule

Year	Book value at beginning of year	Rate	Depreciation for year	Book value at end of year
1	$8300.00	.50	$4150.00	$4150.00
2	4150.00	.50	2075.00	2075.00
3	2075.00	.50	1037.50	1037.50
4	1037.50	.50	518.75	518.75
		Total depreciation $7781.25		

Note that in this example the salvage value ($500) was not attained through the 4 years of depreciation. If the automobile was used beyond the estimated useful life (4 years), the company could claim additional depreciation until book value reaches the salvage value ($518.75 − $500 = $18.75 in this case).

Sum-of-the-Years-Digits Method

Another method of computing depreciation, which assumes that depreciation is greatest during the first year, is the sum-of-the-years-digits method. As with the double-declining-balance method, the depreciation steadily decreases with each year of useful life. The procedure for computing depreciation by the **sum-of-the-years-digits method** follows.

Procedure	Example
To calculate depreciation by the sum-of-the-years-digits:	Use the sum-of-the-years-digits method to compute the depreciation on a $30,500 truck with an estimated useful life of 5 years and salvage value of $500.
1. Subtract the salvage value from the cost to determine the *total* depreciation.	1. The total depreciation is $30,500 − $500 = $30,000.
2. Add the digits representing each of the years of the useful life; this will be used as the denominator of a fraction that will be used in step 3.	2. The sum-of-digits is $1 + 2 + 3 + 4 + 5 = 15$.
3. To find the depreciation for the first year, multiply the *total depreciation* by a fraction that has the number of years of useful life as the numerator and the sum-of-digits (step 2) as the denominator.	3. The depreciation for the first year is $30,000 \cdot \frac{5}{15} = $10,000$.
4. Find the *book value* by subtracting the depreciation from the *cost*.	4. The book value at the end of the first year is $30,500 − 10,000 = $20,500.
5. To find the next year's depreciation, multiply the *total depreciation* by a fraction with the same denominator and a numerator that is one less than the numerator for the previous year. Subtract the depreciation from the old book value to find the new book value.	5. $30,000 \cdot \frac{4}{15} = $8,000$ is the depreciation for the second year. The book value at the end of the second year is $20,500 − $8000 = $12,500.
6. Repeat step 5 until the useful life is finished.	6. $30,000 \cdot \frac{3}{15} = 6000 is the depreciation for the third year. $12,500 − $6000 = 6500 is the book value at the end of the third year. $30,000 \cdot \frac{2}{15} = 4000 is the depreciation for the fourth year. $6500 − $4000 = 2500 is the book value at the end of the fourth year. $30,000 \cdot \frac{1}{15} = 2000 is the depreciation for the fifth year. $2500 − $2000 = 500 is the book value at the end of the fifth year.

     This example can be put in a depreciation schedule (Table 6.5). Note that while the fraction is multiplied times the *total depreciation* (cost minus salvage value) to compute the depreciation, the book value for the first year is found by subtracting the depreciation from the *cost*.

Table 6.5   Sum-of-the-years-digits depreciation schedule

Year	Total depreciation	Rate	Depreciation for year	Book value at end of year
1	$30,000	$\frac{5}{15}$	$10,000	$20,500
2	30,000	$\frac{4}{15}$	8,000	12,500
3	30,000	$\frac{3}{15}$	6,000	6,500
4	30,000	$\frac{2}{15}$	4,000	2,500
5	30,000	$\frac{1}{15}$	2,000	500 (salvage)

EXAMPLE 5   Use the sum-of-the-years-digits to develop a depreciation schedule for machinery costing $64,000 if it is depreciated over a 6-year period and has a salvage value of $1,000.

Solution   The depreciation schedule is given in Table 6.6.

Table 6.6   Sum-of-the-years-digits depreciation schedule

Year	Total depreciation	Rate	Depreciation for year	Book value at end of year
1	$63,000	$\frac{6}{21}$	$18,000	$46,000
2	63,000	$\frac{5}{21}$	15,000	31,000
3	63,000	$\frac{4}{21}$	12,000	19,000
4	63,000	$\frac{3}{21}$	9,000	10,000
5	63,000	$\frac{2}{21}$	6,000	4,000
6	63,000	$\frac{1}{21}$	3,000	1,000 (salvage)

The sum-of-the-years-digits method uses a different type of sequence from the double-declining-balance method to compute its accelerated depreciation. Instead of using a constant rate of depreciation, the yearly rates form the first five terms of an arithmetic sequence whose sum is 1. Looking at Table 6.5, we see that the rates are

$$\frac{5}{15}, \frac{4}{15}, \frac{3}{15}, \frac{2}{15}, \frac{1}{15},$$

which is part of an arithmetic sequence with common difference $-\frac{1}{15}$. The sum of these terms is clearly 1, which we can verify by simply adding them or by using the formula $s_n = (n/2)(a_1 + a_n)$. Using the formula gives

$$s_n = \frac{5}{2}\left(\frac{5}{15} + \frac{1}{15}\right) = 1.$$

The reason this technique for finding the rates works so nicely is that we are seeking an arithmetic sequence of rates whose sum is 1 (so we get 100% of the depreciation) over n years, where the common difference decreases by one part each year. If we let the last term of this sequence be $1/p$, then solving the formula

$$1 = \frac{n}{2}\left(\frac{n}{p} + \frac{1}{p}\right)$$

(where n is the number of years) for p gives us

$$p = \frac{n(n + 1)}{2}.$$

But the sum of the first n terms of the arithmetic sequence

$$1, 2, 3, 4, \ldots, n$$

is

$$s_n = \frac{n}{2}(1 + n) = p$$

so we can find p by simply adding the years digits together! Thus the sum-of-the-years-digits method works for any number of years.

Exercise 6.5

STRAIGHT-LINE METHODS

1. Find the annual depreciation and the annual rate of depreciation of a machine that has a cost of $15,000, a useful life of 10 years, and a salvage value of $1000.
2. Find the annual depreciation and the annual rate of depreciation of a truck with a cost of $25,000, a useful life of 5 years, and a salvage value of $1000.
3. A microcomputer costing $4500 is depreciated over 5 years using the straight-line method. What is the depreciation for each year if the salvage value is $1000?
4. A machine costing $45,000 is depreciated over 5 years using the straight-line method. What is the depreciation for each year if the salvage value is $5000?
5. A truck costing $15,000 is depreciated over 3 years using the straight-line method. What is the depreciation for each year if the salvage value is $3000?
6. A research instrument costing $3500 is depreciated over 3 years using the straight-line method. What is the depreciation for each year if the salvage value is $500?
7. A $300,000 property put into business use is depreciated over 40 years and has a salvage value of $20,000. If it is depreciated using the straight-line method,
   (a) what is the depreciation in the first year?
   (b) what is the depreciation in the tenth year?
8. A $500,000 apartment house is depreciated over 40 years and has a salvage value of $60,000. If it is depreciated using the straight-line method,
   (a) what is the depreciation in the first year?
   (b) what is the depreciation in the eighth year?
9. A machine is expected to produce 2,000,000 units during its lifetime. Its cost was $60,000 and its salvage value is $4000.
   (a) What is the depreciation per unit of production?
   (b) If the machine produces 250,000 units during a given year, what is the depreciation for that year?

10. A machine should produce 50,000,000 decals during its life. Its cost is $30,000 and its salvage value is $5000.
    (a) What is the depreciation per 1000 units of production?
    (b) If the machine produces 4,550,000 decals in a year, what is the depreciation for the year?

DOUBLE-DECLINING-BALANCE METHOD

11. Use the double-declining-balance method to develop a depreciation schedule for an earth-moving machine with a cost of $36,500, a useful life of 4 years, and a salvage value of $2100.
12. Use the double-declining-balance method to develop a depreciation schedule for each year on a machine with a cost of $9000, a useful life of 3 years, and a salvage value of $500.
13. If the microcomputer of problem 3 (costing $4500) is depreciated over 5 years using the double-declining-balance method, develop the depreciation schedule.
14. If the machine of problem 4 (costing $45,000) is depreciated over 5 years using the double-declining-balance method, develop the depreciation schedule.
15. (a) A truck costing $15,000 (see problem 5) is depreciated over 3 years. If the double-declining-balance method is used, develop the depreciation schedule.
    (b) Does this method or the straight-line method (see problem 5) give the depreciation more rapidly?
16. (a) A research instrument costing $3500 (see problem 6) is depreciated over 3 years. If the double-declining-balance method is used, develop the depreciation schedule.
    (b) Does this method or the straight-line method (see problem 6) give depreciation more rapidly?

SUM-OF-THE-YEARS-DIGITS METHOD

17. A truck costing $15,000 is depreciated over 3 years using the sum-of-the-years-digits method. Develop the depreciation schedule for the truck if the salvage value is $3000.
18. A research instrument costing $3500 is depreciated over 3 years using the sum-of-the-years-digits method. Develop a depreciation schedule for the instrument if the salvage value is $500.
19. A $300,000 property with a salvage value of $20,000 is put into business use. If it is depreciated over 40 years using the sum-of-the-years-digit method,
    (a) what is the depreciation in the first year?
    (b) what is the depreciation in the tenth year?
20. If the $500,000 apartment house of problem 8 is depreciated using the sum-of-the-years-digits method,
    (a) what is the depreciation in the first year?
    (b) what is the depreciation in the eighth year?
21. Use the sum-of-the-years-digits method to develop the depreciation schedule for a $7600 company car with a useful life of 3 years and a resale value of $1600.
22. Use the sum-of-the-years-digits method to develop the depreciation schedule for a $16,500 machine with a useful life of 4 years and a salvage value of $3500.

6.6 Depreciation of Property Purchased After 1980 (Optional)

Objectives
- ☐ To compute depreciation on business assets using the ACRS accelerated method
- ☐ To compute depreciation using the ACRS straight-line method
- ☐ To compute deductions using the expensing option
- ☐ To compute depreciation using MACRS

ACRS: 1981–1986

For most depreciable property placed into service during 1981–1986, depreciation must be calculated using the Accelerated Cost Recovery System (ACRS). Salvage value is disregarded under the ACRS for items placed into service after 1980.

Under this system, items that are used for more than one year can be depreciated in one of six classes.

1. 3-year class: automobiles, light duty trucks, and items used for experimentation
2. 5-year class: office fixtures, furniture, equipment, and heavy duty trucks
3. 10-year class: certain public utility property, manufactured residential houses, and railroad tank cars
4. 15-year class: real property, both commercial and residential buildings (land is not depreciable)
5. 18-year class: real property purchased between March 15, 1984, and May 8, 1985
6. 19-year class: real property purchased after May 8, 1985, and before January 1, 1987

Any of the six classes of property that can be depreciated using the ACRS may be depreciated in one of two ways, either by using the accelerated method or straight-line method.

The accelerated method of depreciation could be chosen by a taxpayer seeking the largest deductions in early years. The straight-line method could be used if the taxpayer wishes more depreciation in later years. Once the decision is reached as to which of these methods is more beneficial, you must use it for all depreciable assets put into service in that particular class in the same year. Assets in any of the other classes are not so bound for that year. In following years, assets put into service do not have to be depreciated by the methods chosen in prior years. The depreciation method for property in the 15-year class is decided on a property-by-property basis, rather than on the class as a whole.

Some changes that the ACRS method introduced are the following.

- ☐ In the ACRS method, salvage value is ignored and the useful life has been shortened so that annual depreciation is larger.
- ☐ In contrast to the methods described earlier, the ACRS method utilizes tables of fixed rates.

☐ In the accelerated method, first-year depreciation on 3-, 5-, and 10-year property does not depend on the time during the year the property was placed in service. For 15-, 18-, and 19-year property, the first month of service is needed to determine the first-year depreciation.

Table 6.7 shows the percentage of the original purchase price that is deducted each year under the accelerated method (and the straight-line method) for items in the 3-year category. Table 6.8 shows the percentage for items in the 5-year category. These tables are constructed assuming the property was purchased in the middle of the year (this is called the half-year convention).

Table 6.7   3-year property

Year	Accelerated method	Straight-line method
1	25%	17%
2	38	33
3	37	33
4		17
	100%	100%

Table 6.8   5-year property

Year	Accelerated method bought before 8/1/86	Accelerated method bought after 7/31/86	Straight-line method
1	15%	20%	10%
2	22	32	20
3	21	19	20
4	21	12	20
5	21	12	20
6		5	10
	100%	100%	100%

EXAMPLE 1   A firm places some equipment into service in 1985. If the amount that can be depreciated is $50,000, find the amount of depreciation for each year if the equipment is in the 5-year category and

(a) it is depreciated by the straight-line method.

(b) it is depreciated by the accelerated method.

Solution   (a) Depreciation for year 1: $50,000 · 10% = $ 5,000
Depreciation for each of
     years 2–5: $50,000 · 20% = $10,000
Depreciation for year 6: $50,000 · 10% = $ 5,000
(b) Depreciation for year 1: $50,000 · 15% = $ 7,500
Depreciation for year 2: $50,000 · 22% = $11,000
Depreciation for each of
     years 3–5: $50,000 · 21% = $10,500

If an item is purchased for both personal and business use, then only that part applied to business use can be deducted. For example, if the equipment mentioned above is used 70% of the time for business and 30% of the time for personal purposes, then only 70% of each year's depreciation can be deducted for tax purposes.

EXAMPLE 2   If, in Example 1, the equipment was used 20% of the time for personal purposes, find the straight-line depreciation that would be deductible for tax purposes in the first year.

Solution   The straight-line depreciation for the first year is $5,000. If it was used 20% of the time for personal purposes, 80% of the $5,000, or $4,000, is deductible.

For items that are depreciated in the 15-, 18-, and 19-year classes, the month in which the property is purchased does affect the rate of depreciation. For example, if an apartment building is depreciated over a 15-year period, using the straight-line method, you would deduct $\frac{1}{15}$ of the purchase price for each *full* year of use of the property.

EXAMPLE 3   An apartment building is purchased in October of 1983 for $150,000. How much could be depreciated each year for the building if the straight-line method is used?

Solution   This building is in the 15-year class. The depreciation for the year of purchase would be $\frac{3}{12}$ of the yearly depreciation because it was used only 3 months of that year:

$$\frac{3}{12} \cdot \frac{1}{15} \cdot \$150,000 = \$2500.$$

For each of the next 14 years:

$$\frac{1}{15} \cdot \$150,000 = \$10,000.$$

Nine months of the 15 years remain to be depreciated, so depreciation in the sixteenth year is

$$\frac{9}{12} \cdot \frac{1}{15} \cdot \$150,000 = \$7500.$$

The reason for considering the month of purchase for real properties is to prevent a business from making such purchases in December, obtaining large deductions, and then reselling quickly. Thus, the IRS requires that the month of purchase be considered in the accelerated method as well as the straight-line method.

Table 6.9 gives the percentage of the cost of a property in the 15-year class that may be deducted each year using the accelerated method. The appropriate percentage for each year is found in the column corresponding to the month of purchase (or the month the property is placed into business use). Depreciation tables for 18-year and 19-year properties are given in Tables IX and X in the Appendix.

Table 6.9 15-year deduction, accelerated method

Year	Jan	Feb	Mar	Apr	May	Jun	Jly	Aug	Sep	Oct	Nov	Dec
1	12%	11%	10%	9%	8%	7%	6%	5%	4%	3%	2%	1%
2	10	10	11	11	11	11	11	11	11	11	11	12
3	9	9	9	9	10	10	10	10	10	10	10	10
4	8	8	8	8	8	8	9	9	9	9	9	9
5	7	7	7	7	7	7	8	8	8	8	8	8
6	6	6	6	6	7	7	7	7	7	7	7	7
7	6	6	6	6	6	6	6	6	6	6	6	6
8	6	6	6	6	6	6	5	6	6	6	6	6
9	6	6	6	6	5	6	5	5	5	6	6	6
10	5	6	5	6	5	5	5	5	5	5	6	5
11	5	5	5	5	5	5	5	5	5	5	5	5
12	5	5	5	5	5	5	5	5	5	5	5	5
13	5	5	5	5	5	5	5	5	5	5	5	5
14	5	5	5	5	5	5	5	5	5	5	5	5
15	5	5	5	5	5	5	5	5	5	5	5	5
16	0	0	1	1	2	2	3	3	4	4	4	5

EXAMPLE 4 If the apartment building of Example 3 is depreciated using the accelerated method, what is the depreciation in the

(a) first year?

(b) ninth year?

Solution (a) For 15-year class properties placed into service in October, the first year depreciation is 3% of the cost:

$$\$150{,}000 \cdot 3\% = \$4500.$$

(b) For 15-year class properties placed into service in October, the ninth year depreciation is 6% of the cost:

$$\$150{,}000 \cdot 6\% = \$9000.$$

Expensing

A new option, called the **expensing** option, was also made available by the Economic Recovery Act. The expensing option permits a taxpayer to deduct *in full* up to $5000 on property that was placed into service in 1981 through 1986 in the 3-year and 5-year categories. The expensing option has these conditions.

1. Expensing may be applied to the full cost of the item.

2. Depreciation may not be claimed on items that are expensed, but any amount above the amount expensed may be depreciated.

3. Investment tax credit may not be applied to the amount expensed, but may be applied to the part of the cost that is not expensed.

4. Only items related to self-employment activity or job-related items may be expensed. Investment-related activities do not apply.

EXAMPLE 5   Suppose you purchased an automobile for business use in 1985. If the automobile costs $9600,

(a) how much money can be deducted under the expensing option?

(b) what is the depreciation for the 3-year period after purchase?

Solution   (a) The expensing option permits a deduction of $5000.

(b) All costs over $5000 can be depreciated over the 3-year period,

$$\$9600 - \$5000 = \$4600.$$

Using the accelerated method gives

year 1: $\$4600 \cdot 25\% = \$1150$
year 2: $\$4600 \cdot 38\% = \$1748$
year 3: $\$4600 \cdot 37\% = \$1702$

Note that using the expensing option in Example 5 gives a total deduction of $\$5000 + \$1150 = \$6150$ in the first year.

MACRS: After 1986

The Tax Reform Act of 1986 changed the ACRS method of depreciation. The changes brought about by the Modified ACRS (MACRS) are summarized in the table below.

Old law (ACRS)	New law (MACRS)
Automobiles are depreciated over 3 years.	Automobiles are depreciated over 5 years. Depreciation is limited on cars costing more than $12,800.
Machinery and equipment are depreciated over 5 years.	Machinery and equipment are depreciated over 7 years.
Real estate is depreciated over 15, 18, or 19 years.	Residential real estate is depreciated over 27.5 years, nonresidential real estate over 31.5 years using the straight-line method.
Personal property is depreciated using tables based on the 150% declining balance method.	Personal property is depreciated using the 200% (double) declining-balance method.
Expensing deduction is $5000.	Expensing deduction will be increased to $10,000 by 1990.

Under the new law, most real property is classified as residential, rental, or non-residential real estate property. Depreciation on such property is calculated using the straight-line method and the assumption that the purchase was made in mid-month. Table 6.10 shows the six classes that non-real estate property is placed into, along with the depreciation methods for these classes.

Table 6.10   MACRS depreciation classes and methods

Class	Depreciation method
3 years (certain tractors and race horses) 5 years (computers, office equipment) 7 years (office furniture, single purpose agricultural or horticultural buildings) 10 years (barges, tugs, ships)	Use double-declining (200%)-balance method and a half-year convention, changing to the straight-line method for the first tax year for which that method, when applied to the adjusted basis at the beginning of the year, will yield a larger deduction.
15 years (municipal waste-water treatment plants) 20 years (farm buildings and some municipal sewers)	Use 150% declining-balance method and half-year convention, changing to the straight-line method for the first tax year for which that method, when applied to the adjusted basis at the beginning of the year, will yield a larger deduction.

The half-year convention permits a taxpayer to claim depreciation for half of the year of purchase regardless of when the purchase was made.* Property is then depreciated for a full year in each of the remaining years, with the final half-year of depreciation taken in the year following the recovery period. Thus a 5-year property can be depreciated for one-half year in the year of purchase, depreciated for one year in each of years 2 through 5, and for one-half year in the sixth year.

We see that the double-declining-balance method** is used for property in the 3-, 5-, 7-, and 10-year classes, and that the half-year convention must be used in the year that the property is placed into service.

EXAMPLE 6   An automobile costing $12,000 is purchased for business use in July, 1987. Give the annual depreciation using the MACRS system.

---

*Some restrictions apply.

**See Section 6.5.

Solution   The automobile is a 5-year property, so the double-declining rate of depreciation is $100\%/5 \cdot 2 = 40\%$. The depreciation follows (with the half-year convention for year 1).

Year	Depreciation	Value at end of year
1	$12000(.40) \times \frac{1}{2}$ = \$2400	\$12000 − \$2400 = \$9600
2	$9600(.40)$ = 3840	9600 − 3840 = 5760
3	$5760(.40)$ = 2304	5700 − 2304 = 3456
4	$3456(.40)$ = 1382.40	3456 − 1382.40 = 2073.60
5	$2073.60(.40)$ = 829.44	2073.60 − 829.44 = 1244.16
6	1244.16	

We note, however, that the depreciation deduction can be maximized if we convert to straight-line depreciation when it yields a larger value. The adjusted basis after 3 years is \$3456. The amount that could be deducted in each of the remaining $2\frac{1}{2}$ years is

$$\frac{\$3456}{2.5} = \$1382.40$$

Thus both methods yield the same depreciation in the fourth year and, as we will see, the straight-line method yields a higher depreciation in the fifth year. The adjusted basis at the beginning of the fifth year is \$2073.60, and the amount that could be deducted in each of the remaining $1\frac{1}{2}$ years is

$$\frac{\$2073.60}{1.5} = \$1382.40.$$

Thus a depreciation of \$1382.40 is permitted in year 5, with 1/2 of \$1382.40 permitted in year 6. The depreciation schedule follows.

Year	Depreciation	Value at end of year
1	\$2400	\$9600
2	3840	5760
3	2304	3456
4	1382.40	2073.60
5	1382.40	691.20
6	691.20	0

Note that both the double-declining-balance method and the straight-line method give the same depreciation in year 4 of this example, but this does not happen in other depreciation classes.

We can avoid the drudgery of calculating depreciation as we have in Example 6 by making use of tables that have been developed for depreciating items costing $1. Table XI in the Appendix is such a table.

EXAMPLE 7   Construct a depreciation schedule for a $30,000 tractor (in the 3-year class) purchased in February of 1989.

Solution   Using the percentages from Table XI for a 3-year class item, we have

Year	Percent	Amount of depreciation
1	33	$ 9900
2	45	13500
3	15	4500
4	7	2100
Total	100	$30000

Exercise 6.6

In problems 1–18, assume the properties were purchased in the years 1981–1985.

1. A microcomputer costing $4500 is depreciated over 5 years using the ACRS straight-line method. What is the depreciation for each year?
2. A machine costing $45,000 is depreciated over 5 years using the ACRS straight-line method. What is the depreciation for each year?
3. A truck costing $15,000 is depreciated over 3 years using the ACRS straight-line method. What is the depreciation for each year?
4. A research instrument costing $3500 is depreciated over 3 years. What is the depreciation for each year if the ACRS straight-line method is used?
5. A $300,000 property is put into business use in September, 1983. If it is depreciated over 15 years using the ACRS straight-line method,
   (a) what is the depreciation in the first year?
   (b) what is the depreciation in the tenth year?
6. A $500,000 apartment house is purchased in May, 1983. If it is depreciated over 15 years using the ACRS straight-line method,
   (a) what is the depreciation in the first year?
   (b) what is the depreciation in the eighth year?
7. If the microcomputer (costing $4500) of problem 1 is depreciated over 5 years using the ACRS accelerated method, develop the depreciation schedule.
8. If the machine (costing $45,000) of problem 2 is depreciated over 5 years using the ACRS accelerated method, develop the depreciation schedule.
9. (a) A truck costing $15,000 is depreciated over 3 years. If the ACRS accelerated method is used, develop the depreciation schedule.
   (b) Does this method or the ACRS straight-line method (see problem 3) give the depreciation more rapidly?

10. If the $3500 research instrument of problem 4 is depreciated over 3 years using the ACRS accelerated method, find the depreciation schedule.

11. The $300,000 property of problem 5 is put into business use in September, 1983. If it is depreciated using the ACRS accelerated method,
    (a) what is the depreciation in the first year?
    (b) what is the depreciation in the tenth year?

12. The $500,000 apartment house of problem 6 is purchased in May, 1983. If it is depreciated using the ACRS accelerated method,
    (a) what is the depreciation in the first year?
    (b) what is the depreciation in the eighth year?

13. How much can be expensed under the expensing option if a business purchased an $11,500 microcomputer system in 1984?

14. If the machine of problem 2 was purchased in 1985 and expensed, how much can be expensed?

15. For the microcomputer system of problem 13, what is the largest amount that can be depreciated (including expensing) in the first year? (Use a 5-year class.)

16. For the machine of problem 2 and problem 14, how much depreciation can be claimed in the first year if expensing and the ACRS accelerated method are used?

17. If the expensing option is used in claiming deductions for the $15,000 truck of problem 9, purchased in 1985,
    (a) how much can be expensed?
    (b) after expensing, how much are you permitted to depreciate over 3 years?

18. In problem 17, how much can be depreciated in *each* of the 3 years using the ACRS accelerated method after expensing?

AFTER 1986

Use MACRS to make a depreciation schedule for problems 19–24.

19. A $15,000 computer system is purchased in September, 1988.
20. A truck is purchased for $30,000 in October, 1987.
21. Office furniture costing $20,000 is purchased in July, 1988.
22. A greenhouse is constructed in August, 1988, at a cost of $60,000.
23. A $50,000 race horse (in the 3-year class) is purchased in December, 1988.
24. A 3-year-class tractor is placed into service in July, 1989, with a value of $60,000.

Review Exercises

6.1

1. Find the first 4 terms of the sequence whose nth term is

$$a_n = \frac{1}{n^2}.$$

2. Find the tenth term of the arithmetic sequence with first term -2 and common difference 3.

3. Find the sixth term of the arithmetic sequence with third term 10 and eighth term 25.

4. Find the sum of the first 6 terms of the arithmetic sequence $\frac{1}{3}, \frac{1}{2}, \frac{2}{3}, \ldots$.

6.2

5. Find the fourth term of the geometric sequence with first term 64 and eighth term $\frac{1}{2}$.

6. Find the sum of the first 6 terms of the geometric sequence $\frac{1}{9}, \frac{1}{3}, 1, \ldots$.

APPLICATIONS

6.1

7. If $8000 is borrowed at 12% simple interest for 3 years, what is the amount of the loan at the end of the 3 years?

8. Mary Toy borrowed $2000 from her parents and repaid them $2100 after 9 months. What simple interest rate did she pay?

9. Suppose the winner of a contest receives $10 on the first day of the month, $20 on the second day, $30 on the third day, and so on for a 30-day month. What is the total won?

10. Suppose you are offered two identical jobs: one paying a starting salary of $20,000 with yearly raises of $1000 and one paying a starting salary of $18,000 with yearly raises of $1200. Which job will pay more money over a 10-year period?

6.2

11. If $8000 is invested at 12%, compounded annually, for 3 years, what is the compound amount at the end of the 3 years?

12. If $1000 is invested for 4 years at 8%, compounded quarterly, how much interest will be earned?

13. What is the compound amount if $1000 is invested for 6 years at 8%, compounded semiannually?

14. What is the compound amount if $1000 is invested for 6 years at 8%, compounded continuously?

15. If $8000 is invested at 12% compounded continuously for 3 years, what is the compound amount at the end of the 3 years?

16. What interest is earned in problem 15?

17. Find the effective annual rate equivalent to the nominal rate of 8%, compounded quarterly.

18. Legend has it that when the king of Persia wanted to reward the inventor of chess with whatever he desired, the inventor asked for one grain of wheat on the first square of the chessboard, with the number of grains doubled on each square thereafter for the remaining 63 squares. Find the number of grains on the 64th square. (The sum of all the grains of wheat on all the squares would cover Alaska more than 3 inches deep with wheat!)

19. If, in problem 18, the king granted the inventor's wish for *half* a chessboard, how many grains would the inventor receive?

6.3

20. Find the amount of an ordinary annuity of $800 paid at the end of every 6-month period for 10 years, if it earns interest at 12%, compounded semiannually.

21. Find the amount of an annuity due of $800 paid at the beginning of every 6-month period for 10 years, if it earns interest at 12%, compounded semiannually.

22. If $100 is deposited at the end of each quarterly period for 4 years in an account that pays 8% interest, compounded quarterly, how much money will accrue in the account?

23. What lump sum would have to be invested at 9%, compounded annually, to provide an annuity of $10,000 per year for 10 years?

24. Find the present value of an annuity of $6500 paid semiannually for 4 years after being deferred for 10 years, if money is worth 8% compounded semiannually.

25. A couple wishes to set up an annuity that would provide 6 monthly payments of $3000 while they take an extended cruise. How much of a $15,000 inheritance must be set aside if they plan to leave in 5 years and want the first payment before they leave? Assume money is worth 7.8%, compounded monthly.

6.4

26. A man borrows $3000 for 2 years and makes monthly payments on the loan plus add-on interest at a rate of 12% per year. What are his monthly payments?

27. Debbie Romeo borrows money to purchase a car. If she plans to make monthly payments for 3 years and signs a discounted note for $5200 at a yearly discount rate of 12%, how much money does she receive for her purchase?

28. A debt of $1000 with interest at 12%, compounded monthly, is amortized by 12 monthly payments (of equal size). What is the size of each payment?

29. How much would have to be invested at the end of each year at 6%, compounded annually, to pay off a debt of $80,000 in 10 years?

30. A divorce settlement of $40,000 is paid in 40 monthly payments of $1000 each. What is the present value of this settlement if money is worth 12%, compounded monthly?

6.5
31. Use the straight-line method to find the annual depreciation of a machine purchased before 1981 that has a cost of $100,000, a useful life of 10 years, and a salvage value of $2000.

32. Use the double-declining-balance method to compute the depreciation for the first 4 years on the machine in problem 31.

33. Use the sum-of-the-years-digits to compute the depreciation for the first 4 years on the machine in problem 31.

6.6
34. Use the ACRS straight-line method to find the depreciation schedule for a machine purchased in 1985 at a cost of $100,000 and depreciated over a 5-year period.

35. Use the ACRS accelerated method to find the depreciation schedule for the machine in problem 34.

36. (a) What amount could be deducted under the expensing option for the machine in problem 34?

    (b) What is the total depreciation allowed if the expensing option is used?

    (c) What is the total depreciation allowed in the first year if both expensing and the accelerated method are used?

37. Develop the depreciation schedule for a $10,000 automobile purchased in 1988.

38. If a 7-year property is placed into service in 1988 and has a value of $30,000, what is the depreciation allowed in the third year?

Part Four

Probabilistic Models

WARMUP

	Prerequisite problem type	Answer	Section for review
7.1	(a) The sum of x, $\frac{1}{4}$, and $\frac{2}{3}$ is 1. What is x?	(a) $x = \frac{1}{12}$	1.1 Linear equations
	(b) If the sum of x plus $\frac{1}{3}$ plus $\frac{1}{3}$ is 1, what is x?	(b) $x = \frac{1}{3}$	
7.1	If 12 numbers are weighted so that each of the 12 numbers has an equal weight and the sum of the weights is 1, what weight should be assigned to each number?	$\frac{1}{12}$	1.1 Linear equations
7.1	(a) List the set of integers that satisfies $2 \leq x < 6$.	(a) $\{2, 3, 4, 5\}$	0.1 Sets 3.1 Inequalities
	(b) List the set of integers that satisfies $4 \leq s \leq 12$.	(b) $\{4, 5, 6, 7, 8, 9, 10, 11, 12\}$	
7.8	Find the product: $[.9 \quad .1] \begin{bmatrix} .8 & .2 \\ .3 & .7 \end{bmatrix}$	$[.75 \quad .25]$	2.2 Matrix multiplication
7.8	Solve the system using matrices $.5V_1 + .4V_2 + .3V_3 = V_1$ $.4V_1 + .5V_2 + .3V_3 = V_2$ $.1V_1 + .1V_2 + .4V_3 = V_3$	$V_1 = 3V_3$ $V_2 = 3V_3$	2.3 Gauss-Jordan elimination

7

Introduction to Probability

An economist cannot predict exactly how the gross national product will change, a sociologist cannot determine exactly how group behavior is affected by climatic conditions, and a psychologist cannot determine the exact effect of environment on behavior. Since the behavior of the economy and of people is subject to chance, their prediction involves probability. Answers to questions about the behavioral and life sciences, business, and economics are frequently found by conducting experiments with samples from the larger population and by using statistics (discussed in Chapter 8). The experiments are designed to compare what actually happens with what probability theory predicted would happen. For example, if a rat runs a T-maze, can it learn which way to turn to get food? If the food is on the right and the rat turns right many more times than probability indicates that it should, then we have evidence that it has learned. The conclusions drawn from experiments are usually given in terms of probability because they are extended to larger populations. For example, substances that cause cancer in experimental animals may not be proven to cause cancer in humans, but will be removed from the market because the probability is high that they will.

We will solve a number of problems involving games in this chapter because they lend themselves easily to probability. (In fact, probability theory really started as the result of gambling problems.) We will also see that the theory of probability can be useful in many applications in the management, social, and life sciences.

7.1 Probability

Objectives ☐ To compute the probability of a single event's occurrence
☐ To construct a sample space for a probability experiment

If we toss a coin, it can land in one of two ways, heads or tails. If the coin is a "fair" coin, these two possible **outcomes** have an equal chance of occurring, and we say the outcomes of this **probability experiment** are **equally likely.** If we seek the probability that an experiment has a certain result, that result is called an **event.**

347

Suppose an experiment can have a total of n equally likely outcomes, and that k of these outcomes would be considered successes. Then the probability of achieving a success in the experiment is k/n. That is, the probability of a success in an experiment is the number of ways the experiment can result in a success divided by the total number of possible outcomes. We may state the same idea a different way:

Probability of a Single Event

If an event E can happen in k ways out of a total of n equally likely possibilities, the probability of the occurrence of the event is denoted by

$$\Pr(E) = \frac{k}{n} = \frac{\text{number of successes}}{\text{number of possible outcomes}}.$$

EXAMPLE 1   If we draw a ball from a bag containing 4 white balls and 6 black balls, what is the probability of
(a) getting a white ball?
(b) getting a black ball?
(c) not getting a white ball?

Solution   (a) A white ball can occur (be drawn) in 4 ways out of a total of 10 equally likely possibilities. Thus the probability of drawing a white ball is

$$\Pr(W) = \frac{4}{10} = \frac{2}{5}.$$

(b) We have 6 chances to succeed at drawing a black ball out of a total of 10 possible outcomes. Thus the probability of getting a black ball is

$$\Pr(B) = \frac{6}{10} = \frac{3}{5}.$$

(c) The probability of not getting a white ball is $\Pr(B)$, since not getting a white ball is the same as getting a black ball. Thus $\Pr(\text{not } W) = \Pr(B) = 3/5$.

The probability that event E will fail to occur is denoted by

$$\Pr(\text{not } E) = \frac{n - k}{n} = 1 - \frac{k}{n} = 1 - \Pr(E).$$

An event has probability 0 if and only if it cannot occur, and an event has probability 1 if and only if it is certain to occur. If E is any event,

$$0 \le \Pr(E) \le 1.$$

We summarize these results below:

For an event E,

$$0 \le \text{Pr}(E) \le 1$$
$$\text{Pr}(\text{not } E) = 1 - \text{Pr}(E)$$
$$\text{Pr}(E) = 1 - \text{Pr}(\text{not } E)$$
$$= 0 \text{ if and only if } E \text{ cannot occur}$$
$$= 1 \text{ if and only if } E \text{ is certain to occur}$$

EXAMPLE 2   A dry cleaning firm has 12 employees: 7 women and 5 men. Three of the women and five of the men are 40 years old or older. The remainder are over 20 years of age and under 40. If a person is chosen at random from this firm,* what is the probability that the person is

(a) a woman?   (b) under 40 years of age?   (c) 20 years old?

Solution   (a) There are 7 women, so Pr(woman) = 7/12.

(b) Eight people are 40 or older, so

$$\text{Pr(under 40)} = 1 - \text{Pr}(40+) = 1 - \frac{8}{12} = \frac{4}{12} = \frac{1}{3}.$$

(c) All employees are over 20 years old, so Pr(20) = 0.

EXAMPLE 3   In a sales promotion, a clothing store gives its customers a chance to draw a ticket from a box that contains a discount on their next purchase. The box contains 3000 tickets giving a 10% discount, 500 giving a 30% discount, 100 giving a 50% discount, and 1 giving a 100% discount. What is the probability that a given customer will draw a ticket giving

(a) a 100% discount?
(b) a 50% discount?
(c) a discount of less than 50%?

Solution   (a) There is 1 ticket giving a 100% discount and 3601 tickets in the box, so the probability is

$$\text{Pr(100\% discount)} = \frac{1}{3601}.$$

(b) There are 100 tickets giving a 50% discount, and 3601 tickets, so

$$\text{Pr(50\% discount)} = \frac{100}{3601}.$$

---

*Selecting a person at random means every person has an equal chance of being selected.

(c) There are 3500 tickets giving discounts of less than 50%, so

$$\text{Pr(discount less than 50\%)} = \frac{3500}{3601}.$$

EXAMPLE 4   If a number is to be selected at random from the integers 1 through 12, what is the probability that it is
(a) even?
(b) divisible by 3?
(c) even and divisible by 3?
(d) even or divisible by 3?

Solution   (a) Each number has an equal chance to be selected, and 6 of the 12 numbers are even. Thus

$$\text{Pr(even)} = \frac{6}{12} = \frac{1}{2}.$$

(b) The numbers 3, 6, 9, 12 are divisible by 3. Thus

$$\text{Pr(divisible by 3)} = \frac{4}{12} = \frac{1}{3}.$$

(c) The numbers 1 through 12 that are even *and* divisible by 3 are 6 and 12, so

$$\text{Pr(even and divisible by 3)} = \frac{2}{12} = \frac{1}{6}.$$

(d) The numbers that are even *or* divisible by 3 are 2, 3, 4, 6, 8, 9, 10, 12, so

$$\text{Pr(even or divisible by 3)} = \frac{8}{12} = \frac{2}{3}.$$

In the previous example, it was necessary (at least mentally) to list all the possible outcomes of the experiment (selecting a number at random). A set that contains all the possible outcomes of an experiment is called a **sample space.** In the previous example, a sample space is

$$S = \{1, 2, 3, 4, 5, 6, 7, 8, 9, 10, 11, 12\}.$$

Each element of the sample space is called a **sample point,** and an **event** is a subset of the sample space. Each sample point in the sample space is assigned a **probability measure** or **weight** such that the sum of the weights in the sample space is 1. The probability of an event is the sum of the weights of the sample points in the event's **subspace** (subset of S).

For example, the experiment "drawing a number at random from the numbers 1 through 12" has the sample space S given above. Because each element of S is equally likely to occur, we assign a probability weight of 1/12 to each element. The event "drawing an even number" in this experiment has the subspace

$$E = \{2, 4, 6, 8, 10, 12\}.$$

Because each of the 6 elements in the subspace has weight 1/12, the probability of event E is

$$\text{Pr(even)} = \text{Pr}(E) = \frac{1}{12} + \frac{1}{12} + \frac{1}{12} + \frac{1}{12} + \frac{1}{12} + \frac{1}{12} = \frac{6}{12} = \frac{1}{2}.$$

Note that using the sample space S for this experiment gives the same results as using the formula $\text{Pr}(E) = k/n$ [see Example 4(a)].

Some experiments can have an infinite number of outcomes, but we will concern ourselves only with experiments having finite sample spaces. We can usually construct more than one sample space for an experiment. The sample space in which each sample point is equally likely is called an **equiprobable sample space.**

EXAMPLE 5   Suppose a coin is tossed 3 times. Construct an equiprobable sample space for the experiment.

Solution   Perhaps the most obvious way to record the possibilities for this experiment is to list the number of heads that could result: {0, 1, 2, 3}. But the probability of obtaining 0 heads is different from the probability of obtaining 2 heads, so this sample space does not meet our needs. A sample space in which each outcome is equally likely is {HHH, HHT, HTH, THH, HTT, THT, TTH, TTT}, where HHT indicates the first two tosses were heads and the third was a tail. Because there are 8 equally likely possibilities, each has probability 1/8. Only one of the eight gives 0 heads and three of the eight give 2 heads, so Pr(0 heads) = 1/8 and Pr(2 heads) = 3/8.

To find the probability of obtaining a given sum when a pair of dice is rolled, we need to determine how many outcomes are possible. If we distinguish between the two dice we are rolling, and we record all the possible outcomes for each die, we see that there are 36 possibilities, each of which is equally likely (see Table 7.1).

This list of possible outcomes for finding the sum of two dice is a sample space for the experiment. Because each *element* of this sample space has the same chance of occurring, this is an equiprobable sample space. Because the 36 elements in the sample space are equally likely, we can find the probability that a given sum results by determining the number of ways that sum can occur and dividing that number by 36. Thus the probability that a sum 6 will occur is 5/36, and the probability that a 9 will occur is 4/36 = 1/9. (See the 4 ways the sum 9 can occur in Table 7.1.)

Table 7.1

First die \ Second die	1	2	3	4	5	6
1	(1, 1)	(1, 2)	(1, 3)	(1, 4)	(1, 5)	(1, 6)
2	(2, 1)	(2, 2)	(2, 3)	(2, 4)	(2, 5)	(2, 6)
3	(3, 1)	(3, 2)	(3, 3)	(3, 4)	(3, 5)	(3, 6)
4	(4, 1)	(4, 2)	(4, 3)	(4, 4)	(4, 5)	(4, 6)
5	(5, 1)	(5, 2)	(5, 3)	(5, 4)	(5, 5)	(5, 6)
6	(6, 1)	(6, 2)	(6, 3)	(6, 4)	(6, 5)	(6, 6)

Note that we could have made a sample space for this experiment (finding the sum of a pair of dice) by listing the sums: (2, 3, 4, 5, 6, 7, 8, 9, 10, 11, 12). However, these outcomes are not equally likely; the probability of obtaining a 2 is different from the probability of obtaining a 6. We can see that the probabilities of events can be found more easily if an equiprobable sample space is used to determine the possibilities.

EXAMPLE 6   Use Table 7.1 to find the following probabilities if a pair of distinguishable dice is rolled:

(a) Pr(sum is 5)   (b) Pr(sum is 2)   (c) Pr(sum is 8)

Solution   (a) The sum 5 can occur in four ways: (4, 1), (3, 2), (2, 3), and (1, 4). Therefore Pr(sum is 5) = 4/36 = 1/9.

(b) The sum 2 results only from (1, 1). Thus Pr(sum is 2) = 1/36.

(c) The sample points that give a sum of 8 are in the subspace (6, 2), (5, 3), (4, 4), (3, 5), (2, 6). Thus Pr(sum is 8) = 5/36.

The assignment of the probability of an event is frequently derived from our experiences or from data that has been gathered. Probabilities developed in this way are called **empirical probabilities.** An empirical probability is formed by conducting an experiment or observing a situation a number of times, then noting how many times a certain event occurs.

Empirical Probability of an Event	$\text{Pr(Event)} = \dfrac{\text{Number of observed occurrences of the event}}{\text{Total number of trials or observations}}$

In some cases empirical probability is the only way to assign a probability to an event. For example, life insurance premiums are based on the probability that an individual will live to a certain age. These probabilities are developed empirically and organized into mortality tables.

In other cases, empirical probabilities may have a theoretical framework. For example, in tossing a coin,

$$\text{Pr(Head)} = \text{Pr(Tail)} = \frac{1}{2}$$

gives the theoretical probability. If a coin was actually tossed 1000 times, it might come up heads 517 times and tails 483 times, giving empirical probabilities for these 1000 tosses of

$$\text{Pr(Head)} = \frac{517}{1000} = .517$$

$$\text{Pr(Tail)} = \frac{483}{1000} = .483.$$

On the other hand, if the coin was tossed only 4 times, it might come up heads 3 times and tails once, giving empirical probabilities vastly different from the theoretical ones. In general, empirical probabilities can differ from theoretical probabilities, but they are likely to reflect the theoretical probabilities when the number of observations is large. Moreover, when this is not the case, there may be reason to suspect that the theoretical model does not fit the event (for example, that a coin may be biased).

EXAMPLE 7   Experience has shown that 800 of the 500,000 microcomputer diskettes manufactured by a firm are defective. Based on this evidence, what is the probability that a diskette picked at random from those manufactured by this firm will be defective?

Solution   The 800 defective diskettes occurred in a very large number of diskettes manufactured, so the ratio of the number of defective diskettes to the total number of diskettes manufactured provides the *empirical* probability of a diskette picked at random being defective.

$$\text{Pr(defective)} = \frac{800}{500,000} = \frac{1}{625}$$

Exercise 7.1

1. A die is rolled. What is the probability that
   (a) a 4 will result?
   (b) a 7 will result?
   (c) an odd number will result?
2. A die is rolled. Find the probability of getting a number greater than 3.
3. If the probability that event E will occur is 3/5, what is the probability that E will not occur?
4. If the probability that an event will occur is 7/9, what is the probability that event will not occur?
5. If you draw one card at random from a deck of 12 cards numbered 1 through 12, inclusive, what is the probability that the number you draw is divisible by 4?
6. If you draw one card at random from the deck of problem 5, what is the probability that the number you draw is even and divisible by 3?
7. From a deck of 52 ordinary playing cards, one card is drawn. Find the probability that it is
   (a) a queen.   (b) a red card.   (c) a spade.
8. From a deck of 52 ordinary playing cards, one card is drawn. Find the probability that it is
   (a) a red king.   (b) a king or a black card.
9. One ball is drawn at random from a bag containing 4 red balls and 6 white balls. What is the probability that the ball is
   (a) red?   (b) not red?   (c) red or white?
10. Using the bag of balls in problem 9, what is the probability that a ball drawn at random is
    (a) white   (b) not white   (c) red and white?

11. An urn contains three red balls numbered 1, 2, 3, four white balls numbered 4, 5, 6, 7, and three black balls numbered 8, 9, 10. A ball is drawn from the urn. What is the probability that
    (a) it is red?   (b) it is odd-numbered?
    (c) it is red and odd-numbered?   (d) it is red or odd-numbered?
    (e) it is not black?

12. Using the urn described in problem 11, what is the probability that a ball drawn will be:
    (a) white?   (b) white and odd?   (c) white or even?
    (d) black or white?   (e) black and white?

13. Suppose a fair coin is tossed two times. Construct an equiprobable sample space for the experiment, and determine each of the following probabilities:
    (a) Pr(0 heads)   (b) Pr(1 head)   (c) Pr(2 heads)

14. Suppose a fair coin is tossed four times. Construct an equiprobable sample space for the experiment, and determine each of the following probabilities:
    (a) Pr(2 heads)   (b) Pr(3 heads)   (c) Pr(4 heads)

15. Use Table 7.1 to determine the following probabilities if a distinguishable pair of dice is rolled.
    (a) Pr(sum is 4)   (b) Pr(sum is 10)   (c) Pr(sum is 12)

16. (a) When a pair of distinguishable dice is rolled, what sum is most likely to occur?
    (b) When a pair of distinguishable dice is rolled, what is $\Pr(4 \leq S \leq 8)$, where S represents the sum rolled?

17. If a pair of dice, one green and one red, is rolled, what is
    (a) $\Pr(4 \leq S \leq 7)$, where S is the sum rolled?
    (b) $\Pr(8 \leq S \leq 12)$, where S is the sum rolled?

18. If a green die and a red die are rolled, find
    (a) $\Pr(2 \leq S \leq 6)$, where S is the sum rolled on the two dice.
    (b) $\Pr(4 \leq S)$, where S is the sum rolled on the two dice.

APPLICATIONS

19. A class has 18 boys and 13 girls as students. A student is chosen at random to deliver a report. What is the probability that the person chosen is a girl?

20. A box contains 4 ten dollar bills, 10 five dollar bills, and 1 hundred dollar bill. If you are told you may keep whatever bill you draw randomly from the box, what is the probability that you will receive $100?

21. Three construction companies have bid for a job. Max knows that the two companies he is competing with have probabilities 1/3 and 1/6, respectively, of getting the job. What is the probability Max will get the job?

22. Because three airlines filed for the same air route on the same day, a lottery was held to determine who should get the route. If United Airlines is one of the airlines, what is the probability that
    (a) United is awarded the air route?   (b) United is not awarded the air route?

23. A car rental firm has 350 cars. Seventy of the cars have defective windshield wipers and 25 have defective tail lights. Two hundred of the cars have no defects; the remainder have other defects. What is the probability that a car chosen at random
    (a) has defective windshield wipers?
    (b) has defective tail lights?
    (c) does not have defective tail lights?
    (d) has at least one defect?

24. Forty percent of a company's total output consists of baseballs, 30% consists of softballs, and 10% consists of tennis balls. Its only remaining product is handballs. If they placed

balls in a box in the same proportion as the company's output and selected a ball at random from the box, what is the probability that

(a) the ball is a baseball?   (c) the ball is not a softball?

(b) the ball is a tennis ball?   (d) the ball is a handball?

25. Because of a firm's growth, it is necessary to transfer one of its employees to one of its branch stores. Three of the nine employees are women and each of the nine employees is equally qualified for the transfer. If the person to be transferred is chosen at random, what is the probability that the transferred person is a woman?

26. A firm selling typewriters knows that four of its 100 typewriters will not return properly and that five different ones have a defective key. If none of the other typewriters has a defect, what is the probability of a buyer selecting a defective typewriter from this group of 100?

27. A newly married couple plans to have three children. Assuming the probability of a girl being born equals that of a boy, what is the probability that exactly two of the three children born will be girls? (Hint: Construct the sample space.)

28. A frustrated store manager is asked to make four different yes-no decisions that have no relation to each other. Because he is impatient to leave work, he flips a coin for each decision. If the correct decision in each case was yes, what is the probability that

(a) all of his decisions were correct?

(b) none of his decisions was correct?

(c) half of his decisions were correct?

29. A couple plans to have two children and wants to know the probability of having one boy and one girl.

(a) Does {0, 1, 2} represent an equiprobable sample space for finding the probability of exactly one boy in two children?

(b) Construct an equiprobable sample space for this problem.

(c) What is the probability of getting one boy and one girl in two children?

30. Refer to problem 29. What is the probability that the couple will have

(a) at least one child of each sex?

(b) two children of the same sex?

31. A quiz consists of 6 multiple-choice questions with 5 possible answers for each question. If a student guesses on the first question, what is the probability he will get the correct answer?

32. In the quiz of problem 31, suppose the student knows that two of the possible answers to the first question are not correct. If he guesses among the remaining answers, what is the probability of getting the correct answer to the first question?

33. On the average, 6 articles out of each 250 produced by a certain machine are defective. What is the probability that an article chosen at random is defective?

34. If a baseball player has 1150 at bats and 320 hits, what is the probability he will get a hit his next time at bat?

35. In a certain town, citizens' groups have identified three intersections as potentially dangerous. They collected the following data.

	Intersections		
	A	B	C
Daily traffic flow	25,500	3,890	8,580
Accidents/year	182	51	118

Calculate the probability of having an accident at each intersection in a given year. Which intersection is the most dangerous?

36. A traffic survey showed that 5680 cars entered an intersection of the main street of a city and that 1460 of them turned onto the intersecting street at this intersection.
    (a) What is the empirical probability a car will turn onto the intersecting street?
    (b) What is the probability a car will not turn onto the intersecting street?
37. Prior to an election, a poll of 1200 citizens is taken. Suppose 557 plan to vote for A, 533 plan to vote for B, and the remainder indicated they will not vote.
    (a) If the poll is accurate, find the probability that a citizen chosen at random will vote for A.
    (b) If the poll is accurate, what is the probability that a person picked at random will not vote?
38. Suppose a county has 800,000 registered voters, 480,000 of whom are Democrats and 290,000 of whom are Republicans. If a registered voter is chosen at random, what is the probability that
    (a) he or she is a Democrat?
    (b) he or she is neither a Democrat nor a Republican?
39. Suppose that at a certain hospital the births on a given day consisted of 8 girls and 2 boys. At the same hospital, suppose the births in a given year consisted of 1220 girls and 1194 boys.
    (a) Find the empirical probabilities for the birth of each sex on the given day.
    (b) Find the empirical probabilities for the given year.
    (c) What are the theoretical probabilities, and which empirical probabilities do you think most accurately reflect reality?
40. Suppose a die is tossed 1200 times and a 6 comes up 431 times.
    (a) Find the empirical probability for a 6.
    (b) Based on a comparison of the empirical probability and the theoretical probability, do you think the die is fair or biased?

Suppose the table below summarizes the opinion of various groups on the issue of increased military spending. Use this table to calculate the empirical probabilities in problems 41–44.

| | White | | Non-Whites | | |
Opinion	Republicans	Democrats	Republicans	Democrats	Total
Favor	300	100	25	10	435
Oppose	100	250	25	190	565
Total	400	350	50	200	1000

41. Find the probability that a non-white favors increased military spending.
42. Find the probability that an individual is white and opposes increased military spending.
43. Find the probability that an individual is a white Republican opposed to increased military spending.
44. Find the probability that an individual is a Democrat and opposes increased military spending.

7.2 Independent and Dependent Events

Objectives ☐ To compute the probability that two or more independent events will occur
☐ To compute the probability that two or more dependent events will occur

We may classify two events as independent or dependent. If the occurrence of one event affects the occurrence of the other, the events are said to be **dependent.** If the occurrence of one event does not affect the occurrence of the other, the events are called **independent.**

For example, if a coin is tossed and a die is rolled, the result of the toss of the coin does not affect the result of the roll of the die. Therefore the two events are independent.

In addition, suppose that from a deck of 52 cards, two cards are drawn in succession, without replacement. The result of the first draw will affect the result of the second draw, so the second drawing is dependent on the first. We can see this dependency as follows: Suppose we would like to draw a heart on both draws; the number of hearts available in the deck for the second draw depends on whether or not we received a heart on the first draw.

If E_1 and E_2 are any two events, then the probability that both events occur, denoted $\Pr(E_1E_2)$, is given by

$$\Pr(E_1E_2) = \Pr(E_1) \cdot \Pr(E_2|E_1),$$

where $\Pr(E_2|E_1)$ is the probability that E_2 occurs, given that E_1 has occurred. We call $\Pr(E_2|E_1)$ a **conditional probability.**

Using this formula, we can find the probability that two cards (drawn without replacement) are both kings as follows:

$$\Pr(\text{1st card is a king}) = \frac{4}{52}$$

$$\Pr(\text{2d card is a king}|\text{1st card is a king}) = \frac{3}{51}$$

$$\Pr(\text{2 kings}) = \Pr(\text{1st king}) \cdot \Pr(\text{2d king}|\text{1st king})$$

$$= \frac{4}{52} \cdot \frac{3}{51} = \frac{1}{181}$$

The probability denoted

$$\Pr(\text{2d king}|\text{1st king})$$

is called the conditional probability that the second king will be drawn given that the first king has already been drawn.

EXAMPLE 1   A box contains 3 black balls, 2 red balls, and 5 white balls. One ball is drawn, is *not* replaced, and a second ball is drawn. Find the probability that the first ball is red and the second is black.

Solution   The events are dependent, since both the total number of balls and the number of balls of one color are changed by the first draw. Let E_1 be "red ball first" and E_2 be "black ball second." Then

$$\Pr(E_1 E_2) = \Pr(E_1) \cdot \Pr(E_2 | E_1) = \frac{2}{10} \cdot \frac{3}{9} = \frac{1}{15}.$$

EXAMPLE 2   Suppose a store chain has observed that 80% of its charge accounts have men's names on them and that 16% of the accounts with men's names on them have been delinquent at least once, while 5% of the accounts with women's names have been delinquent at least once. What is the probability that an account selected at random
(a) is in a man's name and is delinquent?
(b) is in a woman's name and is delinquent?

Solution   (a) Pr(man's account) = .80
             Pr(delinquent|man's) = .16
             Pr(man's and delinquent) = (.80)(.16) = .128
         (b) Pr(woman's account) = .20
             Pr(delinquent|woman's) = .05
             Pr(woman's and delinquent) = (.20)(.05) = .01

EXAMPLE 3   All products on an assembly line must pass two inspections. It has been determined that the probability that the first inspector will miss a defective item is .09. If a defective item gets past the first inspector, the probability that the second inspector will not detect it is .01. What is the probability that a defective item will not be rejected by either inspector? (All good items pass both inspections.)

Solution   The two inspections are dependent, for the second inspector only inspects items passed by the first inspector. The probability a defective item will pass both inspections is

$$\Pr(\text{pass both}) = \Pr(\text{pass first}) \cdot \Pr(\text{pass second} | \text{passed first})$$
$$= .09 \cdot .01$$
$$= .0009.$$

EXAMPLE 4   If the probability that a wife watches a certain television show when her husband watches is .45, and if the probability that both watch the show is .30, what is the probability that the husband watches this show?

Solution   Substituting into the formula

$$Pr(\text{both}) = Pr(\text{husband watches}) \cdot Pr(\text{wife watches}|\text{husband watches})$$

gives

$$.30 = Pr(\text{husband watches}) \cdot (.45)$$

so

$$Pr(\text{husband watches}) = .67.$$

If E_1 and E_2 are independent events, the probability that E_2 occurs is not affected by whether E_1 occurred or did not occur. That is,

> $Pr(E_2|E_1) = Pr(E_2)$ *if and only if* E_1 *and* E_2 *are independent events.*
> Thus we may conclude that
>
> $$Pr(E_1E_2) = Pr(E_1) \cdot Pr(E_2)$$
>
> if and only if the events E_1 and E_2 are **independent.**

EXAMPLE 5   A die is rolled and a coin is tossed. Find the probability of getting a 4 on the die and a head on the coin.

Solution   Let E_1 be "4 on the die" and E_2 be "head on the coin." The events are independent because what occurs on the die does not affect what happens to the coin.

$$Pr(E_1) = Pr(4 \text{ on die}) = \frac{1}{6}, \quad \text{and} \quad Pr(E_2) = Pr(\text{head on coin}) = \frac{1}{2}.$$

Then

$$Pr(E_1E_2) = Pr(E_1) \cdot Pr(E_2) = \frac{1}{6} \cdot \frac{1}{2} = \frac{1}{12}.$$

EXAMPLE 6   A pair of dice is rolled, one after the other. What is the probability of getting an odd number on the first die and a 5 on the second?

Solution   What happens on the first die has no effect on what will happen on the second die, so the events are independent. If E_1 is "odd number on first die" and E_2 is "5 on second die," the probability that both will occur is

$$Pr(E_1E_2) = Pr(E_1) \cdot Pr(E_2) = \frac{3}{6} \cdot \frac{1}{6} = \frac{3}{36} = \frac{1}{12}.$$

Note that this is the same probability we would get by using Table 7.1 to answer the question. Use of the appropriate formula will usually permit us to solve probability problems without listing the elements of the sample space. In this case, for example, we can answer the question with the formula and knowledge about the results of rolling one die rather than knowing the results of rolling a pair of dice.

EXAMPLE 7   In a certain country, the probability that a newborn child is a boy is .518. What is the probability that the first two children born in a new year in this country
(a) are both boys?
(b) are both girls?

Solution   (a) The births are independent, so

$$Pr(\text{both boys}) = Pr(\text{boy 1st}) \cdot Pr(\text{boy 2d})$$
$$= (.518)(.518)$$
$$= .268$$

(b) $Pr(\text{girl}) = 1 - .518 = .482$, so

$$Pr(\text{both girls}) = Pr(\text{girl 1st}) \cdot Pr(\text{girl 2d})$$
$$= (.482)(.482)$$
$$= .232$$

These probability formulas can be expanded to include more than two events, as the next example shows.

EXAMPLE 8   A bag contains 3 red marbles, 4 white marbles, and 3 black marbles. Find the probability of getting a red marble on the first draw, a black marble on the second draw, and a white marble on the third draw if (a) the marbles are drawn with replacement, (b) the marbles are drawn without replacement.

Solution   (a) The marbles are replaced after each draw, so the events are independent. Let E_1 be "red on first," E_2 be "black on second," and E_3 be "white on third." Then

$$Pr(E_1 E_2 E_3) = Pr(E_1) \cdot Pr(E_2) \cdot Pr(E_3) = \frac{3}{10} \cdot \frac{3}{10} \cdot \frac{4}{10} = \frac{36}{1000} = \frac{9}{250}.$$

(b) The marbles are not replaced, so the events are dependent.

$$Pr(E_1 E_2 E_3) = Pr(E_1) \cdot Pr(E_2|E_1) \cdot Pr(E_3|E_1 \text{ and } E_2)$$

$$= \frac{3}{10} \cdot \frac{3}{9} \cdot \frac{4}{8} = \frac{1}{20}.$$

EXAMPLE 9   A manager must make decisions about four independent problems. She can make one of three equally likely decisions for each problem, and she makes each decision by guessing. If each problem had only one correct solution, what is the probability she solved every problem correctly?

Solution Her probability of solving each problem correctly by guessing is 1/3. Since the problems are independent, the probability all four decisions are correct is

$$\text{Pr(all correct)} = \frac{1}{3} \cdot \frac{1}{3} \cdot \frac{1}{3} \cdot \frac{1}{3} = \frac{1}{81}.$$

Exercise 7.2

1. A die is thrown twice. What is the probability that a 3 will result the first time and a 6 will result the second time?
2. A die is thrown twice. What is the probability that an even number will result both times?
3. A die is rolled and a coin is tossed. What is the probability that the die results in a 4 and the coin results in a head?
4. The probability that Sam will win in a certain game whenever he plays is 2/5. If he plays two games, what is the probability that he will win just the first game?
5. A coin is tossed three times. What is the probability of getting a head on all three tosses?
6. A coin is tossed four times. What is the probability of getting no heads?
7. A coin is tossed three times. What is the probability of getting at least one tail? (Hint: Use the result of problem 5.)
8. A coin is tossed four times. What is the probability of getting at least one head? (Hint: Use the result of problem 6.)
9. (a) A box contains 3 red balls, 2 white balls, and 5 black balls. Two balls are drawn at random from the box (with replacement of the first before the second is drawn); what is the probability of getting a red ball on the first draw and a white ball on the second draw?
   (b) Answer part (a) if the first ball is not replaced before the second is drawn.
10. (a) One card is drawn at random from a deck of 52 cards. The first card is replaced, and a second card is drawn. Find the probability that both cards are hearts.
    (b) Answer part (a) if the first card is not replaced before the second card is drawn.
11. Two balls are drawn from a bag containing 3 white balls and 2 red balls. If the first ball is replaced before the second is drawn, what is the probability that
    (a) both balls are red?
    (b) both balls are white?
    (c) the first ball is red and the second is white?
    (d) one of the balls is black?
12. Two colored dice, one white and one red, are rolled. Find the probability that the white die is less than 2 and the red die is more than 2.
13. Answer problem 11 if the first ball is not replaced before the second is drawn.
14. A bag contains 6 red balls and 8 green balls. If two balls are drawn together, find the probability that
    (a) both are red.
    (b) both are green.
15. A bag contains 9 nickels, 4 dimes, and 5 quarters. If you draw 3 coins at random from the bag, without replacement, what is the probability that you will get a nickel, a quarter, a nickel, in that order?

16. A red ball and 4 white balls are in a box. If two balls are drawn, without replacement, what is the probability
    (a) of getting a red ball on the first draw and a white ball on the second?
    (b) of getting 2 white balls?
    (c) of getting 2 red balls?

17. From a deck of 52 playing cards two cards are drawn, one after the other without replacement. What is the probability that
    (a) the first will be a king and the second will be a jack?
    (b) the first will be a king and the second will be a jack of the same suit?

18. One card is drawn at random from a deck of 52 cards. The first card is not replaced, and a second card is drawn. Find the probability that
    (a) both cards are spades.
    (b) the first card is a heart and the second is a club.

19. Two cards are drawn from a deck of 52 cards. What is the probability both are aces,
    (a) if the first card was replaced before the second was drawn?
    (b) if the cards were drawn without replacement?

APPLICATIONS

20. If 3% of all light bulbs a company manufactures are defective, the probability of any one bulb being defective is .03. What is the probability that three bulbs drawn independently from the company's stock will be defective?

21. To test its shotgun shells, a company fires 5 of them. What is the probability that all 5 of them will fire properly if 5% of its shells are actually defective?

22. One machine produces 30% of a product for a company. If 10% of the products from this machine are defective and the other machines produce no defective item, what is the probability that an article produced by this company is defective?

23. A company estimates that 30% of the country has seen its commercial and that if a person sees its commercial there is a 20% probability that the person will buy its product. What is the probability that a person chosen at random in the country will have seen the commercial and bought its product?

24. Ronald Lee has been told by a company that the probability that he will be offered a job in the quality control department is .6 and the probability that he will be asked to be foreman of the department, if he is offered the job, is .1. What is the probability that he will be offered the job and asked to be foreman?

25. If a fighter pilot has a 4% chance of being shot down on each mission during a war, is it certain he will be shot down in 25 missions?

26. Suppose a birth control pill is 99% effective in preventing pregnancy.
    (a) What is the probability that none of 100 women using the pill will become pregnant?
    (b) What is the probability that at least one woman per 100 users will become pregnant?

27. The probability that a customer entering a supermarket will buy spaghetti is .1. If she buys spaghetti, the probability she will also buy spaghetti sauce is .4. Whether or not she buys spaghetti, the probability that she will buy milk is .5.
    (a) What is the probability that she will buy both spaghetti and spaghetti sauce?
    (b) What is the probability that she will buy both spaghetti and milk?
    (c) What is the probability she will buy spaghetti, spaghetti sauce, and milk?

28. In a random survey of students concerning student activities, 30 engineering majors, 25 business majors, 20 science majors, and 15 liberal arts majors were selected. If two

students are selected at random, what is the probability of getting
(a) two science majors?
(b) a science and an engineering major?

29. In problem 28, if two students are selected, what is the probability of getting
(a) no science majors?
(b) at least one science major?
(c) at least one liberal arts major?

30. In an actual case,* probability was used to convict a couple of mugging an elderly woman. Shortly after the mugging, a young white woman with blonde hair worn in a ponytail was seen running from the scene of the crime and entering a yellow car that was driven away by a black man with a beard. A couple matching this description was arrested for the crime. A prosecuting attorney argued that the couple arrested had to be the couple at the scene of the crime because the probability of a second couple matching the description was very small. He estimated the probabilities of six events as follows:

> Probability of black-white couple: 1/1000
> Probability of black man: 1/3
> Probability of bearded man: 1/10
> Probability of blonde woman: 1/4
> Probability of hair in ponytail: 1/10
> Probability of yellow car: 1/10

He multiplied these probabilities and concluded that the probability that another couple would have these characteristics is 1/12,000,000. Based on this circumstantial evidence, the couple was convicted and sent to prison. The conviction was overturned by the state supreme court because the prosecutor made an incorrect assumption. What error do you think he made?

31. What is the probability of getting at least one son if a couple plans to have 3 children and if the probability of having a son equals the probability of having a daughter?

32. Suppose that a marksman hits the bullseye 15,000 times in 50,000 shots. If the shots are independent, find the probability that
(a) the next 2 shots hit the bullseye.
(b) the next 5 shots hit the bullseye.
(c) there is at least one miss in the next 5 shots.

33. Assuming there are 365 different birthdays, find the probability that two people chosen at random will have
(a) different birthdays.
(b) the same birthdays.

34. Assuming there are 365 different birthdays, find the probability that of three people chosen randomly,
(a) no two will have the same birthday.
(b) at least two will have the same birthday.

35. Assuming there are 365 different birthdays, find the probability that of 20 people chosen randomly,
(a) no two will have the same birthday.
(b) at least two will have the same birthday.

---

*TIME, January 8, 1965, p. 42, and April 26, 1968, p. 41.

7.3 Mutually Exclusive Events and Nonmutually Exclusive Events

Objectives □ To compute the probability that one or the other of two mutually exclusive events will occur

□ To compute the probability that one or the other of two nonmutually exclusive events will occur

If the occurrence of one event precludes the occurrence of another or others, the events are said to be **mutually exclusive.** This means that if two events are mutually exclusive, the success of one necessitates the failure of the other. If a die is rolled, the event E_1 "rolling a 6" and the event E_2 "rolling a 4" are mutually exclusive because they cannot both result on a single roll of die. Thus if E_1 and E_2 are mutually exclusive events, $\Pr(E_1E_2) = 0$.

If E_1 and E_2 are any two events, then the probability that one event or the other will occur, denoted $\Pr(E_1 \text{ or } E_2)$, is given by

$$\Pr(E_1 \text{ or } E_2) = \Pr(E_1) + \Pr(E_2) - \Pr(E_1E_2).$$

If E_1 and E_2 are **mutually exclusive,** then $\Pr(E_1E_2) = 0$, and

$$\Pr(E_1 \text{ or } E_2) = \Pr(E_1) + \Pr(E_2).$$

EXAMPLE 1 Find the probability of obtaining a 6 or a 4 in one roll of a die.

Solution Rolling a 6 and rolling a 4 on one roll of a die are mutually exclusive events. Let E_1 be the event "rolling a 6" and E_2 be the event "rolling a 4."

$$\Pr(E_1) = \Pr(\text{rolling } 6) = \frac{1}{6} \quad \text{and} \quad \Pr(E_2) = \Pr(\text{rolling } 4) = \frac{1}{6}.$$

Then

$$\Pr(E_1 \text{ or } E_2) = \Pr(E_1) + \Pr(E_2) = \frac{1}{6} + \frac{1}{6} = \frac{1}{3}.$$

EXAMPLE 2 Find the probability of getting a head or a tail in one toss of a coin.

Solution Let E_1 be "tossing a head" and E_2 be "tossing a tail." The events are mutually exclusive, so

$$\Pr(E_1 \text{ or } E_2) = \Pr(E_1) + \Pr(E_2) = \frac{1}{2} + \frac{1}{2} = 1.$$

The result is obvious, since the only possible result is a head or a tail.

The same technique can be used to find the probability of the occurrence of one of three mutually exclusive events.

EXAMPLE 3   Find the probability of tossing 2 distinct dice and obtaining a sum greater than 9.

Solution   Since the event "a sum greater than 9" consists of the mutually exclusive events "sum = 10," "sum = 11," and "sum = 12,"

$$Pr(10 \text{ or } 11 \text{ or } 12) = Pr(10) + Pr(11) + Pr(12)$$

$$= \frac{3}{36} + \frac{2}{36} + \frac{1}{36} = \frac{6}{36} = \frac{1}{6}.$$

These probabilities can be found from Table 7.1.

EXAMPLE 4   Sacco and Rosen are among 3 candidates running for a public office. The probability that Sacco will win is 1/3 and the probability that Rosen will win is 1/2. Only one candidate can win.
(a) What is the probability that Sacco or Rosen will win?
(b) What is the probability that neither Sacco nor Rosen will win?

Solution   (a) The two events are mutually exclusive, so

$$Pr(Sacco \text{ or } Rosen) = Pr(Sacco) + Pr(Rosen) = \frac{1}{3} + \frac{1}{2} = \frac{5}{6}.$$

(b) The probability that neither will win is $1 - 5/6 = 1/6$.

The events E_1 "rolling a number less than 5" and E_2 "rolling an even number" (in one roll of a die) are not mutually exclusive because if we get a 2 or a 4 we get numbers less than 5 *and* even numbers. Thus

$$Pr(E_1 E_2) = Pr(\text{number less than 5 } and \text{ even}) = Pr(2, 4) = \frac{2}{6} = \frac{1}{3}.$$

Then

$$Pr(\text{number less than 5 } or \text{ even}) = Pr(E_1 \text{ or } E_2)$$

$$= Pr(E_1) + Pr(E_2) - Pr(E_1 E_2)$$

$$= \frac{4}{6} + \frac{3}{6} - \frac{2}{6} = \frac{5}{6}.$$

EXAMPLE 5   An integer between 1 and 6 inclusive is chosen at random. What is the probability that it is even or divisible by 3?

Solution   We know that the events are not mutually exclusive because 6 is even and divisible by 3. Therefore, since $Pr(even) = 3/6 = 1/2$, $Pr(\text{divisible by } 3) = 2/6 = 1/3$, and Pr(even *and* divisible by 3) $= $ Pr(6) $= 1/6,$

$$\text{Pr(even or divisible by 3)} = \frac{1}{2} + \frac{1}{3} - \frac{1}{6} = \frac{5}{6} - \frac{1}{6} = \frac{4}{6} = \frac{2}{3}.$$

EXAMPLE 6   The directors of a public school board consist of 8 Democrats, 3 of whom are female, and 4 Republicans, 2 of whom are female. If a director is chosen at random to discuss an issue on television, what is the probability that the person will be a Democrat or female?

Solution   There are 12 directors, of whom 8 are Democrats and 5 are female. But 3 of the directors are Democrats *and* females and cannot be counted twice. Thus

$$\text{Pr(D or f)} = \text{Pr(D)} + \text{Pr(f)} - \text{Pr(D and f)} = \frac{8}{12} + \frac{5}{12} - \frac{3}{12} = \frac{10}{12}.$$

There are some problems in probability that make use of more than one of the formulas we have introduced.

EXAMPLE 7   Suppose a box contains 3 defective transistors and 12 good transistors. If 2 transistors are drawn from the box without replacement, what is the probability that
(a) the first transistor is good and the second is defective?
(b) the first transistor is defective and the second is good?
(c) one of the transistors drawn is good and one of them is defective?

Solution   (a) Pr(good 1st and def. 2d) $= $ Pr(good 1st) $\cdot$ Pr(def. 2d|good 1st)

$$= \frac{12}{15} \cdot \frac{3}{14} = \frac{6}{35}$$

(b) Pr(def. 1st and good 2d) $= $ Pr(def. 1st) $\cdot$ Pr(good 2d|def. 1st)

$$= \frac{3}{15} \cdot \frac{12}{14} = \frac{6}{35}$$

(c) We can draw one good and one defective transistor by drawing the good first and defective second *or* by drawing the defective first and good second. These two events, whose probabilities were found in parts (a) and (b), respectively, are mutually exclusive events. Thus

$$\begin{aligned}
\text{Pr(one good and one def.)} &= \text{Pr(good 1st and def. 2d } or \text{ def. 1st and good 2d)}\\
&= \text{Pr(good 1st and def. 2d)} + \text{Pr(def. 1st and good 2d)}\\
&= \frac{6}{35} + \frac{6}{35} = \frac{12}{35}.
\end{aligned}$$

Exercise 7.3

1. An ordinary die is tossed. What is the probability of getting a 3 or a 4?
2. A card is drawn from a deck of 52. What is the probability that it will be an ace, king, or jack?

3. A bag contains 4 white, 7 black, and 6 green balls. What is the probability that a ball drawn at random from the bag is white or green?

4. In a game where only one player can win, the probability that Jack will win is 1/5 and that Bill will win is 1/4. Find the probability that one of them will win.

5. A cube has 2 faces painted red, 2 painted white, and 2 painted blue. What is the probability of getting a red face or a white face in one roll?

6. A cube has 3 faces painted white, 2 faces painted red, and 1 face painted blue. What is the probability that a roll will result in a red or blue face?

7. If you draw one card from a deck of 12 cards, numbered 1 through 12 inclusive, what is the probability you will get an odd number or a number divisible by 4?

8. Suppose a die is biased (unfair) so that each odd-numbered face has probability 1/4 of resulting, and each even one has probability 1/12 of resulting. Find the probability of getting a number greater than 3.

9. If you draw one card from a deck of 12 cards numbered 1 through 12 inclusive, what is the probability that the card will be odd or divisible by 3?

10. A card is drawn at random from a deck of 52 playing cards. Find the probability that it is either a club or a king.

11. An urn contains 4 red, 5 white, and 6 black balls. One ball is drawn from the urn, replaced, and a second ball is drawn.
    (a) What is the probability that both balls are white?
    (b) What is the probability that one ball is white and one is red?
    (c) What is the probability that neither ball is black?

12. Answer the questions in problem 11 if the two balls were drawn simultaneously from the urn.

13. A bag contains 5 red balls numbered 1, 2, 3, 4, 5 and 9 white balls numbered 6, 7, 8, 9, 10, 11, 12, 13, 14. If a ball is drawn, what is the probability that
    (a) the ball is red and even-numbered?
    (b) the ball is red or even-numbered?

14. In problem 13, what is the probability that the ball is
    (a) white and odd-numbered?
    (b) white or odd-numbered?
    (c) white or even-numbered?

15. A bag contains 4 white balls and 7 red balls. If 2 balls are drawn at random from the bag, with the first ball replaced before the second ball is drawn, what is the probability that
    (a) the first ball is red and the second is white?
    (b) one ball is red and the other is white?

16. Answer problem 15 if the first ball is not replaced before the second is drawn.

17. A bag contains 4 white balls and 6 red balls. What is the probability that if 2 balls are drawn (with replacement):
    (a) the first ball is red and the second is white?
    (b) both balls are red?
    (c) one ball is red and one is white?
    (d) the first ball is red or the second is white?

18. Suppose a fair coin is tossed 3 times.
    (a) What is the probability of obtaining 3 heads?
    (b) What is the probability of obtaining heads on the first two tosses and a tail on the third?
    (c) What is the probability of obtaining 2 heads and a tail?
    (d) What is the probability of obtaining a head and 2 tails?

19. Suppose a coin is tossed twice. What is the probability of getting one head and one tail?

20. If two cards are drawn from a deck without replacement, find the probability of getting a king and a heart.

APPLICATIONS

21. Of 100 students, 24 can speak French, 18 can speak German, and 8 can speak both French and German. If a student is picked at random, what is the probability that he or she can speak French or German?

22. A company employs 65 people. Eight of the 30 men and 21 of the 35 women work in the business office. What is the probability that an employee picked at random is a man or works in the business office?

23. In a group of 35 people, 15 play golf, 12 play tennis, and 6 play both golf and tennis. What is the probability that a person chosen at random can play golf or tennis?

24. A firm is considering three possible locations for a new factory. The probability that site A will be selected is 1/3 and the probability that site B will be selected is 1/5. If only one location will be chosen,
    (a) What is the probability that site A or site B will be chosen?
    (b) What is the probability that neither site A nor site B will be chosen?

25. Maria has ordered a washer and dryer from two different companies. Both the washer and the dryer are to be delivered Thursday. The probability that the washer will be delivered in the morning is .6 and the probability that the dryer will be delivered in the morning is .8. If the probability that either the washer or dryer is delivered in the morning is .9, what is the probability that both will be delivered in the morning?

26. Rob Lee knows his camera will take a good picture unless the flash is defective or the batteries are dead. The probability of having a defective flash is .05, the probability of the battery being dead is .3, and the probability that both these problems occur is .01. What is the probability that the picture will be good?

27. The cognitive complexity of a structure was studied by Scott* using a technique in which a person was asked to specify a number of objects and group them into as many groupings as he or she found meaningful. If a person groups 12 objects into three groups in such a way that

    > 7 objects are in group A,
    > 7 objects are in group B,
    > 8 objects are in group C,
    > 3 objects are in both group A and group B,
    > 5 objects are in both group B and group C,
    > 4 objects are in both group A and group C,
    > 2 objects are in all three groups,

    (a) what is the probability an object chosen at random has been placed into group A or group B?
    (b) what is the probability an object chosen at random has been placed into group B or group C?

28. A group of 100 people contains 60 Democrats and 35 Republicans. If there are 60 women and if 40 of the Democrats are women, what is the probability that a person selected at random is a Democrat or a woman?

29. A mathematics class has 16 engineering majors, 12 science majors, and 4 liberal arts majors. What is the probability that a student selected at random will be a science or liberal arts major?

*W. Scott, "Cognitive Complexity and Cognitive Flexibility," *Sociometry* 25 (1962), pp. 405–414.

30. In problem 29, what is the probability that a student selected at random will be an engineering or science major?
31. In problem 29, 5 of the engineering students, 6 of the science majors, and 2 of the liberal arts majors are female. What is the probability that a student selected at random is an engineering major or is a female?
32. Suppose it is known that two hunters, Jim and Jack, can kill a pheasant on 1/2 and 2/3 of their shots, respectively. What is the probability that they can kill a bird if both shoot at it?
33. A survey questioned 1000 people regarding raising the legal drinking age from 18 to 21. Of the 560 favoring raising the age, 390 were female. Of the 440 opposition responses, 160 were female. If a person is selected at random, what is the probability that the person is a woman or favors raising the age?
34. If a person is selected at random from the group surveyed in problem 33, what is the probability the person is a male or favors raising the age?
35. If a person is selected at random from the group surveyed in problem 33, what is the probability the person is male or opposes raising the age?

Suppose the table below summarizes the opinions of various groups on the issue of increased military spending. Use this table to calculate probabilities in problems 36–39.

Opinion	Whites		Non-Whites		Total
	Republicans	Democrats	Republicans	Democrats	
Favor	300	100	25	10	435
Oppose	100	250	25	190	565
Total	400	350	50	200	1000

36. Find the probability that an individual chosen at random is a Republican or favors increased military spending.
37. Find the probability that an individual selected at random is a Democrat or opposes increased military spending.
38. Find the probability that an individual chosen at random is white or opposes increased military spending.
39. Find the probability that an individual chosen at random is non-white or favors increased military spending.

7.4 Conditional Probability; Bayes' Formula

Objectives
- ☐ To solve probability problems involving conditional probability
- ☐ To use probability trees to solve problems
- ☐ To use Bayes' formula to solve probability problems

We have seen that if one event E_2 is dependent on another event E_1, then the probability both events will occur is

$$\Pr(E_1 E_2) = \Pr(E_1) \cdot \Pr(E_2|E_1),$$

where $\Pr(E_2|E_1)$ denotes the **conditional probability** that E_2 will occur given that E_1 occurs. Solving the equation algebraically for $\Pr(E_2|E_1)$ gives the following.

Conditional Probability	If E_1 and E_2 are any two events then the probability that E_2 occurs, given that E_1 has occurred, is given by

$$Pr(E_2|E_1) = \frac{Pr(E_1 E_2)}{Pr(E_1)}.$$

This formula can be used directly to compute conditional probability.

EXAMPLE 1   A fair die is rolled. Find the probability the result is a 4, given that the result is even.

Solution   Using the conditional probability formula,

$$Pr(4|even) = \frac{Pr(4 \text{ and even})}{Pr(even)}.$$

Since the result "4 and even" is satisfied when the result is a 4, we have

$$Pr(4|even) = \frac{Pr(4 \text{ and even})}{Pr(even)} = \frac{Pr(4)}{Pr(even)} = \frac{1/6}{3/6} = \frac{1}{3}.$$

Note that this is a reasonable result since the die can result in only 3 even numbers, one of which is a 4.

EXAMPLE 2   A red die and a green die are rolled. What is the probability the sum rolled on the dice is 6, given that the sum is less than 7.

Solution   Using the conditional probability formula and the sample space in Table 7.1, we have

$$Pr(\text{sum is } 6|\text{sum} < 7) = \frac{Pr(\text{sum is 6 and sum} < 7)}{Pr(\text{sum} < 7)}.$$

Because

$$Pr(\text{sum is 6 and sum} < 7) = Pr(\text{sum is 6}) = \frac{5}{36},$$

$$Pr(\text{sum is } 6|\text{sum} < 7) = \frac{5/36}{1/36 + 2/36 + 3/36 + 4/36 + 5/36}$$

$$= \frac{5/36}{15/36} = \frac{1}{3}.$$

In dealing with probability problems that involve two or more stages, it is frequently useful to use a **probability tree.**
To illustrate how a tree is constructed, consider the following example.

EXAMPLE 3   A bag contains 5 red balls, 4 blue balls, and 3 white balls. Two balls are drawn, one after the other, without replacement. Draw a tree representing the experiment.

Solution   The first draw could result in a red ball (with probability 5/12), a blue ball (with probability 4/12), or a white ball (with probability 3/12). We can represent the results of the first draw by the tree shown in Figure 7.1.

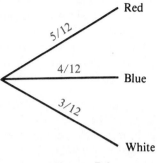

Figure 7.1

The probabilities for red, blue, and white balls occurring on the second draw depend on the result of the first draw. We can represent all the possibilities by adding a second stage to the tree we have drawn, with the conditional probabilities noted (see Figure 7.2).

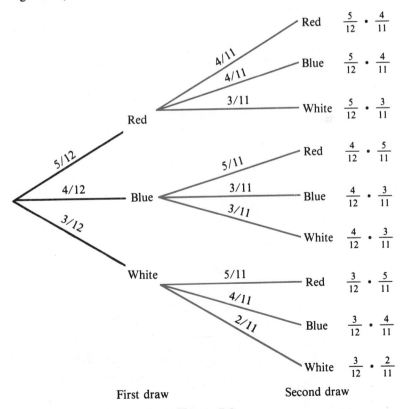

Figure 7.2

The first stage of the experiment in Example 3 has three possible outcomes, so the tree has three branches in the first stage. The second stage has three possible outcomes, so the tree has three branches in its second stage for each first outcome. The total number of possible outcomes in the compound experiment is the same as the total number of terminating branches, so each path through the tree represents a sample point for the experiment. For example, drawing a red ball and then drawing a blue ball is one possible outcome of this experiment, and it is represented by one path through the tree, namely the branch with red on the first draw and blue on the second draw.

> The probability attached to *each branch* of the tree is the *conditional probability* that the specified event will occur, given that the events on the preceding branches have occurred. The probability of a **sample point** for the experiment described by a tree is the **product** of the probabilities attached to the branches **along the path** representing the sample point.

For example, the probability of drawing a red ball first and then a blue ball in the experiment described by Figure 7.2 is the product of 5/12 and 4/11, or 5/33.

EXAMPLE 4   In the experiment described by Example 3 (and Figure 7.2), find
(a) Pr(blue on first draw and white on second draw)
(b) Pr(white on both draws)
(c) Pr(drawing a blue ball and a white ball)
(d) Pr(second ball is red)

Solution   (a) By multiplying the probabilities along the path that represents blue on the first draw and white on the second draw, we obtain

$$\text{Pr(blue on first draw and white on second draw)} = \frac{4}{12} \cdot \frac{3}{11} = \frac{1}{11}.$$

(b) Multiplying the probabilities along the path that represents white on both draws gives

$$\text{Pr(white on both draws)} = \frac{3}{12} \cdot \frac{2}{11} = \frac{1}{22}.$$

(c) This result can occur by drawing a blue ball first, then a white ball *or* by drawing a white ball, then a blue ball. Thus either of two paths leads to this result. Because the results represented by these paths are mutually exclusive, the probability is found by *adding* the probabilities from the two paths. That is, letting B represent a blue ball and W represent a white ball,

$$\text{Pr}(B \text{ and } W) = \text{Pr}(B \text{ first, then } W) + \text{Pr}(W \text{ first, then } B)$$

$$= \frac{4}{12} \cdot \frac{3}{11} + \frac{3}{12} \cdot \frac{4}{11} = \frac{2}{11}.$$

(d) Pr(2d ball is red) = Pr(R then R; *or* B then R; *or* W then R)

$$= \text{Pr}(R \text{ then } R) + \text{Pr}(B \text{ then } R) + \text{Pr}(W \text{ then } R)$$

$$= \frac{5}{12} \cdot \frac{4}{11} + \frac{4}{12} \cdot \frac{5}{11} + \frac{3}{12} \cdot \frac{5}{11} = \frac{5}{12}$$

Using a probability tree permits us to answer more difficult questions regarding conditional probability. For example, in the experiment described by Figure 7.2, we can find the probability that the first ball is red, given that the second ball is blue. To find this probability we recall the formula for conditional probability, which is

$$\text{Pr}(E_2|E_1) = \frac{\text{Pr}(E_1 E_2)}{\text{Pr}(E_1)}.$$

So

$$\text{Pr}(1\text{st is red}|2\text{d is blue}) = \frac{\text{Pr}(1\text{st is red and 2d is blue})}{\text{Pr}(2\text{d is blue})}.$$

Now one path (red-blue) describes "1st is red and 2d is blue" and three paths (red-blue, blue-blue, white-blue) describe "2d is blue," so

$$\text{Pr}(1\text{st is red}|2\text{d is blue}) = \frac{\dfrac{5}{12} \cdot \dfrac{4}{11}}{\dfrac{5}{12} \cdot \dfrac{4}{11} + \dfrac{4}{12} \cdot \dfrac{3}{11} + \dfrac{3}{12} \cdot \dfrac{4}{11}}$$

$$= \frac{5/33}{5/33 + 1/11 + 1/11} = \frac{5}{11}.$$

The preceding example illustrates a special type of problem, which we will call a **Bayes problem.** In this type of problem, we know the result of the second stage of a two-stage experiment and we wish to find the probability of a specified result in the first stage. In the preceding example we knew the second ball drawn was blue and we sought the probability that the first ball was red.

Suppose there are n possible outcomes in the first stage of the experiment, denoted $E_1, E_2, E_3, \ldots, E_n$ and m possible outcomes in the second stage, denoted $F_1, F_2, \ldots, F_m$ (see Figure 7.3 on the following page). Then the probability that event E_1 occurs in the first stage, given that F_1 occurred in the second stage, is

$$\text{Pr}(E_1|F_1) = \frac{\text{Pr}(E_1 \text{ and } F_1)}{\text{Pr}(F_1)}. \qquad (1)$$

By looking at the probability tree in Figure 7.3 we see that

$$\text{Pr}(E_1 \text{ and } F_1) = \text{Pr}(E_1) \cdot \text{Pr}(F_1|E_1)$$

and that

$$\text{Pr}(F_1) = \text{Pr}(E_1 \text{ and } F_1) + \text{Pr}(E_2 \text{ and } F_1) + \cdots + \text{Pr}(E_n \text{ and } F_1).$$

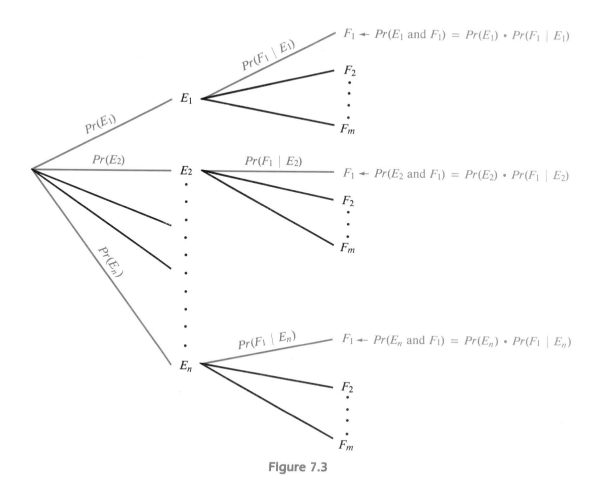

Figure 7.3

Thus using these facts, equation (1) becomes

$$\Pr(E_1|F_1) = \frac{\Pr(E_1) \cdot \Pr(F_1|E_1)}{\Pr(E_1 \text{ and } F_1) + \Pr(E_2 \text{ and } F_1) + \cdots + \Pr(E_n \text{ and } F_1)}. \quad (2)$$

Using the fact that for any E_i, $\Pr(E_i \text{ and } F_1) = \Pr(E_i) \cdot \Pr(F_1|E_i)$, we can rewrite the equation (2) in a form called **Bayes' formula.**

Bayes' Formula	If a probability experiment has n possible outcomes in its first stage given by $E_1, E_2, \ldots , E_n$, and if F_1 is an event in the second stage, then the probability that event E_1 occurs in the first stage, given that F_1 has occurred in the second stage is

$$\Pr(E_1|F_1) = \frac{\Pr(E_1) \cdot \Pr(F_1|E_1)}{\Pr(E_1) \cdot \Pr(F_1|E_1) + \Pr(E_2) \cdot \Pr(F_1|E_2) + \cdots + \Pr(E_n) \cdot \Pr(F_1|E_n)}.$$

Note that Bayes problems can be solved either by this formula or by the use of a probability tree. Of the two methods, many students find using the tree easier because it is less abstract than the formula.

Bayes' Formula and Trees	$\Pr(E_1|F_1) = \dfrac{\text{Product of branch probabilities on path leading to } F_1 \text{ through } E_1}{\text{Sum of all branch products on paths leading to } F_1}$

The following example illustrates both methods of solving a Bayes problem.

EXAMPLE 5   Suppose a test for diagnosing a certain serious disease is successful in detecting the disease in 95% of all persons infected, but that it incorrectly diagnoses 4% of all healthy people as having the serious disease. Suppose also that it incorrectly diagnoses 12% of all people having another minor disease as having the serious disease. If it is known that 2% of the population has the serious disease, 90% of the population is healthy, and 8% has the minor disease, find the probability that a person selected at random has the serious disease if the test indicates that he or she does. Use H to represent healthy, M to represent having the minor disease, and D to represent having the serious disease.

Solution   The tree that represents the health condition of a person chosen at random and the results of the test on that person is shown in Figure 7.4.

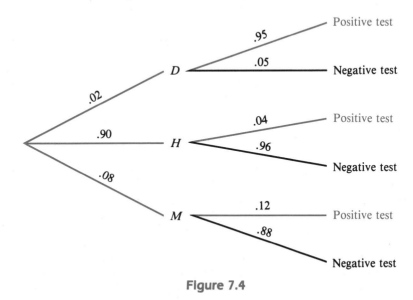

Figure 7.4

We seek $\Pr(D|\text{pos. test})$, where D denotes having the serious disease. Using the tree and the conditional probability formula gives

$$\Pr(D|\text{pos. test}) = \frac{\Pr(D \text{ and pos. test})}{\Pr(\text{pos. test})}$$

$$= \frac{(.02)(.95)}{(.90)(.04) + (.02)(.95) + (.08)(.12)}$$

$$= \frac{.0190}{.0360 + .0190 + .0096}$$

$$= .2941.$$

Using Bayes' formula directly gives the same result.

$$\text{Pr}(D|\text{pos.}) = \frac{\text{Pr}(D) \cdot \text{Pr}(\text{pos. test}|D)}{\text{Pr}(H) \cdot \text{Pr}(\text{pos. test}|H) + \text{Pr}(D) \cdot \text{Pr}(\text{pos. test}|D) + \text{Pr}(M) \cdot \text{Pr}(\text{pos. test}|M)}$$

$$= \frac{(.02)(.95)}{(.90)(.04) + (.02)(.95) + (.08)(.12)} = .2941$$

Exercise 7.4

1. A card is drawn from a deck of 52 playing cards. Given that it is a red card, what is the probability that
   (a) it is a heart?
   (b) it is a king?
2. A card is drawn from a deck of 52 playing cards. Given that it is an ace, king, queen, or jack, what is the probability that it is a jack?
3. A die has been "loaded" so that the probability of rolling any even number is 2/9 and any odd number is 1/9. What is the probability of
   (a) rolling a 6, given that an even number is rolled?
   (b) rolling a 3, given that an odd number is rolled?
4. In problem 3, what is the probability of
   (a) rolling a 5?
   (b) rolling a 5 given that an even number is rolled?
   (c) rolling a 5 given that an odd number is rolled?
5. A bag contains 9 red balls numbered 1, 2, 3, 4, 5, 6, 7, 8, 9, and 6 white balls numbered 10, 11, 12, 13, 14, 15. One ball is drawn from the bag. What is the probability that the ball is even-numbered, given that the ball is red?
6. If one ball is drawn from the bag of problem 5, what is the probability that the ball is white, given that the ball is even-numbered?
7. A bag contains 4 red balls and 6 white balls. Two balls are drawn without replacement.
   (a) What is the probability the second ball is white, given that the first ball is red?
   (b) What is the probability that the second ball is red, given that the first ball is white?
8. Answer problem 7 if the first ball is replaced before the second is drawn.
9. A fair coin is tossed 3 times. Find the probability of
   (a) throwing 3 heads, given that the first toss is a head.
   (b) throwing 3 heads, given that the first two tosses result in heads.
10. A fair coin is tossed 14 times. What is the probability of tossing 14 heads, given that the first 13 tosses are heads?

In problems 11–14, use probability trees to find the probabilities.

11. Two cards are drawn, without replacement, from a regular deck of 52 cards. What is the probability that
    (a) both cards are the same suit?
    (b) both cards are the same suit, given that the first card is the king of hearts?

12. A bag contains 5 coins, 4 of which are fair and 1 that has heads on both sides. If a coin is selected from the box and tossed twice, what is the probability of obtaining 2 heads?

13. Three balls are drawn, without replacement, from a bag containing 4 red balls and 5 white balls. Find the probability that
    (a) three white balls are drawn.
    (b) two white balls and one red ball are drawn.
    (c) the third ball drawn is red.

14. Two cards are drawn, without replacement, from a regular deck of 52 cards. What is the probability that both cards are aces, given that they are the same color?

In problems 15–18, use (I) a probability tree and (II) Bayes' formula to find the probabilities.

15. A pair of dice, 1 red and 1 green, is rolled. What is the probability the red die is a 5, given that the sum of the dice is 10?

16. In problem 15, what is the probability the green die is a 6, given that the sum is 7?

17. There are 3 urns containing coins. Urn I contains 2 gold coins, urn II contains 1 gold coin and 1 silver coin, and urn III contains 2 silver coins. An urn is selected and a coin is drawn from the urn. If the selected coin is gold, what is the probability the urn selected was urn I?

18. In problem 17, what is the probability that the urn selected was urn III if the coin selected was silver?

APPLICATIONS

19. A candidate for public office knows that whoever is nominated from her political party has a 60% chance of winning the election, and that she has a 25% chance of winning her party's nomination. What is the probability that she will win the election?

20. Suppose the probability that a child is a male is 1/2. If a family has 3 children, what is the probability that
    (a) there are 3 girls, given that the first child is a girl?
    (b) there are 2 girls and 1 boy, given that at least 2 of the children are girls?

21. The probability that an individual without a college education earns more than $20,000 is .2, whereas the probability that a person with a B.S. or higher degree will earn more than $20,000 is .6. The probability that a person chosen at random has a B.S. degree is .3. What is the probability a person has at least a B.S. degree if it is known that he or she earns more than $20,000?

22. A small town has 8000 adult males and 6000 adult females. A sociologist conducted a survey and found that 40% of the males and 30% of the females drink heavily. An adult is selected at random from the town.
    (a) What is the probability the person is a male?
    (b) What is the probability the person drinks heavily?
    (c) What is the probability the person is a male or drinks heavily?
    (d) What is the probability the person is a male, if it is known that the person drinks heavily?

23. One hundred boys and one hundred girls were asked if they had ever been frightened by a television program. Thirty of the boys and sixty of the girls said they had been frightened. If one of these children is selected at random,
   (a) what is the probability that he or she has been frightened?
   (b) what is the probability the child is a girl, given that he or she has been frightened?

24. A candidate for public office knows that he has a 60% chance of being elected to the office if he is nominated by his political party, and that his party has a 50% chance of winning with another nominee. If the probability he will be nominated by his party is .25, and his party wins the election, what is the probability that he is the winning candidate?

25. A self-administered pregnancy test detects 85% of those who are pregnant, but does not detect pregnancy in 15%. It is 90% accurate in indicating women who are not pregnant, but indicates 10% of this group as being pregnant. Suppose it is known that 1% of the women in a neighborhood are pregnant. If a woman is chosen at random from those living in this neighborhood and if the test indicates she is pregnant, what is the probability she really is?

26. Of a group of people, $\frac{1}{3}$ are female and $\frac{2}{3}$ are male. Of the males, $\frac{1}{6}$ are blonde, and of the females, $\frac{1}{3}$ are blonde. If a person is picked at random from this group,
   (a) what is the probability that the person will be a blonde?
   (b) what is the probability that the person is a female, given that the person is a blonde?

27. A survey questioned 1000 people regarding raising the legal drinking age from 18 to 21. Of the 560 favoring raising the age, 390 were female. Of the 440 opposition responses, 160 were female.
   (a) What is the probability that a person selected at random is a female?
   (b) What is the probability that a person selected at random favors raising the age if she is a woman?

28. If a person is selected at random from the group in problem 27, what is the probability that this person favors raising the age if the person is a man?

29. In a SAPS (Student Activity Participation Study) survey, 30 engineering majors, 25 business majors, 20 science majors, 15 liberal arts majors, and 10 human development majors were selected. Ten of the engineering, 12 of the science, 6 of the human development, 13 of the business, and 8 of the liberal arts majors selected for the study were female.
   (a) What is the probability of selecting a female if one person from this group is selected randomly?
   (b) What is the probability that a student selected randomly from this group is a science major, given that she is female?

30. If a student is selected at random from the group in problem 29, what is the probability the student is
   (a) an engineering major, given that she is female?
   (b) an engineering major, given that he is male?

Suppose the table below summarizes the opinions of various groups on the issue of increased military spending. Use this table to calculate the empirical probabilities in problems 31–34.

Opinion	Whites		Non-Whites		Totals
	Republicans	Democrats	Republicans	Democrats	
Favor	300	100	25	10	435
Oppose	100	250	25	190	565
Total	400	350	50	200	1000

31. Given that a randomly selected individual is non-white, find the probability that he or she opposes increased military spending.
32. Given that a randomly selected individual is a Democrat, find the probability that he or she opposes increased military spending.
33. Given that a randomly selected individual is in favor of increased military spending, find the probability that he or she is a Republican.
34. Given that a randomly selected individual is opposed to increased military spending, find the probability that he or she is a Democrat.

7.5 Counting; Permutations

Objectives   □ To use the fundamental counting principle and permutations to solve counting problems
□ To solve probability problems involving permutations

Suppose that you decide to dine at a restaurant that offers 3 appetizers, 8 entrees, and 6 desserts. How many different meals can you have? We can answer questions of this type using the **Fundamental Counting Principle.**

| **Fundamental Counting Principle** | If there are m ways in which an event can occur and if there are n ways in which a second event can occur after the first event has occurred, then the two events can occur in $m \cdot n$ ways. |

The fundamental counting principle can be extended to any number of events as long as they are independent. Thus the total number of possible meals at the restaurant is

$$3 \cdot 8 \cdot 6 = 144.$$

EXAMPLE 1   Suppose a person planning a banquet cannot decide how to seat 6 honored guests at the head table. In how many arrangements can they be seated in the six chairs on one side of a table?

Solution   If we think of the six chairs as spaces, we can determine how many ways each space can be filled. The planner could place any one of the 6 people in the first space (say the first chair on the left). One of the 5 remaining persons could then be placed in the second space, one of the 4 remaining persons in the third space, and so on, as follows:

$$\underline{6} \quad \underline{5} \quad \underline{4} \quad \underline{3} \quad \underline{2} \quad \underline{1}$$

By the fundamental counting principle, the total number of arrangements that can be made is the product of these numbers; that is, the total number of possible arrangements is

$$6 \cdot 5 \cdot 4 \cdot 3 \cdot 2 \cdot 1 = 720.$$

Because special products such as $6 \cdot 5 \cdot 4 \cdot 3 \cdot 2 \cdot 1$ frequently occur in counting theory, we use special notation to denote them. We write 6! (read "6 factorial") to denote $6 \cdot 5 \cdot 4 \cdot 3 \cdot 2 \cdot 1$. Likewise $4! = 4 \cdot 3 \cdot 2 \cdot 1$.

> For any positive integer n, we define **n-factorial,** written $n!$, as
>
> $$n! = n(n - 1)(n - 2) \cdots 3 \cdot 2 \cdot 1.$$
>
> We define $0! = 1$.

EXAMPLE 2   Suppose the planner in Example 1 knows that 8 people feel they should be at the head table, but only 6 spaces are available. How many arrangements can be made that place 6 of the 8 people at the head table?

Solution   There are again 6 spaces to fill, but any of 8 people can be placed in the first space, any of 7 people in the second space, and so on. Thus the total number of possible arrangements is

$$\underline{8} \cdot \underline{7} \cdot \underline{6} \cdot \underline{5} \cdot \underline{4} \cdot \underline{3} = 20{,}160.$$

The number of possible arrangements in Example 2 is called the number of **permutations** of 8 things taken 6 at a time, and is denoted $_8P_6$. Note that $_8P_6$ gives the first 6 factors of 8!, so we can use factorial notation to write the product.

$$_8P_6 = \frac{8!}{2!} = \frac{8!}{(8 - 6)!}.$$

In general,

> **Permutations**   The number of possible distinct arrangements of r objects chosen from a set of n objects is called the number of **permutations** of n objects taken r at a time, and equals
>
> $$_nP_r = \frac{n!}{(n - r)!}.$$

EXAMPLE 3   If a state wants each of its license plates to contain 7 different digits (numbers), how many different license plates could it make?

Solution   We seek the number of ways we can arrange 7 different digits from the 10 possible digits (0, 1, 2, 3, . . . , 9). The number is the number of permutations of 10 things taken 7 at a time, or

$$_{10}P_7 = \frac{10!}{(10 - 7)!} = \frac{10!}{3!} = 10 \cdot 9 \cdot 8 \cdot 7 \cdot 6 \cdot 5 \cdot 4 = 604{,}800.$$

Note that we could have answered the question in Example 3 by using the fundamental counting principle or by using permutations. If, in Example 3, the state wanted each of its license plates to have *any* 7 digits rather than 7 *different* digits, the use of permutations would not apply. This is because permutations are used to determine the number of arrangements when each object in the set can be used only once.

We can use the fundamental counting principle to find the number of plates containing any 7 digits. Since any of the 10 digits could be used in each of the 7 places on the plate, the total number of possible plates is

$$10 \cdot 10 \cdot 10 \cdot 10 \cdot 10 \cdot 10 \cdot 10 = 10,000,000.$$

EXAMPLE 4   A psychologist claims she can teach four-year-old children to spell three-letter words very quickly. To test her, one of her students was given cards with the letters A, C, D, K, and T on them and told to spell CAT. What is the probability the child will spell CAT by chance?

Solution   The number of different three-letter "words" that can be formed using these 5 cards is $_5P_3 = 5!/(5 - 3)! = 60$. Since only one of those 60 arrangements will give CAT, the probability that the child will be successful by guessing is 1/60.

Exercise 7.5

1. Compute $_6P_4$.
2. Compute $_8P_5$.
3. Compute $_{10}P_6$.
4. Compute $_7P_4$.
5. Compute $_5P_5$
6. Compute $_4P_1$
7. Compute $_5P_0$
8. Compute $_nP_n$
9. Compute $_nP_0$
10. Compute $_nP_1$
11. Find $\dfrac{(n + 1)!}{n!}$
12. Find $\dfrac{(2n + 2)!}{(2n)!}$
13. If $(n + 1)! = 17n!$, find n.
14. If $(n + 1)! = 30(n - 1)!$, find n.
15. How many four-digit numbers can be formed from the digits 1, 3, 5, 7, 8, and 9
    (a) if each digit may be used once in each number?
    (b) if each digit may be used repeatedly in each number?
16. How many four-digit numbers can be formed from the digits 1, 3, 5, 7, 8, and 9
    (a) if the numbers must be even and digits are not repeated?
    (b) if the numbers are less than 3000 and digits are not repeated?
    Hint: In both parts, begin with the digit where there is a restriction on the choices.

APPLICATIONS

17. The owner of a sailboat received 6 different signal flags when he purchased the sailboat. If the order in which the flags are arranged on the mast determines the signal being sent, how many 3-flag signals can be sent?
18. Eight horses are entered in a race. In how many ways can the horses finish?

19. Four candidates for manager of a department store are ranked according to the weighted average of several criteria. How many different rankings are possible if no two candidates receive the same rank?

20. An examination consists of 12 questions. If 10 questions must be answered, find the number of different orders a student can select the questions to answer.

21. The call letters for radio stations begin with K or W, followed by 3 additional letters. How many sets of call letters having 4 letters are possible?

22. Biologists have identified 4 kinds of small molecules: adenine, cytosine, quanine, and thymine, which link together to form larger molecules in genes. How many 3-molecule chains can be formed if the order or linking is important and each small molecule can occur more than once in a chain?

23. A member of a family of four is asked to rank all members of the family in the order of their power in the family. How many possible rankings are there?

24. A department store manager wants to display 6 brands of a product along one shelf of an aisle. In how many ways can he arrange the brands?

25. How many ways can a 10-question true-false test be answered?

26. How many ways can a 10-question multiple choice test be answered if each question has 4 possible answers?

27. In a 10-part matching question, how many ways can the matches be made if no two parts are used twice and if there are 10 possible matches?

28. Answer problem 27 if there are 10 parts and 15 possible matches.

29. If a child is given cards with A, C, D, G, O, and T on them, what is the probability he or she could spell DOG by guessing the correct arrangement of 3 cards?

30. Eight horses in a race wear numbers 1, 2, 3, 4, 5, 6, 7, and 8. What is the probability that the first three horses to finish the race are numbered 1, 2, 3, respectively?

31. Two men and a woman are lined up to have their picture taken. If they are arranged at random, what is the probability that
    (a) the woman will be on the left in the picture?
    (b) the woman will be in the middle in the picture?

32. If the first digit of a seven-digit telephone number cannot be a 0 or a 1, what is the probability that a number chosen at random will have all seven digits the same?

33. A quiz consists of 10 multiple choice questions with 5 possible choices for each question. If a student guesses the answer to each question, what is the probability that
    (a) she gets all questions correct?
    (b) she gets no questions correct?
    (c) she gets at least one question correct?

34. Suppose in problem 33 that the student was certain of the first 5 questions, and on each of the last 5 she could narrow the answer to one of three choices. Find the probability that
    (a) she scores 50%.
    (b) she scores 100%.
    (c) she passes the test (at least 60%).

35. If a license plate has seven different digits, what is the probability that it contains a zero?

36. A senator asks his constituents to rank 5 issues in order of importance.
    (a) How many rankings are possible?
    (b) What is the probability that one reply chosen at random will rank the issues in alphabetical order?

37. Keys for General Motors cars have six parts, with three patterns for each part.
    (a) How many different key designs are possible?
    (b) If you find a GM key and own a GM car, what is the probability it will fit your trunk?

38. (a) In how many different orders can the letters R, A, N, D, O, M be written?
    (b) If the letters R, A, N, D, O, M are placed in a random order, what is the probability they will spell RANDOM?

7.6 Combinations

Objectives
☐ To use combinations to solve counting problems
☐ To solve probability problems involving combinations

Suppose you are the president of a company and you want to pick 2 secretaries to work for you. If 5 people are qualified, how many different pairs of people can you select? If you select 2 people from the 5 in a specific order, the number of *arrangements* of the 5 people taken 2 at a time would be

$$_5P_2 = 20.$$

But $_5P_2$ gives the number of ways you can select *and* order the pairs, and we seek only the number of ways you can select them. If the names of the people are A, B, C, D, and E, then two of the arrangements, AB and BA, would represent only one pair. Because each of the pairs of people can be arranged in $2! = 2$ ways, the number of pairs that can be selected without regard to order is

$$\frac{_5P_2}{2!} = 10.$$

To find the number of ways you can select 3 people from the 5 without regard to order, we would first find $_5P_3$, then divide by the number of ways the 3 people could be ordered (3!). Thus 3 people can be selected from 5 (without regard for order) in $_5P_3/3! = 10$ ways. We say that the number of combinations of 5 things taken 3 at a time is 10.

Combinations

The number of ways r objects can be chosen from a set of n objects without regard to the order of selection is called the number of **combinations** of n objects taken r at a time, and equals

$$_nC_r = \frac{_nP_r}{r!}.$$

Note that the fundamental difference between permutations and combinations is that permutations are used when order is a factor in the selection, and combinations are used when it is not. Because $_nP_r = n!/(n - r)!$, we have

$$_nC_r = \frac{\dfrac{n!}{(n - r)!}}{r!} = \frac{n!}{(n - r)!r!}.$$

Combination Formula	The number of combinations of n objects taken r at a time is also denoted by $\binom{n}{r}$; that is,

$$\binom{n}{r} = {}_nC_r = \frac{n!}{(n-r)!\,r!}.$$

EXAMPLE 1   An auto dealer is offering any of 6 special options at one price on a specially equipped car being sold. If the dealer will sell as many of these options as you want, and you decide to buy the car with 4 options, how many different choices of specially equipped cars do you have?

Solution   The order in which you choose the options is not relevant, so we seek the number of combinations of 6 things taken 4 at a time. Thus the number of possible choices is

$$_6C_4 = \frac{6!}{(6-4)!\,4!} = \frac{6!}{2!\,4!} = 15.$$

EXAMPLE 2   Suppose you are the junior class president, and you want to pick 4 people to serve on a committee. If 10 people are willing to serve, in how many different ways can you pick your committee?

Solution   Since the order in which the committee members are selected is not important, there are

$$_{10}C_4 = \frac{10!}{6!\,4!} = 210$$

ways in which the committee could be picked.

EXAMPLE 3   Six men and eight women have volunteered to serve on a committee. How many different committees can be formed containing three men and three women?

Solution   Three men can be selected from six in $\binom{6}{3}$ ways, and three women can be selected from eight in $\binom{8}{3}$ ways. Therefore, three men *and* three women can be selected in $\binom{6}{3} \cdot \binom{8}{3} = 1120$ ways.

EXAMPLE 4   A box of 24 shotgun shells contain 4 shells that will not fire. If 8 shells are selected from the box, what is the probability
(a) that all 8 shells will be good?
(b) that 6 shells will be good and 2 will not fire?

Solution (a) The 8 shells can be selected from 24 in $\binom{24}{8}$ ways, and 8 good shells can be selected from the 20 good ones in $\binom{20}{8}$ ways. Thus the probability that all 8 shells will be good is

$$\text{Pr(8 good)} = \frac{\binom{20}{8}}{\binom{24}{8}} = \frac{\frac{20!}{12!8!}}{\frac{24!}{16!8!}} = .17.$$

(b) Six good shells *and* two defective shells can be selected in $\binom{20}{6} \cdot \binom{4}{2}$ ways, so

$$\text{Pr(6 good and 2 defective)} = \frac{\binom{20}{6} \cdot \binom{4}{2}}{\binom{24}{8}} = \frac{\frac{20!}{14!6!} \cdot \frac{4!}{2!2!}}{\frac{24!}{16!8!}} = .316.$$

Exercise 7.6

1. Compute $\binom{6}{2}$.

2. Compute $\binom{8}{6}$.

3. Compute $_7C_5$.

4. Compute $_5C_2$.

5. Compute $\binom{4}{4}$.

6. Compute $\binom{3}{1}$.

7. Compute $\binom{5}{0}$.

8. Compute $\binom{n}{0}$.

9. Compute $\binom{n}{n}$.

10. Compute $\binom{n}{1}$.

11. Verify $_{13}C_{10} = {}_{12}C_9 + {}_{12}C_{10}$.

12. Verify $_{20}C_{15} = {}_{19}C_{14} + {}_{19}C_{15}$.

13. If $_nC_6 = {}_nC_4$, find n.

14. If $_nC_8 = {}_nC_7$, find n.

APPLICATIONS

15. In how many ways can a committee of 5 be selected from 10 people willing to serve?
16. If 8 people are qualified for the next flight to a space station, how many different groups of 3 people can be chosen for the flight?
17. A traveling salesperson has 30 products to sell, but has room in her sample case for only 20 of the products. If all the products are the same size, in how many ways can she select 20 different products for her case?
18. A poker hand consists of 5 cards dealt from a deck of 52 cards. How many different poker hands are possible?
19. A psychological study of outstanding salespeople is to be made. If 5 salespeople are needed and 12 are qualified, in how many ways can the 5 be selected?

20. A company wishes to use the services of 3 different banks in the city. If 15 banks are available, in how many ways can it choose the 3 banks?

21. To determine voters' feelings regarding an issue, a candidate asked a sample of people to pick 4 words out of 10 that they felt best describe the issue. How many different groupings of 4 words are possible?

22. A sociologist wants to pick 3 fifth-grade students from each of four schools. If each of the schools has 50 fifth-grade students, how many different groups of 12 students can he select? (Set up in combination symbols; do not work out.)

23. In how many ways can a committee consisting of 6 men and 6 women be selected from a group consisting of 20 men and 22 women?

24. In how many ways can a hand consisting of 6 spades, 4 hearts, 2 clubs, and 1 diamond be selected from a deck of 52 cards?

25. What is the probability of being dealt a poker hand of 5 cards containing
    (a) 5 spades?   (b) 5 cards of the same suit?

26. A car dealer has 12 different cars he would like to display, but he only has room to display 5.
    (a) In how many ways can he pick 5 cars to display?
    (b) Suppose 8 of the cars are the same color, with the remaining 4 having distinct colors. If the dealer tells a salesperson to display any 5 cars, what is the probability that all 5 cars will be the same color?

27. A box of 12 transistors has 3 defective ones. If 2 transistors are drawn from the box together, what is the probability
    (a) that both transistors are defective?
    (b) that neither transistor is defective?
    (c) that one transistor is defective?

28. A high school principal must select 12 girls at random from the freshman class to serve as hostesses at the junior-senior prom. There are 200 freshman girls, including 20 from minorities, and the principal would like at least one minority girl to have this honor. If he selects the girls at random, what is the probability that
    (a) he will select exactly one minority girl?
    (b) he will select no minority girls?
    (c) he will select at least one minority girl?

29. A box containing 500 central processing units (CPUs) for microcomputers has 20 defective CPUs. If 10 CPUs are selected together from the box, what is the probability that
    (a) all 10 are defective?
    (b) none are defective?
    (c) half of them are defective?

30. Find the probability of being dealt a hand containing 1 spade, 6 hearts, 4 diamonds, and 2 clubs. Assume that a normal deck of 52 cards is used.

31. Suppose that two openings on an appellate court bench are to be filled from current municipal court judges. If the municipal court judges consist of 23 men and 4 women, find the probability
    (a) that both appointees are men.
    (b) that one man and one woman are appointed.
    (c) that at least one woman is appointed.

32. Four men and three women are semifinalists in a lottery. From this group, three finalists are to be selected by a drawing. What is the probability that all three finalists will be men?

33. What is the probability that of three finalists in problem 32, two are men and one is a woman?

34. A task force studying sex discrimination wishes to establish a subcommittee. If the subcommittee is to consist of 11 members chosen from a group of 23 men and 19 women, find the probability that the subcommittee consists of
    (a) 6 men and 5 women.   (b) all women.

35. An insurance company receives 25 claims in a certain month. Company policy mandates that a random selection of 5 of these claims be thoroughly investigated. If 2 of the 25 claims are fraudulent, find the probability that
    (a) both fraudulent claims are thoroughly investigated.
    (b) neither fraudulent claim is thoroughly investigated.

36. Employees of a firm receive annual reviews. In a certain department, 4 employees received excellent ratings, 15 received good ratings, and 1 received a marginal rating. If 3 employees in this department are randomly selected to complete a form for an internal study of the firm, find the probability that
    (a) all 3 selected were rated excellent.
    (b) one from each rating category was selected.

7.7 Expected Value: Decision Making

Objective   ☐   To compute the expected value for an experiment

Many decisions in business and science are made on the basis of what the outcomes of specific decisions will be. One important property that can be developed using probability is expected value. Expected value is very useful in making decisions in business and the sciences. It was originally developed for and is used frequently in gambling, so we will introduce it in this context.

Suppose you toss a coin three times and you receive $1 for each head that results. How much would you expect to win each time you played if you played a large number of times?

The probabilities of 0, 1, 2, and 3 heads are 1/8, 3/8, 3/8, and 1/8, respectively. Thus you would expect to receive 0 dollars 1/8 of the time, 1 dollar 3/8 of the time, 2 dollars 3/8 of the time, and 3 dollars 1/8 of the time. Thus if you played this game a large number of times you would average

$$\$0 \cdot \frac{1}{8} + \$1 \cdot \frac{3}{8} + \$2 \cdot \frac{3}{8} + \$3 \cdot \frac{1}{8} = \$1.50$$

each time you played the game. Thus a fair price to pay to play this game is $1.50, and is called the **expected value** for this game. If a gambling casino offered to let people play this game for $2, the casino could expect to make an average of $.50 for every game that is played. It would have to pay $3 to some people, $2 to some, $1 to some, and $0 to others, but in the long run it could expect to average $.50 for each game that is played.

We define expected value as follows:

Expected Value	If an experiment has n possible numerical outcomes $x_1, x_2, x_3, \ldots, x_n$ with probabilities $\Pr(x_1), \Pr(x_2), \Pr(x_3), \ldots, \Pr(x_n)$, respectively, then the **expected value** for the experiment is $$E(x) = x_1 \cdot \Pr(x_1) + x_2 \cdot \Pr(x_2) + x_3 \cdot \Pr(x_3) + \cdots + x_n \cdot \Pr(x_n).$$

EXAMPLE 1   If a player rolls a die and receives $1 for each dot on the face he rolls, how much money should he expect to receive?

Solution   The following table gives the possible outcomes of the experiment and their probabilities.

x	1	2	3	4	5	6
$\Pr(x)$	1/6	1/6	1/6	1/6	1/6	1/6

Then the expected value (in dollars) is

$$E(x) = 1\left(\frac{1}{6}\right) + 2\left(\frac{1}{6}\right) + 3\left(\frac{1}{6}\right) + 4\left(\frac{1}{6}\right) + 5\left(\frac{1}{6}\right) + 6\left(\frac{1}{6}\right) = \frac{21}{6} = 3.50.$$

He would expect to receive $3.50.

EXAMPLE 2   A fire company sells chances to win a new car, with each ticket costing $5. If the car is worth $8000 and the company sells 3000 tickets, what is the expected value for a person buying one ticket?

Solution   For a person buying one ticket, there are two possible outcomes from the drawing, winning or losing. The probability of winning is 1/3000, and the amount won would be $8000 − $5 (the cost of the ticket). The probability of losing is 2999/3000, and the amount lost is written as a winning of −$5. Thus the expected value is

$$7995\left(\frac{1}{3000}\right) + (-5)\left(\frac{2999}{3000}\right) = \frac{7995}{3000} - \frac{14{,}995}{3000} = -2.33.$$

Thus on the average a person can expect to lose $2.33 every time he or she buys a ticket. It is not possible to lose exactly $2.33 on one ticket—the person will either win an $8000 prize or lose $5; the expected value means that a person who buys large numbers of these tickets can expect to lose an average of $2.33 on each ticket he or she buys. That is, the fire company will make $2.33 on each ticket they sell if they sell all 3000.

EXAMPLE 3   The T. J. Cooper Insurance Company insures 100,000 cars. Their records indicate that during a year they will pay out the following for accidents:

$100,000 with probability .0001
$ 50,000 with probability .001
$ 25,000 with probability .002

$5,000 with probability .008
$1,000 with probability .02

What amount of money would the company expect to pay per car for accidents?

Solution   The expected value of the company's payments is

$$\$100,000(.0001) + \$50,000(.001) + \$25,000(.002) + \$5000(.008) + \$1000(.02)$$
$$= \$10 + \$50 + \$50 + \$40 + \$20 = \$170.$$

Thus the premium the company would charge each driver would be

$$\$170 + \text{operating costs} + \text{profit} + \text{reserve for bad years.}$$

Exercise 7.7

The following tables give the possible numerical outcomes of experiments and the probabilities that they will occur. Find the expected value of each experiment.

1.
x	0	1	2	3
Pr(x)	1/8	1/4	1/4	3/8

2.
x	1	2	3	4
Pr(x)	1/10	1/5	3/10	2/5

3.
x	4	5	6	7
Pr(x)	1/3	1/3	1/3	0

4.
x	1	2	3	4	5	6
Pr(x)	1/12	1/4	1/12	1/4	1/12	1/4

5.
x	0	2	4
Pr(x)	1/6	2/6	3/6

6.
x	3	4	5	6
Pr(x)	3/10	1/5	3/10	1/5

7.
x	1	3	5
Pr(x)	2/3	1/6	1/6

8.
x	1	2	3	4
Pr(x)	1/15	4/15	1/5	7/15

9. An experiment has five possible outcomes for x: 0, 1, 2, 3, 4. The probability that each of these outcomes occurs is $x/10$. What is the expected value of x for the experiment?

10. An experiment has six possible outcomes for x: 0, 1, 2, 3, 4, 5. The probability that each of these outcomes occurs is $x/15$. What is the expected value of x for the experiment?

11. Five slips of paper containing the numbers 0, 1, 2, 3, 4 are placed in a hat. If the experiment consists of drawing one number, and if the experiment is repeated a large number of times, what is the expected value of the number drawn?

12. An experiment consists of rolling a die once. If the experiment is repeated a large number of times, what is the expected value of the number rolled?

APPLICATIONS

13. In studying endangered species, scientists have found that when animals are relocated it takes x years without offspring before the first young are born, where x and the probability of x are given below. What is the expected number of years before the first young are born?

x	0	1	2	3	4
$Pr(x)$	.04	.35	.38	.18	.05

14. If the probability that a newborn child is a male is 1/2, what is the expected number of male children in a family having 4 children?

15. A student is completely unprepared for a 4-choice multiple choice test. If the test has 4 questions and all are guessed at, how many questions should he or she expect to get correct?

16. Suppose the instructor of the student in problem 15 tries to account for guessing on the test by counting the number of questions the student answers correctly and then subtracting from this number 1/4 of the number of questions a student answers. If the student guesses on all 4 problems on this test, for how many problems should he or she expect to get credit?

17. Suppose you are invited to play the following game: You toss 3 coins and receive $1 if one head results, $4 if two heads result, and $9 if three heads result. How much should you pay to play if the game is fair?

18. A charity sells raffle tickets for $1 each. First prize is $500, second prize is $100, third prize is $10. If you bought one of the 1000 tickets sold, what are your expected winnings?

19. Suppose the coin used in problem 17 has been altered so that the probability of a head on any toss is 1/3. How much should you pay to play if the game is fair?

20. Suppose a student is offered a chance to draw a card from an ordinary deck of 52 playing cards and win $10 if he or she draws an ace, $2 for a king, and $1 for a queen. If $2 must be paid to play the game, what is the expected winnings every time the game is played by the student?

21. A young man plans to sell umbrellas at the city's Easter Parade. He knows that he can sell 180 umbrellas at $5 each if it rains hard, he can sell 50 if it rains lightly, and he can sell 10 if it doesn't rain at all. Past records show it rains hard 25% of the time on Easter, rains lightly 20% of the time, and does not rain at all 55% of the time. If he can buy 0, 100, or 200 umbrellas at $2 each and return the unsold ones for $1 each, how many should he buy?

22. If the young man in problem 21 learns from a highly reliable weather forecaster that the probability of a hard rain on Easter is 15%, of a light rain is 20%, and of no rain is 65%, should he still plan to sell umbrellas at the Easter Parade?

23. A candidate must decide if he should spend his time and money on TV commercials or making personal appearances. His staff determines that by using TV he can reach 100,000 people with probability .01, 50,000 people with probability .47, and 25,000 with probability .52; and that by making personal appearances he can reach 80,000 people with probability .02, 50,000 people with probability .47, and 20,000 with probability .51. Which method will reach more people?

24. A car owner must decide if she should take out a $100 deductible collision policy in addition to her liability insurance policy. Records show that each year, in her area, 8% of the drivers have an accident that is their fault or for which no fault is assigned, and

that the average cost of repairs for these types of accidents is $1000. If the $100 deductible collision policy costs $100 per year, would she save money in the long run by buying the insurance or "taking the chance?" (Hint: Find the expected value if she has the policy and if she doesn't have the policy and compare them.)

25. Suppose a youth has a part-time job in an ice cream shop. He receives $20 if he is called to work a full day, and $10 if he is called to work a half day. Over the past year he has been called to work a full day an average of 8 days per month and for a half day an average of 14 days per month. How much can he expect to earn *per day* during a 30-day month?

26. On a multiple choice test with each question having five possible choices, a correct answer earns 4 points, an incorrect answer loses 1 point, and a blank receives 0 points.
   (a) Find the expected point-value earned when a student has no idea of the correct answer but makes a guess on every question.
   (b) Find the expected point-value earned when a student has narrowed the choice by eliminating two of the possible choices on each question, but must guess among the remaining choices.

7.8 Markov Chains

Objectives
   □   To use transition matrices to find specific stages of Markov chains
   □   To write transition matrices for Markov chain problems
   □   To find steady-state vectors for certain Markov chain problems

Certain analyses of price movements, consumer behavior, laboratory animal behavior, and many other processes in business, the social sciences, and the life sciences can be modeled using a technique called **Markov chains.** Markov chains are named for the famous Russian mathematician A. A. Markov, who developed this theory in 1906. Markov chains study a type of repeated trials in which the outcomes on any trial depend *only* on the outcome of the previous trial. Typically each experiment has a finite fixed number of outcomes called **states.**

For example, suppose a department store has determined that a woman who used a credit card last month will use it again this month with probability .8. That is,

Pr(woman will use a charge card this month|she used it last month) = .8

and

Pr(woman will not use card this month|she used it last month) = .2.

Furthermore, suppose the store has determined that the probability that a woman who did not use a credit card last month will not use it this month is .7. That is,

Pr(woman will not use card this month|she did not use it last month) = .7

and

Pr(woman will use card this month|she did not use it last month) = .3.

This is a Markov chain experiment that has two states: using a credit card and not using a credit card. The probability of moving from one state to another is called the **transition** probability; these transition probabilities are the conditional probabilities given above.

Transition probabilities can be organized into a **transition matrix** P, illustrated below.

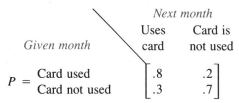

In general, a transition matrix is characterized by the following:

1. The *ij*-entry in the matrix is: Pr(moving from State *i* to State *j*). Note that this is really the probability of moving to State *j* given that you are in State *i*.

2. The entries are nonnegative.

3. The sum of the entries in each row equals 1.

4. The matrix is square.

Now suppose the department store data shows that during the first month a credit card is received the probabilities for each state are as follows:

$$Pr(\text{a woman used a charge card}) = .9$$
$$Pr(\text{a woman did not use a charge card}) = .1.$$

These probabilities determine the **initial-probability vector**

$$A = [.9 \qquad .1],$$

which gives the probabilities for each state at the outset of the trials. Clearly the sum of the entries in a probability vector must be 1, and each entry must be nonnegative.

Notice that of the 90% of women who used the credit card in their initial month, .8 of them will use it again, and of the 10% who didn't use the card, .3 of them will use it next month. Thus

$$
\begin{aligned}
Pr(\text{will use 2d}) &= Pr(\text{used 1st month}) \cdot Pr(\text{will use 2d}|\text{used 1st}) + \\
&\quad\ Pr(\text{not used 1st month}) \cdot Pr(\text{will use 2d}|\text{not used 1st}) \\
&= (.9)(.8) + (.1)(.3) \\
&= .72 + .03 = .75.
\end{aligned}
$$

Note that this is one element of the product matrix AP. Similarly, the second element of the product matrix is the probability that a customer will not use the charge card in the second month.

$$
AP = [.9 \qquad .1] \begin{bmatrix} .8 & .2 \\ .3 & .7 \end{bmatrix} = [.75 \qquad .25]
$$

$$
\underset{\substack{\text{initial} \\ \text{month}}}{} \qquad \underset{\substack{\text{transition} \\ \text{matrix}}}{} \qquad \underset{\substack{\text{second} \\ \text{month}}}{}
$$

Thus

$$\text{Pr(a woman will use a charge card in 2d month)} = .75$$

and

$$\text{Pr(a woman will not use a charge card in 2d month)} = .25.$$

To find the probabilities for each state for the third month, we multiply the second month probability vector times the transition matrix.

$$[.75 \quad .25] \begin{bmatrix} .8 & .2 \\ .3 & .7 \end{bmatrix} = [.675 \quad .325]$$

second   transition   third
month   matrix   month

Continuing in this manner, we can find the probabilities for later months.

EXAMPLE 1   Suppose that in a certain city the Democratic, Republican, and Consumer parties always nominate candidates for mayor. The probability of winning in any election depends on the party in power and is given by the transition matrix P below.

	Party in office next term		
Party in office now	D	R	C
Democrat	.5	.4	.1
Republican	.4	.5	.1
Consumer	.3	.3	.4

Suppose the probability of winning the next election is given by $[.4 \quad .4 \quad .2]$; that is, $\text{Pr(D)} = .4$, $\text{Pr(R)} = .4$, $\text{Pr(C)} = .2$. Find the probability of each party winning the *fourth* election (the third election after this one).

Solution   The probability of each party winning the second election is found using the probabilities given for the first.

$$[.4 \quad .4 \quad .2] \begin{bmatrix} .5 & .4 & .1 \\ .4 & .5 & .1 \\ .3 & .3 & .4 \end{bmatrix} = [.42 \quad .42 \quad .16]$$

Using the probabilities for the second election, we can find the probabilities for the third.

$$[.42 \quad .42 \quad .16] \begin{bmatrix} .5 & .4 & .1 \\ .4 & .5 & .1 \\ .3 & .3 & .4 \end{bmatrix} = [.426 \quad .426 \quad .148]$$

Using the probabilities for the third election, we can find the probabilities for the fourth election.

$$[.426 \quad .426 \quad .148] \begin{bmatrix} .5 & .4 & .1 \\ .4 & .5 & .1 \\ .3 & .3 & .4 \end{bmatrix} = [.4278 \quad .4278 \quad .1444]$$

Notice that the probabilities for the last two elections in Example 1 appear to be very close; that is, the system seems to be stabilizing. In fact, there is a vector $[V_1 \quad V_2 \quad V_3]$ such that

$$[V_1 \quad V_2 \quad V_3] \cdot P = [V_1 \quad V_2 \quad V_3].$$

The specific probability vector for which this is true in Example 1 is $\left[\frac{3}{7} \quad \frac{3}{7} \quad \frac{1}{7}\right]$, since

$$\left[\frac{3}{7} \quad \frac{3}{7} \quad \frac{1}{7}\right] \begin{bmatrix} .5 & .4 & .1 \\ .4 & .5 & .1 \\ .3 & .3 & .4 \end{bmatrix} = \left[\frac{3}{7} \quad \frac{3}{7} \quad \frac{1}{7}\right].$$

This vector is called the **fixed-probability vector** for the given transition matrix. Because this vector is where the process eventually stabilizes, it is also called the **steady-state vector.**

Rather than trying to guess this steady-state vector by repeated multiplication, we can solve the equation

$$[V_1 \quad V_2 \quad V_3] \begin{bmatrix} .5 & .4 & .1 \\ .4 & .5 & .1 \\ .3 & .3 & .4 \end{bmatrix} = [V_1 \quad V_2 \quad V_3]$$

for V_1, V_2, and V_3 as follows.

$$[V_1 \quad V_2 \quad V_3] \begin{bmatrix} .5 & .4 & .1 \\ .4 & .5 & .1 \\ .3 & .3 & .4 \end{bmatrix} = [V_1 \quad V_2 \quad V_3]$$

$$.5V_1 + .4V_2 + .3V_3 = V_1$$
$$.4V_1 + .5V_2 + .3V_3 = V_2$$
$$.1V_1 + .1V_2 + .4V_3 = V_3$$

Solving by Gauss-Jordan elimination gives

$$\begin{bmatrix} -.5 & .4 & .3 & | & 0 \\ .4 & -.5 & .3 & | & 0 \\ .1 & .1 & -.6 & | & 0 \end{bmatrix}$$

$$\begin{bmatrix} 1 & 1 & -6 & | & 0 \\ 0 & -9 & 27 & | & 0 \\ 0 & 9 & -27 & | & 0 \end{bmatrix} \rightarrow \begin{bmatrix} 1 & 1 & -6 & | & 0 \\ 0 & 1 & -3 & | & 0 \\ 0 & 0 & 0 & | & 0 \end{bmatrix} \rightarrow \begin{bmatrix} 1 & 0 & -3 & | & 0 \\ 0 & 1 & -3 & | & 0 \\ 0 & 0 & 0 & | & 0 \end{bmatrix}$$

So

$$V_1 = 3V_3 \qquad V_2 = 3V_3.$$

Any vector satisfying these conditions is a solution to the system. Since $[V_1 \quad V_2 \quad V_3]$ is a probability vector, we have $V_1 + V_2 + V_3 = 1$. Substituting gives $3V_3 + 3V_3 + V_3 = 1$, so $V_3 = \frac{1}{7}$, and the steady-state vector is

$$\left[\frac{3}{7} \quad \frac{3}{7} \quad \frac{1}{7}\right].$$

It can be shown that any transition matrix P such that some power of P, P^m, contains only positive entries is called a **regular transition matrix,** and each Markov chain using a regular transition matrix will have a steady-state vector.

Note that a regular transition matrix P may contain zeros; the only requirement is that some power of P contain all positive entries. In this text we will limit ourselves to regular transition matrices.

Furthermore, if a steady-state vector exists, then the effect of the initial probabilities diminishes as the number of steps in the process increases. This means that the probabilities for the elections would approach

$$\begin{bmatrix} \dfrac{3}{7} & \dfrac{3}{7} & \dfrac{1}{7} \end{bmatrix}$$

regardless of the probabilities for the initial election. For example, even if a Democrat were certain to be elected in the initial election (i.e., the initial vector is [1 0 0]), the probabilities for the fifth election are [.4292 .4291 .1417], which approximates the steady-state vector. (See problem 17 of Exercise 7.8.)

EXAMPLE 2   Suppose that in a certain city the probability that a woman with less than a high school education has a daughter with less than a high school education, a high school degree, or more than a high school education is .2, .6, and .2, respectively. In the same city, the probability that a woman with a high school degree has a daughter with less than a high school education, a high school degree, or more than a high school education is .1, .5, and .4, respectively. Also, the probability that a woman with more than a high school education has a daughter with less than a high school education, a high school degree, or education beyond high school is .1, .1, and .8, respectively. If the population of women in the city is now 60% with less than a high school education, 30% with a high school degree, and 10% with education beyond high school, answer the questions below.
(a) What is the transition matrix for this information?
(b) What is the likely distribution of women according to educational level two generations from now?
(c) What is the steady-state vector for this information?

Solution   (a) The transition matrix is

| | Daughter's educational level | | |
Mother's educational level	Less than H.S.	H.S. degree	More than H.S.
Less than H.S.	.2	.6	.2
H.S. degree	.1	.5	.4
More than H.S.	.1	.1	.8

(b) The likely distribution after one generation is

$$[.6 \quad .3 \quad .1] \begin{bmatrix} .2 & .6 & .2 \\ .1 & .5 & .4 \\ .1 & .1 & .8 \end{bmatrix} = [.16 \quad .52 \quad .32].$$

The likely distribution after two generations is

$$[.16 \quad .52 \quad .32] \begin{bmatrix} .2 & .6 & .2 \\ .1 & .5 & .4 \\ .1 & .1 & .8 \end{bmatrix} = [.116 \quad .388 \quad .496].$$

(c) The steady-state vector is found by solving

$$[V_1 \quad V_2 \quad V_3] \begin{bmatrix} .2 & .6 & .2 \\ .1 & .5 & .4 \\ .1 & .1 & .8 \end{bmatrix} = [V_1 \quad V_2 \quad V_3].$$

$$\begin{cases} .2V_1 + .1V_2 + .1V_3 = V_1 \\ .6V_1 + .5V_2 + .1V_3 = V_2 \\ .2V_1 + .4V_2 + .8V_3 = V_3 \end{cases}$$

$$\begin{cases} -.8V_1 + .1V_2 + .1V_3 = 0 \\ .6V_1 - .5V_2 + .1V_3 = 0 \\ .2V_1 + .4V_2 - .2V_3 = 0 \end{cases}$$

$$\begin{bmatrix} -.8 & .1 & .1 & | & 0 \\ .6 & -.5 & .1 & | & 0 \\ .2 & .4 & -.2 & | & 0 \end{bmatrix} \xrightarrow[R_1 \& R_3]{\text{switch}} \begin{bmatrix} 1 & 2 & -1 & | & 0 \\ 0 & -17 & 7 & | & 0 \\ 0 & 17 & -7 & | & 0 \end{bmatrix}$$

$$\longrightarrow \begin{bmatrix} 1 & 0 & -\frac{3}{17} & | & 0 \\ 0 & 1 & -\frac{7}{17} & | & 0 \\ 0 & 0 & 0 & | & 0 \end{bmatrix}$$

Thus $V_1 = \frac{3}{17} V_3$ and $V_2 = \frac{7}{17} V_3$. The probability vector satisfying these conditions and $V_1 + V_2 + V_3 = 1$ must satisfy

$$\frac{3}{17} V_3 + \frac{7}{17} V_3 + V_3 = 1.$$

Thus

$$\frac{27}{17} V_3 = 1, \text{ so } V_3 = \frac{17}{27},$$

and the steady-state vector is

$$\begin{bmatrix} \dfrac{3}{27} & \dfrac{7}{27} & \dfrac{17}{27} \end{bmatrix}.$$

Exercise 7.8

Which of the vectors in problems 1–4 could *not* be probability vectors?

1. $\begin{bmatrix} \dfrac{1}{4} & \dfrac{3}{4} \end{bmatrix}$ 2. $\begin{bmatrix} \dfrac{5}{6} & \dfrac{2}{3} \end{bmatrix}$

3. $\begin{bmatrix} \dfrac{1}{4} & \dfrac{3}{5} & \dfrac{1}{6} \end{bmatrix}$

4. $\begin{bmatrix} \dfrac{2}{3} & \dfrac{1}{12} & \dfrac{1}{4} \end{bmatrix}$

Which of the matrices in problems 5–8 could *not* be transition matrices?

5. $\begin{bmatrix} .3 & .5 & .2 \\ .1 & .6 & .3 \end{bmatrix}$

6. $\begin{bmatrix} .6 & .2 & .2 \\ .1 & .5 & .4 \\ .3 & .5 & .1 \end{bmatrix}$

7. $\begin{bmatrix} .1 & .3 & .6 \\ .5 & .2 & .3 \\ .1 & .7 & .2 \end{bmatrix}$

8. $\begin{bmatrix} .6 & .5 & -.1 \\ .2 & .6 & .2 \\ .3 & .3 & .4 \end{bmatrix}$

In problems 9–12, use the given transition matrix and the given initial-probability vector to find the probability vector for the third stage (two after the initial stage) of the Markov chain.

$$A = \begin{bmatrix} .1 & .9 \\ .3 & .7 \end{bmatrix} \qquad B = \begin{bmatrix} .5 & .5 \\ .9 & .1 \end{bmatrix}$$

$$C = \begin{bmatrix} .5 & .3 & .2 \\ .3 & .5 & .2 \\ .1 & .1 & .8 \end{bmatrix} \qquad D = \begin{bmatrix} .8 & .1 & .1 \\ .2 & .6 & .2 \\ .3 & .3 & .4 \end{bmatrix}$$

9. Transition matrix A, initial-probability vector [.2   .8].
10. Transition matrix B, initial-probability vector [.6   .4].
11. Transition matrix C, initial-probability vector [.1   .3   .6].
12. Transition matrix D, initial-probability vector [.9   0   .1].

In problems 13–16, find the steady-state vector associated with the given transition matrix from problems 9–12.

13. A 14. B 15. C 16. D

APPLICATIONS

Problems 17 and 18: In a certain city the Democratic, Republican, and Consumer parties always nominate candidates for mayor. The probability of winning in any election depends on the party in power and is given by the transition matrix P below.

Party in office now	\	Party in office next term		
		D	R	C
Democrat		.5	.4	.1
Republican		.4	.5	.1
Consumer		.3	.3	.4

17. Using the transition matrix and assuming the initial-probability vector is [1   0   0], find the probability vectors for the next four steps of the Markov chain. (This initial-probability vector indicates a Democrat is certain to win the initial election.)

18. Using the transition matrix above and assuming that a Republican is certain to win the initial election, find the probability vectors for the next four steps of the Markov chain.

Problems 19–22: The probability that daughters of a mother who attends church regularly will also attend church regularly is .8, while the probability that daughters of a mother who does not attend regularly will attend regularly is .3.

19. What is the transition matrix for this information?
20. If a woman attends church and has one daughter who in turn has one daughter, what is the probability that the granddaughter attends church regularly?
21. If a woman does not attend church, what is the probability that her granddaughter attends church regularly?
22. What is the steady-state vector for this information?

Problems 23–28: A man owns an Audi, a Ford, and a VW. He drives every day and never drives the same car two days in a row. This is the probability that he drives the other cars the next day:

$$\text{Pr(Ford after Audi)} = .7, \quad \text{Pr(VW after Audi)} = .3$$
$$\text{Pr(Audi after Ford)} = .6, \quad \text{Pr(VW after Ford)} = .4$$
$$\text{Pr(Audi after VW)} = .8, \quad \text{Pr(Ford after VW)} = .2$$

23. Write the transition matrix for his selection of a car.
24. If he drove the Ford today, what are the probabilities for the cars that he will drive 2 days from today?
25. If he drove the Ford today, what are the probabilities for the cars that he will drive 4 days from today?
26. If he drove the Audi today, what are the probabilities for the cars that he will drive 4 days from now?
27. What is the steady-state vector for this problem?
28. Would the probabilities for which car he drives 100 days from now depend on whether he drove a Ford or Audi today?
29. Suppose a government study estimated that the probability of successive generations of a rural family remaining in a rural area was .7, and the probability of successive generations of an urban family remaining in an urban area was .9. Assuming a Markov chain applies to these facts, find the steady-state vector.
30. A psychologist found that a laboratory mouse placed in a T-maze will go down the same branch with probability .8 if there was food there on the previous trial, and that it will go down the same branch with probability .6 if there was no food there on the previous trial. Find the steady-state vector for this experiment. If the mouse takes the branches with equal probability when no reward is found, does it appear that the mouse "learns" to choose the food path?
31. The local community-service funding organization in a certain county has classified the population into those who did not give the previous year, those who gave less than their "fair share," and those who met or exceeded their "fair share." Suppose the organization developed the following transition matrix for these groups.

	This year		
Last year	N	L	F
No contribution	.7	.2	.1
Less than fair share	.1	.6	.3
Fair share	0	.1	.9

Find the steady-state vector for this county's contribution habits.

Problems 32 and 33: A local business A has two competitors, B and C. Initially the probability that a customer patronizes A, B, or C is .2, .6, and .2, respectively. Suppose A initiates an advertising campaign to improve its business and finds the following transition matrix to describe the effect.

Last week's customers went to	This week's customers go to		
	A	B	C
A	.7	.2	.1
B	.4	.4	.2
C	.4	.4	.2

32. If A runs the advertising campaign for 3 weeks, find the probability of a customer patronizing each business.
33. Find the steady-state vector for this market, that is, the long-range share of the market that each business can expect if the transition matrix holds.

Problems 34–36: For species that reproduce sexually, characteristics are determined by a gene from each parent. Suppose that for a certain trait there are two possible genes available from each parent, a dominant gene D and a recessive gene r. Then the different gene combinations (called *genotypes*) for the offspring are DD, Dr, rD, and rr, where Dr and rD produce the same trait. Suppose further that these genotypes are the states of a Markov chain with the transition matrix below.

Parent genotype	Offspring genotype		
	DD	Dr	rr
DD	.7	.3	0
Dr	.35	.5	.15
rr	0	.7	.3

34. If the initial occurrence of these genotypes in the population is .5 for DD, .4 for Dr, and .1 for rr, find the distribution (probability) of each type after the first and second generations.
35. Find the fixed-probability vector for this genotype.
36. To which generation(s) does the fixed-probability vector correspond? (See problems 34 and 35.) This is called the Hardy-Weinberg model.

Review Exercises

7.1

1. A bag contains 6 red and 3 blue balls. If 1 ball is drawn at random, what is the probability that it is blue?
2. From a deck of 52 cards, 1 card is to be drawn. What is the probability that it will be a queen?
3. If the probability of winning a game is 1/4 and there can be no ties, what is the probability of losing the game?
4. A card is drawn at random from an ordinary deck of 52 playing cards. What is the probability that it is a queen or a jack?

7.2

5. A deck of 52 cards is shuffled. A card is drawn, then replaced, the pack again shuffled, and a second card drawn. What is the probability that each card drawn is an ace, king, queen, or jack?

6. A bag contains 4 red balls and 3 black balls. Two balls are drawn at random from the bag without replacement. Find the probability that both balls are red.
7. A card is drawn from a deck of 52 playing cards. What is the probability that it is an ace or a 10?
8. A card is drawn at random from a deck of playing cards. What is the probability that it is a king or a red card?

9. A box contains 2 red balls and 3 black balls. Two balls are drawn from the box without replacement. Find the probability that the second ball is red, given that the first ball is black.

10. What is the probability that a letter chosen at random from the word "wooden" is an o?
11. A bag contains 4 red balls numbered 1, 2, 3, 4 and 5 white balls numbered 5, 6, 7, 8, 9. A ball is drawn. What is the probability that the ball
    (a) is red and an even-numbered ball?
    (b) is red or an even number?
    (c) is white or an odd number?

12. How many 3-letter sets of initials are possible?
13. An urn contains 4 red and 6 white balls. One ball is drawn, is not replaced, and a second ball is drawn. What is the probability that one ball is white and one is red?

14. Compute $_6P_2$.
15. Urn I contains 3 red and 4 white balls and urn II contains 5 red and 2 white balls. An urn is selected and a ball drawn.
    (a) What is the probability that urn I is selected and a red ball is drawn?
    (b) What is the probability that a red ball is selected?
    (c) If a red ball is selected, what is the probability that urn I was selected?

16. For the following probability distribution, find the expected value $E(x)$.

x	1	2	3	4
Pr(x)	.2	.3	.4	.1

APPLICATIONS

17. In a certain city, 30,000 citizens out of 80,000 are over 50 years of age. What is the probability that a citizen selected at random will be 50 years old or younger?
18. Of 100 job applicants to the United Nations, 30 speak French, 40 speak German, and 12 speak both French and German. If an applicant is chosen at random, what is the probability the applicant speaks French or German?

19. A personnel director ranks 4 applicants for a job. How many rankings are possible?
20. An organization wants to select a president, vice-president, secretary, and treasurer. If 8 people are willing to serve and each of them is eligible for any of the offices, in how many different ways can the offices be filled?

21. Sixty men out of 1000 and 3 women out of 1000 are color blind. A person is picked at random from a group containing 10 men and 10 women.
    (a) What is the probability that the person is color blind?
    (b) What is the probability the person is a man if the person is color blind?

22. A utility company sends teams of 4 people each to perform repairs. If it has 12 qualified people, how many different ways can people be assigned to a team?
23. An organization wants to select a committee of 4 members from a group of 8 eligible members. How many different committees are possible?

24. A sample of 6 fuses is drawn from a lot containing 10 good fuses and 2 defective fuses. What is the probability that the sample will have
    (a) exactly 1 defective fuse?
    (b) at least 1 defective fuse?
25. A jury can be deadlocked if one person disagrees with the rest. There are 12 ways a jury can be deadlocked if one person disagrees because any one of the 12 jurors could disagree.
    (a) In how many ways can a jury be deadlocked if 2 people disagree?
    (b) If 3 people disagree?

7.7

26. A state lottery pays $500 to anyone who selects the correct 3-digit number from a random drawing. If it costs $1 to play, what are the expected winnings of a person who plays?

Suppose that in a study of leadership style versus industrial productivity, the following data was obtained. Use this empirical data to answer the problems 27–29.

	Leadership style			
Productivity	Democratic	Authoritarian	Laissez-faire	Total
Low	40	15	40	95
Medium	25	75	10	110
High	25	30	20	75
Total	90	120	70	280

7.2

27. Find the probability that a person chosen at random has a democratic style and medium productivity.

7.3

28. Find the probability that an individual chosen at random has high productivity or has an authoritarian style.

7.4

29. Find the probability that an individual chosen at random has an authoritarian style given that he or she has medium productivity.

7.8

Problems 30 and 31: Suppose people in a certain community are classified as being low income, middle income, or high income. Suppose further that the probabilities for children being in any given state depends on which state their parents were in according to the Markov chain transition matrix below.

	Income level of children		
Income level of parents	L	M	H
Low	.15	.6	.25
Middle	.15	.35	.5
High	0	.2	.8

30. If the initial distribution probabilities of families in a certain population are [.7 .2 .1], find the distribution for the next three generations.
31. Find the steady-state vector for the distribution of families by income level.

WARMUP

	Prerequisite problem type	Answer	Section for review
8.5	Expand: (a) $(p + q)^2$ (b) $(p + q)^3$	(a) $p^2 + 2pq + q^2$ (b) $p^3 + 3p^2q + 3pq^2 + q^3$	0.5 Special products
8.8	Identify the graph of $y = -0.33x + 16.43$.	Straight line	1.2 Graphs of first-degree equation
8.6	Graph all real numbers satisfying (a) $100 \le x \le 115$ (b) $-1 \le z \le 2$	(a) (b)	3.1 Linear inequalities
8.4, 8.5	Evaluate: (a) $\binom{4}{3}$ (b) $\binom{5}{2}$ (c) $\binom{24}{0}$	(a) 4 (b) 10 (c) 1	7.6 Combinations
8.4, 8.5, 8.6, 8.7	(a) If 68% of the IQ scores of adults lie between 85 and 115, what is the probability that an adult chosen at random will have an IQ score between 85 and 115? (b) If a fair coin is tossed 3 times, find Pr(2 heads and 1 tail)	(a) .68 (b) $\frac{3}{8}$	7.1 Probability
8.5	If a random variable x for an experiment has probabilities given by the table, $$\begin{array}{c\|ccccccc} x & 0 & 1 & 2 & 3 & 4 & 5 & 6 \\ \hline \text{Pr}(x) & \frac{1}{64} & \frac{6}{64} & \frac{15}{64} & \frac{20}{64} & \frac{15}{64} & \frac{6}{64} & \frac{1}{64} \end{array}$$ find $E(x)$, the expected value for x.	3	7.7 Expected value

8

Introduction to Statistics

In modern business, a vast amount of data is collected for use in making decisions about the production, distribution, and sale of merchandise. Businesses also collect and summarize data about advertising effectiveness, production costs, sales, wages, and profits. Behavioral scientists attempt to reach conclusions about general behavioral characteristics by studying the characteristics of a small sample of people. For example, election predictions are based on a careful sampling of the votes; correct predictions are frequently announced on television even though only 5% of the vote has been counted. Life scientists can use statistical methods with laboratory animals to detect substances that may be dangerous to humans.

A set of data taken from some source of data for the purpose of learning about the source is called a **sample;** the source of the data is called a **population.** The branch of statistics that deals with the collection, organization, summarization, and presentation of sample data is called **descriptive statistics.** The branch that deals with the methods of making estimates, predictions, or inferences about the population from collected sample data is called **inferential statistics.**

The descriptive statistics methods discussed in this chapter include graphical representation of data, measures of central tendency, and measures of dispersion. We will also discuss the binomial and normal probability distributions and use them to solve probability problems and make statistical inferences.

8.1 Frequency Histograms

Objective   □   To set up frequency tables and construct frequency histograms and frequency polygons for sets of data

The first step in statistical work is the collection of data. Data are regarded as statistics data if the numbers collected have some relationship. The heights of all female first-year students are statistical data because a definite relationship exists among the collected numbers.

A *graph* frequently is used to provide a picture of the statistical data that have been gathered and to show relationships among various quantities. The advantage of the graph for showing data is that a person can quickly get an idea of the relationships that exist. The disadvantage is that the data can be shown only approximately on a graph. One type of graph that is used frequently in statistical work is the **frequency histogram.** A histogram is really a bar graph. It is constructed by putting the scores (numbers collected) along the horizontal axis and the frequency with which they occur along the vertical axis. A frequency table is usually set up to prepare the data for the histogram.

EXAMPLE 1   Construct a frequency histogram for the following scores: 38, 37, 36, 40, 35, 40, 38, 37, 36, 37, 39, 38.

Solution   We first construct the frequency table, and then use the table to construct the histogram shown in Figure 8.1.

Score	Frequency
35	1
36	2
37	3
38	3
39	1
40	2

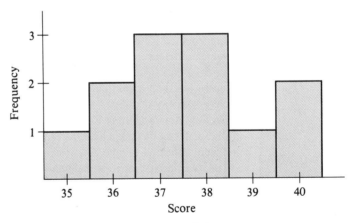

Figure 8.1

EXAMPLE 2   Construct a histogram from the following frequency table:

Interval	Frequency
0–5	0
6–10	2
11–15	5
16–20	1
21–25	3

Solution   The histogram is shown in Figure 8.2.

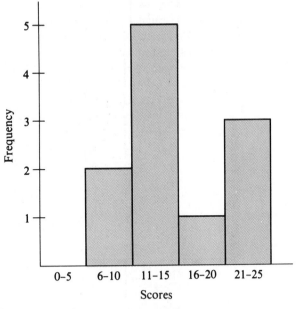

Figure 8.2

By drawing lines connecting the midpoints of the tops of the bars in a frequency histogram, we can construct a line graph called a **frequency polygon.** Figure 8.3 is a frequency polygon for the data in Example 2.

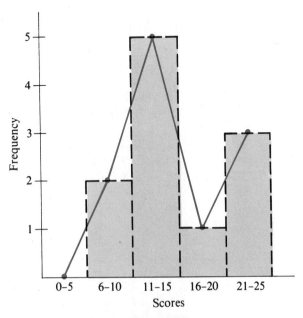

Figure 8.3

If the set of data contains a very large number of different scores, we can construct a frequency table like that in Example 2 by grouping scores into intervals or **classes.** We choose class sizes that make the data easier to handle. It is sometimes convenient to use one number, called a **class mark,** to represent each class of data. The class mark of an interval or class is its midpoint.

EXAMPLE 3   Construct a frequency table and frequency histogram for the data below, using (a) intervals of width 3, (b) five intervals.

$$24, 1, 3, 5, 13, 17, 15, 4, 3, 12$$
$$22, 5, 18, 16, 15, 9, 8, 7, 6, 12$$
$$15, 13, 16, 12, 4, 2, 1, 5, 12, 10$$
$$13, 16, 18, 21, 2, 5, 15, 17, 3, 20$$

Solution   (a)

Classes	Class marks	Frequencies
1–3	2	7
4–6	5	7
7–9	8	3
10–12	11	5
13–15	14	7
16–18	17	7
19–21	20	2
22–24	23	2

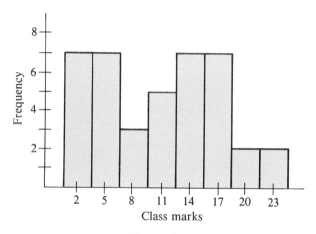

Figure 8.4

(b) The range of scores is from 1 to 24, so the width of each of the five intervals is the smallest integer n where $n \geq \frac{24}{5}$. Thus the width of each interval is 5.

Classes	Class marks	Frequencies
1–5	3	13
6–10	8	5
11–15	13	11
16–20	18	8
21–25	23	3

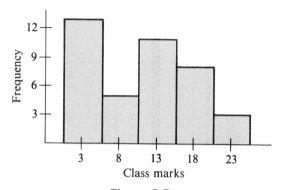

Figure 8.5

If the data are applied to variables such as length, weight, and temperature, which are capable of assuming any value in an interval,* this data can also be recorded in classes. Consider the set of heights of a sample of high school students in Table 8.1. Even though the heights are recorded as whole numbers of inches, it should be recognized that they could represent *any* number in a given interval, and they have been rounded off to the nearest inch.

Since the heights range from a low of 48 inches to a high of 77 inches, the data could be divided into 10 classes, each of which contains a 3-inch interval. The classes and the frequency of scores in each class are given in Table 8.2. Since the heights are measured to the nearest inch, the class containing heights that would round off to 48, 49, or 50 inches extends from 47.5 to 50.5 inches.

The frequency histogram for the data in Table 8.2 is shown in Figure 8.6.

Table 8.1

48	66	63	68	50	51
72	58	68	64	69	56
56	69	77	65	68	63
59	60	74	66	70	64
60	62	59	67	59	63
55	62	69	73	71	64

Table 8.2

Class boundaries	Frequencies
47.5–50.5	2
50.5–53.5	1
53.5–56.5	3
56.5–59.5	4
59.5–62.5	4
62.5–65.5	7
65.5–68.5	6
68.5–71.5	5
71.5–74.5	3
74.5–77.5	1

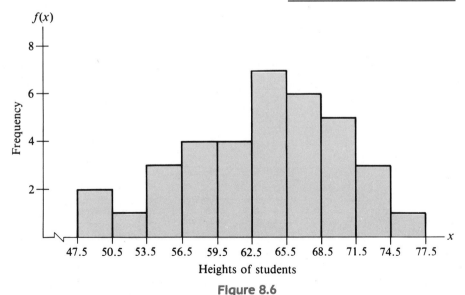

Figure 8.6

*Such a variable is called a **continuous variable**.

Exercise 8.1

Construct a frequency histogram for the data given in the following frequency tables.

1. Score	Frequency
12	2
13	3
14	4
15	3
16	1

2. Score	Frequency
22	1
23	4
24	3
25	2
26	3

3. Score	Frequency
1	3
2	2
3	4
4	1
5	5
6	2

4. Score	Frequency
16	2
17	4
18	3
19	3
20	2
21	4

5.

x	3	4	5	6	7	8	9	10	11	12
$f(x)$	6	0	5	3	4	3	2	1	0	4

6.

x	5	6	8	9	11	12
$f(x)$	3	4	2	7	3	2

7. Interval	Frequency
0–4	1
5–8	0
9–12	2
13–16	3
17–20	1

8. Interval	Frequency
10–14	2
15–19	4
20–24	3
25–29	2
30–34	3

9. Interval	Frequency
20–24	3
25–29	2
30–34	5
35–39	1
40–44	6

10. Interval	Frequency
12–14	2
15–17	4
18–20	3
21–23	5
24–26	3

Construct a frequency histogram for the data in problems 11–16.

11. 3, 2, 5, 6, 3, 2, 6, 5, 4, 2, 1, 6
12. 5, 4, 6, 5, 4, 6, 3, 6, 5, 4, 1, 7
13. 2, 1, 3, 7, 6, 4, 3, 2, 1, 6, 7
14. 14, 15, 14, 15, 15, 16, 18, 17, 16
15. 3, 2, 5, 6, 3, 4, 3, 6
16. 4, 6, 7, 5, 2, 2, 6, 8, 7, 6, 3, 4

17–22. Construct a frequency polygon for the data in each of problems 11–16.

Use the following data for problems 23–26.

$$30, 22, 15, 18, 17, 23, 16, 33, 32, 28$$
$$17, 35, 19, 21, 24, 31, 29, 19, 30, 16$$
$$19, 22, 16, 27, 26, 22, 31, 29, 32, 18$$

23. Construct a frequency histogram with intervals of width 3.
24. Construct a frequency histogram with intervals of width 4.
25. Construct a frequency histogram with four intervals.
26. Construct a frequency histogram with five intervals.

APPLICATIONS

27. Suppose a department store manager has initiated a testing program to determine which employees would make good assistant managers. Use the following table to make a frequency histogram for the classes of scores the employees made on the test.

x	$f(x)$
60–69	9
70–79	10
80–89	12
90–99	3

28. The following table gives the number of hours per week that a group of students study. Construct a frequency histogram for the number of hours.

x(hours)	$f(x)$
$0 \le x < 4$	100
$4 \le x < 8$	250
$8 \le x < 12$	325
$12 \le x < 16$	375
$16 \le x < 20$	300
$20 \le x$	200

29. The following table gives the hours per week worked by students at a given college. Draw a frequency histogram.

x	f(x)
$0 \le x < 6$	5
$6 \le x < 12$	10
$12 \le x < 18$	20
$18 \le x < 24$	10
$24 \le x < 30$	5
$30 \le x < 36$	3
$36 \le x < 42$	2

30. The following table gives the time required for rats to find food in a maze after two successful practice runs. Draw a frequency histogram.

t(min)	f(t)
$0 \le t \le 1$	1
$1 < t \le 2$	3
$2 < t \le 3$	2
$3 < t \le 4$	2
$4 < t \le 5$	1

The data below, used in problems 31 and 32, give the annual income for a sample of residents of a community.

$15,760	$36,400	$27,140
17,340	18,210	60,000
18,210	15,690	14,610
16,410	56,850	17,570
17,570	27,360	24,940
22,300	15,140	35,780
26,320	16,330	11,190
14,790	40,810	72,310
27,560	28,340	22,310
16,800	15,970	32,830

31. Construct a histogram for the incomes using grouped data. Begin the first interval at $9999.50 and use intervals of width $10,000.

32. Construct a histogram for the incomes by beginning with the first interval at $9999.50 and using intervals of width $15,000.

The data on page 411 give the total number of prisoners executed in the United States from 1950 to 1979 and the number of black prisoners executed during the same period. Use this information in problems 33–36. (Source: U.S. Department of Justice, Bureau of Justice Statistics)

Year	Total	Blacks	Year	Total	Blacks	Year	Total	Blacks
1950	82	42	1960	56	35	1970	0	0
1951	105	47	1961	42	22	1971	0	0
1952	83	47	1962	47	19	1972	0	0
1953	62	31	1963	21	8	1973	0	0
1954	81	42	1964	15	7	1974	0	0
1955	76	32	1965	7	1	1975	0	0
1956	65	43	1966	1	0	1976	0	0
1957	65	31	1967	2	1	1977	1	0
1958	49	28	1968	0	0	1978	0	0
1959	49	33	1969	0	0	1979	2	0

33. Construct a histogram for the total number of executions using intervals of length 10.
34. Construct a histogram for the total number of executions each year from 1950 to 1969 using intervals of length 10.
35. Construct a histogram for the number of blacks executed using intervals of length 7.
36. Construct a histogram for the number of blacks executed using 8 intervals.

The following data give the U.S. unemployment rates for selected years from 1948–1980. Use this information in problems 37 and 38. (Source: U.S. Department of Labor, Bureau of Labor Statistics)

Year	Rate	Year	Rate	Year	Rate
1948	3.8%	1963	5.7%	1972	5.6%
1950	5.3	1964	5.2	1973	4.9
1952	3.0	1965	4.5	1974	5.6
1954	5.5	1966	3.8	1975	8.5
1956	4.1	1967	3.8	1976	7.7
1958	6.8	1968	3.6	1977	7.0
1959	5.5	1969	3.5	1978	6.0
1960	5.5	1970	4.9	1979	5.8
1961	6.7	1971	5.9	1980	7.1
1962	5.5				

37. Construct a frequency histogram for the unemployment rates using intervals of length 0.5. Assume the data are discrete.
38. Construct a frequency histogram for the unemployment rates using intervals of length 1.0. Assume the data are discrete.

The following data give U.S. death rates (per 1000 live births) of infants under 28 days of age who were born in selected states and the District of Columbia during 1978. Use this information in problems 39 and 40 on the following page.

11.0	9.6	8.7	12.3	11.4	9.4
9.4	20.2	12.0	10.8	9.2	10.5
9.0	9.3	6.1	7.3	9.0	9.8
10.5	10.3	11.1	9.1	7.7	7.8
7.7	10.9	8.1	8.6	10.5	9.7
6.9	8.6	9.2	9.3	10.6	10.3
9.3	8.9	8.3	10.1	12.4	7.6

39. Construct a frequency histogram for the death rates using intervals of length 2, beginning the first interval at 5.50.
40. Construct a frequency histogram for the death rates using intervals of length 3, beginning the first interval at 5.50.

8.2 Measures of Central Tendency

Objectives
- ☐ To find the mode of a set of scores (numbers)
- ☐ To find the median of a set of scores
- ☐ To find the mean of a set of scores

A set of data can be described by listing all the scores or by drawing a frequency histogram. But we often wish to describe a set of scores by giving the *average score* or the typical score in the set. There are three types of measures that are called "averages," or measures of central tendency. They are the **mode,** the **median,** and the **mean.**

To determine what value represents the most "typical" score in a set of scores, we use the mode of the scores.

> The **mode** of a set of scores is the score that occurs most frequently.

That is, the mode is the most popular score, the one that is most likely to occur. The mode can be readily determined from a frequency table or frequency histogram because it is determined according to the frequency of the scores.

EXAMPLE 1   Find the mode of the following scores: 10, 4, 3, 6, 4, 2, 3, 4, 5, 6, 8, 10, 2, 1, 4, 3.

Solution   The mode is 4, since it occurs more frequently than any other score.

EXAMPLE 2   Determine the mode of the scores shown in the histogram in Figure 8.7.

Solution   The most frequent score, as observed from the histogram, is 2.

EXAMPLE 3   Find the mode of the following scores: 4, 3, 2, 4, 6, 5, 5, 7, 6, 5, 7, 3, 1, 7, 2.

Solution   Both 5 and 7 occur three times. Thus they are both modes. This set of data is said to be *bimodal* because it has two modes.

Although the mode of a set of scores tells us the most frequent score, it does not always represent the typical performance, or central tendency, of the set of

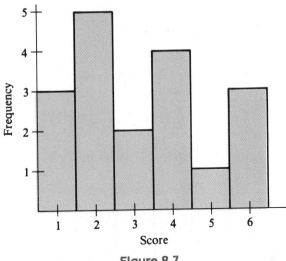

Figure 8.7

scores. For example, the scores 2, 3, 3, 3, 5, 8, 9, 10, 13 have a mode of 3. But 3 is not a good measure of central tendency for this set of scores, for it is nowhere near the middle of the distribution.

One value that gives a better measure of central tendency is the **median.**

> The **median** is the score or point above and below which an equal number of the scores lie.

It is the middle of the distribution of scores. If there is an odd number of scores, we find the median by ranking the scores from smallest to largest and picking the middle score. That score will be the median.

EXAMPLE 4 Find the median of the following scores: 2, 3, 16, 5, 15, 38, 18, 17, 12.

Solution We rank the scores from smallest to largest: 2, 3, 5, 12, 15, 16, 17, 18, 38. The median is the middle score, which is 15. Note that there are 4 scores above and 4 below 15.

EXAMPLE 5 Find the median of the following numbers: 3.1, 2.8, 6.1, 5.4, 2.7, 8.1, 3.2.

Solution The ranking from smallest to largest is 2.7, 2.8, 3.1, 3.2, 5.4, 6.1, 8.1. The median is 3.2.

If the number of scores is even, there will be no middle score when the scores are ranked, so the *median* is the point that is the *average of the two middle scores*.

EXAMPLE 6   Find the median of the following scores: 3, 2, 6, 8, 12, 4, 3, 2, 1, 6.

Solution   We rank the scores from smallest to largest: 1, 2, 2, 3, 3, 4, 6, 6, 8, 12. The two scores that lie in the middle of the distribution are 3 and 4. Thus the median is a point that is midway between 3 and 4; that is, it is the arithmetic average of 3 and 4. The median is

$$\frac{3 + 4}{2} = \frac{7}{2} = 3.5.$$

In this case we say the median is a point because there is no *score* that is 3.5.

It sometimes happens that when the number of scores is even, we find that the two middle scores (after ranking) are the same. When this happens, the median is the value of the two scores.

EXAMPLE 7   Find the median of the following numbers: 2, 3, 6, 7, 4, 6, 8, 3, 7, 8.

Solution   The ranking is 2, 3, 3, 4, 6, 6, 7, 7, 8, 8. The two middle scores are both 6, so the median is 6.

The median is the most easily interpreted measure of central tendency, and it is the best indicator of central tendency when the set of scores contains a few extreme values. However, the most frequently used measure of central tendency is the mean.

> The **mean** of a set of scores is the arithmetic average of the scores.
>
> $$\text{Mean} = \frac{\text{sum of scores}}{\text{number of scores}}$$

The mean is used most often as a measure of central tendency because it is more useful than the median in the general applications of statistics.

The symbol $\bar{x}$ is used to represent the mean of a set of scores in a sample. The expression Σx means the sum of all x's, or in other words, the sum of all the scores. Thus, if n is the number of scores, we can write the formula for the mean as

$$\bar{x} = \frac{\Sigma x}{n}.$$

EXAMPLE 8   Find the mean of the following numbers: 12, 8, 7, 10, 6, 14, 7, 6, 12, 9.

Solution $$\bar{x} = \frac{\Sigma x}{10} = \frac{12 + 8 + 7 + 10 + 6 + 14 + 7 + 6 + 12 + 9}{10}$$

So $\bar{x} = 91/10 = 9.1$.

Note that the mean need not be one of the numbers (scores) given.

EXAMPLE 9   Find the mean of the following numbers: 2.1, 6.3, 7.1, 4.8, 3.2.

Solution
$$\bar{x} = \frac{\Sigma x}{5} = \frac{2.1 + 6.3 + 7.1 + 4.8 + 3.2}{5}$$

So $\bar{x} = 23.5/5 = 4.7$

Any of the three measures of central tendency (mode, median, mean) may be referred to as an average. The measure of central tendency that should be used with data depends on the purpose for which the data were collected. The mode is the number that occurs with the greatest frequency. It is used if we want the most popular value. For example, the mode salary for a company is the salary that is received by most of the employees of the company. The median salary for the company is the salary that falls in the middle of the distribution. The mean salary is the arithmetic average of the salaries. It is quite possible that the mode, median, and mean salaries for a company will be different. Figure 8.8 illustrates how the mode, median, and mean salaries might look for a company.

Payroll of Ace Cap Company

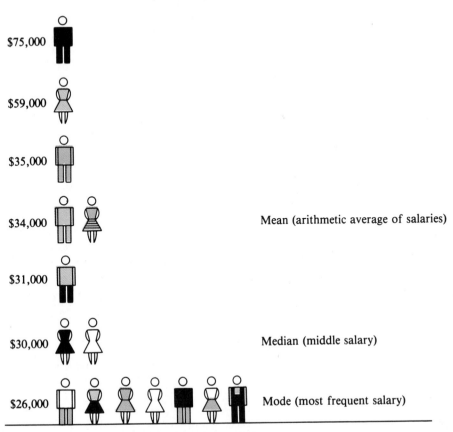

$75,000

$59,000

$35,000

$34,000   Mean (arithmetic average of salaries)

$31,000

$30,000   Median (middle salary)

$26,000   Mode (most frequent salary)

Figure 8.8

Which of the three measures represents the "average" salary? To say the average salary is $34,000 (the mean) helps conceal two things: the bosses' (or owners') very large salaries ($75,000 and $59,000), and the laborers' very small salaries ($26,000). The mode tells us more: The most common salary in this company is $26,000. The median gives us more information about these salaries than any other single figure. It tells us that if the salaries are ranked from lowest to highest, then the salary that lies in the middle is $30,000.

Because any of the three measures may be referred to as the average of a set of data, we must be careful to avoid being misled. The owner of the Ace Cap Company will probably state that the average salary for his company is $34,000 because it makes it appear that he pays high salaries. The local union president will likely claim that the mode ($26,000) is the "average" salary. Advertising agencies may also make use of an "average" that will make their product appear in the best light. We run the danger of being misled if we do not know which average is being cited.

One reason that we may be misled concerning these three measures is that they frequently fall very close to each other, as we shall see in more detail later. Also, since the mean is the most frequently used, we tend to associate it with the word *average*. In fact the mean can be extremely useful if we also have information about how the data vary about the mean. We will discuss measures of variation about the mean in Section 8.3.

If data are given in a frequency table, like

x	1	2	3	4
f	3	1	4	2

we can find the mean $\bar{x}$ by using

$$\bar{x} = \frac{\Sigma x}{n},$$

where 1 is added 3 times, 2 is added once, 3 is added 4 times, and 4 is added twice. Or we can use $\Sigma(x \cdot f)$ and $n = \Sigma f$, so

$$\bar{x} = \frac{\Sigma(x \cdot f)}{\Sigma f},$$

where each value of x is used once.

The mean for the frequency table above is

$$\bar{x} = \frac{1 \cdot 3 + 2 \cdot 1 + 3 \cdot 4 + 4 \cdot 2}{3 + 1 + 4 + 2} = 2.5.$$

EXAMPLE 10   Find the mean of the test scores for a math class.

Scores	Class marks	Frequencies
40–49	44.5	2
50–59	54.5	0
60–69	64.5	6
70–79	74.5	12
80–89	84.5	8
90–99	94.5	2

Solution   For the purpose of finding the mean of interval data, we assume that all scores within an interval are represented by the class mark. Thus

$$\bar{x} = \frac{(44.5)(2) + (54.5)(0) + (64.5)(6) + (74.5)(12) + (84.5)(8) + (94.5)(2)}{30}$$

$$= 74.5$$

Exercise 8.2

Find the modes of the following sets of scores.

1. 3, 4, 3, 2, 2, 3, 5, 7, 6, 2, 3
2. 5, 8, 10, 12, 5, 4, 6, 3, 5
3. 14, 17, 13, 16, 15, 12, 13, 12, 13
4. 38, 37, 36, 32, 34, 32, 33, 37, 31
5. 22, 23, 25, 26, 28, 32, 12

Find the modes of the scores shown in the following histograms.

6.

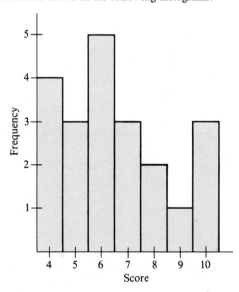

7.

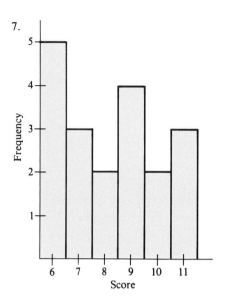

8.

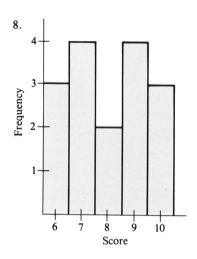

9.

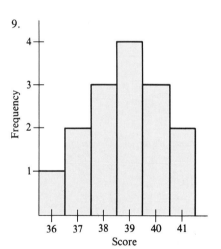

10.

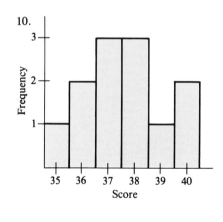

Find the medians of the following sets of scores.

11. 1, 3, 6, 7, 5

12. 2, 1, 3, 4, 2, 1, 2

13. 4, 7, 9, 18, 36, 14, 12

14. 1, 0, 2, 1, 1, 0, 2, 14, 37

15. 6, 7, 8, 4, 3, 6, 8, 2, 1

16. 2, 3, 4, 2, 8, 6, 2, 3

17. 2, 12, 17, 5, 8, 9, 10, 4

18. 1, 3, 2, 4, 4, 9, 10, 12

19. 2, 10, 6, 8, 13, 1, 4, 6

20. 1, 2, 4, 3, 6, 5, 10, 9, 13, 17, 46, 0

Find the mean of the following sets of numbers.

21. 3, 5, 7, 1, 2, 6, 8, 0

22. 9, 10, 8, 7, 5, 13, 11

23. 13, 14, 15, 16, 17, 12, 11

Find the mode, median, and mean of the following scores.

24. 5, 7, 7, 7, 9, 12, 4
25. 3, 2, 1, 6, 8, 12, 14, 2
26. 5, 8, 7, 6, 1, 1, 31
27. 14, 17, 20, 31, 17, 42
28. 3.2, 3.2, 3.5, 3.7, 3.4
29. 2.8, 6.4, 5.3, 5.3, 6.8
30. 1.14, 2.28, 7.58, 6.32, 5.17

In problems 31–38, find the mean.

31.

x	3	4	5	6	7
f	2	4	8	4	2

32.

x	42	43	44	45	46	47	48	49
f	1	2	6	4	8	8	0	1

33.

x	50	100	150	200	250	300
f	12	8	6	4	3	2

34.

x	−3	−2	−1	0	1	2	3
f	1	4	9	15	9	4	1

35.

Scores	Class marks	Frequencies
1–5	3	3
6–10	8	5
11–15	13	8
16–20	18	4
21–25	23	10

36.

Scores	Class marks	Frequencies
100 –110	105	2
111 –121	116	1
122 –132	127	5
133 –143	138	12
144 –154	149	9
155 –165	160	1

37.

Scores	Frequencies
1–3	8
4–6	1
7–9	19
10–12	19
13–15	3

38.

Scores	Frequencies
10,000–19,999	22
20,000–29,999	58
30,000–39,999	104
40,000–49,999	16

APPLICATIONS

39. Suppose a company has 10 employees, 1 earning $80,000, 1 earning $60,000, 2 earning $30,000, 1 earning $20,000, and 5 earning $16,000.
    (a) What is the mean salary for the company?
    (b) What is the median salary?
    (c) What is the mode of the salaries?

40. A taxi company tests a new brand of tires by putting a set of four on each of three taxis. The following table indicates the number of miles the tires lasted. What is the mean number of miles the tires lasted?

Number of miles	Number of tires
15,000	4
16,000	2
17,000	3
18,000	2
19,000	1

Problems 41–43: Suppose you live in a neighborhood with a few expensive homes and many modest homes.

41. If you wanted to impress people with the neighborhood where you lived, which measure would you give as the "average" property value?

42. Which "average" would you cite to the property tax committee if you wanted to convince them that property values aren't very high in your neighborhood?

43. What measure of central tendency would give the most representative "average" property value for your neighborhood?

44. The IQ scores for a class of 30 eighth grade students are given in the table that follows. Find the mean IQ for this class.

Scores	Frequencies
86–90	1
91–95	0
96–100	3
101–105	5
106–110	10
111–115	4
116–120	5
121–125	1
126–130	1

45. In a study of 225 students requiring treatment at a college infirmary, the following data on pulse rates were obtained. Find the mean for the data.

Pulse rates	Frequencies
56–60	1
61–65	4
66–70	23
71–75	56
76–80	76
81–85	34
86–90	17
91–95	9
96–100	2
101–105	3

46. S & S Printing has 15 employees and 5 job classifications. Position and wages for these employees are given in the table.

Job	Number in job	Weekly salary
Supervisor	1	$800
Printers	8	320
Camera-Darkroom	3	500
Secretaries	2	360
Delivery	1	420

(a) What is the mean salary per job classification?

(b) What is the mean salary per person?

8.3 Measures of Variation

Objectives
☐ To find the range of a set of data
☐ To find the variance and standard deviation

Although the mean of a set of data is useful in locating the center of the distribution of the data, it doesn't tell us as much about the distribution as we might think at first. For example, a basketball coach will not be satisfied knowing the mean height of an opposing team. If the mean height of the opposing team is 6 ft, that could mean that every player is 6 ft tall or it could mean that one player is 6 ft tall, two players are 5 ft tall, and two players are 7 ft tall. These two possible teams are quite different. The difference in the distribution of the heights of these teams is not the mean height, but how the heights *vary* from the mean.

One measure of how a distribution varies is the range of the distribution.

> The **range** of a set of numbers is the difference between the largest and smallest numbers in the set.

Consider the following set of heights of a basketball team, in inches: 69, 70, 75, 69, 73, 78, 74, 73, 78, 71. The range of this set of heights is $78 - 69 = 9$ inches.

Note that the range of this set of heights is determined by only two numbers, and does not give any information about how the other heights vary.

If we calculated the deviation of each score from the mean and then attempted to average the deviations, we would immediately see that the deviations add to 0. In an effort to find a meaningful measure of dispersion about the mean, statisticians developed the **variance,** which squares the deviations (to make them all positive) and then averages the squared deviations.

Frequently we do not have all the data for a population and must use a sample of these data. To estimate the variance of a population from a sample, statisticians compensate for the fact that there is usually less variability in a sample than in the population itself by summing the squared deviations and dividing them by $n - 1$ rather than averaging them.

To get a measure comparable to the original deviations before they were squared, the **standard deviation,** which is the square root of the variance, was introduced. The formulas for the variance and standard deviation of sample data follow.

> $$\textit{Variance} \qquad s^2 = \frac{\Sigma(x - \bar{x})^2}{n - 1}$$
>
> $$\textit{Standard Deviation} \qquad s = \sqrt{\frac{\Sigma(x - \bar{x})^2}{n - 1}}$$

The standard deviation is a measure of the concentration of the scores about their mean. The smaller the standard deviation, the closer the scores lie to the mean. For example, the histograms in Figure 8.9 describe two sets of data with the same means and the same ranges. From looking at the histograms we see that more of the data are concentrated about the mean $\bar{x} = 4$ in Figure 8.9(b) than in Figure 8.9(a). We will see that the standard deviation is smaller for the data in 8.9(b) than in Figure 8.9(a).

The standard deviation for sample data is found using the following procedure.

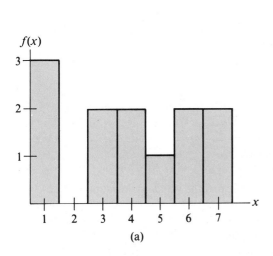

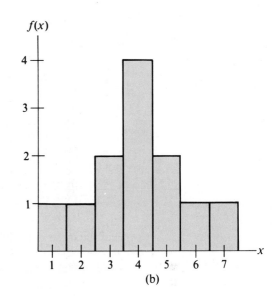

(a)   (b)

Figure 8.9

Procedure	Example
To find the standard deviation of a set of scores:	Find the standard deviation of the scores 4, 6, 8, 9, 3.

1. Find the mean of the scores.

1. $\bar{x} = \dfrac{30}{5} = 6$

2. Calculate the deviation of the scores from the mean by subtracting the mean from each score.

2. $4 - 6 = -2$, $6 - 6 = 0$, $8 - 6 = 2$, $9 - 6 = 3$, $3 - 6 = -3$

3. Square each of these deviations, and add them.

3. $\Sigma(x - \bar{x})^2 = (-2)^2 + 0^2 + 2^2 + 3^2 + (-3)^2$
    $= 4 + 0 + 4 + 9 + 9 = 26$

4. Divide $\Sigma(x - \bar{x})^2$ (from step 3) by $n - 1$, where n is the number of scores. This number is called the **variance** of the scores and is denoted by s^2.

4. $\dfrac{\Sigma(x - \bar{x})^2}{n - 1} = \dfrac{26}{4} = 6.5$, so $s^2 = 6.5$.

5. Take the square root of s^2 (from step 4). This is the **standard deviation,** denoted by s.

5. $s = \sqrt{6.5} = 2.55$.

EXAMPLE 1　Find the mean, variance, and standard deviation of the following: 13, 15, 18, 16, 14, 17, 19.

Solution　1. $\bar{x} = \dfrac{\Sigma x}{n} = \dfrac{112}{7} = 16$

2. $13 - 16 = -3$, $15 - 16 = -1$, $18 - 16 = 2$, $16 - 16 = 0$, $14 - 16 = -2$, $17 - 16 = 1$, $19 - 16 = 3$.

3. $\Sigma(x - \bar{x})^2 = 9 + 1 + 4 + 0 + 4 + 1 + 9 = 28$

4. $s^2 = \dfrac{\Sigma(x - \bar{x})^2}{n - 1} = \dfrac{28}{6} = 4.67$

5. $s = \sqrt{\dfrac{\Sigma(x - \bar{x})^2}{n - 1}} = \sqrt{4.67} = 2.16$

Thus the mean is 16, the variance is 4.67, and the standard deviation is 2.16.

EXAMPLE 2　Figure 8.9(a) is the histogram for the set of data 1, 1, 1, 3, 3, 4, 4, 5, 6, 6, 7, 7. Figure 8.9(b) is the histogram for the data 1, 2, 3, 3, 4, 4, 4, 4, 5, 5, 6, 7. Both sets of data have a range of 6 and a mean of 4. Find their standard deviations.

Solution　For the data of Figure 8.9(a), we have

$\Sigma(x - \bar{x})^2 = (-3)^2 + (-3)^2 + (-3)^2 + (-1)^2 + (-1)^2 + 0^2 + 0^2 + 1^2 + 2^2 + 2^2 + 3^2 + 3^2$

$= 9 + 9 + 9 + 1 + 1 + 0 + 0 + 1 + 4 + 4 + 9 + 9 = 56$

$s^2 = \dfrac{\Sigma(x - \bar{x})^2}{n - 1} = \dfrac{56}{11} = 5.0909$

$s = \sqrt{s^2} = \sqrt{5.0909} = 2.26$

For the data of Figure 8.9(b), we have

$\Sigma(x - \bar{x})^2 = (-3)^2 + (-2)^2 + (-1)^2 + (-1)^2 + 0^2 + 0^2 + 0^2 + 0^2 + 1^2 + 1^2 + 2^2 + 3^2$

$= 9 + 4 + 1 + 1 + 0 + 0 + 0 + 0 + 1 + 1 + 4 + 9 = 30$

$s^2 = \dfrac{30}{11} = 2.7273$

$s = \sqrt{\dfrac{30}{11}} = 1.65$

When a large number of scores is available, the data are usually presented in a frequency table rather than a listing of the scores. We can also use the frequencies with which the scores occur to compute the mean and standard deviation, using the formulas

$$\bar{x} = \frac{\Sigma[x \cdot f(x)]}{n} \quad \text{and} \quad s = \sqrt{\frac{\Sigma[(x - \bar{x})^2 \cdot f(x)]}{n - 1}},$$

where $f(x)$ represents the frequency of the score x. For data in a frequency table, we often write the standard deviation formula using $f = f(x)$ and $\Sigma f = n$.

$$s = \sqrt{\frac{\Sigma[(x - \bar{x})^2 \cdot f]}{\Sigma f - 1}}$$

EXAMPLE 3   Suppose the IQ scores of 20 people working for a company are measured and given by the following table. Find the mean and standard deviation of the IQ for this group.

x	$f(x)$
98	3
105	7
110	2
115	2
120	2
121	1
125	1
130	1
145	1

Solution $\bar{x} = \dfrac{98(3) + 105(7) + 110(2) + 115(2) + 120(2) + 121(1) + 125(1) + 130(1) + 145(1)}{20}$

$= 112$

$s^2 = \dfrac{(-14)^2(3) + (-7)^2(7) + (-2)^2(2) + (3)^2(2) + 8^2(2) + 9^2(1) + 13^2(1) + 18^2(1) + 33^2(1)}{19}$

$= 144.6316$

$s = \sqrt{144.6316} = 12.03$

The calculations performed in Example 3 are routine but tedious, even with the aid of a hand calculator. However, many calculators have statistics functions built in, so that calculation of means and standard deviations can be done by simply entering the data. Consult your calculator manual for details.

If the data in the frequency table are grouped into classes, the class mark is used for x in the formula.

EXAMPLE 4   Find the standard deviation for the data of Example 10, Section 8.2.

Solution   Using the table and mean $\bar{x} = 74.5$ from Example 10 of Section 8.2 and adding columns for $x - \bar{x}$, $(x - \bar{x})^2$, and $(x - \bar{x})^2 \cdot f$, we have the following table.

Scores	Class marks x	Frequencies f	$x - \bar{x}$	$(x - \bar{x})^2$	$(x - \bar{x})^2 \cdot f$
40–49	44.5	2	−30	900	1800
50–59	54.5	0	−20	400	0
60–69	64.5	6	−10	100	600
70–79	74.5	12	0	0	0
80–89	84.5	8	10	100	800
90–99	94.5	2	20	400	800
Totals		30			4000

Using the formula gives

$$s = \sqrt{\frac{\Sigma(x - \bar{x})^2 \cdot f}{\Sigma f - 1}} = \sqrt{\frac{4000}{29}}$$
$$= \sqrt{137.93} = 11.74.$$

Exercise 8.3

In problems 1–4, find the range of the set of numbers given.

1. 3, 5, 7, 8, 2, 11, 6, 5
2. 5, 1, 3, 1.4, 6.3, 8
3. −1, 2, 4, 3, 6, 11, −3, 4, 2
4. 2, 3, 3, 3, 3, 3, 9

Find the mean, variance, and standard deviation of the following sets of data.

5. 5, 7, 1, 3, 0, 8, 6, 2
6. 7, 13, 5, 11, 8, 10, 9
7. 11, 12, 13, 14, 15, 16, 17
8. 4, 3, 6, 7, 8, 9, 12
9. 1, 2, 2, 3, 6, 8, 12, 14
10. 3.1, 3.2, 3.4, 3.6, 3.7
11. 8, 3, 5, 6, 8, 10, 13, 11
12. 2, 3, 5, 6, 8, 4, 2, 2

In problems 13–18, find the mean and standard deviation of the data in the tables.

13.

x	1	2	3	4	5
$f(x)$	3	1	4	2	1

14.

x	3	4	5	6	8
$f(x)$	1	3	4	1	3

15.

x	3	5	7	9	11
$f(x)$	1	0	3	2	6

16.

x	5	8	11	14	17
$f(x)$	3	2	5	4	2

17.

x	3	4	5	6	7	8	9	10	11	12
$f(x)$	6	0	5	3	4	3	2	1	0	4

18.	x	5	6	7	8	9	10	11	12	13	14	15
	$f(x)$	3	2	1	0	2	5	3	1	2	4	6

In problems 19–24, find the standard deviations. The mean for each set is given following the table.

19.

x	3	4	5	6	7
f	2	4	8	4	2

$\bar{x} = 5$

20.

x	42	43	44	45	46	47	48	49
f	1	2	6	4	8	8	0	1

$\bar{x} = 45.5$

21.

x	-3	-2	-1	0	1	2	3
f	1	4	9	15	9	4	1

$\bar{x} = 0$

22.

x	50	100	150	200	250	300
f	12	8	6	4	3	2

$\bar{x} = 127.14$

23.

Scores	Class marks	Frequencies
1–5	3	3
6–10	8	5
11–15	13	8
16–20	18	4
21–25	23	10

$\bar{x} = 15.2$

24.

Scores	Class marks	Frequencies
100–110	105	2
111–121	116	1
122–132	127	5
133–143	138	12
144–154	149	9
155–165	160	1

$\bar{x} = 137.3$

APPLICATIONS

25. A new car with a $9000 list price can be bought for different prices from different dealers. In one city the car can be bought for $8200 from 2 dealers, $8000 from 1 dealer, $7800 from 3 dealers, $7600 from 2 dealers, and $7500 from 2 dealers. What is the mean and standard deviation of the car prices?

26. The birth weights (in kilograms) of 160 children are given in the following table. Find the mean and standard deviation of the weights.

Weights (kg)	Frequencies
2.0	4
2.3	12
2.6	20
2.9	26
3.2	20
3.5	26
3.8	20
4.1	16
4.4	10
4.7	6

27. The following table gives the number of games $f(x)$ in which a baseball team had x hits. Find the mean number of hits they had per game, and the standard deviation.

x	$f(x)$
2	2
3	4
4	0
6	7
7	2
8	3
12	2

28. The fish commission recorded the weights (in pounds) of the fish caught in a lake. Find the mean and standard deviation of these weights, given in the table.

$x(lb)$	$f(x)$
1	3
2	3
3	5
4	2
5	2
6	3
10	2

29. A small company has the following salaries for its 10 employees.

Number	1	1	2	1	5
Salary	80,000	60,000	30,000	20,000	16,000

Find the mean and standard deviation of the salaries for the company.

30. A company tested a sample of a brand of tires and found the number of miles the tires lasted as follows.

Number of tires	4	2	5	1
Number of miles	16,000	18,000	20,000	22,000

Find the mean and standard deviation of the number of miles the tires lasted.

31. In a study of 225 students requiring treatment at a college infirmary, the following data on pulse rates were obtained. The mean pulse rate for this group is 78; find the standard deviation.

Pulse rates	Frequencies
56–60	1
61–65	4
66–70	23
71–75	56
76–80	76
81–85	34
86–90	17
91–95	9
96–100	2
101–105	3

8.4 Binomial Trials

Objective ☐ To solve probability problems related to binomial experiments

Suppose you have a coin that is biased so that when the coin is tossed the probability of getting a head is 2/3 and the probability of getting a tail is 1/3. What is the probability of tossing 2 heads in 3 tosses of this coin?

If the question were, What is the probability that the first two tosses will be heads and the third will be tails?, the answer would be

$$\text{Pr(HHT)} = \frac{2}{3} \cdot \frac{2}{3} \cdot \frac{1}{3} = \frac{4}{27}.$$

However, the original question did not specify the order, so we must consider other orders that will give us 2 heads and 1 tail. We can use a tree to find all the possibilities

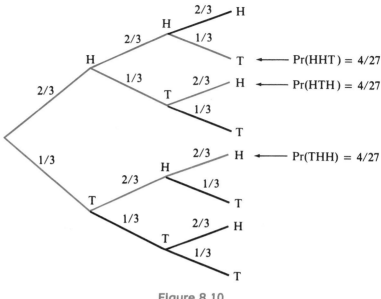

Figure 8.10

(see Figure 8.10). We can see that there are 3 paths through the tree, which correspond to 2 heads and 1 tail in 3 tosses. Since the probability for each successful path is 4/27,

$$Pr(2 \text{ H's and 1 T}) = 3 \cdot \frac{4}{27} = \frac{4}{9}.$$

In this problem we can find the probability of 2 heads in 3 tosses by finding the probability for any one path of the tree (like HHT) and then multiplying that probability by the number of paths that result in 2 heads. We can also determine how many ways 2 heads and 1 tail can result by considering the 3 blanks below:

_____   _____   _____

The number of ways we can pick 2 blanks (for the 2 heads) from the 3 blanks will be equivalent to the number of paths that result in 2 heads. But the number of ways we can select 2 blanks from the 3 blanks is $_3C_2 = \binom{3}{2}$. Thus the probability of 2 heads resulting in 3 tosses is

$$Pr(2 \text{ H's and 1 T}) = \binom{3}{2}\frac{2}{3} \cdot \frac{2}{3} \cdot \frac{1}{3} = \binom{3}{2}\left(\frac{2}{3}\right)^2\left(\frac{1}{3}\right)^1 = \frac{4}{9}.$$

The experiment discussed above (tossing a coin 3 times) is an example of a general class of experiments called **binomial probability experiments.** These experiments are also called **Bernoulli experiments,** or **Bernoulli trials,** after the eighteenth-century mathematician Jacob Bernoulli.

A **binomial probability experiment** satisfies the following properties:

1. There are n repeated trials of the experiment.
2. Each trial results in one of two outcomes, with one denoted success (S) and the other failure (F).
3. The trials are independent, with the probability of success, p, the same for every trial. The probability of failure is $q = 1 - p$ for every trial.
4. The probability of x successes in n trials is

$$Pr(x) = \binom{n}{x} p^x q^{n-x}.$$

$Pr(x)$ is called a **binomial probability.**

EXAMPLE 1   If a die is rolled 4 times and the number of times a 6 results is recorded,
(a) is the experiment a binomial experiment?
(b) what is the probability that three 6's will result?

Solution   (a) Yes. There are 4 trials, resulting in success (a 6) or failure (not a 6). The result of each roll is independent of previous rolls; the probability of success on each roll is 1/6.

(b)
$$Pr(\text{three 6's}) = \binom{4}{3}\left(\frac{1}{6}\right)^3\left(\frac{5}{6}\right)^1 = \frac{4!}{1!3!}\left(\frac{1}{216}\right)\left(\frac{5}{6}\right) = \frac{5}{324}$$

EXAMPLE 2   Suppose it has been determined with probability .1 that any child born in a specific area (near a chemical dump) will have a birth defect. If 5 children are born during a given month,
(a) what is the probability that 2 of them will have a birth defect?
(b) what is the probability that *at least* 2 of them will have a birth defect?

Solution   (a) Note that we may consider a child having a birth defect as a success for this problem even though it is certainly not true in reality. Each of the 5 births is independent with probability of success $p = .1$ and probability of failure $q = .9$. Therefore the experiment is a binomial experiment, and

$$Pr(2) = \binom{5}{2}(.1)^2(.9)^3$$

$$= \frac{5!}{3!2!}(.01)(.729)$$

$$= .0729.$$

(b) The probability of at least 2 of the children having a birth defect is

$$Pr(2) + Pr(3) + Pr(4) + Pr(5)$$

$$= \binom{5}{2}(.1)^2(.9)^3 + \binom{5}{3}(.1)^3(.9)^2 + \binom{5}{4}(.1)^4(.9)^1 + \binom{5}{5}(.1)^5(.9)^0$$

$$= .0729 + .0081 + .00045 + .00001$$

$$= .08146.$$

EXAMPLE 3   A manufacturer of motorcycle parts guarantees that a box of 24 parts will contain at most one defective part. If the records show that the manufacturer's machines produce 1% defective parts, what is the probability that a box of parts will satisfy the guarantee?

Solution   The problem is a binomial experiment problem with $n = 24$ and (considering getting a defective part as a success) $p = .01$. Then the probability the manufacturer will have no more than 1 defective part in a box is

$$Pr(x \le 1) = Pr(0) + Pr(1) = \binom{24}{0}(.01)^0(.99)^{24} + \binom{24}{1}(.01)^1(.99)^{23}$$

$$= 1(1)(.7857) + 24(.01)(.7936) = .9762.$$

Exercise 8.4

1. If the probability of success on each trial of an experiment is .3, what is the probability of 4 successes in 6 independent trials?
2. If the probability of success on each trial of an experiment is .4, what is the probability of 5 successes in 8 trials?
3. Suppose a fair coin is tossed 6 times. What is the probability that
   (a) 6 heads will occur?   (b) 3 heads will occur?   (c) 2 heads will occur?
4. If a fair die is rolled 3 times, what is the probability that
   (a) a 5 will result 2 times out of the 3 rolls?
   (b) an odd number will result 2 times?
   (c) a number divisible by 3 will occur 3 times?
5. Suppose a fair die is rolled 12 times. What is the probability that 5 "aces" (1's) will occur?
6. In problem 5, what is the probability that no aces will occur?
7. A bag contains 6 red balls and 4 black balls. If we draw 5 balls, with each one replaced before the next is drawn,
   (a) what is the probability that 2 balls drawn will be red?
   (b) what is the probability that 5 black balls will be drawn?
   (c) what is the probability that at least 3 black balls will be drawn?

8. A bag contains 6 red balls and 4 black balls. If we draw 5 balls, with each one replaced before the next is drawn, what is the probability that at least 2 balls drawn will be red?

9. Suppose a pair of dice is thrown 4 times. What is the probability that a sum of 9 occurs exactly 2 times?

10. If a pair of dice is thrown 4 times, find the probability that a sum of 7 occurs at least 3 times.

11. Suppose the probability that a marksman will hit a target each time he shoots is .85. If he fires 10 shots at a target, what is the probability he will hit it 8 times?

12. The probability that a sharpshooter will hit a target each time he shoots is .98. What is the probability that he will hit the target 10 times in 10 shots?

APPLICATIONS

13. A family has 4 children. If the probability that each child is a girl is .5, what is the probability that
    (a) half of the children are girls?
    (b) all of the children are girls?

14. A multiple choice test has 10 questions and 5 choices for each question. If a student is totally unprepared and guesses on each question, what is the probability that
    (a) she will answer every question correctly?
    (b) she will answer half of the questions correctly?

15. The manager of a store buys portable radios in lots of 12. Suppose that, on the average, 2 out of each group of 12 are defective. If the manager randomly selects 4 radios out of the group to test,
    (a) what is the probability that he will find 2 defective radios?
    (b) what is the probability he will find no defective radios?

16. A hospital buys thermometers in lots of 1000. On the average, one out of 1000 is defective. If 10 are selected from one lot, what is the probability that none is defective?

17. If the probability that a certain couple will have a blue-eyed child is 1/4 and they have 4 children, what is the probability that
    (a) 1 of their children has blue eyes?
    (b) 2 of their children have blue eyes?
    (c) none of their children has blue eyes?

18. If the probability that a certain couple will have a blue-eyed child is 1/2, and they have 4 children, what is the probability that
    (a) none of the children has blue eyes?
    (b) at least 1 child has blue eyes?

19. Suppose that 10% of the patients having a certain disease die from it. If 5 patients have the disease, what is the probability that
    (a) exactly 2 patients will die from it?
    (b) no patients will die from it?
    (c) no more than 2 patients will die from it?

20. In a certain school district, 3% of the faculty use none of their sick days in a school year. Find the probability that 5 faculty members selected at random used no sick days in a given year.

21. If the ratio of boys born to girls born is 105 to 100, and if 6 children are born in a certain hospital in a day, what is the probability that 4 of them are boys?

22. It has been determined empirically that the probability that a given cell will survive for a given period of time is .4. Find the probability that 3 out of 6 of these cells will survive for this period of time?

23. If records indicate that 4 houses out of 1000 are expected to be damaged by fire in any year, what is the probability that a woman owning 10 houses will have fire damage in 2 of them in a year?

24. Suppose 4 rats are placed in a T-maze in which they must turn right or left. If each rat makes a choice by chance, what is the probability that 2 of the rats will turn to the right?

25. A baseball player has a lifetime batting average of .300. If he comes to bat 5 times in a given game, what is the probability that
    (a) he will get 3 hits?
    (b) he will get more than 3 hits?

26. If the probability of an automobile part being defective is .02, find the probability of getting exactly 3 defective parts in a sample of 12.

27. A company produces shotgun shells in batches of 300. A sample of 10 is tested from each batch, and if more than one defect is found, the entire batch is tested. If 1% of the shells are actually defective,
    (a) what is the probability of 0 defective shells in the sample?
    (b) what is the probability of 1 defective shell?
    (c) what is the probability of more than 1 defective shell?

28. A baseball pitching machine throws a bad pitch with probability .1. What is the probability that the machine will throw 5 or fewer bad pitches out of 20 pitches? (Set up only.)

29. A quiz consists of 10 multiple choice questions with 5 choices for each question. Suppose a student is sure of the first 5 answers and has each of the last 5 questions narrowed to 3 of the possible 5 choices. If the student guesses among the narrowed choices on the last 5 questions, find
    (a) the probability of passing the quiz (getting at least 60%)?
    (b) the probability of getting at least a B (at least 80%)?

30. In a certain community, 10% of the population is Jewish. A study shows that of 7 social service agencies, 4 have board presidents that are Jewish. Find the probability that this could happen by chance.

31. Suppose the probability of suicide among a certain age group is .003. If a randomly selected group of 100 Indians within this age group had no suicides, find the probability of this occurring by chance.

8.5 The Binomial Distribution

Objectives   ☐ To find the mean and standard deviation of a binomial distribution
            ☐ To graph a binomial distribution
            ☐ To expand a binomial to a power, using the binomial formula

One probability distribution that is worthy of special study is the **binomial probability distribution,** defined as follows.

> If x is a variable that assumes the values $0, 1, 2, \ldots, r, \ldots, n$ with probabilities $\binom{n}{0}p^0q^n$, $\binom{n}{1}p^1q^{n-1}$, $\binom{n}{2}p^2q^{n-2}, \ldots, \binom{n}{r}p^rq^{n-r}, \ldots, \binom{n}{n}p^nq^0$, respectively, then x is called a **binomial variable.**
>
> The values of x and their corresponding probabilities described above form the **binomial probability distribution.**

The values of x correspond to the number of successes in the binomial trials and the probabilities are calculated using the methods of the previous section.

For example, suppose a fair coin is tossed 6 times and x represents the number of heads. Then Table 8.3 gives all possible outcomes and their probabilities; that is, Table 8.3 gives the theoretical binomial distribution for the experiment.

Table 8.3

x	0	1	2	3	4	5	6
$Pr(x)$	$\binom{6}{0}\left(\frac{1}{2}\right)^0\left(\frac{1}{2}\right)^6$ $=\frac{1}{64}$	$\binom{6}{1}\left(\frac{1}{2}\right)^1\left(\frac{1}{2}\right)^5$ $=\frac{6}{64}$	$\binom{6}{2}\left(\frac{1}{2}\right)^2\left(\frac{1}{2}\right)^4$ $=\frac{15}{64}$	$\binom{6}{3}\left(\frac{1}{2}\right)^3\left(\frac{1}{2}\right)^3$ $=\frac{20}{64}$	$\binom{6}{4}\left(\frac{1}{2}\right)^4\left(\frac{1}{2}\right)^2$ $=\frac{15}{64}$	$\binom{6}{5}\left(\frac{1}{2}\right)^5\left(\frac{1}{2}\right)^1$ $=\frac{6}{64}$	$\binom{6}{6}\left(\frac{1}{2}\right)^6\left(\frac{1}{2}\right)^0$ $=\frac{1}{64}$

The expected value of the number of successes (expected value was discussed in Section 7.7) is given by

$$E(x) = 0 \cdot \frac{1}{64} + 1 \cdot \frac{6}{64} + 2 \cdot \frac{15}{64} + 3 \cdot \frac{20}{64} + 4 \cdot \frac{15}{64} + 5 \cdot \frac{6}{64} + 6 \cdot \frac{1}{64}$$
$$= \frac{192}{64} = 3.$$

This expected number of successes seems reasonable. If the probability of success is 1/2, we would expect to succeed on half of the 6 trials. For any binomial distribution the expected number of successes is given by np, where n is the number of trials and p is the probability of success. Since the expected value of any probability distribution is defined as the mean of that distribution, we have the following.

Mean of a Binomial Distribution	The theoretical mean of any binomial distribution is $$\mu = np,$$ where n is the number of trials in the corresponding binomial experiment and p is the probability of success on each trial.

The mean of a probability distribution is denoted by the Greek letter μ (mu) rather than $\bar{x}$, as it is for sample data.

A simple formula can also be developed for the standard deviation of a binomial distribution.

Standard Deviation of a Binomial Distribution	The standard deviation of a binomial distribution is $$\sigma = \sqrt{npq},$$ where n is the number of trials, p is the probability of success on each trial, and $q = 1 - p$.

The Greek letter σ (sigma) is used to denote the standard deviation of a probability distribution. The standard deviation of the binomial distribution corresponding to the number of heads resulting when a coin is tossed 16 times is

$$\sigma = \sqrt{16 \cdot \frac{1}{2} \cdot \frac{1}{2}} = \sqrt{4} = 2.$$

EXAMPLE 1   A fair coin is tossed 4 times.

(a) Construct a table with each value of the binomial variable x, where x is the number of heads resulting, and the probability of each value of x.

(b) Graph the distribution.

(c) Find the mean of this binomial distribution.

(d) Find the standard deviation of this distribution.

Solution   (a)

x	$Pr(x)$
0	$\binom{4}{0}\left(\frac{1}{2}\right)^{0}\left(\frac{1}{2}\right)^{4} = \frac{1}{16}$
1	$\binom{4}{1}\left(\frac{1}{2}\right)^{1}\left(\frac{1}{2}\right)^{3} = \frac{4}{16}$
2	$\binom{4}{2}\left(\frac{1}{2}\right)^{2}\left(\frac{1}{2}\right)^{2} = \frac{6}{16}$
3	$\binom{4}{3}\left(\frac{1}{2}\right)^{3}\left(\frac{1}{2}\right)^{1} = \frac{4}{16}$
4	$\binom{4}{4}\left(\frac{1}{2}\right)^{4}\left(\frac{1}{2}\right)^{0} = \frac{1}{16}$

(b)

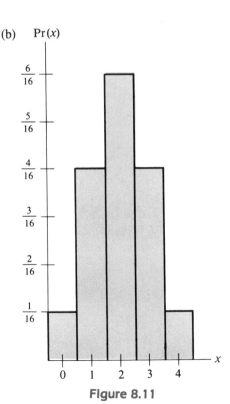

Figure 8.11

(c) The mean of this distribution is

$$\mu = np = 4 \cdot \frac{1}{2} = 2.$$

(d) The standard deviation of this binomial distribution is

$$\sigma = \sqrt{npq} = \sqrt{4 \cdot \frac{1}{2} \cdot \frac{1}{2}} = 1.$$

The binomial probability distribution is closely related to the powers of a binomial. For example, if a binomial experiment has 3 trials with probability of success p on each trial, then the probability distribution is given by Table 8.4 with the values of x written from 3 to 0.

Table 8.4

x	3	2	1	0
Pr(x)	$\binom{3}{3} p^3 q^0 = p^3$	$\binom{3}{2} p^2 q = 3p^2 q$	$\binom{3}{1} pq^2 = 3pq^2$	$\binom{3}{0} p^0 q^3 = q^3$

Now consider the expansion of $(p + q)^3$, which we used earlier.

$$(p + q)^3 = p^3 + 3p^2 q + 3pq^2 + q^3$$

The formula that we can use to expand a binomial $(a + b)$ to any power n is

Binomial Formula

$$(a + b)^n = \binom{n}{n} a^n + \binom{n}{n-1} a^{n-1} b + \binom{n}{n-2} a^{n-2} b^2 + \cdots$$

$$+ \binom{n}{2} a^2 b^{n-2} + \binom{n}{1} ab^{n-1} + \binom{n}{0} b^n$$

EXAMPLE 2 Expand $(x + y)^4$.

Solution

$$(x + y)^4 = \binom{4}{4} x^4 + \binom{4}{3} x^3 y + \binom{4}{2} x^2 y^2 + \binom{4}{1} xy^3 + \binom{4}{0} y^4$$
$$= x^4 + 4x^3 y + 6x^2 y^2 + 4xy^3 + y^4$$

Note that the coefficients in this expansion are related to the probabilities in Example 1.

EXAMPLE 3   (a) If a die is rolled 5 times, what is the probability that exactly 2 faces with 4 on them will result?

(b) What is the coefficient of $p^2 q^3$ in $(p + q)^5$?

Solution   (a) From Section 8.4,

$$\text{Pr(two 4's)} = \binom{5}{2}\left(\frac{1}{6}\right)^2\left(\frac{5}{6}\right)^3 = 10 \cdot \frac{1}{36} \cdot \frac{125}{216} = \frac{625}{3888}.$$

(b) By the binomial formula the coefficient of $p^2 q^3$ is $\binom{5}{2} = 10$.

Exercise 8.5

1. A die is rolled 3 times. If success is rolling a 5,
   (a) construct the binomial distribution for this experiment.
   (b) find the mean of this distribution.
   (c) find the standard deviation of this distribution.
2. A die is rolled 3 times. If success is rolling a number divisible by 3,
   (a) construct the binomial distribution for this experiment.
   (b) write the mean of this distribution.
   (c) write the standard deviation of this distribution.
3. A variable x has a binomial distribution with probability of success .7 for each trial and a total of 60 trials. What is
   (a) the mean and
   (b) the standard deviation of the distribution?
4. A variable x has a binomial distribution with probability .8 for each trial and a total of 40 trials. What is
   (a) the mean and
   (b) the standard deviation of the distribution?
5. Suppose a fair die is rolled 12 times. What is the mean and standard deviation of the number of 5's that occur?
6. Suppose a fair coin is tossed 8 times. What is the mean and standard deviation of the number of tails?
7. Suppose the probability that a certain coin will result in heads is 2/3 when it is tossed. If it is tossed 6 times, how many heads would we expect?
8. A coin is loaded so that the probability of tossing a head is 3/5. If it is tossed 50 times, what is
   (a) the mean and
   (b) the standard deviation of the number of heads that occur?
9. Suppose a pair of dice is thrown 12 times. How many times would we expect a sum of 7 to occur?
10. Suppose a pair of dice is thrown 20 times. How many times would we expect a sum of 6 to occur?
11. Suppose that a die is "loaded" so that the probability of getting each even number is 1/4 and the probability of getting each odd number is 1/12. If it is rolled 24 times, how many times would we expect to get a 3?

12. What is the coefficient of a^3b^5 in the expansion of $(a + b)^8$?
13. What is the coefficient of the term containing a^4b^2 in $(a + b)^6$?
14. (a) What is the coefficient of the term containing a^2b^4 in $(a + b)^6$?
    (b) Does $\binom{6}{4} = \binom{6}{2}$?
15. Expand $(a + b)^6$.
16. Expand $(x + y)^5$.
17. Expand $(x + h)^4$.
18. Write the general expression for $(x + h)^n$.

APPLICATIONS

19. Suppose that 10% of the patients having a certain disease will die from it.
    (a) If 100 people have the disease, how many would we expect to die from it?
    (b) What is the standard deviation of the number of deaths that could occur?
20. Suppose it has been determined that the probability that a rat injected with cancerous cells will live is .6. If 35 rats are injected, how many would be expected to die?
21. A candidate claims 60% of the people in his district will vote for him.
    (a) If his district contains 100,000 voters, how many votes does he expect to get from his district?
    (b) What is the standard deviation of the number of his votes?
22. In a family with 2 children, the probability that both children will be boys is approximately 1/4.
    (a) If 1200 families with two children are selected at random, how many of the families would we expect to have 2 boys?
    (b) What is the standard deviation for the number of families with 2 boys?
23. If the number of votes the candidate in problem 21 gets is 2 standard deviations below what he expected, how many votes did he get (approximately)?
24. If the sample drawn in problem 22 had 315 families with two boys in it, how many standard deviations did the sample data lie above the mean?
25. A multiple choice test has 20 questions and 5 choices for each question. If a student is totally unprepared and guesses on each question, the mean is the number of questions she can expect to answer correctly.
    (a) How many questions can she expect to answer correctly?
    (b) What is the standard deviation of the distribution?
26. Suppose a birth control pill is 99% effective in preventing pregnancy. What number of women would be expected to get pregnant out of 100 women using this pill?
27. A certain calculator circuit board is manufactured in lots of 200. If 1% of the boards are defective, find the mean and standard deviation for the number of defects in each lot.
28. Forty-eight percent of accountants taking exams to become a CPA fail the first time. If 1000 candidates take the exams for the first time, what is the expected number that will pass?
29. A certain type of corn seed has an 85% germination rate. If 2000 seeds are planted, what is the expected number of seeds that would fail to germinate?

8.6 The Normal Distribution

Objectives
☐ To convert normal distribution scores to z-scores
☐ To find the probability that normally distributed scores lie in a certain interval

The binomial variables discussed in Section 8.5 could only assume the values 0, 1, 2, . . . , so a binomial probability distribution is called a **discrete probability distribution** and a binomial variable is called a **discrete random variable.** The binomial distribution is important, but it does not apply to many kinds of measurements. For example, the weights of people, the heights of trees, and the IQ scores of college students cannot be measured with whole numbers because each of them can assume any one of an infinite number of values on a measuring scale. These variables follow a distribution called the normal distribution, which is the most important probability distribution.

The **normal distribution** has the following properties:

1. Its graph is a bell-shaped curve like that of Figure 8.12.* The graph is called the **normal curve.** It approaches the horizontal axis as it extends in both directions, but it never touches it.
2. The curve is symmetric about a vertical centerline. This centerline passes through the value that is the mean, the median, *and* the mode of the distribution. That is, the mean, median, and mode are the same for a normal distribution. (That is why they are all called average.)
3. A normal distribution is completely determined when its mean μ and its standard deviation σ are known.
4. Approximately sixty-eight percent of all scores lie within one standard deviation of the mean. Approximately ninety-five percent of all scores lie within two standard deviations of the mean. More than 99.5% of all scores will lie within three standard deviations of the mean.

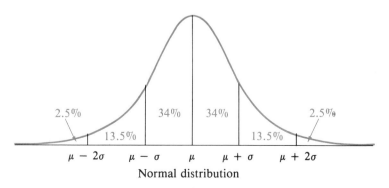

Normal distribution

Figure 8.12

---

*Percentages shown are approximate.

EXAMPLE 1   If IQ scores follow a normal distribution with mean 100 and standard deviation 15, what percentage of the scores will be
(a) between 100 and 115?   (b) between 85 and 115?   (c) between 85 and 130?   (d) between 70 and 130?   (e) greater than 130?

Solution   Figure 8.13 is a graph of the distribution, with approximate percentages shown. We can find the percentages from this graph:
(a) 34%.   (b) 68%.   (c) 81.5%.   (d) 95%.   (e) 2.5%.

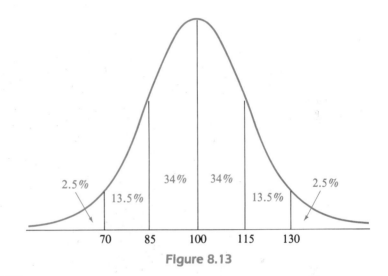

Figure 8.13

The total area under the normal curve is 1. The area under the curve from value x_1 to value x_2 represents the percentage of the scores that lie between x_1 and x_2. Thus the *area* under the curve from x_1 to x_2 *represents the probability* that a score chosen at random will lie between x_1 and x_2. Thus, in Example 1, the probability that a score chosen at random would lie between 85 and 115 is .68, and the probability that it would lie between 70 and 130 is .95.

We have seen that 34% of the scores lie between 100 and 115 in the normal distribution graph in Figure 8.13. As we have mentioned, this also means that the area under the curve from $x = 100$ to $x = 115$ is .34, and that the probability that a score chosen at random from this normal population lies between 100 and 115 is .34. We can write this as

$$\Pr(100 \leq x \leq 115) = .34.$$

Because the probability of obtaining a score from a normal distribution is always related to how many standard deviations the score is away from the mean, it is desirable to convert all scores from a normal distribution to **standard scores,** or **z-scores.** The z-score for any score x is found by determining how many standard deviations x is from the mean μ. This is done using the formula

$$z = \frac{x - \mu}{\sigma}.$$

For example, the normal distribution of IQ scores (graphed in Figure 8.13) has mean $\mu = 100$ and standard deviation $\sigma = 15$. Thus the z-score for 115 is

$$z = \frac{115 - 100}{15} = 1.$$

A z-score of 1 indicates that 115 is 1 standard deviation above the mean.

If we convert all the scores from any normal distribution to z-scores, the distribution of z-scores will always be a normal distribution with mean 0 and standard deviation 1. This distribution is called the **standard normal distribution.**

Figure 8.14 shows the graph of the standard normal distribution, with approximate percentages shown. The total area under the curve is 1, with .5 on either side of the mean 0.

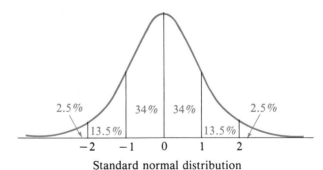

Standard normal distribution

Figure 8.14

By comparing Figure 8.14 with Figure 8.12, we see that each unit from 0 in the standard normal distribution corresponds to one standard deviation from the mean of the normal distribution.

We can use a table to more accurately determine the area under the standard normal curve between two z-scores. Table III in the Appendix gives the area under the normal curve from $z = 0$ to $z = z_0$, for values of z_0 from 0 to 3. As with the normal curve, the area under the curve from $z = 0$ to $z = z_0$ is the probability that a z-score lies between 0 and z_0.

EXAMPLE 2   (a) Find the area under the standard normal curve from $z = 0$ to $z = 1.50$.
             (b) Find $\Pr(0 \le z \le 1.50)$.

Solution   (a) Looking in the column headed by z_0 in Table III, we see 1.50. Across from the 1.50 in the column headed by A is .4332. Thus the area under the standard normal curve between $z = 0$ and $z = 1.50$ is .4332.

(b) The area under the curve from 0 to 1.50 equals the probability z lies between 0 and 1.50, so $\Pr(0 \leq z \leq 1.50) = .4332$.

EXAMPLE 3   (a) Find $\Pr(0 \leq z \leq 2)$.   (b) Find $\Pr(-1 \leq z \leq 0)$.

Solution   (a) $\Pr(0 \leq z \leq 2)$ is found in Table III by looking at the A corresponding to $z = 2$. Thus $\Pr(0 \leq z \leq 2) = .4772$. Figure 8.14 gives the approximate value, but Table III is more accurate.

(b) As shown in Figure 8.15, the area we seek is to the left of the mean (because $z_0 = -1$). Because the normal curve is symmetric, however, the area between $z = -1$ and $z = 0$ is identical to the area between $z = 0$ and $z = 1$. Thus, using $z = 1$ in Table III, we get $\Pr(-1 \leq z \leq 0) = .3413$. Note that the area will always be positive, even if the z-score is negative.

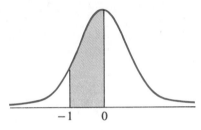

Figure 8.15

EXAMPLE 4   (a) Find $\Pr(-1 \leq z \leq 2)$.   (b) Find $\Pr(1 \leq z \leq 2)$.

Solution   (a) The graph showing the area is in Figure 8.16. Table III only gives areas from 0 on, so we must do the problem in two parts. As we have seen in Example 3, $\Pr(-1 \leq z \leq 0) = .3413$ and $\Pr(0 \leq z \leq 2) = .4772$. From the graph we see the area from $z = -1$ to $z = 2$ is the *sum* of the areas from -1 to 0 and from 0 to 2. Thus $\Pr(-1 \leq z \leq 2) = .3413 + .4772 = .8185$.

(b) The graph showing the area between $z = 1$ and $z = 2$ is in Figure 8.17. This area is the area from $z = 0$ to $z = 2$ minus the area from $z = 0$ to $z = 1$. Thus $\Pr(1 \leq z \leq 2) = \Pr(0 \leq z \leq 2) - \Pr(0 \leq z \leq 1) = .4772 - .3413 = .1359$.

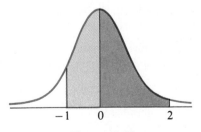

Figure 8.16

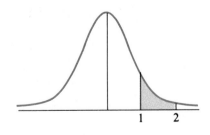

Figure 8.17

> In general, if we seek the area between two z-scores, we find the areas from 0 to each of the z-scores, and then
> (a) add the areas if the two z-scores have opposite signs.
> (b) subtract the areas if the two z-scores have the same signs.

EXAMPLE 5   If the mean height of a population of students is $\mu = 68$ in. with standard deviation $\sigma = 3$ in., what is the probability that a person chosen at random from the population

(a) will be between 68 in. and 74 in. tall?

(b) will be between 65 in. and 74 in. tall?

Solution   (a) To find Pr($68 \leq x \leq 74$), we convert 68 and 74 to z-scores.

$$\text{For 68: } z = \frac{68 - 68}{3} = 0. \qquad \text{For 74: } z = \frac{74 - 68}{3} = 2.$$

Thus Pr($68 \leq x \leq 74$) = Pr($0 \leq z \leq 2$) = .4772.

(b) The z-score for 65 is

$$z = \frac{65 - 68}{3} = -1,$$

and the z-score for 74 is 2. Thus Pr($65 \leq x \leq 74$) = Pr($-1 \leq z \leq 2$), and, as we have seen in Example 4(a), Pr($-1 \leq z \leq 2$) = .8185.

Exercise 8.6

If a population of scores is normally distributed with mean $\mu = 16$ and $\sigma = 3$, how many standard deviations from the mean is each of the following scores?

1. 22

2. 25

3. 13

4. 15

Use Table III in the Appendix to find the probability that a z-score from the standard normal distribution will lie within each of the following intervals.

5. 0 and 1.8

6. 0 and 2.4

7. -1.8 and 0

8. -3 and 0

9. -1.5 and 2.1

10. -1.25 and 3

11. -1.9 and -1.1

12. -2.45 and -1.45

13. 2.1 and 3.0

14. 1.85 and 2.85

If a population of scores is normally distributed with $\mu = 20$ and $\sigma = 5$, use the standard normal distribution to find the following.

15. $\Pr(20 \le x \le 22.5)$

16. $\Pr(20 \le x \le 21.25)$

17. $\Pr(20 \le x \le 26.25)$

18. $\Pr(20 \le x \le 27.75)$

19. $\Pr(13.75 \le x \le 20)$

20. $\Pr(18.5 \le x \le 20)$

21. $\Pr(12.25 \le x \le 21.25)$

22. $\Pr(18.5 \le x \le 27.75)$

23. $\Pr(13.75 \le x \le 18.75)$

24. $\Pr(21.25 \le x \le 25)$

APPLICATIONS

25. If the fish commission states that the mean length of all fish in Spring Run is $\mu = 15$ cm, with a standard deviation of $\sigma = 4$ cm, what is the probability that a fish caught in Spring Run will be
    (a) between 15 cm and 19 cm long?
    (b) between 11 cm and 15 cm long?
    (c) between 11 cm and 19 cm long?
    (d) between 7 cm and 23 cm long?

26. A quart of milk contains a mean of 39 grams of butterfat, with a standard deviation of 2 grams. Use Figure 8.14 to approximate the probability that a quart of milk will contain more than the following:
    (a) 43 grams
    (b) 35 grams

27. The heights of a certain species of plant are normally distributed with a mean $\mu = 20$ cm and $\sigma = 4$ cm. What is the probability that a plant chosen at random will lie between 10 cm and 30 cm?

28. The mean duration of the mating call of a population of tree toads is 189 msec with a standard deviation of 32 msec.
    (a) What proportion of these calls would be expected to last between 157 msec and 221 msec?
    (b) What proportion of these calls would be expected to last between 200 msec and 253 msec?

29. The mean weight of a group of boys is 160 lbs, with a standard deviation of 15 lbs. Find the probability that one of the boys picked at random from the group weighs
    (a) between 160 and 181 lbs.
    (b) more than 190 lbs. (Use Figure 8.14.)
    (c) between 181 and 190 lbs.
    (d) between 130 and 181 lbs.

30. The Scholastic Aptitude Test (SAT) scores are normally distributed with a mean of 500 and a standard deviation of 100. What is the probability that an individual chosen at random has a score
    (a) greater than 700? (Use Figure 8.14)
    (b) less than 300? (Use Figure 8.14)
    (c) between 550 and 600?

31. A certain automobile has its mileage per gallon (mpg) normally distributed with a mean of 28 mpg and a standard deviation of 4 mpg. Find the probability that a car selected at random has gas mileage of
    (a) less than 22 mpg.
    (b) greater than 30 mpg.
    (c) between 26 and 30 mpg.

32. A machine precision cuts tubing such that $\mu = 40.00$ inches and $\sigma = 0.03$ inches. If a piece of tubing is selected at random, find the probability that it measures
    (a) greater than 40.05 inches.
    (b) less than 40.045 inches.
    (c) between 39.95 and 40.05 inches.

33. Blood pressure for a group of women is normally distributed with a mean of 120 and a standard deviation of 12. Find the probability that a woman selected at random has
    (a) blood pressure greater than 140.
    (b) blood pressure less than 110.
    (c) blood pressure between 110 and 130.

34. In a certain state, the daily amounts of industrial waste are normally distributed with a mean of 8000 tons and a standard deviation of 2000 tons. Find the probability that on a randomly selected day the amount of industrial waste is
    (a) greater than 11,000 tons.
    (b) less than 6000 tons.
    (c) between 9000 and 11,000 tons.

35. Reaction time is normally distributed with a mean of 0.7 seconds and a standard deviation of 0.1 seconds. Find the probability that an individual selected at random has a reaction time of
    (a) greater than 0.9 seconds.
    (b) less than 0.6 seconds.
    (c) between 0.6 and 0.9 seconds.

36. Using the reaction times in problem 35, find the reaction time for an individual who is in the
    (a) top 5%.   (b) top 2.5%.

8.7 Samples from Normal Populations; Testing Hypotheses

Objectives   ☐   To find the mean and standard deviation of the distribution of sample means where the samples are drawn from a normal population

☐   To test hypotheses involving samples drawn from normal populations

If all possible samples of size n are drawn from a normal population that has mean μ and standard deviation σ, then the distribution of the means of the samples $\bar{x}$ will also be normally distributed with mean μ, but the sample means will not vary from the population mean as much as the individual scores do. The standard deviation of the distribution of sample means is therefore smaller than the standard deviation of all scores in the population, and is in fact $\sigma/\sqrt{n}$. We denote this standard deviation as $\sigma_{\bar{x}}$.

$$\sigma_{\bar{x}} = \frac{\sigma}{\sqrt{n}}$$

EXAMPLE 1   The height of a certain type of plant is normally distributed with mean $\mu = 30$ cm and standard deviation $\sigma = 5$ cm. If all possible samples of size $n = 100$ are drawn from this population of plants, what are the mean and standard deviation of the distribution of the means of these samples?

Solution   The mean is $\mu = 30$ cm. The standard deviation is $\sigma_{\bar{x}} = 5/\sqrt{100} = 0.5$ cm (see Figure 8.18).

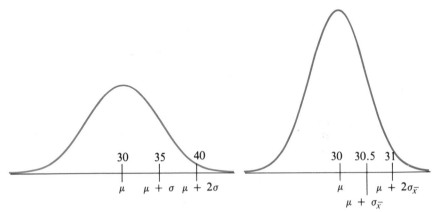

Distribution of heights, x Distribution of sample means, $\bar{x}$

Figure 8.18

Since the distribution of sample means is normally distributed, it follows that approximately 95% of all sample means will lie within 2 standard deviations of the mean. That is, approximately 95% of all $\bar{x}$'s will lie between $\mu - 2\sigma_{\bar{x}}$ and $\mu + 2\sigma_{\bar{x}}$. Thus in Example 1, approximately 95% of all sample means lie between 29 and 31 cm.

The standard deviation of the distribution of sample means is much smaller than that of the original population because the sample means tend to average out the extreme scores in the population. Thus the sample means are more closely concentrated about the mean μ. (See Figure 8.18.)

EXAMPLE 2   In Example 1, what is the probability that a sample of 100 plants chosen at random will have an $\bar{x}$ that lies outside the interval from 29 cm to 31 cm?

Solution   Since approximately 95% of all scores lie between 29 cm and 31 cm, the probability that $\bar{x}$ will lie outside the interval is $1 - .95 = .05$.

Thus if we had a sample of 100 plants whose mean height was greater than 31 cm, and we did not know if they were of the plant type discussed in Example 1 or not, we would be inclined to decide that they were not of that type.

Decisions about whether a random sample represents a desired population or not are a very important part of statistics, and are used every day in *quality control*. For example, suppose you buy a machine that converts tomatoes into tomato juice and squirts 20 oz of juice into cans. If the machine squirts more than 20 oz into each can, you will lose some of your profit; if the machine squirts less than 20 oz into each can, you may be accused of cheating your customers. How can you be reasonably sure your machine is working properly?

One way to test the machine would be to measure every can it produces. Another way would be to take a sample, of, say 100 cans. Suppose you do this and find a sample with $\bar{x} = 20.5$ oz. If you know that the amount squirted into the cans is normally distributed with a standard deviation of 2 oz, you can decide if obtaining a sample whose mean is $\bar{x} = 20.5$ is reasonable when the machine is working properly (that is, has a mean output of 20 oz).

If μ does equal 20 oz, then approximately 95% of all sample means should lie within $\mu \pm 2\sigma_{\bar{x}}$; that is, between $20 - 2 \cdot 2/\sqrt{100}$ and $20 + 2 \cdot 2/\sqrt{100}$, or between 19.6 oz and 20.4 oz. Thus the probability that a sample mean $\bar{x}$ would be outside the interval from 19.6 to 20.4 is approximately .05 *if* $\mu = 20$.

The mean of the sample is 20.5 oz, which lies outside the interval. The probability that this sample mean could occur from a population with a mean of 20 oz is so small that it is reasonable to conclude that the machine is not producing an average of 20 oz per can.

This is an example of a **statistical test,** which forms the basis for **inferential statistics.** An essential ingredient of a statistical test is the **null hypothesis,** which is the assumption or claim that is to be tested. The null hypothesis (denoted H_0) is *assumed* in a statistical test, so it cannot be proved; it can only be shown to be a reasonable or unreasonable assumption. An **alternative hypothesis** H_1 is stated in every statistical test; if the null hypothesis is *rejected* (that is, shown to be unreasonable), then the alternative hypothesis will be accepted as true.

In this example, the null hypothesis is that the machine is working properly, and the alternative hypothesis is that the machine is not working properly. Since the machine squirts 20 oz when it is working properly, the null hypothesis and its alternative may be stated as follows:

$$H_0: \mu = 20$$
$$H_1: \mu \neq 20$$

The test of the null hypothesis consists of deciding the conditions under which we will conclude that the null hypothesis is unreasonable and should be rejected in favor of the alternative hypothesis. In this example, we tested the data to see if the mean $\bar{x}$ of our sample was outside the region from $\mu - 2\sigma/\sqrt{n}$ to $\mu + 2\sigma/\sqrt{n}$ because the probability that this could happen when μ really equals 20 is .05 or less.

Note that it is possible for a machine averaging 20 oz per can to produce a sample of 100 cans with a sample mean of 20.5 oz, but the probability that it could happen is so small that we are willing to take the risk of being wrong. The test we used for this problem was designed so that the probability that we would reject the null hypothesis when it was true would be .05. In such a test we say the α-**level** is .05.* Because we considered the possibility that the sample mean could lie outside 2 standard deviations on either side of the mean, we say this is a **two-tailed test.** The steps used in conducting a two-tailed test with $\alpha = .05$ are shown below.

Statistical test	Example
	Test $\mu = 100$ if $\sigma = 14$ and $\bar{x} = 105$ for a sample of size $n = 49$.
Null Hypothesis: H_0: $\mu = a$	H_0: $\mu = 100$
Alternate Hypothesis: H_1: $\mu \neq a$	H_1: $\mu \neq 100$
TEST: Reject H_0 if the $\bar{x}$ from the sample lies outside the region from $\mu - \dfrac{2\sigma}{\sqrt{n}}$ to $\mu + \dfrac{2\sigma}{\sqrt{n}}$.	TEST: Reject $\mu = 100$ if $\bar{x} = 105$ lies outside the region from $100 - \dfrac{2(14)}{\sqrt{49}}$ to $100 + \dfrac{2(14)}{\sqrt{49}}$ or from 96 to 104. See Figure 8.19.
CONCLUSION: Accept or reject H_0.	CONCLUSION: 105 is in the rejection region. Reject H_0.

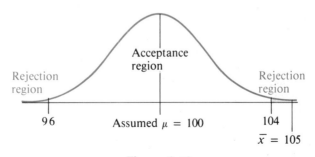

Figure 8.19

EXAMPLE 3   The fish commission claims that the average length of the fish in Spring Lake is $\mu = 15$ cm. The standard deviation of the lengths is $\sigma = 4$ cm and a sample of size 400 has a sample mean $\bar{x} = 14.7$ cm. Test the hypothesis $\mu = 15$ cm to see if their claim is accurate. Use a two-tailed test with an α-level of .05.

*α is "alpha," the first letter of the Greek alphabet.

$H_0: \mu = 15$ $H_1: \mu \neq 15$

Test: Reject H_0 in favor of H_1 if the $\bar{x}$ from the sample lies outside the region from $\mu - 2\sigma/\sqrt{n}$ to $\mu + 2\sigma/\sqrt{n}$.

Data: $\bar{x} = 14.7$, $\sigma = 4$, $n = 400$

Work: $\mu - \dfrac{2\sigma}{\sqrt{n}} = 15 - \dfrac{2(4)}{\sqrt{400}} = 14.6$; $\mu + \dfrac{2\sigma}{\sqrt{n}} = 15 + \dfrac{2(4)}{\sqrt{400}} = 15.4$

Conclusion: $\bar{x} = 14.7$ does not lie outside the interval from 14.6 to 15.4, so we cannot reject the claim. Thus we accept H_0.

It should be noted that the null and alternative hypotheses can have many different forms in inferential statistics, and the statistical tests differ for different forms of hypotheses. We leave the study of these tests to other courses.

Exercise 8.7

1. Samples of size 100 are drawn from a normal population with $\mu = 50$ and $\sigma = 10$.
   (a) Is the set of means of these samples normally distributed?
   (b) What is the mean of the distribution of sample means?
   (c) What is the standard deviation of the distribution of sample means?
2. Samples of size 49 are drawn from a normal population with $\mu = 80$ and $\sigma = 14$.
   (a) What is the mean of the distribution of sample means?
   (b) What is the standard deviation of the distribution of sample means?

In problems 3–6, a sample of size n is drawn from a normal population with mean μ and standard deviation σ. Find the mean and standard deviation of the distribution of sample means in each problem.

3. $n = 25$, $\mu = 60$, $\sigma = 10$ 4. $n = 49$, $\mu = 45$, $\sigma = 7$
5. $n = 100$, $\mu = 30$, $\sigma = 5$ 6. $n = 36$, $\mu = 120$, $\sigma = 3$

In problems 7–10, a sample of size $n = 49$ is drawn from a normal population with mean $\mu = 30$ and $\sigma = 14$.

7. Find $\Pr(30 \leq \bar{x} \leq 35)$.   8. Find $\Pr(28 \leq \bar{x} \leq 33)$.
9. Find $\Pr(33 \leq \bar{x} \leq 35)$.   10. Find $\Pr(29 \leq \bar{x} \leq 31)$.

In problems 11–14, suppose a sample of size n is drawn from a normal population with mean μ and standard deviation σ. In each problem, state in what range 95% of all sample means will lie.

11. $n = 36$, $\mu = 600$, $\sigma = 12$ 12. $n = 49$, $\mu = 350$, $\sigma = 35$
13. $n = 100$, $\mu = 80$, $\sigma = 5$ 14. $n = 25$, $\mu = 50$, $\sigma = 10$

APPLICATIONS

15. IQ scores are normally distributed with $\mu = 100$ and $\sigma = 15$. If samples of size 25 are drawn at random from the population,
    (a) what is the mean of the distribution of means of the samples?
    (b) what is the standard deviation of the distribution of means of the samples?
    (c) is it highly likely that a random sample would have a mean above 109?

16. If the mean height of a population of students is $\mu = 68$ in. with standard deviation $\sigma = 3$ in., what are the mean and standard deviation of the set of sample means of samples of size 100 that can be drawn from this population?

17. The Scholastic Aptitude Test (SAT) scores are normally distributed with a mean of 500 and a standard deviation of 100. What is the probability that a sample of 100 students
    (a) has a mean score of between 480 and 520?
    (b) has a mean score above 520?
    (c) has a mean score outside the range of 480 to 520?

18. When a machine is working properly, it produces bolts that average $\mu = 20$ cm in length, with a standard deviation of $\sigma = 3$ cm. What is the probability that a sample of 9 bolts will have a mean between 18 cm and 22 cm?

19. Refer to problem 17. If a group of 100 students from a high school had a mean SAT score of 525, would you conclude these students were better than average?

20. If the machine in problem 18 is working properly, what is the probability that a sample of 9 bolts will be produced with a sample mean less than 18 cm or greater than 22 cm?

21. A new breed of shrubs has a mean height of 36 in. and a standard deviation of 3 in. Find the probability that a sample of 4 shrubs has a mean height between 37 and 39 in.

22. A soft-drink machine dispenses a mean of 8 oz of drink with a standard deviation of 0.5 oz. What is the probability that a sample of size 16 has a sample mean less than 7.9 oz?

23. Suppose a machine produces a large number of parts that must have a diameter very close to 3 cm, and that experience shows that the standard deviation is $\sigma = .5$ cm. If the mean varies too far from 3 cm, the machine will have to be repaired. To see if the machine is working properly, a sample of size 100 is measured and found to have mean $\bar{x} = 3.15$ cm. Test $H_0: \mu = 3$ cm against $H_1: \mu \neq 3$ cm, using $\alpha = .05$.

24. An automobile was designed to get 30 miles per gallon of gasoline. To test the production models, 36 cars were chosen at random and tested. The mean gasoline mileage was 27.5 miles per gallon, and the standard deviation was known to be $\sigma = 6$ miles per gallon. Use a two-tailed test with $\alpha = .05$ to determine if the cars are performing properly.

25. A firm decides to produce a new type of light bulb. It expects the bulbs to last $\mu = 1600$ hours. A sample of 100 bulbs is tested and found to have a mean $\bar{x} = 1580$. If the standard deviation is known to be $\sigma = 150$ hours, use a two-tailed test with $\alpha = .05$ to determine if 1600 hours is a reasonable estimate.

26. A packing machine is expected to pack $\mu = 25$ cartons per hour, with the number of cartons packed following the normal distribution. To check its efficiency, the number of cartons it packed per hour was recorded for 9 hours. The mean number of cartons packed per hour was $\bar{x} = 24$. Use $\sigma = 2$ and $\alpha = .05$ to determine if the machine is performing differently from its expectations. (Use a two-tailed test.)

27. Blood pressure for women is normally distributed with a mean of 120 and a standard deviation of 12. If a randomly selected group of 49 women who are using a birth control pill have a mean blood pressure of 122.5, use a two-tailed test with $\alpha = .05$ to determine if this is sufficient evidence to conclude that the pill affects blood pressure.

28. If a random sample of 100 women also has a mean blood pressure of 122.5 (see problem 27), use a two-tailed test with $\alpha = .05$ to determine if this is sufficient evidence that the pill affects blood pressure.

29. Braking reaction time for an automobile is normally distributed with a mean of .7 seconds and a standard deviation of .1 seconds. A group of 25 driver-education students has a mean reaction time of .64 seconds. Use a two-tailed test with $\alpha = .05$ to determine if this group's reaction time differs significantly from the mean.

8.8 Linear Regression and Correlation

Objectives   ☐   To write the equation of the line that is the best fit for a set of data points
☐   To compute the correlation coefficient for a set of data points

We have seen in Section 1.5 that it it possible to write the equation of a straight line if we have two points on the line. Business firms frequently like to treat demand functions as though they are linear, even when they are not exactly linear. They do this because linear functions are much easier to handle than other functions. If a firm has more than two points describing the demand for its product, it is likely that the points will not all lie on the same straight line. However, by using a technique called **linear regression** the firm can determine the "best line" that fits these points.

Suppose we have the points shown in Figure 8.20. We seek the line that is the "best fit" for the points. We can eyeball a line that appears to lie along the points.

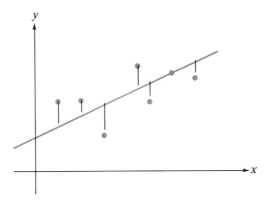

Figure 8.20

Corresponding to each point (x_1, y_1) that we know, we can find a point $(x_1, \hat{y}_1)$ on the line. If the line we have is a good fit for the points, the differences between the y values of the given points and the corresponding $\hat{y}$ values on the line should be small. The line shown is the best line for the points only if the sum of the squares of these differences is a minimum.*

Because we can write the equation of a line as $y = mx + b$, we can find the equation of the line that best fits n given points by assuming the points lie on or near a line with equation

$$\hat{y} = Ax + B.$$

---

*Because linear regression involves minimizing the sum of squared numbers, it is also called the **least squares method.**

For each value of x, we get a value $\hat{y}$, which lies on the line and is an estimate of y. We seek the numbers A and B such that the sum of the squares of the differences,

$$\Sigma(y - \hat{y})^2,$$

is a minimum. If we can find A and B, then we have the equation of the line that describes the data. Using this equation, we can estimate unknown y values for other values of x.

Linear Regression Equation	Using calculus, we can show that $\Sigma(y - \hat{y})^2$ is a minimum, and thus $\hat{y} = Ax + B$ is the equation of the line that is the best fit, if

$$A = \frac{\Sigma x \cdot \Sigma y - n\Sigma xy}{(\Sigma x)^2 - n\Sigma x^2}$$

and

$$B = \frac{\Sigma y - A\Sigma x}{n}.$$

EXAMPLE 1   Suppose the following four points are known. Write the equation of the line that is the best fit for the points.

x	50	25	10	5
y	2	4	10	20

Solution   To find A, and then B, we first find

$$\Sigma x = 50 + 25 + 10 + 5 = 90$$
$$\Sigma x^2 = 2500 + 625 + 100 + 25 = 3250$$
$$\Sigma y = 2 + 4 + 10 + 20 = 36$$
$$\Sigma xy = 100 + 100 + 100 + 100 = 400.$$

Then

$$A = \frac{\Sigma x \cdot \Sigma y - n\,\Sigma xy}{(\Sigma x)^2 - n\Sigma x^2}$$

$$= \frac{90 \cdot 36 - 4 \cdot 400}{90^2 - 4 \cdot 3250}$$

$$= \frac{1640}{-4900}$$

$$= -.33,$$

and

$$B = \frac{\Sigma y - A\Sigma x}{n}$$

$$= \frac{36 - (-.33)(90)}{4}$$

$$= \frac{65.7}{4}$$

$$= 16.43.$$

Thus the line that gives the best fit to these points is

$$\hat{y} = -.33x + 16.43.$$

Figure 8.21 shows the points and the graph of the regression line. Although none of the given points lies on this line, it is the line that best fits the points. If these points represented a demand function, the equation would be written using p and q, as follows:

$$p = -.33q + 16.43.$$

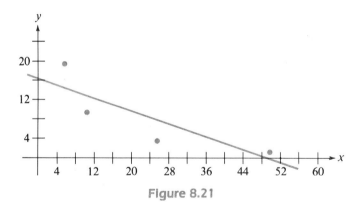

Figure 8.21

EXAMPLE 2   Accountants frequently use linear regression (least squares) to determine a linear equation for their marginal costs. If the following table gives the marginal cost for a product at different levels of production, find the best linear equation for the marginal cost.

x (units)	100	200	300	400
$\overline{MC}$ (Marginal Cost)	2400	4100	6000	8500

Solution   We seek the values A and B such that $\overline{MC} = Ax + B$ is the equation that best fits the points.

$$\Sigma x = 100 + 200 + 300 + 400 = 1000$$
$$\Sigma x^2 = 10{,}000 + 40{,}000 + 90{,}000 + 160{,}000 = 300{,}000$$
$$\Sigma y = 2400 + 4100 + 6000 + 8500 = 21{,}000$$
$$\Sigma xy = 240{,}000 + 820{,}000 + 1{,}800{,}000 + 3{,}400{,}000 = 6{,}260{,}000$$

$$A = \frac{1000(21{,}000) - 4(6{,}260{,}000)}{1000^2 - 4(300{,}000)} = \frac{21{,}000{,}000 - 25{,}040{,}000}{1{,}000{,}000 - 1{,}200{,}000} = 20.2$$

$$B = \frac{21{,}000 - (20.2)(1000)}{4} = \frac{800}{4} = 200$$

Thus the linear equation that best predicts marginal cost is

$$\overline{MC} = 20.2x + 200.$$

Figure 8.22 shows the points and the line.

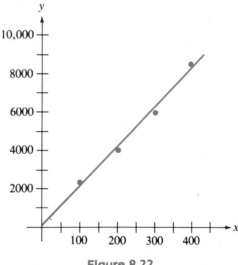

Figure 8.22

This equation gives (approximate) values for marginal cost at different levels of production. For example, at $x = 500$, marginal cost should be approximately

$$\overline{MC} = 20.2(500) + 200 = 10{,}300,$$

and at $x = 250$, it is approximately

$$\overline{MC} = 20.2(250) + 200 = 5250.$$

Linear regression gives us the equation of the line that is the best fit for our data, but it does not tell us how closely our data fit the line. One measure of goodness of fit is the **correlation coefficient,** denoted by r.

> The **correlation coefficient** r is found using
>
> $$r = \frac{n(\Sigma xy) - (\Sigma x)(\Sigma y)}{\sqrt{n(\Sigma x^2) - (\Sigma x)^2}\sqrt{n(\Sigma y^2) - (\Sigma y)^2}}.$$

Although this formula looks very complicated, it is not difficult to use if we have already found the regression line. We have already calculated Σxy, Σx, Σy, and Σx^2 in finding the regression line for Example 1. Thus we need only compute Σy^2 and substitute these values (with $n = 4$) into the formula for r. Since the values are $\Sigma xy = 400$, $\Sigma x = 90$, $\Sigma y = 36$, $\Sigma x^2 = 3250$, and $\Sigma y^2 = 520$,

$$r = \frac{n(\Sigma xy) - (\Sigma x)(\Sigma y)}{\sqrt{n(\Sigma x^2) - (\Sigma x)^2}\sqrt{n(\Sigma y^2) - (\Sigma y)^2}}$$

$$= \frac{4(400) - (90)(36)}{\sqrt{4(3250) - (90)^2}\sqrt{4(520) - (36)^2}}$$

$$= \frac{-1640}{1960}$$

$$= -.84.$$

The formula for the correlation coefficient, developed by Karl Pearson, is designed so that $-1 \le r \le 1$, with a value of r close to 1 meaning the two variables will increase or decrease together, and there is a strong mathematical relationship between them. It does not necessarily mean that one of the variables has a direct effect on the other. For example, there is a high correlation between the increase in the number of ministers in a certain area and the sale of liquor in that area. This does not mean the ministers are drinking the liquor; both increases reflect an increase in population in that area.

A correlation coefficient close to -1 indicates that there is a strong negative correlation; that is, one variable will tend to decrease as the other one increases. It is generally agreed that correlations between -0.2 and 0.2 indicate no significant relation between the variables. (See Figure 8.23.)

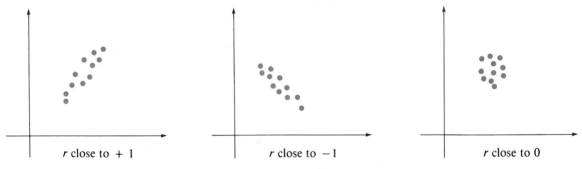

r close to $+1$ r close to -1 r close to 0

Figure 8.23

EXAMPLE 3   Find the correlation coefficient for the data given in Example 2.

Solution   From the data in Example 2, we have $\Sigma xy = 6,260,000$, $\Sigma x = 1000$, $\Sigma y = 21,000$, $\Sigma x^2 = 300,000$, and $\Sigma y^2 = 130,820,000$. Then

$$r = \frac{4(6,260,000) - (1000)(21,000)}{\sqrt{4(300,000) - (1000)^2}\sqrt{4(130,820,000) - (21,000)^2}}$$

$$= \frac{25,040,000 - 21,000,000}{\sqrt{1,200,000 - 1,000,000}\sqrt{523,280,000 - 441,000,000}}$$

$$= \frac{4,040,000}{\sqrt{200,000}\sqrt{82,280,000}} = \frac{4,040,000}{(447.21)(9070.83)}$$

$$= .9959.$$

Exercise 8.8

In problems 1–6, use the points given in the tables to write the equation of the line that is the best fit for the points.

1.
x	3	4	5	6
y	15	22	28	32

2.
x	0	1	2	3
y	6	8	12	15

3.
x	10	20	30	40
y	2	6	5	6

4.
x	60	70	80	90
y	10	20	31	38

5.
x	1	2	3	4
y	1	−4	8	−12

6.
x	2	3	4	5
y	8	25	50	100

7. Find the correlation coefficient for the data in problem 1.
8. Find the correlation coefficient for the data in problem 2.
9. Find the correlation coefficient for the data in problem 3.
10. Find the correlation coefficient for the data in problem 4.
11. Find the correlation coefficient for the data in problem 5.
12. Find the correlation coefficient for the data in problem 6.

APPLICATIONS

13. (a) Write the linear equation (in the form $\hat{p} = Aq + B$) that is the best fit for the following demand schedule.

q	10	20	30	40	50
p	300	250	220	200	180

   (b) Find the correlation coefficient relating quantity demanded and price.

14. (a) Write the linear regression equation for the points in the following supply schedule.

q	10	20	30	40	50
p	100	110	115	125	150

   (b) Find the correlation coefficient relating quantity supplied and price.

15. (a) The following table compares the weekly wages for men and women. Write the linear equation (in the form $\hat{y} = Ax + B$) that is the best fit for the data.

Year	x(Men)	y(Women)
1920	$31.69	$17.71
1930	27.66	15.98
1940	30.64	17.43
1944	54.65	31.21

   (b) Find the correlation between the weekly wages for men and women.

16. The following table shows the temperature readings from two different thermometers placed in water as the temperature of the water changes.

x (thermometer 1)	12	30.5	50	76.5	90
y (thermometer 2)	60	88	110	165	203

   (a) Write the linear equation (in the form $\hat{y} = Ax + B$) that is the best fit for the data.
   (b) How are the thermometers different?
   (c) Find the correlation between the temperatures on the two thermometers.

17. (a) The following table gives the high school and college grade point averages for seven students, where the highest possible grade point in both cases is 4.0. Write the equation of the least squares line for the data.

x (high school)	2.50	3.00	3.25	3.50	3.60	3.75	4.00
y (college)	1.80	2.50	3.50	3.00	2.20	3.20	3.50

   (b) Find the correlation between high school and college grade point averages.

18. (a) The following table compares yearly income for families and their yearly savings. Write the linear regression equation that is the best fit for the data.

Income (x)	20,000	30,000	40,000	50,000	60,000
Savings (y)	1000	1600	2200	3000	3500

   (b) Find the correlation between yearly income and yearly savings.

19. (a) The following table gives the marginal cost for a product at different levels of production. Write the linear regression equation that predicts marginal cost from production.

Units (x)	400	500	600	700	800
Marginal Cost (y)	20	28	27	32	26

(b) Find the correlation between production units and marginal cost.

20. (a) The following table gives the marginal revenue for a product at different levels of sales. Find the regression line relating marginal revenue to sales.

Sales (x)	1000	2000	3000	4000	5000
Marginal Revenue (y)	50	72	86	100	120

(b) Find the correlation between number of sales and marginal revenue.

Review Exercises

Consider the data in the following frequency table, and use the data in problems 1–4.

Score	Frequency
1	4
2	6
3	8
4	3
5	5

8.1–8.3

1. Construct a frequency histogram for the data.
2. What is the mode of the data?
3. What is the mean of the data?
4. What is the median of the data?
5. Construct a frequency histogram for this data, using intervals of length 10:

$$4, 16, 35, 14, 17, 16, 32, 12, 3, 1.$$

6. What is the median of the scores in problem 5?
7. What is the mode of the scores in problem 5?
8. What is the mean of the scores in problem 5?
9. Find the mean, variance, and standard deviation of the following data: 4, 3, 4, 6, 8, 0, 2.
10. Find the mean, variance, and standard deviation of the following data: 3, 2, 1, 5, 1, 4, 0, 2, 1, 1.

8.4

11. Suppose 20% of the population are victims of crime. In a family of 5, find the probability that none of the family is a crime victim.

8.5

12. If one person in 100,000 develops a certain disease, then calculate:
    (a) Pr(exactly one person in 100,000 has the disease).
    (b) Pr(at least one person in 100,000 has the disease).
13. If a die is rolled 4 times, what is the probability that a number greater than 4 is rolled at least 2 times?
14. A coin has been altered so that the probability that a head will occur is 2/3. If the coin is tossed 6 times, give the mean and standard deviation of the distribution of the number of heads.
15. Refer to problem 11.
    (a) What is the expected number of family members that are victims?
    (b) Find the probability that exactly the expected number of family members are victims of crime.
16. Expand $(x + y)^5$.

8.6

17. What is the area under the standard normal curve between $z = -1.6$ and $z = 1.9$?
18. If z is a standard normal score, find $Pr(-1 \leq z \leq -.5)$.
19. Find $Pr(1.23 \leq z \leq 2.55)$.
20. If a variable x is normally distributed with $\mu = 25$ and $\sigma = 5$, find $Pr(25 \leq x \leq 30)$.
21. If a variable x is normally distributed with $\mu = 25$ and $\sigma = 5$, find $Pr(20 \leq x \leq 30)$.
22. If a variable x is normally distributed with $\mu = 25$ and $\sigma = 5$, find $Pr(30 \leq x \leq 35)$.

8.7

23. If a sample of size $n = 100$ is drawn from a normal population with mean $\mu = 25$ and standard deviation $\sigma = 5$, find $Pr(24 \leq \bar{x} \leq 26)$.
24. If a sample of size $n = 100$ is drawn from a normal population with mean $\mu = 25$ and standard deviation $\sigma = 5$, find $Pr(25 \leq \bar{x} \leq 26)$.
25. If a sample of size $n = 100$ is drawn from a normal population with mean $\mu = 25$ and standard deviation $\sigma = 5$, find $Pr(25.5 \leq \bar{x} \leq 26)$.

APPLICATIONS

8.1–8.3

The distribution of farm families (as a percentage of the population) in a 50-county survey revealed the following, to be used in problems 26–28.

Interval	Number of counties
10–19	5
20–29	16
30–39	25
40–49	3
50–59	1

26. Make a frequency histogram for these data.
27. Find the mean percentage of farm families in these 50 counties.
28. Find the standard deviation of the percentage of farm families in these 50 counties.

8.4–8.5

29. Suppose the probability that a certain couple will have a blond child is 1/4. If they have 6 children, what is the probability that 2 of them will be blond?
30. Suppose 70% of a population opposes a proposal and a sample size 5 is drawn from the population. What is the probability the majority of the sample will favor the proposal?

8.7

31. A machine produces a bolt whose mean length is 6 cm, with a standard deviation of 1 cm. To test the machine producing the bolt, a sample of 100 is drawn. Using a two-tailed test with $\alpha = .05$, determine if the machine is working properly if the mean length of the sample is $\bar{x} = 5.91$ cm.

32. A refrigerator manufacturer claims that the interior compartment is held at 38°F with a standard deviation of 1°F. A university that uses these refrigerators in dormitory rooms checks a sample of 100 of the refrigerators and finds the mean to be 37.5°F. Is the manufacturer's claim correct? Use $\alpha = 0.05$ and a two-tailed test.

8.8

33. Consider the following table of values, where x represents the annual income of a man (in thousands of dollars) and y represents his suit size. Use the least-squares method to find the linear equation that best describes suit size as a function of income.

x	20	25	30	35
y	38	40	44	48

34. Find the correlation between income and suit size for the data in problem 33. Does there appear to be a relation between income and suit size?

Part Five

Calculus

WARMUP

	Prerequisite problem type	Answer	Section for review
9.1	If $f(x) = \dfrac{x^2 - x - 6}{x + 2}$, then find (a) $f(-3)$ (b) $f(-2.5)$ (c) $f(-2.1)$ (d) $f(-2)$	(a) -6 (b) -5.5 (c) -5.1 (d) undefined	1.3 Functional notation
9.1, 9.7	Factor: (a) $x^2 - x - 6$ (b) $x^2 - 4$ (c) $x^2 + 3x + 2$ (d) $(x^2 + 1)^5(12x + 1) -$ $12(x^2 + 1)^4(x^3 + x + 1)$	(a) $(x + 2)(x - 3)$ (b) $(x - 2)(x + 2)$ (c) $(x + 1)(x + 2)$ (d) $(x^2 + 1)^4(x^2 - 11)$	0.6 Factoring
9.4, 9.5, 9.6, 9.7	Write as a power: (a) $\sqrt{t}$ (b) $\dfrac{1}{x}$ (c) $\dfrac{1}{\sqrt[3]{x^2 + 1}}$	(a) $t^{1/2}$ (b) x^{-1} (c) $(x^2 + 1)^{-1/3}$	0.3, 0.4 Exponents and radicals
9.3, 9.5, 9.7	Simplify: (a) $\dfrac{4(x + h)^2 - 4x^2}{h}$ (b) $(2x^3 + 3x + 1)(2x) + (x^2 + 4)(6x^2 + 3)$ (c) $\dfrac{x(3x^2) - x^3(1)}{x^2}$	(a) $8x + 4h$ (b) $10x^4 + 33x^2 + 2x + 12$ (c) $2x$	0.5 Simplifying algebraic expressions
9.1, 9.7	Simplify: (a) $\dfrac{x^2 - x - 6}{x + 2}$ if $x \neq -2$ (b) $\dfrac{x^2 - 4}{x - 2}$ if $x \neq 2$ (c) $\dfrac{2(x^2 + 1)^3(x - 1) - 6x(x - 1)^2(x^2 + 1)^2}{(x^2 + 1)^6}$	(a) $x - 3$ (b) $x + 2$ (c) $\dfrac{2(x - 1)(-2x^2 + 3x + 1)}{(x^2 + 1)^4}$	0.7 Simplifying fractions
9.3	If $f(x) = 3x^2 + 2x$, find $\dfrac{f(x + h) - f(x)}{h}$	$6x + 3h + 2$	1.3 Functional notation
9.3	Find the slope of the line passing through $(1, 2)$ and $(2, 4)$.	2	1.5 Slopes
9.3, 9.4, 9.6	Write the equation of the line passing through $(1, 5)$ with slope 8.	$y = 8x - 3$	1.5 Point-slope equation of a line

464

9

Derivatives

If a firm receives $30,000 in revenue during a 30-day month, its average revenue per day is $30,000/30 = $1000. This does not necessarily mean that the actual revenue was $1000 on any one day, just that the average is $1000 per day. Similarly, if a person drives a car 50 miles in an hour's time, the car's average velocity is 50 miles per hour, but the driver could have gotten a speeding ticket for traveling 70 miles per hour on this trip. When we say a car is moving at a velocity of 50 miles per hour, we are talking about the velocity of the car at an instant in time (the instantaneous velocity). We can use the average velocity to find the instantaneous velocity, as follows.

If a car travels in a straight line from the spot y_1 at time x_1 and arrives at spot y_2 at time x_2, then it has traveled the distance $y_2 - y_1$ in the elapsed time $x_2 - x_1$. If we represent the distance traveled by Δy and the elapsed time by Δx, the average velocity is given by

$$V_{av} = \frac{\Delta y}{\Delta x}.$$

The smaller the time interval, the more nearly the average velocity will be to the instantaneous velocity. For example, knowing that a car traveled 50 miles in an hour does not tell us much about its instantaneous velocity at any time during that period of time. But knowing that it traveled 1 mile in 1 minute, or 50 feet in one second, tells us much more about the velocity at a given time. Continuing to decrease the length of the time interval (Δx) will get us closer and closer to the instantaneous velocity.

Some police departments have equipment that measures how fast a car is traveling by measuring how much time elapses while the car travels between two sensors placed 60 inches apart on the road. This is not the instantaneous velocity of the car, but it is an excellent approximation.

We define the **instantaneous velocity** to be the *limit* of $\Delta y/\Delta x$ as Δx approaches 0. We write this as

$$V = \lim_{\Delta x \to 0} \frac{\Delta y}{\Delta x}.$$

Thus we may think of velocity as the instantaneous rate of change of distance with respect to time.

This chapter is concerned with *limits* and *rates of change*. We will see that the *derivative* of a function can be used to determine the rate of change of the dependent variable with respect to the independent variable. In this chapter the derivative will be used to find the marginal profit, marginal cost, and marginal revenue, given the respective profit, total cost, and total revenue functions, and we will find other rates of change, such as rates of change of populations and velocity. We will also use the derivative to determine the slope of a tangent to a curve at a point on the curve. In Chapter 10, more applications of the derivative will be discussed. For example, we will use differentiation to minimize average cost, maximize total revenue, maximize profit, and find the maximum dosage for certain medications.

9.1 Limits: Polynomial and Rational Functions

Objective   □   To find limits of functions, when they exist

Not all functions are as well behaved as the ones we have been discussing up to this point. Some functions have "jumps" or "breaks" in their graphs. For example, the function $f(x) = (x^2 - x - 6)/(x + 2)$ is undefined at $x = -2$. If we substitute -2 for x in the function, we get 0/0, which is meaningless. Thus -2 is not in the domain of this function. To answer the question, What is $f(x)$ close to when x is close, but not equal, to -2?, we introduce the concept of **limit.**

By evaluating the function at values of x on either side of and close to -2, *but not at* -2, we can see what value the function approaches as x approaches -2.

Table 9.1 shows the values of y as x gets close to -2 from the left side and right side of -2.

Table 9.1

Left		Right	
x	y	x	y
-3	-6	-1	-4
-2.5	-5.5	-1.5	-4.5
-2.3	-5.3	-1.7	-4.7
-2.1	-5.1	-1.9	-4.9
-2.01	-5.01	-1.99	-4.99
-2.001	-5.001	-1.999	-4.999

It becomes apparent that *as x approaches -2 from either side, the values of the function approach -5.* We can write this by using the notation

$$f(x) \to -5 \quad \text{as} \quad x \to -2 \quad \text{or} \quad \lim_{x \to -2} f(x) = -5.$$

In general, the notation

$$\lim_{x \to a} f(x) = L$$

means that as x gets "close" to a (but does not equal a), $f(x)$ gets "close" to L.

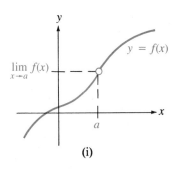

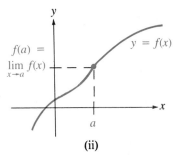

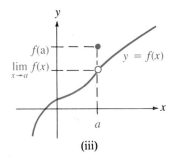

Figure 9.1

Two facts regarding limits must be kept in mind:

1. The limit of a function as x approaches a is independent of the value of the function at a. Even though $\lim_{x \to a} f(x)$ exists, the value of the function at a (i) may be undefined, (ii) may be the same as the limit, or (iii) may be defined but different from the limit (see Figure 9.1). For the function above we have seen that the limit as x approaches -2 exists even though the function is undefined at $x = -2$. That is, $f(-2)$ does not exist, but $\lim_{x \to -2} f(x) = -5$.

2. The limit is said to **exist** only if the following conditions are satisfied:
   (a) The limit L is a finite number.
   (b) The limit as x approaches a from the left [which is written $\lim_{x \to a^-} f(x)$] equals the limit as x approaches a from the right [written $\lim_{x \to a^+} f(x)$]. That is, we must have

$$\lim_{x \to a^-} f(x) = \lim_{x \to a^+} f(x).$$

Figure 9.2 on the following page shows two cases where $\lim_{x \to a} f(x)$ does not exist.

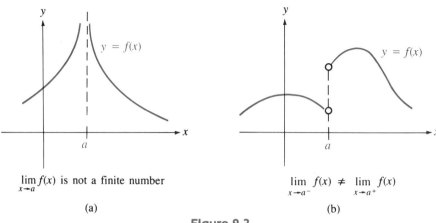

lim $f(x)$ is not a finite number
$x \to a$

(a)

$\lim_{x \to a^-} f(x) \neq \lim_{x \to a^+} f(x)$

(b)

Figure 9.2

For many functions, the value of the limit as $x \to a$ will be the same as the value of the function at $x = a$. But facts 1 and 2 tell us that this will not always be the case. For example, if $f(x) = 2x$, the limit of $f(x)$ as $x \to 2$ is 4, which is the same as $f(2)$. But if

$$f(x) = \frac{x^2 - x - 6}{x + 2},$$

we have seen that $\lim_{x \to -2} f(x) = -5$, while $f(-2)$ is undefined. Those functions f for which the limit as $x \to a$ gives the same value as $f(a)$ for all values of a are special functions, called **continuous functions.** We will discuss continuous functions in the next section.

To evaluate limits we can use the definition and form a table like that used to find

$$\lim_{x \to -2} \frac{x^2 - x - 6}{x + 2} = -5.$$

However, there are several properties of limits that we can use to facilitate our work. These properties follow, and each is illustrated with examples.

Properties of limits

Property	Example
I. $\lim_{x \to a} c = c$, where c is constant	I. (a) $\lim_{x \to 2} 4 = 4$; (b) $\lim_{x \to -1} 5 = 5$
II. $\lim_{x \to a} x = a$	II. (a) $\lim_{x \to 3} x = 3$; (b) $\lim_{x \to -5} x = -5$

III. If $\lim\limits_{x \to a} f(x) = L$ and $\lim\limits_{x \to a} g(x) = M$,

then $\lim\limits_{x \to a} [f(x) \pm g(x)]$

$= \lim\limits_{x \to a} f(x) \pm \lim\limits_{x \to a} g(x) = L \pm M$.

III. (a) $\lim\limits_{x \to 2} (x + 4) = \left(\lim\limits_{x \to 2} x \right) + \left(\lim\limits_{x \to 2} 4 \right)$

$= 2 + 4 = 6$

(b) $\lim\limits_{x \to -1} (x - 1) = \left(\lim\limits_{x \to -1} x \right) - \left(\lim\limits_{x \to -1} 1 \right)$

$= -1 - 1 = -2$

IV. If $\lim\limits_{x \to a} f(x) = L$ and $\lim\limits_{x \to a} g(x) = M$,

then $\lim\limits_{x \to a} [f(x) \cdot g(x)]$

$= \left[\lim\limits_{x \to a} f(x) \right] \left[\lim\limits_{x \to a} g(x) \right] = LM$.

NOTE: $\lim\limits_{x \to a} cf(x) = c \cdot \lim\limits_{x \to a} f(x) = c \cdot L$.

IV. (a) $\lim\limits_{x \to 3} x^2 = \left(\lim\limits_{x \to 3} x \right) \left(\lim\limits_{x \to 3} x \right) = 3 \cdot 3 = 9$

(b) $\lim\limits_{x \to 2} 4x = 4 \left(\lim\limits_{x \to 2} x \right) = 4 \cdot 2 = 8$

(c) $\lim\limits_{x \to -1} 2x^2 = 2 \left(\lim\limits_{x \to -1} x \right) \left(\lim\limits_{x \to -1} x \right)$

$= 2(-1)(-1) = 2$

V. If $\lim\limits_{x \to a} f(x) = L$ and $\lim\limits_{x \to a} g(x) = M$, with

$M \neq 0$ then $\lim\limits_{x \to a} \dfrac{f(x)}{g(x)} = \dfrac{\lim\limits_{x \to a} f(x)}{\lim\limits_{x \to a} g(x)} = \dfrac{L}{M}$.

V. (a) $\lim\limits_{x \to 2} \dfrac{x^2 + 4}{x + 2} = \dfrac{\lim\limits_{x \to 2}(x^2 + 4)}{\lim\limits_{x \to 2} (x + 2)} = \dfrac{8}{4} = 2$

(b) $\lim\limits_{x \to 3} \dfrac{x^2 - 4x}{x - 2} = \dfrac{\lim\limits_{x \to 3} (x^2 - 4x)}{\lim\limits_{x \to 3} (x - 2)}$

$= \dfrac{-3}{1} = -3$

Note that Property V does not apply if the limit of the denominator is 0. This situation occurs frequently in calculus, so we will have to develop methods to deal with it. Before we develop those methods, however, we will consider more examples that use Properties I–V.

EXAMPLE 1   Find $\lim\limits_{x \to 3} (2x^2 + 5)$, if it exists.

Solution

$\lim\limits_{x \to 3} (2x^2 + 5) = \lim\limits_{x \to 3} (2 \cdot x \cdot x + 5)$

$= \lim\limits_{x \to 3} 2 \cdot \lim\limits_{x \to 3} x \cdot \lim\limits_{x \to 3} x + \lim\limits_{x \to 3} 5$

$= 2 \cdot 3 \cdot 3 + 5 = 23$

EXAMPLE 2   Find $\lim\limits_{x \to -2} \dfrac{4 + x^3}{2x + 1}$, if it exists.

Solution

$$\lim_{x \to -2} \frac{4 + x^3}{2x + 1} = \frac{\lim\limits_{x \to -2} (4 + x \cdot x \cdot x)}{\lim\limits_{x \to -2} (2 \cdot x + 1)}$$

$$= \frac{\lim\limits_{x \to -2} 4 + \left(\lim\limits_{x \to -2} x \cdot \lim\limits_{x \to -2} x \cdot \lim\limits_{x \to -2} x \right)}{\left(\lim\limits_{x \to -2} 2 \cdot \lim\limits_{x \to -2} x \right) + \lim\limits_{x \to -2} 1}$$

$$= \frac{4 + (-2)(-2)(-2)}{2(-2) + 1} = \frac{4 - 8}{-4 + 1} = \frac{-4}{-3} = \frac{4}{3}.$$

The function in Example 1 is an example of a **polynomial function.** Polynomial functions have the general form

$$f(x) = a_n x^n + a_{n-1} x^{n-1} + \cdots + a_1 x + a_0.$$

Note that if a function $f(x)$ is a polynomial function, then Properties I through IV imply that $\lim_{x \to a} f(x)$ can be found by evaluating $f(a)$.

Functions formed by the ratio of two polynomials are called **rational functions** (see Example 2). Moreover, if $f(x)$ and $g(x)$ are both polynomials, then Property V implies that for the rational function $f(x)/g(x)$, the limit

$$\lim_{x \to a} \frac{f(x)}{g(x)}$$

can be found by evaluating $f(a)/g(a)$, *as long as* $g(a) \neq 0$. We summarize these facts below.

Function	Definition	Limit
Polynomial Function	The function $f(x) = a_n x^n + a_{n-1} x^{n-1} + \cdots + a_1 x + a_0$, where n is a positive integer, is called a polynomial function.	$\lim\limits_{x \to a} f(x) = f(a)$ for all values a (by Properties I–IV)
Rational Function	The function $h(x) = \dfrac{f(x)}{g(x)}$, where both $f(x)$ and $g(x)$ are polynomial functions, is called a rational function.	$\lim\limits_{x \to a} \dfrac{f(x)}{g(x)} = \dfrac{f(a)}{g(a)}$ when $g(a) \neq 0$ (by Property V)

EXAMPLE 3   Find the following limits, if they exist.

(a) $\lim\limits_{x \to -1} (x^3 - 2x)$ (b) $\lim\limits_{x \to 4} \dfrac{x^2 - 4x}{x - 2}$

Solution   (a) Note that $f(x) = x^3 - 2x$ is a polynomial, so

$$\lim_{x \to -1} f(x) = f(-1) = (-1)^3 - 2(-1) = 1.$$

(b) Note that this limit has the form

$$\lim_{x \to a} \frac{f(x)}{g(x)},$$

where $f(x)$ and $g(x)$ are polynomials and $g(a) \neq 0$. Therefore we have

$$\lim_{x \to 4} \frac{x^2 - 4x}{x - 2} = \frac{4^2 - 4(4)}{4 - 2} = \frac{0}{2} = 0.$$

In Example 3(b), $f(4) = 0$. Note that we cannot use Property V if $g(4) = 0$. To show how to evaluate the limit of a function of this type, let us return to the function

$$f(x) = \frac{x^2 - x - 6}{x + 2}.$$

We cannot use Property V to find

$$\lim_{x \to -2} \frac{x^2 - x - 6}{x + 2}$$

because $\lim_{x \to -2} (x + 2) = 0$. But because taking the limit as $x \to a$ means we are concerned with values close, *but not equal,* to a, we can find

$$\lim_{x \to -2} \frac{x^2 - x - 6}{x + 2}$$

without constructing a table of values. By factoring the numerator, we get

$$\lim_{x \to -2} \frac{x^2 - x - 6}{x + 2} = \lim_{x \to -2} \frac{(x + 2)(x - 3)}{x + 2}.$$

Since the limit is evaluated *near, but not at,* $x = -2$, $x + 2$ is not 0. Thus we can divide numerator and denominator by $x + 2$, giving $\lim_{x \to -2} (x - 3)$. We see that $x - 3$ will approach -5 as x approaches -2. Thus the limit is

$$\lim_{x \to -2} \frac{x^2 - x - 6}{x + 2} = \lim_{x \to -2} (x - 3) = -5.$$

EXAMPLE 4   Find $\lim\limits_{x \to 2} \dfrac{x^2 - 4}{x - 2}$, if it exists.

Solution   We cannot find the limit by using Property V because the denominator is zero at $x = 2$. We can find the limit by factoring the numerator.

$$\lim_{x \to 2} \frac{x^2 - 4}{x - 2} = \lim_{x \to 2} \frac{(x - 2)(x + 2)}{x - 2}$$

$$= \lim_{x \to 2} (x + 2) \qquad \text{We can divide by } x - 2 \text{ because } x$$
$$\text{is approaching 2 but cannot equal}$$
$$= 4 \qquad\qquad\qquad 2, \text{ by the definition of limit.}$$

EXAMPLE 5   Find $\lim\limits_{h \to 0} \dfrac{(x + h)^2 - x^2}{h}$.

Solution   Substituting 0 for h results in 0/0, so we must proceed as follows.

$$\lim_{h \to 0} \frac{(x + h)^2 - x^2}{h} = \lim_{h \to 0} \frac{x^2 + 2xh + h^2 - x^2}{h}$$

$$= \lim_{h \to 0} \frac{2xh + h^2}{h}$$

$$= \lim_{h \to 0} (2x + h) \qquad \text{We can divide by } h \text{ because}$$
$$h \to 0, \text{ but does not equal 0.}$$
$$= 2x$$

EXAMPLE 6   Find $\lim\limits_{x \to 1} \dfrac{x^2 + 3x + 2}{x - 1}$, if it exists.

Solution   Substituting 1 for x in the function results in 6/0, so 1 is not in the domain of the function.

Factoring the numerator of the function gives

$$\lim_{x \to 1} \frac{(x + 1)(x + 2)}{x - 1}.$$

Since $x - 1$ is not a factor of the numerator, we cannot divide numerator and denominator by $x - 1$ as we did before. We see that as x approaches 1 from the right, the numerator will approach 6, and the denominator will approach 0, with each value being larger than 0. Thus as x approaches 1 on its right side, the ratio will become large without bound (see Table 9.2). We write this as

$$\lim_{x \to 1^+} \frac{x^2 + 3x + 2}{x - 1} = +\infty$$

and say the limit does not exist (because it is not a finite number). The symbol $+\infty$ is used to indicate infinity, which is not a number but means that the function is increasing without bound.

Table 9.2

	Left		Right
x	$\dfrac{x^2 + 3x + 2}{x - 1}$	x	$\dfrac{x^2 + 3x + 2}{x - 1}$
0	-2	2	12
0.5	-7.5	1.5	17.5
0.7	-15.3	1.2	35.2
0.9	-55.1	1.1	65.1
0.99	-595.01	1.01	605.01
0.999	-5995.001	1.001	6005.001
0.9999	$-59{,}999.0001$	1.001	60,005.0001
$\displaystyle\lim_{x \to 1^-} \dfrac{x^2 + 3x + 2}{x - 1} = -\infty$		$\displaystyle\lim_{x \to 1^+} \dfrac{x^2 + 3x + 2}{x - 1} = +\infty$	

As x approaches 1 from the left, we see that the numerator of the function will again approach 6, but the denominator will approach 0 through *negative* values. Thus the ratio will again become large without bound, *but* it will be negative (see Table 9.2). Thus we write

$$\lim_{x \to 1^-} \frac{x^2 + 3x + 2}{x - 1} = -\infty.$$

Even though the left-hand and right-hand limits are undefined, the knowledge that they are infinite is helpful in graphing the function. Its graph is shown in Figure 9.3.

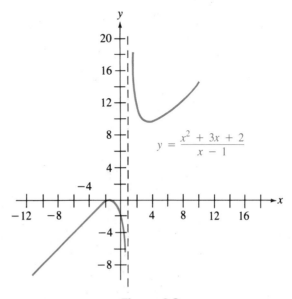

$$y = \frac{x^2 + 3x + 2}{x - 1}$$

Figure 9.3

We have discussed two types of limits that need special consideration. They both result when the denominator of a fraction approaches zero. We summarize as follows.

Evaluating Limits of the Form
$$\lim_{x \to a} \frac{f(x)}{g(x)}, \textbf{ where}$$
$$\lim_{x \to a} g(x) = 0$$

Type I. If $\lim\limits_{x \to a} f(x) = 0$ and $\lim\limits_{x \to a} g(x) = 0$, then we can reduce the fraction $f(x)/g(x)$ by factoring (see Examples 4 and 5).

Type II. If

$$\lim_{x \to a} f(x) \neq 0 \text{ and } \lim_{x \to a} g(x) = 0,$$

then

$$\lim_{x \to a} \frac{f(x)}{g(x)} = \pm \infty.$$

We can test values on both sides of a to determine if the limit gives $+\infty$ or $-\infty$. (See Example 6.)

In Example 6 we wrote

$$\lim_{x \to 1^+} \frac{x^2 + 3x + 2}{x - 1} = +\infty$$

to indicate that the function $(x^2 + 3x + 2)/(x - 1)$ increases without bound as x approaches 1 from values larger than 1.

We say that the limit does not exist (or is undefined) if it is infinite. But as we stated earlier, there is a second situation where the limit does not exist.

If $\lim\limits_{x \to a^+} f(x) \neq \lim\limits_{x \to a^-} f(x)$, then $\lim\limits_{x \to a} f(x)$ does *not* exist.

First-class postage is 25¢ for the first ounce or part of an ounce that a letter weighs, and each additional ounce or part of an ounce above one ounce costs an additional 20¢. Thus we can find the cost of mailing a first-class letter that weighs 5 ounces or less by using Table 9.3. For example, the postage for a letter weighing 3.4 ounces is $f(3.4) = 85$¢ and the postage for a letter weighing 1.2 ounces is $f(1.2) = 45$¢. Notice that any letter weighing more than one ounce but not more than two ounces will cost 45¢ to mail, regardless of how close the weight is to one ounce.

Table 9.3

Weight x	Postage f(x)
$0 < x \le 1$	$0.25
$1 < x \le 2$	0.45
$2 < x \le 3$	0.65
$3 < x \le 4$	0.85
$4 < x \le 5$	1.05

To see if the limit of this post-office function exists as x approaches one ounce, we will examine the function's behavior on either side of $x = 1$ (see Table 9.4).

Table 9.4

Left of x = 1		Right of x = 1	
x	f(x)	x	f(x)
0.5	0.25	1.5	0.45
0.9	0.25	1.1	0.45
0.99	0.25	1.01	0.45
0.999	0.25	1.001	0.45

From Table 9.4 we see that the limit of this function as x approaches 1 from the left is 0.25. We write this

$$\lim_{x \to 1^-} f(x) = 0.25.$$

We also see that the limit as x approaches 1 from the right is 0.45. We write this as

$$\lim_{x \to 1^+} f(x) = 0.45.$$

Since the limit from the left does not equal the limit from the right, the limit does not exist. The graph of the post-office function is shown in Figure 9.4.

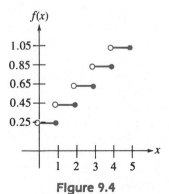

Figure 9.4

It is often interesting and important to see what value(s) the function approaches as x gets large without bound. We write $\lim_{x \to +\infty} f(x)$ to indicate the value the function approaches as the values of x gets very large (or as x increases without bound), and $\lim_{x \to -\infty} f(x)$ to indicate the value the function approaches as x decreases without bound. For many functions, the functional values will become infinitely large as x does, but not all functions behave in this manner. For example, consider the function $f(x) = 1/x$. As x gets very large, the value of $1/x$ will get closer and closer to 0. We write this in limit form as

$$\lim_{x \to +\infty} \frac{1}{x} = 0.$$

The following examples illustrate other infinite limits.

EXAMPLE 7   Find

$$\lim_{x \to +\infty} \frac{2x - 1}{x + 2},$$

if it exists.

Solution   If we let x approach $+\infty$, we see that both the numerator and denominator become very large. But we do not know what the ratio will equal. We can evaluate the limit if we first divide the numerator and denominator by x, giving

$$\lim_{x \to +\infty} \frac{2 - \dfrac{1}{x}}{1 + \dfrac{2}{x}}.$$

Now, the numerator approaches 2 and the denominator approaches 1 because $\lim_{x \to +\infty} \dfrac{1}{x} = 0$ and $\lim_{x \to +\infty} \dfrac{2}{x} = 0$, so

$$\lim_{x \to +\infty} \frac{2x - 1}{x + 2} = \lim_{x \to +\infty} \frac{2 - \dfrac{1}{x}}{1 + \dfrac{2}{x}} = \frac{2}{1} = 2.$$

In finding a limit like the one in Example 7, it is frequently helpful to divide the numerator and denominator by the highest power of x present. In Example 7 we divided both numerator and denominator by x because x^1 was the highest power present.

EXAMPLE 8   Find

$$\lim_{x \to +\infty} \frac{x^3 - 4x}{3x^2 - 1},$$

if it exists.

Solution Both the numerator and denominator will become infinite as $x \to +\infty$. Dividing both numerator and denominator by x^3 gives

$$\lim_{x \to +\infty} \frac{x^3 - 4x}{3x^2 - 1} = \lim_{x \to +\infty} \frac{1 - \dfrac{4}{x^2}}{\dfrac{3}{x} - \dfrac{1}{x^3}} = +\infty.$$

The limit is $+\infty$ because the numerator approaches 1 and the denominator approaches 0 through positive values.

Thus

$$\lim_{x \to +\infty} \frac{x^3 - 4x}{3x^2 - 1}$$

does not exist.

An application that required an infinite limit was an investment problem studied in Section 6.2. It was shown that the compound amount of an investment of $1 at an interest rate of 100%, compounded m times in one year, is

$$S = \left(1 + \frac{1}{m}\right)^m.$$

To find the amount when the interest was compounded continuously, we constructed a table of values of S for increasing values of m. As shown in Table 6.1 (see Section 6.2), as m increases in size, the value of S approaches the special number $e = 2.7182818. \ldots$ In fact, this *limit* defines the number e. That is,

$$e = \lim_{m \to \infty} \left(1 + \frac{1}{m}\right)^m \qquad \text{(by definition)}.$$

We also note that e is sometimes equivalently defined (see problem 53 in Exercise 9.1) as

$$e = \lim_{a \to 0} (1 + a)^{1/a}.$$

Exercise 9.1

Find the following limits, if they exist.

1. $\lim_{x \to 0} 4$

2. $\lim_{x \to 12} e$

3. $\lim_{x \to 3} x$

4. $\lim_{x \to -2} x$

5. $\lim\limits_{x \to 3} 6x$

6. $\lim\limits_{x \to -12} -4x$

7. $\lim\limits_{x \to 2} (x - 3)$

8. $\lim\limits_{x \to 2} (3x - 4)$

9. $\lim\limits_{x \to -1} (4x^2 + 2)$

10. $\lim\limits_{x \to 3} (2x^3 - 12x^2 + 5x + 3)$

11. $\lim\limits_{x \to 2} \dfrac{x^3 - 4}{x - 3}$

12. $\lim\limits_{x \to -1} \dfrac{x^3 - 3x + 1}{x - 1}$

13. $\lim\limits_{x \to 4} \dfrac{4x^2 - 12x - 16}{x + 4}$

14. $\lim\limits_{x \to 3} \dfrac{x^2 - 9}{x + 2}$

15. $\lim\limits_{x \to 3} \dfrac{x^2 - 9}{x - 3}$

16. $\lim\limits_{x \to -4} \dfrac{x^2 - 16}{x + 4}$

17. $\lim\limits_{x \to -2} \dfrac{x^2 + 4x + 4}{x + 2}$

18. $\lim\limits_{x \to 1} \dfrac{x^2 + x - 2}{x - 1}$

19. $\lim\limits_{x. \to 2} \dfrac{x^3 - 4x}{2x^2 - x^3}$

20. $\lim\limits_{x \to 1/2} \dfrac{x^2 - \frac{1}{4}}{2x - 1}$

21. $\lim\limits_{x \to 10} \dfrac{x^2 - 19x + 90}{3x^2 - 30x}$

22. $\lim\limits_{x \to -3} \dfrac{x^4 + 3x^3}{2x^4 - 18x^2}$

23. $\lim\limits_{x \to 2} \dfrac{x^2 + 6x + 9}{x - 2}$

24. $\lim\limits_{x \to 5} \dfrac{x^2 - 6x + 8}{x - 5}$

25. $\lim\limits_{x \to -1} \dfrac{x^2 + 5x + 6}{x + 1}$

26. $\lim\limits_{x \to 3} \dfrac{x^2 + 2x - 3}{x - 3}$

27. $\lim\limits_{x \to 1/3} \dfrac{x^2 - \frac{x}{3}}{9x^2 - 6x + 1}$

28. $\lim\limits_{x \to -5} \dfrac{x^3 + 5x^2}{2x^4 + 20x^3 + 50x^2}$

29. $\lim\limits_{h \to 0} \dfrac{(x + h)^3 - x^3}{h}$

30. $\lim\limits_{h \to 0} \dfrac{2(x + h)^2 - 2x^2}{h}$

31. If $\lim\limits_{x \to 3} f(x) = 4$ and $\lim\limits_{x \to 3} g(x) = -2$, find

(a) $\lim\limits_{x \to 3} [f(x) + g(x)]$.

(b) $\lim\limits_{x \to 3} [f(x) - g(x)]$.

(c) $\lim\limits_{x \to 3} [f(x) \cdot g(x)]$.

(d) $\lim\limits_{x \to 3} \dfrac{g(x)}{f(x)}$.

32. If $\lim\limits_{x \to 2} [f(x) + g(x)] = 5$ and $\lim\limits_{x \to 2} g(x) = 11$, find

(a) $\lim\limits_{x \to 2} f(x)$.

(b) $\lim\limits_{x \to 2} \{[f(x)]^2 - [g(x)]^2\}$.

(c) $\lim\limits_{x \to 2} \dfrac{3g(x)}{[f(x) - g(x)]}$.

33. If $\lim\limits_{x \to 2^+} f(x) = 5$, $\lim\limits_{x \to 2^-} f(x) = 5$, and $f(2) = 0$, find $\lim\limits_{x \to 2} f(x)$, if it exists. Explain your conclusions.

34. If $\lim\limits_{x \to 0^+} f(x) = 3$, $\lim\limits_{x \to 0^-} f(x) = 0$, and $f(0) = 0$, find $\lim\limits_{x \to 0} f(x)$, if it exists. Explain your conclusions.

In problems 35–38, for each given $f(x)$ find the following limits, if they exist:

(a) $\lim\limits_{x \to 1^+} f(x)$ (b) $\lim\limits_{x \to 1^-} f(x)$ (c) $\lim\limits_{x \to 1} f(x)$

35. $f(x) = \begin{cases} 1 + x & \text{if } x \le 1 \\ 2x - 1 & \text{if } x > 1 \end{cases}$

36. $f(x) = \begin{cases} 2x - 3 & \text{if } x < 1 \\ 5 & \text{if } x = 1 \\ \dfrac{2 - 7x}{5} & \text{if } x > 1 \end{cases}$

37. $f(x) = \begin{cases} 3x + 5 & \text{if } x < 0 \\ 4x & \text{if } x > 0 \end{cases}$

38. $f(x) = \begin{cases} \dfrac{2}{x - 7} & \text{if } x \le 2 \\ \dfrac{2}{x} & \text{if } x > 2 \end{cases}$

Evaluate the limits in problems 39–48.

39. $\lim\limits_{x \to +\infty} \dfrac{3}{x + 1}$

40. $\lim\limits_{x \to -\infty} \dfrac{4}{x^2 - 2x}$

41. $\lim\limits_{x \to +\infty} \dfrac{x^3 - 1}{x^3 + 4}$

42. $\lim\limits_{x \to -\infty} \dfrac{3x^2 + 2}{x^2 - 4}$

43. $\lim\limits_{x \to -\infty} \dfrac{5x^3 - 4x}{3x^3 - 2}$

44. $\lim\limits_{x \to +\infty} \dfrac{4x^2 + 5x}{x^2 - 4x}$

45. $\lim\limits_{x \to +\infty} \dfrac{4x + 3}{x^2 - 1}$

46. $\lim\limits_{x \to -\infty} \dfrac{5x^2 + 4x}{2x^3 - 1}$

47. $\lim\limits_{x \to +\infty} \dfrac{3x^2 + 5x}{6x + 1}$

48. $\lim\limits_{x \to -\infty} \dfrac{5x^3 - 8}{4x^2 + 5x}$

The function $f(x) = [\![x]\!]$ is called the **greatest integer function.** For each real value of x, this function gives the greatest integer less than or equal to x. For example, $f(2.5) = 2$, $f(3) = 3$, and $f(-1.5) = -2$.

49. Graph the greatest integer function for $-2 \le x \le 4$.
50. Does $\lim\limits_{x \to 3^+} f(x) = \lim\limits_{x \to 3^-} f(x)$, if $f(x) = [\![x]\!]$?

Find the limits if they exist.

51. $\lim\limits_{x \to 2} f(x)$, where $f(x) = [\![x]\!]$.

52. $\lim\limits_{x \to 1.5} f(x)$, where $f(x) = [\![x]\!]$.

53. Use values 0.1, 0.01, 0.001, 0.0001, and 0.00001 with your calculator to show that

$$(1 + a)^{1/a}$$

approaches e as a approaches 0.

APPLICATIONS

54. The Ace Parking Garage charges $2.00 for parking for 2 hours or less, and 50¢ for each extra hour or part of an hour after the 2-hour minimum. The parking charges for the first 5 hours could be written as a function of the time. The following is a statement of this function, with (a), (b), (c), and (d) to be determined.

$$f(t) = \begin{cases} \text{(a)} & \text{if} \ \ 0 < t \le 2 \\ \$2.50 & \text{if} \ \ 2 < t \le \text{(b)} \\ \text{(c)} & \text{if} \ \ 3 < t \le 4 \\ \text{(d)} & \text{if} \ \ 4 < t \le 5 \end{cases}$$

(e) Find $\lim_{t \to 1} f(t)$, if it exists.

(f) Find $\lim_{t \to 2} f(t)$, if it exists.

55. Suppose the cost C of removing p percent of the particulate pollution from the smokestacks of an industrial plant is given by

$$C(p) = \frac{7300 \, p}{100 - p}$$

(a) Find $\lim_{p \to 100^-} C(p)$, if it exists.

(b) Can 100% of the particulate pollution be removed?

56. Suppose the cost C of obtaining water that contains p percent impurities is given by

$$C(p) = \frac{120,000}{p} - 1200.$$

(a) Find $\lim_{p \to 0^+} C(p)$, if it exists.

(b) Find $\lim_{p \to 100^-} C(p)$, if it exists.

57. The monthly charge for water in a small town is given by

$$f(x) = \begin{cases} 18 & \text{if} \ \ 0 \le x \le 20 \\ 0.1x + 16 & \text{if} \ \ x > 20 \end{cases}$$

Find $\lim_{x \to 20} f(x)$, if it exists.

58. The monthly charge in dollars for x kilowatt hours (kwh) of electricity used by a commercial customer is given by the following function.

$$C(x) = \begin{cases} 7.52 + 0.1079x & \text{if} \ \ 0 \le x \le 5 \\ 19.22 + 0.1079x & \text{if} \ \ 5 < x \le 750 \\ 20.795 + 0.1058x & \text{if} \ \ 750 < x \le 1500 \\ 131.345 + 0.0321x & \text{if} \ \ x > 1500 \end{cases}$$

Find (a) $\lim_{x \to 1500} C(x)$, if it exists.

(b) $\lim_{x \to 5} C(x)$, if it exists.

59. If an annuity makes an infinite series of equal payments at the end of the interest periods, it is called a **perpetuity.** We have seen in Chapter 6 that if a lump-sum investment of A_n is needed to result in n periodic payments of R when the interest rate per period is i, then

$$A_n = R \frac{1 - (1 + i)^{-n}}{i}.$$

Evaluate $\lim\limits_{n \to \infty} A_n$ to show that the lump-sum payment for a perpetuity is

$$A = \frac{R}{i}.$$

60. Find the lump-sum investment needed to make payments of $100 per month in perpetuity if interest is 12%, compounded monthly. Use the formula developed in problem 59.

61. The pressure P of a gas at constant temperature is related to the volume V according to

$$P = \frac{K}{V},$$

where K is a constant. What does P approach as $V \to \infty$?

9.2 Continuous Functions; Asymptotes

Objectives
□ To determine if a function is continuous or discontinuous
□ To determine what type of discontinuity exists at a point where a function is discontinuous
□ To find vertical and horizontal asymptotes of graphs of functions

We have already stated that those functions f for which the limit as $x \to a$ gives the same value as $f(a)$ are continuous functions. Continuous functions can be thought of as those whose graphs can be drawn without lifting the pencil. A more formal definition of continuity follows.

A function f is said to be **continuous at the point** $x = a$ if the following conditions are satisfied:

1. $f(a)$ exists.
2. $\lim\limits_{x \to a} f(x)$ exists.
3. $\lim\limits_{x \to a} f(x) = f(a)$.

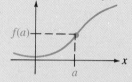

If one or more of these conditions are not satisfied, we say the function is discontinuous at $x = a$. (Figure 9.5 on the following page shows graphs of some functions that are discontinuous at $x = a$.)

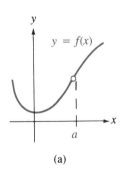

(a)

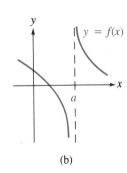

(b)

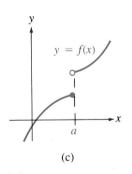

(c)

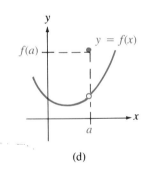

(d)

Figure 9.5

For example, the function $f(x) = 3x + 5$ is continuous at $x = 2$ because

1. $f(2) = 11$

2. $\lim_{x \to 2} f(x) = 11$

3. $\lim_{x \to 2} f(x) = 11 = f(2)$.

Recall that in Section 9.1 we found that we can evaluate $\lim_{x \to a} f(x)$, when $f(x)$ is a polynomial, by evaluating $f(a)$. We can do this because every polynomial is continuous. If a function is not a polynomial, it may have a point where it is not continuous. To determine if a function is continuous, we must investigate the point(s) where it may be discontinuous. As we noted in Section 9.1, a function that can be written as the ratio of two polynomials is called a *rational* function. A rational function may be discontinuous because any value that makes the denominator 0 will be a point of discontinuity. The following examples illustrate methods of determining if a function has any points of discontinuity.

EXAMPLE 1   Is the function $f(x) = \dfrac{x^2 - 1}{x + 1}$ continuous at $x = 1$?

Solution   1. $f(1) = 0$

2. $\lim_{x \to 1} f(x) = 0$

3. $\lim_{x \to 1} f(x) = 0 = f(1)$

Thus $f(x)$ is continuous at $x = 1$.

EXAMPLE 2   Is the function of Example 1 continuous at $x = -1$?

Solution   The function is $f(x) = \dfrac{x^2 - 1}{x + 1}$.

$f(-1)$ is undefined. Thus the function is discontinuous at $x = -1$. Note that $\lim_{x \to -1} f(x)$ does exist, since

$$\lim_{x \to -1} \frac{x^2 - 1}{x + 1} = \lim_{x \to -1} \frac{(x - 1)(x + 1)}{x + 1} = \lim_{x \to -1} (x - 1) = -2.$$

We can see from Example 2 that there is at least one point where the function $f(x) = (x^2 - 1)/(x + 1)$ is discontinuous. The graph of the function of Example 2 is shown in Figure 9.6. Since there is no point corresponding to $x = -1$, this discontinuity is called a **missing point discontinuity.**

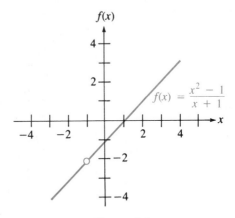

Figure 9.6

If there is *no point of discontinuity* for a function we say it is a **continuous function;** otherwise it is a **discontinuous function.** The function $y = x^2 - 3x + 1$ is a continuous function because there is no point of discontinuity. The function $y = 5/(x - 3)$ is discontinuous because $f(3)$ is undefined.

Sometimes functions cannot be defined by one equation. For example, a function may have a value 0 for all values of x less than 0, and a value equal to x for all values of $x \geq 0$. We can define this function by

$$f(x) = \begin{cases} 0 & \text{if } x < 0 \\ x & \text{if } x \geq 0 \end{cases}.$$

EXAMPLE 3   Is the function $f(x) = \begin{cases} 0 & \text{if } x < 0 \\ x & \text{if } x \geq 0 \end{cases}$ continuous?

Solution   If the function has a point where it is discontinuous, the trouble spot will be at $x = 0$. Since the function is defined differently for $x < 0$ and $x \geq 0$, we must evaluate limits approaching 0 from the left and from the right to test for continuity.

1. $f(0) = 0$
2. $\lim_{x \to 0^-} f(x) = 0$ and $\lim_{x \to 0^+} f(x) = \lim_{x \to 0^+} x = 0$, so $\lim_{x \to 0} f(x) = 0$
3. $\lim_{x \to 0} f(x) = f(0)$

Thus the function is continuous. (See Figure 9.7 on the following page.)

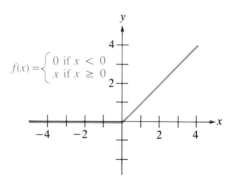

$$f(x) = \begin{cases} 0 \text{ if } x < 0 \\ x \text{ if } x \geq 0 \end{cases}$$

Figure 9.7

EXAMPLE 4   Is the post office function $f(x)$ (see Section 9.1, Table 9.3 on page 475) continuous or discontinuous?

Solution   To show that the function is discontinuous, we only need to show it is discontinuous at one point. Consider the point where $x = 1$.

$$f(1) = 0.25$$
$$\lim_{x \to 1^-} f(x) = 0.25 \quad \text{and} \quad \lim_{x \to 1^+} f(x) = 0.45 \quad \text{Section 9.1, Table 9.4}$$

Since the left and right limits as x approaches 1 disagree, $\lim_{x \to 1} f(x)$ does not exist.
Therefore the post office function is discontinuous. See Figure 9.4 on page 475 for the graph of this function. Note the jumps in the graph. This type of discontinuity is frequently called a **jump discontinuity.**

EXAMPLE 5   Is the function $f(x) = \begin{cases} x & \text{if} \quad x \leq 0 \\ x^2 & \text{if} \quad 0 < x \leq 4 \\ 2x + 4 & \text{if} \quad x > 4 \end{cases}$ continuous?

Solution   There are two trouble spots for this function, one at $x = 0$ and one at $x = 4$. Checking $x = 0$ first, we see

1. $f(0) = 0$

2. $\lim\limits_{x \to 0^-} f(x) = 0 = \lim\limits_{x \to 0^+} f(x)$, so $\lim\limits_{x \to 0} f(x) = 0$

3. $\lim\limits_{x \to 0} f(x) = f(0)$

So $f(x)$ is continuous at $x = 0$.
At $x = 4$, we have

1. $f(4) = 16$

2. $\lim\limits_{x \to 4^-} f(x) = \lim\limits_{x \to 4^-} x^2 = 16$ and $\lim\limits_{x \to 4^+} f(x) = \lim\limits_{x \to 4^+} 2x + 4 = 12$

Thus

$$\lim_{x \to 4^-} f(x) \neq \lim_{x \to 4^+} f(x),$$

so $\lim_{x \to 4} f(x)$ does not exist. Thus the function is discontinuous at $x = 4$.

We have seen two types of discontinuity: missing point and jump. A third type of discontinuity is an **infinite discontinuity.** An infinite discontinuity occurs at $x = c$ if one or more of the following four statements is true.

1. $\lim\limits_{x \to c^-} f(x) = +\infty$

2. $\lim\limits_{x \to c^-} f(x) = -\infty$

3. $\lim\limits_{x \to c^+} f(x) = +\infty$

4. $\lim\limits_{x \to c^+} f(x) = -\infty$

EXAMPLE 6   Is the function $f(x) = 1/(x - 1)$ continuous?

Solution   The denominator of this function will be 0 if $x = 1$, so the trouble spot is at $x = 1$. We see that

1. the function is undefined at $x = 1$.
2. $\lim\limits_{x \to 1^-} f(x) = -\infty$ and $\lim\limits_{x \to 1^+} f(x) = +\infty$

We see that $f(x) = 1/(x - 1)$ has an infinite discontinuity at $x = 1$. The graph of $y = 1/(x - 1)$ (Figure 9.8) shows that the curve approaches $-\infty$ as x approaches 1 from the left and $+\infty$ as x approaches 1 from the right.

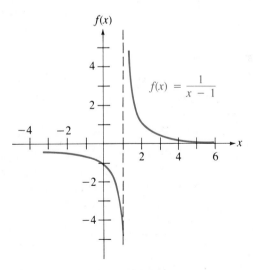

Figure 9.8

When an infinite discontinuity occurs, we say the graph has a **vertical asymptote.** Thus, the graph in Figure 9.8 has a vertical asymptote at $x = 1$.

In general we define the line $x = x_0$ to be a **vertical asymptote** if the limit of the function is $+\infty$ or $-\infty$ as x approaches x_0 (from the left or right).

In other words, the curve will have a vertical asymptote at $x = x_0$ if the denominator of the function approaches 0 but the numerator does not approach 0 as $x \to x_0$.

We also see in Figure 9.8 that the curve approaches the x-axis ($y = 0$) as values of x get large (both positive and negative). We say the x-axis is a **horizontal asymptote** for this curve.

Since the horizontal asymptotes determine behavior at the extremes of the graph, we can find horizontal asymptotes, if they exist, by evaluating the limits $\lim\limits_{x \to +\infty} f(x)$ and $\lim\limits_{x \to -\infty} f(x)$.

If $\lim\limits_{x \to +\infty} f(x)$ or $\lim\limits_{x \to -\infty} f(x)$ exists and equals a number b, then there is a **horizontal asymptote** at $y = b$.

If $\lim\limits_{x \to +\infty} f(x) = \pm\infty$ and $\lim\limits_{x \to -\infty} f(x) = \pm\infty$, then there is no horizontal asymptote.

We see that

$$\lim_{x \to +\infty} \frac{1}{x - 1} = 0 \quad \text{and} \quad \lim_{x \to -\infty} \frac{1}{x - 1} = 0,$$

so the graph of $y = 1/(x - 1)$ has a horizontal asymptote at $y = 0$, as Figure 9.8 shows.

EXAMPLE 7   Find the horizontal and vertical asymptotes of the graph of $y = (2x - 4)/(3x + 6)$.

Solution   The denominator is 0 at $x = -2$. Because the numerator is *not also zero,* we know the limit will be infinite, giving us a vertical asymptote. To determine how the curve approaches the asymptote, we will evaluate the limit as $x \to -2$ from the left and right. As $x \to -2$ from values less than -2, we get very large positive numbers,

$$\lim_{x \to -2^-} \frac{2x - 4}{3x + 6} = +\infty,$$

so the curve increases rapidly to the left of the vertical asymptote. As $x \to -2$ from values greater than -2, we get very large negative numbers,

$$\lim_{x \to -2^+} \frac{2x - 4}{3x + 6} = -\infty,$$

so the graph is very low to the right of the vertical asymptote (see Figure 9.9).

To find horizontal asymptotes, if any exist, we evaluate

$$\lim_{x \to +\infty} \frac{2x - 4}{3x + 6} \quad \text{and} \quad \lim_{x \to -\infty} \frac{2x - 4}{3x + 6}:$$

1. $\displaystyle \lim_{x \to +\infty} \frac{2x - 4}{3x + 6} = \lim_{x \to +\infty} \frac{2 - \dfrac{4}{x}}{3 + \dfrac{6}{x}} = \frac{2}{3}$

2. $\displaystyle \lim_{x \to -\infty} \frac{2x - 4}{3x + 6} = \lim_{x \to -\infty} \frac{2 - \dfrac{4}{x}}{3 + \dfrac{6}{x}} = \frac{2}{3}$

Thus there is a horizontal asymptote at $y = 2/3$.

Plotting a few points (especially the intercepts) and using the information we know about the asymptotes gives the graph, shown in Figure 9.9.

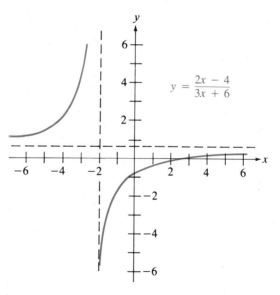

Figure 9.9

The following information is useful in discussing continuity and asymptotes of functions.

A. A polynomial function is continuous everywhere. It has no asymptotes.

B. A rational function is a function of the form $\dfrac{f(x)}{g(x)}$, where $f(x)$ and $g(x)$ are polynomials.

1. If $g(x) \neq 0$ at any value of x, the function is continuous everywhere.

2. If $g(c) = 0$, the function is discontinuous at $x = c$.
   (a) If $g(c) = 0$ and $f(c) \neq 0$, then an infinite discontinuity and a vertical asymptote occur at $x = c$.
   (b) if $g(c) = 0$ and $\lim\limits_{x \to c} \dfrac{f(x)}{g(x)} = L$, then there is a missing point discontinuity at $x = c$.

3. Additional notes regarding rational functions:
   (a) If $\lim\limits_{x \to \infty} \dfrac{f(x)}{g(x)} = L$ or $\lim\limits_{x \to -\infty} \dfrac{f(x)}{g(x)} = L$, where L is a number, then $y = L$ is a horizontal asymptote for the graph of $\dfrac{f(x)}{g(x)}$.
   (b) If $g(d) = 0$ and $f(d) = 0$, then $x - d$ can be factored from $g(x)$ and from $f(x)$ in evaluating $\lim\limits_{x \to d} \dfrac{f(x)}{g(x)}$.

Exercise 9.2

1. Is $f(x) = x^2 - 5x$ continuous at $x = 0$?
2. Is $y = 3x - 5x^3$ continuous at $x = 2$?
3. Is $f(x) = \dfrac{x^2 - 4}{x - 2}$ continuous at $x = -2$?
4. Is $y = \dfrac{x^2 - 9}{x + 3}$ continuous at $x = 3$?
5. Is $y = \dfrac{x^2 - 9}{x + 3}$ continuous at $x = -3$?
6. Is $f(x) = \dfrac{x^2 - 4}{x - 2}$ continuous at $x = 2$?
7. Is $f(x) = \dfrac{x^2 - 2x - 3}{x - 1}$ continuous at $x = 1$?
8. Is $f(x) = \dfrac{x^2 + 5x - 6}{x + 1}$ continuous at $x = 1$?
9. Is $y = \dfrac{x^2 + 5x - 6}{x + 1}$ continuous at $x = -1$?
10. Is $y = \dfrac{x^2 - 8x + 12}{x + 2}$ continuous at $x = -2$?
11. If $f(x) = \begin{cases} 2 & \text{if } x \leq 0 \\ x + 2 & \text{if } x > 0 \end{cases}$, is f continuous at $x = 0$?

12. If $f(x) = \begin{cases} x - 3 & \text{if } x \le 2 \\ 4x - 7 & \text{if } x > 2 \end{cases}$, is f continuous at $x = 2$?

13. If $f(x) = \begin{cases} x^2 + 1 & \text{if } x \le 1 \\ 2x^2 - 1 & \text{if } x > 1 \end{cases}$, is f continuous at $x = 1$?

14. If $f(x) = \begin{cases} x^2 - x & \text{if } x \le 2 \\ 8 - 3x & \text{if } x > 2 \end{cases}$, is f continuous at $x = 2$?

15. Is $f(x) = [\![x]\!]$ continuous at $x = 1$? 16. Is $f(x) = [\![x]\!]$ continuous at $x = 2$?
17. Is $f(x) = [\![x]\!]$ continuous at $x = 1.5$? 18. Is $f(x) = [\![x]\!]$ continuous at $x = 2.98$?

In problems 19–32, determine whether the given function is continuous. If not, identify where it is discontinuous and which type of discontinuity occurs.

19. $f(x) = 4x^2 - 1$

20. $y = 5x^2 - 2x$

21. $y = \dfrac{x^2 - 25}{x - 5}$

22. $f(x) = \dfrac{x^3 - 27}{x - 3}$

23. $g(x) = \dfrac{x^2 + 4x + 4}{x + 2}$

24. $y = \dfrac{x^2 - 5x + 4}{x + 4}$

25. $g(x) = \dfrac{4x^2 + 3x + 2}{x + 2}$

26. $y = \dfrac{4x^2 + 4x + 1}{x + \frac{1}{2}}$

27. $y = \dfrac{x}{x^2 + 1}$

28. $y = \dfrac{2x - 1}{x^2 + 2x + 3}$

29. $f(x) = \begin{cases} 3 & \text{if } x \le 1 \\ x^2 + 2 & \text{if } x > 1 \end{cases}$

30. $f(x) = \begin{cases} x^3 + 1 & \text{if } x \le 1 \\ 2 & \text{if } x > 1 \end{cases}$

31. $f(x) = \begin{cases} x - 4 & \text{if } x \le 3 \\ x^2 - 8 & \text{if } x > 3 \end{cases}$

32. $f(x) = \begin{cases} x^2 + 4 & \text{if } x \ne 1 \\ 5 & \text{if } x = 1 \end{cases}$

In problems 33–36, use the graphs to find each of the following, if they exist:
  (a) vertical asymptotes
  (b) $\lim\limits_{x \to \infty} f(x)$
  (c) $\lim\limits_{x \to -\infty} f(x)$
  (d) horizontal asymptotes

33.

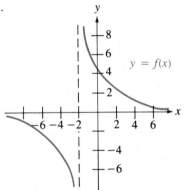

34.

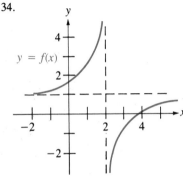

35.

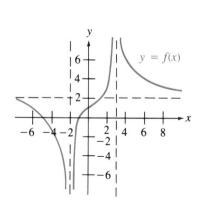

36.

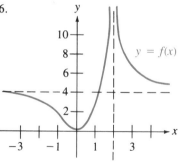

In problems 37–42, find any horizontal and vertical asymptotes for each function.

37. $y = \dfrac{2x}{x - 3}$

38. $y = \dfrac{3x - 1}{x + 5}$

39. $y = \dfrac{x + 1}{x^2 - 4}$

40. $y = \dfrac{4x}{9 - x^2}$

41. $y = \dfrac{3x^2 - 6}{2x - 5}$

42. $y = \dfrac{4x^2 - 1}{4x + 9}$

APPLICATIONS

43. Is the function that describes the Ace Parking Garage's charges (problem 54 of Section 9.1)
    (a) continuous at $t = 1$?
    (b) continuous at $t = 2$?
    (c) continuous?

44. Is the demand function $p = 1/q$ continuous for $q > 0$?

45. Suppose the number of calories of heat required to raise 1 gram of water (or ice) from $-40°C$ to $x°C$ is given by

$$f(x) = \begin{cases} \frac{1}{2}x + 20, & \text{if} \quad -40 \le x < 0 \\ x + 100, & \text{if} \quad 0 \le x. \end{cases}$$

    (a) What can be said about the continuity of the function?
    (b) What accounts for the behavior of the function at $0°C$?

46. Experimental evidence suggests that the response y of the body to the concentration x of injected adrenaline is given by

$$y = \frac{x}{a + bx}$$

    where a and b are experimental constants.
    (a) Is this function continuous for all x?
    (b) Based on your conclusion to (a) and the fact that in reality $x \ge 0$ and $y \ge 0$, must a and b be both positive, both negative, or have opposite signs?

47. The 1986 Tax Reform Act created the following tax schedule for single filers in 1988.

Tax rate	*Taxable income*
15%	0–$17,850
28%	Above $17,850

This means that the tax T is a function of income x as follows:

$$T(x) = \begin{cases} .15x & \text{if } 0 \le x \le 17{,}850 \\ 2677.50 + .28(x - 17{,}850) & \text{if } x > 17{,}850 \end{cases}$$

Is $T(x)$ continuous?

48. Suppose the size of a population of bacteria is given by $P = 1000t/(t + 10)$, where t represents time. Is this function continuous for all values of t? Common sense and nature place certain restrictions on t; is P continuous for all these values of t?

49. Suppose the cost C of removing p percent of the impurities from the waste water in a manufacturing process is given by

$$C(p) = \frac{9800p}{101 - p}.$$

Is this function continuous for all those p-values for which the problem makes sense?

50. Suppose the cost C of removing p percent of the particulate pollution from the exhaust gases at an industrial site is given by

$$C(p) = \frac{8100p}{100 - p}.$$

Describe any discontinuities for $C(p)$.

51. Residential customers in a small town have their monthly charge $f(x)$ for x hundred gallons of water given by

$$f(x) = \begin{cases} 18 & \text{if } 0 \le x \le 20 \\ 18 + 0.1(x - 20) & \text{if } x > 20 \end{cases}$$

Is $f(x)$ continuous?

9.3 The Derivative: Rates of Change; Tangent to a Curve

Objectives
- ☐ To define the derivative as a rate of change
- ☐ To use the definition of derivative to find derivatives of functions
- ☐ To use derivatives to find slopes of tangents to curves

Suppose a firm's revenue is given by the equation

$$f(x) = 100x - x^2, \qquad x \ge 0,$$

where x is the number of units of oil produced per day. (See Figure 9.10 on the following page.)

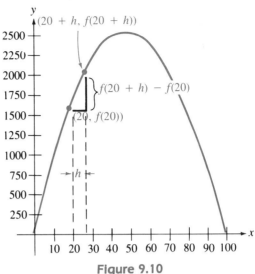

Figure 9.10

If the firm produces and sells 10 units per day, the revenue is

$$f(10) = \$900$$

and if it produces 20 units, its revenue is $f(20) = \$1600$. But if it produces 40 units, its revenue is $f(40) = \$2400$. Thus the revenue the firm receives is different at different levels of production. We can also see that the rate at which the revenue changes is different at different levels of production. For example, if production is increased from 20 units to 40 units, revenue increases from \$1600 to \$2400, so the average rate of change of revenue per unit is

$$\frac{f(40) - f(20)}{40 - 20} = \frac{2400 - 1600}{40 - 20} = \frac{800}{20} = 40.$$

However, if production is increased from 20 units to 30 units, the average rate of change of revenue per unit is

$$\frac{f(30) - f(20)}{30 - 20} = \frac{2100 - 1600}{10} = 50.$$

If production increases from 20 units to 21 units, the average rate of change of revenue per unit is

$$\frac{f(21) - f(20)}{21 - 20} = \frac{1659 - 1600}{1} = 59.$$

In considering the rate of change of the revenue function from some fixed point, as above with $x = 20$, we see that the average rate of change is different for different increases. Thus the average rate of change depends on the size of the increase as well as the level of production. We can find the **instantaneous rate of change,** or more simply, the **rate of change,** that depends upon only the function and the point at which the rate of change is to be found. We find the instantaneous rate of change by computing the average rate of change as x changes by a small amount h, and finding the limit as h approaches 0. Economists call the instantaneous rate of change of revenue the **marginal revenue.**

To find the instantaneous rate of change of revenue at $x = 20$, let us first compute the average rate of change as x increases by the small amount h. If we have $20 + h$ units, the revenue is $f(20 + h) = 100(20 + h) - (20 + h)^2$, so the increase in revenue is $f(20 + h) - f(20)$. (See Figure 9.10.) Since the increase in units is h, the average rate of change is

$$\frac{f(20 + h) - f(20)}{h} = \frac{[100(20 + h) - (20 + h)^2] - [100(20) - 20^2]}{h}$$

$$= \frac{2000 + 100h - (400 + 40h + h^2) - 2000 + 400}{h}$$

$$= \frac{60h - h^2}{h}$$

$$= 60 - h.$$

Now, as h gets smaller and smaller, this average rate of change approaches the instantaneous rate. Using limit notation, the instantaneous rate of change is

$$\lim_{h \to 0} (60 - h) = 60.$$

Thus if the revenue function is $f(x) = 100x - x^2$, $x \geq 0$, the marginal revenue at $x = 20$ units is 60. This means the revenue is increasing at a rate of $60 per unit if production is at 20 units.

To find the instantaneous rate of change of this revenue function at $x = 30$ units of production, we could evaluate

$$\lim_{h \to 0} \frac{f(30 + h) - f(30)}{h} = \lim_{h \to 0} \frac{[100(30 + h) - (30 + h)^2] - [100(30) - 30^2]}{h}$$

$$= \lim_{h \to 0} \frac{40h - h^2}{h}$$

$$= \lim_{h \to 0} (40 - h)$$

$$= 40.$$

Rather than evaluate the rates of change at different levels this way, we can develop a means of evaluating the rate of change at *any* point. If the production increases from any value x to $x + h$, revenue will change from $f(x)$ to $f(x + h)$. Thus the average rate of change in revenue is given by

$$\frac{f(x + h) - f(x)}{h},$$

and the instantaneous rate of change is given by

$$\lim_{h \to 0} \frac{f(x + h) - f(x)}{h}.$$

Thus, for the revenue function $f(x) = 100x - x^2$, the instantaneous rate of change at any point is

$$\lim_{h \to 0} \frac{f(x + h) - f(x)}{h} = \lim_{h \to 0} \frac{[100(x + h) - (x + h)^2] - [100x - x^2]}{h}$$

$$= \lim_{h \to 0} \frac{[100x + 100h - (x^2 + 2xh + h^2)] - [100x - x^2]}{h}$$

$$= \lim_{h \to 0} \frac{100h - 2xh - h^2}{h}$$

$$= \lim_{h \to 0} (100 - 2x - h)$$

$$= 100 - 2x.$$

This new function gives a formula for the *instantaneous rate of change of revenue* (the *marginal revenue*) at any level of production. For example, at $x = 20$ the instantaneous rate of change is $100 - 2(20) = 60$ and at $x = 30$ the rate is $100 - 2(30) = 40$. The function that we have developed to find the instantaneous rate of change of revenue from the revenue function is called the **derivative** of the function $f(x) = 100x - x^2$, and is denoted $f'(x) = 100 - 2x$.

The Derivative

If f is a function defined by $y = f(x)$, then the **derivative** of $f(x)$ at any value x, denoted $f'(x)$, is

$$f'(x) = \lim_{h \to 0} \frac{f(x + h) - f(x)}{h},$$

if it exists. If $f'(x_0)$ exists, we say f is **differentiable** at x_0. The process of finding the derivative is called **differentiation.**

EXAMPLE 1   If $f(x) = 4x^2$,
(a) find $f'(x)$.
(b) evaluate $f'(x)$ at $x = 3$.

Solution   (a) $f'(x) = \lim\limits_{h \to 0} \dfrac{f(x + h) - f(x)}{h}$

$= \lim\limits_{h \to 0} \dfrac{4(x + h)^2 - 4x^2}{h}$

$= \lim\limits_{h \to 0} \dfrac{4(x^2 + 2xh + h^2) - 4x^2}{h}$

$= \lim\limits_{h \to 0} \dfrac{4x^2 + 8xh + 4h^2 - 4x^2}{h}$

$= \lim\limits_{h \to 0} \dfrac{8xh + 4h^2}{h}$

$= \lim\limits_{h \to 0} 8x + 4h$

$= 8x$

(b) $f'(x)$ at $x = 3$ is $f'(3) = 8(3) = 24$.

As was mentioned in the introduction to this chapter, the velocity of a moving object is the instantaneous rate of change of the distance traveled with respect to the elapsed time. Thus, if the distance traveled is given as a function of the time, the derivative of the function will give the velocity at any time. Note that we mentioned that the velocity could be found by evaluating

$$\lim_{\Delta x \to 0} \frac{\Delta y}{\Delta x}.$$

If we represent the change in x values by Δx rather than h, and if we use Δy to denote $f(x + h) - f(x)$, then we can write the definition of derivative in the (shorter) form

$$\lim_{\Delta x \to 0} \frac{\Delta y}{\Delta x}.$$

For this reason the derivative of the function defined by $y = f(x)$ is also denoted by

$$\frac{dy}{dx}.$$

In addition to dy/dx and $f'(x)$, the derivative at any point x may be denoted by y', $\dfrac{d}{dx}f(x)$, $D_x y$, or $D_x f(x)$.

We can, of course, use variables other than x and y to represent functions and their derivatives. For example, we can represent the derivative of the function defined by $p = 2q^2 - 1$ by dp/dq or by $f'(q)$.

EXAMPLE 2   If the profit on a commodity is given by $P(x) = 400x - x^2$, where x is the number of units produced, what is the marginal profit, $P'(x)$,

(a) at $x = 20$ units?

(b) at $x = 100$ units?

(c) at $x = 300$ units? What is happening to profit when 300 units are sold?

Solution   To find the marginal profit at different levels, we will first find the derivative.

$$P'(x) = \lim_{h \to 0} \frac{P(x + h) - P(x)}{h}$$

$$= \lim_{h \to 0} \frac{[400(x + h) - (x + h)^2] - [400x - x^2]}{h}$$

$$= \lim_{h \to 0} \frac{400x + 400h - x^2 - 2xh - h^2 - 400x + x^2}{h}$$

$$= \lim_{h \to 0} \frac{400h - 2xh - h^2}{h}$$

$$= \lim_{h \to 0} 400 - 2x - h$$

$$= 400 - 2x$$

Thus the marginal profit function is $P'(x) = 400 - 2x$. (It is common to denote marginal profit by $\overline{MP}$, so $\overline{MP} = 400 - 2x$.)

(a) The marginal profit at 20 units is

$$P'(20) = 400 - 2(20) = 360.$$

(b) The marginal profit at 100 units is

$$P'(100) = 400 - 2(100) = 200.$$

(c) The marginal profit at 300 units is

$$P'(300) = 400 - 2(300) = -200.$$

A marginal profit of -200 indicates that the profit is decreasing at the rate of $200 per unit. Thus the profit is decreasing rapidly when production is at 300 units. Any increase in production will result in loss of profit.

In Chapter 1 we learned that the rate of change of profit (the marginal profit) for a linear profit function is given by the slope of the line. But will the slope of the profit curve give us the marginal profit if the profit function is not linear? Before we can answer this question, we must define the slope of a curve at a point on the curve. We will define the slope of a curve at a point as the slope of the line tangent to the curve at the point.

In geometry, a tangent to a circle is defined as a line that has one point in common with the circle. (See Figure 9.11(a).) This definition does not apply to all curves, as Figure 9.11(b) shows. Many lines can be drawn through the point A. One of the lines, line l, looks like it is tangent to the curve, but it intersects the curve at two points.

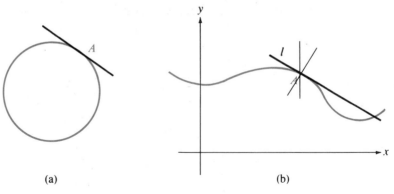

(a)   (b)

Figure 9.11

We can use *secant lines* (lines intersecting the curve at two points) to determine the tangent to a curve at a point A. In Figure 9.12, we have a set of secant lines passing through point A, with the line l representing the tangent to the curve at point A. Note that the secant lines m_1, m_2, m_3, m_4 have their second points (Q_1, Q_2, Q_3, Q_4) approaching A, and that as these points approach A, the secant lines get closer to the tangent line l. We can get a secant line as close as we wish to the tangent line by choosing a "second point" Q sufficiently close to point A.

Since the limiting position of secant lines that pass through point A and points to the left of A will also be the same line (line l), we may say that the common limiting position of the secant lines passing through A is the **tangent line** to the curve at the point A.

We can find the slope of the tangent to the curve at a point A by finding the slope of a secant line passing through A and taking the limit of this slope as the "second point" Q approaches the point A. Consider the function $y = f(x)$, which

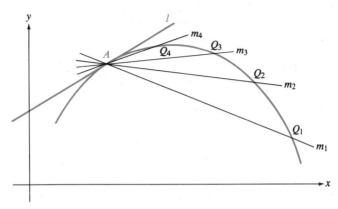

Figure 9.12

passes through the point $A(x_1, y_1)$. To find the slope of the tangent to the graph of $y = f(x)$ at A, we first draw a secant line from point A to a second point Q (x_2, y_2) on the curve (see Figure 9.13(a)).

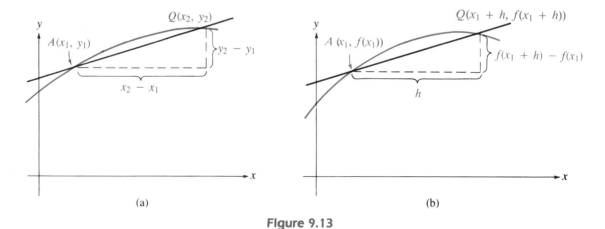

(a)   (b)

Figure 9.13

The slope of this secant line is

$$m_{AQ} = \frac{y_2 - y_1}{x_2 - x_1}.$$

But because we want to find the limit of this slope as Q approaches A, we will write the slope in a different form. Since $y = f(x)$, we can write the coordinates of A as $[x_1, f(x_1)]$. If we represent the difference $x_2 - x_1$ by the letter h, then we can write the coordinates of the point Q as $[x_1 + h, f(x_1 + h)]$. The graph is shown with these new coordinates in Figure 9.13(b). This notation is somewhat awkward, but it will make finding the slope of the tangent line possible. The slope of the secant line (in the new notation) is

$$m_{AQ} = \frac{f(x_1 + h) - f(x_1)}{h}.$$

Now, as the point Q approaches the point A on the curve, the secant line will approach the tangent to the graph of $y = f(x)$ at point A. But how will the slope of the line change as Q approaches A? We see that the difference between their x-values will decrease, so h will approach 0. But we cannot set $h = 0$ to find the slope of the tangent, for the *difference quotient*

$$\frac{f(x_1 + h) - f(x_1)}{h}$$

will be undefined if $h = 0$. Thus the slope of the tangent is the limit of this difference quotient as $h \to 0$.

The **slope of the tangent** to the graph of $y = f(x)$ at point $A[x_1, f(x_1)]$ is

$$m = \lim_{h \to 0} \frac{f(x_1 + h) - f(x_1)}{h}. \tag{1}$$

We can use the formula (1) to find the slope of a tangent to a curve at a point without consideration of the secant lines involved.

EXAMPLE 3   Find the slope of $y = f(x) = x^2$ at the point $A(2, 4)$.

Solution   The formula for the slope of the tangent to $y = f(x)$ at $(2, 4)$ is

$$m = \lim_{h \to 0} \frac{f(2 + h) - f(2)}{h}.$$

So for $f(x) = x^2$, we have

$$m = \lim_{h \to 0} \frac{(2 + h)^2 - 2^2}{h}.$$

Taking the limit immediately would result in both the numerator and the denominator approaching 0. To avoid this, we simplify the fraction before taking the limit.

$$m = \lim_{h \to 0} \frac{4 + 4h + h^2 - 4}{h} = \lim_{h \to 0} \frac{4h + h^2}{h} = \lim_{h \to 0} (4 + h) = 4$$

Thus the slope of the tangent to $y = x^2$ at $(2, 4)$ is 4 (see Figure 9.14).

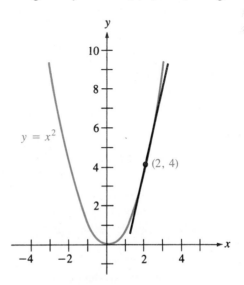

Figure 9.14

The statement "the slope of the tangent to the curve at (2, 4) is 4" is frequently simplified to the statement "the slope of the curve at (2, 4) is 4." Knowledge that the slope is a positive number on an interval tells us that the function is increasing on that interval, which means that a point moving along the graph of the function rises as it moves to the right on that interval. If the derivative (and thus the slope) is negative on an interval, the curve is decreasing on the interval; that is, a point moving along the graph falls as it moves to the right on that interval.

In order to avoid taking the limit of the difference quotient every time we desire the slope of the tangent to a curve at a particular point, we can evaluate the limit at *any* point, denoted $[x, f(x)]$. The resulting limit is

$$\lim_{h \to 0} \frac{f(x + h) - f(x)}{h},$$

which is the *derivative*. Thus we see that *the slope of the graph of a revenue function and the marginal revenue are identical, even when the graph is not a line.*

EXAMPLE 4   Given $y = f(x) = 3x^2 + 2x$, find
(a) the derivative of f at any point $[x, f(x)]$.
(b) the slope of the curve at (1, 5).
(c) the equation of the line tangent to $y = 3x^2 + 2x$ at (1, 5).

Solution   (a) The derivative of f at any value x is denoted by $f'(x)$, and is

$$y' = f'(x) = \lim_{h \to 0} \frac{f(x + h) - f(x)}{h}$$

$$= \lim_{h \to 0} \frac{[3(x + h)^2 + 2(x + h)] - (3x^2 + 2x)}{h}$$

$$= \lim_{h \to 0} \frac{3(x^2 + 2xh + h^2) + 2x + 2h - 3x^2 - 2x}{h}$$

$$= \lim_{h \to 0} \frac{6xh + 3h^2 + 2h}{h}$$

$$= \lim_{h \to 0} (6x + 3h + 2)$$

$$= 6x + 2$$

(b) The derivative is $f'(x) = 6x + 2$, so the slope of the tangent to the curve at (1, 5) is $f'(1) = 6(1) + 2 = 8$.
(c) The equation of the tangent line is $y - 5 = 8(x - 1)$, or $y = 8x - 3$.

Note that we can denote the value of the derivative of $y = f(x)$ at $x = 1$ by either $f'(1)$ or $y'|_{x=1}$.

Exercise 9.3

In problems 1–4, the tangent line to the graph of $f(x)$ at $x = 1$ is shown. In each case, find
(a) $f'(1)$ and (b) the instantaneous rate of change of $f(x)$ at $x = 1$.

1.

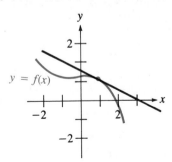

2.

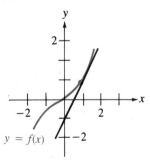

3.

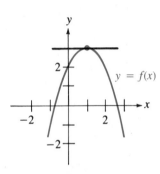

4.

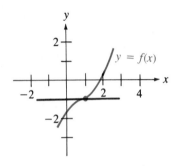

5. If $f(x) = x^2$, find $f'(x)$.
6. If $f(x) = x^2 - 4$, find $f'(x)$.
7. If $p = 3q - 2$, find dp/dq.
8. If $C = 300 + 4x^2$, find C'.
9. If $y = 4x^2 - 2x + 1$, find y'.
10. If $y = 16x^2 - 4x + 2$, find dy/dx.
11. If $y = x^3$, find dy/dx.
12. If $y = 4x^3$, find dy/dx.
13. If $p = q^2 + 4q + 1$, what is the instantaneous rate of change of p with respect to q at $q = 5$?
14. If $p = 2q^2 - 4q + 5$, what is the instantaneous rate of change of p with respect to q at $q = 2$, $p = 5$?
15. If $C = 14x^2 + 5x + 60$, what is the rate of change of C with respect to x when $x = 4$?
16. If $C = 500 + 40x + 0.5x^2$, what is the rate of change of C with respect to x when $x = 5$?
17. (a) What is the slope of the tangent to $y = x$ at any point?
    (b) What is the slope of the tangent to $y = x$ at $(3, 3)$?
18. (a) What function defines the slope of the tangent to the graph of $y = x^2 + 1$ at any point on the curve?
    (b) What is the slope of the tangent to $y = x^2 + 1$ at $(2, 5)$?

19. What is the slope of the tangent to the curve $y = x^2 + x$ at $(2, 6)$?
20. What is the slope of the tangent to the curve $y = x^2 + 3x$ at $(-1, -2)$?
21. Find the slope of the tangent to $f(x) = x^2$ at the point $(3, 9)$.
22. Find the slope of the tangent to $f(x) = x^3$ at the point $(2, 8)$.
23. Find the equation of the line tangent to $y = x^2$ at $(3, 9)$. (See problem 21.)
24. Find the equation of the line tangent to $y = x^3$ at $(2, 8)$. (See problem 22.)
25. Find the equation of the line tangent to $y = 3x^2 + 1$ at $(1, 4)$.
26. Find the equation of the line tangent to $y = x^2 - 5x$ at $(2, -6)$.

In problems 27–30, a point (a, b) on the graph of $y = f(x)$ is given and the equation of the line tangent to the graph of $f(x)$ at (a, b) is given. In each case, find $f'(a)$ and $f(a)$.

27. $(1, 4)$; $y = -3x + 7$ \hspace{2cm} 28. $(3, 1)$; $y = 1$
29. $(-3, -9)$; $5x - 2y = 3$ \hspace{1.3cm} 30. $(-1, 6)$; $x + 10y = 59$
31. If the instantaneous rate of change of $f(x)$ at $(1, -1)$ is 3, write the equation of the line tangent to the graph of $f(x)$ at $x = 1$.
32. If the instantaneous rate of change of $g(x)$ at $(-1, -2)$ is 1/2, write the equation of the line tangent to the graph of $g(x)$ at $x = -1$.

Since the derivative of a function represents both the slope of the tangent to the curve and the instantaneous rate of change of the function, it is possible to use information about one to gain information about the other. In problems 33–38, use the graph of a function $y = f(x)$ given by Figure 9.15.

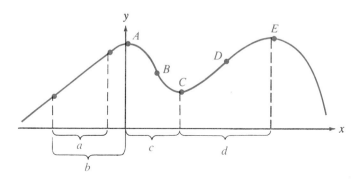

Figure 9.15

33. Over what interval(s) (a) through (d) is the rate of change of $f(x)$ constant?
34. Over what interval(s) (a) through (d) is the rate of change of $f(x)$ positive?
35. At what point(s) A through E is the rate of change of $f(x)$ equal to zero?
36. Over what interval(s) (a) through (d) is the rate of change of $f(x)$ negative?
37. At what point(s) A through E does the rate of change of $f(x)$ change from positive to negative?
38. At what point(s) A through E does the rate of change of $f(x)$ change from negative to positive?

APPLICATIONS

39. If the revenue function for a stereo system is

$$R(x) = 300x - x^2,$$

where x denotes the number of units sold,
(a) what is the marginal revenue if 50 units are sold?
(b) what is the marginal revenue if 100 units are sold?
(c) what is the marginal revenue if 150 units are sold?
(d) what is happening to revenue when 150 units are sold?

40. If the total revenue function for a blender is

$$R(x) = 36x - 0.01x^2,$$

where x is the number of units sold,
(a) what function gives the marginal revenue?
(b) what is the marginal revenue when 600 units are sold?
(c) what is the marginal revenue when 2000 units are sold?
(d) what is the marginal revenue when 1800 units are sold?

41. If the profit function for a car is

$$P(x) = 500x - x^2 - 100,$$

(a) what is the marginal profit if 200 units are sold?
(b) what is the marginal profit when 300 units are sold?
(c) what is happening to profit when 300 units are sold?

42. If the profit function for a truck is

$$P(x) = 1000x - 0.2x^2 - 100,$$

(a) what is the marginal profit function?
(b) what is the marginal profit when 1000 units are sold?
(c) what is the marginal profit when 2500 units are sold?

43. If the total revenue function for a toy is

$$R(x) = 2x,$$

and the total cost function is

$$C(x) = 100 + 0.2x^2 + x,$$

(a) what is the marginal profit function?
(b) what is the marginal profit if 10 units are produced and sold?

44. If the total revenue function for a personal computer is $R(x) = 88x$, and the total cost function is $C(x) = 3x^2 + 40x + 200$,
(a) what is the marginal profit function?
(b) what is the marginal profit if 7 units are produced and sold?

45. If 0.05 second elapses while a car travels over two sensors on the road which are 5 feet apart, what is the average velocity (*in miles per hour*) of the car as it travels between the sensors (88 feet per second is equivalent to 60 miles per hour)?

46. One speed-check system used by local police measures the elapsed time between two marks 0.1 mile apart. If 5.85 seconds elapse while a car on the highway travels between the two marks, find the average velocity of the car (in miles per hour) as it travels between the two marks.

47. The weight of a culture of bacteria is given by the following chart.

time (hrs)	0	1	2	3	4
weight (g)	5	10	20	40	80

Find the average rate of change of the weight in
(a) the first hour.
(b) the first 2 hours.
(c) the first 4 hours.
(d) the period from 2 to 4 hours.

48. When a ball is dropped from a height of 256 ft, the distance it travels in t seconds is given by

$$s = 16t^2.$$

(a) Find the average rate of change of the distance (average velocity) in the first 2 seconds of the fall.
(b) Find the average rate in the next 2 seconds.
(c) Find the instantaneous rate at $t = 2$ seconds.

49. On an 80-mile trip, a driver averages 40 mph for the first 40 miles and 60 mph for the last 40 miles. What is the average speed for the trip? Careful!

9.4 Derivative Formulas

Objectives
- ☐ To find derivatives of constant functions
- ☐ To find derivatives of powers of x
- ☐ To find derivatives of functions involving constant coefficients
- ☐ To find the derivatives of sums and differences of functions

We have already used the definition of derivative to find the following derivatives:

If $f(x) = x^2$, then $f'(x) = 2x$.   Problem 5, Exercise 9.3
If $f(x) = x^3$, then $f'(x) = 3x^2$.   Problem 11, Exercise 9.3

In addition, it can be shown that

If $f(x) = x^4$, $f'(x) = 4x^3$.
If $f(x) = x^5$, $f'(x) = 5x^4$.

Do you recognize a pattern that could be used to find the derivative of $f(x) = x^6$? What is the derivative of $f(x) = x^n$? If you said that the derivative of $f(x) = x^6$ is $f'(x) = 6x^5$ and the derivative of $f(x) = x^n$ is $f'(x) = nx^{n-1}$, you're right. We can use the definition of derivative to show this. If n is a positive integer, then

$$f'(x) = \lim_{h \to 0} \frac{f(x + h) - f(x)}{h}$$

$$= \lim_{h \to 0} \frac{(x + h)^n - x^n}{h}.$$

Since we are assuming n is a positive integer, we can use the binomial formula (see Chapter 8) to expand $(x + h)^n$.

$$f'(x) = \lim_{h \to 0} \frac{\left[x^n + \frac{n}{1}x^{n-1}h + \frac{n(n-1)}{1 \cdot 2}x^{n-2}h^2 + \cdots + h^n \right] - x^n}{h}$$

$$= \lim_{h \to 0} \left[nx^{n-1} + \frac{n(n-1)}{1 \cdot 2}x^{n-2}h + \cdots + h^{n-1} \right]$$

Now, each term after nx^{n-1} contains h as a factor, so all terms except nx^{n-1} will approach 0 as $h \to 0$. Thus

$$f'(x) = nx^{n-1}.$$

We state this derivative rule formally as follows.

Powers of x Rule   If $f(x) = x^n$, where n is a real number, then $f'(x) = nx^{n-1}$.

Note that the rule applies for any real number n even though we proved it only for the case when n is a positive integer.

EXAMPLE 1   Find the derivatives of the following functions.

(a) $f(x) = x^2$ (b) $g(x) = x^6$ (c) $y = x^{1/3}$ (d) $y = \dfrac{1}{x}$

Solution   (a) If $f(x) = x^2$, then $f'(x) = 2x^{2-1} = 2x$.

(b) If $g(x) = x^6$, then $g'(x) = 6x^{6-1} = 6x^5$.

(c) The rule was proved only for positive integers, but it applies for all real values of n. Thus

$$y' = \frac{1}{3}x^{1/3-1} = \frac{1}{3}x^{-2/3} = \frac{1}{3x^{2/3}} .$$

(d) The function must be expressed in the form $y = x^n$, so we will rewrite the equation.

$$y = \frac{1}{x} = x^{-1}$$

Then

$$\frac{dy}{dx} = -1x^{-1-1} = -x^{-2}.$$

We can rewrite this derivative in a form similar to that of the original function, as follows.

$$\frac{dy}{dx} = -\frac{1}{x^2} .$$

Since the derivative of $y = 1/x$ is $dy/dx = -1/x^2$, the slope of the tangent to $y = 1/x$ at $(2, \frac{1}{2})$ is

$$\left.\frac{dy}{dx}\right|_{x=2} = -\frac{1}{2^2} = -\frac{1}{4}.$$

The graph and tangent line are shown in Figure 9.16. Note that neither the function nor its derivative exists when $x = 0$.

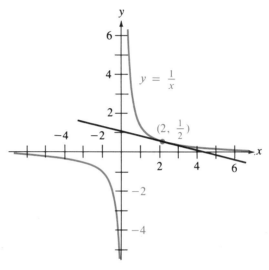

Figure 9.16

The differentiation rules are stated and proved for the independent variable x, but they also apply to other independent variables. The following examples illustrate differentiation with variables other than x.

EXAMPLE 2   Find the derivatives of the following functions.

(a) $u(s) = s^3$ (b) $p = q^{2/3}$ (c) $C(t) = \sqrt{t}$ (d) $s = \dfrac{1}{\sqrt{t}}$

Solution   (a) If $u(s) = s^3$, then $u'(s) = 3s^{3-1} = 3s^2$.

(b) If $p = q^{2/3}$, then $dp/dq = \frac{2}{3}q^{2/3-1} = \frac{2}{3}q^{-1/3} = 2/(3q^{1/3})$.

(c) Writing $\sqrt{t}$ in its equivalent form, $t^{1/2}$, permits us to use the derivative formula:

$$C'(t) = \frac{1}{2}t^{1/2-1} = \frac{1}{2}t^{-1/2}.$$

Writing the derivative in radical form gives

$$C'(t) = \frac{1}{2} \cdot \frac{1}{t^{1/2}} = \frac{1}{2\sqrt{t}}.$$

(d) Writing $1/\sqrt{t}$ as a power of t gives

$$s = \frac{1}{t^{1/2}} = t^{-1/2}, \quad \text{so} \quad \frac{ds}{dt} = -\frac{1}{2}t^{-1/2-1} = -\frac{1}{2}t^{-3/2}.$$

Writing the derivative in a form similar to that of the original function gives

$$\frac{ds}{dt} = -\frac{1}{2} \cdot \frac{1}{t^{3/2}} = -\frac{1}{2\sqrt{t^3}}.$$

EXAMPLE 3 Find the slope of the tangent to the curve $y = x^3$ at $x = 1$.

Solution The derivative of $y = x^3$ is $y' = f'(x) = 3x^2$. The slope of the tangent to $y = x^3$ at $x = 1$ is $y'|_{x=1} = f'(1) = 3(1)^2 = 3$. The graph and the tangent line are shown in Figure 9.17.

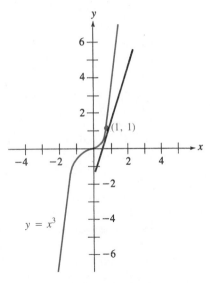

Figure 9.17

A function of the form $y = f(x) = c$, where c is a constant, is called a constant function. We can easily show that the derivative of a constant function is 0, as follows.

$$f'(x) = \lim_{h \to 0} \frac{f(x + h) - f(x)}{h} = \lim_{h \to 0} \frac{c - c}{h} = \lim_{h \to 0} 0 = 0$$

We can state this rule formally.

Constant-Function Rule	If $f(x) = c$, where c is a constant, then $f'(x) = 0$.

EXAMPLE 4   Find the derivative of the function defined by $y = 4$.

Solution
$$\frac{dy}{dx} = 0$$

Recall that the function defined by $y = 4$ has a horizontal line as its graph. Thus the slope of the line (and the derivative of the function) is 0.

We now can take derivatives of constant functions and powers of x. But we do not yet have a rule for taking derivatives of functions of the form $f(x) = 4x^5$ or $g(t) = \frac{1}{2}t^2$. The following rule provides a method for handling functions of this type.

Coefficient Rule	If $f(x) = c \cdot u(x)$, where c is a constant, then $f'(x) = c \cdot u'(x)$.

The above formula says that the derivative of a constant times a function is the constant times the derivative of the function.

We can use the fact that

$$\lim_{h \to 0} c \cdot g(h) = c \cdot \lim_{h \to 0} g(h),$$

which was discussed in Section 9.1, to verify the coefficient rule. If $f(x) = c \cdot u(x)$, then

$$f'(x) = \lim_{h \to 0} \frac{f(x + h) - f(x)}{h}$$

$$= \lim_{h \to 0} \frac{c \cdot u(x + h) - c \cdot u(x)}{h}$$

$$= \lim_{h \to 0} c \cdot \left[\frac{u(x + h) - u(x)}{h} \right]$$

$$= c \cdot \lim_{h \to 0} \frac{u(x + h) - u(x)}{h}.$$

So
$$f'(x) = c \cdot u'(x).$$

EXAMPLE 5   Find the derivatives of the following functions.

(a) $f(x) = 4x^5$ (b) $g(t) = \frac{1}{2}t^2$ (c) $p = \dfrac{5}{\sqrt{q}}$

Solution   (a) $f'(x) = 4(5x^4) = 20x^4$

(b) $g'(t) = \frac{1}{2}(2t) = t$

(c) $p = \dfrac{5}{\sqrt{q}} = 5q^{-1/2}$, so

$$\frac{dp}{dq} = 5\left(-\frac{1}{2}q^{-3/2}\right) = -\frac{5}{2\sqrt{q^3}}$$

In Example 4 of Section 9.3, we found the derivative of $y = 3x^2 + 2x$ to be $y' = 6x + 2$. In Exercise 9.3, we found that the derivative of $p = 3q - 2$ was $dp/dq = 3 - 0 = 3$ (in problem 7) and that the derivative of $C = 300 + 4x^2$ is $C' = 0 + 8x = 8x$. These results suggest that we can find the derivative of a polynomial by finding the derivatives of its terms and combining them. The following rules, which are easily proved, state this formally.

Sum Rule   If $f(x) = u(x) + v(x)$, where u and v are functions of x, then

$$f'(x) = u'(x) + v'(x).$$

Thus, the derivative of a sum of two functions is the sum of their derivatives.

Difference Rule   If $f(x) = u(x) - v(x)$, where u and v are functions of x, then

$$f'(x) = u'(x) - v'(x).$$

EXAMPLE 6   Find the derivatives of the following functions.

(a) $y = x^2 + 3$ (b) $p = q^2 - 4q$ (c) $y = 3x + 5$

Solution   (a) $y' = 2 \cdot x + 0 = 2x$

(b) $dp/dq = 2 \cdot q - 4 \cdot 1 = 2q - 4$

(c) $y' = 3 \cdot 1 + 0 = 3$

In Example 6(c) we saw that the derivative of $y = 3x + 5$ is 3. Because the slope of a line is the same at all points on the line, it is reasonable that the derivative of a linear equation is a constant. In particular, the slope of the graph of the equation $y = mx + b$ is m at all points on its graph because the derivative of $y = mx + b$ is $y' = f'(x) = m$.

The rules regarding the derivatives of sums and differences of two functions also apply if more than two functions are involved. For example, the derivative of $f(x) = 4x^3 - 2x^2 + 5x - 3$ is $f'(x) = 12x^2 - 4x + 5$. We may think of the functions that are added and subtracted as terms of the function f. Then it would be correct to say that we may take the derivative of a function term by term.

EXAMPLE 7   Find the derivatives of the following functions.
(a) $y = 3x^3 - 4x^2$ (b) $p = \frac{1}{3}q^3 + 2q^2 - 3$ (c) $u(x) = 5x^4 + x^{1/3}$

Solution   (a) $y' = 3(3x^2) - 4(2x) = 9x^2 - 8x$

(b) $\dfrac{dp}{dq} = \frac{1}{3}(3q^2) + 2(2q) - 0 = q^2 + 4q$

(c) $u'(x) = 5(4x^3) + \frac{1}{3}x^{-2/3} = 20x^3 + \dfrac{1}{3x^{2/3}}$

EXAMPLE 8   Find the derivatives of the following functions.
(a) $y = 4x^3 + \sqrt{x}$ (b) $s = 5t^6 - \dfrac{1}{t^2}$

Solution   (a) We may write the equation as

$$y = 4x^3 + x^{1/2},$$

so

$$y' = 4(3x^2) + \frac{1}{2}x^{-1/2} = 12x^2 + \dfrac{1}{2x^{1/2}},$$

or

$$y' = 12x^2 + \dfrac{1}{2\sqrt{x}}.$$

(b) We may write $s = 5t^6 - 1/t^2$ as

$$s = 5t^6 - t^{-2},$$

so

$$\dfrac{ds}{dt} = 5(6t^5) - (-2t^{-3}) = 30t^5 + 2t^{-3},$$

or

$$\dfrac{ds}{dt} = 30t^5 + \dfrac{2}{t^3}.$$

EXAMPLE 9   Find the slope of the tangent to $f(x) = \frac{1}{2}x^2 + 5x$ at each of the following.
(a) $x = 2$ (b) $x = -5$

Solution The derivative of $f(x) = \frac{1}{2}x^2 + 5x$ is $f'(x) = x + 5$.
(a) At $x = 2$, the slope is $f'(2) = 2 + 5 = 7$.
(b) At $x = -5$, the slope is $f'(-5) = -5 + 5 = 0$. Thus the tangent to the curve is a horizontal line at $x = -5$.

EXAMPLE 10 Suppose a businessperson wants to ship instruments in a shock-proof package. To test the packaging material, a package is dropped off the top of a 144-foot building. If the distance (in feet) that the package falls from the top of the building in x seconds is given by

$$y = f(x) = 16x^2,$$

what will be the velocity of the package when it hits the ground?

Solution We can answer this question by finding the derivative

$$f'(x) = 32x.$$

Since it will take 3 seconds to fall the 144 feet $[16(3)^2 = 144]$, the velocity of the package will be

$$f'(3) = 32(3) = 96$$

feet per second when the package hits the ground.

Exercise 9.4

Find the derivatives of the following functions.

1. $y = 4$

2. $f(s) = 6$

3. $y = x$

4. $s = t^2$

5. $c(x) = x^3$

6. $u(x) = x^5$

7. $y = 4x^3$

8. $y = 8x^5$

9. $p = 5q^8$

10. $f(q) = 8q^3$

11. $f(x) = 3x + 8$

12. $y = 5x^3 - 3x^2$

13. $y = 3x^6 - 12x^2$

14. $f(s) = s^2 + 4s + 1$

15. $p = 5q^3 + 4q^2 + 2$

16. $c(x) = x^3 - 5x^2 + 4x$

17. $y = x^{-3}$

18. $y = x^{-1}$

19. $y = \dfrac{1}{x^2}$

20. $y = \dfrac{1}{x^5}$

21. $y = x^{2/3}$

22. $f(q) = q^{11/5}$

23. $f(x) = x^{-4/5}$

24. $y = x^{-8/3}$

25. $p = \sqrt[3]{q^2}$

26. $f(q) = \sqrt[5]{q^3}$

27. $y = 5x^{-4/5} + 2x^{1/5}$

28. $y = 6x^{-8/3} - x^{-2/3}$

29. $y = 3x^3 - \dfrac{2}{x^5}$

30. $y = 4x^2 - \dfrac{2}{x^2}$

31. $y = \dfrac{3}{x^3} - \dfrac{1}{x^{1/3}} - 5\sqrt{x}$

32. $y = \dfrac{3}{x^4} - \dfrac{2}{3x} + 5$

33. $y = 2\sqrt{x} + 4\sqrt{x^3} - 3$

34. $y = \sqrt[3]{x} + 6\sqrt[3]{x^4} - 5$

In problems 35–38, find the slopes of the tangents to the following curves at the indicated points.

35. $y = 4x^2 + 3x$, $x = 2$

36. $C(x) = 3x^2 - 5$, $(3, 22)$

37. $P(x) = x^2 - 4x$, $(2, -4)$

38. $R(x) = 16x + x^2$, $x = 1$

In problems 39–42, write the equations of the tangent lines to the curves at the indicated points.

39. $y = 3x^2 + 2x$, $(1, 5)$

40. $y = 4x - x^2$, $(5, -5)$

41. $f(x) = 4x^2 - \dfrac{1}{x}$ at $x = -\dfrac{1}{2}$

42. $f(x) = \dfrac{x^3}{3} - \dfrac{3}{x^3}$ at $x = -1$

43. At what point(s) will the slope of the tangent to $y = x^2 - 4x + 3$ be 0?

44. At what point(s) will the slope of the tangent to $y = x^3 - 5x^2 - 8x + 5$ be 0?

APPLICATIONS

45. A ball is thrown into the air according to the equation

$$s = 112t - 16t^2,$$

where t is in seconds and s is in feet.
(a) What equation describes the velocity of the ball?
(b) What is the velocity when $t = 2$? Is the ball going up or going down?

46. A projectile is shot vertically into the air, with its height described by

$$s = 960t - 16t^2 + 100,$$

where s is in feet and t is in seconds.
(a) What equation describes the velocity of the projectile?
(b) What is the velocity when $t = 20$?

47. The population size y of a certain organism at time t is given by

$$y = 4t^2 + 2t.$$

Find the rate of change of population.

48. The number of organisms of a certain bacteria at time t can be modeled according to the equation

$$N(t) = 2500(1 + 2t^2).$$

Find the rate of change of the number.

49. A swimming pool is filled by an inlet pipe. The number of gallons N in the pool at time t is

$$N = 2t^2 + 30t,$$

where t is in minutes. At what rate is the pool filling when t is 10?

50. Pressure P of a gas is related to volume V according to Boyle's law, and this relationship is expressed by the equation

$$P = \frac{C}{V},$$

where C is constant. Find the rate of change of pressure with respect to volume.

51. The total revenue for a commodity is described by the function

$$R = 300x - 0.02x^2.$$

(a) What is the marginal revenue when 40 units are sold?
(b) Interpret your answer to part (a).

52. Suppose the profit function for a product is

$$P = 400x - 0.1x^2 + 0.01x^3 - 3000.$$

(a) What is the marginal profit when 100 units are sold?
(b) Is profit increasing or decreasing when 100 units are sold?

In problems 53 and 54, use the fact that the average cost of producing x items is given by

$$\overline{C}(x) = \frac{\text{Total cost}}{x} = \frac{C(x)}{x}.$$

53. Suppose the total cost function for the production of x units of a product is given by

$$C(x) = 4000 + 55x + 0.1x^2$$

(a) Find the instantaneous rate of change of average costs with respect to the number of units produced.
(b) Find the level of production at which this rate of change equals zero.

54. Suppose the total cost function for a certain commodity is given by

$$C(x) = 40{,}500 + 190x + 0.2x^2$$

(a) Find the instantaneous rate of change of average costs with respect to the number of units produced.
(b) Find the level of production at which this rate of change equals zero.

55. Suppose the cost C to a city of obtaining drinking water that contains p percent impurities (by volume) is given by

$$C = \frac{120{,}000}{p} - 1200.$$

Find the rate of change of cost with respect to p when impurities account for 1% (by volume).

9.5 Product and Quotient Rules

Objectives
- ☐ To use the Product Rule to find the derivative of certain functions
- ☐ To use the Quotient Rule to find the derivative of certain functions
- ☐ To find the differential of a function

We have formulas that permit us to find the derivatives of the sums and differences of functions easily. But we are not so lucky with products. The derivative of a product is *not* the product of the derivatives. To see this, we consider the function $f(x) = x \cdot x$. Since this function is $f(x) = x^2$, its derivative is $f'(x) = 2x$. But the product of the derivatives of x and x would give $1 \cdot 1 = 1 \neq 2x$. Thus we need a different formula to find the derivative of a product. This formula is given by the **Product Rule.**

Product Rule	If $f(x) = u(x) \cdot v(x)$, where u and v are differentiable functions of x, then
	$$f'(x) = u(x) \cdot v'(x) + v(x) \cdot u'(x).$$

Thus, the derivative of a product of two functions is the first function times the derivative of the second plus the second function times the derivative of the first.

EXAMPLE 1   Use the Product Rule to find the derivative of $f(x) = x^2 \cdot x$.

Solution   Using the formula with $u(x) = x^2$, $v(x) = x$, we have

$$
\begin{aligned}
f'(x) &= u(x) \cdot v'(x) + v(x) \cdot u'(x) \\
&= x^2 \cdot 1 + x(2x) \\
&= x^2 + 2x^2 \\
&= 3x^2.
\end{aligned}
$$

Note that we could have found the same result by multiplying the factors and finding the derivative of $f(x) = x^3$. But we will soon see how valuable the Product Rule is.

EXAMPLE 2   Find dy/dx if $y = (2x^3 + 3x + 1)(x^2 + 4)$.

Solution   Using the Product Rule with $u(x) = 2x^3 + 3x + 1$ and $v(x) = x^2 + 4$, we have

$$
\begin{aligned}
\frac{dy}{dx} &= (2x^3 + 3x + 1)(2x) + (x^2 + 4)(6x^2 + 3) \\
&= 4x^4 + 6x^2 + 2x + 6x^4 + 3x^2 + 24x^2 + 12 \\
&= 10x^4 + 33x^2 + 2x + 12.
\end{aligned}
$$

We could, of course, avoid using the Product Rule by multiplying the two factors before taking the derivative. But multiplying the factors first may involve more work than using the Product Rule.

EXAMPLE 3   Given $f(x) = (4x^3 + 5x^2 - 6x + 5)(x^3 - 4x^2 + 1)$, find the slope of the tangent to $f(x)$ at $x = 1$.

Solution $f'(x) = (4x^3 + 5x^2 - 6x + 5)(3x^2 - 8x) + (x^3 - 4x^2 + 1)(12x^2 + 10x - 6)$. If we substitute $x = 1$ into the equation above, we find that the slope of the curve at $x = 1$ is $f'(1) = 8(-5) + (-2)(16) = -72$.

The rule for finding the derivative of a function that is the quotient of two polynomials requires a new formula.

Quotient Rule

If $f(x) = u(x)/v(x)$, where u and v are differentiable functions of x, with $v(x) \neq 0$, then

$$f'(x) = \frac{v(x) \cdot u'(x) - u(x) \cdot v'(x)}{[v(x)]^2}.$$

The above formula says that the derivative of a quotient is the denominator times the derivative of the numerator minus the numerator times the derivative of the denominator, all divided by the square of the denominator.

To see that this rule is reasonable, consider the function $f(x) = x^3/x$, $x \neq 0$. Using the Quotient Rule, with $u(x) = x^3$ and $v(x) = x$, we get

$$f'(x) = \frac{x(3x^2) - x^3(1)}{x^2} = \frac{3x^3 - x^3}{x^2} = \frac{2x^3}{x^2} = 2x.$$

Since $f(x) = x^3/x = x^2$ if $x \neq 0$, we see that $f'(x) = 2x$ is the correct derivative.

EXAMPLE 4   If $f(x) = \dfrac{x^2 - 4x}{x + 5}$, find $f'(x)$.

Solution   Using the Quotient Rule with $u(x) = x^2 - 4x$ and $v(x) = x + 5$, we get

$$f'(x) = \frac{(x + 5)(2x - 4) - (x^2 - 4x)(1)}{(x + 5)^2}$$

$$= \frac{2x^2 + 6x - 20 - x^2 + 4x}{(x + 5)^2}$$

$$= \frac{x^2 + 10x - 20}{(x + 5)^2}.$$

EXAMPLE 5   If $f(x) = \dfrac{x^3 - 3x^2 + 2}{x^2 - 4}$, find $f'(x)$.

Solution   Using the Quotient Rule, with $u(x) = x^3 - 3x^2 + 2$ and $v(x) = x^2 - 4$, we get

$$f'(x) = \frac{(x^2 - 4)(3x^2 - 6x) - (x^3 - 3x^2 + 2)(2x)}{(x^2 - 4)^2}$$

$$= \frac{(3x^4 - 6x^3 - 12x^2 + 24x) - (2x^4 - 6x^3 + 4x)}{(x^2 - 4)^2}$$

$$= \frac{x^4 - 12x^2 + 20x}{(x^2 - 4)^2}.$$

EXAMPLE 6   Use the Quotient Rule to find the derivative of $y = 1/x^3$.

Solution   Letting $u(x) = 1$ and $v(x) = x^3$, we get

$$y' = \frac{x^3(0) - 1(3x^2)}{(x^3)^2}$$

$$= -\frac{3x^2}{x^6}$$

$$= -\frac{3}{x^4}.$$

Note that we could have found the derivative more easily by writing

$$y = 1/x^3 = x^{-3},$$

so

$$y' = -3x^{-4} = -\frac{3}{x^4}.$$

It is not necessary to use the Quotient Rule when the denominator of the function in question contains only a constant. For example, the function $y = (x^3 - 3x)/3$ can be written $y = \frac{1}{3}(x^3 - 3x)$, so the derivative is $y' = \frac{1}{3}(3x^2 - 3) = x^2 - 1$.

We have used the symbol dy/dx as one of the symbols to denote the derivative of $y = f(x)$ with respect to x, but there are advantages to using the symbols dy and dx separately. We can define the **differential** dy as follows.

The Differential   If $f'(x)$ is the derivative of $y = f(x)$, then the **differential** of y is

$$dy = f'(x)\, dx.$$

EXAMPLE 7   If $y = x^3 - 4x^2 + 5$, find dy.

Solution $dy = f'(x) \cdot dx = (3x^2 - 8x)\, dx$

EXAMPLE 8   If $y = \dfrac{x - 2}{x^2}$, find

(a) $\dfrac{dy}{dx}$.   (b) dy.

Solution   (a) Using the Quotient Rule gives

$$\frac{dy}{dx} = \frac{x^2(1) - (x - 2)2x}{(x^2)^2}$$

$$= \frac{x^2 - 2x^2 + 4x}{x^4}$$

$$= \frac{-x^2 + 4x}{x^4} = \frac{-x + 4}{x^3}.$$

(b) $dy = \dfrac{-x + 4}{x^3}\, dx$

Exercise 9.5

1. Find y' if $y = (x + 3)(x^2 - 2x)$.
2. Find $f'(x)$ if $f(x) = (3x - 1)(x^3 + 1)$.
3. Find $\dfrac{dp}{dq}$ if $p = (3q - 1)(q^2 + 2)$.
4. Find $\dfrac{ds}{dt}$ if $s = (t^4 + 1)(t^3 - 1)$.
5. If $f(x) = (x^{12} + 3x^4 + 4)(4x^3 - 1)$, find $f'(x)$.
6. If $y = (3x^7 + 4)(8x^6 - 6x^4 - 9)$, find $\dfrac{dy}{dx}$.
7. If $R(x) = (3x - 1)(100 + 2x^2)$, find $R'(x)$.
8. If $C(x) = (34x + 300)(25 + x^2)$, find $C'(x)$.
9. If $y = (x + 1)\sqrt{x}$, find y'.
10. If $y = \sqrt[3]{x}(x^2 + 1)$, find $\dfrac{dy}{dx}$.
11. If $y = \left(4\sqrt{x} + \dfrac{3}{x}\right)\left(3\sqrt[3]{x} - \dfrac{5}{x^2} - 5^2\right)$, find $\dfrac{dy}{dx}$.
12. If $y = \left(3\sqrt[4]{x^5} - \sqrt[5]{x^4} - 1\right)\left(\dfrac{2}{x^3} - \dfrac{1}{\sqrt{x}}\right)$, find y'.
13. What is the slope of the tangent to $y = (x^2 + 1)(x^3 - 4x)$ at $(1, -6)$?
14. What is the slope of the tangent to $y = (x^3 - 3)(x^2 - 4x + 1)$ at $(2, -15)$?
15. Find y' if $y = \dfrac{x}{x^2 - 1}$.

16. Find $f'(x)$ if $f(x) = \dfrac{x^2}{x - 3}$.
17. Find $\dfrac{dp}{dq}$ if $p = \dfrac{q^2 + 1}{q - 2}$.
18. Find $C'(x)$ if $C(x) = \dfrac{x^2 + 1}{x^2 - 1}$.

19. Find $\dfrac{dy}{dx}$ if $y = \dfrac{1 - x^4}{x^3 + 1}$

20. Find $\dfrac{dz}{dt}$ if $z = \dfrac{t^3 - 4t}{16 - t^4}$

21. Find $\dfrac{dp}{dq}$ if $p = \dfrac{3\sqrt[3]{q}}{1 - q}$

22. Find $\dfrac{dy}{dx}$ if $y = \dfrac{2\sqrt{x} - 1}{1 - 4\sqrt{x^3}}$

23. Find y' if $y = \dfrac{x(x^2 + 4)}{x - 2}$.

24. Find $f'(x)$ if $f(x) = \dfrac{(x + 1)(x - 2)}{x^2 + 1}$.

25. Find the derivative of $y = \dfrac{x - 2}{x + 1}$ at $\left(1, -\dfrac{1}{2}\right)$.

26. Find the derivative of $y = \dfrac{x^2 + 1}{x - 2}$ at $(1, -2)$.

27. Find the slope of the tangent to $y = \dfrac{x^2 + 1}{x + 3}$ at $(2, 1)$.

28. Find the slope of the tangent to $y = \dfrac{x^2 - 4x}{x^2 + 2x}$ at $\left(2, -\dfrac{1}{2}\right)$.

29. Write the equation of the tangent line to $y = \dfrac{3x^4 - 2x - 1}{4 - x^2}$ at $x = 1$.

30. Write the equation of the tangent line to $y = \dfrac{x^2 - 4x}{2x - x^3}$ at $x = 2$.

31. At what point(s) will the slope of the tangent to $y = (x^2 + 1)(x - 2)$ be 0?

32. At what point(s) will the slope of the tangent to $y = \dfrac{x^2}{x - 2}$ be 0?

33. If $y = x^3 + 4x^2 + 5x + 5$, find dy.

34. If $p = q^4 - 5q^2$, find dp.

35. If $s = x^2(x + 1)$, find ds.

36. If $y = \dfrac{x + 1}{x - 1}$, find dy.

37. If $y = \dfrac{\sqrt{x}}{2x + 1}$, find dy.

38. If $y = \sqrt{x}\,(2x + 1)$, find dy.

APPLICATIONS

39. If the cost C of removing p percent of the particulate pollution from the exhaust gases at an industrial site is given by

$$C(p) = \dfrac{8100p}{100 - p},$$

find the rate of change of C with respect to p.

40. If the cost C of removing p percent of the impurities from the waste water in a manufacturing process is given by

$$C(p) = \frac{9800p}{101 - p},$$

find the rate of change of C with respect to p.

41. Suppose the revenue function for a product is given by

$$R(x) = \frac{6x^2 - 27x}{2x + 1}.$$

Find the marginal revenue function.

42. The number of action potentials produced by a nerve, t seconds after a stimulus, is given by

$$N(t) = 25t + \frac{4}{t^2 + 2} - 2.$$

Find the rate at which the action potentials are produced.

43. The reaction R to an injection of a drug is related to the dosage x according to

$$R(x) = x^2\left(500 - \frac{x}{3}\right),$$

where 1000 mg is the maximum dosage. If the rate of reaction with respect to the dosage defines the sensitivity to the drug, find the sensitivity.

44. Experimental evidence has shown that the concentration of injected adrenaline, x, is related to the response, y, of a muscle according to the equation

$$y = \frac{x}{a + bx},$$

where a and b are constants. Find the rate of change of response with respect to the concentration.

45. Suppose

$$P = \frac{1000t}{t + 10}$$

represents the size of a population of bacteria, where t represents time. What is the rate of growth of the population?

46. It is determined that a wildlife refuge can support a group of up to 120 of a certain endangered species. If 75 are introduced on the refuge and their population after t years is given by

$$p(t) = 75\left(1 + \frac{4t}{t^2 + 16}\right),$$

find the rate of population growth after t years. Find the rate after each of the first seven years.

47. If a test having reliability r is lengthened by a factor n, the reliability of the new test is given by

$$R = \frac{nr}{1 + (n - 1)r}, \qquad 0 < r \le 1.$$

Find the rate at which R changes with respect to n.

9.6 The Chain Rule and Power Rule

Objectives
- ☐ To form the composite of two functions
- ☐ To use the chain rule to differentiate functions
- ☐ To use the power rule to differentiate functions

Up to this point, we have found derivatives of sums of functions, differences of functions, products of functions, and quotients of functions. We will now consider a new way to combine two functions and a method of finding the derivative of the new function that is formed. This new function is called a composite function. Just as we can substitute a number for the independent variable in a function, we can substitute a second function for the variable. This creates a new function, called a **composite function.**

Composite Functions

The **composite function** g of f is the function $g \circ f$ defined by

$$(g \circ f)(x) = g[f(x)].$$

The domain of $g \circ f$ is the subset of the domain of f for which $g \circ f$ is defined.

EXAMPLE 1 If $f(x) = 2x$ and $g(x) = x^2$, find $g[f(x)]$.

Solution Substituting $f(x) = 2x$ for x in $g(x)$ gives $g[f(x)] = g[2x] = [2x]^2 = 4x^2$.

Figure 9.18 illustrates how the composite function $g \circ f$ is created from f and g, where $f(x) = 2x$ and $g(x) = x^2$.

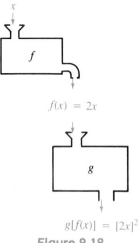

$$f(x) = 2x$$

$$g[f(x)] = [2x]^2$$

Figure 9.18

EXAMPLE 2   If $f(x) = 3x^2$ and $g(x) = 2x - 1$, find $F(x) = f[g(x)]$.

Solution   Substituting $g(x) = 2x - 1$ for x in $f(x)$ gives

$$f[g(x)] = f(2x - 1) = 3(2x - 1)^2.$$

Thus $F(x) = 3(2x - 1)^2$.

We could find the derivative of the function $F(x) = 3(2x - 1)^2$ by multiplying out the expression $3(2x - 1)^2$. Then

$$F(x) = 3(4x^2 - 4x + 1) = 12x^2 - 12x + 3,$$

so $F'(x) = 24x - 12$. But we can also use a very powerful rule, called the Chain Rule, to find derivatives of functions of this type. If we write the composite function $y = f[g(x)]$ in the form $y = f(u)$, where $u = g(x)$, we can state the **Chain Rule** as follows.

Chain Rule	If f and g are differentiable functions with $y = f(u)$ and $u = g(x)$, then y is a differentiable function of x, and

$$\frac{dy}{dx} = \frac{d}{du} f(u) \cdot \frac{d}{dx} g(x)$$

or, written another way,

$$\frac{dy}{dx} = \frac{dy}{du} \cdot \frac{du}{dx}.$$

Note that dy/du represents the derivative of $y = f(u)$ *with respect to u* and du/dx represents the derivative of $u = g(x)$ *with respect to x*. For example, if $y = 3(2x - 1)^2$, we may write $y = f(u) = 3u^2$, where $u = 2x - 1$. Then the derivative is

$$\frac{dy}{dx} = \frac{dy}{du} \cdot \frac{du}{dx} = 6u \cdot 2 = 12u.$$

To write the derivative in terms of x, we substitute $2x - 1$ for u. Thus

$$\frac{dy}{dx} = 12(2x - 1) = 24x - 12.$$

Note that we get the same result by using the Chain Rule as we did by multiplying out $F(x) = 3(2x - 1)^2$. The Chain Rule is important because it is not always possible to rewrite the function as a polynomial. Consider the following example.

EXAMPLE 3   If $y = \sqrt{x^2 - 1}$, find $\dfrac{dy}{dx}$.

Solution   If we write this function as $y = f(u) = \sqrt{u}$, where $u = x^2 - 1$, we can find the derivative.

$$\frac{dy}{dx} = \frac{dy}{du} \cdot \frac{du}{dx} = \frac{1}{2} \cdot u^{-1/2} \cdot 2x$$

$$= u^{-1/2} \cdot x = \frac{1}{\sqrt{u}} \cdot x = \frac{x}{\sqrt{u}}$$

To write the derivative in terms of x alone, we substitute $x^2 - 1$ for u. Then

$$\frac{dy}{dx} = \frac{x}{\sqrt{x^2 - 1}} .$$

Note that we could not find the derivative of a function like that of Example 3 by the methods learned previously.

EXAMPLE 4   If $y = \dfrac{1}{(x^2 + 3x + 1)^2}$, find $\dfrac{dy}{dx}$.

Solution   If we let $u = x^2 + 3x + 1$, we can write $y = f(u) = \dfrac{1}{u^2}$, or $y = u^{-2}$. Then

$$\frac{dy}{dx} = \frac{dy}{du} \cdot \frac{du}{dx} = -2u^{-3}(2x + 3) = \frac{-4x - 6}{u^3} .$$

Substituting for u gives

$$\frac{dy}{dx} = \frac{-4x - 6}{(x^2 + 3x + 1)^3} .$$

A direct result of the Chain Rule is a very useful rule, called the **Power Rule.**

Power Rule   If $y = u^n$, where u is a differentiable function of x, then

$$\frac{dy}{dx} = nu^{n-1} \cdot \frac{du}{dx} .$$

EXAMPLE 5   If $y = (x^2 - 4x)^6$, find $\dfrac{dy}{dx}$.

Solution   The right side of the equation is in the form u^n, with $u = x^2 - 4x$. Thus by the Power Rule,

$$\frac{dy}{dx} = nu^{n-1} \cdot \frac{du}{dx} = 6u^5(2x - 4).$$

Substituting for u gives

$$\frac{dy}{dx} = 6(x^2 - 4x)^5(2x - 4)$$

$$= (12x - 24)(x^2 - 4x)^5.$$

EXAMPLE 6   If $y = 3\sqrt[3]{x^2 - 3x + 1}$, find y'.

Solution   Since $y = 3(x^2 - 3x + 1)^{1/3}$, we can use the Power Rule with $u = x^2 - 3x + 1$.

$$y' = 3\left[nu^{n-1}\frac{du}{dx} \right]$$

$$= 3\left[\frac{1}{3}u^{-2/3}(2x - 3) \right]$$

$$= (x^2 - 3x + 1)^{-2/3}(2x - 3)$$

$$= \frac{2x - 3}{(x^2 - 3x + 1)^{2/3}}$$

EXAMPLE 7   If $p = \dfrac{4}{3q^2 + 1}$, find $\dfrac{dp}{dq}$.

Solution   We can use the Power Rule to find dp/dq if we write the equation in the form

$$p = 4(3q^2 + 1)^{-1}.$$

Then

$$\frac{dp}{dq} = 4[-1(3q^2 + 1)^{-2}(6q)]$$

$$= \frac{-24q}{(3q^2 + 1)^2}.$$

The derivative of the function in Example 7 can also be found by using the Quotient Rule, but the Power Rule provides a more efficient method.

EXAMPLE 8   Find the derivative of $g(x) = \dfrac{1}{\sqrt{(x^2 + 1)^3}}$.

Solution   Writing $g(x)$ as a power gives

$$g(x) = (x^2 + 1)^{-3/2}.$$

Then

$$g'(x) = -\frac{3}{2}(x^2 + 1)^{-5/2}(2x)$$

$$= -3x \cdot \frac{1}{(x^2 + 1)^{5/2}}$$

$$= \frac{-3x}{\sqrt{(x^2 + 1)^5}}.$$

Exercise 9.6

Differentiate the functions in problems 1–20.

1. $y = (x^2 + 1)^3$

2. $p = (q^2 + 4q)^4$

3. $y = (4x^2 - 4x + 1)^4$

4. $r = (s^2 + 5s)^{10}$

5. $f(x) = \dfrac{1}{(x^2 + 2)^3}$

6. $g(x) = \dfrac{1}{4x^3 + 1}$

7. $g(x) = (x^2 + 4x)^{-2}$

8. $p = (q^3 + 1)^{-5}$

9. $c(x) = (x^2 + 3x + 4)^{-3}$

10. $y = (x^2 - 8x)^{2/3}$

11. $g(x) = \dfrac{1}{(2x^3 + 3x + 5)^{3/4}}$

12. $y = \dfrac{1}{(3x^3 + 4x + 1)^{3/2}}$

13. $y = \sqrt{x^2 + 4x + 5}$

14. $y = \sqrt{x^2 + 3x}$

15. $s = 4\sqrt{3x - x^2}$

16. $y = 3\sqrt[3]{(x - 1)^2}$

17. $y = \dfrac{8(x^2 - 3)^5}{5}$

18. $y = \dfrac{5\sqrt{1 - x^3}}{6}$

19. $y = \dfrac{(3x + 1)^5 - 3x}{7}$

20. $y = \dfrac{\sqrt{2x - 1} - \sqrt{x}}{2}$

21. Find the slope of the tangent to $y = (x^3 + 2x)^4$ at $x = 2$.

22. Find the slope of the tangent to $y = \sqrt{5x^2 + 2x}$ at $x = 1$.

23. Find the slope of the tangent to $y = \sqrt{x^3 + 1}$ at $(2, 3)$.

24. Find the slope of the tangent to $y = (4x^3 - 5x + 1)^3$ at $(1, 0)$.

25. Write the equation of the tangent to $y = (x^2 - 3x + 3)^3$ at $(1, 1)$.

26. Write the equation of the tangent to $y = (x^2 + 1)^3$ at $(2,125)$.

27. Write the equation of the tangent to $y = \sqrt{3x^2 - 2}$ at $x = 3$.

28. Write the equation of the tangent to $y = \left(\dfrac{1}{x^3 - x}\right)^3$ at $x = 2$.

29. At what values of x will the slope of the tangent to $y = (x^2 - 4)^3$ be 0?

30. At what value(s) of x will the slope of the tangent to $y = \sqrt{4 - x^2}$ be 0?

31. If $y = \sqrt{x^2 + 10}$ and $\dfrac{dx}{dt} = -4$, find $\dfrac{dy}{dt}$. Hint: $\dfrac{dy}{dt} = \dfrac{dy}{dx} \cdot \dfrac{dx}{dt}$.

32. If $y = (2x - 1)^{10}$ and $\dfrac{dx}{dt} = 3$, find $\dfrac{dy}{dt}$.

APPLICATIONS

33. The area of a circle is given by $A = \pi r^2$. If the rate of change of the radius with respect to time (i.e., dr/dt) is 4 in./min., find the rate of change of the area (dA/dt)
    (a) when $r = 1$ in.
    (b) when $r = 10$ in.

34. The volume of a cube of side x is given by $V = x^3$. If the length of the sides is changing at 2 in./min., find the rate of change of the volume (dV/dt)
    (a) when $x = 3$ in.
    (b) when $x = 4$ in.

35. Suppose the number of grams of bacteria in a population is given by $y = (t^2 + 1)^2$, where t is the number of hours of growth. Find the rate of growth of the bacteria
    (a) at time t.
    (b) at $t = 10$.
36. The description of body heat loss due to convection involves a coefficient of convection, K_c, which depends on wind velocity according to the equation

$$K_c = 4\sqrt{4v + 1}.$$

Find the rate of change of the coefficient with respect to the wind velocity.
37. The Schütz-Borisoff law relates the amount of substrate, y, transformed by an enzyme as a function of time, t, according to the equation

$$y = k\sqrt{cat},$$

where k, a, and c are constants. Find the rate at which the substrate is transformed.

The relation between the magnitude of a sensation y and the magnitude of the stimulus, x, is given by

$$y = k(x - x_0)^n,$$

where k is a constant and x_0 is the threshold of effective stimulus, and n depends on the type of stimulus. Find the rate of change of sensation with respect to the amount of stimulus for each of problems 38–40.

38. For the stimulus of visual brightness $y = k(x - x_0)^{1/3}$.
39. For the stimulus of warmth $y = k(x - x_0)^{8/5}$.
40. For the stimulus of electrical stimulation $y = k(x - x_0)^{7/2}$.
41. Ballistics experts are able to identify the weapon that fired a certain bullet by studying the markings on the bullet. Tests are conducted by firing into a bale of paper. If the distance (in inches) that the bullet travels into the paper is given by

$$S = 27 - (3 - 10t)^3$$

for $0 \leq t \leq 0.3$ seconds, find the velocity of the bullet one-tenth of a second after hitting the paper.
42. Suppose the population of a certain microorganism at time t (in minutes) is given by

$$P = 1000 - 1000(t + 10)^{-1}.$$

Find the rate of change of population.
43. The concentration C of a substance in the body depends on the quantity of the substance, Q, and the volume, V, through which it is distributed. For a static substance this is given by

$$C = \frac{Q}{V}.$$

For a situation like that in the kidneys, where the fluids are moving, the concentration is the ratio of the rate of change of quantity with respect to time and the rate of change of volume with respect to time.
    (a) Formulate the equation for concentration of a moving substance.
    (b) Show this is equal to the rate of change of quantity with respect to volume.

9.7 Using Derivative Formulas

Objective   □   To use derivative formulas separately and in combination with each other

We have used the Power Rule to find the derivative of functions like

$$y = (x^3 - 3x^2 + x + 1)^5,$$

but we have not found the derivative of functions like

$$y = [(x^2 + 1)(x^3 + x + 1)]^5.$$

This function is different because the function u (which is raised to the fifth power) is the product of two functions ($x^2 + 1$ and $x^3 + x + 1$). The equation is of the form $y = u^5$, where $u = (x^2 + 1)(x^3 + x + 1)$. This means that the Product Rule should be used to find du/dx. Then

$$\frac{dy}{dx} = 5u^4 \cdot \frac{du}{dx}$$

$$= 5[(x^2 + 1)(x^3 + x + 1)]^4[(x^2 + 1)(3x^2 + 1) + (x^3 + x + 1)(2x)]$$

$$= 5[(x^2 + 1)(x^3 + x + 1)]^4(5x^4 + 6x^2 + 2x + 1)$$

$$= (25x^4 + 30x^2 + 10x + 5)[(x^2 + 1)(x^3 + x + 1)]^4.$$

A different type of problem involving the Power Rule and the Product Rule is finding the derivative of $y = (x^2 + 1)^5(x^3 + x + 1)$. We may think of y as the *product* of two functions, one of which is a power. Thus the fundamental formula we should use is the Product Rule. The two functions are $u(x) = (x^2 + 1)^5$ and $v(x) = x^3 + x + 1$. The Product Rule is

$$\frac{dy}{dx} = u(x) \cdot v'(x) + v(x) \cdot u'(x)$$

$$= (x^2 + 1)^5(3x^2 + 1) + (x^3 + x + 1) \cdot 5(x^2 + 1)^4 2x.$$

Note that the Power Rule was used to find $u'(x)$, since $u(x) = (x^2 + 1)^5$.
We can simplify dy/dx by factoring out $(x^2 + 1)^4$:

$$\frac{dy}{dx} = (x^2 + 1)^4[(x^2 + 1)(3x^2 + 1) + (x^3 + x + 1) \cdot 5 \cdot 2x]$$

$$= (x^2 + 1)^4(13x^4 + 14x^2 + 10x + 1).$$

EXAMPLE 1   If $y = \left(\dfrac{x^2}{x - 1}\right)^2$, find y'.

Solution   We again have an equation of the form $y = u^n$, but this time u is a quotient. Thus we will need the Quotient Rule to find du/dx.

$$y' = nu^{n-1} \cdot \frac{du}{dx}$$

$$= 2u^1 \frac{(x - 1) \cdot 2x - x^2 \cdot 1}{(x - 1)^2}$$

Substituting for u and simplifying gives

$$y' = 2 \cdot \frac{x^2}{x-1} \cdot \frac{2x^2 - 2x - x^2}{(x-1)^2}$$

$$= \frac{2x^2(x^2 - 2x)}{(x-1)^3}$$

$$= \frac{2x^4 - 4x^3}{(x-1)^3} \cdot$$

EXAMPLE 2   Find $f'(x)$ if $f(x) = \dfrac{(x-1)^2}{(x^2+1)^3}$.

Solution   The function is the quotient of two functions, $(x-1)^2$ and $(x^2+1)^3$, so we must use the Quotient Rule to find the derivative of $f(x)$. *But* taking the derivative of $(x-1)^2$ and $(x^2+1)^3$ will require the Power Rule.

$$f'(x) = [v(x) \cdot u'(x) - u(x) \cdot v'(x)]/[v(x)]^2$$

$$= \frac{(x^2+1)^3[2(x-1)] - (x-1)^2[3(x^2+1)^2 2x]}{[(x^2+1)^3]^2}$$

$$= \frac{2(x^2+1)^3(x-1) - 6x(x-1)^2(x^2+1)^2}{(x^2+1)^6}$$

We see that 2, $(x^2+1)^2$, and $(x-1)$ are all factors in both terms of the numerator, so we can factor them out.

$$f'(x) = \frac{2(x^2+1)^2(x-1)[(x^2+1) - 3x(x-1)]}{(x^2+1)^6}$$

$$= \frac{2(x-1)(-2x^2 + 3x + 1)}{(x^2+1)^4}$$

EXAMPLE 3   Find $f'(x)$ if $f(x) = (x^2 - 1)\sqrt{3 - x^2}$.

Solution   The function is the product of two functions, $x^2 - 1$ and $\sqrt{3 - x^2}$. Therefore we will use the Product Rule to find the derivative of $f(x)$. *But* the derivative of $\sqrt{3 - x^2} = (3 - x^2)^{1/2}$ will require the Power Rule.

$$f'(x) = u(x) \cdot v'(x) + v(x) \cdot u'(x)$$

$$= (x^2 - 1)[\tfrac{1}{2}(3 - x^2)^{-1/2}(-2x)] + (3 - x^2)^{1/2}(2x)$$

$$= (x^2 - 1)[-x(3 - x^2)^{-1/2}] + (3 - x^2)^{1/2}(2x)$$

$$= \frac{-x^3 + x}{(3 - x^2)^{1/2}} + 2x(3 - x^2)^{1/2}$$

We can combine these terms over the common denominator $(3 - x^2)^{1/2}$ as follows.

$$f'(x) = \frac{-x^3 + x}{(3 - x^2)^{1/2}} + \frac{2x(3 - x^2)^1}{(3 - x^2)^{1/2}}$$

$$= \frac{-x^3 + x + 6x - 2x^3}{(3 - x^2)^{1/2}}$$

$$= \frac{-3x^3 + 7x}{(3 - x^2)^{1/2}}$$

We should note that in Example 3 we could have written $f'(x)$ in the form

$$f'(x) = (-x^3 + x)(3 - x^2)^{-1/2} + 2x(3 - x^2)^{1/2}.$$

Now, the factor $(3 - x^2)$, to different powers, is contained in both terms of the expression. Thus we can factor $(3 - x^2)^{-1/2}$ from both terms. (We choose the $-1/2$ power because it is the smaller of the two powers.) Dividing $(3 - x^2)^{-1/2}$ into the first term gives $(-x^3 + x)$ and dividing it into the second term gives $2x(3 - x^2)^1$. Why? Thus we have

$$f'(x) = (3 - x^2)^{-1/2}[(-x^3 + x) + 2x(3 - x^2)]$$

$$= \frac{-3x^2 + 7x}{(3 - x^2)^{1/2}},$$

which agrees with our previous answer.

It may be helpful to review the formulas needed to find the derivatives of various types of functions. Table 9.5 has examples of different types of functions and the formulas needed to find their derivatives.

Table 9.5

Example	Formula
$f(x) = 14$	If $f(x) = c$, $f'(x) = 0$
$y = x^4$	If $f(x) = x^n$, $f'(x) = nx^{n-1}$
$g(x) = 5x^3$	If $g(x) = cf(x)$, $g'(x) = cf'(x)$
$y = 3x^2 + 4x$	If $f(x) = u(x) + v(x)$, $f'(x) = u'(x) + v'(x)$
$y = (x^2 - 2)(x + 4)$	If $f(x) = u(x) \cdot v(x)$, $f'(x) = u(x) \cdot v'(x) + v(x) \cdot u'(x)$
$f(x) = \dfrac{x^3 + 1}{x^2}$	If $f(x) = \dfrac{u(x)}{v(x)}$, $f'(x) = \dfrac{v(x) \cdot u'(x) - u(x) \cdot v'(x)}{[v(x)]^2}$
$y = (x^3 - 4x)^{10}$	If $y = u^n$, $u = g(x)$, $\dfrac{dy}{dx} = nu^{n-1} \cdot \dfrac{du}{dx}$
$y = \left(\dfrac{x - 1}{x^2 + 3}\right)^3$	Power Rule, then Quotient Rule to find $\dfrac{du}{dx}$, $u = \dfrac{x - 1}{x^2 + 3}$
$y = (x + 1)\sqrt{x^3 + 1}$	Product Rule, then Power Rule to find $v'(x)$, $v(x) = \sqrt{x^3 + 1}$
$y = \dfrac{(x^2 - 3)^4}{x}$	Quotient Rule, then Power Rule to find the derivative of the numerator

Exercise 9.7

Find the derivatives of the following functions. Simplify and express the answer using positive exponents only.

1. $f(x) = \pi^4$

2. $f(x) = \dfrac{1}{4}$

3. $g(x) = \dfrac{4}{x^4}$

4. $y = \dfrac{x^4}{4}$

5. $g(x) = 5x^3 + \dfrac{4}{x}$

6. $y = 3x^2 + 4\sqrt{x}$

7. $y = (x^2 - 2)(x + 4)$

8. $y = (x^3 - 5x^2 + 1)(x^3 - 3)$

9. $f(x) = \dfrac{x^3 + 1}{x^2}$

10. $y = \dfrac{1 + x^2 - x^4}{1 + x^4}$

11. $y = \dfrac{(x^3 - 4x)^{10}}{10}$

12. $y = \dfrac{5}{2}(3x^4 - 6x^2 + 2)^5$

13. $y = \dfrac{5}{3}x^3(4x^5 - 5)^3$

14. $y = 3(x^2 + 4x)(x^5 + 1)^3$

15. $y = (x - 1)^2(x^2 + 1)$

16. $f(x) = (5x^3 + 1)(x^4 + 5x)^2$

17. $y = \dfrac{(x^2 - 4)^3}{x^2 + 1}$

18. $y = \dfrac{(x^2 - 3)^4}{x}$

19. $p = [(q + 1)(q^3 - 3)]^3$

20. $y = [(4 - x^2)(x^2 + 5x)]^4$

21. $R(x) = [x^2(x^2 + 3x)]^4$

22. $c(x) = [x^3(x^2 + 1)]^{-3}$

23. $y = \left(\dfrac{2x - 1}{x^2 + x}\right)^4$

24. $y = \left(\dfrac{5 - x^2}{x^4}\right)^3$

25. $g(x) = (8x^4 + 3)^2(x^3 - 4x)^3$

26. $y = (3x^3 - 4x)^3(4x^2 - 8)^2$

27. $f(x) = \dfrac{\sqrt[3]{x^2 + 5}}{4 - x^2}$

28. $g(x) = \dfrac{\sqrt[3]{2x - 1}}{2x + 1}$

29. $y = x^2\sqrt[4]{4x - 3}$

30. $y = 3x^3\sqrt{x^4 + 3}$

31. $c(x) = 2x\sqrt{x^3 + 1}$

32. $R(x) = x\sqrt[3]{3x^3 + 2}$

APPLICATIONS

33. The total physical output P of workers is a function of the number of workers, x. The function $P = f(x)$ is called the physical productivity function. Suppose the physical productivity of x construction workers is given by

$$P = 10(3x + 1)^3 - 10.$$

Find marginal physical productivity, dP/dx.

34. Suppose the revenue function for a certain product is given by

$$R(x) = 15(2x + 1)^{-1} + 30x - 15,$$

where x is in thousands of units and R is in thousands of dollars.
(a) Find the marginal revenue when 2000 units are sold.
(b) How is revenue changing when 2000 units are sold?

35. Suppose the revenue function for a computer is given by

$$R(x) = 60,000x + 40,000(10 + x)^{-1} - 4000.$$

(a) Find the marginal revenue when 10 units are sold.
(b) How is revenue changing when 10 units are sold?

36. Suppose the production of x items of a new line of products is given by

$$x = 200[(t + 10) - 400(t + 40)^{-1}],$$

where t is the number of weeks the line has been in production. Find the rate of production.

37. If the national consumption function is given by

$$C(y) = 2(y + 1)^{1/2} + 0.4y + 4,$$

find the marginal propensity to consume.

38. Suppose the demand function for an appliance is given by

$$p = \frac{400 \, (q + 1)}{(q + 2)^2}.$$

Find the rate of change of price with respect to the number of appliances.

39. When squares of side x are cut from the corners of a 12-inch square piece of cardboard, an open top box can be formed by folding up the sides. The volume of this box is given by

$$V = x(12 - 2x)^2.$$

Find the rate of change of volume with respect to the size of the squares.

9.8 Applications of Derivatives in Business and Economics

Objectives
- ☐ To find the marginal cost and marginal revenue at different levels of production
- ☐ To find the marginal profit function, given information about total cost and total revenue

In Chapter 1, we defined marginal cost as the rate of change of the total cost function. For a linear total cost function, the marginal cost was defined as the slope of the function's graph. For any total cost function defined by an equation, we can find the instantaneous rate of change of cost (the marginal cost) at any level of production by finding the derivative of the function.

> If $C = C(x)$ is a total cost function for a commodity, then its derivative, $\overline{MC} = C'(x)$ is the **marginal cost function.**

The linear cost function with equation

$$C(x) = 300 + 6x \qquad \text{(in dollars)}$$

has marginal cost \$6 because its slope is 6. Taking the derivative of $C(x)$ gives

$$\overline{MC} = C'(x) = 6,$$

which verifies that the marginal cost is \$6 at all levels of production.
The cost function

$$C(x) = 1000 + 6x + x^2$$

has derivative

$$C'(x) = 6 + 2x.$$

Then the marginal cost at x = 10 (when 10 units are produced) is

$$C'(10) = 6 + 2(10) = 26,$$

and the marginal cost at 40 units is

$$C'(40) = 6 + 2(40) = 86.$$

Thus the marginal cost is \$26 at 10 units and \$86 at 40 units of production.

As noted previously, when the derivative of a function is positive (and thus the slope of the tangent to the curve is positive), the function is increasing, and the value of the derivative gives us a measure of how fast it is increasing. Since marginal cost is the derivative of total cost, we can use marginal cost to measure increases in the total cost function. For example, the marginal cost for

$$C(x) = 1000 + 6x + x^2$$

is 86 at $x = 40$ and 26 at $x = 10$. This tells us the cost is increasing faster at $x = 40$ than it is at $x = 10$.

Since producing more units can never reduce the total cost of production, the following properties are valid:

1. The total cost can never be negative. If there are fixed costs, the cost of producing 0 units is positive; otherwise, the cost of producing 0 units is 0.

2. The total cost function is always increasing; the more units produced, the higher the total cost. Thus the marginal cost is always positive.

3. There may be limitations on the units produced, by factors such as plant space.

The graphs of many marginal cost functions tend to be U-shaped; they eventually will rise, even though there may be an initial interval where they decrease.

EXAMPLE 1   If the total cost function for a commodity is $C(x) = x^3 - 9x^2 + 33x + 30$, find the marginal cost and sketch its graph.

Solution   The marginal cost is

$$\overline{MC} = C'(x) = 3x^2 - 18x + 33.$$

The graph of the total cost function is shown in Figure 9.19(a) on the following page, and the graph of the marginal cost function is shown in Figure 9.19(b).

As we have seen in Section 9.3, the instantaneous rate of change (the derivative) of the revenue function is the marginal revenue.

If $R = R(x)$ is the total revenue function for a commodity, then the **marginal revenue function** is $\overline{MR} = R'(x)$.

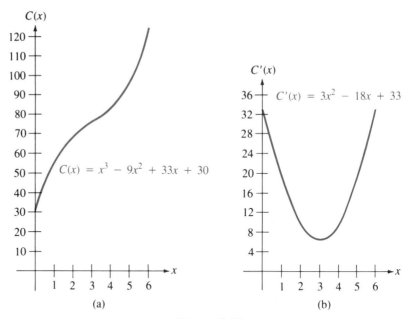

Figure 9.19

EXAMPLE 2 (a) Find the marginal revenue function for the total revenue function
$$R(x) = 16x - 0.02x^2.$$
(b) Find the marginal revenue for this product at $x = 40$.

Solution (a) The marginal revenue function is
$$\overline{MR} = R'(x) = 16 - 0.04x.$$
(b) At $x = 40$, $R'(40) = 16 - 1.6 = 14.40$. Thus the forty-first item sold will increase the total revenue by approximately $14.40.

EXAMPLE 3 Graph the total revenue and marginal revenue functions of Example 2.

Solution The graphs are shown in Figures 9.20 and 9.21, respectively. Note that the total revenue function has a maximum value at $x = 400$. After that, the total revenue function decreases. This means that, because of a discount, the total revenue will be reduced each time a unit is sold if more than 400 are produced and sold. The graph of the marginal revenue function (Figure 9.21) shows the marginal revenue is positive to the left of 400. This indicates that the rate at which the total revenue is changing is positive until 400 units are sold. Thus the total revenue is increasing. Then, at 400 units, the rate of change is 0. After 400 units are sold, the marginal revenue is negative, which indicates that the total revenue is now decreasing. It is clear from looking at either graph that no more than 400 units should be produced and sold if the total revenue function is $R(x) = 16 - 0.02x^2$. That is, the *total revenue* function has its maximum at $x = 400$.

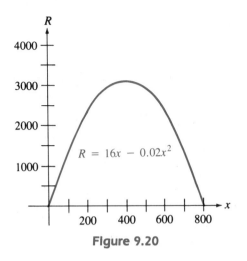

Figure 9.20

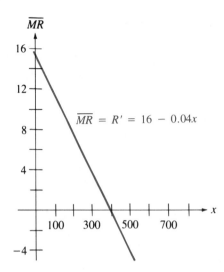

Figure 9.21

As with marginal cost and marginal revenue, the derivative of a profit function for a commodity gives us the marginal profit function for the commodity.

> If $P = P(x)$ is the profit function for a commodity, then the **marginal profit function** is $\overline{MP} = P'(x)$.

EXAMPLE 4 If the total profit for a product is given by $P(x) = 20\sqrt{x + 1} - 2x$, what is the marginal profit at a production level of 15 units?

Solution The marginal profit function is

$$P'(x) = 20 \cdot \frac{1}{2}(x + 1)^{-1/2} - 2 = \frac{10}{\sqrt{x + 1}} - 2.$$

If 15 units are produced, the marginal profit is

$$P'(15) = \frac{10}{\sqrt{15 + 1}} - 2 = \frac{1}{2}.$$

EXAMPLE 5 If the total revenue function for a commodity is $R(x) = 47x$ and the total cost function is $C(x) = 100 + x + x^2$, $0 \leq x \leq 25$, find the marginal profit function.

Solution The total profit function is

$$P(x) = 47x - (100 + x + x^2)$$

or

$$P(x) = 46x - 100 - x^2.$$

The marginal profit function is

$$P'(x) = 46 - 2x.$$

The marginal profit in Example 5 is not always positive, so producing and selling a certain number of items will maximize profit. Note that the marginal profit will be negative (that is, profit will decrease) if more than 23 items are produced. We will discuss methods of maximizing total revenue and profit, and for minimizing average cost, in Chapter 10.

Exercise 9.8

Find the marginal cost functions related to the cost functions in problems 1–8.

1. $C(x) = 40 + 8x$
2. $C(x) = 200 + 16x$
3. $C(x) = 500 + 13x + x^2$
4. $C(x) = 300 + 10x + \frac{1}{100}x^2$
5. $C = x^3 - 6x^2 + 24x + 10$
6. $C = x^3 - 12x^2 + 63x + 15$
7. $C = 400 + 27x + x^3$
8. $C(x) = 50 + 48x + x^3$
9. If the cost function for a commodity is $C(x) = 40 + x^2$, find the marginal cost at $x = 5$ and tell what this predicts about the cost of producing one additional unit.
10. If the cost function for a commodity is $C(x) = 300 + 6x + \frac{1}{20}x^2$, find the marginal cost at $x = 8$ and tell what this predicts about the cost of producing one additional unit.
11. If the cost function for a commodity is $C(x) = x^3 - 4x^2 + 30x + 20$, find the marginal cost at $x = 4$ and tell what this predicts about the cost of producing one additional unit.
12. If the cost function for a commodity is $C(x) = \frac{1}{90}x^3 + 4x^2 + 4x + 10$, find the marginal cost at $x = 3$ and tell what this predicts about the cost of producing one additional unit.
13. If the cost function for a commodity is $C(x) = 300 + 4x + x^2$, graph the marginal cost function.
14. If the cost function for a commodity is $C(x) = x^3 - 12x^2 + 63x + 15$, graph the marginal cost function.
15. (a) If the total revenue function for a product is $R(x) = 4x$, what is the marginal revenue function?
    (b) What does this marginal revenue function tell us?
16. If the total revenue function for a product is $R(x) = 32x$, what is the marginal revenue for the product?
17. Suppose the total revenue function for a commodity is $R = 36x - 0.01x^2$.
    (a) Find $R(100)$ and tell what it represents.
    (b) Find the marginal revenue function.
    (c) Find the marginal revenue at $x = 100$, and tell what it predicts about the sale of the next unit.
18. Suppose the total revenue function for a commodity is $R(x) = 25x - 0.05x^2$.
    (a) Find $R(50)$ and tell what it represents.
    (b) Find the marginal revenue function.
    (c) Find the marginal revenue at $x = 50$, and tell what it predicts about the sale of the next unit.

19. (a) Graph the marginal revenue function from problem 17.
    (b) At what value of x will total revenue be maximized?
    (c) What is the maximum revenue?
20. (a) Graph the marginal revenue function from problem 18.
    (b) Sale of how many units will maximize total revenue?
    (c) What is the maximum revenue?
21. If the total profit function is $P(x) = 5x - 25$, find the marginal profit.
22. If the total profit function is $P(x) = 16x - 32$, find the marginal profit.
23. Suppose the total revenue function for a product is $R(x) = 32x$ and the total cost function is $C(x) = 200 + 2x + x^2$.
    (a) Find the profit from the production and sales of 20 units.
    (b) Find the marginal profit function.
    (c) Find $\overline{MP}$ at $x = 20$ and tell what it predicts.
24. Suppose the total revenue function is given by $R(x) = 46x$ and the total cost function is given by $C(x) = 100 + 30x + \frac{1}{10}x^2$.
    (a) Find $P(100)$.
    (b) Find the marginal profit function.
    (c) Find $\overline{MP}$ at $x = 100$ and tell what it predicts.
25. (a) Graph the marginal profit function for the profit function $P(x) = 30x - x^2 - 200$.
    (b) What level of production will give a 0 marginal profit?
    (c) At what level of production will profit be a maximum?
    (d) What is the maximum profit?
26. (a) Graph the marginal profit function for the profit function $P(x) = 16x - 0.1x^2 - 100$.
    (b) What level of production will give a 0 marginal profit?
    (c) At what level of production will profit be a maximum?
    (d) What is the maximum profit?

Review Exercises

9.1

In problems 1–12, find each limit, if it exists.

1. $\lim\limits_{x \to 4} (3x^2 + x + 3)$

2. $\lim\limits_{x \to 4} \dfrac{x^2 - 16}{x + 4}$

3. $\lim\limits_{x \to -1} \dfrac{x^2 - 1}{x + 1}$

4. $\lim\limits_{x \to 3} \dfrac{x^2 - 9}{x - 3}$

5. $\lim\limits_{x \to 2} \dfrac{4x^3 - 8x^2}{4x^3 - 16x}$

6. $\lim\limits_{x \to -\frac{1}{2}} \dfrac{x^2 - \frac{1}{4}}{6x^2 + x - 1}$

7. $\lim\limits_{x \to 3} \dfrac{x^2 - 16}{x - 3}$

8. $\lim\limits_{x \to -3} \dfrac{x^2 - 9}{x - 3}$

9. $\lim\limits_{x \to 1} \dfrac{x^2 - 9}{x - 3}$

10. $\lim\limits_{x \to 2} \dfrac{x^2 - 8}{x - 2}$

11. $\lim\limits_{h. \to 0} \dfrac{3(x + h)^2 - 3x^2}{h}$

12. $\lim\limits_{h \to 0} \dfrac{[(x + h) - 2(x + h)^2] - [x - 2x^2]}{h}$

In problems 13–18, suppose

$$f(x) = \begin{cases} x^2 + 1 & \text{if } x \le 0 \\ x & \text{if } 0 < x < 1. \\ 2x^2 - 1 & \text{if } x \ge 1 \end{cases}$$

13. What is $\lim\limits_{x \to -1} f(x)$?

14. What is $\lim\limits_{x \to 0} f(x)$, if it exists?

15. What is $\lim\limits_{x \to 1} f(x)$, if it exists?

16. Is $f(x)$ continuous at $x = 0$?

17. Is $f(x)$ continuous at $x = 1$?

18. Is $f(x)$ continuous at $x = -1$?

Are each of the functions in problems 19–22 continuous? If not, which type of discontinuity occurs?

19. $y = \dfrac{x^2 + 25}{x - 5}$

20. $y = \dfrac{x^2 - 3x + 2}{x - 2}$

21. $f(x) = \begin{cases} x + 2 & \text{if } x \le 2 \\ 5x - 6 & \text{if } x > 2 \end{cases}$

22. $y = \begin{cases} x^4 - 3 & \text{if } x \le 1 \\ 2x - 3 & \text{if } x > 1 \end{cases}$

In problems 23 and 24, find any horizontal asymptotes and any vertical asymptotes.

23. $y = \dfrac{3x + 2}{2x - 4}$

24. $y = \dfrac{x^2}{1 - x^2}$

In problems 25 and 26, use the graphs to find the following:
   (a) vertical asymptotes
   (b) horizontal asymptotes
   (c) points of discontinuity (identify the type)

25.

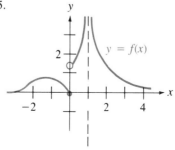

26.

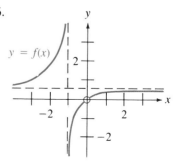

27. Decide whether each of the following is true or false.

   (a) $\lim\limits_{h \to 0} \dfrac{f(x + h) - f(x)}{h}$ gives the formula for the slope of the tangent and the instantaneous rate of change of $f(x)$ at any value of x.

   (b) $\lim\limits_{h \to 0} \dfrac{f(c + h) - f(c)}{h}$ gives the equation of the tangent line to $f(x)$ at $x = c$.

28. Use the definition of derivative to find $f'(x)$ for $f(x) = 3x^2 + 2x - 1$.

29. If $c = 4x^5 - 6x^3$, find c'.

30. If $f(x) = 4x^2 - 1$, find $f'(x)$.

31. If $p = 3q + \sqrt{7}$, find dp/dq.

32. If $y = \sqrt{x}$, find y'.

33. If $f(z) = \sqrt[3]{2^4}$, find $f'(z)$.

34. If $v(x) = 4/\sqrt[3]{x}$, find $v'(x)$.

35. If $y = \dfrac{1}{x} - \dfrac{1}{\sqrt{x}}$, find y'.

36. If $f(x) = \dfrac{3}{2x^2} - \sqrt[3]{x} + 4^5$, find $f'(x)$.

37. Write the equation of the tangent to $y = 3x^5 - 6$ at $x = 1$.

38. Write the equation of the line tangent to the curve $y = 3x^3 - 2x$ at the point $(2, 20)$.

In problems 39 and 40, find all x-values where the slope of the tangent equals zero.

39. $f(x) = x^3 - 3x^2 + 1$

40. $f(x) = x^6 - 6x^4 + 8$

9.5

41. If $g(x) = (3x - 1)(x^2 - 4x)$, find $g'(x)$.

42. Find y' if $y = (x^2 + 1)(3x^3 + 1)$.

43. If $p = \dfrac{2q - 1}{q^2}$, find $\dfrac{dp}{dq}$.

44. Find $\dfrac{ds}{dt}$ if $s = \dfrac{\sqrt{t}}{(3t + 1)}$.

45. Find dy for $y = \sqrt{x}\,(3x + 2)$.

46. Find dC for $C = \dfrac{5x^4 - 2x^2 + 1}{x^3 + 1}$.

9.6

47. If $y = (x^3 - 4x^2)^3$, find y'.

48. If $y = (5x^6 + 6x^4 + 5)^6$, find y'.

49. If $y = (x^3 - 4x^2)^3$, find $\dfrac{dy}{dx}$.

50. Find $g'(x)$ if $g(x) = \dfrac{1}{\sqrt{x^3 - 4x}}$.

9.7

51. Find $f'(x)$ if $f(x) = x^2(2x^4 + 5)^8$.

52. Find S' if $S = \dfrac{(3x + 1)^2}{x^2 - 4}$.

53. Find $\dfrac{dy}{dx}$ if $y = [(3x + 1)(2x^3 - 1)]^{12}$.

54. Find y' if $y = \left(\dfrac{x + 1}{1 - x^2}\right)^3$.

55. Find y' if $y = x\sqrt{x^2 - 4}$.

56. Find $\dfrac{dy}{dx}$ if $y = \dfrac{x}{\sqrt[3]{3x - 1}}$.

APPLICATIONS

9.8

57. If the cost function for a good is $C(x) = 3x^2 + 6x + 600$,
   (a) what is the marginal cost function?
   (b) what is the marginal cost if 30 units are produced?

58. If the total cost function for a commodity is $C(x) = 400 + 5x + x^3$, what is the marginal cost when 4 units are produced?

59. If the total revenue function for a commodity is $R = 40x - 0.02x^2$, with x representing the number of units,
   (a) find the marginal revenue function.
   (b) at what level of production will marginal revenue be 0?

60. If the total revenue function is given by $R(x) = 60x$ and the total cost function is given by $C = 200 + 10x + 0.1x^2$, what is the marginal profit at $x = 10$?

61. If the total revenue function for a commodity is given by $R = 80x - 0.04x^2$,
   (a) find the marginal revenue function.
   (b) what is the marginal revenue at $x = 100$?

62. If the revenue function for a product is

$$R(x) = \dfrac{60x^2}{2x + 1},$$

find the marginal revenue.

WARMUP

	Prerequisite problem type	Answer	Section for review
10.2	Write $\frac{1}{3}(x^2 - 1)^{-2/3}(2x)$ with positive exponents.	$\dfrac{2x}{3(x^2 - 1)^{2/3}}$	0.3, 0.4 Exponents and radicals
10.1, 10.3	Factor: (a) $x^3 - x^2 - 6x$ (b) $8000 - 80x - 3x^2$	(a) $x(x - 3)(x + 2)$ (b) $(40 - x)(200 + 3x)$	0.6 Factoring
10.2	(a) For what values of x is $\dfrac{2}{3\sqrt[3]{x + 2}}$ undefined? (b) For what values of x is $\frac{1}{3}(x^2 - 1)^{-2/3}(2x)$ undefined?	(a) $x = -2$ (b) $x = -1,\ x = 1$	1.3 Domains of functions
10.1	If $f(x) = \frac{1}{3}x^3 - x^2 - 3x + 2$, and $f'(x) = x^2 - 2x - 3$, (a) find $f(-1)$. (b) find $f'(-2)$.	(a) $\frac{11}{3}$ (b) 5	1.3 Functional notation
10.1	(a) Solve $0 = x^2 - 2x - 3$ (b) If $f'(x) = 3x^2 - 3$, what values of x make $f'(x) = 0$?	(a) $x = -1,\ x = 3$ (b) $x = -1,\ x = 1$	4.1 Solving quadratic equations
10.2	(a) Is the function $y = x^{1/3}$ continuous at $x = 0$? (b) Is the function $y = \dfrac{1}{x^2}$ continuous at $x = 0$?	(a) Yes (b) No	9.2 Continuity
10.1, 10.2, 10.3, 10.4	Find the derivatives: (a) $y = \frac{1}{3}x^3 - x^2 - 3x + 2$ (b) $f(x) = x^{1/3}$ (c) $f = x + 2\left(\dfrac{80,000}{x}\right)$ (d) $p(t) = 1 + \dfrac{4t}{t^2 + 16}$ (e) $y = (x + 2)^{2/3}$ (f) $y = \sqrt[3]{x^2 - 1}$	(a) $y' = x^2 - 2x - 3$ (b) $f'(x) = \frac{1}{3}x^{-2/3}$ (c) $\dfrac{df}{dx} = 1 - \dfrac{160,000}{x^2}$ (d) $p'(t) = \dfrac{64 - 4t^2}{(t^2 + 16)^2}$ (e) $\dfrac{2}{3(x + 2)^{1/3}}$ (f) $\dfrac{2x}{3(x^2 - 1)^{2/3}}$	9.4, 9.5, 9.6 Derivatives

10

Applications of Derivatives

In Chapter 9 we learned that the derivative could be used to determine rates of change, including velocity, marginal cost, marginal revenue, marginal profit, and rates of growth. We also used the derivative to determine the slope of the tangent to a curve at a given point.

In this chapter we will consider methods of determining when functions are maximized and minimized. We will see that the derivative can be used to determine the "turning points" of the graph of a function, so we can determine when a curve reaches its highest (or lowest) point. Knowledge of where a curve has a relative maximum and/or relative minimum will be very helpful in sketching its graph.

The relative maximum of a function can be useful in determining the levels of production that will maximize profit functions and revenue functions, the maximum dosage for certain medications, and maximum sizes of some changing populations. The relative minimum of an average cost function can be used to find the level of production that will minimize the average cost per unit.

10.1 Relative Maxima and Minima; Curve Sketching

Objectives
- [ ] To find relative maxima and minima and horizontal points of inflection of functions
- [ ] To sketch graphs of functions by using information about maxima, minima, and horizontal points of inflection

Except for very simple graphs (straight lines and parabolas, for example), plotting points will not give a very accurate graph of a function. In addition to intercepts and asymptotes, we can use the first derivative as an aid in graphing. The first derivative identifies the "turning points" of a curve, which will help determine the general shape of the curve.

In Figure 10.1 on the next page, we see the graph of $y = \frac{1}{3}x^3 - x^2 - 3x + 2$ has two "turning points," at $\left(-1, \frac{11}{3}\right)$ and $(3, -7)$. The curve has a relative maximum at $\left(-1, \frac{11}{3}\right)$ because this point is higher than any other point "near" it on the

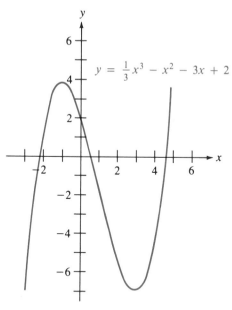

$$y = \frac{1}{3}x^3 - x^2 - 3x + 2$$

Figure 10.1

"near" it on the curve; the curve has a relative minimum at $(3, -7)$ because this point is lower than any other point "near" it on the curve. A formal definition follows.

A function f has a **relative maximum** at $x = x_1$ if there is an interval around x_1 on which $f(x_1) \geq f(x)$ for all x in the interval. A function f has a **relative minimum** at $x = x_2$ if there is an interval around x_2 on which $f(x_2) \leq f(x)$ for all x in the interval.

A function f is said to be *increasing* over an interval in its domain if for every x_1 and x_2 in the interval, $f(x_2) > f(x_1)$ if $x_2 > x_1$. A function f is *decreasing* over an interval if for every x_1 and x_2 in the interval, $f(x_2) < f(x_1)$ if $x_2 > x_1$.

If a function f is increasing, the slope of the tangent to the curve is positive, and if f is decreasing, the slope of the tangent to the curve is negative. This leads us to conclude the following.

If f is a function that is differentiable on an interval (a, b), then

if $f'(x) > 0$ for all x in (a, b), f is increasing on (a, b).
if $f'(x) < 0$ for all x in (a, b), f is decreasing on (a, b).

The derivative $f'(x)$ can change signs only at values of x where $f'(x) = 0$ or $f'(x)$ is undefined. We call these values of x **critical values.** The point corresponding to a critical value for x is a **critical point.** Because a curve changes from increasing to decreasing at a relative maximum (see Figure 10.1), we have the following fact.

> If f has a relative maximum at $x = x_0$, then $f'(x_0) = 0$ or $f'(x_0)$ is undefined.

Figure 10.2 shows the graph of a function with two relative maxima, one at $x = x_1$ and the second at $x = x_3$. At $x = x_1$ the derivative is 0, and at $x = x_3$ the derivative does not exist.

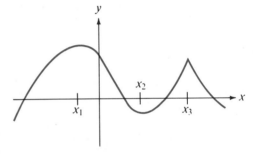

Figure 10.2

As Figure 10.2 shows, the function changes from decreasing to increasing at a relative minimum. Thus we have the following fact.

> If f has a relative minimum at $x = x_0$, then $f'(x_0) = 0$ or $f'(x_0)$ is undefined.

Thus we can find relative maxima and minima for a curve by finding values of x for which the first derivative* is 0 or undefined. The behavior of the derivative to the left and right (and near) these values will tell us if they are relative maxima or relative minima, or neither one.

Suppose the point (x_1, y_1) is a critical point. If $f'(x)$ is positive to the left of, and near, this critical point, and if $f'(x)$ is negative to the right of, and near, this critical point, then the curve is increasing to the left of the point and decreasing to the right. This means that a relative maximum occurs at the point. If we draw tangent

---

*The derivatives we have been discussing thus far are called *first* derivatives. We will discuss higher-order derivatives in Chapter 11.

lines to the curve to the left of and to the right of this critical point, they would be as follows.

To the left, $f'(x) > 0$:

To the right, $f'(x) < 0$:

If $f'(x_1) = 0$, the tangent line is horizontal there. Thus these tangent lines form the pattern,

which shows us the curve has the shape

with a relative maximum at (x_1, y_1).

This can be *illustrated* as follows*:

Left of critical point, $f'(x) > 0$.
At critical point, $f'(x_1) = 0$. $\Rightarrow$
Right of critical point, $f'(x) < 0$.

 rel. max.

Similarly, suppose the point (x_2, y_2) is a critical point, $f'(x)$ is negative to the left of, and near, (x_2, y_2), and $f'(x)$ is positive to the right of, and near, this critical point. Then the curve is decreasing to the left of the point and increasing to the right, and a relative minimum occurs at the point. If we draw tangent lines to the curve to the left of and to the right of this critical point, they would be as follows.

To the left, $f'(x) < 0$:

To the right, $f'(x) > 0$:

If $f'(x_2) = 0$, the tangent line is horizontal there. Thus these tangent lines form the pattern,

----

*The word "implies" is symbolized by "$\Rightarrow$."

which shows us the curve has the shape

with a relative minimum at (x_2, y_2).

This can be illustrated as follows:

$\left.\begin{array}{l}\text{Left of critical point, } f'(x) < 0. \\ \text{At critical point, } f'(x_2) = 0. \\ \text{Right of critical point, } f'(x) > 0.\end{array}\right\} \Rightarrow$

If $f'(x)$ does not change signs as x passes from one side of a critical point (x_3, y_3) to the other, the critical point is neither a maximum nor a minimum. Such a point is called a **horizontal point of inflection**. If $f'(x_3) = 0$, we can illustrate the two possible cases as follows:

$\left.\begin{array}{l}\text{Left of critical point, } f'(x) > 0. \\ \text{At critical point, } f'(x_3) = 0. \\ \text{Right of critical point, } f'(x) > 0.\end{array}\right\} \Rightarrow$ horizontal point of inflection

or

$\left.\begin{array}{l}\text{Left of critical point, } f'(x) < 0. \\ \text{At critical point, } f'(x_3) = 0. \\ \text{Right of critical point, } f'(x) < 0.\end{array}\right\} \Rightarrow$ horizontal point of inflection

The preceding discussion suggests the following procedure for finding relative maxima and minima of a function.

First-derivative test

Procedure	Example
To find relative maxima and minima of a function:	Find the relative maxima and minima of $f(x) = \frac{1}{3}x^3 - x^2 - 3x + 2$.
1. Find the first derivative of the function.	1. $f'(x) = x^2 - 2x - 3$
2. Set the derivative equal to 0, and solve for values of x that satisfy $f'(x) = 0$. These are called *critical values*. Values that make $f'(x)$ undefined are also critical values.	2. $0 = x^2 - 2x - 3$ has solutions $x = -1$, $x = 3$. No values of x make $x^2 - 2x - 3$ undefined. Critical values are -1 and 3.
3. Substitute the critical values into the *original function* to find the *critical points*.	3. $f(-1) = \frac{11}{3}$ $f(3) = -7$ The critical points are $\left(-1, \frac{11}{3}\right)$ and $(3, -7)$.

4. Evaluate $f'(x)$ at some value of x to the left and right of each critical value:
   (a) If $f'(x) > 0$ to the left and $f'(x) < 0$ to the right of the critical value, the critical point is a relative maximum.
   (b) If $f'(x) < 0$ to the left and $f'(x) > 0$ to the right of the critical value, the critical point is a relative minimum.

4. $f'(-2) = 5 > 0$ and
   $f'(0) = -3 < 0$
   Thus $(-1, 11/3)$ is a relative maximum.
   $f'(2) = -3 < 0$ and $f'(4) = 5 > 0$
   Thus $(3, -7)$ is a relative minimum.

The graph of this function is shown in Figure 10.3.

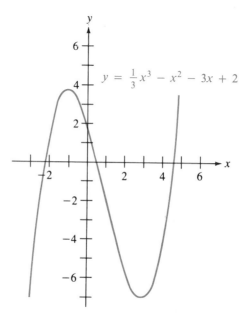

$$y = \frac{1}{3}x^3 - x^2 - 3x + 2$$

Figure 10.3

We can test to the left and right of each critical value by testing to the left of the smallest critical value, then testing a value *between* each critical value, then testing to the right of the largest critical value. The following example illustrates this procedure.

EXAMPLE 1   Find the relative maxima and minima of $y = x^3 - 3x + 6$.

Solution   1. The first derivative of $y = f(x)$ is $y' = f'(x) = 3x^2 - 3$.
2. Setting $f'(x) = 0$ gives $0 = 3x^2 - 3$.
   Solving for x gives

$$0 = 3(x - 1)(x + 1)$$
$$x = -1, \qquad x = 1.$$

3. Substituting the critical values ($x = -1$ and $x = 1$) into the original function gives the critical points: $f(-1) = 8$, so $(-1,8)$ is a critical point; $f(1) = 4$, so $(1, 4)$ is a critical point.

4. Testing $f'(x)$ to the left of the smaller critical value, then between the two critical values, then to the right of the larger critical value gives

$$f'(-2) = 3(-2)^2 - 3 = 9 > 0$$
$$\text{Critical value } f'(-1) = 0$$
$$f'(0) = 3(0)^2 - 3 = -3 < 0$$

$$\Rightarrow \text{rel. max. at } (-1, 8).$$

$$\text{Critical value } f'(1) = 0$$
$$f'(2) = 3(2)^2 - 3 = 9 > 0$$

$$\Rightarrow \text{rel. min. at } (1, 4).$$

Thus $(-1, 8)$ is a relative maximum and $(1, 4)$ is a relative minimum. The relative maximum and relative minimum are shown in Figure 10.4(a) and the graph of the curve is given in Figure 10.4(b). Notice how easy it is to graph the equation once the relative maxima and minima are graphed.

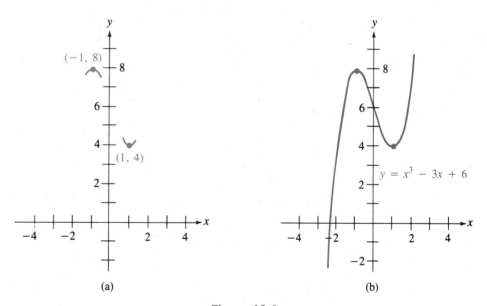

$$y = x^3 - 3x + 6$$

(a)   (b)

Figure 10.4

Note that we substitute the critical values into the *original function* $f(x)$ to find the y-values of the critical points, but we test for relative maxima and minima by substituting values near the critical values into the *derivative of the function*, $f'(x)$.

EXAMPLE 2   Find the relative maxima and minima of $f(x) = \frac{1}{4}x^4 - \frac{1}{3}x^3 - 3x^2 + 8$, and sketch its graph.

Solution
1. $f'(x) = x^3 - x^2 - 6x$
2. $0 = x^3 - x^2 - 6x$
   $0 = x(x - 3)(x + 2)$

$x = 0$	$x - 3 = 0$	$x + 2 = 0$
	$x = 3$	$x = -2$

Thus, the critical values are $x = 0$, $x = 3$, and $x = -2$.

3. $f(-2) = \frac{8}{3}$, so $\left(-2, \frac{8}{3}\right)$ is a critical point.
   $f(0) = 8$, so $(0, 8)$ is a critical point.
   $f(3) = -\frac{31}{4}$, so $\left(3, -\frac{31}{4}\right)$ is a critical point.

4. $\left.\begin{array}{l} f'(-3) = -18 < 0 \\ f'(-2) = 0 \\ f'(-1) = 4 > 0 \end{array}\right\} \Rightarrow$ ⌣ $\left(-2, \frac{8}{3}\right)$ is a relative minimum.

   $\left.\begin{array}{l} f'(0) = 0 \\ f'(1) = -6 < 0 \end{array}\right\} \Rightarrow$ ⌢ $(0, 8)$ is a relative maximum.

   $\left.\begin{array}{l} f'(3) = 0 \\ f'(4) = 24 > 0 \end{array}\right\} \Rightarrow$ ⌣ $\left(3, -\frac{31}{4}\right)$ is a relative minimum.

Figure 10.5(a) shows the graph of the function near the critical points, and Figure 10.5(b) shows the graph of the function.

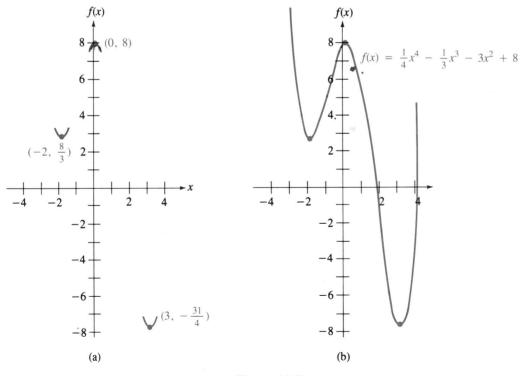

(a)   (b)

Figure 10.5

NOTE: Only four values were needed to test three critical points in Example 2. This method will work *only if* the critical values are tested in order from smallest to largest.

Recall that if the first derivative of f is 0 at x_0, but does not change from positive to negative or negative to positive as x passes through x_0, then we say f has a **horizontal point of inflection** at x_0.

EXAMPLE 3   Find the relative maxima, relative minima, and horizontal points of inflection of $h(x) = \frac{1}{4}x^4 - \frac{2}{3}x^3 - 2x^2 + 8x + 4$, and sketch its graph.

Solution   1. $h'(x) = x^3 - 2x^2 - 4x + 8$
2. $0 = x^3 - 2x^2 - 4x + 8$ or $0 = x^2(x - 2) - 4(x - 2)$. Therefore, we have $0 = (x - 2)(x^2 - 4)$. Thus $x = -2$ and $x = 2$ are solutions.
3. The critical points are $\left(-2, -\frac{32}{3}\right)$ and $\left(2, \frac{32}{3}\right)$.

4. $\left.\begin{array}{l} h'(-3) = -25 < 0 \\ h'(-2) = 0 \\ h'(0) = 8 > 0 \\ h'(2) = 0 \\ h'(3) = 5 > 0 \end{array}\right\}$ $\Rightarrow \left(-2, -\frac{32}{3}\right)$ is a relative minimum.

$\Rightarrow \left(2, \frac{32}{3}\right)$ is a horizontal point of inflection.

The graph of $y = h(x)$ is shown in Figure 10.6.

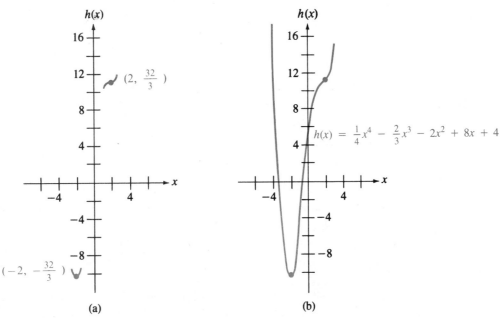

(a)   (b)

Figure 10.6

Exercise 10.1

For each function in problems 1–6,
(a) find dy/dx.
(b) find the critical values.
(c) find the critical points.
(d) classify the critical points as relative maxima, relative minima, or horizontal points of inflection.

1. $y = \frac{1}{2}x^2 - x$

2. $y = x^2 + 4x$

3. $y = 2x - x^2$

4. $y = 9 - x^2$

5. $y = x^3 + 3x^2 + 3x$

6. $y = x^3 - 6x^2 + 12x$

For each function in problems 7–10,
(a) find dy/dx.
(b) find the critical values.
(c) find the critical points.
(d) classify the critical points as relative maxima, relative minima, or horizontal points of inflection.
(e) sketch the graph.

7. $y = \dfrac{x^3}{3} + \dfrac{x^2}{2} - 2x + 1$

8. $y = \dfrac{x^4}{4} - \dfrac{x^3}{3}$

9. $y = x^3 - 3x^2$

10. $y = x^4 - 2x^2$

For each function in problems 11–26, find the relative maxima, relative minima, and horizontal points of inflection, and sketch the graphs.

11. $y = \frac{1}{3}x^3 - x^2 + x + 1$

12. $y = \frac{1}{4}x^4 - \frac{2}{3}x^3 + \frac{1}{2}x^2 - 2$

13. $y = x^4 - 4x^3$

14. $y = x^3(x - 1)$

15. $y = (x^2 - 2x)^2$

16. $y = x(x - 1)^2$

17. $y = x(x - 2)^3$

18. $y = (x^2 - 4)^2$

19. $p = q^3 - 3q^2 + 4$

20. $p = \frac{1}{3}q^3 - 2q^2 - 12q$

21. $p = q^3 + q^2 - 8q + 3$

22. $C(x) = x^3 - \frac{3}{2}x^2 - 6x + 4$

23. $y = 3x^5 - 5x^3 + 1$

24. $y = \frac{1}{2}x^6 - 3x^4 + 7$

25. $y = \dfrac{x^3(x - 5)^2}{27}$

26. $y = \dfrac{x^2(x - 5)^3}{27}$

APPLICATIONS

27. The number of milligrams x of a medication in the bloodstream t hours after taking a dosage can be modeled by

$$x(t) = \frac{2000t}{t^2 + 16}.$$

(a) For what t-values is x increasing?
(b) Find the t-value at which x is maximum.
(c) Find the maximum value for x. Do not graph.

28. Suppose the concentration C of a medication in the bloodstream t hours after an injection is given by

$$C(t) = \frac{0.2t}{t^2 + 1}.$$

(a) Find the number of hours before C attains its maximum.
(b) Find the maximum concentration. Do not graph.

29. Suppose that the proportion P of voters who recognize a candidate's name t months after the start of the campaign is given by

$$P(t) = \frac{13t}{t^2 + 100} + 0.18.$$

(a) How many months after the start of the campaign is recognition at its maximum?
(b) To have greatest recognition on November 1, when should a campaign be launched?

10.2   More Maxima and Minima; Undefined Derivatives

Objectives   ☐   To use information from derivatives to sketch graphs
☐   To find absolute maxima and minima of functions

As we mentioned in the First Derivative Test in Section 10.1, values of x that make the first derivative undefined are also critical values for a function. The first derivative may be undefined at the point $x = x_0$ because

1. The function is undefined at x_0.

2. The point $x = x_0$ is not in the domain of the derivative even though it is in the domain of the function.

3. The limit of the difference quotient

$$\frac{f(x + h) - f(x)}{h}$$

is different from the left than it is from the right; thus

$$f'(x) = \lim_{h \to 0} \frac{f(x + h) - f(x)}{h}$$

does not exist.

Figure 10.7 is the graph of $y = f(x) = 1/x^2$. Since $f'(x) = -2/x^3$, both $f(x)$ and $f'(x)$ are undefined at $x = 0$.

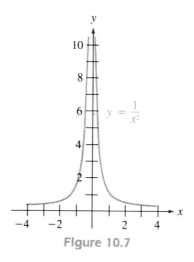

Figure 10.7

Figure 10.8 is the graph of $y = f(x) = x^{1/3}$. Since $f'(x) = 1/(3x^{2/3})$, the function $f(x) = x^{1/3}$ is defined at $x = 0$, but $f'(x)$ is not defined at $x = 0$.

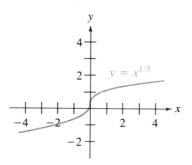

Figure 10.8

Figure 10.9 is the graph of $y = f(x) = |x|$. The function $f(x)$ is defined at $x = 0$, but $f'(x)$ does not exist at $x = 0$. Slopes (derivatives) for $x < 0$ are all -1, and slopes for $x > 0$ are all $+1$.

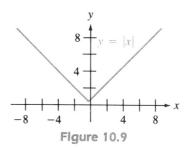

Figure 10.9

Several observations can be made using these figures.

First note that in Figures 10.8 and 10.9, the functions are continuous at $x = 0$, but do not have derivatives at $x = 0$. What is the relationship between differentiability and continuity? The answer is as follows.

> If a function f is differentiable at $x = a$, then f is continuous at $x = a$.

Also note that the equations graphed in Figures 10.8 and 10.9 show that the converse of this statement is false. That is, they show functions that are continuous at $x = 0$ but whose derivatives at $x = 0$ do not exist.

Finally, note that in Figure 10.8, the value at $x = 0$ is neither maximum nor minimum, and in Figure 10.9, the value $x = 0$ yields a minimum. How do we classify these cases? The answer is to use the First Derivative Test just as we did in Section 10.1. Some further examples will be helpful.

EXAMPLE 1   Find the relative maxima and minima (if any) of the graph of $y = (x + 2)^{2/3}$.

Solution   1. $y' = f'(x) = \frac{2}{3}(x + 2)^{-1/3} = \dfrac{2}{3\sqrt[3]{x + 2}}$

2. $0 = \dfrac{2}{3\sqrt[3]{x + 2}}$ has no solutions; $f'(x)$ is undefined at $x = -2$.

3. $f(-2) = 0$, so the critical point is $(-2, 0)$.

4. $\left. \begin{array}{l} f'(-3) = -\frac{2}{3} \\ f'(-1) = \frac{2}{3} \end{array} \right\} \Rightarrow$ a relative minimum occurs at $(-2, 0)$.

The graph is shown in Figure 10.10.

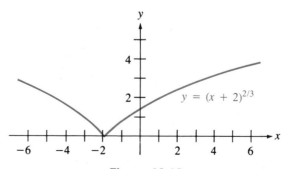

Figure 10.10

EXAMPLE 2   Find the relative maxima and relative minima of

$$y = \frac{x^2 + 1}{x}$$

and sketch its graph.

Solution   1. $y' = f'(x) = \dfrac{x(2x) - (x^2 + 1)(1)}{x^2}$

$$= \frac{x^2 - 1}{x^2}$$

2. $0 = \dfrac{x^2 - 1}{x^2}$ has solutions $x = -1$ and $x = 1$, and $f'(x)$ is undefined at
$x = 0$. Thus the critical values are $-1, 1,$ and 0.

3. Critical points occur at $(-1, -2)$ and $(1, 2)$, but y is undefined at $x = 0$. Thus
the function has a discontinuity at $x = 0$. Investigating limits shows the graph
has a vertical asymptote at $x = 0$.

4. $\left.\begin{array}{l} f'(-2) > 0 \\ f'\left(-\frac{1}{2}\right) < 0 \end{array}\right\} \Rightarrow$ relative maximum at $(-1, -2)$

$\left.\begin{array}{l} f'\left(-\frac{1}{2}\right) < 0 \\ f'\left(\frac{1}{2}\right) < 0 \end{array}\right\} \Rightarrow$ vertical asymptote at $x = 0$

$\left.\begin{array}{l} f'\left(\frac{1}{2}\right) < 0 \\ f'(2) > 0 \end{array}\right\} \Rightarrow$ relative minimum at $(1, 2)$

The graph is shown in Figure 10.11.

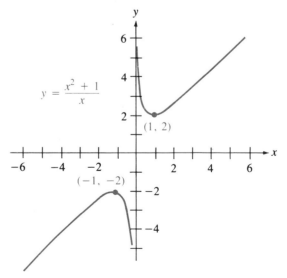

Figure 10.11

EXAMPLE 3   Find the relative maxima and minima of the function $g(x) = \sqrt[3]{x^2 - 1}$.

Solution

1. $g'(x) = \frac{1}{3}(x^2 - 1)^{-2/3}(2x) = \dfrac{2x}{3(x^2 - 1)^{2/3}}$

2. $0 = \dfrac{2x}{3(x^2 - 1)^{2/3}}$ has solution $x = 0$. But $g'(x)$ is undefined at $x = -1$ and $x = 1$. Thus the critical values are -1, 0, and 1.

3. The critical points are $(-1, 0)$, $(0, -1)$, and $(1, 0)$.

4. $\left.\begin{array}{l} g'(-2) < 0 \\ g'\left(-\frac{1}{2}\right) < 0 \end{array}\right\} \Rightarrow$ no maximum or minimum at $(-1, 0)$.

   $\left.\begin{array}{l} g'\left(\frac{1}{2}\right) > 0 \\ g'(2) > 0 \end{array}\right\} \Rightarrow (0, -1)$ is a relative minimum.

   $\Rightarrow$ no maximum or minimum at $(1, 0)$.

The graph of g is shown in Figure 10.12.

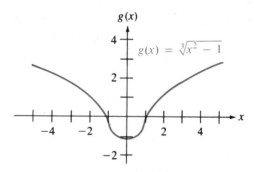

Figure 10.12

Notice that in Figure 10.12 the relative minimum is the lowest point on the graph. In this case we call the point an **absolute minimum** for the function. Similarly, when there is a point that is the highest point on the graph over the domain of the function, then we call the point an **absolute maximum** for the function.

In Figure 10.12, we see that there is no relative maximum. However, if the domain of the function is restricted to the interval $\left[-\frac{1}{2}, 1\right]$, then there is an absolute maximum at the point $(1, 0)$, and the absolute minimum is still at $(0, -1)$. If we consider the function in Figure 10.12 with the domain restricted to the interval $[1, 3]$, then its absolute minimum would occur at the point $(1, 0)$, and its absolute maximum at $(3, 2)$.

As the above discussion indicates, if the domain of a function is limited, an absolute maximum or minimum may occur at the endpoints of the domain. In testing functions with limited domains for absolute maxima and minima, we must compare the endpoints of the domain with the relative maxima and minima found by taking derivatives. In applications to the management, life, and social sciences, a limited domain occurs very often, since many quantities are required to be positive, or at least nonnegative.

EXAMPLE 4   Find the absolute maximum and absolute minimum of the function

$$y = x^2 - 1. \qquad (-1 \le x \le 2)$$

Solution   We first find points where the derivative is 0.
1. $y' = f'(x) = 2x$
2. $0 = 2x$ has solution $x = 0$.
3. The critical point is $(0, -1)$.
4. $\left. \begin{array}{l} f'(-1) = -2 < 0 \\ f'(1) = 2 > 0 \end{array} \right\} \Rightarrow (0, -1)$ is a relative minimum.

We now compare the values of the function at the endpoints of the domain with this relative minimum.

$$f(-1) = 0; \; f(2) = 3$$

Thus we see that $(0, -1)$ is the absolute minimum and $(2, 3)$ is the absolute maximum. The graph of the function is shown in Figure 10.13.

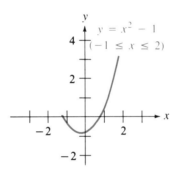

Figure 10.13

Exercise 10.2

In problems 1–10, determine where each function has undefined derivatives.

1. $y = \dfrac{1}{x}$

2. $y = \dfrac{1}{x - 2}$

3. $y = \sqrt{x}$

4. $y = \sqrt[3]{x - 3}$

5. $y = \dfrac{x^2 - 4}{x - 1}$

6. $y = \dfrac{x^2 + 3}{x}$

7. $y = (x - 1)^{2/3}$

8. $f(x) = \sqrt{4 - x^2}$

9. $f(x) = \begin{cases} 3x + 4 & \text{if } x \le 0 \\ 4 - \frac{1}{2}x & \text{if } x > 0 \end{cases}$

10. $y = \begin{cases} x + 2 & \text{if } x < 0 \\ 2 - x & \text{if } x \ge 0 \end{cases}$

Use information about their derivatives to sketch the graphs of the functions in problems 11–24.

11. $y = 1/x^2$

12. $y = 4/(x - 4)^2$

13. $y = 1/(x - 1)^2$

14. $y = 1/x^3$

15. $y = \dfrac{x^2 + 4}{x}$

16. $y = \dfrac{4}{(x + 4)^2}$

17. $y = \sqrt[3]{x^2 - 4}$

18. $y = \sqrt{x} + 3$

19. $c(x) = \sqrt{x}(x - 1)^2$

20. $R(x) = x^{2/3}(x - 1)^2$

21. $y = \dfrac{x^{1/3}(x - 7)^2}{6}$

22. $y = x^{2/3}(x - 5)$

23. $f(x) = \begin{cases} x + 2 & \text{if } x \le 2 \\ 4 & \text{if } x > 2 \end{cases}$

24. $f(x) = \begin{cases} 3 & \text{if } x \le 0 \\ x + 1 & \text{if } x > 0 \end{cases}$

Find the absolute maxima and minima, if they occur, for the functions in problems 25–30.

25. $f(x) = 16 - x^2$

26. $f(x) = x^2 - 2x$

27. $g(x) = 2x^2 - x$ $(0 \le x \le 3)$

28. $h(x) = 2x^2 - x$ $(1 \le x \le 4)$

29. $f(x) = 16 - x^2$ $(0 \le x \le 3)$

30. $f(x) = 6x^2 - x^3$ $(0 \le x \le 7)$

31. Will every function that is differentiable at $x = a$ also be continuous at $x = a$?

32. Will every function that is continuous at $x = a$ also be differentiable at $x = a$?

APPLICATIONS

33. Residential customers in a small town have their charge, C in dollars, for water given by

$$C = \begin{cases} 18 & \text{if } 0 \le x \le 20 \\ 0.1x + 16 & \text{if } x > 20 \end{cases}$$

where x is in hundreds of gallons of usage.
(a) Find the rate of change of C with respect to usage at $x = 15$ and at $x = 30$.
(b) Does the rate of change of C with respect to x exist at $x = 20$?

34. The 1988 federal income tax T (in dollars) for a single filer whose taxable income is x dollars is

$$T = \begin{cases} 0.15x & \text{if } 0 \le x \le \$17,850. \\ 2677.50 + 0.28(x - 17,850) & \text{if } x > \$17,850. \end{cases}$$

(a) Find the rate of change of T with respect to x (the tax rate) when $x = \$15,000$ and when $x = \$30,000$.
(b) Does the derivative of T with respect to x exist at $x = \$17,850$?
(c) What happens at $x = \$17,850$ to explain your answer to (b)?

35. The percentage p of particulate pollution that can be removed from the smokestacks of an industrial plant by spending C dollars is given by

$$p = \frac{100C}{7300 + C}.$$

(a) Find any C-values where the rate of change of p with respect to C does not exist. Make sure these make sense in the problem.

(b) Find C-values for which p is increasing.

(c) Find $\lim\limits_{C \to \infty} \dfrac{dp}{dC}$.

(d) Can 100% of the pollution be removed?

36. The percentage p of impurities that can be removed from the waste water of a manufacturing process at a cost of C dollars is given by

$$p = \frac{100C}{8100 + C}.$$

(a) Find any C-values where the rate of change of p with respect to C does not exist. Make sure these make sense in the problem.

(b) Find C-values for which p is increasing.

(c) Find $\lim\limits_{C \to \infty} \dfrac{dp}{dC}$.

(d) Can 100% of the pollution be removed?

10.3 Applications of Maxima and Minima to Business and Economics

Objectives
- ☐ To maximize revenue, given the total revenue function
- ☐ To minimize the average cost, given the total cost function
- ☐ To find the maximum profit from total cost and total revenue functions, or from a profit function

The techniques used to find maxima and minima as an aid in curve sketching can be used to maximize revenue and profit and to minimize average cost when the appropriate functions are known.

Maximizing Revenue

Since the marginal revenue is the first derivative of the total revenue, it should be obvious that the total revenue function will have a critical point at the point where the marginal revenue equals 0. With the total revenue function $R(x) = 16x - 0.02x^2$, the point where $R'(x) = 0$ is clearly a maximum since $R(x)$ is a parabola that opens downward. But the revenue function may not always be a parabola and the critical point may not always be a maximum, so it is wise to verify that the maximum value occurs at the critical point.

EXAMPLE 1   If total revenue for a firm is given by

$$R(x) = 8000x - 40x^2 - x^3,$$

where x is the number of units sold, find the number of units that must be sold to maximize revenue. Find the maximum revenue.

Solution $R'(x) = 8000 - 80x - 3x^2$ so we must solve $8000 - 80x - 3x^2 = 0$ for x.

$$(40 - x)(200 + 3x) = 0$$
$$40 - x = 0 \qquad 200 + 3x = 0$$

so

$$x = 40 \text{ or } x = -\frac{200}{3}$$

Now, we reject the negative value for x, but we must verify that $x = 40$ will yield maximum revenue.

$$\left. \begin{array}{l} R'(0) = 8000 > 0 \\ R'(100) = 8000 - 8000 - 30{,}000 < 0 \end{array} \right\} \Rightarrow \text{relative maximum}$$

This test shows that $x = 40$ yields the maximum revenue when $x \geq 0$. The maximum revenue is

$$R(40) = 8000(40) - 40(40)^2 - (40)^3 = \$192{,}000.$$

EXAMPLE 2   A travel agency will plan a group tour for groups of size 25 or larger. If the group contains exactly 25 people, the cost is \$300 per person. However, each person's cost is reduced by \$10 for each additional person above the 25. What size group will produce the largest revenue for the agency?

Solution   The total revenue is

$$R = (\text{number of people})(\text{cost per person}).$$

If 25 people go, the total revenue will be

$$R = 25 \cdot \$300 = \$7500.$$

But if x additional people go, the number of people will be $25 + x$, and the cost per person will be $(300 - 10x)$ dollars. Then the total revenue will be a function of x,

$$R = R(x) = (25 + x)(300 - 10x),$$

or

$$R(x) = 7500 + 50x - 10x^2.$$

This function will have its maximum where $\overline{MR} = R'(x) = 0$; $R'(x) = 50 - 20x$, and the solution to $0 = 50 - 20x$ is $x = 2.5$. Thus adding 2.5 people to the group should maximize the total revenue. But we cannot add half a person. So we will test the total revenue function for 27 people and 28 people. This will determine the most profitable number.

   For $x = 2$ (giving 27 people) we get $R(2) = 7500 + 50(2) - 10(2)^2 = 7560$.
For $x = 3$ (giving 28 people) we get $R(3) = 7500 + 50(3) - 10(3)^2 = 7560$.
Note that both 27 and 28 people give the same total revenue, and that this revenue is greater than the revenue for 25 people. Thus the revenue is maximized at either 27 or 28 people in the group.

Minimizing Average Cost

Since the total cost function is always increasing, we cannot find the number of units that will make the total cost a minimum (except for producing 0 units, which is an absolute minimum). However, we usually can find the number of units that will make the average cost per unit a minimum.

> If the total cost is represented by $C = C(x)$, then the **average cost per unit** is
>
> $$\overline{C} = \frac{C(x)}{x}.$$

For example, if $C = 3x^2 + 4x + 2$ is the total cost function for a commodity, the *average cost function* is

$$\overline{C} = \frac{3x^2 + 4x + 2}{x} = 3x + 4 + \frac{2}{x}.$$

Note that the average cost per unit is undefined if no units are produced.

We can use the first-derivative test to find the minimum of the average cost function, as the following example shows.

EXAMPLE 3   If the total cost function for a commodity is given by $C = \frac{1}{4}x^2 + 4x + 100$, where x represents the number of units produced, producing how many units will result in a minimum *average cost* per unit? Find the minimum average cost.

Solution   The *average cost* function is given by

$$\overline{C} = \frac{\frac{1}{4}x^2 + 4x + 100}{x} = \frac{x}{4} + 4 + \frac{100}{x}.$$

Then

$$\overline{C}' = \overline{C}'(x) = \frac{1}{4} - \frac{100}{x^2}.$$

Setting $\overline{C}' = 0$ gives

$$0 = \frac{1}{4} - \frac{100}{x^2},$$

so $0 = x^2 - 400$, or $x = \pm 20$.

Since the quantity produced must be positive, 20 units should minimize the average cost per unit. We show it is a minimum by testing derivatives to the right and left of $x = 20$.

$$\left. \begin{array}{l} \overline{C}'(10) = -\frac{3}{4} < 0 \\ \overline{C}'(30) = \frac{5}{36} > 0 \end{array} \right\} \Rightarrow \text{relative minimum}$$

Thus the minimum average cost per unit occurs if 20 units are produced. The graph of the average cost per unit is shown in Figure 10.14. The minimum average cost per unit is $\overline{C}(20) = \$14$.

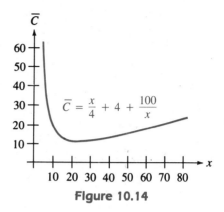

Figure 10.14

Maximizing Profit

In Chapter 9, we defined the marginal profit function as the derivative of the profit function. That is,

$$\overline{MP} = P'(x).$$

In this chapter we have seen how to use the derivative to find maxima and minima for various functions. Now we can apply those same techniques, in the context of marginal profit, in order to maximize profit functions.

EXAMPLE 4   If the total cost function for a certain period for an item is $C(x) = 100 + 2x + x^2$ and the total revenue function is $R(x) = 36x$, how many items will produce a maximum profit? Find the maximum profit.

Solution   The profit function is

$$P(x) = R(x) - C(x) = 36x - (100 + 2x + x^2),$$
or $P(x) = 34x - 100 - x^2.$

Then the marginal profit is

$$\overline{MP} = P'(x) = 34 - 2x.$$

Setting marginal profit equal to 0 and solving gives

$$0 = 34 - 2x$$
$$x = 17.$$

The profit function has a parabola as its graph, so the relative maximum at $x = 17$ is the maximum. Thus the maximum profit of $P(17) = \$189$ occurs if 17 items are produced and sold per period.

If there is a physical limitation on the number of units that can be produced in a given period of time, then the endpoints of the interval caused by these limitations should also be checked.

EXAMPLE 5   The total profit function for a commodity is

$$P(x) = 4x^3 - 210x^2 + 3600x - 200 \qquad (0 \leq x \leq 30),$$

where x is the number of units sold. Find the number of items that will maximize profit.

Solution   The marginal profit function is

$$P'(x) = 12x^2 - 420x + 3600.$$

Setting it equal to 0, we get

$$0 = 12(x - 15)(x - 20),$$

so $P'(x) = 0$ at $x = 15$ *and* $x = 20$. Testing to the right and left of these values (as in the first-derivative test) we get

$$
\left.
\begin{array}{l}
P'(0) = 3600 > 0 \\
P'(18) = -72 < 0 \\
P'(25) = 600 > 0
\end{array}
\right\}
\left.
\right\}
\begin{array}{l}
\Rightarrow \text{relative maximum at } x = 15 \\
\Rightarrow \text{relative minimum at } x = 20
\end{array}
$$

Thus the total profit function has a *relative* maximum at (15, 20050) but we must check the endpoints (0 and 30) before deciding if it is the absolute maximum.

$$P(0) = -200 \qquad \text{and} \qquad P(30) = \$26{,}800$$

Thus the absolute maximum occurs at the endpoint, $x = 30$. Figure 10.15 shows the graph of the profit function.

x	P
0	−200
10	18,800
15	20,050
20	19,800
25	21,050
30	26,800

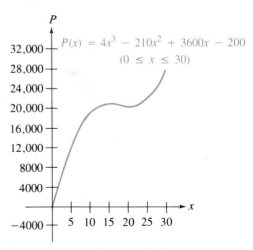

Figure 10.15

Recall that in Chapter 9 we showed that if

$$h(x) = f(x) \pm g(x)$$

then

$$h'(x) = f'(x) \pm g'(x).$$

In particular, if

$$P(x) = R(x) - C(x)$$

then

$$P'(x) = R'(x) - C'(x).$$

But since these derivatives represent marginal profit, marginal revenue and marginal cost, respectively, we may write $\overline{MP} = \overline{MR} - \overline{MC}$.

Now, we know that marginal profit is 0 when profit is maximized, so we may write

$$0 = \overline{MR} - \overline{MC}$$

or

$$\overline{MR} = \overline{MC}.$$

That is, *marginal profit will be 0 when marginal revenue equals marginal cost.*

The statement that "profit will be maximized when marginal revenue equals marginal cost" is found frequently in economics texts, and is true in *many* cases.* But we should always check the point where $\overline{MR} = \overline{MC}$ to make sure this critical point is the absolute maximum on the interval determined by the physical limitations.

EXAMPLE 6 The total cost per day to produce Ace electric shavers is

$$C(x) = 360 + 10x + \tfrac{1}{5}x^2.$$

Physical limitations permit only 80 shavers to be produced each day. If the total revenue function for the shavers is

$$R(x) = 45x - \tfrac{1}{2}x^2,$$

at what level of production will profit be maximized?

Solution To maximize the profit, we will find $\overline{MR}$ and $\overline{MC}$ and find the value of x that makes them equal.

$$\overline{MR} = 45 - x$$
$$\overline{MC} = 10 + \tfrac{2}{5}x$$

---

*Most profit curves developed by companies for their products will not be as complex as the one in Example 5, so the points where $\overline{MR} = \overline{MC}$ are the points of maximum profit for them.

Solving $\overline{MR} = \overline{MC}$ gives

$$45 - x = 10 + \tfrac{2}{5}x$$
$$35 = \tfrac{7}{5}x$$
$$x = 25.$$

Thus the maximum profit appears to occur when 25 shavers are produced. Since the profit function,

$$P(x) = R(x) - C(x) = 35x - \tfrac{7}{10}x^2 - 360$$

has as its graph a parabola opening downward, and because 25 is within the firm's physical limitations, the maximum profit will occur when 25 shavers are produced.

Exercise 10.3

MAXIMIZING REVENUE

1. If the total revenue function for a radio is $R = 36x - 0.01x^2$, sale of how many units will maximize the total revenue? Find the maximum revenue.
2. If the total revenue function for a blender is $R(x) = 25x - 0.05x^2$, sale of how many units will provide the maximum total revenue? Find the maximum revenue.
3. If the total revenue function for a computer is $R(x) = 2000x - 20x^2 - x^3$, find the level of sales that maximizes revenue and find the maximum revenue.
4. A firm has total revenues given by

$$R(x) = 2800x - 8x^2 - x^3$$

for a product. Find the maximum revenue from sales of that product.
5. An agency charges $10 per person for a trip to a concert if 30 people travel in a group. But for each person above the 30, the charge will be reduced by $.20. How many people will maximize the total revenue for the agency?
6. A company handles an apartment building with 50 units. Experience has shown that if the rent for each of the units is $360 per month, all of the units will be filled, but one unit will become vacant for each $10 increase in the monthly rate. What rent should be charged to maximize the total revenue from the building?
7. A cable TV company has 1000 customers paying $20 each month. If each $1 reduction in price attracts 100 new customers, find the price that yields maximum revenue. Find the maximum revenue.
8. A company has determined that its monthly sales revenue S is related to the number of dollars x spent on advertising, with

$$S = 5000 + 8000x - 0.2x^2.$$

Spending how much money on advertising will maximize their revenue? Find the maximum sales revenue.
9. The function $\overline{R}(x) = R(x)/x$ defines the average revenue for selling x units. For

$$R(x) = 2000x + 20x^2 - x^3,$$

(a) find the maximum average revenue.

(b) show that $\bar{R}(x)$ attains its maximum at the x-value where $\bar{R}(x) = \overline{MR}$.

10. For the revenue function given by

$$R(x) = 2800x + 8x^2 - x^3,$$

(a) find the maximum average revenue.

(b) show that $\bar{R}(x)$ attains its maximum at the x-value where $\bar{R}(x) = \overline{MR}$.

MINIMIZING AVERAGE COST

11. If the total cost function for a lamp is $C(x) = 25 + 13x + x^2$, producing how many units will result in a minimum average cost per unit? Find the minimum average cost.

12. If the total cost function for a motorcycle is $C(x) = 300 + 10x + 0.03x^2$, producing how many units will result in a minimum average cost per unit? Find the minimum average cost.

13. If the total cost function for a product is $C(x) = 100 + x^2$, producing how many units will result in a minimum average cost per unit? Find the minimum average cost.

14. If the total cost function for a product is $C(x) = 250 + 6x + 0.1x^2$, producing how many units will minimize the average cost? Find the minimum average cost.

15. If the total cost function for a product is $C(x) = (x + 4)^3$, where x represents the number of hundreds of units produced, producing how many units will minimize average cost? Find the minimum average cost.

16. If the total cost function for a product is $C(x) = (x + 5)^3$, where x represents the number of hundreds of units produced, producing how many units will minimize average cost? Find the minimum average cost.

17. For the cost function in problem 11, show that average costs are minimized at the x-value where

$$\bar{C}(x) = \overline{MC}.$$

18. For the cost function in problem 12, show that average costs are minimized at the x-value where

$$\bar{C}(x) = \overline{MC}.$$

MAXIMIZING PROFIT

19. If the profit function is $P(x) = 5x^2 - 250$, find the number of units (x) that will maximize the profit.

20. If the profit function is $P(x) = 16x - 320$, find the number of units that will maximize the profit.

21. If the total revenue function is given by $R(x) = 32x$ and the total cost function is given by $C(x) = 200 + 2x + x^2$, selling how many units will maximize profit? Find the maximum profit.

22. If the total revenue function is given by $R(x) = 46x$ and the total cost function is given by $C(x) = 100 + 30x + \frac{1}{10}x^2$, find the number of units that should be produced and sold to maximize profit. Find the maximum profit.

23. If the profit function for a product is $P(x) = 5600x + 85x^2 - x^3 - 200,000$, selling how many items will produce a maximum profit? Find the maximum profit.

24. If the profit function for a commodity is $P = 6400x - 18x^2 - \frac{1}{3}x^3 - 40,000$, selling how many units will result in a maximum profit? Find the maximum profit.

25. A manufacturer estimates that x units of its product can be produced at a total cost of $C(x) = 45,000 + 100x + x^3$. If the manufacturer's total revenue from the sale of x units is $R(x) = 4600x$, determine the level of production x that will maximize the profit. Find the maximum profit.

26. A product can be produced at a total cost $C(x) = 800 + 100x^2 + x^3$, where x is the number produced. If the total revenue is given by $R(x) = 60,000x - 50x^2$, determine the level of production that will maximize the profit. Find the maximum profit.

27. A firm can produce only 1000 units per month. The monthly total cost is given by $C(x) = 300 + 200x$, where x is the number produced. If the total revenue is given by $R(x) = 250x - \frac{1}{100}x^2$, how many items should they produce for maximum profit? Find the maximum profit.

28. A firm can produce 100 units per week. If its total cost function is $C = 500 + 1500x$ and its total revenue function is $R = 1600x - x^2$, how many units should it produce to maximize its profit? Find the maximum profit.

29. A company handles an apartment building with 50 units. Experience has shown that if the rent of each of the units is $360 per month, all of the units will be filled, but one unit will become vacant for each $10 increase in this monthly rate. If the monthly cost of maintaining the apartment building is $6 per rented unit, what rent should be charged per month to maximize the profit?

30. A travel agency will plan a group tour for groups of size 25 or larger. If the group contains exactly 25 people, the cost is $500 per person. However, each person's cost is reduced by $10 for each additional person above the 25. If the travel agency incurs a cost of $125 per person for the tour, what size group will give the agency the maximum profit?

10.4 Applications of Maxima and Minima

Objective   ☐   To apply the procedures for finding maxima and minima to solve problems from the management, life, and social sciences

One of the most important applications of calculus in applied situations is in finding maxima and minima. As individuals, workers, or consumers, we may be interested in such things as maximum population, maximum area, maximum revenue, minimum cost, minimum competency, or maximum dosage. If we have a function that models population, area, or revenue, we can apply the methods of this chapter to find maxima or minima for that function.

EXAMPLE 1   Population of an endangered species at a wildlife refuge is a function of time, given by

$$p(t) = 80\left(1 + \frac{4t}{t^2 + 16}\right).$$

If the species is introduced to the refuge at time $t = 0$, find the maximum number of individuals that will populate the refuge.

Solution   This function will have a relative maximum when $p'(t) = 0$.

$$p'(t) = 80\left[\frac{(t^2 + 16)(4) - (4t)(2t)}{(t^2 + 16)^2}\right]$$

$$p'(t) = 80\left[\frac{4t^2 + 64 - 8t^2}{(t^2 + 16)^2}\right]$$

$$p'(t) = 80\left[\frac{64 - 4t^2}{(t^2 + 16)^2}\right]$$

Now, $p'(t) = 0$ when its numerator is 0 (note the denominator is never 0), so we must solve

$$64 - 4t^2 = 0$$
$$4(4 + t)(4 - t) = 0$$
so $$t = -4 \text{ or } t = 4$$

We are only interested in positive t-values, so we test $t = 4$.

$$\left.\begin{array}{l} p'(0) = 80\left(\dfrac{64}{256}\right) > 0 \\[2mm] p'(10) = 80\left[-\dfrac{336}{(116)^2}\right] < 0 \end{array}\right\} \Rightarrow \text{relative maximum}$$

The relative maximum is $p(4) = 80\left(1 + \frac{16}{32}\right) = 120$. At $t = 0$, the population is $p(0)$, and it increases to $p(4) = 120$. After $t = 4$, $p(t)$ decreases, so $p(4) = 120$ is the maximum population.

EXAMPLE 2   The rate of change of photosynthesis depends on the intensity of light x according to the equation

$$R(x) = 270x - 90x^2.$$

Find the intensity that maximizes this rate.

Solution $R'(x) = 270 - 180x$, so we must solve $270 - 180x = 0$ for x. Hence

$$x = \frac{270}{180} = \frac{3}{2}.$$

Now we verify that $x = \frac{3}{2}$ yields the maximum rate.

$$\left.\begin{array}{l} R'(0) = 270 > 0 \\ R'(2) = -90 < 0 \end{array}\right\} \Rightarrow \text{relative maximum}$$

In fact, we could also note that $R(x) = 270x - 90x^2$ is a parabola that opens downward, so $x = \frac{3}{2}$ must yield the maximum value for R. The maximum rate is

$$R\left(\frac{3}{2}\right) = 270\left(\frac{3}{2}\right) - 90\left(\frac{3}{2}\right)^2 = 202\frac{1}{2}.$$

Sometimes we must develop the function we need from the statement of the problem. In this case it is important to understand what is to be maximized or minimized, and to express that quantity as a function of *one* variable.

EXAMPLE 3   A farmer wants to make a rectangular pasture with 80,000 square feet. If the pasture lies along a river and he fences the remaining three sides, what dimensions should he use to minimize the amount of fence needed?

Solution   In Figure 10.16, if x represents the length of the pasture (parallel to the river), and y represents the width, then the length of fence needed is

$$f = y + x + y = x + 2y.$$

Since the length of the fence is to be minimized, this is the desired function, but we must express the length as a function of either x or y only.

Returning to the problem we see that the area is given by $xy = 80{,}000$. Solving for y and substituting gives

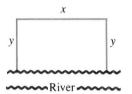

Figure 10.16

$$f = x + 2\left(\frac{80{,}000}{x}\right) = x + \frac{160{,}000}{x}.$$

The derivative of f is

$$\frac{df}{dx} = 1 - \frac{160{,}000}{x^2},$$

so

$$0 = 1 - \frac{160{,}000}{x^2}$$
$$x^2 = 160{,}000$$
$$x = \pm 400.$$

Of course, only $x = 400$ applies to this problem. Testing, we see that

$$\left.\begin{array}{l} f'(200) = 1 - 4 < 0 \\ f'(400) = 0 \\ f'(800) = 1 - \frac{1}{4} > 0 \end{array}\right\} \Rightarrow \text{relative minimum at } x = 400.$$

Notice that for $x > 0$, the function decreases until $x = 400$ and increases thereafter, so $x = 400$ yields the minimum fence.

Since $x = 400$ gives $y = \dfrac{80{,}000}{x} = 200$, the minimum amount of fence needed is $f = 800$ feet.

EXAMPLE 4   Postal restrictions limit the size of packages sent through the mails. If the restrictions are that the length plus the girth may not exceed 108 in., find the volume of the largest box with square cross-section that can be mailed.

Solution   Let l equal the length of the box and s equal a side of the square end. The volume we seek to maximize is given by

$$V = s^2 l.$$

We can use the restriction girth plus length equals 108,

$$4s + l = 108,$$

to express V as a function of s or l. Since it is easier to eliminate l, we write

$$V = s^2(108 - 4s)$$

or

$$V = 108s^2 - 4s^3.$$

Thus

$$\frac{dV}{ds} = 216s - 12s^2$$

$$0 = s(216 - 12s).$$

Critical values are $s = 0$, $s = \dfrac{216}{12} = 18.$

The critical value $s = 0$ will not maximize the volume for, in this case, $V = 0$. Testing to the left and right of $s = 18$ gives

$$V'(17) > 0 \qquad \text{and} \qquad V'(19) < 0.$$

Thus, $s = 18$ in. and $l = 36$ in. yield a maximum volume of 11,664 cubic inches.

Exercise 10.4

1. The amount of photosynthesis that takes place in a certain plant depends on the intensity of light x according to the equation

$$f(x) = 145x^2 - 30x^3.$$

   Find the intensity of light for which photosynthesis is greatest.
2. A ball thrown into the air from a building 100 ft high travels along a path described by

$$y = \frac{-x^2}{110} + x + 100,$$

   where y is its height and x is the horizontal distance from the building. What is the maximum height the ball will reach?
3. Sensitivity to a drug depends on the dosage size x according to the equation

$$S = 1000x - x^2.$$

   Find the dosage that maximizes sensitivity.

4. The efficiency E of a muscle performing a maximal contraction is a function of the time of the contraction t, and has been found to satisfy the following equation:

$$E = \frac{1 - 0.24t}{2 + t}.$$

Find the maximum efficiency.

5. The yield from a grove of orange trees is given by $x(800 - x)$, where x is the number of orange trees per acre. How many trees per acre will maximize the yield?

6. The velocity v of an autocatalytic reaction can be represented by the equation

$$v = x(a - x),$$

where a is the amount of material originally present and x is the amount that has been decomposed at any given time. Find the maximum velocity of the reaction.

7. According to B. F. Visser, the velocity v of air in the trachea during a cough is related to the radius r of the trachea according to

$$v = ar^2(r_0 - r),$$

where a is constant and r_0 is the radius of the trachea in a relaxed state. Find the radius r that produces the maximum velocity of air in the trachea during a cough.

8. Suppose in an election year the proportion p of voters that recognize a certain candidate's name t months after the campaign started is given by

$$p(t) = \frac{7.2t}{t^2 + 36} + 0.2.$$

After how many months is the proportion maximized?

9. Suppose the percentage p (as a decimal) of people who could correctly identify 2 of 8 defendants in an espionage case t days after their trial began is given by

$$p(t) = \frac{6.4t}{t^2 + 64} + 0.05.$$

Find the number of days before awareness is maximized, and find the maximum percentage.

10. If $x + y = 12$, find x and y that maximizes xy.
11. Find the two positive numbers whose sum is 100 and whose product is a maximum.
12. Find the two positive numbers whose product is 50 and whose sum is a minimum.
13. A farmer has 2500 feet of fence to enclose a rectangular lot. If all four sides are fenced in, what dimensions will give a maximum area for the lot?
14. A farmer wishes to make a rectangular lot containing 1600 square feet. What dimensions will require the minimum amount of fence?
15. A farmer has 2500 feet of fence to enclose a rectangular lot along a river. If he uses fence to enclose three sides of the lot, what dimensions will give a maximum area for the lot?
16. Two equal rectangular lots are enclosed by fencing the perimeter of a rectangular lot and then putting a fence across its middle. If each lot is to contain 1200 square feet, what is the minimum amount of fence needed to enclose the lots (include the fence across the middle)?
17. If the product of the concentrations of hydrogen ions $[H^+]$ and hydroxyl ions $[OH^-]$ in a certain solution is known to be 10^{-12}, what is the hydrogen ion concentration at which the sum of the hydrogen and hydroxyl ion concentrations is a minimum? Hint: Represent $[H^+]$ by x and $[OH^-]$ by y.

18. The running yard for a dog kennel must contain at least 900 square feet. If a 20-foot side of the kennel is used as part of one side of a rectangular yard with 900 square feet, what dimensions will use the least amount of fencing?

19. A rectangular box with a square base is to be formed from a square piece of metal with 12-inch sides. If a square piece with side x is cut from the corners of the metal and the sides are folded up to form an open box, the volume of the box is $V = (12 - 2x)^2 x$ (see Figure 10.17). What value of x will maximize the volume of the box?

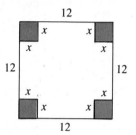

Figure 10.17

20. A square piece of cardboard 36 cm on a side is to be formed into a rectangular box by cutting squares with length x from each corner and folding up the sides. What is the maximum volume possible for the box?

21. The owner of an orange grove must decide when to pick one variety of oranges. She can sell them for $8 a bushel if she sells them now, with each tree yielding an average of 5 bushels. The yield increases by one half bushel per week for the next 5 weeks, but the price per bushel decreases by $.50 per bushel each week. When should the oranges be picked for maximum return?

22. A box with an open top and a square base is to be constructed to contain 4000 cubic inches. Find the dimensions that will require the minimum amount of material to construct the box.

23. A printer has a contract to print 100,000 posters for a political candidate. He can run the posters by using any number of plates from one to 30 on his press. If he uses x metal plates, they will produce x copies of the poster with each impression of the press. The metal plates cost $2.00 to prepare, and it costs $12.50 per hour to run the press. If the press can make 1000 impressions per hour, how many metal plates should he make to minimize his costs?

24. A garden consists of a rectangle with semicircles at each end. Find the largest area that can be enclosed by 800 feet of fence.

25. A rectangular area is to be enclosed and divided into thirds. The family has $800 to spend for the fencing material. The outside fence costs $10 per running foot installed, and the dividers cost $20 per running foot installed. What are the dimensions that will maximize the area enclosed? (Answer has a fraction.)

26. A kennel of 640 square feet is to be constructed as shown in Figure 10.18. The cost is $4 per running foot for the sides and $1 per running foot for the ends and dividers. What are the dimensions of the kennel that will minimize the cost?

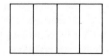

Figure 10.18

27. The base of a rectangular box is to be twice as long as it is wide. The volume of the box is 256 cubic inches. Material for the top costs $10 per square inch and the material for the sides and bottom costs $5 per square inch. Find the dimensions that will make the cost a minimum.

28. A vacationer on an island 8 miles offshore from a point that is 48 miles from town must travel to town occasionally. (See Figure 10.19.) The vacationer has a boat capable of traveling 30 mph and can go by auto along the coast at 55 mph. At what point should the car be left to minimize the time it takes to get to town?

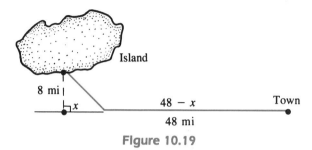

Figure 10.19

29. A homeowner has to pay for utility line installation to his house from a transformer on the street at the corner of his property. Because of local restrictions the lines must be underground on his property. Suppose the costs are $5/foot along the street and $10/foot underground. How far from the transformer should he enter the property to minimize installation costs? See Figure 10.20.

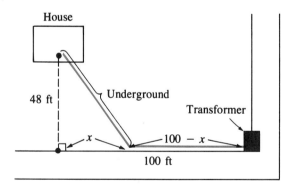

Figure 10.20

30. A boat is 1 mile offshore from a point B that is 10 miles from a town. If the line from the boat to B is perpendicular to the line from B to town, and if the person in the boat can row at 3 mph and walk at 5 mph, find the point A so that rowing to A and walking from there to town minimizes the time it takes to get to town.

31. Manufacturers make production runs to restock their inventories. Since there are costs associated with both the production of items and their storage (placement into inventory), a typical question in these **inventory cost models** is "How many items should be produced in each production run to minimize the total costs of production and storage?" If x items are produced in each run, and items are removed from inventory at a fixed constant rate, then the units in storage changes with time and is illustrated in Figure 10.21.

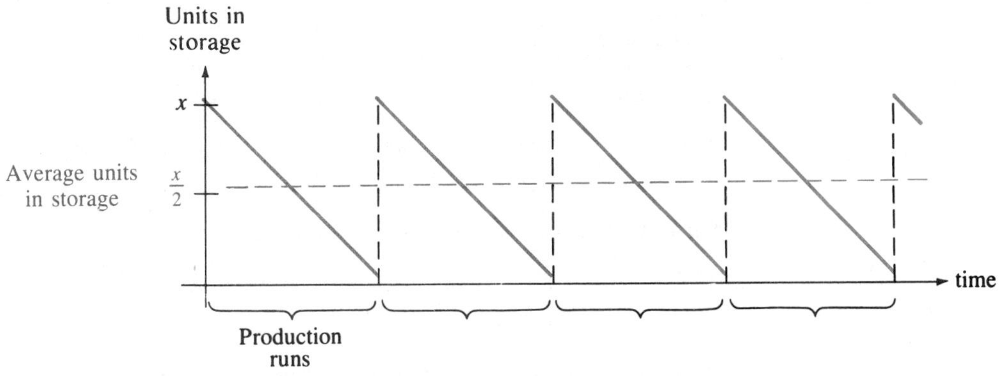

Figure 10.21

To see how these models work, consider the following. Suppose a company needs 1,000,000 items during a year. If it costs the company $800 to prepare each production run and $6 for each item produced, then total production costs are given by

$$\text{(\# runs)(cost per run)} + \text{(\# items)(cost per item)}$$
$$= \left[\frac{1,000,000}{x} \right] (\$800) + (1,000,000)(\$6).$$

If it costs the company $1 for each item stored, then total storage costs are

$$\text{(average \# stored)(cost per item)} = \left(\frac{x}{2} \right) (\$1).$$

Thus the total costs of production and storage are

$$C = \left[\frac{1,000,000}{x} \right] (800) + 6,000,000 + \frac{x}{2}.$$

Find x so that C is minimized.

32. Suppose a company needs 60,000 items during a year and that preparation for each production run costs $400. Suppose further than it costs $4 to produce each item and 75¢ to store each one. Use the inventory-cost model in problem 31 to find the number of items in each production run that will minimize the total costs of production and storage.

Review Exercises

10.1

In problems 1–4, find all critical points and determine whether they are relative maxima, relative minima, or horizontal points of inflection. Do not sketch.

1. $y = -x^2$

2. $p = q^2 - 4q - 5$

3. $f(x) = 1 - 3x + 3x^2 - x^3$

4. $f(x) = \dfrac{3x}{x^2 + 1}$

In problems 5–8,
(a) find the relative maxima and minima, if any exist.
(b) find the horizontal points of inflection, if any exist.
(c) sketch the graph.

5. $y = x^3 + x^2 - x - 1$ 6. $f(x) = 4x^3 - x^4$

7. $f(x) = x^3 - \dfrac{15}{2}x^2 - 18x + \dfrac{3}{2}$ 8. $y = 5x^7 - 7x^5 - 1$

In problems 9 and 10, determine where $f'(x)$ is undefined.

9. $f(x) = x - 3\sqrt[3]{x}$ 10. $f(x) = \begin{cases} 25 - x & \text{if } x \le 25 \\ 0 & \text{if } x > 25 \end{cases}$

In problems 11–14,
(a) find all critical points, including those where $f'(x)$ is undefined.
(b) find any relative maxima and minima.
(c) sketch each graph.

11. $y = \dfrac{1}{x}$ 12. $y = x^{2/3} - 1$

13. $y = \sqrt[3]{x - 4}$ 14. $y = x^{2/3}(x - 4)^2$

15. Given $R = 280x - x^2$, find the absolute maximum and minimum for R on
    (a) $0 \le x \le 200$ and   (b) $0 \le x \le 100$.

16. Given $y = 6400x - 18x^2 - \dfrac{x^3}{3}$, find the absolute maximum and minimum for y on
    (a) $0 \le x \le 50$ and   (b) $0 \le x \le 100$.

APPLICATIONS

17. If the total cost function for a product is

$$C(x) = 3x^2 + 15x + 75,$$

how many units will minimize the average cost? Find the minimum average cost.

18. If the total revenue function for a product is given by

$$R(x) = 32x - 0.01x^2,$$

how many units will maximize the total revenue? Find the maximum revenue.

19. Suppose the profit function for a product is given by

$$P(x) = 1080x + 9.6x^2 - 0.1x^3 - 50,000.$$

Find the maximum profit.

20. If $R(x) = 46x - x^2$ and $C(x) = 5x^2 + 10x + 3$, how many units (x) maximize profit?

21. A product can be produced at a total cost $C(x) = 800 + 4x$, where x is the number produced. If the total revenue is given by $R(x) = 80x - \frac{1}{4}x^2$, determine the level of production that will maximize the profit.

22. The total cost function for a product is $C = 2x^2 + 54x + 98$. Producing how many units will minimize average cost?

23. McRobert's TV Shop sells 200 sets per month at a price of $400 per unit. Market research indicates that they can sell one additional set for each $1 they reduce the price. At what selling price will they maximize revenue?

10.4

24. If, in problem 23, the sets cost the shop $250 each, when will profit be maximized?
25. The reaction R to an injection of a drug is related to the dosage x according to

$$R(x) = x^2\left(500 - \frac{x}{3}\right).$$

• Find the dosage that yields maximum reaction.
26. The number of parts produced per hour by a worker is given by

$$N = 4 + 3t^2 - t^3,$$

where t is the number of hours on the job without a break. If the worker starts at 8 A.M., when will she be at maximum production during the morning?
27. Population estimates show that the equation $P = 300 + 10t - t^2$ represents the size of the graduating class of a high school, with t representing the number of years after 1990, $0 \le t \le 10$. What will be the largest graduating class in the decade?
28. Suppose an observatory is to be built between cities A and B that are 30 miles apart. For the best viewing, the observatory should be located where the night brightness from these cities is minimum. If the night brightness of city A is 8 times that of city B, then the night brightness b between the two cities and x miles from A is given by

$$b = \frac{8k}{x^2} + \frac{k}{(30 - x)^2},$$

where k is a constant. Find the best location for the observatory; that is, find x that minimizes b.
29. A playpen manufacturer wants to make a rectangular enclosure with maximum play area. To remain competitive, he wants the perimeter of the base to be only 16 feet. What dimensions should the playpen have?
30. A printed page is to contain 56 square inches and have a $\frac{3}{4}$-inch margin at the bottom and a 1-inch margin on the top and on both sides. Find the dimensions that minimize the size of the page (and hence the costs for paper).

WARMUP

	Prerequisite problem type	Answer	Section for review
11.4	(a) Simplify: $\dfrac{1}{(3x)^{1/2}} \cdot \dfrac{1}{2}(3x)^{-1/2} \cdot 3$ (b) Write with a positive exponent: $\sqrt{x^2 - 1}$	(a) $\dfrac{1}{2x}$ (b) $(x^2 - 1)^{1/2}$	0.4 Rational Exponents
11.1, 11.3	If $f''(x) = 36x^2 + 36x - 6$, what is $f''(1)$?	66	1.3 Functional notation
11.3	(a) Vertical lines have _____ slopes. (b) Horizontal lines have _____ slopes.	(a) Undefined (b) 0	1.5 Slopes
11.3	Write the equation of the line passing through $(-2, -2)$ with slope 5.	$y = 5x + 8$	1.5 Equations of lines
11.2, 11.3	Solve: (a) $0 = 12x^3 - 12x^2$ (b) $x^2 + y^2 - 9 = 0$, for y.	(a) $x = 1, x = 0$ (b) $y = \pm\sqrt{9 - x^2}$	4.1 Quadratic equations
11.4	(a) Write $\log_a(x + h) - \log_a x$ as an expression involving one log function. (b) Does $\ln x^4 = 4\ln x$? (c) Does $\dfrac{x}{h}\log_a\left(\dfrac{x + h}{x}\right)$ $= \log_a\left(1 + \dfrac{h}{x}\right)^{x/h}$? (d) Expand $\ln(xy)$ to separate x and y. (e) If $y = a^x$, then $x = $ _____. (f) Simplify $e^{\ln x^2}$	(a) $\log_a\left(\dfrac{x + h}{x}\right)$ (b) Yes (c) Yes (d) $\ln x + \ln y$ (e) $\log_a y$ (f) x^2	5.2 Logarithms
11.1, 11.2, 11.3	Find the derivative of (a) $y = x^4 - 3x^2 + x^{-2}$ (b) $y = (2x - 1)^{1/2}$ (c) $y = \sqrt{9 - x^2}$	(a) $4x^3 - 6x - 2x^{-3}$ (b) $(2x - 1)^{-1/2}$ (c) $-x(9 - x^2)^{-1/2}$	9.3, 9.5 Derivatives

Derivatives Continued

In Chapter 9 we developed formulas to find the (first) derivative of certain functions, and in Chapter 10 we used (first) derivatives to sketch curves and to find the relative maxima and minima of functions. In this chapter we will see that the derivative formulas can be used to find derivatives of first derivatives, which we call second derivatives. In a similar manner we can also find higher derivatives.

The second derivative can be used to determine where the graph of an equation will be concave up, where it will be concave down, and where the graph will change from concave up to concave down, or vice versa. (Points where this occurs are called points of inflection.) The second-derivative test uses concavity to determine where the graph of an equation has a relative maximum or minimum.

In this chapter we will also develop derivative formulas for logarithmic and exponential functions, and apply them to problems in the management, life, and social sciences. We will also develop methods for finding derivatives of one variable with respect to another variable even though the relationship between them may not be functional. This method is called implicit differentiation.

The special business and economics applications include profit maximization in competitive and monopoly markets, elasticity of demand, and maximization of taxation revenue.

11.1 Higher-Order Derivatives

Objective ☐ To find second derivatives and higher derivatives of certain functions

In Chapter 9 we introduced the first derivative of a function. Because the derivative of a function is itself a function, we can take a derivative of the derivative. The derivative of a first derivative is called a **second derivative.** We can find the second derivative of a function f by differentiating it twice. If f' represents the first derivative of a function, then f'' represents the second derivative of that function.

EXAMPLE 1   If $f(x) = 3x^3 - 4x^2 + 5$, find $f''(x)$.

Solution   The first derivative is $f'(x) = 9x^2 - 8x$.
The second derivative is $f''(x) = 18x - 8$.

EXAMPLE 2   Find the second derivative of $y = x^4 - 3x^2 + x^{-2}$.

Solution   The first derivative is $y' = 4x^3 - 6x - 2x^{-3}$.
The second derivative, which we may denote by y'', is

$$y'' = 12x^2 - 6 + 6x^{-4}.$$

It is also common to use $\dfrac{d^2y}{dx^2}$ and $\dfrac{d^2}{dx^2} f(x)$ to denote the second derivative of a function.

EXAMPLE 3   If $y = \sqrt{2x - 1}$, find d^2y/dx^2.

Solution   The first derivative is

$$\frac{dy}{dx} = \frac{1}{2}(2x - 1)^{-1/2}(2) = (2x - 1)^{-1/2}.$$

The second derivative is

$$\begin{aligned}
\frac{d^2y}{dx^2} &= -\frac{1}{2}(2x - 1)^{-3/2}(2) \\
&= -(2x - 1)^{-3/2} \\
&= \frac{-1}{(2x - 1)^{3/2}} = \frac{-1}{\sqrt{(2x - 1)^3}}.
\end{aligned}$$

We can also find third, fourth, fifth, and higher derivatives, continuing indefinitely. The third, fourth, and fifth derivatives of a function f are denoted by f''', $f^{(4)}$, and $f^{(5)}$, respectively. Other notations for the third and fourth derivatives include:

$$\begin{array}{cc}
y''' & y^{(4)} \\
\dfrac{d^3y}{dx^3} & \dfrac{d^4y}{dx^4} \\
\dfrac{d^3f(x)}{dx^3} & \dfrac{d^4f(x)}{dx^4}
\end{array}$$

EXAMPLE 4   Find the first four derivatives of $f(x) = 4x^3 + 5x^2 + 3$.

Solution
$$\begin{aligned}
f'(x) &= 12x^2 + 10x \\
f''(x) &= 24x + 10 \\
f'''(x) &= 24 \\
f^{(4)}(x) &= 0
\end{aligned}$$

Just as the first derivative, $f'(x)$, can be used to determine the rate of change of a function $f(x)$, the second derivative $f''(x)$ can be used to determine the rate of change of $f'(x)$.

EXAMPLE 5   If $f(x) = 3x^4 + 6x^3 - 3x^2 + 4$,
(a) how fast is $f(x)$ changing at $(1, 10)$?
(b) how fast is $f'(x)$ changing at $(1, 10)$?
(c) is $f'(x)$ increasing or decreasing at $(1, 10)$?

Solution   (a) Since $f'(x) = 12x^3 + 18x^2 - 6x$, we have $f'(1) = 12 + 18 - 6 = 24$. Thus the rate of change of $f(x)$ at $(1, 10)$ is 24.
(b) Since $f''(x) = 36x^2 + 36x - 6$, we have $f''(1) = 66$. Thus the rate of change of $f'(x)$ at $(1, 10)$ is 66.
(c) Since $f''(1) = 66 > 0$, $f'(x)$ is increasing at $(1, 10)$.

EXAMPLE 6   Suppose a particle travels according to the equation $s = 100t - 16t^2 + 200$, where s is the distance and t is the time. Then ds/dt is the velocity, and $d^2s/dt^2 = dv/dt$ is the acceleration of the particle. Find the acceleration.

Solution   The velocity is $v = ds/dt = 100 - 32t$, and the acceleration is

$$\frac{dv}{dt} = \frac{d^2s}{dt^2} = -32.$$

Exercise 11.1

In problems 1–8, find the second derivative.

1. $f(x) = 4x^3 - 15x^2 + 3x + 2$
2. $f(x) = 2x^{10} - 18x^5 - 12x^3 + 4$
3. $y = 10x^3 - x^2 + 14x + 3$
4. $y = 6x^5 - 3x^4 + 12x^2$
5. $g(x) = x^3 - \dfrac{1}{x}$
6. $h(x) = x^2 - \dfrac{1}{x^2}$
7. $y = x^3 - \sqrt{x}$
8. $y = 3x^2 - \sqrt[3]{x^2}$
9. If $y = x^5 - x^{1/2}$, find $\dfrac{d^2y}{dx^2}$.
10. If $y = x^4 + x^{1/3}$, find $\dfrac{d^2y}{dx^2}$.
11. If $f(x) = \sqrt{x - 1}$, find $\dfrac{d^2}{dx^2} f(x)$.
12. If $f(x) = \sqrt[3]{x + 2}$, find $\dfrac{d^2}{dx^2} f(x)$.
13. If $y = \sqrt{x^2 + 4}$, find y''.
14. If $f(x) = \sqrt{4x^2 - 2}$, find $f''(x)$.
15. If $y = x(x + 1)^{-1}$, find y''.
16. If $y = \dfrac{2x}{x^2 + 1}$, find y''.

In problems 17–28, find the third derivative.

17. $y = x^5 - 16x^3 + 12$
18. $y = 6x^3 - 12x^2 + 6x$
19. $f(x) = 2x^9 - 6x^6$
20. $f(x) = 3x^5 - x^6$
21. $y = 1/x$
22. $y = 1/x^2$
23. $y = \sqrt{x}$
24. $y = \sqrt[3]{x}$
25. $f(x) = \sqrt{x + 1}$
26. $f(x) = \sqrt{x - 5}$
27. $y = \sqrt{x^2 + 4}$ (see problem 13)
28. $y = x(x + 1)^{-1}$ (see problem 15)

29. Find $\dfrac{d^4y}{dx^4}$ if $y = 4x^3 - 16x$.

30. Find $y^{(4)}$ if $y = x^6 - 15x^3$.

31. Find $f^{(4)}(x)$ if $f(x) = \sqrt{x}$.

32. Find $f^{(4)}(x)$ if $f(x) = 1/x$.

33. If $f(x) = 16x^2 - x^3$, what is the rate of change of $f'(x)$ at $(1, 15)$?

34. If $y = 36x^2 - 6x^3 + x$, what is the rate of change of y' at $(1, 31)$?

APPLICATIONS

35. The amount of photosynthesis that takes place in a certain plant depends on the intensity of light x according to the equation

$$f(x) = 145x^2 - 30x^3.$$

   (a) Find the rate of change of photosynthesis with respect to the intensity.
   (b) What is the rate of change when $x = 1$? when $x = 3$?
   (c) How fast is the rate of change changing when $x = 1$? when $x = 3$?

36. The reaction R to an injection of a drug is related to the dosage x according to

$$R(x) = x^2\left(500 - \frac{x}{3}\right).$$

   (a) If the sensitivity is defined as dR/dx, what is the sensitivity when $x = 350$? when $x = 700$?
   (b) What is the rate of change of sensitivity when $x = 350$? when $x = 700$?

37. If a particle travels as a function of time according to the formula $s = 100 + 80t - t^2$, find the acceleration of the particle.

38. If the formula describing the distance an object travels as a function of time is

$$s = 100 + 160t - 16t^2,$$

   (a) what is the acceleration of the object when $t = 4$?
   (b) is the velocity of the object increasing or decreasing at $t = 4$?

39. If the revenue from sales of a product can be described by $R(x) = 100x - 0.01x^2$, is the marginal revenue for the product increasing or decreasing?

40. If the total cost of producing the product of problem 39 is $C(x) = 100 + 30x + 0.02x^2$, does the marginal cost increase or decrease?

41. Does the marginal profit for the product mentioned in problems 39 and 40 increase or decrease?

42. The reaction R to an injection of a drug is related to the dosage x according to

$$R(x) = x^2\left(500 - \frac{x}{3}\right).$$

   The sensitivity to the drug is defined by dR/dx, and was found in problem 36. Find the dosage that maximizes sensitivity.

43. The amount of photosynthesis that takes place in a certain plant depends on the intensity of light x according to the equation

$$f(x) = 145x^2 - 30x^3.$$

   The rate of change of the amount of photosynthesis with respect to the intensity was found in problem 35. Find the intensity that maximizes the rate of change.

11.2 Concavity; Points of Inflection

Objectives
☐ To find points of inflection of graphs of functions
☐ To use the second-derivative test to graph functions

Just as we used the first derivative to determine if a curve was increasing or decreasing on a given interval, we can use the second derivative to determine if the curve is concave up or concave down on an interval.

A curve is said to be **concave up** on an interval [a, b] if at each point on the interval the curve is above its tangent at that point (Figure 11.1). If the curve is below all its tangents on a given interval, it is **concave down** on the interval (Figure 11.2).

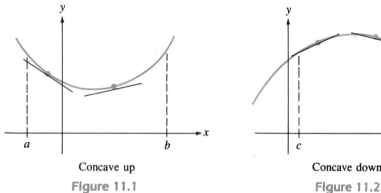

Concave up

Figure 11.1

Concave down

Figure 11.2

The second derivative can be used to determine the concavity of a curve.

Assume the first and second derivatives of function f exist. Then if $f''(x) > 0$ on an interval I, the graph of f is **concave up** on the interval. If $f''(x) < 0$ on an interval I, then the graph of f is **concave down** on I.

EXAMPLE 1 Is the graph of $f(x) = x^3 - 4x^2 + 3$
(a) concave up or down at $(1, 0)$?
(b) concave up or down at $(2, -5)$?

Solution (a) We must find $f''(x)$ before we can answer this question.

$$f'(x) = 3x^2 - 8x$$
$$f''(x) = 6x - 8$$

Then $f''(1) = 6(1) - 8 = -2$, so the graph is concave down at $(1, 0)$.

(b) Since $f''(2) = 6(2) - 8 = 4$, the graph is concave up at $(2, -5)$. The graph of $f(x) = x^3 - 4x^2 + 3$ is shown in Figure 11.3.

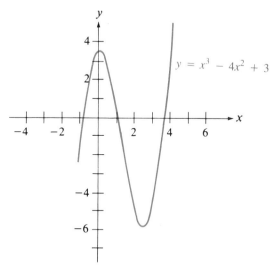

Figure 11.3

Looking at the graph of $y = x^3 - 4x^2 + 3$ (Figure 11.3) we see that the curve is concave down on the left and concave up on the right. Thus it has changed from concave down to concave up at some point. But at what point? According to the discussion earlier, it is the point where the second derivative changes from negative to positive. This point is called a **point of inflection.**

> A point (x_0, y_0) on the graph of a function f is called a **point of inflection** if the curve is concave up on one side of the point and concave down on the other side. The second derivative at this point, $f''(x_0)$, will be 0 or undefined.

In general, we can find points of inflection as follows.

Procedure	Example

To find the point(s) of inflection of a curve:

Find the points of inflection of the graph of
$$y = \frac{x^4}{2} - x^3 + 5.$$

1. Find the second derivative of the function.

1. $y' = f'(x) = 2x^3 - 3x^2$
   $y'' = f''(x) = 6x^2 - 6x$

2. Set the second derivative equal to 0, and solve for x. Potential points of inflection occur at these values of x or at values of x where $f(x)$ is defined and $f''(x)$ is undefined.

2. $0 = 6x^2 - 6x$ has solutions $x = 0$, $x = 1$. $f''(x)$ is defined everywhere.

3. Find the potential points of inflection.

3. $(0, 5)$ and $(1, 9/2)$ are potential points of inflection.

4. If the second derivative has opposite signs on the two sides of one of these values of x, a point of inflection occurs.

4. $f''(-1) = 12 > 0$

$f''\left(\frac{1}{2}\right) = -\frac{3}{2} < 0$

$f''(2) = 12 > 0$

$\left.\begin{array}{l}\end{array}\right\}$ $\Rightarrow$ $(0, 5)$ is a point of inflection

$\left.\begin{array}{l}\end{array}\right\}$ $(1, \frac{9}{2})$ is a $\Rightarrow$ point of inflection

See the graph in Figure 11.4.

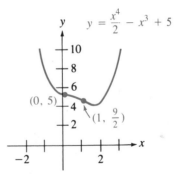

$$y = \frac{x^4}{2} - x^3 + 5$$

$(0, 5)$ $(1, \frac{9}{2})$

Figure 11.4

The graph of $y = \frac{1}{2}x^4 - x^3 + 5$ is shown in Figure 11.4. Note the points of inflection at $(0, 5)$ and $\left(1, \frac{9}{2}\right)$. The point of inflection at $(0, 5)$ is a horizontal point of inflection because $f'(x)$ is also 0 at $x = 0$.

We can use information about points of inflection and concavity to help sketch graphs. For example, if we know the curve is concave up at a critical point, then the point must be a relative minimum because the tangent to the curve is horizontal at the critical point, and only a point at the bottom of a "concave up" curve could have a horizontal tangent (see Figure 11.5 on the following page).

On the other hand, if the curve is concave down at a critical point, then the point is a relative maximum (see Figure 11.6 on the following page).

Thus we can use the **second-derivative test** to determine if a critical point is a relative maximum or minimum.

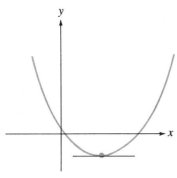

Figure 11.5   **Figure 11.6**

Second-derivative test

Procedure	Example
To find relative maxima and minima of a function:	Find the relative maxima and minima of $y = f(x) = \frac{1}{3}x^3 - x^2 - 3x + 2$.
1. Find the critical values of the function.	1. $f'(x) = x^2 - 2x - 3$ $0 = (x - 3)(x + 1)$ has solutions $x = -1$ and $x = 3$. No values of x make $x^2 - 2x - 3$ undefined.
2. Substitute the critical values into $f(x)$ to find the critical points.	2. $f(-1) = \frac{11}{3}$ $f(3) = -7$ The critical points are $\left(-1, \frac{11}{3}\right)$ and $(3, -7)$.
3. Evaluate $f''(x)$ at each critical value. (a) If $f''(x_0) < 0$, a relative maximum occurs at x_0. (b) If $f''(x_0) > 0$, a relative minimum occurs at x_0. (c) If $f''(x_0) = 0$, or if $f''(x_0)$ is undefined, the second-derivative test fails; use the first-derivative test.	3. $f''(x) = 2x - 2$ $f''(-1) = 2(-1) - 2 = -4 < 0$ $\left(-1, \frac{11}{3}\right)$ is a relative maximum. $f''(3) = 2(3) - 2 = 4 > 0$ $(3, -7)$ is a relative minimum. (The graph is shown in Figure 11.7.)

EXAMPLE 2   Find the relative maxima and minima and points of inflection of $y = 3x^4 - 4x^3$.

Solution
$$y' = f'(x) = 12x^3 - 12x^2$$

Solving $0 = 12x^3 - 12x^2$ gives $x = 1$ and $x = 0$. Thus the critical points are $(1, -1)$ and $(0, 0)$.

$$y'' = f''(x) = 36x^2 - 24x$$
$$f''(1) = 12 > 0 \Rightarrow (1, -1) \text{ is a relative minimum}$$
$$f''(0) = 0 \Rightarrow \text{the Second-Derivative Test fails}$$

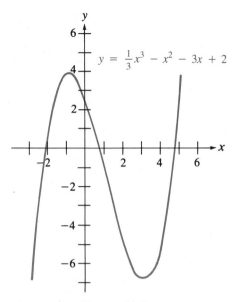

Figure 11.7

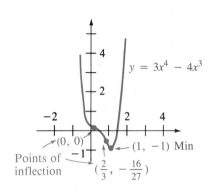

Figure 11.8

Since the Second-Derivative Test fails, we must use the First-Derivative Test at the critical point $(0, 0)$.

$$\left.\begin{array}{l} f'(-1) = -24 < 0 \\ f'(\tfrac{1}{2}) = -\tfrac{3}{2} < 0 \end{array}\right\} \Rightarrow (0, 0) \text{ is a horizontal point of inflection}$$

We look for points of inflection by setting $f''(x) = 0$ and solving for x. We find $0 = 36x^2 - 24x$ has solutions $x = 0$ and $x = \tfrac{2}{3}$.

Testing for concavity at $x = 0$ gives

$$\left.\begin{array}{l} f''(-1) = 60 > 0 \\ f''(\tfrac{1}{2}) = -3 < 0 \end{array}\right\} \Rightarrow (0, 0) \text{ is a point of inflection}$$

Thus we see again that $(0, 0)$ is a horizontal point of inflection. This is a special point, where the curve changes concavity *and* has a horizontal tangent (see Figure 11.8). Testing for concavity at $x = \tfrac{2}{3}$ gives

$$\left.\begin{array}{l} f''(\tfrac{1}{2}) = -3 < 0 \\ f''(1) = 12 > 0 \end{array}\right\} \Rightarrow (\tfrac{2}{3}, -\tfrac{16}{27}) \text{ is a point of inflection.}$$

Exercise 11.2

Find the points of inflection of the graphs of the following functions, if they exist.

1. $y = x^3 - 3x^2$
2. $y = x^3 + 6x$
3. $y = 2x^3 + 4x$
4. $y = 4x^3 - 3x^2$
5. $y = x^2 - 4x + 3$
6. $y = 4x^2 + 5x + 6$

7. $f(x) = x^3 - 6x^2 + 5x + 6$

8. $f(x) = 2x^3 - 4x^2 + 5x - 2$

9. $y = \frac{1}{4}x^4 + \frac{1}{2}x^3 - 3x^2 + 3$

10. $f(x) = \dfrac{x^4}{4} + 2x^3 - 48x^2 + 8x + 4$

11. $p = q^3 - 9q^2$

12. $p = 2q^4 - 6q^2 + 4$

13. $y = x^{1/3}$

14. $y = x^{2/3}$

15. $y = x^{4/3} - 4x^{1/3}$

16. $y = x^{7/3} - 7x^{4/3}$

17. $y = \dfrac{4x}{x^2 + 1}$

18. $y = \dfrac{8x}{x^2 + 4}$

Find the relative maxima, relative minima, and points of inflection, and sketch the graph of the following functions.

19. $y = x^2 - 4x + 2$

20. $y = x^3 - x^2$

21. $y = x^3 - 3x^2 + 6$

22. $y = x^4 - 8x^3 + 16x^2$

23. $y = x^4 - 16x^2$

24. $y = x^3 + 1$

25. $y = x^4 - 4$

26. $y = \frac{1}{3}x^3 - 2x^2 + 3x + 2$

27. $p = 3q^4 - 4q^3 + 1$

28. $p = \dfrac{q^2}{4} - \dfrac{1}{q}$

29. $w = \dfrac{z^2}{8} - \dfrac{1}{z}$

30. $f(w) = 4w^3 - 6w^2 - 24w$

31. $y = \dfrac{4x}{x^2 + 1}$ (see problem 17)

32. $y = \dfrac{8x}{x^2 + 4}$ (see problem 18)

33. $y = x^{4/3} - 4x^{1/3}$ (see problem 15)

34. $y = x^{7/3} - 7x^{4/3}$ (see problem 16)

APPLICATIONS

35. Figure 11.9 is a typical graph of worker productivity as a function of time on the job.
    (a) If P represents the productivity and t represents the time, write a symbol that represents the rate of change of productivity with respect to time.
    (b) Which of A, B, or C is the critical point for the rate of change found in part (a)? This point actually corresponds to the point at which the rate of production is maximized, or the point for maximum worker efficiency. In economics, this is called the **point of diminishing returns.**
    (c) Which of A, B, or C corresponds to the maximum production?

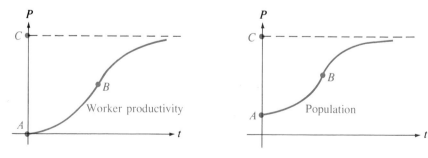

Figure 11.9   Figure 11.10

36. Figure 11.10 shows the growth of a population as a function of time.
   (a) If P represents the population and t represents the time, write a symbol that represents the rate of change (growth rate) of the population with respect to time.
   (b) Which of A, B, or C corresponds to the point at which the growth rate attains its maximum?
   (c) Which of A, B, or C corresponds to the maximum population?
37. Figure 11.11 shows the oxygen level P (for purity) in a lake t months after an oil spill.
   (a) Which of A, B, or C is the point of inflection for the graph in Figure 11.11?
   (b) On which side of C is $\dfrac{d^2P}{dt^2} < 0$?
   (c) Does the *rate of change* of purity attain its maximum at C?

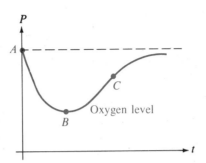

Figure 11.11

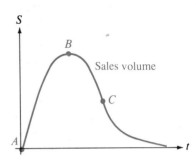

Figure 11.12

38. Figure 11.12 shows the daily sales volume S as a function of time t since an ad campaign.
   (a) Which of A, B, or C is the point of inflection for the graph in Figure 11.12?
   (b) On which side of C is $\dfrac{d^2S}{dt^2} > 0$?
   (c) Does the *rate of change* of sales volume attain its minimum at C?
39. Suppose that the rate of change R of the number of people affected by a flu virus in a community of 10,000 is given by

$$R = kN(10,000 - N),$$

   where N is the number affected and k is a constant. Find the number N at which the rate of spread (that is, R) is maximized.
40. According to Poiseulle's law, the speed S of blood through an artery of radius r at a distance x from the artery wall is given by

$$S = k[r^2 - (r - x)^2],$$

   where k is constant. Find the distance x that maximizes the speed.
41. Suppose the oxygen level P (for purity) in a body of water t months after an oil spill is given by

$$P(t) = 500\left[1 - \frac{4}{t + 4} + \frac{16}{(t + 4)^2}\right].$$

(a) How long before the oxygen level reaches its minimum?

(b) How long before the rate of change of P is maximized?

42. Suppose a company's daily sales volume attributed to an advertising campaign is given by

$$S(t) = \frac{3}{t + 3} - \frac{18}{(t + 3)^2}.$$

(a) How long before sales volume is maximized?

(b) How long before the rate of change of sales volume is minimized?

43. Suppose the total number of units produced by a worker in t hours of an 8-hour shift can be modeled by the **production function** $P(t)$:

$$P(t) = 27t + 12t^2 - t^3.$$

(a) Find the number of hours before production is maximized.

(b) Find the number of hours before the rate of production is maximized. That is, find the point of diminishing returns.

44. Suppose the total number of children's phonographs assembled by a worker in t hours is given by

$$N(t) = 64 - \frac{128(t + 3)}{(t + 3)^2 + 9}, \qquad 0 \le t \le 8.$$

Find the number of hours until the rate of production is maximized. That is, find the point of diminishing returns.

11.3 Implicit Differentiation

Objectives   □   To find derivatives by using implicit differentiation
           □   To find slopes of tangents by using implicit differentiation

Up to this point, we have taken derivatives of functions of the form $y = f(x)$. Some functions are given in equations of the form $F(x, y) = 0$. For example, the equation $xy - 4x + 1 = 0$ is in the form $F(x, y) = 0$, but we can solve for y to write the equation in the form $y = (4x - 1)/x$. We can say that $xy - 4x + 1 = 0$ defines y **implicitly** as a function of x, while $y = (4x - 1)/x$ defines the function explicitly.

The equation $x^2 + y^2 - 9 = 0$ has a circle as it graph. If we solve the equation for y, we get $y = \pm\sqrt{9 - x^2}$, which indicates that y is not a function of x. We can, however, consider the equation as defining *two* functions, $y = \sqrt{9 - x^2}$ and $y = -\sqrt{9 - x^2}$ (see Figure 11.13). We say that the equation $x^2 + y^2 - 9 = 0$ defines the two functions implicitly.

Even though an equation like $\ln xy + xe^y + x - 3 = 0$ may be difficult or even impossible to solve for y, and even though the equation may not represent y as a single function of x, we can use a technique called **implicit differentiation** to find the derivative of y with respect to x. The word *implicit* means we are implying that y is a function of x without verifying it. We simply take the derivative of both sides of $f(x, y) = 0$ and then solve algebraically for dy/dx.

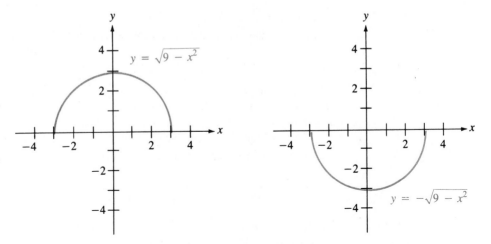

Figure 11.13

For example, we can find the derivative dy/dx from $x^2 + y^2 - 9 = 0$ by taking the derivative of both sides of the equation.

$$\frac{d}{dx}(x^2 + y^2 - 9) = \frac{d}{dx}(0)$$

$$\frac{d}{dx}(x^2) + \frac{d}{dx}(y^2) + \frac{d}{dx}(-9) = \frac{d}{dx}(0)$$

We have assumed y is a function of x; the derivative of y^2 is treated like the derivative of u^n, where u is a function of x. Thus the derivative is

$$2x + 2y^1 \cdot \frac{dy}{dx} + 0 = 0.$$

Solving for dy/dx gives

$$\frac{dy}{dx} = -\frac{2x}{2y} = -\frac{x}{y}.$$

Let us now compare this derivative with the derivatives of the two functions $y = \sqrt{9 - x^2}$ and $y = -\sqrt{9 - x^2}$. The derivative of $y = \sqrt{9 - x^2}$ is

$$\frac{dy}{dx} = \frac{1}{2}(9 - x^2)^{-1/2}(-2x) = \frac{-x}{\sqrt{9 - x^2}}$$

and the derivative of $y = -\sqrt{9 - x^2}$ is

$$\frac{dy}{dx} = -\frac{1}{2}(9 - x^2)^{-1/2}(-2x) = \frac{x}{\sqrt{9 - x^2}}.$$

Note that if we substitute $\pm\sqrt{9 - x^2}$ for y in our "implicit" derivative, we would get the two derivatives that were derived from the "explicit" functions.

EXAMPLE 1   Find the slope of the tangent to the graph of $x^2 + y^2 - 9 = 0$ at $(\sqrt{5}, 2)$.

Solution   The slope of the tangent to the curve is the derivative of the equation, evaluated at the given point. Taking the derivative implicitly gives us $dy/dx = -x/y$. Evaluating the derivative at $(\sqrt{5}, 2)$ gives the slope of the tangent as $-\sqrt{5}/2$.

We also found the derivative of $x^2 + y^2 - 9 = 0$ by solving for y explicitly. The function whose graph contains $(\sqrt{5}, 2)$ is $y = \sqrt{9 - x^2}$, and its derivative is

$$\frac{dy}{dx} = \frac{-x}{\sqrt{9 - x^2}}.$$

Evaluating the derivative at $(\sqrt{5}, 2)$, we get the slope of the tangent: $-\sqrt{5}/2$.

Thus we see that both methods give us the same slope for the tangent, but that the implicit method is easier to use.

EXAMPLE 2   Find dy/dx if $x^2 + 4x - 3y^2 + 4y = 0$.

Solution   Taking the derivative implicitly gives

$$\frac{d}{dx}(x^2) + \frac{d}{dx}(4x) + \frac{d}{dx}(-3y^2) + \frac{d}{dx}(4y) = \frac{d}{dx}(0).$$

Now, $\dfrac{d}{dx}(x^2) = 2x$

$\dfrac{d}{dx}(4x) = 4$

$\dfrac{d}{dx}(-3y^2) = -3(2y)\dfrac{dy}{dx} = -6y\dfrac{dy}{dx}$

$\dfrac{d}{dx}(4y) = 4(1)\dfrac{dy}{dx} = 4\dfrac{dy}{dx}$

and $\dfrac{d}{dx}(0) = 0.$

So $2x + 4 - 6y\dfrac{dy}{dx} + 4\dfrac{dy}{dx} = 0$

or $(-6y + 4)\dfrac{dy}{dx} = -2x - 4,$

which gives $\dfrac{dy}{dx} = \dfrac{-2x - 4}{-6y + 4}$

or $\dfrac{dy}{dx} = \dfrac{x + 2}{3y - 2}.$

EXAMPLE 3   Write the equation of the tangent to the graph of $x^3 + xy + 4 = 0$ at the point $(-2, -2)$.

Solution   Taking the derivative implicitly gives

$$\frac{d}{dx}(x^3) + \frac{d}{dx}(xy) + \frac{d}{dx}(4) = \frac{d}{dx}(0).$$

The $\frac{d}{dx}(xy)$ indicates that we should take the derivative of the *product* of x and y. Since we are assuming y is a function of x and since x is a function of x, we must use the Product Rule to find $\frac{d}{dx}(xy)$.

$$\frac{d}{dx}(xy) = x \cdot 1\frac{dy}{dx} + y \cdot 1 = x\frac{dy}{dx} + y$$

Thus we have

$$3x^2 + \left(x\frac{dy}{dx} + y\right) + 0 = 0.$$

Solving for dy/dx gives

$$\frac{dy}{dx} = \frac{-3x^2 - y}{x}.$$

The slope of the tangent to the curve at $x = -2$, $y = -2$ is

$$m = \frac{-3(-2)^2 - (-2)}{-2} = 5.$$

The equation of the tangent line is

$$y - (-2) = 5[x - (-2)], \qquad \text{or} \qquad y = 5x + 8.$$

EXAMPLE 4   At what point(s) does $x^2 + 4y^2 - 2x + 4y - 2 = 0$ have a horizontal tangent? At what point(s) does it have a vertical tangent?

Solution   First we find the derivative implicitly:

$$2x + 8y \cdot y' - 2 + 4y' - 0 = 0$$

$$y' = \frac{2 - 2x}{8y + 4} = \frac{1 - x}{4y + 2}$$

Horizontal tangents will occur where $y' = 0$; that is, where $x = 1$. We can now find the corresponding y value(s) by substituting 1 for x in the original equation and solving.

$$1 + 4y^2 - 2 + 4y - 2 = 0$$
$$4y^2 + 4y - 3 = 0$$
$$(2y - 1)(2y + 3) = 0$$
$$y = \tfrac{1}{2}, \qquad y = -\tfrac{3}{2}$$

Thus horizontal tangents occur at $\left(1, \frac{1}{2}\right)$, and $\left(1, -\frac{3}{2}\right)$ (see Figure 11.14).

Vertical tangents will occur where the derivative is undefined; that is, where $y = -\frac{1}{2}$. To find the corresponding x value(s), we substitute $-\frac{1}{2}$ in the equation for y and solve for x.

$$x^2 + 4\left(-\frac{1}{2}\right)^2 - 2x + 4\left(-\frac{1}{2}\right) - 2 = 0$$
$$x^2 - 2x - 3 = 0$$
$$(x - 3)(x + 1) = 0$$
$$x = 3, \qquad x = -1$$

Thus vertical tangents occur at $\left(3, -\frac{1}{2}\right)$ and $\left(-1, -\frac{1}{2}\right)$ (see Figure 11.14).

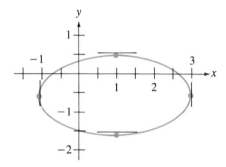

Figure 11.14

Exercise 11.3

Find dy/dx for the functions in problems 1–4.

1. $x^2 + 2y^2 - 4 = 0$
2. $x + y^2 - 4y + 6 = 0$
3. $x^2 + 4x + y^2 - 3y + 1 = 0$
4. $x^2 - 5x + y^3 - 3y - 3 = 0$

5. If $x^2 + y^2 = 4$, find y'.
6. If $p^2 + 4p - q = 4$, find dp/dq.
7. If $x^2 + 3xy = 4$, find y'.
8. If $xy^2 - y^2 = 1$, find y'.
9. If $pq = 4$, find dp/dq.
10. If $pq = 4p - 2$, find dp/dq.
11. If $\sqrt{x^2 + y^2} = 4$, find $\dfrac{dy}{dx}$.
12. If $p\sqrt{q} = 5$, find dp/dq.
13. If $\dfrac{\sqrt{p}}{q} - 4 = 0$, find dp/dq.
14. If $\dfrac{x - y}{y} = 9$, find y'.

15. If $\dfrac{x + y}{xy} = 5$, find y'.

16. If $x^{1/3} + y^{1/3} = xy$, find y'.

17. Find dy/dx for $x^4 + 3x^3y^2 - 2y^5 = (2x + 3y)^2$.

18. Find y' for $2x + 2y = \sqrt{x^2 + y^2}$.

19. Find the slope of the tangent to the curve $x^2 + 4x + y^2 + 2y - 4 = 0$ at $(1, -1)$.

20. Find the slope of the tangent to the curve $x^2 - 4x + 2y^2 - 4 = 0$ at $(2, 2)$.

21. Find the slope of the tangent to the curve $x^2 + 2xy + 3 = 0$ at $(-1, 2)$.

22. Find the slope of the tangent to the curve $y + x^2 = 4$ at $(0, 4)$.

23. Write the equation of the tangent to the curve $x^2 - 2y^2 + 4 = 0$ at $(2, 2)$.

24. Write the equation of the tangent to the curve $x^2 + y^2 + 2x - 3 = 0$ at $(-1, 2)$.

25. Write the equation of the tangent to the curve $4x^2 + 3y^2 - 4y - 3 = 0$ at $(-1, 1)$.

26. Write the equation of the tangent to the curve $xy + y = 0$ at $(3, 0)$.

27. At what points does the curve defined by $x^2 + 4y^2 - 4x - 4 = 0$ have
    (a) horizontal tangents?
    (b) vertical tangents?

28. At what points does the curve defined by $x^2 + 4y^2 - 4 = 0$ have
    (a) horizontal tangents?
    (b) vertical tangents?

29. In problem 5, the derivative was found to be

$$y' = \frac{-x}{y}.$$

Take the implicit derivative of both sides of this equation to show

$$y'' = \frac{-y + xy'}{y^2}.$$

30. Find y' implicitly for $x^3 - y^3 = 8$. Then, by taking derivatives implicitly, use it to show

$$y'' = \frac{2x(y - xy')}{y^3}.$$

31. Use the result of problem 29 in parts (a) and (b) below.
    (a) Substitute $-x/y$ for y' in the expression for y'' and simplify to show

$$y'' = -\frac{(x^2 + y^2)}{y^3}.$$

    (b) Does $y'' = -4/y^3$? Why or why not?

32. Use the result of problem 30.
    (a) Substitute x^2/y^2 for y' in the expression for y'' and simplify to show

$$y'' = \frac{2x(y^3 - x^3)}{y^5}.$$

    (b) Does $y'' = -16x/y^5$? Why or why not?

33. Find y'' for $\sqrt{x} + \sqrt{y} = 1$, and simplify.

34. Find y'' for $\dfrac{1}{x} - \dfrac{1}{y} = 1$.

APPLICATIONS

35. Suppose that a company's sales volume y (in thousands of dollars) is related to its advertising expenditures x (in thousands of dollars) according to

$$xy - 20x + 10y = 0.$$

Find the rate of change of sales volume with respect to advertising expenditures when $x = 10$ (thousand dollars).

36. Suppose that the number of mosquitoes N (in thousands) in a certain swampy area near a community is related to the number of pounds of insecticide x sprayed on the nesting areas according to

$$Nx - 10x + N = 300.$$

Find the rate of change of N with respect to x when 49 lb of insecticide are used.

37. Suppose that a company can produce 12,000 units when the number of hours of skilled labor y and unskilled labor x satisfy

$$384 = (x + 1)^{3/4} (y + 2)^{1/3}.$$

Find the rate of change of skilled labor hours with respect to unskilled labor hours when $x = 255$ and $y = 214$. This can be used to approximate the change in skilled labor hours required to maintain the same production level when unskilled labor hours are increased by one hour.

38. Suppose that production of 10,000 units of a certain agricultural crop is related to the number of hours of labor x and the number of acres of the crop y according to

$$300x + 30{,}000y = 11xy - 0.0002x^2 - 5y.$$

Find the rate of change of the number of hours with respect to the number of acres.

39. If the demand function for a product is given by

$$p(q + 1)^2 = 200{,}000,$$

find the rate of change of quantity with respect to price when $p = \$80$. Interpret this result.

40. If the demand function for a commodity is given by

$$p^2(2q + 1) = 100{,}000,$$

find the rate of change of quantity with respect to price when $p = \$50$. Interpret this result.

11.4 Derivatives of Logarithmic Functions

Objective   ☐   To find derivatives of logarithmic functions

In Chapter 5, we discussed the exponential function $y = a^x$ and the logarithmic function $y = \log_a x$. We have seen the importance of functions of the form $y = e^x$. In this section we will develop the derivative of the function $y = \log_a x$, which will again show the importance of the number e.

Derivative of a Logarithmic Function	If $y = \log_a x$, then $$\frac{dy}{dx} = \frac{1}{x} \log_a e, \quad \text{or} \quad \frac{dy}{dx} = \frac{1}{x \ln a}*.$$

The proof of $\dfrac{dy}{dx} = \dfrac{1}{x} \log_a e$ follows.

If $y = f(x) = \log_a x$,

$$\frac{dy}{dx} = \lim_{h \to 0} \frac{f(x + h) - f(x)}{h}$$

$$= \lim_{h \to 0} \frac{\log_a (x + h) - \log_a x}{h}.$$

Because $\log_a M - \log_a N = \log_a \dfrac{M}{N}$, we have

$$\frac{dy}{dx} = \lim_{h \to 0} \frac{\log_a \left(\dfrac{x + h}{x} \right)}{h}.$$

Introducing the factor x/x gives

$$\frac{dy}{dx} = \lim_{h \to 0} \frac{x}{x} \cdot \frac{1}{h} \log_a \left(\frac{x + h}{x} \right)$$

$$= \lim_{h \to 0} \frac{1}{x} \cdot \frac{x}{h} \log_a \left(1 + \frac{h}{x} \right).$$

Using $N \log_a M = \log_a M^N$ gives

$$\frac{dy}{dx} = \lim_{h \to 0} \frac{1}{x} \log_a \left(1 + \frac{h}{x} \right)^{x/h},$$

so

$$\frac{dy}{dx} = \frac{1}{x} \lim_{h \to 0} \log_a \left(1 + \frac{h}{x} \right)^{x/h}.$$

---

*This alternate formula is the result of using $b = e$ in the change of base formula: $\log_a b = \dfrac{\ln b}{\ln a}$.

The logarithmic function is continuous when it is defined, so

$$\frac{dy}{dx} = \frac{1}{x} \log_a \left[\lim_{h \to 0} \left(1 + \frac{h}{x} \right)^{x/h} \right].$$

Now

$$\lim_{h \to 0} \left(1 + \frac{h}{x} \right)^{x/h}$$

is of the same form as

$$\lim_{a \to 0} (1 + a)^{1/a} = e,$$

so

$$\frac{dy}{dx} = \frac{1}{x} \log_a e.$$

Thus we have

$$\frac{d}{dx} \log_a x = \frac{1}{x} \log_a e.$$

Recall that $\log_e e = 1$; this means that if the logarithm were to the base e, the derivative would be $1/x$. That is,

$$\frac{d}{dx} (\log_e x) = \frac{d}{dx} (\ln x) = \frac{1}{x}.$$

If $y = \ln x$, then $\dfrac{dy}{dx} = \dfrac{1}{x}$.

We see the derivatives of logarithmic functions have a simpler form if the base of the logarithm is e.

EXAMPLE 1   If $y = x^3 + 3 \ln x$, find dy/dx.

Solution

$$\frac{dy}{dx} = 3x^2 + 3 \left(\frac{1}{x} \right) = 3x^2 + \frac{3}{x}$$

EXAMPLE 2   If $y = x^2 \ln x$, find y'.

Solution   By the Product Rule,

$$y' = x^2 \cdot \frac{1}{x} + (\ln x)(2x) = x + 2x \ln x.$$

We can use the Chain Rule to find the formula for the derivatives of $y = \log_a u$ and $y = \ln u$, where $u = f(x)$.

Derivatives of Logarithmic Functions

If $y = \log_a u$, where $u = f(x)$, then

$$\frac{dy}{dx} = \frac{1}{u} (\log_a e) \frac{du}{dx} = \frac{1}{u} \cdot \frac{1}{\ln a} \cdot \frac{du}{dx}.$$

If $y = \ln u$, where $u = f(x)$, then

$$\frac{dy}{dx} = \frac{1}{u} \cdot \frac{du}{dx}.$$

EXAMPLE 3   If $y = \log_4 (x^3 + 1)$, find dy/dx.

Solution   The function is of the form $y = \log_4 u$, where $u = x^3 + 1$. Thus

$$\frac{dy}{dx} = \frac{1}{x^3 + 1} (\log_4 e) 3x^2$$

$$= \frac{3x^2}{x^3 + 1} \log_4 e.$$

The derivative could also be written in the form

$$\frac{dy}{dx} = \frac{3x^2}{(x^3 + 1)\ln 4}.$$

EXAMPLE 4   If $f(x) = \ln x^4$, find $f'(x)$.

Solution   The function is of the form $f(x) = \ln u$, where $u = x^4$. Then

$$f'(x) = \frac{1}{x^4} \cdot 4x^3 = \frac{4}{x}.$$

Note that we could have found the derivative by first writing $f(x) = \ln x^4 = 4 \ln x$. Then,

$$f'(x) = 4 \cdot \frac{1}{x} = \frac{4}{x}.$$

EXAMPLE 5   If $y = \ln \sqrt{3x}$, find y'.

Solution   Letting $u = \sqrt{3x} = (3x)^{1/2}$, we have

$$y' = \frac{1}{(3x)^{1/2}} \cdot \frac{1}{2} (3x)^{-1/2} \cdot 3 = \frac{3}{2(3x)} = \frac{1}{2x}.$$

Or, writing $y = \frac{1}{2} \ln 3x$ gives

$$y' = \frac{1}{2} \cdot \frac{1}{3x} \cdot 3 = \frac{1}{2x}.$$

EXAMPLE 6   If $\ln xy = 6$, find dy/dx.

Solution   Using the properties of logarithms, we have

$$\ln x + \ln y = 6,$$

which leads to the implicit derivative.

$$\frac{1}{x} + \frac{1}{y}\frac{dy}{dx} = 0$$

Solving gives

$$\frac{dy}{dx} = -\frac{y}{x}.$$

Exercise 11.4

Find the derivatives of the functions in problems 1–16.

1. $y = \log_4 x$
2. $y = \log_5 x$
3. $y = \ln x$
4. $y = \ln (2x)$
5. $y = \ln (x^3 - 4x)$
6. $y = \log_e (x^5 - x^4)$
7. $y = \ln (4x - 1) - 3 \ln x$
8. $y = 3 \ln x - \ln (x + 1)$
9. $y = \ln \left(\dfrac{4x - 1}{x^3}\right)$
10. $y = \ln \left(\dfrac{x^3}{x + 1}\right)$
11. $y = 3 \ln x + \dfrac{1}{2} \ln (x + 1)$
12. $y = 2 \ln x + \ln (x^4 - x + 1)$
13. $y = \ln (x^3 \sqrt{x + 1})$
14. $y = \ln [x^2(x^4 - x + 1)]$
15. $y = \ln \sqrt{2}$
16. $y = \ln \sqrt{e}$

17. Find dp/dq if $p = \ln (q^2 + 1)$.

18. Find ds/dq if $s = \ln \left(\dfrac{q^2}{4} + 1\right)$.

19. Find $\dfrac{dp}{dq}$ if $p = \ln \left(\dfrac{q^2 - 1}{q}\right)$.

20. Find $\dfrac{ds}{dt}$ if $s = \ln [t^3(t^2 - 1)]$.

21. Find $\dfrac{dy}{dt}$ if $y = \ln \left[\dfrac{t^2 + 3}{\sqrt{1 - t}}\right]$.

22. Find $\dfrac{dy}{dx}$ if $y = \ln \left[\dfrac{3x + 2}{x^2 - 5}\right]^{1/4}$.

In problems 23–32, find dy/dx.

23. $y = x \ln x - x$
24. $y = x^2 \ln (2x + 3)$
25. $y = \dfrac{\ln x}{x}$
26. $y = \dfrac{1 + \ln x}{x^2}$
27. $y = \ln (x^4 + 3)^2$
28. $y = \ln (3x + 1)^{1/2}$

29. $y = [\ln (x^4 + 3)]^2$

30. $y = \sqrt{\ln (3x + 1)}$

31. $\ln y = x$

32. $\log y = x$

33. If $x \ln y = 4$, find dy/dx.

34. If $\ln xy = 2$, find dy/dx.

35. Find the slope of the tangent to the curve $x^2 + \ln y = 4$ at the point $(2, 1)$.

36. Write the equation of the tangent to the curve $x \ln y + 2xy = 2$ at the point $(1, 1)$.

APPLICATIONS

37. If the pH of a solution is given by

$$pH = -\log [H^+],$$

where $[H^+]$ is the concentration of hydrogen ions (in gram atoms per liter), what is the rate of change of pH with respect to $[H^+]$?

38. Suppose the proportion of people affected by a certain disease is described by

$$\ln \left(\frac{P}{1 - P}\right) = 0.5t,$$

where t is the time in months. Use implicit differentiation to find dP/dt, which represents the rate at which P grows.

39. If the Reynolds number relating to the flow of blood exceeds

$$R = A \ln r - Br,$$

where r is the radius of the aorta and A and B are positive constants, the blood flow becomes turbulent. What is the radius r that makes R a maximum?

40. The demand function for a product is given by $p = 4000/\ln (x + 10)$, where p is the price per unit when x units are demanded.
    (a) Find the rate of change of price with respect to the number of units sold when 40 units are sold.
    (b) Find the rate of change of price with respect to the number of units sold when 90 units are sold.
    (c) Find the second derivative to see if the rate at which the price is changing at 40 units is increasing or decreasing.

41. The number of grams of radium, y, that will remain after t years if 100 grams existed originally can be found using the equation

$$-0.000436t = \ln \left(\frac{y}{100}\right).$$

Use implicit differentiation to find the rate of change of y with respect to t, that is, the rate at which the radium will decay.

11.5 Derivatives of Exponential Functions

Objective ☐ To find derivatives of exponential functions

In the previous section we found derivatives of logarithmic functions. In this section we turn our attention to exponential functions. The formula for the derivative of $y = a^x$ follows.

$$\text{If } y = a^x, \text{ then } \frac{dy}{dx} = \frac{a^x}{\log_a e}.$$

$$\text{Alternate form: } \frac{dy}{dx} = a^x \ln a$$

We can verify that the derivative of $y = a^x$ is $dy/dx = a^x/\log_a e$ as follows. We can write the function $y = a^x$ in the logarithmic form

$$\log_a y = x.$$

Taking the derivatives with respect to x of both sides of this equation, we get

$$\frac{1}{y} \cdot \frac{dy}{dx} \cdot \log_a e = 1.$$

Solving this equation for dy/dx gives $dy/dx = y/\log_a e$. But $y = a^x$, so

$$\frac{dy}{dx} = \frac{a^x}{\log_a e}.$$

We can find the alternate form by taking the natural logarithm of both sides of $y = a^x$, getting

$$\ln y = \ln a^x = x \ln a$$
$$\frac{1}{y} \cdot y' = 1 \cdot \ln a$$
$$y' = y \ln a = a^x \ln a.$$

EXAMPLE 1   If $y = 4^x$, find dy/dx.

Solution
$$\frac{dy}{dx} = \frac{4^x}{\log_4 e} \left(\text{or } \frac{dy}{dx} = 4^x \ln 4 \right)$$

Using the derivative formula with $y = e^x$ gives

$$\frac{dy}{dx} = \frac{e^x}{\log_e e} = e^x,$$

since $\log_e e = 1$.

$$\text{If } y = e^x, \text{ then } dy/dx = e^x.$$

EXAMPLE 2   If $p = e^q$, find dp/dq.

Solution
$$dp/dq = e^q$$

As with the logarithmic functions, the Chain Rule will permit us to expand our derivative formulas.

Derivatives of Exponential Functions

If $y = a^u$, where u is a function of x, then

$$\frac{dy}{dx} = \frac{a^u}{\log_a e} \cdot \frac{du}{dx} = a^u \frac{du}{dx} \ln a$$

If $y = e^u$, where u is a function of x, then

$$\frac{dy}{dx} = e^u \cdot \frac{du}{dx}.$$

EXAMPLE 3   If $y = 10^{x^2}$, find dy/dx.

Solution
$$\frac{dy}{dx} = 10^{x^2} \cdot 2x \cdot \frac{1}{\log e} = \frac{2x \cdot 10^{x^2}}{\log e}$$

This answer could also be written as $\dfrac{dy}{dx} = 2x \cdot 10^{x^2} \ln 10$.

EXAMPLE 4   If $f(x) = e^{4x^3}$, find $f'(x)$.

Solution
$$f'(x) = e^{4x^3} \cdot 12x^2 = 12x^2 e^{4x^3}$$

EXAMPLE 5   If $p = qe^{5q}$, find dp/dq.

Solution
$$\frac{dp}{dq} = (q \cdot e^{5q} \cdot 5) + (e^{5q} \cdot 1)$$
$$= 5qe^{5q} + e^{5q}$$

EXAMPLE 6   If $s = 3te^{3t^2 + 5t}$, find ds/dt.

Solution
$$\frac{ds}{dt} = 3t \cdot e^{3t^2 + 5t}(6t + 5) + e^{3t^2 + 5t} \cdot 3$$
$$= (18t^2 + 15t)e^{3t^2 + 5t} + 3e^{3t^2 + 5t}$$

EXAMPLE 7   If $y = e^{\ln x^2}$, find y'.

Solution
$$y' = e^{\ln x^2} \cdot \frac{1}{x^2} \cdot 2x = \frac{2}{x} e^{\ln x^2}$$

But by Property II of logarithms (Section 5.2) $e^{\ln u} = u$, so we can simplify the derivative to

$$y' = \frac{2}{x} \cdot x^2 = 2x.$$

Note that if we had used this property *before* taking the derivative, we would have

$$y = e^{\ln x^2} = x^2. \text{ Then the derivative is } y' = 2x.$$

EXAMPLE 8   If $u = w/e^{3w}$, find u'.

Solution   The function is a quotient, with the denominator equal to e^{3w}. Using the Quotient Rule gives

$$u' = \frac{e^{3w} \cdot 1 - w \cdot e^{3w} \cdot 3}{(e^{3w})^2}$$

$$= \frac{e^{3w} - 3we^{3w}}{e^{6w}}$$

$$= \frac{1 - 3w}{e^{3w}}.$$

EXAMPLE 9   If $q = e^{-p}$ describes the demand for a product, find dq/dp.

Solution
$$\frac{dq}{dp} = e^{-p}(-1) = -e^{-p}$$

Exercise 11.5

Find the derivatives of the functions in problems 1–24.

1. $y = 4^{x^2}$
2. $y = 5^{x-1}$
3. $y = 6e^{3x^2}$
4. $y = 1 - 2e^{-x^3}$
5. $y = e^{-1/x}$
6. $y = 2e^{\sqrt{x}}$
7. $y = 2e^{(x^2+1)^3}$
8. $y = e^{\sqrt{x^2-9}}$
9. $y = e^{-1/x^2} + e^{-x^2}$
10. $y = \frac{2}{e^{2x}} + \frac{e^{2x}}{2}$
11. $s = t^2e^t$
12. $p = 4qe^{q^3}$
13. $y = e^3 + e^{\ln x}$
14. $s = x \ln e^{x^3}$
15. $y = 2\sqrt{e^x} + e^{\sqrt{x}}$
16. $y = e^{x^4} - (e^x)^4$
17. $y = \ln(e^{2x} + 1)$
18. $y = \ln(e^{4x} + 2)$
19. $y = e^{-3x} \ln(2x)$
20. $y = e^{2x^2} \ln(4x)$
21. $y = \frac{1 + e^{5x}}{e^{3x}}$
22. $y = \frac{x}{1 + e^{2x}}$
23. $y = (e^{3x} + 4)^{10}$
24. $y = \frac{e^x - e^{-x}}{e^x + e^{-x}}$

25. If $xe^y = 6$, find dy/dx.

26. If $x + e^{xy} = 10$, find dy/dx.

27. If $e^{xy} = 4$, find dy/dx.

28. If $x - xe^y = 3$, find dy/dx.

29. If $ye^x - y = 3$, find dy/dx.

30. If $x^2y = e^{x+y}$, find dy/dx.

31. Find the slope of the line tangent to the graph of $y = xe^{-x}$ at $x = 1$.

32. Find the slope of the line tangent to the curve $ye^x = 4$ at $(0, 4)$.

33. Write the equation of the line tangent to the curve $xe^y = 3$ at $(3, 0)$.

34. Write the equation of the line tangent to the graph of $y = \dfrac{e^{-x}}{1 + e^{-x}}$ at $x = 0$.

35. The equation for the standard normal probability distribution is

$$y = \frac{1}{\sqrt{2\pi}} e^{-z^2/2}.$$

At what value of z will the curve be at its highest point?

36. (a) Find the mode of the normal distribution* given by

$$y = \frac{1}{\sqrt{2\pi}} e^{-(x-10)^2/4}.$$

(b) What is the mean of this normal distribution?

APPLICATIONS

37. The compound amount that accrues when $100 is invested at 8%, compounded continuously, is $S(t) = 100e^{0.08t}$, where t is the number of years.
    (a) At what rate is the money in this account growing when $t = 1$?
    (b) At what rate is it growing when $t = 10$?

38. Suppose that world population can be considered as growing according to the equation $N = N_0(1 + r)^t$, where N_0 and r are constants. Find the rate of change of N with respect to t.

39. The number of molecules of a certain substance that have enough energy to activate a reaction is given by $y = 100{,}000e^{-1/x}$, where y is the number of molecules and x is the (absolute) temperature of the substance. What is the rate of change of y with respect to temperature?

40. When a body is moved from one medium to another, its temperature T will change according to the equation

$$T = T_0 + Ce^{kt},$$

where T_0 is the temperature of the new medium, C the temperature difference between the mediums (old − new), t the time in the new medium, and k a constant. If T_0, C, and k are held constant, what is the rate of change of T with respect to time?

41. We have seen (in Section 6.2) that if P is invested for n years at 10%, compounded continuously, the compound amount is given by the function

$$S = Pe^{0.1\,n}.$$

(a) At what rate is the compound amount growing at any time (for any n)?
(b) At what rate is the compound amount growing after 1 year ($n = 1$)?
(c) Is the rate of growth of the compound amount greater than 10%? Why?

---

*The mode occurs at the highest point on normal curves, and equals the mean.

42. Medical research has shown that between heartbeats the pressure in the aorta of normal adults is a function of time and can be modeled by the equation

$$P = 95e^{-0.491t}.$$

(a) Use the derivative to find the rate at which the pressure changes at any time t.
(b) Use the derivative to find the rate at which the pressure changes after 0.1 seconds.
(c) Is the pressure increasing or decreasing?
(d) Find the rate of pressure change when the pressure is 80.

43. The concentration y of a certain drug in the bloodstream at any time t (in hours) is given by $y = 100(1 - e^{-0.462t})$. Find the rate of change of the concentration after one hour. Give your answer to 3 decimal places.

44. The amount of the radioactive isotope thorium-234 present at time t is given by

$$Q(t) = 100e^{-0.02828t}.$$

Find the rate of radioactive decay of the isotope.

45. The number of people $N(t)$ in a community who are reached by a particular rumor at time t (in days) is given by

$$N(t) = \frac{50,500}{1 + 100e^{-0.7t}}.$$

Find the rate of change of $N(t)$.

46. Suppose the spread of a disease through the student body at an isolated college campus can be modeled by

$$y = \frac{10,000}{1 + 9999e^{-0.99t}},$$

where y is the total number affected at time t (in days). Find the rate of change of y.

11.6 Applications in Business and Economics

Objectives   □ To find the maximum profit, given the average cost and price in a competitive market
□ To find the maximum profit, given the demand function and average cost function in a monopoly
□ To find the tax per unit that will maximize tax revenue
□ To find the elasticity of demand

Profit Maximization in a Competitive Market

We have discussed total cost, total revenue, and profit functions in previous chapters, and we have also discussed demand functions. But we have not discussed how the demand for a product affects the total revenue of a firm and thus the firm's profit. In a *competitive market*, each firm is so small in the market that its actions cannot affect the price of the product. The price of the product is determined in the market by the intersection of the market demand curve (from all consumers) and market supply curve (from all firms that supply this product). The firm can sell as little or as much as it desires at the given market price, which it cannot change.

Therefore, a firm in a competitive market has a total revenue function given by $R(x) = px$, where p is the price that is the market equilibrium price for the product and x is the quantity it sells.

EXAMPLE 1 A firm in a competitive market must sell its product for \$200 per unit. The average cost per unit (per month) is $\overline{C} = 80 + x$, where x represents the number of units sold per month. How many units should be sold to maximize profit?

Solution If the average cost per unit is $\overline{C} = 80 + x$, then the total cost of x units is given by $C(x) = (80 + x)x = 80x + x^2$. The revenue per unit is \$200, so the total revenue is given by $R(x) = 200x$. Thus the profit function is

$$P(x) = R(x) - C(x) = 200x - (80x + x^2), \quad \text{or} \quad P(x) = 120x - x^2.$$

Then $P'(x) = 120 - 2x$. Setting $P'(x) = 0$ and solving for x gives $x = 60$. Since $P''(60) = -2$, the profit is maximized when the firm sells 60 units per month.

Profit Maximization in a Monopolistic Market

We have seen that a seller in a competitive market cannot change the market price. But a seller who has a monopoly can control the price by regulating the supply of the product. Since the seller controls the supply, he or she can force the price higher by limiting supply. If the seller increases the supply, prices will fall. Figure 11.15 shows the graph of the demand function $p = 3300/x$.

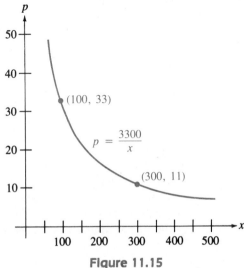

Figure 11.15

For a price of $33 per unit for a product whose demand curve is given in Figure 11.15, the monopolist will only supply 100 units. To sell 300 units, the monopolist will have to settle for $11 per unit. That is, if the monopolist wants to sell all that he or she produces, the price charged will have to be the price consistent with that level of output on the demand curve.

If the demand function for the product is $p = f(x)$, the total revenue for the sale of x units is $R(x) = px = f(x) \cdot x$. Note that the price p is fixed by the market in a competitive market, but varies with output for the monopolist.

If $\overline{C} = \overline{C}(x)$ represents the average cost per unit sold, then the total cost for the x units sold is $C = \overline{C}x$. Since we have both total cost and total revenue as a function of the quantity, x, we can maximize the profit function, $P(x) = px - \overline{C}x$, where p represents the demand function $p = f(x)$ and $\overline{C}$ represents the average cost function $\overline{C} = \overline{C}(x)$.

EXAMPLE 2   The daily demand function for a product is

$$p = 168 - 0.2x.$$

If a monopolist finds the average cost is

$$\overline{C} = 120 + x,$$

(a) how many units must be sold to maximize profit?
(b) what is the selling price at this "optimal" level of production?
(c) what is the maximum possible profit?

Solution   (a) The total revenue function for the product is

$$R(x) = px = (168 - 0.2x)x = 168x - 0.2x^2,$$

and the total cost function is

$$C(x) = \overline{C}x = (120 + x)x = 120x + x^2.$$

Thus the profit function is

$$P(x) = R(x) - C(x) = 168x - 0.2x^2 - (120x + x^2),$$

or $P(x) = 48x - 1.2x^2$. Then $P'(x) = 48 - 2.4x$, so $P'(x) = 0$ when $x = 20$.

We see that $P''(20) = -2.4$, so by the second-derivative test, $P(x)$ is a maximum at $x = 20$. That is, selling 20 units will maximize profit.
(b) The selling price is determined by $p = 168 - 0.2x$, so the price that will result from supplying 20 units per day is $p = 168 - 0.2(20) = 164$. That is, the "optimal" selling price is $164 per unit.
(c) The profit at $x = 20$ is $P(20) = 48(20) - 1.2(20)^2 = 960 - 480 = 480$. Thus the maximum possible profit is $480 per day.

Taxation in a Competitive Market

Many taxes imposed by governments are "hidden." That is, the tax is levied on goods produced, and the producers must pay the tax. Of course, the tax becomes a cost to the producers, and they pass the tax on to the consumer in the form of higher prices for goods. But it isn't quite that simple, as the following discussion shows.

Suppose the government imposes a tax of t dollars on each unit produced and sold by producers. If we are in pure competition in which the consumers' demand depends only on price, the *demand function* will not change. The tax will change the supply function, of course, because at each level of output q, the firm will want to charge a price higher by the amount of the tax. This will shift the entire supply curve upward by the amount of the tax t, and market equilibrium will occur at a point where quantity demanded is lower.

The graph of the market demand function, the original market supply function, and the market supply function after taxes is shown in Figure 11.16. Since the tax added to each item is constant, the supply function is parallel to the original supply function and t units above it.

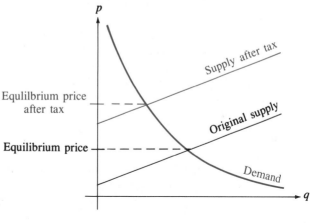

Figure 11.16

Note in this case that after the taxes are imposed, *no* items are supplied at the price that was the equilibrium price before taxation. After the taxes are imposed, the consumers will simply have to pay more for the product. Since taxation does not change the demand curve, the quantity purchased at market equilibrium will be less than it was before taxation. Thus governments planning taxes should recognize that they will not collect taxes on the original equilibrium quantity. They will collect on the *new* equilibrium quantity, a quantity reduced by their taxation. Thus a large tax on each item may reduce the quantity demanded at the new market equilibrium so much that very little revenue would result from the tax.

If the tax revenue is represented by $T = tq$, where t is the tax per unit and q is the equilibrium quantity of the supply and demand functions after taxation, we can use the following procedure for maximizing the total tax revenue.

Procedure	Example
To find the tax per item (under pure competition) that will maximize total tax revenue:	If the demand and supply functions are given by $p = 600 - q$ and $p = 200 + \frac{1}{3}q$, respectively, find the tax rate t that will maximize the total tax revenue T.
1. Write the supply function after taxation.	1. $p = 200 + \frac{1}{3}q + t$
2. Set the demand and (new) supply functions equal, and solve for t.	2. $600 - q = 200 + \frac{1}{3}q + t$ $400 - \frac{4}{3}q = t$
3. Form the total tax revenue function, $T = tq$, and take its derivative with respect to q.	3. $T = tq = 400q - \frac{4}{3}q^2$ $T'(q) = \dfrac{dT}{dq} = 400 - \dfrac{8}{3}q$
4. Set $T' = 0$, solve for q. This is the q that should maximize T. Use the second-derivative test to verify it.	4. $0 = 400 - \frac{8}{3}q$ $q = 150$ $T''(q) = -\frac{8}{3}$. Thus T is maximized at $q = 150$.
5. Substitute the value of q into the equation for t (in step 2). This is the value of t that will maximize T.	5. $t = 400 - \frac{4}{3}(150) = 200$ A tax of \$200 per item will maximize the total tax revenue. The total tax revenue for the period would be $200 \cdot (150) = \$30,000$.

Note that in the example just given, if a tax of \$300 were imposed, the total tax revenue the government would receive would be

$$(\$300)(75) = \$22,500.$$

This means that consumers would spend \$100 more for each item, suppliers would sell 75 fewer items, and the government would lost \$7500 in tax revenue. Thus everyone would suffer if the tax rate were raised above \$200.

Elasticity of Demand

We know from the law of demand that consumers will respond to changes in prices; if prices increase, the quantity demanded will decrease. But the degree of responsiveness of the consumers to price changes will vary widely for different products. For example, a price increase in insulin will not decrease greatly the demand for it by diabetics, but a price increase in clothes may cause consumers to buy considerably less and wear their old clothes longer. When the response to price changes is considerable, we say the demand is *elastic*. When price changes cause relatively small changes in demand for a product, the demand is said to be *inelastic* for that product.

The *elasticity of demand* is measured by economists by dividing the rate of change in demand by the rate of change in price. We may write this as

$$E_d = -\frac{\text{change in quantity demanded}}{\text{original quantity demanded}} \div \frac{\text{change in price}}{\text{original price}}$$

or

$$E_d = -\frac{\Delta q}{q} \div \frac{\Delta p}{p}.$$

The demand curve usually has a negative slope, so we have introduced a negative sign into the formula to give us a positive elasticity.

We can write the equation for elasticity as

$$E_d = -\frac{p}{q} \cdot \frac{\Delta q}{\Delta p},$$

and define the **point elasticity of demand** as

$$\eta = \lim_{\Delta p \to 0} \left(-\frac{p}{q} \cdot \frac{\Delta q}{\Delta p} \right) = -\frac{p}{q} \cdot \frac{dq}{dp}.$$

The **point elasticity of demand** at the point (q_A, p_A) is

$$\eta = -\frac{p}{q} \cdot \frac{dq}{dp} \bigg|_{(q_A, p_A)}$$

EXAMPLE 3   If a commodity has a demand curve given by $p + 5q = 100$, find the point elasticity of demand at $q = 8, p = 60$.

Solution   We can find dq/dp by using implicit differentiation with respect to p.

$$1 + 5 \frac{dq}{dp} = 0$$

$$\frac{dq}{dp} = -\frac{1}{5}.$$

Thus

$$\eta = -\frac{p}{q} \left(-\frac{1}{5} \right) \bigg|_{(8, \, 60)} = -\frac{60}{8} \left(-\frac{1}{5} \right) = \frac{3}{2}.$$

In the next example, we will see that the derivative dq/dp for $p + 5q = 100$ is also $-\frac{1}{5}$ when it is found by first solving for q.

EXAMPLE 4   Find the point elasticity of the demand function $p + 5q = 100$ at $(10, 50)$.

Solution   Solving the demand function for q gives $q = 20 - \frac{1}{5}p$. Then $dq/dp = -\frac{1}{5}$, and

$$\eta = -\frac{p}{q}\left(-\frac{1}{5}\right)\Bigg|_{(10,\ 50)} = -\frac{50}{10}\left(-\frac{1}{5}\right) = 1.$$

Note that in Examples 3 and 4 the demand equation was $p + 5q = 100$, so the demand "curve" is a straight line, with slope $m = -5$. But the elasticity was $\eta = 3/2$ at $(8, 60)$ and $\eta = 1$ at $(10, 50)$. The elasticity for this same demand curve is $\eta = 2/3$ at $(12, 40)$. This illustrates that the elasticity of demand may be different at different points on the demand curve, even though the slope of the demand "curve" is constant. (See Figure 11.17.)

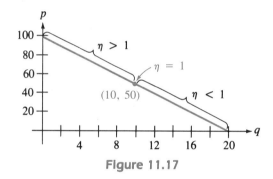

Figure 11.17

These examples show that the elasticity of demand is more than just the slope of the demand curve, which is the rate at which the demand is changing. Recall that the elasticity measures the consumers' degree of responsiveness to a price change. We can look at the relation between elasticity and a firm's total revenue as follows:

1. If $\eta > 1$, the demand is **elastic,** and an increase in price will result in decrease in total revenue. On the other hand, a decrease in price will increase total revenue.

2. If $\eta < 1$, the demand is **inelastic,** and an increase in price will result in an increase in total revenue. A decrease in price will lead to a decrease in revenue.

3. If $\eta = 1$, the demand is **unitary elastic,** and neither an increase nor decrease in price will change total revenue.

Exercise 11.6

PROFIT MAXIMIZATION IN A COMPETITIVE MARKET

1. The price of a product in a competitive market is $300. If the average cost of producing the product is $\overline{C} = 160 + x$, where x is the number of units produced per month, how many units should the firm produce and sell to maximize its profit?

2. The average cost of producing a product is $\overline{C} = 60 + 2x$, where x represents the number of units produced per week. If the equilibrium price determined by a competitive market is $220, how many units should the firm produce and sell each week to maximize its profit?

3. If the daily average cost of producing a product by the Ace Company is $\overline{C} = 10 + 2x$, and if the price on the competitive market is $50, what is the maximum daily profit the Ace Company can expect on this product?

4. The Mary Ellen Candy Company produces chocolate Easter bunnies at an average cost of $\overline{C} = 0.10 + 0.01x$, where x is the number produced. If the price on the competitive market for this size bunny is $2.50, how many should it produce to maximize its profit?

5. A firm has monthly average costs given by

$$\overline{C} = \frac{45{,}000}{x} + 100 + x^2,$$

where x is the number of units produced per month. The firm can sell its product in a competitive market for $4600 per unit. Find the number of units that gives maximum profit, and find the maximum profit.

6. A small business has weekly average costs of

$$\overline{C} = \frac{100}{x} + 30 + \frac{x}{10},$$

where x is the number of units produced each week. The competitive market price for this business' product is $46 per unit. Find the level of production that yields maximum profit, and find the maximum profit.

PROFIT MAXIMIZATION IN A MONOPOLISTIC MARKET

7. The weekly demand function for a product sold by only one firm is $p = 600 - \frac{1}{2}x$ and the average cost of production and sale is $\overline{C} = 300 + 2x$.
   (a) Find the quantity that will maximize profit.
   (b) Find the selling price at this optimal level of production.
   (c) What is the maximum profit?

8. The monthly demand function for a product sold by a monopoly is $p = 8000 - x$, and its average cost is $\overline{C} = 4000 + 5x$. Determine
   (a) the quantity that will maximize profit.
   (b) the selling price at the optimal quantity.
   (c) the maximum profit.

9. If the monthly demand function for a product sold by a monopoly is $p = 1960 - \frac{1}{3}x^2$, and the average cost is $\overline{C} = 1000 + 2x + x^2$, find
   (a) the quantity that will give maximum profit.
   (b) the maximum profit.

10. The monthly demand function for a product sold by a monopoly is $p = 5900 - \frac{1}{2}x^2$, and its average cost is $\overline{C} = 3020 + 2x$. Will the firm make a profit or loss?

11. An industry having a monopoly on a product has its average weekly costs given by

$$\overline{C} = \frac{10,000}{x} + 60 - 0.03x + 0.00001x^2.$$

The weekly demand for the product is given by $p = 120 - 0.015x$. Find the price the industry should set and the number of units it should produce to obtain maximum profit. Find the maximum profit.

12. A large corporation having monopolistic control in the marketplace has its average daily costs given by

$$\overline{C} = \frac{800}{x} + 100x + x^2.$$

The daily demand for its product is given by $p = 60,000 - 50x$. Find the quantity that gives maximum profit, and find the maximum profit. What selling price should the corporation set for its product?

TAXATION IN A COMPETITIVE MARKET

13. If the weekly demand function is $p = 30 - q$ and the supply function before taxation is $p = 6 + 2q$, what tax per item will maximize the total tax revenue?

14. If the demand function for a fixed period of time is $p = 38 - 2q$ and the supply function before taxation is $p = 8 + 3q$, what tax per item will maximize the total tax revenue?

15. If the weekly demand function is $p = 200 - 2q^2$ and the supply function before taxation is $p = 20 + 3q$, what tax per item will maximize the total tax revenue?

16. If the monthly demand function is $p = 7230 - 5q^2$ and the supply function before taxation is $p = 30 + 30q^2$, what tax per item will maximize the total tax revenue?

17. Suppose the weekly demand for a product is given by $p + 2q = 840$, and the weekly supply before taxation is given by $p = 0.02q^2 + 0.55q + 7.4$. Find the tax per item that produces maximum tax revenue. Find the tax revenue.

18. If the daily demand for a product is given by $p + q = 1000$, and the daily supply before taxation is given by $p = q^2/30 + 2.5q + 920$, find the tax per item that maximizes tax revenue. Find the tax revenue.

ELASTICITY OF DEMAND

19. (a) Find the point elasticity of the demand function $p + 4q = 80$ at $(10, 40)$.
    (b) How will a price increase affect total revenue?

20. (a) Find the point elasticity of the demand function $2p + 3q = 150$ at the price $p = 15$.
    (b) How will a price increase affect total revenue?

21. (a) Find the point elasticity of the demand function $p^2 + 2p + q = 49$ at $p = 6$.
    (b) How will a price increase affect total revenue?

22. (a) Find the point elasticity of the demand function $pq = 81$ at $p = 3$.
    (b) How will a price increase affect total revenue?

23. Find the point elasticity of the demand curve defined by $q = 100e^{-2p}$ when $p = 4$.

24. Find the point elasticity of the demand function $q = 80e^{-p/2}$ if the price is \$4.

25. If the demand function for a product is $q = 12 - \ln p$, find the point elasticity of demand when the price is \$405 and the quantity is 6.
26. If the demand function for a product is $q = 15 - \frac{1}{3} \ln p$, find the point elasticity of demand when price is \$20, quantity is 14.
27. We have stated that when

$$\eta = -\frac{p}{q} \cdot \frac{dq}{dp} = 1,$$

the total revenue is unchanged as price increases. Given the total revenue function

$$R = p \cdot q, \qquad \text{with } q = f(p),$$

use implicit differentiation with respect to p to show that R is unchanged $(dR/dp = 0)$ when $\eta = 1$.
28. We have stated that when

$$\eta = -\frac{p}{q} \cdot \frac{dq}{dp} > 1,$$

the total revenue is decreasing as price increases. Given the total revenue function

$$R = p \cdot q, \qquad \text{with } q = f(p),$$

use implicit differentiation with respect to p to show that R is decreasing $(dR/dp < 0)$ when $\eta > 1$.
29. Show that $R = p \cdot q$ is increasing $(dR/dp > 0)$ when $\eta < 1$.

Review Exercises

11.1

Find the second derivative.

1. $y = \sqrt{x} - x^2$

2. $y = x^4 - \dfrac{1}{x}$

Find the fifth derivative.

3. $y = (2x + 1)^4$

4. $y = \dfrac{(1 - x)^6}{24}$

5. If $\dfrac{dy}{dx} = \sqrt{x^2 - 4}$, find $\dfrac{d^3y}{dx^3}$.

6. If $\dfrac{d^2y}{dx^2} = \dfrac{x}{x^2 + 1}$, find $\dfrac{d^4y}{dx^4}$.

11.2

7. Is the graph of $y = x^4 - 3x^3 + 2x - 1$ concave up or concave down at $x = 2$?
8. Find the points of inflection of the graph of $y = x^4 - 2x^3 - 12x^2 + 6$.
9. Find the relative maxima, relative minima, and points of inflection of the graph of $y = x^3 - 3x^2 - 9x + 10$.

In problems 10–12, find any relative maxima, relative minima, points of inflection, and sketch each graph.

10. $y = x^3 - 12x$
11. $y = 2 + 5x^3 - 3x^5$
12. $y = x^{7/3} - 7x^{1/3} + 2$

13. Find $\dfrac{dy}{dx}$ for $y^2 = 4x - 1$.

14. Find $\dfrac{dy}{dx}$ if $x^2 + 3y^2 + 2x - 3y + 2 = 0$.

15. Find $\dfrac{dy}{dx}$ for $3x^2 + 2x^3y^2 - y^5 = 7$.

16. Find the second derivative of $x^2 + y^2 = 1$.

17. Find the slope of the tangent to the curve $x^2 + 4x - 3y^2 + 6 = 0$ at $(3, 3)$.

18. Find the points where tangents to the graph of the equation in problem 17 are horizontal.

In problems 19–30, find the derivative of each function.

19. If $y = x^2e^x$, find dy/dx.

20. If $y = \ln e^{x^2}$, find y'.

21. If $p = \ln\left(\dfrac{q}{q^2 - 1}\right)$, find $\dfrac{dp}{dq}$.

22. If $y = e^{x^2}$, find dy/dx.

23. If $y = 3^{3x-4}$, find dy/dx.

24. If $y = (1 + \ln x)^{10}$, find dy/dx.

25. If $y = \dfrac{\ln x}{x}$, find $\dfrac{dy}{dx}$.

26. If $y = \dfrac{1 + e^{-x}}{1 - e^{-x}}$, find $\dfrac{dy}{dx}$.

27. If $y = \dfrac{\ln (2x + 1)}{2x + 1}$, find $\dfrac{dy}{dx}$.

28. If $x = e^t(t^2 + 4)^2$, find $\dfrac{dx}{dt}$.

29. If $y \ln x = 5$, find $\dfrac{dy}{dx}$.

30. Find $\dfrac{dy}{dx}$ for $e^{xy} = y$.

APPLICATIONS

31. If the compound amount of $1000 invested for n years at 12%, compounded continuously, is given by

$$S = 1000e^{0.12n},$$

find the rate at which the compound amount is growing after 1 year.

32. (a) In problem 31, find the rate of growth of the compound amount after 2 years.
    (b) How much faster is the compound amount growing at the end of 2 years than after 1 year?

33. A breeder reactor converts stable uranium-238 into the isotope plutonium-239. The decay of this isotope is given by

$$A(t) = A_0e^{-0.00002876t},$$

where $A(t)$ is the amount of isotope at time t, in years, and A_0 is the original amount. This isotope has a half-life of 24,101 years (that is, half of it will decay away in 24,101 years).
    (a) At what rate is $A(t)$ decaying at this point in time?
    (b) At what rate is $A(t)$ decaying after 1 year?
    (c) Is the rate of decay at its half-life greater or less than after 1 year?

34. The average cost of producing a product is $\overline{C} = 600e^{x/600}$. What is the marginal cost when 600 units are produced?

35. The price of a product in a competitive market is $250. The average cost of producing the product is $\overline{C} = 70 + 3x$, where x is the number of units produced per week. How many units will have to be produced to maximize profit?

36. Suppose for a product in a competitive market, the demand function is $p = 1200 - 2x$ and the supply function is $p = 200 + 2x$, where x is the number of units. If a firm's average cost function for this product is

$$\overline{C}(x) = \frac{12,000}{x} + 50 + x,$$

find the maximum profit. *Hint:* First find the equilibrium price.

37. The monthly demand function for a product sold by a monopoly is $p = 800 - x$, and its average cost is $\overline{C} = 200 + x$. Determine
    (a) the quantity that will maximize profit.
    (b) the selling price at the optimal quantity.

38. Suppose in a monopolistic market that the demand function for a commodity is

$$p = 7000 - 10x - \frac{x^2}{3}.$$

If a company's average cost function for this commodity is

$$\overline{C}(x) = \frac{40,000}{x} + 600 + 8x,$$

find the maximum profit.

39. Can increasing the tax per unit sold actually lead to a decrease in tax revenues?

40. If the supply and demand functions for a product are

$$p = 40 + 20q \quad \text{and} \quad p = \frac{5000}{q + 1},$$

respectively, find the tax t that maximizes tax revenue.

41. (a) Find the point elasticity of the demand function $pq = 27$ at $(9, 3)$.
    (b) How will a price increase affect total revenue?

42. Suppose the demand for a product is given by

$$p^2(2q + 1) = 10,000.$$

Find the elasticity of demand when $p = \$20$.

WARMUP

	Prerequisite problem type	Answer	Section for review
12.1–12.4	Write as a power: (a) $\sqrt{x}$ (b) $\sqrt{x^2 - 9}$	(a) $x^{1/2}$ (b) $(x^2 - 9)^{1/2}$	0.4 Radicals
12.2	Expand $(x^2 + 4)^2$.	$x^4 + 8x^2 + 16$	0.5 Special powers
12.3	Divide $x^4 - 2x^3 + 4x^2 - 7x - 1$ by $x^2 - 2x$.	$x^2 + 4 + \dfrac{x - 1}{x^2 - 2x}$	0.5 Division
12.1, 12.2, 12.3	Find the derivative of (a) $f(x) = 2x^{1/2}$ (b) $u = x^3 - 3x$	(a) $f'(x) = x^{-1/2}$ (b) $u' = 3x^2 - 3$	9.4 Derivatives
12.2	If $y = \dfrac{(x^2 + 4)^6}{6}$, what is y'?	$(x^2 + 4)^5 2x$	9.6 Derivatives
12.3	(a) If $y = \ln u$, what is y'? (b) If $y = e^u$, what is y'?	(a) $y' = \dfrac{1}{u} \cdot u'$ (b) $y' = e^u \cdot u'$	11.4, 11.5 Derivatives
12.2	If $u = x^2 + 4$, what is du?	$2x\,dx$	9.5 Differentials
12.5	Solve for y: $\ln y = kt + C$	$y = e^{kt + C}$	5.2 Logarithmic functions
12.5	Solve for k: $0.5 = e^{5600k}$	$k = -0.00012378$	5.3 Exponential equations

12

Indefinite Integrals

If the marginal cost for a product is \$36 at all levels of production, we know that the total cost function is a linear function. In particular $C(x) = 36x + \text{FC}$, where FC is the fixed cost. But if the marginal cost changes at different levels of production, the total cost function cannot be linear. In this chapter we will use integration to find total cost functions, given information about marginal costs and fixed costs.

Accountants can use linear regression to translate information about marginal cost into a linear equation defining (approximately) the marginal cost function. By integrating this marginal cost function, it is possible to find an (approximate) function that defines the total cost.

We can also use integration to find total revenue functions from marginal revenue functions, to optimize profit from information about marginal cost and marginal revenue, and to find national consumption functions from information about marginal propensity to consume.

Integration can be used in the social and life sciences to predict growth or decay from expressions giving rates of change. For example, we can determine equations for population size from the rate of growth; we can write equations for the number of radioactive atoms remaining in a substance if we know the rate of disintegration of the substance; and we can determine the volume of blood flow from information about the rate of flow.

12.1 The Indefinite Integral

Objective   □   To find certain indefinite integrals

We have discussed methods for finding derivatives of functions in the previous chapters. We will now turn our attention to reversing the operation of differentiation. Given the derivative of a function, we can find the function. This process is called **antidifferentiation.** For example, if the derivative of a function is $2x$, we know the function could be $f(x) = x^2$ because $\dfrac{d}{dx}(x^2) = 2x$. But the function could also be

$f(x) = x^2 + 4$ because $\dfrac{d}{dx}(x^2 + 4) = 2x$. It is clear that any function of the form

615

$f(x) = x^2 + C$, where C is a constant, will have $f'(x) = 2x$ as its derivative. Thus we say the **antiderivative** of $f'(x) = 2x$ is $f(x) = x^2 + C$, where C is an arbitrary constant.

EXAMPLE 1   If $f'(x) = 3x^2$, what is $f(x)$?

Solution   The derivative of the function $f(x) = x^3$ is $f'(x) = 3x^2$. But other functions also have this derivative. They will all be of the form $f(x) = x^3 + C$, where C is a constant. Thus we say $f(x) = x^3 + C$ is the antiderivative of $f'(x) = 3x^2$.

EXAMPLE 2   If $f'(x) = x^3$, what is $f(x)$?

Solution   We know that the derivative of $f(x) = x^4$ is $4x^3$, so the derivative of $f(x) = x^4/4$ is $f'(x) = x^3$. Thus any function of the form $f(x) = x^4/4 + C$ will have the derivative $f'(x) = x^3$.

It is easily seen that

$$\text{if } f'(x) = x^4, \quad \text{then } f(x) = \frac{x^5}{5} + C;$$

$$\text{if } f'(x) = x^5, \quad \text{then } f(x) = \frac{x^6}{6} + C.$$

In general,

$$\text{If } f'(x) = x^n, \text{ then } f(x) = \frac{x^{n+1}}{n+1} + C, \text{ for } n \neq -1.$$

We can see that this general formula applies for any $n \neq -1$ by noting that the derivative of

$$f(x) = \frac{x^{n+1}}{n+1} + C \quad \text{is} \quad f'(x) = \frac{(n+1)x^n}{n+1} + 0 = x^n.$$

We will discuss the case when $n = -1$ later.

EXAMPLE 3   What is the antiderivative of $f'(x) = x^{-1/2}$?

Solution   Using the formula, we get

$$f(x) = \frac{x^{1/2}}{1/2} + C = 2x^{1/2} + C.$$

We can check by noting that the derivative of $2x^{1/2} + C$ is $x^{-1/2}$.

The process of finding an antiderivative is called **integration.** The function that results when integration takes place is called an **indefinite integral,** or more simply, an **integral.** We can denote the indefinite integral (that is, the antiderivative) of a function $f(x)$ by $\int f(x)\,dx$. Thus we can write $\int x^2\,dx$ to indicate the antiderivative of the function $f(x) = x^2$. The expression is read as "the integral of x^2 with respect to x." In this case, x^2 is called the **integrand.** The **integral sign,** $\int$, indicates the process of integration, and the dx indicates that the integral is to be taken with respect to x. Since the antiderivative of x^2 is $x^3/3 + C$, we can write

$$\int x^2\,dx = \frac{x^3}{3} + C.$$

Note that integration results in a function (actually a number of functions, one for each value of C). This is reasonable, since the derivative of a function is a function.

We can now use the integral sign and rewrite the formula for integrating powers of x.

Powers of x Formula	$\int x^n\,dx = \dfrac{x^{n+1}}{n+1} + C \qquad (\text{for } n \neq -1)$

EXAMPLE 4   Find $\int \sqrt[3]{x}\,dx$.

Solution

$$\int \sqrt[3]{x}\,dx = \int x^{1/3}\,dx = \frac{x^{4/3}}{\frac{4}{3}} + C$$

$$= \frac{3}{4}x^{4/3} + C = \frac{3}{4}\sqrt[3]{x^4} + C.$$

Other formulas will be useful in evaluating integrals. The table below shows how some new integration formulas result from differentiation formulas.

Derivative	Integral
$\dfrac{d}{dx}(x) = 1$	$\Rightarrow \int dx = x + C$
$\dfrac{d}{dx}[c \cdot u(x)] = c \cdot \dfrac{d}{dx}u(x)$	$\Rightarrow \int c\,u(x)\,dx = c \int u(x)\,dx$
$\dfrac{d}{dx}[u(x) \pm v(x)] = \dfrac{d}{dx}u(x) \pm \dfrac{d}{dx}v(x)$	$\Rightarrow \int [u(x) \pm v(x)]\,dx = \int u(x)\,dx \pm \int v(x)\,dx$

The formulas above indicate that we can integrate functions term-by-term just as we were able to take derivatives term-by-term.

EXAMPLE 5   Evaluate $\int 4 \, dx$.

Solution
$$\int 4 \, dx = 4 \int dx = 4(x + C_1) = 4x + C$$

(Since C_1 is an unknown constant, we can write $4C_1$ as the unknown constant C.)

EXAMPLE 6   Evaluate $\int 8x^5 \, dx$.

Solution
$$\int 8x^5 \, dx = 8 \int x^5 \, dx = 8\left(\frac{x^6}{6} + C_1\right) = \frac{4x^6}{3} + C$$

EXAMPLE 7   Evaluate $\int (x^3 + 4x) \, dx$.

Solution
$$\int (x^3 + 4x) \, dx = \int x^3 \, dx + \int 4x \, dx$$
$$= \left(\frac{x^4}{4} + C_1\right) + \left(4 \cdot \frac{x^2}{2} + C_2\right)$$
$$= \frac{x^4}{4} + 2x^2 + C_1 + C_2$$
$$= \frac{x^4}{4} + 2x^2 + C$$

Note that we need only one constant because the sum of C_1 and C_2 is just a new constant.

EXAMPLE 8   Evaluate $\int (x - 4)^2 \, dx$.

Solution   We can multiply out the square before we integrate.
$$\int (x - 4)^2 \, dx = \int (x^2 - 8x + 16) \, dx = \frac{x^3}{3} - 4x^2 + 16x + C$$

EXAMPLE 9   Sales records show that the rate of change of the revenue (that is, the marginal revenue) for a product is $\overline{MR} = 300 - 0.2x$, where x represents the quantity sold. Find the total revenue function for the product.

Solution   We know that the marginal revenue can be found by differentiating the total revenue function. That is,
$$R'(x) = 300 - 0.2x.$$

Thus integrating the marginal revenue function will give the total revenue function.
$$R(x) = \int (300 - 0.2x) \, dx = 300x - 0.1x^2 + K*$$

---

*We are using K rather than C here to represent the constant of integration to avoid confusion between the constant C and the cost function $C = C(x)$.

We can use the fact that there is no revenue when no units are sold to evaluate K. Setting $x = 0$ and $R = 0$ gives $0 = 300(0) - 0.1(0)^2 + K$, so $K = 0$. Thus the total revenue function is

$$R(x) = 300x - 0.1x^2.$$

Exercise 12.1

1. If $f'(x) = 4x^3$, what is $f(x)$?
2. If $f'(x) = 5x^4$, what is $f(x)$?
3. If $f'(x) = x^6$, what is $f(x)$?
4. If $g'(x) = x^4$, what is $g(x)$?

Evaluate the following integrals.

5. $\int x^7\,dx$
6. $\int x^5\,dx$
7. $\int 5x^3\,dx$
8. $\int 4x^5\,dx$
9. $\int 8x^5\,dx$
10. $\int 16x^9\,dx$
11. $\int 5\,dx$
12. $\int 6\,dx$
13. $\int 3^3\,dx$
14. $\int 5^2\,dx$
15. $\int x^{3/2}\,dx$
16. $\int x^{2/3}\,dx$
17. $\int \frac{1}{2}x^{2/3}\,dx$
18. $\int \frac{2}{3}x^{3/2}\,dx$
19. $\int \sqrt{x}\,dx$
20. $\int \sqrt{x^3}\,dx$
21. $\int 6\sqrt{x}\,dx$
22. $\int 3\sqrt[3]{x^2}\,dx$
23. $\int (x^4 - 3x^2)\,dx$
24. $\int (3x^2 - 4x)\,dx$
25. $\int (x^3 - 3x^2 + 4)\,dx$
26. $\int (x^3 - 4x + 3)\,dx$
27. $\int (x^4 - 2x + \sqrt{x})\,dx$
28. $\int (3x^3 - x^2 - \sqrt[3]{x})\,dx$
29. $\int (x + 5)^2\,dx$
30. $\int (2x + 1)^2\,dx$
31. $\int (4x^2 - 1)^2\,dx$
32. $\int (x^3 + 1)^2\,dx$
33. $\int (x^2 + 1)^3\,dx$
34. $\int (x - 1)^3\,dx$

APPLICATIONS

35. If the marginal revenue for a month for a commodity is $\overline{MR} = 3$, what is the total revenue function?
36. If the marginal revenue for a month for a commodity is $\overline{MR} = 5$, what is the total revenue function?
37. If the marginal revenue for a month for a commodity is $\overline{MR} = 4x - 3$, find the total revenue function.
38. If the marginal revenue for a month for a commodity is $\overline{MR} = 5x - 2$, find the total revenue function.
39. If the marginal revenue for a month is given by $\overline{MR} = 3x - 1$, what is the total revenue from the production and sale of 50 units?
40. If the marginal revenue for a month is given by $\overline{MR} = 5x - 3$, find the total revenue from the sale of 75 units.
41. Suppose that when a sense organ receives a stimulus at time t, the total number of action potentials is $P(t)$. If the rate at which action potentials are produced is $t^3 + 4t^2 + 6$, and if there are 0 action potentials when $t = 0$, find the formula for $P(t)$.

42. Suppose a particle has been shot into the air in such a way that the rate at which its height is changing is $v = 320 - 32t$, in feet per second, and suppose that it is 1600 feet high when $t = 10$. Write the equation that describes the height of the particle at any time t.

43. A factory is dumping pollutants into a river at a rate given by $dx/dt = t^{3/4}/600$ tons per week, where t is the time in weeks since they began dumping and x is the number of tons of pollutants.
    (a) Find the equation for total tons of pollutants dumped.
    (b) How many tons were dumped during the first year?

44. The rate at which the radius of an oil slick is spreading from an offshore oil well is 4 feet per hour. If the radius is 100 feet when $t = 25$ hours, write the radius of the oil slick as a function of time.

45. The DeWitt Company has found that the rate of change of its average cost for a product is

$$\overline{C}'(x) = \frac{1}{4} - \frac{100}{x^2}, \text{ in dollars, where } x \text{ is the number of units.}$$

    If the average cost of producing 20 units is $40.00, find
    (a) the average cost function for the product.
    (b) the average cost of 100 units of the product.

46. The rate of growth of the population of a city is predicted to be

$$\frac{dp}{dt} = 1000t^{1.08},$$

    where p is the population at time t, and t is measured in years from the present. Suppose the current population is 100,000.
    (a) What is the predicted rate of growth 5 years from the present?
    (b) What is the predicted population 5 years from the present?

47. An oil tanker hits a reef and begins to leak. The efforts of the workers repairing the leak cause the rate at which the oil is leaking to decrease. If the oil was leaking at a rate of 31 barrels per hour at the end of the first hour after the accident, and if the rate is decreasing at a rate of one barrel per hour,
    (a) what function describes the rate of loss?
    (b) how many barrels of oil will leak in the first 6 hours?
    (c) when will the oil leak be stopped? How much will have leaked altogether?

12.2 The Power Rule

Objective   □   To evaluate integrals of the form $\int u^n \cdot u' \, dx$ if $n \neq -1$

In Example 8 of Section 12.1, we evaluated

$$\int (x - 4)^2 \, dx$$

by squaring $x - 4$ and integrating the resulting polynomial term-by-term. In this section we will attempt to integrate powers of some functions without multiplying out the powers.

Recall that if $y = [u(x)]^n$, the derivative of y is

$$\frac{dy}{dx} = n[u(x)]^{n-1} \cdot u'(x).$$

Using this formula for derivatives, we can see that

$$\int n[u(x)]^{n-1} \cdot u'(x) \, dx = [u(x)]^n + C.$$

It is easy to see that this formula is equivalent to the following formula, called the **Power Rule.**

Power Rule

$$\int [u(x)]^n \cdot u'(x) \, dx = \frac{[u(x)]^{n+1}}{n+1} + C, \quad \text{if } n \neq -1.$$

Note that the Power Rule is similar to the formula

$$\int x^n \, dx = \frac{x^{n+1}}{n+1} + C,$$

except that the Power Rule requires that $u'(x)$ be present in the integral. However, if $u(x) = x$, then $u'(x) = 1$, so the Power Rule is actually an extension of the powers of x rule.

Recalling that the differential

$$du = u'(x) \, dx,$$

we can write the Power Rule in the form

$$\int u^n \, du = \frac{u^{n+1}}{n+1} + C, \quad \text{if } n \neq -1.$$

EXAMPLE 1   Evaluate $\int (x^2 + 4)^5 \cdot 2x \, dx$.

Solution   To use the Power Rule, we must be sure we have the function $u(x)$, its derivative $u'(x)$, and n.

$$u = x^2 + 4, \quad n = 5$$
$$u' = 2x$$

All required parts are present, so the integral is of the form

$$\int (x^2 + 4)^5 2x \, dx = \int u^5 \cdot u' \, dx = \int u^5 \, du$$

$$= \frac{u^6}{6} + C = \frac{(x^2 + 4)^6}{6} + C.$$

We can check the integration by noting that the derivative of

$$\frac{(x^2 + 4)^6}{6} + C \quad \text{is} \quad (x^2 + 4)^5 \cdot 2x.$$

EXAMPLE 2   Evaluate $\int \sqrt{2x + 3} \cdot 2\ dx$.

Solution   If we let $u = 2x + 3$, then $u' = 2$ and $du = 2\ dx$, so we have

$$\int \sqrt{2x + 3} \cdot 2\ dx = \int \sqrt{u}\ du$$

$$= \int u^{1/2}\ du$$

$$= \frac{u^{3/2}}{3/2} + C.$$

Since $u = 2x + 3$, we have

$$\int \sqrt{2x + 3} \cdot 2\ dx = \frac{2}{3}(2x + 3)^{3/2} + C.$$

CHECK: The derivative of $\frac{2}{3}(2x + 3)^{3/2} + C$ is $(2x + 3)^{1/2} \cdot 2$.

EXAMPLE 3   Evaluate $\int (x^2 + 4)^4 \cdot x\ dx$.

Solution   If we let $u = x^2 + 4$, then $u' = 2x$. Thus we do not have an integral of the form $\int u^n \cdot u'\ dx$, as we did in Example 1. But since we are missing *only the constant factor* 2 to make it the correct form, we can multiply by 2 and divide it out as follows:

$$\int (x^2 + 4)^4 \cdot x\ dx = \int (x^2 + 4)^4 \cdot \frac{1}{2}(2x)\ dx.$$

We can then factor the $\frac{1}{2}$ outside the integral sign since it is a constant, getting

$$\tfrac{1}{2}\int (x^2 + 4)^4 \cdot 2x\ dx.$$

Now the integral is in the form $\frac{1}{2}\int u^4 \cdot u'\ dx$. Thus

$$\int (x^2 + 4)^4 \cdot x\ dx = \frac{1}{2} \int (x^2 + 4)^4 \cdot 2x\ dx$$

$$= \frac{1}{2} \frac{(x^2 + 4)^5}{5} + C$$

$$= \frac{1}{10} (x^2 + 4)^5 + C.$$

EXAMPLE 4   Evaluate $\int \sqrt{x^3 - 4} \cdot x^2\ dx$.

Solution   If we let $u = x^3 - 4$, then $u' = 3x^2$. Thus if we multiply by the constant factor 3 (and divide it out) we have

$$\int \sqrt{x^3 - 4} \cdot x^2\ dx = \int \sqrt{x^3 - 4} \cdot \frac{1}{3}(3x^2)\ dx$$

$$= \frac{1}{3} \int (x^3 - 4)^{1/2} \cdot 3x^2\ dx.$$

This integral is of the form $\frac{1}{3}\int u^{1/2} \cdot u' \, dx$, resulting in

$$\frac{1}{3} \cdot \frac{u^{3/2}}{3/2} + C = \frac{1}{3} \cdot \frac{(x^3 - 4)^{3/2}}{3/2} + C$$

$$= \frac{2}{9} (x^3 - 4)^{3/2} + C.$$

Note that we can introduce *only a constant factor* to get the integral into the proper form. If the integral requires the introduction of a *variable* to get it into the form $u^n \cdot u' \, dx$, we *cannot* use the form, and must try something else.

EXAMPLE 5   Evaluate $\int (x^2 + 4)^2 \, dx$.

Solution   If we let $u = x^2 + 4$, then $u' = 2x$. Since we would have to introduce a variable to get u' in the integral, we cannot solve this problem by using the Power Rule. We must find another method. We can evaluate this integral by squaring the factor and then integrating term-by-term.

$$\int (x^2 + 4)^2 \, dx = \int (x^4 + 8x^2 + 16) \, dx$$

$$= \frac{x^5}{5} + \frac{8x^3}{3} + 16x + C$$

Note that if we had tried to introduce the factor $2x$ into the integral, we would get

$$\int (x^2 + 4)^2 \, dx = \int (x^2 + 4)^2 \cdot \frac{1}{2x} (2x) \, dx$$

$$= \frac{1}{2} \int (x^2 + 4)^2 \cdot \frac{1}{x} (2x) \, dx.$$

But we cannot factor the $1/x$ outside the integral, so we do not have the proper form. Again, we can only introduce *a constant factor* to get an integral in the proper form.

EXAMPLE 6   Evaluate $\int (2x^2 - 4x)^2 (x - 1) \, dx$.

Solution   If we want to treat this as an integral of the form $\int u^n u' \, dx$, we will have to let $u = 2x^2 - 4x$. Then u' will be $4x - 4$. Multiplying and dividing by 4 will give us this form, as follows.

$$\int (2x^2 - 4x)^2 (x - 1) \, dx = \int (2x^2 - 4x)^2 \cdot \frac{1}{4} \cdot 4(x - 1) \, dx$$

$$= \frac{1}{4} \int (2x^2 - 4x)^2 (4x - 4) \, dx$$

$$= \frac{1}{4} \frac{(2x^2 - 4x)^3}{3} + C$$

$$= \frac{1}{12} (2x^2 - 4x)^3 + C$$

EXAMPLE 7   Evaluate $\displaystyle\int \frac{x^2 - 1}{(x^3 - 3x)^3}\, dx$.

Solution   This integral can be treated as $\int u^{-3} u'\, dx$ if we let $u = x^3 - 3x$. Then we can multiply (and divide) by 3 to get $u' = 3(x^2 - 1)$.

$$\int \frac{x^2 - 1}{(x^3 - 3x)^3}\, dx = \int (x^3 - 3x)^{-3} \cdot \frac{1}{3} \cdot 3(x^2 - 1)\, dx$$

$$= \frac{1}{3} \int (x^3 - 3x)^{-3} (3x^2 - 3)\, dx$$

$$= \frac{1}{3} \left[\frac{(x^3 - 3x)^{-2}}{-2} \right] + C$$

$$= \frac{-1}{6(x^3 - 3x)^2} + C$$

Exercise 12.2

Evaluate the following integrals.

1. $\int (x^2 + 3)^3 2x\, dx$

2. $\int (3x^3 + 1)^4 9x^2\, dx$

3. $\int (15x^2 + 10)^4 (30x)\, dx$

4. $\int (8x^4 + 5)^3 (32x^3)\, dx$

5. $\int (3x - x^3)^2 (3 - 3x^2)\, dx$

6. $\int (4x^2 - 3x)^4 (8x - 3)\, dx$

7. $\int (x^2 + 5)^3 x\, dx$

8. $\int (3x^2 - 4)^6 x\, dx$

9. $\int \sqrt{x^4 + 6}\, x^3\, dx$

10. $\int \sqrt{5 - x^2}\, x\, dx$

11. $\int (3 - x^2)^2\, dx$

12. $\int (x^2 - 5)^2\, dx$

13. $\int (4x - 1)^6\, dx$

14. $\int (5 - x)^3\, dx$

15. $\int (x^2 + 1)^3 x\, dx$

16. $\int (x^2 - 3)^3\, dx$

17. $\int (x^2 - 2x)^4 (x - 1)\, dx$

18. $\int \sqrt{x^3 - 3x}\, (x^2 - 1)\, dx$

19. $\int (x + 1) \sqrt[3]{x^2 + 2x}\, dx$

20. $\int (x^4 - x^2)^6 (2x^3 - x)\, dx$

21. $\displaystyle\int \frac{x^2}{(x^3 - 1)^2}\, dx$

22. $\displaystyle\int \frac{x}{(x^2 - 1)^3}\, dx$

23. $\displaystyle\int \frac{x^2}{(x^3 - 5)^4}\, dx$

24. $\displaystyle\int \frac{x^3}{\sqrt[3]{x^4 + 5}}\, dx$

25. $\displaystyle\int \frac{x^2 - 4x}{\sqrt{x^3 - 6x^2}}\, dx$

26. $\displaystyle\int \frac{3x^5 - 2x^3}{(x^6 - x^4)^5}\, dx$

27. $\int \dfrac{8x^2}{(x^3 - 4)^2}\, dx$

28. $\int \dfrac{5x^3}{(x^4 - 8)^3}\, dx$

29. $\int \dfrac{x^3 - 1}{(x^4 - 4x)^3}\, dx$

30. $\int \dfrac{x^2 + 1}{\sqrt{x^3 + 3x}}\, dx$

APPLICATIONS

31. The total physical output of a number of machines or workers is called *physical productivity,* and is a function of the number of machines or workers. If $P = f(x)$ is the productivity, dP/dx is the marginal physical productivity. If the marginal physical productivity for bricklayers is $dP/dx = 90(x + 1)^2$, where P is the number of bricks laid per day, find the physical productivity of 4 bricklayers.

32. Suppose the marginal revenue for a product is given by

$$\overline{\text{MR}} = \dfrac{-30}{(2x + 1)^2} + 30.$$

Find the total revenue.

33. The marginal revenue for a new calculator is given by

$$\overline{\text{MR}} = 60,000 - \dfrac{40,000}{(10 + x)^2},$$

where x represents hundreds of calculators. Find the total revenue function for these calculators.

34. The rate of production of a new line of products is given by

$$\dfrac{dx}{dt} = 200\left[1 + \dfrac{400}{(t + 40)^2}\right],$$

where x is the number of items and t is the number of weeks the product has been in production.

(a) Assuming $x = 0$ when $t = 0$, find the equation that represents the total number of items produced as a function of time t.

(b) How many items were produced in the fifth week?

35. The rate of change in typing speed of the average student is $\dfrac{ds}{dx} = 5(x + 1)^{-1/2}$, where x is the number of typing lessons the student has had.

(a) Find the function that gives typing speed as a function of the number of lessons if the average student can type 10 words per minute with no lessons ($x = 0$).

(b) How many words per minute can the average student type after 24 lessons?

36. Because a new employee must learn his assigned task, his production will increase with time. Suppose that for the average new employee, the rate of performance is given by

$$\dfrac{dN}{dt} = \dfrac{1}{2\sqrt{t + 1}},$$

where N is the number of units completed t hours after beginning a new task. If 2 units are completed after 3 hours, how many units are completed after 8 hours?

37. An excellent film with a very small advertising budget must depend largely on word-of-mouth advertising. In this case, the rate at which weekly attendance might grow can be given by

$$\dfrac{dA}{dt} = \dfrac{-100}{(t + 10)^2} + \dfrac{2000}{(t + 10)^3},$$

where t is the time in weeks since release and A is attendance in millions.

(a) Find the function that describes weekly attendance for this film.

(b) Find the attendance at this film in the 10th week.

38. An inferior product with a large advertising budget does well at the beginning, but sales fall off as people discontinue use of the product. Suppose the rate of monthly sales is given by

$$S'(t) = \frac{400}{(t+1)^3} - \frac{200}{(t+1)^2},$$

where S is sales in millions and t is time in weeks.
(a) Find the function that describes the weekly sales.
(b) Find the sales for the first week and for the 9th week.

39. Because of the decline of the steel industry, a western Pennsylvania town predicts that its public school population will decrease at the rate

$$\frac{dN}{dx} = \frac{-300}{\sqrt{x+9}},$$

where x is the number of years and N is the total school population. If the present population ($x = 0$) is 8000, what size population is planned for in seven years?

40. A new fast-food firm predicts that the number of franchises for its products will grow at the rate

$$\frac{dn}{dt} = 9\sqrt{t+1},$$

where t is the number of years, $0 \le t \le 10$. If they have one franchise ($n = 1$) at present ($t = 0$), how many franchises are predicted for 8 years from now?

12.3 Integrals Involving Logarithmic and Exponential Functions

Objectives ☐ To evaluate integrals of the form $\int \dfrac{u'}{u}\, dx$

☐ To evaluate integrals of the form $\int e^u u'\, dx$

Recall that the Power Rule for integrals applies only if $n \ne -1$. That is,

$$\int u^n u'\, dx = \frac{u^{n+1}}{n+1} + C \qquad \text{if } n \ne -1.$$

The following formula applies when $n = -1$.

$$\int u^{-1} u'\, dx = \int \frac{u'}{u}\, dx = \int \frac{du}{u} = \ln |u| + C$$

This formula is a direct result of the fact that

$$\frac{d}{dx}(\ln u) = \frac{1}{u} \cdot u'.$$

The absolute value is used with the natural logarithm because u may be positive or negative, but the logarithm is defined only when the quantity is positive.

EXAMPLE 1   Evaluate $\displaystyle\int \frac{4}{4x + 1}\, dx.$

Solution   This integral is of the form

$$\int \frac{u'}{u}\, dx, = \ln |u| + C$$

with $u = 4x + 1$ and $u' = 4$. Thus

$$\int \frac{4}{4x + 1}\, dx = \ln |4x + 1| + C.$$

EXAMPLE 2   Evaluate $\displaystyle\int \frac{x - 3}{x^2 - 6x + 1}\, dx.$

Solution   This integral is of the form $\int (u'/u)\, dx$, *almost.* If we let $u = x^2 - 6x + 1$, then $u' = 2x - 6$. If we multiply (and divide) the numerator by 2, we get

$$\int \frac{x - 3}{x^2 - 6x + 1}\, dx = \frac{1}{2} \int \frac{2(x - 3)}{x^2 - 6x + 1}\, dx$$

$$= \frac{1}{2} \int \frac{2x - 6}{x^2 - 6x + 1}\, dx$$

$$= \frac{1}{2} \ln |x^2 - 6x + 1| + C.$$

If an integral contains a fraction in which the degree of the numerator is equal to or greater than that of the denominator, we should divide the denominator into the numerator as a first step.

EXAMPLE 3   Evaluate $\displaystyle\int \frac{x^4 - 2x^3 + 4x^2 - 7x - 1}{x^2 - 2x}\, dx.$

Solution   Since the numerator is of higher degree than the denominator, we begin by dividing $x^2 - 2x$ into the numerator, which gives the integral in the form

$$\int \left(x^2 + 4 + \frac{x - 1}{x^2 - 2x} \right) dx$$

Integrating gives

$$\frac{x^3}{3} + 4x + \frac{1}{2} \ln |x^2 - 2x| + C.$$

We know that

$$\frac{d}{dx}(e^u) = e^u \cdot u'.$$

The corresponding integral is given by the following.

> If u is a function of x, then $\int e^u \cdot u' \, dx = e^u + C$.

EXAMPLE 4   Evaluate $\int 2xe^{x^2} \, dx$.

Solution   This is of the form $\int e^u \cdot u' \, dx$. Letting $u = x^2$ implies $u' = 2x$. Thus

$$\int 2xe^{x^2} \, dx = \int e^{x^2}(2x) \, dx$$
$$= e^{x^2} + C.$$

EXAMPLE 5   Evaluate $\int x^2 e^{x^3} \, dx$.

Solution   This is *almost* of the form $\int e^u \cdot u' \, dx$. Letting $u = x^3$ implies $u' = 3x^2$. Thus

$$\int x^2 e^{x^3} \, dx = \frac{1}{3} \int e^{x^3}(3x^2) \, dx = \frac{1}{3} e^{x^3} + C.$$

We can also integrate functions of variables other than x. For example,

$$\int 2e^{2y} \, dy = e^{2y} + C.$$

EXAMPLE 6   Evaluate $\displaystyle\int \frac{z}{z^2 + 1} \, dz$.

Solution   This integral is almost of the form $\displaystyle\int \frac{du}{u}$. Letting $u = z^2 + 1$, we see that du must be $2z \, dz$. So

$$\int \frac{z}{z^2 + 1} \, dz = \frac{1}{2} \int \frac{2z}{z^2 + 1} \, dz = \frac{1}{2} \ln |z^2 + 1| + C.$$

Exercise 12.3

Evaluate the following integrals.

1. $\displaystyle\int \frac{3x^2}{x^3 + 4} \, dx$

2. $\displaystyle\int \frac{8x^7}{x^8 - 1} \, dx$

3. $\displaystyle\int \frac{3x^2 - 2}{x^3 - 2x} \, dx$

4. $\displaystyle\int \frac{4x^3 + 2x}{x^4 + x^2} \, dx$

5. $\int \dfrac{x^3}{x^4 + 1}\, dx$

6. $\int \dfrac{x^2}{x^3 - 9}\, dx$

7. $\int \dfrac{4x}{x^2 - 4}\, dx$

8. $\int \dfrac{5x^2}{x^3 - 1}\, dx$

9. $\int \dfrac{dz}{4z + 1}$

10. $\int \dfrac{y}{y^2 + 1}\, dy$

11. $\int \dfrac{z^2 + 1}{z^3 + 3z}\, dz$

12. $\int \dfrac{x + 2}{x^2 + 4x}\, dx$

13. $\int \dfrac{x^3 - x^2 + 1}{x - 1}\, dx$

14. $\int \dfrac{2x^3 + x^2 + 2x + 3}{2x + 1}\, dx$

15. $\int \dfrac{x^2 + x + 3}{x^2 + 3}\, dx$

16. $\int \dfrac{x^4 - 2x^2 + x}{x^2 - 2}\, dx$

17. $\int 3e^{3x}\, dx$

18. $\int 4e^{4x}\, dx$

19. $\int e^{-x}\, dx$

20. $\int e^{2x}\, dx$

21. $\int x^3 e^{3x^4}\, dx$

22. $\int xe^{2x^2}\, dx$

23. $\int x^3 e^{x^4}\, dx$

24. $\int (e^x + e^{-x})\, dx$

25. $\int ye^{y^2}\, dy$

26. $\int 6e^{3y}\, dy$

27. $\int 3e^{5x}\, dx$

28. $\int 2e^{x/2}\, dx$

APPLICATIONS

29. Suppose the marginal revenue from the sale of a product is $\overline{MR} = R'(x) = 6e^{0.01x}$. What is the revenue on the sale of 100 units of the product?

30. Suppose the rate at which the concentration of a drug in the blood changes with respect to time t is given by

$$C'(t) = \frac{c}{b - a}(be^{-bt} - ae^{-at}), \qquad t \geq 0,$$

where a, b, and c are constants depending on the drug administered, with $b > a$. Assuming $C(t) = 0$ when $t = 0$, find the formula for the concentration of the drug in the blood at any time t.

31. The rate of disintegration of a radioactive substance can be described by

$$\frac{dn}{dt} = n_0(-K)e^{-Kt},$$

where n_0 is the number of radioactive atoms present when time t is 0, and K is a positive constant that depends on the substance involved. Using the fact that the constant of integration is 0, integrate dn/dt to find the number of atoms n that are still radioactive after time t.

32. Since the world contains only about 10 billion acres of arable land, world population is limited. Suppose the world population is limited to 40 billion people and that the rate of population growth is proportional to how close the world is to this upper limit. Then the rate of growth would be $dP/dt = K(40 - P)$, where K is a positive constant. This means

$$t = \frac{1}{K}\int \frac{1}{40 - P}\, dP.$$

(a) Evaluate this integral to find an expression relating P and t.

(b) Use the properties relating logarithms and exponential functions to write P as a function of t.

33. The rate of vocabulary memorization of the average student in a foreign language is given by

$$\frac{dv}{dt} = \frac{40}{t + 1},$$

where t is the number of continuous hours of study, $0 < t \le 4$. How many words would the average student memorize in 3 hours?

34. The rate of growth of world population can be modeled by

$$\frac{dn}{dt} = \frac{N_0(1 + r)^t}{\log_{(1+r)}e}, r < 1,$$

where t is the time in years from the present and N_0 and r are constants. What function describes world population if the present population is N_0?

35. If \$$P$ are invested for n years at 10%, compounded continuously, the rate at which the compound amount is growing is

$$\frac{dS}{dn} = 0.1Pe^{0.1n}.$$

(a) What function describes the compound amount at the end of n years?

(b) In how many years will the compound amount double?

36. When an object is moved from one environment to another, its temperature T changes at a rate given by

$$\frac{dT}{dt} = kCe^{kt},$$

where t is the time in the new environment (in hours), C is the temperature difference (old − new) between the two environments, and k is a constant. If the temperature of the body (and the old environment) is 70°F, and $C = -10$°F, what function describes the temperature T of the object t hours after it is moved?

37. The rate at which blood pressure decreases in the aorta of normal adults after a heartbeat is

$$\frac{dp}{dt} = -46.645e^{-0.491t},$$

where t is time in seconds.

(a) What function describes the blood pressure in the aorta?

(b) What is the blood pressure 0.1 seconds after a heartbeat?

38. A store finds that its sales decline after the end of an advertising campaign, with its total sales for the period declining at the rate $S'(t) = -147.78e^{-0.2t}$, $0 < t \le 100$, where t is the number of days since the end of the campaign. Suppose $S = 7389$ when $t = 0$.

(a) Find the function that describes the total number of sales t days after the end of the campaign.

(b) Find the total number of sales 10 days after the end of the advertising campaign.

12.4 Applications of the Indefinite Integral in Business and Economics

Objectives □ To use integration to find total cost functions from information involving marginal cost
□ To optimize profit, given information regarding marginal cost and marginal revenue
□ To use integration to find national consumption functions from information about marginal propensity to consume and marginal propensity to save

We again turn our attention to applications involving cost, profit, and consumption. We have been continually returning to these and other basic applications because a thorough understanding of these concepts is imperative for success in any study of economics and business.

Total Cost and Profit

We can use integration to derive total cost and profit functions from the marginal cost and marginal revenue functions. One of the reasons for the marginal approach in economics is that firms can observe marginal changes in real life. If they know the marginal cost and the total cost when a given quantity is sold, they can develop their total cost function.

We know that the marginal cost for a commodity is $\overline{MC} = C'(x)$, where $C(x)$ is the total cost function. Thus if we have the marginal cost function, we can integrate to find the total cost. That is, $C(x) = \int \overline{MC}\, dx$.

If, for example, the marginal cost is $\overline{MC} = 4x + 3$, the total cost is given by

$$C(x) = \int \overline{MC}\, dx$$
$$= \int (4x + 3)\, dx$$
$$= 2x^2 + 3x + K,$$

where K represents the constant of integration. Now, we know that the total revenue is 0 if no items are produced, but the total cost may not be 0 if nothing is produced. The fixed costs accrue whether goods are produced or not. Thus, in this case, the constant of integration that results corresponds to the fixed costs FC of production.

Thus we cannot determine the total cost function from the marginal cost unless additional information is available to help us determine the fixed costs.

EXAMPLE 1   If the marginal cost function for a month for a certain product is $\overline{MC} = 3x + 50$, and if the fixed costs related to the product amount to $100 per month, find the total cost function for the month.

Solution   The total cost function is

$$C(x) = \int (3x + 50)\, dx$$
$$= \frac{3x^2}{2} + 50x + K.$$

But the constant of integration K is found by using the fact that $C(0) = FC = 100$. Thus

$$3(0)^2 + 50(0) + K = 100, \text{ so } K = 100.$$

Thus, the total cost for the month is given by

$$C(x) = \frac{3x^2}{2} + 50x + 100.$$

EXAMPLE 2   If the monthly records show that the rate of change of the cost (that is, the marginal cost) for a product is $\overline{MC} = 10x + 40$, and that the total cost of producing 100 items in the month is $60,000$, what would be the total cost of producing 400 items per month?

Solution   We can integrate the marginal cost to find the total cost function.

$$C(x) = \int \overline{MC}\, dx = \int (10x + 40)\, dx$$
$$= 5x^2 + 40x + K$$

We can find K by using the fact that the cost for 100 items is $60,000$.

$$C(100) = 60,000 = 5(100)^2 + 40(100) + K,$$

so

$$K = 6000$$

Thus the total cost function is $C(x) = 5x^2 + 40x + 6000$, and the cost of producing 400 items is

$$C(400) = 800,000 + 16,000 + 6000$$
$$= 822,000 \quad \text{(dollars)}.$$

We stated in an earlier chapter that the profit is usually maximized when $\overline{MR} = \overline{MC}$. To see that this does not always give us a maximum *positive* profit, consider the following facts concerning the manufacture of widgets over the period of a month:
(a) The marginal revenue is $\overline{MR} = 400 - 30x$.
(b) The marginal cost is $\overline{MC} = 20x + 50$.
(c) When 5 widgets are produced and sold, the total cost is 1750. The profit *should* be maximized when $\overline{MR} = \overline{MC}$, or when $400 - 30x = 20x + 50$. Solving for x gives $x = 7$. To see if our profit is maximized when 7 units are produced and sold, let us examine the profit function.

The profit function is given by $P(x) = R(x) - C(x)$, where

$$R(x) = \int \overline{MR} \, dx \quad \text{and} \quad C(x) = \int \overline{MC} \, dx.$$

Integrating, we get

$$R(x) = \int (400 - 30x) \, dx = 400x - 15x^2 + K,$$

but $K = 0$ for this total revenue function, so

$$R(x) = 400x - 15x^2.$$

The total cost function is

$$C(x) = \int (20x + 50) \, dx = 10x^2 + 50x + K.$$

The value of fixed cost can be determined by using the fact that 5 widgets cost $1750. This tells us $C(5) = 1750 = 250 + 250 + K$, so $K = 1250$. Thus the total cost is $C(x) = 10x^2 + 50x + 1250$. Now, the profit is

$$P(x) = R(x) - C(x),$$

or

$$P(x) = (400x - 15x^2) - (10x^2 + 50x + 1250).$$

Simplifying gives

$$P(x) = 350x - 25x^2 - 1250.$$

We have found that $\overline{MR} = \overline{MC}$ if $x = 7$. But if $x = 7$, profit is

$$P(7) = 2450 - 1225 - 1250 = -25.$$

That is, the production and sale of 7 items results in a loss of $25.

The discussion above indicates that, although setting $\overline{MR} = \overline{MC}$ may optimize profit, it does not indicate the level of profit or loss, as forming the profit function does.

If the widget firm is in a competitive market, and its optimal level of production results in a loss, it has two options. It can continue to produce at the optimal level in the short run until it can lower or eliminate its fixed costs, even though it is losing money; or it can take a larger loss (its fixed cost) by stopping production. Producing 7 units causes a loss of $25 per month, and ceasing production results in a loss of $1250 (the fixed cost) per month. If this firm and many others like it cease production, the supply will be reduced, causing an eventual increase in price. The firm can resume production when the price increase indicates it can make a profit.

EXAMPLE 3   Given that $\overline{MR} = 200 - 4x$, $\overline{MC} = 50 + 2x$, and the total cost of producing 10 Wagbats is $700, at what level should the Wagbat firm hold production in order to maximize the profits?

Solution   Setting $\overline{MR} = \overline{MC}$, we can solve for the production level that maximizes profit.

$$200 - 4x = 50 + 2x$$
$$150 = 6x$$
$$25 = x$$

The level of production that should optimize profit is 25 units. To see whether 25 units maximizes profits or minimizes the losses (in the short run), we must find the total revenue and total cost functions.

$$R(x) = \int (200 - 4x)\, dx = 200x - 2x^2 + K$$
$$= 200x - 2x^2, \quad \text{since } K = 0$$

$$C(x) = \int (50 + 2x)\, dx = 50x + x^2 + K$$

We find K by noting $C(x) = 700$ when $x = 10$.

$$700 = 50(10) + (10)^2 + K,$$

so $K = 100$.

Thus, the cost is given by

$$C = C(x) = 50x + x^2 + 100.$$

At $x = 25$,

$$R = R(25) = 200(25) - 2(25)^2 = \$3750$$

and

$$C = C(25) = 50(25) + (25)^2 + 100 = \$1975.$$

We see that the total revenue is greater than the total cost, so production should be held at 25 units, which results in a maximum profit.

National Consumption and Savings

In Chapter 1 we discussed the **national consumption function,** $C = f(y)$, where y is the disposable national income. The **marginal propensity to consume** is the derivative of the consumption function with respect to y, $dC/dy = f'(y)$.

If we know the marginal propensity to consume, we can integrate with respect to y to find

$$C = \int f'(y)\, dy = f(y) + K.$$

We can find the unique national consumption function if we have additional information to help us determine the value of K, the constant of integration.

EXAMPLE 4   If consumption is $6 billion when disposable income is 0, and if the marginal propensity to consume is $dC/dy = 0.3 + 0.4/\sqrt{y}$ (in billions of dollars), then find the national consumption function.

Solution   If

$$\frac{dC}{dy} = 0.3 + \frac{0.4}{\sqrt{y}},$$

then

$$C = \int \left(0.3 + \frac{0.4}{\sqrt{y}} \right) dy = 0.3y + 0.8y^{1/2} + K.$$

Now, if $C = 6$ when $y = 0$, then $6 = 0.3(0) + 0.8\sqrt{0} + K$. Thus the constant of integration is $K = 6$, and the consumption function is

$$C = 0.3y + 0.8\sqrt{y} + 6 \qquad \text{(billions of dollars)}.$$

If S represents national savings, we can assume the disposable national income is given by $y = C + S$, or $S = y - C$. Then the **marginal propensity to save** is $dS/dy = 1 - dC/dy$.

EXAMPLE 5   If the consumption is $9 billion when income is 0, and if the marginal propensity to save is 0.25, find the consumption function.

Solution   If $dS/dy = 0.25$, then $0.25 = 1 - dC/dy$, or $dC/dy = 0.75$ Thus,

$$C = \int 0.75 \, dy = 0.75y + K.$$

If $C = 9$ when $y = 0$, then $9 = 0.75(0) + K$, or $K = 9$. Then the consumption function is $C = 0.75y + 9$ (billions of dollars).

Exercise 12.4

TOTAL COST AND PROFIT

1. If the monthly marginal cost for a product is $\overline{MC} = 2x + 100$, with fixed costs amounting to $200, find the total cost function for the month.
2. If the monthly marginal cost for a product is $\overline{MC} = x + 30$, and the related fixed costs are $50, find the total cost function for the month.
3. If the marginal cost for a product is $\overline{MC} = 4x + 2$, and the production of 10 units results in a total cost of $300, find the total cost function.
4. If the marginal cost for a product is $\overline{MC} = 3x + 50$, and the total cost of producing 20 units is $2000, what will be the total cost function?
5. If the marginal cost for a product is $\overline{MC} = 4x + 40$, and the total cost of producing 25 units is $3000, what will be the cost of producing 30 units?

6. If the marginal cost for producing a product is $\overline{MC} = 5x + 10$, with a fixed cost of $800, what will be the cost of producing 20 units?

7. A firm knows that its marginal cost for a product is $\overline{MC} = 3x + 20$, that its marginal revenue is $\overline{MR} = 44 - 5x$, and that the cost of production and sale of 80 units is $11,400. Given this information, find
   (a) the optimal level of production.
   (b) the profit function.
   (c) the profit or loss at the optimal level.

8. A certain firm's marginal cost for a product is $\overline{MC} = 6x + 60$, its marginal revenue is $\overline{MR} = 180 - 2x$, and its total cost of production of 10 items is $1000. Given this information,
   (a) find the optimal level of production.
   (b) find the profit function.
   (c) find the profit or loss at the optimal level of production.
   (d) should production be continued for the short run?
   (e) should production be continued for the long run?

9. Suppose the marginal revenue for a product is $\overline{MR} = 900$ and the marginal cost is $\overline{MC} = 30\sqrt{x} + 4$, with a fixed cost of $1,000.
   (a) Find the profit or loss from the production and sale of 5 units.
   (b) How many units will result in a maximum profit?

10. Suppose the marginal cost for a product is $\overline{MC} = 60\sqrt{x} + 1$ and its fixed cost is $340.00. If the marginal revenue for it is $\overline{MR} = 80x$, find the profit or loss from production and sale of the following number of units.
    (a) 3
    (b) 8

11. If the average cost of a product changes at the rate

$$\overline{C}'(x) = -6x^{-2} + 1/6,$$

and if the average cost of 10 units is $20.00, find
   (a) What is the average cost function?
   (b) What is the average cost of 20 units?

12. If the average cost of a product changes at the rate

$$\overline{C}'(x) = \frac{-10}{x^2} + \frac{1}{10},$$

and if the average cost of 10 units is $20.00, find
   (a) the average cost function.
   (b) the average cost of 20 units.

NATIONAL CONSUMPTION AND SAVINGS

13. If consumption is $5 billion when disposable income is 0, and if the marginal propensity to consume is

$$\frac{dC}{dy} = 0.4 + \frac{0.3}{\sqrt{y}} \quad \text{(in billion of dollars),}$$

then find the national consumption function.

14. If consumption is $7 billion when disposable income is 0, and if the marginal propensity to consume is 0.80, find the national consumption function (in billions of dollars).

15. If consumption is $8 billion when income is 0, and if the marginal propensity to consume is

$$\frac{dC}{dy} = 0.3 + \frac{0.2}{\sqrt{y}} \qquad \text{(in billions of dollars),}$$

find the national consumption function.

16. If national consumption is $9 billion when income is 0, and if the marginal propensity to consume is 0.30, what is consumption when disposable income is $20 billion?

17. If consumption is $6 billion when disposable income is 0, and if the marginal propensity to consume is

$$\frac{dC}{dy} = \frac{1}{\sqrt{y+1}} + 0.4 \qquad \text{(in billions of dollars),}$$

find the national consumption function.

18. If consumption is $5.8 billion when disposable income is 0, and if the marginal propensity to consume is

$$\frac{dC}{dy} = \frac{1}{\sqrt{2y+9}} + 0.8 \qquad \text{(in billions of dollars),}$$

find the national consumption function.

19. Suppose the marginal propensity to consume is

$$\frac{dC}{dy} = 0.7 - e^{-2y} \qquad \text{(in billions of dollars),}$$

and that consumption is $5.65 billion when disposable income is 0. Find the national consumption function.

20. Suppose the marginal propensity to consume is

$$\frac{dC}{dy} = 0.04 + \frac{\ln(y+1)}{y+1} \qquad \text{(in billions of dollars),}$$

and that consumption is $6.04 billion when disposable income is 0. Find the national consumption function.

21. Suppose the marginal propensity to save is

$$\frac{dS}{dy} = 0.15 \qquad \text{(in billions of dollars)}$$

and consumption is $5.15 billion when disposable income is 0. Find the national consumption function.

22. Suppose the marginal propensity to save is

$$\frac{dS}{dy} = 0.22 \qquad \text{(in billions of dollars)}$$

and consumption is $8.6 billion when disposable income is 0. Find the national consumption function.

23. Suppose the marginal propensity to save is

$$\frac{dS}{dy} = 0.2 - \frac{1}{\sqrt{3y+7}} \qquad \text{(in billions of dollars)}$$

and consumption is $6 billion when disposable income is 0. Find the national consumption function.

24. If consumption is $3 billion when disposable income is 0, and if the marginal propensity to save is

$$\frac{dS}{dy} = 0.2 + e^{-1.5y} \qquad \text{(in billions of dollars),}$$

find the national consumption function.

12.5 Differential Equations

Objectives   ☐   To find the general solutions of separable differential equations
☐   To find particular solutions of separable differential equations

Recall that we introduced the derivative as an instantaneous rate of change and denoted the instantaneous rate of change of y with respect to time as dy/dt. For many growth processes, the rate of change of the amount of a substance with respect to time is proportional to the amount present. This can be represented by the equation

$$\frac{dy}{dt} = ky \qquad (k = \text{constant}).$$

An equation of this type is called a **differential equation** because it contains derivatives (or differentials). Other examples of differential equations are

(a) $f'(x) = \dfrac{1}{x + 1}$,   (b) $\dfrac{dy}{dt} = 2t$,   and   (c) $x \, dy = (y + 1) \, dx$.

The solution to a differential equation is a function that satisfies the original differential equation. As we saw in Section 12.1, a function satisfying (a) above is an antiderivative of $f'(x)$, and a solution to (b) is the function $y = t^2$ because if $y = t^2$, then $dy/dt = 2t$. Other functions, such as $y = t^2 + 4$ and $y = t^2 - 3$ are also solutions to $dy/dt = 2t$. We can find the **general solution** by integrating both sides of $dy/dt = 2t$.

$$\int \frac{dy}{dt} \, dt = \int 2t \, dt$$

$$y = t^2 + C$$

Thus $y = t^2 + C$ is the general solution to the differential equation $dy/dt = 2t$. If a specific value of C is found, then the resulting solution is called a **particular solution.**

Any equation that contains a first derivative (such as dy/dx or dy/dt) and no higher derivative is called a **first-order** differential equation.

Not every differential equation can be solved as easily as $dy/dt = 2t$. For example, the equation

$$\frac{dy}{dt} = ky$$

cannot be solved by simply integrating both sides of the equation with respect to t. We cannot evaluate $\int ky\, dt$ unless we can express y as a function of t, but $y = f(t)$ is the solution we seek.

However, we can rewrite $dy/dt = ky$ so that all terms containing y are on one side of the equation and all terms containing t are on the other side. That is,

$$\frac{dy}{y} = k\, dt.$$

In general, when a differential equation can be rewritten in the form

$$A(y)\, dy = B(t)\, dt \qquad \text{or} \qquad g(y)\, dy = f(x)\, dx,$$

we say the equation is **separable.** The solution of a separable differential equation is obtained by integrating both sides of the equation after the variables have been separated.

Thus to solve the equation

$$\frac{dy}{dt} = ky,$$

we write it in separated form as

$$\frac{dy}{y} = k\, dt$$

and integrate both sides as follows:

$$\int \frac{dy}{y} = \int k\, dt$$

$$\ln |y| + C_1 = kt + C_2.$$

Combining C_1 and C_2 gives

$$\ln |y| = kt + C_3.$$

Assuming $y > 0$ and writing this equation in exponential form gives

$$y = e^{kt + C_3}$$
$$y = e^{kt} \cdot e^{C_3} = Ce^{kt}, \qquad \text{where } C = e^{C_3}.$$

This solution

$$y = Ce^{kt}$$

is the general solution of the differential equation $dy/dt = ky$ because all solutions have this form, with different values of C giving different particular solutions.

EXAMPLE 1   Solve the equation

$$\frac{dy}{dx} = x^2 y.$$

Solution　The equation can be solved by considering dy/dx as a quotient of differentials and separating variables. Multiplying both sides of this equation by dx/y, we can rewrite the equation as

$$\frac{dy}{y} = x^2\, dx.$$

Integrating both sides gives

$$\ln|y| + C_1 = \frac{x^3}{3} + C_2$$

or

$$\ln|y| = \frac{x^3}{3} + C, \text{ where } C = C_2 - C_1.$$

Writing the equation in exponential form gives

$$e^{x^3/3 + C} = |y|.$$

So　　　　　$y = e^{x^3/3} \cdot e^C = Ae^{x^3/3}$, using $y > 0$ and $A = e^C$.

We can verify that $y = Ae^{x^3/3}$ is a solution of $dy/dx = x^2 y$ on any interval where y is defined.

$$y = Ae^{x^3/3} \Rightarrow \frac{dy}{dx} = Ae^{x^3/3}(x^2)$$

Replacing y by $Ae^{x^3/3}$ and dy/dx by $Ax^2 e^{x^3/3}$ gives

$$Ax^2 e^{x^3/3} = x^2(Ae^{x^3/3}).$$

EXAMPLE 2　A liquid carries a drug into an organ of volume 300 cc at a rate of 5 cc/sec, and the liquid leaves the organ at the same rate. If the concentration of the drug in the entering liquid is 0.1 g/cc, and if x represents the amount of drug in the organ at any time t, then using the fact that the rate of change of the amount of the drug in the organ, dx/dt, equals the rate at which the drug enters minus the rate at which it leaves, we have

$$\frac{dx}{dt} = \left(\frac{5\text{ cc}}{\text{sec}}\right)\left(\frac{0.1\text{ g}}{\text{cc}}\right) - \left(\frac{5\text{ cc}}{\text{sec}}\right)\left(\frac{x\text{ g}}{300\text{ cc}}\right)$$

or

$$\frac{dx}{dt} = 0.5 - \frac{x}{60} = \frac{30}{60} - \frac{x}{60} = \frac{30 - x}{60}.$$

Find the amount of the drug in the organ as a function of time t.

Solution　Multiplying both sides of the equation $\dfrac{dx}{dt} = \dfrac{30 - x}{60}$ by $\dfrac{dt}{(30 - x)}$ gives

$$\frac{dx}{30 - x} = \frac{1}{60}\, dt.$$

The equation is now separated, so we can integrate both sides.

$$\int \frac{dx}{30 - x} = \int \frac{1}{60} \, dt$$

$$-\ln (30 - x) = \frac{1}{60} t + C_1 \qquad (30 - x > 0)$$

$$\ln (30 - x) = -\frac{1}{60} t - C_1$$

Rewriting this in exponential form gives

$$30 - x = e^{-t/60 - C_1} = e^{-t/60} \cdot e^{-C_1}.$$

Letting $C = e^{-C_1}$ we have

$$30 - x = Ce^{-t/60}$$

so

$$x = 30 - Ce^{-t/60},$$

and we have the desired function.

For many equations, conditions are present that allow us to determine a value of C and hence a particular solution. For example, suppose that in Example 2 we knew that at $t = 0$ there was none of the drug present in the organ; that is, when $t = 0, x = 0$. Substituting these values into the general solution gives

$$x = 30 - Ce^{-t/60}$$
$$0 = 30 - C(e^0)$$
$$C = 30.$$

Replacing C by 30 in the general solution gives the particular solution

$$x = 30 - 30e^{-t/60}.$$

This solution describes the amount of drug in the organ as a function of t, if the **initial condition** $x = 0$ when $t = 0$ is true.

In many applied problems that can be modeled using differential equations, we have access to conditions that allow us to obtain a particular solution.

EXAMPLE 3 Carbon 14 dating, used to determine the age of fossils, is based on three facts. First, the amount of carbon 14 in any living organism is essentially constant (suppose that amount is 100 units). Second, when an organism dies, the rate of change of carbon 14 in the organism is proportional to the amount present; that is, if y is the amount present, then

$$\frac{dy}{dt} = ky \qquad (t \text{ in years}).$$

Third, the half-life of carbon 14 is 5600 years.

Suppose anthropologists discover a fossil that contains 1 unit of carbon 14. Find the age of the fossil.

Solution   We must find a particular solution to

$$\frac{dy}{dt} = ky$$

subject to the fact that when $t = 0$, $y = 100$, and we must determine the value of k based on the half-life of carbon 14 (i.e., $t = 5600$, $y = 50$). From our previous discussion in this section, the general solution to the differential equation $dy/dt = ky$ is $y = Ce^{kt}$. Using the initial condition $y = 100$ when $t = 0$, we have

$$100 = Ce^{k(0)} \Rightarrow 100 = C,$$

so the equation becomes

$$y = 100e^{kt}.$$

Now, using $y = 50$ when $t = 5600$ in this equation gives

$$50 = 100e^{5600k}$$

or

$$0.5 = e^{5600k}.$$

Rewriting this equation in logarithmic form gives

$$\ln (0.5) = 5600k$$
$$-0.69315 = 5600k$$
$$-0.00012378 = k.$$

Thus the equation we seek is

$$y = 100e^{-0.00012378t}.$$

Using the fact that $y = 1$ when the fossil was discovered, we can find its age, t, by solving

$$1 = 100e^{-0.00012378t}$$

or

$$0.01 = e^{-0.00012378t}.$$

Rewriting this in logarithmic form gives

$$\ln (0.01) = -0.00012378t$$
$$-4.6051702 = -0.00012378t$$
$$37,204 = t.$$

Thus, the fossil is approximately 37,200 years old.

———————

If p is the price of a given commodity at time t, then we can think of price as a function of time. Similarly, the number of units demanded by consumers, q_d, at any time, and the number of units supplied by producers, q_s, at any time, may also be considered as functions of time.

Both the quantity demanded and the quantity supplied depend not only on the price at the time, but on the direction and rate of change that consumers and producers feel that prices may be moving. For example, even when prices are high, if consumers feel that prices are rising, the demand may rise. Similarly, if prices are low but producers feel they may go lower, the supply may rise.

If we assume that prices are determined in the marketplace by supply and demand, then the equilibrium price is the one we seek. Equating the number of units supplied with the number demanded gives rise to a first-order differential equation, as the following example shows.

EXAMPLE 4   Suppose the supply and demand functions for a certain commodity are given in hundreds of units by

$$q_s = 30 + p + 5\frac{dp}{dt}$$

$$q_d = 51 - 2p + 4\frac{dp}{dt},$$

where dp/dt denotes the rate of change of the price with respect to time. If, at $t = 0$, the price is 12, express price as a function of time.

Solution   Setting $q_s = q_d$ gives

$$30 + p + 5\frac{dp}{dt} = 51 - 2p + 4\frac{dp}{dt}$$

$$\frac{dp}{dt} = 21 - 3p = 3(7 - p).$$

Separating the variables and solving gives

$$\frac{dp}{7 - p} = 3\,dt$$
$$-\ln(7 - p) = 3t + C_1$$
$$\ln(7 - p) = -3t - C_1$$
$$7 - p = e^{-3t - C_1} = Ce^{-3t}$$
$$7 - Ce^{-3t} = p.$$

Now, using $t = 0$ and $p = 12$ gives $7 - C = 12$, or $C = -5$, so $p = 7 + 5e^{-3t}$ gives the price as a function of time.

Notice in Example 4 that $\lim\limits_{t \to \infty} p = 7$. This means that in this marketplace there is price stability for this item, and we can expect the price of this commodity to approach 7. If $\lim\limits_{t \to \infty} p = \infty$, then prices are increasing as time passes, and we have price instability (inflation) until the equations modeling supply and demand are altered by economic factors.

Exercise 12.5

In problems 1–16, find the general solution to the given differential equation.

1. $\dfrac{dy}{dx} = x^3$

2. $\dfrac{dy}{dx} = 12$

3. $x^2\,dx = y\,dy$

4. $x^3\,dx = \dfrac{dy}{y^3}$

5. $\dfrac{dx}{x^3} = y\,dy$

6. $\dfrac{dy}{y^3} = x^2\,dx$

7. $\dfrac{dx}{x^2} = (y^2 + 1)\,dy$

8. $\dfrac{dy}{y^3} = (x^2 + x)\,dx$

9. $\dfrac{dx}{x} = \dfrac{dy}{y^2}$

10. $\dfrac{dx}{x} = \dfrac{dy}{y}$

11. $\dfrac{dy}{dx} = \dfrac{x}{y}$

12. $\dfrac{dy}{dx} = \dfrac{x^2 + x}{y + 1}$

13. $(x + 1)\dfrac{dy}{dx} = y$

14. $x^2 y\dfrac{dy}{dx} = y^2 + 1$

15. $e^{2x}y\,dy = (y + 1)\,dx$

16. $e^{4x}(y + 1)\,dx + e^{2x}y\,dy = 0$

In problems 17–24, find the particular solution to each differential equation.

17. $\dfrac{dy}{dx} = \dfrac{x^2}{y^3}$, when $x = 1$, $y = 1$

18. $\dfrac{dy}{dx} = \dfrac{x + 1}{xy}$, when $x = 1$, $y = 3$

19. $2y^2\,dx = 3x^2\,dy$, when $x = 2$, $y = -1$

20. $(x + 1)\,dy = y^2\,dx$, when $x = 0$, $y = 2$

21. $x^2 e^{2y}\,dy = (x^3 + 1)\,dx$, when $x = 1$, $y = 0$

22. $y' = \dfrac{1}{xy}$, when $x = 1$, $y = 3$

23. $2xy\dfrac{dy}{dx} = y^2 + 1$, when $x = 1$, $y = 2$

24. $xe^y\,dx = (x + 1)\,dy$, when $x = 0$, $y = 0$

APPLICATIONS

25. If x and y are measurements of parts of an organism, then the rate of change in y with respect to x is proportional to the ratio of y to x. That is, these measurements satisfy

$$\dfrac{dy}{dx} = k\dfrac{y}{x},$$

which is referred to as an allometric law of growth. Solve this differential equation.

26. Suppose the chemical conversion of a substance satisfies

$$\frac{dx}{dt} = \frac{x^3}{10},$$

where x is the amount of unconverted substance. If 100 g of this substance are present initially, find x as a function of t.

27. A bimolecular chemical reaction is one where two molecules react to give another substance. Suppose that two molecules of a certain substance containing A molecules initially react to form two molecules of a new substance. If x represents the number of molecules of the new substance, then the rate of change of x is proportional to the square of the number of molecules of the original substance available to be converted. That is,

$$\frac{dx}{dt} = k(A - x)^2.$$

If 40% of the initial amount is converted after 1 hour, how long before 90% is converted?

28. When glucose is infused into the bloodstream, the concentration C of the glucose satisfies

$$\frac{dC}{dt} = a - bC$$

where a and b are constants. Find a formula for C as a function of time. Find $\lim_{t \to \infty} C(t)$.

29. Suppose for a certain commodity the supply and demand functions are given by

$$q_d = 60 - p - 3\frac{dp}{dt}$$

$$q_s = 100 + p - 4\frac{dp}{dt},$$

where p is the price. If at $t = 0$, $p = 8$ units, find price as a function of time.

30. Suppose for a certain product, the demand function is

$$q_d = 50 - 2p - 3\frac{dp}{dt}$$

and the supply function is

$$q_s = 40 + 2p + \frac{dp}{dt}.$$

If at $t = 0$, $p = 15$ units, find the price as a function of time.

31. Suppose a liquid carries a drug into a 100 cc organ at a rate of 5 cc/sec and leaves at the same rate. Suppose the concentration of the drug entering is 0.06 g/cc. If initially there is no drug in the organ, find the amount of drug in the organ as a function of time.

32. Suppose a liquid carries a drug into a 250 cc organ at a rate of 10 cc/sec and leaves the organ at 8 cc/sec. Suppose the concentration of the drug is 0.15 g/cc. Find the amount of drug in the organ as a function of time if initially there is none in the organ.

33. Suppose the growth of a certain bacteria satisfies

$$\frac{dy}{dt} = ky,$$

where y is the number of organisms and t is the number of hours. If initially there are 10,000 organisms and the number triples every 2 hours, how long before there is 100 times the original population?

34. Suppose for a certain bacteria, growth occurs according to

$$\frac{dy}{dt} = ky \qquad (t \text{ in hours}).$$

If the doubling rate depends on temperature, find how long it takes for the number of bacteria to reach 50 times the original number at each given temperature in (a) and (b).

(a) At 90°, the number doubles every 30 min. $\left(\frac{1}{2} \text{ hour}\right)$.

(b) At 40°, the number doubles every 3 hours.

35. A breeder reactor converts uranium-238 into an isotope of plutonium-239. After 10 years, 0.03% of the radioactivity has dissipated (that is, 0.9997 of the initial amount remains). Suppose that initially there are 100 lbs of this substance. Find the half-life.

36. A certain radioactive substance has a half-life of 50 hours. How long does it take for 90% of the radioactivity to be dissipated if the amount of material x satisfies

$$\frac{dx}{dt} = kx, \qquad (t \text{ in hours})?$$

37. Let V denote the volume of a tumor, and suppose the growth rate of the tumor satisfies

$$\frac{dV}{dt} = 0.2Ve^{-0.1t}.$$

If the initial volume of the tumor is 1.86 units, find an equation for V as a function of t.

38. The differential equation

$$\frac{dx}{dt} = x(a - b \ln x),$$

where x represents the number of objects at time t and a and b are constants, is the model for Gompertz curves. Recall from Section 5.3 that Gompertz curves can be used in studies of growth or decline of populations, organizations, and revenue from sales of a product. Solve this differential equation to obtain the Gompertz curve formula

$$x = e^{a/b}e^{-ce^{-bt}}.$$

39. Newton's law of cooling states that the rate of change of temperature $u = u(t)$ of an object is proportional to the temperature difference between the object and its surroundings, where T is the constant temperature of the surroundings. That is,

$$\frac{du}{dt} = k(u - T).$$

Suppose an object at 0°C is placed in a room where the temperature is 20°C. If the temperature of the object is 8°C after 1 hour, how long will it take for the object to reach 18°C?

40. The rate of change of atmospheric pressure P with respect to the altitude above sea level h is proportional to the pressure. That is,

$$\frac{dP}{dh} = kP.$$

Suppose the pressure at sea level is denoted by P_0, and at 18,000 ft the pressure is half what it is at sea level. Find the pressure, as a percentage of P_0, at 25,000 ft.

41. Newton's law of cooling can be used to estimate time of death of a corpse. (Actually the estimate may be quite rough because cooling does not begin until metabolic processes have ceased.) Suppose a corpse is discovered at noon in a 70° room, and at that time the body temperature is 96.1°F. If at 1:00 P.M. the temperature is 94.6°F, use Newton's law of cooling to estimate the time of death.

Review Exercises

12.1–12.3

Evaluate the following integrals.

1. $\int x^6 \, dx$

2. $\int x^{1/2} \, dx$

3. $\int (x^3 - 3x^2 + 4x + 5) \, dx$

4. $\int (x^2 - 1)^2 \, dx$

5. $\int (x^2 - 1)^2 x \, dx$

6. $\int (x^3 - 3x^2)(x^2 - 2x) \, dx$

7. $\int (x^3 + 4)^2 \, x \, dx$

8. $\int (x^3 + 4)^6 x^2 \, dx$

9. $\int \frac{x^2}{x^3 + 1} \, dx$

10. $\int \frac{x^2}{(x^3 + 1)^2} \, dx$

11. $\int \frac{x^2 \, dx}{\sqrt[3]{x^3 - 4}}$

12. $\int \frac{x^2 \, dx}{x^3 - 4}$

13. $\int \frac{x^3 + 1}{x^2} \, dx$

14. $\int \frac{x^3 - 3x + 1}{x - 1} \, dx$

15. $\int (x^3 + 4x) \, dx$

16. $\int (x - 1)^2 \, dx$

17. $\int \frac{x^2}{2x^3 - 7} \, dx$

18. $\int (x - 1) \, dx$

19. $\int (x^3 - e^{3x}) \, dx$

20. $\int xe^{x^2 + 1} \, dx$

21. $\int \frac{x^2}{(x^3 + 1)^2} \, dx$

22. $\int \frac{7x^3}{\sqrt{1 - x^4}} \, dx$

23. $\int y^2 e^{y^3} \, dy$

24. $\int \left(x - \frac{1}{(x + 1)^2} \right) dx$

12.5

Solve the following differential equations.

25. $x^2 dy = y^3 \, dx$

26. $y' = \dfrac{3y + 1}{x^2}$

27. $(x - 4)y^4 \, dx - x^3(y^2 - 3) \, dy = 0$

28. Find the particular solution of the equation in problem 27 if $y = 1$ when $x = 1$.

29. Find the particular solution of

$$y' = \frac{2x}{1 + 2y}$$

if $y = 0$ when $x = 2$.

APPLICATIONS

12.1

30. If the marginal revenue for a month for a product is $\overline{MR} = 6x - 12$, find the total revenue from the sale of 4 units of the product.
31. Suppose the rate of change of production of the average worker at a factory is given by

$$\frac{dp}{dt} = 27 + 24t - 3t^2, \qquad 0 \le t \le 8,$$

where p is the number of units produced by the worker in t hours. How many units will the average worker produce in an 8-hour shift? (Assume $p = 0$ when $t = 0$.)

12.2

32. The rate of change of the oxygen level in a body of water after an oil spill is given by

$$P'(t) = 400\left[\frac{5}{(t + 5)^2} - \frac{50}{(t + 5)^3}\right],$$

where t is the number of months since the spill. What function gives the oxygen level P at any time t if $P = 400$ when $t = 0$?
33. A population of bacteria grows at the rate

$$r = \frac{100,000}{(t + 100)^2},$$

where t is time. If the population is 1000 when $t = 1$, write the equation that gives the size of the population at any time t.

12.3

34. The rate of change of the market share (as a percent) a firm expects for a new product is

$$\frac{dy}{dt} = 2.4e^{-0.04t},$$

where t is the number of months after the product is introduced.
    (a) Write the equation that gives the expected market share y at any time t. (Note that $y = 0$ when $t = 0$.)
    (b) What market share does the firm expect after one year?
35. If the marginal revenue for a product is $\overline{MR} = \frac{800}{x + 1}$, find the total revenue function.

12.4

36. If the marginal cost for a product is $\overline{MC} = 6x + 4$ and the cost of producing 100 items is $31,400,
    (a) find the fixed costs.
    (b) find the total cost function.
37. Suppose a product has a daily marginal revenue $\overline{MR} = 46$ and a daily marginal cost $\overline{MC} = 30 + \frac{1}{5}x$. If the daily fixed cost is $200.00, how many units will give maximum profit and what is the maximum profit?

12.5

38. Radioactive beryllium is sometimes used to date fossils found in deep-sea sediment. The amount of radioactive material x satisfies

$$\frac{dx}{dt} = kx.$$

Suppose that 10 units of beryllium are present in a living organism and that the half-life of beryllium is 4.6 million years. Find the age of a fossil if 20% of the original radioactivity is present when the fossil is discovered.

WARMUP

	Prerequisite problem type	Answer	Section for review
13.1	Simplify: $$\frac{1}{n^3}\left[\frac{n(n+1)(2n+1)}{6} - \frac{2n(n+1)}{2} + n\right]$$	$$\frac{2n^2 - 3n + 1}{6n^2}$$	0.7 Fractions
13.2, 13.5	(a) If $F(x) = \frac{x^4}{4} + 4x + C$, what is $F(4) - F(2)$? (b) If $F(x) = -\frac{1}{9}\ln\frac{9 + \sqrt{81 - 9x^2}}{3x}$, what is $F(3) - F(2)$?	(a) 68 (b) $\frac{1}{9}\ln\left(\frac{3 + \sqrt{5}}{2}\right)$	1.3 Functional notation
13.1, 13.7	Find the limit: (a) $\lim\limits_{n \to +\infty} \frac{n^2 + n}{2n^2}$ (b) $\lim\limits_{n \to +\infty} \frac{2n^2 - 3n + 1}{6n^2}$ (c) $\lim\limits_{b \to \infty}\left(1 - \frac{1}{b}\right)$ (d) $\lim\limits_{b \to \infty}\left(\frac{-100{,}000}{e^{0.10b}} + 100{,}000\right)$	(a) $\frac{1}{2}$ (b) $\frac{1}{3}$ (c) 1 (d) 100,000	9.1 Limits
13.6	Find the derivative of $y = \ln x$.	$\frac{1}{x}$	11.4 Derivatives of logarithmic functions
13.2–13.7	Integrate (a) $\int (x^3 + 4)\,dx$ (b) $\int x\sqrt{x^2 - 9}\,dx$ (c) $\int e^{2x}\,dx$	(a) $\frac{x^4}{4} + 4x + C$ (b) $\frac{1}{2}\left[\frac{2}{3}(x^2 - 9)^{3/2}\right] + C$ (c) $\frac{1}{2}e^{2x} + C$	12.1, 12.2, 12.3 Integration

650

13

Definite Integrals

We have seen some applications of the indefinite integral in Chapter 12. In this chapter we define the definite integral and discuss a theorem that is useful for evaluating it. We will also see how it can be used to find the area under certain curves. The definite integral is used to solve many interesting types of problems from economics, finance, and probability.

Some consumers are willing to pay more than the market equilibrium price, and some producers are willing to sell for less than this price. The savings are called **consumer's surplus** and **producer's surplus,** respectively, and areas under the demand and supply curves are used to calculate them. The area under certain curves can also be used to solve probability problems.

If interest is compounded continuously, definite integrals can be used to approximate the income from and the present value of a continuous income stream. Improper integrals can be used to find the capital value of continuous income streams.

Evaluating improper integrals is one of three new techniques of integration introduced in this chapter. The other two are use of integral tables and integration by parts.

13.1 Area Under a Curve

Objective □ To use the sum of areas of rectangles to approximate the area under a curve

One way to find the accumulated production (such as the production of ore from a mine) over a period of time is to graph the rate of production as a function of time, and find the area under the resulting curve over a specified time interval. For example, if a coal mine produced at a rate of 30 tons per day, the production over 10 days ($30 \cdot 10 = 300$) could be represented by the area under the line $y = 30$ between $x = 0$ and $x = 10$ (see Figure 13.1 on the following page).

Although we did not need area to find the total production in this case, using area to determine the accumulated production is very useful when the rate of production function varies at different points in time. For example, if the rate of production is represented by

$$y = 100e^{-0.1x}, \qquad 0 \le x \le 20,$$

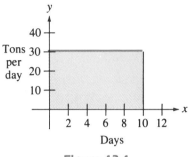

Figure 13.1

where x represents the number of days, then the area under the curve (and above the x-axis) from $x = 0$ to $x = 10$ represents the total production over the 10-day period (see Figure 13.2).

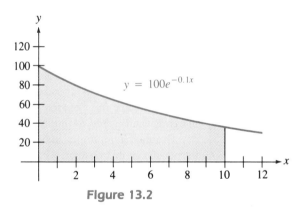

Figure 13.2

In order to determine the accumulated production and solve other types of problems, we need a method for finding areas under curves. For example, suppose we wish to find the area between the curve $y = x$ and the x-axis from $x = 0$ to $x = 1$ (see Figure 13.3). One way to approximate this area is to use the areas of rectangles whose bases are on the x-axis and whose heights are the vertical distances from points on their bases to the curve. We can divide the interval $[0, 1]$ into n equal subintervals and use them as the bases of n rectangles whose heights are determined by the curve (see Figure 13.4). The width of each of these rectangles is $1/n$. Using the functional value at the right endpoint of each subinterval as the height of the rectangle, we get n rectangles as shown in Figure 13.4. Because part of each rectangle lies above the curve, the sum of the areas of the rectangles will overestimate the area.

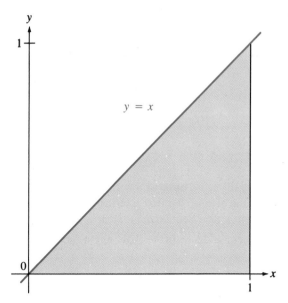

Figure 13.3

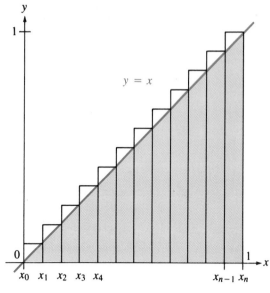

Figure 13.4

Then, with $y = f(x) = x$ and subinterval width $1/n$, we have

$$x_1 = \frac{1}{n}, \ f(x_1) = \frac{1}{n}, \text{ so the area of the 1st rectangle is } \frac{1}{n} \cdot \frac{1}{n} = \frac{1}{n^2}$$

$$x_2 = \frac{2}{n}, \ f(x_2) = \frac{2}{n}, \text{ so the area of the 2d rectangle is } \frac{2}{n} \cdot \frac{1}{n} = \frac{2}{n^2}$$

$$\vdots$$

$$x_i = \frac{i}{n}, \ f(x_i) = \frac{i}{n}, \text{ so the area of the } i\text{th rectangle is } \frac{i}{n} \cdot \frac{1}{n} = \frac{i}{n^2}$$

$$\vdots$$

$$x_n = \frac{n}{n}, \ f(x_n) = \frac{n}{n}, \text{ so the area of the } n\text{th rectangle is } \frac{n}{n} \cdot \frac{1}{n} = \frac{n}{n^2}.$$

Note that i/n^2 gives the area of the ith rectangle for *any* value of i. Thus for any value of n, this area can be approximated by the sum

$$A \approx \frac{1}{n^2} + \frac{2}{n^2} + \frac{3}{n^2} + \cdots + \frac{i}{n^2} + \cdots + \frac{n}{n^2}.$$

In particular, we have the following approximations of this area for specific values of n (the number of rectangles).

$$n = 5: \quad A \approx \frac{1}{25} + \frac{2}{25} + \frac{3}{25} + \frac{4}{25} + \frac{5}{25} = \frac{15}{25} = 0.60$$

$$n = 10: \quad A \approx \frac{1}{100} + \frac{2}{100} + \frac{3}{100} + \cdots + \frac{10}{100} = \frac{55}{100} = 0.55$$

$$n = 100: A \approx \frac{1}{10,000} + \frac{2}{10,000} + \frac{3}{10,000} + \cdots + \frac{100}{10,000} = \frac{5050}{10,000} = 0.505$$

We can find this sum for any n more easily if we observe that the common denominator is n^2 and that the numerator is the sum of the first n terms of an arithmetic sequence with first term 1 and last term n (see Section 6.1). Hence, as we proved in Section 6.1, the terms in the numerator add to $\frac{n}{2}(n + 1)$ for any n, and the area is approximated by

$$A \approx \frac{1 + 2 + 3 + \cdots + n}{n^2} = \frac{\frac{n}{2}(n + 1)}{n^2} = \frac{n + 1}{2n}.$$

Using this formula, we see the following.

$$n = 5: \quad A \approx \frac{5 + 1}{2(5)} = \frac{6}{10} = 0.60$$

$$n = 10: \quad A \approx \frac{10 + 1}{2(10)} = \frac{11}{20} = 0.55$$

$$n = 100: A \approx \frac{100 + 1}{2(100)} = \frac{101}{200} = 0.505$$

Note that as n gets larger, the number of rectangles will increase, their area will decrease, and the approximation will become more accurate. To get the best approximation possible, we will let n increase without bound. This gives

$$A = \lim_{n \to +\infty} \frac{n + 1}{2n} = \lim_{n \to +\infty} \frac{1 + 1/n}{2} = \frac{1}{2}.$$

We can see that this area is correct, for we are computing the area of a triangle with base 1 and height 1. The formula for the area of a triangle gives

$$A = \frac{1}{2}bh = \frac{1}{2} \cdot 1 \cdot 1 = \frac{1}{2}.$$

A special notation exists that uses the Greek letter Σ (sigma) to express the sum of numbers or expressions. For example, we may indicate the sum of the n numbers $a_1, a_2, a_3, a_4, \ldots, a_n$ by

$$\sum_{i=1}^{n} a_i = a_1 + a_2 + a_3 + \cdots + a_n.$$

This may be read as "The sum of a_i as i goes from 1 to n." The subscript i in a_i is replaced, first by 1, then by 2, then by 3, . . . , until it reaches the value above sigma. The i is called the **index of summation,** and it starts with the lower limit, 1, and ends with the upper limit, n. For example, if $x_1 = 2$, $x_2 = 3$, $x_3 = -1$, and $x_4 = -2$, then

$$\sum_{i=1}^{4} x_i = x_1 + x_2 + x_3 + x_4 = 2 + 3 + (-1) + (-2) = 2.$$

The area of the triangle discussed above was approximated by

$$A \approx \frac{1}{n^2} + \frac{2}{n^2} + \frac{3}{n^2} + \cdots + \frac{i}{n^2} + \cdots + \frac{n}{n^2}.$$

Using **sigma notation** we can write this sum as

$$A \approx \sum_{i=1}^{n} \left(\frac{i}{n^2} \right).$$

Sigma notation allows us to represent the sums of the areas of the rectangles in an abbreviated fashion. Some formulas that simplify computations involving sums follow.

Sum Formulas

I. $\displaystyle\sum_{i=1}^{n} 1 = n$

II. $\displaystyle\sum_{i=1}^{n} cx_i = c \sum_{i=1}^{n} x_i \qquad (c = \text{constant})$

III. $\displaystyle\sum_{i=1}^{n} (x_i + y_i) = \sum_{i=1}^{n} x_i + \sum_{i=1}^{n} y_i$

IV. $\displaystyle\sum_{i=1}^{n} i = \frac{n(n+1)}{2}$

V. $\displaystyle\sum_{i=1}^{n} i^2 = \frac{n(n+1)(2n+1)}{6}$

We have found that the area of the triangle discussed above was approximated by

$$A \approx \sum_{i=1}^{n} \frac{i}{n^2}.$$

We can use these formulas to simplify this sum as follows.

$$\sum_{i=1}^{n} \frac{i}{n^2} = \frac{1}{n^2} \sum_{i=1}^{n} i \qquad \text{Formula II}$$

$$= \frac{1}{n^2} \left[\frac{n(n+1)}{2} \right] \qquad \text{Formula IV}$$

$$= \frac{n+1}{2n}$$

Note that this is the same formula we obtained using other methods.

The following example shows we can find the area by evaluating the function at the left-hand endpoints of the subintervals.

EXAMPLE 1   Use rectangles to find the area under $y = x^2$ (and above the x-axis) from $x = 0$ to $x = 1$.

Solution   We again divide the interval $[0, 1]$ into n equal subintervals of length $1/n$. If we evaluate the function at the left-hand endpoints of these subintervals to determine the heights of the rectangles, the sum of the areas of the rectangles will underestimate the area (see Figure 13.5).

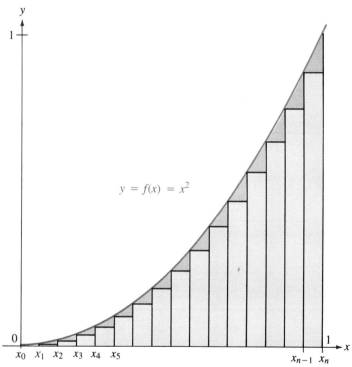

Figure 13.5

Then

$$x_0 = \frac{0}{n} = 0, \; f(x_0) = 0, \qquad \text{so the area of 1st rectangle is } 0 \cdot 0 = 0;$$

$$x_1 = \frac{1}{n}, \qquad f(x_1) = \left(\frac{1}{n}\right)^2 = \frac{1}{n^2}, \text{ so the area of 2d rectangle is } \frac{1}{n^2} \cdot \frac{1}{n} = \frac{1}{n^3};$$

$$x_2 = \frac{2}{n}, \qquad f(x_2) = \left(\frac{2}{n}\right)^2 = \frac{4}{n^2}, \text{ so the area of 3d rectangle is } \frac{4}{n^2} \cdot \frac{1}{n} = \frac{4}{n^3};$$

$$x_3 = \frac{3}{n}, \qquad f(x_3) = \left(\frac{3}{n}\right)^2 = \frac{9}{n^2}, \text{ so the area of 4th rectangle is } \frac{9}{n^2} \cdot \frac{1}{n} = \frac{9}{n^3};$$

$$x_{i-1} = \frac{i-1}{n}, \quad f(x_{i-1}) = \left(\frac{i-1}{n}\right)^2, \text{ so the area of the } i\text{th rectangle is}$$

$$\frac{(i-1)^2}{n^2} \cdot \frac{1}{n} = \frac{i^2 - 2i + 1}{n^3} \, ;$$

$$\vdots$$

$$x_{n-1} = \frac{n-1}{n}, \quad f(x_{n-1}) = \left(\frac{n-1}{n}\right)^2, \text{ so the area of the } n\text{th rectangle is}$$

$$\frac{(n-1)^2}{n^2} \cdot \frac{1}{n} = \frac{(n-1)^2}{n^3} \, .$$

Note that $(i^2 - 2i + 1)/n^3$ gives the area of the ith rectangle for *any* value of i.

The sum of these areas may be written as

$$S = \sum_{i=1}^{n} \frac{i^2 - 2i + 1}{n^3} = \frac{1}{n^3}\left(\sum_{i=1}^{n} i^2 - 2\sum_{i=1}^{n} i + \sum_{i=1}^{n} 1\right)$$

$$= \frac{1}{n^3}\left[\frac{n(n+1)(2n+1)}{6} - \frac{2n(n+1)}{2} + n\right]$$

$$= \frac{2n^3 + 3n^2 + n}{6n^3} - \frac{n^2 + n}{n^3} + \frac{n}{n^3}$$

$$= \frac{2n^2 - 3n + 1}{6n^2} \, .$$

If n is large, there will be a large number of smaller rectangles and the approximation of the area under the curve will be good; the larger n, the better the approximation. For example, if $n = 10$, the area approximation is

$$S(10) = \frac{200 - 30 + 1}{600} = 0.285,$$

while if $n = 100$,

$$S(100) = \frac{20,000 - 300 + 1}{60,000} = 0.328.$$

To get the best approximation possible, we let n increase without bound. This gives

$$A = \lim_{n \to \infty}\left(\frac{2n^2 - 3n + 1}{6n^2}\right)$$

$$= \lim_{n \to \infty}\left(\frac{2 - \dfrac{3}{n} + \dfrac{1}{n^2}}{6}\right) = \frac{1}{3} \, .$$

Note that the approximations with $n = 10$ and $n = 100$ were less than $\frac{1}{3}$. This is because all the rectangles were *under* the curve (see Figure 13.5).

Thus we see that we can determine the area under a curve $y = f(x)$ from $x = a$ to $x = b$ by dividing the interval $[a, b]$ into n equal subintervals of width $(b - a)/n$ and evaluating

$$A = \lim_{n \to \infty} \sum_{i=1}^{n} f(x_i)\left[\frac{b - a}{n}\right] \qquad \text{(using right-hand endpoints)}$$

or

$$A = \lim_{n \to \infty} \sum_{i=1}^{n} f(x_{i-1})\left[\frac{b - a}{n}\right] \qquad \text{(using left-hand endpoints).}$$

Exercise 13.1

In problems 1–4, approximate the area under each curve over the interval specified by using the indicated number of subintervals (or rectangles) and evaluating the function at the *right-hand* endpoints of the subintervals.

1. $f(x) = 4x - x^2$ from $x = 0$ to $x = 2$; 4 subintervals
2. $f(x) = x^3$ from $x = 0$ to $x = 3$; 6 subintervals
3. $f(x) = 9 - x^2$ from $x = 1$ to $x = 3$; 8 subintervals
4. $f(x) = x^2 + x + 1$ from $x = -1$ to $x = 1$; 4 subintervals

In problems 5–8, approximate the area under each curve by evaluating the function at the *left-hand* endpoints of the subintervals.

5. $f(x) = 4x - x^2$ from $x = 0$ to $x = 2$; 4 subintervals
6. $f(x) = x^3$ from $x = 0$ to $x = 3$; 6 subintervals
7. $f(x) = 9 - x^2$ from $x = 1$ to $x = 3$; 8 subintervals
8. $f(x) = x^2 + x + 1$ from $x = -1$ to $x = 1$; 4 subintervals

When the area under $f(x) = x^2 + x$ from $x = 0$ to $x = 2$ is approximated, the formulas for the sum of n rectangles using *left-hand* endpoints and *right-hand* endpoints are as follows:

$$\text{Left-hand endpoints:} \qquad S_L = \frac{14}{3} - \frac{6}{n} + \frac{4}{3n^2}$$

$$\text{Right-hand endpoints:} \qquad S_R = \frac{14n^2 + 18n + 4}{3n^2}$$

Use these formulas to answer problems 9–13.

9. Find $S_L(10)$ and $S_R(10)$.
10. Find $S_L(100)$ and $S_R(100)$.
11. Find $\lim_{n \to \infty} S_L$ and $\lim_{n \to \infty} S_R$.
12. Compare the right-hand and left-hand values by finding $S_R - S_L$ for $n = 10$, $n = 100$, and as $n \to \infty$. (Use problems 9–11.)
13. Since $f(x) = x^2 + x$ is increasing over the interval from $x = 0$ to $x = 2$, functional values at the right-hand endpoints are maximum values for each subinterval, and functional values at the left-hand endpoints are minimum values for each subinterval. How would the approximate area using $n = 10$ and *any* other point within each subinterval compare with $S_L(10)$ and $S_R(10)$? What would happen to the area result as $n \to \infty$ if any other point in each subinterval was used?

In problems 14–23, find the value of each sum.

14. $\sum\limits_{k=1}^{3} x_k$, if $x_1 = 1, x_2 = 3, x_3 = -1, x_4 = 5$.

15. $\sum\limits_{i=1}^{4} x_i$, if $x_1 = 3, x_2 = -1, x_3 = 3, x_4 = -2$.

16. $\sum\limits_{i=3}^{5} (i^2 + 1)$
17. $\sum\limits_{j=2}^{5} (j^2 - 3)$

18. $\sum\limits_{i=4}^{7} \left(\dfrac{i - 3}{i^2} \right)$
19. $\sum\limits_{j=0}^{4} (j^2 - 4j + 1)$

20. $\sum\limits_{k=1}^{50} 1$
21. $\sum\limits_{j=1}^{60} 3$

22. $\sum\limits_{k=1}^{50} (6k^2 + 5)$
23. $\sum\limits_{k=1}^{30} (k^2 + 4k)$

In problems 24 and 25, use the Sum Formulas I–IV to express each of the following without the summation symbol.

24. $\sum\limits_{i=1}^{n} \left(1 + \dfrac{i^2}{n^2} \right) \left(\dfrac{2}{n} \right)$
25. $\sum\limits_{i=1}^{n} \left(1 - \dfrac{2i}{n} + \dfrac{i^2}{n^2} \right) \left(\dfrac{3}{n} \right)$

Use the function $y = x$ from $x = 0$ to $x = 1$ and n equal subintervals with the function evaluated at the *left-hand* endpoint of each subinterval for problems 26–32.

26. What is the area of
    (a) the first rectangle?
    (b) the second rectangle?
    (c) the ith rectangle?
27. Find a formula for the sum of the areas of the n rectangles (call this S).
28. Find $S(10)$.
29. Find $S(100)$.
30. Find $S(1000)$.
31. Find $\lim\limits_{n \to \infty} S$.
32. How do your answers to problems 28–31 compare to the corresponding calculations in the discussion (before Example 1) of the area under $y = x$ using *right-hand* endpoints?

For problems 33–38, use the function $y = x^2$ from $x = 0$ to $x = 1$ and n equal subintervals with the function evaluated at the *right-hand* endpoints.

33. Find a formula for the sum of the areas of the n rectangles (call this S).
34. Find $S(10)$.
35. Find $S(100)$.
36. Find $S(1000)$.
37. Find $\lim\limits_{n \to \infty} S$.
38. How do your answers to problems 34–37 compare to the corresponding calculations in Example 1?
39. Use rectangles to find the area between $y = x^2 - 6x + 8$ and the x-axis from $x = 0$ to $x = 2$. Divide the interval $[0, 2]$ into n equal subintervals, so each subinterval has length $2/n$.

40. Use rectangles to find the area between $y = 4x - x^2$ and the x-axis from $x = 0$ to $x = 4$. Divide the interval $[0, 4]$ into n equal subintervals, so each subinterval has length $4/n$.

13.2 The Definite Integral; The Fundamental Theorem of Calculus

Objectives
- ☐ To evaluate definite integrals using the Fundamental Theorem of Calculus
- ☐ To find probabilities for certain continuous probability density functions

In the previous section we saw that we could determine the area under a curve using equal subintervals and the functional values at either the left-hand endpoints or the right-hand endpoints of the subintervals. In fact, we can use subintervals that are not of equal length, and we can use any point within each subinterval to determine the height of each rectangle. Suppose we wish to find the area above the x-axis and under the curve $y = f(x)$ over a closed interval $[a, b]$. We can divide the interval into n subintervals (not necessarily equal), with the endpoints of these intervals at $x_0 = a, x_1, x_2, \ldots, x_n = b$. We now choose a point (*any* point) in each subinterval, and denote the points $x_1{}^*, x_2{}^*, \ldots, x_i{}^*, \ldots, x_n{}^*$. Then the ith rectangle (for any i) has height $f(x_i{}^*)$ and width $x_i - x_{i-1}$, so its area is $f(x_i{}^*)(x_i - x_{i-1})$. Then the sum of the areas of the n rectangles is

$$S = \sum_{i=1}^{n} f(x_i{}^*)(x_i - x_{i-1})$$

$$= \sum_{i=1}^{n} f(x_i{}^*) \, \Delta x_i, \qquad \text{where } \Delta x_i = x_i - x_{i-1}.$$

Because the points in the subinterval may be chosen anywhere in the subinterval, we cannot be sure if the rectangles will underestimate or overestimate the area under the curve. But increasing the number of subintervals (increasing n) and making sure that every interval becomes smaller (just increasing n will not guarantee this if the subintervals are unequal) will improve the estimation. Thus for any subdivision of $[a, b]$ and any $x_i{}^*$ the area is given by

$$A = \lim_{\substack{n \to \infty \\ \max \, \Delta x_i \to 0}} \sum_{i=1}^{n} f(x_i{}^*) \, \Delta x_i, \qquad \text{provided this limit exists.}$$

Because of the special importance of this limit and its applications beyond area determination, we give it a special definition.

Definite Integral	If f is a function on the interval $[a, b]$, then the *definite integral* of f from a to b is

$$\int_a^b f(x)\, dx = \lim_{\substack{n \to \infty \\ \max \Delta x \to 0}} \sum_{i=1}^{n} f(x_i^*)\, \Delta x_i .$$

If the limit exists, then the definite integral exists and we say f is integrable on $[a, b]$.

The obvious question is, How is this definite integral related to the indefinite integral (antiderivative) we have been studying? The answer to this question is given by the **Fundamental Theorem of Calculus.**

Fundamental Theorem of Calculus	Let f be a continuous function on the closed interval $[a, b]$; then the definite integral of f exists on this interval, and

$$\int_a^b f(x)\, dx = F(b) - F(a),$$

where F is any function such that $F'(x) = f(x)$ for all x in $[a, b]$.

Stated differently, the theorem says that if the function F is an indefinite integral of a function f that is continuous on the interval $[a, b]$, then

$$\int_a^b f(x)\, dx = F(b) - F(a).$$

We denote $F(b) - F(a)$ by $F(x)\Big|_a^b$.

EXAMPLE 1   Evaluate $\displaystyle\int_2^4 (x^3 + 4)\, dx.$

Solution
$$\int_2^4 (x^3 + 4)\, dx = \frac{x^4}{4} + 4x + C \,\Big|_2^4$$

$$= \left[\frac{(4)^4}{4} + 4(4) + C\right] - \left[\frac{(2)^4}{4} + 4(2) + C\right]$$

$$= (64 + 16 + C) - (4 + 8 + C)$$

$$= 68$$

Note that the Fundamental Theorem states that F can be *any* indefinite integral of f, so we need not add the constant of integration to the integral. The constant C that could be added would always subtract out. (See Example 1.)

EXAMPLE 2   Evaluate $\displaystyle\int_1^3 (3x^2 + 6x)\,dx$.

Solution

$$\int_1^3 (3x^2 + 6x)\,dx = x^3 + 3x^2 \Big|_1^3$$
$$= (3^3 + 3 \cdot 3^2) - (1^3 + 3 \cdot 1^2)$$
$$= 54 - 4 = 50$$

EXAMPLE 3   Evaluate $\displaystyle\int_3^5 x\sqrt{x^2 - 9}\,dx$

Solution

$$\int_3^5 x\sqrt{x^2 - 9}\,dx = \frac{1}{2}\int_3^5 (x^2 - 9)^{1/2}(2x)\,dx$$
$$= \frac{1}{2}\left[\frac{2}{3}(x^2 - 9)^{3/2}\right]\Big|_3^5$$
$$= \frac{1}{2}\left[\frac{2}{3}\cdot 16^{3/2} - \frac{2}{3}\cdot 0\right]$$
$$= \frac{1}{3}\cdot 64 = \frac{64}{3}$$

In the integral $\int_a^b f(x)\,dx$, we call a the *lower limit* and b the *upper limit* of integration. Although we developed the definite integral with the assumption that the lower limit was less than the upper limit, the following properties permit us to evaluate the definite integral even when that is not the case.

1. $\displaystyle\int_a^a f(x)\,dx = 0$

2. If f is integrable on $[a, b]$, then

$$\int_b^a f(x)\,dx = -\int_a^b f(x)\,dx.$$

The following examples illustrate these definitions.

EXAMPLE 4   Evaluate $\displaystyle\int_4^4 x^2\,dx$.

Solution

$$\int_4^4 x^2\,dx = \frac{x^3}{3}\Big|_4^4 = \frac{4^3}{3} - \frac{4^3}{3} = 0$$

EXAMPLE 5   Compare $\int_{2}^{4} 3x^2 \, dx$ and $\int_{4}^{2} 3x^2 \, dx$.

Solution
$$\int_{2}^{4} 3x^2 \, dx = x^3 \Big|_{2}^{4} = 4^3 - 2^3 = 56$$

$$\int_{4}^{2} 3x^2 \, dx = x^3 \Big|_{4}^{2} = 2^3 - 4^3 = -56$$

Thus

$$\int_{4}^{2} 3x^2 \, dx = -\int_{2}^{4} 3x^2 \, dx.$$

Another property of definite integrals is called the additive property:

If f is continuous on some interval containing a, b, and c, then

$$\int_{a}^{b} f(x) \, dx = \int_{a}^{c} f(x) \, dx + \int_{c}^{b} f(x) \, dx.$$

EXAMPLE 6   Show $\int_{2}^{3} 4x \, dx + \int_{3}^{5} 4x \, dx = \int_{2}^{5} 4x \, dx.$

Solution
$$\int_{2}^{3} 4x \, dx = 2x^2 \Big|_{2}^{3} = 18 - 8 = 10$$

$$\int_{3}^{5} 4x \, dx = 2x^2 \Big|_{3}^{5} = 50 - 18 = 32$$

$$\int_{2}^{5} 4x \, dx = 2x^2 \Big|_{2}^{5} = 50 - 8 = 42$$

Thus

$$\int_{2}^{3} 4x \, dx + \int_{3}^{5} 4x \, dx = \int_{2}^{5} 4x \, dx.$$

Let us now return to area problems, to see the relationship between the definite integral and the area under a curve. By the formula for the area of a triangle and by summing areas of rectangles, we found the area under the curve (line) $y = x$ from

$x = 0$ to $x = 1$ to be $\frac{1}{2}$ (see Figure 13.6(a)). Using the definite integral to find the area gives

$$A = \int_0^1 x \, dx = \frac{x^2}{2} \Big|_0^1 = \frac{1}{2} - 0 = \frac{1}{2}.$$

In Example 1 of Section 13.1 we used rectangles to find that the area under $y = x^2$ from $x = 0$ to $x = 1$ was $\frac{1}{3}$ (see Figure 13.6(b)). Using the definite integral, we get

$$A = \int_0^1 x^2 \, dx = \frac{x^3}{3} \Big|_0^1 = \frac{1}{3} - 0 = \frac{1}{3},$$

which agrees with the answer obtained in Example 1.

However, not every definite integral represents the area between the curve and the x-axis over an interval. For example,

$$\int_0^2 (x - 2) \, dx = \frac{x^2}{2} - 2x \Big|_0^2 = (2 - 4) - (0) = -2.$$

This would indicate that the area between the curve and the x-axis is negative, but area must be positive. A look at the graph of $y = x - 2$ (see Figure 13.6(c)) shows us what is happening. The region bounded by $y = x - 2$ and the x-axis between $x = 0$ and $x = 2$ is a triangle whose base is 2 and height is 2, so its area is $\frac{1}{2}bh = \frac{1}{2}(2)(2) = 2$. The reason the integral has value -2 is because $y = x - 2$ lies below the x-axis from $x = 0$ to $x = 2$, so the functional values over the interval $[0, 2]$ are negative. Thus the value of the definite integral over *this* interval does not represent the area between the curve and the x-axis.

In general, the definite integral will give the area under the curve and above the x-axis only when $f(x) \geq 0$ for all x in $[a, b]$.

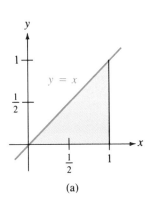

(a)

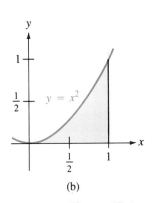

(b)

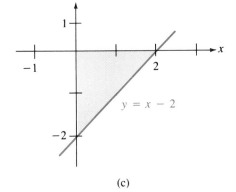

(c)

Figure 13.6

the x-axis only when $f(x) \geq 0$ for all x in $[a, b]$.

Area Under a Curve	If f is a continuous function on $[a, b]$ and $f(x) \geq 0$ on $[a, b]$, then the exact area between $y = f(x)$ and the x-axis from $x = a$ to $x = b$ is given by

$$\text{Area} \atop \text{(shaded)} = \int_a^b f(x)\, dx.$$

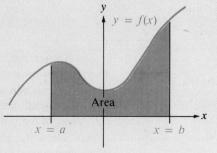

If the rate of growth with respect to time, $f'(t)$, of some function (such as the amount of money at compound interest) is known, then the integral of that rate of growth gives the function $f(t)$ (that gives accumulated money, for example). The value of this function at $t = k$ is the total amount at this time, and the value at $t = 0$ is the amount at the beginning of the time period. Thus the total growth during this period is

$$f(k) - f(0).$$

This value can be found by evaluating the definite integral

$$\int_0^k f'(t)\, dt.$$

For non-negative rates of growth, this definite integral (and growth) is the same as the area under the graph of $f'(t)$ from $t = 0$ to $t = k$.

EXAMPLE 7   Suppose that money flows continuously into a slot machine at a casino and grows at a rate given by

$$A' = 100e^{0.1t}$$

where t is time in hours and $0 \leq t \leq 10$. Find the total amount of money that accumulates in the machine during the 10-hour period.

Solution   The total amount is given by

$$A = \int_0^{10} 100e^{0.1t}\, dt$$

$$= \frac{100}{0.1} \int_0^{10} e^{0.1t}(0.1)\, dt$$

$$= 1000e^{0.1t} \Big|_0^{10}$$

$$= 1000e - 1000$$

$$\approx 1718.28 \text{ (dollars)}.$$

In Section 8.6, we stated that the total area under the normal curve is 1, and that the area under the curve from value x_1 to value x_2 represents the probability that a score chosen at random will lie between x_1 and x_2.

The normal distribution is an example of a **continuous distribution** because the values of the random variable vary continuously rather than assuming discrete values. The above statements relating probability and area under the graph apply to other continuous probability distributions (frequently called **probability density functions**). Thus we can use the definite integral to find the probability that a random variable lies within a given interval. Consider the following example.

EXAMPLE 8   Suppose the probability density function for the life of a computer component is $f(x) = 0.10e^{-0.10x}$, where x is the number of years the component is in use. Find the probability that the component will last between 3 and 5 years.

Solution   The probability that the component will last between 3 and 5 years is the area under the graph of the function between $x = 3$ and $x = 5$. The probability is given by the integral

$$\int_3^5 0.10e^{-0.10x} \, dx = -e^{-0.10x} \Big|_3^5$$

$$= -e^{-0.5} + e^{-0.3}$$

$$\approx -0.6065 + 0.7408$$

$$= 0.1343$$

Exercise 13.2

Evaluate the following definite integrals.

1. $\displaystyle\int_2^4 x^3 \, dx$

2. $\displaystyle\int_0^5 x^2 \, dx$

3. $\displaystyle\int_{-1}^2 5x^4 \, dx$

4. $\displaystyle\int_{-2}^4 4x^3 \, dx$

5. $\displaystyle\int_{-2}^3 5 \, dx$

6. $\displaystyle\int_{-8}^{-5} 7 \, dx$

7. $\displaystyle\int_0^5 4\sqrt[3]{x^2} \, dx$

8. $\displaystyle\int_2^4 3\sqrt{x} \, dx$

9. $\displaystyle\int_2^4 (4x^3 - 6x^2 - 5x) \, dx$

10. $\displaystyle\int_0^2 (x^4 - 5x^3 + 2x) \, dx$

11. $\displaystyle\int_2^3 (x - 4)^2 \, dx$

12. $\displaystyle\int_{-1}^3 (x + 2)^3 \, dx$

13. $\displaystyle\int_2^4 (x^2 + 2)^3 x \, dx$

14. $\displaystyle\int_0^3 (2x - x^2)^4 (1 - x) \, dx$

15. $\displaystyle\int_{-1}^2 (x^3 - 3x^2)^3 (x^2 - 2x) \, dx$

16. $\displaystyle\int_0^4 (3x^2 - 2)^4 x \, dx$

17. $\displaystyle\int_2^3 x\sqrt{x^2 + 3} \, dx$

18. $\displaystyle\int_{-1}^2 x\sqrt[3]{x^2 - 5} \, dx$

19. $\displaystyle\int_4^6 \sqrt{x^2 - 2} \, dx$

20. $\displaystyle\int_2^2 (x^3 - 4x) \, dx$

21. $\displaystyle\int_3^6 \frac{x}{3x^2 + 4} \, dx$

22. $\displaystyle\int_0^2 \frac{x}{x^2 + 4} \, dx$

23. In Figure 13.7, which of the shaded regions A, B, C, or D has the area given by
$\displaystyle\int_a^b f(x) \, dx$?

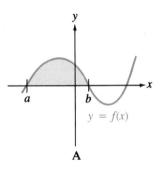

A

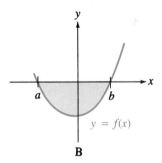

B

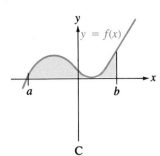

C

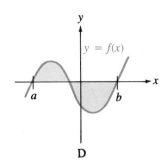

D

Figure 13.7

24. For which of the following functions $f(x)$ does $\displaystyle\int_0^2 f(x) \, dx$ give the area between the graph of $f(x)$ and the x-axis from $x = 0$ to $x = 2$?
(a) $f(x) = x^2 + 1$ (b) $f(x) = -x^2$ (c) $f(x) = x - 1$

In problems 25–28,
(a) write the integral that describes the area of the shaded region.
(b) find the area.

25.

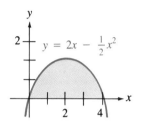

26.

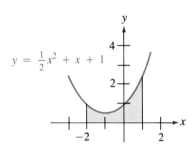

27.

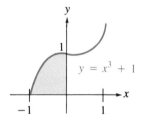

28.

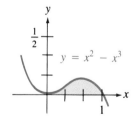

29. Find the area between the curve $y = -x^2 + 3x - 2$ and the x-axis from $x = 1$ to $x = 2$.

30. Find the area between the curve $y = x^2 + 3x + 2$ and the x-axis from $x = -1$ to $x = 3$.

31. Find the area between the curve $y = xe^{x^2}$ and the x-axis from $x = 1$ to $x = 3$.

32. Find the area between the curve $y = e^{-x}$ and the x-axis from $x = -1$ to $x = 1$.

33. How does $\int_{-1}^{-3} x\sqrt{x^2 + 1}\, dx$ compare with $\int_{-3}^{-1} x\sqrt{x^2 + 1}\, dx$?

34. If $\int_{-1}^{0} x^3\, dx = -\frac{1}{4}$ and $\int_{0}^{1} x^3\, dx = \frac{1}{4}$, what does $\int_{-1}^{1} x^3\, dx$ equal?

35. If $\int_{1}^{2} (2x - x^2)\, dx = \frac{2}{3}$ and $\int_{2}^{4} (2x - x^2)\, dx = -\frac{20}{3}$, what does $\int_{1}^{4} (x^2 - 2x)\, dx$ equal?

36. If $\int_{1}^{2} (2x - x^2)\, dx = \frac{2}{3}$, what does $\int_{1}^{2} (12x - 6x^2)\, dx$ equal?

APPLICATIONS

In problems 37 and 38, the velocity of blood through a vessel is given by $v = K(R^2 - r^2)$, where K is the (constant) maximum velocity of the blood, R the (constant) radius of the vessel, and r the distance of the particular corpuscle from the center of the vessel. The rate of flow can be found by measuring the volume of blood that flows past a point in a given time period. This volume, V, is given by

$$V = \int_{0}^{R} v(2\pi r\, dr).$$

37. Find the volume if $R = 0.30$ cm and $v = (0.30 - 3.33r^2)$ cm/sec.
38. Develop a general formula for V by evaluating

$$V = \int_{0}^{R} v(2\pi r\, dr)$$

using $v = K(R^2 - r^2)$.

In problems 39 and 40, the rate of production of a new line of products is given by

$$\frac{dx}{dt} = 200\left[1 + \frac{400}{(t + 40)^2}\right],$$

where x is the number of items produced and t is the number of weeks the products have been in production.

39. How many units were produced in the first five weeks?
40. How many units were produced in the sixth week?
41. If the rate of depreciation of a building is given by $D'(t) = 3000(20 - t)$, $0 \le t \le 20$, what is the total depreciation of the building over the first 10 years ($t = 0$ to $t = 10$)?
42. What is the total depreciation of the building of problem 41 during the next 10 years ($t = 10$ to $t = 20$)?
43. Suppose the probability density function for the life of a light bulb is

$$f(x) = 0.5e^{-0.5x},$$

where x is the number of years it is in service. What is the probability that the light bulb lasts between 1 and 2 years?

44. What is the probability that the light bulb of problem 43 will last 1 year or less?
45. Suppose the probability density function for the life span of a microwave unit is

$$f(t) = 0.2e^{-0.2t},$$

where t is the number of years the unit is in service. What is the probability that the microwave unit will last 1 year or less?

46. What is the probability that the microwave unit described in problem 45 will last between 1 and 10 years?
47. A store finds that its sales change at a rate given by

$$S'(t) = -3t^2 + 300t,$$

where t is the number of days after an advertising campaign ends and $0 \le t \le 30$. If daily sales are $S(0) = 500$ at the end of the campaign, find
   (a) the total sales for the first week after the campaign ends ($t = 0$ to $t = 7$).
   (b) the total number of sales for the second week after the campaign ends ($t = 7$ to $t = 14$).

13.3 Area Between Two Curves

Objectives
   ☐ To find the area between two curves
   ☐ To find the average value of a function

We have used the definite integral to find the area of the region between a curve and the x-axis over an interval where the curve lies above the x-axis. We can easily extend this technique to finding the area between two curves over an interval where one curve lies above the other. (See Figure 13.8.)

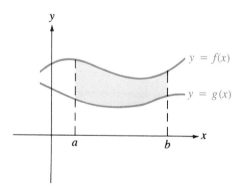

Figure 13.8

Suppose that the graphs of both $y = f(x)$ and $y = g(x)$ lie above the x-axis, and that the graph of $y = f(x)$ lies above $y = g(x)$ throughout the interval from $x = a$ to $x = b$; that is, $f(x) \ge g(x)$ on $[a, b]$.

Then $\displaystyle\int_a^b f(x)\, dx$ gives the area between the graph of $y = f(x)$ and the x-axis (see Figure 13.9 (a)), and $\displaystyle\int_a^b g(x)\, dx$ gives the area between the graph of $y = g(x)$

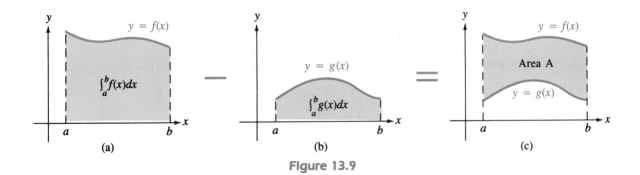

Figure 13.9

and the x-axis (see Figure 13.9 (b)). As Figure 13.9 (c) shows, the area of the region between the graphs of $y = f(x)$ and $y = g(x)$ is the difference of these two areas. That is,

$$\text{Area between the curves} = \int_a^b f(x)\, dx - \int_a^b g(x)\, dx.$$

Although Figure 13.9 (c) shows the graphs of both $y = f(x)$ and $y = g(x)$ lying above the x-axis, this difference of their integrals will always give the area between their graphs if both functions are continuous and if $f(x) \geq g(x)$ on the interval $[a, b]$.

Using the fact that

$$\int_a^b f(x)\, dx - \int_a^b g(x)\, dx = \int_a^b [f(x) - g(x)]\, dx,$$

we have the following result.

Area Between Two Curves	If f and g are continuous functions on $[a, b]$ and if $f(x) \geq g(x)$ on $[a, b]$, then the area of the region bounded by $y = f(x)$, $y = g(x)$, $x = a$, and $x = b$ is $$A = \int_a^b [f(x) - g(x)]\, dx.$$

EXAMPLE 1   Find the area of the region bounded by $y = x^2 + 4$, $y = x$, $x = 0$, and $x = 3$.

Solution   We first sketch the graphs of the functions. The graph of the region is shown in Figure 13.10. Since $y = x^2 + 4$ lies above $y = x$ in the interval from $x = 0$ to $x = 3$, the area is

$$A = \int_0^3 [(x^2 + 4) - x]\, dx$$

$$= \frac{x^3}{3} + 4x - \frac{x^2}{2}\, \Big|_0^3$$

$$= \left[9 + 12 - \frac{9}{2}\right] - (0 + 0 - 0)$$

$$= 16\tfrac{1}{2} \text{ square units.}$$

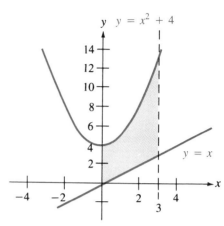

Figure 13.10

EXAMPLE 2   Find the area between $y = -x^2$ and the x-axis from $x = -1$ to $x = 1$.

Solution   Graphing $y = -x^2$ gives us the region shown in Figure 13.11. Clearly $y = -x^2$ is below the x-axis ($y = 0$). Using $f(x) = 0$ and $g(x) = -x^2$, we have $f(x) \geq g(x)$, so the area of the region from $x = -1$ to $x = 1$ is

$$A = \int_{-1}^1 [0 - (-x^2)]\, dx$$

$$= \int_{-1}^1 x^2\, dx$$

$$= \frac{x^3}{3}\, \Big|_{-1}^1$$

$$= \frac{1}{3} - \left[-\frac{1}{3}\right] = \frac{2}{3} \text{ square units.}$$

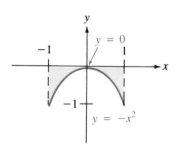

Figure 13.11

We are sometimes asked to find the area enclosed by two curves. In this case, we find the points of intersection of the curves to determine a and b.

EXAMPLE 3   Find the area enclosed by $y = x^2$ and $y = 2x + 3$.

Solution   We first find a and b by finding the x-coordinates of the points of intersection of the graphs. Setting the y-values equal gives

$$x^2 = 2x + 3$$
$$x^2 - 2x - 3 = 0$$
$$(x - 3)(x + 1) = 0$$
$$x = 3, x = -1.$$

Thus $a = -1$ and $b = 3$.

We next sketch the graphs of these functions on the same set of axes. (If you do not recognize the graphs of these functions, it suffices to plot enough points to determine which function is above the other on the interval $[-1, 3]$.) Figure 13.12 shows the region between the graphs, with $2x + 3 \geq x^2$ from $x = -1$ to $x = 3$.

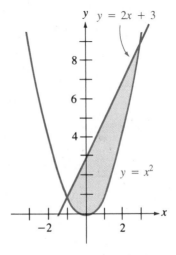

Figure 13.12

The area of the enclosed region is

$$A = \int_{-1}^{3} [(2x + 3) - x^2] \, dx$$

$$= x^2 + 3x - \frac{x^3}{3} \Big|_{-1}^{3}$$

$$= (9 + 9 - 9) - \left(1 - 3 + \frac{1}{3}\right)$$

$$= 10\tfrac{2}{3} \text{ square units.}$$

Some graphs enclose two or more regions because they have more than two points of intersection.

EXAMPLE 4   Find the area of the region enclosed by the graphs of

$$y = f(x) = x^3 - x^2 \text{ and } y = g(x) = 2x.$$

Solution   To find the points of intersection of the graphs, we set the y-values equal and solve for x.

$$x^3 - x^2 = 2x$$
$$x^3 - x^2 - 2x = 0$$
$$x(x - 2)(x + 1) = 0$$
$$x = 0, x = 2, x = -1$$

Graphing these functions between $x = -1$ and $x = 2$, we see that $f(x) \geq g(x)$ for the region enclosed by the curves from $x = -1$ to $x = 0$, but that $f(x) \leq g(x)$ for the region enclosed by the curves from $x = 0$ to $x = 2$. See Figure 13.13.

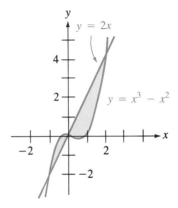

Figure 13.13

We need one integral to find the area of the region from $x = -1$ to $x = 0$ and a second integral to find the area from $x = 0$ to $x = 2$. The area is found by summing these two integrals.

$$A = \int_{-1}^{0} [(x^3 - x^2) - (2x)] \, dx + \int_{0}^{2} [(2x) - (x^3 - x^2)] \, dx$$

$$= \int_{-1}^{0} (x^3 - x^2 - 2x) \, dx + \int_{0}^{2} (2x - x^3 + x^2) \, dx$$

$$= \left(\frac{x^4}{4} - \frac{x^3}{3} - x^2 \right) \Big|_{-1}^{0} + \left(x^2 - \frac{x^4}{4} + \frac{x^3}{3} \right) \Big|_{0}^{2}$$

$$= \left[(0) - \left(\frac{1}{4} - \frac{-1}{3} - 1 \right) \right] + \left[\left(4 - \frac{16}{4} + \frac{8}{3} \right) - (0) \right] = \frac{37}{12}$$

Thus, the area between the curves is $\dfrac{37}{12}$ square units.

If the graph of $y = f(x)$ lies on or above the x-axis from $x = a$ to $x = b$, then the area between the graph and the x-axis is

$$A = \int_a^b f(x)\, dx.$$

The area A is also the area of a rectangle with base equal to $b - a$ and height equal to the *average value* (or average height) of the function $y = f(x)$ (see Figure 13.14).

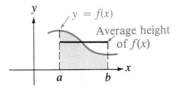

Figure 13.14

Thus the average value of the function is

$$\frac{A}{b - a} = \frac{1}{b - a}\int_a^b f(x)\, dx.$$

Even if $f(x) \le 0$ on all or part of the interval $[a, b]$, we can find the average value by using the integral. Thus we have the following.

Average Value   The average value of a continuous function $y = f(x)$ over the interval $[a, b]$ is

$$\frac{1}{b - a}\int_a^b f(x)\, dx.$$

EXAMPLE 5   Suppose the cost function for a product is $C(x) = 400 + x + 0.3x^2$.
(a) What is the average value of $C(x)$ for $x = 10$ to $x = 20$ units?
(b) Find the average cost per unit if 40 units are produced.

Solution   (a) The average value of $C(x)$ is

$$\frac{1}{20 - 10}\int_{10}^{20}(400 + x + 0.3x^2)\, dx = \frac{1}{10}\left[400x + \frac{x^2}{2} + 0.1x^3\right]_{10}^{20}$$

$$= \frac{1}{10}[(8000 + 200 + 800) - (4000 + 50 + 100)]$$

$$= 485 \text{ (dollars)}.$$

(b) The average cost function is

$$\bar{C}(x) = \frac{C(x)}{x} = \frac{400}{x} + 1 + 0.3x.$$

The average cost per unit if 40 units are produced is

$$\bar{C}(40) = \frac{400}{40} + 1 + 0.3(40)$$

$$= 23 \text{ (dollars)}.$$

Exercise 13.3

In problems 1–24, find the areas of the described regions.

1. Between $y = x^2$ and $y = x + 2$ from $x = 1$ to $x = 2$
2. Between $y = 4 - x^2$ and $y = x^2 - 4x - 2$ from $x = -1$ to $x = 3$
3. Between $y = x^2 + 2x$ and $y = 4 - x^2$ from $x = 1$ to $x = 3$
4. Between $y = x^2 + 2x$ and $y = 4 - x^2$ from $x = 0$ to $x = 1$
5. Between $y = x^2 - 8$ and $y = 6x - x^2$ from $x = 0$ to $x = 4$
6. Between $y = x^2 - 8$ and $y = 6x - x^2$ from $x = 4$ to $x = 5$
7. Between $y = x^3$ and $y = x^2$ from $x = -1$ to $x = 0$
8. Between $y = x^3 - x$ and $y = 3x$ from $x = -2$ to $x = 0$
9. Between $y = x^3$ and $y = x^2$ from $x = 0$ to $x = 1$
10. Between $y = x^3 - x$ and $y = 3x$ from $x = 0$ to $x = 2$

11. Enclosed by $y = x^2$ and $y = \sqrt{x}$
12. Enclosed by $y = x^2$ and $y = 4x - x^2$
13. Enclosed by $y = x^3 - x^2$ and $y = x^2$
14. Enclosed by $y = 1 - x^2$ and $y = x^2 + x$
15. Enclosed by $y = 2x^2 - 9x$ and $y = 10 - x$
16. Enclosed by $y = x^3 + 1$ and $y = x^2 + x$
17. Enclosed by $y = x^3$ and $y = x$
18. Enclosed by $y = x^3$ and $y = 2x - x^2$
19. Enclosed by $y = x^3$ and $y = x^2 + 2x$
20. Enclosed by $y = \frac{1}{2}x^2$ and $y = x^2 - 2x$
21. Enclosed by $y = x^4 - 2x^2 + 1$ and $y = 1 - x^2$
22. Enclosed by $y = \frac{4}{x^2}$ and $y = 5 - x^2$
23. Enclosed by $y = \frac{3}{x}$ and $y = 4 - x$
24. Enclosed by $y = \frac{6}{x}$ and $y = -x - 5$

APPLICATIONS

25. If the cost of producing x units of an item is $C(x) = x^2 + 400x + 2000$,
    (a) use $\bar{C}(x)$ to find the average cost of producing 1000 units.
    (b) find the average value of the cost function $C(x)$ over the interval from 0 to 1000.

26. Figure 13.15 shows how an inventory of a product is depleted each quarter of a given
    year. What is the average inventory per month for the first three months for this product?
    [Assume the graph is a line joining (0, 1300) and (3, 100).]

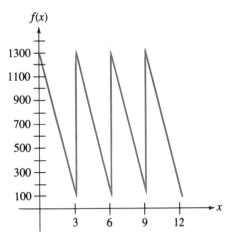

Figure 13.15

27. The number of daily sales of a product was found to be given by

$$S = 100xe^{-x^2} + 100$$

x days after the start of an advertising campaign for it. Find the average daily sales during
the first 20 days of the campaign, that is, from $x = 0$ to $x = 20$.

28. If no new advertising campaign is begun for the product of problem 27, what is the
average number of sales per day for the next 10 days?

29. If the demand function for a product is given by

$$p = 500 + \frac{1000}{q + 1},$$

where p is the price and q is the number of units demanded, find the average price as
demand ranges from 49 to 99 units.

30. Suppose that the income from a slot machine in a casino flows continuously at a rate

$$f(t) = 100e^{0.1t},$$

where t is the time in hours since the casino opened. Then the total income during the
first 10 hours is given by

$$\int_0^{10} 100e^{0.1t} \, dt.$$

Find the average income over the first 10 hours.

31. A drug manufacturer has developed a time-release capsule with the number of milligrams
of the drug in the bloodstream given by

$$S = 30x^{18/7} - 240x^{11/7} + 480x^{4/7},$$

where t is in hours and $0 \leq t \leq 4$. Find the average number of milligrams of the drug
in the bloodstream for the first four hours after a capsule is taken.

13.4 Applications of Definite Integrals in Business and Economics; Consumer's Surplus, Producer's Surplus, and Continuous Income Streams

Objectives
- ☐ To use definite integrals to find consumer's surplus
- ☐ To use definite integrals to find producer's surplus
- ☐ To use definite integrals to find total income and present value of continuous income streams

The definite integral can be used in a number of applications in business and economics, including price discrimination, revenue versus cost, consumer's surplus, and producer's surplus. In this section we will consider three applications, **consumer's surplus**, **producer's surplus**, and **continuous income streams**.

Consumer's Surplus

Suppose the demand for a product is given by $p = f(x)$, while supply of the product is described by $p = q(x)$. The price p_1 where the graphs of these functions intersect is the **equilibrium price** (see Figure 13.16). As the demand curve shows, some consumers (but not all) would be willing to pay more than $\$p_1$ for the product. For

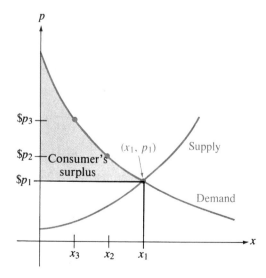

Figure 13.16

example, some consumers would be willing to buy x_3 units if the price is $\$p_3$. Those consumers willing to pay more than $\$p_1$ are benefiting from the lower price. The total gain for all those consumers willing to pay more than $\$p_1$ is called the **consumer's surplus,** and under proper assumptions the area of the shaded region in Figure 13.16 represents this consumer's surplus.

Looking at Figure 13.17, we see that if the demand curve has equation $p = f(x)$, the consumer's surplus is given by the area between $f(x)$ and the x-axis from 0 to x_1, *minus* the area of the rectangle denoted TR:

$$CS = \int_0^{x_1} f(x)\, dx - p_1 x_1.$$

Note that $p_1 x_1$ is the area of the rectangle that represents the total revenue (see Figure 13.17).

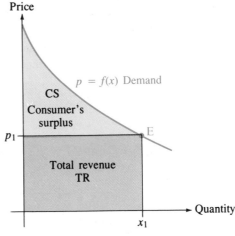

Figure 13.17

EXAMPLE 1   The demand function for a product is $p = 100/(x + 1)$. If the equilibrium price is $20, what is the consumer's surplus?

Solution   We must first find the quantity that will be purchased at this price. Letting $p = 20$, and solving for x gives

$$20 = \frac{100}{x + 1}$$
$$20(x + 1) = 100$$
$$x + 1 = 5$$
$$x = 4.$$

Thus the equilibrium point is (4, 20). The consumer's surplus is given by the formula

$$CS = \int_0^{x_1} f(x)\,dx - p_1 x_1$$

$$= \int_0^4 \frac{100}{x+1}\,dx - 20 \cdot 4$$

$$= 100 \ln |x+1| \ \Big|_0^4 - 80$$

$$= 100\,(\ln 5 - \ln 1) - 80$$

$$\approx 100\,(1.6094 - 0) - 80$$

$$= 160.94 - 80$$

$$= 80.94.$$

The consumer's surplus is $80.94.

EXAMPLE 2   The demand function for a product is $p = \sqrt{49 - 6x}$ and the supply function is $p = x + 1$. Find the equilibrium point and the consumer's surplus there.

Solution   The graphs of the supply and demand functions are shown in Figure 13.18.

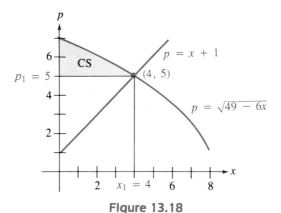

Figure 13.18

We can find the equilibrium point by solving the two equations simultaneously.

$$\sqrt{49 - 6x} = x + 1$$

$$49 - 6x = (x + 1)^2$$

$$0 = x^2 + 8x - 48$$

$$0 = (x + 12)(x - 4)$$

$$x = 4 \text{ or } x = -12$$

Thus the equilibrium quantity is 4 and the equilibrium price is \$5 (because $x = -12$ is not a solution). The consumer's surplus is given by

$$CS = \int_0^4 f(x)\, dx - p_1 x_1$$

$$= \int_0^4 \sqrt{49 - 6x}\, dx - 5 \cdot 4$$

$$= -\frac{1}{6} \int_0^4 \sqrt{49 - 6x}(-6\, dx) - 20$$

$$= -\frac{1}{9} (49 - 6x)^{3/2} \Big|_0^4 - 20$$

$$= -\frac{1}{9} [(25)^{3/2} - (49)^{3/2}] - 20$$

$$= -\frac{1}{9} (125 - 343) - 20$$

$$\approx 24.22 - 20 = 4.22.$$

The consumer's surplus is \$4.22.

EXAMPLE 3 If a monopoly has a total cost function $C(x) = 60 + 2x^2$ for a product whose demand is given by $p = 30 - x$, find the consumer's surplus at the point where the monopoly has maximum profit.

Solution We must first find the point where the profit function is maximized. Since the demand for x units is $p = 30 - x$, the total revenue is $R(x) = (30 - x)x = 30x - x^2$. Thus the profit function is

$$P(x) = R(x) - C(x)$$
$$P(x) = 30x - x^2 - (60 + 2x^2)$$
$$P(x) = 30x - 60 - 3x^2.$$

Then $\qquad P'(x) = 30 - 6x.$

So $\qquad 0 = 30 - 6x$ has solution $x = 5$.

Since $P''(5) = -6 < 0$, the profit for the monopolist is maximized when $x = 5$ units are sold at price $p = 25$.

The consumer's surplus at $x = 5$, $p = 25$ is given by

$$CS = \int_0^5 f(x)\, dx - 5 \cdot 25,$$

where $f(x)$ is the demand function.

$$CS = \int_0^5 (30 - x)\, dx - 125$$

$$= 30x - \left. \frac{x^2}{2} \right|_0^5 - 125$$

$$= \left(150 - \frac{25}{2} \right) - 125$$

$$= \frac{25}{2} = 12.50$$

The consumer's surplus is $12.50.

Producer's Surplus

When a product is sold at the equilibrium price, some producers will also benefit, for they would have sold the product at a lower price. The area between the line $p = p_1$ and the supply curve (from $x = 0$ to $x = x_1$) gives the producer's surplus (see Figure 13.19).

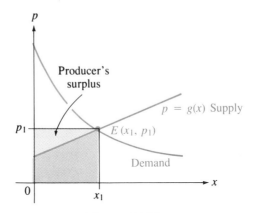

Figure 13.19

If the supply function is $p = g(x)$, the **producer's surplus** is given by the area between the graph of $p = g(x)$ and the x-axis from 0 to x_1 *subtracted from* the area of the rectangle $0x_1Ep_1$.

$$\text{PS} = p_1x_1 - \int_0^{x_1} g(x) \, dx$$

Note that p_1x_1 represents the total revenue at the equilibrium point.

EXAMPLE 4   Suppose the supply function for a product is $p = x^2 + x$. If the equilibrium price is $20, what is the producer's surplus?

Solution   Since $p = 20$, we can find x as follows:

$$20 = x^2 + x$$
$$0 = x^2 + x - 20$$
$$0 = (x + 5)(x - 4)$$
$$x = -5, x = 4.$$

The equilibrium point is $x = 4$, $p = 20$. The producer's surplus is given by

$$PS = 20 \cdot 4 - \int_0^4 (x^2 + x) \, dx$$

$$= 80 - \left(\frac{x^3}{3} + \frac{x^2}{2} \right) \Big|_0^4$$

$$= 80 - \left(\frac{64}{3} + 8 \right)$$

$$\approx 50.67.$$

The producer's surplus is $50.67. See Figure 13.20.

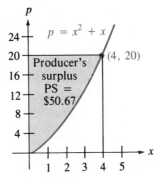

Figure 13.20

EXAMPLE 5   The demand function for a product is $p = \sqrt{49 - 6x}$ and the supply function is $p = x + 1$. Find the producer's surplus.

Solution   We found the equilibrium point for these functions to be $(4, 5)$ in Example 2 (see Figure 13.18). The producer's surplus is

$$PS = 5 \cdot 4 - \int_0^4 (x + 1) \, dx$$

$$= 20 - \left(\frac{x^2}{2} + x \right) \Big|_0^4$$

$$= 20 - (8 + 4) = 8.$$

The producer's surplus is $8.

Continuous Income Streams

An oil company's profits depend upon the amount of oil that can be pumped from a well. Thus, we can consider a pump at an oil field as producing a continuous stream of income for the owner. Since both the pump and the oil field "wear out" with time, the continuous stream of income is a function of time. Suppose $f(t)$ is the (annual) *rate* of flow of income from this pump; then we can find the total income from the rate of income by using integration. In particular, the total income for k years is given by

$$\text{Total income} = \int_0^k f(t) \, dt.$$

EXAMPLE 6   A small oil company considers the continuous pumping of oil from a well as a continuous income stream with its annual rate of flow at time t given by

$$f(t) = 600e^{-0.2t}$$

in thousands of dollars. Find an estimate of the total income from this well over the next 10 years.

Solution
$$\begin{aligned}
\text{Total income} &= \int_0^{10} f(t) \, dt \\
&= \int_0^{10} 600e^{-0.2t} \, dt \\
&= \frac{600}{-0.2} e^{-0.2t} \Big|_0^{10} \\
&= -3000(e^{-2} - 1) \\
&\approx 2594 \text{ (to the nearest integer)}
\end{aligned}$$

Thus, the total income is approximately $2,594,000.

Besides the total income from a continuous income stream, the present value of the stream is also important. The present value is useful in deciding when to replace machinery (such as the oil pump in the example) or what new equipment to select.

To find the present value of a continuous stream of income with rate of flow $f(t)$, we first graph the function $f(t)$ and divide the time interval from 0 to k into n subintervals of width Δt_i, $i = 1$ to n.

The total amount of income is the area under this curve between $t = 0$ and $t = k$. We can approximate the amount of income in each subinterval by finding the area of the rectangle in that subinterval. (See Figure 13.21.)

We have shown that the compound amount S that accrues if P is invested for t years at an annual rate r, compounded continuously, is

$$S = Pe^{rt}.$$

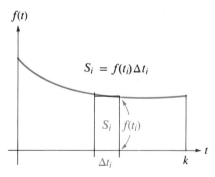

Figure 13.21

Thus the present value of the investment or annuity that yields the single payment of $S after t years is

$$P = \frac{S}{e^{rt}} = Se^{-rt}.$$

The contribution to S in the ith subinterval is $S_i = f(t_i)\,\Delta t_i$, and the present value of this amount is

$$P_i = f(t_i)\Delta t_i e^{-rt_i}.$$

Thus the total present value of S can be approximated by

$$\sum_{i=1}^{n} f(t_i)\Delta t_i e^{-rt_i}.$$

This approximation improves as $\Delta t_i \to 0$ with the present value given by

$$\lim_{\Delta t_i \to 0} \sum_{i=1}^{n} f(t_i)\Delta t_i e^{-rt_i}.$$

This limit gives the present value as a definite integral.

Present Value of a Continuous Income Stream	If $f(t)$ is the rate of continuous income flow at interest rate r, compounded continuously, then the present value of the continuous income stream is $$\text{Present value} = \int_0^k f(t)e^{-rt}\,dt,$$ where $t = 0$ to $t = k$ is the time interval.

EXAMPLE 7   Suppose that the oil company in Example 6 is planning to sell the well due to its remote location. Suppose further that the company wants to use the present value

of the well over the next 10 years to help establish its selling price. If they determine that the annual rate of flow is

$$f(t) = 600e^{-0.2(t+5)}$$

in thousands of dollars, and if money is worth 10%, compounded continuously, find this present value.

Solution

$$\text{Present value} = \int_0^{10} f(t)e^{-rt}\, dt$$

$$= \int_0^{10} 600e^{-0.2(t+5)}\, e^{-0.1t}\, dt$$

$$= \int_0^{10} 600e^{-0.3t-1}\, dt$$

$$= \frac{600}{-0.3} e^{-0.3t-1} \Big|_0^{10}$$

$$= -2000(e^{-4} - e^{-1})$$

$$\approx 699 \text{ (to the nearest integer)}$$

Thus, the present value is $699,000.

Exercise 13.4

CONSUMER'S SURPLUS

1. The demand function for a product is $p = 34 - x^2$. If the equilibrium price is $9, what is the consumer's surplus?
2. The demand function for a product is $p = 100 - 4x$. If the equilibrium price is $40, what is the consumer's surplus?
3. The demand function for a product is $p = 200/(x + 2)$. If the equilibrium quantity is 8 units, what is the consumer's surplus?
4. The demand function for a product is $p = 100/(1 + 2x)$. If the equilibrium quantity is 12 units, what is the consumer's surplus?
5. The demand function for a certain product is $p = 81 - x^2$ and the supply function is $p = x^2 + 4x + 11$. Find the equilibrium point and the consumer's surplus there.
6. The demand function for a certain product is $p = 49 - x^2$ and the supply function is $p = 4x + 4$. Find the equilibrium point and the consumer's surplus there.
7. If the demand function for a product is $p = 12/(x + 1)$ and the supply function for it is $p = 1 + 0.2x$, find the consumer's surplus under pure competition.
8. If the demand function for a good is $p = 110 - x^2$ and the supply function for it is $p = 2 - \frac{6}{5}x + \frac{1}{5}x^2$, find the consumer's surplus under pure competition.
9. A monopoly has a total cost function $C = 1000 + 120x + 6x^2$ for its product, which has demand function $p = 360 - 3x - 2x^2$. Find the consumer's surplus at the point where the monopoly has maximum profit.
10. A monopoly has a total cost function $C = 500 + 2x^2 + 10x$ for its product, which has demand function $p = -\frac{1}{3}x^2 - 2x + 30$. Find the consumer's surplus at the point where the monopoly has a maximum profit.

PRODUCER'S SURPLUS

11. Suppose the supply function for a good is $p = 4x^2 + 2x + 2$. If the equilibrium price is $422, what is the producer's surplus there?

12. Suppose the supply function for a good is $p = 0.1x^2 + 3x + 20$. If the equilibrium price is $36, what is the producer's surplus there?

13. If the supply function for a commodity is $p = 10e^{x/3}$, what is the producer's surplus when 15 units are sold?

14. If the supply function for a commodity is $p = 40 + 100(x + 1)^2$, what is the producer's surplus at $x = 20$?

15. Find the producer's surplus for a product if its demand function is $p = 81 - x^2$ and its supply function is $p = x^2 + 4x + 11$.

16. Find the producer's surplus for a product if its demand function is $p = 49 - x^2$ and its supply function is $p = 4x + 4$.

17. Find the producer's surplus for a product with demand function $p = 12/(x + 1)$ and supply function $p = 1 + 0.2x$.

18. Find the producer's surplus for a product with demand function $p = 110 - x^2$ and supply function $p = 2 - \frac{6}{5}x + \frac{1}{5}x^2$.

19. The demand function for a certain product is $p = 144 - 2x^2$ and the supply function is $p = x^2 + 33x + 48$. Find the producer's surplus at the equilibrium point.

20. The demand function for a product is $p = 280 - 4x - x^2$ and the supply function for it is $p = 160 + 4x + x^2$. Find the producer's surplus at the equilibrium point.

CONTINUOUS INCOME STREAMS

21. Find the total income over the next 10 years from a continuous income stream that has an annual rate of flow at time t given by $f(t) = 12,000$ (dollars).

22. Find the total income over the next 8 years from a continuous income stream with an annual rate of flow at time t given by $f(t) = 8500$ (dollars).

23. Suppose a steel company views the production of its continuous caster as a continuous income stream with a monthly rate of flow at time t given by

$$f(t) = 24,000e^{0.03t} \text{ (dollars)}.$$

Find the total income from this caster in the first year.

24. Suppose that the Quick-Fix Car Service franchise finds that the income generated by its stores can be modeled by assuming the income is a continuous stream with monthly rate of flow at time t given by

$$f(t) = 10,000e^{0.02t} \text{ (dollars)}.$$

Find the total income from a Quick-Fix store for the first two years of operation.

25. A small brewery considers the output of its bottling machine as a continuous income stream with annual rate of flow at time t given by

$$f(t) = 80e^{-0.1t}$$

in thousands of dollars. Find the total income from this stream for the next 10 years.

26. A company that services a number of vending machines considers their income as a continuous stream with its annual rate of flow at time t given by

$$f(t) = 120e^{-0.4t}$$

in thousands of dollars. Find the income from this stream over the next 5 years.

27. A franchise models the profit from its store as a continuous income stream with monthly rate of flow at time t given by

$$f(t) = 3000e^{0.004t} \text{ (dollars).}$$

When a new store opens, its manager is judged against the model, with special emphasis on the second half of the first year. Find the total profit for the second six-month period ($t = 6$ to $t = 12$).

28. The Quick-Fix Car Service franchise has a continuous income stream with a monthly rate of flow modeled by $f(t) = 10{,}000e^{0.02t}$ (dollars). Find the total income for years 2 through 5.

29. A continuous income stream has its annual rate of flow at time t given by

$$f(t) = 12{,}000e^{0.04t} \text{ (dollars).}$$

If money is worth 8%, compounded continuously, find the present value of this stream for the next 8 years.

30. A continuous income stream has an annual rate of flow at time t given by

$$f(t) = 9000e^{0.12t} \text{ (dollars).}$$

Find the present value of this stream for the next 10 years, if money is worth 6%, compounded continuously.

31. The income from an established chain of laundromats is a continuous stream with its annual rate of flow at time t given by $f(t) = 63{,}000$ (dollars). If money is worth 7%, compounded continuously, find the present value of this chain over the next 5 years.

32. The profit from an insurance agency can be considered as a continuous income stream with annual rate of flow at time t given by $f(t) = 84{,}000$ (dollars). Find the present value of this agency over the next 12 years, if money is worth 8%, compounded continuously.

33. Suppose a printing firm considers the production of its presses as a continuous income stream. If the annual rate of flow at time t is given by

$$f(t) = 97.5e^{-0.2(t+3)}$$

in thousands of dollars, and if money is worth 6%, compounded continuously, find the present value of the presses over the next 10 years.

34. Suppose that a vending machine company is considering selling some of its machines. Suppose further that the income from these particular machines is a continuous stream with annual rate of flow at time t given by

$$f(t) = 12e^{-0.4(t+3)}$$

in thousands of dollars. Find the present value of these machines over the next 5 years if money is worth 10%, compounded continuously.

35. A 58-year old couple is considering opening a business of their own. They will purchase either an established Gift and Card Shoppe or open a new Video Rental Palace. The Gift Shoppe has a continuous income stream with an annual rate of flow at time t given by

$$G(t) = 30{,}000 \text{ (dollars),}$$

and the Video Palace has a continuous income stream with a projected annual rate of flow at time t given by

$$V(t) = 21{,}600e^{0.08t} \text{ (dollars).}$$

The initial investment for each business is the same, and money is worth 10%, compounded continuously. Find the present value of each business over the next 7 years (until the couple reaches age 65), to see which is the better buy.

36. If the couple in problem 35 plans to keep the business until age 70 (for the next 12 years), find each present value to see which business is the better buy in this case.

13.5   Using Tables of Integrals

Objective ☐ To use tables of integrals to evaluate certain integrals

We have used some special integration formulas to evaluate integrals, but many integration problems exist that require additional formulas or methods. In this section we will learn how to use a table of integration formulas already developed for us. Table 13.1 contains a selected number of integration formulas (many more exist). Using the formulas is not quite as easy as it may sound, for finding the correct formula and using it properly may present some problems. The following examples illustrate how these formulas are used.

Table 13.1   Integration formulas

1. $\displaystyle\int u^n \, du = \frac{u^{n+1}}{n+1} + C, \qquad \text{for } n \neq -1$

2. $\displaystyle\int \frac{du}{u} = \int u^{-1} \, du = \ln |u| + C$

3. $\displaystyle\int a^u \, du = a^u \log_a e + C = \frac{a^u}{\ln a} + C$

4. $\displaystyle\int e^u \, du = e^u + C$

5. $\displaystyle\int \frac{du}{a^2 - u^2} = \frac{1}{2a} \ln \left| \frac{a+u}{a-u} \right| + C$

6. $\displaystyle\int \sqrt{u^2 + a^2} \, du = \frac{1}{2} (u\sqrt{u^2 + a^2} + a^2 \ln |u + \sqrt{u^2 + a^2}|) + C$

7. $\displaystyle\int \sqrt{u^2 - a^2} \, du = \frac{1}{2} (u\sqrt{u^2 - a^2} - a^2 \ln |u + \sqrt{u^2 - a^2}|) + C$

8. $\displaystyle\int \frac{du}{\sqrt{u^2 + a^2}} = \ln |u + \sqrt{u^2 + a^2}| + C$

9. $\displaystyle\int \frac{du}{u\sqrt{a^2 - u^2}} = -\frac{1}{a} \ln \left| \frac{a + \sqrt{a^2 - u^2}}{u} \right| + C$

10. $\displaystyle\int \frac{du}{\sqrt{u^2 - a^2}} = \ln |u + \sqrt{u^2 - a^2}| + C$

11. $\displaystyle\int \frac{du}{u\sqrt{a^2 + u^2}} = -\frac{1}{a} \ln \left| \frac{a + \sqrt{a^2 + u^2}}{u} \right| + C$

12. $\displaystyle\int \frac{u \, du}{au + b} = \frac{u}{a} - \frac{b}{a^2} \ln |au + b| + C$

13. $\displaystyle\int \frac{du}{u(au + b)} = \frac{1}{b} \ln \left| \frac{u}{au + b} \right| + C$

14. $\displaystyle\int \ln u \, du = u(\ln u - 1) + C$

15. $\displaystyle\int \frac{u \, du}{(au + b)^2} = \frac{1}{a^2} \left(\ln |au + b| + \frac{b}{au + b} \right) + C$

16. $\displaystyle\int u\sqrt{au + b} \, du = \frac{2(3au - 2b)(au + b)^{3/2}}{15a^2} + C$

17. $\displaystyle\int u \, dv = uv - \int v \, du$

EXAMPLE 1   Evaluate $\displaystyle\int \frac{dx}{\sqrt{x^2 + 4}}$.

Solution   We must find a formula in the table that is of the same form as this integral. We see that formula 8 has the desired form, *if* we let $u = x$ and $a = 2$. Thus

$$\int \frac{dx}{\sqrt{x^2 + 4}} = \ln |x + \sqrt{x^2 + 4}| + C.$$

EXAMPLE 2   Evaluate $\displaystyle\int_1^2 \frac{dx}{x^2 + 2x}$.

Solution   There does not appear to be any formula having exactly the same form as our integral. But if we rewrite our integral as

$$\int_1^2 \frac{dx}{x(x + 2)} ,$$

we see that formula 13 will work. Letting $u = x$, $a = 1$, and $b = 2$, we get

$$\int_1^2 \frac{dx}{x(x + 2)} = \frac{1}{2} \ln \left| \frac{x}{x + 2} \right|_1^2$$

$$= \frac{1}{2} \ln \left| \frac{2}{4} \right| - \frac{1}{2} \ln \left| \frac{1}{3} \right|$$

$$= \frac{1}{2} \left(\ln \frac{1}{2} - \ln \frac{1}{3} \right)$$

$$= \frac{1}{2} \ln \frac{3}{2}$$

$$= \frac{1}{2} \ln 1.5.$$

Although the formulas are given in terms of the variable u, they may be used with any variable.

EXAMPLE 3   Evaluate $\displaystyle\int \frac{dq}{9 - q^2}$.

Solution   The formula that applies in this case is formula 5, with $a = 3$ and $u = q$. Then

$$\int \frac{dq}{9 - q^2} = \frac{1}{2 \cdot 3} \ln \left| \frac{3 + q}{3 - q} \right| + C = \frac{1}{6} \ln \left| \frac{3 + q}{3 - q} \right| + C$$

EXAMPLE 4   Evaluate $\displaystyle\int \ln (2x + 1) \, dx$.

Solution   This integral has the form of formula 14, with $u = 2x + 1$. But if $u = 2x + 1$, du must be represented by the differential of $2x + 1$ (that is, $2\,dx$). Thus

$$\int \ln (2x + 1)\, dx = \frac{1}{2} \int \ln (2x + 1)(2\, dx)$$

$$= \frac{1}{2} (2x + 1)[\ln (2x + 1) - 1] + C.$$

EXAMPLE 5   Evaluate $\displaystyle\int_2^3 \frac{dx}{x\sqrt{81 - 9x^2}}$.

Solution   This integral is similar to that of formula 9 in Table 13.1. Letting $a = 9$ and $u = 3x$, and multiplying the numerator and denominator by 3 gives the proper form.

$$\int_2^3 \frac{dx}{x\sqrt{81 - 9x^2}} = \int_2^3 \frac{3\,dx}{3x\sqrt{81 - 9x^2}}$$

$$= -\frac{1}{9} \ln \left|\frac{9 + \sqrt{81 - 9x^2}}{3x}\right|_2^3$$

$$= -\frac{1}{9} \ln \left(\frac{9 + \sqrt{0}}{9}\right) - \left[-\frac{1}{9} \ln \left(\frac{9 + \sqrt{45}}{6}\right)\right]$$

$$= \frac{1}{9} \left[\ln \left(\frac{9 + \sqrt{45}}{6}\right) - \ln (1)\right] = \frac{1}{9} \ln \left(\frac{3 + \sqrt{5}}{2}\right)$$

It should be pointed out again that the formulas given in Table 13.1 represent a very small sample of the integration formulas. Additional formulas may be found in books of mathematical tables.

Exercise 13.5

Evaluate the following integrals.

1. $\displaystyle\int \frac{dx}{16 - x^2}$

2. $\displaystyle\int \frac{dx}{x(3x + 5)}$

3. $\displaystyle\int_1^4 \frac{dx}{x\sqrt{9 + x^2}}$

4. $\displaystyle\int \frac{dx}{x\sqrt{9 - x^2}}$

5. $\displaystyle\int \ln w\, dw$

6. $\displaystyle\int \frac{dv}{v(3v + 8)}$

7. $\displaystyle\int_0^2 \frac{q\, dq}{6q + 9}$

8. $\displaystyle\int_1^5 \frac{dq}{q\sqrt{25 + q^2}}$

9. $\displaystyle\int 3^x\, dx$

10. $\displaystyle\int_0^3 \sqrt{x^2 + 16}\, dx$

11. $\displaystyle\int_5^7 \sqrt{x^2 - 25}\, dx$

12. $\displaystyle\int \frac{x\, dx}{(3x + 2)^2}$

13. $\int w\sqrt{4w + 5}\, dw$

14. $\int \dfrac{dy}{\sqrt{9 + y^2}}$

15. $\int x\, 5^{x^2}\, dx$

16. $\int \sqrt{9x^2 + 4}\, dx$

17. $\int_0^3 x\sqrt{x^2 + 4}\, dx$

18. $\int x\sqrt{x^4 - 36}\, dx$

19. $\int \dfrac{5\, dx}{x\sqrt{8 - x^2}}$

20. $\int x\, e^{x^2}\, dx$

21. $\int \dfrac{dx}{\sqrt{9x^2 - 4}}$

22. $\int \dfrac{dx}{16 - 4x^2}$

23. $\int_5^6 \dfrac{dx}{x^2 - 16}$

24. $\int_0^1 \dfrac{x\, dx}{6 - 5x}$

25. $\int \dfrac{dx}{\sqrt{(3x + 1)^2 + 1}}$

26. $\int \dfrac{dx}{9 - (2x + 3)^2}$

27. $\int_0^3 x\sqrt{(x^2 + 1)^2 + 9}\, dx$

28. $\int_1^e x \ln x^2\, dx$

29. $\int \dfrac{x\, dx}{7 - 3x^2}$

30. $\int_0^1 \dfrac{e^x}{1 + e^x}\, dx$

31. $\int \dfrac{dx}{\sqrt{4x^2 + 7}}$

32. $\int e^{2x}\sqrt{3e^x + 1}\, dx$

33. $\int \dfrac{e^{\sqrt{x-1}}}{\sqrt{x - 1}}\, dx$

34. $\int \dfrac{3x}{\sqrt{x^4 - 9}}\, dx$

35. $\int \dfrac{x^3\, dx}{(4x^2 + 5)^2}$

36. $\int (e^x + 1)^3\, e^x\, dx$

APPLICATIONS

37. If the supply function for a commodity is $p = 40 + 100 \ln (x + 1)^2$, what is the producer's surplus at $x = 20$?

38. If the demand function for a good is $p = 5000e^{-x} + 4$, where x is the number of hundreds of bushels of wheat, what is the consumer's surplus at $x = 7$, $p = 9.10$?

39. If the marginal cost for a good is $\overline{MC} = \sqrt{x^2 + 9}$ and if the fixed cost is $300, what is the total cost function?

40. What is the total cost of producing 4 units for the good in problem 39?

41. Suppose the demand function for an appliance is

$$p = \frac{400q + 400}{(q + 2)^2}.$$

What is the consumer's surplus if the equilibrium price is $19 and the equilibrium quantity is 18?

42. An isolated community of 1000 people susceptible to a certain disease is exposed when one member returns carrying the disease. If x represents the number infected with the disease at time t (in days), then the rate of change of x is proportional to the product of the number infected, x, and the number still susceptible, $1000 - x$. That is,

$$\frac{dx}{dt} = kx(1000 - x).$$

(a) If $k = 0.01$, solve this differential equation.

(b) Find how long before half the population of the community is affected.

(c) Find the rate of new cases, dx/dt, after every other day for the first 13 days.

43. Suppose that in 1982, the rate of increase of new AIDS cases was predicted to be

$$\frac{dN}{dt} = 2^t(700),$$

where t is the number of years from 1982. If the number of AIDS cases was 1012 in 1982 ($t = 0$), what would be the predicted number of cases for 1986 ($t = 4$)? (The actual number of new cases in 1986 was 13,898.)

13.6   Integration by Parts

Objective   ☐   To evaluate integrals using the method of integration by parts

Formula 17 in Table 13.1 is the formula for **integration by parts:**

$$\int u \, dv = u \cdot v - \int v \, du.$$

This formula is very useful if the integral we seek to evaluate can be treated as the product of one function, u, and the differential dv of a second function, so that the two integrals $\int dv$ and $\int v \cdot du$ can be found. Let us consider an example using this method.

EXAMPLE 1   Evaluate $\int xe^x \, dx$.

Solution   We cannot evaluate this integral using methods we have learned up to now. But we can "split" the integrand into two parts, setting one part equal to u and the second part equal to dv. This "split" must be done in such a way that $\int dv$ and $\int v \, du$ can be evaluated. Letting $u = x$ and $dv = e^x \, dx$ are possible choices. If we make these choices, we have

$$u = x \qquad dv = e^x \, dx$$
$$du = 1 \, dx \qquad v = e^x$$

Then

$$\int xe^x \, dx = u \cdot v - \int v \, du$$
$$= x \cdot e^x - \int e^x \, dx$$
$$= xe^x - e^x + C.$$

We see that choosing $u = x$ and $dv = e^x \, dx$ worked in evaluating $\int xe^x \, dx$ in Example 1. If we had chosen $u = e^x$ and $dv = x \, dx$, the results would not have been so successful.

How can we select u and dv to make integration by parts work? There are no general rules for separating the integrand into u and dv, but the goal is to select a dv that is integrable and will result in an $\int v \, du$ that is also integrable. There are usually just two reasonable choices, and it may be necessary to try both. Practice will increase your insight and lead to increasingly successful educated guesses. Consider the following examples.

EXAMPLE 2   Evaluate $\int x \ln x \, dx$.

Solution   Let $u = \ln x$ and $dv = x \, dx$. Then

$$du = \frac{1}{x} \, dx \quad \text{and} \quad v = \frac{x^2}{2}.$$

So

$$\int x \ln x \, dx = u \cdot v - \int v \, du$$

$$= (\ln x) \frac{x^2}{2} - \int \frac{x^2}{2} \cdot \frac{1}{x} \, dx$$

$$= \frac{x^2}{2} \ln x - \int \frac{x}{2} \, dx$$

$$= \frac{x^2}{2} \ln x - \frac{x^2}{4} + C.$$

Note that letting $dv = \ln x \, dx$ would lead to great difficulty in evaluating $\int dv$ and $\int v \, du$, so it would not be a wise choice.

EXAMPLE 3   Evaluate $\int \ln x^2 \, dx$.

Solution   It is frequently good practice to let expressions involving logarithms be part of u in integrating by parts, as the derivatives of logarithmic expressions are usually simple.

In this problem, we can let $u = \ln x^2 = 2 \ln x$ and $dv = dx$, so $du = 2 \cdot \frac{1}{x} \, dx$ and $v = x$. Then

$$\int \ln x^2 \, dx = x \ln x^2 - \int x \cdot \frac{2}{x} \, dx$$

$$= x \ln x^2 - 2x + C.$$

Note that if we write $\ln x^2$ as $2 \ln x$, we can evaluate this integral using formula 14 of Table 13.1.

Sometimes it is necessary to repeat the integration by parts to complete the evaluation. As before, the goal is to produce a new integral that is simpler.

EXAMPLE 4   Evaluate $\int x^2 e^{2x}\, dx$.

Solution   Let $u = x^2$ and $dv = e^{2x}\, dx$, so $du = 2x\, dx$ and $v = \frac{1}{2}e^{2x}$. Then

$$\int x^2 e^{2x}\, dx = \frac{1}{2} x^2 e^{2x} - \int xe^{2x}\, dx.$$

We cannot evaluate $\int xe^{2x}\, dx$ directly, but this new integral is simpler than the original, and a second integration by parts will be successful. Letting $u = x$ and $dv = e^{2x}\, dx$ gives $du = dx$ and $v = \frac{1}{2}e^{2x}$. So

$$\int x^2 e^{2x}\, dx = \frac{1}{2} x^2 e^{2x} - \left(\frac{1}{2} xe^{2x} - \int \frac{1}{2} e^{2x}\, dx \right)$$

$$= \frac{1}{2} x^2 e^{2x} - \frac{1}{2} xe^{2x} + \frac{1}{4} e^{2x} + C$$

$$= \frac{1}{4} e^{2x}(2x^2 - 2x + 1) + C.$$

The most obvious choices for u and dv are not always the correct ones, as the following example shows. Integration by parts still requires some trial and error.

EXAMPLE 5   Evaluate $\int x^3 \sqrt{x^2 + 1}\, dx$.

Solution   Since x^3 can be integrated easily, it may appear that the new integral would be simplified if we let $u = \sqrt{x^2 + 1}$ and $dv = x^3$. But then du would be $\frac{1}{2}(x^2 + 1)^{-1/2}\, 2x$, making $\int v\, du$ more complicated than the original integral. However, we can use $\sqrt{x^2 + 1}$ as part of dv; we can evaluate $\int dv$ if we let $dv = x\sqrt{x^2 + 1}\, dx$. Then $u = x^2$ and $dv = x(x^2 + 1)^{1/2}\, dx$, so $du = 2x\, dx$ and $v = \frac{1}{3}(x^2 + 1)^{3/2}$. Thus

$$\int x^3 \sqrt{x^2 + 1}\, dx = \frac{x^2}{3}(x^2 + 1)^{3/2} - \int \frac{2x}{3}(x^2 + 1)^{3/2}\, dx$$

$$= \frac{x^2}{3}(x^2 + 1)^{3/2} - \frac{2}{15}(x^2 + 1)^{5/2} + C$$

$$= \frac{1}{15}(x^2 + 1)^{3/2}[5x^2 - 2(x^2 + 1)] + C$$

$$= \frac{1}{15}(x^2 + 1)^{3/2}(3x^2 - 2) + C.$$

One further note about integration by parts. It can be very useful on certain types of problems, but not on all types. Don't attempt to use integration by parts when easier methods are available.

Exercise 13.6

Evaluate the following integrals.

1. $\displaystyle\int xe^{2x}\,dx$

2. $\displaystyle\int xe^{-x}\,dx$

3. $\displaystyle\int x^2 \ln x\,dx$

4. $\displaystyle\int x^3 \ln x\,dx$

5. $\displaystyle\int_4^6 q\sqrt{q-4}\,dq$

6. $\displaystyle\int_0^1 y(1-y)^{3/2}\,dy$

7. $\displaystyle\int_0^1 x^2 e^x\,dx$

8. $\displaystyle\int x^3 e^x\,dx$

9. $\displaystyle\int \frac{\ln x}{x^2}\,dx$

10. $\displaystyle\int \frac{\ln (x-1)}{\sqrt{x-1}}\,dx$

11. $\displaystyle\int xe^{x^2}\,dx$

12. $\displaystyle\int x^2 e^{-x}\,dx$

13. $\displaystyle\int \frac{x}{\sqrt{x-3}}\,dx$

14. $\displaystyle\int \frac{x^2}{\sqrt{x-3}}\,dx$

15. $\displaystyle\int_1^e \ln x\,dx$

16. $\displaystyle\int_0^4 \frac{t}{e^t}\,dt$

17. $\displaystyle\int x \ln (2x-3)\,dx$

18. $\displaystyle\int x \ln (4x)\,dx$

19. $\displaystyle\int q^3 \sqrt{q^2-3}\,dq$

20. $\displaystyle\int \frac{x^3}{\sqrt{9-x^2}}\,dx$

21. $\displaystyle\int_0^4 x^3\sqrt{x^2+9}\,dx$

22. $\displaystyle\int_0^2 x^3 e^{x^2}\,dx$ (use problem 11)

23. $\displaystyle\int \sqrt{x}\,\ln x\,dx$

24. $\displaystyle\int_1^2 (\ln x)^2\,dx$

25. $\displaystyle\int x^3 \ln^2 x\,dx$

26. $\displaystyle\int e^{2x}\sqrt{e^x+1}\,dx$

APPLICATIONS

27. If the supply function for a commodity is $p = 30 + 50 \ln (2x+1)^2$, what is the producer's surplus at $x = 30$?

28. If the marginal cost function for a product is $\overline{MC} = 1 + 3 \ln (x+1)$, and if the fixed cost is $100, find the total cost function.

29. Suppose that a machine's production can be considered as a continuous income stream with annual rate of flow at time t given by

$$f(t) = 10{,}000 - 500t \quad \text{(dollars)}.$$

If money is worth 10%, compounded continuously, find the present value of the machine over the next 5 years.

30. Suppose that the production of a machine used to mine coal is considered as a continuous income stream with annual rate of flow at time t given by

$$f(t) = 280{,}000 - 14{,}000t \quad \text{(dollars)}.$$

If money is worth 7%, compounded continuously, find the present value of this machine over the next 8 years.

13.7 Improper Integrals and Their Applications

Objectives
- ☐ To evaluate improper integrals
- ☐ To apply improper integrals to probability density functions and continuous income streams

One application of calculus to business and to statistics involves finding the area of a region that extends infinitely to the left or right along the *x*-axis (see Figure 13.22). The areas of regions of this type can be found using **improper integrals.**

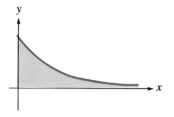 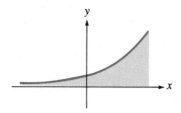 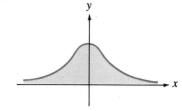

Figure 13.22

Let us consider how to find the area between the curve $y = 1/x^2$ and the *x*-axis to the right of $x = 1$.

To find the area under this curve from $x = 1$ and $x = b$, where *b* is any number greater than 1 (see Figure 13.23), we evaluate

$$A = \int_1^b \frac{1}{x^2}\, dx = \frac{-1}{x}\Big|_1^b = \frac{-1}{b} - \left(\frac{-1}{1}\right)$$

$$= 1 - \frac{1}{b}.$$

Note that the larger *b* is, the closer the area is to 1. If $b = 100$, $A = 99/100$, if $b = 1000$, $A = 999/1000$, and if $b = 1,000,000$, $A = 999,999/1,000,000$.

We can represent the area of the region under $1/x^2$ to the right of 1 using the notation

$$\lim_{b \to \infty} \int_1^b \frac{1}{x^2}\, dx = \lim_{b \to \infty}\left(1 - \frac{1}{b}\right),$$

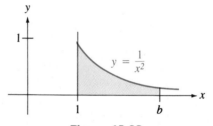

Figure 13.23

where $\lim\limits_{b\to\infty}$ represents the limit as b gets larger without bound. Clearly

$$\lim_{b\to\infty}\frac{1}{b} = 0,$$

so

$$\lim_{b\to\infty}\left(1 - \frac{1}{b}\right) = 1.$$

Thus the area under the curve $y = 1/x^2$ to the right of $x = 1$ is 1.

In general, we define the area under a curve $y = f(x)$ to the right of $x = a$, with $f(x) \geq 0$, to be

$$\text{Area} = \lim_{b\to\infty}(\text{area from } a \text{ to } b) = \lim_{b\to\infty}\int_a^b f(x)\,dx.$$

This motivates the definition of the improper integral.

Improper Integral

$$\int_a^\infty f(x)\,dx = \lim_{b\to\infty}\int_a^b f(x)\,dx$$

If the limit defining the improper integral is a finite number, we say the integral *converges;* if the limit is not a finite number, we say the integral *diverges.*

EXAMPLE 1   Evaluate the following improper integrals, if they converge.

(a) $\displaystyle\int_1^\infty \frac{1}{x^3}\,dx$ (b) $\displaystyle\int_1^\infty \frac{1}{x}\,dx$

Solution   (a) $\displaystyle\int_1^\infty \frac{1}{x^3}\,dx = \lim_{b\to\infty}\int_1^b \frac{1}{x^3}\,dx$

$$= \lim_{b\to\infty}\left[\frac{x^{-2}}{-2}\right]_1^b$$

$$= \lim_{b\to\infty}\left[\frac{-1}{2b^2} - \left(\frac{-1}{2(1)^2}\right)\right]$$

$$= \lim_{b\to\infty}\left(\frac{-1}{2b^2} + \frac{1}{2}\right)$$

Now as $b \to \infty$, $\dfrac{-1}{2b^2} \to 0$, so the limit, and the integral, converge to $\dfrac{1}{2}$. That is,

$$\int_1^\infty \frac{1}{x^3}\,dx = \frac{1}{2}.$$

(b) $\displaystyle\int_1^\infty \frac{1}{x}\,dx = \lim_{b\to\infty}\int_1^b \frac{1}{x}\,dx$

$\displaystyle\qquad = \lim_{b\to\infty}\left[\ln x\right]_1^b$

$\displaystyle\qquad = \lim_{b\to\infty}(\ln b - \ln 1)$

Now $\ln b$ increases without bound as $b \to \infty$, so the limit, and the integral, diverge. We write this as

$$\int_1^\infty \frac{1}{x}\,dx = \infty.$$

From Example 1 we can conclude that the area under the curve $y = 1/x^3$ to the right of $x = 1$ is $\frac{1}{2}$, while the corresponding area under the curve $y = 1/x$ is infinite. (We have already seen that the corresponding area under $y = 1/x^2$ is 1.)

As Figure 13.24 shows, the graphs of the curves look similar, but the graph of $1/x^2$ gets "close" to the x-axis much more rapidly than the graph of $1/x$. The area under $y = 1/x$ does not converge to a finite number because as $x \to \infty$ the graph of $1/x$ does not approach the x-axis rapidly enough.

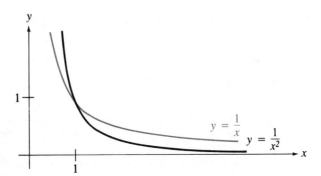

Figure 13.24

We have seen in Section 13.4 that the present value of a continuous income stream over a fixed number of years can be found using a definite integral. When this notion is extended to an infinite time interval, the result is called the **capital value** of the income stream and is given by

$$\text{Capital value} = \int_0^\infty f(t)\, e^{-rt}\, dt,$$

where $f(t)$ is the annual rate of flow at time t and r is the annual interest rate, compounded continuously.

EXAMPLE 2   Suppose an organization wants to establish a trust fund that will provide a continuous income stream with an annual rate of flow at time t given by $f(t) = 10,000$. If the interest rate remains at 10%, compounded continuously, find the capital value of the fund.

Solution   The capital value of the fund is given by

$$\int_0^\infty 10,000e^{-0.10t}\, dt = \lim_{b \to \infty} \int_0^b 10,000e^{-0.10t}\, dt$$

$$= \lim_{b \to \infty} \left[-100,000e^{-0.10t} \right]_0^b$$

$$= \lim_{b \to \infty} \left[\frac{-100,000}{e^{0.10b}} + 100,000 \right]$$

$$= 100,000.$$

Thus, the capital value of the fund is $100,000.

Another term for a fund such as the one in Example 2 is a **perpetuity.** Usually the rate of flow of a perpetuity is a constant. If the rate of flow is a constant A, it can be shown that the capital value is given by A/r (see problem 17 in the exercise set).

A second improper integral has the form

$$\int_{-\infty}^b f(x)\, dx$$

and is defined by:

$$\int_{-\infty}^b f(x)\, dx = \lim_{a \to \infty} \int_{-a}^b f(x)\, dx.$$

The integral converges if the limit on the right is finite. In addition, the improper integral

$$\int_{-\infty}^\infty f(x)\, dx$$

is defined by:

$$\int_{-\infty}^\infty f(x)\, dx = \lim_{a \to \infty} \int_{-a}^0 f(x)\, dx + \lim_{b \to \infty} \int_0^b f(x)\, dx$$

If both limits on the right are finite, the improper integral converges; otherwise, it diverges.

EXAMPLE 3   Evaluate the following integrals.

(a) $\displaystyle\int_{-\infty}^{4} e^{3x}\, dx$ (b) $\displaystyle\int_{-\infty}^{\infty} \frac{x^3}{(x^4 + 3)^2}\, dx$

Solution   (a) $\displaystyle\int_{-\infty}^{4} e^{3x}\, dx = \lim_{a \to \infty} \int_{-a}^{4} e^{3x}\, dx$

$$= \lim_{a \to \infty} \left[\left(\frac{1}{3}\right)e^{3x}\right]_{-a}^{4}$$

$$= \lim_{a \to \infty} \left[\left(\frac{1}{3}\right)e^{12} - \left(\frac{1}{3}\right)e^{-3a}\right]$$

$$= \lim_{a \to \infty} \left[\left(\frac{1}{3}\right)e^{12} - \left(\frac{1}{3}\right)\left(\frac{1}{e^{3a}}\right)\right]$$

$$= \frac{1}{3}\, e^{12}$$

(because $1/e^{3a} \to 0$ as $a \to \infty$)

(b) $\displaystyle\int_{-\infty}^{\infty} \frac{x^3}{(x^4 + 3)^2}\, dx = \lim_{a \to \infty} \int_{-a}^{0} \frac{x^3}{(x^4 + 3)^2}\, dx + \lim_{b \to \infty} \int_{0}^{b} \frac{x^3}{(x^4 + 3)^2}\, dx$

$$= \lim_{a \to \infty} \left[\frac{1}{4}\frac{(x^4 + 3)^{-1}}{-1}\right]_{-a}^{0} + \lim_{b \to \infty} \left[\frac{1}{4}\frac{(x^4 + 3)^{-1}}{-1}\right]_{0}^{b}$$

$$= \lim_{a \to \infty} \left[-\frac{1}{4}\left(\frac{1}{3} - \frac{1}{a^4 + 3}\right)\right] + \lim_{b \to \infty} \left[-\frac{1}{4}\left(\frac{1}{b^4 + 3} - \frac{1}{3}\right)\right]$$

$$= -\frac{1}{12} + 0 + 0 + \frac{1}{12} = 0$$

(since $\displaystyle\lim_{a \to \infty} \frac{1}{a^4 + 3} = 0$ and $\displaystyle\lim_{b \to \infty} \frac{1}{b^4 + 3} = 0$)

In Section 13.2, we calculated the probability that a computer component would last between 3 and 5 years when the probability density function for the life span is $f(x) = 0.10e^{-0.10x}$, where x is the number of years, $x \ge 0$. The probability that the component will last more than 3 years is given by the improper integral

$$\int_{3}^{\infty} 0.10e^{-0.10x}\, dx,$$

which gives

$$\lim_{b \to \infty} \int_{3}^{b} 0.10e^{-0.10x}\, dx = \lim_{b \to \infty} \left[-e^{-0.10x}\right]_{3}^{b}$$

$$= \lim_{b \to \infty} \left[-e^{-0.10b} + e^{-0.3}\right]$$

$$= e^{-0.3} = 0.7408.$$

We noted in Chapter 8 that the sum of the probabilities for a probability distribution (i.e., probability density function) equals 1. In particular, we stated that the area under the normal probability curve is 1.

In general, if $f(x) \geq 0$ for all x, then f is a probability density function for a continuous random variable if and only if

$$\int_{-\infty}^{\infty} f(x) \, dx = 1.$$

The complete probability density function for the life span of the computer component mentioned above is

$$f(x) = \begin{cases} 0.10e^{-0.10x} & \text{if } x \geq 0 \\ 0 & \text{if } x < 0. \end{cases}$$

We can verify that

$$\int_{-\infty}^{\infty} f(x) \, dx = 1$$

for this function.

$$\int_{-\infty}^{\infty} f(x) \, dx = \int_{-\infty}^{0} f(x) \, dx + \int_{0}^{\infty} f(x) \, dx = \int_{-\infty}^{0} 0 \, dx + \int_{0}^{\infty} 0.10e^{-0.10x} \, dx$$

$$= 0 + \lim_{b \to \infty} \int_{0}^{b} 0.1e^{-0.10x} \, dx$$

$$= \lim_{b \to \infty} \left[-e^{-0.10x} \right]_{0}^{b}$$

$$= \lim_{b \to \infty} \left[-e^{-0.10b} + 1 \right]$$

$$= 1.$$

In Section 8.5, we found the expected value (mean) of the binomial probability distribution using the formula

$$E(x) = \sum_{i=1}^{n} x \Pr(x).$$

For continuous probability distributions, like the normal probability distribution, the expected value, or mean, can be found by evaluating the improper integral

$$\int_{-\infty}^{\infty} x f(x) \, dx.$$

Expected Value (Mean)	If x is a continuous random variable with probability density function f, then the mean of the probability distribution is $$\int_{-\infty}^{\infty} xf(x)\,dx.$$

The normal distribution density function, in standard form, is

$$f(x) = \frac{1}{\sqrt{2\pi}}\, e^{-x^2/2},$$

so the mean of the normal probability distribution is given by

$$\mu = \int_{-\infty}^{\infty} x\left(\frac{1}{\sqrt{2\pi}}\, e^{-x^2/2}\right) dx$$

$$= \lim_{a\to\infty} \int_{-a}^{0} \frac{1}{\sqrt{2\pi}}\, xe^{-x^2/2}\, dx + \lim_{b\to\infty} \int_{0}^{b} \frac{1}{\sqrt{2\pi}}\, xe^{-x^2/2}\, dx$$

$$= \lim_{a\to\infty} \frac{1}{\sqrt{2\pi}}\left[-e^{-x^2/2}\right]_{-a}^{0} + \lim_{b\to\infty} \frac{1}{\sqrt{2\pi}}\left[-e^{-x^2/2}\right]_{0}^{b}$$

$$= \frac{1}{\sqrt{2\pi}}(-1 + 0) + \frac{1}{\sqrt{2\pi}}(0 + 1) = 0.$$

This verifies the statement in Chapter 8 that the mean of the standard normal distribution is 0.

Exercise 13.7

In problems 1–16, evaluate the improper integrals where possible.

1. $\int_{1}^{\infty} e^{-x}\, dx$

2. $\int_{0}^{\infty} x^2 e^{-x^3}\, dx$

3. $\int_{1}^{\infty} \frac{1}{x^4}\, dx$

4. $\int_{0}^{\infty} e^{3x}\, dx$

5. $\int_{1}^{\infty} \frac{1}{\sqrt{x}}\, dx$

6. $\int_{5}^{\infty} \frac{dx}{(x-1)^3}$

7. $\int_{-\infty}^{-1} \frac{10}{x^2}\, dx$

8. $\int_{-\infty}^{-2} \frac{x}{\sqrt{x^2-1}}\, dx$

9. $\int_{-\infty}^{0} x^2 e^{-x^3}\, dx$

10. $\int_{-\infty}^{0} \frac{x}{(x^2+1)^2}\, dx$

11. $\int_{-\infty}^{-1} \frac{6}{x}\, dx$

12. $\int_{-\infty}^{-2} \frac{3x}{x^2+1}\, dx$

13. $\displaystyle\int_{-\infty}^{\infty} \frac{2x}{x^2 + 1}\, dx$

14. $\displaystyle\int_{-\infty}^{\infty} \frac{x}{(x^2 + 1)^2}\, dx$

15. $\displaystyle\int_{-\infty}^{\infty} x^3 e^{-x^4}\, dx$

16. $\displaystyle\int_{-\infty}^{\infty} x^4 e^{-x^5}\, dx$

APPLICATIONS

17. Suppose that a continuous income stream has an annual rate of flow at time t given by $f(t) = A$, where A is a constant. If the interest rate is r (as a decimal, $r > 0$), compounded continuously, show that the capital value of the stream is A/r.

18. Suppose that a donor wishes to provide a cash gift to a hospital that will generate a continuous income stream with an annual rate of flow at time t given by $f(t) = \$20{,}000$. If money is worth 12%, compounded continuously, find the capital value of this perpetuity.

19. Suppose that a business provides a continuous income stream with an annual rate of flow at time t given by $f(t) = 120e^{0.04t}$ in thousands of dollars. If the interest rate is 9%, compounded continuously, find the capital value of the business.

20. Suppose that the output of the machinery in a factory can be considered as a continuous income stream with annual rate of flow at time t given by $f(t) = 450e^{-0.09t}$ in thousands of dollars. If the annual interest rate is 6%, compounded continuously, find the capital value of the machinery.

21. Suppose that the rate at which a nuclear power plant produces radioactive waste is proportional to the number of years it has been operating, according to $f(t) = 500t$ in pounds per year. Suppose also that the waste decays exponentially at a rate of 3% per year. Then the amount of radioactive waste that will accumulate in b years is given by

$$\int_0^b 500te^{-0.03(b-t)}\, dt.$$

(a) Evaluate this integral.
(b) How much waste will accumulate in the long run? Take the limit as $b \to \infty$ in part (a).

22. The field intensity around an (infinitely) long straight electrical wire is

$$F = \frac{\mu IM}{10} \int_{-\infty}^{\infty} \frac{dx}{(x^2 + r^2)^{3/2}},$$

where μ, r, I, and M are constants. Evaluate this integral.

23. The probability density function for the life span of an electronics part is $f(t) = 0.08e^{-0.08t}$, where t is the number of months in service. Find the probability that any given part of this type lasts longer than 24 months.

24. A transmission repair firm, desiring to offer a lifetime warranty on its repairs, has determined that the probability density function for transmission failure after repair is $f(t) = 0.3e^{-0.3t}$, where t is the number of months after repair. What is the probability that a transmission chosen at random will last
(a) 3 months or less?
(b) more than 3 months?

25. Show that the function

$$f(x) = \begin{cases} \dfrac{200}{x^3} & \text{if } x \geq 10 \\ 0 & \text{otherwise} \end{cases}$$

is a probability density function.

26. Show that

$$f(x) = \begin{cases} 3e^{-3t} & \text{if } t \geq 0 \\ 0 & \text{if } t < 0 \end{cases}$$

is a probability density function.

27. For what value of c is the function

$$f(x) = \begin{cases} c/x^2 & \text{if } x \geq 1 \\ 0 & \text{otherwise} \end{cases}$$

a probability density function?

28. For what value of c is the function

$$f(x) = \begin{cases} c/x^3 & \text{if } x \geq 100 \\ 0 & \text{otherwise} \end{cases}$$

a probability density function?

29. If

$$f(x) = \begin{cases} ce^{-0.5x}, & x \geq 0 \\ 0, & x < 0 \end{cases}$$

is a probability density function, what must be the value of c?

30. If

$$f(x) = \begin{cases} ce^{-kx} & \text{if } x \geq 0 \\ 0 & \text{if } x < 0 \end{cases}$$

is a probability density function, what must be the value of c?

31. Find the mean of the probability distribution if the probability density function is

$$f(x) = \begin{cases} \dfrac{200}{x^3} & \text{if } x \geq 10 \\ 0 & \text{otherwise.} \end{cases}$$

32. Find the mean of the probability distribution if the probability density function is

$$f(x) = \begin{cases} c/x^3 & \text{if } x \geq 100 \\ 0 & \text{otherwise.} \end{cases}$$

Review Exercises

13.1

1. Calculate $\displaystyle\sum_{k=1}^{8} (k^2 + 1)$.

2. Use formulas to simplify

$$\sum_{i=1}^{n} \frac{3i}{n^3}.$$

3. Use 6 subintervals of the same size to approximate the area under the graph of $y = 3x^2$ from $x = 0$ to $x = 1$. Use the right-hand endpoints of the subintervals to find the heights of the rectangles.

4. Use rectangles to find the area under the graph of $y = 3x^2$ from $x = 0$ to $x = 1$. Use n equal subintervals.

13.2

5. Use a definite integral to find the area under the graph of $y = 3x^2$ from $x = 0$ to $x = 1$.

6. Find the area between the graph of $y = x^3 - 4x + 5$ and the x-axis from $x = 1$ to $x = 3$.

Evaluate the following integrals.

7. $\int_1^4 4\sqrt{x^3}\, dx$

8. $\int_{-3}^2 (x^3 - 3x^2 + 4x + 2)\, dx$

9. $\int_0^5 (x^3 + 4x)\, dx$

10. $\int_{-2}^3 (x + 2)^2\, dx$

11. $\int_{-3}^{-1} (x + 1)\, dx$

12. $\int_2^3 \frac{x^2}{2x^3 - 7}\, dx$

13. $\int_{-1}^2 (x^2 + x)\, dx$

14. $\int_1^4 \left(\frac{1}{x} + \sqrt{x}\right) dx$

15. $\int_0^4 (2x + 1)^{1/2}\, dx$

16. $\int_0^1 \frac{x}{x^2 + 1}\, dx$

17. $\int_0^1 e^{-2x}\, dx$

18. $\int_0^1 xe^{x^2}\, dx$

13.3

Find the area between the following curves.

19. $y = x^2 - 3x + 2$ and $y = x^2 + 4$ from $x = 0$ to $x = 5$
20. $y = x^2$ and $y = 4x + 5$
21. $y = x^3$ and $y = x$ from $x = -1$ to $x = 0$
22. $y = x^3 - 1$ and $y = x - 1$

13.5

Evaluate the integrals, using integral tables.

23. $\int \sqrt{x^2 - 4}\, dx$

24. $\int_0^1 3^x\, dx$

25. $\int x \ln x^2\, dx$

26. $\int \frac{dx}{x(3x + 2)}$

13.6

Use integration by parts to evaluate the following.

27. $\int x^5 \ln x\, dx$

28. $\int xe^{-2x}\, dx$

29. $\int \frac{x\, dx}{\sqrt{x + 5}}$

30. $\int_1^e \ln x\, dx$

13.7

Evaluate the following improper integrals.

31. $\int_1^\infty \frac{1}{x}\, dx$

32. $\int_{-\infty}^{-1} \frac{200}{x^3}\, dx$

33. $\int_0^\infty 5e^{-3x}\, dx$

34. $\int_{-\infty}^0 \frac{x}{(x^2 + 1)^2}\, dx$

APPLICATIONS

13.2

35. Maintenance costs for buildings increase as the buildings age. If the rate of increase in maintenance costs for a building is

$$M'(t) = \frac{14,000}{\sqrt{t + 16}},$$

where M is in dollars and t is time in years, $0 \leq t \leq 15$, find the total maintenance cost for the first nine years ($t = 0$ to $t = 9$).

36. Suppose the probability density function for the life expectancy of a "disposable" telephone is

$$f(x) = \begin{cases} 1.4e^{-1.4x}, & x \geq 0 \\ 0, & x < 0. \end{cases}$$

Find the probability that the telephone lasts at least 2 years.

13.3

37. The compound amount of $1000 invested in a savings account at 10%, compounded continuously, is $A = 1000e^{0.1t}$, where t is in years. Find the average amount in the savings account during the first five years.

38. Suppose the total income from a video machine is given by

$$I = 50e^{0.2t}, \ 0 \leq t \leq 4, \ t \text{ in hours.}$$

Find the average income over this four-hour period.

13.4

39. The demand function for a product under pure competition is $p = \sqrt{64 - 4x}$, and the supply function is $p = x - 1$.
    (a) Find the market equilibrium.
    (b) Find the consumer's surplus at market equilibrium.

40. Find the producer's surplus at market equilibrium for problem 39.

41. Find the total income over the next 10 years from a continuous income stream that has an annual flow rate at time t given by

$$f(t) = 125e^{0.05t},$$

in thousands of dollars.

42. Suppose that a machine's production is considered as a continuous income stream with an annual rate of flow at time t given by

$$f(t) = 150e^{-0.2t},$$

in thousands of dollars. If money is worth 8%, compounded continuously, find the present value of the machine over the next 5 years.

13.5

43. Suppose the cost function for a product is given by $C(x) = \sqrt{40{,}000 + x^2}$. Find the average cost over the first 150 units.

13.6

44. Suppose the present value of a continuous income stream over the next 5 years is given by

$$P = 9000 \int_0^5 te^{-0.08t} \, dt, \ P \text{ in dollars, } t \text{ in years.}$$

Find the present value.

45. If the marginal cost for a product is $\overline{MC} = 3 + x \ln(x + 1)$ and if the fixed cost is $2000, find the total cost function.

13.7

46. Find the probability that a telephone lasts more than 1 year, if the probability density function for its life expectancy is given by

$$f(x) = \begin{cases} 1.4e^{-1.4x} & \text{if } x \geq 0 \\ 0 & \text{if } x < 0. \end{cases}$$

WARMUP

	Prerequisite problem type	Answer	Section for review
14.1	If $y = f(x)$, x is the independent variable and y is the _____variable.	Dependable	1.3 Functions
14.1	What is the domain of $f(x) = \dfrac{3x}{x-1}$?	All reals except $x = 1$	1.3 Domains
14.1	If $C(x) = 5 + 5x$, what is $f(0.20)$?	6	1.3 Functional notation
14.5, 14.6	(a) Solve for x and y: $\begin{cases} 0 = 50 - 2x - 2y \\ 0 = 60 - 2x - 4y \end{cases}$ (b) Solve for x and y: $\begin{cases} x = 2y \\ x + y - 9 = 0 \end{cases}$	(a) $y = 5$, $x = 20$ (b) $x = 6$, $y = 3$	1.6 Systems of equations
14.2, 14.4, 14.5, 14.6	If $z = 4x^2 + 5x^3 - 7$, what is $\dfrac{dz}{dx}$?	$\dfrac{dz}{dx} = 8x + 15x^2$	9.4 Derivatives
14.2	If $f(x) = (x^2 - 1)^2$, what is $f'(x)$?	$f'(x) = 4x(x^2 - 1)$	9.6 Derivatives
14.2, 14.4	If $z = 10y - \ln y$, what is $\dfrac{dz}{dy}$?	$\dfrac{dz}{dy} = 10 - \dfrac{1}{y}$	11.4 Derivatives of logarithmic functions
14.2, 14.4	If $z = 5x^2 + e^x$, what is $\dfrac{dz}{dx}$?	$\dfrac{dz}{dx} = 10x + e^x$	11.5 Derivatives of exponential functions
14.2	Find the slope of the tangent to $y = 4x^3 - 4e^x$ at $(0, -4)$.	-4	9.3, 9.4, 9.5 Derivatives

14

Functions of
Two or More Variables

Although we have been dealing primarily with functions of one variable, many real-life situations involve a variable that is a function of two or more variables. For example, the grade you receive in a course is a function of several test grades. The cost of manufacturing a product may involve the cost of labor, the cost of materials, and overhead expenses. The concentration of a substance at any point in a vein after an injection is a function of time since the injection t, the velocity of the blood v, and the distance the point is from the point of injection.

In this chapter we will extend our study to functions of two or more variables. We will extend the derivative concept to functions of several variables by taking partial derivatives, and we will learn how to maximize functions of two variables. We will use these concepts to solve problems in the management, social, and life sciences. In particular, we will discuss joint cost functions, marginal cost, marginal productivity, and marginal demand functions. We will use Lagrange multipliers to maximize functions of two variables subject to a condition that constrains the variables.

14.1 Functions of Two or More Variables

Objectives ☐ To find the domain and range of a function of two or more variables
          ☐ To evaluate a function of two or more variables given values for the independent variables

The relations we have studied up to this point have been limited to two variables, with one of the variables assumed to be a function of the other. But there are many instances where one variable may depend on two or more other variables. For example, the volume of a gas depends on the temperature and the pressure to which the gas is subjected. The universal gas law is $V = nRT/P$, where V is the volume, P is the pressure, n is the number of moles of gas, R is a constant, and T is the absolute temperature. (The constant R is called the universal gas constant.)

In economics, the demand function for a commodity frequently depends on the price of the commodity, available income, and prices of competing goods. Other examples from economics will be presented later in this chapter.

709

We write $z = f(x, y)$ to state that z is a function of both x and y. The variables x and y are called the **independent variables** and z is called the **dependent variable.** Thus the function f associates with each pair of possible values for the independent variables (x and y) exactly one value of the dependent variable (z).

The equation $z = x^2 - xy$ defines z as a function of x and y. We can denote this by writing $z = f(x, y) = x^2 - xy$. The domain of the function is the set of all ordered pairs (of real numbers) and the range is the set of all real numbers.

EXAMPLE 1　Give the domain of the function

$$g(x, y) = \frac{x^2 - 3y}{x - y}.$$

Solution　The domain of the function is the set of ordered pairs that do not give a 0 denominator. That is, the domain is the set of all ordered pairs where the first and second elements are not equal (that is, where $x \neq y$).

We graph the function $z = f(x, y)$ by using three dimensions. We can construct a three-dimensional coordinate space by drawing three mutually perpendicular axes as in Figure 14.1. By setting up a scale of measurement along the three axes from the origin 0, we can determine the three coordinates (x, y, z) for any point P. The point shown in Figure 14.1 is $+2$ units in the x-direction, $+3$ units in the y-direction, and $+4$ units in the z-direction, so the coordinates of the point are $(2, 3, 4)$.

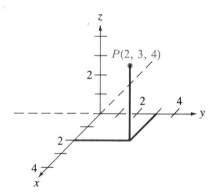

Figure 14.1

The pairs of axes determine the three **coordinate planes;** the xy-plane, the yz-plane, and the xz-plane. The planes divide the space into eight octants. The point $P(2, 3, 4)$ is in the first octant.

If we are given a function $z = f(x, y)$, we can find the z-value corresponding to $x = a$ and $y = b$ by evaluating $f(a, b)$.

EXAMPLE 2　If $z = f(x, y) = x^2 - 4xy + xy^3$, find the following.
(a) $f(1,2)$　　(b) $f(2, 5)$　　(c) $f(-1, 3)$

Solution (a) $f(1, 2) = 1^2 - 4(1)(2) + (1)(2)^3 = 1$
(b) $f(2, 5) = 2^2 - 4(2)(5) + (2)(5)^3 = 214$
(c) $f(-1, 3) = (-1)^2 - 4(-1)(3) + (-1)(3)^3 = -14$

EXAMPLE 3 The cost of manufacturing a Wosh is given by

$$C(x, y) = 5 + 5x + 2y,$$

where x represents the cost of one ounce of material used and y represents the cost of labor in dollars per hour. If the material cost is $.20 per ounce and labor costs $3.50 per hour, what is the cost of manufacturing one Wosh?

Solution The cost is

$$C(0.20, 3.50) = 5 + 5(0.20) + 2(3.50)$$
$$= 13 \text{ (dollars)}.$$

For a given function $z = f(x, y)$, we can construct a table of values by assigning values to x and y and finding the corresponding values of z. To each pair of values for x and y there corresponds a unique value of z, and thus a unique point in space. From a table of values such as this, a finite number of points can be plotted. All points that satisfy the equation form a "surface" in space. Since z is a function of x and y, lines parallel to the z-axis will intersect such a surface in at most one point. The graph of the equation $z = 4 - x^2 - y^2$ is a surface like that shown in Figure 14.2. The portion of the surface above the xy-plane is like a bullet and is called a **paraboloid.**

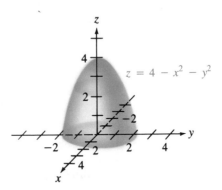

Figure 14.2

In practical applications of functions of two variables, we will have little need to construct the graphs of the surfaces. For this reason, we will not discuss methods of sketching the graphs. Although you will not be asked to sketch graphs of these surfaces, the fact that the graphs do *exist* will be used in studying relative maxima and minima of functions of two variables.

The properties of functions of one variable can be extended to functions of two variables. The precise definition of continuity for functions of two variables is technical, and may be found in more advanced books. We will limit our study to functions that are continuous and have continuous derivatives in the domain of interest to us. We may think of continuous functions as functions whose graphs consist of surfaces without "holes" or "breaks" in them.

Let the function $U = f(x, y)$ represent the **utility** (that is, satisfaction) derived by a consumer from the consumption of two goods, X and Y, where x and y represent the amounts of X and Y, respectively. Since we will assume the utility function is continuous, a given level of utility can be derived from an infinite number of combinations of x and y. The graph of all points (x, y) that give the same utility is called an **indifference curve.** A set of indifference curves corresponding to different levels of utility is called an **indifference map** (see Figure 14.3).

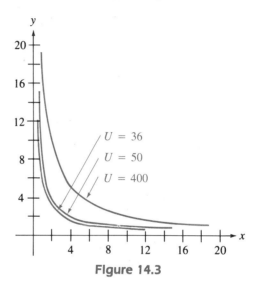

Figure 14.3

EXAMPLE 4   Suppose the utility function for two goods, X and Y, is $U = x^2y^2$ and a consumer purchases 10 units of X and 2 units of Y.
(a) If the consumer purchases 5 units of X, how many units of Y must be purchased to retain the same level of utility?
(b) Graph the indifference curve for this level of utility.
(c) Graph the indifference curves for this utility function if $U = 50$ and if $U = 36$.

Solution   (a) If $x = 10$ and $y = 2$ satisfy the utility function, then $U = 10^2 \cdot 2^2 = 400$. Thus if x is 5, y must satisfy $400 = 5^2y^2$; so $y = 4$.
(b) The indifference curve for $U = 400$ is $400 = x^2y^2$. The graph for positive x and y is shown in Figure 14.3.
(c) The indifference map in Figure 14.3 contains these indifference curves.

We can easily extend the concept of a function of two variables to that of a function of three or more variables. For example, $w = f(x, y, z)$ states that w is a function of the three variables, x, y, and z. The implicit function relating the five variables x, y, z, w, and u is denoted by $f(x, y, z, w, u) = 0$.

In general, we can represent y as a function of n independent variables x_1, x_2, x_3, ..., x_n by $y = f(x_1, x_2, x_3, \ldots, x_n)$. Of course it is no longer possible to "graph" the functions of three or more variables, since we would need more than three dimensions to represent the graphs. This does not imply that there is little use for functions of n variables. The applications in mathematics, science, and economics are numerous.

Exercise 14.1

Give the domain of the following functions.

1. $z = x^2 + y^2$

2. $z = 4x - 3y$

3. $z = \dfrac{4x - 3}{y}$

4. $z = \dfrac{x + y^2}{\sqrt{x}}$

5. $z = \dfrac{4x^3y - x}{2x - y}$

6. $z = \sqrt{x} - y$

7. $q = \sqrt{p_1} + 3p_2$

8. $q = \dfrac{p_1 + p_2}{\sqrt{p_1}}$

Evaluate the following functions at the given values of the independent variables.

9. $z = x^3 + 4xy + y^2$; $x = 1$, $y = -1$

10. $z = 4x^2 - 3xy^3$; $x = 2$, $y = 2$

11. $z = \dfrac{x - y}{x + y}$; $x = 4$, $y = -1$

12. $z = \dfrac{x^2 + xy}{x - y}$; $x = 3$, $y = 2$

13. $C(x_1, x_2) = 600 + 4x_1 + 6x_2$; $x_1 = 400$, $x_2 = 50$

14. $C(x_1, x_2) = 500 + 5x_1 + 7x_2$; find $C(200, 300)$.

15. $q_1(p_1, p_2) = \dfrac{p_1 + 4p_2}{p_1 - p_2}$; find $q_1(40, 35)$.

16. $q_1(p_1, p_2) = \dfrac{5p_1 - p_2}{p_1 + 3p_2}$; find $q_1(50, 10)$.

17. $z(x, y) = xe^{x+y}$; find $z(3, -3)$.

18. $f(x, y) = ye^{2x} + y^2$; find $f(0, 7)$.

19. $f(x, y) = \dfrac{\ln (xy)}{x^2 + y^2}$; find $f(-3, -4)$.

20. $z(x, y) = x \ln y - y \ln x$; find $z(1, 1)$.

21. $w = \dfrac{x^2 + 4yz}{xyz}$ at $(1, 3, 1)$

22. $u = f(w, x, y, z) = \dfrac{wx - yz^2}{xy - wz}$ at $(2, 3, 1, -1)$

23. Suppose the utility function for two goods X and Y is given by $U = xy^2$, and a consumer purchases 9 units of X and 6 units of Y.
    (a) If the consumer purchases 9 units of Y, how many units of X must be purchased to retain the same level of utility?
    (b) If the consumer purchases 81 units of X, how many units of Y must be purchased to retain the same level of utility?

24. Suppose an indifference curve for two goods, X and Y, has equation $xy = 400$. If 20 units of X are purchased, how many units of Y must be purchased to remain on this indifference curve?

25. Suppose the number of units of a good produced, z, is given by $z = 20xy$, where x is the number of machines working properly and y is the average number of work-hours per machine. Find the production for a week in which
    (a) 12 machines are working properly and the average number of work-hours per machine is 30.
    (b) 10 machines are working properly and the average number of work-hours per machine is 25.

26. The Kirk Kelly Kandy Company makes two kinds of candy, Kisses and Kreams. The profit function for the company is

    $$P(x, y) = 100x + 64y - 0.01x^2 - 0.25y^2,$$

    where x is the number of pounds of Kisses sold per week and y is the number of pounds of Kreams. What is their profit if they sell
    (a) 20 pounds of Kisses and 10 pounds of Kreams?
    (b) 100 pounds of Kisses and 16 pounds of Kreams?
    (c) 10,000 pounds of Kisses and 256 pounds of Kreams?

27. The cost per day to society of an epidemic is

    $$C(x, y) = 20x + 200y,$$

    where C is in dollars, x is the number of people infected on a given day, and y is the number of people who die on a given day. If 14,000 people are infected and 20 people die on a given day, what is the cost to society?

28. An area of land is to be sprayed with two brands of pesticide: x liters of brand 1 and y liters of brand 2. If the number of insects killed is given by

    $$f(x, y) = 10,000 - 6500e^{-0.01x} - 3500e^{-0.02y},$$

    how many insects would be killed if 80 liters of brand 1 and 120 liters of brand 2 were used?

29. The amount S of an investment earning 6%, compounded continuously, is a function of the principal P and the length of time t that the principal has been invested, and is given by

    $$S = f(P, t) = Pe^{0.06t}.$$

    Find $f(2000, 20)$, and interpret your answer.

30. Suppose a gas satisfies the universal gas law, $V = nRT/P$, with n equal to 10 moles of the gas and R, the universal gas constant, equal to 0.082054. What is V if $T = 10°K$ and $P = 1$ atmosphere?

The output or production Q (for quantity) of a company can be modeled according to the equation

$$Q = AK^\alpha L^{1-\alpha},$$

where A is a constant, K is the company's capital investment, L is the size of the labor force (in work hours), and α is a constant with $0 < \alpha < 1$. Functions of this type are called **Cobb-Douglas production functions,** and they are frequently used in economics.

31. Suppose a company's production is given by the Cobb-Douglas production function

$$Q = 30K^{1/4} L^{3/4}.$$

(a) Find Q if $K = \$10,000$ and $L = 625$ hours.
(b) Show that if *both* K and L are doubled, then the output is doubled.

32. Suppose the production of a company is given by the Cobb-Douglas production function

$$Q = 70K^{2/3} L^{1/3}.$$

(a) Find Q if $K = \$64,000$ and $L = 512$ hours.
(b) Show that if both K and L are halved, then Q is also halved.

14.2 Partial Differentiation

Objectives
- ☐ To find partial derivatives of functions of two or more variables
- ☐ To evaluate partial derivatives of functions of two or more variables at given points
- ☐ To use partial derivatives to find slopes of tangents to surfaces

We have used derivatives to find the rate of change of cost with respect to the quantity produced (in Chapter 9). If cost is given as a function of two variables (such as material costs x and labor costs y), we can find the rate of change of cost with respect to *one* of these independent variables. This is done by finding the **partial derivative** of the function with respect to one variable, while holding the other one constant.

For example, suppose the cost of manufacturing a good is given by

$$C(x, y) = 5 + 5x + 2y,$$

where x represents the cost of one ounce of material used and y represents the labor cost in dollars per hour. To find the rate at which the cost changes with respect to material used x, we treat the y variable as though it were a constant and take the derivative of C with respect to x. This derivative is

$$\frac{\partial C}{\partial x} = 0 + 5 + 0, \qquad \text{or} \qquad \frac{\partial C}{\partial x} = 5.$$

Note that the partial derivative of $2y$ with respect to x is 0 because y is treated as a constant. Since the partial derivative is a new type of derivative, we use a new symbol to denote it, $\partial C/\partial x$.

The partial derivative $\partial C/\partial x = 5$ tells us that the total cost C changes at a rate 5 times that of the cost of materials *if* labor costs remain constant. To see the rate at which total cost changes with respect to labor costs, we find $\partial C/\partial y = 0 + 0 + 2$, or $\partial C/\partial y = 2$. Thus if material costs are held constant, an increase of \$1 in labor costs will cause an increase of \$2 in the total cost of the good.

In general, if $z = f(x, y)$ we denote the partial derivative of z with respect to x as $\partial z/\partial x$ and the partial derivative of z with respect to y as $\partial z/\partial y$. Note that dz/dx represents the derivative of a function of one variable, x, and that $\partial z/\partial x$ represents the partial derivative of a function of two or more variables.

Other notations used to represent the partial derivative of $z = f(x, y)$ with respect to x are

$$\frac{\partial f}{\partial x}, \qquad \frac{\partial}{\partial x}f(x, y), \qquad f_x(x, y), \qquad f_x, \qquad \text{and} \qquad z_x.$$

If x is held constant in the function $z = f(x, y)$ and the derivative is taken with respect to y, we have the partial derivative of z with respect to y, denoted by

$$\frac{\partial z}{\partial y}, \qquad \frac{\partial f}{\partial y}, \qquad \frac{\partial}{\partial y}f(x, y), \qquad f_y(x, y), \qquad f_y, \qquad \text{or} \qquad z_y.$$

EXAMPLE 1   If $z = 4x^2 + 5x^2y^2 + 6y^3 - 7$, find $\partial z/\partial x$ and $\partial z/\partial y$.

Solution
$$\frac{\partial z}{\partial x} = 8x + 10y^2x$$

$$\frac{\partial z}{\partial y} = 10x^2y + 18y^2$$

EXAMPLE 2   If $z = x^2y + e^x - \ln y$, find z_x and z_y.

Solution
$$z_x = \frac{\partial z}{\partial x} = 2yx + e^x$$

$$z_y = \frac{\partial z}{\partial y} = x^2 - \frac{1}{y}$$

EXAMPLE 3   If $f(x, y) = (x^2 - y^2)^2$, find the following.
(a) f_x (b) f_y

Solution   (a) $f_x = 2(x^2 - y^2)2x = 4x^3 - 4xy^2$
(b) $f_y = 2(x^2 - y^2)(-2y) = -4x^2y + 4y^3$

EXAMPLE 4   If $q = \dfrac{p_1p_2 + 2p_1}{p_1p_2 - 2p_2}$, find $\partial q/\partial p_1$.

Solution
$$\frac{\partial q}{\partial p_1} = \frac{(p_1p_2 - 2p_2)(p_2 + 2) - (p_1p_2 + 2p_1)p_2}{(p_1p_2 - 2p_2)^2}$$

$$= \frac{p_1p_2^2 + 2p_1p_2 - 2p_2^2 - 4p_2 - p_1p_2^2 - 2p_1p_2}{(p_1p_2 - 2p_2)^2}$$

$$= \frac{-2p_2^2 - 4p_2}{p_2^2(p_1 - 2)^2}$$

$$= \frac{-2p_2(p_2 + 2)}{p_2^2(p_1 - 2)^2}$$

$$= \frac{-2(p_2 + 2)}{p_2(p_1 - 2)^2}$$

We may evaluate partial derivatives by substituting values for x *and* y in the same manner we did with derivatives of functions of one variable. For example, if $\partial z/\partial x = 2x - xy$, the value of the derivative at $x = 2$, $y = 3$ is

$$\frac{\partial z}{\partial x}\Big|_{(2,\ 3)} = 2(2) - 2 \cdot 3 = -2.$$

Other notations used to denote evaluation of partial derivatives with respect to x at (a, b) are

$$\frac{\partial}{\partial x} f(a, b) \qquad \text{and} \qquad f_x(a, b).$$

We denote the evaluation of partial derivatives with respect to y at (a, b) by

$$\frac{\partial z}{\partial y}\Big|_{(a,\ b)}, \qquad \frac{\partial}{\partial y} f(a, b), \qquad \text{or} \qquad f_y(a, b).$$

EXAMPLE 5   Find the partial derivative of $f(x, y) = x^2 + 3xy + 4$ with respect to x at the point $(1, 2, 11)$.

Solution
$$f_x(x, y) = 2x + 3y$$
$$f_x(1, 2) = 2(1) + 3(2) = 8$$

EXAMPLE 6   Suppose a company's sales are related to its television advertising by

$$s = 20{,}000 + 10nt + 20n^2,$$

where n is the number of commercials per day and t is the length of the commercials in seconds. Find the partial derivative of s with respect to n and use the result to find the instantaneous rate of change of sales with respect to the number of commercials per day, if they are currently running ten 30-second commercials.

Solution   The partial derivative of s with respect to n is $\partial s/\partial n = 10t + 40n$. At $n = 10$ and $t = 30$, the rate of change in sales is approximately

$$\frac{\partial s}{\partial n}\Big|_{\substack{n=10 \\ t=30}} = 700.$$

Thus increasing the number of commercials by one would result in approximately 700 additional sales.

We have seen that the partial derivative $\partial z/\partial x$ is found by holding y constant and taking the derivative of z with respect to x, using the usual differentiation rules. The formal definition of $\partial z/\partial x$ is as follows.

> The partial derivative of $z = f(x, y)$ with respect to x at the point (x, y) is
>
> $$\frac{\partial z}{\partial x} = \frac{\partial}{\partial x} f(x, y) = \lim_{h \to 0} \frac{f(x + h, y) - f(x, y)}{h}.$$

To find $\dfrac{\partial}{\partial y} f(x, y)$, we hold x constant, and use the formula

$$\frac{\partial z}{\partial y} = \frac{\partial}{\partial y} f(x, y) = \lim_{h \to 0} \frac{f(x, y + h) - f(x, y)}{h}.$$

We have already stated that the graph of $z = f(x, y)$ is a surface in three dimensions. The partial derivative with respect to x of such a function may be thought of as the slope of the tangent to the surface at a point (x, y, z) on the surface *in the direction of the x-axis*. That is, if a plane parallel to the x-axis cuts the surface, passing through the point (x_0, y_0, z_0), the line in the plane that is tangent to the surface will have a slope equal to $\partial z/\partial x$ evaluated at the point. Thus

$$\left. \frac{\partial z}{\partial x} \right|_{(x_0, y_0)}$$

represents the slope of the tangent to the surface in the direction of the x-axis (see Figure 14.4).

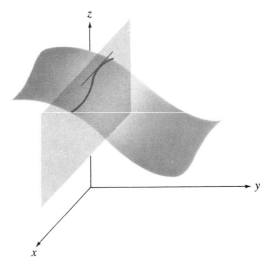

Figure 14.4

Similarly,

$$\frac{\partial z}{\partial y}\bigg|_{(x_0,\ y_0)} = \frac{\partial}{\partial y} f(x_0,\ y_0)$$

represents the slope of the tangent to the surface at $(x_0,\ y_0,\ z_0)$ in the direction of the y-axis (see Figure 14.5).

EXAMPLE 7   Find the slope of the tangent in the x-direction to the surface $z = 4x^3 - 4e^x + 4y^2$ at the point $(0, 2, 12)$ on the surface.

Solution

$$\frac{\partial z}{\partial x} = 12x^2 - 4e^x$$

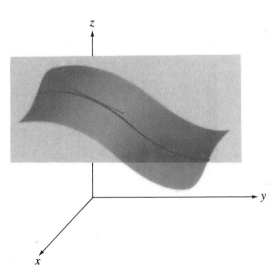

Figure 14.5

Evaluating the partial derivative at the given point, we find the slope of the tangent.

$$\frac{\partial z}{\partial x}\bigg|_{(0,\ 2)} = 12(0)^2 - 4e^0 = -4$$

This tells us that z is *decreasing* at a rate of approximately 4 units for each increase of 1 unit in x at this point. That is, the slope of the tangent to the surface in the x-direction is negative at $(0, 2, 12)$.

EXAMPLE 8   Using the same function and point as that of Example 7, find the slope of the tangent in the y-direction to the surface at the point.

Solution
$$\frac{\partial z}{\partial y} = 8y$$

$$\left.\frac{\partial z}{\partial y}\right|_{(0,\ 2)} = 8(2) = 16$$

So the slope of the tangent in the y-direction is increasing at a rate of 16 units in the z-value for each unit change in y.

Up to this point we have considered derivatives of functions of two variables. We can easily extend the concept to functions of three or more variables. We can find the partial derivative with respect to any one independent variable by taking the derivative of the function with respect to that variable while holding all other independent variables constant.

EXAMPLE 9   If $u = f(w, x, y, z) = 3x^2y + w^3 - 4xyz$, find the following.

(a) $\dfrac{\partial u}{\partial w}$ (b) $\dfrac{\partial u}{\partial x}$ (c) $\dfrac{\partial u}{\partial y}$ (d) $\dfrac{\partial u}{\partial z}$

Solution   (a) $\dfrac{\partial u}{\partial w} = 3w^2$ (b) $\dfrac{\partial u}{\partial x} = 6xy - 4yz$ (c) $\dfrac{\partial u}{\partial y} = 3x^2 - 4xz$

(d) $\dfrac{\partial u}{\partial z} = -4xy$

EXAMPLE 10   If $C = 4x_1 + 2x_1^2 + 3x_2 - x_1x_2 + x_3^2$, find the following.

(a) $\dfrac{\partial C}{\partial x_1}$ (b) $\dfrac{\partial C}{\partial x_2}$ (c) $\dfrac{\partial C}{\partial x_3}$

Solution   (a) $\dfrac{\partial C}{\partial x_1} = 4 + 4x_1 - x_2$ (b) $\dfrac{\partial C}{\partial x_2} = 3 - x_1$ (c) $\dfrac{\partial C}{\partial x_3} = 2x_3$

Exercise 14.2

1. Find $\dfrac{\partial z}{\partial x}$ if $z = x^4 - 5x^2 + 4x + 3y^3 - 5y$.

2. Find $\dfrac{\partial z}{\partial y}$ if $z = x^5 - 6x + 4y^3 - y$.

3. Find $\dfrac{\partial z}{\partial x}$ if $z = x^2 - 5y + y$.   4. Find $\dfrac{\partial z}{\partial y}$ if $z = x^2 - 5y + y$.

5. If $z = x^3 + 4xy + 6y$, find z_y.   6. If $z = x^2 + 4xt + 6y$, find z_x.

7. If $z = 4x^2 - 5xy + 6y^2$, find z_y.

8. If $z = 4x^2 + 6xy^2 - y$, find z_x.

9. If $z = xy + y^2$, find z_x.

10. If $z = xy + y^2$, find z_y.

11. If $z = e^x + y \ln x$, find $\dfrac{\partial z}{\partial x}$.

12. If $z = e^x + y \ln x$, find $\dfrac{\partial z}{\partial y}$.

13. If $z = e^{xy}$, find z_y.

14. If $z = \ln(xy)$, find z_x.

15. If $z = (x^3 + y^2)^3$, find $\dfrac{\partial z}{\partial x}$.

16. If $z = \sqrt{x - y}$, find z_y.

17. If $f(x, y) = (xy + y)^2$, find $\dfrac{\partial f}{\partial y}$.

18. If $f(x, y) = x\sqrt{y - x}$, find $\dfrac{\partial f}{\partial x}$.

19. If $C(x, y) = 600 - 4xy + 10x^2y$, find $\dfrac{\partial C}{\partial x}$.

20. If $C(x, y) = 1000 - 4x + xy^2$, find $\dfrac{\partial C}{\partial y}$.

21. If $q = \dfrac{5p_1 + 4p_2}{p_1 + p_2}$, find $\dfrac{\partial q}{\partial p_1}$.

22. If $q = \dfrac{5p_1 + 4p_2}{p_1 + p_2}$, find $\dfrac{\partial q}{\partial p_2}$.

23. If $Q(x, y) = 1500 + x^2 + 4xy + y^2$, find $\dfrac{\partial Q}{\partial x}$.

24. If $Q(x, y) = 1500 + x^2 + 4xy + y^2$, find $\dfrac{\partial Q}{\partial y}$.

25. Find the partial derivative of $f(x, y) = 4x^3 - 5xy + y^2$ with respect to x at the point $(1, 2, -2)$.

26. Find the partial derivative of $f(x, y) = 3x^2 + 4x + 6xy$ with respect to y at $x = 2$, $y = -1$.

27. Find the slope of the tangent in the x-direction to the surface $z = 5x^3 - 4xy$ at the point $(1, 2, -3)$.

28. Find the slope of the tangent in the y-direction to the surface $z = x^3 - 5xy$ at $(2, 1, -2)$.

29. Find the slope of the tangent in the y-direction to the surface $z = e^{xy}$ at $(0, 1, 1)$.

30. Find the slope of the tangent in the x-direction to the surface $z = \ln(xy)$ at $(1, 1, 0)$.

31. If $u = f(w, x, y, z) = y^2 - x^2z + 4x$, find the following.

   (a) $\dfrac{\partial u}{\partial w}$ (b) $\dfrac{\partial u}{\partial x}$ (c) $\dfrac{\partial u}{\partial y}$ (d) $\dfrac{\partial u}{\partial z}$

32. If $u = x^2 + 3xy + xz$, find the following.

   (a) u_x (b) u_y (c) u_z

33. If $C(x_1, x_2, x_3) = 4x_1^2 + 5x_1x_2 + 6x_2^2 + x_3$, find the following.

   (a) $\dfrac{\partial C}{\partial x_1}$ (b) $\dfrac{\partial C}{\partial x_2}$ (c) $\dfrac{\partial C}{\partial x_3}$

34. If $f(x, y, z) = 2x\sqrt{yz - 1} + x^2z^3$, find the following.

   (a) $\dfrac{\partial f}{\partial x}$ (b) $\dfrac{\partial f}{\partial y}$ (c) $\dfrac{\partial f}{\partial z}$

APPLICATIONS

35. When a homeowner has a 25-year variable rate mortgage loan, the monthly payment R is a function of the amount of the loan A and the current interest rate i (as a decimal); that is, $R = f(A, i)$. Interpret each of the following.
    (a) $f(100,000, 0.08) = 1289$
    (b) $\dfrac{\partial f}{\partial i} (100,000, 0.08) = 62.51$

36. Suppose the total cost of producing a product is $C(x, y) = 25 + 2x^2 + 3y^2$, where x is the cost per pound for material and y is cost per hour for labor.
    (a) If material costs are held constant, at what rate will the total cost increase for each $1 per hour increase in labor?
    (b) If the labor costs are held constant, at what rate will the total cost increase for each increase of $1 in material cost?

37. Suppose the number of insects killed by two brands of pesticide is given by

$$f(x, y) = 10,000 - 6500e^{-0.01x} - 3500e^{-0.02y},$$

where x is the number of liters of brand 1 and y is the number of liters of brand 2.
    (a) What is the rate of change of insect deaths with respect to the number of liters of brand 1?
    (b) What is the rate of change of insect deaths with respect to the number of liters of brand 2?

38. Suppose the profit from the sale of Kisses and Kreams is given by

$$P(x, y) = 100x + 64y - 0.01x^2 - 0.25y^2,$$

where x is the number of pounds of Kisses and y is the number of pounds of Kreams.
    (a) Find $\partial P/\partial x$, and give the approximate rate of change of profit with respect to the number of pounds of Kisses if present sales are 20 pounds of Kisses and 10 pounds of Kreams.
    (b) Find $\partial P/\partial y$, and give the approximate rate of change of profit with respect to the number of pounds of Kreams that are sold if 100 pounds of Kisses and 16 pounds of Kreams are currently being sold.

39. If $U = f(x, y)$ is the utility function for goods X and Y, the *marginal utility* of X is $\partial U/\partial x$ and the *marginal utility* of Y is $\partial U/\partial y$. If $U = x^2y^2$,
    (a) find the marginal utility of X.
    (b) find the marginal utility of Y.

40. If the utility function for goods X and Y is $U = xy + y^2$,
    (a) find the marginal utility of X.
    (b) find the marginal utility of Y.

41. Suppose the output Q (in thousands of units) of a certain company is $Q = 75K^{1/3}L^{2/3}$, where K is the capital expenditures in thousands of dollars and L is the number of labor hours. Find $\partial Q/\partial K$ and $\partial Q/\partial L$ when capital expenditures are $729,000 and the labor hours total 1728.

42. Suppose the production Q (in hundreds of gallons of paint) of a paint manufacturer can be modeled by $Q = 140K^{1/2}L^{1/2}$, where K is the company's capital expenditures in thousands of dollars and L is the size of the labor force (in hours worked). Find $\partial Q/\partial K$ and $\partial Q/\partial L$ when capital expenditures are $250,000 and the labor hours are 1225.

14.3 Applications of Functions of Two Variables in Business and Economics

Objectives   ☐   To evaluate cost functions at given levels of production
  ☐   To find marginal costs from total cost and joint cost functions
  ☐   To find marginal productivity for given production functions
  ☐   To find marginal demand functions from demand functions for a pair of related products

Joint Cost and Marginal Cost

Suppose a firm produces two commodities using the same inputs in different proportions. In such a case the **joint cost function** is of the form $C = Q(x, y)$, where x and y represent the quantities of each commodity and C represents the total cost for the two commodities. Then $\partial C/\partial x$ is the **marginal cost** with respect to product x and $\partial C/\partial y$ is the **marginal cost** with respect to product y.

EXAMPLE 1 If the joint cost function for two products is

$$C = Q(x, y) = 50 + x^2 + 8xy + y^3,$$

(a) find the marginal cost with respect to x.
(b) find the marginal cost with respect to y.
(c) find the marginal cost with respect to x at $(5, 3)$.
(d) find the marginal cost with respect to y at $(5, 3)$.

Solution (a) The marginal cost with respect to x is $\partial C/\partial x = 2x + 8y$.

(b) $\dfrac{\partial C}{\partial y} = 8x + 3y^2$

(c) $\dfrac{\partial C}{\partial x}\bigg|_{(5,\ 3)} = 2(5) + 8(3) = 34$

Thus, if 5 units of product x and 3 units of product y are produced, the total cost will increase approximately \$34 for each unit increase in product x if y is held constant.

(d) $\dfrac{\partial C}{\partial y}\bigg|_{(5,\ 3)} = 8(5) + 3(3)^2 = 67$

Thus, if 5 units of product x and 3 units of product y are produced, the total cost will increase approximately \$67 for each unit increase in product y if x is held constant.

Production Functions

An important problem in economics concerns how the factors necessary for production determine the output of a product. For example, the output of a product depends on available labor, land, capital, material, and machines. If the amount of output z of a product depends on the amounts of two inputs x and y, then the quantity z is given by the **production function** $z = f(x, y)$.

EXAMPLE 2   Suppose it is known that z bushels of a crop can be harvested according to the function

$$z = (21) \frac{6xy - 4x^2 - 3y}{2x + 0.01y}$$

when $100x$ work-hours of labor are employed on y acres of land.

What would be the output (in bushels) if 200 work-hours were used on 300 acres?

Solution   Since $z = f(x, y)$,

$$f(2, 300) = (21) \frac{6(2)(300) + 4(2)^2 - 3(300)}{2(2) + 3}$$

$$= (21) \frac{3600 + 16 - 900}{7} = 8148 \text{ (bushels)}.$$

If $z = f(x, y)$ is a production function, $\partial z/\partial x$ represents the change in the output z with respect to input x while input y remains constant. This partial derivative is called the **marginal productivity of x**. The partial derivative $\partial z/\partial y$ is the **marginal productivity of y**, and measures the rate of change of z with respect to input y.

Marginal productivity (for either input) will be positive over a wide range of inputs, but it increases at a decreasing rate, and may eventually reach a point where it no longer increases, and begins to decrease.

EXAMPLE 3   If a production function is given by $z = 5x^{1/2}y^{1/4}$,
(a) find the marginal productivity of x.
(b) find the marginal productivity of y.

Solution   (a) $\dfrac{\partial z}{\partial x} = \dfrac{5}{2} x^{-1/2} y^{1/4}$

(b) $\dfrac{\partial z}{\partial y} = \dfrac{5}{4} x^{1/2} y^{-3/4}$

Note that the marginal productivity of x is positive for all values of x, but that it decreases as x gets larger (because of the negative exponent). The same is true for the marginal productivity of y.

Demand Functions

Suppose that two products are sold at prices p_1 and p_2, respectively, on a competitive market consisting of a fixed number of consumers with given tastes and incomes. Then the amount of each *one* of the products demanded by the consumers is dependent on the prices of *both* products on the market. If q_1 represents the demand for the first product, then $q_1 = f(p_1, p_2)$ is the **demand function** for that product. The graph of such a function is called a **demand surface.** An example of a demand function in two variables is $q_1 = 400 - 2p_1 - 4p_2$. Here q_1 is a function of two variables p_1 and p_2. If $p_1 = \$10$ and $p_2 = \$20$, the demand would equal $400 - 2(10) - 4(20) = 300$.

EXAMPLE 4   The demand functions for two products are

$$q_1 = 50 - 5p_1 - 2p_2$$
$$q_2 = 100 - 3p_1 - 8p_2.$$

What is the demand for each of the products if the price of the first is $p_1 = \$5$ and the price of the second is $p_2 = \$8$?

Solution
$$q_1 = 50 - 5(5) - 2(8) = 9$$
$$q_2 = 100 - 3(5) - 8(8) = 21$$

Thus, if these are the prices, the demand for product 2 is higher than the demand for product 1.

EXAMPLE 5   Using the demand equations in Example 4, find a pair of prices p_1 and p_2 such that the demands for product 1 and product 2 are equal.

Solution   We want q_1 to equal q_2. Setting $q_1 = q_2$, we see that

$$50 - 5p_1 - 2p_2 = 100 - 3p_1 - 8p_2$$
$$6p_2 - 50 = 2p_1$$
$$p_1 = 3p_2 - 25$$

Now, any pair of values that satisfies this equation will make the demands equal. Letting $p_2 = 10$, we see $p_1 = 5$ will satisfy the equation. Thus the prices $p_1 = 5$ and $p_2 = 10$ will make the demands equal. The prices $p_1 = 2$ and $p_2 = 9$ will also make the demands equal. Many pairs of values (that is, all those satisfying $p_1 = 3p_2 - 25$) will equalize the demands.

If the demand functions for a pair of related products, product 1 and product 2, are $q_1 = f(p_1, p_2)$ and $q_2 = g(p_1, p_2)$, respectively, then the partial derivatives of q_1 and q_2 are called **marginal demand functions.**

$\dfrac{\partial q_1}{\partial p_1}$ is the marginal demand of q_1 with respect to p_1.

$\dfrac{\partial q_1}{\partial p_2}$ is the marginal demand of q_1 with respect to p_2.

$\dfrac{\partial q_2}{\partial p_1}$ is the marginal demand of q_2 with respect to p_1.

$\dfrac{\partial q_2}{\partial p_2}$ is the marginal demand of q_2 with respect to p_2.

For typical demand functions, if the price of product 2 is fixed, the demand for product 1 will decrease as its price p_1 increases. In this case the marginal demand of q_1 with respect to p_1 will be negative; that is, $\partial q_1/\partial p_1 < 0$. Similarly, $\partial q_2/\partial p_2 < 0$.

But what about $\partial q_2/\partial p_1$ and $\partial q_1/\partial p_2$? If $\partial q_2/\partial p_1$ and $\partial q_1/\partial p_2$ are both positive, the two products are **competitive** because an increase in price p_1 will result in an increase in demand for product 2 (q_2) if the price p_2 is held constant, while an increase in price p_2 will increase the demand for product 1 if p_1 is held constant. Stated more simply, an increase in the price of one of the two products will result in an increased demand for the other, so the products are in competition. For example, an increase in the price of a Japanese automobile will result in an increase in demand for an American automobile if the price of the American automobile is held constant.

If $\partial q_2/\partial p_1$ and $\partial q_1/\partial p_2$ are both negative, the products are **complementary** because an increase in the price of one product will cause a decrease in demand for the other product if the price of the second product doesn't change. Under these conditions, a *decrease* in the price of product 1 would result in an *increase* in the demand for product 2, and a decrease in the price of product 2 would result in an increase in the demand for product 1. For example, a decrease in the price of gasoline would result in an increase in the demand for large automobiles.

If the signs of $\partial q_2/\partial p_1$ and $\partial q_1/\partial p_2$ are different, the products are neither competitive nor complementary. This situation rarely occurs, but is possible.

EXAMPLE 6   The demand functions for two related products, product 1 and product 2, are given by

$$q_1 = 400 - 5p_1 + 6p_2$$
$$q_2 = 250 + 4p_1 - 5p_2$$

(a) Determine the four marginal demands.
(b) Are product 1 and product 2 complementary or competitive?

Solution   (a) $\dfrac{\partial q_1}{\partial p_1} = -5$ $\dfrac{\partial q_2}{\partial p_2} = -5$

$\dfrac{\partial q_1}{\partial p_2} = 6$ $\dfrac{\partial q_2}{\partial p_1} = 4$

(b) Since $\partial q_1/\partial p_2$ and $\partial q_2/\partial p_1$ are both positive, they are competitive.

Exercise 14.3

JOINT COST AND MARGINAL COST

1. The cost of manufacturing one item is given by

$$C(x, y) = 30 + 3x + 5y,$$

where x is the cost of one hour of labor and y is the cost of one pound of material. If the hourly cost of labor is $4, and the material costs $3 per pound, what is the cost of manufacturing one of these items?

2. The manufacture of one unit of a product has cost given by

$$C(x, y, z) = 10 + 8x + 3y + z,$$

where x is the cost of one pound of one raw material, y is the cost of one pound of a second material, and z is the cost of one work-hour of labor. If the cost of the first raw material is $16 per pound, the cost of the second raw material is $8 per pound, and labor costs $8 per work-hour, what will it cost to produce one unit of the product?

3. The total cost of producing one unit of a product is

$$C(x, y) = 30 + 2x + 4y + \frac{xy}{50},$$

where x is the cost per pound of raw materials and y is the cost per hour of labor.
   (a) If labor costs are held constant, at what rate will the total cost increase for each increase of $1 per pound in material cost?
   (b) If material costs are held constant, at what rate will the total cost increase for each $1 per hour increase in labor costs?

4. The total cost of producing an item is

$$C(x, y) = 40 + 4x + 6y + \frac{x^2 y}{100},$$

where x is the cost per pound of raw materials and y is the cost per hour for labor.
   (a) How will an increase of $1 per pound of raw materials affect the total cost?
   (b) How will an increase of $1 per hour in labor costs affect the total cost?

5. The total cost of producing one unit of a product is given by

$$C(x, y) = 20x + 70y + \frac{x^2}{1000} + \frac{xy^2}{100},$$

where x represents the cost per pound of raw materials and y represents the hourly rate for labor. The present cost for raw materials is $10 per pound and the present hourly rate for labor is $4.
   (a) How will an increase of $1 per pound for raw materials affect the total cost?
   (b) How will an increase of $1 per hour in labor costs affect the total cost?

6. The total cost from the sale of one unit of a product is given by

$$C(x, y) = 30 + 10x^2 + 20y - xy,$$

where x is the hourly labor rate and y is the cost per pound of raw materials. The current hourly rate is $5, and the raw materials cost $6 per pound.
   (a) How will an increase of $1 per pound for the raw materials affect the total cost?
   (b) How will an increase of $1 in the hourly labor rate affect the total cost?

7. The joint cost function for two products is

$$C(x, y) = 30 + x^2 + 3y + 2xy,$$

where x represents the quantity of product X produced and y represents the quantity of product Y produced.
   (a) Find the marginal cost with respect to x if 8 units of product X and 10 units of product Y are produced.
   (b) Find the marginal cost with respect to y if 8 units of product X and 10 units of product Y are produced.

8. The joint cost function for products X and Y is

$$C(x, y) = 40 + 3x^2 + y^2 + xy,$$

where x represents the quantity of X and y represents the quantity of Y.
   (a) Find the marginal cost with respect to x if 20 units of product X and 15 units of product Y are produced.
   (b) Find the marginal cost with respect to y if 20 units of X and 15 units of Y are produced.

9. If the joint cost function for two products is

$$C(x, y) = x\sqrt{y^2 + 1},$$

   (a) Find the marginal cost (function) with respect to x.
   (b) Find the marginal cost with respect to y.

10. Suppose the joint cost function for x units of product X and y units of product Y is given by

$$C(x, y) = 2500 \sqrt{xy + 1}.$$

   (a) Find the marginal cost with respect to x.
   (b) Find the marginal cost with respect to y.

11. Suppose the joint cost function for two products is

$$C(x, y) = 1200 \ln (xy + 1) + 10{,}000.$$

   (a) Find the marginal cost with respect to x.
   (b) Find the marginal cost with respect to y.

12. Suppose the joint cost function for two products is

$$C(x, y) = y \ln (x + 1).$$

   (a) Find the marginal cost with respect to x.
   (b) Find the marginal cost with respect to y.

PRODUCTION FUNCTIONS

13. Suppose the production function for a product is $z = \sqrt{4xy}$, where x represents the number of work-hours per month and y is the number of available machines.
   (a) Determine the marginal productivity of x.
   (b) Determine the marginal productivity of y.

14. Suppose the production function for a product is

$$z = 60x^{2/5}y^{3/5},$$

where x is the capital expenditures and y is the number of labor hours.
   (a) Find the marginal productivity of x.
   (b) Find the marginal productivity of y.

15. Suppose the production function for a product is $z = \sqrt{x} \ln (y + 1)$, where x represents the number of work-hours and y represents the available capital (per week).
    (a) Find the marginal productivity of x.
    (b) Find the marginal productivity of y.

16. Suppose a company's production function for a certain product is

$$z = (x + 1)^{1/2} \ln (y^2 + 1),$$

where x is the number of work hours of unskilled labor and y is the number of work hours of skilled labor.
    (a) Find the marginal productivity of x.
    (b) Find the marginal productivity of y.

For problems 17–19, suppose the production function for an agricultural product is given by

$$z = \frac{11xy - 0.0002x^2 - 5y}{0.03x + 3y},$$

where x is the number of hours of labor and y is the number of acres of the crop.

17. Find the output when $x = 300$ and $y = 500$.

18. Find the marginal productivity of the number of acres of the crop (y) when $x = 300$ and $y = 500$.

19. Find the marginal productivity of the number of hours of labor (x) when $x = 300$ and $y = 500$.

20. If a production function is given by $z = 12x^{3/4}y^{1/3}$,
    (a) find the marginal productivity of x.
    (b) find the marginal productivity of y.

DEMAND FUNCTIONS

21. The demand functions for two products are given by

$$q_1 = 300 - 8p_1 - 4p_2$$
$$q_2 = 400 - 5p_1 - 10p_2.$$

Find the demand for each of the products if the price of the first is $p_1 = 10$ and the price of the second is $p_2 = 8$.

22. The demand functions for two products are given by

$$q_1 = 900 - 9p_1 + 2p_2$$
$$q_2 = 1200 + 6p_1 - 10p_2.$$

Find the demands q_1 and q_2 if $p_1 = \$10$ and $p_2 = \$12$.

23. Find a pair of prices p_1 and p_2 such that the demands for the two products of problem 21 will be equal.

24. Find a pair of prices p_1 and p_2 such that the demands for the two products of problem 22 will be equal.

In each of problems 25–28, the demand functions for two related products, A and B, are given. Complete parts (a)–(e) for each problem.
    (a) Find the marginal demand of q_A with respect to p_A.
    (b) Find the marginal demand of q_A with respect to p_B.
    (c) Find the marginal demand of q_B with respect to p_B.
    (d) Find the marginal demand of q_B with respect to p_A.
    (e) Are the two goods competitive or complementary?

25. $\begin{cases} q_A = 400 - 3p_A - 2p_B \\ q_B = 250 - 5p_A - 6p_B \end{cases}$

26. $\begin{cases} q_A = 600 - 4p_A + 6p_B \\ q_B = 1200 + 8p_A - 4p_B \end{cases}$

27. $\begin{cases} q_A = 5000 - 50p_A - \dfrac{600}{p_B + 1} \\ q_B = 10{,}000 - \dfrac{400}{p_A + 4} + \dfrac{400}{p_B + 4} \end{cases}$

28. $\begin{cases} q_A = 2500 + \dfrac{600}{p_A + 2} - 40p_B \\ q_B = 3000 - 100p_A + \dfrac{400}{p_B + 5} \end{cases}$

14.4 Higher-Order Partial Derivatives

Objective   ☐   To find and evaluate second and higher-order partial derivatives of functions of two variables

Just as each derivative of a function of one variable in turn may have second, third, and higher derivatives, partial derivatives may also have partial derivatives. A function of two variables, such as $z = f(x, y)$, has *four* second partial derivatives. The notations for these second partial derivatives follow.

$$z_{xx} = \frac{\partial^2 z}{\partial x^2} = \frac{\partial}{\partial x}\left(\frac{\partial z}{\partial x}\right): \text{ both derivatives taken with respect to } x.$$

$$z_{yy} = \frac{\partial^2 z}{\partial y^2} = \frac{\partial}{\partial y}\left(\frac{\partial z}{\partial y}\right): \text{ both derivatives taken with respect to } y.$$

$$z_{xy} = \frac{\partial^2 z}{\partial y\, \partial x} = \frac{\partial}{\partial y}\left(\frac{\partial z}{\partial x}\right): \begin{array}{l} \text{first derivative taken with respect to } x, \\ \text{second with respect to } y. \end{array}$$

$$z_{yx} = \frac{\partial^2 z}{\partial x\, \partial y} = \frac{\partial}{\partial x}\left(\frac{\partial z}{\partial y}\right): \begin{array}{l} \text{first derivative taken with respect to } y, \\ \text{second with respect to } x. \end{array}$$

EXAMPLE 1   If $z = x^3 y - 3xy^2 + 4$, find each of the second partial derivatives of the function.

Solution   Since

$$z_x = 3x^2 y - 3y^2 \text{ and } z_y = x^3 - 6xy,$$

$$z_{xx} = \frac{\partial}{\partial x}(3x^2 y - 3y^2) = 6xy$$

$$z_{xy} = \frac{\partial}{\partial y}(3x^2\, y - 3y^2) = 3x^2 - 6y$$

$$z_{yy} = \frac{\partial}{\partial y} (x^3 - 6xy) = -6x$$

$$z_{yx} = \frac{\partial}{\partial x} (x^3 - 6xy) = 3x^2 - 6y.$$

Note that z_{xy} and z_{yx} are equal for the function of Example 1. This will always occur if the derivatives of this function are continuous.

> If the second partial derivatives z_{xy} and z_{yx} of a function $z = f(x, y)$ are continuous at a point, they are equal there.

EXAMPLE 2 Find each of the second partial derivatives of $z = x^2y + e^{xy}$.

Solution Since
$$z_x = 2xy + e^{xy} \cdot y,$$
$$z_{xx} = 2y + e^{xy} \cdot y^2 = 2y + y^2e^{xy}$$
$$z_{xy} = 2x + (e^{xy} \cdot 1 + ye^{xy} \cdot x)$$
$$= 2x + e^{xy} + xye^{xy}.$$

Since
$$z_y = x^2 + e^{xy} \cdot x,$$
$$z_{yx} = 2x + (e^{xy} \cdot 1 + xe^{xy} \cdot y)$$
$$= 2x + e^{xy} + xye^{xy}$$
$$z_{yy} = 0 + xe^{xy} \cdot x = x^2e^{xy}.$$

EXAMPLE 3 If $z = x^2y + \ln x$, find $z_{xy}|_{(1, 1)}$.

Solution
$$z_x = 2xy + \frac{1}{x}$$
$$z_{xy} = 2x$$
$$z_{xy}|_{(1, 1)} = 2(1) = 2$$

We can find partial derivatives of order higher than the second. For example, we can find the third-order partial derivatives z_{xyx} and z_{xyy} for the function in Example 1 from the second derivative $z_{xy} = 3x^2 - 6y$:

$$z_{xyx} = 6x$$
$$z_{xyy} = -6.$$

EXAMPLE 4 If $z = x^3y^2 + 4 \ln x$, find z_{xyy}.

Solution
$$z_x = 3x^2y^2 + 4 \cdot \frac{1}{x}$$
$$z_{xy} = 3x^2(2y) + 0 = 6x^2y$$
$$z_{xyy} = 6x^2$$

Exercise 14.4

1. If $z = x^2 + 4x - 5y^3$, find the following.
   (a) z_{xx} (b) z_{xy} (c) z_{yx} (d) z_{yy}

2. If $z = x^3 - 5y^2 + 4y + 1$, find the following.
   (a) z_{xx} (b) z_{xy} (c) z_{yx} (d) z_{yy}

3. If $z = x^2y - 4xy^2$, find the following.
   (a) z_{xx} (b) z_{xy} (c) z_{yx} (d) z_{yy}

4. If $z = xy^2 + 4xy - 5$, find the following.
   (a) z_{xx} (b) z_{xy} (c) z_{yx} (d) z_{yy}

5. If $z = x^2 - xy + 4y^3$, find z_{xyx}.

6. If $z = x^3 - 4x^2y + 5y^3$, find z_{yyx}.

7. If $z = x^4 + x \ln y + y^2$, find z_{xyy}.

8. If $z = x^2y^3 + ye^x - y^2$, find z_{yxy}.

9. If $f(x, y) = x^3y + 4xy^4$, find $\dfrac{\partial^2}{\partial x^2} f(x, y)\big|_{(1, -1)}$.

10. If $f(x, y) = x^4y^2 + 4xy$, find $\dfrac{\partial^2}{\partial y^2} f(x, y)\big|_{(1, 2)}$.

11. If $f(x_1, x_2) = 3x_1^2 - 2x_1x_2$, find the following.
   (a) $\dfrac{\partial^2 f(x_1, x_2)}{\partial x_1^2}\bigg|_{(3, 2)}$ (b) $\dfrac{\partial^2 f(x_1, x_2)}{\partial x_2^2}\bigg|_{(3, 2)}$

12. If $f(x, y) = x^3y^2 + 4xy^3$, find the following.
   (a) $\dfrac{\partial^2 f(x, y)}{\partial x^2}\bigg|_{(1, 3)}$ (b) $\dfrac{\partial^2 f(x, y)}{\partial y^2}\bigg|_{(1, 3)}$

13. If $z = x^2y + ye^{x^2}$, find $z_{yx}\big|_{(1, 2)}$.

14. If $z = xy^3 + x \ln y^2$, find $z_{xy}\big|_{(2, 1)}$.

15. If $f(x, y) = x^2 + e^{xy}$, find the following.
   (a) $\dfrac{\partial^2 f}{\partial x^2}$ (b) $\dfrac{\partial^2 f}{\partial y\, \partial x}$ (c) $\dfrac{\partial^2 f}{\partial x\, \partial y}$ (d) $\dfrac{\partial^2 f}{\partial y^2}$

16. If $z = xe^{xy}$, find the following.
   (a) z_{xx} (b) z_{yy} (c) z_{xy} (d) z_{yx}

17. If $f(x, y) = y^2 - \ln xy$, find the following.
   (a) $\dfrac{\partial^2 f}{\partial x^2}$ (b) $\dfrac{\partial^2 f}{\partial y\, \partial x}$ (c) $\dfrac{\partial^2 f}{\partial x\, \partial y}$ (d) $\dfrac{\partial^2 f}{\partial y^2}$

18. If $f(x, y) = x^3 + \ln (xy - 1)$, find the following.
   (a) $\dfrac{\partial^2 f}{\partial x^2}$ (b) $\dfrac{\partial^2 f}{\partial y^2}$ (c) $\dfrac{\partial^2 f}{\partial x\, \partial y}$ (d) $\dfrac{\partial^2 f}{\partial y\, \partial x}$

19. If $z = \dfrac{\ln (x^2 + y^2)}{x^2}$, find z_{yy}.

20. If $z = \ln (x^2 + 4y^2)$, find z_{xx}.

21. If $z = \sqrt{4x^2 + y^2}$, find z_{xx}.

22. If $z = \ln (x^2 + 4y^2)$, find z_{yy}.

23. If $w = 4x^3y + y^2z + z^3$, find the following.
   (a) w_{xxy} (b) w_{xyx} (c) w_{xyz}

24. If $w = 4xyz + x^3y^2z + x^3$, find the following.
   (a) w_{xyz} (b) w_{xzz} (c) w_{yyz}

14.5 Maxima and Minima

Objective   ☐   To find relative maxima, minima, and saddle points of functions of two variables

In our study of differentiable functions of one variable, we saw that for a relative maximum or minimum to occur at a point, the tangent line to the curve had to be horizontal at that point. The function $z = f(x, y)$ describes a surface in three dimensions. If all partial derivatives of $f(x, y)$ exist, then the surface described by $z = f(x, y)$ must have a horizontal plane tangent to the surface at a point in order to have a relative maximum or minimum at that point (see Figure 14.6). But if the plane tangent to the surface at the point is horizontal, then all the tangent lines to the surface at that point must also be horizontal, for they lie in the tangent plane. In particular, the tangent line in the direction of the x-axis will be horizontal, so $\partial z/\partial x = 0$ at the point; and the tangent line in the direction of the y-axis will be horizontal, so $\partial z/\partial y = 0$ at the point. Thus we can determine the *critical points* for a surface by finding those points where *both* $\partial z/\partial x = 0$ and $\partial z/\partial y = 0$.

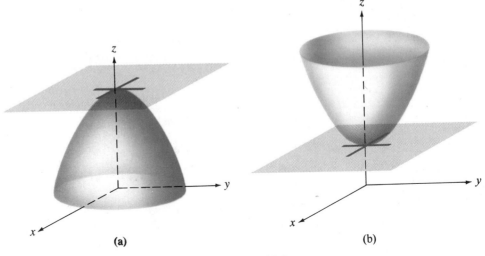

(a)   (b)

Figure 14.6

How can we determine whether a critical point is a relative maximum or relative minimum, or neither of these? Finding that $\partial^2 z/\partial x^2 < 0$ and $\partial^2 z/\partial y^2 < 0$ is not enough to tell us we have a relative maximum. The "second derivative" test we must use involves the values of the second partial derivatives and the value of D at the critical point (a, b), where D is defined as follows:

$$D = \frac{\partial^2 z}{\partial x^2} \cdot \frac{\partial^2 z}{\partial y^2} - \left(\frac{\partial^2 z}{\partial x\, \partial y}\right)^2.$$

We shall state, without proof, the result that determines whether there is a relative maximum or minimum or neither at a point (a, b).

Test for Maxima and Minima	Let $z = f(x, y)$ be a function for which

$$\frac{\partial z}{\partial x} = \frac{\partial z}{\partial y} = 0 \text{ at a point } (a, b),$$

and suppose all second partial derivatives are continuous there. For

$$D = z_{xx} \cdot z_{yy} - (z_{xy})^2:$$

(a) If $D > 0$ and $\partial^2 z / \partial x^2 > 0$ at (a, b), then a relative minimum occurs at (a, b). In this case, $\partial^2 z / \partial y^2 > 0$ at (a, b) also.

(b) If $D > 0$ and $\partial^2 z / \partial x^2 < 0$ at (a, b), then a relative maximum occurs at (a, b). In this case, $\partial^2 z / \partial y^2 < 0$ at (a, b) also.

(c) If $D < 0$ at (a, b), there is neither a relative maximum nor minimum at (a, b).

(d) If $D = 0$ at (a, b), then the test fails; the function must be investigated near the point.

We can test for relative maxima and minima by using the following procedure.

Procedure	Example
To find relative maxima and minima of $z = f(x, y)$.	Test $z = 4 - 4x^2 - y^2$ for relative maxima and minima.
1. Find $\partial z / \partial x$ and $\partial z / \partial y$.	1. $\dfrac{\partial z}{\partial x} = -8x; \quad \dfrac{\partial z}{\partial y} = -2y$
2. Find the point(s) that satisfy *both* $\partial z / \partial x = 0$ and $\partial z / \partial y = 0$. These are the critical points.	2. $\dfrac{\partial z}{\partial x} = 0$ if $x = 0$. $\dfrac{\partial z}{\partial y} = 0$ if $y = 0$. The critical point is $(0, 0, 4)$.
3. Find all second partial derivatives.	3. $\dfrac{\partial^2 z}{\partial x^2} = -8; \quad \dfrac{\partial^2 z}{\partial y^2} = -2$ $\dfrac{\partial^2 z}{\partial x\, \partial y} = \dfrac{\partial^2 z}{\partial y\, \partial x} = 0$
4. Evaluate D at the critical point(s).	4. At $(0, 0)$, $D = (-8)(-2) - 0^2 = 16.$
5. Use the test for maxima and minima to determine if relative maxima or minima occur.	5. $D > 0$, $\partial^2 z / \partial x^2 < 0$, and $\partial^2 z / \partial y^2 < 0$. A relative maximum occurs at $(0, 0)$. The graph is shown in Figure 14.7.

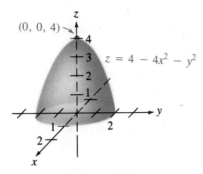

$(0, 0, 4)$

$z = 4 - 4x^2 - y^2$

Figure 14.7

EXAMPLE 1   Test $z = x^2 + y^2 - 2x + 1$ for relative maxima and minima.

Solution   1. $\dfrac{\partial z}{\partial x} = 2x - 2;$ $\dfrac{\partial z}{\partial y} = 2y$

2. $\dfrac{\partial z}{\partial x} = 0$ if $x = 1.$

$\dfrac{\partial z}{\partial y} = 0$ if $y = 0.$

Both are 0 if $x = 1$ *and* $y = 0$, so the critical point is $(1, 0, 0)$.

3. $\dfrac{\partial^2 z}{\partial x^2} = 2;$ $\dfrac{\partial^2 z}{\partial y^2} = 2$

$\dfrac{\partial^2 z}{\partial x\, \partial y} = \dfrac{\partial^2 z}{\partial y\, \partial x} = 0$

4. At $(1, 0)$, $D = 2 \cdot 2 - 0^2 = 4.$

5. $D > 0$, $\partial^2 z/\partial x^2 > 0$, and $\partial^2 z/\partial y^2 > 0$. A relative minimum occurs at $(1, 0)$. (See Figure 14.8.)

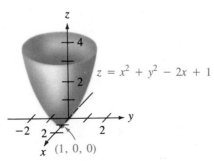

$z = x^2 + y^2 - 2x + 1$

$(1, 0, 0)$

Figure 14.8

EXAMPLE 2   Test $z = y^2 - x^2$ for relative maxima and minima.

Solution   1. $\dfrac{\partial z}{\partial x} = -2x;$ $\dfrac{\partial z}{\partial y} = 2y$

2. $\dfrac{\partial z}{\partial x} = 0$ if $x = 0;$ $\dfrac{\partial z}{\partial y} = 0$ if $y = 0.$

So both equal 0 if $x = 0$, $y = 0$. The critical point is $(0, 0, 0)$.

3. $\dfrac{\partial^2 z}{\partial x^2} = -2;$ $\dfrac{\partial^2 z}{\partial y^2} = 2;$ $\dfrac{\partial^2 z}{\partial x \, \partial y} = \dfrac{\partial^2 z}{\partial y \, \partial x} = 0$

4. $D = (-2)(2) - 0 = -4$

5. $D < 0$, so the critical point is neither a relative maximum nor minimum. As Figure 14.9 shows, the surface formed has the shape of a saddle. For this reason, critical points that are neither relative maxima nor minima are called **saddle points.**

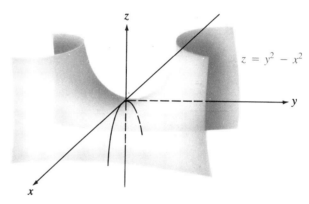

$z = y^2 - x^2$

Figure 14.9

The following example involves a surface with two critical points.

EXAMPLE 3   Test $z = x^3 + y^3 + 6xy$ for relative maxima and minima.

Solution   1. $\dfrac{\partial z}{\partial x} = 3x^2 + 6y;$ $\dfrac{\partial z}{\partial y} = 3y^2 + 6x$

2. $\dfrac{\partial z}{\partial x} = 0$ if $0 = 3x^2 + 6y;$ that is, if $y = -\tfrac{1}{2}x^2.$

$\dfrac{\partial z}{\partial y} = 0$ if $0 = 3y^2 + 6x;$ that is, if $x = -\tfrac{1}{2}y^2.$

Since *both* conditions must be satisfied, we can substitute $-\frac{1}{2}y^2$ for x in $y = -\frac{1}{2}x^2$, and obtain

$$y = -\frac{1}{2}\left(-\frac{1}{2}y^2\right)^2,$$

$$y = -\frac{1}{8}y^4$$

$$y + \frac{1}{8}y^4 = 0$$

$$y(8 + y^3) = 0.$$

So $y = 0$ or $y^3 = -8$; thus, $y = 0$ or $y = -2$. If $y = 0$, $x = -\frac{1}{2}(0)^2 = 0$, so one critical point is $(0, 0, 0)$. If $y = -2$, $x = -\frac{1}{2}(-2)^2 = -2$, so the second critical point is $(-2, -2, 8)$.

3. $\dfrac{\partial^2 z}{\partial x^2} = 6x;$ $\quad \dfrac{\partial^2 z}{\partial y^2} = 6y;$ $\quad \dfrac{\partial^2 z}{\partial x\,\partial y} = \dfrac{\partial^2 z}{\partial y\,\partial x} = 6$

Thus $D = (6x)(6y) - (6)^2$.

4. At $(0, 0)$, $D = 0 \cdot 0 - (6)^2 = -36 < 0$.

At $(-2, -2)$, $D = (-12)(-12) - 36 = 108 > 0$.

5. At $(0, 0)$, $D < 0$, so a saddle point occurs at $(0, 0, 0)$.

At $(-2, -2)$, $D > 0$, $\partial^2 z/\partial x^2 = 6(-2) = -12$, and $\partial^2 z/\partial y^2 = 6(-2) = -12$, so a relative maximum is 8 at $(-2, -2)$.

EXAMPLE 4   Maximize the profit if the demand functions for products X and Y are $p_1 = 50 - x$ and $p_2 = 60 - 2y$, and if the joint cost function for the products is $C(x, y) = 2xy$.

Solution   The profit function is $P(x, y) = p_1 x + p_2 y - C(x, y)$, so

$$P(x, y) = (50 - x)x + (60 - 2y)y - 2xy$$
$$= 50x - x^2 + 60y - 2y^2 - 2xy.$$

To maximize the profit, we proceed as follows.

$$P_x = 50 - 2x - 2y \quad \text{and} \quad P_y = 60 - 4y - 2x.$$

Solving simultaneously $P_x = 0$ and $P_y = 0$, we have

$$\begin{cases} 0 = 50 - 2x - 2y \\ 0 = 60 - 2x - 4y \end{cases}$$

or $-10 + 2y = 0$, so $y = 5$. Thus $0 = 40 - 2x$, so $x = 20$. Now $P_{xx} = -2$, $P_{yy} = -4$, and $P_{xy} = -2$, and

$$D = (P_{xx})(P_{yy}) - (P_{xy})^2 = (-2)(-4) - (-2)^2 = +4.$$

Since $P_{xx} < 0$, $P_{yy} < 0$ and $D > 0$, the values $x = 20$ and $y = 5$ yield maximum profit. Therefore, when $x = 20$ and $y = 5$, $p_1 = 30$, $p_2 = 50$, and the maximum profit is

$P(20, 5) = 600 + 250 - 200 = 650$ (dollars).

Exercise 14.5

In the following problems, test for relative maxima and minima.

1. $z = 9 - x^2 - y^2$
2. $z = 16 - 4x^2 - 9y^2$
3. $z = x^2 + y^2 + 4$
4. $z = x^2 + y^2 - 4$
5. $z = x^2 + y^2 - 2x + 4y + 5$
6. $z = 4x^2 + y^2 + 4x + 1$
7. $z = x^2 + 6xy + y^2 + 16x$
8. $z = x^2 - 4xy + y^2 - 6y$
9. $z = \dfrac{x^2 - y^2}{9}$
10. $z = \dfrac{y^2}{4} - \dfrac{x^2}{9}$
11. $z = 24 - x^2 + xy - y^2 + 36y$
12. $z = 46 - x^2 + 2xy - 4y^2$
13. $z = x^2 + xy + y^2 - 4y + 10x$
14. $z = x^2 + 5xy + 10y^2 + 8x - 40y$
15. $z = x^3 + y^3 - 6xy$
16. $z = x^3 + y^3 + 3xy$

APPLICATIONS

17. Suppose the profit from the sale of Kisses and Kreams is given by

$$P(x, y) = 100x + 64y - 0.01x^2 - 0.25y^2,$$

where x is the number of pounds of Kisses and y is the number of pounds of Kreams. Selling how many pounds of Kisses and Kreams will maximize profit?

18. The profit from the sales of two products is given by

$$P(x, y) = 20x + 70y - x^2 - y^2,$$

where x is the number of units of product 1 sold and y is the number of units of product 2. Selling how much of each product will maximize profit?

19. A new food is designed to add weight to mature beef cattle. The increase in weight is given by $W = xy(20 - x - 2y)$, where x is the number of units of the first ingredient and y is the number of units of the second ingredient. How many units of each ingredient will maximize the weight gain?

20. The profit for a grain crop is related to fertilizer and labor. If the profit per acre is

$$P = 100x + 40y - 5x^2 - 2y^2,$$

where x is the number of units of fertilizer and y is the number of work-hours, what values of x and y will maximize the profit?

21. Suppose $P = 3.78x^2 + 1.5y^2 - 0.09x^3 - 0.01y^3$ is the production function for a product with x units of one input and y units of a second input. Find the values of x and y that will maximize production.

22. Suppose x units of one input and y units of a second input result in

$$P = 40x + 50y - x^2 - y^2 - xy$$

units of a product. Determine the inputs x and y that will maximize P.

23. Suppose a manufacturer produces two brands of a product, brand 1 and brand 2. If the demand for brand 1 is $p_1 = 10 - x$, the demand for brand 2 is $p_2 = 40 - 2y$, and if the joint cost function is $C = xy$, how many of each brand should be produced to maximize profit?

24. Suppose a firm produces two products, A and B, that sell for $a and $b, respectively, with the total cost of producing x units of A and y units of B equal to $C(x, y)$. Show that profit from these products is maximized when

$$\frac{\partial C}{\partial x}(x, y) = a \quad \text{and} \quad \frac{\partial C}{\partial y}(x, y) = b.$$

25. Find the values for each of the dimensions of an open-top box of length x, width y, and height $\dfrac{500,000}{xy}$ such that the box requires the least amount of material to make.

26. Find the values for each of the dimensions of a closed-top box of length x, width y, and height z if the volume equals 27,000 cubic inches and the box requires the least amount of material to make. (Hint: First write z in terms of x and y as in problem 25.)

27. A company manufactures two products, A and B. If x is the number of units of A and y is the number of units of B, then the cost and revenue functions are

$$C(x, y) = 2x^2 - 2xy + y^2 - 7x + 10y + 11$$
$$R(x, y) = 5x + 4y.$$

Find the number of each type of product that should be manufactured to maximize profit.

28. Let x be the number of worker hours required and y be the amount of capital required to produce z units of a product. Show that the average production per worker hour, z/x, is maximized when

$$\frac{\partial z}{\partial x} = \frac{z}{x}.$$

Use $z = f(x, y)$ and assume a maximum exists.

14.6 Maxima and Minima of Functions Subject to Constraints; Lagrange Multipliers

Objective ☐ To find the maximum or minimum value of a function of two or more variables subject to a condition that constrains the variables

Many practical problems require that a function of two or more variables be maximized or minimized subject to certain conditions, or constraints, that limit the variables involved. For example, a firm will want to maximize its profits within the limits (constraints) imposed by its production capacity. Similarly, a city planner may want to locate a new building to maximize access to public transportation, yet may be constrained by the availability and cost of building sites.

We can obtain maxima and minima for a function $z = f(x, y)$ subject to the constraint $g(x, y) = 0$ by using the method of **Lagrange multipliers,** named for the famous eighteenth century mathematician Joseph Louis Lagrange. Lagrange multipliers can be used with functions of two or more variables when the constraints are given by an equation.

In order to find the critical values of a function $f(x, y)$ subject to the constraint $g(x, y) = 0$ we will use the new variable λ to form the **objective function**

$$F(x, y, \lambda) = f(x, y) + \lambda g(x, y).$$

It can be shown that the critical values of $F(x, y, \lambda)$ will satisfy the constraint $g(x, y,)$ and will also be critical points of $f(x, y)$. Thus we need only find the critical points of $F(x, y, \lambda)$ to find the required critical points.

To find the critical points of $F(x, y, \lambda)$, we must find the points that make all the partial derivatives equal to 0. That is, the points must satisfy

$$\partial F/\partial x = 0, \qquad \partial F/\partial y = 0, \qquad \text{and} \qquad \partial F/\partial \lambda = 0.$$

Since $F(x, y, \lambda) = f(x, y) + \lambda g(x, y)$, these equations may be written as

$$\frac{\partial f}{\partial x} + \lambda \frac{\partial g}{\partial x} = 0$$

$$\frac{\partial f}{\partial y} + \lambda \frac{\partial g}{\partial y} = 0$$

$$g(x, y) = 0.$$

Finding the values of x and y that satisfy these three equations simultaneously gives the critical values.

This method will not tell us if the critical points correspond to maxima or minima, but this can either be determined from the physical setting for the problem or by testing according to a procedure similar to that used for unconstrained maxima and minima. The following examples will illustrate the use of Lagrange multipliers.

EXAMPLE 1   Find the maximum value of $z = x^2 y$ subject to the condition $x + y = 9$, $x \geq 0$, $y \geq 0$.

Solution   The function to be maximized is $f(x, y) = x^2 y$.
The constraint is $g(x, y) = 0$, where $g(x, y) = x + y - 9$.
The objective function is

$$F(x, y, \lambda) = f(x, y) + \lambda g(x, y),$$

or

$$F(x, y, \lambda) = x^2 y + \lambda(x + y - 9).$$

Thus

$$\frac{\partial F}{\partial x} = 2xy + \lambda(1) = 0, \qquad \text{or} \qquad 2xy + \lambda = 0$$

$$\frac{\partial F}{\partial y} = x^2 + \lambda(1) = 0, \qquad \text{or} \qquad x^2 + \lambda = 0$$

$$\frac{\partial F}{\partial \lambda} = 0 + 1(x + y - 9) = 0, \qquad \text{or} \qquad x + y - 9 = 0.$$

Solving the first two equations for λ and substituting gives

$$\lambda = -2xy$$
$$\lambda = -x^2$$
$$2xy = x^2$$
$$2xy - x^2 = 0$$
$$x(2y - x) = 0.$$

So $\qquad x = 0 \qquad$ or $\qquad x = 2y.$

Since $x = 0$ could not make $z = x^2y$ a maximum, we substitute $x = 2y$ into $x + y - 9 = 0$.

$$2y + y = 9$$
$$y = 3$$
$$x = 6$$

Thus the function $z = x^2y$ is maximized at 108 when $x = 6$, $y = 3$, if the constraint is $x + y = 9$. Testing values near $x = 6$, $y = 3$, and satisfying the constraint shows the function is maximized there. (Try $x = 5.5$, $y = 3.5$, $x = 7$, $y = 2$, and so on.)

EXAMPLE 2 Find the minimum value of the function $z = x^3 + y^3 + xy$ subject to the constraint $x + y - 4 = 0$.

Solution The function to be minimized is $f(x, y) = x^3 + y^3 + xy$.
The constraint function is $g(x, y) = x + y - 4$.
The objective function is

$$F(x, y, \lambda) = f(x, y) + \lambda g(x, y),$$

or

$$F(x, y, \lambda) = x^3 + y^3 + xy + \lambda(x + y - 4).$$

Then

$$\frac{\partial F}{\partial x} = 3x^2 + y + \lambda = 0$$

$$\frac{\partial F}{\partial y} = 3y^2 + x + \lambda = 0$$

$$\frac{\partial F}{\partial \lambda} = x + y - 4 = 0.$$

Solving the first two equations for λ and substituting gives the following.

$$\lambda = -(3x^2 + y)$$
$$\lambda = -(3y^2 + x)$$
$$3x^2 + y = 3y^2 + x \qquad (1)$$

Solving $x + y - 4 = 0$ for y gives $y = 4 - x$. Substituting into equation (1) for y, we get

$$3x^2 + (4 - x) = 3(4 - x)^2 + x$$
$$3x^2 + 4 - x = 48 - 24x + 3x^2 + x$$
$$22x = 44 \qquad \text{or} \qquad x = 2.$$

Thus when $x + y - 4 = 0$, $x = 2$ and $y = 2$ give the miminum value $z = 20$.

EXAMPLE 3 Find the maximum value of the function $z = 2xy - 2x^2 - 2y^2$ subject to the constraint $2x + y = 7$.

Solution   The constraint function is $g(x, y) = 2x + y - 7$, so the objective function is

$$F(x, y, \lambda) = 2xy - 2x^2 - 2y^2 + \lambda(2x + y - 7).$$

Then

$$\frac{\partial F}{\partial x} = 2y - 4x + 2\lambda = 0$$

$$\frac{\partial F}{\partial y} = 2x - 4y + \lambda = 0$$

$$\frac{\partial F}{\partial \lambda} = 2x + y - 7 = 0.$$

Solving the first two equations for λ gives

$$\lambda = -y + 2x$$
$$\lambda = -2x + 4y$$
$$-y + 2x = -2x + 4y$$
$$4x = 5y$$
$$x = \frac{5y}{4}.$$

Substituting for x in $2x + y - 7 = 0$ gives $\frac{5}{2}y + y - 7 = 0$, so the critical values are $y = 2$, $x = \frac{5}{2}$. Testing values near $x = \frac{5}{2}$, $y = 2$, shows the function has a relative maximum there. The maximum value is $-21/2$.

We can also use Lagrange multipliers to find the maxima and minima of functions of three (or more) variables subject to two (or more) constraints. The method involves using two multipliers, one for each constraint, getting an objective function $F = f + \lambda g_1 + \mu g_2$. We leave further discussion for more advanced courses.

We can easily extend the method to functions of three or more variables, as the following example shows.

EXAMPLE 4   Find the minimum value of the function $w = x + y^2 + z^2$, subject to the constraint $x + y + z = 1$.

Solution   The function to be minimized is $f(x, y, z) = x + y^2 + z^2$. The constraint is $g(x, y, z) = 0$, where $g(x, y, z) = x + y + z - 1$.

The objective function is

$$F(x, y, z, \lambda) = f(x, y, z) + \lambda g(x, y, z),$$

or

$$F(x, y, z, \lambda) = x + y^2 + z^2 + \lambda(x + y + z - 1).$$

Then

$$\frac{\partial F}{\partial x} = 1 + \lambda = 0$$

$$\frac{\partial F}{\partial y} = 2y + \lambda = 0$$

$$\frac{\partial F}{\partial z} = 2z + \lambda = 0$$

$$\frac{\partial F}{\partial \lambda} = x + y + z - 1 = 0.$$

Solving the first three equations simultaneously gives

$$\lambda = -1$$

$$y = \tfrac{1}{2}$$

$$z = \tfrac{1}{2}.$$

Substituting these values in the fourth equation (which is the constraint), we get $x + \tfrac{1}{2} + \tfrac{1}{2} - 1 = 0$, so $x = 0$, $y = \tfrac{1}{2}$, $z = \tfrac{1}{2}$. Thus, $w = \tfrac{1}{2}$ is the minimum value since other values of x, y, and z satisfying $x + y + z = 1$ give larger values for w.

EXAMPLE 5 Suppose the utility function for commodities X and Y is given by $U = x^2y^2$, where x and y are the amounts of X and Y, respectively. If p_1 and p_2 represent the prices of X and Y, respectively, and I represents the consumer's income available to purchase these two commodities, the equation $p_1x + p_2y = I$ is called the *budget constraint*. If the price of X is \$2, the price of Y is \$4, and the income available is \$40, find the x and y that maximizes utility.

Solution The utility function is $U = x^2y^2$ and the budget constraint is $2x + 4y = 40$. The objective function is

$$F(x, y, \lambda) = x^2y^2 + \lambda(2x + 4y - 40).$$

$$\frac{\partial F}{\partial x} = 2xy^2 + 2\lambda, \qquad \frac{\partial F}{\partial y} = 2x^2y + 4\lambda, \qquad \frac{\partial F}{\partial \lambda} = 2x + 4y - 40$$

Setting these partial derivatives equal to 0 and solving gives

$$-\lambda = xy^2 = x^2y/2, \qquad \text{or} \qquad xy^2 - x^2y/2 = 0,$$

so
$$xy(y - x/2) = 0$$

yields $x = 0$, $y = 0$, or $x = 2y$. Neither $x = 0$ nor $y = 0$ maximizes utility. If $x = 2y$, we have

$$0 = 4y + 4y - 40.$$

Thus $y = 5$ and $x = 10$.

Testing values near $x = 10$, $y = 5$ shows these values maximize utility, at $U = 2500$.

Exercise 14.6

1. Find the minimum value of $z = x^2 + y^2$ subject to the condition $x + y = 6$.
2. Find the minimum value of $z = 4x^2 + y^2$ subject to the constraint $x + y = 5$.
3. Find the minimum value of $z = 3x^2 + 5y^2 - 2xy$ subject to the constraint $x + y = 5$.

4. Find the maximum value of $z = 2xy - 3x^2 - 5y^2$ subject to the constraint $x + y = 5$.
5. Find the maximum value of $z = x^2y$ subject to the constraint $x + y = 6$, $x \geq 0$, $y \geq 0$.
6. Find the maximum value of the function $z = x^3y^2$ subject to the condition $x + y = 10$, $x \geq 0$, $y \geq 0$.
7. Find the maximum value of the function $z = 2xy - 2x^2 - 4y^2$ subject to the condition $x + 2y = 8$.
8. Find the minimum value of $z = 2x^2 + y^2 - xy$ subject to the constraint $2x + y = 8$.
9. Find the minimum value of $z = x^2 + y^2$ subject to the condition $2x + y + 1 = 0$.
10. Find the minimum value of $z = x^2 + y^2$ subject to the condition $xy = 1$.
11. Find the minimum value of the function $w = x^2 + y^2 + z^2$ subject to the constraint $x + y + z = 3$.
12. Find the minimum value of the function $w = x^2 + y^2 + z^2$, subject to the condition $2x - 4y + z = 21$.
13. Find the maximum value of $w = xz + y$, subject to the constraint $x^2 + y^2 + z^2 = 1$.
14. Find the maximum value of $w = x^2yz$ subject to $4x + y + z = 4$, $x \geq 0$, $y \geq 0$, and $z \geq 0$.

APPLICATIONS

15. Suppose the utility function for two commodities is given by $U = x^2y$ and that the budget constraint is $3x + 6y = 18$. What values of x and y will maximize utility?
16. Suppose the budget constraint in problem 15 is $5x + 20y = 80$. What values of x and y will maximize $U = x^2y$?
17. Suppose the utility function for two products is given by $U = x^2y$, and the budget constraint is $2x + 3y = 120$. Find the values of x and y that maximize utility.
18. Suppose the utility function for two commodities is given by $U = x^2y^3$, and the budget constraint is $10x + 15y = 250$. Find the values of x and y that maximize utility.
19. A firm has two plants, X and Y. Suppose the cost of producing x units at plant X is $x^2 + 1200$ and the cost of producing y units of the same product at plant Y is given by $3y^2 + 800$. If they have an order for 1200 units, how many should they produce at each plant to fill this order and minimize the cost of production?
20. Suppose the cost of producing x units at plant X is $(3x + 4)x$ and the cost of producing y units of the same product at plant Y is $(2y + 8)y$. If the firm owning the plants has an order for 149 units, how many should it produce at each plant to fill this order and minimize its cost of production?
21. On the basis of past experience a company has determined that its sales revenue is related to its advertising according to the formula $s = 20x + y^2 + 4xy$, where x is the amount spent in radio advertising and y is the amount spent in television advertising. If the company plans to spend $30,000 on these two means of advertising, how much should they spend on each method to maximize their sales revenue?
22. Find the dimensions x, y, and z of the rectangular box with largest volume that satisfies

$$3x + 4y + 12z = 12.$$

23. Find the dimensions of the box with square base, open top, and volume 500,000 cc that requires the least materials.
24. Show that a box with a square base, open top, and a fixed volume requires the least material to build if it has a height equal to one-half the length of one side of the base.

Review Exercises

14.1

1. What is the domain of $z = \dfrac{3}{2x - y}$?

2. What is the domain of $z = \dfrac{3x + 2\sqrt{y}}{x^2 + y^2}$?

3. If $w(x, y, z) = x^2 - 3yz$, find $w(2, 3, 1)$.

4. If $Q(K, L) = 70K^{2/3}L^{1/3}$, find $Q(64,000, 512)$.

14.2

5. Find $\dfrac{\partial z}{\partial x}$ if $z = 5x^3 + 6xy + y^2$.

6. Find $\dfrac{\partial z}{\partial y}$ if $z = 12x^5 - 14x^3y^3 + 6y^4 - 1$.

In problems 7–12, find z_x and z_y.

7. $z = 4x^2y^3 + \dfrac{x}{y}$

8. $z = \sqrt{x^2 + 2y^2}$

9. $z = (xy + 1)^{-2}$

10. $z = e^{x^2y^3}$

11. $z = e^{xy} + y \ln x$

12. $z = e^{\ln xy}$

13. Find the partial derivative of $f(x, y) = 4x^3 + 5xy^2 + y^3$ with respect to x at the point $(1, 2, -8)$.

14. Find the slope of the tangent in the x-direction to the surface $z = 5x^4 - 3xy^2 + y^2$ at $(1, 2, -3)$.

14.4

In problems 15–18, find the second partials (a) z_{xx} (b) z_{yy} (c) z_{xy} (d) z_{yx}.

15. $z = x^2y - 3xy$

16. $z = 3x^3y^4 - \dfrac{x^2}{y^2}$

17. $z = x^2e^{y^2}$

18. $z = \ln (xy + 1)$

14.5

19. Test $z = 16 - x^2 - xy - y^2 + 24y$ for maxima and minima.

20. Test $z = x^3 + y^3 - 3xy$ for maxima and minima.

14.6

21. Find the minimum value of $z = 4x^2 + y^2$ subject to the constraint $x + y = 10$.

22. Find the maximum value of $z = x^4y^2$ subject to the constraint $x + y = 9$, $x \geq 0$, $y \geq 0$.

APPLICATIONS

14.1

23. Suppose the utility function for two goods X and Y is given by $U = x^2y$, and a consumer purchases 6 units of X and 15 units of Y. If the consumer purchases 60 units of Y, how many units of X must be purchased to retain the same level of utility?

24. Suppose an indifference curve for two products, X and Y, has the equation $xy = 1600$. If 80 units of X are purchased, how many units of Y must be purchased?

14.3

25. The joint cost function for two products is $C(x, y) = x^2\sqrt{y^2 + 13}$.
   (a) Find the marginal cost with respect to x if 20 units of x and 6 units of y are produced.
   (b) Find the marginal cost with respect to y if 20 units of x and 6 units of y are produced.

26. Suppose the production function for a company is given by

$$Q = 80K^{1/4} L^{3/4},$$

where Q is the output (in hundreds of units), K is the capital expenditures (in thousands of dollars), and L is the labor hours. Find $\partial Q/\partial K$ and $\partial Q/\partial L$ when expenditures are $625,000 and total labor hours are 4096.

27. The demand functions for two related products, product A and product B, are given by

$$q_A = 400 - 2p_A - 3p_B$$
$$q_B = 300 - 5p_A - 6p_B.$$

(a) Find the marginal demand of q_A with respect to p_A.
(b) Find the marginal demand of q_B with respect to p_B.
(c) Are the two products complementary or competitive?

28. Suppose the demand functions for two related products, A and B, are given by

$$q_A = 800 - 40p_A - \frac{2}{p_B + 1}$$

$$q_B = 1000 - \frac{10}{p_A + 4} - 30p_B.$$

Determine whether the products are competitive or complementary.

14.5

29. The profit from the sale of two products is given by $P(x, y) = 40x + 80y - x^2 - y^2$, where x is the number of units of product 1 and y is the number of units of product 2. Selling how much of each product will maximize profit?

14.6

30. If the utility function for two commodities is $U = x^2y$, and the budget constraint is $4x + 5y = 60$, find the values of x and y that maximize utility.

Appendix

Table 1 Exponential Functions

x	e^x	e^{-x}	x	e^x	e^{-x}
0.0	1.000	1.000	3.0	20.09	0.0498
0.1	1.105	0.9048	3.1	22.20	0.0450
0.2	1.221	0.8187	3.2	24.53	0.0408
0.3	1.350	0.7408	3.3	27.11	0.0369
0.4	1.492	0.6703	3.4	29.96	0.0334
0.5	1.649	0.6065	3.5	33.12	0.0302
0.6	1.822	0.5488	3.6	36.60	0.0273
0.7	2.014	0.4966	3.7	40.45	0.0247
0.8	2.226	0.4493	3.8	44.70	0.0224
0.9	2.460	0.4066	3.9	49.40	0.0202
1.0	2.718	0.3679	4.0	54.60	0.0183
1.1	3.004	0.3329	4.1	60.34	0.0166
1.2	3.320	0.3012	4.2	66.69	0.0150
1.3	3.669	0.2725	4.3	73.70	0.0136
1.4	4.055	0.2466	4.4	81.45	0.0123
1.5	4.482	0.2231	4.5	90.02	0.0111
1.6	4.953	0.2019	4.6	99.48	0.0101
1.7	5.474	0.1827	4.7	109.9	0.0091
1.8	6.050	0.1653	4.8	121.5	0.0082
1.9	6.686	0.1496	4.9	134.3	0.0074
2.0	7.389	0.1353	5.0	148.4	0.0067
2.1	8.166	0.1225	5.1	164.0	0.0061
2.2	9.025	0.1108	5.2	181.3	0.0055
2.3	9.974	0.1003	5.3	200.3	0.0050
2.4	11.02	0.0907	5.4	221.4	0.0045
2.5	12.18	0.0821	5.5	244.7	0.0041
2.6	13.46	0.0743	5.6	270.4	0.0037
2.7	14.88	0.0672	5.7	298.9	0.0033
2.8	16.44	0.0608	5.8	330.3	0.0030
2.9	18.17	0.0550	5.9	365.0	0.0027
			6.0	403.4	0.0025
			7.0	1097	0.0009
			8.0	2981	0.0003
			9.0	8103	0.0001

Table II   Selected Values of Log$_e$ x

x	ln x	x	ln x	x	ln x
.002	−6.215	1.40	0.336	600	6.397
.004	−5.521	1.50	0.405	700	6.551
.010	−4.605	2	0.693	800	6.685
.015	−4.200	3	1.099	900	6.802
.018	−4.017	5	1.609	1000	6.908
.020	−3.912	7	1.946	1300	7.170
.023	−3.772	10	2.303	1600	7.378
.027	−3.612	20	2.996	2000	7.601
.030	−3.507	30	3.401	2300	7.741
.040	−3.219	50	3.912	2600	7.863
.045	−3.101	80	4.382	3000	8.006
.050	−2.996	100	4.605	3500	8.161
.080	−2.526	110	4.700	4000	8.294
.10	−2.303	130	4.868	4600	8.434
.20	−1.609	150	5.011	5100	8.537
.30	−1.204	170	5.136	5700	8.648
.40	−0.916	200	5.298	6300	8.748
.41	−0.892	230	5.438	6900	8.839
.48	−0.734	250	5.521	7500	8.923
.50	−0.693	280	5.635	8100	9.000
.52	−0.654	300	5.704	8700	9.071
.60	−0.511	350	5.858	9300	9.138
.70	−0.357	400	5.991	10000	9.210
.80	−0.223	410	6.016	11000	9.306
.90	−0.105	460	6.131	12000	9.363
1.00	0.0	500	6.215	13000	9.473
1.30	0.262	520	6.254	14000	9.547
1.35	0.300	580	6.363	15000	9.616

Table III   Areas Under the Standard
Normal Curve

The value of A is the area under the standard normal
curve between $z = 0$ and $z = z_0$, for $z_0 \geq 0$. Areas for
negative values of z_0 are obtained by symmetry.

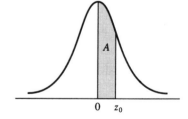

z_0	A	z_0	A	z_0	A	z_0	A
.00	.0000	.06	.0239	.12	.0478	.18	.0714
.01	.0040	.07	.0279	.13	.0517	.19	.0754
.02	.0080	.08	.0319	.14	.0557	.20	.0793
.03	.0120	.09	.0359	.15	.0596	.21	.0832
.04	.0160	.10	.0398	.16	.0636	.22	.0871
.05	.0199	.11	.0438	.17	.0675	.23	.0910

Table III Areas Under the Standard Normal Curve (Continued)

z_0	A	z_0	A	z_0	A	z_0	A
.24	.0948	.70	.2580	1.16	.3770	1.62	.4474
.25	.0987	.71	.2612	1.17	.3790	1.63	.4485
.26	.1026	.72	.2642	1.18	.3810	1.64	.4495
.27	.1064	.73	.2673	1.19	.3830	1.65	.4505
.28	.1103	.74	.2704	1.20	.3849	1.66	.4515
.29	.1141	.75	.2734	1.21	.3869	1.67	.4525
.30	.1179	.76	.2764	1.22	.3888	1.68	.4535
.31	.1217	.77	.2794	1.23	.3907	1.69	.4545
.32	.1255	.78	.2823	1.24	.3925	1.70	.4554
.33	.1293	.79	.2852	1.25	.3944	1.71	.4564
.34	.1331	.80	.2881	1.26	.3962	1.72	.4573
.35	.1368	.81	.2910	1.27	.3980	1.73	.4582
.36	.1406	.82	.2939	1.28	.3997	1.74	.4591
.37	.1443	.83	.2967	1.29	.4015	1.75	.4599
.38	.1480	.84	.2996	1.30	.4032	1.76	.4608
.39	.1517	.85	.3023	1.31	.4049	1.77	.4616
.40	.1554	.86	.3051	1.32	.4066	1.78	.4625
.41	.1591	.87	.3079	1.33	.4082	1.79	.4633
.42	.1628	.88	.3106	1.34	.4099	1.80	.4641
.43	.1664	.89	.3133	1.35	.4115	1.81	.4649
.44	.1700	.90	.3159	1.36	.4131	1.82	.4656
.45	.1736	.91	.3186	1.37	.4147	1.83	.4664
.46	.1772	.92	.3212	1.38	.4162	1.84	.4671
.47	.1808	.93	.3238	1.39	.4177	1.85	.4678
.48	.1844	.94	.3264	1.40	.4192	1.86	.4686
.49	.1879	.95	.3289	1.41	.4207	1.87	.4693
.50	.1915	.96	.3315	1.42	.4222	1.88	.4700
.51	.1950	.97	.3340	1.43	.4236	1.89	.4706
.52	.1985	.98	.3365	1.44	.4251	1.90	.4713
.53	.2019	.99	.3389	1.45	.4265	1.91	.4719
.54	.2054	1.00	.3413	1.46	.4279	1.92	.4726
.55	.2088	1.01	.3438	1.47	.4292	1.93	.4732
.56	.2123	1.02	.3461	1.48	.4306	1.94	.4738
.57	.2157	1.03	.3485	1.49	.4319	1.95	.4744
.58	.2190	1.04	.3508	1.50	.4332	1.96	.4750
.59	.2224	1.05	.3531	1.51	.4345	1.97	.4756
.60	.2258	1.06	.3554	1.52	.4357	1.98	.4762
.61	.2291	1.07	.3577	1.53	.4370	1.99	.4767
.62	.2324	1.08	.3599	1.54	.4382	2.00	.4773
.63	.2357	1.09	.3621	1.55	.4394	2.01	.4778
.64	.2389	1.10	.3643	1.56	.4406	2.02	.4783
.65	.2422	1.11	.3665	1.57	.4418	2.03	.4788
.66	.2454	1.12	.3686	1.58	.4430	2.04	.4793
.67	.2486	1.13	.3708	1.59	.4441	2.05	.4798
.68	.2518	1.14	.3729	1.60	.4452	2.06	.4803
.69	.2549	1.15	.3749	1.61	.4463	2.07	.4808

Table III Areas Under the Standard Normal Curve (Continued)

z_0	A	z_0	A	z_0	A	z_0	A
2.08	.4812	2.54	.4945	3.00	.4987	3.46	.4997
2.09	.4817	2.55	.4946	3.01	.4987	3.47	.4997
2.10	.4821	2.56	.4948	3.02	.4987	3.48	.4998
2.11	.4826	2.57	.4949	3.03	.4988	3.49	.4998
2.12	.4830	2.58	.4951	3.04	.4988	3.50	.4998
2.13	.4834	2.59	.4952	3.05	.4989	3.51	.4998
2.14	.4838	2.60	.4953	3.06	.4989	3.52	.4998
2.15	.4842	2.61	.4955	3.07	.4989	3.53	.4998
2.16	.4846	2.62	.4956	3.08	.4990	3.54	.4998
2.17	.4850	2.63	.4957	3.09	.4990	3.55	.4998
2.18	.4854	2.64	.4959	3.10	.4990	3.56	.4998
2.19	.4857	2.65	.4960	3.11	.4991	3.57	.4998
2.20	.4861	2.66	.4961	3.12	.4991	3.58	.4998
2.21	.4865	2.67	.4962	3.13	.4991	3.59	.4998
2.22	.4868	2.68	.4963	3.14	.4992	3.60	.4998
2.23	.4871	2.69	.4964	3.15	.4992	3.61	.4999
2.24	.4875	2.70	.4965	3.16	.4992	3.62	.4999
2.25	.4878	2.71	.4966	3.17	.4992	3.63	.4999
2.26	.4881	2.72	.4967	3.18	.4993	3.64	.4999
2.27	.4884	2.73	.4968	3.19	.4993	3.65	.4999
2.28	.4887	2.74	.4969	3.20	.4993	3.66	.4999
2.29	.4890	2.75	.4970	3.21	.4993	3.67	.4999
2.30	.4893	2.76	.4971	3.22	.4994	3.68	.4999
2.31	.4896	2.77	.4972	3.23	.4994	3.69	.4999
2.32	.4898	2.78	.4973	3.24	.4994	3.70	.4999
2.33	.4901	2.79	.4974	3.25	.4994	3.71	.4999
2.34	.4904	2.80	.4974	3.26	.4994	3.72	.4999
2.35	.4906	2.81	.4975	3.27	.4995	3.73	.4999
2.36	.4909	2.82	.4976	3.28	.4995	3.74	.4999
2.37	.4911	2.83	.4977	3.29	.4995	3.75	.4999
2.38	.4913	2.84	.4977	3.30	.4995	3.76	.4999
2.39	.4916	2.85	.4978	3.31	.4995	3.77	.4999
2.40	.4918	2.86	.4979	3.32	.4996	3.78	.4999
2.41	.4920	2.87	.4980	3.33	.4996	3.79	.4999
2.42	.4922	2.88	.4980	3.34	.4996	3.80	.4999
2.43	.4925	2.89	.4981	3.35	.4996	3.81	.4999
2.44	.4927	2.90	.4981	3.36	.4996	3.82	.4999
2.45	.4929	2.91	.4982	3.37	.4996	3.83	.4999
2.46	.4931	2.92	.4983	3.38	.4996	3.84	.4999
2.47	.4932	2.93	.4983	3.39	.4997	3.85	.4999
2.48	.4934	2.94	.4984	3.40	.4997	3.86	.4999
2.49	.4936	2.95	.4984	3.41	.4997	3.87	.5000
2.50	.4938	2.96	.4985	3.42	.4997	3.88	.5000
2.51	.4940	2.97	.4985	3.43	.4997	3.89	.5000
2.52	.4941	2.98	.4986	3.44	.4997		
2.53	.4943	2.99	.4986	3.45	.4997		

Table IV   AMOUNT OF $1 AT COMPOUND INTEREST $\left(1 + \dfrac{i}{k}\right)^{kn}$

Periods	$\frac{1}{2}\%$	$\frac{3}{4}\%$	1%	$1\frac{1}{2}\%$	2%
1	1.005 000	1.007 500	1.010 000	1.015 000	1.020 000
2	1.010 025	1.015 056	1.020 100	1.030 225	1.040 400
3	1.015 075	1.022 669	1.030 301	1.045 678	1.061 208
4	1.020 151	1.030 339	1.040 604	1.061 364	1.082 432
5	1.025 251	1.038 067	1.051 010	1.077 284	1.104 081
6	1.030 378	1.045 852	1.061 520	1.093 443	1.126 162
7	1.035 529	1.053 696	1.072 135	1.109 845	1.148 686
8	1.040 707	1.061 599	1.082 857	1.126 493	1.171 659
9	1.045 911	1.069 561	1.093 685	1.143 390	1.195 093
10	1.051 140	1.077 583	1.104 622	1.160 541	1.218 994
11	1.056 396	1.085 664	1.115 668	1.177 949	1.243 374
12	1.061 678	1.093 807	1.126 825	1.195 618	1.268 242
13	1.066 986	1.102 010	1.138 093	1.213 552	1.293 607
14	1.072 321	1.110 276	1.149 474	1.231 756	1.319 479
15	1.077 683	1.118 603	1.160 969	1.250 232	1.345 868
16	1.083 071	1.126 992	1.172 579	1.268 986	1.372 786
17	1.088 487	1.135 445	1.184 304	1.288 020	1.400 241
18	1.093 929	1.143 960	1.196 147	1.307 341	1.428 246
19	1.099 399	1.152 540	1.208 109	1.326 951	1.456 811
20	1.104 896	1.161 184	1.220 190	1.346 855	1.485 947
21	1.110 420	1.169 893	1.232 392	1.367 058	1.515 666
22	1.115 972	1.178 667	1.244 716	1.387 564	1.545 980
23	1.121 552	1.187 507	1.257 163	1.408 377	1.576 899
24	1.127 160	1.196 414	1.269 735	1.429 503	1.608 437
25	1.132 796	1.205 387	1.282 432	1.450 945	1.640 606
26	1.138 460	1.214 427	1.295 256	1.472 710	1.673 418
27	1.144 152	1.223 535	1.308 209	1.494 800	1.706 886
28	1.149 873	1.232 712	1.321 291	1.517 222	1.741 024
29	1.155 622	1.241 957	1.354 504	1.539 981	1.775 845
30	1.161 400	1.251 272	1.347 849	1.563 080	1.811 362
31	1.167 207	1.260 656	1.361 327	1.586 526	1.847 589
32	1.173 043	1.270 111	1.374 941	1.610 324	1.884 541
33	1.178 908	1.279 637	1.388 690	1.634 479	1.922 231
34	1.184 803	1.289 234	1.402 577	1.658 996	1.960 676
35	1.190 727	1.298 904	1.416 603	1.683 881	1.999 890
36	1.196 681	1.308 645	1.430 769	1.709 140	2.039 887
37	1.202 664	1.318 460	1.445 076	1.734 777	2.080 685
38	1.208 677	1.328 349	1.459 527	1.760 798	2.122 299
39	1.214 721	1.338 311	1.474 123	1.787 210	2.164 745
40	1.220 794	1.348 349	1.488 864	1.814 018	2.208 040

Table IV AMOUNT OF $1 AT COMPOUND INTEREST $\left(1 + \dfrac{i}{k}\right)^{kn}$ (Continued)

Periods	3%	4%	5%	6%	7%
1	1.030 000	1.040 000	1.050 000	1.060 000	1.070 000
2	1.060 900	1.081 600	1.102 500	1.123 600	1.144 900
3	1.092 727	1.124 864	1.157 625	1.191 016	1.225 043
4	1.125 509	1.169 859	1.215 506	1.262 477	1.310 796
5	1.159 274	1.216 653	1.276 282	1.338 226	1.402 552
6	1.194 052	1.265 319	1.340 096	1.418 519	1.500 730
7	1.229 874	1.315 932	1.407 100	1.503 630	1.605 781
8	1.266 770	1.368 569	1.477 455	1.593 848	1.718 186
9	1.304 773	1.423 312	1.551 328	1.689 479	1.838 459
10	1.343 916	1.480 244	1.628 895	1.790 848	1.967 151
11	1.384 234	1.539 454	1.710 339	1.898 299	2.104 852
12	1.425 761	1.601 032	1.795 856	2.012 196	2.252 192
13	1.468 534	1.665 074	1.885 649	2.132 928	2.409 845
14	1.512 590	1.731 676	1.979 932	2.260 904	2.578 534
15	1.557 967	1.800 944	2.078 928	2.396 558	2.759 032
16	1.604 706	1.872 981	2.182 875	2.540 352	2.952 164
17	1.652 848	1.947 901	2.292 018	2.692 773	3.158 815
18	1.702 433	2.025 817	2.406 619	2.854 339	3.379 932
19	1.753 506	2.106 849	2.526 950	3.025 600	3.616 528
20	1.806 111	2.191 123	2.653 298	3.207 135	3.869 684
21	1.860 295	2.278 768	2.785 963	3.399 564	4.140 562
22	1.916 103	2.369 919	2.925 261	3.603 537	4.430 402
23	1.973 587	2.464 716	3.071 524	3.819 750	4.740 530
24	2.032 794	2.563 304	3.225 100	4.048 935	5.072 367
25	2.093 778	2.665 836	3.386 355	4.291 871	5.427 433
26	2.156 591	2.772 470	3.555 673	4.549 383	5.807 353
27	2.221 289	2.883 369	3.733 456	4.822 346	6.213 868
28	2.287 928	2.998 703	3.920 129	5.111 687	6.648 838
29	2.356 566	3.118 651	4.116 136	5.418 388	7.114 257
30	2.427 262	3.243 398	4.321 942	5.743 491	7.612 255
31	2.500 080	3.373 133	4.538 039	6.088 101	8.145 113
32	2.575 083	3.508 059	4.764 941	6.453 387	8.715 271
33	2.652 335	3.648 381	5.003 189	6.840 590	9.325 340
34	2.731 905	3.794 316	5.253 348	7.251 025	9.978 114
35	2.813 862	3.946 089	5.516 015	7.686 087	10.676 582
36	2.898 278	4.103 933	5.791 816	8.147 252	11.423 942
37	2.985 227	4.268 090	6.081 407	8.636 087	12.223 618
38	3.074 783	4.438 813	6.385 477	9.154 252	13.079 272
39	3.167 027	4.616 366	6.704 751	9.703 507	13.994 821
40	3.262 038	4.801 021	7.039 989	10.285 718	14.974 458

Table IV AMOUNT OF \$1 AT COMPOUND INTEREST $\left(1 + \dfrac{i}{k}\right)^{kn}$ (Continued)

Periods	8%	9%	10%	11%	12%
1	1.080 000	1.090 000	1.100 000	1.110 000	1.120 000
2	1.166 400	1.188 100	1.210 000	1.232 100	1.254 400
3	1.259 712	1.295 029	1.331 000	1.367 631	1.404 928
4	1.360 489	1.411 582	1.464 100	1.518 070	1.573 519
5	1.469 328	1.538 624	1.610 510	1.685 058	1.762 342
6	1.586 874	1.677 100	1.771 561	1.870 415	1.973 823
7	1.713 824	1.828 039	1.948 717	2.076 160	2.210 681
8	1.850 930	1.992 563	2.143 589	2.304 538	2.475 963
9	1.999 005	2.171 893	2.357 948	2.558 037	2.773 079
10	2.158 925	2.367 364	2.593 742	2.839 421	3.105 848
11	2.331 639	2.580 426	2.853 117	3.151 757	3.478 550
12	2.518 170	2.812 665	3.138 428	3.498 451	3.895 976
13	2.719 624	3.065 805	3.452 271	3.883 280	4.363 493
14	2.937 194	3.341 727	3.797 498	4.310 441	4.887 112
15	3.172 169	3.642 482	4.177 248	4.784 590	5.473 566
16	3.425 943	3.970 306	4.594 973	5.310 894	6.130 394
17	3.700 018	4.327 633	5.054 470	5.895 093	6.866 041
18	3.996 020	4.717 120	5.559 917	6.543 553	7.689 966
19	4.315 701	5.141 661	6.115 909	7.263 344	8.612 762
20	4.660 957	5.604 411	6.727 500	8.062 312	9.646 293
21	5.033 834	6.108 808	7.400 250	8.949 166	10.803 848
22	5.436 540	6.658 600	8.140 275	9.933 574	12.100 310
23	5.871 464	7.257 874	8.954 303	11.026 267	13.552 347
24	6.341 181	7.911 083	9.849 733	12.239 157	15.178 629
25	6.848 475	8.623 081	10.834 706	13.585 464	17.000 064
26	7.396 353	9.399 158	11.918 177	15.079 865	19.040 072
27	7.988 062	10.245 082	13.109 994	16.738 650	21.324 881
28	8.627 106	11.167 140	14.420 994	18.579 902	23.883 867
29	9.317 275	12.172 182	15.863 093	20.623 691	26.749 931
30	10.062 657	13.267 678	17.449 403	22.892 297	29.959 922
31	10.867 670	14.461 770	19.194 343	25.410 450	33.555 113
32	11.737 083	15.763 329	21.113 777	28.205 599	37.581 726
33	12.676 050	17.182 028	23.225 155	31.308 215	42.091 534
34	13.690 134	18.728 411	25.547 670	34.752 119	47.142 518
35	14.785 344	20.413 968	28.102 437	38.574 852	52.799 620
36	15.968 172	22.251 225	30.912 681	42.818 085	59.135 574
37	17.245 626	24.253 835	34.003 948	47.528 075	66.231 843
38	18.625 276	26.436 680	37.404 344	52.756 163	74.179 664
39	20.115 298	28.815 982	41.144 779	58.559 341	83.081 224
40	21.724 522	31.409 420	45.259 257	65.000 868	93.050 971

8%

Table V   Amount of an Ordinary Annuity of $1 $(s_{\overline{n}|i})$

Periods	1%	2%	3%	4%	5%	6%
1	1.000 000	1.000 000	1.000 000	1.000 000	1.000 000	1.000 000
2	2.010 000	2.020 000	2.030 000	2.040 000	2.050 000	2.060 000
3	3.030 100	3.060 400	3.090 900	3.121 600	3.152 500	3.183 600
4	4.060 401	4.121 608	4.183 627	4.246 464	4.310 125	4.374 616
5	5.101 005	5.204 040	5.309 136	5.416 323	5.525 631	5.637 093
6	6.152 015	6.308 121	6.468 410	6.632 975	6.801 913	6.975 319
7	7.213 535	7.434 284	7.662 462	7.898 294	8.142 008	8.393 838
8	8.285 670	8.582 969	8.892 336	9.214 226	9.549 109	9.897 468
9	9.368 527	9.754 629	10.159 106	10.582 795	11.026 564	11.491 316
10	10.462 212	10.949 721	11.463 879	12.006 107	12.577 893	13.180 795
11	11.566 834	12.168 716	12.807 796	13.486 351	14.206 787	14.971 643
12	12.682 503	13.412 090	14.192 030	15.025 805	15.917 126	16.869 941
13	13.809 328	14.680 332	15.617 790	16.626 838	17.712 983	18.882 138
14	14.947 421	15.973 939	17.086 324	18.291 911	19.598 632	21.015 066
15	16.096 895	17.293 418	18.598 914	20.023 588	21.578 564	23.275 970
16	17.257 864	18.639 286	20.156 881	21.824 531	23.657 492	25.672 529
17	18.430 443	20.012 072	21.761 588	23.697 512	25.840 366	28.212 880
18	19.614 747	21.412 313	23.414 435	26.645 413	28.132 385	30.905 653
19	20.810 895	22.840 559	25.116 869	27.671 229	30.539 004	33.759 992
20	22.019 004	24.297 371	26.870 375	29.778 079	33.065 954	36.785 592
21	23.239 194	25.783 318	28.676 486	31.969 202	35.719 252	39.992 727
22	24.471 586	27.298 985	30.536 780	34.247 970	38.505 214	43.392 291
23	25.716 301	28.844 964	32.452 884	36.617 889	41.430 475	46.995 829
24	26.973 464	30.421 864	34.426 470	39.082 604	44.501 999	50.815 578
25	28.243 199	32.030 301	36.459 264	41.645 908	47.727 099	54.864 513
26	29.525 631	33.670 907	38.553 042	44.311 745	51.113 454	59.156 384
27	30.820 887	35.344 325	40.709 634	47.084 214	54.669 126	63.705 767
28	32.129 096	37.051 212	42.930 923	49.967 583	58.402 583	68.528 113
29	33.450 387	38.792 236	45.218 850	52.966 286	62.322 712	73.639 800
30	34.784 891	40.568 081	47.575 416	56.084 938	66.438 847	79.058 188
31	36.132 740	42.379 443	50.002 678	59.328 335	70.760 790	84.801 679
32	37.494 067	44.227 031	52.502 759	62.701 469	75.298 829	90.889 780
33	38.869 008	46.111 572	55.077 842	66.209 528	80.063 771	97.343 167
34	40.257 698	48.033 804	57.730 177	69.857 909	85.066 959	104.183 757
35	41.660 275	49.994 480	60.462 082	73.652 225	90.320 307	111.434 783
36	43.076 878	51.994 369	63.275 945	77.598 314	95.836 323	119.120 870
37	44.507 646	54.034 257	66.174 223	81.702 247	101.628 139	127.268 122
38	45.952 723	56.114 942	69.159 450	85.970 336	107.709 546	135.904 209
39	47.412 250	58.237 241	72.234 233	90.409 150	114.095 023	145.058 462
40	48.886 373	60.401 986	75.401 260	95.025 516	120.799 774	154.761 970

Table V   Amount of an Ordinary Annuity of $1 $(s_{\overline{n}|i})$ (Continued)

Periods	7%	8%	9%	10%	11%	12%
1	1.000 000	1.000 000	1.000 000	1.000 000	1.000 000	1.000 000
2	2.070 000	2.080 000	2.090 000	2.100 000	2.110 000	2.120 000
3	3.214 900	3.246 400	3.278 100	3.310 000	3.342 100	3.374 400
4	4.439 943	4.506 112	4.573 129	4.641 000	4.709 731	4.779 328
5	5.750 739	5.866 601	5.984 711	6.105 100	6.227 801	6.352 847
6	7.153 291	7.335 929	7.523 335	7.715 610	7.912 860	8.115 189
7	8.654 021	8.922 803	9.200 435	9.487 171	9.783 274	10.089 012
8	10.259 803	10.636 628	11.028 474	11.435 888	11.859 434	12.299 693
9	11.977 989	12.487 558	13.021 036	13.579 477	14.136 972	14.775 656
10	13.816 448	14.486 563	15.192 930	15.937 425	16.722 009	17.548 735
11	15.783 599	16.645 488	17.560 293	18.531 167	19.561 430	20.654 583
12	17.888 451	18.977 127	20.140 720	21.384 284	22.713 187	24.133 133
13	20.140 643	21.495 297	22.953 385	24.522 712	26.211 638	28.029 109
14	22.550 488	24.214 920	26.019 189	27.974 984	30.094 918	32.392 602
15	25.129 022	27.152 114	29.360 916	31.772 482	34.405 359	37.279 715
16	27.888 054	30.324 283	33.003 399	35.949 730	39.189 949	42.753 281
17	30.840 218	33.750 226	36.973 705	40.544 703	44.500 843	48.883 674
18	33.999 033	37.450 244	41.301 338	45.599 174	50.395 936	55.749 715
19	37.378 965	41.446 263	46.018 458	51.159 091	56.939 489	63.439 681
20	40.995 493	45.761 965	51.160 120	57.275 000	64.202 833	72.052 443
21	44.865 177	50.422 922	56.764 530	64.002 501	72.265 145	81.698 736
22	49.005 740	55.456 756	62.873 338	71.402 750	81.214 310	92.502 584
23	53.436 142	60.893 296	69.531 939	79.543 025	91.147 885	104.602 894
24	58.176 672	66.764 760	76.789 813	88.497 328	102.174 152	118.155 242
25	63.249 039	73.105 940	84.700 896	98.347 061	114.413 309	133.333 871
26	68.676 471	79.954 416	93.323 977	109.181 767	127.998 773	150.333 935
27	74.483 824	87.350 769	102.723 135	121.099 944	143.078 638	169.374 007
28	80.697 692	95.338 831	112.968 217	134.209 938	159.817 288	190.698 888
29	87.346 531	103.965 937	124.135 357	148.630 932	178.397 190	214.582 755
30	94.460 788	113.283 212	136.307 539	164.494 026	199.020 881	241.332 686
31	102.073 043	123.345 869	149.575 217	181.943 428	221.913 178	271.292 608
32	110.218 156	134.213 539	164.036 987	201.137 771	247.323 628	304.847 721
33	118.933 427	145.950 622	179.800 316	222.251 548	275.529 227	342.429 447
34	128.258 767	158.626 671	196.982 344	245.476 703	306.837 442	384.520 981
35	138.236 881	172.316 805	215.710 755	271.024 374	341.589 561	431.663 499
36	148.913 462	187.102 150	236.124 723	299.126 811	380.164 413	484.463 119
37	160.337 405	203.070 322	258.375 948	330.039 493	422.982 498	543.598 693
38	172.561 023	220.315 948	282.629 783	364.043 442	470.510 573	609.830 536
39	185.640 295	238.941 223	309.066 464	401.447 787	523.266 737	684.010 201
40	199.635 116	259.056 521	337.882 446	442.592 566	581.826 078	767.091 425

Table VI   Present Value of an Annuity of \$1 $(a_{\overline{n}|i})$

Periods	1%	2%	3%	4%	5%	6%
1	0.990 099	0.980 392	0.970 874	0.961 538	0.952 381	0.943 396
2	1.970 395	1.941 561	1.913 470	1.886 095	1.859 410	1.833 393
3	2.940 985	2.883 883	2.828 611	2.775 091	2.723 248	2.673 012
4	3.901 965	3.807 729	3.717 098	3.629 895	3.545 951	3.465 106
5	4.853 431	4.713 460	4.579 707	4.451 822	4.329 477	4.212 364
6	5.795 476	5.601 431	5.417 191	5.242 137	5.075 692	4.917 324
7	6.728 194	6.471 991	6.230 283	6.002 055	5.786 373	5.582 381
8	7.651 678	7.325 482	7.019 692	6.732 745	6.463 213	6.209 794
9	8.566 017	8.162 237	7.786 109	7.435 332	7.107 822	6.801 692
10	9.471 304	8.982 585	8.530 203	8.110 896	7.721 735	7.360 087
11	10.367 628	9.786 848	9.252 624	8.760 477	8.306 414	7.886 875
12	11.255 077	10.575 342	9.954 004	9.385 074	8.863 252	8.383 844
13	12.133 740	11.348 374	10.634 955	9.985 648	9.393 573	8.852 683
14	13.003 703	12.106 249	11.296 073	10.563 123	9.898 641	9.294 984
15	13.865 052	12.849 264	11.937 935	11.118 387	10.379 658	9.712 249
16	14.717 874	13.577 710	12.561 102	11.652 296	10.837 770	10.105 895
17	15.562 251	14.291 872	13.166 118	12.165 669	11.274 066	10.477 260
18	16.398 268	14.992 032	13.753 513	12.659 297	11.689 587	10.827 604
19	17.226 008	15.678 462	14.323 799	13.133 939	12.085 321	11.158 117
20	18.045 553	16.351 434	14.877 475	13.590 326	12.462 210	11.469 921
21	18.856 983	17.011 210	15.415 024	14.029 160	12.821 153	11.764 077
22	18.660 379	17.658 049	15.936 917	14.451 115	13.163 003	12.041 582
23	20.455 821	18.292 205	16.443 608	14.856 842	13.488 574	12.303 379
24	21.243 387	18.913 926	16.935 542	15.246 963	13.798 642	12.550 358
25	22.023 155	19.523 457	17.413 148	15.622 080	14.093 945	12.783 356
26	22.795 203	20.121 036	17.876 842	15.982 769	14.375 185	13.003 166
27	23.559 607	20.706 898	18.327 032	16.329 586	14.643 034	13.210 534
28	24.316 443	21.281 273	18.764 108	16.663 063	14.898 127	13.406 164
29	25.065 785	21.844 385	19.188 455	16.983 715	15.141 074	13.590 721
30	25.807 708	22.396 456	19.600 441	17.292 033	15.372 451	13.764 831
31	26.542 285	22.937 702	20.000 429	17.588 494	15.592 810	13.929 086
32	27.269 589	23.468 335	20.388 766	17.873 552	15.802 677	14.084 043
33	27.989 692	23.988 564	20.765 792	18.147 646	16.002 549	14.230 230
34	28.702 666	24.498 592	21.131 837	18.411 198	16.192 904	14.368 141
35	28.408 580	24.998 620	21.487 220	18.664 613	16.374 194	14.498 246
36	30.107 505	25.488 843	21.832 253	18.908 282	16.546 852	14.620 987
37	30.799 510	25.969 454	22.167 235	19.142 579	16.711 287	14.736 780
38	31.484 663	26.440 641	22.492 462	19.367 864	16.867 893	14.846 019
39	32.163 033	26.902 589	22.808 215	19.584 485	17.017 041	14.949 075
40	32.834 686	27.355 480	23.114 772	19.792 774	17.159 086	15.046 297

Table VI   Present Value of an Annuity of $1 $(a_{\overline{n}|i})$ (Continued)

Periods	7%	8%	9%	10%	11%	12%
1	0.934 579	0.925 926	0.917 431	0.909 091	0.900 901	0.892 857
2	1.808 018	1.783 265	1.759 111	1.735 537	1.712 523	1.690 051
3	2.624 316	2.577 097	2.531 295	2.486 852	2.443 715	2.401 831
4	3.387 211	3.312 127	3.239 720	3.169 865	3.102 446	3.037 349
5	4.100 197	3.992 710	3.889 651	3.790 787	3.695 897	3.604 776
6	4.766 540	4.622 880	4.485 919	4.355 261	4.230 538	4.111 407
7	5.389 289	5.206 370	5.032 953	4.868 419	4.712 196	4.563 757
8	5.971 299	5.746 639	5.534 819	5.334 926	5.146 123	4.967 640
9	6.515 232	6.246 888	5.995 247	5.759 024	5.537 048	5.328 250
10	7.023 582	6.710 081	6.417 658	6.144 567	5.889 232	5.650 223
11	7.498 674	7.138 964	6.805 191	6.495 061	6.206 515	5.937 699
12	7.942 686	7.536 078	7.160 725	6.813 692	6.492 356	6.194 374
13	8.357 651	7.903 776	7.486 904	7.103 356	6.749 870	6.423 548
14	8.745 468	8.244 237	7.786 150	7.366 687	6.981 865	6.628 168
15	9.107 914	8.559 479	8.060 688	7.606 080	7.190 870	6.810 864
16	9.446 649	8.851 369	8.312 558	7.823 709	7.379 162	6.973 986
17	9.763 223	9.121 638	8.543 631	8.021 553	7.548 794	7.119 630
18	10.059 087	9.371 887	8.755 625	8.201 412	7.701 617	7.249 670
19	10.335 595	9.603 599	8.950 115	8.364 920	7.839 294	7.365 777
20	10.594 014	9.818 147	9.128 546	8.513 564	7.963 328	7.469 444
21	10.835 527	10.016 803	9.292 244	8.648 694	8.075 070	7.562 003
22	11.061 241	10.200 744	9.442 425	8.771 540	8.175 739	7.644 646
23	11.272 187	10.371 059	9.580 207	8.883 218	8.266 432	7.718 434
24	11.469 334	10.528 758	9.706 612	8.984 744	8.348 137	7.784 316
25	11.653 583	10.674 776	9.822 580	9.077 040	8.421 745	7.843 139
26	11.825 779	10.809 978	9.928 972	9.160 945	8.488 058	7.895 660
27	11.986 709	10.935 165	10.026 580	9.237 223	8.547 800	7.942 554
28	12.137 111	11.051 079	10.116 128	9.306 567	8.601 622	7.984 423
29	12.277 674	11.158 406	10.198 283	9.369 606	8.650 110	8.021 806
30	12.409 041	11.257 783	10.273 654	9.426 914	8.693 793	8.055 184
31	12.531 814	11.349 799	10.342 802	9.479 013	8.733 146	8.084 986
32	12.646 555	11.434 999	10.406 240	9.526 376	8.768 600	8.111 594
33	12.753 790	11.513 888	10.464 441	9.569 432	8.800 541	8.135 352
34	12.854 009	11.586 934	10.517 835	9.608 575	8.829 316	8.156 564
35	12.947 672	11.654 568	10.566 821	9.644 159	8.855 240	8.175 504
36	13.035 208	11.717 193	10.611 763	9.676 508	8.878 594	8.192 414
37	13.117 017	11.775 179	10.652 993	9.705 917	8.899 635	8.207 513
38	13.193 473	11.828 869	10.690 820	9.732 651	8.918 590	8.220 993
39	13.264 928	11.878 582	10.725 523	9.756 956	8.935 666	8.233 030
40	13.331 709	11.924 613	10.757 360	9.779 051	8.951 051	8.243 777

Table VII   Periodic Payment to Amortize \$1 at the End of n Periods $\left(\dfrac{1}{a_{\overline{n}|i}}\right)$

Periods	1%	2%	3%	4%	5%	6%
1	1.010 000	1.020 000	1.030 000	1.040 000	1.050 000	1.060 000
2	0.507 512	0.515 049	0.522 611	0.530 196	0.537 805	0.545 437
3	0.340 022	0.346 755	0.353 530	0.360 349	0.367 209	0.374 110
4	0.256 281	0.262 624	0.269 027	0.275 490	0.282 012	0.288 591
5	0.206 040	0.212 158	0.218 355	0.224 627	0.230 975	0.237 396
6	0.172 548	0.178 526	0.184 598	0.190 762	0.197 017	0.203 363
7	0.148 628	0.154 512	0.160 506	0.166 610	0.172 820	0.179 135
8	0.130 690	0.136 510	0.142 456	0.148 528	0.154 722	0.161 036
9	0.116 740	0.122 515	0.128 434	0.134 493	0.140 690	0.147 022
10	0.105 582	0.111 327	0.117 231	0.123 291	0.129 505	0.135 868
11	0.096 454	0.102 178	0.108 077	0.114 149	0.120 389	0.126 793
12	0.088 849	0.094 560	0.100 462	0.106 552	0.112 825	0.119 277
13	0.082 415	0.088 118	0.094 030	0.100 144	0.106 456	0.112 960
14	0.076 901	0.082 602	0.088 526	0.094 669	0.101 024	0.107 585
15	0.072 124	0.077 825	0.083 767	0.089 941	0.096 342	0.102 963
16	0.067 945	0.073 650	0.079 611	0.085 820	0.092 270	0.098 952
17	0.064 258	0.069 970	0.075 953	0.082 199	0.088 699	0.095 445
18	0.060 982	0.066 702	0.072 709	0.078 993	0.085 546	0.092 357
19	0.058 052	0.063 782	0.069 814	0.076 139	0.082 745	0.089 621
20	0.055 415	0.061 157	0.067 216	0.073 582	0.080 243	0.087 185
21	0.053 031	0.058 785	0.064 872	0.071 280	0.077 996	0.085 005
22	0.050 864	0.056 631	0.062 747	0.069 199	0.075 971	0.083 046
23	0.048 886	0.054 668	0.060 814	0.067 309	0.074 137	0.081 278
24	0.047 073	0.052 871	0.059 047	0.065 587	0.072 471	0.079 679
25	0.045 407	0.051 220	0.057 428	0.064 012	0.070 952	0.078 227
26	0.043 869	0.049 699	0.055 938	0.062 567	0.069 564	0.076 904
27	0.042 446	0.048 293	0.054 564	0.061 239	0.068 292	0.075 697
28	0.041 124	0.046 990	0.053 293	0.060 013	0.067 123	0.074 593
29	0.039 895	0.045 778	0.052 115	0.058 880	0.066 046	0.073 580
30	0.038 748	0.044 650	0.051 019	0.057 830	0.065 051	0.072 649
31	0.037 676	0.043 596	0.049 999	0.056 855	0.064 132	0.071 792
32	0.036 671	0.042 611	0.049 047	0.055 949	0.063 280	0.071 002
33	0.035 727	0.041 687	0.048 156	0.055 104	0.062 490	0.070 273
34	0.034 840	0.040 819	0.047 322	0.054 315	0.061 755	0.069 598
35	0.034 004	0.040 002	0.046 539	0.053 577	0.061 072	0.068 974
36	0.033 214	0.039 233	0.045 804	0.052 887	0.060 434	0.068 395
37	0.032 468	0.038 507	0.045 112	0.052 240	0.059 840	0.067 857
38	0.031 761	0.037 821	0.044 459	0.051 632	0.059 284	0.067 358
39	0.031 092	0.037 171	0.043 844	0.051 061	0.058 765	0.066 894
40	0.030 456	0.036 556	0.043 262	0.050 523	0.058 278	0.066 462

Table VII Periodic Payment to Amortize $1 at the End of *n* Periods $\left(\dfrac{1}{a_{\overline{n}|i}}\right)$ (Continued)

Periods	7%	8%	9%	10%	11%	12%
1	1.070 000	1.080 000	1.090 000	1.100 000	1.110 000	1.120 000
2	0.553 092	0.560 769	0.568 469	0.576 190	0.583 934	0.591 698
3	0.381 052	0.388 034	0.395 055	0.402 115	0.409 213	0.416 349
4	0.295 228	0.301 921	0.308 669	0.315 471	0.322 326	0.329 234
5	0.243 891	0.250 456	0.257 092	0.263 797	0.270 570	0.277 410
6	0.209 796	0.216 315	0.222 920	0.229 607	0.236 377	0.243 226
7	0.185 553	0.192 072	0.198 691	0.205 405	0.212 215	0.219 118
8	0.167 468	0.174 015	0.180 674	0.187 444	0.194 321	0.201 303
9	0.153 486	0.160 080	0.166 799	0.173 641	0.180 602	0.187 679
10	0.142 378	0.149 029	0.155 820	0.162 745	0.169 801	0.176 984
11	0.133 357	0.140 076	0.146 947	0.153 963	0.161 121	0.168 415
12	0.125 902	0.132 695	0.139 651	0.146 763	0.154 027	0.161 437
13	0.119 651	0.126 522	0.133 567	0.140 779	0.148 151	0.155 677
14	0.114 345	0.121 297	0.128 433	0.135 746	0.143 228	0.150 871
15	0.109 795	0.116 830	0.124 059	0.131 474	0.139 065	0.146 824
16	0.105 858	0.112 977	0.120 300	0.127 817	0.135 517	0.143 390
17	0.102 425	0.109 629	0.117 046	0.124 664	0.132 471	0.140 457
18	0.099 413	0.106 702	0.114 212	0.121 930	0.129 843	0.137 937
19	0.096 753	0.104 128	0.111 730	0.119 547	0.127 563	0.135 763
20	0.094 393	0.101 852	0.109 546	0.117 460	0.125 576	0.133 879
21	0.092 289	0.099 832	0.107 617	0.115 624	0.123 838	0.132 240
22	0.090 406	0.098 032	0.105 905	0.114 005	0.122 313	0.130 811
23	0.088 714	0.096 422	0.104 382	0.112 572	0.120 971	0.129 560
24	0.087 189	0.094 978	0.103 023	0.111 300	0.119 787	0.128 463
25	0.085 811	0.093 679	0.101 806	0.110 168	0.118 740	0.127 500
26	0.084 561	0.092 507	0.100 715	0.109 159	0.117 813	0.126 652
27	0.083 426	0.091 448	0.099 735	0.108 258	0.116 989	0.125 904
28	0.082 392	0.090 489	0.098 852	0.107 451	0.116 257	0.125 244
29	0.081 449	0.089 619	0.098 056	0.106 728	0.115 605	0.124 660
30	0.080 586	0.088 827	0.097 336	0.106 079	0.115 025	0.124 144
31	0.079 797	0.088 107	0.096 686	0.105 496	0.114 506	0.123 686
32	0.079 073	0.087 451	0.096 096	0.104 972	0.114 043	0.123 280
33	0.078 408	0.086 852	0.095 562	0.104 499	0.113 629	0.122 920
34	0.077 797	0.086 304	0.095 077	0.104 074	0.113 259	0.122 601
35	0.077 234	0.085 803	0.094 636	0.103 690	0.112 927	0.122 317
36	0.076 715	0.085 345	0.094 235	0.103 343	0.112 630	0.122 064
37	0.076 237	0.084 924	0.093 870	0.103 030	0.112 364	0.121 840
38	0.075 795	0.084 539	0.093 538	0.102 747	0.112 125	0.121 640
39	0.075 387	0.084 185	0.093 236	0.102 491	0.111 911	0.121 462
40	0.075 009	0.083 860	0.092 960	0.102 259	0.111 719	0.121 304

Table VIII   Periodic Payment for a Sinking Fund of $1 at the End of n Periods $\left(\dfrac{1}{s_{\overline{n}|i}}\right)$

Periods	1%	2%	3%	4%	5%	6%
1	1.000 000	1.000 000	1.000 000	1.000 000	1.000 000	1.000 000
2	0.497 512	0.495 049	0.492 611	0.490 196	0.487 805	0.485 437
3	0.330 022	0.326 755	0.323 530	0.320 349	0.317 209	0.314 110
4	0.246 281	0.242 624	0.239 027	0.235 490	0.232 012	0.228 591
5	0.196 040	0.192 158	0.188 355	0.184 627	0.180 975	0.177 396
6	0.162 548	0.158 526	0.154 598	0.150 762	0.147 017	0.143 363
7	0.138 628	0.134 512	0.130 506	0.126 610	0.122 820	0.119 135
8	0.120 690	0.116 510	0.112 456	0.108 528	0.104 722	0.101 036
9	0.106 740	0.102 515	0.098 434	0.094 493	0.090 690	0.087 022
10	0.095 582	0.091 327	0.087 231	0.083 291	0.079 505	0.075 868
11	0.086 454	0.082 178	0.078 077	0.074 149	0.070 389	0.066 793
12	0.078 849	0.074 560	0.070 462	0.066 552	0.062 825	0.059 277
13	0.072 415	0.068 118	0.064 030	0.060 144	0.056 456	0.052 960
14	0.066 901	0.062 602	0.058 526	0.054 669	0.051 024	0.047 585
15	0.062 124	0.057 825	0.053 767	0.049 941	0.046 342	0.042 963
16	0.057 945	0.053 650	0.049 611	0.045 820	0.042 270	0.038 952
17	0.054 258	0.049 970	0.045 953	0.042 199	0.038 699	0.035 445
18	0.050 982	0.046 702	0.042 709	0.038 993	0.035 546	0.032 357
19	0.048 052	0.043 782	0.039 814	0.036 139	0.032 745	0.029 621
20	0.045 415	0.041 157	0.037 216	0.033 582	0.030 243	0.027 185
21	0.043 031	0.038 785	0.034 872	0.031 280	0.027 996	0.025 005
22	0.040 864	0.036 631	0.032 747	0.029 199	0.025 971	0.023 046
23	0.038 886	0.034 668	0.030 814	0.027 309	0.024 137	0.021 278
24	0.037 073	0.032 871	0.029 047	0.025 587	0.022 471	0.019 679
25	0.035 407	0.031 220	0.027 428	0.024 012	0.020 952	0.018 227
26	0.033 869	0.029 699	0.025 938	0.022 567	0.019 564	0.016 904
27	0.032 446	0.028 293	0.024 564	0.021 239	0.018 292	0.015 697
28	0.031 124	0.026 990	0.023 293	0.020 013	0.017 123	0.014 593
29	0.029 895	0.025 778	0.022 115	0.018 880	0.016 046	0.013 580
30	0.028 748	0.024 650	0.021 019	0.017 830	0.015 051	0.012 649
31	0.027 676	0.023 596	0.019 999	0.016 855	0.014 132	0.011 792
32	0.026 671	0.022 611	0.019 047	0.015 949	0.013 280	0.011 002
33	0.025 727	0.021 687	0.018 156	0.015 104	0.012 490	0.010 273
34	0.024 840	0.020 819	0.017 322	0.014 315	0.011 755	0.009 598
35	0.024 004	0.020 002	0.016 539	0.013 577	0.011 072	0.008 974
36	0.023 214	0.019 233	0.015 804	0.012 887	0.010 434	0.008 395
37	0.022 468	0.018 507	0.015 112	0.012 240	0.009 840	0.007 857
38	0.021 761	0.017 821	0.014 459	0.011 632	0.009 284	0.007 358
39	0.021 092	0.017 171	0.013 844	0.011 061	0.008 764	0.006 894
40	0.020 456	0.016 556	0.013 262	0.010 523	0.008 278	0.006 462

Table VIII Periodic Payment for a Sinking Fund of \$1 at the End of n Periods $\left(\dfrac{1}{s_{\overline{n}|\,i}}\right)$
(Continued)

Periods	7%	8%	9%	10%	11%	12%
1	1.000 000	1.000 000	1.000 000	1.000 000	1.000 000	1.000 000
2	0.483 092	0.480 769	0.478 469	0.476 190	0.473 934	0.471 698
3	0.311 052	0.308 034	0.305 055	0.302 115	0.299 213	0.296 349
4	0.225 228	0.221 921	0.218 669	0.215 471	0.212 326	0.209 234
5	0.173 891	0.170 456	0.167 092	0.163 797	0.160 570	0.157 410
6	0.139 796	0.136 315	0.132 920	0.129 607	0.126 377	0.123 226
7	0.115 553	0.112 072	0.108 691	0.105 405	0.102 215	0.099 118
8	0.097 468	0.094 015	0.090 674	0.087 444	0.084 321	0.081 303
9	0.083 486	0.080 080	0.076 799	0.073 641	0.070 602	0.067 679
10	0.072 378	0.069 029	0.065 820	0.062 745	0.059 801	0.056 984
11	0.063 357	0.060 076	0.056 947	0.053 963	0.051 121	0.048 415
12	0.055 902	0.052 695	0.049 651	0.046 763	0.044 027	0.041 437
13	0.049 651	0.046 522	0.043 567	0.040 779	0.038 151	0.035 677
14	0.044 345	0.041 297	0.038 433	0.035 746	0.033 228	0.030 871
15	0.039 795	0.036 830	0.034 059	0.031 474	0.029 065	0.026 824
16	0.035 858	0.032 977	0.030 300	0.027 817	0.025 517	0.023 390
17	0.032 425	0.029 629	0.027 046	0.024 664	0.022 471	0.020 457
18	0.029 413	0.026 702	0.024 212	0.021 930	0.019 843	0.017 937
19	0.026 753	0.024 128	0.021 730	0.019 547	0.017 563	0.015 763
20	0.024 393	0.021 852	0.019 546	0.017 460	0.015 576	0.013 879
21	0.022 289	0.019 832	0.017 617	0.015 624	0.013 838	0.012 240
22	0.020 406	0.018 032	0.015 905	0.014 005	0.012 313	0.010 811
23	0.018 714	0.016 422	0.014 382	0.012 572	0.010 971	0.009 560
24	0.017 189	0.014 978	0.013 023	0.011 300	0.009 787	0.008 463
25	0.015 811	0.013 679	0.011 806	0.010 168	0.008 740	0.007 500
26	0.014 561	0.012 507	0.010 715	0.009 159	0.007 813	0.006 652
27	0.013 426	0.011 448	0.009 735	0.008 258	0.006 989	0.005 904
28	0.012 392	0.010 489	0.008 852	0.007 451	0.006 257	0.005 244
29	0.011 449	0.009 619	0.008 056	0.006 728	0.005 605	0.004 660
30	0.010 586	0.008 827	0.007 336	0.006 079	0.005 025	0.004 144
31	0.009 797	0.008 107	0.006 686	0.005 496	0.004 506	0.003 686
32	0.009 073	0.007 451	0.006 096	0.004 972	0.004 043	0.003 280
33	0.008 408	0.006 852	0.005 562	0.004 499	0.003 629	0.002 920
34	0.007 797	0.006 304	0.005 077	0.004 074	0.003 259	0.002 601
35	0.007 234	0.005 803	0.004 636	0.003 690	0.002 927	0.002 317
36	0.006 715	0.005 345	0.004 235	0.003 343	0.002 630	0.002 064
37	0.006 237	0.004 924	0.003 870	0.003 030	0.002 364	0.001 840
38	0.005 795	0.004 539	0.003 538	0.002 747	0.002 125	0.001 640
39	0.005 387	0.004 185	0.003 236	0.002 491	0.001 911	0.001 462
40	0.005 009	0.003 860	0.002 960	0.002 259	0.001 719	0.001 304

Table IX 18-Year Property Deduction—Accelerated Method
(Use column for the first month in the year the property is used for business purposes.)

Year	Jan	Feb	Mar	Apl	May	Jun	Jly	Aug	Sep	Oct	Nov	Dec
1	9	9	8	7	6	5	4	4	3	2	1	0.4
2	9	9	9	9	9	9	9	9	9	10	10	10.0
3	8	8	8	8	8	8	8	8	9	9	9	9.0
4	7	7	7	7	7	8	8	8	8	8	8	8.0
5	7	7	7	7	7	7	7	7	7	7	7	7.0
6	6	6	6	6	6	6	6	6	6	6	6	6.0
7	5	5	5	5	6	6	6	6	6	6	6	6.0
8	5	5	5	5	5	5	5	5	5	5	5	5.0
9	5	5	5	5	5	5	5	5	5	5	5	5.0
10	5	5	5	5	5	5	5	5	5	5	5	5.0
11	5	5.	5	5	5	5	5	5	5	5	5	5.0
12	5	5	5	5	5	5	5	5	5	5	5	5.0
13	4	4	4	4	4	4	5	4	4	4	5	5.0
14	4	4	4	4	4	4	4	4	4	4	4	4.0
15	4	4	4	4	4	4	4	4	4	4	4	4.0
16	4	4	4	4	4	4	4	4	4	4	4	4.0
17	4	4	4	4	4	4	4	4	4	4	4	4.0
18	4	3	4	4	4	4	4	4	4	4	4	4.0
19		1	1	1	2	2	2	3	3	3	3	3.6

Table X 19-Year Property Deduction—Accelerated Method
(Use column for the first month in the year the property is used for business purposes.)

Year	Jan	Feb	Mar	Apl	May	Jun	Jly	Aug	Sep	Oct	Nov	Dec
1	8.8	8.1	7.3	6.5	5.8	5.0	4.2	3.5	2.7	1.9	1.1	0.4
2	8.4	8.5	8.5	8.6	8.7	8.8	8.8	8.9	9.0	9.0	9.1	9.2
3	7.6	7.7	7.7	7.8	7.9	7.9	8.0	8.1	8.1	8.2	8.3	8.3
4	6.9	7.0	7.0	7.1	7.1	7.2	7.3	7.3	7.4	7.4	7.5	7.6
5	6.3	6.3	6.4	6.4	6.5	6.5	6.6	6.6	6.7	6.8	6.8	6.9
6	5.7	5.7	5.8	5.9	5.9	5.9	6.0	6.0	6.1	6.1	6.2	6.2
7	5.2	5.2	5.3	5.3	5.3	5.4	5.4	5.5	5.5	5.6	5.6	5.6
8	4.7	4.7	4.8	4.8	4.8	4.9	4.9	5.0	5.0	5.1	5.1	5.1
9	4.2	4.3	4.3	4.4	4.4	4.5	4.5	4.5	4.5	4.6	4.6	4.7
10	4.2	4.2	4.2	4.2	4.2	4.2	4.2	4.2	4.2	4.2	4.2	4.2
11	4.2	4.2	4.2	4.2	4.2	4.2	4.2	4.2	4.2	4.2	4.2	4.2
12	4.2	4.2	4.2	4.2	4.2	4.2	4.2	4.2	4.2	4.2	4.2	4.2
13	4.2	4.2	4.2	4.2	4.2	4.2	4.2	4.2	4.2	4.2	4.2	4.2
14	4.2	4.2	4.2	4.2	4.2	4.2	4.2	4.2	4.2	4.2	4.2	4.2
15	4.2	4.2	4.2	4.2	4.2	4.2	4.2	4.2	4.2	4.2	4.2	4.2
16	4.2	4.2	4.2	4.2	4.2	4.2	4.2	4.2	4.2	4.2	4.2	4.2
17	4.2	4.2	4.2	4.2	4.2	4.2	4.2	4.2	4.2	4.2	4.2	4.2
18	4.2	4.2	4.2	4.2	4.2	4.2	4.2	4.2	4.2	4.2	4.2	4.2
19	4.2	4.2	4.2	4.2	4.2	4.2	4.2	4.2	4.2	4.2	4.2	4.2
20	0.2	0.5	0.9	1.2	1.6	1.9	2.3	2.6	3.0	3.3	3.7	4.0

TABLE XI   Annual Depreciation (Percent of Original Depreciable Basis)

Year	3-Year Class	5-Year Class	7-Year Class	10-Year Class	15-Year Class	20-Year Class
	(200% declining balance)			(150% declining balance)		
1	33.00	20.00	14.28	10.00	5.00	3.75
2	45.00	32.00	24.49	18.00	9.50	7.22
3	15.00*	19.20	17.49	14.40	8.55	6.68
4	7.00	11.52	12.49	11.52	7.69	6.18
5		11.52*	8.93*	9.22	6.93	5.71
6		5.76	8.93	7.37	6.23	5.28
7			8.93	6.55*	5.90*	4.89
8			4.46	6.55	5.90	4.52
9				6.55	5.90	4.46*
10				6.55	5.90	4.46
11				3.29	5.90	4.46
12					5.90	4.46
13					5.90	4.46
14					5.90	4.46
15					5.90	4.46
16					3.00	4.46
17						4.46
18						4.46
19						4.46
20						4.46
21						2.25

*Year of switch to straight-line to maximize depreciation deduction.

Source: Ignacio Bello, *Contemporary Business Mathematics*
         (Lexington: D.C. Heath, 1988) p. 344.

Answers

Following are the answers to all Chapter Review Exercises and to odd-numbered Section Exercises.

EXERCISE 0.1

1. $\in$ 3. $\in$ 5. $\notin$ 7. $\{1, 2, 3, 4, 5, 6, 7\}$ 9. $\{\ \}$ or $\varnothing$ 11. $\{x : x$ is a natural number greater than 2 and less than 8$\}$ 13. yes   15. no   17. $D \subseteq C$ 19. $D \subseteq A$ 21. $A \subseteq B$ or $B \subseteq A$
23. yes   25. no   27. A and B, B and D, C and D 29. $A \cap B = \{4, 6\}$ 31. $A \cap B = \varnothing$
33. $A \cup B = \{1, 2, 3, 4, 5\}$ 35. $A \cup B = \{1, 2, 3, 4\} = B$ 37. $A' = \{4, 6, 9, 10\}$
39. $(A \cup B)' = \{6, 9\}$ 41. $A \cap B' = \{1, 2, 5, 7\}$ 43. $A' \cup B' = \{1, 2, 4, 5, 6, 7, 9, 10\}$
45. $A - B = \{1, 7\}$ 47. $A - B = \varnothing$ or $\{\ \}$ 49. (a) {Robbins, Swartz, Gonzalas, Barth, McRoberts} all people running for judge   (b) {Robbins} running on both tickets

51. (a) 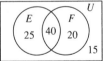   (b) 40   (c) 85   (d) 25

53. 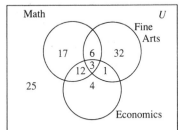   (a) 25   (b) 43   (c) 53

EXERCISE 0.2

1. irrational   3. rational, integer, natural   5. meaningless   7. rational   9. commutative property of addition   11. associative property of addition   13. associative property of multiplication
15. distributive property   17. [number line from -7 to 11]   19. $<$

21. $<$ 23. $<$ 25. 6   27. 5   29. -13 31. -16 33. $+13$ 35. -17 37. $+60$
39. -22 41. $<$ 43. $>$ 45. $>$ 47. -6 49. -9 51. 4   53. $10/3$ 55. $-4/3$
57. 10.846764   59. -0.000038585 61. 9122.387471   63. 20.59077463   65. -0.00250793

EXERCISE 0.3

1. -64 3. -16 5. $1/9$ 7. $-9/4$ 9. 6^8 11. $1/10$ 13. 3^9 15. $(3/2)^2 = 9/4$
17. $1/x^6$ 19. x/y^2 21. x^7 23. $x^{-2} = 1/x^2$ 25. $2^{-7} = 1/2^7$ 27. x^4 29. y^{12}
31. x^{12} 33. x^2y^2 35. $16/x^4$ 37. $x^8/(16y^4)$ 39. $-16a^2/b^2$ 41. $2/(xy^2)$ 43. $1/x^9y^6$
45. $(a^{18}c^{12})/b^6$ 47. x^{-1} 49. $8x^3$ 51. $\frac{1}{4}x^{-2}$ 53. $-\frac{1}{8}x^3$ 55. 2.0736 57. -7776
59. $A = \$2114.81; I = \$914.81$ 61. $A = \$9607.70; I = \$4607.70$

EXERCISE 0.4

1. $16/3$ 3. -8 5. -2 7. 8 9. $m^{3/2}$ 11. $(m^2n^5)^{1/4}$ 13. $\sqrt[4]{x^7}$ 15. $-1/4\sqrt[4]{x^5}$
17. $y^{3/4}$ 19. $z^{19/4}$ 21. $1/y^{5/2}$ 23. x 25. $1/y^{21/10}$ 27. $x^{1/2}$ 29. $1/x$ 31. $8x^2$
33. $8x^2y^2\sqrt{2y}$ 35. $2x^2y\sqrt[3]{5x^2y^2}$ 37. $6x^2y\sqrt{x}$ 39. $42x^3y^2\sqrt{x}$ 41. $2xy^5/3$
43. $2b\sqrt[4]{b}/(3a^2)$ 45. $\sqrt{6}/3$ 47. $\sqrt{mx}/x$ 49. $\sqrt[3]{mx^2}/x^2$ 51. $-\frac{2}{3}x^{-2/3}$ 53. $3x^{3/2}$
55. $3\sqrt{x}/2$ 57. $1/(2\sqrt{x})$ 59. 74 kg

EXERCISE 0.5

1. (a) 2 (b) -1 (c) 10 (d) one   3. (a) 5 (b) -14 (c) 0 (d) several
5. $11x^2 + 19x - 6$ 7. $7x^2y^2 - 4x^3$ 9. $a + 8b - c$ 11. $-q - 1$ 13. $x^2 - 1$ 15. $35x^5$
17. $3rs$ 19. $2m^2x^3$ 21. $2ax^4 + a^2x^3 + a^2bx^2$ 23. $6y^2 - y - 12$ 25. $2 - 5x^2 + 2x^4$
27. $16x^2 + 24x + 9$ 29. $x^4 - x^2 + 1/4$ 31. $4x^2 - 1$ 33. $0.01 - 16x^2$ 35. $x^3 - 8$
37. $x^8 + 3x^6 - 10x^4 + 5x^3 + 25x$ 39. $3 + m + 2m^2n$ 41. $8x^3y^2/3 + 5/(3y) - 2x^2/(3y)$
43. $x^3 + 3x^2 + 3x + 1$ 45. $8x^3 - 36x^2 + 54x - 27$ 47. $0.1x^2 - 1.995x - 0.1$
49. $x^2 - 2x + 5 + -11/(x + 2)$ 51. $x^2 + 3x - 1 + (-4x + 2)/(x^2 + 1)$ 53. $x + 2x^2$
55. $x - x^{1/2} - 2$ 57. $x - 9$ 59. $4x^2 + 4x$

EXERCISE 0.6

1. $3b(3a - 4a^2 + 6b)$ 3. $2x(2x + 4y^2 + y^3)$ 5. $(5 - x^2)(y - 4)$ 7. $(6 + y)(x - m)$
9. $(x + 2)(x + 6)$ 11. $(x - 3)(x + 2)$ 13. $2(x - 7)(x + 3)$ 15. $(7x + 4)(x - 2)$ 17. $(x - 5)^2$
19. $(7a + 12b)(7a - 12b)$ 21. $2x(x - 2)^2$ 23. $(2x - 3)(x + 2)$ 25. $3(x + 4)(x - 3)$
27. $2x(x + 2)(x - 2)$ 29. $(5x + 2)(2x + 3)$ 31. $(5x - 1)(2x - 9)$ 33. $(3x - 1)(3x + 8)$
35. $(y^2 + 4x^2)(y + 2x)(y - 2x)$ 37. $(x + 2)^2(x - 2)^2$ 39. $(2x + 1)(2x - 1)(x + 1)(x - 1)$
41. $(x + 1)^3$ 43. $(x - 4)^3$ 45. $(x - 4)(x^2 + 4x + 16)$ 47. $(3 + 2x)(9 - 6x + 4x^2)$ 49. $x + 1$
51. $1 + x$ 53. $7x - 3x^3$ 55. $4x(4 - x)^2$

EXERCISE 0.7

1. $2y^3/z$ 3. $1/3$ 5. $(x - 1)/(x - 3)$ 7. $(2xy^2 - 5)/(y + 3)$ 9. $20x/y$ 11. $32/3$
13. $2x^2 - 7x + 6$ 15. $-(x + 1)(x + 3)/(x - 1)(x - 3)$ 17. $15bc^2/2$ 19. $5y/(y - 3)$
21. $\dfrac{-x(x-3)(x+2)}{x+3}$ 23. $\dfrac{4a - 4}{a(a - 2)}$ 25. $(x^2 + 3x + 1)/(x + 1)$ 27. $\dfrac{16a + 15a^2}{12(x + 2)}$
29. $\dfrac{-5x + 17}{(x - 4)(x - 1)(x - 5)}$ 31. $\dfrac{85x - 39}{30(x - 2)}$ 33. $\dfrac{-4y}{(x - 2y)^2(x + 2y)}$ 35. $\dfrac{7x + 8}{(x - 2)(x + 2)(x + 1)}$
37. $(7x - 3x^3)/\sqrt{3 - x^2}$ 39. $(\sqrt{5} + 3)/(-4)$ 41. $(1 - 2\sqrt{x} + x)/(1 - x)$
43. $1/(\sqrt{(x + h} + \sqrt{x})$ 45. $(bc + ac + ab)/abc$

CHAPTER 0 REVIEW EXERCISES

1. yes   2. no   3. no   4. {1, 2, 3, 5, 6, 7, 8, 9, 10}   5. {1, 3}   6. {4, 5, 6, 7, 8, 10}   7. {2, 9}

8. (a)   (b) 10   (c) 100

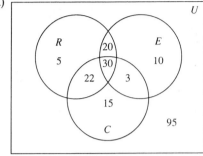

R: recognized
E: exercise
C: community involvement

9. (a) commutative property of addition   (b) associative property of multiplication   (c) distributive law
10. irrational   11. rational, integer   12. meaningless   13. 6   14. 142   15. 10   16. 5/4
17. 9   18. -29 19. $-13/4$ 20. 10.62857888   21. (a) 1   (b) $2^7 = 128$ (c) 4^6 (d) 7
22. (a) $1/x^2$ (b) x^{10} (c) x^9 (d) $1/y^8$ (e) y^6 23. $-x^2y^2/36$ 24. $9y^8/(4x^4)$
25. $y^2/(4x^4)$ 26. $-x^8z^4/y^4$ 27. $3x/(y^7z)$ 28. $x^5/(2y^3)$ 29. (a) 4   (b) 2/7
30. (a) $x^{1/2}$ (b) $x^{2/3}$ (c) $x^{-1/4}$ 31. (a) $\sqrt[3]{x^2}$ (b) $1/\sqrt{x} = \sqrt{x}/x$ (c) $-x\sqrt{x}$
32. (a) $5y\sqrt{2x}/2$ (b) $\sqrt[3]{x^2y}/x^2$ 33. $x^{5/6}$ 34. y 35. $x^{17/4}$ 36. $x^{11/3}$ 37. $x^{2/5}$
38. x^2y^8 39. $216x^2/125y^{7/4}$ 40. $2xy^2\sqrt{3xy}$ 41. $25x^3y^4\sqrt{2y}$ 42. $6x^2y^4\sqrt[3]{5x^2y^2}$
43. $8a^2b^4\sqrt{2a}$ 44. $2xy$ 45. $4x\sqrt{x}/(y^3\sqrt{3y}) = 4x\sqrt{3xy}/3y^4$ 46. $-x - 2$ 47. $-x^2 - x$
48. $4x^3 + xy + 4y - 4$ 49. $24x^5y^5$ 50. $3y^5/x^6$ 51. $3x^2 - 7x + 4$ 52. $3x^2 + 5x - 2$
53. $4x^2 - 7x - 2$ 54. $6x^2 - 11x - 7$ 55. $4x^2 - 12x + 9$ 56. $16x^2 - 9$
57. $2x^4 + 2x^3 - 5x^2 + x - 3$ 58. $8x^3 - 12x^2 + 6x - 1$ 59. $x^3 - y^3$ 60. $(2/y) - (3xy/2) - 3x^2$
61. $3x^2 + 2x - 3 + (-3x + 7)/(x^2 + 1)$ 62. $x^3 - x^2 + 2x + 7 + 21/(x - 3)$ 63. $x^2 - x$
64. $2x - a$ 65. $x^3(2x - 1)$ 66. $2(x^2 + 1)^2(1 + x)(1 - x)$ 67. $(x + 1)^2(x - 1)$ 68. $(2x - 1)^2$
69. $(4 + 3x)(4 - 3x)$ 70. $2x^2(x + 2)(x - 2)$ 71. $(x - 7)(x + 3)$ 72. $(3x + 2)(x - 1)$
73. $(4x + 3)(3x - 8)$ 74. $(2x + 3)^2(2x - 3)^2$ 75. $(2 + x^3)(2 - x)(4 + 2x + x^2)$ 76. $x^{2/3} + 1$

77. (a) $x/(x + 2)$ (b) $\dfrac{2xy(2 - 3xy)}{2x - 3y}$ 78. $\dfrac{x^2 - 4}{x(x + 4)}$ 79. $(x + 3)/(x - 3)$ 80. $\dfrac{x(x - 3)}{(x + 1)(2x + 1)}$

81. $\dfrac{x^2(3x - 2)}{(x - 1)(x + 2)}$ 82. $(6x^2 + 9x - 1)/(6x^2)$ 83. $\dfrac{4x - x^2}{4(x - 2)}$ 84. $\dfrac{x^2 - x + 12}{3(x + 2)(x - 1)}$

85. $-\dfrac{x^2 + 2x + 2}{x(x - 1)^2}$ 86. $\dfrac{x(x - 4)}{(x - 2)(x + 1)(x - 3)}$ 87. $3(\sqrt{x} + 1)$ 88. $2/(\sqrt{x} + \sqrt{x - 4})$

EXERCISE 1.1

1. $x = 9$ 3. $x = 4$ 5. $x = -5/4$ 7. $x = 9/2$ 9. $x = 0$ 11. $x = 5/2$ 13. $x = 17/13$
15. $x = 13/5$ 17. $x = 40$ 19. $x = 1.7$ 21. $x = -29/2$ 23. $x = -1$ 25. $x = -1/3$
27. $x = 1$ 29. $x = 0$ 31. $x \approx -0.279$ 33. $x \approx -1147.362$ 35. (a) 3333 approx.
(b) 15,873   37. $-40°$ 39. (a) 132 lb   (b) $73\frac{7}{11}$ in   41. $31.88   43. 9000   45. $85,000
47. $307   49. $246   51. $300   53. 96   55. lost $40   57. $8800

EXERCISE 1.2

1.

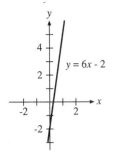

$y = 6x - 2$

3.

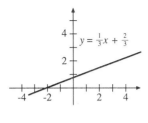

$y = \frac{1}{3}x + \frac{2}{3}$

5.

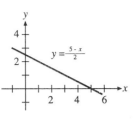

$y = \frac{5 - x}{2}$

7.

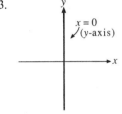

$2x - 3y = 12$

9.

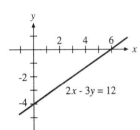

$6x + 5y = 9$

11.

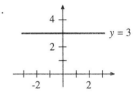

$y = 3$

13.

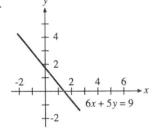

$x = 0$
$(y\text{-axis})$

15.

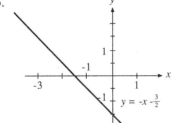

$y = -x - \frac{3}{2}$

17.

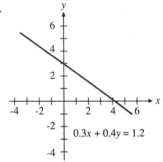

$0.3x + 0.4y = 1.2$

19.

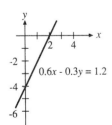

$0.6x - 0.3y = 1.2$

21.

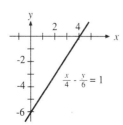

$\frac{x}{4} - \frac{y}{6} = 1$

23.

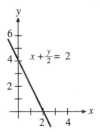

$x + \frac{y}{2} = 2$

25. See Exercise 19. $x/2 - y/4 = 1$ is equivalent to $0.6x - 0.3y = 1.2$.

27. (a)

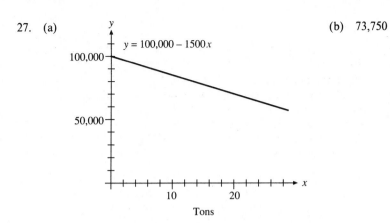

$$y = 100,000 - 1500x$$

Tons

(b) 73,750

29.

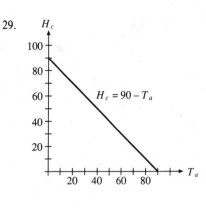

$$H_c = 90 - T_a$$

31.

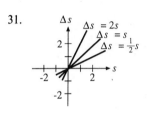

$$\Delta s = 2s$$
$$\Delta s = s$$
$$\Delta s = \tfrac{1}{2}s$$

33.

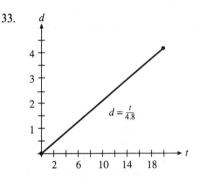

$$d = \frac{t}{4.8}$$

35. (a)

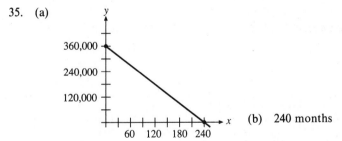

(b) 240 months

EXERCISE 1.3

1. yes   3. no   5. yes   7. no   9. (a) -10 (b) 6   (c) -34 (d) 2.8   11. (a) -3
(b) 1   (c) 13   (d) 6   13. (a) $63/8$ (b) $17/24$ (c) -24.996 15. (a) -1 (b) 1
(c) 1   (d) no   17. (a) 37   (b) undefined   (c) 2.99   (d) 1.81   19. (a) 13
(b) $x^2 + 3x + 3$ (c) $x^2 + 2xh + h^2 + x + h + 1$ 21. (a) $-2x^2 - 4xh - 2h^2 + x + h$
(b) $-4xh - 2h^2 + h$ (c) $-4x - 2h + 1$ 23. yes   25. no   27. 2   29. 0
31. (a) $b = a^2 - 4a$ (b) $(1, -3)$, yes   (c) $(3, -3)$, yes   (d) $x = 0, x = 4$, yes   33. D: all reals;
R: reals $y \geqslant 4$ 35. D: reals $x \geqslant 1$; R: reals $y \geqslant 0$ 37. all reals except $x = 0$ 39. reals $x \geqslant 1$
and $x \neq 2$ 41. (a) yes   (b) $v \geqslant -1/4$ (c) $v \geqslant 0$ 43. (a) yes   (b) all reals
(c) D: $32° \leqslant F \leqslant 212°$; R: $0° \leqslant C \leqslant 100°$ (d) 4.44°C   45. (a) 6   (b) 20   (c) 42
47. (a) $N(2) = 48\frac{2}{3}$; number is 48   (b) $N(10) = 248\frac{4}{102}$; number is 248   49. (a) $0 \leqslant p < 100$
(b) $5972.73   (c) $65,700   (d) $722,700   (e) $1,817,700   51. (a) yes
(b) $A(2) = 96; A(30) = 600$ (c) $0 < x < 50$ 53. (a) $18   (b) $19   (c) $20

EXERCISE 1.4

1. (a) $3 billion   (c)   C
   (b) $7.2 billion

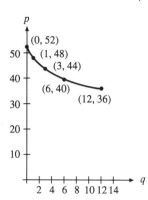

3. (a) $5.6 billion   (c)   C
   (b) $14.6 billion

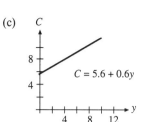

5. (a) $16 billion   (b) $16.5 billion   (c) 47%   7.

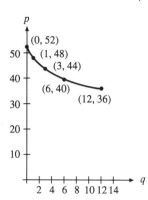

9.

11. demand decreases   13. (a) 600   (b) 200   (c) shortage

15. 16 demanded, 25 supplied; surplus   17. (a) $C(x) = 17x + 3400$ (b) $6800
19. (a) $C(x) = 43x + 1850$ (b) $1850   (c) $3441   21. (a) $R(x) = 34x$ (b) $10,200
23. (a) $R(x) = 80x$ (b) $6000   25. (a) $P(x) = 17x - 3400$ (b) $1700   (c) 200
27. (a) $P(x) = 37x - 1850$ (b) $-$740, loss of $740   (c) 50   29. (a) 50 and 550 units
(b) 300 units   (c) $5000

wrong

EXERCISE 1.5

1. $m = 2$ 3. $m = -5$ 5. $m = 0$ 7. $m = 7/3, b = -1/4$ 9. $m = 0, b = 3$
11. $m = -1/2, b = -2/3$ 13. no slope, no y-intercept   15. $m = 1/4, b = 0$ 17. $m = -2/3, b = 2$

19. $m \approx -0.831, b \approx 29.2$ 21.

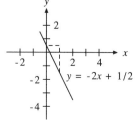

23.

25.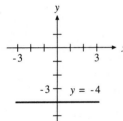

27.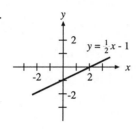

29.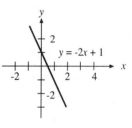

31.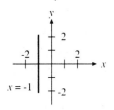

33. $y = 2x - 4$ 35. $-x + 13y = 32$ 37. $y = 2$ 39. $y = -\frac{3}{5}x - \frac{41}{5}$

41. $y = -\frac{6}{5}x + \frac{23}{5}$ 43. $y = -\frac{8}{5}x + \frac{128}{5}$ 45. $y = 5.19 + 0.5191x$ 47. $p = 85{,}000 - 1700x$; Domain: $0 \leqslant x \leqslant 50$ 49. (a) $m = 5$, C-intercept 250   (b) $\overline{MC} = 5$ means each additional unit produced adds \$5 to total costs.   (c) \$250   (d) $m = \overline{MC} = 5$; C-intercept = fixed costs = 250
(e) \$5, \$5   51. (a) 27   (b) $\overline{MR} = 27$ means each additional unit sold adds \$27 to total revenues.
(c) \$27, \$27   53. R-intercept = 0 in both because there can be no revenue when no units are sold (i.e., when $x = 0$).   55. (a) $P(x) = 22x - 250$ (b) 22   (c) $\overline{MP} = 22$ (d) Each unit sold adds \$22 to profits at all levels of production, so produce and sell as much as possible.   57. $C(x) = 27x + 3000$

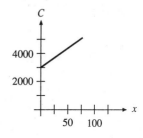

59. $R = 3.2t - 0.2$ 61. $P = 50x - 10{,}000$ 63.

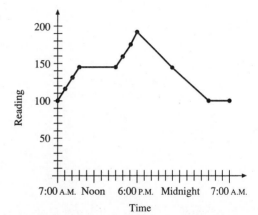

EXERCISE 1.6

1. $x = 2, y = 2$ 3. no solution   5. $x = 2, y = 5$ 7. $x = 14/11, y = 6/11$ 9. $x = 10/3, y = 2$
11. $x = 2, y = 1$ 13. $x = 1, y = 1$ 15. no solution   17. $x = -52/7, y = -128/7$ 19. dependent
21. $x = 1, y = 7$ 23. $x = 1, y = 1, z = -1$ 25. $x = 3, y = 2, z = 1$ 27. $r = 1, s = 1, t = 1$
29. \$68,000 at 18%; \$77,600 at 10%   31. \$13,500 at 10%; \$10,000 at 12%   33. $A = 4$ oz, $B = 6\frac{2}{3}$ oz
35. $A = 4550, B = 1500$ 37. 7 cc of 20%; 3 cc of 5%   39. 5 oz of A, 1 oz of B, 5 oz of C
41. $A = 200, B = 100, C = 200$

EXERCISE 1.7

1. (a) $C(y) = 0.6y + 8$ (b) 0.6   3.   5. (a) 0.65   (b) \$5 billion

7.

9. They are equal.   11. (a) demand falls; supply rises   (b) (30, \$25)

13. (a) $q = 20$ (b) $q = 40$ (c) shortage   15. shortage   17.

19. $p = -\frac{1}{2}q + 28$ 21.   23. $p = \frac{1}{3}q + \frac{34}{3}$ 25. $q = 20, p = \$18$

27. $q = 10, p = \$180$ 29. $q = 100, p = \$325$ 31. (a) \$15   (b) $q = 100, p = \$100$
(c) $q = 50, p = \$110$ (d) yes   33. $q = 8; p = \$188$ 35. (a) Revenue passes through the origin.

(b) $2000   (c) 400 units   (d) $\overline{MC} = 2.5; \overline{MR} = 7.5$ 37. 33   39. (a) $R(x) = 12x$; $C(x) = 8x + 1600$ (b) 400 units   41. (a) $P(x) = 4x - 1600$ (b) $x = 400$ units to break even   43. 20,000 units

CHAPTER 1 REVIEW EXERCISES

1. $x = 7$ 2. $x = 31/3$ 3. $x = -13$ 4. $-29/8$ 5. $x = -1/9$ 6. $x = 10.05$ 7. $x = 2/5$
8. $x \approx 1.11$ 9.

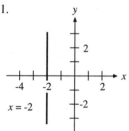

10.

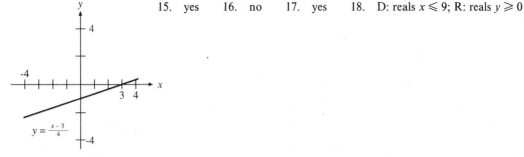

11.

12.

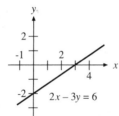

13.

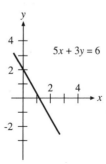

14.

15. yes   16. no   17. yes   18. D: reals $x \leqslant 9$; R: reals $y \geqslant 0$

19. reals $x \geqslant -3$ except $x = 0$ 20. (a) 2   (b) 37   (c) 29/4   21. (a) 0   (b) 9/4
(c) 10.01   22. (a) 0   (b) 10,000   (c) -25 (d) 0.1   23. (a) -36 (b) $-x^2 + 7x + 8$
(c) $-x^2 - 2xh - h^2 + 9x + 9h$ 24. $9 - 2x - h$ 25. yes   26. no   27. 4   28. $x = 0, x = 4$
29. $y = 1, y = -1$ 30. $m = -3/4$ 31. $m = 1$ 32. undefined   33. $m = -2/5, b = 2$
34. $m = -4/3, b = 2$ 35. $y = 4x + 2$ 36. $y = -\frac{1}{2}x + 3$ 37. $y = \frac{2}{5}x + \frac{9}{5}$ 38. $y = -x - 5$
39. $y = -\frac{11}{8}x + \frac{17}{4}$ 40. $x = -1$ 41. $y = 4x + 2$ 42. $y = \frac{4}{3}x + \frac{10}{3}$

43. $x = 2, y = 1$ 44. $x = 10, y = -1$ 45. $x = 3, y = -2$ 46. no solution
47. $x = 10, y = -71$ 48. $x = 2, y = 1$ 49. $x = 1, y = -1, z = 2$ 50. $x = 1, y = 10, z = 9$
51. 95%   52. 40,000 mi. He would normally drive more than 40,000 miles in 5 years so he should buy diesel.

53. (a) \$2 billion   (b) \$6 billion   54. C(y)   55. (a) 12 supplied; 14 demanded

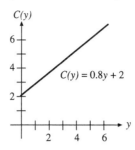

$C(y) = 0.8y + 2$

(b) shortage   (c) increase   56. (a) $C(x) = 2x + 500$ (b) \$700   57. (a) $R(x) = 4x$ (b) \$400
58. (a) $P(x) = 2x - 500$ (b) loss of \$300   (c) 250   59. \$100,000 at 9.5%; \$50,000 at 11%
60. 2.8 liters of 20%; 1.2 liters of 70%   61.

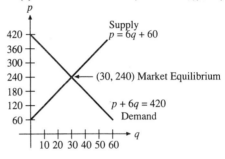

Supply
$p = 6q + 60$

$(30, 240)$ Market Equilibrium

$p + 6q = 420$
Demand

62. (a) \$4 billion   (b) 0.6   (c) $C(y) = 4 + 0.6y$ C   63. (a) 38.80

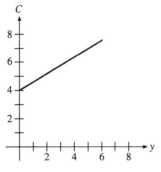

(b) 61.30   (c) 22.50   (d) 200   64. (a) $C(x) = 22x + 1500$ (b) $R(x) = 52x$
(c) $P(x) = 30x - 1500$ (d) $\overline{MC} = 22$ (e) $\overline{MR} = 52$ (f) $\overline{MP} = 30$ (g) $x = 50$
65. $q = 300, p = \$150$

EXERCISE 2.1

1. $x = 3, y = 2, z = 3, w = 4$ 3. $x = 4, y = 1, w = 3, z = 3$ 5. A, C, D, F, Z   7. A, F, Z;
C and D   9. (a) 1   (b) $a_{31} = 4, a_{32} = 0, a_{33} = 3$ (c) 2   (d) 1 or 3   (e) $i = 1, j = 1$
or $i = 2, j = 3$

11. $-A = \begin{bmatrix} -1 & 0 & -2 \\ -3 & -2 & -1 \\ -4 & 0 & -3 \end{bmatrix}$ 13. $\begin{bmatrix} 0 & 0 & 0 & 0 & 0 \\ 0 & 0 & 0 & 0 & 0 \end{bmatrix}$ 15. $\begin{bmatrix} 9 & 5 \\ 4 & 7 \end{bmatrix}$ 17. $\begin{bmatrix} 0 & -2 & -1 \\ 4 & 2 & 0 \\ 2 & 3 & 7 \end{bmatrix}$

19. impossible   21. impossible   23. A 25. impossible   27. $x = 2, y = 2, z = -3$ 29. 80

31. 86   33. $\begin{bmatrix} 80 & 75 \\ 58 & 106 \end{bmatrix}$ 35. A 37. $D = \begin{bmatrix} 10 & 4 \\ 7 & 2 \end{bmatrix}$

39. $\begin{array}{c} \\ \text{I} \\ \text{II} \\ \text{III} \end{array}\begin{bmatrix} \text{wt} & 1 \\ 140 & 5.5 \\ 151 & 5.7 \\ 141 & 5.5 \end{bmatrix}$ or $\begin{array}{c} \\ \text{wt} \\ 1 \end{array}\begin{bmatrix} \text{I} & \text{II} & \text{III} \\ 140 & 151 & 141 \\ 5.5 & 5.7 & 5.5 \end{bmatrix}$

41. $\begin{bmatrix} 110 & 7 \\ 64 & 6.1 \\ 49 & 4.3 \end{bmatrix}$ or $\begin{bmatrix} 110 & 64 & 49 \\ 7 & 6.1 & 4.3 \end{bmatrix}$

43. (a) $A = \begin{bmatrix} 122{,}822 & 135{,}884 & 134{,}018 \\ 72{,}342 & 74{,}421 & 72{,}673 \\ 5{,}085 & 7{,}214 & 7{,}091 \\ 289 & 369 & 365 \end{bmatrix}$

(b) $B = \begin{bmatrix} 152{,}117 & 200{,}714 & 223{,}314 \\ 102{,}266 & 119{,}790 & 116{,}161 \\ 3{,}604 & 5{,}221 & 5{,}801 \\ 1 & 1 & 0 \end{bmatrix}$

(c) $A - B = \begin{bmatrix} -29{,}295 & -64{,}830 & -89{,}296 \\ -29{,}924 & -45{,}369 & -43{,}488 \\ 1{,}481 & 1{,}993 & 1{,}290 \\ 288 & 368 & 365 \end{bmatrix}$

EXERCISE 2.2

1. no   3. $\begin{bmatrix} 3 & 0 & 6 \\ 9 & 6 & 3 \\ 12 & 0 & 9 \end{bmatrix}$ 5. $\begin{bmatrix} 28 & 16 \\ 10 & 18 \end{bmatrix}$ 7. impossible   9. $\begin{bmatrix} 29 & 25 \\ 10 & 12 \end{bmatrix}$ 11. $\begin{bmatrix} 22 & 16 \\ 20 & 19 \end{bmatrix}$

13. no   15. $\begin{bmatrix} 7 & 5 & 3 & 2 \\ 14 & 9 & 11 & 3 \\ 13 & 10 & 12 & 3 \end{bmatrix}$ 17. impossible   19. $\begin{bmatrix} 13 & 9 & 3 & 4 \\ 9 & 7 & 16 & 1 \end{bmatrix}$ 21. $\begin{bmatrix} 17 & 0 & 14 \\ 8 & 2 & 11 \end{bmatrix}$

23. $\begin{bmatrix} 9 & 0 & 8 \\ 13 & 4 & 11 \\ 16 & 0 & 17 \end{bmatrix}$ 25. $\begin{bmatrix} 161 & 126 \\ 42 & 35 \end{bmatrix}$ 27. yes   29. $\begin{bmatrix} -55 & 88 & 0 \\ -42 & 67 & 0 \\ 28 & -44 & 1 \end{bmatrix}$ 31. $\begin{bmatrix} 0 & 0 & 0 \\ 0 & 0 & 0 \\ 0 & 0 & 0 \end{bmatrix}$

33. $\begin{bmatrix} 0 & 0 & 0 \\ 0 & 0 & 0 \\ 0 & 0 & 0 \end{bmatrix}$ 35. A 37. Z 39. no (see Exercise 31)   41. $AB = \begin{bmatrix} 1 & 0 \\ 0 & 1 \end{bmatrix}, BA = \begin{bmatrix} 1 & 0 \\ 0 & 1 \end{bmatrix}$

43. $\begin{bmatrix} 23.10 & 42 & 105 & 5.25 \\ 21 & 42 & 21 & 0 \\ 29.40 & 73.50 & 47.25 & 0 \\ 15.75 & 73.50 & 21 & 10.5 \\ 21 & 0 & 105 & 5.25 \end{bmatrix}$

45. (a) $\begin{bmatrix} 13{,}500 & 12{,}400 \\ 10{,}500 & 10{,}600 \end{bmatrix}$ (b) A: from Kink; B: from Ace 47. (a) $\begin{bmatrix} 5 \\ 3 \\ 4 \\ 4 \end{bmatrix}$ (b) [$1,030,000]

49. (a) $\begin{bmatrix} 2.5 & 50 \\ .826 & 15.05 \\ 0 & 0 \end{bmatrix}$ (b) $\begin{bmatrix} 15 & 300 \\ 12.63 & 230.05 \\ 9.8 & 190 \end{bmatrix}$ 51. $\begin{bmatrix} .08 & .22 & .12 \\ .10 & .08 & .19 \\ .05 & .07 & .09 \\ .10 & .26 & .15 \\ .12 & .04 & .24 \end{bmatrix}$

53. carnivore 1: plant 5; carnivore 2: plant 4; carnivore 3: plant 5

EXERCISE 2.3

1. $\begin{bmatrix} 3 & 2 & 4 & | & 0 \\ 2 & -1 & 2 & | & 0 \\ 1 & -2 & -4 & | & 0 \end{bmatrix}$ 3. $\begin{bmatrix} 1 & -3 & 4 & | & 2 \\ 2 & 0 & 2 & | & 1 \\ 1 & 2 & 1 & | & 1 \end{bmatrix}$ 5. $x = 2, y = 3$ 7. $x = 1/3, y = 5/3$

9. $x = 15, y = -13, z = 2$ 11. $x = 15, y = 0, z = 2$ 13. $x = 1, y = -1, z = 1$ 15. $x_1 = 1,$ $x_2 = 0, x_3 = 1, x_4 = 0$ 17. $x = 1, y = 3, z = 1, w = 0$ 19. $x = (b_2 c_1 - b_1 c_2)/(a_1 b_2 - a_2 b_1)$

21. $x = 0, y = -z$ 23. $x = \frac{5}{3} + \frac{1}{3}z, y = \frac{1}{3} + \frac{2}{3}z$ 25. $x = 1 - z, y = \frac{1}{2}z$ 27. no solution

29. $x = 0, y = 0, z = 0$ 31. $x = 2z - 2, y = 1 + z$ 33. $x = 9/2, y = -1/2, z = -1$

35. $x_1 = \frac{23}{38}x_3, x_2 = \frac{12}{19}x_3$ 37. no solution 39. $x_1 = \frac{41}{26} - \frac{6}{13}x_4; x_2 = \frac{7}{26} + \frac{5}{13}x_4; x_3 = -\frac{9}{26} + \frac{1}{13}x_4$

41. $76,500 to A; 42,000 to B 43. 254 Type I, 385 Type II, 19 Type III 45. I $= 80$g, II $= 50$g, III $= 50$ g

47. 3 passenger, 4 transport, 4 jumbo 49. 2 of Portfolio I, 2 of Portfolio II 51. 3/8 lb of red meat, 6 slices of bread, 4 glasses of milk 53. (a) A: $200 + x_4 = 100 + x_1$ C: $200 + x_2 = 100 + x_3$ B: $300 + x_1 = 200 + x_2$ D: $500 + x_3 = 800 + x_4$

(b) $x_1 = x_4 + 100, x_2 = x_4 + 200, x_3 = x_4 + 300$ 55. any amount of bacteria III between 1800 and 2300; amount of bacteria I $= 6900 - 3$(bacteria III); amount of bacteria II $= 1/2$(bacteria III) $- 900$ 57. 4 Type I and 2 Type II; 5 Type I, 1 Type II, and 1 Type III; or 6 Type I and 2 Type III

EXERCISE 2.4

1. yes 3. $\begin{bmatrix} \frac{1}{3} & 0 & 0 \\ 0 & \frac{1}{3} & 0 \\ 0 & 0 & \frac{1}{3} \end{bmatrix}$ 5. $\begin{bmatrix} 2 & -7 \\ -1 & 4 \end{bmatrix}$ 7. no inverse 9. $\begin{bmatrix} \frac{5}{2} & -1 \\ -2 & 1 \end{bmatrix}$ 11. $\begin{bmatrix} -\frac{1}{10} & \frac{7}{10} \\ \frac{1}{5} & -\frac{2}{5} \end{bmatrix}$

13. $\begin{bmatrix} -1 & 1 & 0 \\ 1 & 0 & 0 \\ -1 & 0 & 1 \end{bmatrix}$ 15. $\begin{bmatrix} \frac{1}{3} & -\frac{1}{3} & \frac{1}{3} \\ -\frac{2}{3} & -\frac{1}{3} & \frac{7}{3} \\ \frac{1}{3} & \frac{2}{3} & -\frac{5}{3} \end{bmatrix}$ 17. no inverse 19. no inverse 21. $\begin{bmatrix} x \\ y \\ z \end{bmatrix} = \begin{bmatrix} 1 \\ 1 \\ 2 \end{bmatrix}$

23. $x = 2, y = 1$ 25. $x = 1, y = 2$ 27. $x = 1, y = 1, z = 1$ 29. $x = 1, y = 3, z = 2$

31. 172, 208, 268, 327, 101, 123, 268, 327, 216, 263, 162, 195, 176, 215, 343, 417 33. Hang on.

35. Answers in back. 37. 15cc at 40%; 10cc at 10% 39. A $= 5.5$ mg and B $= 8.8$ mg for Patient I; A $= 10$ mg and B $= 16$ mg for Patient II

EXERCISE 2.5

1. 8   3. 40   5. most: raw materials; least: fuels   7. raw materials, manufacturing, service
9. farm products $= 200$; machinery $= 40$ 11. agricultural products $= 100$; oil $= 700$ 13. agricultural
goods $= 400$; manufactured goods $= 500$; fuels $= 400$ 15. electronics $= 1240$; steel $= 1260$; autos $= 720$
17. products $= 7/17$ households; machinery $= 1/17$ household   19. government $= 10/19$ households;
industry $= 11/19$ households

21. $\begin{bmatrix} 24 \\ 96 \\ 24 \\ 120 \\ 492 \\ 3456 \end{bmatrix}$ 3456 bolts, 492 braces, 120 sheets   23. $\begin{bmatrix} 10 \\ 10 \\ 20 \\ 56 \\ 20 \\ 26 \\ 300 \end{bmatrix}$ 56 2 × 4's, 20 braces, 26 clamps, 300 nails

25. development $= \$21,000$; promotional $= \$12,000$ 27. engineering $= \$15,000$; computer $= \$13,000$

CHAPTER 2 REVIEW EXERCISES

1. 4   2. 0   3. A, B 4. none   5. $\begin{bmatrix} 6 & -1 & -9 & 3 \\ 10 & 3 & -1 & 4 \\ -2 & -2 & -2 & 14 \end{bmatrix}$ 6. $\begin{bmatrix} 3 & -3 \\ 4 & -1 \\ 2 & -6 \\ 1 & -2 \end{bmatrix}$ 7. $\begin{bmatrix} 8 & 8 & 4 & -10 \\ 12 & 6 & -2 & 0 \\ 0 & 0 & -6 & 10 \end{bmatrix}$

8. $\begin{bmatrix} 12 & -6 \\ 15 & 0 \\ 18 & 0 \\ 3 & 9 \end{bmatrix}$ 9. $\begin{bmatrix} 4 & 0 \\ 0 & 4 \end{bmatrix}$ 10. $\begin{bmatrix} 2 & -12 \\ -8 & -22 \end{bmatrix}$ 11. $\begin{bmatrix} 2 & 5 \\ 1 & 1 \end{bmatrix}$ 12. $\begin{bmatrix} 5 & 16 \\ 6 & 15 \end{bmatrix}$ 13. $\begin{bmatrix} 2 & 37 & 61 & -55 \\ -2 & 9 & -3 & -20 \\ 10 & 10 & -14 & -30 \end{bmatrix}$

14. $\begin{bmatrix} 43 & -23 \\ 33 & -12 \\ -13 & 15 \end{bmatrix}$ 15. $\begin{bmatrix} 10 & 16 \\ 15 & 25 \\ 18 & 30 \\ 6 & 11 \end{bmatrix}$ 16. $\begin{bmatrix} 17 & 73 \\ 7 & 28 \end{bmatrix}$ 17. $\begin{bmatrix} 3 & 7 \\ 23 & 42 \end{bmatrix}$ 18. F 19. F 20. $\begin{bmatrix} 1 & 0 \\ 0 & 1 \end{bmatrix}$

21. F 22. yes   23. $x = 22, y = 9$ 24. $x = -3, y = 3, z = 4$ 25. $x = -3/2, y = 7, z = -11/2$

26. no solution   27. $x = 2 - 2z; y = -1 - 2z$ 28. $x_1 = 1, x_2 = 11, x_3 = -4, x_4 = -5$ 29. $\begin{bmatrix} \frac{1}{2} & \frac{1}{4} \\ \frac{5}{2} & \frac{7}{4} \end{bmatrix}$

30. $\begin{bmatrix} -1 & -2 & 8 \\ 1 & 2 & -7 \\ 1 & 1 & -4 \end{bmatrix}$ 31. $\begin{bmatrix} 2 & 1 & -2 \\ 7 & 5 & -8 \\ -13 & -9 & 15 \end{bmatrix}$ 32. $\begin{bmatrix} -33 \\ 30 \\ 19 \end{bmatrix}$ 33. $\begin{bmatrix} 4 \\ 5 \\ -13 \end{bmatrix}$

34. $A^{-1} = \begin{bmatrix} -41 & 32 & 5 \\ 17 & -13 & -2 \\ -9 & 7 & 1 \end{bmatrix}$; $x = 4, y = -2, z = 2$ 35. $\begin{bmatrix} 250 & 140 \\ 480 & 700 \end{bmatrix}$ 36. $\begin{bmatrix} 1030 & 800 \\ 700 & 1200 \end{bmatrix}$

37. (a) higher in June   (b) higher in July   38. $\begin{matrix} \text{men} & \text{women} \\ \begin{bmatrix} 865 & 885 \\ 210 & 270 \end{bmatrix} \end{matrix} \begin{matrix} \text{Robes} \\ \text{Hoods} \end{matrix}$ 39. $\begin{bmatrix} 1750 \\ 480 \end{bmatrix} \begin{matrix} \text{Robes} \\ \text{Hoods} \end{matrix}$

40. $[2230]$ 41. 400 fast food, 700 computer, 200 pharmaceutical   42. $A = 2C, B = 2000 - 4C$

43. $X = \begin{bmatrix} 366 \\ 322 \\ 402 \end{bmatrix}$, approx.   44. $G = \frac{64}{93} H; A = \frac{59}{93} H; M = \frac{40}{93} H$

EXERCISE 3.1

1. $x < 2$ 3. $x \leqslant -4$ 5. $x < 2$ 7. $x < -3$ 9. $x < 3/2$ 11. $x \leqslant -1$ 13. $x \leqslant 5/28$

15. $x > 1.949$ 17. $x < -4$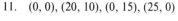

19. $x < 3$ 21. $x \geqslant -7/2$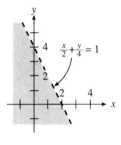

23. $x < 2$ 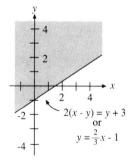   25. $x < 20/17$ 27. $(1, 3]$, half-open

29. $(2, 10)$, open   31. $[-3, 2]$, closed   33. $(-4, 3)$, open   35. $[4, 6]$, closed   37. $[4, 9)$, half-open

39. $1 < x < 4$ 41. $x > 4$ 43. $C \geqslant 37$ 45. (a) (1) $x_4 \leqslant 1100$,   (2) $x_4 \leqslant 1000$,   (3) $x_4 \leqslant 900$,

(4) $x \geqslant 0$ (b) $0 \leqslant x_4 \leqslant 900$ (c) $x_1 \in [100, 1000]$, $x_2 \in [200, 1100]$, $x_3 \in [300, 1200]$

EXERCISE 3.2

1.

3.

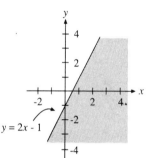

5.

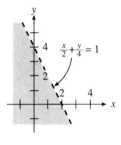

7.

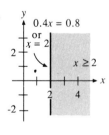

9.

11. $(0, 0)$, $(20, 10)$, $(0, 15)$, $(25, 0)$

13. $(0, 0)$, $(7, 0)$, $(5, 5)$, $(2, 6)$, $(0, 4)$ 15. $(0, 5)$, $(1, 2)$, $(3, 1)$, $(6, 0)$ 17.

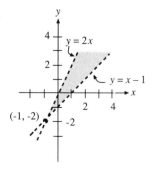

19.

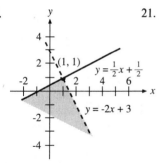

21.

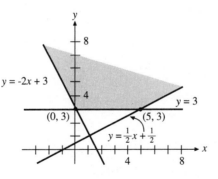

23.

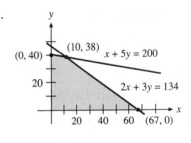

25.

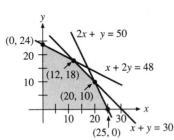

27.

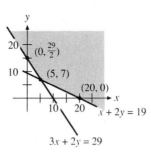

29. $2x + y = 3$

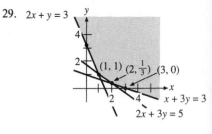

31.

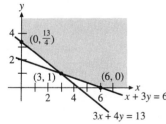

33. Let x = cord-type trimmer and y = cordless trimmer.

(a) Constraints are:
$$x + y \leqslant 300$$
$$2x + 4y \leqslant 800$$
$$x \geqslant 0, y \geqslant 0$$

(b)

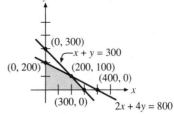

35. Let x = minutes of radio, and y = minutes of television.

(a) Constraints are:
$$x + y \geqslant 80$$
$$0.006x + 0.09y \geqslant 2.16$$
$$x \geqslant 0, y \geqslant 0$$

(b)

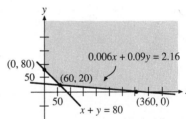

EXERCISE 3.3

1. max $= 20$ at $(4, 4)$; min $= 0$ at $(0, 0)$ 3. max $= 68$ at $(12, 4)$; min $= 14$ at $(2, 2)$ 5. no max; min $= 10$ at $(2, 1)$ 7. $(0, 0), (0, 20), (10, 18), (15, 10), (20, 0)$; max $= 66$ at $(10, 18)$
9. $(0, 60), (10, 30), (20, 20), (70, 0)$; min $= 90$ at $(10, 30)$ 11. max $= 382$ at $x = 10, y = 38$
13. max $= 80$ at $x = 20, y = 10$ 15. min $= 115$ at $x = 5, y = 7$ 17. min $= 36$ at $x = 3, y = 0$
19. max $= 6$ at $(0, 2)$ 21. max $= 10$ at $(2, 4)$ 23. max $= 22$ at $(2, 4)$ 25. max $= 30$ on line between $(0, 5)$ and $(3, 4)$ 27. min $= 32$ at $(2, 3)$ 29. min $= 9$ at $(2, 3)$ 31. min $= 20$ at $(4, 2)$
33. min $= 1870$ on line between $(10, 40)$ and $(30, 10)$ 35. max $= \$10,000$ at 200 cord-type, 100 cordless
37. 250 fish: 150 of I, 100 of II   39. $R = \$366,000$ with 6 satellite and 17 full-service branches
41. radio $= 60$, TV $= 20$, $C = \$16,000$ 43. 30 days for Factory 1 and 20 days for Factory 2; cost $= \$700,000$ 45. 60 days for Location I and 70 days for Location II; cost $= \$86,000$

EXERCISE 3.4

1. $\begin{bmatrix} 2 & 5 & 1 & 0 & 0 & 30 \\ 1 & 5 & 0 & 1 & 0 & 25 \\ -2 & -4 & 0 & 0 & 1 & 0 \end{bmatrix}$ 3. $\begin{bmatrix} 1 & 5 & 1 & 0 & 0 & 200 \\ 2 & 3 & 0 & 1 & 0 & 134 \\ -4 & -9 & 0 & 0 & 1 & 0 \end{bmatrix}$ 5. $\begin{bmatrix} 2 & 7 & 9 & 1 & 0 & 0 & 0 & 100 \\ 6 & 5 & 1 & 0 & 1 & 0 & 0 & 145 \\ 1 & 2 & 7 & 0 & 0 & 1 & 0 & 90 \\ -2 & -5 & -2 & 0 & 0 & 0 & 1 & 0 \end{bmatrix}$

7. $\begin{bmatrix} 2 & 4 & 1 & 0 & 0 & 24 \\ 1 & ① & 0 & 1 & 0 & 5 \\ -4 & -11 & 0 & 0 & 1 & 0 \end{bmatrix}$ 9. $\begin{bmatrix} 10 & ㉗ & 1 & 0 & 0 & 0 & 200 \\ 4 & 51 & 0 & 1 & 0 & 0 & 400 \\ 15 & 27 & 0 & 0 & 1 & 0 & 350 \\ -6 & -7 & 0 & 0 & 0 & 1 & 0 \end{bmatrix}$ 11. $\begin{bmatrix} 2 & 0 & 1 & -\frac{3}{4} & 0 & 12 \\ ③ & 1 & 0 & \frac{1}{3} & 0 & 15 \\ -4 & 0 & 0 & 3 & 1 & 15 \end{bmatrix}$

13. Solution is complete   15. $\begin{bmatrix} 4 & 4 & 1 & 0 & 0 & 2 & 0 & 12 \\ ② & ④ & 0 & 1 & 0 & -1 & 0 & 4 \\ -3 & -11 & 0 & 0 & 1 & -1 & 0 & 6 \\ -3 & -3 & 0 & 0 & 0 & 4 & 1 & 150 \end{bmatrix}$ 17. No solution is possible.

Either circled number may act as the next pivot, but only one of them.

19. $x = 11, y = 9; f = 20$ 21. $x = 0, y = 14, z = 11; f = 525$ 23. $x = 50, y = 10, z = 0, f = 100$. Multiple solutions are possible.   25. $x = 0, y = 5, f = 50$ 27. $x = 4, y = 3, f = 17$
29. $x = 2, y = 5, f = 17$ 31. $x = 4, y = 3, f = 11$ 33. $x = 0, y = 2, z = 5, f = 40$
35. $x = 15, y = 15, z = 25, f = 780$ 37. $x = 6, y = 2, z = 26, f = 206$ 39. $x = 8, y = 16, f = 32$
41. no solution   43. $x = 0, y = 50$ or $x = 40, y = 40, f = 600$ 45. 15 males, 20 females; $f = 35$ animals
47. 500 tomatoes, 1800 peaches; $P = 4100$ 49. 21 newspaper, 13 radio   51. Medium 1 $= 10$, Medium 2 $= 10$, Medium 3 $= 12$ 53. \$1650 profit with 46A, 20B, 6C

EXERCISE 3.5

1. $\begin{bmatrix} 1 & 1 & 9 \\ 1 & 3 & 15 \\ 5 & 2 & g \end{bmatrix}$ transpose $= \begin{bmatrix} 1 & 1 & 5 \\ 1 & 3 & 2 \\ 9 & 15 & g \end{bmatrix}$ 3. $\begin{bmatrix} 4 & 1 & 11 \\ 3 & 2 & 12 \\ 3 & 1 & 6 \\ 3 & 1 & g \end{bmatrix}$ transpose $= \begin{bmatrix} 4 & 3 & 3 & 3 \\ 1 & 2 & 1 & 1 \\ 11 & 12 & 6 & g \end{bmatrix}$

5. $\begin{bmatrix} 1 & 3 & 0 & 1 \\ 4 & 6 & 1 & 3 \\ 0 & 4 & 1 & 1 \\ 12 & 48 & 8 & g \end{bmatrix}$ transpose $= \begin{bmatrix} 1 & 4 & 0 & 12 \\ 3 & 6 & 4 & 48 \\ 0 & 1 & 1 & 8 \\ 1 & 3 & 1 & g \end{bmatrix}$ 7. Maximize $f = 9x_1 + 15x_2$ subject to
$$x_1 + x_2 \leqslant 5$$
$$x_1 + 3x_2 \leqslant 2$$

9. Maximize $f = 11x_1 + 12x_2 + 6x_3$
    subject to $4x_1 + 3x_2 + 3x_3 \leqslant 3$
    $\qquad\qquad x_1 + 2x_2 + \ x_3 \leqslant 1$

11. Maximize $f = x_1 + 3x_2 + x_3$
    subject to $\qquad\quad x_1 + 4x_2 \leqslant 12$
    $\qquad\qquad 3x_1 + 6x_2 + 4x_3 \leqslant 48$
    $\qquad\qquad\qquad x_2 + \ x_3 \leqslant 8$

13. $y_1 = 0, y_2 = 9; g = 18$ (min)   15. $y_1 = 2, y_2 = 3; g = 9$ (min)   17. $y_1 = 2/5, y_2 = 1/5, y_3 = 1/5;$
$g = 16$ (min)   19. min $= 32$ at $x = 16, y = 0$ 21. min $= 28$ at $x = 2, y = 0, z = 1$
23. food I $= 0$ oz, food II $= 3$ oz; $C = \$.60$ (min)   25. diet A $= 4$ servings, diet B $= 10$ servings;
min $= 1.42$ oz   27. food 1 $= 4$ g, food 2 $= 3$ g; $C = 15$ units (min)   29. mine I $= 4$ days, mine II $= 3$
days, mine III $= 2$ days; $C = \$72,000$ (min)   31. (a) Minimize $g = y_1 + y_2 + y_3 + y_4 + y_5 + y_6$
subject to $y_1 \geqslant 40 - y_6$ (b) $y_1 = 40; y_2 = 0; y_3 = 30; y_4 = 10; y_5 = 10; y_6 = 0;$ 90 nurses total
$\qquad\qquad y_2 \geqslant 20 - y_1$
$\qquad\qquad y_3 \geqslant 30 - y_2$
$\qquad\qquad y_4 \geqslant 40 - y_3$
$\qquad\qquad y_5 \geqslant 20 - y_4$
$\qquad\qquad y_6 \geqslant 10 - y_5$

CHAPTER 3 REVIEW EXERCISES

1. $x \leqslant 3$

2. $x \geqslant -20/3$

3. $x \geqslant -15/13$

4. $x \leqslant -3/2$

5. (a) closed; [0, 5]

(b) half-open; [3, 7)   (c) open; (−3, 2)   6. (a) $-1 < x < 16$ (b) $-12 < x \leqslant 8$ (c) $x < -1$

7.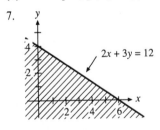

8.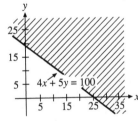

9.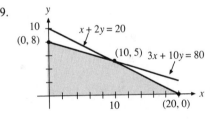

10.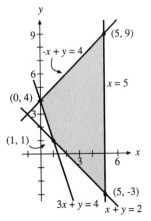

11. $f = 66$ at (6, 6)   12. $f = 91$ at (9, 2)   13. $f = 43$ at (7, 9)

14. $f = 31$ at $(12, 7)$ 15. $g = 24$ at $(3, 3)$ 16. $g = 20$ at $(5, 1)$ 17. $g = 247/3$ at $(212/3, 7/3)$
18. $g = 80$ at $(5, 45)$ 19. $f = 168$ at $(12, 7)$ 20. $f = 260$ at $(60, 20)$ 21. $f = 360$ at $(40, 30)$
22. $f = 270$ at $(5, 3, 2)$ 23. $f = 640$ on the line between $(160, 0)$ and $(90, 70)$ 24. no solution
25. $g = 32$ at $y_1 = 2, y_2 = 3$ 26. $g = 20$ at $y_1 = 4, y_2 = 2$ 27. $g = 7$ at $y_1 = 1, y_2 = 5$
28. $g = 16$ at $y_1 = 2/5, y_2 = 1/5, y_3 = 1/5$ 29. $P = 590$ when smaller $= 75$, larger $= 110$
30. $C = \$300,000$ when #1 operates 30 days, #2 operates 25 days   31. $P = \$320; I = 40, II = 20$
32. $f = 32,000$ at $(8000, 0, 1000)$ 33. Cost $= \$5.60; A = 40$ lb, $B = 0$ lb   34. Cost $= \$8500$;
$A = 20$ days, $B = 15$ days, $C = 0$ days

EXERCISE 4.1

1. $x^2 + 5x - 3 = 0$ 3. $x^2 + 2x - 1 = 0$ 5. $y^2 + 3y - 2 = 0$ 7. $3/2, -3/2$ 9. $0, 1$
11. $0, 140$ 13. $-1, 3$ 15. $-7, 3$ 17. $1/2$ 19. $-6, 2$ 21. (a) $-1/3, 1/2$
(b) $-0.33, 0.50$ 23. (a) $2 + 2\sqrt{2}, 2 - 2\sqrt{2}$ (b) $4.83, -0.83$ 25. no real solutions
27. (a) $-7/4, 3/4$ (b) $-1.75, 0.75$ 29. (a) $(1 \pm \sqrt{31})/5$ (b) $1.31, -0.91$ 31. $\sqrt{7}, -\sqrt{7}$
33. no real solutions   35. $-2/7$ 37. $-2, 5$ 39. no real solutions   41. $2/3, 3$
43. $-300, 100$ 45. $0.69, -0.06$ 47. $(5 + \sqrt{37})/2, (5 - \sqrt{37})/2$ 49. (a) $v = 28\sqrt{30}$
(b) $v = 28\sqrt{70}$ (c) $h = v^2/1960 - 10$ 51. (a) $r = R/\sqrt{2}$ (b) $r = R\sqrt{3}/2$ (c) $v_r = 0$
53. 4 ft   55. 219 ft   57. $80

EXERCISE 4.2

1. $(-1, -1/2)$; min   3. $(1, 9)$; max
5. zeros $(-2, 0), (0, 0)$ 7. zeros $(-2, 0)$ $(4, 0)$ 9. vertex $(0, -4)$; zeros $(-2, 0), (2, 0)$

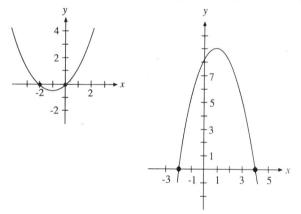

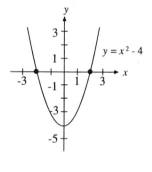

11. vertex $(2, 1)$; zeros $(0, 0), (4, 0)$ 13. vertex $(-2, 0)$; zero $(-2, 0)$

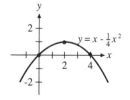

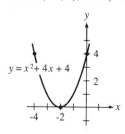

15.   vertex $(-5/2, -9/4)$; zeros $(-1, 0)$, $(-4, 0)$

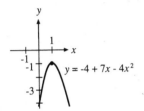

$x^2 + 5x - y + 4 = 0$

17.   vertex $(-2, 3)$; no zeros

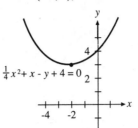

$\frac{1}{4}x^2 + x - y + 4 = 0$

19.   no zeros; vertex $(0, 5)$

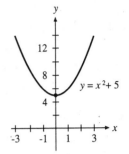

$y = x^2 + 5$

21.   no zeros; vertex $(7/8, -15/16)$

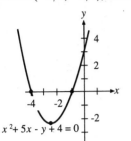

$y = -4 + 7x - 4x^2$

23.   zeros $(10, 0)$, $(30, 0)$; vertex $(20, 10)$

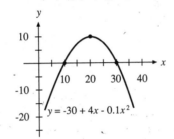

$y = -30 + 4x - 0.1x^2$

25.   no zeros; vertex $(-1, 8/5)$

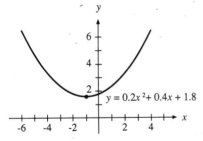

$y = 0.2x^2 + 0.4x + 1.8$

27.   (a)   zero $(0, 0)$; vertex $(0, 0)$

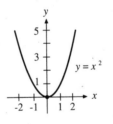

$y = x^2$

(b)   zero $(0, 0)$; vertex $(0, 0)$

$y = -x^2$

(c)   zeros $(-1, 0)$, $(1, 0)$; vertex $(0, -1)$

$y = x^2 - 1$

(d)   zero $(1, 0)$; vertex $(1, 0)$

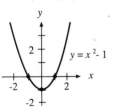

$y = (x - 1)^2$

29.

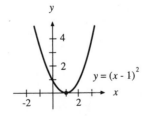

$(0, 20)$ Vertex

$x = 20 - 0.01v^2$

$20\sqrt{5}$

31. 400   33. 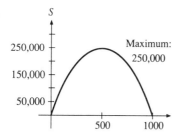   35.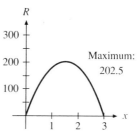

37. Equation   (a) (384.62, 202.31)   (b) (54, 46) Projectile (a) goes higher.

39. 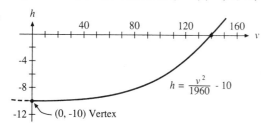   41. $A = (900x - 3x^2)/4$, 16,875 sq ft

EXERCISE 4.3

1. (a), (b) 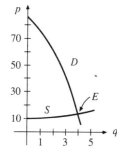   (c) See E on graph.   (d) $q = 4, p = \$14$

3. (a), (b) 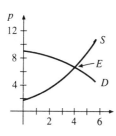   (c) See E on graph.   (d) $q = 4, p = \$6.60$ 5. $q = 10, p = \$196$

7. $p = \$27.08, q = 216\frac{2}{3}$ 9. $p = \$40, q = 30$ 11. $q = 90, p = \$50$ 13. $q = 70, p = \$62$
15. $x = 40$ units, $x = 50$ units   17. $x = 50, x = 300$ 19. $x = 15$ units; reject $x = 100$
21. \$41,173.61   23. \$356   25. $x = 55, P(55) = 2025$ 27. (a) $P(x) = -x^2 + 350x - 15,000$;
max is \$15,625   (b) no   (c) x-values agree   29. (a) $x = 28$ units, $x = 1000$ units   (b) \$651,041.67
(c) $P(x) = -x^2 + 1028x - 28,000$; max is \$236,196   (d) no

CHAPTER 4 REVIEW EXERCISES

1. $x = 0, x = -5/3$ 2. $x = 0, x = 4/3$ 3. $x = -2, x = -3$ 4. $x = (-5 + \sqrt{47})/2,$
$x = (-5 - \sqrt{47})/2$ 5. no real solutions   6. $x = \sqrt{3}/2, x = -\sqrt{3}/2$ 7. no real solutions
8. $z = -9, z = 3$ 9. $x = 8, x = -2$ 10. $x = 3, x = -1$ 11. $5/7, -4/5$ 12. $(-1 + \sqrt{2})/4,$
$(-1 - \sqrt{2})/4$ 13. $7/2, 100$ 14. $13/5, 90$ 15. $x = (-a \pm \sqrt{a^2 - 4b})/2$
16. $r = (2a \pm \sqrt{4a^2 + x^3 c})x$ 17. $1.64, -7051.64$ 18. $0.41, -2.38$

19. vertex $(-2, -2)$; zeros $(0, 0), (-4, 0)$ 20. vertex $(0, 4)$; zeros $(4, 0), (-4, 0)$

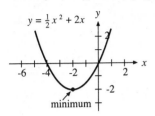

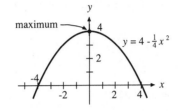

21. vertex $(1/2, 25/4)$; zeros $(-2, 0), (3, 0)$ 22. vertex $(2, 1)$; no real zeros

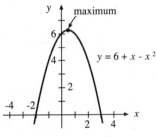

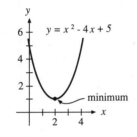

23. vertex $(-3, 0)$; zero $(-3, 0)$ 24. vertex $(3/2, 0)$; zero $(3/2, 0)$ 25. vertex $(0, -3)$; zeros $(-3, 0), (3, 0)$

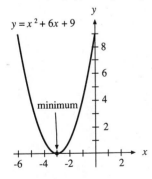

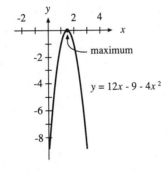

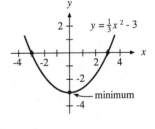

26. vertex $(0, 2)$; no real zeros   27. vertex $(-1, 4)$; no real zeros   28. vertex $(7/2, 9/4)$; zeros $(2, 0), (5, 0)$

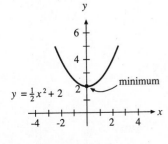

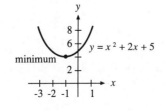

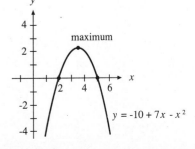

29. vertex (100, 1000); zeros (0, 0), (200, 0)

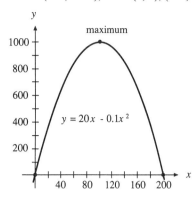

30. vertex (75, 6.25); zeros (50, 0), (100, 0)

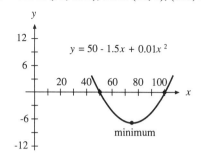

31. (a) $x = 200$ ft   (b) $A = 30{,}000$ sq ft

32.

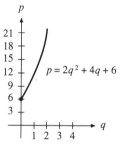

33.

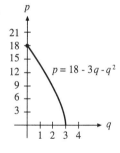

34. (a)

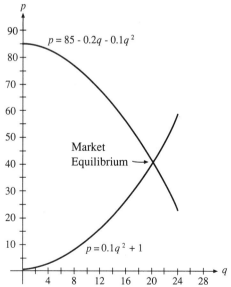

(b) $p = 41, q = 20$

35. $p = 400, q = 10$ 36. $p = 10, q = 20$ 37. $x = 46 + 2\sqrt{89}, x = 46 - 2\sqrt{89}$

38. (15, 1275), (60, 2400)   39. max revenue $= \$2500$; max profit $= \$506.25$

40. max profit = 12.25; break-even $x = 100$, $x = 30$ 41. $x = 50$, $P(50) = 640$

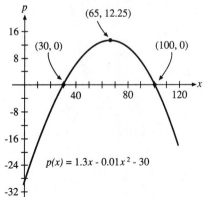

$p(x) = 1.3x - 0.01x^2 - 30$

42. (a) $C = 15,000 + 140x + 0.04x^2$; $R = 300x - 0.06x^2$ (b) 100, 1500   (c) 2500
     (d) $P = 160x - 15,000 - 0.1x^2$; max at 800   (e) at 2500: $P = -240,000$; at 800: $P = 49,000$

EXERCISE 5.1

1. 3.162278   3. 0.01296525   5. 1.44225   7. 7.3891   9. 0.04979

11.

$y = 4^x$

13.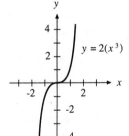

$y = 2(x^3)$

15.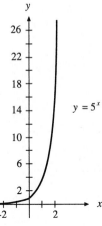

$y = 5^x$

17.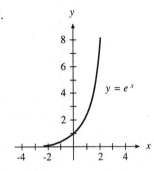

$y = e^x$

19.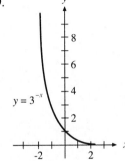

$y = 3^{-x}$

21.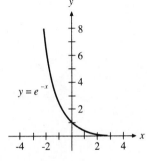

$y = e^{-x}$

23.
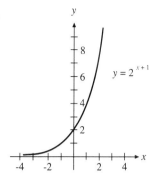
$y = 2^{x+1}$

25.
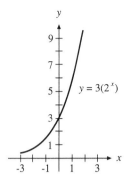
$y = 3(2^x)$

27.
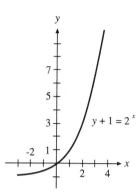
$y + 1 = 2^x$

29.
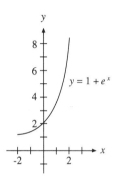
$y = 1 + e^x$

31.   Identical shape, 1 unit higher

33.
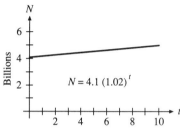
$N = 4.1\,(1.02)^t$

35.
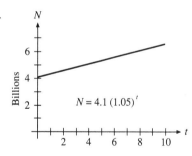
$N = 4.1\,(1.05)^t$

37.
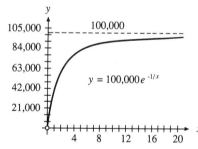
$y = 100{,}000e^{-1/x}$

39.
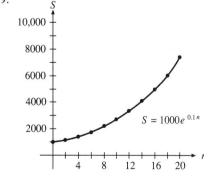
$S = 1000e^{0.1n}$

41.
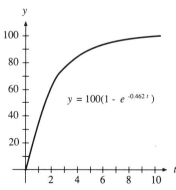
$y = 100(1 - e^{-0.462\,t})$

43.
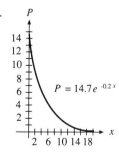
$P = 14.7e^{-0.2\,x}$

EXERCISE 5.2

1. $2^4 = 16$ 3. $4^{1/2} = 2$ 5. $x = 8$ 7. $x = 1/2$ 9. $\log_2 32 = 5$ 11. $\log_4 (1/4) = -1$

13. 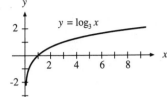   15. 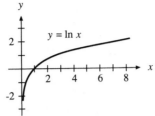   17.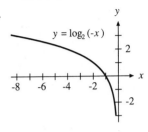

19. 3   21. 1/2   23. 4   25. x 27. 1   29. 2   31. x 33. 2   35. 1.0792
37. 0.5118   39. -2.4082 41. 8.319   43. $\log x - \log (x + 1)$ 45. $\log_7 x + \frac{1}{3} \log_7 (x + 4)$
47. $\log_a a^x = x$. Let $v = \log_a a^x$. In exp form: $a^v = a^x$; $\therefore v = x$.   49. $\log_a (MN) = \log_a M + \log_a N$.
Let $u = \log_a M$; $v = \log_a N$. In exp form $a^u = M$ and $a^v = N$; $\therefore MN = a^u \cdot a^v = a^{u+v}$.
In log form $\log_a (MN) = u + v = \log_a M + \log_a N$.   51. 5.903   53. 15.8   55. 4:1
57. 140 decibels   59. 2512:1   61. (a) 7.4   (b) 4.2   (c) 2.2   63. (a) 0.001
(b) 1.62×10^{-8} (c) 0.0000001

EXERCISE 5.3

1. 128,402   3. (a) 600   (b) 2119   (c) 3000   (d)   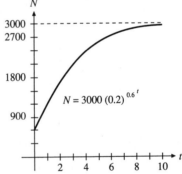   5. 1979

7. (a) 37   (b) 1.5 hours   9. (a) 52   (b) tenth   11. (a) 2038   (b) 4.9 months
13. (a) 69%   (b) 37,204 years (approx.)   15. (a) \$4.98   (b) 8   17. \$502   19. (a) \$333.81
(b) 147   21. \$420.09   23. \$2707   25. (a) 0 lb   (b) 29.95 lb   (c) 0.21 min   27. (a) $x = 16, 0.2\%$
(b) 10.56 min   (c) 0.06%   29. (a) \$5469.03   (b) 7 yr, 9 mo (approx.)

CHAPTER 5 REVIEW EXERCISES

1. (a) $\log_2 y = x$ (b) $\log_3 2x = y$ 2. (a) $7^{-2} = 1/49$ (b) $4^{-1} = x$

3. A.

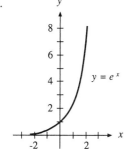

$y = e^x$

4. A.

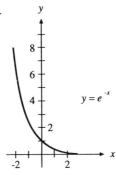

$y = e^{-x}$

5.

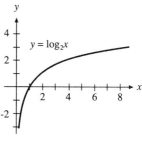

$y = \log_2 x$

6.

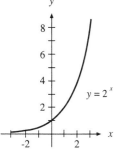

$y = 2^x$

7.

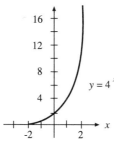

$y = 4^x$

8.

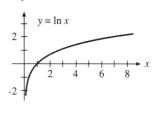

$y = \ln x$

9.

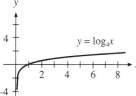

$y = \log_4 x$

10.

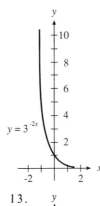

$y = 3^{-2x}$

11.

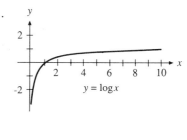

$y = \log x$

12.

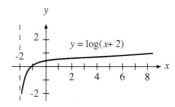

$y = \log(x + 2)$

13.

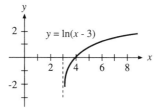

$y = \ln(x - 3)$

14.

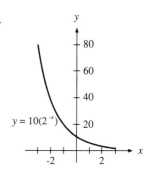

$y = 10(2^{-x})$

15. 0   16. 2   17. 1/2   18. −1   19. 8   20. 1   21. 5   22. 3.15   23. 0.6020
24. 0.6021   25. 1.8062   26. 1.8063   27. $\log y + \log z$ 28. $\frac{1}{2}\ln(x+1) - \frac{1}{2}\ln x$ 29. no
30. −2   31. 5   32. 1   33. 0   34. (a) −3.9   (b) 0.14 B_0 (c) 0.004 B_0 (d) yes
35. (a) 3000   (b) 8603   (c) 10,000   36. (a) $27,440.58   (b) 12 weeks   37. $1366.19
38. 5.8 years   39. (a) $5532.77   (b) 5.13 years

EXERCISE 6.1

1. (a) $9600   (b) $19,600   3. (a) $30   (b) $1030   5. $864   7. $3850   9. 13%
11. (a) 6.5%   (b) 5.65%   13. $1631.07   15. pay on time   17. 3, 6, 9, 12, 15, 18, 21, 24, 27, 30
19. 1/3, 2/3, 1, 4/3, 5/3, 2, 7/3, 8/3   21. −1/4, 1/4, −1/4, 1/4, −1/4, 1/4   23. −1/2, 1/4, −1/6, 1/8,
−1/10, 1/12   25. −1, −1/4, −1/15, 0; $a_{10} = 1/20$ 27. 11, 14, 17   29. 15/2, 9, 21/2, 12   31. 25
33. 5/2   35. 15   37. 100   39. 67.5   41. 30   43. 6   45. 21, 34, 55   47. $2400
49. the job starting at $20,000   51. (a) $3000   (b) $4500   (c) Plan II, by $1500   (d) $10,000
(e) $13,500   (f) Plan II, by $3500   (g) Plan II

EXERCISE 6.2

(Minor differences may occur if calculators are used.)

1. $24,846.78   3. $3086.45   5. $4755.03   7. $6844.36   9. $7309.98   11. $502.47
13. $50.26 more at 8%   15. 8.24%   17. 6.18%   19. 3 years   21. 4%   23. $3996.02
25. $63,128.75   27. 5.12 years (approx.)   29. 24, 48, 96, 192   31. 24, 16, 32/3   33. 320
35. 81/4   37. 2184   39. 2.625   41. 121   43. 422/27   45. $350,580 (approx.)
47. 24.4 million (approx.)   49. 35 years   51. 40.5 ft   53. $4096   55. 320,000
57. $7,231,366   59. $1801.14   61. 15,625   63. 305,175,780

EXERCISE 6.3

1. $14.49   3. $7328.22   5. $1072.97   7. $1074.82   9. $6042.22   11. $4774.55
13. $103,213.29   15. $6.153291, or $6.15   17. $1180.78   19. $4152.32   21. $26,517.13
23. $976.32   25. $1165.23   27. $2115.07   29. $11,689.59   31. $2,128,391
33. $7957.86   35. $74,993.20   37. $19,922.97   39. $1317.98

EXERCISE 6.4

1. (a) $180   (b) $1980   (c) $165   3. (a) $400   (b) $100   (c) no   5. (a) $400
(b) $1600   (c) worse deal   7. (a) $1945.95   (b) $216.22 for 8 payments; last payment is $216.19
9. 18.5%   11. 19.5%   13. $2504.56   15. $1288.29

17.

Period	Payment	Interest	Balance reduction	Unpaid balance
				$100,000.00
1	$39.505.50	$9000.00	$30,505.50	69,494.50
2	39,505.50	6254.51	33,250.99	36,243.51
3	39,505.43	3261.92	36,243.51	0.00
	118,516.43	18,516.43	100,000.00	

19.

Period	Payment	Interest	Balance reduction	Unpaid balance
				$20,000.00
1	$5380.54	$600.00	$4780.54	15,219.46
2	5380.54	456.58	4923.96	10,295.50
3	5380.54	308.87	5071.67	5,223.83
4	5380.54	156.71	5223.83	0.00
	21,522.16	1522.16	20,000.00	

21. $4466.29   23. $3443.61   25. $4359.23   27. $1237.78   29. $2967.75
31. $62,473.28   33. $32.084.31   35. $6274.50   37. $4372.20   39. $2921.40
41. $265.24   43. sinking fund saves $423.90

EXERCISE 6.5

1. $1400/yr, 9.3%   3. $700   5. $4000   7. (a) $7000   (b) $7000   9. (a) 2.8¢/unit
(b) $7000   11. 1st: $18,250; 2nd: $9125; 3rd: $4562.50; 4th: $2281.51   13. 1st: $1800; 2nd: $1080;
3rd: $620; 4th: $0; 5th: $0   15. (a) 1st: $10,000; 2nd: $2000; 3rd: $0   (b) this method
17. 1st year: $6000; 2nd year: $4000; 3rd year: $2000   19. (a) $13,658.54   (b) $10,585.37
21. 1st: $3000; 2nd: $2000; 3rd: $1000

EXERCISE 6.6

1. 1st: $450; 2nd: $900; 3rd: $900; 4th: $900; 5th: $900; 6th: $450   3. 1st: $2550; 2nd: $4950; 3rd: $4950;
4th: $2550   5. (a) $6666.67   (b) $20,000   7. 1st: $675; 2nd: $990; 3rd: $945; 4th: $945; 5th: $945
9. (a) 1st: $3750; 2nd: $5700; 3rd: $5550   (b) this method   11. (a) $12,000   (b) $15,000
13. $5000   15. $5975   17. (a) $5000   (b) $10,000   19.

Year	Depreciation
1	$3000
2	4800
3	2880
4	1728
5	1728
6	864

21.

Year	Depreciation
1	$2856
2	4898
3	3498
4	2498
5	1786
6	1786
7	1786
8	892

23.

Year	Depreciation
1	$16,500
2	22,500
3	7,500
4	3,500

CHAPTER 6 REVIEW EXERCISES

1. 1, 1/4, 1/9, 1/16   2. 25   3. 19   4. $4\frac{1}{2}$ 5. 8   6. $40\frac{4}{9}$ 7. $10,880   8. $6\frac{2}{3}\%$
9. $4650   10. the $20,000 job ($245,000 vs. $234,000)   11. $11,239.42   12. $372.79
13. $1601.03   14. $1616.06   15. $11,466.64   16. $3466.64   17. 8.24%   18. 2^{63}

19. $2^{32} - 1$ 20. $29,428.47   21. $31,194.18   22. $1863.93   23. $64,176.58   24. $19,972.79
25. $12,007.09   26. $155   27. $3328   28. $88.85   29. $6069.44   30. $32,834.69
31. $9800/yr   32. 1st: $20,000; 2nd: $16,000; 3rd: $12,800; 4th: $10,240   33. 1st: $17,818.18;
2nd: $16,036.36; 3rd: $14,254.54; 4th: $12,472.73   34. 1st: $10,000; 2nd: $20,000; 3rd: $20,000; 4th: $20,000;
5th: $20,000; 6th: $10,000   35. 1st: $15,000; 2nd: $22,000; 3rd: $21,000; 4th: $21,000; 5th: $21,000.
36. (a) $5000   (b) $95,000   (c) $19,250

37. Year	Depreciation
1	$2000
2	3200
3	1920
4	1152
5	1152
6	576

38. Year	Depreciation
1	$4284
2	7347
3	5247
4	3747
5	2679
6	2679
7	2679
8	1338

EXERCISE 7.1

1. (a) $1/6$ (b) 0   (c) $1/2$ 3. $2/5$ 5. $1/4$ 7. (a) $1/13$ (b) $1/2$ (c) $1/4$
9. (a) $2/5$ (b) $3/5$ (c) 1   11. (a) $3/10$ (b) $1/2$ (c) $1/5$ (d) $3/5$ (e) $7/10$
13. {HH, HT, TH, TT};   (a) $1/4$ (b) $1/2$ (c) $1/4$ 15. (a) $1/12$ (b) $1/12$ (c) $1/36$
17. (a) $1/2$ (b) $5/12$ 19. $13/31$ 21. $1/2$ 23. (a) $1/5$ (b) $1/14$ (c) $13/14$
(d) $3/7$ 25. $1/3$ 27. $3/8$ 29. (a) no   (b) {BB, BG, GB, GG}   (c) $1/2$ 31. $1/5$
33. $3/125$ 35. Pr(A) = 0.000019554 or approx. 1.9 accidents per 100,000
Pr(B) = 0.000035919 or approx. 3.6 accidents per 100,000
Pr(C) = 0.000037679 or approx. 3.8 accidents per 100,000
Intersection C is the most dangerous.
37. (a) $557/1200$ (b) $11/120$ 39. (a) boy: $1/5$; girl: $4/5$ (b) boy: .4946; girl: .5054   (c) part b
41. $35/250 = 7/50$ 43. $1/10$

EXERCISE 7.2

1. $1/36$ 3. $1/12$ 5. $1/8$ 7. $7/8$ 9. (a) $3/50$ (b) $1/15$ 11. (a) $4/25$ (b) $9/25$
(c) $6/25$ (d) 0   13. (a) $1/10$ (b) $3/10$ (c) $3/10$ (d) 0   15. $5/68$ 17. (a) $4/663$
(b) $1/663$ 19. (a) $1/169$ (b) $1/221$ 21. $(.95)^5 = .774$ 23. .06   25. no   27. (a) .04
(b) .05   (c) .02   29. (a) .603   (b) .397   (c) .307   31. $7/8$ 33. (a) $364/365$
(b) $1/365$ 35. (a) .59   (b) .41

EXERCISE 7.3

1. $1/3$ 3. $10/17$ 5. $2/3$ 7. $3/4$ 9. $2/3$ 11. (a) $(5/15) \cdot (5/15) = 1/9$
(b) $(5/15) \cdot (4/15) + (4/15) \cdot (5/15) = 8/45$ (c) $(9/15) \cdot (9/15) = 9/25$ 13. (a) $1/7$ (b) $5/7$
15. (a) $28/121$ (b) $56/121$ 17. (a) $6/25$ (b) $9/25$ (c) $12/25$ (d) $19/25$ 19. $1/2$
21. $34/100$ 23. $21/35$ 25. .5   27. (a) $11/12$ (b) $5/6$ 29. $1/2$ 31. $3/4$ 33. .72
35. $61/100$ 37. $27/40$ 39. $13/20$

EXERCISE 7.4

1. (a) $1/2$ (b) $1/13$ 3. (a) $1/3$ (b) $1/3$ 5. $4/9$ 7. (a) $2/3$ (b) $4/9$ 9. (a) $1/4$
(b) $1/2$ 11. (a) $4/17$ (b) $4/17$ 13. (a) $(5/9) \cdot (4/8) \cdot (3/7) = 5/42$

(b) $(5/9) \cdot (4/8) \cdot (4/7) + (5/9) \cdot (4/8) \cdot (4/7) + (4/9) \cdot (5/8) \cdot (4/7) = 10/21$
(c) $(5/9) \cdot (4/8) \cdot (4/7) + (5/9) \cdot (4/8) \cdot (3/7) + (4/9) \cdot (3/8) \cdot (2/7) + (4/9) \cdot (5/8) \cdot (3/7) = 4/9$ 15. $1/3$
17. $2/3$ 19. $.15$ 21. $9/16$ 23. (a) $9/20$ (b) $2/3$ 25. $.079$ 27. (a) $11/20$
(b) $39/55$ 29. (a) $49/100$ (b) $12/49$ 31. $43/50$ 33. $65/87$

EXERCISE 7.5

1. 360 3. $151{,}200$ 5. $5! = 120$ 7. 1 9. 1 11. $n + 1$ 13. 16
15. (a) $6 \cdot 5 \cdot 4 \cdot 3 = 360$ (b) $6^4 = 1296$ 17. 120 19. 24 21. $35{,}152$ 23. 24
25. $2^{10} = 1024$ 27. $10! = 3{,}628{,}800$ 29. $1/120$ 31. (a) $1/3$ (b) $1/3$

33. (a) $(1/5)^{10} = 1/9{,}765{,}625$ (b) $(4/5)^{10} = .107$ (c) $.893$ 35. $\dfrac{7(9 \cdot 8 \cdot 7 \cdot 6 \cdot 5 \cdot 4)}{10 \cdot 9 \cdot 8 \cdot 7 \cdot 6 \cdot 5 \cdot 4} = \dfrac{7}{10}$
37. (a) $3^6 = 729$ (b) $1/729$

EXERCISE 7.6

1. 15 3. 21 5. 1 7. 1 9. 1 11. $_{13}C_{10} = 286; \; _{12}C_9 + \, _{12}C_{10} = 220 + 66 = 286$ 13. 10
15. 252 17. $30{,}045{,}015$ 19. 792 21. 210 23. $2{,}891{,}999{,}880$ 25. (a) $.0005$ (b) $.002$
27. (a) $1/22$ (b) $6/11$ (c) $9/22$ 29. (a) 7.5162×10^{-16} approx.   (b) $.66231$ approx.
(c) 1.3115×10^{-5} 31. (a) $.721$ (b) $.262$ (c) $.279$ 33. $18/35$ 35. (a) $.033$ (b) $.633$

EXERCISE 7.7

1. $15/8$ 3. 5 5. $8/3$ 7. 2 9. 3 11. 2 13. 1.85 15. 1 17. $\$3$ 19. $\$1.67$
21. If he buys 0, his profit is 0. If he buys 100, his expected profit is
$\$3(100)(.25) + \$3(50)(.20) + \$3(10)(.55) + \$(-1)50(.20) + \$(-1)90(.55) = \$62$. If he buys 200, his expected profit
is $\$3(180)(.25) + \$3(50)(.20) + \$3(10)(.55) + (-\$1)(20)(.25) + (-\$1)(150)(.20) + (-\$1)(190)(.55) = \$42$. He
should buy 100.   23. TV: 37,500; personal: 35,300; TV   25. $\$10$

EXERCISE 7.8

1. can   3. cannot   5. cannot   7. can   9. $[.248 \quad .752]$ 11. $[.228 \quad .236 \quad .536]$ 13. $[1/4 \quad 3/$
15. $[1/4 \quad 1/4 \quad 1/2]$ 17. $[.5 \quad .4 \quad .1]; [.44 \quad .43 \quad .13]; [.431 \quad .43 \quad .139]; [.4292 \quad .4291 \quad .1417]$

19. $\begin{array}{c} \\ R \\ N \end{array}\begin{array}{cc} R & N \\ \begin{bmatrix} .8 & .2 \\ .3 & .7 \end{bmatrix} \end{array}$ 21. $.45$ 23. $\begin{array}{c} \\ A \\ F \\ V \end{array}\begin{array}{ccc} A & F & V \\ \begin{bmatrix} 0 & .7 & .3 \\ .6 & 0 & .4 \\ .8 & .2 & 0 \end{bmatrix} \end{array}$ 25. $[.3928 \quad .37 \quad .2372]$

27. $[46/113 \quad 38/113 \quad 29/113]$ 29. $\begin{array}{c} \\ r \\ u \end{array}\begin{array}{cc} r & u \\ \begin{bmatrix} .7 & .3 \\ .1 & .9 \end{bmatrix} \end{array}; [1/4 \quad 3/4]$ 31. $[1/14 \quad 3/14 \quad 5/7]$ 33. $[4/7 \quad 2/7 \quad 1/7]$

35. $49/100 \quad 42/100 \quad 9/100]$

CHAPTER 7 REVIEW EXERCISES

1. $1/3$ 2. $1/13$ 3. $3/4$ 4. $2/13$ 5. $16/169$ 6. $2/7$ 7. $2/13$ 8. $7/13$ 9. $1/2$
10. $1/3$ 11. (a) $2/9$ (b) $2/3$ (c) $7/9$ 12. 26^3 13. $8/15$ 14. 30 15. (a) $3/14$
(b) $4/7$ (c) $3/8$ 16. 2.4 17. $5/8$ 18. $58/100$ 19. $4! = 24$ 20. $_8P_4 = 1680$
21. (a) $63/2000$ (b) $60/63$ 22. $_{12}C_4 = 495$ 23. $_8C_4 = 70$ 24. (a) $(_{10}C_5)(_2C_1)/\,_{12}C_6$

(b) $\dfrac{(_{10}C_5)(_2C_1) + (_{10}C_4)(_2C_2)}{_{12}C_6}$ 25. (a) $_{12}C_2 = 66$ (b) $_{12}C_3 = 220$ 26. $-50¢$ 27. $5/56$

28. $33/56$ 29. $15/22$ 30. $[.135 \quad .51 \quad .355][.09675 \quad .3305 \quad .57275][.0640875 \quad .288275 \quad .6476375]$
31. $[12/265 \quad 68/265 \quad 37/53]$

EXERCISE 8.1

1.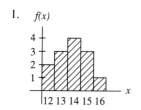

3.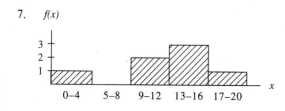

5.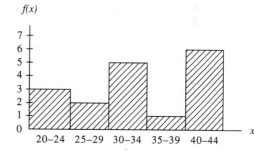

7.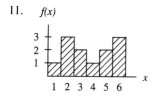

9.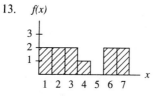

11.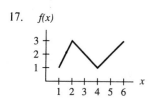

13.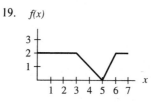

15.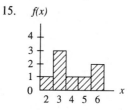

17.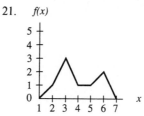

23.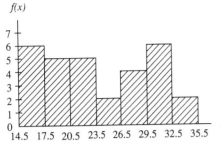

25.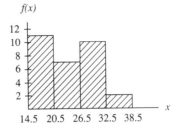

27.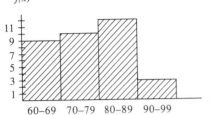

29.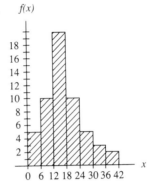

31.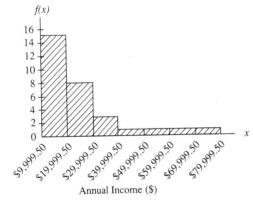

33.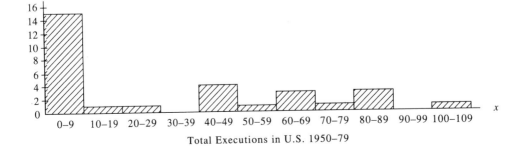

35.   *f(x)*

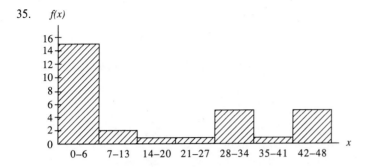

Number of Blacks Executed in U.S. 1950–79

37.   *f(x)*

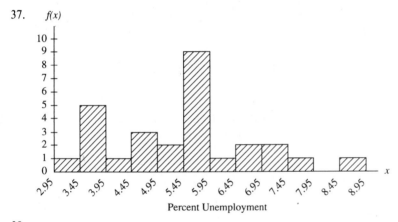

Percent Unemployment

39.   *f(x)*

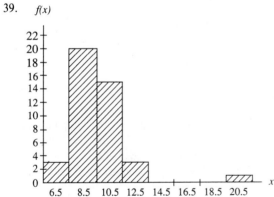

Number of Deaths per 1000 Live Births

EXERCISE 8.2

1. 3   3. 13   5. no mode   7. 6   9. 39   11. 5   13. 12   15. 6   17. 8.5   19. 6
21. 4   23. 14   25. mode = 2, median = 4.5, mean = 6   27. mode = 17, median = 18.5,
mean = 23.5   29. mode = 5.3, median = 5.3, mean = 5.32   31. 5   33. 127.1   35. 15.2
37. 8.48   39. (a) $30,000   (b) $18,000   (c) $16,000   41. mean   43. median   45. 78

EXERCISE 8.3

1. 9   3. 14   5. 4, 8.5714, 2.9277   7. 14, 4.6667, 2.1602   9. 6, 24.2857, 4.9281
11. 8, 10.8571, 3.2950   13. 2.73, 1.35   15. 9, 2.56   17. 6.75, 2.96   19. 1.12   21. 1.27
23. 6.91   25. $\bar{x} = \$7800, s = \$262.47$ 27. $\bar{x} = 6, s = 2.847$ 29. $30,000; $22,310.93   31. 7.40

EXERCISE 8.4

1. .0595   3. (a) 1/64   (b) 5/16   (c) 15/64   5. .0284   7. (a) .2304   (b) .0102
(c) .3174   9. .0585   11. .2759   13. (a) .375   (b) .0625   15. (a) .1157   (b) .4823
17. (a) 27/64   (b) 27/128   (c) 81/256   19. (a) .0729   (b) .5905   (c) .9914   21. .2457
23. .0007   25. (a) .1323   (b) .0308   27. (a) .9044   (b) .0914   (c) .0043   29. (a) .8683
(b) .2099   31. .740

EXERCISE 8.5

1. (a)

x	0	1	2	3
Pr(x)	125/216	25/72	5/72	1/216

(b) $3(1/6) = 1/2$ (c) $\sqrt{3(1/6)(5/6)} = (1/6)\sqrt{15}$

3. (a) 42   (b) 3.55   5. 2, 1.29   7. 4   9. 2   11. 2   13. 15
15. $a^6 + 6a^5b + 15a^4b^2 + 20a^3b^3 + 15a^2b^4 + 6ab^5 + b^6$ 17. $x^4 + 4x^3h + 6x^2h^2 + 4xh^3 + h^4$
19. (a) $100(.10) = 10$ (b) $\sqrt{100(.10)(.90)} = 3$ 21. (a) 60,000   (b) $\sqrt{24,000} = 154.919$
23. 59,690   25. (a) 4   (b) 1.79   27. 2, 1.41   29. 300

EXERCISE 8.6

1. 2   3. 1   5. .4641   7. .4641   9. $.4332 + .4821 = .9153$ 11. $.4713 - .3643 = .1070$
13. $.4987 - .4821 = .0166$ 15. .1915   17. .3944   19. .3944   21. .5381   23. .2957
25. (a) .3413   (b) .3413   (c) .6826   (d) .9546   27. $.4938 + .4938 = .9876$ 29. (a) .4192
(b) .025   (c) .0581   (d) .8965   31. (a) .0668   (b) .3085   (c) .3830   33. (a) .0475
(b) .2033   (c) .5934   35. (a) .0227   (b) .1587   (c) .8186

EXERCISE 8.7

1. (a) yes   (b) 50   (c) 1   3. 60, 2   5. 30, .5   7. .4938   9. .0606   11. 596 through 604
13. 79 through 81   15. (a) 100   (b) 3   (c) no   17. (a) .9546   (b) $.5 - .4773 = .0227$
(c) .0454   19. yes   21. .2287   23. Reject H_0. (The machine needs to be repaired.)
25. Accept H_0. (1600 hours is a reasonable estimate.)   27. Accept H_0; (not sufficient evidence the pill affects
blood pressure)   29. Reject H_0; (group's reaction time is faster than mean)

EXERCISE 8.8

1. $\hat{y} = 5.7x - 1.4$ 3. $\hat{y} = .11x + 2$ 5. $\hat{y} = -2.7x + 5$ 7. $r = .993$ 9. $r = .750$
11. $r = -.414$ 13. (a) $\hat{p} = -2.9q + 317$ (b) $r = -.978$ 15. (a) $\hat{y} = .57x - .0287$
(b) $r = .999$ 17. (a) $\hat{y} = .91x - .24$ (b) $r = .689$ 19. (a) $\hat{y} = .016x + 17$ (b) $r = 583$

CHAPTER 8 REVIEW EXERCISES

1. $f(x)$ 2. 3   3. $77/26 = 2.96$ 4. 3   5. $f(x)$

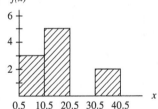

6. 15   7. 16   8. 15   9. $\bar{x} = 3.86$; $s^2 = 6.81$; $s = 2.61$ 10. $\bar{x} = 2$; $s^2 = 2.44$; $s = 1.56$
11. $(4/5)^5$ 12. (a) $(99{,}999/100{,}000)^{99{,}999} \approx 0.37$ (b) $1 - (99{,}999/100{,}000)^{100{,}000} \approx 0.63$ 13. $33/81$
14. $\mu = 4$, $\sigma = (2\sqrt{3}/3$ 15. (a) 1   (b) $(4/5)^4$ 16. $x^5 + 5x^4y + 10x^3y^2 + 10x^2y^3 + 5xy^4 + y^5$
17. .9165   18. .1498   19. .1039   20. .3413   21. .6826   22. .1360   23. .9546
24. .4773   25. .1360   26. $f(x)$ 27. 30.3%   28. 8.35%

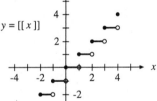

Class Marks

29. .297   30. .16308   31. Accept H_0; the machine appears to be working properly.   32. Reject H_0; the manufacturer's claim is not correct.   33. $\hat{y} = 0.68x + 23.8$ 34. $r = 0.99$. Based on this very small sample, there is a mathematical relationship between the values for these variables.

EXERCISE 9.1

1. 4   3. 3   5. 18   7. -1 9. 6   11. -4 13. 0   15. 6   17. 0   19. -2
21. $1/30$ 23. no limit ($\pm\infty$)   25. no limit ($\pm\infty$)   27. no limit ($\pm\infty$)   29. $3x^2$ 31. (a) 2
(b) 6   (c) -8 (d) $-1/2$ 33. $\lim_{x \to 2} f(x) = 5$ 35. (a) 1   (b) 2   (c) doesn't exist
37. (a) 4   (b) 4   (c) 4   39. 0   41. 1   43. $5/3$ 45. 0   47. ∞
49.   51. no limit   55. (a) doesn't exist   (b) no

$y = [[x]]$

57. 18   61. 0

EXERCISE 9.2

1. yes   3. yes   5. no, $f(-3)$ undefined   7. no, $f(1)$ undefined   9. no, $f(-1)$ undefined
11. yes   13. no, $\lim_{x \to -1} f(x) \neq \lim_{x \to -1} f(x)$ 15. no   17. yes   19. continuous
21. missing point discontinuity at $x = 5$.   23. missing point discontinuity at $x = -2$.
25. infinite discontinuity at $x = -2$.   27. continuous   29. continuous   31. jump discontinuity
at $x = 3$.   33. (a) $x = -2$ (b) 0 (c) 0 (d) $y = 0$ 35. (a) $x = -2, x = 3$ (b) 2 (c) 2
(d) $y = 2$ 37. vert: $x = 3$; horiz: $y = 2$ 39. vert: $x = 2$, $x = -2$; horiz: $y = 0$ 41. vert: $x = 5/2$;
horiz: none   43. (a) yes (b) no (c) no   45. (a) jump discontinuity at $x = 0$
(b) It changes from ice to water, or from solid to liquid.   47. yes   49. yes   51. yes

EXERCISE 9.3

1. $-1/2$ 3. 0   5. $2x$ 7. 3   9. $8x - 2$ 11. $3x^2$ 13. 14   15. 117   17. (a) 1
(b) 1   19. 5   21. 6   23. $y = 6x - 9$ 25. $y = 6x - 2$ 27. $-3; 4$ 29. $5/2; -9$
31. $y = 3x - 4$ 33. a 35. A, C, E   37. A, E   39. (a) 200 (b) 100 (c) 0
(d) changing from increasing to decreasing   41. (a) 100 (b) -100 (c) decreasing
43. (a) $1 - 0.4x$ (b) -3 45. 68 mph   47. (a) 5 g/hr (b) 7.5 g/hr (c) 18.75 g/hr
(d) 30 g/hr   49. 48 mph

EXERCISE 9.4

1. 0   3. 1   5. $3x^2$ 7. $12x^2$ 9. $40q^7$ 11. 3   13. $18x^5 - 24x$ 15. $15q^2 + 8q$
17. $-3x^{-4}$ 19. $-2x^{-3} = -2/x^3$ 21. $\frac{2}{3}x^{-1/3} = 2/(3x^{1/3})$ 23. $-\frac{4}{5}x^{-9/5} = -4/(5x^{9/5})$
25. $\frac{2}{3}q^{-1/3} = 2/(3\sqrt[3]{q})$ 27. $-4x^{-9/5} + \frac{2}{5}x^{-4/5}$ 29. $9x^2 + 10/x^6$ 31. $-9/x^4 + 1/(3x^{4/3}) - 5/(2\sqrt{x})$
33. $1/\sqrt{x} + 6\sqrt{x}$ 35. 19   37. 0   39. $y = 8x - 3$ 41. $y = 3$ 43. $(2, -1)$
45. (a) $v = 112 - 32t$ (b) $48 = v$ when $t = 2$; up   47. $dy/dt = 8t + 2$ 49. 70 gal/min
51. (a) $298.40 (b) Sale of the next unit yields approx. $298.40.   53. (a) $\bar{C}'(x) = -4000/x^2 + 0.1$
(b) 200 units   55. $-$120,000

EXERCISE 9.5

1. $y' = 3x^2 + 2x - 6$ 3. $dp/dq = 9q^2 - 2q + 6$
5. $f'(x) = (x^{12} + 3x^4 + 4)(12x^2) + (4x^3 - 1)(12x^{11} + 12x^3)$ 7. $R'(x) = 18x^2 - 4x + 300$
9. $y' = (3x + 1)/(2\sqrt{x})$ 11. $y' = (4\sqrt{x} + 3/x)(1/\sqrt[3]{x^2} + 10/x^3) + (3\sqrt[3]{x} - 5/x^2 - 5^2)(2/\sqrt{x} - 3/x^2)$
13. -8 15. $y' = (-x^2 - 1)/(x^2 - 1)^2$ 17. $\dfrac{dp}{dq} = (q^2 - 4q - 1)/(q - 2)^2$
19. $y' = (-x^6 - 4x^3 - 3x^2)/(x^3 + 1)^2$ 21. $dp/dq = (2q + 1)/[\sqrt[3]{q^2}(1 - q)^2]$
23. $y' = (2x^3 - 6x^2 - 8)/(x - 2)^2$ 25. $3/4$ 27. $3/5$ 29. $y = \frac{10}{3}x - \frac{10}{3}$ 31. $(1/3, -50/27)$
and $(1, -2)$ 33. $dy = (3x^2 + 8x + 5)dx$ 35. $ds = (3x^2 + 2x)dx$ 37. $(1 - 2x)dx/[2\sqrt{x}(2x + 1)^2]$
39. $C'(p) = 810,000/(100 - p)^2$ 41. $R'(x) = (12x^2 + 12x - 27)/(2x + 1)^2$ 43. $S = 1000x - x^2$
45. $dp/dt = 10,000/(t + 10)^2$ 47. $dR/dn = r(1 - r)/[1 + (n - 1)r]^2$

EXERCISE 9.6

1. $6x(x^2 + 1)^2$ 3. $4(8x - 4)(4x^2 - 4x + 1)^3 = 16(2x - 1)^7$ 5. $-6x/(x^2 + 2)^4$ 7. $-4(x + 2)(x^2 + 4x)^{-3}$
9. $-3(2x + 3)(x^2 + 3x + 4)^{-4}$ 11. $\dfrac{-3(6x^2 + 3)}{4(2x^3 + 3x + 5)^{7/4}}$ 13. $(x + 2)/\sqrt{x^2 + 4x + 5}$

15. $(6 - 4x)/\sqrt{3x - x^2}$ 17. $16x(x^2 - 3)^4$ 19. $\dfrac{15(3x + 1)^4 - 3}{7}$ 21. $96{,}768$ 23. 2

25. $y = -3x + 4$ 27. $9x - 5y = 2$ 29. $x = 0, x = -2, x = 2$ 31. $-4x/\sqrt{x^2 + 10}$

33. (a) $8\pi\ \text{in}^2/\text{min}$ (b) $80\pi\ \text{in}^2/\text{min}$ 35. (a) $dy/dt = 4t(t^2 + 1)$ (b) 4040

37. $y' = kac/(2\sqrt{cat}\,)$ 39. $dy/dx = (8k/5)(x - x_0)^{3/5}$ 41. $10\ \text{ft/sec}$

43. (a) $C = (dQ/dt)/(dV/dt)$ (b) $dQ/dV = dQ/dt \cdot dt/dV = (dQ/dt)/(dV/dt)$

EXERCISE 9.7

1. 0 3. $4(-4x^{-5}); -16/x^5$ 5. $15x^2 + 4(-x^{-2}); 15x^2 - 4/x^2$

7. $(x^2 - 2)1 + (x + 4)(2x); 3x^2 + 8x - 2$ 9. $\dfrac{x^2(3x^2) - (x^3 + 1)(2x)}{(x^2)^2}; (x^3 - 2)/x^3$

11. $(3x^2 - 4)(x^3 - 4x)^9$ 13. $\frac{5}{3}x^3[3(4x^5 - 5)^2(20x^4)] + (4x^5 - 5)^3(5x^2); 5x^2(4x^5 - 5)^2(24x^5 - 5)$

15. $(x - 1)^2(2x) + (x^2 + 1)\,2(x - 1); 2(x - 1)(2x^2 - x + 1)$

17. $\dfrac{(x^2 + 1)\,3(x^2 - 4)^2(2x) - (x^2 - 4)^3(2x)}{(x^2 + 1)^2}; \dfrac{2x(x^2 - 4)^2(2x^2 + 7)}{(x^2 + 1)^2}$

19. $3[(q + 1)(q^3 - 3)]^2[(q + 1)\,3q^2 + (q^3 - 3)1]; 3(4q^3 + 3q^2 - 3)[(q + 1)(q^3 - 3)]^2$

21. $4[x^2(x^2 + 3x)]^3[x^2(2x + 3) + (x^2 + 3x)(2x)]; 4x^2(4x + 9)[x^2(x^2 + 3x)]^3$

23. $4\left(\dfrac{2x - 1}{x^2 + x}\right)^3\left[\dfrac{(x^2 + x)2 - (2x - 1)(2x + 1)}{(x^2 + x)^2}\right]; \dfrac{4(-2x^2 + 2x + 1)(2x - 1)^3}{(x^2 + x)^5}$

25. $(8x^4 + 3)^2\,3(x^3 - 4x)^2(3x^2 - 4) + (x^3 - 4x)^3\,2(8x^4 + 3)(32x^3);$
$(8x^4 + 3)(x^3 - 4x)^2(136x^6 - 352x^4 + 27x^2 - 36)$

27. $\dfrac{(4 - x^2)\frac{1}{3}(x^2 + 5)^{-2/3}(2x) - (x^2 + 5)^{1/3}(-2x)}{(4 - x^2)^2}; \dfrac{2x(2x^2 + 19)}{3\sqrt[3]{(x^2 + 5)^2} \cdot (4 - x^2)^2}$

29. $(x^2)\frac{1}{4}(4x - 3)^{-3/4}(4) + (4x - 3)^{1/4}(2x); (9x^2 - 6x)/\sqrt[4]{(4x - 3)^3}$

31. $(2x)\frac{1}{2}(x^3 + 1)^{-1/2}(3x^2) + (x^3 + 1)^{1/2}(2); (5x^3 + 2)/\sqrt{x^3 + 1}$ 33. $dp/dx = 90(3x + 1)^2$

35. (a) $\$59{,}900$ (b) It is increasing.   37. $C'(y) = 1/\sqrt{y + 1} + 0.4$ 39. $dV/dx = 144 - 96x + 12x^2$

EXERCISE 9.8

1. $\overline{MC} = 8$ 3. $\overline{MC} = 13 + 2x$ 5. $\overline{MC} = 3x^2 - 12x + 24$ 7. $\overline{MC} = 27 + 3x^2$ 9. $\$10$; the cost will increase by $\$10$.   11. $\$46$; the cost will increase by $\$46$.   13. $\overline{MC}$

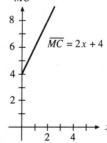

15. (a) $\overline{MR} = 4$ (b) The sale of each additional item brings in $\$4$ revenue at all levels of production.

17.   (a)   \$3500; this is revenue from the sale of 100 units.   (b) $\overline{MR} = 36 - 0.02x$
(c)   \$34; Revenue will increase by \$34.   19.   (a) $\overline{MR} = 36 - 0.02x$ (b) $x = 1800$ (c)   \$32,400

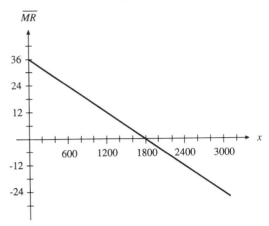

21. $\overline{MP} = 5$ 23.   (a)   \$0   (b) $\overline{MP} = 30 - 2x$ (c) $-\$10$; profit will decrease by \$10 if one additional
unit is sold.   25.   (a)   (b) $x = 15$ (c) $x = 15$ (d)   \$25

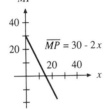

CHAPTER 9 REVIEW EXERCISES

1.   55   2.   0   3. -2 4.   6   5. $\frac{1}{2}$ 6. $\frac{1}{5}$ 7.   no limit ($\pm \infty$)   8.   0   9.   4
10.   no limit   11. $6x$ 12. $1 - 4x$ 13.   2   14.   no limit   15.   1   16.   no   17.   yes
18.   yes   19.   infinite discontinuity at $x = 5$ 20.   missing point discontinuity at $x = 2$
21.   continuous   22.   jump discontinuity at $x = 1$ 23.   horiz: $y = \frac{3}{2}$, vert: $x = 2$ 24.   horiz: $y = -1$,
vert: $x = -1, x = 1$ 25.   (a) $x = 1$ (b) $y = 0$ (c)   jump at $x = 0$, infinite at $x = 1$
26.   (a) $x = -1$ (b) $y = \frac{1}{2}$ (c)   infinite at $x = -1$, missing point at $x = 0$ 27.   (a)   true   (b)   false
28. $f'(x) = 6x + 2$ 29. $20x^4 - 18x^2$ 30. $8x$ 31.   3   32. $\frac{1}{2}\sqrt{x}$ 33.   0   34. $-\frac{4}{3}\sqrt[3]{x^4}$
35. $-\dfrac{1}{x^2} + \dfrac{1}{2\sqrt{x^3}}$ 36. $\dfrac{-3}{x^3} - \dfrac{1}{3\sqrt[3]{x^2}}$ 37. $y = 15x - 18$ 38. $y = 34x - 48$ 39. $x = 0, x = 2$
40. $x = 0, x = 2, x = -2$ 41. $9x^2 - 26x + 4$ 42. $15x^4 + 9x^2 + 2x$ 43. $\dfrac{2(1 - q)}{q^3}$
44. $\dfrac{1 - 3t}{[2\sqrt{t}(3t + 1)^2]}$ 45. $\dfrac{9x + 2}{2\sqrt{x}}\,dx$ 46. $\dfrac{5x^6 + 2x^4 + 20x^3 - 3x^2 - 4x}{(x^3 + 1)^2}\,dx$
47. $(9x^2 - 24x)(x^3 - 4x^2)^2$ 48. $6(30x^5 + 24x^3)(5x^6 + 6x^4 + 5)^5$ 49. $(9x^2 - 24x)(x^3 - 4x^2)^2$
50. $\dfrac{-(3x^2 - 4)}{2\sqrt{(x^3 - 4x)^3}}$ 51. $2x(2x^4 + 5)^7(34x^4 + 5)$ 52. $\dfrac{-2(3x + 1)(x + 12)}{(x^2 - 4)^2}$

53. $36[(3x + 1)(2x^3 - 1)]^{11}(8x^3 + 2x^2 - 1)$ 54. $\dfrac{3}{(1 - x)^4}$ 55. $\dfrac{(2x^2 - 4)}{\sqrt{x^2 - 4}}$ 56. $\dfrac{2x - 1}{(3x - 1)^{4/3}}$

57. (a) $\overline{MC} = 6x + 6$ (b) 186   58. 53   59. (a) $\overline{MR} = 40 - 0.04x$ (b) $x = 1000$ units

60. 48   61. (a) $\overline{MR} = 80 - 0.08x$ (b) 72   62. $\dfrac{120x(x + 1)}{(2x + 1)^2}$

EXERCISE 10.1

1. (a) $dy/dx = x - 1$ (b) $x = 1$ (c) $(1, -\tfrac{1}{2})$ (d) relative minimum   3. (a) $dy/dx = 2 - 2x$
(b) $x = 1$ (c) $(1, 1)$ (d) relative maximum   5. (a) $dy/dx = 3x^2 + 6x + 3$ (b) $x = -1$
(c) $(-1, -1)$ (d) horizontal point of inflection   7. (a) $dy/dx = x^2 + x - 2$ (b) $x = -2, x = 1$

(c) $(-2, 13/3), (1, -1/6)$ (d) $(-2, 13/3)$ rel max; $(1, -1/6)$ rel min   (e)

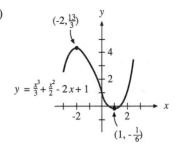

9. (a) $dy/dx = 3x^2 - 6x$ (b) $x = 0, x = 2$ (c) $(0, 0), (2, -4)$ (d) $(0, 0)$ max; $(2, -4)$ min

(e)

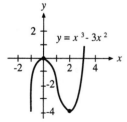

11. $(1, 4/3)$ HPI; no max nor min

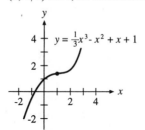

13. $(0, 0)$ HPI; $(3, -27)$ min

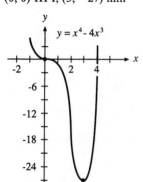

15. $(1, 1)$ rel max; $(0, 0), (2, 0)$ rel min

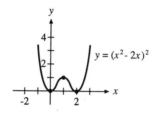

17. $(1/2, -27/16)$ min;
    $(2, 0)$ HPI

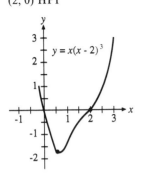

19. $(0, 4)$ rel max;
    $(2, 0)$ rel min

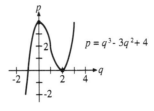

21. $(4/3, -95/27)$ min;
    $(-2, 15)$ max

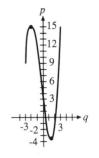

23. $(-1, 3)$ rel max; $(1, -1)$ rel min;
    HPI $(0, 1)$

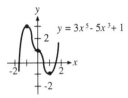

25. $(3, 4)$ rel max; $(5, 0)$ rel min;
    HPI $(0, 0)$

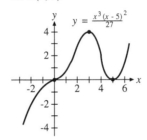

27. (a) $0 \leqslant t < 4$ 29. (a) 10   (b) Jan. 1
    (b) $t = 4$
    (c) 250 mg

EXERCISE 10.2

1. $x = 0$ 3. $x \leqslant 0$ 5. $x = 1$ 7. $x = 1$ 9. $x = 0$ 11. No derivative at $x = 0$;
    no max, no min

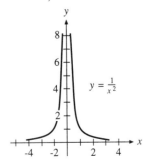

13. No derivative at $x = 1$; no max, no min   15.

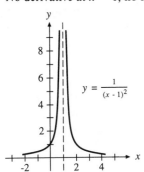

$y = \frac{1}{(x-1)^2}$

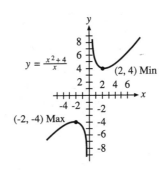

$y = \frac{x^2+4}{x}$

(2, 4) Min

(-2, -4) Max

17. $(0, -\sqrt[3]{4})$ min; derivative does not exist at $x = 2$, $x = -2$.   19. Domain: $x \geqslant 0$

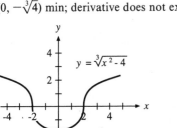

$y = \sqrt[3]{x^2 - 4}$

$(0,-\sqrt[3]{4})$ Min

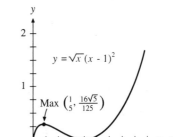

$y = \sqrt{x}\,(x-1)^2$

Max $\left(\frac{1}{5}, \frac{16\sqrt{5}}{125}\right)$

Min (0, 0)   Min (1, 0)

21.   23. No derivative at (2, 4)

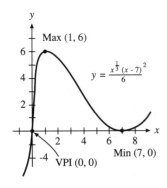

Max (1, 6)

$y = \frac{x^{\frac{1}{3}}(x-7)^2}{6}$

Min (7, 0)

VPI (0, 0)

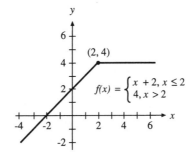

(2, 4)

$f(x) = \begin{cases} x + 2, x \leq 2 \\ 4, x > 2 \end{cases}$

25. (0, 16) absolute max   27. $\left(\frac{1}{4}, -\frac{1}{8}\right)$ absolute min; (3, 15) absolute max   29. (0, 16) absolute max;
(3, 7) absolute min   31. yes   33. (a) 0 at $x = 15$, 0.1 at $x = 30$ (b) No, slope different on either side
of $x = 20$.   35. (a) none   (b) $C \geqslant 0$ (c) 0   (d) no

EXERCISE 10.3

1. $x = 1800$ units, $R = \$32,400$ 3. $x = 20$ units, $R = \$24,000$ 5. 40 people
7. $p = \$15$, $R = \$22,500$ 9. (a) max $= \$2100$ (b) $x = 10$ 11. $x = 5$ units, $\overline{C} = \$23$

13. $x = 10$ units, $\overline{C} = \$20$ 15.   200 units ($x = 2$), $\overline{C} = \$1.08$ 17. $x = 5$
19.   no maximum; produce as much as possible   21. $x = 15$ units, $P = \$25$ 23. $x = 80$ units,
$P = \$280,000$ 25. $x = 10\sqrt{15} \approx 39$ units, $P \approx \$71,181$ (using $x = 39$)   27. $x = 1000$ units, $P = \$39,700$
29.   rent $= \$430$

EXERCISE 10.4

1. $x = 29/9$ 3. $x = 500$ 5.   400 trees   7. $r = \frac{2}{3} r_0$ 9. $t = 8, p = 45\%$ 11.   50, 50
13.   625 ft $\times$ 625 ft   15.   625 ft $\times$ 1250 ft   17. $10^{-6} = $ hydrogen ion concentration   19. $x = 2$
21.   3 weeks from now   23.   25 plates   25.   20 ft long, $6\frac{2}{3}$ ft across (dividers run across)
27. $4'' \times 8'' \times 8''$ high   29.   72.3 ft   31. $x = 40,000$

CHAPTER 10 REVIEW EXERCISES

1. $(0, 0)$ max   2. $(2, -9)$ min   3.   HPI $(1, 0)$ 4. $(1, \frac{3}{2})$ max, $(-1, -\frac{3}{2})$ min

5.

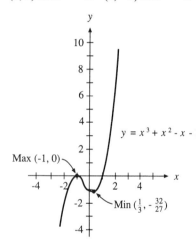

$y = x^3 + x^2 - x - 1$

Max $(-1, 0)$

Min $(\frac{1}{3}, -\frac{32}{27})$

6.

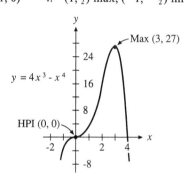

Max $(3, 27)$

$y = 4x^3 - x^4$

HPI $(0, 0)$

7.

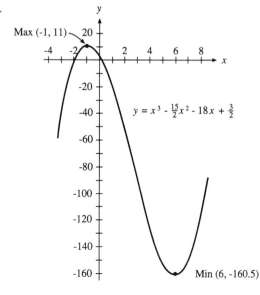

Max $(-1, 11)$

$y = x^3 - \frac{15}{2}x^2 - 18x + \frac{3}{2}$

Min $(6, -160.5)$

8.

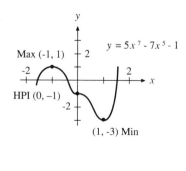

$y = 5x^7 - 7x^5 - 1$

Max $(-1, 1)$

HPI $(0, -1)$

$(1, -3)$ Min

9. f' does not exist at $x = 0$ 10. f' does not exist at $x = 25$ 11. no critical points; no max nor min

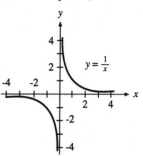

12.

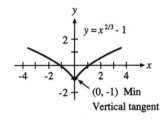

13.

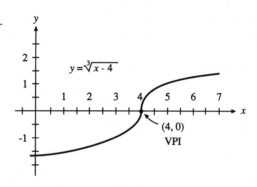

14.

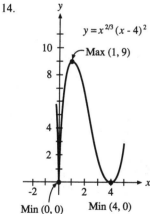

15. (a) $(0, 0)$ absolute min; $(140, 19{,}600)$ absolute max
     (b) $(0, 0)$ absolute min; $(100, 18{,}000)$ absolute max

16. (a) $(50; 233{,}333)$ absolute max; $(0, 0)$ absolute min   (b) $(64; 248{,}491)$ absolute max; $(0, 0)$ absolute min
17. $x = 5$ units, $\overline{C} = \$45$ 18. $x = 1600$ units, $R = \$25{,}600$ 19. $P = \$54{,}000$ at $x = 100$ units
20. $x = 3$ units   21. $x = 152$ units   22. $x = 7$ units   23. $\$300$ 24. selling 175 sets at $\$425$ each
25. $x = 1000$ units   26. 10:00 A.M.   27. 325 in 1995   28. 20 mi from A, 10 mi from B
29. 4 ft $\times$ 4 ft   30. $8\frac{3}{4}'' \times 10''$

EXERCISE 11.1

1. $24x - 30$ 3. $60x - 2$ 5. $6x - 2x^{-3}$ 7. $6x + \frac{1}{4}x^{-3/2}$ 9. $20x^3 + \frac{1}{4}x^{-3/2}$ 11. $\dfrac{-1}{4(x-1)^{3/2}}$

13. $\dfrac{4}{(x^2+4)^{3/2}}$ 15. $\dfrac{-2}{(x+1)^3}$ 17. $60x^2 - 96$ 19. $1008x^6 - 720x^3$ 21. $-6/x^4$ 23. $\frac{3}{8}x^{-5/2}$

25. $\frac{3}{8}(x+1)^{-5/2}$ 27. $-12x(x^2+4)^{-5/2}$ 29. 0   31. $-15/16x^{7/2}$ 33. 26

35. (a) $290x - 90x^2$ (b) 200, 60   (c) 110, -250 37. -2 39. decreasing   41. decrease

43. $x = 29/18$

EXERCISE 11.2

1. $(1, -2)$ 3. $(0, 0)$ 5. none   7. $(2, 0)$ 9. $(-2, -9)$ and $(1, \frac{3}{4})$ 11. $(3, -54)$

13. $(0, 0)$ 15. $(0, 0)$ and $(-2, 7.6)$ 17. $(0, 0), (\sqrt{3}, \sqrt{3})$, and $(-\sqrt{3}, -\sqrt{3})$

19. no points of inflection   21.

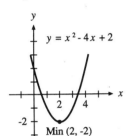

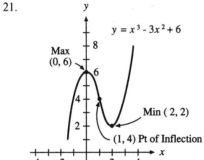

23. $(0, 0)$ max; $(2\sqrt{2}, -64), (-2\sqrt{2}, -64)$ min; $(2\sqrt{6}/3, -320/9), (-2\sqrt{6}/3, 320/9)$ pts of inflection

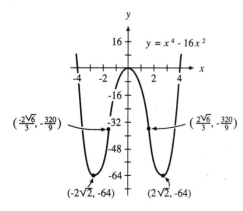

25. $y = x^4 - 4$; no points of inflection

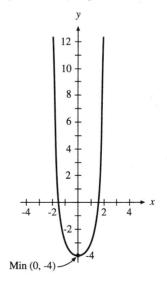

27. $p = 3q^4 - 4q^3 + 1$; points of inflection:
     $(0, 1)$ and $(2/3, 11/27)$; min: $(1, 0)$

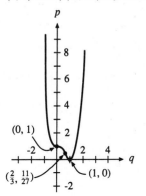

29. $w = z^2/8 - 1/z$; point of inflection: $(2, 0)$;
     min: $(-\sqrt[3]{4}, 3\sqrt[3]{16}/8)$; vertical asymptote: $z = 0$

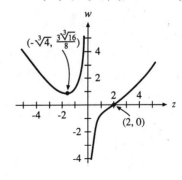

31.

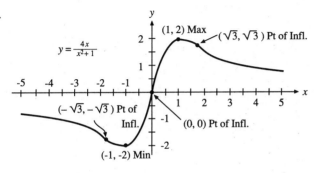

33.

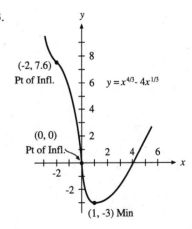

35. (a) $P'(t)$ (b) B (c) C 37. (a) C (b) the right side   (c) yes   39. 5000
41. (a) 4 months   (b) 8 months   43. (a) in an 8-hour shift, max when $t = 8$ (b) 4 hr.

EXERCISE 11.3

1. $-x/2y$ 3. $-(2x + 4)/(2y - 3)$ 5. $-x/y$ 7. $-(2x + 3y)/3x$ 9. $-p/q$ 11. $-x/y$

13. $8\sqrt{p}$ 15. $(5y - 1)/(1 - 5x)$ 17. $(4x^3 + 9x^2y^2 - 8x - 12y)/(18y + 12x - 6x^3y + 10y^4)$

19. undefined   21. 1   23. $y = \frac{1}{2}x + 1$ 25. $y = 4x + 5$ 27. horizontal: $(2, \sqrt{2}), (2, -\sqrt{2})$;

vertical: $(2 + 2\sqrt{2}, 0), (2 - 2\sqrt{2}, 0)$ 31. (b) yes, because $x^2 + y^2 = 4$ 33. $1/2x\sqrt{x}$ 35. 1/2

37. $-243/128$ 39. At $p = \$80$, $q = 49$ and $dq/dp = -5/16$, which means that if the price is increased to
$\$81$, quantity demanded will decrease by approximately 5/16 units.

EXERCISE 11.4

1. $(1/x) \log_4 e$ 3. $1/x$ 5. $(3x^2 - 4)/(x^3 - 4x)$ 7. $y' = \dfrac{4}{4x - 1} - \dfrac{3}{x} = \dfrac{3 - 8x}{x(4x - 1)}$

9. $y' = \dfrac{4}{4x - 1} - \dfrac{3}{x} = \dfrac{3 - 8x}{x(4x - 1)}$ 11. $\dfrac{7x + 6}{2x(x + 1)}$ 13. $\dfrac{7x + 6}{2x(x + 1)}$ 15. $y' = 0$

17. $dp/dq = 2q/(q^2 + 1)$ 19. $\dfrac{dp}{dq} = \dfrac{(q^2 + 1)}{q(q^2 - 1)}$ 21. $\dfrac{dy}{dt} = -\dfrac{(3t^2 - 4t - 3)}{2(1 - t)(t^2 + 3)}$ 23. $\ln x$

25. $(1 - \ln x)/x^2$ 27. $8x^3/(x^4 + 3)$ 29. $\dfrac{8x^3 \ln (x^4 + 3)}{x^4 + 3}$ 31. y 33. $\dfrac{-y \ln y}{x}$, or $\dfrac{-4y}{x^2}$

35. -4 37. $\left(-\dfrac{1}{[\mathrm{H}^+]}\right) \log e$ 39. A/B 41. $dy/dt = -0.000436y$

EXERCISE 11.5

1. $y' = 2x(4^{x^2})/\log_4 e$ 3. $y' = 36xe^{3x^2}$ 5. $y' = e^{-1/x}/x^2$ 7. $y' = 12x(x^2 + 1)^2 e^{(x^2 + 1)^3}$

9. $y' = \dfrac{2}{x^3} e^{-1/x^2} - 2xe^{-x^2}$ 11. $ds/dt = te^t(t + 2)$ 13. $y' = 1$ 15. $y' = e^{\frac{1}{2}x} + e^{\sqrt{x}}/(2\sqrt{x})$

17. $y' = 2e^{2x}/(e^{2x} + 1)$ 19. $y' = e^{-3x}/x - 3e^{-3x} \ln (2x)$ 21. $y' = (2e^{5x} - 3)/e^{3x} = 2e^{2x} - 3e^{-3x}$

23. $y' = 30e^{3x}(e^{3x} + 4)^9$ 25. $-1/x$ 27. $-y/x$ 29. $ye^x/(1 - e^x)$ 31. 0

33. $y = -\frac{1}{3}x + 1$ 35. $z = 0$ 37. (a) 8.67 (b) 17.80 39. $100{,}000e^{-1/x}/x^2$

41. (a) $0.1(Pe^{0.1n})$ (b) $0.1(Pe^{0.1}) \approx 0.1105P$ (c) yes; because of the compounding   43. 29.107

45. $N'(t) = 3{,}535{,}000\, e^{-0.7t}/(1 + 100\, e^{-0.7t})^2$

EXERCISE 11.6

1. 70 3. $\$200$ 5. 39 units; $P(39) = \$71{,}181$ 7. (a) 60 (b) $\$570$ (c) $\$9000$
9. (a) 15 (b) $\$9450$ 11. 2000 units priced at $\$90/$unit. Max profit is $\$90{,}000/$wk   13. $\$12/$item
15. $\$115$ per item   17. $\$483$ per item; $\$40{,}100$ 19. (a) 1 (b) no change   21. (a) 84
(b) Revenue will decrease   23. 8 25. $\frac{1}{6}$
27. $dR/dp = p\,(dq/dp) + q$; $\eta = 1 \Rightarrow dq/dp = -q/p$; $\therefore dR/dp = p(-q/p) + q = -q + q = 0$
29. $dR/dp = p(dq/dp) + q$; $\eta < 1 \Rightarrow (-p/q)(dq/dp) < 1 \Rightarrow dq/dp > -q/p$;
$\therefore dR/dp = p(dq/dp) + q > p(-q/p) + q = 0$ so $dR/dp > 0$

CHAPTER 11 REVIEW EXERCISES

1. $y'' = -1/(4x^{3/2}) - 2$ 2. $y'' = 12x^2 - 2/x^3$ 3. $d^5y/dx^5 = 0$ 4. $d^5y/dx^5 = -30(1 - x)$
5. $d^3y/dx^3 = -4/(x^2 - 4)^{3/2}$ 6. $\dfrac{d^4y}{dx^4} = \dfrac{2x(x^2 - 3)}{(x^2 + 1)^3}$ 7. concave up   8. $(-1, -3), (2, -42)$
9. $(-1, 15)$ rel max; $(3, -17)$ rel min; $(1, -1)$ point of inflection

10. $y = x^3 - 12x$; $(-2, 16)$ max;
    $(2, -16)$ min; $(0, 0)$ point of inflection

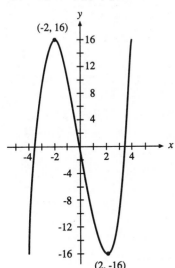

11.

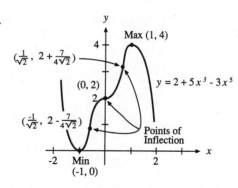

$\left(\frac{1}{\sqrt{2}}, 2 + \frac{7}{4\sqrt{2}}\right)$

Max $(1, 4)$

$(0, 2)$

$y = 2 + 5x^3 - 3x^5$

$\left(\frac{1}{\sqrt{2}}, 2 - \frac{7}{4\sqrt{2}}\right)$

Points of Inflection

Min $(-1, 0)$

12.

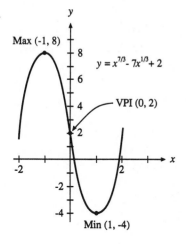

Max $(-1, 8)$

$y = x^{7/3} - 7x^{1/3} + 2$

VPI $(0, 2)$

Min $(1, -4)$

13. $dy/dx = 2/y$

14. $\dfrac{dy}{dx} = \dfrac{2(x + 1)}{3(1 - 2y)}$

15. $y' = \dfrac{6x(1 + xy^2)}{y(5y^3 - 4x^3)}$

16. $d^2y/dx^2 = -(x^2 + y^2)/y^3$

17. $5/9$

18. $(-2, \pm\sqrt{\frac{2}{3}})$

19. $x^2e^x + 2xe^x$

20. $2x$

21. $1/q - \left[\dfrac{2q}{(q^2 - 1)}\right]$

22. $dy/dx = 2xe^{x^2}$

23. $dy/dx = 3^{3x-3}/\log_3 e$

24. $y' = \dfrac{10(1 + \ln x)^9}{x}$

25. $y' = \dfrac{1 - \ln x}{x^2}$

26. $dy/dx = -2e^{-x}/(1 - e^{-x})^2$

27. $dy/dx = \dfrac{2[1 - \ln(2x + 1)]}{(2x + 1)^2}$

28. $dx/dt = e^t(t^2 + 4)(t + 2)^2$

29. $y' = \dfrac{-y}{x \ln x}$

30. $dy/dx = ye^{xy}/(1 - xe^{xy})$

31. 135.3

32. (a) 152.5 (b) 1.13 times faster

33. (a) $-0.00002876\,A_0$　(b) $-0.00002876\,A_0$　(c) less　34. $1200e$　35. 30
36. \$93,625 at 325 units　37. (a) 150　(b) \$650　38. \$208,490.67 at 64 units　39. yes
40. \$880　41. (a) 1　(b) no change　42. 25/12, elastic

EXERCISE 12.1

1. $x^4 + C$　3. $\frac{1}{7}x^7 + C$　5. $\frac{1}{8}x^8 + C$　7. $\frac{5}{4}x^4 + C$　9. $\frac{4}{3}x^6 + C$　11. $5x + C$　13. $27x + C$

15. $\frac{2}{5}x^{5/2} + C$　17. $\frac{3}{10}x^{5/3} + C$　19. $\frac{2}{3}x^{3/2} + C$　21. $4x^{3/2} + C$　23. $\frac{1}{5}x^5 - x^3 + C$

25. $\frac{1}{4}x^4 - x^3 + 4x + C$　27. $\frac{1}{5}x^5 - x^2 + \frac{2}{3}x^{3/2} + C$　29. $\frac{1}{3}x^3 + 5x^2 + 25x + C$ or $\frac{1}{3}(x + 5)^3 + C$

31. $\frac{16}{5}x^5 - \frac{8}{3}x^3 + x + C$　33. $\frac{1}{7}x^7 + \frac{3}{5}x^5 + x^3 + x + C$　35. $R(x) = 3x$　37. $R(x) = 2x^2 - 3x$

39. \$3700　41. $P(t) = \frac{1}{4}t^4 + \frac{4}{3}t^3 + 6t$　43. (a) $x = t^{7/4}/1050$　(b) 0.96 tons

45. (a) $x/4 + 100/x + 30$　(b) \$56　47. (a) $r = -t + 32$　(b) 174　(c) $r = 0$ at $t = 32$
(d) 512 barrels

EXERCISE 12.2

1. $\frac{1}{4}(x^2 + 3)^4 + C$　3. $(15x^2 + 10)^5/5 + C$　5. $\frac{1}{3}(3x - x^3)^3 + C$　7. $\frac{1}{8}(x^2 + 5)^4 + C$

9. $\frac{1}{6}(x^4 + 6)^{3/2} + C$　11. $9x - 2x^3 + \frac{1}{5}x^5 + C$　13. $(4x - 1)^7/28 + C$　15. $\frac{1}{8}(x^2 + 1)^4 + C$

17. $\frac{1}{10}(x^2 - 2x)^5 + C$　19. $\frac{3}{8}(x^2 + 2x)^{4/3} + C$　21. $-1/[3(x^3 - 1)] + C$　23. $-1/[9(x^3 - 5)^3] + C$

25. $\frac{2}{3}\sqrt{x^3 - 6x^2} + C$　27. $-8/[3(x^3 - 4)] + C$　29. $-1/[8(x^4 - 4x)^2] + C$　31. 3720

33. $R(x) = 60{,}000x + \left[\dfrac{40{,}000}{(10 + x)}\right] - 4000$　35. (a) $s = 10\sqrt{x + 1}$　(b) 50

37. (a) $100/(t + 10) - 1000/(t + 10)^2$　(b) 2.5 million　39. 7400

EXERCISE 12.3

1. $\ln |x^3 + 4| + C$　3. $\ln |x^3 - 2x| + C$　5. $\frac{1}{4}\ln |x^4 + 1| + C$　7. $2\ln |x^2 - 4| + C$

9. $\frac{1}{4}\ln |4z + 1| + C$　11. $\frac{1}{3}\ln |z^3 + 3z| + C$　13. $\frac{1}{3}x^3 + \ln |x - 1| + C$　15. $x + \frac{1}{2}\ln |x^2 + 3| + C$

17. $e^{3x} + C$　19. $-e^{-x} + C$　21. $\frac{1}{12}e^{3x^4} + C$　23. $\frac{1}{4}e^{x^4} + C$　25. $\frac{1}{2}e^{y^2} + C$　27. $\frac{3}{5}e^{5x} + C$

29. \$1030.97　31. $n = n_0 e^{-Kt}$　33. 55　35. (a) $Pe^{0.1\,n}$　(b) approx. 7 yr
37. (a) $P = 95e^{-0.491t}$　(b) ≈ 90.45

EXERCISE 12.4

1. $C(x) = x^2 + 100x + 200$　3. $C(x) = 2x^2 + 2x + 80$　5. \$3750
7. (a) $x = 3$ units is optimal level　(b) $P(x) = -4x^2 + 24x - 200$　(c) loss of \$164
9. (a) \$2960　(b) 896　11. (a) $\overline{C}(x) = 6/x + x/6 + 200$　(b) \$203.63

13. $C(y) = 0.4y + 0.6\sqrt{y} + 5$　15. $C(y) = 0.3y + 0.4\sqrt{y} + 8$　17. $C = 2\sqrt{y + 1} + 0.4y + 4$

19. $C = 0.7y + 0.5e^{-2y} + 5.15$　21. $C = 0.85y + 5.15$　23. $C = 0.8y + \dfrac{2\sqrt{3y + 7}}{3} + 4.24$

EXERCISE 12.5

1. $y = x^4/4 + C$ 3. $x^3/3 = y^2/2 + C$ 5. $-1/(2x^2) = y^2/2 + C$ 7. $-1/x = y^3/3 + y + C$

9. $\ln|x| + 1/y = C$ 11. $x^2/2 - y^2/2 = C$ 13. $y = C(x + 1)$ 15. $y - \ln|y + 1| = -\frac{1}{2}e^{-2x} + C$

17. $3y^4 = 4x^3 - 1$ 19. $y = 3x/(2 - 4x)$ 21. $xe^{2y} = x^3 + 2x - 2$ 23. $y^2 + 1 = 5x$

25. $y = cx^k$ 27. $13\frac{1}{2}$ hr   29. $p = 28e^{2t} - 20$ 31. $x = 6(1 - e^{-t/20})$ 33. $t = 8.4$ hr

35. 23,100 yrs (approximately)   37. $V = 1.86e^{2 - 2e^{-0.1t}}$ 39. $t = 4.5$ hr   41. 10:24 A.M.

CHAPTER 12 REVIEW EXERCISES

1. $\frac{1}{7}x^7 + C$ 2. $\frac{2}{3}x^{3/2} + C$ 3. $\frac{1}{4}x^4 - x^3 + 2x^2 + 5x + C$ 4. $\frac{1}{5}x^5 - \frac{2}{3}x^3 + x + C$

5. $\frac{1}{6}(x^2 - 1)^3 + C$ 6. $\frac{1}{6}(x^3 - 3x^2)^2 + C$ 7. $\frac{1}{8}x^8 + \frac{8}{5}x^5 + 8x^2 + C$ 8. $\frac{1}{21}(x^3 + 4)^7 + C$

9. $\frac{1}{3}\ln|x^3 + 1| + C$ 10. $\dfrac{-1}{3(x^3 + 1)} + C$ 11. $\frac{1}{2}(x^3 - 4)^{2/3} + C$ 12. $\frac{1}{3}\ln|x^3 - 4| + C$

13. $\frac{1}{2}x^2 - \frac{1}{x} + C$ 14. $\frac{1}{3}x^3 + \frac{1}{2}x^2 - 2x - \ln|x - 1| + C$ 15. $x^4/4 + 2x^2 + C$

16. $x^3/3 - x^2 + x + C$ 17. $\frac{1}{6}\ln|2x^3 - 7| + C$ 18. $x^2/2 - x + C$ 19. $x^4/4 - e^{3x}/3 + C$

20. $\frac{1}{2}e^{x^2+1} + C$ 21. $\dfrac{-1}{3(x^3 + 1)} + C$ 22. $-\frac{7}{2}\sqrt{1 - x^4} + C$ 23. $\frac{1}{3}e^{y^3} + C$

24. $x^2/2 + 1/(x + 1) + C$ 25. $C = 1/x - 1/(2y^2)$ 26. $y = Ce^{-3/x} - \frac{1}{3}$

27. $-1/x + 2/x^2 + 1/y - 1/y^3 = C$ 28. $-1/x + 2/x^2 + 1/y - 1/y^3 = 1$ 29. $y^2 + y + 4 = x^2$

30. 0   31. 472   32. $400[1 - 5/(t + 5) + 25/(t + 5)^2]$ 33. $p = 1990.099 - 100,000/(t + 100)$

34. (a) $y = -60e^{-0.04t} + 60$ (b) 23%   35. $R = 800\ln(x + 1)$

36. (a) $1000   (b) $C(x) = 3x^2 + 4x + 1000$ 37. 80 units, $440   38. 10,680,870 yrs approx

EXERCISE 13.1

1. 6.25   3. 8.3125   5. 4.25   7. 10.3125   9. $S_L(10) = 4.08$; $S_R(10) = 5.28$

11. both equal 14/3   13. It would lie between $S_L(10)$ and $S_R(10)$. It would equal 14/3.   15. 3

17. 42   19. -5 21. 180   23. 11,315   25. $3 - \dfrac{3(n + 1)}{n} + \dfrac{(n + 1)(2n + 1)}{2n^2} = \dfrac{2n^2 - 3n + 1}{2n^2}$

27. $S = (n - 1)/2n$ 29. 99/200   31. $\frac{1}{2}$ 33. $S = \dfrac{(n + 1)(2n + 1)}{6n^2}$ 35. $6767/20,000 \approx 0.3384$

37. $\frac{1}{3}$ 39. $\frac{20}{3}$

EXERCISE 13.2

1. 60   3. 33   5. 25   7. $12\sqrt[3]{25}$ 9. 98   11. $\frac{7}{3}$ 13. 12,960   15. 0

17. $8\sqrt{3} - \frac{7}{3}\sqrt{7}$ 19. 0   21. $\frac{1}{6}\ln(112/31)$ 23. A, C 25. (a) $\int_0^4 (2x - \frac{1}{2}x^2)dx$ (b) 16/3

27. (a) $\int_{-1}^0 (x^3 + 1)dx$ (b) 3/4   29. $\frac{1}{6}$ 31. $\frac{1}{2}(e^9 - e)$ 33. same absolute values, opposite signs

35. 6   37. 0.04 cm³   39. 1222 (approx)   41. $450,000   43. $e^{-0.5} - e^{-1} \approx 0.2387$

45. $1 - e^{-0.2} \approx 0.1813$ 47. (a) $7007   (b) $19,649

EXERCISE 13.3

1. $7/6$　　3. $\frac{52}{3}$　　5. $\frac{112}{3}$　　7. $7/12$　　9. $1/12$　　11. $1/3$　　13. $4/3$　　15. 72　　17. $1/2$
19. $37/12$　　21. $4/15$　　23. $4 - 3\ln 3$　　25. (a) $\$1402$　(b) $\$535{,}333.33$　　27. 102.5 units
29. $\$513.86$　　31. 147 mg

EXERCISE 13.4

1. $\$83.33$　　3. $\$161.89$　　5. $(5, 56)$; $\$83.33$　　7. $\$11.50$　　9. $\$204.17$　　11. $\$2766.67$
13. $\$17{,}839.58$　　15. $\$133.33$　　17. $\$2.50$　　19. $\$103.35$　　21. $\$120{,}000$
23. $\$346{,}664$ (nearest dollar)　　25. $\$506{,}000$ (nearest thousand)　　27. $\$18{,}660$ (nearest dollar)
29. $\$82{,}155$ (nearest dollar)　　31. $\$265{,}781$ (nearest dollar)　　33. $\$190{,}519$ (nearest dollar)
35. Gift shop: $\$151{,}024$; Video Rental: $\$141{,}093$; Gift shop is a better buy.

EXERCISE 13.5

1. $\frac{1}{8}\ln|(4 + x)/(4 - x)| + C$　　3. $\frac{1}{3}\ln[(3 + \sqrt{10})/2]$　　5. $w(\ln w - 1) + C$　　7. $\frac{1}{3} + \frac{1}{4}\ln\left(\frac{3}{7}\right)$

9. $3^x\log_3 e + C$ or $3^x/\ln 3 + C$　　11. $\frac{1}{2}[7\sqrt{24} - 25\ln(7 + \sqrt{24}) + 25\ln 5]$　　13. $\dfrac{(6x - 5)(4x + 5)^{3/2}}{60} + C$

15. $\frac{1}{2}(5^{x^2})\log_5 e + C$　　17. $\frac{1}{3}(13^{3/2} - 8)$　　19. $\dfrac{-5}{\sqrt{8}}\ln\left|\dfrac{\sqrt{8} + \sqrt{8 - x^2}}{x}\right| + C$

21. $\frac{1}{3}\ln|3x + \sqrt{9x^2 - 4}| + C$　　23. $\frac{1}{8}\ln\left(\frac{9}{5}\right)$　　25. $\frac{1}{3}\ln|3x + 1 + \sqrt{(3x + 1)^2 + 1}| + C$

27. $\frac{1}{4}[10\sqrt{109} - \sqrt{10} + 9\ln(10 + \sqrt{109}) - 9\ln(1 + \sqrt{10})]$　　29. $-\frac{1}{6}\ln|7 - 3x^2| + C$

31. $\frac{1}{2}\ln|2x + \sqrt{4x^2 + 7}| + C$　　33. $2e^{\sqrt{x-1}} + C$　　35. $\frac{1}{32}[\ln|4x^2 + 5| + 5/(4x^2 + 5)] + C$

37. $\$3391.10$　　39. $C = \frac{1}{2}x\sqrt{x^2 + 9} + \frac{9}{2}\ln\left|\dfrac{x + \sqrt{x^2 + 9}}{3}\right| + 300$　　41. $CS = \$399$ approx

43. $16{,}160$

EXERCISE 13.6

1. $\frac{1}{2}xe^{2x} - \frac{1}{4}e^{2x} + C$　　3. $\frac{1}{3}x^3\ln x - \frac{1}{9}x^3 + C$　　5. $\dfrac{104\sqrt{2}}{15}$　　7. $e - 2$　　9. $-(1 + \ln x)/x + C$

11. $\frac{1}{2}e^{x^2} + C$　　13. $(x - 3)^{1/2}(\frac{2}{3}x + 4) + C$　　15. 1

17. $\dfrac{x^2}{2}\ln(2x - 3) - \frac{1}{4}x^2 - \frac{3}{4}x - \frac{9}{8}\ln(2x - 3) + C$　　19. $\frac{1}{5}(q^2 - 3)^{3/2}(q^2 + 2) + C$　　21. 282.4

23. $\frac{2}{3}x^{3/2}\ln x - \frac{4}{9}x^{3/2} + C$　　25. $\frac{1}{4}x^4\ln^2 x - \frac{1}{8}x^4\ln x + \frac{1}{32}x^4 + C$　　27. $\$2794.46$　　29. $\$34{,}836.73$

EXERCISE 13.7

1. $1/e$　　3. $\frac{1}{3}$　　5. diverges　　7. 10　　9. diverges　　11. diverges　　13. diverges　　15. 0

17. $\int_0^\infty Ae^{-rt}dt = A/r$　　19. $\$2{,}400{,}000$　　21. (a) $500\left[\dfrac{e^{-0.03b} + 0.03b - 1}{0.0009}\right]$　　(b) limit $= \infty$

23. 0.147　　25. 1　　27. $c = 1$　　29. $c = \frac{1}{2}$　　31. 20

CHAPTER 13 REVIEW EXERCISES

1. 212   2. $\dfrac{3(n+1)}{2n^2}$ 3. $91/72$ 4. 1   5. 1   6. 14   7. $248/5$ 8. $-205/4$

9. $825/4$ 10. $125/3$ 11. -2 12. $\frac{1}{6}\ln 47 - \frac{1}{6}\ln 9$ 13. $9/2$ 14. $\ln 4 + 14/3$ 15. $26/3$

16. $\frac{1}{2}\ln 2$ 17. $(1 - e^{-2})/2$ 18. $(e-1)/2$ 19. $95/2$ 20. 36   21. $\frac{1}{4}$ 22. $\frac{1}{2}$

23. $\frac{1}{2}x\sqrt{x^2 - 4} - 2\ln|x + \sqrt{x^2 - 4}| + C$ 24. $2\log_3 e$ 25. $\frac{1}{2}x^2(\ln x^2 - 1) + C$

26. $\frac{1}{2}\ln|x| - \frac{1}{2}\ln|3x + 2| + C$ 27. $\frac{1}{6}x^6 \ln x - \frac{1}{36}x^6 + C$ 28. $(-xe^{-2x}/2) - (e^{-2x}/4) + C$

29. $2x\sqrt{x+5} - \frac{4}{3}(x+5)^{3/2} + C$ 30. 1   31. ∞ 32. -100 33. $\frac{5}{3}$ 34. $-\frac{1}{2}$ 35. $\$28,000$

36. $e^{-2.8} \approx 0.061$ 37. $\$1297.44$ 38. $\$76.60$ 39. (a) $(7, 6)$ (b) $\$7.33$ 40. $\$24.50$
41. $\$1,621,803$ 42. $\$403,609$ 43. $\$217.42$ 44. $\$86,557.41$

45. $-\dfrac{x^2}{4} + \dfrac{7}{2}x + \dfrac{x^2 - 1}{2}\ln(x+1) + 2000$ 46. $e^{-1.4} \approx 0.247$

EXERCISE 14.1

1. $\{(x, y): x$ and y are real numbers$\}$ 3. $\{(x, y): x$ is any real number and y is any real number except $0\}$
5. $\{(x, y): x$ and y are real numbers and $2x - y \neq 0\}$ 7. $\{(p_1, p_2): p_1$ and p_2 are real numbers and $p_1 \geq 0\}$

9. -2 11. $\frac{5}{3}$ 13. 2500   15. 36   17. 3   19. $\frac{1}{25}\ln(12)$ 21. $\frac{13}{3}$ 23. (a) $x = 4$
(b) $y = 2$ 25. (a) 7200   (b) 5000   27. $\$284,000$ 29. $\$6640.23$; the amount that results when
$\$2000$ is invested for 20 years   31. (a) 37,500   (b) $30(2K)^{1/4}(2L)^{3/4} = 30(2^{1/4})(2^{3/4})K^{1/4}L^{3/4} = 2[30K^{1/4}L^{3/4}]$

EXERCISE 14.2

1. $4x^3 - 10x + 4$ 3. $2x$ 5. $4x + 6$ 7. $12y - 5x$ 9. y 11. $e^x + y/x$ 13. xe^{xy}
15. $9x^2(x^3 + y^2)^2$ 17. $2y(x + 1)^2$ 19. $-4y + 20xy$ 21. $p_2/(p_1 + p_2)^2$ 23. $2x + 4y$ 25. 2
27. 7   29. 0   31. (a) 0   (b) $-2xz + 4$ (c) $2y$ (d) $-x^2$ 33. (a) $8x_1 + 5x_2$
(b) $5x_1 + 12x_2$ (c) 1   35. (a) For a mortage of $\$100,000$ and an 8% interest rate, the monthly payment
is $\$1289$.   (b) The rate of change of the payment with respect to the interest rate is $\$62.51$. That is, if the rate
goes from 8% to 9% on a $\$100,000$ mortage, the approximate increase in the monthly payment is $\$62.51$.
37. (a) $65e^{-0.01x}$ (b) $70e^{-0.02y}$ 39. (a) $2xy^2$ (b) $2x^2y$ 41. $\partial Q/\partial K = 44\frac{4}{9}$ $\partial Q/\partial L = 37\frac{1}{2}$

EXERCISE 14.3

1. 57   3. (a) $2 + y/50$ (b) $4 + x/50$ 5. (a) 20.18   (b) 70.80   7. (a) 36   (b) 19
9. (a) $\sqrt{y^2 + 1}$ (b) $xy/\sqrt{y^2 + 1}$ 11. (a) $1200y/(xy + 1)$ (b) $1200x/(xy + 1)$
13. (a) $\sqrt{y/x}$ (b) $\sqrt{x/y}$ 15. (a) $\ln(y + 1)/(2\sqrt{x})$ (b) $\sqrt{x}/(y + 1)$ 17. $z = 1092$ approx
19. $z_x = 3.6$ 21. $q_1 = 188; q_2 = 270$ 23. any values for p_1 and p_2 that satisfy $6p_2 - 3p_1 = 100$ and that
make q_1 and q_2 nonnegative, such as $p_1 = 10, p_2 = 21\frac{2}{3}$ 25. (a) -3 (b) -2 (c) -6 (d) -5
(e) complementary   27. (a) -50 (b) $600/(p_B + 1)^2$ (c) $-400/(p_B + 4)^2$ (d) $400/(p_A + 4)^2$
(e) competitive

EXERCISE 14.4

1. (a) 2   (b) 0   (c) 0   (d) $-30y$ 3. (a) $2y$ (b) $2x - 8y$ (c) $2x - 8y$ (d) $-8x$ 5. 0
7. $-1/y^2$ 9. -6 11. (a) 6   (b) 0   13. $2 + 2e$ 15. (a) $2 + y^2e^{xy}$ (b) $xye^{xy} + e^{xy}$

(c) $xye^{xy} + e^{xy}$ (d) x^2e^{xy} 17. (a) $1/x^2$ (b) 0   (c) 0   (d) $2 + 1/y^2$ 19. $\dfrac{2x^2 - 2y^2}{x^2(x^2 + y^2)^2}$

21. $4y^2/(4x^2 + y^2)^{3/2}$ 23. (a) $24x$ (b) $24x$ (c) 0

EXERCISE 14.5

1. max $(0, 0, 9)$ 3. min $(0, 0, 4)$ 5. min $(1, -2, 0)$ 7. saddle $(1, -3, 8)$ 9. saddle $(0, 0, 0)$
11. max $(12, 24, 456)$ 13. min $(-8, 6, -52)$ 15. saddle $(0, 0, 0)$; min $(2, 2, -8)$
17. $x = 5000, y = 128$ 19. $x = \frac{20}{3}, y = \frac{10}{3}$ 21. $x = 28, y = 100$ 23. $x = 0, y = 10$
25. length $= 100$, width $= 100$, height $= 50$ 27. $x = 3, y = 0$

EXERCISE 14.6

1. 18 at $(3, 3)$ 3. 35 at $(3, 2)$ 5. 32 at $(4, 2)$ 7. -28 at $(3, \frac{5}{2})$ 9. $\frac{1}{5}$ at $(-\frac{2}{5}, -\frac{1}{5})$
11. 3 at $(1, 1, 1)$ 13. 1 at $(0, 1, 0)$ 15. $x = 4, y = 1$ 17. $x = 40, y = \frac{40}{3}$
19. $x = 900, y = 300$ 21. $x = \$10,003.33, y = \$19,996.67$ 23. length $= 100$ cm, width $= 100$ cm, height $= 50$ cm

CHAPTER 14 REVIEW EXERCISES

1. $\{(x, y): x$ and y are real numbers and $y \neq 2x\}$ 2. $\{(x, y): x$ and y are real numbers with $y \geq 0$ and $(x, y) \neq (0, 0)\}$ 3. -5 4. $896,000$ 5. $15x^2 + 6y$ 6. $24y^3 - 42x^3y^2$
7. $z_x = 8xy^3 + 1/y; z_y = 12x^2y^2 - x/y^2$ 8. $z_x = x/\sqrt{x^2 + 2y^2}; z_y = 2y/\sqrt{x^2 + 2y^2}$
9. $z_x = -2y/(xy + 1)^3; z_y = -2x/(xy + 1)^3$ 10. $z_x = 2xy^3e^{x^2y^3}; z_y = 3x^2y^2e^{x^2y^3}$
11. (a) $ye^{xy} + y/x$ (b) $xe^{xy} + \ln x$ 12. (a) y (b) x 13. -8 14. 8
15. (a) $2y$ (b) 0   (c) $2x - 3$ (d) $2x - 3$ 16. (a) $18xy^4 - 2/y^2$ (b) $36x^3y^2 - 6x^2/y^4$
(c) $36x^2y^3 + 4x/y^3$ (d) $36x^2y^3 + 4x/y^3$ 17. (a) $2e^{y^2}$ (b) $4x^2y^2e^{y^2} + 2x^2e^{y^2}$
(c) $4xye^{y^2}$ (d) $4xye^{y^2}$ 18. (a) $-y^2/(xy + 1)^2$ (b) $-x^2/(xy + 1)^2$ (c) $1/(xy + 1)^2$
(d) $1/(xy + 1)^2$ 19. max $(-8, 16, 208)$ 20. saddle $(0, 0, 0)$; min $(1, 1, -1)$ 21. 80 at $(2, 8)$
22. 11,664 at $(6, 3)$ 23. 3 units   24. 20   25. (a) 280   (b) $2400/7$
26. $\partial Q/\partial K = 81.92; \partial Q/\partial L = 37.5$ 27. (a) -2 (b) -6 (c) complementary   28. competitive
29. $x = 20, y = 40$ 30. $x = 10, y = 4$

Index